# TOP TITLES FOR THE ENTHUSIAST

## WORLD AIRLINE COLOURS
### *of yesteryear*

This new addition to the popular World Airline Colours series takes a nostalgic look at colour schemes and airliners of yesteryear, with coverage of 100 airlines and over 40 different aircraft types. Entries include: BOAC/BKS/Monarch/Cunard Eagle Britannias, BEA Vanguard/Herald, BUA Carvair/VC-10, Eagle Airways Viking, Autair Ambassador, Dan Air DC-7/1-11/707/Comet, BMA Argonaut, BAF Carvair, Laker 707/DC-10, TMAC DC-7/CL-44, BEA Airtours Comet, Euravia L-049, BKS Trident, Cambrian DC-3/1-11, Aer Turas Bristol 170/DC-4/DC-7, Aer Lingus F-27, Lufthansa/Flying Tigers C-46s, Iberia/Varig/National/BOAC/Eastern Super Constellations, Northeast Viscount, TWA Starliner, Aeroflot Tu-104, SAS/TMA/UTA/Balair/Kar Air/SAM/Pan Am/Sabena DC-6s, plus many others.

148 full colour illustrations - casebound.

## AIRLINES & AIRLINERS
### TRIDENT

The first in a new series of airliner monographs featuring quality photographic coverage and comprehensive operational/production histories. All Trident operators illustrated, including the air forces of China and Pakistan, plus many derelict/damaged aircraft - some rarely seen or photographed. Nearly 50 illustrations in colour and mono record the Trident's history from beginning to end. Issue No.2 of Airlines & Airliners is dedicated to the **VC-10** - same format etc. as above.

## WORLD AIRLINE COLOURS
### VOLUME 1

Last published in 1985 as the first in the original four-volume series, this new and completely updated edition follows the established format with coverage of 148 of the world's major airlines. Full colour photographic coverage focuses on many new generation types such as the Boeing 747-400, McDonnell Douglas MD-11, Airbus A320, and the CFM-powered Boeing 737 family etc., most of which were still in the development stage when the original World Airline Colours 1 was published. This new volume also features many newly-created airlines such as Air Ukraine, Lithuanian Airlines and Croatia Airlines etc.

148 full colour illustrations - casebound
Available May/June 1993

## BUCHairPORTS

The new 1993 edition of this popular handbook is arguably the best yet, with coverage of 679 airports worldwide. Includes spectator facilities, radio frequencies, over 100 airport layouts/maps, plus much more.

## WORLD AIRLINE FLEETS NEWS

Published monthly, World Airline Fleets News features over 60 quality illustrations in both colour and mono, plus a round up of all the latest airline news, new deliveries/allocations, and articles to suit a variety of tastes. UK subscriptions are post FREE.

### Please add the following for postage & packing
**UK:** Add 10% to the value of your order (minimum charge £1-50)
**EUROPE:** Add 20% (minimum £2-00)
**OUTSIDE EUROPE (surface):** Add 20% (minimum £2-00)
**OUTSIDE EUROPE (airmail):** Add 50% (minimum £5-00)

### ORDER FORM

| | | |
|---|---|---|
| World Airline Colours of Yesteryear | | £13-95 ..... |
| World Airline Colours Volume 1 | (June) | £13-95 ..... |
| Airlines & Airliners No.1 – Trident | | £ 4-95 ..... |
| Airlines & Airliners No.2 – VC-10 | | £ 4-95 ..... |
| BUCHairPorts | | £12-95 ..... |
| Jet & Propjet Corporate Directory 1993 | | £10-95 ..... |
| Biz Jet 1993 | | £ 8-95 ..... |
| Airlines 1993 | | £ 7-50 ..... |
| Jet Airliner Production List | | £11-95 ..... |
| Turboprop Airliner Production List | | £ 8-95 ..... |
| Piston Airliner Production List | | £ 8-95 ..... |
| High in the Sky | | £ 5-95 ..... |
| | | |
| World Airline Fleets News (single copy – post free) | | £ 2-75 ..... |
| annual subscription (UK) | | £30-00 ..... |

Full catalogue/price list available on request

How to pay: Cheques made payable to 'The Aviation Data Centre Ltd', Access or VISA credit cards, Postal Order, IMO or Eurocheque.

Name: _____

Address: _____

_____

_____

Card no: _____ Exp. _____

**Send your order to:**
**The Aviation Data Centre Ltd.,**
**PO Box 92, Feltham,**
**Middlesex TW13 4SA, England**

# AIRCRAFT illustrated abc CIVIL Aircraft Markings

## ALAN J. WRIGHT

**IAN ALLAN** *Publishing*

# Contents

This forty-fourth edition published 1993

ISBN 0 7110 2129 5

Published by Ian Allan Ltd, Shepperton, Surrey;
and printed in Great Britain by Ian Allan Printing Ltd,
Coombelands House, Addlestone, Surrey KT15 1HY.

*Front cover:* EC-DLG, Airbus A300B4-120. *Peter R. March (PRM)*
*Rear cover, top:* G-ACSS, DH88 Comet. *PRM*
*Rear cover, bottom:* G-ASND, PA-23 Aztec 250. *PRM*

# Introduction

The 'G' prefixed four letter registration system was adopted in 1919 after a short-lived spell of about three months with serial numbers beginning at K-100. Until July 1928 the UK allocations were in the G-Exxx range, but as a result of further International agreements, this series was ended at G-EBZZ, the replacement being G-Axxx. From this point the registrations were issued in a reasonably orderly manner through to G-AZZZ, reached in July 1972. There were two exceptions. To avoid possible confusion with signal codes, the G-AQxx sequence was omitted, while G-AUxx was reserved for Australian use originally. In recent years however, an individual request for a mark in the latter range has been granted by the Authorities.

Although the next logical sequence was started at G-Bxxx, it was not long before the strictly applied rules relating to aircraft registration began to be relaxed. Permission was readily given for personalised marks to be issued incorporating virtually any four letter combination, while re-registration has also become a common feature, a practice almost unheard of in the past. In this book, where this has taken place at some time, the previous UK civil identity appears in parenthesis after the owner's/operator's name. An example of this is One-Eleven G-BBMG which originally carried G-AWEJ.

Some aircraft have also been allowed to wear military markings without displaying their civil identity. In this case the serial number actually carried is shown in parenthesis after the type's name. For example Mosquito G-ASKH flies as RR299 in RAF colours. As an aid to the identification of these machines, a military conversion list is provided.

Other factors caused a sudden acceleration in the number of registrations allocated by the Civil Aviation Authority in the early 1980s. The first surge came with the discovery that it was possible to register plastic bags and other items even less likely to fly, on payment of the standard fee. This erosion of the main register was checked in early 1982 by the issue of a special sequence for such devices commencing at G-FYAA. Powered hang-gliders provided the second glut of allocations as a result of the decision that these types should now be officially registered. Although a few of the early examples penetrated the normal in-sequence register, the vast majority were given marks in other special ranges, this time G-MBxx, G-MGxx, G-MJxx, G-MMxx, G-MNxx, G-MTxx, G-MVxx, G-MWxx, G-MYxx and G-MZxx. At first it was common practice for microlights to ignore the requirement to carry their official identity. However the vast majority now display their registration somewhere on the structure, the size and position depending on the dimensions of the component to which it is applied.

Throughout the UK section of this book, there are many instances where the probable base of the aircraft has been included. This is positioned at the end of the owner/operator details preceded by an oblique stroke. It must of course be borne in mind that changes do take place and that no attempt has been made to record the residents at the many private strips. The base of airline equipment has been given as the company's headquarter's airport, although frequently aircraft are outstationed for long periods.

Non-airworthy preserved aircraft are shown with a star after the type.

The three-letter codes used by airlines to prefix flight numbers are included for those carriers appearing in the book. Radio frequencies for the larger airfields/airports are also listed.

**Acknowledgements**
Once again thanks are extended to the Registration Department of the Civil Aviation Authority for its assistance and allowing access to its files. The comments and amendments flowing from Wal Gandy have as always proved of considerable value, while Richard Lawsey also contributed useful facts. The help given by numerous airlines or their information agencies has been much appreciated. The work of A. S. Wright and C. P. Wright during the update of this edition must not go unrecorded, since without it, deadlines would probably become impossible. **AJW**

# International Civil Aircraft Markings

| | | | |
|---|---|---|---|
| A2- | Botswana | OK- | Czech Republic & Slovakia |
| A3- | Tonga | OO- | Belgium |
| A5- | Bhutan | OY- | Denmark |
| A6- | United Arab Emirates | P- | Korea (North) |
| A7- | Qatar | P2- | Papua New Guinea |
| A9C- | Bahrain | P4- | Aruba |
| A40- | Oman | PH- | Netherlands |
| AP- | Pakistan | PJ- | Netherlands Antilles |
| B- | China/Taiwan | PK- | Indonesia and West Irian |
| BNMAU- | Mongolia | PP-, PT- | Brazil |
| C-F, C-G | Canada | PZ- | Surinam |
| C2- | Nauru | RA- | Russia |
| C3 | Andora | RDPL- | Laos |
| C5- | Gambia | RP- | Philippine Republic |
| C6- | Bahamas | S2- | Bangladesh |
| C9- | Mozambique | S7- | Seychelles |
| CC- | Chile | S9- | São Tomé |
| CCCP-* | C.I.S. (Ceased officially 1 Jan 1993) | SE- | Sweden |
| CN- | Morocco | SL- | Slovenia |
| CP- | Bolivia | SP- | Poland |
| CS- | Portugal | ST- | Sudan |
| CU- | Cuba | SU- | Egypt |
| CX- | Uruguay | SX- | Greece |
| D- | Germany | T2- | Tuvalu |
| D2- | Angola | T3- | Kiribati |
| D4 | Cape Verde Islands | T7- | San Marino |
| D6- | Comores Islands | TC- | Turkey |
| DQ- | Fiji | TF- | Iceland |
| EC- | Spain | TG- | Guatemala |
| EI- | Republic of Ireland | TI- | Costa Rica |
| EL- | Liberia | TJ- | United Republic of Cameroon |
| EP- | Iran | TL- | Central African Republic |
| ES | Estonia | TN- | Republic of Congo (Brazzaville) |
| ET- | Ethiopia | TR- | Gabon |
| F- | France, Colonies and Protectorates | TS- | Tunisia |
| G- | United Kingdom | TT- | Chad |
| H4- | Solomon Islands | TU- | Ivory Coast |
| HA- | Hungary | TY- | Benin |
| HB- | Switzerland and Liechtenstein | TZ- | Mali |
| HC- | Ecuador | UR- | Ukraine |
| HH- | Haiti | V2- | Antigua |
| HI- | Dominican Republic | V3- | Belize |
| HK- | Colombia | V5- | Namibia |
| HL- | Korea (South) | V8- | Brunei |
| HP- | Panama | VH- | Australia |
| HR- | Honduras | VN- | Vietnam |
| HS- | Thailand | VP-F | Falkland Islands |
| HV- | The Vatican | VP-LA | Anguilla |
| HZ- | Saudi Arabia | VP-LMA | Montserrat |
| I- | Italy | VP-LV | Virgin Islands |
| J2- | Djibouti | VQ-T | Turks & Caicos Islands |
| J3- | Grenada | VR-B | Bermuda |
| J5- | Guinea Bissau | VR-C | Cayman Islands |
| J6- | St Lucia | VR-G | Gibraltar |
| J7- | Dominica | VR-H | Hong Kong |
| J8- | St Vincent | VT- | India |
| JA- | Japan | XA-, XB-, | |
| JY- | Jordan | XC-, | Mexico |
| LN- | Norway | XT- | Burkina Faso |
| LV- | Argentine Republic | XU- | Kampuchea |
| LX- | Luxembourg | XY- | Myanmar |
| LY- | Lithuania | YA- | Afghanistan |
| LZ- | Bulgaria | YI- | Iraq |
| MI- | Marshall Islands | YJ- | Vanuatu |
| N- | United States of America | YK- | Syria |
| OB- | Peru | YL- | Latvia |
| OD- | Lebanon | YN- | Nicaragua |
| OE- | Austria | YR- | Romania |
| OH- | Finland | YS- | El Salvador |

| | | | | |
|---|---|---|---|---|
| YU- | Yugoslavia | | 5Y- | Kenya |
| YV- | Venezuela | | 6O- | Somalia |
| Z- | Zimbabwe | | 6V- | Senegal |
| ZA- | Albania | | 6Y- | Jamaica |
| ZK- | New Zealand | | 7O- | Yemen |
| ZP- | Paraguay | | 7P- | Lesotho |
| ZS- | South Africa | | 7Q- | Malawi |
| 3A- | Monaco | | 7T- | Algeria |
| 3B- | Mauritius | | 8P- | Barbados |
| 3C- | Equatorial Guinea | | 8Q- | Maldives |
| 3D- | Swaziland | | 8R- | Guyana |
| 3X- | Guinea | | 9A | Croatia |
| 4R- | Sri Lanka | | 9G- | Ghana |
| 4U | United Nations Organisation | | 9H- | Malta |
| 4X- | Israel | | 9J- | Zambia |
| 5A- | Libya | | 9K- | Kuwait |
| 5B- | Cyprus | | 9L- | Sierra Leone |
| 5H- | Tanzania | | 9M- | Malaysia |
| 5N- | Nigeria | | 9N- | Nepal |
| 5R- | Malagasy Republic (Madagascar) | | 9Q- | Zaïre |
| 5T- | Mauritania | | 9U- | Burundi |
| 5U- | Niger | | 9V- | Singapore |
| 5V- | Togo | | 9XR- | Rwanda |
| 5W- | Western Samoa (Polynesia) | | 9Y- | Trinidad and Tobago |
| 5X- | Uganda | | * Cyrillic letters for SSSR. |

# Aircraft Type Designations & Abbreviations

(eg PA-28 Piper Type 28)

| | | | | |
|---|---|---|---|---|
| A. | Beagle, Auster | | G.C. | Globe |
| AA- | American Aviation, Grumman American | | GY | Gardan |
| | | | H | Helio |
| AB | Agusta-Bell | | HM. | Henri Mignet |
| AG | American General | | HP. | Handley Page |
| AS | Aérospatiale | | HR. | Robin |
| A.S. | Airspeed | | H.S. | Hawker Siddeley |
| ATI | Aero Trasporti Italiani | | IL | Ilyushin |
| A.W. | Armstrong Whitworth | | IMCO | Intermountain Manufacturing Co |
| B. | Blackburn, Bristol Boeing, Beagle | | J. | Auster |
| | | | L. | Lockheed |
| BAC | British Aircraft Corporation | | L.A. | Luton |
| BAe | British Aerospace | | M. | Miles, Mooney |
| BAT | British Aerial Transport | | MBB | Messerschmitt-Bölkow-Blohm |
| B.K. | British Klemm | | MJ | Jurca |
| BN | Britten-Norman | | M.S. | Morane-Saulnier |
| Bo | Bolkow | | NA | North American |
| Bu | Bucker | | P. | Hunting (formerly Percival), Piaggio |
| CAARP | Co-operative des Ateliers Aer de la Région Parisienne | | PA- | Piper |
| | | | PC. | Pilatus |
| CCF | Canadian Car & Foundry Co | | QAC | Quickie Aircraft Co |
| C.H. | Chrislea | | R. | Rockwell |
| CHABA | Cambridge Hot-Air Ballooning Association | | RAFGSA | Royal Air Force Gliding & Soaring Association |
| CLA | Comper | | S. | Short, Sikorsky |
| CP. | Piel | | SA., SE, SO. | Sud-Aviation, Aérospatiale, Scottish Aviation |
| D. | Druine | | | |
| DC- | Douglas Commercial | | SC | Short |
| D.H. | de Havilland | | SCD | Side Cargo Door |
| D.H.C. | de Havilland Canada | | Soc | Society |
| DR. | Jodel (Robin-built) | | S.R. | Saunders-Roe, Stinson |
| EMB | Embraer | | ST | SOCATA |
| EoN | Elliotts of Newbury | | T. | Tipsy |
| EP | Edgar Percival | | TB | SOCATA |
| F. | Fairchild, Fokker | | Tu | Tupolev |
| FFA | Flug und Fahrzeugwerke AG | | UH. | United Helicopters (Hiller) |
| FH | Fairchild-Hiller | | UTA | Union de Transports Aérien |
| G. | Grumman | | V. | Vickers-Armstrongs, BAC |
| GA | Gulfstream American | | V.S. | Vickers-Supermarine |
| G.A.L. | General Aircraft | | WAR | War Aircraft Replicas |
| | | | W.S. | Westland |
| | | | Z. | Zlin |

G-AEZJ, P.10 Vega Gull. A/W

# British Civil Aircraft Registrations

| Reg. | Type (†False registration) | Owner or Operator | Notes |
|------|----------------------------|-------------------|-------|
| G-EACN | BAT BK23 Bantam (K123) ★ | Shuttleworth Trust/O. Warden | |
| G-EAGA | Sopwith Dove | R. H. Reeves | |
| G-EASD | Avro 504L | AJD Engineering Ltd | |
| G-EASQ | Bristol Babe (replica) (BAPC87) ★ | Bomber County Museum/Hemswell | |
| G-EAVX | Sopwith Pup (B1807) | K. A. M. Baker | |
| G-EBHX | D.H.53 Humming Bird | Shuttleworth Trust/O. Warden | |
| G-EBIA | RAF SE-5A (F904) | Shuttleworth Trust/O. Warden | |
| G-EBIB | RAF SE-5A (F939) ★ | Science Museum | |
| G-EBIC | RAF SE-5A (F938) ★ | RAF Museum | |
| G-EBIR | D.H.51 | Shuttleworth Trust/O. Warden | |
| G-EBJE | Avro 504K (E449)★ | RAF Museum | |
| G-EBJG | Parnall Pixie III ★ | Midland Aircraft Preservation Soc | |
| G-EBJO | ANEC II ★ | Shuttleworth Trust/O. Warden | |
| G-EBKY | Sopwith Pup (N5180) | Shuttleworth Trust/O. Warden | |
| G-EBLV | D.H.60 Cirrus Moth | British Aerospace/Hatfield | |
| G-EBMB | Hawker Cygnet I ★ | RAF Museum | |
| G-EBNV | English Electric Wren | Shuttleworth Trust/O. Warden | |
| G-EBQP | D.H.53 Humming Bird (J7326)★ | Russavia Collection | |
| G-EBWD | D.H.60X Hermes Moth | Shuttleworth Trust/O. Warden | |
| G-EBXU | D.H.60X Moth Seaplane | D. E. Cooper-Maguire | |
| G-EBYY | Cierva C.8L ★ | Musée de l'Air, Paris | |
| G-EBZM | Avro 594 Avian IIIA ★ | Greater Manchester Museum of Science & Technology | |
| G-EBZN | D.H.60X Moth | J. Hodgkinson (G-UAAP) | |
| G-AAAH | D.H.60G Gipsy Moth (replica) (BAPC 168) ★ | Hilton Hotel/Gatwick | |
| G-AAAH | D.H.60G Gipsy Moth Jason ★ | Science Museum | |
| G-AACN | H.P.39 Gugnunc ★ | Science Museum/Wroughton | |
| G-AADR | D.H.60GM Moth | H. F. Moffatt | |
| G-AAHY | D.H.60M Moth | M. E. Vaisey | |
| G-AAIN | Parnall Elf II | Shuttleworth Trust/O. Warden | |
| G-AAMX | D.H.60GM Moth | R. J. Parkhouse | |
| G-AAMY | D.H.60M Moth | R. M. Brooks | |
| G-AAMZ | D.H.60G Moth | C. C. & J. M. Lovell | |
| G-AANG | Blériot XI | Shuttleworth Trust/O. Warden | |
| G-AANH | Deperdussin Monoplane | Shuttleworth Trust/O. Warden | |
| G-AANI | Blackburn Monoplane | Shuttleworth Trust/O. Warden | |
| G-AANJ | L.V.G.-C VI (7198/18) | Shuttleworth Trust/O. Warden | |
| G-AANL | D.H.60M Moth | D. & P. Ellis | |
| G-AANM | Bristol 96A F.2B (D7889) | Aero Vintage Ltd | |
| G-AANO | D.H.60GMW Moth | A. W. & M. E. Jenkins | |
| G-AANV | D.H.60G Moth | R. I. Souch | |
| G-AAOK | Curtiss Wright Travel Air 12Q | Shipping & Airlines Ltd/Biggin Hill | |
| G-AAOR | D.H.60G Moth (EM-01) | J. A. Pothecary/Shoreham | |
| G-AAPZ | Desoutter I (mod.) ★ | Shuttleworth Trust/O. Warden | |
| G-AAUP | Klemm L.25-1A | J. I. Cooper | |
| G-AAVJ | D.H.60GMW Moth | R. M. Brooks | |
| G-AAWO | D.H.60G Gipsy Moth | N. J. W. Reid & L. A. Fenwick | |
| G-AAXK | Klemm L.25-1A | C. C. Russell-Vick (stored) | |
| G-AAYX | Southern Martlet | Shuttleworth Trust/O. Warden | |
| G-AAZP | D.H.80A Puss Moth | R. P. Williams | |
| G-ABAA | Avro 504K (H2311) ★ | Greater Manchester Museum of Science & Technology | |
| G-ABAG | D.H.60G Moth | Shuttleworth Trust/O. Warden | |
| G-ABDA | D.H.60G-III Moth Major | I. M. Castle | |
| G-ABDW | D.H.80A Puss Moth (VH-UQB) ★ | Museum of Flight/E. Fortune | |
| G-ABDX | D.H.60G Moth | M. D. Souch | |
| G-ABEE | Avro 594 Avian IVM (Sports) ★ | Aeroplane Collection Ltd | |
| G-ABEV | D.H.60G Moth | Wessex Aviation & Transport Ltd | |
| G-ABLM | Cierva C.24 ★ | Mosquito Aircraft Museum | |
| G-ABLS | D.H.80A Puss Moth | R. C. F. Bailey | |
| G-ABMR | Hart 2 (J9941)★ | RAF Museum | |
| G-ABNT | Civilian C.A.C.1 Coupe | Shipping & Airlines Ltd/Biggin Hill | |
| G-ABNX | Redwing 2 | J. Pothecary (stored) | |
| G-ABOI | Wheeler Slymph ★ | Midland Air Museum | |
| G-ABOX | Sopwith Pup (N5195) | Museum of Army Flying/Middle Wallop | |

| Notes | Reg. | Type | Owner or Operator |
|---|---|---|---|
| | G-ABSD | D.H.60G Moth | M. E. Vaisey |
| | G-ABTC | CLA.7 Swift | P. Channon (*stored*) |
| | G-ABUS | CLA.7 Swift | R. C. F. Bailey |
| | G-ABUL† | D.H.82A Tiger Moth ★ | FAA Museum (G-AOXG)/Yeovilton |
| | G-ABUU | CLA.7 Swift | H. B. Fox |
| | G-ABVE | Arrow Active 2 | J. D. Penrose |
| | G-ABWP | Spartan Arrow | R. E. Blain/Barton |
| | G-ABXL | Granger Archaeopteryx ★ | Shuttleworth Trust/O. Warden |
| | G-ABYN | Spartan Three Seater II | R. I. & J. O. Souch |
| | G-ABZB | D.H.60G-III Moth Major | R. E. & B. A. Ogden |
| | G-ACAA | Bristol 96A F.2B (D8084) | Patina Ltd/Duxford |
| | G-ACBH | Blackburn B.2 ★ | R. Coles |
| | G-ACCB | D.H.83 Fox Moth | E. A. Gautrey |
| | G-ACDA | D.H.82A Tiger Moth | R. J. Biddle |
| | G-ACDC | D.H.82A Tiger Moth | Tiger Club Ltd/Headcorn |
| | G-ACDJ | D.H.82A Tiger Moth | P. Henley & J. K. Moorhouse |
| | G-ACEJ | D.H.83 Fox Moth | J. I. Cooper |
| | G-ACET | D.H.84 Dragon | M. C. Russell |
| | G-ACGT | Avro 594 Avian IIIA ★ | Yorkshire Light Aircraft Ltd/Leeds |
| | G-ACIT | D.H.84 Dragon ★ | Science Museum/Wroughton |
| | G-ACLL | D.H.85 Leopard Moth | D. C. M. & V. M. Stiles |
| | G-ACMA | D.H.85 Leopard Moth | S. J. Filhol/Sherburn |
| | G-ACMD | D.H.82A Tiger Moth | J. A. Pothecary/Shoreham |
| | G-ACMN | D.H.85 Leopard Moth | H. D. Labouchere |
| | G-ACOJ | D.H.85 Leopard Moth | Aviation Heritage Ltd |
| | G-ACOL | D.H.85 Leopard Moth | M. J. Abbott |
| | G-ACSP | D.H.88 Comet | Saltair Ltd/Staverton |
| | G-ACSS | D.H.88 Comet | Shuttleworth Trust *Grosvenor House*/ Hatfield |
| | G-ACTF | CLA.7 Swift ★ | Brooklands Museum of Aviation/ Weybridge |
| | G-ACUS | D.H.85 Leopard Moth | T. P. A. Norman/Panshanger |
| | G-ACUU | Cierva C.30A (HM580)★ | G. S. Baker/Duxford |
| | G-ACUX | S.16 Scion (VH-UUP) ★ | Ulster Folk & Transport Museum |
| | G-ACVA | Kay Gyroplane★ | Glasgow Museum of Transport |
| | G-ACWM | Cierva C.30A ★ | International Helicopter Museum/ Weston-s-Mare |
| | G-ACWP | Cierva C.30A (AP507) ★ | Science Museum |
| | G-ACXB | D.H.60G-III Moth Major | D. F. Hodgkinson |
| | G-ACXE | B.K.L-25C Swallow | J. C. Wakeford |
| | G-ACYK | Spartan Cruiser III ★ | Museum of Flight (front fuselage)/ E. Fortune |
| | G-ACZE | D.H.89A Dragon Rapide | Wessex Aviation & Transport Ltd (G-AJGS)/Henstridge |
| | G-ADAH | D.H.89A Dragon Rapide ★ | Greater Manchester Museum of Science & Technology |
| | G-ADCG | D.H.82A Tiger Moth | A. J. Wilson & M. D. Lowe |
| | G-ADEV | Avro 504K (H5199) | Shuttleworth Trust (G-ACNB)/O. Warden |
| | G-ADFO | Blackburn B-2 ★ | R. Cole |
| | G-ADFV | Blackburn B-2 ★ | Humberside Aircraft Preservation Soc |
| | G-ADGP | M.2L Hawk Speed Six | R. I. Souch |
| | G-ADGT | D.H.82A Tiger Moth | D. R. & Mrs M. Wood |
| | G-ADGV | D.H.82A Tiger Moth | K. J. Whitehead |
| | G-ADHA | D.H.83 Fox Moth | Wessex Aviation & Transport Ltd |
| | G-ADHD | D.H.60G-III Moth Major | M. E. Vaisey |
| | G-ADIA | D.H.82A Tiger Moth | M. F. W. B. Maunsell/Goodwood |
| | G-ADJJ | D.H.82A Tiger Moth | J. M. Preston |
| | G-ADKC | D.H.87B Hornet Moth | L. E. Day/Carlisle |
| | G-ADKK | D.H.87B Hornet Moth | C. P. B. Horsley & R. G. Anniss |
| | G-ADKL | D.H.87B Hornet Moth | A. de Cadenet |
| | G-ADKM | D.H.87B Hornet Moth | L. V. Mayhead |
| | G-ADLY | D.H.87B Hornet Moth | R. M. Brooks |
| | G-ADMT | D.H.87B Hornet Moth | M. A. Livett |
| | G-ADMW | M.2H Hawk Major (DG590) ★ | Museum of Army Flying/Middle Wallop |
| | G-ADND | D.H.87B Hornet Moth | Shuttleworth Trust/O. Warden |
| | G-ADNE | D.H.87B Hornet Moth | Aviation Heritage Ltd |
| | G-ADNL | M.5 Sparrowhawk | K. D. Dunkerley |
| | G-ADNZ | D.H.82A Tiger Moth | C. A. Pullan |
| | G-ADOT | D.H.87B Hornet Moth ★ | Mosquito Aircraft Museum |
| | G-ADPC | D.H.82A Tiger Moth | N. J. Baker & J. Beattie |
| | G-ADPJ | B.A.C. Drone | N. H. Ponsford |

| Notes | Reg. | Type | Owner or Operator |
|---|---|---|---|
| | G-ADPR | P.3 Gull | Shuttleworth Trust *Jean*/O. Warden |
| | G-ADPS | B.A. Swallow 2 | Wessex Aviation & Transport Ltd |
| | G-ADRA | Pietenpol Air Camper | A. J. Mason |
| | G-ADRC | K. & S. Jungster J-1 | J. J. Penney & L. R. Williams |
| | G-ADRG† | Mignet HM.14 (replica) (BAPC77) ★ | Stratford Aircraft Collection |
| | G-ADRR | Aeronca C.3 | D. S. Morgan |
| | G-ADRY† | Mignet HM.14 (replica) (BAPC29) ★ | Brooklands Museum of Aviation/ Weybridge |
| | G-ADUR | D.H.87B Hornet Moth | Wessex Aviation & Transport Ltd |
| | G-ADWJ | D.H.82A Tiger Moth | C. R. Hardiman |
| | G-ADWO | D.H.82A Tiger Moth (BB807) | Wessex Aviation Soc |
| | G-ADXS | Mignet HM.14 ★ | Thameside Aviation Museum/E. Tilbury |
| | G-ADXT | D.H.82A Tiger Moth | R. G. Hanauer/Goodwood |
| | G-ADYS | Aeronca C.3 | B. C. Cooper |
| | | | |
| | G-AEBB | Mignet HM.14 ★ | Shuttleworth Trust/O. Warden |
| | G-AEBJ | Blackburn B-2 | British Aerospace PLC/Brough |
| | G-AEDB | B.A.C. Drone 2 | M. C. Russell |
| | G-AEDT | D.H.90 Dragonfly | Wessex Aviation & Transport Ltd |
| | G-AEDU | D.H.90 Dragonfly | T. P. A. Norman |
| | G-AEEG | M.3A Falcon | Skysport Engineering Ltd |
| | G-AEEH | Mignet HM.14 ★ | RAF Museum/St Athan |
| | G-AEFG | Mignet HM.14 (BAPC75) ★ | N. Ponsford |
| | G-AEFT | Aeronca C.3 | C. E. Humphreys & ptnrs/Henstridge |
| | G-AEGV | Mignet HM.14 ★ | Midland Aircraft Preservation Soc |
| | G-AEHM | Mignet HM.14 ★ | Science Museum/Wroughton |
| | G-AEJZ | Mignet HM.14 (BAPC120) ★ | Bomber County Museum/Hemswell |
| | G-AEKR | Mignet HM.14 (BAPC121) ★ | S. Yorks Aviation Soc |
| | G-AEKV | Kronfeld Drone ★ | Brooklands Museum of Aviation/ Weybridge |
| | G-AELO | D.H.87B Hornet Moth | D. E. Wells |
| | G-AEML | D.H.89 Dragon Rapide | Proteus Holdings Ltd |
| | G-AENP | Hawker Hind (K5414) (BAPC78) | Shuttleworth Trust/O. Warden |
| | G-AEOA | D.H.80A Puss Moth | P. & A. Wood/O. Warden |
| | G-AEOF† | Mignet HM.14 (BAPC22) ★ | Aviodome/Schiphol, Holland |
| | G-AEOF | Rearwin 8500 | Shipping & Airlines Ltd/Biggin Hill |
| | G-AEOH | Mignet HM.14 ★ | Midland Air Museum |
| | G-AEPH | Bristol F.2B (D8096) | Shuttleworth Trust/O. Warden |
| | G-AERV | M.11A Whitney Straight ★ | Ulster Folk & Transport Museum |
| | G-AESB | Aeronca C.3 | D. S. & I. M. Morgan |
| | G-AESE | D.H.87B Hornet Moth | J. G. Green/Redhill |
| | G-AESZ | Chilton D.W.1 | R. E. Nerou |
| | G-AETA | Caudron G.3 (3066) ★ | RAF Museum |
| | G-AEUJ | M.11A Whitney Straight | R. E. Mitchell |
| | G-AEVS | Aeronca 100 | A. J. E. Smith |
| | G-AEVZ | B. A. Swallow 2 | J. R. H. Ealand |
| | G-AEXD | Aeronca 100 | Mrs M. A. & R. W. Mills |
| | G-AEXF | P.6 Mew Gull | J. D. Penrose/Old Warden |
| | G-AEXT | Dart Kitten II | A. J. Hartfield |
| | G-AEXZ | Piper J-2 Cub | Mrs M. & J. R. Dowson/Leicester |
| | G-AEYY | Martin Monoplane ★ | Martin Monoplane Syndicate/Hatfield |
| | G-AEZF | S.16 Scion 2 ★ | Southend Historic Aircraft Soc |
| | G-AEZJ | P.10 Vega Gull | R. A. J. Spurrell/White Waltham |
| | G-AEZX | Bucker Bu133C Jungmeister | A. J. E. Ditheridge |
| | | | |
| | G-AFAP† | C.A.S.A. C.352L ★ | Aerospace Museum/Cosford |
| | G-AFAX | B. A. Eagle 2 | J. G. Green |
| | G-AFBS | M.14A Hawk Trainer ★ | G. D. Durbridge-Freeman (G-AKKU)/ Duxford |
| | G-AFCL | B. A. Swallow 2 | A. M. Dowson/O. Warden |
| | G-AFDO | Piper J-3F-60 Cub | R. Wald |
| | G-AFDX | Hanriot HD.1 (75) ★ | RAF Museum |
| | G-AFEL | Monocoupe 90A | Daryll Group |
| | G-AFFD | Percival Q-6 ★ | B. D. Greenwood |
| | G-AFFH | Piper J-2 Cub | M. J. Honeychurch |
| | G-AFFI | Mignet HM.14 (replica) (BAPC76) ★ | Yorkshire Air Museum/Elvington |
| | G-AFGC | B. A. Swallow 2 | H. Plain |
| | G-AFGD | B. A. Swallow 2 | A. T. Williams & ptnrs/Shobdon |
| | G-AFGE | B. A. Swallow 2 | G. R. French |
| | G-AFGH | Chilton D.W.1. | M. L. & G. L. Joseph |
| | G-AFGI | Chilton D.W.1. | J. E. McDonald |

## The Aviation Shop

Right on the terraces at Manchester Airport and the only one of its type, this Aladdin's cave sells everything the Enthusiast could wish for at very attractive prices. This is a shop run by enthusiasts for enthusiasts and all customers are warmly welcomed. Call, phone, or mail your orders. Visa and Access accepted. Just send a large SAE for our current list of main items to:

The Aviation Shop, Dept CM
Spectator Terraces,
Manchester Airport, Manchester M22 5SZ.
Phone:  061 499 0303   Fax:061 436 3030

## The Aviation Society

T.A.S offers **everything** an enthusiast could ever want!

The Society's exclusive monthly magazine *Winged Words* contains all Manchester movements, regular feature articles on civil and military, the most comprehensive SELCAL tie-up service etc. The fortnightly social meetings feature prominent aviation personalities, video presentations and much more.

T.A.S specialist low-cost flights and trips are World famous covering England, Europe and beyond. If you want the most out of your hobby you **MUST** join T.A.S! Just send an SAE to:

The Registrar, T.A.S. The Airport Tour Centre
———— Manchester Airport, Manchester M22 5SZ ————

| Notes | Reg. | Type | Owner or Operator |
|---|---|---|---|
| | G-AFGM | Piper J-4A Cub Coupé | A. J. P. Marshall/Carlisle |
| | G-AFGZ | D.H.82A Tiger Moth | M. R. Paul (G-AMHI) |
| | G-AFHA | Mosscraft M.A.1. ★ | C. V. Butler |
| | G-AFIN | Chrislea Airguard ★ | Aeroplane Collection Ltd |
| | G-AFIU | Parker C.A.4 Parasol (LA-3 Minor)★ | Aeroplane Collection Ltd/Warmingham |
| | G-AFJA | Watkinson Dingbat ★ | K. Woolley |
| | G-AFJB | Foster-Wikner G.M.1. Wicko (DR613) ★ | K. Woolley |
| | G-AFJR | Tipsy Trainer 1 | M. E. Vaisey (*Stored*) |
| | G-AFJV | Mosscraft MA.2 | C. V. Butler |
| | G-AFLW | M.17 Monarch | N. I. Dalziel/Biggin Hill |
| | G-AFNG | D.H.94 Moth Minor | T. E. G. Buckett & J. L. Phipps/ White Waltham |
| | G-AFNI | D.H.94 Moth Minor | B. M. Welford |
| | G-AFOB | D.H.94 Moth Minor | Wessex Aviation & Transport Ltd |
| | G-AFOJ | D.H.94 Moth Minor | Mosquito Aircraft Museum |
| | G-AFPN | D.H.94 Moth Minor | J. W. & A. R. Davy/Carlisle |
| | G-AFPR | D.H.94 Moth Minor | J. A. Livett |
| | G-AFRZ | M.17 Monarch | R. E. Mitchell (G-AIDE) |
| | G-AFSC | Tipsy Trainer 1 | R. V. & M. H. Smith |
| | G-AFSV | Chilton D.W.1A | R. Nerou |
| | G-AFSW | Chilton D.W.2 ★ | R. I. Souch |
| | G-AFTA | Hawker Tomtit (K1786) | Shuttleworth Trust/O. Warden |
| | G-AFTN | Taylorcraft Plus C2 | Leicestershire County Council Museums |
| | G-AFUP | Luscombe 8A Silvaire | Trust Me Airtours |
| | G-AFVE | D.H.82 Tiger Moth (T7230) | P. A. Shaw & M. R. Paul |
| | G-AFVN | Tipsy Trainer 1 | D. F. Lingard |
| | G-AFWH | Piper J-4A Cub Coupé | J. R. Edwards & D. D. Smith |
| | G-AFWI | D.H.82A Tiger Moth | E. Newbigin |
| | G-AFWT | Tipsy Trainer 1 | J. S. Barker/Redhill |
| | G-AFYD | Luscombe 8E Silvaire | J. D. Iliffe |
| | G-AFYO | Stinson H.W.75 | R. N. Wright |
| | G-AFZA | Piper J-4A Cub Coupé | J. R. Joiner & M. L. Ryan |
| | G-AFZE | Heath Parasol | K. C. D. St Cyrien |
| | G-AFZK | Luscombe 8A Silvaire | M. G. Byrnes |
| | G-AFZL | Porterfield CP.50 | P. G. Lucas & S. H. Sharpe/ White Waltham |
| | G-AFZN | Luscombe 8A Silvaire | A. L. Young/Henstridge |
| | G-AGAT | Piper J-3F-50 Cub | R. I. & J. O. Souch |
| | G-AGBN | G.A.L.42 Cygnet 2 ★ | Museum of Flight/E. Fortune |
| | G-AGEG | D.H.82A Tiger Moth | T. P. A. Norman |
| | G-AGFT | Avia FL.3 | P. A. Smith |
| | G-AGHY | D.H.82A Tiger Moth | P. Groves |
| | G-AGIV | Piper J-3C-65 Cub | P. C. & F. M. Gill |
| | G-AGJG | D.H.89A Dragon Rapide | M. J. & D. J. T. Miller/Duxford |
| | G-AGLK | Auster 5D | L. Colliver/Shoreham |
| | G-AGMI | Luscombe 8A Silvaire | Ebork Ltd |
| | G-AGNJ | D.H.82A Tiger Moth | B. P. Borsberry & ptnrs |
| | G-AGNV | Avro 685 York 1 (TS798) ★ | Aerospace Museum/Cosford |
| | G-AGOH | J/1 Autocrat | Leicestershire County Council Museums |
| | G-AGOS | R.S.4 Desford Trainer (VZ728) | Museum of Flight/E. Fortune |
| | G-AGOY | M.48 Messenger 3 (U-0247) | P. A. Brooks |
| | G-AGPG | Avro 19 Srs 2 ★ | Brenzett Aviation Museum |
| | G-AGPK | D.H.82A Tiger Moth | P. D. Castle |
| | G-AGRU | V.498 Viking 1A ★ | Brooklands Museum of Aviation/Weybridge |
| | G-AGSH | D.H.89A Dragon Rapide 6 | Venom Jet Promotions Ltd/Bournemouth |
| | G-AGTM | D.H.89A Dragon Rapide 6 (NF875) | Russavia Ltd |
| | G-AGTO | J/1 Autocrat | M. J. Barnett & D. J. T. Miller/Duxford |
| | G-AGTT | J/1 Autocrat | R. Farrer |
| | G-AGVG | J/1 Autocrat | S. J. Riddington/Leicester |
| | G-AGVN | J/1 Autocrat | R. J. Hirst |
| | G-AGVV | Piper J-3C-65 Cub | P. R. Lewis |
| | G-AGXN | J/1N Alpha | I. R. Walters/Cranwell |
| | G-AGXT | J/1N Alpha ★ | Nene Valley Aircraft Museum |
| | G-AGXU | J/1N Alpha | R. J. Guess/Sibson |
| | G-AGXV | J/1 Autocrat | B. S. Dowsett |
| | G-AGYD | J/1N Alpha | P. D. Hodson |
| | G-AGYH | J/1N Alpha | W. R. V. Marklew |
| | G-AGYK | J/1 Autocrat | D. A. Smith |
| | G-AGYL | J/1 Autocrat ★ | Military Vehicle Conservation Group |

| Reg. | Type | Owner or Operator | Notes |
|------|------|-------------------|-------|
| G-AGYT | J/1N Alpha | P. J. Barrett | |
| G-AGYU | DH.82A Tiger Moth (DE208) | A. Grimshaw | |
| G-AGYY | Ryan ST.3KR | D. S. & I. M. Morgan | |
| G-AGZZ | D.H.82A Tiger Moth | G. P. P. Shea-Simonds/Netheravon | |
| G-AHAL | J/1N Alpha | Wickenby Flying Club Ltd | |
| G-AHAM | J/1 Autocrat | P. J. Stock/Goodwood | |
| G-AHAN | D.H.82A Tiger Moth | A. J. Clarry & S. F. Bancroft/Redhill | |
| G-AHAP | J/1 Autocrat | V. H. Bellamy | |
| G-AHAU | J/1 Auto\crat | B. W. Webb | |
| G-AHAV | J/1 Autocrat | C. J. Freeman/Headcorn | |
| G-AHBL | D.H.87B Hornet Moth | Dr Ursula H. Hamilton | |
| G-AHBM | D.H.87B Hornet Moth | P. A. & E. P. Gliddon | |
| G-AHCK | J/1N Alpha | Skegness Air Taxi Service Ltd | |
| G-AHCL | J/1N Alpha | Electronic Precision Ltd (G-OJVC) | |
| G-AHCR | Gould-Taylorcraft Plus D Special | D. E. H. Balmford & D. R. Shepherd/Dunkeswell | |
| G-AHEC | Luscombe 8A Silvaire | Luscombe EC Group | |
| G-AHED | D.H.89A Dragon Rapide (RL962) ★ | RAF Museum Storage & Restoration Centre/Cardington | |
| G-AHGD | D.H.89A Dragon Rapide | R. Jones | |
| G-AHGW | Taylorcraft Plus D (LB375) | C. V. Butler/Coventry | |
| G-AHGZ | Taylorcraft Plus D | M. Pocock | |
| G-AHHH | J/1 Autocrat | H. A. Jones/Norwich | |
| G-AHHP | J/1N Alpha | D. J. Hutcheson (G-SIME) | |
| G-AHHT | J/1N Alpha | A. C. Barber & N. J. Hudson | |
| G-AHHU | J/1N Alpha ★ | L. Groves & I. R. F. Hammond | |
| G-AHIP | Piper J-3C-65 Cub | R. T. & D. H. Tanner | |
| G-AHIZ | D.H.82A Tiger Moth | C.F.G. Flying Ltd/Cambridge | |
| G-AHKX | Avro 19 Srs 2 | British Aerospace PLC/Woodford | |
| G-AHKY | Miles M.18 Series 2 | Museum of Flight/E. Fortune | |
| G-AHLI | Auster 3 | G. A. Leathers | |
| G-AHLK | Auster 3 | E. T. Brackenbury/Leicester | |
| G-AHLT | D.H.82A Tiger Moth | R. C. F. Bailey | |
| G-AHMJ | Cierva C.30A (K4235) ★ | Shuttleworth Trust/O. Warden | |
| G-AHMN | D.H.82A Tiger Moth (N6985) | Museum of Army Flying/Middle Wallop | |
| G-AHNR | Bucker Bu181 Bestmann | R. A. Anderson | |
| G-AHNR | Taylorcraft BC-12D | M. L. Balding & J. M. Oakins/Biggin Hill | |
| G-AHOO | D.H.82A Tiger Moth | G. W. Bisshopp | |
| G-AHRI | D.H.104 Dove 1 ★ | Newark Aviation Museum | |
| G-AHRO | Cessna 140 | R. H. Screen/Kidlington | |
| G-AHSA | Avro 621 Tutor (K3215) | Shuttleworth Trust/O. Warden | |
| G-AHSD | Taylorcraft Plus D | A. Tucker | |
| G-AHSO | J/1N Alpha | W. P. Miller | |
| G-AHSP | J/1 Autocrat | N. J. Hudson & A. C. Barber | |
| G-AHSS | J/1N Alpha | Felthorpe Auster Group | |
| G-AHST | J/1N Alpha | C. H. Smith | |
| G-AHTE | P.44 Proctor V | J. G. H. Hassell (stored) | |
| G-AHTW | A.S.40 Oxford (V3388) ★ | Skyfame Collection/Duxford | |
| G-AHUF | D.H.82A Tiger Moth | D. S. & I. M. Morgan | |
| G-AHUG | Taylorcraft Plus D | D. Nieman | |
| G-AHUI | M.38 Messenger 2A ★ | Berkshire Aviation Group | |
| G-AHUJ | M.14A Hawk Trainer 3 (R1914) | — | |
| G-AHUN | Globe GC-1B Swift | A. G. Craig | |
| G-AHUV | D.H.82A Tiger Moth | W. G. Gordon | |
| G-AHVU | D.H.82A Tiger Moth (T6313) | Foley Farm Flying Group | |
| G-AHVV | D.H.82A Tiger Moth | R. Jones | |
| G-AHWJ | Taylorcraft Plus D (LB294) | Museum of Army Flying/Middle Wallop | |
| G-AHXE | Taylorcraft Plus D (LB312) | J. Pothecary/Shoreham | |
| G-AIBE | Fulmar II (N1854) ★ | F.A.A. Museum/Yeovilton | |
| G-AIBH | J/1N Alpha | M. J. Bonnick | |
| G-AIBM | J/1 Autocrat | D. G. Greatrex | |
| G-AIBR | J/1 Autocrat | A. A. Marshall | |
| G-AIBW | J/1N Alpha | W. E. Bateson/Blackpool | |
| G-AIBX | J/1 Autocrat | Wasp Flying Group | |
| G-AIBY | J/1 Autocrat | D. Morris/Sherburn | |
| G-AICX | Luscombe 8A Silvaire | R. V. Smith/Henstridge | |
| G-AIDL | D.H.89A Dragon Rapide 6 | Snowdon Mountain Aviation Ltd | |
| G-AIDS | D.H.82A Tiger Moth | K. D. Pogmore & T. Dann | |
| G-AIEK | M.38 Messenger 2A (RG333) | J. Buckingham | |
| G-AIFZ | J/1N Alpha | C. P. Humphries | |

| Notes | Reg. | Type | Owner or Operator |
|---|---|---|---|
| | G-AIGD | J/1 Autocrat | R. B. Webber & P. K. Pike |
| | G-AIGF | J/1N Alpha | A. R. C. Mathie |
| | G-AIGM | J/1N Alpha | Wickenby Flying Club Ltd |
| | G-AIGT | J/1N Alpha | P. R. & J. S. Johnson |
| | G-AIGU | J/1N Alpha | N. K. Geddes |
| | G-AIIH | Piper J-3C-65 Cub | J. A. de Salis |
| | G-AIJI | J/1N Alpha ★ | C. J. Baker |
| | G-AIJM | Auster J/4 | N. Huxtable |
| | G-AIJR | Auster J/4 | B. A. Harris/Halfpenny Green |
| | G-AIJS | Auster J/4 ★ | *stored* |
| | G-AIJT | Auster J/4 srs 100 | Aberdeen Auster Flying Group |
| | G-AIJZ | J/1 Autocrat | *stored* |
| | G-AIKE | Auster 5 | C. J. Baker |
| | G-AIPR | Auster J/4 | MPM Flying Group/Booker |
| | G-AIPV | J/1 Autocrat | W. P. Miller |
| | G-AIPW | J/1 Autocrat | B. Hillman |
| | G-AIRC | J/1 Autocrat | R. C. Tebbett |
| | G-AIRI | D.H.82A Tiger Moth | E. R. Goodwin (*stored*) |
| | G-AIRK | D.H.82A Tiger Moth | R. C. Teverson & ptnrs |
| | G-AISA | Tipsy B Srs 1 | J. W. Thomson & R. P. Aston |
| | G-AISC | Tipsy B Srs 1 | Wagtail Flying Group |
| | G-AISS | Piper J-3C-65 Cub | K. W. Wood & F. Watson |
| | G-AIST | V.S.300 Spitfire IA (AR213) | Proteus Holdings Ltd/Goodwood |
| | G-AISX | Piper J-3C-65 Cub | V. Luck |
| | G-AITB | A.S.10 Oxford (MP425) ★ | Newark Air Museum |
| | G-AIUA | M.14A Hawk Trainer 3 | P. A. Brook |
| | G-AIUL | D.H.89A Dragon Rapide 6 | I. Jones |
| | G-AIXA | Taylorcraft Plus D | A. A. & M. J. Copse |
| | G-AIXD | D.H.82A Tiger Moth | Sark International Airways/Guernsey |
| | G-AIXJ | D.H.82A Tiger Moth | D. Green |
| | G-AIXN | Benes-Mraz M.1c Sokol | P. Knott |
| | G-AIYG | SNCAN Stampe SV-4B | J. F. Hopkins/Old Sarum |
| | G-AIYR | D.H.89A Dragon Rapide | Clacton Aero Club (1988) Ltd |
| | G-AIYS | D.H.85 Leopard Moth | Wessex Aviation & Transport Ltd |
| | G-AIZE | F.24W Argus 2 ★ | RAF Museum/Henlow |
| | G-AIZF | D.H.82A Tiger Moth ★ | *stored* |
| | G-AIZG | V.S. Walrus 1 (L2301) ★ | F.A.A. Museum/Yeovilton |
| | G-AIZU | J/1 Autocrat | C. J. & J. G. B. Morley |
| | G-AIZZ | J/1 Autocrat | M. J. Murphy |
| | | | |
| | G-AJAC | J/1N Alpha | N. J. Mortimore & H. A. Bridgman |
| | G-AJAD | Piper J-3C-65 Cub | R. A. C. Hoppenbrouwers |
| | G-AJAE | J/1N Alpha | M. G. Stops |
| | G-AJAJ | J/1N Alpha | R. B. Lawrence |
| | G-AJAM | J/2 Arrow | D. A. Porter |
| | G-AJAO | Piper J-3C-65 Cub | P. L. Jones |
| | G-AJAP | Luscombe 8A Silvaire | R. J. Thomas |
| | G-AJAS | J/1N Alpha | C. J. Baker |
| | G-AJCP | D.31 Turbulent | B. R. Pearson |
| | G-AJDW | J/1 Autocrat | D. R. Hunt |
| | G-AJDY | J/1 Autocrat | Truck Panels Ltd |
| | G-AJEB | J/1N Alpha ★ | Aeroplane Collection Ltd/Warmingham |
| | G-AJEE | J/1 Autocrat | A. R. C. De Albanoz/Bournemouth |
| | G-AJEH | J/1N Alpha | J. T. Powell-Tuck |
| | G-AJEI | J/1N Alpha | W. P. Miller |
| | G-AJEM | J/1 Autocrat | J. C. Greenslade |
| | G-AJES | Piper J-3C-65 Cub (330485) | D. Silsbury |
| | G-AJGJ | Auster 5 (RT486) | S. C. Challis |
| | G-AJHJ | Auster 5 | *stored* |
| | G-AJHS | D.H.82A Tiger Moth | S. R. N. Higgins/Holland |
| | G-AJHU | D.H.82A Tiger Moth | M. E. R. Coghlan |
| | G-AJIH | J/1 Autocrat | T. Boyd & A. H. Diver |
| | G-AJIS | J/1N Alpha | K. J. Slattery |
| | G-AJIT | J/1 Kingsland Autocrat | A. J. Kay |
| | G-AJIU | J/1 Autocrat | W. Greenhalgh & Son Ltd/Doncaster |
| | G-AJIW | J/1N Alpha | N. A. Roberts |
| | G-AJJP | Jet Gyrodyne (XJ389) ★ | Aerospace Museum/Cosford |
| | G-AJJS | Cessna 120 | Robhurst Flying Group |
| | G-AJJT | Cessna 120 | J. S. Robson |
| | G-AJJU | Luscombe 8E Silvaire | L. C. Moon |
| | G-AJKB | Luscombe 8E Silvaire | A. F. Hall & P. S. Hatwell/Ipswich |
| | G-AJOA | D.H.82A Tiger Moth (T5424) | F. P. Le Coyte |
| | G-AJOC | M.38 Messenger 2A ★ | Ulster Folk & Transport Museum |

| Reg. | Type | Owner or Operator | Notes |
|------|------|-------------------|-------|
| G-AJOE | M.38 Messenger 2A | Cotswold Aircraft Restoration Group | |
| G-AJON | Aeronca 7AC Champion | A. Biggs & J. L. Broad/Booker | |
| G-AJOV† | Sikorsky S-51 ★ | Aerospace Museum/Cosford | |
| G-AJOZ | F.24W Argus 2 ★ | Lincolnshire Aviation Museum | |
| G-AJPI | F.24R-41a Argus 3 (314887) | M. R. Keen/Liverpool | |
| G-AJPZ | J/1 Autocrat ★ | Wessex Aviation Soc | |
| G-AJRB | J/1 Autocrat | S. C. Luck/Sywell | |
| G-AJRC | J/1 Autocrat | S. W. Watkins & ptnrs | |
| G-AJRE | J/1 Autocrat (Lycoming) | T. A. Hodges | |
| G-AJRH | J/1N Alpha | Leicestershire County Council Museums | |
| G-AJRS | M.14A Hawk Trainer 3 (P6382) | Shuttleworth Trust/O. Warden | |
| G-AJTW | D.H.82A Tiger Moth (N6965) | J. A. Barker | |
| G-AJUD | J/1 Autocrat | C. L. Sawyer | |
| G-AJUE | J/1 Autocrat | P. H. B. Cole | |
| G-AJUL | J/1N Alpha | M. J. Crees | |
| G-AJVE | D.H.82A Tiger Moth | Red Baron Aviation Ltd/Shipdham | |
| G-AJXC | Auster 5 | J. E. Graves | |
| G-AJXV | Auster 4 (NJ695) | B. A. Farries/Leicester | |
| G-AJXY | Auster 4 | G. B. Morris | |
| G-AJYB | J/1N Alpha | P. J. Shotbolt | |
| | | | |
| G-AKAA | Piper J-3C-65 Cub | G. J. C. Ball | |
| G-AKAT | M.14A Magister (T9738) | A. J. E. Smith | |
| G-AKAZ | Piper J-3C-65 Cub | AKAZ Group | |
| G-AKBM | M.38 Messenger 2A ★ | Bristol Plane Preservation Unit | |
| G-AKBO | M.38 Messenger 2A | B. du Cros | |
| G-AKDN | D.H.C. 1A Chipmunk 10 | D. S. Backhouse | |
| G-AKEL | M.65 Gemini 1A ★ | Ulster Folk & Transport Museum | |
| G-AKER | M.65 Gemini 1A ★ | Berkshire Aviation Group | |
| G-AKEZ | M.38 Messenger 2A (RG333) | P. G. Lee | |
| G-AKGD | M.65 Gemini 1A ★ | Berkshire Aviation Group | |
| G-AKGE | M.65 Gemini 3C ★ | Ulster Folk & Transport Museum | |
| G-AKHP | M.65 Gemini 1A | P. G. Lee | |
| G-AKHZ | M.65 Gemini 7 ★ | Berkshire Aviation Group | |
| G-AKIB | Piper J-3C-90 Cub (480015) | M. C. Bennett | |
| G-AKIF | D.H.89A Dragon Rapide | Airborne Taxi Services Ltd/Booker | |
| G-AKIN | M.38 Messenger 2A | R. Spiller & Sons/Sywell | |
| G-AKIU | P.44 Proctor V | J. N. Sharman | |
| G-AKKB | M.65 Gemini 1A | J. Buckingham | |
| G-AKKH | M.65 Gemini 1A | M. C. Russell | |
| G-AKKR | M.14A Magister (T9707) ★ | Greater Manchester Museum of Science & Technology | |
| G-AKKY | M.14A Hawk Trainer 3 (L6906) (BAPC44) ★ | Berkshire Aviation Group/Woodley | |
| G-AKLW | SA.6 Sealand 1 ★ | Ulster Folk & Transport Museum | |
| G-AKOE | D.H.89A Dragon Rapide 4 | J. E. Pierce/Chirk | |
| G-AKOT | Auster 5 ★ | C. J. Baker | |
| G-AKOW | Auster 5 (TJ569) ★ | Museum of Army Flying/Middle Wallop | |
| G-AKPF | M.14A Hawk Trainer 3 (V1075) | P. A. Brook/Shoreham | |
| G-AKPI | Auster 5 (NJ703) | B. H. Hargrave/Doncaster | |
| G-AKRA | Piper J-3C-65 Cub | W. R. Savin | |
| G-AKSY | Auster 5 | Aerofab Flying Group | |
| G-AKSZ | Auster 5 | A. R. C. Mathie | |
| G-AKTH | Piper J-3C-65 Cub | A. L. Wickens | |
| G-AKTI | Luscombe 8A Silvaire | N. C. W. N. Lester | |
| G-AKTK | Aeronca 11AC Chief | N. G. Gullis | |
| G-AKTM | Luscombe 8F Silvaire | B. Bayley | |
| G-AKTN | Luscombe 8A Silvaire | R. G. Morris | |
| G-AKTO | Aeronca 7AC Champion | D. C. Murray | |
| G-AKTP | PA-17 Vagabond | L. A. Maynard | |
| G-AKTR | Aeronca 7AC Champion | C. & G. Fielder | |
| G-AKTS | Cessna 120 | J. Greenaway | |
| G-AKTT | Luscombe 8A Silvaire | S. J. Charters | |
| G-AKUE | D.H.82A Tiger Moth | D. F. Hodgkinson | |
| G-AKUF | Luscombe 8A Silvaire | A. G. Palmer | |
| G-AKUG | Luscombe 8A Silvaire | P. & L. A. Groves | |
| G-AKUH | Luscombe 8E Silvaire | I. M. Bower | |
| G-AKUI | Luscombe 8E Silvaire | J. A. Pothecary | |
| G-AKUJ | Luscombe 8E Silvaire | D. Delaney & C. L. Cooper | |
| G-AKUK | Luscombe 8A Silvaire | Leckhampstead Flying Group | |
| G-AKUL | Luscombe 8A Silvaire | E. A. Taylor | |
| G-AKUM | Luscombe 8F Silvaire | R. J. Willies | |
| G-AKUN | Piper J-3F-65 Cub | W. A. Savin | |

| Notes | Reg. | Type | Owner or Operator |
|---|---|---|---|
| | G-AKUO | Aeronca 11AC Chief | KUO Flying Group/White Waltham |
| | G-AKUP | Luscombe 8E Silvaire | R. J. Williams |
| | G-AKUR | Cessna 140 | P. Power & L. P. Z. Yelland |
| | G-AKUW | C.H.3 Super Ace | D. R. Bean |
| | G-AKVF | C.H.3 Super Ace | P. V. B. Longthorp/Bodmin |
| | G-AKVM | Cessna 120 | C120 Group/Norwich |
| | G-AKVN | Aeronca 11AC Chief | S. R. Napthen & J. Moore |
| | G-AKVO | Taylorcraft BC-12D | R. J. Whybrow & S. R. Roberts |
| | G-AKVP | Luscombe 8A Silvaire | R. M. Shipp |
| | G-AKVZ | M.38 Messenger 4B | Shipping & Airlines Ltd/Biggin Hill |
| | G-AKWS | Auster 5-160 | J. E. Homewood |
| | G-AKWT | Auster 5 ★ | Loughborough & Leicester Aircraft Preservation Soc |
| | G-AKXP | Auster 5 | F. E. Telling & G. R. Attwell |
| | G-AKXS | D.H.82A Tiger Moth | P. A. Colman |
| | G-AKZN | P.34A Proctor 3 (Z7197) ★ | RAF Museum/St Athan |
| | G-ALAH | M.38 Messenger 4A (RH377) ★ | RAF Museum/Henlow |
| | G-ALAX | D.H.89A Dragon Rapide ★ | Durney Aeronautical Collection/Andover |
| | G-ALBJ | Auster 5 | P. N. Elkington |
| | G-ALBK | Auster 5 | S. J. Wright & Co (Farmers) Ltd |
| | G-ALBN | Bristol 173 (XF785) ★ | RAF Museum/Henlow |
| | G-ALCK | P.34A Proctor 3 (LZ766) ★ | Skyfame Collection/Duxford |
| | G-ALCS | M.65 Gemini 3C ★ | Stored |
| | G-ALCU | D.H.104 Dove 2 ★ | Midland Air Museum/Coventry |
| | G-ALDG | HP.81 Hermes 4 ★ | Duxford Aviation Soc (Fuselage only) |
| | G-ALEH | PA-17 Vagabond | A. D. Pearce/Redhill |
| | G-ALFA | Auster 5 | H&B Auster Group |
| | G-ALFM | D.H.104 Devon C.2 | C. Charalambous |
| | G-ALFT | D.H.104 Dove 6 ★ | Snowdon Mountain Aviation Museum |
| | G-ALFU | D.H.104 Dove 6 ★ | Duxford Aviation Soc |
| | G-ALGA | PA-15 Vagabond | M. J. Markey/Biggin Hill |
| | G-ALIJ | PA-17 Vagabond | Popham Flying Group/Popham |
| | G-ALIW | D.H.82A Tiger Moth | D. I. M. Geddes & F. Curry/Booker |
| | G-ALJF | P.34A Proctor 3 | J. F. Moore/Biggin Hill |
| | G-ALJL | D.H.82A Tiger Moth | C. G. Clarke |
| | G-ALLF | Slingsby T.31A Kirby Prefect | N. J. Churcher |
| | G-ALNA | D.H.82A Tiger Moth | P. D. Castle |
| | G-ALND | D.H.82A Tiger Moth (N9191) | J. T. Powell-Tuck |
| | G-ALNV | Auster 5 ★ | stored |
| | G-ALOD | Cessna 140 | J. R. Stainer |
| | G-ALRH | EoN Type 8 Baby (AST) | P. D. Moran/Chipping |
| | G-ALRI | D.H.82A Tiger Moth (T5672) | Wessex Aviation & Transport Ltd |
| | G-ALSP | Bristol 171 (WV783) Sycamore ★ | RN Fleetlands Museum |
| | G-ALSS | Bristol 171 (WA576) Sycamore ★ | E. Fortune |
| | G-ALST | Bristol 171 (WA577) Sycamore ★ | N.E. Aircraft Museum/Usworth |
| | G-ALSW | Bristol 171 (WT933) Sycamore ★ | Newark Air Museum |
| | G-ALSX | Bristol 171 (G-48-1) Sycamore ★ | International Helicopter Museum/ Weston-s-Mare |
| | G-ALTO | Cessna 140 | J. P. Bell |
| | G-ALTW | D.H.82A Tiger Moth ★ | A. Mangham |
| | G-ALUC | D.H.82A Tiger Moth | D. R. & M. Wood/Shipdham |
| | G-ALVP | D.H.82A Tiger Moth ★ | V. & R. Wheele (stored) |
| | G-ALWB | D.H.C.1 Chipmunk 22A | M. L. & J. M. Soper/Perth |
| | G-ALWF | V.701 Viscount ★ | Viscount Preservation Trust RMA Sir John Franklin/Duxford |
| | G-ALWS | D.H.82A Tiger Moth ★ | Air Service Training Ltd/Perth |
| | G-ALWW | D.H.82A Tiger Moth ★ | F. W. Fay & ptnrs |
| | G-ALXT | D.H.89A Dragon Rapide ★ | Science Museum/Wroughton |
| | G-ALXZ | Auster 5-150 | B. J. W. Thomas & R. A. E. Witheridge |
| | G-ALYB | Auster 5 (RT520)★ | S. Yorks Aircraft Preservation Soc |
| | G-ALYG | Auster 5D | A. L. Young/Henstridge |
| | G-ALYW | D.H.106 Comet 1 ★ | RAF Exhibition Flight (fuselage converted to Nimrod) |
| | G-ALZE | BN-1F ★ | M. R. Short/Southampton Hall of Aviation |
| | G-ALZO | A.S.57 Ambassador★ | Duxford Aviation Soc |
| | G-AMAW | Luton LA-4 Minor | R. H. Coates |
| | G-AMBB | D.H.82A Tiger Moth | J. Eagles |
| | G-AMCA | Dakota 3 | Air Atlantique Ltd/Coventry |
| | G-AMCK | D.H.82A Tiger Moth | D. L. Frankel |
| | G-AMCM | D.H.82A Tiger Moth | G. C. Masterton |
| | G-AMDA | Avro 652A Anson 1 (N4877)★ | Skyfame Collection/Duxford |

| Reg. | Type | Owner or Operator | Notes |
|------|------|-------------------|-------|
| G-AMEN | PA-18 Super Cub 95 | A. Lovejoy & W. Cook | |
| G-AMHF | D.H.82A Tiger Moth | A. J. West | |
| G-AMHJ | Dakota 6 | Air Atlantique Ltd/Coventry | |
| G-AMIU | D.H.82A Tiger Moth | R. & Mrs J. L. Jones | |
| G-AMKU | J/1B Aiglet | Southdown Flying Group (stored) | |
| G-AMLZ | P.50 Prince 6E ★ | J. F. Coggins/Coventry | |
| G-AMMS | J/5F Aiglet Trainer | A. J. Large | |
| G-AMNN | D.H.82A Tiger Moth | M. Thrower/Shoreham | |
| G-AMOG | V.701 Viscount ★ | Aerospace Museum/Cosford | |
| G-AMOU | D.H.82A Tiger Moth (T6269) | Fortress Wastecare (Spa) Ltd | |
| G-AMPG | PA-12 Super Cruiser | R. Simpson | |
| G-AMPI | SNCAN Stampe SV-4C | J. Hewett | |
| G-AMPO | Dakota 4 | Air Atlantique Ltd/Coventry | |
| G-AMPP | Dakota 3 (G-AMSU) ★ | Aces High Ltd/North Weald | |
| G-AMPY | Dakota 4 | Air Atlantique Ltd/Coventry | |
| G-AMPZ | Dakota 4 | Air Atlantique Ltd/Coventry | |
| G-AMRA | Dakota 6 | Air Atlantique Ltd/Coventry | |
| G-AMRF | J/5F Aiglet Trainer | A. I. Topps/E. Midlands | |
| G-AMRK | G.37 Gladiator I (N2308) | Shuttleworth Trust/O. Warden | |
| G-AMSG | SIPA 903 | S. W. Markham | |
| G-AMSV | Dakota 4 | Air Atlantique Ltd/Coventry | |
| G-AMTA | J/5F Aiglet Trainer | H. J. Jauncey/Rochester | |
| G-AMTD | J/5F Aiglet Trainer | Leicestershire Aero Club Ltd | |
| G-AMTK | D.H.82A Tiger Moth | S. W. McKay & M. E. Vaisey | |
| G-AMTM | J/1 Autocrat | R. Stobo & D. Clewley | |
| G-AMTV | D.H.82A Tiger Moth | K. J. Slattery | |
| G-AMUF | D.H.C.1 Chipmunk 21 | Redhill Tailwheel Flying Club Ltd | |
| G-AMUI | J/5F Aiglet Trainer | D. P. Copse | |
| G-AMVD | Auster 5 | R. F. Tolhurst | |
| G-AMVP | Tipsy Junior | A. R. Wershat | |
| G-AMVS | D.H.82A Tiger Moth | J. T. Powell-Tuck | |
| G-AMXP | D.H.104 Sea Devon C.20 | M. A. Knowles | |
| G-AMXT | D.H.104 Sea Devon C.20 | W. Gentle & P. C. Gill | |
| G-AMYA | Zlin Z.381 | D. M. Fenton | |
| G-AMYD | J/5L Aiglet Trainer | G. H. Maskell | |
| G-AMYJ | Dakota 6 | Air Atlantique Ltd/Coventry | |
| G-AMYL | PA-17 Vagabond | P. J. Penn-Sayers/Shoreham | |
| G-AMZI | J/5F Aiglet Trainer | J. F. Moore/Biggin Hill | |
| G-AMZT | J/5F Aiglet Trainer | D. Hyde & J. W. Saull/Cranfield | |
| G-AMZU | J/5F Aiglet Trainer | J. A. Longworth & ptnrs | |
| | | | |
| G-ANAF | Dakota 3 | Air Atlantique Ltd/Coventry | |
| G-ANAP | D.H.104 Dove 6 ★ | Brunel Technical College/Lulsgate | |
| G-ANCF | B.175 Britannia 308 ★ | Proteus Aero Services | |
| G-ANCS | D.H.82A Tiger Moth (R4907) | P. G. Wright | |
| G-ANCX | D.H.82A Tiger Moth | D. R. Wood/Biggin Hill | |
| G-ANDE | D.H.82A Tiger Moth | The Vintage Aeroplane Co Ltd | |
| G-ANDM | D.H.82A Tiger Moth | J. G. Green | |
| G-ANDP | D.H.82A Tiger Moth | A. H. Diver | |
| G-ANDX | D.H.104 Devon C.2 | L. Richards | |
| G-ANEC | D.H.82A Tiger Moth ★ | (stored) | |
| G-ANEF | D.H.82A Tiger Moth (T5493) | RAF College Flying Club Co Ltd/Cranwell | |
| G-ANEH | D.H.82A Tiger Moth | P. L. Gaze | |
| G-ANEL | D.H.82A Tiger Moth | Chauffair Ltd | |
| G-ANEM | D.H.82A Tiger Moth | P. J. Benest (stored) | |
| G-ANEN | D.H.82A Tiger Moth | M. D. Souch | |
| G-ANEW | D.H.82A Tiger Moth | A. L. Young | |
| G-ANEZ | D.H.82A Tiger Moth | C. D. J. Bland & T. S. Warren/Sandown | |
| G-ANFC | D.H.82A Tiger Moth (DE363) | H. J. Jauncey | |
| G-ANFH | Westland S-55 ★ | International Helicopter Museum/ Weston-s-Mare | |
| G-ANFI | D.H.82A Tiger Moth (DE623) | G. P. Graham | |
| G-ANFL | D.H.82A Tiger Moth | R. P. Whitby & ptnrs | |
| G-ANFM | D.H.82A Tiger Moth | S. A. Brook & ptnrs/Booker | |
| G-ANFP | D.H.82A Tiger Moth ★ | Mosquito Aircraft Museum | |
| G-ANFU | Auster 5 (NJ719)★ | N.E. Aircraft Museum | |
| G-ANFV | D.H.82A Tiger Moth (DF155) | R. A. L. Falconer | |
| G-ANFW | D.H.82A Tiger Moth | G. M. Fraser/Denham | |
| G-ANGK | Cessna 140A | D. W. Munday | |
| G-ANHK | D.H.82A Tiger Moth | J. D. Iliffe | |
| G-ANHR | Auster 5 | C. G. Winch | |
| G-ANHS | Auster 4 | Tango Uniform Group | |
| G-ANHU | Auster 4 | D. J. Baker (stored) | |

| Notes | Reg. | Type | Owner or Operator |
|---|---|---|---|
| | G-ANHX | Auster 5D | D. J. Baker |
| | G-ANHZ | Auster 5 (TW384) | D. W. Pennell |
| | G-ANIE | Auster 5 (TW467) | S. J. Partridge |
| | G-ANIJ | Auster 5D (TJ672) | M. Pocock & R. Eastmann |
| | G-ANIS | Auster 5 | J. Clarke-Cockburn |
| | G-ANJA | D.H.82A Tiger Moth (N9389) | J. J. Young |
| | G-ANJD | D.H.82A Tiger Moth | H. J. Jauncey/(stored) |
| | G-ANJK | D.H.82A Tiger Moth | A. D. Williams |
| | G-ANJV | W.S.55 Whirlwind 3 (VR-BET)★ | International Helicopter Museum/ Weston-s-Mare |
| | G-ANKK | D.H.82A Tiger Moth (T5854) | Halfpenny Green Tiger Group |
| | G-ANKT | D.H.82A Tiger Moth (T6818) | Shuttleworth Trust/O. Warden |
| | G-ANKZ | D.H.82A Tiger Moth (N6466) | R. Stephens |
| | G-ANLD | D.H.82A Tiger Moth | K. Peters |
| | G-ANLH | D.H.82A Tiger Moth | Wessex Aviation & Transport Ltd |
| | G-ANLS | D.H.82A Tiger Moth | P. A. Gliddon |
| | G-ANLU | Auster 5 | S. C. Challis & G. Guinn |
| | G-ANLW | W.B.1. Widgeon (MD497) ★ | Wilkie Museum Collection/Blackpool |
| | G-ANLX | D.H.82A Tiger Moth | B. J. Borsberry & ptnrs |
| | G-ANMO | D.H.82A Tiger Moth | E. Lay |
| | G-ANMV | D.H.82A Tiger Moth (T7404) | J. W. Davy/Cardiff |
| | G-ANMY | D.H.82A Tiger Moth | D. J. Elliott |
| | G-ANNB | D.H.82A Tiger Moth | Cormack (Aircraft Services) Ltd |
| | G-ANNG | D.H.82A Tiger Moth | P. F. Walter |
| | G-ANNI | D.H.82A Tiger Moth | A. R. Brett |
| | G-ANNK | D.H.82A Tiger Moth | P. J. Wilcox/Cranfield |
| | G-ANNN | D.H.82A Tiger Moth | T. Pate |
| | G-ANOA | Hiller UH-12A ★ | Redhill Technical College |
| | G-ANOD | D.H.82A Tiger Moth | P. G. Watson |
| | G-ANOH | D.H.82A Tiger Moth | N. Parkhouse/White Waltham |
| | G-ANOK | Saab S.91C Safir ★ | A. F. Galt & Co (stored) |
| | G-ANOM | D.H.82A Tiger Moth | P. A. Colman |
| | G-ANON | D.H.82A Tiger Moth (T7909) | A. C. Mercer/Sherburn |
| | G-ANOO | D.H.82A Tiger Moth | R. K. Packman |
| | G-ANOR | D.H.82A Tiger Moth (T6991) | C. L. Keith-Lucas & Aero Vintage Ltd |
| | G-ANOV | D.H.104 Dove 6 ★ | Museum of Flight/E. Fortune |
| | G-ANPE | D.H.82A Tiger Moth | I. E. S. Huddleston (G-IESH) |
| | G-ANPK | D.H.82A Tiger Moth | The D. & P. Group |
| | G-ANPP | P.34A Proctor 3 | C. P. A. & J. Jeffery |
| | G-ANRF | D.H.82A Tiger Moth | C. D. Cyster |
| | G-ANRM | D.H.82A Tiger Moth | Clacton Aero Club (1988) Ltd & A. B. Cutting |
| | G-ANRN | D.H.82A Tiger Moth | J. J. V. Elwes |
| | G-ANRP | Auster 5 (TW439) | C. T. K. Lane |
| | G-ANRS | V.372 Viscount ★ | Wales Aircraft Museum/Cardiff |
| | G-ANRX | D.H.82A Tiger Moth ★ | Mosquito Aircraft Museum |
| | G-ANSM | D.H.82A Tiger Moth | J. L. Bond |
| | G-ANTE | D.H.82A Tiger Moth | T. I. Sutton & B. J. Champion/Chester |
| | G-ANTK | Avro 685 York ★ | Duxford Aviation Soc |
| | G-ANTS | D.H.82A Tiger Moth (N6532) | J. G. Green |
| | G-ANUO | D.H.114 Heron 2D | Avtech Ltd/Biggin Hill |
| | G-ANUW | D.H.104 Dove 6 ★ | (stored)/Stansted |
| | G-ANWB | D.H.C.1 Chipmunk 21 | G. Briggs/Blackpool |
| | G-ANWO | M.14A Hawk Trainer 3 ★ | P. A. Brook |
| | G-ANWX | J/5L Aiglet Trainer | L. P. Mullins |
| | G-ANXB | D.H.114 Heron 1B ★ | Newark Air Museum |
| | G-ANXC | J/5R Alpine | C. J. Repek & ptnrs |
| | G-ANXR | P.31C Proctor 4 (RM221) | L. H. Oakins/Biggin Hill |
| | G-ANYP | P.31C Proctor 4 (NP184) | R. A. Anderson |
| | G-ANZJ | P.31C Proctor 4 (NP303) ★ | A. Hillyard |
| | G-ANZT | Thruxton Jackaroo | D. J. Neville & P. A. Dear |
| | G-ANZU | D.H.82A Tiger Moth | P. A. Jackson |
| | G-ANZZ | D.H.82A Tiger Moth | D. L. Frankel |
| | G-AOAA | D.H.82A Tiger Moth | R. C. P. Brookhouse |
| | G-AOAR | P.31C Proctor 4 (NP181) ★ | Historic Aircraft Preservation Soc |
| | G-AOBG | Somers-Kendall SK.1 ★ | stored |
| | G-AOBH | D.H.82A Tiger Moth (T7997) | D. S. & I. M. Morgan |
| | G-AOBJ | D.H.82A Tiger Moth | D. H. R. Jenkins |
| | G-AOBO | D.H.82A Tiger Moth | P. A. Brook |
| | G-AOBU | P.84 Jet Provost | T. J. Manna |
| | G-AOBV | J/5P Autocar | P. E. Champney |
| | G-AOBX | D.H.82A Tiger Moth | P. G. Watson |

| Reg. | Type | Owner or Operator | Notes |
|------|------|-------------------|-------|
| G-AOCP | Auster 5 ★ | C. Baker (stored) | |
| G-AOCR | Auster 5D | J. M. Edis | |
| G-AOCU | Auster 5 | S. J. Ball/Leicester | |
| G-AODA | Westland S-55 Srs 3 | Bristow Helicopters Ltd | |
| G-AODT | D.H.82A Tiger Moth | A. H. Warminger | |
| G-AOEH | Aeronca 7AC Champion | R. P. Clark | |
| G-AOEI | D.H.82A Tiger Moth | C.F.G. Flying Ltd/Cambridge | |
| G-AOEL | D.H.82A Tiger Moth ★ | Museum of Flight/E. Fortune | |
| G-AOES | D.H.82A Tiger Moth | A. Twemlow & G. A. Cordery | |
| G-AOET | D.H.82A Tiger Moth | Venom Jet Promotions Ltd/Bournemouth | |
| G-AOEX | Thruxton Jackaroo | A. T. Christian | |
| G-AOFE | D.H.C.1 Chipmunk 22A (WB702) | R. A. Roberts | |
| G-AOFM | J/5P Autocar | N. P. Beaumont | |
| G-AOFS | J/5L Aiglet Trainer | P. N. A. Whitehead | |
| G-AOGA | M.75 Aries ★ | Irish Aviation Museum (stored) | |
| G-AOGE | P.34A Proctor 3 | N. I. Dalziel/Biggin Hill | |
| G-AOGI | D.H.82A Tiger Moth | W. J. Taylor | |
| G-AOGR | D.H.82A Tiger Moth (T6099) | M. I. Edwards | |
| G-AOGV | J/5R Alpine | R. E. Heading | |
| G-AOHL | V.802 Viscount ★ | British Air Ferries (Cabin Trainer)/Southend | |
| G-AOHM | V.802 Viscount | British Air Ferries Viscount Sir George Edwards/Southend | |
| G-AOHY | D.H.82A Tiger Moth | C. R. & S. A. Hardiman/Shobdon | |
| G-AOHZ | J/5P Autocar | A. D. Hodgkinson | |
| G-AOIL | D.H.82A Tiger Moth | T. C. Lawless | |
| G-AOIM | D.H.82A Tiger Moth | C. R. Hardiman/Shobdon | |
| G-AOIR | Thruxton Jackaroo | L. H. Smith | |
| G-AOIS | D.H.82A Tiger Moth | V. B. & R. G. Wheele/Shoreham | |
| G-AOIY | J/5G Autocar | C. N. Towers | |
| G-AOJC | V.802 Viscount (fuselage only) ★ | Wales Aircraft Museum/Cardiff | |
| G-AOJH | D.H.83C Fox Moth | R. M. Brooks | |
| G-AOJJ | D.H.82A Tiger Moth (DF128) | E. Lay | |
| G-AOJK | D.H.82A Tiger Moth | P. A. de Courcy Swoffer | |
| G-AOJS | D.H.C.1 Chipmunk 22A | R. H. Cooper | |
| G-AOJT | D.H.106 Comet 1 ★ | Mosquito Aircraft Museum | |
| G-AOKH | P.40 Prentice 1 | J. F. Moore/Biggin Hill | |
| G-AOKL | P.40 Prentice 1 (VS610) | J. K. Cook | |
| G-AOKO | P.40 Prentice 1 ★ | J. F. Coggins/Coventry | |
| G-AOKZ | P.40 Prentice 1 (VS623) ★ | Midland Air Museum | |
| G-AOLK | P.40 Prentice 1 | Hilton Aviation Ltd/Southend | |
| G-AOLU | P.40 Prentice 1 (VS356) ★ | — | |
| G-AORB | Cessna 170B | Eaglescott Parachute Centre | |
| G-AORG | D.H.114 Heron 2 | Duchess of Brittany (Jersey) Ltd | |
| G-AORW | D.H.C.1 Chipmunk 22A | V. P. Butler/Biggin Hill | |
| G-AOSF | D.H.C.1 Chipmunk 22 | D. Mercer | |
| G-AOSK | D.H.C.1 Chipmunk 22 | A. M. S. Cullen | |
| G-AOSO | D.H.C.1 Chipmunk 22 | Earl of Suffolk & Berkshire & J. Hoerner | |
| G-AOSU | D.H.C.1 Chipmunk 22 (Lycoming) | RAFGSA/Bicester | |
| G-AOSY | D.H.C.1 Chipmunk 22 (WB585) | Franbrave Ltd | |
| G-AOTD | D.H.C.1 Chipmunk 22 (WB588) | Shuttleworth Trust/O. Warden | |
| G-AOTF | D.H.C.1 Chipmunk 23 (Lycoming) | RAFGSA/Bicester | |
| G-AOTI | D.H.114 Heron 2D | Avtech Ltd/Biggin Hill | |
| G-AOTK | D.53 Turbi | The T. K. Flying Group/Hatfield | |
| G-AOTR | D.H.C.1 Chipmunk 22 | Ulster ChipmunkGroup/Newtownards | |
| G-AOTY | D.H.C.1 Chipmunk 22A (WG472) | P. D. Harrison | |
| G-AOUJ | Fairey Ultra-Light ★ | International Helicopter Museum/Weston-s-Mare | |
| G-AOUO | D.H.C.1 Chipmunk 22 (Lycoming) | RAFGSA/Bicester | |
| G-AOUP | D.H.C.1 Chipmunk 22 | Wessex Flying Group | |
| G-AOUR | D.H.82A Tiger Moth ★ | Ulster Folk & Transport Museum | |
| G-AOVF | B.175 Britannia 312F ★ | Aerospace Museum/Cosford | |
| G-AOVT | B.175 Britannia 312F ★ | Duxford Aviation Soc | |
| G-AOVW | Auster 5 | B. Marriott/Cranwell | |
| G-AOXG | D.H.82A Tiger Moth (G-ABUL) ★ | FAA Museum/Yeovilton | |
| G-AOXN | D.H.82A Tiger Moth | S. L. G. Darch | |
| G-AOYG | V.806 Viscount | British Air Ferries Viscount Sir Peter Masefield/Southend | |
| G-AOYL | V.806 Viscount | British Air Ferries Viscount Churchill/Southend | |
| G-AOYN | V.806 Viscount | British Air Ferries/Southend | |
| G-AOYP | V.806 Viscount | British Air Ferries/Southend | |
| G-AOYR | V.806 Viscount | British Air Ferries/Southend | |

| Notes | Reg. | Type | Owner or Operator |
|-------|------|------|-------------------|
| | G-AOZH | D.H.82A Tiger Moth (K2572) | V. B. & R. G. Wheele/Shoreham |
| | G-AOZL | J/5Q Alpine | E. A. Taylor/Southend |
| | G-AOZP | D.H.C.1 Chipmunk 22 | M. Darlington |
| | G-AOZU | D.H.C.1 Chipmunk 22A | R. H. Cooper |
| | | | |
| | G-APAA | J/5R Alpine ★ | L. A. Groves (stored) |
| | G-APAF | Auster 5 (TW511) | J. E. Allen (G-CMAL) |
| | G-APAH | Auster 5 | P. A. Wensak |
| | G-APAL | D.H.82A Tiger Moth (N6847) | P. S. & R. A. Chapman |
| | G-APAM | D.H.82A Tiger Moth | R. P. Williams |
| | G-APAO | D.H.82A Tiger Moth | F. J. Longe |
| | G-APAP | D.H.82A Tiger Moth | R. A. Slade |
| | G-APAS | D.H.106 Comet 1XB ★ | Aerospace Museum/Cosford |
| | G-APBE | Auster 5 | C. W. Wilkinson/Panshanger |
| | G-APBI | D.H.82A Tiger Moth (EM903) | R. Devaney & ptnrs/Audley End |
| | G-APBO | D.53 Turbi | R. C. Hibberd |
| | G-APBW | Auster 5 | N. Huxtable |
| | G-APCB | J/5Q Alpine | A. A. Beswick & I. A. Freeman |
| | G-APCC | D.H.82A Tiger Moth | L. J. Rice/Henstridge |
| | G-APDB | D.H.106 Comet 4 ★ | Duxford Aviation Soc |
| | G-APEG | V.953C Merchantman ★ | Airport Fire Service/E. Midlands |
| | G-APEJ | V.953C Merchantman | Hunting Cargo Airlines Ltd Ajax |
| | G-APEM | V.953C Merchantman | Hunting Cargo Airlines Ltd/ DHL Agamemnon |
| | G-APEP | V.953C Merchantman | Hunting Cargo Airlines Ltd Superb |
| | G-APES | V.953C Merchantman | Hunting Cargo Airlines Ltd Swiftsure |
| | G-APEY | V.806 Viscount | British Air Ferries/Southend |
| | G-APFA | D.54 Turbi | A. Eastelow & F. J. Keitch/Dunkeswell |
| | G-APFG | Boeing 707-436 ★ | Cabin water spray tests/Cardington |
| | G-APFJ | Boeing 707-436 ★ | Aerospace Museum/Cosford |
| | G-APFU | D.H.82A Tiger Moth | Mithril Racing Ltd/Goodwood |
| | G-APGL | D.H.82A Tiger Moth | K. A. Broomfield |
| | G-APHV | Avro 19 Srs 2 (VM360) ★ | Museum of Flight/E. Fortune |
| | G-APIE | Tipsy Belfair B | P. A. Smith |
| | G-APIH | D.H.82A Tiger Moth (R5086) | C. R. Kirby |
| | G-APIK | J/1N Alpha | N. D. Voce |
| | G-APIM | V.806 Viscount ★ | Brooklands Museum of Aviation/ Weybridge |
| | G-APIT | P.40 Prentice 1 (VR192) ★ | WWII Aircraft Preservation Soc/Lasham |
| | G-APIU | P.40 Prentice 1 ★ | J. F. Coggins/Coventry |
| | G-APIY | P.40 Prentice 1 (VR249) ★ | Newark Air Museum |
| | G-APIZ | D.31 Turbulent | M. J. Whatley/Booker |
| | G-APJB | P.40 Prentice 1 (VR259) ★ | City Airways/Coventry |
| | G-APJJ | Fairey Ultra-light ★ | Midland Aircraft Preservation Soc |
| | G-APJO | D.H.82A Tiger Moth | D. R. & M. Wood |
| | G-APJZ | J/1N Alpha | P. G. Lipman |
| | G-APKH | D.H.85 Leopard Moth | R. G. Grocott (G-ACGS) |
| | G-APKM | J/1N Alpha | D. E. A. Huggins |
| | G-APKN | J/1N Alpha | Felthorpe Auster Group |
| | G-APKY | Hiller UH-12B | D. A. George (stored) |
| | G-APLG | J/5L Aiglet Trainer | G. R. W. Brown |
| | G-APLK | Miles M.100 Student 2 | A. S. Topen (G-MIOO)/Cranfield |
| | G-APLO | D.H.C.1 Chipmunk 22A (WD379) | Lindholme Aircraft Ltd/Jersey |
| | G-APLU | D.H.82A Tiger Moth | The Intrepid Flying Group |
| | G-APMB | D.H.106 Comet 4B ★ | Gatwick Handling Ltd (ground trainer) |
| | G-APMH | J/1U Workmaster | R. E. Neal & E. R. Stevens/Leicester |
| | G-APML | Dakota 6 | Air Atlantique Ltd |
| | G-APMM | D.H.82A Tiger Moth (K2568) | R. K. J. Hadlow |
| | G-APMX | D.H.82A Tiger Moth | G. A. Broughton |
| | G-APMY | PA-23 Apache 160 ★ | NE Wales Institute of Higher Education (instructional airframe)/Clwyd |
| | G-APNJ | Cessna 310 ★ | Chelsea College/Shoreham |
| | G-APNS | Garland-Bianchi Linnet | Paul Penn-Sayers Model Services Ltd |
| | G-APNT | Currie Wot | J. W. Salter |
| | G-APNZ | D.31 Turbulent | Tiger Club (1990) Ltd/Headcorn |
| | G-APOA | J/1N Alpha | C. R. Harris/Biggin Hill |
| | G-APOD | Tipsy Belfair | L. F. Potts |
| | G-APOI | Saro Skeeter Srs 8 ★ | Wilkie Museum Collection/Blackpool |
| | G-APOL | D.31 Turbulent | A. Gregori & S. Tinker |
| | G-APPA | D.H.C.1 Chipmunk 22 | I. R. Young/Glasgow |
| | G-APPL | P.40 Prentice 1 | S. J. Saggers/Biggin Hill |
| | G-APPM | D.H.C.1 Chipmunk 22 | Freston Aviation Ltd |
| | G-APRF | Auster 5 | D. R. Slade |

| Reg. | Type | Owner or Operator | Notes |
|------|------|-------------------|-------|
| G-APRJ | Avro 694 Lincoln B.2 ★ | Aces High Ltd/North Weald | |
| G-APRL | AW.650 Argosy 101 ★ | Midland Air Museum | |
| G-APRR | Super Aero 45 | R. H. Jowett | |
| G-APRT | Taylor JT.1 Monoplane | J. P. Leigh | |
| G-APSA | Douglas DC-6A | Instone Air Line Ltd/Coventry | |
| G-APSR | J/1U Workmaster | D. & K. Aero Services Ltd/Shobdon | |
| G-APTP | PA-22 Tri-Pacer 150 | R. J. & F. A. Fox | |
| G-APTR | J/1N Alpha | C. J. & D. J. Baker | |
| G-APTS | D.H.C.1 Chipmunk 22A | G. T. Grimward/Booker | |
| G-APTU | Auster 5 | G-APTU Flying Group | |
| G-APTW | W.B.1 Widgeon ★ | Cornwall Aero Park/Helston | |
| G-APTY | Beech G.35 Bonanza | G. E. Brennand & ptnrs | |
| G-APTZ | D.31 Turbulent | F. R. Hutchings | |
| G-APUD | Bensen B.7M (modified) ★ | Greater Manchester Museum of Science & Technology | |
| G-APUE | L-40 Meta Sokol | S. E. & M. J. Aherne | |
| G-APUK | J/1 Autocrat | P. L. Morley | |
| G-APUP | Sopwith Pup (replica) (N5182) ★ | RAF Museum/Hendon | |
| G-APUR | PA-22 Tri-Pacer 160 | P. J. Hewitt | |
| G-APUW | J/5V-160 Autocar | Anglia Auster Syndicate | |
| G-APUY | D.31 Turbulent | C. Jones & ptnrs/Barton | |
| G-APUZ | PA-24 Comanche 250 | P. A. Brook | |
| G-APVF | Putzer Elster B (97+04) | B. W. Griffiths & A. J. Robinson | |
| G-APVG | J/5L Aiglet Trainer | C. M. Daggett/Cranfield | |
| G-APVN | D.31 Turbulent | R. Sherwin/Shoreham | |
| G-APVS | Cessna 170B | N. Simpson | |
| G-APVY | PA-25 Pawnee 150 | KK Aviation (stored) | |
| G-APVZ | D.31 Turbulent | H. R. Oldland | |
| G-APWA | HPR-7 Herald 101 ★ | Museum of Berkshire Aviation/Woodley | |
| G-APWJ | HPR-7 Herald 201 ★ | Duxford Aviation Soc | |
| G-APWN | WS-55 Whirlwind 3 ★ | Midland Air Museum | |
| G-APWY | Piaggio P.166 ★ | Science Museum/Wroughton | |
| G-APWZ | EP.9 Prospector ★ | Museum of Army Flying/Middle Wallop | |
| G-APXJ | PA-24 Comanche 250 | T. Wildsmith/Netherthorpe | |
| G-APXM | PA-22 Tri-Pacer 160 | R. J. Chinn | |
| G-APXR | PA-22 Tri-Pacer 160 | A. Troughton | |
| G-APXT | PA-22 Tri-Pacer 150 (modified) | J. W. & I. Daniels | |
| G-APXU | PA-22 Tri-Pacer 125 | Medway Aircraft Preservation Soc Ltd | |
| G-APXW | EP.9 Prospector ★ | Museum of Army Flying/Middle Wallop | |
| G-APXX | D.H.A.3 Drover 2 (VH-FDT) ★ | WWII Aircraft Preservation Soc/Lasham | |
| G-APXY | Cessna 150 | Merlin Flying Club Ltd/Hucknall | |
| G-APYB | Tipsy T.66 Nipper 3 | B. O. Smith | |
| G-APYD | D.H.106 Comet 4B ★ | Science Museum/Wroughton | |
| G-APYG | D.H.C.1 Chipmunk 22 | E. J. I. Musty & P. A. Colman | |
| G-APYI | PA-22 Tri-Pacer 135 | G. K. Hare/Fenland | |
| G-APYN | PA-22 Tri-Pacer 160 | W. D. Stephens | |
| G-APYT | Champion 7FC Tri-Traveller | B. J. Anning | |
| G-APYW | PA-22 Tri-Pacer 150 | Fiddian Ltd | |
| G-APZJ | PA-18 Super Cub 150 | Southern Sailplanes | |
| G-APZK | PA-18 Super Cub 95 | W. T. Knapton | |
| G-APZL | PA-22 Tri-Pacer 160 | R. T. Evans | |
| G-APZR | Cessna 150 ★ | Engine test-bed/Biggin Hill | |
| G-APZS | Cessna 175A | G. A. Nash/Booker | |
| G-APZX | PA-22 Tri-Pacer 150 | Applied Signs Ltd | |
| G-ARAM | PA-18 Super Cub 150 | Clacton Aero Club (1988) Ltd | |
| G-ARAN | PA-18 Super Cub 150 | A. P. Docherty/Redhill | |
| G-ARAO | PA-18 Super Cub 95 (607327) | R. T. Bennett & N. Tyler | |
| G-ARAS | Champion 7EC Traveller | Clipgate Flying Group | |
| G-ARAT | Cessna 180C | Eaglescott Parachute Centre | |
| G-ARAU | Cessna 150 | S. Lynn/Sibson | |
| G-ARAW | Cessna 182C Skylane | P. Channon | |
| G-ARAX | PA-22 Tri-Pacer 150 | S. J. Kew/Booker | |
| G-ARAZ | D.H.82A Tiger Moth | R. M. Brooks | |
| G-ARBE | D.H.104 Dove 8 | A. Freeman & T. Howe | |
| G-ARBG | Tipsy T.66 Nipper 2 | J. Horovitz & J. McLeod | |
| G-ARBM | J/1B Aiglet | Aerofab Flying Group | |
| G-ARBN | PA-23 Apache 160 | H. Norden & H. J. Liggins | |
| G-ARBO | PA-24 Comanche 250 | D. M. Harbottle & I. S. Graham/Goodwood | |
| G-ARBP | Tipsy T.66 Nipper 2 | F. W. Kirk | |
| G-ARBS | PA-22 Tri-Pacer 160 (tailwheel) | S. D. Rowell | |
| G-ARBV | PA-22 Tri-Pacer 150 | Oaksey Pacers | |
| G-ARBZ | D.31 Turbulent | J. Mickleburgh | |

| Notes | Reg. | Type | Owner or Operator |
|---|---|---|---|
| | G-ARCC | PA-22 Tri-Pacer 150 | Popham Flying Group/Popham |
| | G-ARCF | PA-22 Tri-Pacer 150 | R. E. Ryan |
| | G-ARCH | Cessna 310D ★ | *Instructional airframe*/Perth |
| | G-ARCS | Auster D6/180 | E. A. Matty/Shobdon |
| | G-ARCT | PA-18 Super Cub 95 | M. J. Kirk |
| | G-ARCV | Cessna 175A | R. Francis & C. Campbell |
| | G-ARCW | PA-23 Apache 160 | D. R. C. Reeves |
| | G-ARCX | AW Meteor 14 ★ | Museum of Flight/E. Fortune |
| | G-ARDB | PA-24 Comanche 250 | R. A. Sareen/Booker |
| | G-ARDD | CP.301C1 Emeraude | R. M. Shipp |
| | G-ARDE | D.H.104 Dove 6 | R. J. H. Small/North Weald |
| | G-ARDG | EP.9 Prospector ★ | Museum of Army Flying/Middle Wallop |
| | G-ARDJ | Auster D.6/180 | RN Aviation (Leicester Airport) Ltd |
| | G-ARDO | Jodel D.112 | W. R. Prescott |
| | G-ARDP | PA-22 Tri-Pacer 150 | G. M. Jones |
| | G-ARDS | PA-22 Caribbean 150 | A. C. Donaldson & C. I. Lavery |
| | G-ARDT | PA-22 Tri-Pacer 160 | M. Henderson |
| | G-ARDV | PA-22 Tri-Pacer 160 | B. R. Griffiths |
| | G-ARDY | Tipsy T.66 Nipper 2 | M. J. Mann |
| | G-ARDZ | Jodel D.140A | M. J. Wright |
| | G-AREA | D.H.104 Dove 8 ★ | Mosquito Aircraft Museum |
| | G-AREB | Cessna 175B Skylark | R. J. Postlethwaite & ptnrs/Wellesbourne |
| | G-AREF | PA-23 Aztec 250 ★ | Southall College of Technology |
| | G-AREH | D.H.82A Tiger Moth | T. Pate |
| | G-AREI | Auster 3 (MT438) | J. A. Vetch |
| | G-AREL | PA-22 Caribbean 150 | H. H. Cousins/Fenland |
| | G-AREO | PA-18 Super Cub 150 | DRA (Farnborough) Gliding Club Ltd |
| | G-ARET | PA-22 Tri-Pacer 160 | D. T. Daniels |
| | G-AREV | PA-22 Tri-Pacer 160 | Spatrek Ltd/Barton |
| | G-AREX | Aeronca 15AC Sedan | R. J. Middleton-Turnbull & P. Lowndes |
| | G-AREZ | D.31 Turbulent | J. St. Clair-Quentin/Shobdon |
| | G-ARFB | PA-22 Caribbean 150 | C. T. Woodward & ptnrs |
| | G-ARFD | PA-22 Tri-Pacer 160 | P. C. Hambilton & G. F. Martin/Blackpool |
| | G-ARFG | Cessna 175A Skylark | R. J. Fray/Sibson |
| | G-ARFH | PA-24 Comanche 250 | L. M. Walton |
| | G-ARFI | Cessna 150A | J. H. Fisher |
| | G-ARFL | Cessna 175B Skylark | D. J. Mason |
| | G-ARFN | Cessna 150A ★ | *Instructional airframe*/Perth |
| | G-ARFO | Cessna 150A | Moray Flying Club Ltd |
| | G-ARFT | Jodel DR. 1050 | R. Shaw |
| | G-ARFV | Tipsy T.66 Nipper 2 | C. G. Stone/Biggin Hill |
| | G-ARGB | Auster 6A ★ | C. Baker (*stored*) |
| | G-ARGG | D.H.C.1 Chipmunk 22 (WD305) | Willpower Garage Ltd |
| | G-ARGO | PA-22 Colt 108 | B. E. Goodman/Liverpool |
| | G-ARGV | PA-18 Super Cub 150 | Deeside Gliding Club (Aberdeenshire) Ltd/ Aboyne |
| | G-ARGY | PA-22 Tri-Pacer 160 (G-JEST) | G. K. Hare (G-JEST) |
| | G-ARGZ | D.31 Turbulent | J. C. Mansell |
| | G-ARHB | Forney F-1A Aircoupe | A. V. Rash & D. R. Wickes |
| | G-ARHC | Forney F-1A Aircoupe | A. P. Gardner/Elstree |
| | G-ARHF | Forney F-1A Aircoupe | R. A. Nesbitt-Dufort |
| | G-ARHI | PA-24 Comanche 180 | W. H. Entress/Swansea |
| | G-ARHL | PA-23 Aztec 250 | J. J. Freeman & Co Ltd/Headcorn |
| | G-ARHM | Auster 6A | D. Hollowell & ptnrs/Finmere |
| | G-ARHN | PA-22 Caribbean 150 | D. B. Furniss & A. Munro/Doncaster |
| | G-ARHP | PA-22 Tri-Pacer 160 | W. Wardle |
| | G-ARHR | PA-22 Caribbean 150 | J. A. Hargraves/Fairoaks |
| | G-ARHT | PA-22 Caribbean 150 ★ | Moston Technical College |
| | G-ARHU | PA-22 Tri-Pacer 160 | B. L. Newbold & H. Streets |
| | G-ARHW | D.H.104 Dove 8 | R. M. Brooks |
| | G-ARHX | D.H.104 Dove 8 ★ | —/Booker |
| | G-ARHZ | D.62 Condor | Condor Hotel Zulu Group |
| | G-ARID | Cessna 172B | A. Taylor |
| | G-ARIE | PA-24 Comanche 250 | W. Radwanski (*stored*)/Coventry |
| | G-ARIF | Ord-Hume O-H.7 Minor Coupé | N. H. Ponsford |
| | G-ARIH | Auster 6A (TW591) | India Hotel Ltd |
| | G-ARIK | PA-22 Caribbean 150 | C. J. Berry |
| | G-ARIL | PA-22 Caribbean 150 | K. Knight |
| | G-ARIV | Cessna 172B | G-ARIV Flying Group |
| | G-ARJB | D.H.104 Dove 8 ★ | J. C. Bamford (*stored*) |
| | G-ARJC | PA-22 Colt 108 | F. W. H. Dulles |
| | G-ARJE | PA-22 Colt 108 | C. I. Fray |
| | G-ARJF | PA-22 Colt 108 | M. J. Collins |

| Reg. | Type | Owner or Operator | Notes |
|------|------|-------------------|-------|
| G-ARJH | PA-22 Colt 108 | G. P. A. Elborough | |
| G-ARJR | PA-23 Apache 160G ★ | *Instructional airframe*/Kidlington | |
| G-ARJS | PA-23 Apache 160G | Bencray Ltd/Blackpool | |
| G-ARJT | PA-23 Apache 160G | Hiveland Ltd | |
| G-ARJU | PA-23 Apache 160G | Chantaco Ltd/Biggin Hill | |
| G-ARJV | PA-23 Apache 160G | Economic Insulations Ltd | |
| G-ARJW | PA-23 Apache 160G | *stored*/Bristol | |
| G-ARJZ | D.31 Turbulent | N. H. Jones | |
| G-ARKG | J/5G Autocar | C. M. Milborrow | |
| G-ARKJ | Beech N35 Bonanza | T. Cust | |
| G-ARKK | PA-22 Colt 108 | A. T. J. Hyatt | |
| G-ARKM | PA-22 Colt 108 | B. V. & E. A. Howes/Earls Colne | |
| G-ARKN | PA-22 Colt 108 | R. A. & N. L. E. Dupee | |
| G-ARKP | PA-22 Colt 108 | C. J. & J. Freeman/Headcorn | |
| G-ARKR | PA-22 Colt 108 | B. J. M. Montegut | |
| G-ARKS | PA-22 Colt 108 | J. Dickenson | |
| G-ARLG | Auster D.4/108 | Auster D4 Group | |
| G-ARLK | PA-24 Comanche 250 | M. Walker | |
| G-ARLO | A.61 Terrier 1 ★ | *stored* | |
| G-ARLP | A.61 Terrier 1 | Gemini Flying Group | |
| G-ARLR | A.61 Terrier 2 | W. H. Dyozinski | |
| G-ARLU | Cessna 172B Skyhawk ★ | *Instructional airframe*/Irish AC | |
| G-ARLV | Cessna 172B Skyhawk | P. D. Lowdon | |
| G-ARLW | Cessna 172B Skyhawk ★ | *(spares source)*/Barton | |
| G-ARLX | Jodel D.140B | Shipping & Airlines Ltd/Biggin Hill | |
| G-ARLZ | D.31A Turbulent | R. S. Hatwell & A. F. Hall | |
| G-ARMA | PA-23 Apache 160G ★ | *Instructional airframe*/Kidlington | |
| G-ARMB | D.H.C.1 Chipmunk 22A (WB660) | Red Baron Aviation Ltd/Shipdham | |
| G-ARMC | D.H.C.1 Chipmunk 22A (WB703) | West London Aero Services Ltd/ White Waltham | |
| G-ARMD | D.H.C.1 Chipmunk 22A ★ | K. & L. Aero Services (*stored*) | |
| G-ARMF | D.H.C.1 Chipmunk 22A | Chipmunk G-BCIW Syndicate | |
| G-ARMG | D.H.C.1 Chipmunk 22A | Chipmunk Preservation Group Ltd/ Wellesbourne | |
| G-ARML | Cessna 175B Skylark | R. C. Convine | |
| G-ARMN | Cessna 175B Skylark ★ | Southall College of Technology | |
| G-ARMO | Cessna 172B Skyhawk | G. R. E. Evans & D. J. Clark | |
| G-ARMR | Cessna 172B Skyhawk | Sunsaver Ltd/Barton | |
| G-ARMZ | D.31 Turbulent | J. E. M. B. Millns | |
| G-ARNB | J/5G Autocar | R. F. Tolhurst | |
| G-ARND | PA-22 Colt 108 | E. J. Clarke | |
| G-ARNE | PA-22 Colt 108 | T. D. L. Bowden/Shipdham | |
| G-ARNG | PA-22 Colt 108 | S. S. Delwarte/Shoreham | |
| G-ARNI | PA-22 Colt 108 | P. R. Monk & A. C. Savage | |
| G-ARNJ | PA-22 Colt 108 | Colt Flying Group | |
| G-ARNK | PA-22 Colt 108 (tailwheel) | G. K. Hare | |
| G-ARNL | PA-22 Colt 108 | J. A. & J. A. Dodsworth/White Waltham | |
| G-ARNO | A.61 Terrier 1 | *(stored)* | |
| G-ARNP | A.109 Airedale | S. W. & M. Isbister | |
| G-ARNY | Jodel D.117 | D. J. Lockett | |
| G-ARNZ | D.31 Turbulent | N. J. Mathias | |
| G-AROA | Cessna 172B Skyhawk | D. E. Partridge | |
| G-AROE | Aero 145 | Gooney Bird Trading Ltd | |
| G-AROF | L.40 Meta-Sokol | G. D. H. Crawford | |
| G-AROJ | A.109 Airedale ★ | D. J. Shaw (*stored*) | |
| G-AROM | PA-22 Colt 108 | J. R. Colthurst | |
| G-ARON | PA-22 Colt 108 | R. W. Curtis | |
| G-AROO | Forney F-1A Aircoupe | W. J. McMeekan/Newtownards | |
| G-AROW | Jodel D.140B | Acebell Aviation Ltd/Redhill | |
| G-AROY | Boeing Stearman A.75N.1 | W. A. Jordan | |
| G-ARPH | H.S.121 Trident 1C ★ | Aerospace Museum, Cosford | |
| G-ARPK | H.S.121 Trident 1C ★ | Manchester Airport Authority | |
| G-ARPL | H.S.121 Trident 1C ★ | BAA Airport Fire Service/Edinburgh | |
| G-ARPN | H.S.121 Trident 1C ★ | BAA Airport Fire Service/Aberdeen | |
| G-ARPP | H.S.121 Trident 1C ★ | BAA Airport Fire Service/Glasgow | |
| G-ARPX | H.S.121 Trident 1C ★ | Airwork Services Ltd/Perth | |
| G-ARPZ | H.S.121 Trident 1C ★ | RFD Ltd/Dunsfold | |
| G-ARRD | Jodel DR.1050 | C. M. Fitton | |
| G-ARRE | Jodel DR.1050 | A. Luty & M. P. Edwards/Barton | |
| G-ARRF | Cessna 150A | Electrical Engineering Services | |
| G-ARRL | J/1N Alpha | G. N. Smith & C. Webb | |
| G-ARRM | Beagle B.206-X ★ | Shoreham Airport Museum | |
| G-ARRS | CP.301A Emeraude | E. H. Booker | |

| Notes | Reg. | Type | Owner or Operator |
|---|---|---|---|
| | G-ARRT | Wallis WA-116-1 | K. H. Wallis |
| | G-ARRU | D.31 Turbulent | N. C. Lowes |
| | G-ARRX | Auster 6A | J. E. D. Mackie |
| | G-ARRY | Jodel D.140B | Fictionview Ltd |
| | G-ARRZ | D.31 Turbulent | C. I. Jefferson |
| | G-ARSB | Cessna 150A | B. T. White/Andrewsfield |
| | G-ARSG | Roe Triplane Type IV replica | Shuttleworth Trust/O. Warden |
| | G-ARSJ | CP.301-C2 Emeraude | R. J. Lewis |
| | G-ARSL | A.61 Terrier 2 | R. A. Hutchinson & P. T. M. Hardy |
| | G-ARSP | L.40 Meta-Sokol | R. E. Carpenter |
| | G-ARSU | PA-22 Colt 108 | W. H. & D. Gough |
| | G-ARSW | PA-22 Colt 108 | Sierra Whisky Flying Group/Sibson |
| | G-ARSX | PA-22 Tri-Pacer 160 | S. Hutchinson |
| | G-ARTD | PA-23 Apache 160 | Dr. D. A. Jones |
| | G-ARTG | Hiller UH-12C ★ | White Hart Inn/Stockbridge |
| | G-ARTH | PA-12 Super Cruiser | L. D. Johnston |
| | G-ARTJ | Bensen B.8 ★ | Museum of Flight/E. Fortune |
| | G-ARTL | D.H.82A Tiger Moth (T7281) | P. A. Jackson |
| | G-ARTT | M.S.880B Rallye Club | R. N. Scott |
| | G-ARTW | Cessna 150B ★ | Instructional airframe/Perth |
| | G-ARTX | Cessna 150B ★ | Instructional airframe/Perth |
| | G-ARTY | Cessna 150B ★ | Instructional airframe/Perth |
| | G-ARTZ | McCandless M.4 Gyrocopter | W. E. Partridge (stored) |
| | G-ARUG | J/5G Autocar | D. P. H. Hulme/Biggin Hill |
| | G-ARUH | Jodel DR.1050 | PFA Group/Denham |
| | G-ARUI | A.61 Terrier | A. C. Ladd |
| | G-ARUL | Cosmic Wind | P. G. Kynsey |
| | G-ARUO | PA-24 Comanche 180 | Uniform Oscar Group/Elstree |
| | G-ARUV | CP.301A Emeraude | J. Tanswell |
| | G-ARUY | J/1N Alpha | D. L. Webley |
| | G-ARUZ | Cessna 175C Skylark | Cardiff Skylark Group |
| | G-ARVM | V.1101 VC10 ★ | Aerospace Museum/Cosford |
| | G-ARVO | PA-18 Super Cub 95 | Deltair Ltd |
| | G-ARVS | PA-28 Cherokee 160 | Skyscraper Ltd/Stapleford |
| | G-ARVT | PA-28 Cherokee 160 | Red Rose Aviation Ltd/Liverpool |
| | G-ARVU | PA-28 Cherokee 160 | D. J. Hockings/Biggin Hill |
| | G-ARVV | PA-28 Cherokee 160 | G. E. Hopkins |
| | G-ARVZ | D.62B Condor | G. Smith |
| | G-ARWB | D.H.C.1 Chipmunk 22 (WK611) | L. J. Willcocks |
| | G-ARWH | Cessna 172C Skyhawk ★ | — |
| | G-ARWO | Cessna 172C Skyhawk | J. P. Stafford |
| | G-ARWR | Cessna 172C Skyhawk | The Devanha Flying Group Ltd |
| | G-ARWS | Cessna 175C Skylark | E. N. Skinner |
| | G-ARXD | A.109 Airedale | D. Howden |
| | G-ARXG | PA-24 Comanche 250 | I. M. Callier |
| | G-ARXH | Bell 47G | A. B. Searle |
| | G-ARXP | Luton LA-4A Minor | W. C. Hymas |
| | G-ARXT | Jodel DR.1050 | CJM Flying Group |
| | G-ARXU | Auster 6A | The A Team |
| | G-ARXW | M.S.885 Super Rallye | Bond Glen Flying Club Ltd/Londonderry |
| | G-ARXX | M.S.880B Rallye Club | P. S. E. Clifton |
| | G-ARYB | H.S.125 Srs 1★ | British Aerospace PLC/Hatfield |
| | G-ARYC | H.S.125 Srs 1 ★ | The Mosquito Aircraft Museum |
| | G-ARYD | Auster AOP.6 (WJ358) ★ | Museum of Army Flying/Middle Wallop |
| | G-ARYF | PA-23 Aztec 250B | I. J. T. Branson/Biggin Hill |
| | G-ARYH | PA-22 Tri-Pacer 160 | Filtration (Water Treatment Engineers) Ltd |
| | G-ARYI | Cessna 172C | J. Rhodes |
| | G-ARYK | Cessna 172C | J. H. Emery |
| | G-ARYR | PA-28 Cherokee 180 | R. J. Gerrard & C. S. Wilkinson/Booker |
| | G-ARYS | Cessna 172C Skyhawk | Guildbrook Associates Ltd |
| | G-ARYV | PA-24 Comanche 250 | Ilford Business Machines Ltd |
| | G-ARYZ | A.109 Airedale | V. J. Reid |
| | G-ARZB | Wallis WA-116 Srs 1 | K. H. Wallis |
| | G-ARZE | Cessna 172C ★ | Parachute jump trainer/Cockerham |
| | G-ARZM | D.31 Turbulent | Tiger Club (1990) Ltd/Headcorn |
| | G-ARZN | Beech N35 Bonanza | D. W. Mickleburgh/Leicester |
| | G-ARZP | A.109 Airedale | G. B. O'Neill (stored)/Booker |
| | G-ARZW | Currie Wot | J. H. Blake |
| | G-ARZX | Cessna 150B | P. H. Slade |
| | G-ASAA | Luton LA-4A Minor | R. J. Moore |
| | G-ASAI | A.109 Airedale | K. R Howden & ptnrs |
| | G-ASAJ | A.61 Terrier 2 (WE569) | S. J. B. White & ptnrs |

28

| Reg. | Type | Owner or Operator | Notes |
|------|------|-------------------|-------|
| G-ASAK | A.61 Terrier 2 | Rochford Hundred Flying Group/Southend | |
| G-ASAL | SAL Bulldog 120 | British Aerospace PLC/Prestwick | |
| G-ASAM | D.31 Turbulent | Tiger Club (1990) Ltd/Headcorn | |
| G-ASAN | A.61 Terrier 2 | D. R. Godfrey | |
| G-ASAT | M.S.880B Rallye Club | M. Cutovic | |
| G-ASAU | M.S.880B Rallye Club | T. C. & R. Edwards | |
| G-ASAX | A.61 Terrier 2 | G. Strathdee | |
| G-ASAZ | Hiller UH-12E4 | Pan-Air Ltd | |
| G-ASBA | Currie Wot | M. A. Kaye | |
| G-ASBB | Beech 23 Musketeer | D. Silver/Southend | |
| G-ASBH | A.109 Airedale | D. T. Smollett | |
| G-ASBY | A.109 Airedale | M. R. H. Wheatley & R. K. Wilson | |
| G-ASCC | Beagle E.3 AOP Mk 11 | Old Training Plane Co | |
| G-ASCM | Isaacs Fury II (K2050) | D. Biggs | |
| G-ASCU | PA-18A Super Cub 150 | Farm Aviation Services Ltd | |
| G-ASCZ | CP.301A Emeraude | J. O. R. Penman/France | |
| G-ASDF | Edwards Gyrocopter ★ | B. King | |
| G-ASDK | A.61 Terrier 2 | M. L. Rose | |
| G-ASDL | A.61 Terrier 2 | C. E. Mason | |
| G-ASDO | Beech 95-A55 Baron ★ | No 2498 Sqn ATC/Jersey | |
| G-ASDY | Wallis WA-116/F | K. H. Wallis | |
| G-ASEA | Luton LA-4A Minor | G. C. Jones | |
| G-ASEB | Luton LA-4A Minor | S. R. P. Harper | |
| G-ASEG | A.61 Terrier (VF548) | R .S. O. B. Evans & J. P. P. A. Midgley | |
| G-ASEO | PA-24 Comanche 250 | Planetalk Ltd | |
| G-ASEP | PA-23 Apache 235 | Arrowstate Ltd/Denham | |
| G-ASEU | D.62A Condor | W. Grant | |
| G-ASFA | Cessna 172D | APS Worldwide/Cranfield | |
| G-ASFD | L-200A Morava | M. Emery/Bournemouth | |
| G-ASFK | J/5G Autocar | R. W. & M. Struth | |
| G-ASFL | PA-28 Cherokee 180 | D. F. Ranger/Popham | |
| G-ASFR | Bo.208A1 Junior | S. T. Dauncey | |
| G-ASFX | D.31 Turbulent | E. F. Clapham & W. B. S. Dobie | |
| G-ASGC | V.1151 Super VC10 ★ | Duxford Aviation Soc | |
| G-ASHB | Cessna 182F | Sport Parachute Centre Ltd/Tilstock | |
| G-ASHD | Brantly B-2A ★ | International Helicopter Museum/ Weston-s-Mare | |
| G-ASHH | PA-23 Aztec 250 | Leicestershire Thread & Trimming Manufacturers Ltd/Sibson | |
| G-ASHS | SNCAN Stampe SV-4B | Three Point Flying Ltd | |
| G-ASHT | D.31 Turbulent | C. W. N. Huke | |
| G-ASHU | PA-15 Vagabond | G. J. Romanes | |
| G-ASHV | PA-23 Aztec 250B | R. J. Ashley & G. O'Gorman | |
| G-ASHX | PA-28 Cherokee 180 | Powertheme Ltd/Barton | |
| G-ASIB | Cessna F.172D | G-ASIB Flying Group | |
| G-ASII | PA-28 Cherokee 180 | T. R. Hart & Natocars Ltd | |
| G-ASIJ | PA-28 Cherokee 180 | Precision Products Ltd & D. Beadle | |
| G-ASIL | PA-28 Cherokee 180 | N. M. Barker & ptnrs/Leicester | |
| G-ASIS | Jodel D.112 | E. F. Hazel | |
| G-ASIT | Cessna 180 | A. & P. A. Wood | |
| G-ASIY | PA-25 Pawnee 235 | RAFGSA/Bicester | |
| G-ASJC | BAC One-Eleven 201AC | British Air Ferries Ltd/Southend | |
| G-ASJL | Beech H.35 Bonanza | MLP Aviation Ltd/Elstree | |
| G-ASJM | PA-30 Twin Comanche 160 ★ | Via Nova Ltd (stored) | |
| G-ASJO | Beech B.23 Musketeer | S. Boon/Sandown | |
| G-ASJV | V.S.361 Spitfire IX (MH434) | Nalfire Aviation Ltd/Duxford | |
| G-ASJY | GY-80 Horizon 160 | A. H. Wooffindin | |
| G-ASJZ | Jodel D.117A | P. J. & M. Edwards | |
| G-ASKC | D.H.98 Mosquito 35 (TA719) ★ | Skyfame Collection/Duxford | |
| G-ASKH | D.H.98 Mosquito T.3 (RR299) | British Aerospace PLC/Chester | |
| G-ASKJ | A.61 Terrier 1 (VX926) | N. K. & M. D. Freestone | |
| G-ASKK | HPR-7 Herald 211 ★ | Norwich Aviation Museum | |
| G-ASKL | Jodel D.150A | J. M. Graty | |
| G-ASKP | D.H.82A Tiger Moth | Tiger Club (1990) Ltd/Headcorn | |
| G-ASKS | Cessna 336 Skymaster | M. J. Godwin | |
| G-ASKT | PA-28 Cherokee 180 | A. Mattacks & T. Hood | |
| G-ASKV | PA-25 Pawnee 235 | Southdown Gliding Club Ltd | |
| G-ASLH | Cessna 182F | R. W. Boote | |
| G-ASLK | PA-25 Pawnee 235 | Bristol Gliding Club (Pty) Ltd/Nympsfield | |
| G-ASLL | Cessna 336 ★ | stored/Bournemouth | |
| G-ASLR | Agusta-Bell 47J-2 | Leeds & Manchester Group Ltd | |
| G-ASLV | PA-28 Cherokee 235 | Sackville Flying Group | |
| G-ASLX | CP.301A Emeraude | T. J. Caton | |

# G-ASMA – G-ASUL

| Notes | Reg. | Type | Owner or Operator |
|---|---|---|---|
| | G-ASMA | PA-30 Twin Comanche 160 C/R | B. D. Glynn/Redhill |
| | G-ASMC | P.56 Provost T.1. | W. Walker (stored) |
| | G-ASME | Bensen B.8M | D. A. Farnworth |
| | G-ASMF | Beech D.95A Travel Air | M. J. A. Hornblower |
| | G-ASMJ | Cessna F.172E | Mike Juliet Group/Audley End |
| | G-ASML | Luton LA-4A Minor | Fenland Strut Flying Group |
| | G-ASMM | D.31 Tubulent | G. E. Arthur |
| | G-ASMO | PA-23 Apache 160G ★ | Aviation Enterprises/Fairoaks |
| | G-ASMS | Cessna 150A | M. B. & G. T. Cocks |
| | G-ASMT | Fairtravel Linnet 2 | A. F. Cashin |
| | G-ASMU | Cessna 150D | Telepoint Ltd/Barton |
| | G-ASMV | CP.1310-C3 Super Emeraude | P. F. D. Waltham/Leicester |
| | G-ASMW | Cessna 150D | Yorkshire Light Aircraft Ltd/Leeds |
| | G-ASMY | PA-23 Apache 160H | R. D. & E. Forster |
| | G-ASMZ | A.61 Terrier 2 (VF516) | R. C. Burden |
| | G-ASNB | Auster 6A (VX118) | M. Pocock & ptnrs |
| | G-ASNC | D.5/180 Husky | Peterborough & Spalding Gliding Club/ Boston |
| | G-ASND | PA-23 Aztec 250 | Sky Leisure Aviation Ltd/Shoreham |
| | G-ASNH | PA-23 Aztec 250B | J. Hoerner & The Earl of Suffolk & Berkshire |
| | G-ASNI | CP.1310-C3 Super Emeraude | D. Chapman |
| | G-ASNK | Cessna 205 | Justgold Ltd |
| | G-ASNN | Cessna 185F ★ | (parachute jump trainer)/Tilstock |
| | G-ASNU | H.S.125 Srs. 1 | Flintgrange Ltd |
| | G-ASNW | Cessna F.172E | J. A. Gibbs |
| | G-ASOC | Auster 6A | J. A. Rayment/Hinton-in-the-Hedges |
| | G-ASOH | Beech 95-B55A Baron | GMD Group |
| | G-ASOI | A.61 Terrier 2 | N. K. & C. M. Geddes |
| | G-ASOK | Cessna F.172E | Okay Flying Group/Denham |
| | G-ASOM | A.61 Terrier 2 | J. E. Tootell (G-JETS) |
| | G-ASON | PA-30 Twin Comanche 160 | Follandbeech Ltd |
| | G-ASOO | PA-30 Twin Comanche 160 | K. H. Acketts |
| | G-ASOP | Sopwith F.1 Camel (B6291) | K. C. D. St Cyrien/Middle Wallop |
| | G-ASOX | Cessna 205A | Border Parachute Centre |
| | G-ASPF | Jodel D.120 | T. J. Bates |
| | G-ASPI | Cessna F.172E | Icarus Flying Group/Rochester |
| | G-ASPK | PA-28 Cherokee 140 | Westward Airways (Lands End) Ltd/St Just |
| | G-ASPP | Bristol Boxkite (replica) | Shuttleworth Trust/O. Warden |
| | G-ASPS | Piper J-3C-90 Cub | A. J. Chalkley/Blackbushe |
| | G-ASPU | D.31 Turbulent | I. Maclennan |
| | G-ASPV | D.H.82A Tiger Moth | B. S. Charters/Shipdham |
| | G-ASRB | D.62B Condor | T. J. McRae & H. C. Palmer/Shoreham |
| | G-ASRC | D.62B Condor | J. Knight |
| | G-ASRF | Jenny Wren | G. W. Gowland (stored) |
| | G-ASRH | PA-30 Twin Comanche 160 | Island Aviation & Travel Ltd |
| | G-ASRI | PA-23 Aztec 250B ★ | Graham Collins Associates Ltd |
| | G-ASRK | A.109 Airedale ★ | R. K. Wilson & M. R. H. Wheatley |
| | G-ASRO | PA-30 Twin Comanche 160 | D. W. Blake |
| | G-ASRR | Cessna 182G | J. A. Rees |
| | G-ASRT | Jodel D.150 | P. Turton |
| | G-ASRW | PA-28 Cherokee 180 | Astro Electrical & Heating Ltd/Shoreham |
| | G-ASSE | PA-22 Colt 108 | J. B. King/Goodwood |
| | G-ASSF | Cessna 182G Skylane | Burbage Farms Ltd/Lutterworth |
| | G-ASSM | H.S.125 Srs 1/522 ★ | Science Museum/S. Kensington |
| | G-ASSP | PA-30 Twin Comanche 160 | P. H. Tavener |
| | G-ASSS | Cessna 172E | D. H. N. Squires & P. R. March/Bristol |
| | G-ASST | Cessna 150D | F. R. H. Parker |
| | G-ASSU | CP.301A Emeraude | R. W. Millward (stored)/Redhill |
| | G-ASSV | Kensinger KF | C. I. Jefferson |
| | G-ASSW | PA-28 Cherokee 140 | W. G. R. Wunderlich/Biggin Hill |
| | G-ASTA | D.31 Turbulent | R. N. Steel |
| | G-ASTH | Mooney M.20C ★ | E. Martin (stored) |
| | G-ASTI | Auster 6A | M. Pocock |
| | G-ASTL | Fairey Firefly 1 (Z2033) ★ | Skyfame Collection/Duxford |
| | G-ASTP | Hiller UH-12C ★ | International Helicopter Museum/ Weston-s-Mare |
| | G-ASTV | Cessna 150D (tailwheel) ★ | stored |
| | G-ASUB | Mooney M.20E Super 21 | P. K. Pemberton |
| | G-ASUD | PA-28 Cherokee 180 | S. J. Rogers & M. N. Petchey |
| | G-ASUE | Cessna 150D | D. Huckle/Panshanger |
| | G-ASUG | Beech E18S ★ | Museum of Flight/E. Fortune |
| | G-ASUI | A.61 Terrier 2 | K. W. Chigwell & D. R. Lee |
| | G-ASUL | Cessna 182G Skylane | Blackpool & Fylde Aero Club Ltd |

| Reg. | Type | Owner or Operator | Notes |
|------|------|-------------------|-------|
| G-ASUP | Cessna F.172E | GASUP Air/Cardiff | |
| G-ASUR | Dornier Do 28A-1 | Sheffair Ltd | |
| G-ASUS | Jurca MJ.2B Tempete | D. G. Jones/Coventry | |
| G-ASVG | CP.301B Emeraude | K. R. Jackson | |
| G-ASVM | Cessna F.172E | GATRL Flying Group | |
| G-ASVN | Cessna U.206 Super Skywagon | L. Rawson | |
| G-ASVO | HPR-7 Herald 214 | British Air Ferries Ltd/Southend | |
| G-ASVP | PA-25 Pawnee 235 | Aquila Gliding Club Ltd | |
| G-ASVZ | PA-28 Cherokee 140 | P. Cowey | |
| G-ASWB | A.109 Airedale | C. Gene & G. Taylor/Teesside | |
| G-ASWH | Luton LA-5A Major | J. T. Powell-Tuck | |
| G-ASWJ | Beagle 206 Srs 1 (8449M) ★ | RAF Halton | |
| G-ASWL | Cessna F.172F | Bagby Aviation Flying Group | |
| G-ASWN | Bensen B.8M | D. R. Shepherd | |
| G-ASWP | Beech A.23 Musketeer | MLP Aviation Ltd/Elstree | |
| G-ASWW | PA-30 Twin Comanche 160 | D. M. White | |
| G-ASWX | PA-28 Cherokee 180 | A. F. Dadds | |
| G-ASXC | SIPA 901 | M. K. Dartford & M. Cookson | |
| G-ASXD | Brantly B.2B | Lousada PLC | |
| G-ASXI | Tipsy T.66 Nipper 3 | P. F. J. Wells | |
| G-ASXJ | Luton LA-4A Minor | J. S. Allison/Halton | |
| G-ASXR | Cessna 210 | A. Schofield | |
| G-ASXS | Jodel DR.1050 | R. A. Hunter | |
| G-ASXU | Jodel D.120A | G. W. Worley & D. J. Buffham | |
| G-ASXX | Avro 683 Lancaster 7 (NX611) ★ | Lincolnshire Aviation Heritage Centre/ E. Kirkby | |
| G-ASXY | Jodel D.117A | P. A. Davies & ptnrs/Cardiff | |
| G-ASXZ | Cessna 182G Skylane | P. M. Robertson/Perth | |
| G-ASYD | BAC One-Eleven 670 | British Aerospace | |
| G-ASYG | A.61 Terrier 2 ★ | stored/Hinton-in-the-Hedges | |
| G-ASYJ | Beech D.95A Travel Air | Crosby Aviation (Jersey) Ltd | |
| G-ASYK | PA-30 Twin Comanche 160 | M. S. Harvell | |
| G-ASYP | Cessna 150E | Henlow Flying Group | |
| G-ASYW | Bell 47G-2 | Bristow Helicopters Ltd | |
| G-ASYZ | Victa Airtourer 100 | N. C. Grayson | |
| G-ASZB | Cessna 150E | W. A. Smale/Exeter | |
| G-ASZD | Bo 208A2 Junior | A. J. Watson & ptnrs/O. Warden | |
| G-ASZE | A.61 Terrier 2 | P. J. Moore | |
| G-ASZJ | S.C.7 Skyvan 3A-100 | GEC Marconi Ltd/Luton | |
| G-ASZR | Fairtravel Linnet | H. C. D. & F. J. Garner | |
| G-ASZS | GY.80 Horizon 160 | J. M. B. Duncan | |
| G-ASZU | Cessna 150E | T. H. Milburn | |
| G-ASZV | Tipsy T.66 Nipper 2 | R. L. Mitcham/Elstree | |
| G-ASZX | A.61 Terrier 1 | C. A. Bailey | |
| | | | |
| G-ATAF | Cessna F.172F | S. Lancashire Flyers Ltd | |
| G-ATAG | Jodel DR. 1050 | T. M. Dawes-Gamble | |
| G-ATAI | D.H.104 Dove 8 | L. A. Wootton/France | |
| G-ATAS | PA-28 Cherokee 180 | E. J. Titterrell | |
| G-ATAT | Cessna 150E | The Derek Pointon Group (stored) | |
| G-ATAU | D.62B Condor | M. A. Peare/Redhill | |
| G-ATAV | D.62C Condor | R. W. H. Watson & K. J. Gallagher | |
| G-ATBG | Nord 1002 (NJ-C11) | L. M. Walton | |
| G-ATBH | Aero 145 | P. D. Aberbach | |
| G-ATBI | Beech A.23 Musketeer | R. F. G. Dent/Staverton | |
| G-ATBJ | Sikorsky S-61N | British International Helicopters Ltd | |
| G-ATBL | D.H.60G Moth | J. M. Greenland | |
| G-ATBP | Fournier RF-3 | K. McBride | |
| G-ATBS | D.31 Turbulent | D. R. Keene & J. A. Lear | |
| G-ATBU | A.61 Terrier 2 | P. R. Anderson | |
| G-ATBW | Tipsy T.66 Nipper 2 | Stapleford Nipper Group | |
| G-ATBX | PA-20 Pacer 135 | G. D. & P. M. Thomson | |
| G-ATBZ | W.S.58 Wessex 60 ★ | International Helicopter Museum/ Weston-s-Mare | |
| G-ATCC | A.109 Airedale | J. F. Moore & ptnrs/Biggin Hill | |
| G-ATCD | D.5/180 Husky | Oxford Flying & Gliding Group/Enstone | |
| G-ATCE | Cessna U.206 | J. Fletcher & D. Hickling/Langar | |
| G-ATCJ | Luton LA-4A Minor | R. M. Sharphouse | |
| G-ATCL | Victa Airtourer 100 | A. D. Goodall | |
| G-ATCN | Luton LA-4A Minor | J. C. Gates & C. Neilson | |
| G-ATCR | Cessna 310 ★ | ITD Aviation Ltd/Denham | |
| G-ATCU | Cessna 337 | University of Cambridge | |
| G-ATCX | Cessna 182H Skylane | K. J. Fisher/Bodmin | |

| Notes | Reg. | Type | Owner or Operator |
|---|---|---|---|
| | G-ATDA | PA-28 Cherokee 160 | Global Aircraft Services Ltd |
| | G-ATDN | A.61 Terrier 2 (TW641) | S. J. Saggers/Biggin Hill |
| | G-ATDO | Bo 208C Junior | H. Swift |
| | G-ATEF | Cessna 150E | Swans Aviation |
| | G-ATEG | Cessna 150E | A. W. Woodward/Biggin Hill |
| | G-ATEK | H.S. 748 Srs 2B | STH Sales Ltd |
| | G-ATEM | PA-28 Cherokee 180 | Chiltern Valley Aviation Ltd |
| | G-ATEP | EAA Biplane ★ | E. L. Martin (*stored*)/Guernsey |
| | G-ATES | PA-32 Cherokee Six 260 ★ | *Parachute jump trainer*/Ipswich |
| | G-ATET | PA-30 Twin Comanche 160 | P. W. Bayliss |
| | G-ATEV | Jodel DR. 1050 | R. A. Smith |
| | G-ATEW | PA-30 Twin Comanche 160 | Air Northumbria Group/Newcastle |
| | G-ATEX | Victa Airtourer 100 | Medway Victa Group |
| | G-ATEZ | PA-28 Cherokee 140 | J. A. Burton/E. Midlands |
| | G-ATFD | Jodel DR. 1050 | V. Usher |
| | G-ATFF | PA-23 Aztec 250C | Neatspin Ltd |
| | G-ATFG | Brantly B.2B ★ | Museum of Flight/E. Fortune |
| | G-ATFK | PA-30 Twin Comanche 160 | D. J. Crinnon/White Waltham |
| | G-ATFM | Sikorsky S-61N | British International Helicopters Ltd/ Aberdeen |
| | G-ATFR | PA-25 Pawnee 150 | R. R. Harris |
| | G-ATFU | D.H.85 Leopard Moth | A. de Cadenet |
| | G-ATFV | Agusta-Bell 47J-2A | Alexander Warren & Co Ltd |
| | G-ATFW | Luton LA-4A Minor | C. W. Uldale |
| | G-ATFX | Cessna F.172G | Isabella Properties Ltd |
| | G-ATFY | Cessna F.172G | H. Cowan |
| | G-ATGE | Jodel DR.1050 | J. R. Roberts |
| | G-ATGH | Brantly B.2B | Helihire Ltd |
| | G-ATGN | Thorn Coal Gas balloon | British Balloon Museum |
| | G-ATGO | Cessna F.172G | P. J. Spedding & M. Johnston |
| | G-ATGP | Jodel DR.1050 | Madley Flying Group |
| | G-ATGY | GY.80 Horizon | P. W. Gibberson/Birmingham |
| | G-ATGZ | Griffiths GH-4 Gyroplane | G. Griffiths |
| | G-ATHA | PA-23 Apache 235 ★ | Brunel Technical College/Bristol |
| | G-ATHD | D.H.C.1 Chipmunk 22 (WP971) | Spartan Flying Group Ltd/Denham |
| | G-ATHF | Cessna 150F ★ | Lincolnshire Aircraft Museum |
| | G-ATHI | PA-28 Cherokee 180 ★ | *Instructional airframe*/Dublin |
| | G-ATHK | Aeronca 7AC Champion | N. S. Chittenden |
| | G-ATHM | Wallis WA-116 Srs 1 | Wallis Autogyros Ltd |
| | G-ATHN | Nord 1101 Noralpha | E. L. Martin (*stored*)/Guernsey |
| | G-ATHR | PA-28 Cherokee 180 | Britannia Airways Ltd/Luton |
| | G-ATHT | Victa Airtourer 115 | H. C. G. Munroe |
| | G-ATHU | A.61 Terrier 1 | J. A. L. Irwin |
| | G-ATHV | Cessna 150F | P. Cooper |
| | G-ATHX | Jodel DR. 100A | I. M. Hursey |
| | G-ATHZ | Cessna 150F | E. & R. D. Forster |
| | G-ATIA | PA-24 Comanche 260 | L. A. Brown |
| | G-ATIC | Jodel DR.1050 ★ | *stored* |
| | G-ATID | Cessna 337 | M. R. Tarrant/Bourn |
| | G-ATIE | Cessna 150F ★ | *Parachute jump trainer*/Chetwynd |
| | G-ATIG | HPR-7 Herald 214 | Janes Aviation Ltd/Blackpool |
| | G-ATIN | Jodel D.117 | D. R. Upton & J. G. Kay/Barton |
| | G-ATIR | AIA Stampe SV-4C | N. M. Bloom |
| | G-ATIS | PA-28 Cherokee 160 | P. J. Fydelor |
| | G-ATIZ | Jodel D.117 | R. Frith & ptnrs |
| | G-ATJA | Jodel DR.1050 | Bicester Flying Group |
| | G-ATJC | Victa Airtourer 100 | Aviation West Ltd |
| | G-ATJG | PA-28 Cherokee 140 | Royal Aircraft Establishment Dept/ Thurleigh |
| | G-ATJL | PA-24 Comanche 260 | M. J. Berry & T. R. Quinn/Blackbushe |
| | G-ATJM | Fokker Dr.1 replica (152/17) | R. Lamplough/Duxford |
| | G-ATJN | Jodel D.119 | R. F. Bradshaw |
| | G-ATJR | PA-E23 Aztec 250C | S. Lightbown |
| | G-ATJT | GY.80 Horizon 160 | N. Huxtable |
| | G-ATJV | PA-32 Cherokee Six 260 | SMK Engineers Ltd |
| | G-ATKF | Cessna 150F | A. F. G. Clutterbuck |
| | G-ATKH | Luton LA-4A Minor | H. E. Jenner |
| | G-ATKI | Piper J-3C-65 Cub | J. H. Allistone/Booker |
| | G-ATKS | Cessna F.172G | Blois Aviation Ltd |
| | G-ATKT | Cessna F.172G | P. J. Megson |
| | G-ATKU | Cessna F.172G | Heatherlake Ltd |
| | G-ATKX | Jodel D.140C | A. J. White & G. A. Piper/Biggin Hill |
| | G-ATKZ | Tipsy T.66 Nipper 2 | M. W. Knights |

| Reg. | Type | Owner or Operator | Notes |
|------|------|-------------------|-------|
| G-ATLA | Cessna 182J Skylane | Shefford Transport Engineers Ltd/Luton | |
| G-ATLB | Jodel DR.1050/M1 | La Petit Oiseau Syndicate/Sherburn | |
| G-ATLC | PA-23 Aztec 250C ★ | Alderney Air Charter Ltd (stored) | |
| G-ATLG | Hiller UH-12B | Bristow Helicopters Ltd | |
| G-ATLM | Cessna F.172G | Air Fotos Aviation Ltd/Newcastle | |
| G-ATLP | Bensen B.8M | C. D. Julian | |
| G-ATLT | Cessna U-206A | Army Parachute Association/Netheravon | |
| G-ATLV | Jodel D.120 | W. H. Greenwood | |
| G-ATLW | PA-28 Cherokee 180 | Lima Whisky Flying Group | |
| G-ATMC | Cessna F.150F | C. J. & E. J. Leigh | |
| G-ATMG | M.S.893 Rallye Commodore 180 | D. R. Wilkinson & T. Coldwell | |
| G-ATMH | D.5/180 Husky | Devon & Somerset Gliding Club Ltd | |
| G-ATMI | H.S.748 Srs 2A | Janes Aviation 748 Ltd/Blackpool | |
| G-ATMJ | H.S.748 Srs 2A | Janes Aviation 748 Ltd/Blackpool | |
| G-ATML | Cessna F.150F | B. A. Pickers | |
| G-ATMM | Cessna F.150F | R. Jacobs & R. Felton | |
| G-ATMT | PA-30 Twin Comanche 160 | D. H. T. Bain/Newcastle | |
| G-ATMU | PA-23 Apache 160G | P. K. Martin & R. W. Harris | |
| G-ATMW | PA-28 Cherokee 140 | Bencray Ltd/Blackpool | |
| G-ATMX | Cessna F.150F | A. A. Spirling | |
| G-ATMY | Cessna 150F | C. F. Read/Doncaster | |
| G-ATNB | PA-28 Cherokee 180 | R. F. Hill | |
| G-ATNE | Cessna F.150F | J. & S. Brew | |
| G-ATNJ | Cessna F.150F ★ | Instructional airframe/Perth | |
| G-ATNK | Cessna F.150F | Pegasus Aviation Ltd | |
| G-ATNL | Cessna F.150F | S. M. Kemp & ptnrs | |
| G-ATNV | PA-24 Comanche 260 | B. S. Reynolds & P. R. Fortescue/Bourn | |
| G-ATNX | Cessna F.150F | P. Jenkins | |
| G-ATOA | PA-23 Apache 160G | K. White | |
| G-ATOD | Cessna F.150F | E. Watson & ptnrs/St Just | |
| G-ATOE | Cessna F.150F | S. Armstrong | |
| G-ATOF | Cessna F-150F ★ | Instructional airframe/Perth | |
| G-ATOG | Cessna F-150F ★ | Instructional airframe/Perth | |
| G-ATOH | D.62B Condor | L. S. Thorne | |
| G-ATOI | PA-28 Cherokee 140 | O. & E. Flying Ltd/Stapleford | |
| G-ATOJ | PA-28 Cherokee 140 | Firefly Aviation Ltd/Glasgow | |
| G-ATOK | PA-28 Cherokee 140 | ILC Flying Group | |
| G-ATOL | PA-28 Cherokee 140 | L. J. Nation & G. Alford | |
| G-ATOM | PA-28 Cherokee 140 | R. W. Mason/Kidlington | |
| G-ATON | PA-28 Cherokee 140 | R. G. Walters | |
| G-ATOO | PA-28 Cherokee 140 ★ | Instructional airframe/Moston Centre | |
| G-ATOP | PA-28 Cherokee 140 | P. R. Coombs/Blackbushe | |
| G-ATOR | PA-28 Cherokee 140 | D. Palmer & V. G. Whitehead | |
| G-ATOS | PA-28 Cherokee 140 | E. Alexander | |
| G-ATOT | PA-28 Cherokee 180 | J. B. Waterfield & G. L. Birch | |
| G-ATOU | Mooney M.20E Super 21 | M20 Flying Group | |
| G-ATOY | PA-24 Comanche 260 ★ | Museum of Flight/E. Fortune | |
| G-ATOZ | Bensen B.8M | J. Jordan | |
| G-ATPD | H.S.125 Srs 1B | G. M. Kay | |
| G-ATPN | PA-28 Cherokee 140 | M. F. Hatt & ptnrs/Southend | |
| G-ATPT | Cessna 182J Skylane | Western Models Ltd/Redhill | |
| G-ATPV | JB.01 Minicab | I. A. J. Lappin | |
| G-ATRA | LET L.13 Blanik | Blanik Sydincate | |
| G-ATRC | Beech B.95A Travel Air | P. J. Simmons | |
| G-ATRG | PA-18 Super Cub 150 | Lasham Gliding Soc Ltd | |
| G-ATRI | Bo 208C Junior | Chertwood Ltd | |
| G-ATRK | Cessna F.150F | J. Rees & F. Doncaster | |
| G-ATRL | Cessna F.150F | S. S. Delwarte/Shoreham | |
| G-ATRO | PA-28 Cherokee 140 | 390th Flying Group | |
| G-ATRR | PA-28 Cherokee 140 | Marnham Investments Ltd | |
| G-ATRW | PA-32 Cherokee Six 260 | Moxley & Frankl Ltd | |
| G-ATRX | PA-32 Cherokee Six 260 | J. W. Stow | |
| G-ATSI | Bo 208C Junior | M. R. Reynolds & B. A. Riseborough | |
| G-ATSL | Cessna F.172G | D. Le Cheminant/Guernsey | |
| G-ATSM | Cessna 337A | Landscape & Ground Maintenance | |
| G-ATSR | Beech M.35 Bonanza | Bonanza International Ltd | |
| G-ATSX | Bo 208C Junior | R. J. C. Campbell & M. H. Goley | |
| G-ATSY | Wassmer WA41 Super Baladou IV | Baladou Flying Group | |
| G-ATTB | Wallis WA-116-1 (XR944) | D. A. Wallis | |
| G-ATTD | Cessna 182J Skylane | K. M. Brennan & ptnrs | |
| G-ATTF | PA-28 Cherokee 140 | D. H. Fear | |
| G-ATTG | PA-28 Cherokee 140 | Arrow Air Services Engineering Ltd/ Shipdham | |

| Notes | Reg. | Type | Owner or Operator |
|---|---|---|---|
| | G-ATTI | PA-28 Cherokee 140 | D. J. Skidmore |
| | G-ATTK | PA-28 Cherokee 140 | G-ATTK Flying Group/Southend |
| | G-ATTM | Jodel DR.250-160 | R. W. Tomkinson |
| | G-ATTR | Bo 208C Junior 3 | S. Luck |
| | G-ATTV | PA-28 Cherokee 140 | G-ATTV Group |
| | G-ATTX | PA-28 Cherokee 180 | Ipac Aviation Ltd |
| | G-ATTY | PA-32 Cherokee Six 260 | F. J. Wadia |
| | G-ATUB | PA-28 Cherokee 140 | R. H. Partington & M. J. Porter |
| | G-ATUD | PA-28 Cherokee 140 | E. J. Clempson |
| | G-ATUF | Cessna F.150F | A. R. Hawes/Ipswich |
| | G-ATUG | D.62B Condor | HMW Aviation |
| | G-ATUH | Tipsy T.66 Nipper 1 | D. G. Spruce |
| | G-ATUI | Bo 208C Junior | A. W. Wakefield |
| | G-ATUL | PA-28 Cherokee 180 | H. M. Synge |
| | G-ATVF | D.H.C.1 Chipmunk 22 (Lycoming) | RAFGSA/Dishforth |
| | G-ATVK | PA-28 Cherokee 140 | JRB Aviation Ltd/Southend |
| | G-ATVL | PA-28 Cherokee 140 | West London Aero Services Ltd/ White Waltham |
| | G-ATVO | PA-28 Cherokee 140 | D. L. Claydon |
| | G-ATVP | F.B.5 Gunbus (2345) ★ | RAF Museum/Hendon |
| | G-ATVS | PA-28 Cherokee 180 | Markel Aviation |
| | G-ATVW | D.62B Condor | J. P. Coulter & J. Chidley/Panshanger |
| | G-ATVX | Bo 208C Junior | G. & G. E. F. Warren |
| | G-ATWA | Jodel DR.1050 | Jodel Syndicate |
| | G-ATWB | Jodel D.117 | W. Bampton & ptnrs/Andrewsfield |
| | G-ATWE | M.S.892A Rallye Commodore | D. I. Murray |
| | G-ATWJ | Cessna F.172F | C. J. & J. Freeman/Headcorn |
| | G-ATWP | Alon A-2 Aircoupe | H. Dodd & I. Wilson |
| | G-ATWR | PA-30 Twin Comanche 160B | Lubair (Transport Services) Ltd/ E. Midlands |
| | G-ATXA | PA-22 Tri-Pacer 150 | R. C. Teverson |
| | G-ATXD | PA-30 Twin Comanche 160B | Jet Heritage Ltd/Bournemouth |
| | G-ATXF | GY-80 Horizon 150 | D. C. Hyde |
| | G-ATXJ | H.P.137 Jetstream 300 ★ | British Aerospace (*display mock-up*)/ Prestwick |
| | G-ATXM | PA-28 Cherokee 180 | D. J. Bates |
| | G-ATXN | Mitchell-Proctor Kittiwake | D. W. Kent |
| | G-ATXO | SIPA 903 | M. Hillam/Sherburn |
| | G-ATXZ | Bo 208C Junior | M. W. Hurst |
| | G-ATYM | Cessna F.150G | J. F. Perry & Co |
| | G-ATYN | Cessna F.150G | Skegness Air Taxi Services Ltd |
| | G-ATYS | PA-28 Cherokee 180 | R. V. Waite |
| | G-ATZA | Bo 208C Junior | Skyward Services Ltd/Jersey |
| | G-ATZG | AFB2 gas balloon | Flt Lt S. Cameron *Aeolis* |
| | G-ATZK | PA-28 Cherokee 180 | R. W. Nash & J. A. Gibbs/Kidlington |
| | G-ATZM | Piper J-3C-65 Cub | R. W. Davison |
| | G-ATZS | Wassmer WA41 Super Baladou IV | G. R. Outwin & D. P. Bennett |
| | G-ATZY | Cessna F.150G | J. Easson/Edinburgh |
| | G-ATZZ | Cessna F.150G | Matthews Air Trading Services/Southend |
| | G-AVAA | Cessna F.150G | LAR Aviation Ltd/Shoreham |
| | G-AVAK | M.S.893A Rallye Commodore 180 | W. K. Anderson (*stored*)/Perth |
| | G-AVAP | Cessna F.150G | Seawing Flying Club Ltd/Southend |
| | G-AVAR | Cessna F.150G | J. A. Rees & F. Doncaster |
| | G-AVAU | PA-30 Twin Comanche 160B | L. Batin/Fairoaks |
| | G-AVAW | D.62B Condor | Avato Flying Group |
| | G-AVAX | PA-28 Cherokee 180 | J. J. Parkes |
| | G-AVBG | PA-28 Cherokee 180 | G-AVBG Flying Group/White Waltham |
| | G-AVBH | PA-28 Cherokee 180 | T. R. Smith (Agricultural Machinery) Ltd |
| | G-AVBP | PA-28 Cherokee 140 | Bristol & Wessex Aeroplane Club |
| | G-AVBS | PA-28 Cherokee 180 | Piper Aircraft Club/St Just |
| | G-AVBT | PA-28 Cherokee 180 | J. F. Mitchell |
| | G-AVBZ | Cessna F.172H | M. Byl |
| | G-AVCE | Cessna F.172H | Doncaster Aero Club Ltd |
| | G-AVCM | PA-24 Comanche 260 | F. Smith & Sons Ltd/Stapleford |
| | G-AVCS | A.61 Terrier 1 | A. Topen/Cranfield |
| | G-AVCT | Cessna F.150G | M. L. Biggs/Shobdon |
| | G-AVCU | Cessna F.150G | Farley Aviation Ltd |
| | G-AVCV | Cessna 182J Skylane | University of Manchester Institute of Science & Technology/Woodford |
| | G-AVCX | PA-30 Twin Comanche 160B | T. Barge |
| | G-AVCY | PA-30 Twin Comanche 160B | R. C. Pugsley/Cardiff |
| | G-AVDA | Cessna 182K Skylane | F. W. Ellis & M. C. Burnett |

| Reg. | Type | Owner or Operator | Notes |
|------|------|-------------------|-------|
| G-AVDF | Beagle Pup 100 ★ | Shoreham Airport Museum | |
| G-AVDG | Wallis WA-116 Srs 1 | K. H. Wallis | |
| G-AVDT | Aeronca 7AC Champion | D. Cheney & J. G. Woods | |
| G-AVDV | PA-22 Tri-Pacer 150 (tailwheel) | S. C. Brooks/Slinfold | |
| G-AVDW | D.62B Condor | Druine Condor G-AVDW Group | |
| G-AVDY | Luton LA-4A Minor | D. E. Evans & ptnrs | |
| G-AVEB | Morane MS 230 (157) | T. McG. Leaver | |
| G-AVEC | Cessna F.172H | W. H. Ekin (Engineering) Co Ltd | |
| G-AVEF | Jodel D.150 | Tiger Club (1990) Ltd/Headcorn | |
| G-AVEH | SIAI-Marchetti S.205 | Bob Crowe Aircraft Sales Ltd | |
| G-AVEM | Cessna F.150G | P. Brown | |
| G-AVEN | Cessna F.150G | N. J. Budd/Aberdeen | |
| G-AVEO | Cessna F.150G | H. I. Matthews/Southend | |
| G-AVER | Cessna F.150G | Howells Group PLC | |
| G-AVET | Beech 95-C55A Baron | L. D. Taylor | |
| G-AVEU | Wassmer WA.41 Baladou IV | G. J. Richardson | |
| G-AVEX | D.62B Condor | Cotswold Roller Hire Ltd/Long Marston | |
| G-AVEY | Currie Super Wot | A. Eastelow/Dunkeswell | |
| G-AVEZ | HPR-7 Herald 210 ★ | *Rescue Trainer*/Norwich | |
| G-AVFB | H.S.121 Trident 2E ★ | Duxford Aviation Soc | |
| G-AVFE | H.S.121 Trident 2E ★ | Belfast Airport Authority | |
| G-AVFG | H.S.121 Trident 2E ★ | *Ground handling trainer*/Heathrow | |
| G-AVFH | H.S.121 Trident 2E ★ | Mosquito Aircraft Museum (Fuselage only) | |
| G-AVFK | H.S.121 Trident 2E ★ | Metropolitan Police Training Centre/ Hounslow | |
| G-AVFM | H.S.121 Trident 2E ★ | Brunel Technical College/Bristol | |
| G-AVFP | PA-28 Cherokee 140 | H. D. Vince Ltd/Woodvale | |
| G-AVFR | PA-28 Cherokee 140 | VFR Flying Group/Newtownards | |
| G-AVFS | PA-32 Cherokee Six 300 | Comed Aviation Ltd/Blackpool | |
| G-AVFU | PA-32 Cherokee Six 300 | Ashley Gardner Flying Club Ltd | |
| G-AVFX | PA-28 Cherokee 140 | D. J. Young & H. Weldon | |
| G-AVFZ | PA-28 Cherokee 140 | H. H. Elder | |
| G-AVGA | PA-24 Comanche 260 | Conram Aviation/Biggin Hill | |
| G-AVGB | PA-28 Cherokee 140 | D. J. Hill/Fowlmere | |
| G-AVGC | PA-28 Cherokee 140 | P. A. Hill | |
| G-AVGD | PA-28 Cherokee 140 | S. & G. W. Jacobs | |
| G-AVGE | PA-28 Cherokee 140 | H. H. T. Wolf | |
| G-AVGH | PA-28 Cherokee 140 | Phoenix Aviation Services Ltd | |
| G-AVGI | PA-28 Cherokee 140 | D. G. Smith & C. D. Barden | |
| G-AVGJ | Jodel DR.1050 | S. T. Gilbert & D. J. Kirkwood | |
| G-AVGK | PA-28 Cherokee 180 | Golf Kilo Flying Group | |
| G-AVGP | BAC One-Eleven 408EF | Brymon European Airways Ltd *City of Coventry* | |
| G-AVGV | Cessna F.150G | Bagby Aviation Flying Group | |
| G-AVGY | Cessna 182K Skylane | Clifford F. Cross (Wisbech) Ltd/Fenland | |
| G-AVGZ | Jodel DR.1050 | D. C. Webb | |
| G-AVHH | Cessna F.172H | M. J. Mann & J. Hickinbotom | |
| G-AVHL | Jodel DR.105A | Jodel G-AVHL Flying Group | |
| G-AVHM | Cessna F.150G | A. G. Wintle & J. Knight/Elstree | |
| G-AVHN | Cessna F.150F ★ | Brunel Technical College/Bristol | |
| G-AVHT | Auster AOP.9 (WZ711) | M. Somerton-Rayner/Middle Wallop | |
| G-AVHY | Fournier RF.4D | J. Connelly | |
| G-AVIA | Cessna F.150G | Cheshire Air Training School (Merseyside) Ltd/Liverpool | |
| G-AVIB | Cessna F.150G | Group India Bravo | |
| G-AVIC | Cessna F.172H | Pembrokeshire Air Ltd/Haverfordwest | |
| G-AVID | Cessna 182J | T. D. Boyle | |
| G-AVIE | Cessna F.172H | M. P. Parker | |
| G-AVII | AB-206A JetRanger | Bristow Helicopters Ltd | |
| G-AVIL | Alon A.2 Aircoupe (VX147) | M. J. Close | |
| G-AVIN | M.S.880B Rallye Club | G. I. J. Thomson/Norwich | |
| G-AVIO | M.S.880B Rallye Club | P. I. Thomas | |
| G-AVIP | Brantly B.2B | P. J. Troy-Davies | |
| G-AVIS | Cessna F.172H | R. T. Jones/Rochester | |
| G-AVIT | Cessna F.150G | Shropshire Aero Club Ltd/Sleap | |
| G-AVIZ | Scheibe SF.25A Motorfalke | D. C. Pattison & D. A. Wilson | |
| G-AVJE | Cessna F.150G | G-AVJE Syndicate | |
| G-AVJF | Cessna F.172H | J. A. & G. M. Rees | |
| G-AVJG | Cessna 337B | Alderney Air Charter | |
| G-AVJI | Cessna F.172H | M. A. Kempson | |
| G-AVJJ | PA-30 Twin Comanche 160B | A. H. Manser | |
| G-AVJK | Jodel DR.1050/M1 | G. Wylde | |
| G-AVJO | Fokker E.III (replica) (422-15) | Bianchi Aviation Film Services Ltd | |

| Notes | Reg. | Type | Owner or Operator |
|---|---|---|---|
| | G-AVJV | Wallis WA-117 Srs 1 | K. H. Wallis (G-ATCV) |
| | G-AVJW | Wallis WA-118 Srs 2 | K. H. Wallis (G-ATPW) |
| | G-AVKB | MB.50 Pipistrelle | B. H. Pickard |
| | G-AVKD | Fournier RF-4D | Lasham RF4 Group |
| | G-AVKE | Gadfly HDW.1 ★ | International Helicopter Museum/ Weston-s-Mare |
| | G-AVKG | Cessna F.172H | P. E. P. Sheppard |
| | G-AVKI | Slingsby T.66 Nipper 3 | J. Fisher |
| | G-AVKJ | Slingsby T.66 Nipper 3 | J. M. Greenway |
| | G-AVKK | Slingsby T.66 Nipper 3 | C. Watson |
| | G-AVKL | PA-30 Twin Comanche 160B | C. Matthews |
| | G-AVKN | Cessna 401 | Law Leasing Ltd |
| | G-AVKP | A.109 Airedale | D. R. Williams |
| | G-AVKR | Bo 208C Junior | C. W. Grant |
| | G-AVKY | Hiller UH-12E | Agricopters Ltd/Chilbolton |
| | G-AVKZ | PA-23 Aztec 250C | Tindon Ltd/Little Snoring |
| | G-AVLB | PA-28 Cherokee 140 | J. A. Overton Ltd/Andrewsfield |
| | G-AVLC | PA-28 Cherokee 140 | F. C. V. Hopkins/Swansea |
| | G-AVLD | PA-28 Cherokee 140 | WLS Flying Group/White Waltham |
| | G-AVLE | PA-28 Cherokee 140 | Video Security Services/Tollerton |
| | G-AVLF | PA-28 Cherokee 140 | G. H. Hughesdon |
| | G-AVLG | PA-28 Cherokee 140 | R. Friedlander & D. C. Raymond |
| | G-AVLH | PA-28 Cherokee 140 | Menai Flying Group |
| | G-AVLI | PA-28 Cherokee 140 | J. V. White |
| | G-AVLJ | PA-28 Cherokee 140 | E. Berks Boat Company Ltd |
| | G-AVLN | B.121 Pup 2 | C. A. Thorpe |
| | G-AVLO | Bo 208C Junior | J. A. Webb & K. F. Barnard/Popham |
| | G-AVLR | PA-28 Cherokee 140 | Group 140/Panshanger |
| | G-AVLT | PA-28 Cherokee 140 | R. W. Harris & ptnrs/Southend |
| | G-AVLU | PA-28 Cherokee 140 | London Transport (CRS) Sports Association Flying Club/Fairoaks |
| | G-AVLW | Fournier RF-4D | F. Mumford |
| | G-AVLY | Jodel D.120A | G-AVLY Flying Group |
| | G-AVMA | GY-80 Horizon 180 | B. R. Hildick |
| | G-AVMB | D.62B Condor | J. C. Mansell |
| | G-AVMD | Cessna 150G | Bagby Aviation Flying Group |
| | G-AVMF | Cessna F. 150G | J. F. Marsh |
| | G-AVMJ | BAC One-Eleven 510ED | British Airways *Strathclyde Region* |
| | G-AVMN | BAC One-Eleven 510ED | British Airways *County of Essex* |
| | G-AVMO | BAC One-Eleven 510ED | British Airways *Lothian Region* |
| | G-AVMS | BAC One-Eleven 510ED | British Airways *County of West Sussex* |
| | G-AVMV | BAC One-Eleven 510ED | British Airways *Greater Manchester County* |
| | G-AVMW | BAC One-Eleven 510ED | British Airways *Grampian Region* |
| | G-AVNC | Cessna F.150G | J. Turner |
| | G-AVNE | W.S.58 Wessex Mk 60 Srs 1 ★ | International Helicopter Museum/ Weston-s-Mare |
| | G-AVNN | PA-28 Cherokee 180 | B. Andrews & C. S. Mitchell |
| | G-AVNO | PA-28 Cherokee 180 | Allister Flight Ltd/Stapleford |
| | G-AVNP | PA-28 Cherokee 180 | R. W. Harris & ptnrs |
| | G-AVNR | PA-28 Cherokee 180 | R. R. Livingstone |
| | G-AVNS | PA-28 Cherokee 180 | November Sierra Flying Group |
| | G-AVNU | PA-28 Cherokee 180 | O. Durrani |
| | G-AVNW | PA-28 Cherokee 180 | Len Smith's School & Sports Ltd |
| | G-AVNX | Fournier RF-4D | Nymphsfield RF-4 Group |
| | G-AVNY | Fournier RF-4D | V. S. E. Norman/Staverton |
| | G-AVNZ | Fournier RF-4D | Shipping & Airlines Ltd/Biggin Hill |
| | G-AVOA | Jodel DR.1050 | D. A. Willies/Cranwell |
| | G-AVOH | D.62B Condor | D. F. Ranger/Popham |
| | G-AVOM | Jodel DR.221 | M. A. Mountford/Headcorn |
| | G-AVOO | PA-18 Super Cub 150 | London Gliding Club Ltd/ Dunstable |
| | G-AVOZ | PA-28 Cherokee 180 | J. R. Winning/Booker |
| | G-AVPC | D.31 Turbulent | J. Sharp (*stored*) |
| | G-AVPD | D.9 Bebe | S. W. McKay (*stored*) |
| | G-AVPH | Cessna F.150G | W. Lancashire Aero Club/Woodvale |
| | G-AVPI | Cessna F.172H | R. W. Cope |
| | G-AVPJ | D.H.82A Tiger Moth | C. C. Silk |
| | G-AVPK | M.S.892A Rallye Commodore | B. A. Bridgewater/Halfpenny Green |
| | G-AVPM | Jodel D.117 | J. Houghton/Brighton |
| | G-AVPN | HPR-7 Herald 213 | Channel Express (Air Services) Ltd/ Bournemouth |
| | G-AVPO | Hindustan HAL-26 Pushpak | J. A. Rimell |
| | G-AVPR | PA-30 Twin Comanche 160B | Cold Storage (Jersey) Ltd |

| Reg. | Type | Owner or Operator | Notes |
|------|------|-------------------|-------|
| G-AVPS | PA-30 Twin Comanche 160B | J. M. Bisco/Staverton | |
| G-AVPT | PA-18 Super Cub 150 | Tiger Club (1990) Ltd/Headcorn | |
| G-AVPV | PA-28 Cherokee 180 | MLP Aviation Ltd/Elstree | |
| G-AVRK | PA-28 Cherokee 180 | J. Gama | |
| G-AVRN | Boeing 737-204 | Britannia Airways Ltd *Capt James Cook* | |
| G-AVRP | PA-28 Cherokee 140 | T. Hiscox | |
| G-AVRS | GY-80 Horizon 180 | Air Venturas Ltd | |
| G-AVRT | PA-28 Cherokee 140 | Star Aviation Trust Group/Stapleford | |
| G-AVRU | PA-28 Cherokee 180 | G-AVRU Partnership/Clacton | |
| G-AVRW | GY-20 Minicab | Kestrel Flying Group/Tollerton | |
| G-AVRY | PA-28 Cherokee 180 | Brigfast Ltd/Blackbushe | |
| G-AVRZ | PA-28 Cherokee 180 | Mantavia Group Ltd | |
| G-AVSA | PA-28 Cherokee 180 | G-AVSA Flying Group | |
| G-AVSB | PA-28 Cherokee 180 | White House Garage Ashford Ltd | |
| G-AVSC | PA-28 Cherokee 180 | Medidata Ltd | |
| G-AVSD | PA-28 Cherokee 180 | Landmate Ltd | |
| G-AVSE | PA-28 Cherokee 180 | Yorkshire Aeroplane Club Ltd/Leeds | |
| G-AVSF | PA-28 Cherokee 180 | Monday Club/Blackbushe | |
| G-AVSI | PA-28 Cherokee 140 | CR Aviation Ltd | |
| G-AVSP | PA-28 Cherokee 180 | Devon School of Flying/Dunkeswell | |
| G-AVSR | D.5/180 Husky | A. L. Young | |
| G-AVSZ | AB-206B JetRanger | Bristow Helicopters Ltd | |
| G-AVTC | Slingsby T.66 Nipper 3 | M. K. Field | |
| G-AVTJ | PA-32 Cherokee Six 260 | Itenson Aviation | |
| G-AVTK | PA-32 Cherokee Six 260 | Malu Aviation Ltd/Alderney | |
| G-AVTP | Cessna F.172H | W. Murphy | |
| G-AVTT | Ercoupe 415D | Wright's Farm Eggs Ltd/Andrewsfield | |
| G-AVTV | M.S.893A Rallye Commodore | D. B. Meeks | |
| G-AVUD | PA-30 Twin Comanche 160B | F. M. Aviation/Biggin Hill | |
| G-AVUG | Cessna F.150H | Skyways Flying Group/Netherthorpe | |
| G-AVUH | Cessna F.150H | G-AVUH Group | |
| G-AVUL | Cessna F.172H | R. Bilson & R. D. Turner | |
| G-AVUS | PA-28 Cherokee 140 | R. Groat/Glasgow | |
| G-AVUT | PA-28 Cherokee 140 | Bencray Ltd/Blackpool | |
| G-AVUU | PA-28 Cherokee 140 | A. Jahanfar & ptnrs/Southend | |
| G-AVUZ | PA-32 Cherokee Six 300 | Ceesix Ltd/Jersey | |
| G-AVVC | Cessna F.172H | J. S. M. Cattle | |
| G-AVVE | Cessna F.150H ★ | R. Windley (*stored*) | |
| G-AVVI | PA-30 Twin Comanche 160B | H. E. Boulter & D. G. Bligh | |
| G-AVVJ | M.S.893A Rallye Commodore | Herefordshire Gliding Club Ltd/ Shobdon | |
| G-AVVL | Cessna F.150H | N. E. Sams/Cranfield | |
| G-AVVO | Avro 652A Anson 19 (VL348) ★ | Newark Air Museum | |
| G-AVVV | PA-28 Cherokee 180 | A. H. Lavender & D. M. Smith | |
| G-AVVX | Cessna F.150H | Hatfield Flying Club | |
| G-AVWA | PA-28 Cherokee 140 | M. Jarrett | |
| G-AVWD | PA-28 Cherokee 140 | M. P. Briggs | |
| G-AVWE | PA-28 Cherokee 140 | W. C. C. Meyer (*stored*)/Biggin Hill | |
| G-AVWG | PA-28 Cherokee 140 | Bencray Ltd/Blackpool | |
| G-AVWH | PA-28 Cherokee 140 | G-OHOG Flying Ltd | |
| G-AVWI | PA-28 Cherokee 140 | L. M. Veitch | |
| G-AVWJ | PA-28 Cherokee 140 | M. J. Steer/Biggin Hill | |
| G-AVWL | PA-28 Cherokee 140 | P. J. Pratt/Dunkeswell | |
| G-AVWM | PA-28 Cherokee 140 | P. E. Preston & ptnrs/Southend | |
| G-AVWN | PA-28R Cherokee Arrow 180 | Vawn Air Ltd/Jersey | |
| G-AVWO | PA-28R Cherokee Arrow 180 | P. D. Cahill/Biggin Hill | |
| G-AVWR | PA-28R Cherokee Arrow 180 | D. A. Howe | |
| G-AVWT | PA-28R Cherokee Arrow 180 | Cloud Base Aviation Group | |
| G-AVWU | PA-28R Cherokee Arrow 180 | Arrow Flyers Ltd | |
| G-AVWV | PA-28R Cherokee Arrow 180 | Strathtay Flying Group | |
| G-AVWY | Fournier RF-4D | B. Houghton | |
| G-AVXA | PA-25 Pawnee 235 | S. Wales Gliding Club Ltd | |
| G-AVXC | Slingsby T.66 Nipper 3 | S. D. Todd | |
| G-AVXD | Slingsby T.66 Nipper 3 | D. A. Davidson | |
| G-AVXF | PA-28R Cherokee Arrow 180 | JDR Arrow Group | |
| G-AVXI | H.S.748 Srs 2A | Civil Aviation Authority/Teesside | |
| G-AVXJ | H.S.748 Srs 2A | Civil Aviation Authority/Teesside | |
| G-AVXX | Cessna FR.172E | Goldensimple Ltd | |
| G-AVXY | Auster AOP.9 (XK417) ★ | R. Windley (*on rebuild*)/Leicester | |
| G-AVXZ | PA-28 Cherokee 140 ★ | ATC Hangar (*instructional airframe*) | |
| G-AVYB | H.S.121 Trident 1E-140 ★ | *SAS training airframe*/Hereford | |
| G-AVYE | H.S.121 Trident 1E-140 ★ | *Test airframe*/Hatfield | |
| G-AVYK | A.61 Terrier 3 | A. R. Wright/Booker | |
| G-AVYL | PA-28 Cherokee 180 | Cherokee G-AVYL Flying Group | |

| Notes | Reg. | Type | Owner or Operator |
|---|---|---|---|
| | G-AVYM | PA-28 Cherokee 180 | Carlisle Aviation (1985) Ltd/Crosby |
| | G-AVYP | PA-28 Cherokee 140 | T. D. Reid (Braids) Ltd/Newtownards |
| | G-AVYR | PA-28 Cherokee 140 | D.R. Flying Club Ltd/Staverton |
| | G-AVYS | PA-28R Cherokee Arrow 180 | D. H. Saunders/Ipswich |
| | G-AVYT | PA-28R Cherokee Arrow 180 | Blackpool & Fylde Aero Club |
| | G-AVYV | Jodel D.120 | A. J. Sephton |
| | G-AVZB | Aero Z-37 Cmelak ★ | Science Museum/Wroughton |
| | G-AVZI | Bo 208C Junior | C. F. Rogers |
| | G-AVZM | B.121 Pup 1 | ARAZ Group/Elstree |
| | G-AVZN | B.121 Pup 1 | E. M. Lewis & C. A. Homewood |
| | G-AVZO | B.121 Pup 1 ★ | Thameside Aviation Museum/E. Tilbury |
| | G-AVZP | B.121 Pup 1 | T. A. White |
| | G-AVZR | PA-28 Cherokee 180 | Lincoln Aero Club Ltd/Sturgate |
| | G-AVZU | Cessna F.150H | R. D. & E. Forster/Swanton Morley |
| | G-AVZV | Cessna F.172H | E. M. & D. S. Lightbown |
| | G-AVZW | EAA Biplane Model P | R. G. Maidment & G. R. Edmundson/ Goodwood |
| | G-AVZX | M.S.880B Rallye Club | A. F. K. Horne |
| | G-AWAA | M.S.880B Rallye Club | P. A. Cairns/Dunkeswell |
| | G-AWAC | GY-80 Horizon 180 | R. D. Harper |
| | G-AWAD | Beech 95-D55 Baron | Aero Lease Ltd/Bournemouth |
| | G-AWAH | Beech 95-D55 Baron | B. J. S. Grey |
| | G-AWAI | Beech 95-D55 Baron | Executive Displays Ltd |
| | G-AWAJ | Beech 95-D55 Baron | Standard Hose Ltd/Leeds |
| | G-AWAT | D.62B Condor | Tarwood Ltd/Redhill |
| | G-AWAU | Vickers F.B.27A Vimy (replica) (F8614) ★ | Bomber Command Museum/Hendon |
| | G-AWAW | Cessna F.150F ★ | Science Museum/S. Kensington |
| | G-AWAZ | PA-28R Cherokee Arrow 180 | A. & A. A. Buckley |
| | G-AWBA | PA-28R Cherokee Arrow 180 | March Flying Group/Stapleford |
| | G-AWBB | PA-28R Cherokee Arrow 180 | M. D. Parker & J. Lowe |
| | G-AWBC | PA-28R Cherokee Arrow 180 | Anglo Aviation (UK) Ltd |
| | G-AWBE | PA-28 Cherokee 140 | B. E. Boyle |
| | G-AWBH | PA-28 Cherokee 140 | R. C. A. Mackworth |
| | G-AWBJ | Fournier RF-4D | J. M. Adams |
| | G-AWBL | BAC One-Eleven 416EK | Brymon European Airways Ltd *City of Birmingham* |
| | G-AWBM | D.31 Turbulent | A. D. Pratt |
| | G-AWBN | PA-30 Twin Comanche 160B | Stourfield Investments Ltd/Jersey |
| | G-AWBP | Cessna 182L Skylane | Xaxanaka Aviation Ltd/Thruxton |
| | G-AWBS | PA-28 Cherokee 140 | W. London Aero Services Ltd/ White Waltham |
| | G-AWBT | PA-30 Twin Comanche 160B ★ | *Instructional airframe*/Cranfield |
| | G-AWBU | Morane-Saulnier N (replica) (M.S.50) | Personal Plane Services Ltd/ Booker |
| | G-AWBV | Cessna 182L Skylane | Aerofilms Ltd/Elstree |
| | G-AWBW | Cessna F.172H ★ | Brunel Technical College/Bristol |
| | G-AWBX | Cessna F.150H | D. F. Ranger |
| | G-AWCM | Cessna F.150H | Cheshire Air Training School (Merseyside) Ltd/Liverpool |
| | G-AWCN | Cessna FR.172E | LEC Refrigeration Ltd |
| | G-AWCP | Cessna F.150H (tailwheel) | C. E. Mason/Shobdon |
| | G-AWDA | Slingsby T.66 Nipper 3 | J. A. Cheesebrough |
| | G-AWDD | Slingsby T.66 Nipper 3 | P. F. J. Wells |
| | G-AWDI | PA-23 Aztec 250C | *(stored)* |
| | G-AWDO | D.31 Turbulent | R. N. Crosland |
| | G-AWDP | PA-28 Cherokee 180 | B. H. & P. M. Illston/Shipdham |
| | G-AWDR | Cessna FR.172E | B. A. Wallace |
| | G-AWDU | Brantly B.2B | G. E. J. Redwood |
| | G-AWEF | SNCAN Stampe SV-4B | Tiger Club (1990) Ltd/Headcorn |
| | G-AWEI | D.62B Condor | M. J. Steer |
| | G-AWEL | Fournier RF-4D | A. B. Clymo/Halfpenny Green |
| | G-AWEM | Fournier RF-4D | B. J. Griffin/Wickenby |
| | G-AWEN | Jodel DR.1050 | L. G. Earnshaw & ptnrs |
| | G-AWEP | Ord-Hume JB-01 Minicab | J. A. Stewart & S. N. Askey |
| | G-AWER | PA-23 Aztec 250C | H. McC. Clarke/Ronaldsway |
| | G-AWET | PA-28 Cherokee 180 | Broadland Flying Group Ltd/ Shipdham |
| | G-AWEV | PA-28 Cherokee 140 | Broxbow Ltd |
| | G-AWEX | PA-28 Cherokee 140 | R. Badham |
| | G-AWEZ | PA-28R Cherokee Arrow 180 | Topcruise Ltd |
| | G-AWFB | PA-28R Cherokee Arrow 180 | Luke Aviation Ltd/Bristol |
| | G-AWFC | PA-28R Cherokee Arrow 180 | K. A. Goodchild/Southend |

| Reg. | Type | Owner or Operator | Notes |
|---|---|---|---|
| G-AWFD | PA-28R Cherokee Arrow 180 | D. J. Hill | |
| G-AWFF | Cessna F.150H | Shobdon Aircraft Maintenance | |
| G-AWFJ | PA-28R Cherokee Arrow 180 | K. Barr | |
| G-AWFK | PA-28R Cherokee Arrow 180 | Steepletone Products Ltd | |
| G-AWFN | D.62B Condor | R. James | |
| G-AWFO | D.62B Condor | T. A. Major | |
| G-AWFP | D.62B Condor | Blackbushe Flying Club | |
| G-AWFR | D.31 Turbulent | L. W. Usherwood | |
| G-AWFT | Jodel D.9 Bebe | W. H. Cole | |
| G-AWFW | Jodel D.117 | F. H. Greenwell | |
| G-AWFZ | Beech A23 Musketeer | R. Sweet & B D. Corbett | |
| G-AWGA | A.109 Airedale ★ | stored/Sevenoaks | |
| G-AWGD | Cessna F.172H | Aero Marine Technology Ltd | |
| G-AWGJ | Cessna F.172H | J. & C. J. Freeman/Headcorn | |
| G-AWGK | Cessna F.150H | G. R. Brown/Shoreham | |
| G-AWGM | Arkle Kittiwake 2 | M. K. Field | |
| G-AWGN | Fournier RF-4D | R. H. Ashforth/Staverton | |
| G-AWGP | Cessna T.210H | S. Harcourt/Elstree | |
| G-AWGR | Cessna F.172H | P. A. Hallam | |
| G-AWGZ | Taylor JT.1 Monoplane | J. A. L. Parton | |
| G-AWHB | C.A.S.A. 2-111D (6J+PR) ★ | Aces High Ltd/North Weald | |
| G-AWHV | Rollason Beta B.2A | V. W. B. Davies | |
| G-AWHX | Rollason Beta B.2 | S. G. Jones | |
| G-AWHY | Falconar F.11-3 | J. R. Riley-Gale (G-BDPB) | |
| G-AWIF | Brookland Mosquito 2 | —/Husbands Bosworth | |
| G-AWII | V.S.349 Spitfire VC (AR501) | Shuttleworth Trust/Duxford | |
| G-AWIO | Brantly B.2B | J. K. Davies (G-OBPG) | |
| G-AWIP | Luton LA-4A Minor | J. Houghton | |
| G-AWIR | Midget Mustang | K. E. Sword/Leicester | |
| G-AWIT | PA-28 Cherokee 180 | Manco Ltd | |
| G-AWIV | Airmark TSR.3 | D. J. & F. M. Nunn | |
| G-AWIW | SNCAN Stampe SV-4B | R. E. Mitchell | |
| G-AWIY | PA-23 Aztec 250C | B. Anderson/Belfast | |
| G-AWJE | Slingsby T.66 Nipper 3 | T. Mosedale | |
| G-AWJF | Slingsby T.66 Nipper 3 | R. Wilcock/Shoreham | |
| G-AWJI | M.S.880B Rallye Club | D. V. Tyler/Southend | |
| G-AWJV | D.H.98 Mosquito TT Mk 35 (TA634) ★ | Mosquito Aircraft Museum | |
| G-AWJX | Zlin Z.526 Akrobat | Aerobatics International Ltd | |
| G-AWJY | Zlin Z.526 Akrobat | Elco Manufacturing Co | |
| G-AWKB | M.J.5 Sirocco F2/39 | G. D. Claxton | |
| G-AWKD | PA-17 Vagabond | A. T. & M. R. Dowie/ White Waltham | |
| G-AWKM | B.121 Pup 1 | D. M. G. Jenkins/Swansea | |
| G-AWKO | B.121 Pup 1 | Bustard Flying Club Ltd | |
| G-AWKP | Jodel DR.253 | D. A. Hood | |
| G-AWKT | M.S.880B Rallye Club | J. Strain/Portadown | |
| G-AWKX | Beech A65 Queen Air ★ | (Instructional airframe)/Shoreham | |
| G-AWLA | Cessna F.150H | Royal Artillery Aero Club Ltd/Middle Wallop | |
| G-AWLE | Cessna F.172H | H. Mendelsohn & H. I. Shott | |
| G-AWLF | Cessna F.172H | Gannet Aviation Ltd | |
| G-AWLG | SIPA 903 | S. W. Markham | |
| G-AWLI | PA-22 Tri-Pacer 150 | J. S. Lewery/Shoreham | |
| G-AWLL | AB-206B JetRanger 2 | Base Helicopters Ltd | |
| G-AWLO | Boeing Stearman E.75 | N. D. Pickard/Shoreham | |
| G-AWLP | Mooney M.20F | Petratek Ltd | |
| G-AWLR | Slingsby T.66 Nipper 3 | C. F. O'Neill | |
| G-AWLS | Slingsby T.66 Nipper 3 | Stapleford Nipper Group | |
| G-AWLZ | Fournier RF-4D | E. V. Goodwin & C. R. Williamson | |
| G-AWMD | Jodel D.11 | G. E. Valler | |
| G-AWMF | PA-18 Super Cub 150 (modified) | Booker Gliding Club Ltd | |
| G-AWMI | Glos-Airtourer 115 | Airtourer Group 86/Cardiff | |
| G-AWMK | AB-206B JetRanger | Bristow Helicopters Ltd | |
| G-AWMM | M.S.893A Rallye Commodore 180 | D. P. & S. White | |
| G-AWMN | Luton LA-4A Minor | C. F. O'Neill | |
| G-AWMP | Cessna F.172H | Blois Aviation Ltd | |
| G-AWMR | D.31 Turbulent | C. F. Kennedy | |
| G-AWMT | Cessna F.150H | R. V. Grocott/Sleap | |
| G-AWMZ | Cessna F.172H ★ | Parachute jump trainer/Cark | |
| G-AWNA | Boeing 747-136 | British Airways Colliford Lake | |
| G-AWNB | Boeing 747-136 | British Airways Llangorse Lake | |
| G-AWNC | Boeing 747-136 | British Airways Lake Windermere | |
| G-AWNE | Boeing 747-136 | British Airways Derwent Water | |
| G-AWNF | Boeing 747-136 | British Airways Blagdon Water | |

| Notes | Reg. | Type | Owner or Operator |
|---|---|---|---|
| | G-AWNG | Boeing 747-136 | British Airways *Rutland Water* |
| | G-AWNH | Boeing 747-136 | British Airways *Devoke Water* |
| | G-AWNJ | Boeing 747-136 | British Airways *Bassenthwaite Lake* |
| | G-AWNL | Boeing 747-136 | British Airways *Ennerdale Water* |
| | G-AWNM | Boeing 747-136 | British Airways *Ullswater* |
| | G-AWNN | Boeing 747-136 | British Airways *Loweswater* |
| | G-AWNO | Boeing 747-136 | British Airways *Grafham Water* |
| | G-AWNP | Boeing 747-136 | British Airways *Hanningfield Water* |
| | G-AWNT | BN-2A Islander | Aerofilms Ltd/Elstree |
| | G-AWOA | M.S.880B Rallye Club | M. Craven & ptnrs/Barton |
| | G-AWOE | Aero Commander 680E | J. M. Houlder/Elstree |
| | G-AWOF | PA-15 Vagabond | J. K. Davies |
| | G-AWOH | PA-17 Vagabond | The High Flats Flying Group |
| | G-AWOT | Cessna F.150H | J. M. Montgomerie & J. Ferguson |
| | G-AWOU | Cessna 170B | S. Billington/Denham |
| | G-AWOX | W.S.58 Wessex 60 ★ | International Helicopters Museum/ Weston-s-Mare |
| | G-AWPH | P.56 Provost T.1 | J. A. D. Bradshaw |
| | G-AWPJ | Cessna F.150H | W. J. Greenfield |
| | G-AWPN | Shield Xyla | M. J. Herlihy |
| | G-AWPP | Cessna F.150H | Croxley Flying Group/Denham |
| | G-AWPS | PA-28 Cherokee 140 | K. J. Steele & D. J. Hewitt |
| | G-AWPU | Cessna F.150J | Howells Group PLC |
| | G-AWPW | PA-12 Super Cruiser | J. E. Davies/Sandown |
| | G-AWPY | Bensen B.8M | J. Jordan |
| | G-AWPZ | Andreasson BA-4B | J. M. Vening |
| | G-AWRK | Cessna F.150J | Southern Strut Flying Group/Shoreham |
| | G-AWRL | Cessna F.172H | B. Welsh |
| | G-AWRS | Avro 19 Srs. 2 ★ | N. E. Aircraft Museum |
| | G-AWRY | P.56 Provost T.1 (XF836) | Slymar Aviation & Services Ltd |
| | G-AWRZ | Bell 47G-5 | Hammond Aerial Spraying Ltd |
| | G-AWSA | Avro 652A Anson 19 (VL349) ★ | Norfolk & Suffolk Aviation Museum |
| | G-AWSD | Cessna F.150J | British Skysports *(stored)* |
| | G-AWSL | PA-28 Cherokee 180D | Fascia Ltd/Southend |
| | G-AWSM | PA-28 Cherokee 235 | S. J. Green |
| | G-AWSN | D.62B Condor | J. Leader |
| | G-AWSP | D.62B Condor | R. Q. & A. S. Bond/Wellesbourne |
| | G-AWSS | D.62C Condor | G. Bruce/Inverness |
| | G-AWST | D.62B Condor | Humberside Aviation/Doncaster |
| | G-AWSV | Skeeter 12 (XM553) | Maj. M. Somerton-Rayner/Middle Wallop |
| | G-AWSW | D.5/180 Husky (XW635) | RAF College Flying Club/Cranwell |
| | G-AWSY | Boeing 737-204 | Britannia Airways Ltd *General James Wolfe*/ Luton |
| | G-AWTA | Cessna E.310N | Heliscott Ltd |
| | G-AWTJ | Cessna F.150J | B. L. Wratten & D. G. Williams |
| | G-AWTL | PA-28 Cherokee 180D | D. M. Bailey |
| | G-AWTS | Beech A.23 Musketeer | G-AWTS Flying Group |
| | G-AWTV | Beech A.23 Musketeer | A. Johnston/Blackbushe |
| | G-AWTW | Beech 95-B55 Baron | R. W. Davies/Staverton |
| | G-AWTX | Cessna F.150J | R. D. & E. Forster |
| | G-AWUB | GY-201 Minicab | H. P. Burrill |
| | G-AWUE | Jodel DR.1050 | S. Bichan |
| | G-AWUG | Cessna F.150H | J. Easson/Edinburgh |
| | G-AWUH | Cessna F.150H | Airtime (Hampshire) Ltd |
| | G-AWUJ | Cessna F.150H | W. Lawton/Doncaster |
| | G-AWUL | Cessna F.150H | Alderquest Ltd |
| | G-AWUN | Cessna F.150H | D. King |
| | G-AWUO | Cessna F.150H | Air Fenland Ltd |
| | G-AWUS | Cessna F.150J | Recreational Flying Centre (Popham) Ltd |
| | G-AWUT | Cessna F.150J | S. J. Black/Leeds |
| | G-AWUU | Cessna F.150J | D. G. Burden |
| | G-AWUW | Cessna F.172H | B. Stewart/Panshanger |
| | G-AWUX | Cessna F.172H | D. K. Brian & ptrs |
| | G-AWUZ | Cessna F.172H | G. F. Burling |
| | G-AWVA | Cessna F.172H | Barton Air Ltd |
| | G-AWVB | Jodel D.117 | Gower Taildraggers/Swansea |
| | G-AWVC | B.121 Pup 1 | J. H. Marshall & J. J. West |
| | G-AWVE | Jodel DR.1050/M1 | E. A. Taylor/Southend |
| | G-AWVF | P.56 Provost T.1 (XF877) | Hunter Wing Ltd/Bournemouth |
| | G-AWVG | AESL Airtourer T.2 | C. J. Schofield |
| | G-AWVN | Aeronca 7AC Champion | W. S. & W. A. Bowker/Rush Green |
| | G-AWVZ | Jodel D.112 | D. C. Stokes |
| | G-AWWE | B.121 Pup 2 | J. M. Randle/Coventry |

| Reg. | Type | Owner or Operator | Notes |
|---|---|---|---|
| G-AWWF | B.121 Pup 1 | N. M. Morris/Denham | |
| G-AWWI | Jodel D.117 | J. C. Hatton | |
| G-AWWM | GY-201 Minicab | J. S. Brayshaw | |
| G-AWWN | Jodel DR.1051 | T. W. M. Beck & ptnrs | |
| G-AWWO | Jodel DR.1050 | Whiskey Oscar Group/Barton | |
| G-AWWP | Aerosport Woody Pusher III | M. S. Bird & R. D. Bird | |
| G-AWWT | D.31 Turbulent | P. J. Simpson | |
| G-AWWU | Cessna FR.172F | Westward Airways (Lands End) Ltd | |
| G-AWWW | Cessna 401 | Air Charter & Travel Ltd | |
| G-AWWX | BAC One-Eleven 509EW | British Air Ferries/Southend | |
| G-AWXA | Cessna 182M | P. Cannon | |
| G-AWXO | H.S.125 Srs. 400B | Twinjet Aircraft Sales Ltd/Luton | |
| G-AWXR | PA-28 Cherokee 180D | J. D. Williams | |
| G-AWXS | PA-28 Cherokee 180D | Rayhenro Flying Group/Shobdon | |
| G-AWXU | Cessna F.150J | Howe Aviation Group | |
| G-AWXY | M.S.885 Super Rallye | Sussex Spraying Services Ltd/Shoreham | |
| G-AWXZ | SNCAN Stampe SV-4C | Personal Plane Services Ltd/Booker | |
| G-AWYB | Cessna FR.172F | C. W. Larkin/Southend | |
| G-AWYF | G.159 Gulfstream 1 | Ford Motor Co Ltd/Stansted | |
| G-AWYJ | B.121 Pup 2 | H. C. Taylor | |
| G-AWYL | Jodel DR.253B | M. J. McRobert | |
| G-AWYO | B.121 Pup 1 | B. R. C. Wild/Popham | |
| G-AWYR | BAC One-Eleven 501EX | British Airways Birmingham County of Suffolk | |
| G-AWYS | BAC One-Eleven 501EX | British Airways Birmingham County of Norfolk | |
| G-AWYT | BAC One-Eleven 501EX | British Airways Birmingham County of Gwynedd | |
| G-AWYU | BAC One-Eleven 501EX | British Airways Birmingham County of Avon | |
| G-AWYV | BAC One-Eleven 501EX | British Airways Birmingham County of Powys | |
| G-AWYX | M.S.880B Rallye Club | J. M. L. Edwards/Exeter | |
| G-AWYY | T.57 Camel replica (B6401) ★ | FAA Museum/Yeovilton | |
| G-AWZE | H.S.121 Trident 3B ★ | *Instructional airframe*/Heathrow | |
| G-AWZI | H.S.121 Trident 3B ★ | Surrey Fire Brigade (*instructional airframe*)/Reigate | |
| G-AWZJ | H.S.121 Trident 3B ★ | British Airports Authority/Prestwick | |
| G-AWZK | H.S.121 Trident 3B ★ | *Ground trainer*/Heathrow | |
| G-AWZM | H.S.121 Trident 3B ★ | Science Museum/Wroughton | |
| G-AWZN | H.S.121 Trident 3B ★ | Cranfield | |
| G-AWZO | H.S.121 Trident 3B ★ | British Aerospace PLC/Hatfield | |
| G-AWZP | H.S.121 Trident 3B ★ | Greater Manchester Museum of Science & Technology (*nose only*) | |
| G-AWZR | H.S.121 Trident 3B ★ | CAA Fire School/Teesside | |
| G-AWZU | H.S.121 Trident 3B ★ | BAA Airport Fire Service/Stansted | |
| G-AWZX | H.S.121 Trident 3B ★ | BAA Airport Fire Services/Gatwick | |
| G-AWZZ | H.S.121 Trident 3B ★ | Airport Fire Services/Birmingham | |
| G-AXAB | PA-28 Cherokee 140 | Bencray Ltd/Blackpool | |
| G-AXAK | M.S.880B Rallye Club | R. L. & C. Stewart | |
| G-AXAN | D.H.82A Tiger Moth (EM720) | M. E. Carrell | |
| G-AXAO | Omega 56 balloon | P. D. Furlong | |
| G-AXAS | Wallis WA-116T | K. H. Wallis (G-AVDH) | |
| G-AXAT | Jodel D.117A | P. S. Wilkinson | |
| G-AXAU | PA-30 Twin Comanche 160C | Bartcourt Ltd (*derelict*)/Bournemouth | |
| G-AXAX | PA-23 Aztec 250D | Air Navigation & Trading Co Ltd/Blackpool | |
| G-AXBF | D.5/180 Husky | C. H. Barnes | |
| G-AXBH | Cessna F.172H | Photoair Ltd/Sibson | |
| G-AXBJ | Cessna F.172H | Bravo Juliet Group/Leicester | |
| G-AXBW | D.H.82A Tiger Moth (T5879) | R. Venning | |
| G-AXBZ | D.H.82A Tiger Moth | D. H. McWhir | |
| G-AXCA | PA-28R Cherokee Arrow 200 | D. T. Wright | |
| G-AXCG | Jodel D.117 | Charlie Golf Group/Andrewsfield | |
| G-AXCI | Bensen B.8M ★ | Loughborough & Leicester Aircraft Museum | |
| G-AXCL | M.S.880B Rallye Club | L. A. Christie & D. P. Barclay | |
| G-AXCM | M.S.880B Rallye Club | J. R. Hammett | |
| G-AXCN | M.S.880B Rallye Club | J. E. Compton | |
| G-AXCX | B.121 Pup 2 | L. A. Pink | |
| G-AXCY | Jodel D.117 | R. Thwaites & P. G. Bumpus/Shoreham | |
| G-AXDB | Piper J-3C-65 Cub | J. R. Wraight | |
| G-AXDC | PA-23 Aztec 250D | N. J. Lilley/Bodmin | |

| Notes | Reg. | Type | Owner or Operator |
|---|---|---|---|
| | G-AXDI | Cessna F.172H | M. F. & J. R. Leusby/Conington |
| | G-AXDK | Jodel DR.315 | Delta Kilo Flying Group/Sywell |
| | G-AXDM | H.S.125 Srs 400B | GEC Ferranti Defence Systems Ltd/ Edinburgh |
| | G-AXDN | BAC-Sud Concorde 01 ★ | Duxford Aviation Soc |
| | G-AXDU | B.121 Pup 2 | J. R. Clegg |
| | G-AXDV | B.121 Pup 1 | C. N. G. Hobbs & J. J. Teagle |
| | G-AXDW | B.121 Pup 1 | Cranfield Institute of Technology |
| | G-AXDY | Falconar F-II | J. Nunn |
| | G-AXDZ | Cassutt Racer Srs IIIM | A. Chadwick/Little Staughton |
| | G-AXEB | Cassutt Racer Srs IIIM | G. E. Horder/Redhill |
| | G-AXEC | Cessna 182M | H. S. Mulligan & E. R. Wilson |
| | G-AXED | PA-25 Pawnee 235 | Wolds Gliding Club Ltd/Pocklington |
| | G-AXEH | B.121 Pup ★ | Museum of Flight/E. Fortune |
| | G-AXEI | Ward Gnome ★ | Lincolnshire Aviation Museum |
| | G-AXEO | Scheibe SF.25B Falke | Newcastle & Tees-side Gliding Club Ltd |
| | G-AXES | B.121 Pup 2 | P. A. G. Field/Nairobi |
| | G-AXEV | B.121 Pup 2 | D. S. Russell |
| | G-AXFG | Cessna 337D | C. Keane |
| | G-AXFH | D.H.114 Heron 1B/C | (stored)/Southend |
| | G-AXFN | Jodel D.119 | M. C. Lee & A. M. Westley |
| | G-AXGC | M.S.880B Rallye Club | Ian Richard Transport Services Ltd |
| | G-AXGE | M.S.880B Rallye Club | R. P. Loxton |
| | G-AXGG | Cessna F.150J | G. L. Carpenter & S. C. May |
| | G-AXGP | Piper J-3C-65 Cub | W. K. Butler |
| | G-AXGR | Luton LA-4A Minor | B. Thomas |
| | G-AXGS | D.62B Condor | B. W. Haston |
| | G-AXGV | D.62B Condor | R. J. Wrixon |
| | G-AXGZ | D.62B Condor | Lincoln Condor Group/Sturgate |
| | G-AXHA | Cessna 337A | G. Evans |
| | G-AXHC | SNCAN Stampe SV-4C | D. L. Webley |
| | G-AXHE | BN-2A Islander | NW Parachute Centre Ltd/Cark |
| | G-AXHI | M.S.880B Rallye Club | J. M. Whittard (stored)/Sandown |
| | G-AXHO | B.121 Pup 2 | L. W. Grundy/Stapleford |
| | G-AXHP | Piper J-3C-65 Cub | P. J. Acreman |
| | G-AXHR | Piper J-3C-65 Cub (329601) | G-AXHR Cub Group |
| | G-AXHS | M.S.880B Rallye Club | B. & A. Swales |
| | G-AXHT | M.S.880B Rallye Club | D. E. Guck |
| | G-AXHV | Jodel D.117A | D. M. Cashmore |
| | G-AXHX | M.S.892A Rallye Commodore | D. W. Weever |
| | G-AXIA | B.121 Pup 1 | Cranfield Institute of Technology |
| | G-AXIE | B.121 Pup 2 | G. A. Ponsford/Goodwood |
| | G-AXIF | B.121 Pup 2 | T. G. Hiscock & R. G. Knapp |
| | G-AXIG | B.125 Bulldog 104 | George House (Holdings) Ltd |
| | G-AXIO | PA-28 Cherokee 140B | W. London Aero Services Ltd/ White Waltham |
| | G-AXIR | PA-28 Cherokee 140B | J. E. T. Lock |
| | G-AXIT | M.S.893A Rallye Commodore 180 | T. J. Price |
| | G-AXIW | Scheibe SF.25B Falke | Sailplane Services/Nympsfield |
| | G-AXIX | Glos-Airtourer 150 | J. C. Wood |
| | G-AXIY | Bird Gyrocopter ★ | Motor Museum/Chudleigh |
| | G-AXJB | Omega 84 balloon | Southern Balloon Group |
| | G-AXJH | B.121 Pup 2 | J. S. Chillingworth |
| | G-AXJI | B.121 Pup 2 | Cole Aviation Ltd/Southend |
| | G-AXJJ | B.121 Pup 2 | Bumpf Group |
| | G-AXJK | BAC One-Eleven 501EX | British Airways Birmingham County of Hereford |
| | G-AXJM | BAC One-Eleven 501EX | British Airways Birmingham County Durham |
| | G-AXJN | B.121 Pup 2 | D. M. Jenkins & D. F. Jenvey/Shoreham |
| | G-AXJO | B.121 Pup 2 | J. A. D. Bradshaw |
| | G-AXJR | Scheibe SF.25B Falke | D. R. Chatterton |
| | G-AXJV | PA-28 Cherokee 140B | Mona Aviation Ltd |
| | G-AXJX | PA-28 Cherokee 140B | Patrolwatch Ltd |
| | G-AXJY | Cessna U-206D | B. W. Wells |
| | G-AXKD | PA-23 Aztec 250D | Levenmere Ltd/Norwich |
| | G-AXKH | Luton LA-4A Minor | M. E. Vaisey |
| | G-AXKI | Jodel D.9 Bebe | M. R. M. Welch |
| | G-AXKJ | Jodel D.9 Bebe | C. C. Gordon |
| | G-AXKK | Westland Bell 47G-4A | Alan Mann Helicopters Ltd/Fairoaks |
| | G-AXKO | Westland-Bell 47G-4A | Alan Mann Helicopters Ltd/Fairoaks |
| | G-AXKR | Westland Bell 47G-4A | F. C. Owen |
| | G-AXKS | Westland Bell 47G-4A ★ | Museum of Army Flying/Middle Wallop |

| Reg. | Type | Owner or Operator | Notes |
|------|------|-------------------|-------|
| G-AXKW | Westland-Bell 47G-4A | A. C. Watson | |
| G-AXKX | Westland Bell 47G-4A | Alan Mann Helicopters Ltd/Fairoaks | |
| G-AXKY | Westland Bell 47G-4A | L. Goddard | |
| G-AXLG | Cessna 310K | Smiths (Outdrives) Ltd | |
| G-AXLI | Slingsby T.66 Nipper 3 | N. J. Arthur/Finmere | |
| G-AXLL | BAC One-Eleven 523FJ | British Airways *County of Yorkshire* | |
| G-AXLS | Jodel DR.105A | E. Gee/Southampton | |
| G-AXLZ | PA-18 Super Cub 95 | J. C. Quantrell/Shipdham | |
| G-AXMA | PA-24 Comanche 180 | Tegrel Products Ltd/Newcastle | |
| G-AXMB | Slingsby T.7 Motor Cadet 2 | I. G. Smith/Langar | |
| G-AXMD | Omega O-56 balloon ★ | British Balloon Museum | |
| G-AXMN | J/5B Autocar | A. Phillips | |
| G-AXMP | PA-28 Cherokee 180 | T. M. P. Tomsett | |
| G-AXMS | PA-30 Twin Comanche 160C | G. J. Mendes | |
| G-AXMW | B.121 Pup 1 | DJP Engineering (Knebworth) Ltd | |
| G-AXMX | B.121 Pup 2 | Susan A. Jones/Cannes | |
| G-AXNC | Boeing 737-204 | Britannia Airways Ltd *Isambard Kingdom Brunel* | |
| G-AXNJ | Wassmer Jodel D.120 | Clive Flying Group/Sleap | |
| G-AXNL | B.121 Pup 1 | Northamptonshire School of Flying Ltd/Sywell | |
| G-AXNM | B.121 Pup 1 | J. & F. E. Green | |
| G-AXNN | B.121 Pup 2 | Gabrielle Aviation Ltd/Shoreham | |
| G-AXNP | B.121 Pup 2 | J. W. Ellis | |
| G-AXNR | B.121 Pup 2 | S. T. Raby & ptnrs | |
| G-AXNS | B.121 Pup 2 | Derwent Aero/Netherthorpe | |
| G-AXNW | SNCAN Stampe SV-4C | C. S. Grace | |
| G-AXNX | Cessna 182M | Cast High Ltd | |
| G-AXNZ | Pitts S.1C Special | W. A. Jordan | |
| G-AXOG | PA-E23 Aztec 250D | R. W. Diggens/Denham | |
| G-AXOH | M.S.894 Rallye Minerva | Bristol Cars Ltd/White Waltham | |
| G-AXOI | Jodel D.9 Bebe | D. G. Garner | |
| G-AXOJ | B.121 Pup 2 | Pup Flying Group | |
| G-AXOL | Currie Wot | R. G. Boyes | |
| G-AXOR | PA-28 Cherokee 180D | Oscar Romeo Aviation | |
| G-AXOS | M.S.894A Rallye Minerva | D. R. C. Bell | |
| G-AXOT | M.S.893 Rallye Commodore 180 | P. Evans & J. C. Graves | |
| G-AXOV | Beech 95-B55A Baron | S. Brod/Elstree | |
| G-AXOZ | B.121 Pup 1 | Touchdown Aviation Ltd | |
| G-AXPB | B.121 Pup 1 | M. J. K. Seary | |
| G-AXPF | Cessna F.150K | D. R. Marks/Denham | |
| G-AXPG | Mignet HM-293 | W. H. Cole (*stored*) | |
| G-AXPM | B.121 Pup 1 | M. J. Coton | |
| G-AXPN | B.121 Pup 2 | D. J. Elbourn & ptnrs | |
| G-AXPZ | Campbell Cricket | W. R. Partridge | |
| G-AXRC | Campbell Cricket | K. W. Hayr (*stored*) | |
| G-AXRL | PA-28 Cherokee 160 | T. W. Clark/Headcorn | |
| G-AXRO | PA-30 Twin Comanche 160C | S. M. Bogdiukiewicz/Staverton | |
| G-AXRP | SNCAN Stampe SV-4C | C. C. Manning | |
| G-AXRR | Auster AOP.9 (XR241) | The Aircraft Restoration Co/Duxford | |
| G-AXRT | Cessna FA.150K (tailwheel) | W. R. Pickett/Southampton | |
| G-AXRU | Cessna FA.150K | Arrival Enterprises Ltd | |
| G-AXSC | B.121 Pup 1 | T. R. Golding & C. Spencer | |
| G-AXSD | B.121 Pup 1 | A. C. Townend | |
| G-AXSF | Nash Petrel | Nash Aircraft Ltd/Lasham | |
| G-AXSG | PA-28 Cherokee 180 | J. Montgomery | |
| G-AXSI | Cessna F.172H | R. I. Chantrey (G-SNIP) | |
| G-AXSM | Jodel DR.1051 | K. D. Doyle | |
| G-AXSV | Jodel DR.340 | Leonard F. Jollye Ltd/Panshanger | |
| G-AXSW | Cessna FA.150K | Furness Aviation Ltd/Walney Island | |
| G-AXSZ | PA-28 Cherokee 140B | Kilo Foxtrot Group/Sandown | |
| G-AXTA | PA-28 Cherokee 140B | G-AXTA Syndicate | |
| G-AXTC | PA-28 Cherokee 140B | B. Mellor & J. Hutchinson | |
| G-AXTD | PA-28 Cherokee 140B | G. R. Walker/Southend | |
| G-AXTH | PA-28 Cherokee 140B | W. London Aero Services Ltd/White Waltham | |
| G-AXTI | PA-28 Cherokee 140B | London Transport (CRS) Sports Association Flying Club/Fairoaks | |
| G-AXTJ | PA-28 Cherokee 140B | A. P. Merrifield/Stapleford | |
| G-AXTL | PA-28 Cherokee 140B | Jenrick Flying Group | |
| G-AXTO | PA-24 Comanche 260 | J. L. Wright | |
| G-AXTP | PA-28 Cherokee 180 | E. R. Moore/Elstree | |
| G-AXTX | Jodel D.112 | J. J. Penney | |

| Notes | Reg. | Type | Owner or Operator |
|---|---|---|---|
| | G-AXUA | B.121 Pup 1 | F. R. Blennerhassett & ptnrs |
| | G-AXUB | BN-2A Islander | Headcorn Parachute Club |
| | G-AXUC | PA-12 Super Cruiser | J. J. Bunton |
| | G-AXUE | Jodel DR.105A | L. Lewis |
| | G-AXUF | Cessna FA.150K | A. D. McLeod |
| | G-AXUI | H.P.137 Jetstream 1 | Cranfield Institute of Technology |
| | G-AXUJ | J/1 Autocrat | R. G. Earp & J. W. H. Lee/Sibson |
| | G-AXUK | Jodel DR.1050 | North Oxford Flying Co |
| | G-AXUM | H.P.137 Jetstream 1 | Cranfield Institute of Technology |
| | G-AXUW | Cessna FA.150K | Coventry Air Training School |
| | G-AXVB | Cessna F.172H | C. Gabbitas/Staverton |
| | G-AXVK | Campbell Cricket | L. W. Harding |
| | G-AXVM | Campbell Cricket | D. M. Organ |
| | G-AXVN | McCandless M.4 | W. R. Partridge |
| | G-AXVS | Jodel DR.1050 | D. T. J. Harwood |
| | G-AXVV | Piper J-3C-65 Cub | J. MacCarthy |
| | G-AXVW | Cessna F.150K | J. M. R. Layton |
| | G-AXWA | Auster AOP.9 (XN437) | M. L. & C. M. Edwards/Biggin Hill |
| | G-AXWB | Omega 65 balloon | A. Robinson & M. J. Moore *Ezekiel* |
| | G-AXWH | BN-2A Islander | Midland Parachute Centre Ltd |
| | G-AXWP | BN-2A Islander | Isles of Scilly Skybus Ltd/St Just |
| | G-AXWR | BN-2A Islander | Isles of Scilly Skybus Ltd/St Just |
| | G-AXWT | Jodel D.11 | R. C. Owen |
| | G-AXWV | Jodel DR.253 | J. R. D. Bygraves/O. Warden |
| | G-AXWZ | PA-28R Cherokee Arrow 200 | E. J. M. Kroes |
| | G-AXXV | D.H.82A Tiger Moth (DE992) | C. N. Wookey & S. G. Jones |
| | G-AXXW | Jodel D.117 | A. Szep/Netherthorpe |
| | G-AXYD | BAC One-Eleven 509EW | British Air Ferries/Southend |
| | G-AXYK | Taylor JT.1 Monoplane | T. W. M. Beck & M. J. Smith |
| | G-AXYY | WHE Airbuggy | R. A. A. Chiles |
| | G-AXYZ | WHE Airbuggy | W. B. Lumb |
| | G-AXZA | WHE Airbuggy | B. Gunn |
| | G-AXZB | WHE Airbuggy | D. R. C. Pugh |
| | G-AXZD | PA-28 Cherokee 180E | M. D. & V. A. Callaghan |
| | G-AXZF | PA-28 Cherokee 180E | E. P. C. & W. R. Rabson/Southampton |
| | G-AXZK | BN-2A Islander | M. E. Mortlock/Pampisford |
| | G-AXZM | Slingsby T.66 Nipper 3 | G. R. Harlow |
| | G-AXZO | Cessna 180 | G. James |
| | G-AXZP | PA-E23 Aztec 250D | J. Durkin |
| | G-AXZT | Jodel D.117 | N. Batty |
| | G-AXZU | Cessna 182N | The Biplane Co Ltd |
| | | | |
| | G-AYAA | PA-28 Cherokee 180E | Alpha-Alpha Ltd |
| | G-AYAB | PA-28 Cherokee 180E | J. A. & J. C. Cunningham |
| | G-AYAC | PA-28R Cherokee Arrow 200 | Fersfield Flying Group |
| | G-AYAJ | Cameron O-84 balloon | E. T. Hall |
| | G-AYAL | Omega 56 balloon ★ | British Balloon Museum |
| | G-AYAN | Slingsby Motor Cadet III | A. Nelson |
| | G-AYAR | PA-28 Cherokee 180E | D. M. Markscheffel/Stapleford |
| | G-AYAT | PA-28 Cherokee 180E | AYAT Flying Group |
| | G-AYAU | PA-28 Cherokee 180E | Tiarco Ltd |
| | G-AYAV | PA-28 Cherokee 180E | Tee Tee Aviation Ltd/Biggin Hill |
| | G-AYAW | PA-28 Cherokee 180E | R. C. Pendle & M. J. Rose |
| | G-AYBD | Cessna F.150K | F. A. Fox/Southampton |
| | G-AYBG | Scheibe SF.25B Falke | D. J. Rickman |
| | G-AYBO | PA-23 Aztec 250D | Twinguard Aviation Ltd/Elstree |
| | G-AYBP | Jodel D.112 | G-AYBP Group |
| | G-AYBR | Jodel D.112 | D. H. Nourish |
| | G-AYBU | Western 84 balloon | D. R. Gibbons |
| | G-AYBV | Chasle YC-12 Tourbillon | B. A. Mills |
| | G-AYCC | Campbell Cricket | D. J. M. Charity |
| | G-AYCE | CP.301C Emeraude | R. A. Austin/Bodmin |
| | G-AYCF | Cessna FA.150K | E. J. Atkins/Popham |
| | G-AYCG | SNCAN Stampe SV-4C | N. Bignall/Booker |
| | G-AYCJ | Cessna TP.206D | H. O. Holm/Bournemouth |
| | G-AYCN | Piper J-3C-65 Cub | W. R. & B. M. Young |
| | G-AYCO | CEA DR.360 | G. T. Birks & T. M. Curry/Booker |
| | G-AYCP | Jodel D.112 | D. J. Nunn |
| | G-AYCT | Cessna F.172H | Charlie Tango Flying Group |
| | G-AYDG | M.S.894A Rallye Minerva | Rallye Minerva Group |
| | G-AYDI | D.H.82A Tiger Moth | R. B. Woods & ptnrs |
| | G-AYDR | SNCAN Stampe SV-4C | A. J. Mcluskie |
| | G-AYDV | Coates SA.II-1 Swalesong | J. R. Coates/Rush Green |

| Reg. | Type | Owner or Operator | Notes |
|---|---|---|---|
| G-AYDW | A.61 Terrier 2 | A. Topen/Cranfield | |
| G-AYDX | A.61 Terrier 2 | J. Tyers | |
| G-AYDY | Luton LA-4A Minor | T. Littlefair & N. Clark | |
| G-AYDZ | Jodel DR.200 | F. M. Ward/Sherburn | |
| G-AYEB | Jodel D.112 | M. A. Watts | |
| G-AYEC | CP.301A Emeraude | R. S. Needham | |
| G-AYED | PA-24 Comanche 260 | G. N. Snell | |
| G-AYEE | PA-28 Cherokee 180E | D. J. Beale | |
| G-AYEF | PA-28 Cherokee 180E | S. R. J. Attwood | |
| G-AYEG | Falconar F-9 | B. E. Trinder | |
| G-AYEH | Jodel DR.1050 | S. Penson | |
| G-AYEI | PA-31 Turbo Navajo | Stewart McDonald & Co | |
| G-AYEJ | Jodel DR.1050 | J. M. Newbold | |
| G-AYEN | Piper J-3C-65 Cub | P. Warde & C. F. Morris | |
| G-AYET | M.S.892A Rallye Commodore 150 | R. N. Jones | |
| G-AYEV | Jodel DR.1050 | L. G. Evans/Headcorn | |
| G-AYEW | Jodel DR.1051 | Taildragger Group/Halfpenny Green | |
| G-AYEY | Cessna F.150K | W. J. Moyse | |
| G-AYFA | SA Twin Pioneer 3 | Flight One Ltd/Shobdon | |
| G-AYFC | D.62B Condor | P. A. Wensak & D. J. Wilson | |
| G-AYFD | D.62B Condor | B. G. Manning | |
| G-AYFE | D.62C Condor | D. I. H. Johnstone & W. T. Barnard | |
| G-AYFF | D.62B Condor | A. F. S. Caldecourt | |
| G-AYFG | D.62C Condor | W. A. Braim | |
| G-AYFJ | M.S.880B Rallye Club | Rallye FJ Group | |
| G-AYFP | Jodel D.140 | S. K. Minocha/Sherburn | |
| G-AYFT | PA-39 Twin Comanche 160 C/R | G. A. Barber/Blackbushe | |
| G-AYFV | Crosby BA-4B | A. R. C. Mathie/Norwich | |
| G-AYGA | Jodel D.117 | R. L. E. Horrell | |
| G-AYGB | Cessna 310Q ★ | Instructional airframe/Perth | |
| G-AYGC | Cessna F.150K | Alpha Aviation Group/Barton | |
| G-AYGD | Jodel DR.1051 | B. A. James | |
| G-AYGE | SNCAN Stampe SV-4C | The Hon A. M. J. Rothschild/Booker | |
| G-AYGG | Jodel D.120 | G-AYGG Group | |
| G-AYGK | BN-2A Islander | Pathcircle Ltd/Langar | |
| G-AYGX | Cessna FR.172G | A. Douglas & J. K. Brockley | |
| G-AYHA | AA-1 Yankee | Elstree Emus Flying Group | |
| G-AYHI | Campbell Cricket | J. F. MacKay/Inverness | |
| G-AYHX | Jodel D.117A | L. J. E. Goldfinch | |
| G-AYHY | Fournier RF-4D | P. M. & S. M. Wells | |
| G-AYIA | Hughes 369HS ★ | G. D. E. Bilton/Sywell | |
| G-AYIF | PA-28 Cherokee 140C | The Hare Flying Group/Elstree | |
| G-AYIG | PA-28 Cherokee 140C | Snowdon Mountain Aviation Ltd | |
| G-AYII | PA-28R Cherokee Arrow 200 | Devon Growers Ltd & A. L. Bacon/Exeter | |
| G-AYIJ | SNCAN Stampe SV-4B | K. B. Palmer/Headcorn | |
| G-AYIT | D.H.82A Tiger Moth | Ulster Tiger Group/Newtownards | |
| G-AYJA | Jodel DR.1050 | G. I. Doake | |
| G-AYJB | SNCAN Stampe SV-4C | F. J. M. & J. P. Esson/Middle Wallop | |
| G-AYJD | Alpavia-Fournier RF-3 | E. Shouler | |
| G-AYJP | PA-28 Cherokee 140C | RAF Brize Norton Flying Club Ltd | |
| G-AYJR | PA-28 Cherokee 140C | RAF Brize Norton Flying Club Ltd | |
| G-AYJU | Cessna TP-206A | D. N. Crank | |
| G-AYJW | Cessna FR.172G | R. T. Burton | |
| G-AYJY | Isaacs Fury II | A. V. Francis | |
| G-AYKA | Beech 95-B55A Baron | Walsh Bros (Tunnelling) Ltd/Elstree | |
| G-AYKD | Jodel DR.1050 | B. P. Irish | |
| G-AYKF | M.S.880B Rallye Club | F. A. Lemon | |
| G-AYKJ | Jodel D.117A | Juliet Group/Shoreham | |
| G-AYKK | Jodel D.117 | D. M. Whitham | |
| G-AYKL | Cessna F.150L | M. A. Judge | |
| G-AYKS | Leopoldoff L-7 | C. E. & W. B. Cooper | |
| G-AYKT | Jodel D.117 | G. Wright/Sherburn | |
| G-AYKW | PA-28 Cherokee 140C | T. A. Hird | |
| G-AYKX | PA-28 Cherokee 140C | Robin Flying Group | |
| G-AYKZ | SAI KZ-8 | R. E. Mitchell/Coventry | |
| G-AYLA | Glos-Airtourer 115 | R. E. Parker | |
| G-AYLB | PA-39 Twin Comanche 160 C/R | Penny (Mechanical Services) Ltd | |
| G-AYLE | M.S.880B Rallye Club | G-AYLE Syndicate | |
| G-AYLF | Jodel DR.1051 | Sicile Group | |
| G-AYLL | Jodel DR.1050 | B. R. Cornes | |
| G-AYLP | AA-1 Yankee | D. Nairn & E. Y. Hawkins | |
| G-AYLV | Jodel D.120 | M. R. Henham | |
| G-AYLX | Hughes 269C | J. Lloyd | |

| Notes | Reg. | Type | Owner or Operator |
|---|---|---|---|
| | G-AYME | Fournier RF-5 | R. D. Goodger/Biggin Hill |
| | G-AYMG | HPR-7 Herald 213 | Channel Express (Air Services) Ltd/ Bournemouth |
| | G-AYMK | PA-28 Cherokee 140C | The Piper Flying Group |
| | G-AYMO | PA-23 Aztec 250C | Supreme Windows |
| | G-AYMP | Currie Wot Special | H. F. Moffatt |
| | G-AYMR | Lederlin 380L Ladybug | J. S. Brayshaw |
| | G-AYMT | Jodel DR.1050 | Merlin Flying Club Ltd/Hucknall |
| | G-AYMU | Jodel D.112 | M. R. Baker |
| | G-AYMV | Western 20 balloon | G. F. Turnbull |
| | G-AYMW | Bell 206A JetRanger 2 | Dollar Air Services Ltd/Coventry |
| | G-AYMZ | PA-28 Cherokee 140C | T. H. & M. G. Weetman/Prestwick |
| | G-AYNA | Currie Wot | J. M. Lister |
| | G-AYNC | W.S. 58 Wessex 60 Srs 1 ★ | International Helicopter Museum/ Weston-s-Mare |
| | G-AYND | Cessna 310Q | Source Premium & Promotional Consultants Ltd/Fairoaks |
| | G-AYNF | PA-28 Cherokee 140C | W. S. Bath |
| | G-AYNJ | PA-28 Cherokee 140C | Lion Flying Group Ltd/Elstree |
| | G-AYNN | Cessna 185B Skywagon | Bencray Ltd/Blackpool |
| | G-AYNP | W.S.55 Whirlwind Srs 3 | Bristow Helicopters Ltd |
| | G-AYOM | Sikorsky S-61N Mk 2 | British International Helicopters Ltd/ Aberdeen |
| | G-AYOP | BAC One-Eleven 530FX | British Airways Birmingham *County of Humberside* |
| | G-AYOW | Cessna 182N Skylane | A. T. Jay |
| | G-AYOY | Sikorsky S-61N Mk 2 | British International Helicopters Ltd/ Aberdeen |
| | G-AYOZ | Cessna FA.150L | Exeter Flying Club Ltd |
| | G-AYPD | Beech 95-B55A Baron | F. Sherwood & Sons (Transport) Ltd |
| | G-AYPE | Bo 209 Monsun | Papa Echo Ltd/Biggin Hill |
| | G-AYPF | Cessna F.177RG | S. J. Westley |
| | G-AYPG | Cessna F.177RG | D. Davies |
| | G-AYPH | Cessna F.177RG | W. J. D. Tollett |
| | G-AYPI | Cessna F.177RG | Cardinal Aviation Ltd/Guernsey |
| | G-AYPJ | PA-28 Cherokee 180 | Mona Aviation Ltd |
| | G-AYPM | PA-18 Super Cub 95 | N. H. Chapman |
| | G-AYPO | PA-18 Super Cub 95 | A. W. Knowles |
| | G-AYPR | PA-18 Super Cub 95 | E. H. Booker |
| | G-AYPS | PA-18 Super Cub 95 | Tony Dyer Television |
| | G-AYPT | PA-18 Super Cub 95 | P. Shires |
| | G-AYPU | PA-28R Cherokee Arrow 200 | Alpine Ltd/Jersey |
| | G-AYPV | PA-28 Cherokee 140D | R. J. & J. M. Charlton |
| | G-AYPZ | Campbell Cricket | A. Melody |
| | G-AYRF | Cessna F.150L | D. T. A. Rees |
| | G-AYRG | Cessna F.172K | W. I. Robinson |
| | G-AYRH | M.S.892A Rallye Commodore 150 | J. D. Watt |
| | G-AYRI | PA-28R Cherokee Arrow 200 | E. P. Van Mechelen & Delta Motor Co (Windsor) Sales Ltd/White Waltham |
| | G-AYRM | PA-28 Cherokee 140D | E. S. Dignam/Biggin Hill |
| | G-AYRO | Cessna FA.150L Aerobat | Thruxton Flight Centre |
| | G-AYRR | H.S.125 Srs 403B | Duke of Westminster |
| | G-AYRS | Jodel D.120A | K. Heeley |
| | G-AYRT | Cessna F.172K | K. W. J. & A. B. L. Hayward |
| | G-AYRU | BN-2A-6 Islander | Joint Service Parachute Centre/ Netheravon |
| | G-AYSA | PA-23 Aztec 250C | N. Parkinson & W. Smith |
| | G-AYSB | PA-30 Twin Comanche 160C | R. K. Buckle/Booker |
| | G-AYSD | Slingsby T.61A Falke | G-AYSD Flying Group |
| | G-AYSH | Taylor JT.1 Monoplane | C. J. Lodge |
| | G-AYSJ | Bucker Bu133 Jungmeister (LG+01) | Patina Ltd/Duxford |
| | G-AYSK | Luton LA-4A Minor | Luton Minor Group |
| | G-AYSX | Cessna F.177RG | C. P. Heptonstall |
| | G-AYSY | Cessna F.177RG | Horizon Flyers Ltd/Denham |
| | G-AYTA | M.S.880B Rallye Club | Kemps Corrosion Services Ltd |
| | G-AYTJ | Cessna 207 Super Skywagon | Foxair/Perth |
| | G-AYTN | Cameron O-65 balloon | P. G. Hall & R. F. Jessett Prometheus |
| | G-AYTR | CP.301A Emeraude | P. J. Hall |
| | G-AYTT | Phoenix PM-3 Duet | H. E. Jenner |
| | G-AYTV | MJ.2A Tempete | D. Perry |
| | G-AYTY | Bensen B.8 | J. H. Wood & J. S. Knight |
| | G-AYUA | Auster AOP.9 (XK416) ★ | A. Topen *(stored)* |

| Reg. | Type | Owner or Operator | Notes |
|------|------|-------------------|-------|
| G-AYUB | CEA DR.253B | D. J. Brook | |
| G-AYUH | PA-28 Cherokee 180F | G-AYUH Group | |
| G-AYUI | PA-28 Cherokee 180 | Ansair Aviation Ltd/Andrewsfield | |
| G-AYUJ | Evans VP-1 Volksplane | S. W. Cross & M. A. Farrelly | |
| G-AYUM | Slingsby T.61A Falke | Hereward Flying Group/Sibson | |
| G-AYUN | Slingsby T.61A Falke | C. W. Vigar & R. J. Watts | |
| G-AYUP | Slingsby T.61A Falke | Cranwell Gliding Club | |
| G-AYUR | Slingsby T.61A Falke | K. E. Ballington | |
| G-AYUS | Taylor JT.1 Monoplane | R. R. McKinnon | |
| G-AYUT | Jodel DR.1050 | R. Norris | |
| G-AYUV | Cessna F.172H | Snowdon Mountain Aviation Ltd/ Caernarfon | |
| G-AYUW | BAC One-Eleven 476FM★ | AIM Aviation Ltd (cabin water spray tests)/ Bournemouth | |
| G-AYVA | Cameron O-84 balloon | A. Kirk April Fool | |
| G-AYVO | Wallis WA120 Srs 1 | K. H. Wallis | |
| G-AYVP | Woody Pusher | J. R. Wraight | |
| G-AYVT | Brochet MB.84 ★ | Dunelm Flying Group (stored) | |
| G-AYVU | Cameron O-56 balloon | Shell-Mex & B.P. Ltd Hot Potato | |
| G-AYWA | Avro 19 Srs 2 ★ | Strathallan Aircraft Collection | |
| G-AYWD | Cessna 182N | Chartec Ltd | |
| G-AYWE | PA-28 Cherokee 140 | N. Roberson | |
| G-AYWH | Jodel D.117A | D. Kynaston & J. Deakin | |
| G-AYWM | Glos-Airtourer Super 150 | The Star Flying Group/Staverton | |
| G-AYWT | AIA Stampe SV-4C | B. K. Lecomber/Denham | |
| G-AYXP | Jodel D.117A | G. N. Davies | |
| G-AYXS | SIAI-Marchetti S205-18R | J. J. Barnett/Old Sarum | |
| G-AYXT | W.S. 55 Whirlwind Srs 2 (XK940) | Wilkie Museum Collection/Blackpool | |
| G-AYXU | Champion 7KCAB Citabria | Norfolk Gliding Club Ltd/Tibenham | |
| G-AYXV | Cessna FA.150L | Wreck/Popham | |
| G-AYXW | Evans VP-1 | J. S. Penny/Doncaster | |
| G-AYYK | Slingsby T.61A Falke | Cornish Gliding & Flying Club Ltd/ Perranporth | |
| G-AYYL | Slingsby T.61A Falke | C. Wood | |
| G-AYYO | Jodel DR.1050/M1 | Bustard Flying Club Ltd/Old Sarum | |
| G-AYYT | Jodel DR.1050/M1 | Sicile Flying Group/Sandown | |
| G-AYYU | Beech C23 Musketeer | P. Peck | |
| G-AYYW | BN-2A Islander | RN & R. Marines Sport Parachute Association/Dunkeswell | |
| G-AYYX | M.S.880B Rallye Club | J. Turnbull & P. W. Robinson | |
| G-AYYY | M.S.880B Rallye Club | T. W. Heffer/Elstree | |
| G-AYZE | PA-39 Twin Comanche 160 C/R | J. E. Palmer/Staverton | |
| G-AYZH | Taylor JT.2 Titch | P. J. G. Goddard | |
| G-AYZI | SNCAN Stampe SV-4C | W. H. Smout & C. W. A. Simmons | |
| G-AYZJ | W.S. 55 Whirlwind Srs 2 (XM685) ★ | Newark Air Museum | |
| G-AYZK | Jodel DR.1050/M1 | D. G. Hesketh & D. Lees | |
| G-AYZN | PA-23 Aztec 250D | D. J. Sewell/Nigeria | |
| G-AYZS | D.62B Condor | P. E. J. Huntley & M. N. Thrush | |
| G-AYZU | Slingsby T.61A Falke | The Falcon Gliding Group/Enstone | |
| G-AYZW | Slingsby T.61A Falke | J. A. Dandie & R. J. M. Clement | |
| G-AZAB | PA-30 Twin Comanche 160B | T. W. P. Sheffield/Humberside | |
| G-AZAD | Jodel DR.1051 | Cawdor Flying Group/Inverness | |
| G-AZAJ | PA-28R Cherokee Arrow 200B | J. McHugh & ptnrs/Stapleford | |
| G-AZAV | Cessna 337F | J. R. Surbey | |
| G-AZAW | GY-80 Horizon 160 | E. P. Sadler | |
| G-AZAZ | Bensen B.8M ★ | FAA Museum/Yeovilton | |
| G-AZBA | T.66 Nipper 3 | Nipper Aerobatic Flying Group | |
| G-AZBB | MBB Bo 209 Monsun 160FV | G. N. Richardson/Staverton | |
| G-AZBC | PA-39 Twin Comanche 160 C/R | H. G. Orchin | |
| G-AZBE | Glos-Airtourer Super 150 | F. B. Miles | |
| G-AZBH | Cameron O-84 balloon | Serendipity Balloon Group | |
| G-AZBI | Jodel D.150 | C. A. Bailey & L. J. Cudd | |
| G-AZBK | PA-23 Aztec 250E | Vulcan Aviation Ltd | |
| G-AZBL | Jodel D.9 Bebe | West Midlands Flying Group | |
| G-AZBN | AT-16 Harvard IIB (FT391) | Swaygate Ltd/Shoreham | |
| G-AZBT | Western O-65 balloon | D. J. Harris Hermes | |
| G-AZBU | Auster AOP.9 | K. H. Wallis | |
| G-AZBY | W.S.58 Wessex 60 Srs 1 ★ | International Helicopter Museum/ Weston-s-Mare | |
| G-AZBZ | W.S.58 Wessex 60 Srs 1 ★ | International Helicopter Museum/ Weston-s-Mare | |

| Notes | Reg. | Type | Owner or Operator |
|---|---|---|---|
| | G-AZCB | SNCAN Stampe SV-4C | M. J. Cowburn/Redhill |
| | G-AZCK | B.121 Pup 2 | G. C. B. Weir |
| | G-AZCL | B.121 Pup 2 | E. G. A. Prance |
| | G-AZCP | B.121 Pup 1 | Pup Group 87/Elstree |
| | G-AZCT | B.121 Pup 1 | Northamptonshire School of Flying Ltd |
| | G-AZCU | B.121 Pup 1 | A. A. Harris |
| | G-AZCV | B.121 Pup 2 | N. R. W. Long/Elstree |
| | G-AZCZ | B.121 Pup 2 | P. R. Moorehead |
| | G-AZDA | B.121 Pup 1 | G. H. G. Bishop/Shoreham |
| | G-AZDD | MBB Bo 209 Monsun 150FF | Double Delta Flying Group/Biggin Hill |
| | G-AZDE | PA-28R Cherokee Arrow 200B | Electro-Motion UK (Export) Ltd/ |
| | | | E. Midlands |
| | G-AZDF | Cameron O-84 balloon | K. L. C. M. Busemeyer |
| | G-AZDG | B.121 Pup 2 | D. J. Sage/Coventry |
| | G-AZDK | Beech 95-B55 Baron | C. C. Forrester |
| | G-AZDX | PA-28 Cherokee 180F | M. Cowan |
| | G-AZDY | D.H.82A Tiger Moth | J. B. Mills |
| | G-AZEE | M.S.880B Rallye Club | P. L. Clements |
| | G-AZEF | Jodel D.120 | J. R. Legge |
| | G-AZEG | PA-28 Cherokee 140D | Ashley Gardner Flying Club Ltd |
| | G-AZER | Cameron O-42 balloon | M. P. Dokk-Olsen & P. L. Jaye |
| | G-AZEU | B.121 Pup 2 | P. Tonkin & R. S. Kinman |
| | G-AZEV | B.121 Pup 2 | G. P. Martin/Shoreham |
| | G-AZEW | B.121 Pup 2 | K. Cameron |
| | G-AZEY | B.121 Pup 2 | B. F. Hill |
| | G-AZFA | B.121 Pup 2 | K. F. Plummer |
| | G-AZFC | PA-28 Cherokee 140D | M. L. Hannah/Blackbushe |
| | G-AZFF | Jodel D.112 | C. R. Greenaway |
| | G-AZFI | PA-28R Cherokee Arrow 200B | G-AZFI Ltd/Sherburn |
| | G-AZFM | PA-28R Cherokee Arrow 200B | Linco (Holdings) Ltd |
| | G-AZFP | Cessna F.177RG | Allen Aviation Ltd/Goodwood |
| | G-AZFR | Cessna 401B | Westair Flying Services Ltd/Blackpool |
| | G-AZFZ | Cessna 414 | Redapple Ltd/Fairoaks |
| | G-AZGA | Jodel D.120 | D. H. Pattison |
| | G-AZGC | SNCAN Stampe SV-4C (No 120) | V. Lindsay |
| | G-AZGE | SNCAN Stampe SV-4A | M. R. L. Astor/Booker |
| | G-AZGF | B.121 Pup 2 | K. Singh |
| | G-AZGI | M.S.880B Rallye Club | B. McIntyre |
| | G-AZGJ | M.S.880B Rallye Club | P. Rose |
| | G-AZGL | M.S.894A Rallye Minerva | The Cambridge Aero Club Ltd |
| | G-AZGY | CP.301B Emeraude | J. R. Riley-Gale |
| | G-AZGZ | D.H.82A Tiger Moth (NM181) | F. R. Manning |
| | G-AZHB | Robin HR.100-200 | C. & P. P. Scarlett/Sywell |
| | G-AZHC | Jodel D.112 | J. A. Summer & A. Burton/Netherthorpe |
| | G-AZHD | Slingsby T.61A Falke | J. Sentance |
| | G-AZHH | SA 102.5 Cavalier | D. W. Buckle |
| | G-AZHI | Glos-Airtourer Super 150 | H. J. Douglas/Biggin Hill |
| | G-AZHJ | S.A. Twin Pioneer Srs 3 | Prestwick Pioneer Preservation Soc Ltd |
| | G-AZHK | Robin HR.100/200B | D. J. Sage (G-ILEG) |
| | G-AZHR | Piccard Ax6 balloon | G. Fisher |
| | G-AZHT | Glos-Airtourer T.3 | Aviation West Ltd/Glasgow |
| | G-AZHU | Luton LA-4A Minor | W. Cawrey/Netherthorpe |
| | G-AZIB | ST-10 Diplomate | Diplomate Group |
| | G-AZID | Cessna FA.150L | Exeter Flying Club Ltd |
| | G-AZII | Jodel D.117A | J. S. Brayshaw |
| | G-AZIJ | Jodel DR.360 | Rob Airway Ltd/Guernsey |
| | G-AZIK | PA-34-200 Seneca II | Caseright Ltd |
| | G-AZIL | Slingsby T.61A Falke | D. W. Savage |
| | G-AZIO | SNCAN Stampe SV-4C (Lycoming) ★ | /Booker |
| | G-AZIP | Cameron O-65 balloon | Dante Balloon Group *Dante* |
| | G-AZJC | Fournier RF-5 | W. St. G. V. Stoney/Italy |
| | G-AZJE | Ord-Hume JB-01 Minicab | J. B. Evans/Sandown |
| | G-AZJI | Western O-65 balloon | W. Davison *Peek-a-Boo* |
| | G-AZJN | Robin DR.300/140 | Wright Farm Eggs Ltd |
| | G-AZJV | Cessna F.172L | J. A. & A. J. Boyd/Cardiff |
| | G-AZJY | Cessna FRA.150L | G. Firbank |
| | G-AZJZ | PA-23 Aztec 250E | Encee Services Ltd/Cardiff |
| | G-AZKC | M.S.880B Rallye Club | L. J. Martin/Redhill |
| | G-AZKD | M.S.880B Rallye Club | P. Feeney/Kidlington |
| | G-AZKE | M.S.880B Rallye Club | B. S. Rowden & W. L. Rogers |
| | G-AZKK | Cameron O-56 balloon | Gemini Balloon Group *Gemini* |
| | G-AZKN | Robin HR.100/200 | Wonderful Flying Circus |

| Reg. | Type | Owner or Operator | Notes |
|------|------|-------------------|-------|
| G-AZKO | Cessna F.337F | Crispair Aviation Services Ltd | |
| G-AZKP | Jodel D.117 | J. Lowe | |
| G-AZKR | PA-24 Comanche 180 | S. McGovern | |
| G-AZKS | AA-1A Trainer | M. D. Henson | |
| G-AZKW | Cessna F.172L | J. C. C. Wright | |
| G-AZKZ | Cessna F.172L | R. D. & E. Forster/Swanton Morley | |
| G-AZLE | Boeing N2S-5 Kaydet | P. J. Wenman | |
| G-AZLF | Jodel D.120 | M. S. C. Ball | |
| G-AZLH | Cessna F.150L | Skegness Air Taxi Service Ltd/Boston | |
| G-AZLL | Cessna FRA.150L | Air Service Training Ltd/Perth | |
| G-AZLN | PA-28 Cherokee 180F | Liteflite Ltd/Kidlington | |
| G-AZLO | Cessna F.337F | Stored/Bourn | |
| G-AZLV | Cessna 172K | B. L. F. Karthaus | |
| G-AZLY | Cessna F.150L | Cleveland Flying School Ltd/Tees-side | |
| G-AZLZ | Cessna F.150L | Exeter Flying Club Ltd | |
| G-AZMB | Bell 47G-3B | Helitech (Luton) Ltd | |
| G-AZMC | Slingsby T.61A Falke | Essex Gliding Club Ltd | |
| G-AZMD | Slingsby T.61C Falke | R. A. Rice | |
| G-AZMF | BAC One-Eleven 530FX | British Airways Birmingham County of Northumberland | |
| G-AZMH | Morane-Saulnier M.S.500 (ZA+WN) | Wessex Aviation & Transport Ltd | |
| G-AZMJ | AA-5 Traveler | R. T. Love/Bodmin | |
| G-AZMN | Glos-Airtourer T.5 | W. Crozier & I. Young/Glasgow | |
| G-AZMX | PA-28 Cherokee 140 ★ | NE Wales Institute of Higher Education (Instructional airframe)/Clwyd | |
| G-AZMZ | M.S.893A Rallye Commodore 150 | P. J. Wilcox/Cranfield | |
| G-AZNK | SNCAN Stampe SV-4A | P. D. Jackson | |
| G-AZNL | PA-28R Cherokee Arrow 200D | P. L. Buckley Ltd | |
| G-AZNO | Cessna 182P | M&D Aviation/Bournemouth | |
| G-AZNT | Cameron O-84 balloon | N. Tasker | |
| G-AZOA | MBB Bo 209 Monsun 150FF | R. P. Wilson | |
| G-AZOB | MBB Bo 209 Monsun 150FF | G. N. Richardson/Staverton | |
| G-AZOE | Glos-Airtourer 115 | R. J. Zukowski | |
| G-AZOF | Glos-Airtourer Super 150 | D. C. Macdonald | |
| G-AZOG | PA-28R Cherokee Arrow 200D | J. G. Collins/Cambridge | |
| G-AZOH | Beech 65-B90 Queen Air | Genoex UK Ltd | |
| G-AZOL | PA-34-200 Seneca II | St Bridgets Aviation Ltd & ptnrs | |
| G-AZOO | Western O-65 balloon | Southern Balloon Group Carousel | |
| G-AZOR | MBB Bo 105D | Bond Helicopters Ltd/Bourn | |
| G-AZOS | Jurca MJ.5-F1 Sirocco | O. R. B. Dixon/Barton | |
| G-AZOT | PA-34-200 Seneca II | G. S. Jenkins & M. R. C. Smerald | |
| G-AZOU | Jodel DR.1051 | Horsham Flying Group/Slinfold | |
| G-AZOZ | Cessna FRA.150L | Seawing Flying Club Ltd/Southend | |
| G-AZPA | PA-25 Pawnee 235 | Black Mountain Gliding Co Ltd | |
| G-AZPC | Slingsby T.61C Falke | M. F. Cuming | |
| G-AZPF | Fournier RF-5 | R. Pye/Blackpool | |
| G-AZPH | Craft-Pitts S-1S Special ★ | Science Museum/London | |
| G-AZPV | Luton LA-4A Minor | G. D. S. Rumble | |
| G-AZPX | Western O-31 balloon | Eugena Rex Balloon Group | |
| G-AZPZ | BAC One-Eleven 515FB | British Airways Dumfries and Galloway Region | |
| G-AZRA | MBB Bo 209 Monsun 150FF | Alpha Flying Ltd/Denham | |
| G-AZRD | Cessna 401B | Morbaine Ltd | |
| G-AZRG | PA-23 Aztec 250D | Woodgate Aviation (IOM) Ltd/Ronaldsway | |
| G-AZRH | PA-28 Cherokee 140D | Joseph Carter & Sons (Jersey) Ltd | |
| G-AZRI | Payne balloon | Aardvark Balloon Co | |
| G-AZRK | Fournier RF-5 | Thurleigh Flying Group | |
| G-AZRL | PA-18 Super Cub 95 | B. J. Stead | |
| G-AZRM | Fournier RF-5 | A. R. Dearden & R. Speer/Shoreham | |
| G-AZRN | Cameron O-84 balloon | C. A. Butter & J. J. T. Cooke | |
| G-AZRP | Glos-Airtourer 115 | B. F. Strawford | |
| G-AZRR | Cessna 310Q | Routarrow Ltd/Norwich | |
| G-AZRS | PA-22 Tri-Pacer 150 | T. W. R. Case | |
| G-AZRV | PA-28R Cherokee Arrow 200B | Designed for Sound Ltd | |
| G-AZRW | Cessna T.337C | R. C. Frazle/Southend | |
| G-AZRX | GY-80 Horizon 160 | Horizon Flying Group | |
| G-AZRZ | Cessna U.206F | M. E. Bolton | |
| G-AZSA | Stampe SV-4B | J. K. Faulkner/Biggin Hill | |
| G-AZSC | AT-16 Harvard IIB | Machine Music Ltd/Fairoaks | |
| G-AZSD | Slingsby T.29B Motor Tutor | R. G. Boynton | |
| G-AZSF | PA-28R Cherokee Arrow 200D | W. T. Northorpe & R. J. Mills/Coventry | |
| G-AZSH | PA-28R Cherokee Arrow 180 | C. & G. Clarke | |
| G-AZSN | PA-28R Cherokee Arrow 200 | Jetstream Air Couriers Ltd/Bristol | |

49

| Notes | Reg. | Type | Owner or Operator |
|---|---|---|---|
| | G-AZSU | H.S.748 Srs 2A | Euroair Transport Ltd |
| | G-AZSW | B.121 Pup 1 | Northamptonshire School of Flying Ltd/Sywell |
| | G-AZSZ | PA-23 Aztec 250D | Strata Surveys Ltd |
| | G-AZTA | MBB Bo 209 Monsun 150FF | M. E. F. Reynolds/Goodwood |
| | G-AZTD | PA-32 Cherokee Six 300D | Presshouse Publications Ltd/Enstone |
| | G-AZTF | Cessna F.177RG | J. Bolson & Son Ltd/Bournemouth |
| | G-AZTI | MBB Bo 105D | Bond Helicopters Ltd |
| | G-AZTK | Cessna F.172F | C. O. Simpson |
| | G-AZTO | PA-34-200 Seneca II | Bulldog Aviation Ltd |
| | G-AZTR | SNCAN Stampe SV-4C | P. G. Palumbo/Booker |
| | G-AZTS | Cessna F.172L | C. E. Stringer |
| | G-AZTV | Stolp SA.500 Starlet | G. R. Rowland |
| | G-AZTW | Cessna F.177RG | R. M. Clarke/Leicester |
| | G-AZUK | BAC One-Eleven 476FM | British Air Ferries/Southend |
| | G-AZUM | Cessna F.172L | Fowlmere Fliers |
| | G-AZUP | Cameron O-65 balloon | R. S. Bailey & ptnrs |
| | G-AZUT | M.S.893A Rallye Commodore 180 | Rallye Flying Group |
| | G-AZUV | Cameron O-65 balloon ★ | British Balloon Museum |
| | G-AZUX | Western O-56 balloon | M. W. H. Henton |
| | G-AZUY | Cessna E.310L | Drawline Transport Group PLC |
| | G-AZUZ | Cessna FRA.150L | D. J. Parker/Netherthorpe |
| | G-AZVA | MBB Bo 209 Monsun 150FF | J. Nivison |
| | G-AZVB | MBB Bo 209 Monsun 150FF | P. C. Logsdon/Dunkeswell |
| | G-AZVE | AA-5 Traveler | G-AZVE Flying Group/Rochester |
| | G-AZVF | M.S.894A Rallye Minerva | P. D. Lloyd |
| | G-AZVG | AA-5 Traveler | Grumair Flying Group |
| | G-AZVH | M.S.894A Rallye Minerva | Bristol Cars Ltd/White Waltham |
| | G-AZVI | M.S.892A Rallye Commodore | Shobdon Flying Group |
| | G-AZVJ | PA-34-200 Seneca II | Skyfotos Ltd/Lydd |
| | G-AZVL | Jodel D.119 | Forest Flying Group/Stapleford |
| | G-AZVM | Hughes 369HS | Diagnostic Reagents Ltd |
| | G-AZVP | Cessna F.177RG | Horizon Flyers Ltd |
| | G-AZVT | Cameron O-84 balloon | Sky Soarer Ltd *Jules Verne* |
| | G-AZWB | PA-28 Cherokee 140 | Skyscraper Ltd |
| | G-AZWD | PA-28 Cherokee 140 | BM Aviation (Winchester) |
| | G-AZWE | PA-28 Cherokee 140 | Devon School of Flying/Dunkeswell |
| | G-AZWF | SAN Jodel DR.1050 | G-AZWF Jodel Syndicate |
| | G-AZWS | PA-28R Cherokee Arrow 180 | J. E. Shepherd & C. A. Douglas |
| | G-AZWT | Westland Lysander IIIA (V9441) | Strathallan Aircraft Collection |
| | G-AZWW | PA-23 Aztec 250E | Phoenix Aviation (Flight Training) Ltd/Cranfield |
| | G-AZWY | PA-24 Comanche 260 | Keymer Son & Co Ltd/Biggin Hill |
| | G-AZXA | Beech 95-C55 Baron | F.R. Aviation Ltd/Bournemouth |
| | G-AZXB | Cameron O-65 balloon | R. J. Mitchener & P. F.Smart |
| | G-AZXC | Cessna F.150L | S. Redfearn/Netherthorpe |
| | G-AZXD | Cessna F.172L | Birdlake Ltd/Wellesbourne |
| | G-AZXG | PA-23 Aztec 250D | N. J. Le Fevre & M. J. Leeder/Norwich |
| | G-AZXR | BN-2A-9 Islander | Fenchurch Leasing Ltd |
| | G-AZYA | GY-80 Horizon 160 | T. Poole & ptnrs/Sywell |
| | G-AZYB | Bell 47H-1 ★ | International Helicopter Museum/Weston-s-Mare |
| | G-AZYD | M.S.893A Rallye Commodore | Buckminster Gliding Club Ltd/Saltby |
| | G-AZYF | PA-28 Cherokee 180 | J. C. Glynn/E. Midlands |
| | G-AZYM | Cessna E.310Q | Kingswinford Engineering Co Ltd |
| | G-AZYS | CP.301C-1 Emeraude | F. P. L. Clauson |
| | G-AZYU | PA-23 Aztec 250E | L. J. Martin/Biggin Hill |
| | G-AZYV | Burns O-77 balloon | B. F. G. Ribbans *Contrary Mary* |
| | G-AZYY | Slingsby T.61A Falke | J. A. Towers |
| | G-AZYZ | WA.51A Pacific | Yankee Zulu Ltd/Biggin Hill |
| | G-AZZG | Cessna 188 Agwagon | N. C. Kensington |
| | G-AZZH | Practavia Pilot Sprite 115 | K. G. Stewart |
| | G-AZZK | Cessna 414 | D. O. McIntyre |
| | G-AZZO | PA-28 Cherokee 140 | R. J. Hind/Elstree |
| | G-AZZP | Cessna F.172H | M. Bell & ptnrs/Exeter |
| | G-AZZR | Cessna F.150L | R. J. Doughton |
| | G-AZZS | PA-34-200 Seneca II | Robin Cook Aviation/Shoreham |
| | G-AZZT | PA-28 Cherokee 180 ★ | *Ground instruction airframe*/Cranfield |
| | G-AZZV | Cessna F.172L | D. M. Charrington |
| | G-AZZW | Fournier RF-5 | R. G. Trute |
| | G-AZZX | Cessna FRA.150L | J. E. Uprichard & ptnrs/Newtownards |
| | G-AZZZ | D.H.82A Tiger Moth | S. W. McKay |

| Reg. | Type | Owner or Operator | Notes |
|------|------|-------------------|-------|
| G-BAAD | Evans Super VP-1 | R. A. Martin | |
| G-BAAF | Manning-Flanders MF1 (replica) | Aviation Film Services Ltd/Booker | |
| G-BAAI | M.S.893A Rallye Commodore | R. D. Taylor/Thruxton | |
| G-BAAK | Cessna 207 | B. W. Wells | |
| G-BAAL | Cessna 172A | Rochester Aviation Ltd | |
| G-BAAP | PA-28R Cherokee Arrow 200 | J. C. Flashman | |
| G-BAAT | Cessna 182P Skylane | A. H. Hunt/St Just | |
| G-BAAU | Enstrom F-28C-UK | M. Upton | |
| G-BAAW | Jodel D.119 | K. J. Cockrill/Ipswich | |
| G-BAAX | Cameron O-84 balloon | The New Holker Estate Co Ltd *Holker Hall* | |
| G-BAAZ | PA-28R Cherokee Arrow 200D | A. W. Rix/Guernsey | |
| G-BABB | Cessna F.150L | Seawing Flying Club Ltd/Southend | |
| G-BABC | Cessna F.150L | Suffolk Aero Club Ltd/Ipswich | |
| G-BABD | Cessna FRA.150L | C. J. Hopewell | |
| G-BABE | Taylor JT.2 Titch | P. D. G. Grist/Sibson | |
| G-BABG | PA-28 Cherokee 180 | Mendip Flying Group/Bristol | |
| G-BABK | PA-34-200 Seneca II | D. F. J. Flashman/Biggin Hill | |
| G-BABY | Taylor JT.2 Titch | R. E. Finlay | |
| G-BACB | PA-34-200 Seneca II | London Flight Centre (Stansted) Ltd | |
| G-BACC | Cessna FRA.150L | C. M. & J. H. Cooper/Cranfield | |
| G-BACE | Fournier RF-5 | R. W. K. Stead/Perranporth | |
| G-BACH | Enstrom F-28A | M. & P. Food Products Ltd | |
| G-BACJ | Jodel D.120 | Wearside Flying Association/Newcastle | |
| G-BACL | Jodel D.150 | M. L. Sargeant/Biggin Hill | |
| G-BACN | Cessna FRA.150L | Air Service Training Ltd/Perth | |
| G-BACO | Cessna FRA.150L | W. R. Burgess & ptnrs/Sibson | |
| G-BACP | Cessna FRA.150L | B. A. Mills | |
| G-BADC | Luton Beta B.2A | H. M. Mackenzie | |
| G-BADH | Slingsby T.61A Falke | Falke Flying Group | |
| G-BADI | PA-23 Aztec 250D | W. London Aero Services Ltd/ White Waltham | |
| G-BADJ | PA-E23 Aztec 250E | CKS Air Ltd/Southend | |
| G-BADL | PA-34-200 Seneca II | K. Smith & M. Corbett | |
| G-BADM | D.62B Condor | M. Harris & J. Taylor | |
| G-BADO | PA-32 Cherokee Six 300E | B. J. Haylor & ptnrs/Southampton | |
| G-BADU | Cameron O-56 balloon | J. Philp *Dream Machine* | |
| G-BADV | Brochet MB-50 | P. A. Cairns/Dunkeswell | |
| G-BADW | Pitts S-2A Special | R. E. Mitchell/Coventry | |
| G-BADZ | Pitts S-2A Special | Tiger Club (1990) Ltd/Headcorn | |
| G-BAEB | Robin DR.400/160 | P. D. W. King | |
| G-BAEC | Robin HR.100/210 | Robin Travel & Designways (Interior Design) Ltd | |
| G-BAED | PA-23 Aztec 250C | Advanced Airship Corp. Ltd/Jurby | |
| G-BAEE | Jodel DR.1050/M1 | R. Little | |
| G-BAEM | Robin DR.400/125 | M. A. Webb/Booker | |
| G-BAEN | Robin DR.400/180 | B. T. & L. M. Spreckley/Shoreham | |
| G-BAEP | Cessna FRA.150L (modified) | A. M. Lynn | |
| G-BAER | Cosmic Wind | R. S. Voice/Redhill | |
| G-BAET | Piper J-3C-65 Cub | C. J. Rees | |
| G-BAEU | Cessna F.150L | Skyviews & General Ltd | |
| G-BAEV | Cessna FRA.150L | N. J. Wiszowaty/Blackbushe | |
| G-BAEW | Cessna F.172M | Northamptonshire School of Flying Ltd/ Sywell | |
| G-BAEY | Cessna F.172M | R. Fursman/Southampton | |
| G-BAEZ | Cessna FRA.150L | E. Bannister | |
| G-BAFA | AA-5 Traveler | C. F. Mackley/Stapleford | |
| G-BAFD | MBB Bo 105D | Bond Helicopters Ltd/Aberdeen | |
| G-BAFG | D.H.82A Tiger Moth | J. E. & P. J. Shaw | |
| G-BAFH | Evans VP-1 | C. M. Gibson | |
| G-BAFI | Cessna F.177RG | Gloucestershire Flying Club | |
| G-BAFL | Cessna 182P | D. P. Holland | |
| G-BAFM | AT-16 Harvard IIB (FS728) | N. G. R. Moffat | |
| G-BAFP | Robin DR.400/160 | A. S. Langdale & J. Bevis-Lawson/ Shoreham | |
| G-BAFS | PA-18 Super Cub 150 | M. D. Morris/Sandown | |
| G-BAFT | PA-18 Super Cub 150 | T. J. Wilkinson | |
| G-BAFU | PA-28 Cherokee 140 | R. C. Saunders/Gamston | |
| G-BAFV | PA-18 Super Cub 95 | T. F. & S. J. Thorpe | |
| G-BAFW | PA-28 Cherokee 140 | American Aviation Technologies Ltd | |
| G-BAFX | Robin DR.400/140 | Nicholas Advertising Ltd | |
| G-BAGB | SIAI-Marchetti SF.260 | British Midland Airways Ltd/E. Midlands | |
| G-BAGC | Robin DR.400/140 | Caseright Ltd | |
| G-BAGF | Jodel D.92 Bebe | E. Evans | |

| Notes | Reg. | Type | Owner or Operator |
|---|---|---|---|
| | G-BAGG | PA-32 Cherokee Six 300E | Hornair Ltd |
| | G-BAGI | Cameron O-31 balloon | D. C. & S. J. Boxall |
| | G-BAGL | SA.341G Gazelle Srs 1 | Autokraft Ltd |
| | G-BAGN | Cessna F.177RG | R. W. J. Andrews |
| | G-BAGO | Cessna 421B | Jadealto (Sales & Marketing) Ltd |
| | G-BAGR | Robin DR.400/140 | F. C. Aris & J. D. Last/Mona |
| | G-BAGS | Robin DR.400/180 2+2 | Headcorn Flying School Ltd |
| | G-BAGT | Helio H.295 Courier | B. J. C. Woodall Ltd |
| | G-BAGV | Cessna U.206F | Scottish Parachute Club/Strathallan |
| | G-BAGX | PA-28 Cherokee 140 | Klingair Ltd/Conington |
| | G-BAGY | Cameron O-84 balloon | P. G. Dunnington *Beatrice* |
| | G-BAHD | Cessna 182P Skylane | G. G. Ferriman |
| | G-BAHE | PA-28 Cherokee 140 | A. H. Evans & A. O. Jones/Sleap |
| | G-BAHF | PA-28 Cherokee 140 | S. J. Green/Halfpenny Green |
| | G-BAHG | PA-24 Comanche 260 | Friendly Aviation (Jersey) Ltd |
| | G-BAHH | Wallis WA-121 | K. H. Wallis |
| | G-BAHI | Cessna F.150H | A. G. Brindle/Blackpool |
| | G-BAHJ | PA-24 Comanche 250 | K. Cooper |
| | G-BAHL | Robin DR.400/160 | R. E. Thorns & G. W. Dimmer/Old Sarum |
| | G-BAHN | Beech 95-58TC Baron | Remoteassist Ltd |
| | G-BAHO | Beech C.23 Sundowner | G-ATJG Private Aircraft Syndicate Ltd |
| | G-BAHP | Volmer VJ.22 Sportsman | J. F. Morris |
| | G-BAHS | PA-28R Cherokee Arrow 200-II | A. A. Wild & ptnrs |
| | G-BAHX | Cessna 182P | PP Dupost Group |
| | G-BAHZ | PA-28R Cherokee Arrow 200-II | J. H. Reynolds |
| | G-BAIA | PA-32 Cherokee Six 300E | J. Barham |
| | G-BAIB | Enstrom F-28A | Farmax Helicopters |
| | G-BAIH | PA-28R Cherokee Arrow 200-II | G. J. Williamson |
| | G-BAII | Cessna FRA.150L | Air Service Training Ltd/Perth |
| | G-BAIK | Cessna F.150L | Wickenby Aviation Ltd |
| | G-BAIL | Cessna FR.172J | G. Greenall |
| | G-BAIN | Cessna FRA.150L | Air Service Training Ltd/Perth |
| | G-BAIP | Cessna F.150L | W. D. Cliffe & J. F. Platt/Wellesbourne |
| | G-BAIR | Thunder Ax7-77 balloon | P. A. & Mrs M. Hutchins |
| | G-BAIS | Cessna F.177RG | A. J. Everex & T. W. Goodall |
| | G-BAIW | Cessna F.172M | Humber Aviation Ltd |
| | G-BAIX | Cessna F.172M | R. A. Nichols/Elstree |
| | G-BAIY | Cameron O-65 balloon | Budget Rent A Car (UK) Ltd |
| | G-BAIZ | Slingsby T.61A Falke | Falke Syndicate |
| | G-BAJA | Cessna F.177RG | Don Ward Productions Ltd/Biggin Hill |
| | G-BAJB | Cessna F.177RG | G. J. Banfield |
| | G-BAJC | Evans VP-1 | R. A. Hazelton |
| | G-BAJE | Cessna 177 Cardinal | N. C. Butcher |
| | G-BAJN | AA-5 Traveler | Janacrew Flying Group |
| | G-BAJO | AA-5 Traveler | J. R. Howard/Blackpool |
| | G-BAJR | PA-28 Cherokee 180 | Chosen Few Flying Group/Newtownards |
| | G-BAJY | Robin DR.400/180 | F. Birch & K. J. Pike/Sturgate |
| | G-BAJZ | Robin DR.400/125 | Rochester Aviation Ltd |
| | G-BAKD | PA-34-200 Seneca II | Andrews Professional Colour Laboratories/Elstree |
| | G-BAKH | PA-28 Cherokee 140 | Woodgate Air Services (IoM) Ltd/Ronaldsway |
| | G-BAKJ | PA-30 Twin Comanche 160B | M. F. Fisher & W. R. Lawes/Biggin Hill |
| | G-BAKK | Cessna F.172H ★ | *Parachute jump trainer*/Coventry |
| | G-BAKL | F.27 Friendship Mk 200 | Air UK Ltd/Norwich |
| | G-BAKM | Robin DR.400/140 | MKS Syndicate |
| | G-BAKN | SNCAN Stampe SV-4C | M. Holloway |
| | G-BAKO | Cameron O-84 balloon | D. C. Dokk-Olsen *Pied Piper* |
| | G-BAKR | Jodel D.117 | A. B. Bailey/White Waltham |
| | G-BAKS | AB-206B JetRanger 2 | Dollar Air Services Ltd/Coventry |
| | G-BAKV | PA-18 Super Cub 150 | Pounds Marine Shipping Ltd/Goodwood |
| | G-BAKW | B.121 Pup 2 | Oakley Motor Units Ltd & J. P. Baudrier |
| | G-BAKY | Slingsby T.61C Falke | G. A. Schulz & A. Jones/Leicester |
| | G-BALF | Robin DR.400/140 | F. A. Spear/Panshanger |
| | G-BALG | Robin DR.400/180 | R. Jones |
| | G-BALH | Robin DR.400/140B | J. D. Copsey |
| | G-BALI | Robin DR.400 2+2 | Robin Flying Group |
| | G-BALJ | Robin DR.400/180 | D. A. Bett & D. de Lacey-Rowe |
| | G-BALK | SNCAN Stampe SV-4C | L. J. Rice |
| | G-BALN | Cessna T.310Q | O'Brien Properties Ltd/Shoreham |
| | G-BALT | Enstrom F-28A | Codnor Pet-Aquatics |
| | G-BALX | D.H.82A Tiger Moth (N6848) | Toadair |
| | G-BALY | Practavia Pilot Sprite 150 | A. L. Young |

| Reg. | Type | Owner or Operator | Notes |
|------|------|-------------------|-------|
| G-BALZ | Bell 212 | B.E.A.S. Ltd/Redhill | |
| G-BAMB | Slingsby T.61C Falke | Bambi Aircraft Club | |
| G-BAMC | Cessna F.150L | Barry Aviation Ltd | |
| G-BAME | Volmer VJ-22 Sportsman | A. McLeod | |
| G-BAMF | MBB Bo 105D | Bond Helicopters Ltd/Bourn | |
| G-BAMJ | Cessna 182P | A. E. Kedros | |
| G-BAMK | Cameron D-96 airship | D. W. Liddiard | |
| G-BAML | Bell 206B JetRanger 2 | Heliscott Ltd | |
| G-BAMM | PA-28 Cherokee 235 | G-BAMM Group | |
| G-BAMR | PA-16 Clipper | H. Royce | |
| G-BAMS | Robin DR.400/160 | G-BAMS Ltd/Headcorn | |
| G-BAMU | Robin DR.400/160 | The Alternative Flying Group/Sywell | |
| G-BAMV | Robin DR.400/180 | B. F. Hill | |
| G-BAMY | PA-28R Cherokee Arrow 200-II | G-BAMY Group/Birmingham | |
| G-BANA | Robin DR.221 | G. T. Pryor | |
| G-BANB | Robin DR.400/180 | Time Electronics Ltd/Biggin Hill | |
| G-BANC | GY-201 Minicab | J. T. S. Lewis & J. E. Williams | |
| G-BAND | Cameron O-84 balloon | Mid-Bucks Farmers Balloon Group *Clover* | |
| G-BANE | Cessna FRA.150L | Spectrum Flying Group/Newtownards | |
| G-BANF | Luton LA-4A Minor | W. J. McCollum | |
| G-BANG | Cameron O-84 balloon | R. F. Harrower | |
| G-BANK | PA-34-200 Seneca II | Cleveland Flying School Ltd/Teesside | |
| G-BANT | Cameron O-65 balloon | M. A. Dworski & R. M. Bishop | |
| G-BANU | Wassmer Jodel D.120 | C. E. McKinney | |
| G-BANV | Phoenix Currie Wot | K. Knight | |
| G-BANW | CP.1330 Super Emeraude | P. S. Milner | |
| G-BANX | Cessna F.172M | J. F. Davis/Badminton | |
| G-BAOB | Cessna F.172M | V. B. Cheesewright/Earls Court | |
| G-BAOG | M.S.880B Rallye Club | G. W. Simpson | |
| G-BAOH | M.S.880B Rallye Club | A. Devery | |
| G-BAOJ | M.S.880B Rallye Club | BAOJ Ltd | |
| G-BAOM | M.S.880B Rallye Club | D. H. Tonkin | |
| G-BAOP | Cessna FRA.150L | M. K. Field | |
| G-BAOS | Cessna F.172M | F. W. Ellis & ptnrs | |
| G-BAOU | AA-5 Traveler | C. J. Earle & I. S. Hacon | |
| G-BAOV | AA-5A Cheetah | A. Kerridge | |
| G-BAOW | Cameron O-65 balloon | P. I. White *Winslow Boy* | |
| G-BAOY | Cameron S-31 balloon | Shell-Mex BP Ltd *New Potato* | |
| G-BAPA | Fournier RF-5B Sperber | Nuthampstead G-BAPA Group | |
| G-BAPB | D.H.C.1 Chipmunk 22 | R. C. P. Brookhouse/Redhill | |
| G-BAPC | Luton LA-4A Minor ★ | Midland Aircraft Preservation Soc | |
| G-BAPF | V.814 Viscount | British Air Ferries/Southend | |
| G-BAPI | Cessna FRA.150L | Industrial Supplies (Peterborough) Ltd/Sibson | |
| G-BAPJ | Cessna FRA.150L | M. D. Page/Manston | |
| G-BAPK | Cessna F.150L | Andrewsfield Flying Club Ltd | |
| G-BAPL | PA-23 Turbo Aztec 250E | Medici Spa Marine & Exploration Ltd | |
| G-BAPM | Fuji FA.200-160 | R. P. Munday/Biggin Hill | |
| G-BAPP | Evans VP-1 | N. H. Eastwood | |
| G-BAPR | Jodel D.11 | R. G. Marshall | |
| G-BAPS | Campbell Cougar ★ | International Helicopter Museum/Weston-s-Mare | |
| G-BAPV | Robin DR.400/160 | J. D. & M. Millne | |
| G-BAPW | PA-28R Cherokee Arrow 180 | Papa Whisky Flying Group | |
| G-BAPX | Robin DR.400/160 | M. A. Musselwhite | |
| G-BAPY | Robin HR.100/210 | Gloria Baby Aviation Ltd | |
| G-BARB | PA-34-200 Seneca II | S. Wood | |
| G-BARC | Cessna FR.172J | G. N. Hopcraft | |
| G-BARD | Cessna 337C | D. W. Horton | |
| G-BARF | Jodel D.112 Club | P. G. Rose | |
| G-BARG | Cessna E.310Q | Sally Marine Ltd | |
| G-BARH | Beech C.23 Sundowner | G. A. Davitt | |
| G-BARJ | Bell 212 | Autair International Ltd/Panshanger | |
| G-BARN | Taylor JT.2 Titch | R. G. W. Newton | |
| G-BARP | Bell 206B JetRanger 2 | S.W. Electricity Board/Bristol | |
| G-BARS | D.H.C.1 Chipmunk 22 | T. I. Sutton/Chester | |
| G-BARV | Cessna 310Q | Old England Watches Ltd/Elstree | |
| G-BARZ | Scheibe SF.28A Tandem Falke | K. Kiely | |
| G-BASB | Enstrom F-28A | GTS Engineering (Coventry) Ltd | |
| G-BASD | B.121 Pup 2 | C. C. Brown/Leicester | |
| G-BASG | AA-5 Traveler | ASG Aviation Group/Glenrothes | |
| G-BASH | AA-5 Traveler | J. J. Woodhouse | |
| G-BASJ | PA-28 Cherokee 180 | W. Brown | |

| Notes | Reg. | Type | Owner or Operator |
|---|---|---|---|
| | G-BASL | PA-28 Cherokee 140 | Air Navigation & Trading Ltd/Blackpool |
| | G-BASM | PA-34-200 Seneca II | Poplar Aviation Group/Ipswich |
| | G-BASN | Beech C.23 Sundowner | M. F. Fisher |
| | G-BASO | Lake LA-4 Amphibian | R. J. Willies |
| | G-BASP | B.121 Pup 1 | B. J. Coutts/Sywell |
| | G-BASX | PA-34-200 Seneca II | J. W. Anstee & Anstee & Ware Ltd |
| | G-BATC | MBB Bo 105D | Bond Helicopters Ltd/Swansea |
| | G-BATJ | Jodel D.119 | E. G. Waite/Shobdon |
| | G-BATM | PA-32 Cherokee Six 300E | Patgrove Ltd/Bolney |
| | G-BATN | PA-23 Aztec 250E | Marshall of Cambridge Ltd |
| | G-BATR | PA-34-200 Seneca II | Aerohire Ltd/Halfpenny Green |
| | G-BATT | Hughes 269C | Pennine Helicopters |
| | G-BATV | PA-28 Cherokee 180D | J. N. Rudsdale |
| | G-BATW | PA-28 Cherokee 140 | C. R. Lambert/Earls Colne |
| | G-BATX | PA-23 Aztec 250E | Tayside Aviation Ltd/Dundee |
| | G-BAUA | PA-23 Aztec 250D | David Parr & Associates Ltd/Shobdon |
| | G-BAUC | PA-25 Pawnee 235 | Southdown Gliding Club Ltd |
| | G-BAUE | Cessna 310Q | A. J. Dyer/Elstree |
| | G-BAUH | Jodel D.112 | G. A. & D. Shepherd |
| | G-BAUI | PA-23 Aztec 250D | SFT Aviation Ltd/Bournemouth |
| | G-BAUJ | PA-23 Aztec 250E | S. J. & C. J. Westley/Cranfield |
| | G-BAUK | Hughes 269C | Curtis Engineering (Frome) Ltd |
| | G-BAUN | Bell 206B Jet Ranger | Bristow Helicopters Ltd |
| | G-BAUR | F.27 Friendship Mk 200 | Air UK Ltd *Robert Louis Stevenson*/ Norwich |
| | G-BAUV | Cessna F.150L | Skyviews & General Ltd |
| | G-BAUW | PA-23 Aztec 250E | R. E. Myson |
| | G-BAUY | Cessna FRA.150L | The PMM Group/Glenrothes |
| | G-BAUZ | SNCAN NC.854S | W. A. Ashley & D. Horne |
| | G-BAVB | Cessna F.172M | T. J. Nokes & T. V. Phillips |
| | G-BAVC | Cessna F.150L | Tayside Aviation Ltd/Dundee |
| | G-BAVH | D.H.C.1 Chipmunk 22 | Portsmouth Naval Gliding Club/ Lee-on-Solent |
| | G-BAVL | PA-23 Aztec 250E | S. P. & A. V. Chillott |
| | G-BAVO | Boeing Stearman N2S (26) | V. A. Holliday & T. E. W. Terrell |
| | G-BAVR | AA-5 Traveler | E. R. Pyatt |
| | G-BAVS | AA-5 Traveler | V. J. Peake/Headcorn |
| | G-BAVU | Cameron A-105 balloon | J. D. Michaelis |
| | G-BAVZ | PA-23 Aztec 250E | Ravenair/Manchester |
| | G-BAWB | PA-23 Aztec 250C | Emberden Ltd/Biggin Hill |
| | G-BAWG | PA-28R Cherokee Arrow 200-II | Solent Air Ltd |
| | G-BAWI | Enstrom F-28A-UK | M. & P. Food Products Ltd |
| | G-BAWK | PA-28 Cherokee 140 | Newcastle-upon-Tyne Aero Club Ltd |
| | G-BAWN | PA-30 Twin Comanche 160C | R. A. & J. M. Nunn |
| | G-BAWR | Robin HR.100/210 | T. Taylor |
| | G-BAWU | PA-30 Twin Comanche 160B | CCH Aviation Ltd |
| | G-BAWW | Thunder Ax7-77 balloon | M. L. C. Hutchins *Taurus*/Holland |
| | G-BAXD | BN-2A Mk III Trislander | Aurigny Air Services/Guernsey |
| | G-BAXE | Hughes 269A | Reethorpe Engineering Ltd |
| | G-BAXF | Cameron O-77 balloon | R. D. Sargeant & M. F. Lasson |
| | G-BAXH | Cessna 310Q | D. A. Williamson |
| | G-BAXJ | PA-32 Cherokee Six 300B | UK Parachute Services/Ipswich |
| | G-BAXK | Thunder Ax7-77 balloon | T. J. Orchard & A. R. Snook |
| | G-BAXP | PA-23 Aztec 250E | Ashcombe Ltd |
| | G-BAXS | Bell 47G-5 | LRC Leisure Ltd |
| | G-BAXT | PA-28R Cherokee Arrow 200-II | P. R. Phealon/Old Sarum |
| | G-BAXU | Cessna F.150L | W. Lancs Aero Club Ltd/Woodvale |
| | G-BAXY | Cessna F.172M | Galaxy Enterprises Ltd |
| | G-BAXZ | PA-28 Cherokee 140 | H. Martin & D. Norris/Halton |
| | G-BAYC | Cameron O-65 balloon | D. Whitlock & R. T. F. Mitchell |
| | G-BAYL | Nord 1203/III Norecrin | D. M. Fincham |
| | G-BAYO | Cessna 150L | Cheshire Air Training School (Merseyside) Ltd/Liverpool |
| | G-BAYP | Cessna 150L | Three Counties Aero Engineering Ltd/ Lasham |
| | G-BAYR | Robin HR.100/210 | L. A. Christie/Stapleford |
| | G-BAYV | SNCAN 1101 Noralpha (1480)★ | Booker Aircraft Museum |
| | G-BAYZ | Bellanca 7GCBC Citabria | Cambridge University Gliding Trust Ltd/ Gransdon |
| | G-BAZC | Robin DR.400/160 | Southern Sailplanes |
| | G-BAZH | Boeing 737-204 | Britannia Airways Ltd *Sir Frederick Handley Page* |
| | G-BAZJ | HPR-7 Herald 209 ★ | Guernsey Airport Fire Services |

| Reg. | Type | Owner or Operator | Notes |
|------|------|-------------------|-------|
| G-BAZM | Jodel D.11 | Bingley Flying Group/Leeds | |
| G-BAZS | Cessna F.150L | Sherburn Aero Club Ltd | |
| G-BAZT | Cessna F.172M | M. Fraser/Exeter | |
| G-BAZU | PA-28R Cherokee Arrow 200 | S. C. Simmons/White Waltham | |
| G-BBAE | L.1011-385 TriStar 100 | Caledonian Airways *Loch Earn*/Gatwick | |
| G-BBAF | L.1011-385 TriStar 100 | Caledonian Airways/Gatwick | |
| G-BBAG | L.1011-385 TriStar 1 | British Airways *Bridgwater Bay*/Heathrow | |
| G-BBAH | L.1011-385 TriStar 100 | Caledonian Airways/Gatwick | |
| G-BBAI | L.1011-385 TriStar 1 | Caledonian Airways *Loch Inver*/Gatwick | |
| G-BBAJ | L.1011-385 TriStar 100 | Caledonian Airways *Loch Rannoch*/Gatwick | |
| G-BBAK | M.S.894A Rallye Minerva | R. B. Hemsworth & C. L. Hill/Exeter | |
| G-BBAW | Robin HR.100/210 | Scoba Ltd/Goodwood | |
| G-BBAX | Robin DR.400/140 | S. R. Young | |
| G-BBAY | Robin DR.400/140 | Rothwell Group | |
| G-BBAZ | Hiller UH-12E | Copley Farms Ltd | |
| G-BBBC | Cessna F.150L | W. J. Greenfield | |
| G-BBBI | AA-5 Traveler | C. S. Jenks | |
| G-BBBK | PA-28 Cherokee 140 | Bencray Ltd/Blackpool | |
| G-BBBM | Bell 206B JetRanger 2 | Express Newspapers PLC | |
| G-BBBN | PA-28 Cherokee 180 | BT Flying Group | |
| G-BBBO | SIPA 903 | J. S. Hemmings & C. R. Steer | |
| G-BBBW | FRED Series 2 | C. Briggs | |
| G-BBBX | Cessna E310L | Atlantic Air Transport Ltd/Coventry | |
| G-BBBY | PA-28 Cherokee 140 | J. L. Yourell/Luton | |
| G-BBCA | Bell 206B JetRanger 2 | E. Wootton | |
| G-BBCB | Western O-65 balloon | G. M. Bulmer | |
| G-BBCC | PA-23 Aztec 250D | Northamptonshire School of Flying Ltd/Sywell | |
| G-BBCD | Beech 95-B55 Baron | L. M. Tulloch | |
| G-BBCH | Robin DR.400/2+2 | Headcorn Flying School Ltd | |
| G-BBCI | Cessna 150H | P. T. W. Sheffield | |
| G-BBCK | Cameron O-77 balloon | R. J. Leathart *The Mary Gloster* | |
| G-BBCN | Robin HR.100/210 | K. T. G. Atkins/Teesside | |
| G-BBCP | Thunder Ax6-56 balloon | J. M. Robinson *Jack Frost* | |
| G-BBCS | Robin DR.400/140 | A. R. G. Besler | |
| G-BBCW | PA-23 Aztec 250E | JDT Holdings Ltd/Sturgate | |
| G-BBCY | Luton LA-4A Minor | D. C. Stokes | |
| G-BBCZ | AA-5 Traveler | P. J. Kember | |
| G-BBDB | PA-28 Cherokee 180 | T. D. Strange/Newtownards | |
| G-BBDC | PA-28 Cherokee 140 | A. Dunk | |
| G-BBDD | PA-28 Cherokee 140 | Midland Air Training School | |
| G-BBDE | PA-28R Cherokee Arrow 200-II | R. L. Coleman & A. E. Stevens | |
| G-BBDG | Concorde 100 ★ | British Aerospace PLC/Filton | |
| G-BBDH | Cessna F.172M | P. S. C. & B. J. Comina | |
| G-BBDJ | Thunder Ax6-56 balloon | S. W. D. & H. B. Ashby *Jack Tar* | |
| G-BBDK | V.808C Viscount Freightmaster | British Air Ferries *Viscount Linley*/Southend | |
| G-BBDL | AA-5 Traveler | D. G. Hopkins & W. Woods/Coventry | |
| G-BBDM | AA-5 Traveler | D. J. & P. L. Hazell | |
| G-BBDN | Taylor JT.1 Monoplane | T. Barnes | |
| G-BBDO | PA-23 Turbo Aztec 250E | R. Long/Bristol | |
| G-BBDP | Robin DR.400/160 | Robin Lance Aviation Associates Ltd | |
| G-BBDT | Cessna 150H | U. K. Mercer & J. K. Sibbald | |
| G-BBDV | SIPA S.903 | W. McAndrew | |
| G-BBEA | Luton LA-4A Minor | Mid Suffolk Flying Group | |
| G-BBEB | PA-28R Cherokee Arrow 200-II | R. D. Rippingale/Thruxton | |
| G-BBEC | PA-28 Cherokee 180 | C. F. Bishop/Clacton | |
| G-BBED | M.S.894A Rallye Minerva 220 | Sky-Ad Ltd/Birmingham | |
| G-BBEF | PA-28 Cherokee 140 | Air Navigation & Trading Co Ltd/Blackpool | |
| G-BBEI | PA-31 Turbo Navajo | BKS Surveys Ltd/Exeter | |
| G-BBEL | PA-28R Cherokee Arrow 180 | G. R. Cole & A. Grimshaw/Ronaldsway | |
| G-BBEN | Bellanca 7GCBC Citabria | C. A. G. Schofield | |
| G-BBEO | Cessna FRA.150L | R. H. Ford | |
| G-BBEV | PA-28 Cherokee 140 | Comed Aviation Ltd/Blackpool | |
| G-BBEX | Cessna 185A Skywagon | Westward Airways (Lands End) Ltd | |
| G-BBEY | PA-23 Aztec 250E | Cormack (Aircraft Services) Ltd/Glasgow | |
| G-BBFC | AA-1B Trainer | T. F. Shorter/Lydd | |
| G-BBFD | PA-28R Cherokee Arrow 200-II | CR Aviation Ltd | |
| G-BBFL | GY-201 Minicab | D. B. Busfield | |
| G-BBFS | Van Den Bemden gas balloon | A. J. F. Smith *Le Tomate* | |
| G-BBFV | PA-32 Cherokee Six 260 | C. J. Janson | |

55

| Notes | Reg. | Type | Owner or Operator |
|---|---|---|---|
| | G-BBGB | PA-E23 Aztec 250E | Ravenair/Manchester |
| | G-BBGC | M.S.893E Rallye 180GT | Mark Thorpe & ptnrs |
| | G-BBGE | PA-23 Aztec 250D | B. Jones |
| | G-BBGH | AA-5 Traveler | L. W. Mitchell & D. Abbiss |
| | G-BBGI | Fuji FA.200-160 | D. T. C. Pollock |
| | G-BBGJ | Cessna 180 | B. W. Wells & Burbage Farms Ltd |
| | G-BBGL | Baby Great Lakes | F. Ball |
| | G-BBGR | Cameron O-65 balloon | M. L. & L. P. Willoughby |
| | G-BBGX | Cessna 182P Skylane | WOC Hire Ltd |
| | G-BBGZ | CHABA 42 balloon | G. Laslett & ptnrs |
| | G-BBHC | Enstrom F-28A | Blades Helicopters Ltd/Goodwood |
| | G-BBHD | Enstrom F-28A | R. E. Harvey |
| | G-BBHF | PA-23 Aztec 250E | Bevan Lynch Aviation Ltd/Birmingham |
| | G-BBHG | Cessna E310Q | G. P. Williams |
| | G-BBHI | Cessna 177RG | T. G. W. Bunce |
| | G-BBHJ | Piper J-3C-65 Cub | R. V. Miller & J. Stanbridge |
| | G-BBHK | AT-16 Harvard IIB (FH153) | Bob Warner Aviation/Exeter |
| | G-BBHL | Sikorsky S-61N Mk II | Bristow Helicopters Ltd *Glamis* |
| | G-BBHX | M.S.893E Rallye Commodore | JKP Aviation |
| | G-BBHY | PA-28 Cherokee 180 | Air Operations Ltd/Guernsey |
| | G-BBIA | PA-28R Cherokee Arrow 200-II | A. G. (Commodities) Ltd/Stapleford |
| | G-BBIC | Cessna 310Q | H. Bollmann Manufacturers Ltd |
| | G-BBID | PA-28 Cherokee 140 | M. & J. M. McCormac |
| | G-BBIF | PA-23 Aztec 250E | Ingold Resources Ltd |
| | G-BBIH | Enstrom F-28A-UK | Pyramid Precision Engineering Ltd |
| | G-BBII | Fiat G-46-3B (14) | V. S. E. Norman |
| | G-BBIL | PA-28 Cherokee 140 | India Lima Flying Group |
| | G-BBIN | Enstrom F-28A | Southern Air Ltd/Shoreham |
| | G-BBIO | Robin HR.100/210 | R. A. King/Headcorn |
| | G-BBIT | Hughes 269B | Contract Development & Projects (Leeds) Ltd (*stored*) |
| | G-BBIV | Hughes 269C | A. Harvey |
| | G-BBIX | PA-28 Cherokee 140 | Sterling Contract Hire Ltd |
| | G-BBJB | Thunder Ax7-77 balloon | St Crispin Balloon Group *Dick Darby* |
| | G-BBJI | Isaacs Spitfire (RN218) | A. N. R. Houghton & ptnrs |
| | G-BBJU | Robin DR.400/140 | J. C. Lister |
| | G-BBJV | Cessna F.177RG | Pilot Magazine/Biggin Hill |
| | G-BBJX | Cessna F.150L | Yorkshire Flying Services Ltd/Leeds |
| | G-BBJY | Cessna F.172M | J. Lucketti/Barton |
| | G-BBJZ | Cessna F.172M | Burks, Green & ptnrs |
| | G-BBKA | Cessna F.150L | R. Hall & L. W. Scattergood |
| | G-BBKB | Cessna F.150L | Justgtold Ltd/Blackpool |
| | G-BBKC | Cessna F.172M | W. F. Hall |
| | G-BBKE | Cessna F.150L | Wickenby Aviation Ltd |
| | G-BBKF | Cessna FRA.150L | Compton Abbas Airfield Ltd |
| | G-BBKG | Cessna FR.172J | R. Windley/Tattershall |
| | G-BBKI | Cessna F.172M | C. W. & S.A . Burman |
| | G-BBKL | CP.301A Emeraude | D. W. Paton |
| | G-BBKR | Scheibe SF.24A Motorspatz | P. I. Morgans |
| | G-BBKU | Cessna FRA.150L | Penguin Group |
| | G-BBKX | PA-28 Cherokee 180 | RAE Flying Club Ltd/Farnborough |
| | G-BBKY | Cessna F.150L | Howells Group PLC |
| | G-BBKZ | Cessna 172M | Exeter Flying Club Ltd |
| | G-BBLA | PA-28 Cherokee 140 | Woodgate Aviation Co Ltd/Woodvale |
| | G-BBLE | Hiller UH-12E | Agricopters Ltd/Chilbolton |
| | G-BBLH | Piper J-3C-65 Cub | Shipping & Airlines Ltd/Biggin Hill |
| | G-BBLL | Cameron O-84 balloon | University of East Anglia Hot-Air Ballooning Club *Boadicea* |
| | G-BBLM | SOCATA Rallye 100S | M. & J. Grafton |
| | G-BBLP | PA-23 Aztec 250D | Donington Aviation Ltd/E. Midlands |
| | G-BBLS | AA-5 Traveler | D. A. Reid/Prestwick |
| | G-BBLU | PA-34-200 Seneca II | F. Tranter/Manchester |
| | G-BBMB | Robin DR.400/180 | J. T. M. Ball/Biggin Hill |
| | G-BBME | BAC One-Eleven 401AK | Brymon European Airways Ltd (G-AZMI)/*City of Nottingham* |
| | G-BBMG | BAC One-Eleven 408EF | Brymon European Airways Ltd (G-AWEJ)/*Stratford upon Avon* |
| | G-BBMH | EAA. Sports Biplane Model P.1 | K. Dawson |
| | G-BBMJ | PA-23 Aztec 250E | Tindon Ltd/Little Snoring |
| | G-BBMK | PA-31 Turbo Navajo | Steer Aviation Ltd/Biggin Hill |
| | G-BBMN | D.H.C.1 Chipmunk 22 | R. Steiner/Panshanger |
| | G-BBMO | D.H.C.1 Chipmunk 22 | Holland Aerobatics Ltd |
| | G-BBMR | D.H.C.1 Chipmunk T.10 | Southall Technical College |

| Reg. | Type | Owner or Operator | Notes |
|------|------|-------------------|-------|
| | (WB763) ★ | | |
| G-BBMT | D.H.C.1 Chipmunk 22 | V. F. J. Falconer & W. A. Lee/Dunstable | |
| G-BBMV | D.H.C.1 Chipmunk 22 (WG348) | P. J. Morgan (Aviation) Ltd | |
| G-BBMW | D.H.C.1 Chipmunk 22 (WK628) | Mike Whisky Group/Shoreham | |
| G-BBMX | D.H.C.1 Chipmunk 22 | A. L. Brown & P. S. Murchison | |
| G-BBMZ | D.H.C.1 Chipmunk 22 | Wycombe Gliding School Syndicate/ Booker | |
| G-BBNA | D.H.C.1 Chipmunk 22 (Lycoming) | Coventry Gliding Club Ltd/ Husbands Bosworth | |
| G-BBNC | D.H.C.1 Chipmunk T.10 (WP790) ★ | Mosquito Aircraft Museum | |
| G-BBND | D.H.C.1 Chipmunk 22 (WD286) | A. J. Organ/Bourn | |
| G-BBNG | Bell 206B JetRanger 2 | Helicopter Crop Spraying Ltd | |
| G-BBNH | PA-34-200 Seneca II | Lawrence Goodwin Machine Tools Ltd/ Coventry | |
| G-BBNI | PA-34-200 Seneca II | Channel Aviation (UK) Ltd | |
| G-BBNJ | Cessna F.150L | Sherburn Aero Club Ltd | |
| G-BBNN | PA-23 Aztec 250D | Woodgate Executive Air Charter Ltd | |
| G-BBNO | PA-23 Aztec 250E | Falcon Flying Services/Biggin Hill | |
| G-BBNT | PA-31-350 Navajo Chieftain | Northern Executive Aviation Ltd/ Manchester | |
| G-BBNX | Fuji FA.200-160 | G. C. Thomas/Kidlington | |
| G-BBNX | Cessna FRA.150L | General Airline Ltd | |
| G-BBNY | Cessna FRA.150L | Air Tows Ltd/Lasham | |
| G-BBNZ | Cessna F.172M | R. J. Nunn | |
| G-BBOA | Cessna F.172M | J. W. J. Adkins/Southend | |
| G-BBOC | Cameron O-77 balloon | J. A. B. Gray | |
| G-BBOD | Thunder O-45 balloon | B. R. & M. Boyle | |
| G-BBOE | Robin HR.200/100 | Aberdeen Flying Group | |
| G-BBOH | Pitts S-1S Special | Venom Jet Promotions Ltd/Bournemouth | |
| G-BBOJ | PA-23 Aztec 250E ★ | Instructional airframe/Cranfield | |
| G-BBOL | PA-18 Super Cub 150 | Lakes Gliding Club Ltd | |
| G-BBOO | Thunder Ax-56 balloon | K. Meehan Tigerjack | |
| G-BBOX | Thunder Ax7-77 balloon | R. C. Weyda Rocinante | |
| G-BBOY | Thunder Ax6-56A balloon | N. C. Faithfull Eric of Titchfield | |
| G-BBPJ | Cessna F.172M | B. W. Aviation Ltd/Cardiff | |
| G-BBPK | Evans VP-1 | G. D. E. Macdonald | |
| G-BBPM | Enstrom F-28A | D. Newman | |
| G-BBPN | Enstrom F-28A | Selecting Ltd | |
| G-BBPO | Enstrom F-28A | Southern Air Ltd/Shoreham | |
| G-BBPS | Jodel D.117 | A. Appleby/Redhill | |
| G-BBPU | Boeing 747-136 | British Airways Virginia Water | |
| G-BBPW | Robin HR.100/210 | D. H. Smith | |
| G-BBPX | PA-34-200 Seneca II | Richel Investments Ltd/Guernsey | |
| G-BBPY | PA-28 Cherokee 180 | Sunsaver Ltd | |
| G-BBRA | PA-23 Aztec 250D | G. Cataldo | |
| G-BBRB | D.H.82A Tiger Moth (DF198) | R. Barham/Biggin Hill | |
| G-BBRC | Fuji FA.200-180 | BBRC Ltd | |
| G-BBRH | Bell 47G-5A | Helicopter Supplies & Engineering Ltd | |
| G-BBRI | Bell 47G-5A | Alan Mann Helicopters Ltd/Fairoaks | |
| G-BBRJ | PA-23 Aztec 250E | C. G. Wilson | |
| G-BBRN | Procter Kittiwake (XW784) | J. A. Rees/Haverfordwest | |
| G-BBRV | D.H.C.1 Chipmunk 22 | HSA (Chester) Sports & Social Club | |
| G-BBRX | SIAI-Marchetti S.205-18F | A. L. Cogswell & R. C. West | |
| G-BBRZ | AA-5 Traveler | C. P. Osbourne | |
| G-BBSA | AA-5 Traveler | K. Lynn | |
| G-BBSB | Beech C23 Sundowner | Sundowner Group/Manchester | |
| G-BBSC | Beech B24R Sierra | Beechcombers Flying Group | |
| G-BBSM | PA-32 Cherokee Six 300E | Wardle/Smith Group | |
| G-BBSS | D.H.C.1A Chipmunk 22 | Coventry Gliding Club Ltd/ Husbands Bosworth | |
| G-BBSU | Cessna 421B | Holding & Barnes PLC/Southend | |
| G-BBSW | Pietenpol Air Camper | J. K. S. Wills | |
| G-BBTG | Cessna FRA.150L | C. M. Vlieland-Boddy/Compton Abbas | |
| G-BBTG | Cessna F.172M | D. H. Laws | |
| G-BBTH | Cessna F.172M | S. Gilmore/Newtownards | |
| G-BBTJ | PA-23 Aztec 250E | Geonex Ltd | |
| G-BBTK | Cessna FRA.150L | Air Service Training Ltd/Perth | |
| G-BBTL | PA-23 Aztec 250C | Air Navigation & Trading Co Ltd/Blackpool | |
| G-BBTS | Beech V35B Bonanza | P. S. Bubbear & J. M. Glanville | |
| G-BBTU | ST-10 Diplomate | P. Campion/Stapleford | |
| G-BBTX | Beech C23 Sundowner | K. Harding/Blackbushe | |
| G-BBTY | Beech C23 Sundowner | TY Club/Biggin Hill | |

| Notes | Reg. | Type | Owner or Operator |
|---|---|---|---|
| | G-BBTZ | Cessna F.150L | Woodgate Air Services Ltd |
| | G-BBUD | Sikorsky S-61N Mk II | British International Helicopters Ltd/ Aberdeen |
| | G-BBUE | AA-5 Traveler | Hebog (Mon) Cyfyngedig |
| | G-BBUF | AA-5 Traveler | W. McLaren |
| | G-BBUG | PA-16 Clipper | J. Dolan |
| | G-BBUJ | Cessna 421B | D. M. Charrington |
| | G-BBUL | Mitchell-Procter Kittiwake 1 | R. Bull |
| | G-BBUT | Western O-65 balloon | G. F. Turnbull |
| | G-BBUU | Piper J-3C-65 Cub | O. J. J. Rogers |
| | G-BBVA | Sikorsky S-61N Mk II | Bristow Helicopters Ltd *Vega* |
| | G-BBVE | Cessna 340 | Beechair Ltd/Biggin Hill |
| | G-BBVF | SA Twin Pioneer III ★ | Museum of Flight/E. Fortune |
| | G-BBVG | PA-23 Aztec 250C | *(stored)*/Little Staughton |
| | G-BBVI | Enstrom F-28A ★ | *Ground trainer*/Kidlington |
| | G-BBVJ | Beech B24R Sierra | A. R. Mead |
| | G-BBVO | Isaacs Fury II (S1579) | C. M. Barnes |
| | G-BBVP | Westland-Bell 47G-3B1 | CKS Air Ltd/Southend |
| | G-BBWM | PA-E23 Aztec 250E | Guernsey Air Search Ltd |
| | G-BBWN | D.H.C.1 Chipmunk 22 (WZ876) | D. C. Budd |
| | G-BBXB | Cessna FRA.150L | M. L. Swain *(stored)*/Bourn |
| | G-BBXG | PA-34-200 Seneca II | London Flight Centre (Stansted) Ltd |
| | G-BBXH | Cessna FR.172F | H. H. Metal Finishing (Wales) Ltd |
| | G-BBXK | PA-34-200 Seneca II | Poyston Aviation |
| | G-BBXL | Cessna E310Q | Chatsworth Studios Ltd/Newcastle |
| | G-BBXO | Enstrom F-28A | Repetek Ltd |
| | G-BBXS | Piper J-3C-65 Cub | M. J. Butler (G-ALMA)/Langham |
| | G-BBXU | Beech B24R Sierra | B. M. Russell/Coventry |
| | G-BBXW | PA-28-151 Warrior | Shropshire Aero Club Ltd |
| | G-BBXX | PA-31-350 Navajo Chieftain | Natural Environment Research Council |
| | G-BBXY | Bellanca 7GCBC Citabria | J. Turner/Shoreham |
| | G-BBXZ | Evans VP-1 | L. A. Edwards |
| | G-BBYB | PA-18 Super Cub 95 | Tiger Club (1990) Ltd/Headcorn |
| | G-BBYE | Cessna 195 | Profile Productions Ltd & TAC Productions Ltd |
| | G-BBYH | Cessna 182P | Croftmarsh Ltd |
| | G-BBYK | PA-23 Aztec 250E | Kraken Air/Cardiff |
| | G-BBYL | Cameron O-77 balloon | Buckingham Balloon Club *Jammy* |
| | G-BBYM | H.P.137 Jetstream 200 | British Aerospace PLC (G-AYWR)/Warton |
| | G-BBYO | BN-2A Mk III Trislander | Aurigny Air Services (G-BBWR)/Guernsey |
| | G-BBYP | PA-28 Cherokee 140 | R. A. Wakefield |
| | G-BBYS | Cessna 182P Skylane | I. M. Jones |
| | G-BBZF | PA-28 Cherokee 140 | J. A. Havers & M. G. West/Elstree |
| | G-BBZH | PA-28R Cherokee Arrow 200-II | Zulu Hotel Club |
| | G-BBZI | PA-31-310 Turbo Navajo | Air Care (South West) Ltd |
| | G-BBZJ | PA-34-200 Seneca II | Sentry Courier Ltd/Blackbushe |
| | G-BBZN | Fuji FA.200-180 | J. Westwood & P. D. Wedd |
| | G-BBZO | Fuji FA.200-160 | G-BBZO Group |
| | G-BBZS | Enstrom F-28A | Southern Air Ltd/Shoreham |
| | G-BBZV | PA-28R Cherokee Arrow 200-II | Unicol Engineering/Kidlington |
| | G-BCAC | M.S.894A Rallye Minerva 220 | R. S. Rogers/Cardiff |
| | G-BCAH | D.H.C.1 Chipmunk 22 (WG316) | V. B. Wheele/Shoreham |
| | G-BCAN | Thunder Ax7-77 balloon | Wessex Hot-Air Team |
| | G-BCAP | Cameron O-56 balloon | S. R. Seager |
| | G-BCAR | Thunder Ax7-77 balloon ★ | British Balloon Museum |
| | G-BCAT | PA-31-310 Turbo Navajo | Hubbardair Ltd |
| | G-BCAZ | PA-12 Super Cruiser | A. D. Williams |
| | G-BCBD | Bede BD-5B | Brockmore-Bede Aircraft (UK) Ltd/ Shobdon |
| | G-BCBG | PA-23 Aztec 250E | M. J. L. Batt/Booker |
| | G-BCBH | Fairchild 24R-46A Argus III | Ebork Ltd |
| | G-BCBJ | PA-25 Pawnee 235 | Deeside Gliding Club (Aberdeenshire) Ltd |
| | G-BCBK | Cessna 421B | Munford Development Co Ltd |
| | G-BCBL | Fairchild 24R-46A Argus III (HB751) | F. J. Cox |
| | G-BCBM | PA-23 Aztec 250C | S. Lightbrown & M. Kavanagh |
| | G-BCBR | AJEP/Wittman W.8 Tailwind | D. A. Hood |
| | G-BCBW | Cessna 182P | Teesside Aero Club Ltd |
| | G-BCBX | Cessna F.150L | J. Kelly/Newtownards |
| | G-BCBY | Cessna F.150L | Scottish Airways Flyers (Prestwick) Ltd |
| | G-BCBZ | Cessna 337C | J. J. Zwetsloot |
| | G-BCCB | Robin HR.200/100 | M. J. Ellis |

| Reg. | Type | Owner or Operator | Notes |
|---|---|---|---|
| -BCCC | Cessna F.150L | Fleeting Moments Ltd | |
| -BCCD | Cessna F.172M | Austin Aviation Ltd | |
| -BCCE | PA-23 Aztec 250E | Falcon Flying Services/Biggin Hill | |
| -BCCF | PA-28 Cherokee 180 | J. T. Friskney Ltd/Skegness | |
| -BCCG | Thunder Ax7-65 balloon | N. H. Ponsford | |
| -BCCJ | AA-5 Traveler | T. Needham/Manchester | |
| -BCCK | AA-5 Traveler | Prospect Air Ltd/Barton | |
| -BCCR | CP.301A Emeraude (modified) | J. H. & C. J. Waterman | |
| -BCCU | BN-2A Mk.III-1 Trislander | Cormack (Aircraft Services) Ltd | |
| -BCCX | D.H.C.1 Chipmunk 22 (Lycoming) | RAFGSA/Dishforth | |
| -BCCY | Robin HR.200/100 | Bristol Strut Flying Group | |
| -BCDA | Boeing 727-46 | — | |
| -BCDB | PA-34-200 Seneca II | A. & G. Aviation Ltd/Bournemouth | |
| -BCDC | PA-18 Super Cub 95 | Cotswold Aero Club Ltd/Staverton | |
| -BCDJ | PA-28 Cherokee 140 | C. Wren/Southend | |
| -BCDK | Partenavia P.68B | Truman Aviation Ltd/Tollerton | |
| -BCDL | Cameron O-42 balloon | D. P. & Mrs B. O. Turner *Chums* | |
| -BCDN | F.27 Friendship Mk 200 | Air UK/Norwich | |
| -BCDR | Thunder Ax7-77 balloon | W. G. Johnston & ptnrs *Obelix* | |
| -BCDY | Cessna FRA.150L | Air Service Training Ltd/Perth | |
| -BCEA | Sikorsky S-61N Mk II | British International Helicopters Ltd/ Aberdeen | |
| -BCEB | Sikorsky S-61N Mk II | British International Helicopters Ltd/ Penzance | |
| -BCEC | Cessna F.172M | United Propedent Ltd/Manchester | |
| -BCEE | AA-5 Traveler | Echo Echo Ltd/Bournemouth | |
| -BCEF | AA-5 Traveler | Forest Aviation Ltd/Guernsey | |
| -BCEN | BN-2A Islander | Atlantic Air Transport Ltd/Coventry | |
| -BCEO | AA-5 Traveler | N. F. Lyons | |
| -BCEP | AA-5 Traveler | D. V. Reynolds | |
| -BCER | GY-201 Minicab | D. Beaumont/Sherburn | |
| -BCEU | Cameron O-42 balloon | Entertainment Services Ltd *Harlequin* | |
| -BCEX | PA-23 Aztec 250E | Weekes Bros (Welling) Ltd/Biggin Hill | |
| -BCEY | D.H.C.1 Chipmunk 22 | Gopher Flying Group | |
| -BCEZ | Cameron O-84 balloon | Anglia Aeronauts Ascension Association | |
| -BCFB | Cameron O-77 balloon | J. J. Harris & P. Pryce-Jones | |
| -BCFC | Cameron O-65 balloon | B. H. Mead *Candy Twist* | |
| -BCFD | West balloon ★ | British Balloon Museum *Hellfire* | |
| -BCFF | Fuji FA-200-160 | G. W. Brown & M. R. Gibbons | |
| -BCFN | Cameron O-65 balloon | W. G. Johnson & H. M. Savage | |
| -BCFO | PA-18 Super Cub 150 | Portsmouth Naval Gliding Club/ Lee-on-Solent | |
| -BCFR | Cessna FRA.150L | J. J. Baumhardt/Southend | |
| -BCFW | Saab 91D Safir | D. R. Williams | |
| -BCFY | Luton LA-4A Minor | J. Knight | |
| -BCGB | Bensen B.8 | A. Melody | |
| -BCGC | D.H.C.1 Chipmunk 22 (WP903) | Culdrose Gliding Club | |
| -BCGG | Jodel DR.250 Srs 160 | C. G. Gray (G-ATZL) | |
| -BCGH | SNCAN NC.854S | Nord Flying Group | |
| -BCGI | PA-28 Cherokee 140 | A. Dodd/Redhill | |
| -BCGJ | PA-28 Cherokee 140 | J. Miller & J. L. Hunter/Edinburgh | |
| -BCGL | Jodel D.112 | J. Harris | |
| -BCGM | Jodel D.120 | D. N. K. & M. A. Symon | |
| -BCGN | PA-28 Cherokee 140 | Oxford Flyers Ltd/Kidlington | |
| -BCGS | PA-28R Cherokee Arrow 200 | Arrow Aviation | |
| -BCGT | PA-28 Cherokee 140 | T. D. Bugg | |
| -BCGW | Jodel D.11 | G. H. & M. D. Chittenden | |
| -BCGX | Bede BD-5A/B | R. Hodgson | |
| -BCHK | Cessna F.172H | E. C. & A. K. Shimmin | |
| -BCHL | D.H.C.1 Chipmunk 22A (WP788) | Shropshire Soaring Ltd/Sleap | |
| -BCHM | SA.341G Gazelle 1 | Westland Helicopters Ltd/Yeovil | |
| -BCHP | CP.1310-C3 Super Emeraude | R. F. Sothcott (G-JOSI) | |
| -BCHT | Schleicher ASK.16 | D. E. Cadisch & K. A. Lillywhite/Dunstable | |
| -BCHV | D.H.C.1 Chipmunk 22 | N. F. Charles/Sywell | |
| -BCHX | SF.23A Sperling | *(stored)*/Rufforth | |
| -BCID | PA-34-200 Seneca II | C. J. Freeman/Headcorn | |
| -BCIE | PA-28-151 Warrior | J. A. & J. V. Bridger/Exeter | |
| -BCIF | PA-28 Cherokee 140 | Fryer-Robins Aviation Ltd/E. Midlands | |
| -BCIH | D.H.C.1 Chipmunk 22 (WD363) | J. M. Hosey/Stansted | |
| -BCIJ | AA-5 Traveler | I. J. Bond & D. J. McCooke | |
| -BCIK | AA-5 Traveler | Trent Aviation Ltd | |
| -BCIN | Thunder Ax7-77 balloon | P. G & R. A. Vale | |
| -BCIO | PA-39 Twin Comanche 160 C/R | F. Duckworth | |

| Notes | Reg. | Type | Owner or Operator |
|---|---|---|---|
| | G-BCIR | PA-28-151 Warrior | P. J. Brennan |
| | G-BCIT | CIT/A1 Srs 1 | Cranfield Institute of Technology |
| | G-BCJF | Beagle B.206 Srs 1 | (stored)/Biggin Hill |
| | G-BCJH | Mooney M.20F | P. B. Bossard |
| | G-BCJM | PA-28 Cherokee 140 | Top Cat Aviation Ltd |
| | G-BCJN | PA-28 Cherokee 140 | A. J. Steed/Goodwood |
| | G-BCJO | PA-28R Cherokee Arrow 200 | Tomcat Aviation/Norwich |
| | G-BCJP | PA-28 Cherokee 140 | K. E. Tolliday & ptnrs |
| | G-BCJS | PA-23 Aztec 250C ★ | derelict/Ronaldsway |
| | G-BCKN | D.H.C.1A Chipmunk 22 | RAFGSA/Cranwell |
| | G-BCKO | PA-23 Aztec 250E | Geonex UK Ltd |
| | G-BCKP | Luton LA-5A Major | D. & W. H. Gough |
| | G-BCKS | Fuji FA.200-180 | J. T. Hicks/Goodwood |
| | G-BCKT | Fuji FA.200-180 | Littlewick Green Service Station Ltd/ Booker |
| | G-BCKU | Cessna FRA.150L | Air Service Training Ltd/Perth |
| | G-BCKV | Cessna FRA.150L | Air Service Training Ltd/Perth |
| | G-BCLC | Sikorsky S-61N | Bristow Helicopters/HM Coastguard |
| | G-BCLD | Sikorsky S-61N | Bristow Helicopters Ltd |
| | G-BCLI | AA-5 Traveler | Albemotive Ltd |
| | G-BCLJ | AA-5 Traveler | E. A. A. A. Wiltens |
| | G-BCLL | PA-28 Cherokee 180 | K. J. Scamp |
| | G-BCLS | Cessna 170B | Teesside Flight Centre Ltd |
| | G-BCLT | M.S.894A Rallye Minerva 220 | S. Clough |
| | G-BCLU | Jodel D.117 | N. A. Wallace |
| | G-BCLW | AA-1B Trainer | E. J. McMillan |
| | G-BCMD | PA-18 Super Cub 95 | R. G. Brooks/Dunkeswell |
| | G-BCMJ | SA.102.5 Cavalier (tailwheel) | R. G. Sykes/Shoreham |
| | G-BCMT | Isaacs Fury II | M. H. Turner |
| | G-BCNC | GY.201 Minicab | J. R. Wraight |
| | G-BCNP | Cameron O-77 balloon | M. L. J. Ritchie |
| | G-BCNR | Thunder Ax7-77A balloon | S. J. Miliken & ptnrs |
| | G-BCNT | Partenavia P.68B | Welsh Airways Ltd |
| | G-BCNX | Piper J-3C-65 Cub | K. J. Lord/Ipswich |
| | G-BCNZ | Fuji FA.200-160 | J. Bruton & A. Lincoln/Manchester |
| | G-BCOB | Piper J-3C-65 Cub | R. W. & Mrs J. W. Marjoram |
| | G-BCOE | H.S.748 Srs 2B | British Aerospace PLC/Woodford |
| | G-BCOF | H.S.748 Srs 2B | British Aerospace PLC/Woodford |
| | G-BCOG | Jodel D.112 | C. Hughes & W. K. Rose/Kidlington |
| | G-BCOH | Avro 683 Lancaster 10 (KB976) | Bitteswell Ltd/Biggin Hill |
| | G-BCOI | D.H.C.1 Chipmunk 22 | D. S. McGregor & A. T. Letham |
| | G-BCOJ | Cameron O-56 balloon | T. J. Knott & M. J. Webber |
| | G-BCOL | Cessna F.172M | A. H. Creaser |
| | G-BCOM | Piper J-3C-65 Cub | Dougal Flying Group/Shoreham |
| | G-BCOO | D.H.C.1 Chipmunk 22 | T. G. Fielding & M. S. Morton/Blackpool |
| | G-BCOP | PA-28R Cherokee Arrow 200-II | E. A. Saunders/Halfpenny Green |
| | G-BCOR | SOCATA Rallye 100ST | R. G. Trute |
| | G-BCOU | D.H.C.1 Chipmunk 22 (WK522) | P. J. Loweth |
| | G-BCOX | Bede BD-5A | H. J. Cox |
| | G-BCOY | D.H.C.1 Chipmunk 22 (Lycoming) | Coventry Gliding Club Ltd/Husbands Bosworth |
| | G-BCPB | Howes radio-controlled model free balloon | R. B. & Mrs C. Howes Posbee 1 |
| | G-BCPD | GY-201 Minicab | A. H. K. Denniss/Halfpenny Green |
| | G-BCPE | Cessna F.150M | Semloh Aviation Services/Andrewsfield |
| | G-BCPF | PA-23 Aztec 250D | Chapman Commercials Ltd |
| | G-BCPG | PA-28R Cherokee Arrow 200-II | Roses Flying Group/Liverpool |
| | G-BCPH | Piper J-3C-65 Cub (329934) | M. J. Janaway |
| | G-BCPJ | Piper J-3C-65 Cub | Piper Cub Group/Popham |
| | G-BCPK | Cessna F.172M | J. G. Bell |
| | G-BCPN | AA-5 Traveler | B.W. Agricultural Equipments Ltd |
| | G-BCPO | Partenavia P.68B | H. Russell |
| | G-BCPU | D.H.C.1 Chipmunk T.10 | P. Waller/Booker |
| | G-BCPX | Szep HFC.125 | A. Szep/Netherthorpe |
| | G-BCRB | Cessna F.172M | Specialised Laboratory Equipment Ltd |
| | G-BCRE | Cameron O-77 balloon | A. R. Langton |
| | G-BCRH | Alaparma Baldo B.75 | A. L. Scadding/(stored) |
| | G-BCRI | Cameron O-65 balloon | V. J. Thorne Joseph |
| | G-BCRJ | Taylor JT.1 Monoplane | S. Wolstenholme |
| | G-BCRK | SA.102.5 Cavalier | R. Simpson |
| | G-BCRL | PA-28-151 Warrior | F. N. Garland/Biggin Hill |
| | G-BCRN | Cessna FRA.150L | Air Service Training Ltd/Perth |
| | G-BCRP | PA-E23 Aztec 250E | ReFair/Sibson |

| Reg. | Type | Owner or Operator | Notes |
|---|---|---|---|
| G-BCRR | AA-5B Tiger | Capulet Flying Group/Elstree | |
| G-BCRT | Cessna F.150M | Suffolk Aero Club Ltd/Ipswich | |
| G-BCRX | D.H.C.1 Chipmunk 22 (WD292) | J. R. Chapman & ptnrs | |
| G-BCSA | D.H.C.1 Chipmunk 22 | RAFGSA/Kinloss | |
| G-BCSB | D.H.C.1 Chipmunk 22 (Lycoming) | RAFGSA/Cosford | |
| G-BCSL | D.H.C.1 Chipmunk 22 | Jalawain Ltd/Barton | |
| G-BCSM | Bellanca 8GCBC Scout | B. T. Spreckley/Southampton | |
| G-BCST | M.S.893A Rallye Commodore 180 | P. J. Wilcox/Cranfield | |
| G-BCSX | Thunder Ax7-77 balloon | A. T. Wood Whoopski | |
| G-BCSY | Taylor JT.2 Titch | T. Hartwell & D. Wilkinson | |
| G-BCTA | PA-28-151 Warrior | T. G. Aviation Ltd/Manston | |
| G-BCTF | PA-28-151 Warrior | Premier Plane Leasing Co Ltd | |
| G-BCTI | Schleicher ASK.16 | Tango India Syndicate/Cranfield | |
| G-BCTJ | Cessna 310Q | TJ Flying Group | |
| G-BCTK | Cessna FR.172J | G-BCTK Group | |
| G-BCTT | Evans VP-1 | B. J. Boughton | |
| G-BCTU | Cessna FRA.150M | J. H. Fisher & N. D. Hall | |
| G-BCUB | Piper J-3C-65 Cub | A. L. Brown & G. Attwell/Bourn | |
| G-BCUF | Cessna F.172M | G. H. Kirke Ltd | |
| G-BCUH | Cessna F.150M | M. G. Montgomerie | |
| G-BCUI | Cessna F.172M | Hillhouse Estates Ltd | |
| G-BCUJ | Cessna F.150M | Sandtoft Air Services (1985) Ltd | |
| G-BCUL | SOCATA Rallye 100ST | C. A. Ussher & Fountain Estates Ltd | |
| G-BCUW | Cessna F.177RG | S. J. Westley | |
| G-BCUY | Cessna FRA.150M | S. R. Cameron | |
| G-BCVA | Cameron O-65 balloon | J. C. Bass & ptnrs Crepe Suzette | |
| G-BCVB | PA-17 Vagabond | A. T. Nowak/Popham | |
| G-BCVC | SOCATA Rallye 100ST | J. L. & T. A. Hodges | |
| G-BCVE | Evans VP-2 | D. Masterson & D. B. Winstanley | |
| G-BCVF | Practavia Pilot Sprite | D. G. Hammersley | |
| G-BCVG | Cessna FRA.150L | Air Service Training Ltd/Perth | |
| G-BCVH | Cessna FRA.150L | Yorkshire Light Aircraft Ltd/Leeds | |
| G-BCVI | Cessna FR.172J | Roger Savage (Photography) | |
| G-BCVJ | Cessna F.172M | Rothland Ltd | |
| G-BCVW | GY-80 Horizon 180 | P. M. A. Parrett/Dunkeswell | |
| G-BCVY | PA-34-200T Seneca II | C.S.E. Aviation Ltd/Kidlington | |
| G-BCWA | BAC One-Eleven 518 FG | British Air Ferries (G-AXMK)/Southend | |
| G-BCWB | Cessna 182P | G. McCabe | |
| G-BCWF | S.A. Twin Pioneer 1 | Flight One Ltd (G-APRS)/Staverton | |
| G-BCWH | Practavia Pilot Sprite | R. Tasker/Blackpool | |
| G-BCWK | Alpavia Fournier RF-3 | D. I. Nickolls & ptnrs | |
| G-BCWL | Westland Lysander III (V9281) | Wessex Aviation & Transport Ltd | |
| G-BCWR | BN-2A-21 Islander | Pilatus BN Ltd/Bembridge | |
| G-BCXB | SOCATA Rallye 100ST | A. Smails | |
| G-BCXE | Robin DR.400/2+2 | C. J. Freeman | |
| G-BCXF | H.S.125 Srs 600B | Aravco Ltd/Heathrow | |
| G-BCXJ | Piper J-3C-65 Cub (413048) | W. F. Stockdale/Compton Abbas | |
| G-BCXN | D.H.C.1 Chipmunk 22 (WP800) | G. M. Turner/Duxford | |
| G-BCXO | MBB Bo 105D | Bond Helicopters Ltd/Bourn | |
| G-BCXR | BAC One-Eleven 517FE | British Air Ferries (G-BCCV)/Southend | |
| G-BCYH | DAW Privateer Mk. 2 | D. B. Limbert | |
| G-BCYI | Schleicher ASK-16 | Lasham K16 Syndicate | |
| G-BCYJ | D.H.C.1 Chipmunk 22 (WG307) | R. A. L. Falconer | |
| G-BCYK | Avro CF.100 Mk 4 Canuck (18393) ★ | Imperial War Museum/Duxford | |
| G-BCYM | D.H.C.1 Chipmunk 22 | C. R. R. Eagleton/Headcorn | |
| G-BCYR | Cessna F.172M | Donne Enterprises | |
| G-BCZH | D.H.C.1 Chipmunk 22 (WK622) | A. C. Byrne & D. Featherby/Norwich | |
| G-BCZI | Thunder Ax7-77 balloon | R. G. Griffin & R. Blackwell | |
| G-BCZM | Cessna F.172M | Cornwall Flying Club Ltd/Bodmin | |
| G-BCZN | Cessna F.150M | Mona Aviation Ltd | |
| G-BCZO | Cameron O-77 balloon | W. O. T. Holmes Leo | |
| G-BDAB | SA.102.5 Cavalier | A. H. Brown | |
| G-BDAC | Cameron O-77 balloon | D. Fowler & J. Goody Chocolate Ripple | |
| G-BDAD | Taylor JT.1 Monoplane | G-BDAD Group | |
| G-BDAE | BAC One-Eleven 518FG | British Air Ferries (G-AMXI)/Southend | |
| G-BDAG | Taylor JT-1 Monoplane | R. S. Basinger | |
| G-BDAH | Evans VP-1 | A. M. Carter | |
| G-BDAI | Cessna FRA.150M | A. Sharma | |
| G-BDAK | R. Commander 112A | C. Boydon | |
| G-BDAL | R. 500S Shrike Commander | Quantel Ltd | |
| G-BDAM | AT-16 Harvard IIB (FE992) | N. A. Lees & E. C. English | |

| Notes | Reg. | Type | Owner or Operator |
|---|---|---|---|
| | G-BDAO | SIPA S.91 | A. L. Rose |
| | G-BDAP | AJEP Tailwind | J. Whiting |
| | G-BDAR | Evans VP-1 | R. B. Valler |
| | G-BDAV | PA-23 Aztec 250C | Acketts Ltd |
| | G-BDAX | PA-23 Aztec 250C | P. G. Lawrence |
| | G-BDAY | Thunder Ax5-42A balloon | T. M. Donnelly *Meconium* |
| | G-BDBD | Wittman W.8 Tailwind | E. D. Bond |
| | G-BDBF | FRED Srs 2 | R. G. Boyton |
| | G-BDBH | Bellanca 7GCBC Citabria | Inkpen Gliding Club Ltd/Thruxton |
| | G-BDBI | Cameron O-77 balloon | C. A. Butter & J. J. Cook |
| | G-BDBJ | Cessna 182P | H. C. Wilson |
| | G-BDBL | D.H.C.1 Chipmunk 22 | R. J. Fox |
| | G-BDBP | D.H.C.1 Chipmunk 22 (WP843) | R. M. Brooks |
| | G-BDBS | Short SD3-30 | Short Bros PLC/Belfast City |
| | G-BDBU | Cessna F.150M | Andrewsfield Flying Club Ltd |
| | G-BDBA | Jodel D.11A | Seething Jodel Group |
| | G-BDBZ | W.S.55 Whirlwind Srs 2 ★ | *Ground instruction airframe*/Kidlington |
| | G-BDCB | D.H.C.1 Chipmunk 22 (WP835) | R. F. Tolhurst |
| | G-BDCC | D.H.C.1 Chipmunk 22 (Lycoming) | Coventry Gliding Club Ltd/ Husbands Bosworth |
| | G-BDCD | Piper J-3C-85 Cub (480133) | Suzanne C. Brooks/Slinfold |
| | G-BDCE | Cessna F.172H | P. R. George |
| | G-BDCI | CP.301A Emeraude | D. L. Sentance |
| | G-BDCK | AA-5 Traveler | Northfield Garage Ltd |
| | G-BDCL | AA-5 Traveler | J. Crowe |
| | G-BDCM | Cessna F.177RG | P. R. Gunnel/Gamston |
| | G-BDCO | B.121 Pup 1 | K. R. Knapp |
| | G-BDCS | Cessna 421B | British Aerospace PLC/Warton |
| | G-BDCU | Cameron O-77 balloon | H. P. Carlton |
| | G-BDDD | D.H.C.1 Chipmunk 22 | RAE Aero Club Ltd/Farnborough |
| | G-BDDF | Jodel D.120 | Sywell Skyriders Flying Group |
| | G-BDDG | Jodel D.112 | Wandering Imp Group |
| | G-BDDS | PA-25 Pawnee 235 | Vale of Neath Gliding Club |
| | G-BDDT | PA-25 Pawnee 235 | Boston Aviation Services |
| | G-BDDX | Whittaker MW.2B Excalibur ★ | Cornwall Aero Park/Helston |
| | G-BDDZ | CP.301A Emeraude | V. W. Smith & E. C. Mort |
| | G-BDEC | SOCATA Rallye 100ST | L. J. R. C. Bolingbroke |
| | G-BDEF | PA-34-200T Seneca II | Haylock Son & Hunter |
| | G-BDEH | Jodel D.120A | EH Flying Group/Bristol |
| | G-BDEI | Jodel D.9 Bebe | P. M. Bowden/Barton |
| | G-BDET | D.H.C.1 Chipmunk 22 | D. Algra |
| | G-BDEU | D.H.C.1 Chipmunk 22 (WP808) | A. Taylor |
| | G-BDEV | Taylor JT.1 Monoplane | D. A. Bass |
| | G-BDEW | Cessna FRA.150M | C. M. Vlieland-Boddy/Compton Abbas |
| | G-BDEX | Cessna FRA.150M | C. M. Vlieland-Boddy/Compton Abbas |
| | G-BDEY | Piper J-3C-65 Cub | Ducksworth Flying Club |
| | G-BDEZ | Piper J-3C-65 Cub | R. J. K. Spurrell |
| | G-BDFB | Currie Wot | J. Jennings |
| | G-BDFC | R. Commander 112A | R. Fletcher |
| | G-BDFG | Cameron O-65 balloon | N. A. Robertson *Golly II* |
| | G-BDFH | Auster AOP.9 (XR240) | R. O. Holden/Booker |
| | G-BDFI | Cessna F.150M | LAR Aviation Ltd/Shoreham |
| | G-BDFJ | Cessna F.150M | T. J. Lynn/Sibson |
| | G-BDFM | Caudron C.270 Luciole | G. V. Gower |
| | G-BDFR | Fuji FA.200-160 | A. Wright |
| | G-BDFS | Fuji FA.200-160 | B. Sharbati & B. Lawrence |
| | G-BDFU | Dragonfly MPA Mk 1 ★ | Museum of Flight/E. Fortune |
| | G-BDFW | R. Commander 112A | M. & D. A. Doubleday |
| | G-BDFX | Auster 5 (TW517) | Bee Flight Flying Group |
| | G-BDFY | AA-5 Traveler | Edinburgh Flying Club Ltd |
| | G-BDFZ | Cessna F.150M | Skyviews & General Ltd |
| | G-BDGA | Bushby-Long Midget Mustang | J. R. Owen |
| | G-BDGB | GY-20 Minicab | D. G. Burden |
| | G-BDGH | Thunder Ax7-77 balloon | R. J. Mitchener & P. F. Smart |
| | G-BDGM | PA-28-151 Warrior | B. Whiting |
| | G-BDGN | AA-5B Tiger | R. Stone |
| | G-BDGO | Thunder Ax7-77 balloon | International Distillers & Vintners Ltd |
| | G-BDGP | Cameron V-65 balloon | Warwick Balloons Ltd |
| | G-BDGY | PA-28 Cherokee 140 | R. E. Woolridge/Staverton |
| | G-BDHJ | Pazmany PL.1 | C. T. Millner |
| | G-BDHK | Piper J-3C-65 Cub (329417) | A. Liddiard |
| | G-BDHL | PA-23 Aztec 250E | Cheshire Flying Services Ltd/Manchester |
| | G-BDIC | D.H.C.1 Chipmunk 22 (WD388) | Woodvale Aviation Co Ltd |

| Reg. | Type | Owner or Operator |
|------|------|-------------------|
| G-BDIE | R. Commander 112A | C. A. Ringrose & H. J. Bendiksen |
| G-BDIG | Cessna 182P | D. P. Cranston & Bob Crowe Aircraft Sales Ltd/Cranfield |
| G-BDIH | Jodel D.117 | N. D. H. Stokes |
| G-BDIJ | Sikorsky S-61N | Bristow Helicopters Ltd |
| G-BDIM | D.H.C.1 Chipmunk 22 | Historic Flying Ltd/Cambridge |
| G-BDIX | D.H.106 Comet 4C ★ | Museum of Flight/E. Fortune |
| G-BDJB | Taylor JT.1 Monoplane | J. F. Barber |
| G-BDJC | AJEP W.8 Tailwind | J. H. Medforth |
| G-BDJD | Jodel D.112 | Drem Sport Aviation Group |
| G-BDJF | Bensen B.8MV | R. P. White |
| G-BDJG | Luton LA-4A Minor | A. W. Anderson & A. J. Short |
| G-BDJN | Robin HR.200/100 | Northampton School of Flying Ltd/Sywell |
| G-BDJP | Piper J-3C-90 Cub | J. M. Pothecary (stored)/Shoreham |
| G-BDJR | SNCAN NC.858 | R. F. M. Marson & P. M. Harmer |
| G-BDKB | SOCATA Rallye 150ST | N. C. Anderson |
| G-BDKC | Cessna A185F | Bridge of Tilt Co Ltd |
| G-BDKD | Enstrom F-28A | TR Bitz |
| G-BDKH | CP.301A Emeraude | P. G. & F. M. Morris |
| G-BDKI | Sikorsky S-61N | British International Helicopters Ltd |
| G-BDKJ | K. & S. SA.102.5 Cavalier | B. D. Battman |
| G-BDKK | Bede BD-5B | A. W. Odell (stored)/Headcorn |
| G-BDKM | SIPA 903 | S. W. Markham |
| G-BDKU | Taylor JT.1 Monoplane | C. M. Harding & J. Ball |
| G-BDKV | PA-28R Cherokee Arrow 200-II | B. Carter |
| G-BDKW | R. Commander 112A | Denny Bros Printing Ltd |
| G-BDLO | AA-5A Cheetah | S. & J. Dolan/Denham |
| G-BDLR | AA-5B Tiger | MAGEC Aviation Ltd/Luton |
| G-BDLS | AA-1B Trainer | P. W. Vaughan & M. D. Harling/Andrewsfield |
| G-BDLT | R. Commander 112A | Wintergrain Ltd/Exeter |
| G-BDLY | SA.102.5 Cavalier | P. R. Stevens/Southampton |
| G-BDMB | Robin HR.100/210 | R. J. Hitchman & Son |
| G-BDMM | Jodel D.11 | P. N. Marshall |
| G-BDMO | Thunder Ax7-77A ballon | G. C. Elson |
| G-BDMS | Piper J-3C-65 Cub | A. T. H. Martin & K. G. Harris |
| G-BDMW | Jodel DR.100 | R. O. F. Harper |
| G-BDNC | Taylor JT.1 Monoplane | G. A. Stanley |
| G-BDNG | Taylor JT.1 Monoplane | J. M. Fforde |
| G-BDNO | Taylor JT.1 Monoplane | W. R. Partridge |
| G-BDNP | BN-2A Islander ★ | Ground parachute trainer/Headcorn |
| G-BDNR | Cessna FRA.150M | Cheshire Air Training School Ltd/Liverpool |
| G-BDNT | Jodel D.92 | R. F. Morton |
| G-BDNU | Cessna F.172M | C. H. P. Bell |
| G-BDNW | AA-1B Trainer | T. D. Saveker |
| G-BDNX | AA-1B Trainer | R. M. North |
| G-BDNZ | Cameron O-77 balloon | I. L. McHale |
| G-BDOC | Sikorsky S-61N Mk II | Bristow Helicopters Ltd |
| G-BDOD | Cessna F.150M | Latharp Ltd/Booker |
| G-BDOE | Cessna FR.172J | Rocket Partnership |
| G-BDOF | Cameron O-56 balloon | New Holker Estates Co Fred Cavendish |
| G-BDOG | SA Bulldog Srs 200/2100 | D. C. Bonsall/Netherthorpe |
| G-BDOI | Hiller UH-12E | T. J. Clark |
| G-BDOL | Piper J-3C-65 Cub | U. E. Allman & M. C. Jordan/Shoreham |
| G-BDON | Thunder Ax7-77A balloon | J. R. Henderson & ptnrs |
| G-BDOR | Thunder Ax6-56A balloon | M. S. Drinkwater & G. Fitzpatrick |
| G-BDOW | Cessna FRA.150M | TT & Co |
| G-BDPA | PA-28-151 Warrior | Noon (Aircraft Leasing) Ltd/Shoreham |
| G-BDPF | Cessna F.172M | Semloh Aviation Services/Andrewsfield |
| G-BDPK | Cameron O-56 balloon | Rango Balloon & Kite Co |
| G-BDPV | Boeing 747-136 | British Airways Blea Water |
| G-BDRB | AA-5B Tiger | Dorset Air Ltd |
| G-BDRC | V.724 Viscount ★ | Fire School/Manston |
| G-BDRD | Cessna FRA.150M | Air Service Training Ltd/Perth |
| G-BDRF | Taylor JT.1 Monoplane | B. R. Ratcliffe |
| G-BDRG | Taylor JT.2 Titch | D. R. Gray |
| G-BDRJ | D.H.C.1 Chipmunk 22 (WP857) | J. C. Schooling |
| G-BDRK | Cameron O-65 balloon | D. L. Smith Smirk |
| G-BDRL | Stitts SA-3A Playboy | W. McNally & J. L. Clarke |
| G-BDSB | PA-28-181 Archer II | Testair Ltd/Blackbushe |
| G-BDSE | Cameron O-77 balloon | British Airways Concorde |
| G-BDSF | Cameron O-56 balloon | A. R. Greensides & B. H. Osbourne |
| G-BDSH | PA-28 Cherokee 140 | P. M. Ireland |

| Notes | Reg. | Type | Owner or Operator |
|---|---|---|---|
| | G-BDSK | Cameron O-65 balloon | Southern Balloon Group *Carousel II* |
| | G-BDSL | Cessna F.150M | Cleveland Flying School Ltd/Tees-side |
| | G-BDSM | Slingsby T.31B Cadet III | J. A. L. Parton |
| | G-BDSN | Wassmer WA.52 Europa | Sierra November Group (G-BADN) |
| | G-BDSO | Cameron O-31 balloon | Budget Rent-a-Car *Baby Budget* |
| | G-BDTB | Evans VP-1 | S. Pearl |
| | G-BDTL | Evans VP-1 | A. K. Lang |
| | G-BDTN | BN-2A Mk III-2 Trislander | Aurigny Air Services Ltd/Guernsey |
| | G-BDTU | Omega III gas balloon | G. F. Turnbull |
| | G-BDTV | Mooney M.20F | S. Redfearn |
| | G-BDTW | Cassutt Racer | B. E. Smith & C. S. Thompson/Redhill |
| | G-BDTX | Cessna F.150M | A. A. & R. N. Croxford/Southend |
| | G-BDUI | Cameron V-56 balloon | D. C. Johnson |
| | G-BDUJ | PA-31-310 Turbo Navajo | Club Air (Europe) Ltd |
| | G-BDUL | Evans VP-1 | J. T. Taylor |
| | G-BDUM | Cessna F.150M | SFG Ltd/Shipdham |
| | G-BDUN | PA-34-200T Seneca II | Air Medical Ltd |
| | G-BDUO | Cessna F.150M | Sandown Aero Club |
| | G-BDUX | Slingsby T.31B Cadet III | J. C. Anderson/Cranfield |
| | G-BDUY | Robin DR.400/140B | J. M. Dean & A. L. Jubb |
| | G-BDUZ | Cameron V-56 balloon | Zebedee Balloon Service |
| | G-BDVA | PA-17 Vagabond | I. M. Callier |
| | G-BDVB | PA-15 (PA-17) Vagabond | B. P. Gardner |
| | G-BDVC | PA-17 Vagabond | A. R. Caveen |
| | G-BDVG | Thunder Ax6-56A balloon | R. F. Pollard *Argonaut* |
| | G-BDVS | F.27 Friendship Mk 200 | Air UK *Eric Gandar Dower*/Norwich |
| | G-BDVU | Mooney M.20F | Digital Duplication Ltd/Stapleford |
| | G-BDWA | SOCATA Rallye 150ST | J. T. Wilson/Bann Foot |
| | G-BDWE | Flaglor Scooter | D. W. Evernden |
| | G-BDWG | BN-2A Islander | Wilsons Transport Ltd |
| | G-BDWH | SOCATA Rallye 150ST | M. A. Jones |
| | G-BDWJ | SE-5A (replica) (F8010) | S. M. Smith/Booker |
| | G-BDWK | Beech 95-58 Baron | Cammac Coal Ltd |
| | G-BDWL | PA-25 Pawnee 235 | Peterborough & Spalding Gliding Club |
| | G-BDWM | Mustang scale replica (FB226) | D. C. Bonsall |
| | G-BDWO | Howes Ax6 balloon | R. B. & Mrs C. Howes *Griffin* |
| | G-BDWP | PA-32R Cherokee Lance 300 | W. M. Brown & B. J. Wood/Birmingham |
| | G-BDWV | BN-2A Mk III-2 Trislander | Aurigny Air Services Ltd/Guernsey |
| | G-BDWX | Jodel D.120A | J. P. Lassey |
| | G-BDWY | PA-28 Cherokee 140 | Comed Aviation Ltd/Blackpool |
| | G-BDXA | Boeing 747-236B | British Airways *City of Peterborough* |
| | G-BDXB | Boeing 747-236B | British Airways *City of Liverpool* |
| | G-BDXC | Boeing 747-236B | British Airways *City of Manchester* |
| | G-BDXD | Boeing 747-236B | British Airways *City of Plymouth* |
| | G-BDXE | Boeing 747-236B | British Airways *City of Glasgow* |
| | G-BDXF | Boeing 747-236B | British Airways *City of York* |
| | G-BDXG | Boeing 747-236B | British Airways *City of Oxford* |
| | G-BDXH | Boeing 747-236B | British Airways *City of Elgin* |
| | G-BDXI | Boeing 747-236B | British Airways *City of Cambridge* |
| | G-BDXJ | Boeing 747-236B | British Airways *City of Birmingham* |
| | G-BDXK | Boeing 747-236B | British Airways *City of Canterbury* |
| | G-BDXL | Boeing 747-236B | British Airways *City of Winchester* |
| | G-BDXM | Boeing 747-236B (SCD) | British Airways *City of Derby* |
| | G-BDXN | Boeing 747-236B (SCD) | British Airways *City of Stoke-on-Trent* |
| | G-BDXO | Boeing 747-236B | British Airways *City of Bath* |
| | G-BDXP | Boeing 747-236B (SCD) | British Airways *City of Salisbury* |
| | G-BDXX | SNCAN NC.858S | J. R. Rowell & J. E. Hobbs/Sandown |
| | G-BDYD | R. Commander 114 | SRS Aviation |
| | G-BDYF | Cessna 421C | Simco 408 Ltd |
| | G-BDYG | P.56 Provost T.1 (WV493) ★ | Museum of Flight/E. Fortune |
| | G-BDYH | Cameron V-56 balloon | B. J. Godding |
| | G-BDYM | Skysales S-31 balloon | Miss A. I. Smith & M. J. Moore *Cheeky Devil* |
| | G-BDZA | Scheibe SF.25E Super Falket | Norfolk Gliding Club Ltd/Tibenham |
| | G-BDZB | Cameron S-31 balloon | Kenning Motor Group Ltd *Kenning* |
| | G-BDZD | Cessna F.172M | Three Counties Aero Engineering Ltd/ Lasham |
| | G-BDZS | Scheibe SF.25E Super Falke | S. Sagar |
| | G-BDZU | Cessna 421C | E. E. Smith Contracts Ltd |
| | G-BDZX | PA-28-151 Warrior | Catalina Seaplanes Ltd |
| | G-BDZY | Luton LA-4A Minor | P. J. Dalby |
| | G-BEAB | Jodel DR.1051 | C. Fitton |

| Reg. | Type | Owner or Operator | Notes |
|------|------|-------------------|-------|
| G-BEAC | PA-28 Cherokee 140 | D. J. Hockings/Biggin Hill | |
| G-BEAD | WG.13 Lynx ★ | *Instructional airframe*/Middle Wallop | |
| G-BEAG | PA-34-200T Seneca II | C.S.E. Aviation Ltd/Kidlington | |
| G-BEAH | J/2 Arrow | W. J. & Mrs M. D. Horler | |
| G-BEAK | L-1011-385 TriStar 50 | British Airways *Carmarthen Bay* | |
| G-BEAL | L-1011-385 TriStar 50 | Caledonian Airways Ltd *Loch Moy* | |
| G-BEAM | L-1011-385 TriStar 50 | British Airways *Swansea Bay* | |
| G-BEBC | W.S.55 Whirlwind 3 (XP355) ★ | Norwich Aviation Museum | |
| G-BEBE | AA-5A Cheetah | Bills Aviation Ltd | |
| G-BEBF | Auster AOP.9 | M. D. N. & Mrs A. C. Fisher | |
| G-BEBG | WSK-PZL SDZ-45A Ogar | The Ogar Syndicate | |
| G-BEBI | Cessna F.172M | Calder Equipment Ltd/Hatfield | |
| G-BEBL | Douglas DC-10-30 | British Airways *Forest of Dean*/Gatwick | |
| G-BEBM | Douglas DC-10-30 | British Airways *Sherwood Forest*/Gatwick | |
| G-BEBN | Cessna 177B | A. J. Franchi & Franchi Aviation Ltd | |
| G-BEBO | Turner TSW-2 Wot | The Turner Special Flying Group | |
| G-BEBR | GY-201 Minicab | A. S. Jones & D. R. Upton | |
| G-BEBS | Andreasson BA-4B | J. S. Mortimer | |
| G-BEBT | Andreasson BA-4B | A. Horsfall | |
| G-BEBU | R. Commander 112A | M. Rowland & J. K. Woodford | |
| G-BEBZ | PA-28-151 Warrior | Goodwood Terrena Ltd/Goodwood | |
| G-BECA | SOCATA Rallye 100ST | Bredon Flying Group | |
| G-BECB | SOCATA Rallye 100ST | A. J. Trible | |
| G-BECC | SOCATA Rallye 150ST | Golf Charlie Group/Booker | |
| G-BECD | SOCATA Rallye 150ST | A. J. Liddle & A. S. du Feu | |
| G-BECF | Scheibe SF.25A Falke | D. A. Wilson & ptnrs | |
| G-BECG | Boeing 737-204ADV | Britannia Airways Ltd *Amy Johnson*/Luton | |
| G-BECH | Boeing 737-204ADV | Britannia Airways Ltd *Viscount Montgomery of Alamein*/Luton | |
| G-BECJ | Partenavia P.68B | Covex PLC | |
| G-BECK | Cameron V-56 balloon | D. W. & P. Allum | |
| G-BECN | Piper J-3C-65 Cub (480480) | R. C. Partridge & M. Oliver | |
| G-BECO | Beech A.36 Bonanza | Euro Aviation Ltd/ Conington | |
| G-BECT | C.A.S.A.1.131 Jungmann | Shoreham 131 Group | |
| G-BECW | C.A.S.A.1.131 Jungmann | N. C. Jensen/Redhill | |
| G-BECZ | CAARP CAP.10B | Aerobatic Associates Ltd | |
| G-BEDA | C.A.S.A.1.131 Jungmann | M. G. Kates & D. J. Berry | |
| G-BEDB | Nord 1203 Norecrin (5) | B. F. G. Lister *(stored)*/Chirk | |
| G-BEDD | Jodel D.117A | A. T. Croy/Kirkwall | |
| G-BEDF | Boeing B-17G-105-VE (124485) | B-17 Preservation Ltd/Duxford | |
| G-BEDG | R. Commander 112A | L. E. Blackburn | |
| G-BEDI | Sikorsky S-61N | British International Helicopters Ltd | |
| G-BEDJ | Piper J-3C-65 Cub (44-80594) | D. J. Elliott | |
| G-BEDK | Hiller UH-12E | Agricopters Ltd/Chilbolton | |
| G-BEDL | Cessna T.337D | T. J. Brammer & R. Masterman | |
| G-BEDV | V.668 Varsity T.1 (WJ945) ★ | D. S. Selway/Duxford | |
| G-BEDZ | BN-2A Islander | Loganair Ltd/Glasgow | |
| G-BEEE | Thunder Ax6-56A balloon | I. R. M. Jacobs *Avia* | |
| G-BEEG | BN-2A Islander | Telair Manchester Ltd/Barton | |
| G-BEEH | Cameron V-56 balloon | B. & N. V. Moreton | |
| G-BEEI | Cameron N-77 balloon | P. S. & G. G. Rankin | |
| G-BEEJ | Cameron O-77 balloon | DAL (Builders Merchants) Ltd *Dal's Pal* | |
| G-BEEP | Thunder Ax5-42 balloon | B. C. Faithfull/Holland | |
| G-BEER | Isaacs Fury II | Baycol Aviation | |
| G-BEEU | PA-28 Cherokee 140E | Touch & Go Ltd | |
| G-BEEW | Taylor JT.1 Monoplane | K. Wigglesworth/Breighton | |
| G-BEFA | PA-28-151 Warrior | Firmbeam Ltd/Booker | |
| G-BEFC | AA-5B Tiger | Portway Aviation/Shobdon | |
| G-BEFF | PA-28 Cherokee 140 | C. Haymes & G. M. Thurlow/Shipdham | |
| G-BEFR | Fokker DR.1/(replica) (425/17) | R. A. Bowes & P. A. Crawford | |
| G-BEFV | Evans VP-2 | D. A. Cotton | |
| G-BEGA | Westland-Bell 47G-3B1 | Flight 47 Ltd | |
| G-BEGG | Scheibe SF.25E Super Falke | G-BEGG Flying Group | |
| G-BEGV | PA-23 Aztec 250F | Flamex Ltd | |
| G-BEHH | PA-32R Cherokee Lance 300 | SMK Engineering Ltd/Leeds | |
| G-BEHS | PA-25 Pawnee 260C | S. L. Robinson | |
| G-BEHU | PA-34-200T Seneca II | ANT Aviation/Cambridge | |
| G-BEHV | Cessna F.172N | J. Easson/Edinburgh | |
| G-BEHW | Cessna F.150M | W. Lancashire Aero Club Ltd/Woodvale | |
| G-BEHX | Evans VP-2 | G. S. Adams | |
| G-BEIA | Cessna FRA.150M | Air Service Training Ltd/Perth | |
| G-BEIB | Cessna F.172N | Sheltons of Wollaston (Garages) Ltd | |
| G-BEIC | Sikorsky S-61N | British International Helicopters Ltd/ | |

| Notes | Reg. | Type | Owner or Operator |
|---|---|---|---|
| | | | Aberdeen |
| | G-BEIF | Cameron O-65 balloon | C. Vening |
| | G-BEIG | Cessna F.150M | Herefordshire Aero Club Ltd/Shobdon |
| | G-BEII | PA-25 Pawnee 235D | Burn Gliding Club Ltd |
| | G-BEIL | SOCATA Rallye 150T | The Rallye Flying Group |
| | G-BEIP | PA-28-181 Archer II | C. Royale |
| | G-BEIS | Evans VP-1 | P. J. Hunt |
| | G-BEJA | Thunder Ax6-56A balloon | P. A. Hutchins *Jackson* |
| | G-BEJB | Thunder Ax6-56A balloon | International Distillers & Vinters Ltd |
| | G-BEJD | H.S.748 Srs 1 | Janes Aviation 748 Ltd/Blackpool |
| | G-BEJE | H.S.748 Srs 1 | Janes Aviation 748 Ltd/Blackpool |
| | G-BEJK | Cameron S-31 balloon | Rango Balloon & Kite Co |
| | G-BEJL | Sikorsky S-61N | British International Helicopters Ltd/ |
| | | | Aberdeen |
| | G-BEJM | BAC One-Eleven 423ET | Ford Motor Co Ltd/Stansted |
| | G-BEJP | D.H.C.6 Twin Otter 310 | Loganair Ltd/Glasgow |
| | G-BEJV | PA-34-200T Seneca II | C.S.E. Aviation Ltd/Kidlington |
| | G-BEJW | BAC One-Eleven 423ET | — |
| | G-BEKE | H.S.748 Srs 1 | Janes Aviation 748 Ltd/Blackpool |
| | G-BEKL | Bede BD-4E | H. B. Carter |
| | G-BEKM | Evans VP-1 | G. J. McDill/Glenrothes |
| | G-BEKN | Cessna FRA.150M | RFC (Bourn) Ltd |
| | G-BEKO | Cessna F.182Q | Tyler International |
| | G-BEKR | Rand KR-2 | A. N. Purchase |
| | G-BELF | BN-2A Islander | Activity Aviation Ltd |
| | G-BELP | PA-28-151 Warrior | Devon School of Flying/Dunkeswell |
| | G-BELR | PA-28 Cherokee 140 | H. M. Clarke |
| | G-BELP | PA-28-151 Warrior | Devon School of Flying/Dunkeswell |
| | G-BELT | Cessna F.150J | Yorkshire Light Aircraft Ltd (G-AWUV)/ |
| | | | Leeds |
| | G-BELX | Cameron V-56 balloon | P. A. & N. J. Foot |
| | G-BEMB | Cessna F.172M | Stocklaunch Ltd |
| | G-BEMD | Beech 95-B55 Baron | A. G. Perkins |
| | G-BEMM | Slingsby T.31B Motor Cadet | M. N. Martin |
| | G-BEMU | Thunder Ax5-42 balloon | I. J. Liddiard & A. Merritt |
| | G-BEMW | PA-28-181 Archer II | J. A. Pothecary |
| | G-BEMY | Cessna FRA.150M | L. G. Sawyer/Blackbushe |
| | G-BEND | Cameron V-56 balloon | Dante Balloon Group *Le Billet* |
| | G-BENJ | R. Commander 112B | R. C. Wilcox/Blackbushe |
| | G-BENK | Cessna F.172M | Graham Churchill Plant Ltd |
| | G-BENN | Cameron V-56 balloon | S. H. Budd |
| | G-BENT | Cameron N-77 balloon | N. Tasker |
| | G-BEOD | Cessna 180 | Avionics Research Ltd/Cranfield |
| | G-BEOE | Cessna FRA.150M | W. J. Henderson |
| | G-BEOH | PA-28R-201T Turbo Arrow III | G-BEOH Group |
| | G-BEOI | PA-18 Super Cub 150 | Southdown Gliding Club Ltd |
| | G-BEOK | Cessna F.150M | Stardial Ltd/Southend |
| | G-BEOO | Sikorsky S-61N Mk. II | British International Helicopters Ltd |
| | G-BEOX | L-414 Hudson IV (A16-199) ★ | RAF Museum/Hendon |
| | G-BEOY | Cessna FRA.150L | R. W. Denny |
| | G-BEOZ | A.W.650 Argosy 101 ★ | Aeropark/E. Midlands |
| | G-BEPB | Pereira Osprey II | J. J. & A. J. C. Zwetsloot/Bourn |
| | G-BEPC | SNCAN Stampe SV-4C | Andy Foan Aviation Services Ltd |
| | G-BEPE | SC.5 Belfast | HeavyLift Cargo Airlines Ltd (G-ASKE) |
| | | | *(withdrawn)*/Southend |
| | G-BEPF | SNCAN Stampe SV-4A | L. J. Rice |
| | G-BEPH | BN-2A Mk III-2 Trislander | Aurigny Air Services Ltd/Guernsey |
| | G-BEPI | BN-2A Mk III-2 Trislander | Aurigny Air Services Ltd/Guernsey |
| | G-BEPO | Cameron N-77 balloon | G. Camplin & V. Aitken |
| | G-BEPS | SC.5 Belfast | HeavyLift Cargo Airlines Ltd/Stansted |
| | G-BEPV | Fokker S.11-1 Instructor | L. C. MacKnight |
| | G-BEPY | R. Commander 112B | Emin Aviation Ltd/Biggin Hill |
| | G-BEPZ | Cameron D-96 hot-air airship | D. W. Liddiard |
| | G-BERA | SOCATA Rallye 150ST | Air Touring Services Ltd/Biggin Hill |
| | G-BERC | SOCATA Rallye 150ST | Severn Valley Aero Group |
| | G-BERD | Thunder Ax6-56A balloon | P. M. Gaines |
| | G-BERI | R. Commander 114 | K. B. Harper/Blackbushe |
| | G-BERN | Saffrey S-330 balloon | B. Martin *Beeze* |
| | G-BERT | Cameron V-56 balloon | Southern Balloon Group *Bert* |
| | G-BERW | R. Commander 114 | Malvern Holdings Ltd |
| | G-BERY | AA-1B Trainer | R. H. J. Levi |
| | G-BESO | BN-2A Islander | Isles of Scilly Skybus Ltd/St Just |
| | G-BETD | Robin HR.200/100 | R. A. Parsons/Bourn |

| Reg. | Type | Owner or Operator | Notes |
|---|---|---|---|
| G-BETE | Rollason B.2A Beta | T. M. Jones/Tatenhill | |
| G-BETF | Cameron 'Champion' balloon | Balloon Stable Ltd *Champion* | |
| G-BETG | Cessna 180K Skywagon | T. P. A. Norman/Panshanger | |
| G-BETI | Pitts S-1D Special | P. Metcalfe/Teesside | |
| G-BETL | PA-25 Pawnee 235D | Boston Aviation Services | |
| G-BETM | PA-25 Pawnee 235D | Yorkshire Gliding Club (Pty) Ltd | |
| G-BETO | M.S.885 Super Rallye | BETO Group | |
| G-BETP | Cameron O-65 balloon | J. R. Rix & Sons Ltd | |
| G-BETT | PA-34-200 Seneca II | Andrews Professional Colour Laboratories Ltd/Headcorn | |
| G-BETV | HS.125 Srs 600B | Rolls-Royce PLC/Filton | |
| G-BEUA | PA-18 Super Cub 150 | London Gliding Club (Pty) Ltd/Dunstable | |
| G-BEUD | Robin HR.100/285R | E. A. & L. M. C. Payton/Cranfield | |
| G-BEUI | Piper J-3C-65 Cub | M. J. Whatley | |
| G-BEUK | Fuji FA.200-160 | Euro Marine Group Ltd | |
| G-BEUL | Beech 95-58 Baron | Foyle Flyers Ltd/Eglinton | |
| G-BEUM | Taylor JT.1 Monoplane | M. T. Taylor | |
| G-BEUN | Cassutt Racer IIIm | R. S. Voice/Redhill | |
| G-BEUP | Robin DR.400/180 | A. V. Pound & Co Ltd | |
| G-BEUR | Cessna F.172M | M. E. Moore/Compton Abbas | |
| G-BEUS | AIA Stampe SV-4C | G-BEUS Flying Group | |
| G-BEUU | PA-18 Super Cub 95 | F. Sharples/Sandown | |
| G-BEUV | Thunder Ax6-56A balloon | Silhouette Balloon Group | |
| G-BEUX | Cessna F.172N | Ladel Ltd | |
| G-BEUY | Cameron N-31 balloon | M. W. A. Shemilt | |
| G-BEVA | SOCATA Rallye 150ST | The Rallye Group | |
| G-BEVB | SOCATA Rallye 150ST | N. R. Haines | |
| G-BEVC | SOCATA Rallye 150ST | B. W. Walpole | |
| G-BEVG | PA-34-200T-2 Seneca | Pullploy Ltd/Bournemouth | |
| G-BEVI | Thunder Ax7-77A balloon | The Painted Clouds Balloon Co Ltd | |
| G-BEVO | Sportavia-Pützer RF-5 | T. Barlow | |
| G-BEVP | Evans VP-2 | G. Moscrop & R. C. Crowley | |
| G-BEVS | Taylor JT.1 Monoplane | D. Hunter | |
| G-BEVT | BN-2A Mk III-2 Trislander | Aurigny Air Services Ltd/Guernsey | |
| G-BEVW | SOCATA Rallye 150ST | P. C. Goodwin | |
| G-BEWJ | Westland-Bell 47G-3B1 | Ropeleyville Ltd | |
| G-BEWM | Sikorsky S-61N Mk II | British International Helicopters Ltd | |
| G-BEWN | D.H.82A Tiger Moth | H. D. Labouchere | |
| G-BEWO | Zlin Z.326 Trener Master | Nimrod Group Ltd/Staverton | |
| G-BEWR | Cessna F.172N | Cheshire Air Training School (Merseyside) Ltd/Liverpool | |
| G-BEWX | PA-28R-201 Arrow III | A. Vickers | |
| G-BEXK | PA-25 Pawnee 235D | Howard Avis (Aviation) Ltd | |
| G-BEXN | AA-1C Lynx | Lynx Flying Group | |
| G-BEXO | PA-23 Apache 160 | Man-Air | |
| G-BEXR | Mudry/CAARP CAP-10B | Man-Air | |
| G-BEXS | Cessna F.150M | Firecrest Aviation Ltd | |
| G-BEXW | PA-28-181 Archer II | R. P. Crozier | |
| G-BEXX | Cameron V-56 balloon | K. A. Schlussler | |
| G-BEXY | PA-28 Cherokee 140 | G. J. Jenkins & D. L. James | |
| G-BEXZ | Cameron N-56 balloon | D. C. Eager & G. C. Clark | |
| G-BEYA | Enstrom 280C Shark | Aspleys Antiques Ltd | |
| G-BEYB | Fairey Flycatcher (replica) (S1287) | John S. Fairey/Duxford | |
| G-BEYD | HPR-7 Herald 401 | *Stored*/Southend | |
| G-BEYF | HPR-7 Herald 401 | Channel Express (Air Services) Ltd/Bournemouth | |
| G-BEYK | HPR-7 Herald 401 | Janes Aviation Ltd/Blackpool | |
| G-BEYL | PA-28 Cherokee 180 | B. G. & G. Airlines Ltd/Jersey | |
| G-BEYO | PA-28 Cherokee 140 | Mersey Control Systems Ltd | |
| G-BEYT | PA-28 Cherokee 140 | H. Foulds | |
| G-BEYV | Cessna T.210M | Forth Engineering Ltd | |
| G-BEYW | Taylor JT.1 Monoplane | R. A. Abrahams/Barton | |
| G-BEYZ | Jodel DR.1051/M1 | M. J. McCarthy & S. Aarons/Biggin Hill | |
| G-BEZA | Zlin Z.226T Trener | L. Bezak | |
| G-BEZC | AA-5 Traveler | P. N. & S. E. Field | |
| G-BEZE | Rutan Vari-Eze | H. C. Mackinnon | |
| G-BEZF | AA-5 Traveler | G. A. Randall/Exeter | |
| G-BEZG | AA-5 Traveler | B. A. & P. G. Osburn/Biggin Hill | |
| G-BEZH | AA-5 Traveler | L. & S. M. Sims | |
| G-BEZI | AA-5 Traveler | BEZI Flying Group/Cranfield | |
| G-BEZJ | MBB Bo 105D | Bond Helicopters Ltd/Bourn | |
| G-BEZK | Cessna F.172H | Zulu Kilo Flying Group | |
| G-BEZL | PA-31-310 Turbo Navajo C | London Flight Centre (Stansted) Ltd | |

| Notes | Reg. | Type | Owner or Operator |
|---|---|---|---|
| | G-BEZM | Cessna F.182Q | Ashcombe Ltd (G-WALK) |
| | G-BEZO | Cessna F.172M | Staverton Flying Services Ltd |
| | G-BEZP | PA-32 Cherokee Six 300D | Falcon Styles Ltd/Booker |
| | G-BEZR | Cessna F.172M | Kirmington Aviation Ltd |
| | G-BEZS | Cessna FR.172J | B. A. Wallace |
| | G-BEZV | Cessna F.172M | Insch Flying Group/Aberdeen |
| | G-BEZY | Rutan Vari-Eze | R. J. Jones |
| | G-BEZZ | Jodel D.112 | G-BEZZ Jodel Group |
| | | | |
| | G-BFAA | GY-80 Horizon 160 | Mary Poppins Ltd |
| | G-BFAB | Cameron N-56 balloon | Phonogram Ltd *Phonogram* |
| | G-BFAC | Cessna F.177RG | J. J. Baumhardt/Southend |
| | G-BFAF | Aeronca 7BCM (7797) | D. C. W. Harper/Finmere |
| | G-BFAH | Phoenix Currie Wot | R. W. Clarke |
| | G-BFAI | R. Commander 114 | D. S. Innes/Guernsey |
| | G-BFAK | M.S.892A Rallye Commodore 150 | P. G. Wells & J. D. Hensby |
| | G-BFAM | PA-31P Pressurised Navajo | CMH Management Services |
| | G-BFAN | H.S.125 Srs 600F | British Aerospace (G-AZHS)/Hatfield |
| | G-BFAO | PA-20 Pacer 135 | J. Day & ptnrs/Goodwood |
| | G-BFAP | SIAI-Marchetti S.205-20R | A. O. Broin |
| | G-BFAR | Cessna 500-1 Citation | Club Air (Europe) Ltd |
| | G-BFAS | Evans VP-1 | A. I. Sutherland |
| | G-BFAW | D.H.C.1 Chipmunk 22 | R. V. Bowles |
| | G-BFAX | D.H.C.1 Chipmunk 22 (WG422) | B. Earl/Biggin Hill |
| | G-BFBA | Jodel DR.100A | A. Brown & R. Wood |
| | G-BFBB | PA-23 Aztec 250E | Alpha-Air |
| | G-BFBD | Partenavia P.68B | Calmsafe Ltd |
| | G-BFBE | Robin HR.200/100 | D. V. Pell & J. Dyson |
| | G-BFBF | PA-28 Cherokee 140 | Marnham Investments Ltd |
| | G-BFBM | Saffery S.330 balloon | B. Martin *Beeze II* |
| | G-BFBR | PA-28-161 Warrior II | Lowery Holdings Ltd/Fairoaks |
| | G-BFBU | Partenavia P.68B | W. Holmes & Son Ltd |
| | G-BFBY | Piper J-3C-65 Cub | L. W. Usherwood |
| | G-BFCT | Cessna TU.206F | Cecil Aviation Ltd/Cambridge |
| | G-BFCZ | Sopwith Camel (B7270) ★ | Brooklands Museum Trust Ltd/Weybridge |
| | G-BFDC | D.H.C.1 Chipmunk 22 | N. F. O'Neill/Newtownards |
| | G-BFDE | Sopwith Tabloid (replica) (168) ★ | RAF Museum Storage & Restoration Centre/Cardington |
| | G-BFDF | SOCATA Rallye 235E | J. H. Atkinson/Skegness |
| | G-BFDG | PA-28R-201T Turbo-Arrow III | Richard Pearson Ltd |
| | G-BFDI | PA-28-181 Archer II | Truman Aviation Ltd/Tollerton |
| | G-BFDK | PA-28-161 Warrior II | C.S.E. Aviation Ltd/Kidlington |
| | G-BFDL | Piper J-3C-65 Cub (454537) | P. B. Rice & A. White |
| | G-BFDM | Jodel D.120 | Worcestershire Gliding Ltd |
| | G-BFDN | PA-31-350 Navajo Chieftain | Genoex Ltd |
| | G-BFDO | PA-28R-201T Turbo Arrow III | M. I. & D. G. Goss |
| | G-BFDZ | Taylor JT.1 Monoplane | L. J. Greenhough |
| | G-BFEB | Jodel D.150 | S. Russell |
| | G-BFEC | PA-23 Aztec 250F | P. V. Naylor-Leyland |
| | G-BFEE | Beech 95-E55 Baron | Interair (Aviation) Ltd/Bournemouth |
| | G-BFEF | Agusta-Bell 47G-3B1 | R. J. Chilton |
| | G-BFEH | Jodel D.117A | C. V. & S. J. Philpott |
| | G-BFEI | Westland-Bell 47G-3B1 | Trent Air Services Ltd/Cranfield |
| | G-BFEK | Cessna F.152 | Staverton Flying Services Ltd |
| | G-BFER | Bell 212 | Bristow Helicopters Ltd |
| | G-BFEV | PA-25 Pawnee 235 | B. Walker & Co (Dursley) Ltd |
| | G-BFEW | PA-25 Pawnee 235 | B. Walker & Co (Dursley) Ltd |
| | G-BFEY | PA-25 Pawnee 235 | Howard Avis Aviation Ltd |
| | G-BFFC | Cessna F.152-II | Yorkshire Flying Services Ltd/Leeds |
| | G-BFFE | Cessna F.152-II | Doncaster Aero Club |
| | G-BFFG | Beech 95-B55 Baron | V. Westley |
| | G-BFFJ | Sikorsky S-61N Mk II | British International Helicopters Ltd/ Aberdeen |
| | G-BFFK | Sikorsky S-61N Mk II | British International Helicopters Ltd/ Aberdeen |
| | G-BFFP | PA-18 Super Cub 150 (modified) | Booker Gliding Club Ltd |
| | G-BFFT | Cameron V-56 balloon | R. I. M. Kerr & D. C. Boxall |
| | G-BFFW | Cessna F.152 | Tayside Aviation Ltd/Dundee |
| | G-BFFY | Cessna F.150M | Northside Aviation Ltd/Liverpool |
| | G-BFFZ | Cessna FR.172 Hawk XP | Bravo Aviation Ltd |
| | G-BFGD | Cessna F.172N-II | Falcon Flying Services/Biggin Hill |
| | G-BFGF | Cessna F.177RG | Keelex 121 Ltd |
| | G-BFGG | Cessna FRA.150M | Far North Flight Training Ltd/Wick |

| Reg. | Type | Owner or Operator | Notes |
|---|---|---|---|
| G-BFGH | Cessna F.337G | T. Perkins/Sherburn | |
| G-BFGK | Jodel D.117 | B. F. J. Hope | |
| G-BFGL | Cessna FA.152 | Yorkshire Flying Services Ltd/Leeds | |
| G-BFGO | Fuji FA.200-160 | Butane Buzzard Aviation Corporation Ltd | |
| G-BFGS | M.S.893E Rallye 180GT | K. M. & H. Bowen | |
| G-BFGW | Cessna F.150H | C. E. Stringer | |
| G-BFGX | Cessna FRA.150M | Air Service Training Ltd/Perth | |
| G-BFGZ | Cessna FRA.150M | Air Service Training Ltd/Perth | |
| G-BFHH | D.H.82A Tiger Moth | P. Harrison & M. J. Gambrell/Redhill | |
| G-BFHI | Piper J-3C-65 Cub | J. M. Robinson | |
| G-BFHP | Champion 7GCAA Citabria | T. A. Holding | |
| G-BFHR | Jodel DR.220/2+2 | T. W. Greaves | |
| G-BFHT | Cessna F.152-II | Riger Ltd/Luton | |
| G-BFHU | Cessna F.152-II | Deltair Ltd/Chester | |
| G-BFHV | Cessna F.152-II | Aerohire Ltd | |
| G-BFHX | Evans VP-1 | P. Johnson | |
| G-BFIB | PA-31 Turbo Navajo | Mann Aviation Ltd/Fairoaks | |
| G-BFID | Taylor JT.2 Titch Mk III | G. Hunter | |
| G-BFIE | Cessna FRA.150M | RFC (Bourn) Ltd | |
| G-BFIF | Cessna FR.172K XPII | Falcon Flight Training Ltd/Eglinton | |
| G-BFIG | Cessna FR.172K XPII | Tenair Ltd | |
| G-BFIJ | AA-5A Cheetah | J. H. Wise/Redhill | |
| G-BFIN | AA-5A Cheetah | G-BFIN Group | |
| G-BFIP | Wallbro Monoplane 1909 replica | K. H. Wallis/Swanton Morley | |
| G-BFIR | Avro 652A Anson 21 (WD413) | G. M. K. Fraser (stored)/Arbroath | |
| G-BFIT | Thunder Ax6-56Z balloon | J. A. G. Tyson | |
| G-BFIU | Cessna FR.172K XP | B. M. Jobling | |
| G-BFIV | Cessna F.177RG | Kingfishair Ltd/Blackbushe | |
| G-BFIX | Thunder Ax7-77A balloon | R. Owen | |
| G-BFJA | AA-5B Tiger | Sentry Courier Ltd/Blackbushe | |
| G-BFJH | SA.102-5 Cavalier | B. F. J. Hope | |
| G-BFJI | Robin HR.100/250 | Financial Services Training Ltd | |
| G-BFJJ | Evans VP-1 | M. J. Collins | |
| G-BFJK | PA-23 Aztec 250F | R. Marsden & P. E. T. Price | |
| G-BFJN | Westland-Bell 47G-3B1 | Howden Helicopters | |
| G-BFJR | Cessna F.337G | Mannix Aviation/E. Midlands | |
| G-BFJV | Cessna F.172H | Southport & Merseyside Aero Club Ltd | |
| G-BFJW | AB-206B JetRanger | European Aviation Ltd | |
| G-BFJZ | Robin DR.400/140B | Rochester Aviation Ltd | |
| G-BFKA | Cessna F.172N | D. J. A. Seagram | |
| G-BFKB | Cessna F.172N | R. E. Speigel | |
| G-BFKC | Rand KR.2 | L. H. S. Stephens & I. S. Hewitt | |
| G-BFKD | R. Commander 114B | M. D. Faiers | |
| G-BFKF | Cessna FA.152 | Klingair Ltd/Conington | |
| G-BFKG | Cessna F.152 | Luton Flight Training Ltd | |
| G-BFKH | Cessna F.152 | T. G. Aviation Ltd/Manston | |
| G-BFKL | Cameron N-56 balloon | Merrythought Toys Ltd Merrythought | |
| G-BFKY | PA-34-200 Seneca II | S.L.H. Construction Ltd/Biggin Hill | |
| G-BFLH | PA-34-200T Seneca II | C.S.E. Aviation Ltd/Kidlington | |
| G-BFLI | PA-28R-201T Turbo Arrow III | Cowley (Recruitment) Ltd | |
| G-BFLK | Cessna F.152 | Galaxy Enterprises Ltd | |
| G-BFLL | H.S.748 Srs 2A | Euroair Transport Ltd | |
| G-BFLM | Cessna 150M | Cornwall Flying Club Ltd/Bodmin | |
| G-BFLN | Cessna 150M | Sherburn Aero Club Ltd | |
| G-BFLP | Amethyst Ax6 balloon | K. J. Hendry Amethyst | |
| G-BFLU | Cessna F.152 | Inverness Flying Services Ltd | |
| G-BFLV | Cessna F.172N | Cheshire Air Training School (Merseyside) Ltd/Liverpool | |
| G-BFLX | AA-5A Cheetah | Abraxas Aviation Ltd/Denham | |
| G-BFLZ | Beech 95-A55 Baron | W. G. Thompson | |
| G-BFMC | BAC One-Eleven 414FG | — | |
| G-BFME | Cameron V-56 balloon | Warwick Balloons Ltd | |
| G-BFMF | Cassutt Racer Mk IIIM | P. H. Lewis | |
| G-BFMG | PA-28-161 Warrior II | Bailey Aviation Ltd | |
| G-BFMH | Cessna 177B | Span Aviation Ltd/Newcastle | |
| G-BFMK | Cessna FA.152 | RAF Halton Aeroplane Club Ltd | |
| G-BFMM | PA-28-181 Archer II | Bristol & Wessex Aeroplane Club Ltd | |
| G-BFMR | PA-20 Pacer 125 | J. E. Cummings | |
| G-BFMX | Cessna F.172N | Jureen Aviation | |
| G-BFMY | Sikorsky S-61N | Bristow Helicopters Ltd | |
| G-BFMZ | Payne Ax6 balloon | G. F. Payne | |
| G-BFNC | AS.350B Ecureuil | Dollar Air Services Ltd/Coventry | |
| G-BFNG | Jodel D.112 | E. N. & L. K. Simmons | |

69

| Notes | Reg. | Type | Owner or Operator |
|---|---|---|---|
| | G-BFNI | PA-28-161 Warrior II | P. Elliott/Biggin Hill |
| | G-BFNJ | PA-28-161 Warrior II | C.S.E. Aviation Ltd/Kidlington |
| | G-BFNK | PA-28-161 Warrior II | C.S.E. Aviation Ltd/Kidlington |
| | G-BFNM | Globe GC.1 Swift | Nottingham Flying Group/Tatenhill |
| | G-BFNU | BN-2B Islander | Isle of Scilly Sky Bus Ltd/St Just |
| | G-BFOD | Cessna F.182Q | G. N. Clarke |
| | G-BFOE | Cessna F.152 | Holmes Rentals |
| | G-BFOF | Cessna F.152 | Staverton Flying School Ltd |
| | G-BFOG | Cessna 150M | W. J. Pinches & M. D. Bayliss |
| | G-BFOJ | AA-1 Yankee | A. J. Morton/Bournemouth |
| | G-BFOP | Jodel D.120 | R. J. Wesley & G. D. Western/Ipswich |
| | G-BFOS | Thunder Ax6-56A balloon | N. T. Petty |
| | G-BFOU | Taylor JT.1 Monoplane | G. Bee |
| | G-BFOV | Cessna F.172N | D. J. Walker |
| | G-BFOZ | Thunder Ax6-56 balloon | R. L. Harbord |
| | G-BFPA | Scheibe SF.25B Super Falke | Yorkshire Gliding Club (Pty) Ltd/ Sutton Bank |
| | G-BFPB | AA-5B Tiger | Guernsey Aero Club |
| | G-BFPH | Cessna F.172K | J. M. Reid |
| | G-BFPL | Fokker D.VII (replica) (4253/18) | A. E. Hutton/North Weald |
| | G-BFPM | Cessna F.172M | N. R. Havercroft |
| | G-BFPO | R. Commander 112B | J. G. Hale Ltd |
| | G-BFPP | Bell 47J-2 | J. F. Kelly |
| | G-BFPS | PA-25 Pawnee 235D | Kent Gliding Club Ltd/Challock |
| | G-BFPZ | Cessna F.177RG | R. P. Nash/Norwich |
| | G-BFRA | R. Commander 114 | Sabre Engines Ltd/Bournemouth |
| | G-BFRD | Bowers Flybaby 1A | F. R. Donaldson |
| | G-BFRF | Taylor JT.1 Monoplane | E. R. Bailey |
| | G-BFRI | Sikorsky S-61N | Bristow Helicopters Ltd |
| | G-BFRL | Cessna F.152 | M. K. Barnes & G. N. Olsen |
| | G-BFRM | Cessna 550 Citation II | Marshall of Cambridge (Engineering) Ltd |
| | G-BFRO | Cessna F.150M | Skyviews & General Ltd/Carlisle |
| | G-BFRR | Cessna FRA.150M | Interair Aviation Ltd/Bournemouth |
| | G-BFRS | Cessna F.172N | Poplar Toys Ltd |
| | G-BFRV | Cessna FA.152 | Turnhouse Flying Club |
| | G-BFRX | PA-25 Pawnee 260 | Yorkshire Gliding Club (Pty) Ltd/ Sutton Bank |
| | G-BFRY | PA-25 Pawnee 260 | B. Walker & Co (Dursley) Ltd |
| | G-BFSA | Cessna F.182Q | Clark Masts Ltd/Sandown |
| | G-BFSB | Cessna F.152 | Tatenhill Aviation |
| | G-BFSC | PA-25 Pawnee 235D | Farm Aviation Services Ltd/Enstone |
| | G-BFSD | PA-25 Pawnee 235D | Deeside Gliding Club Ltd/Aboyne |
| | G-BFSK | PA-23 Apache 160 ★ | Oxford Air Training School/Kidlington |
| | G-BFSP | H.S.125 Srs 700B | Corporate Jets Ltd/Hatfield |
| | G-BFSR | Cessna F.150J | Air Fenland Ltd |
| | G-BFSS | Cessna FR.172G | Minerva Services |
| | G-BFSY | PA-28-181 Archer II | Downland Aviation |
| | G-BFTC | PA-28R-201T Turbo Arrow III | D. Hughes/Sherburn |
| | G-BFTF | AA-5B Tiger | F. C. Burrow Ltd/Leeds |
| | G-BFTG | AA-5B Tiger | D. Hepburn & G. R. Montgomery |
| | G-BFTH | Cessna F.172N | Bath Stone Co Ltd |
| | G-BFTT | Cessna 421C | P&B Metal Components Ltd/Manston |
| | G-BFTX | Cessna F.172N | E. Kent Flying Group |
| | G-BFTY | Cameron V-77 balloon | Regal Motors (Bilston) Ltd *Regal Motors* |
| | G-BFTZ | MS.880B Rallye Club | R. & B. Legge Ltd |
| | G-BFUB | PA-32RT-300 Lance II | Jolida Holdings Ltd |
| | G-BFUD | Scheibe SF.25E Super Falke | S. H. Hart |
| | G-BFUG | Cameron N-77 balloon | Headland Services Ltd |
| | G-BFUZ | Cameron V-77 balloon | Skysales Ltd |
| | G-BFVB | Boeing 737-204ADV | Britannia Airways Ltd *Sir Thomas Sopwith* |
| | G-BFVF | PA-38-112 Tomahawk | Ipswich School of Flying Ltd |
| | G-BFVG | PA-28-181 Archer II | G-BFVG Flying Group/Blackpool |
| | G-BFVH | D.H.2 Replica (5894) | Wessex Aviation & Transport Ltd |
| | G-BFVI | H.S.125 Srs 700B | Bristow Helicopters Ltd |
| | G-BFVM | Westland-Bell 47G-3B1 | K. R. Dossett |
| | G-BFVO | Partenavia P.68B | Airmark Aviation Services Ltd |
| | G-BFVP | PA-23 Aztec 250F | Litton Aviation Services Ltd |
| | G-BFVS | AA-5B Tiger | S. W. Biroth & T. Chapman/Denham |
| | G-BFVU | Cessna 150L | Thruxton Flight Centre Ltd |
| | G-BFWB | PA-28-161 Warrior II | C.S.E. Aviation Ltd/Kidlington |
| | G-BFWD | Currie Wot | F. E. Nuthall |
| | G-BFWE | PA-23 Aztec 250E | Air Navigation & Trading Co Ltd/Blackpool |
| | G-BFWK | PA-28-161 Warrior II | Woodgate Air Services (IoM) Ltd |

| Reg. | Type | Owner or Operator | Notes |
|------|------|-------------------|-------|
| G-BFWL | Cessna F.150L | Howells Group PLC | |
| G-BFWW | Robin HR.100/210 | Willingair Ltd | |
| G-BFXC | Mooney M.20C | Kent Engraving Ltd | |
| G-BFXD | PA-28-161 Warrior II | C.S.E. Aviation Ltd/Kidlington | |
| G-BFXE | PA-28-161 Warrior II | C.S.E. Aviation Ltd/Kidlington | |
| G-BFXF | Andreasson BA.4B | A. Brown/Sherburn | |
| G-BFXH | Cessna F.152 | M. Entwistle | |
| G-BFXI | Cessna F.172M | Thanet Electronics/Manston | |
| G-BFXK | PA-28 Cherokee 140 | G. S. & Mrs M. T. Pritchard/Southend | |
| G-BFXL | Albatross D.5A (D5397/17) | FAA Museum/Yeovilton | |
| G-BFXR | Jodel D.112 | G. Barthorpe | |
| G-BFXS | R. Commander 114 | Keats Printing Ltd | |
| G-BFXW | AA-5B Tiger | Crosswind Aviation Ltd/Leeds | |
| G-BFXX | AA-5B Tiger | M. J. Porter | |
| G-BFYA | MBB Bo 105DB | Mennak Ltd | |
| G-BFYB | PA-28-161 Warrior II | C.S.E. Aviation Ltd/Kidlington | |
| G-BFYC | PA-32RT-300 Lance II | A. A. Barnes | |
| G-BFYE | Robin HR.100/285 ★ | stored/Sywell | |
| G-BFYI | Westland-Bell 47G-3B1 | B. Walker & Co (Dursley) Ltd | |
| G-BFYJ | Hughes 369HE | S. M. Ridgley | |
| G-BFYK | Cameron V-77 balloon | D. M. Williams | |
| G-BFYL | Evans VP-2 | A. G. Wilford | |
| G-BFYM | PA-28-161 Warrior II | C.S.E. Aviation Ltd/Kidlington | |
| G-BFYN | Cessna FA.152 | Phoenix Flying Services Ltd/Glasgow | |
| G-BFYO | Spad XIII (replica) (3398) ★ | FAA Museum/Yeovilton | |
| G-BFYP | Bensen B.7 | A. J. Philpotts | |
| G-BFYU | SC.5 Belfast | HeavyLift Cargo Airlines Ltd/Southend | |
| G-BFZB | Piper J-3C-85 Cub | Zebedee Flying Group/Shoreham | |
| G-BFZD | Cessna FR.182RG | R. B. Lewis & Co/Sleap | |
| G-BFZG | PA-28-161 Warrior II | C.S.E. Aviation Ltd/Kidlington | |
| G-BFZH | PA-28R Cherokee Arrow 200 | K. E. Miles | |
| G-BFZL | V.836 Viscount | British Air Ferries/Southend | |
| G-BFZM | R. Commander 112TC | Rolls-Royce Ltd/Filton | |
| G-BFZN | Cessna FA.152 | Falcon Flying Services/Biggin Hill | |
| G-BFZO | AA-5A Cheetah | Heald Air Ltd/Manchester | |
| G-BFZT | Cessna FA.152 | Zulu Tango Ltd/Guernsey | |
| G-BFZU | Cessna FA.152 | R. T. Love | |
| G-BFZV | Cessna F.172M | R. Thomas | |
| | | | |
| G-BGAA | Cessna 152 II | PJC Leasing Ltd | |
| G-BGAB | Cessna F.152 II | TG Aviation Ltd/Manston | |
| G-BGAD | Cessna F.152 II | J. G. Bell | |
| G-BGAE | Cessna F.152 II | Klingair Ltd/Conington | |
| G-BGAF | Cessna FA.152 | Suffolk Aero Club Ltd/Ipswich | |
| G-BGAG | Cessna F.172N | Semloh Aviation Services/Andrewsfield | |
| G-BGAJ | Cessna F.182Q II | Ground Airport Services Ltd/Guernsey | |
| G-BGAK | Cessna F.182Q II | Safari World Services Ltd | |
| G-BGAX | PA-28 Cherokee 140 | Devon School of Flying/Dunkeswell | |
| G-BGAY | Cameron O-77 balloon | S. W. C. & P. C. A. Hall | |
| G-BGAZ | Cameron V-77 balloon | Cameron Balloons Ltd Silicon Chip | |
| G-BGBA | Robin R.2100A | D. Faulkner/Redhill | |
| G-BGBC | L.1011-385 TriStar 200 | British Airways St Andrews Bay | |
| G-BGBE | Jodel DR.1050 | J. A. & B. Mawby | |
| G-BGBF | D.31A Turbulent | S. P. Wakeham | |
| G-BGBG | PA-28-181 Archer II | Harlow Printing Ltd/Newcastle | |
| G-BGBI | Cessna F.150L | Bugby Flying Group | |
| G-BGBK | PA-38-112 Tomahawk | F. Marshall & R. C. Priest/Netherthorpe | |
| G-BGBN | PA-38-112 Tomahawk | Leavesden Flight Centre Ltd | |
| G-BGBP | Cessna F.152 | Stapleford Flying Club Ltd | |
| G-BGBR | Cessna F.172N | Falcon Flying Services/Biggin Hill | |
| G-BGBU | Auster AOP.9 (XN435) | P. Neilson | |
| G-BGBW | PA-38-112 Tomahawk | Truman Aviation Ltd/Tollerton | |
| G-BGBX | PA-38-112 Tomahawk | Ipswich School of Flying Ltd | |
| G-BGBY | PA-38-112 Tomahawk | Ravenair Ltd/Manchester | |
| G-BGBZ | R. Commander 114 | R. S. Fenwick/Biggin Hill | |
| G-BGCG | Douglas C-47A | on rebuild | |
| G-BGCL | AA-5A Cheetah | AIG Air Services Ltd | |
| G-BGCM | AA-5A Cheetah | Deltaflight Ltd | |
| G-BGCO | PA-44-180 Seminole | J. R. Henderson | |
| G-BGCX | Taylor JT.1 Monoplane | G. M. R. Walters | |
| G-BGCY | Taylor JT.1 Monoplane | M. T. Taylor | |
| G-BGCZ | Bell 212 | Bristow Helicopters Ltd | |
| G-BGDA | Boeing 737-236 | British Airways Manchester River Tamar | |

| Notes | Reg. | Type | Owner or Operator |
|---|---|---|---|
| | G-BGDB | Boeing 737-236 | GB Airways Ltd *Mons Veleta* |
| | G-BGDC | Boeing 737-236 | British Airways *River Humber* |
| | G-BGDD | Boeing 737-236 | British Airways *River Tees* |
| | G-BGDE | Boeing 737-236 | British Airways Birmingham *River Avon* |
| | G-BGDF | Boeing 737-236 | British Airways Manchester *River Thames* |
| | G-BGDG | Boeing 737-236 | British Airways Manchester *River Medway* |
| | G-BGDH | Boeing 737-236 | British Airways Manchester *River Clyde* |
| | G-BGDI | Boeing 737-236 | British Airways Birmingham *River Ouse* |
| | G-BGDJ | Boeing 737-236 | British Airways Manchester *River Trent* |
| | G-BGDK | Boeing 737-236 | British Airways Manchester *River Mersey* |
| | G-BGDL | Boeing 737-236 | British Airways Manchester *River Don* |
| | G-BGDN | Boeing 737-236 | British Airways Manchester *River Tyne* |
| | G-BGDO | Boeing 737-236 | GB Airways Ltd |
| | G-BGDP | Boeing 737-236 | British Airways *River Taff* |
| | G-BGDR | Boeing 737-236 | British Airways *River Bann* |
| | G-BGDS | Boeing 737-236 | GB Airways Ltd *Mons Calpe* |
| | G-BGDT | Boeing 737-236 | British Airways Manchester *River Forth* |
| | G-BGDU | Boeing 737-236 | GB Airways Ltd *Mons Abyala* |
| | G-BGEA | Cessna F.150M | Agricultural & General Aviation Ltd |
| | G-BGED | Cessna U.206F | Chapman Aviation Ltd |
| | G-BGEE | Evans VP-1 | D. P. Byatt |
| | G-BGEF | Jodel D.112 | G. G. Johnson & S. J. Davies |
| | G-BGEH | Monnet Sonerai II | A. Dodd |
| | G-BGEI | Baby Great Lakes | I. D. Trask |
| | G-BGEK | PA-38-112 Tomahawk | Cheshire Flying Services Ltd/Manchester |
| | G-BGEL | PA-38-112 Tomahawk | Ravenair Ltd/Manchester |
| | G-BGEM | Partenavia P.68B | Meridian Air Services Ltd/Staverton |
| | G-BGEP | Cameron D-38 balloon | Cameron Balloons Ltd |
| | G-BGEW | SNCAN NC.854S | Tavair Ltd |
| | G-BGEX | Brookland Mosquito 2 | R. T. Gough |
| | G-BGFC | Evans VP-2 | S. W. C. Hollins |
| | G-BGFF | FRED Srs 2 | F. Bolton/Blackpool |
| | G-BGFG | AA-5A Cheetah | Fletcher Aviation Ltd/Biggin Hill |
| | G-BGFH | Cessna F.182Q | Sunseeker Leisure PLC |
| | G-BGFI | AA-5A Cheetah | I. J. Hay & A. Nayyar/Biggin Hill |
| | G-BGFJ | Jodel D.9 Bebe | C. M. Fitton |
| | G-BGFK | Evans VP-1 | I. N. M. Cameron |
| | G-BGFT | PA-34-200T Seneca II | C.S.E. Aviation Ltd/Kidlington |
| | G-BGFX | Cessna F.152 | A. W. Fay/Cranfield |
| | G-BGGA | Bellanca 7GCBC Citabria | L. A. King |
| | G-BGGB | Bellanca 7GCBC Citabria | M. D. Cowburn |
| | G-BGGC | Bellanca 7GCBC Citabria | R. P. Ashfield & J. P. Stone |
| | G-BGGD | Bellanca 8GCBC Scout | Bristol & Gloucestershire Gliding Club/ Nympsfield |
| | G-BGGE | PA-38-112 Tomahawk | Truman Aviation Ltd/Tollerton |
| | G-BGGF | PA-38-112 Tomahawk | Truman Aviation Ltd/Tollerton |
| | G-BGGG | PA-38-112 Tomahawk | Teesside Flight Centre Ltd |
| | G-BGGI | PA-38-112 Tomahawk | Truman Aviation Ltd/Tollerton |
| | G-BGGL | PA-38-112 Tomahawk | Pan-Air Ltd/Leavesden |
| | G-BGGM | PA-38-112 Tomahawk | Pan-Air Ltd/Leavesden |
| | G-BGGN | PA-38-112 Tomahawk | Domeastral Ltd/Elstree |
| | G-BGGO | Cessna F.152 | E. Midlands Flying School Ltd |
| | G-BGGP | Cessna F.152 | E. Midlands Flying School Ltd |
| | G-BGGU | Wallis WA-116R-R | K. H. Wallis |
| | G-BGGV | Wallis WA-120 Srs 2 | K. H. Wallis |
| | G-BGGW | Wallis WA-112 | K. H. Wallis |
| | G-BGGY | AB-206B Jet Ranger ★ | *Instructional airframe*/Cranfield |
| | G-BGHE | Convair L-13A | J. Davis/USA |
| | G-BGHF | Westland WG.30 ★ | International Helicopter Museum/ Weston-s-Mare |
| | G-BGHI | Cessna F.152 | Taxon Ltd/Shoreham |
| | G-BGHM | Robin R.1180T | H. Price |
| | G-BGHP | Beech 76 Duchess | Net Supply Co Ltd |
| | G-BGHS | Cameron N-31 balloon | W. R. Teasdale |
| | G-BGHT | Falconar F-12 | C. R. Coates |
| | G-BGHU | NA T-6G Texan (115042) | C. E. Bellhouse |
| | G-BGHV | Cameron V-77 balloon | E. Davies |
| | G-BGHW | Thunder Ax8-90 balloon | Edinburgh University Balloon Group |
| | G-BGHY | Taylor JT.1 Monoplane | R. A. Hand |
| | G-BGHZ | FRED Srs 2 | A. Smith |
| | G-BGIB | Cessna 152 II | Mona Aviation Ltd |
| | G-BGIC | Cessna 172N | T. R. Sinclair |
| | G-BGID | Westland-Bell 47G-3B1 | M. J. Cuttell |

| Reg. | Type | Owner or Operator | Notes |
|------|------|-------------------|-------|
| G-BGIG | PA-38-112 Tomahawk | Scotia Safari Ltd/Prestwick | |
| G-BGII | PA-32 Cherokee Six 300E | D. L. P. Milligan | |
| G-BGIO | Bensen B.8M | C. G. Johns | |
| G-BGIP | Colt 56A balloon | J. G. N. Perfect | |
| G-BGIU | Cessna F.172H | MG Services | |
| G-BGIV | Bell 47G-5 | Abraxas Aviation Ltd | |
| G-BGIX | H.295 Super Courier | C. M. Lee/Andrewsfield | |
| G-BGIY | Cessna F.172N | G. Gormack/Glasgow | |
| G-BGIZ | Cessna F.152 | Creaton Aviation Services Ltd | |
| G-BGJB | PA-44-180 Seminole | Oxford Management Ltd | |
| G-BGJE | Boeing 737-236 | British Airways *River Wear*/Gatwick | |
| G-BGJF | Boeing 737-236 | British Airways *River Axe*/Gatwick | |
| G-BGJG | Boeing 737-236 | British Airways *River Arun*/Gatwick | |
| G-BGJH | Boeing 737-236 | British Airways *River Lyne*/Gatwick | |
| G-BGJI | Boeing 737-236 | British Airways *River Wey*/Gatwick | |
| G-BGJJ | Boeing 737-236 | British Airways *River Swale*/Gatwick | |
| G-BGJK | Boeing 737-236 | British Airways *River Cherwell*/Gatwick | |
| G-BGJM | Boeing 737-236 | British Airways *River Ribble*/Gatwick | |
| G-BGJU | Cameron V-65 Balloon | J. A Folkes | |
| G-BGJW | GA-7 Cougar | Lambill Ltd | |
| G-BGKC | SOCATA Rallye 110ST | J. H. Cranmer & T. A. Timms | |
| G-BGKD | SOCATA Rallye 110ST | W. G. Dunn & A. G. Cameron | |
| G-BGKE | BAC One-Eleven 539GL | GEC Ferranti Defence Systems Ltd | |
| G-BGKJ | MBB Bo 105C | Bond Helicopters Ltd | |
| G-BGKO | GY-20 Minicab | R. B. Webber | |
| G-BGKS | PA-28-161 Warrior II | Marnham Investments Ltd | |
| G-BGKT | Auster AOP.9 (XN441) | K. H. Wallis | |
| G-BGKU | PA-28R-201 Arrow III | Caplane Ltd | |
| G-BGKV | PA-28R-201 Arrow III | R. Haverson & R. G. Watson | |
| G-BGKY | PA-38-112 Tomahawk | Prospect Air Ltd | |
| G-BGKZ | J/5F Aiglet Trainer | J. K. Cook | |
| G-BGLA | PA-38-112 Tomahawk | Norwich School of Flying | |
| G-BGLB | Bede BD-5B | W. Sawney | |
| G-BGLE | Saffrey S.330 balloon | C. J. Dodd & ptnrs | |
| G-BGLF | Evans VP-1 Srs 2 | M. Hartigan/Fenland | |
| G-BGLG | Cessna 152 | Skyviews & General Ltd/Bourn | |
| G-BGLH | Cessna 152 | Deltair Ltd/Chester | |
| G-BGLI | Cessna 152 | Luton Flying Club (*stored*) | |
| G-BGLK | Monnet Sonerai II | N. M. Smorthit | |
| G-BGLN | Cessna FA.152 | Bournemouth Flying Club | |
| G-BGLO | Cessna F.172N | A. H. Slaughter/Southend | |
| G-BGLS | Oldfield Super Baby Lakes | J. F. Dowe | |
| G-BGLW | PA-34-200 Seneca | Stapleford Flying Club Ltd | |
| G-BGLX | Cameron N-56 balloon | Sara A. G. Williams | |
| G-BGLZ | Stits SA-3A Playboy | B. G. Ell | |
| G-BGMA | D.31 Turbulent | G. C. Masterton | |
| G-BGME | SIPA S.903 | M. Emery & C. A. Suckling (G-BCML)/ Redhill | |
| G-BGMJ | GY-201 Minicab | S. L. Wakefield & ptnrs | |
| G-BGMO | H.S.748 Srs 2A | — | |
| G-BGMP | Cessna F.172G | D. Rowe | |
| G-BGMR | GY-201 Minicab | T. J. D. Hodge & ptnrs | |
| G-BGMS | Taylor JT.2 Titch | M. A. J. Spice | |
| G-BGMT | MS.894E Rallye 235GT | J. Murray | |
| G-BGMU | Westland-Bell 47G-3B1 | V. L. J. & V. English | |
| G-BGMV | Scheibe SF.25B Falke | Mendip Falke Flying Group | |
| G-BGNB | Short SD3-30 Variant 100 | Gill Aviation Ltd/Newcastle | |
| G-BGND | Cessna F.172N | Stansted Fluid Power (Products) Ltd | |
| G-BGNG | Short SD3-30 | Gill Aviation Ltd/Newcastle | |
| G-BGNR | Cessna F.172N | Picturama Group Ltd | |
| G-BGNT | Cessna F.152 | Klingair Ltd/Conington | |
| G-BGNV | GA-7 Cougar | E. C. & C. E. E. Craven Walker | |
| G-BGNZ | Cessna FRA.150L | G. P. Grant-Suttie | |
| G-BGOD | Colt 77A balloon | C. Allen & M. D. Steuer | |
| G-BGOG | PA-28-161 Warrior II | W. D. Moore | |
| G-BGOI | Cameron O-56 balloon | S. H. Budd | |
| G-BGOL | PA-28R-201T Turbo Arrow III | Clark Aviation Services Ltd | |
| G-BGOM | PA-31-310 Turbo Navajo | Oxford Aero Charter Ltd/Kidlington | |
| G-BGON | GA-7 Cougar | BLS Aviation Ltd/Elstree | |
| G-BGOO | Colt 56 SS balloon | British Gas Corporation | |
| G-BGOP | Dassault Falcon 20F | Nissan (UK) Ltd/Heathrow | |
| G-BGOR | AT-6D Harvard III (14863) | M. L. Sargeant | |
| G-BGOX | PA-31-350 Navajo Chieftain | Woodgate Aviation (IoM) Ltd | |

| Notes | Reg. | Type | Owner or Operator |
|---|---|---|---|
| | G-BGPA | Cessna 182Q | Guildcroft Enterprises Ltd |
| | G-BGPB | CCF T-6J Texan (20385) | Aircraft Restorations Ltd/Duxford |
| | G-BGPD | Piper J-3C-65 Cub | P. D. Whiteman |
| | G-BGPH | AA-5B Tiger | A. J. Dales |
| | G-BGPI | Plumb BGP-1 | B. G. Plumb |
| | G-BGPJ | PA-28-161 Warrior II | W. Lancs Warrior Co Ltd |
| | G-BGPK | AA-5B Tiger | G. A. Platon/Bournemouth |
| | G-BGPL | PA-28-161 Warrior II | T. G. Aviation Ltd/Manston |
| | G-BGPM | Evans VP-2 | M. G. Reilly |
| | G-BGPN | PA-18 Super Cub 150 | Clacton Aero Club (1988) Ltd |
| | G-BGPU | PA-28 Cherokee 140 | Air Navigation & Trading Co Ltd/Blackpool |
| | G-BGPZ | M.S.890A Rallye Commodore | Popham Flying Group |
| | G-BGRC | PA-28 Cherokee 140 | Arrow Air Centre Ltd/Shipdham |
| | G-BGRD | Beech 200 Super King Air | Flightline Ltd (G-IPRA)/Southend |
| | G-BGRE | Beech A200 Super King Air | Martin-Baker (Engineering) Ltd/Chalgrove |
| | G-BGRG | Beech 76 Duchess | Arrows Aviation Co Ltd/Manchester |
| | G-BGRH | Robin DR.400/22 | Rochester Aviation Ltd |
| | G-BGRI | Jodel DR.1051 | B. Gunn & K. L. Burnett |
| | G-BGRK | PA-38-112 Tomahawk | Goodwood Terrena Ltd |
| | G-BGRL | PA-38-112 Tomahawk | Goodwood Terrena Ltd |
| | G-BGRM | PA-38-112 Tomahawk | Goodwood Terrena Ltd |
| | G-BGRN | PA-38-112 Tomahawk | Goodwood Terrena Ltd |
| | G-BGRO | Cessna F.172M | Northfield Garage Ltd/Prestwick |
| | G-BGRR | PA-38-112 Tomahawk | Prospect Air Ltd |
| | G-BGRS | Thunder Ax7-77Z balloon | A. N. Casperd |
| | G-BGRT | Steen Skybolt | R. C. Nichols & ptnrs/Stapleford |
| | G-BGRX | PA-38-112 Tomahawk | Leavesden Flight Centre Ltd |
| | G-BGSA | M.S.892E Rallye 150GT | W. E. Taylor & Son Ltd/Exeter |
| | G-BGSG | PA-44-180 Seminole | D. J. McSorley |
| | G-BGSH | PA-38-112 Tomahawk | Scotia Safari Ltd/Prestwick |
| | G-BGSI | PA-38-112 Tomahawk | Cheshire Flying Services Ltd/Manchester |
| | G-BGSJ | Piper J-3C-65 Cub | W. J. Higgins/Dunkeswell |
| | G-BGST | Thunder Ax7-65 balloon | J. L. Bond |
| | G-BGSV | Cessna F.172N | Southwell Air Services Ltd |
| | G-BGSW | Beech F33 Debonair | Marketprior Ltd/Swansea |
| | G-BGSX | Cessna F.152 | Holmes Rentals |
| | G-BGSY | GA-7 Cougar | Van Allen Ltd/Guernsey |
| | G-BGTB | SOCATA TB.10 Tobago ★ | D. Pope (stored) |
| | G-BGTC | Auster AOP.9 (XP282) | P. T. Bolton/Tollerton |
| | G-BGTF | PA-44-180 Seminole | New Guarantee Trust Properties Ltd |
| | G-BGTG | PA-23 Aztec 250F | R. J. Howard/Sherburn |
| | G-BGTI | Piper J-3C-65 Cub | A. P. Broad |
| | G-BGTJ | PA-28 Cherokee 180 | Serendipity Aviation/Staverton |
| | G-BGTK | Cessna FR.182RG | Barmoor Aviation |
| | G-BGTP | Robin HR.100/210 | J. C. Parker |
| | G-BGTR | PA-28 Cherokee 140 | Liverpool Flying School Ltd |
| | G-BGTT | Cessna 310R | Aviation Beauport Ltd/Jersey |
| | G-BGTU | BAC One-Eleven 409AY | Turbo Union Ltd/Filton |
| | G-BGTX | Jodel D.117 | Madley Flying Group/Shobdon |
| | G-BGUA | PA-38-112 Tomahawk | Rhodair Maintenance Ltd/Cardiff |
| | G-BGUB | PA-32 Cherokee Six 300E | R. Howton |
| | G-BGUY | Cameron V-56 balloon | J. L. Guy |
| | G-BGVB | Robin DR.315 | Victor Bravo Group |
| | G-BGVE | CP.1310-C3 Super Emeraude | Victor Echo Group |
| | G-BGVH | Beech 76 Duchess | Velco Marketing |
| | G-BGVK | PA-28-161 Warrior II | D. S. Wells |
| | G-BGVL | PA-38-112 Tomahawk | R. A. Crook/Norwich |
| | G-BGVN | PA-28RT-201 Arrow IV | Essex Aviation Ltd/Stapleford |
| | G-BGVR | Thunder Ax6-56Z balloon | A. N. G. Howie |
| | G-BGVS | Cessna F.172M | P. D. A. Aviation Ltd/Tollerton |
| | G-BGVT | Cessna R.182RG | D. C. Massey |
| | G-BGVU | PA-28 Cherokee 180 | P. E. Toleman |
| | G-BGVV | AA-5A Cheetah | A. H. McVicar |
| | G-BGVW | AA-5A Cheetah | London Aviation Ltd |
| | G-BGVY | AA-5B Tiger | Porter Bell Ltd/Goodwood |
| | G-BGVZ | PA-28-181 Archer II | MS 124 Ltd |
| | G-BGWA | GA-7 Cougar | Lough Erne Aviation Ltd |
| | G-BGWC | Robin DR.400/180 | E. F. Braddon & D. C. Shepherd/ Rochester |
| | G-BGWF | PA-18 Super Cub 150 | D. B. Meeks |
| | G-BGWH | PA-18 Super Cub 150 | Clacton Aero Club (1988) Ltd |
| | G-BGWI | Cameron V-65 balloon | Army Balloon Club/Germany |
| | G-BGWJ | Sikorsky S-61N | British Executive Air Services Ltd |

| Reg. | Type | Owner or Operator | Notes |
|------|------|-------------------|-------|
| G-BGWK | Sikorsky S-61N | Bristow Helicopters Ltd | |
| G-BGWM | PA-28-181 Archer II | Thames Valley Flying Club Ltd | |
| G-BGWN | PA-38-112 Tomahawk | Teesside Flight Centre Ltd | |
| G-BGWO | Jodel D.112 | K. McBride | |
| G-BGWS | Enstrom 280C Shark | Parish Developments Ltd | |
| G-BGWU | PA-38-112 Tomahawk | R. J. Howard | |
| G-BGWV | Aeronca 7AC Champion | RFC Flying Group/Popham | |
| G-BGWW | PA-23 Turbo Aztec 250E | L. B. Pegg | |
| G-BGWY | Thunder Ax6-56Z balloon | J. G. O'Connel | |
| G-BGWZ | Eclipse Super Eagle ★ | FAA Museum/Yeovilton | |
| G-BGXA | Piper J-3C-65 Cub (329471) | K. Nicholls | |
| G-BGXB | PA-38-112 Tomahawk | AT Aviation Ltd/Cardiff | |
| G-BGXC | SOCATA TB.10 Tobago | N. N. Tullah/Cranfield | |
| G-BGXD | SOCATA TB.10 Tobago | Selles Dispensing Chemists Ltd | |
| G-BGXJ | Partenavia P.68B | Cecil Aviation Ltd/Cambridge | |
| G-BGXK | Cessna 310R | Air Service Training Ltd/Perth | |
| G-BGXL | Bensen B.8MV | B. P. Triefus | |
| G-BGXN | PA-38-112 Tomahawk | Panshanger School of Flying Ltd | |
| G-BGXO | PA-38-112 Tomahawk | Goodwood Terrena Ltd | |
| G-BGXP | Westland-Bell 47G-3B1 | Ace Motor Salvage (Norfolk) | |
| G-BGXR | Robin HR.200/100 | J. P. Kistner & E. G. Cleobury | |
| G-BGXS | PA-28-236 Dakota | Bawtry Road Service Station Ltd | |
| G-BGXT | SOCATA TB.10 Tobago | D. A. H. Morris | |
| G-BGXU | WMB-1 balloon | C. J. Dodd & ptnrs | |
| G-BGXZ | Cessna FA.152 | Alouette Flying Club Ltd/Biggin Hill | |
| G-BGYG | PA-28-161 Warrior II | C.S.E. Aviation Ltd/Kidlington | |
| G-BGYH | PA-28-161 Warrior II | C.S.E. Aviation Ltd/Kidlington | |
| G-BGYJ | Boeing 737-204ADV | Britannia Airways Ltd Sir Barnes Wallis | |
| G-BGYK | Boeing 737-204ADV | Britannia Airways Ltd R. J. Mitchell | |
| G-BGYN | PA-18 Super Cub 150 | A. G. Walker | |
| G-BGYR | H.S.125 Srs 600B | British Aerospace PLC/Warton | |
| G-BGYT | EMB-110P1 Bandeirante | — | |
| G-BGYV | EMB-110P1 Bandeirante | — | |
| G-BGZF | PA-38-112 Tomahawk | Cambrian Flying Club/Swansea | |
| G-BGZJ | PA-38-112 Tomahawk | W. R. C. M. Foyle | |
| G-BGZK | Westland-Bell 47G-3B1 | Dawnville Ltd | |
| G-BGZL | Eiri PIK-20E | G-BGZL Flying Group/Enstone | |
| G-BGZN | WMB.2 Windtracker balloon | S. R. Woolfries | |
| G-BGZO | M.S.880B Rallye Club | G-BGZO Flying Group | |
| G-BGZR | Meagher Model balloon Mk.1 | S. C. Meagher | |
| G-BGZS | Keirs Heated Air Tube | M. N. J. Kirby | |
| G-BGZW | PA-38-112 Tomahawk | Ravenair Ltd/Manchester | |
| G-BGZY | Jodel D.120 | M. Hale | |
| G-BGZZ | Thunder Ax6-56 balloon | J. M. Robinson | |
| | | | |
| G-BHAA | Cessna 152 | Herefordshire Aero Club Ltd/Shobdon | |
| G-BHAC | Cessna A.152 | Herefordshire Aero Club Ltd/Shobdon | |
| G-BHAD | Cessna A.152 | Shropshire Aero Club Ltd/Sleap | |
| G-BHAF | PA-38-112 Tomahawk | Notelevel Ltd | |
| G-BHAI | Cessna F.152 | P. P. D. Howard-Johnston/Edinburgh | |
| G-BHAJ | Robin DR.400/160 | Rowantask Ltd | |
| G-BHAL | Rango Saffery S.200 SS | A. M. Lindsay Anneky Panky | |
| G-BHAM | Thunder Ax6-56 balloon | D. Sampson | |
| G-BHAR | Westland-Bell 47G-3B1 | E. A. L. Sturmer | |
| G-BHAT | Thunder Ax7-77 balloon | C. P. Witter Ltd Witter | |
| G-BHAV | Cessna F.152 | Iceni Leasing | |
| G-BHAW | Cessna F.172N | K. E. Willis/Manston | |
| G-BHAX | Enstrom F-28C-UK-2 | PVS (Barnsley) Ltd | |
| G-BHAY | PA-28RT-201 Arrow IV | Alpha Yankee Group/Newcastle | |
| G-BHBA | Campbell Cricket | S. M. Irwin | |
| G-BHBB | Colt 77A balloon | S. D. Bellew | |
| G-BHBE | Westland-Bell 47G-3B1 (Soloy) | T. R. Smith (Agricultural Machinery) Ltd | |
| G-BHBF | Sikorsky S-76A | Bristow Helicopters Ltd | |
| G-BHBG | PA-32R Cherokee Lance 300 | R. W. F. Warner | |
| G-BHBI | Mooney M.20J | B. K. Arthur/Exeter | |
| G-BHBL | L.1011-385 TriStar 200 | British Airways Largs Bay | |
| G-BHBM | L.1011-385 TriStar 200 | British Airways Poole Bay | |
| G-BHBN | L.1011-385 TriStar 200 | British Airways Bideford Bay | |
| G-BHBO | L.1011-385 TriStar 200 | British Airways St Magnus Bay | |
| G-BHBR | L.1011-385 TriStar 200 | British Airways Bude Bay | |
| G-BHBS | PA-28RT-201T Turbo Arrow IV | B. C. Oates/Barton | |
| G-BHBT | Marquart MA.5 Charger | R. G. & C. J. Maidment/Shoreham | |
| G-BHBZ | Partenavia P.68B | T. Hayselden (Doncaster) Ltd | |

| Notes | Reg. | Type | Owner or Operator |
|-------|------|------|-------------------|
| | G-BHCC | Cessna 172M | T. Howard |
| | G-BHCE | Jodel D.112 | D. M. Parsons |
| | G-BHCF | WMB.2 Windtracker balloon | C. J. Dodd & ptnrs |
| | G-BHCM | Cessna F.172H | The English Connection Ltd/Panshanger |
| | G-BHCP | Cessna F.152 | Sherburn Aero Club Ltd |
| | G-BHCW | PA-22 Tri-Pacer 150 | B. Brooks |
| | G-BHCX | Cessna F.152 | A. S. Bamrah/Biggin Hill |
| | G-BHCZ | PA-38-112 Tomahawk | J. E. Abbott |
| | G-BHDD | V.668 Varsity T.1 (WL626) ★ | Aeropark/E. Midlands |
| | G-BHDE | SOCATA TB.10 Tobago | A. A. Dooley/Popham |
| | G-BHDH | Douglas DC-10-30 | British Airways Benmore Forest/Gatwick |
| | G-BHDI | Douglas DC-10-30 | British Airways Forest of Ae/Gatwick |
| | G-BHDJ | Douglas DC-10-30 | British Airways Glengap Forest/Gatwick |
| | G-BHDK | Boeing B-29A-BN (461748) ★ | Imperial War Museum/Duxford |
| | G-BHDL | Bell 212 | Bristow Helicopters Ltd |
| | G-BHDM | Cessna F.152 II | Tayside Aviation Ltd/Dundee |
| | G-BHDP | Cessna F.182Q II | P. S. Blackledge |
| | G-BHDR | Cessna F.152 II | Tayside Aviation Ltd/Dundee |
| | G-BHDS | Cessna F.152 II | Tayside Aviation Ltd/Dundee |
| | G-BHDT | SOCATA TB.10 Tobago | R. D. Hill |
| | G-BHDU | Cessna F.152 II | Falcon Flying Services/Biggin Hill |
| | G-BHDV | Cameron V-77 balloon | P. Glydon |
| | G-BHDW | Cessna F.152 | Tayside Aviation Ltd/Dundee |
| | G-BHDX | Cessna F.172N | Skyhawk DX Group |
| | G-BHDZ | Cessna F.172N | J. B. Roberts |
| | G-BHEC | Cessna F.152 | W. R. C. Foyle |
| | G-BHED | Cessna FA.152 | TG Aviation Ltd/Manston |
| | G-BHEG | Jodel D.150 | P. R. Underhill |
| | G-BHEH | Cessna 310G | Thorney Machinery Co Ltd/Conington |
| | G-BHEK | CP.1315-C3 Super Emeraude | D. B. Winstanley/Barton |
| | G-BHEL | Jodel D.117 | J. F. Dowe |
| | G-BHEM | Bensen B.8M | A. M. Sands |
| | G-BHEN | Cessna FA.152 | Leicestershire Aero Club Ltd |
| | G-BHEO | Cessna FR.182RG | M. C. Costin |
| | G-BHEP | Cessna 172 RG Cutlass | Full Sutton Flying Centre Ltd |
| | G-BHER | SOCATA TB.10 Tobago | Vale Aviation Ltd |
| | G-BHET | SOCATA TB.10 Tobago | Claude Hooper Ltd |
| | G-BHEU | Thunder Ax7-65 balloon | M. H. R. Govett |
| | G-BHEV | PA-28R Cherokee Arrow 200 | E. & G. H. Kelk |
| | G-BHEX | Colt 56A balloon | A. S. Dear & ptnrs Super Wasp |
| | G-BHEZ | Jodel D.150 | D. R. Elpick/O. Warden |
| | G-BHFC | Cessna F.152 | T. G. Aviation Ltd/Manston |
| | G-BHFE | PA-44-180 Seminole | Grunwick Ltd/Elstree |
| | G-BHFF | Jodel D.112 | P. J. Swain |
| | G-BHFG | SNCAN Stampe SV-4C (45) | Stormswift Ltd |
| | G-BHFH | PA-34-200T Seneca II | Hendefern Ltd/Goodwood |
| | G-BHFI | Cessna F.152 | BAe (Warton) Flying Group/Blackpool |
| | G-BHFJ | PA-28RT-201T Turbo Arrow IV | T. L. P. Delaney |
| | G-BHFK | PA-28-151 Warrior | Ilkeston Car Sales Ltd |
| | G-BHFM | Murphy S.200 balloon | M. Murphy |
| | G-BHFR | Eiri PIK-20E-1 | J. MacWilliam & T. Dalrymple-Smith |
| | G-BHFS | Robin DR.400/180 | D. S. Chandler |
| | G-BHGA | PA-31-310 Turbo Navajo | Heltor Ltd |
| | G-BHGC | PA-18 Super Cub 150 | Portsmouth Naval Gliding Club/ Lee-on-Solent |
| | G-BHGF | Cameron V-56 balloon | P. Smallward |
| | G-BHGJ | Jodel D.120 | Q. M. B. Oswell |
| | G-BHGK | Sikorsky S-76A | Bond Helicopters Ltd |
| | G-BHGM | Beech 76 Duchess | T. Hayselden |
| | G-BHGO | PA-32 Cherokee Six 260 | Sydney House Communities/Manston |
| | G-BHGP | SOCATA TB.10 Tobago | C. Flanagan |
| | G-BHGX | Colt 56B balloon | M. N. Dixon |
| | G-BHGY | PA-28R Cherokee Arrow 200 | V. Humphries/Gamston |
| | G-BHHB | Cameron V-77 balloon | R. Powell & K. G. Betts |
| | G-BHHE | Jodel DR.1051/M1 | P. Bridges |
| | G-BHHG | Cessna F.152 | Northamptonshire School of Flying Ltd/ Sywell |
| | G-BHHH | Thunder Ax7-65 balloon | C. A. Hendley (Essex) Ltd |
| | G-BHHI | Cessna F.152 | Semloh Aviation Services/Andrewsfield |
| | G-BHHK | Cameron N-77 balloon | I. S. Bridge |
| | G-BHHN | Cameron V-77 balloon | Itchen Valley Balloon Group |
| | G-BHHU | Short SD3-30 | Gill Aviation Ltd/Newcastle |
| | G-BHHX | Jodel D.112 | D. I. Walker |

| Reg. | Type | Owner or Operator | Notes |
|---|---|---|---|
| G-BHHZ | Rotorway Scorpion 133 | L. W. & O. Usherwood | |
| G-BHIB | Cessna F.182Q | Gogood Ltd | |
| G-BHIC | Cessna F.182Q | General Building Services Ltd/Leeds | |
| G-BHIG | Colt 31A balloon | P. A. Lindstrand | |
| G-BHIH | Cessna F.172N | K. R. Gough & W. J. Baker | |
| G-BHII | Cameron V-77 balloon | R. V. Brown | |
| G-BHIJ | Eiri PIK-20E-1 | I. W. Patterson | |
| G-BHIK | Adam RA-14 Loisirs | L. Lewis | |
| G-BHIN | Cessna F.152 | P. Skinner/Netherthorpe | |
| G-BHIR | PA-28R Cherokee Arrow 200 | Lightstrong Ltd/Manchester | |
| G-BHIS | Thunder Ax7-65 balloon | Hedgehoppers Balloon Group | |
| G-BHIT | SOCATA TB.9 Tampico | Air Touring Services Ltd/Biggin Hill | |
| G-BHIY | Cessna F.150K | Westfield Flying Group | |
| G-BHJA | Cessna A.152 | Cornwall Flying Club Ltd/Bodmin | |
| G-BHJB | Cessna A.152 | Thruxton Flight Centre Ltd | |
| G-BHJF | SOCATA TB.10 Tobago | D. G. Dedman/Leavesden | |
| G-BHJI | Mooney M.20J | S. F. Lister | |
| G-BHJK | Maule M5-235C Lunar Rocket | P. F. Hall & R. L. Sambell/Coventry | |
| G-BHJN | Fournier RF-4D | RF-4 Flying Group | |
| G-BHJO | PA-28-161 Warrior II | Inverness Flying Services Ltd | |
| G-BHJS | Partenavia P.68B | Sound Technology PLC | |
| G-BHJU | Robin DR.400/2+2 | Harlow Transport Services Ltd/Headcorn | |
| G-BHJZ | EMB-110P2 Bandeirante | Streamline Aviation/E. Midlands | |
| G-BHKA | Evans VP-1 | M. L. Perry | |
| G-BHKH | Cameron O-65 balloon | D. G. Body | |
| G-BHKJ | Cessna 421C | Crosslee PLC | |
| G-BHKR | Colt 12A balloon ★ | British Balloon Museum | |
| G-BHKT | Jodel D.112 | M. L. & P. J. Moore | |
| G-BHKV | AA-5A Cheetah | Alouette Flying Club Ltd/Biggin Hill | |
| G-BHKX | Beech 76 Duchess | Jetstream Air Couriers Ltd | |
| G-BHKY | Cessna 310R II | Air Service Training Ltd/Perth | |
| G-BHLE | Robin DR.400/180 | L. H. Mayall | |
| G-BHLH | Robin DR.400/180 | W. A. Clark | |
| G-BHLJ | Saffery-Rigg S.200 balloon | I. A. Rigg | |
| G-BHLK | GA-7 Cougar | Autair Ltd | |
| G-BHLT | D.H.82A Tiger Moth | P. J. & A. J. Borsberry | |
| G-BHLU | Fournier RF-3 | M. C. Roper | |
| G-BHLW | Cessna 120 | R. E. & E. P. Nerou | |
| G-BHLX | AA-5B Tiger | Tiger Aviation (Jersey) Ltd | |
| G-BHLY | Sikorsky S-76A | Bristow Helicopters Ltd | |
| G-BHMA | SIPA 903 | H. J. Taggart | |
| G-BHMC | M.S.880B Rallye Club | The G-BHMC Group | |
| G-BHME | WMB.2 Windtracker balloon | I. R. Bell & ptnrs | |
| G-BHMG | Cessna FA.152 | R. D. Smith | |
| G-BHMI | Cessna F.172N | W. Lancs Aero Club Ltd (G-WADE)/ Woodvale | |
| G-BHMJ | Avenger T.200-2112 balloon | R. Light *Lord Anthony 1* | |
| G-BHMK | Avenger T.200-2112 balloon | P. Kinder *Lord Anthony 2* | |
| G-BHML | Avenger T.200-2112 balloon | L. Caulfield *Lord Anthony 3* | |
| G-BHMM | Avenger T.200-2112 balloon | M. Murphy *Lord Anthony 4* | |
| G-BHMO | PA-20M Cerpa Special (Pacer) | A. B. Holloway & ptnrs | |
| G-BHMR | Stinson 108-3 | D. G. French/Sandown | |
| G-BHMT | Evans VP-1 | P. E. J. Sturgeon | |
| G-BHMU | Colt 21A balloon | J. R. Parkington & Co Ltd | |
| G-BHMW | F.27 Friendship Mk 200 | Air UK *Amy Johnson*/Norwich | |
| G-BHMX | F.27 Friendship Mk 200 | Air UK *Fred Truman*/Norwich | |
| G-BHMY | F.27 Friendship Mk 200 | Air UK/Norwich | |
| G-BHMZ | F.27 Friendship Mk 200 | Air UK *R. J. Mitchell*/Norwich | |
| G-BHNA | Cessna F.152 | Sheffield Aero Club Ltd/Netherthorpe | |
| G-BHNC | Cameron O-65 balloon | D. & C. Bareford | |
| G-BHND | Cameron N-65 balloon | Hunter & Sons (Wells) Ltd | |
| G-BHNL | Jodel D.112 | G. van der Gaag | |
| G-BHNM | PA-44-180 Seminole | Standby One Flight Services Ltd | |
| G-BHNO | PA-28-181 Archer II | Davison Plant Hire Co/Compton Abbas | |
| G-BHNP | Eiri PIK-20E-1 | J. T. Morgan | |
| G-BHNU | Cessna F.172N | B. Swindell (Haulage) Ltd/Barton | |
| G-BHNV | Westland-Bell 47G-3B1 | Leyline Helicopters Ltd | |
| G-BHNX | Jodel D.117 | R. V. Rendall | |
| G-BHOA | Robin DR.400/160 | M. J. Ferguson | |
| G-BHOF | Sikorsky S-61N | Bristow Helicopters Ltd | |
| G-BHOG | Sikorsky S-61N | Bristow Helicopters Ltd | |
| G-BHOH | Sikorsky S-61N | Bristow Helicopters Ltd | |
| G-BHOL | Jodel DR.1050 | D. G. Hart | |

| Notes | Reg. | Type | Owner or Operator |
|---|---|---|---|
| | G-BHOM | PA-18 Super Cub 95 | C. H. A. Bott |
| | G-BHOO | Thunder Ax7-65 balloon | D. Livesey & J. M. Purves *Scraps* |
| | G-BHOP | Thunder Ax3 balloon | B. Meeson |
| | G-BHOR | PA-28-161 Warrior II. | Oscar Romeo Flying Group/Biggin Hill |
| | G-BHOT | Cameron V-65 balloon | Dante Balloon Group |
| | G-BHOU | Cameron V-65 balloon | F. W. Barnes |
| | G-BHOW | Beech 95-58PA Baron | Anglo-African Machinery Ltd/Coventry |
| | G-BHOZ | SOCATA TB.9 Tampico | M. Brown |
| | G-BHPJ | Eagle Microlite | G. Breen/Enstone |
| | G-BHPK | Piper J-3C-65 Cub (236800) | H. W. Sage/Sywell |
| | G-BHPL | C.A.S.A. 1.131E Jungmann | M. G. Jeffries |
| | G-BHPM | PA-18 Super Cub 95 | P. I. Morgans |
| | G-BHPO | Colt 14A balloon | C. J. Boxall |
| | G-BHPS | Jodel D.120A | J. P. Leigh |
| | G-BHPT | Piper J-3C-65 Cub | D. I. Cooke |
| | G-BHPX | Cessna 152 | J. A. Pothecary/Shoreham |
| | G-BHPY | Cessna 152 | Cloudshire Ltd/Wellesbourne |
| | G-BHPZ | Cessna 172N | O'Brian Properties Ltd/Redhill |
| | G-BHRA | R. Commander 114A | P. A. Warner |
| | G-BHRB | Cessna F.152 | Howells Group PLC |
| | G-BHRC | PA-28-161 Warrior II | Sherwood Flying Club Ltd/Tollerton |
| | G-BHRD | D.H.C.1 Chipmunk 22 (WP977) | A. J. Dunstan & P. R. Joshua/Kidlington |
| | G-BHRH | Cessna FA.150K | Merlin Flying Club Ltd/Hucknall |
| | G-BHRI | Saffery S.200 balloon | N. J. & H. L. Dunnington |
| | G-BHRM | Cessna F.152 | Aerohire Ltd/Halfpenny Green |
| | G-BHRN | Cessna F.152 | J. Easson/Edinburgh |
| | G-BHRO | R. Commander 112A | John Raymond Transport Ltd/Cardiff |
| | G-BHRP | PA-44-180 Seminole | E. Midlands Flying School Ltd |
| | G-BHRR | CP.301A Emeraude | T. W. Offen |
| | G-BHRW | Jodel DR.221 | Dauphin Flying Group |
| | G-BHRY | Colt 56A balloon | A. S. Davidson |
| | G-BHSA | Cessna 152 | Skyviews & General Ltd/Sherburn |
| | G-BHSB | Cessna 172N | Saunders Caravans Ltd |
| | G-BHSD | Scheibe SF.25E Super Falke | Lasham Gliding Soc Ltd |
| | G-BHSE | R. Commander 114 | 604 Sqdn Flying Group Ltd |
| | G-BHSL | C.A.S.A. 1.131 Jungmann | Cotswold Flying Group |
| | G-BHSN | Cameron N-56 balloon | I. Bentley |
| | G-BHSP | Thunder Ax7-77Z balloon | Out-Of-The-Blue |
| | G-BHSS | Pitts S-1C Special | C. I. Fray |
| | G-BHST | Hughes 369D | Acme Jewellery Ltd |
| | G-BHSU | H.S.125 Srs 700B | Shell Aircraft Ltd/Heathrow |
| | G-BHSV | H.S.125 Srs 700B | Shell Aircraft Ltd/Heathrow |
| | G-BHSW | H.S.125 Srs 700B | Shell Aircraft Ltd/Heathrow |
| | G-BHSY | Jodel DR.1050 | S. R. Orwin & T. R. Allebone |
| | G-BHTA | PA-28-236 Dakota | Dakota Ltd |
| | G-BHTC | Jodel DR.1050/M1 | G. Clark |
| | G-BHTD | Cessna T.188C AgHusky | ADS (Aerial) Ltd/Southend |
| | G-BHTG | Thunder Ax6-56 balloon | F. R. & Mrs S. H. MacDonald |
| | G-BHTH | NA T-6G Texan (2807) | J. J. Woodhouse |
| | G-BHTJ | H.S.125 Srs 700B | British Aerospace PLC (G-BRDI/ G-HHOI) |
| | G-BHTM | Cameron 80 Can SS balloon | BP Oil Ltd |
| | G-BHTR | Bell 206B JetRanger 3 | Huktra (UK) Ltd |
| | G-BHTT | Cessna 500 Citation | Paycourt Ltd |
| | G-BHTV | Cessna 310R | Brenair Ltd/Cardiff |
| | G-BHUB | Douglas C-47A (315509) ★ | Imperial War Museum/Duxford |
| | G-BHUE | Jodel DR.1050 | M. J. Harris |
| | G-BHUG | Cessna 172N | P. Hartley |
| | G-BHUI | Cessna 152 | Cheshire Air Training School Ltd |
| | G-BHUJ | Cessna 172N | Three Counties Aero Engineering Ltd/ Lasham |
| | G-BHUM | D.H.82A Tiger Moth | S. G. Towers |
| | G-BHUO | Evans VP-2 | D. A. Wood |
| | G-BHUP | Cessna F.152 | Stapleford Flying Club Ltd |
| | G-BHUR | Thunder Ax3 balloon | B. F. G. Ribbons |
| | G-BHUU | PA-25 Pawnee 235 | Pawnee Aviation/Boston |
| | G-BHVB | PA-28-161 Warrior II | Bobbington Air Training School Ltd/ Halfpenny Green |
| | G-BHVC | Cessna 172RG Cutlass | I. B. Willis/Panshanger |
| | G-BHVE | Saffery S.330 balloon | P. M. Randles |
| | G-BHVF | Jodel D.150A | C. A. Parker & ptnrs/Sywell |
| | G-BHVN | Cessna 152 | Three Counties Aero Engineering Ltd/ Lasham |

| Reg. | Type | Owner or Operator | Notes |
|------|------|-------------------|-------|
| G-BHVP | Cessna 182Q | Air Tows/Lasham | |
| G-BHVR | Cessna 172N | Three Counties Aero Engineering Ltd/ Lasham | |
| G-BHVV | Piper J-3C-65 Cub | W. A. N. Jenkins | |
| G-BHVZ | Cessna 180 | R. Moore/Blackpool | |
| G-BHWA | Cessna F.152 | Wickenby Aviation Ltd | |
| G-BHWB | Cessna F.152 | Wickenby Aviation Ltd | |
| G-BHWE | Boeing 737-204ADV | Britannia Airways Ltd/Sir Sidney Camm | |
| G-BHWF | Boeing 737-204ADV | Britannia Airways Ltd/Lord Brabazon of Tara | |
| G-BHWG | Mahatma S.200SR balloon | H. W. Gandy Spectrum | |
| G-BHWH | Weedhopper JC-24A | G. A. Clephane | |
| G-BHWK | M.S.880B Rallye Club | Arrow Flying Group | |
| G-BHWN | WMB.3 Windtracker 200 balloon | C. J. Dodd & G. J. Luckett | |
| G-BHWS | Cessna F.152 | Turnhouse Flying Club | |
| G-BHWW | Cessna U.206G | Fife Airport Management Ltd | |
| G-BHWY | PA-28R Cherokee Arrow 200-II | Piper Arrow Group | |
| G-BHWZ | PA-28-181 Archer II | I. R. McCue | |
| G-BHXA | SA Bulldog Srs 120/1210 | SAYF Aviation Ltd | |
| G-BHXB | SA Bulldog Srs 120/1210 | SAYF Aviation Ltd | |
| G-BHXD | Jodel D.120 | K. B. Sutton & D. R. Taylor/Cranfield | |
| G-BHXK | PA-28 Cherokee 140 | GXK Flying Group | |
| G-BHXL | Evans VP-2 | R. S. Wharton | |
| G-BHXS | Jodel D.120 | I. R. Willis | |
| G-BHXT | Thunder Ax6-56Z balloon | Ocean Traffic Services Ltd | |
| G-BHXU | AB-206B JetRanger 3 | Castle Air Charters Ltd | |
| G-BHXV | AB-206B JetRanger 3 | Compass Aviation Ltd (G-OWJM) | |
| G-BHXY | Piper J-3C-65 Cub (44-79609) | Grasshopper Flyers | |
| G-BHYA | Cessna R.182RG II | Stainless Steel Profile Cutters Ltd | |
| G-BHYB | Sikorsky S-76A | British International Helicopters Ltd/ Beccles | |
| G-BHYC | Cessna 172RG Cutlass | J. D. B. Hamilton & J. McW. Henderson | |
| G-BHYD | Cessna R.172K XP II | Sylmar Aviation Services Ltd | |
| G-BHYE | PA-34-200T Seneca II | C.S.E. Aviation Ltd/Kidlington | |
| G-BHYF | PA-34-200T Seneca II | C.S.E. Aviation Ltd/Kidlington | |
| G-BHYG | PA-34-200T Seneca II | C.S.E. Aviation Ltd/Kidlington | |
| G-BHYI | SNCAN Stampe SV-4A | P. A. Irwin | |
| G-BHYN | Evans VP-2 | D. Cromie | |
| G-BHYO | Cameron N-77 balloon | C. Sisson | |
| G-BHYP | Cessna F.172M | G-BHYP Flying Group/Blackpool | |
| G-BHYR | Cessna F.172M | Alumvale Ltd/Stapleford | |
| G-BHYV | Evans VP-1 | L. Chiappi/Blackpool | |
| G-BHYW | AB-206B JetRanger | Lakeside Helicopters Ltd | |
| G-BHYX | Cessna 152 II | Stapleford Flying Club Ltd | |
| G-BHZE | PA-28-181 Archer II | Northfield Garage Ltd | |
| G-BHZF | Evans VP-2 | P. Jenkins | |
| G-BHZH | Cessna F.152 | 1013 Ltd/Guernsey | |
| G-BHZK | AA-5B Tiger | N. K. Margolis/Elstree | |
| G-BHZM | Jodel DR.1050 | G. H. Wylde/Manchester | |
| G-BHZO | AA-5A Cheetah | Scotia Safari Ltd/Prestwick | |
| G-BHZR | SA Bulldog Srs 120/1210 | SAYF Aviation Ltd | |
| G-BHZS | SA Bulldog Srs 120/1210 | SAYF Aviation Ltd | |
| G-BHZT | SA Bulldog Srs 120/1210 | SAYF Aviation Ltd | |
| G-BHZU | Piper J-3C-65 Cub | J. K. Tomkinson | |
| G-BHZV | Jodel D.120A | J. G. Munro/Perth | |
| G-BHZX | Thunder Ax7-65A balloon | R. J. & H. M. Beattie | |
| G-BIAA | SOCATA TB.9 Tampico | T. Smith | |
| G-BIAB | SOCATA TB.9 Tampico | H. W. A. Thirlway | |
| G-BIAC | SOCATA Rallye 235E | Anpal Finance Ltd & Aerial Facilities Ltd/ Biggin Hill | |
| G-BIAH | Jodel D.112 | D. Mitchell | |
| G-BIAI | WMB.2 Windtracker balloon | I. Chadwick | |
| G-BIAK | SOCATA TB.10 Tobago | Air Tobago Ltd | |
| G-BIAL | Rango NA.8 balloon | A. M. Lindsay | |
| G-BIAO | Evans VP-2 | P. J. Hall | |
| G-BIAP | PA-16 Clipper | I. M. Callier & P. J. Bish/White Waltham | |
| G-BIAR | Rigg Skyliner II balloon | I. A. Rigg | |
| G-BIAU | Sopwith Pup (replica) (N6452) | FAA Museum/Yeovilton | |
| G-BIAX | Taylor JT.2 Titch | G. F. Rowley | |
| G-BIAY | AA-5 Traveler | M. D. Dupay & ptnrs | |
| G-BIBA | SOCATA TB.9 Tampico | TB Aviation Ltd | |
| G-BIBB | Mooney M.20C | J. R. Gardiner | |
| G-BIBC | Cessna 310R | Air Service Training Ltd/Perth | |

| Notes | Reg. | Type | Owner or Operator |
|---|---|---|---|
| | G-BIBD | Rotec Rally 2B | A. Clarke |
| | G-BIBG | Sikorsky S-76A | Bristow Helicopters Ltd |
| | G-BIBJ | Enstrom 280C-UK-2 Shark | Tindon Ltd/Little Snoring |
| | G-BIBK | Taylor JT.2 Titch | J. G. McTaggart |
| | G-BIBN | Cessna FA.150K | P. H. Lewis |
| | G-BIBO | Cameron V-65 balloon | I. Harris |
| | G-BIBP | AA-5A Cheetah | Scotia Safari Ltd/Prestwick |
| | G-BIBS | Cameron P-20 balloon | Cameron Balloons Ltd |
| | G-BIBT | AA-5B Tiger | Fergusons (Blyth) Ltd/Newcastle |
| | G-BIBU | Morris Ax7-77 balloon | K. Morris |
| | G-BIBV | WMB.3 Windtracker balloon | P. B. Street |
| | G-BIBW | Cessna F.172N | Deltair Ltd/Chester |
| | G-BIBX | WMB.2 Windtracker balloon | I. A. Rigg |
| | G-BIBY | Beech F33A Bonanza | Baythorne Ltd/Fairoaks |
| | G-BIBZ | Thunder Ax3 balloon | F. W. Barnes |
| | G-BICC | Vulture Tx3 balloon | C. P. Clitheroe |
| | G-BICD | Auster 5 | R. T. Parsons |
| | G-BICE | AT-6C Harvard IIA (41-33275) | C. M. L. Edwards/Ipswich |
| | G-BICG | Cessna F.152 | Falcon Flying Services/Biggin Hill |
| | G-BICJ | Monnet Sonerai II | D. J. Marks |
| | G-BICM | Colt 56A balloon | Avon Advertiser Balloon Club |
| | G-BICN | F.8L Falco | R. J. Barber |
| | G-BICP | Robin DR.360 | Bravo India Flying Group/Woodvale |
| | G-BICR | Jodel D.120A | Beehive Flying Group/White Waltham |
| | G-BICS | Robin R.2100A | G-BICS Group/Sibson |
| | G-BICT | Evans VP-1 | A. S. Coombe & D. L. Tribe |
| | G-BICU | Cameron V-56 balloon | K. C. Tanner |
| | G-BICW | PA-28-161 Warrior II | D. Gellhorn |
| | G-BICX | Maule M5-235C Lunar Rocket | A. T. Jeans & I. Best-Devereux/Old Sarum |
| | G-BICY | PA-23 Apache 160 | A. M. Lynn/Sibson |
| | G-BIDD | Evans VP-1 | T. Edwards |
| | G-BIDE | CP.301A Emeraude | D. Elliott |
| | G-BIDF | Cessna F.172P | J. J. Baumhardt/Southend |
| | G-BIDG | Jodel D.150A | D. R. Gray/Barton |
| | G-BIDH | Cessna 152 II | Cumbria Aero Club (G-DONA)/Carlisle |
| | G-BIDI | PA-28R-201 Arrow III | LBE Contract Tooling Ltd |
| | G-BIDJ | PA-18A Super Cub 150 | AB Plant (Bristol) Ltd |
| | G-BIDK | PA-18 Super Cub 150 | Scottish Gliding Union Ltd |
| | G-BIDM | Cessna F.172H | *(stored)*/Ingoldmells |
| | G-BIDO | CP.301A Emeraude | A. R. Plumb |
| | G-BIDP | PA-28-181 Archer II | Sky Aviation Ltd |
| | G-BIDU | Cameron V-77 balloon | E. Eleazor |
| | G-BIDV | Colt 14A balloon | International Distillers & Vintners (House Trade) Ltd |
| | G-BIDW | Sopwith 11/2 Strutter (replica) (A8226) ★ | RAF Museum/Hendon |
| | G-BIDX | Jodel D.112 | H. N. Nuttall & R. P. Walley |
| | G-BIDY | WMB.2 Windtracker balloon | D. M. Campion |
| | G-BIEC | AB-206A JetRanger 2 | Autair Helicopters Ltd |
| | G-BIEF | Cameron V-77 balloon | D. S. Bush |
| | G-BIEH | Sikorsky S-76A | Bond Helicopters Ltd/Bourn |
| | G-BIEJ | Sikorsky S-76A | Bristow Helicopters Ltd |
| | G-BIEK | WMB.4 Windtracker balloon | P. B. Street |
| | G-BIEN | Jodel D.120A | Echo November Flight/Bristol |
| | G-BIEO | Jodel D.112 | Woodside Flying Group |
| | G-BIES | Maule M5-235C Lunar Rocket | William Proctor Farms |
| | G-BIET | Cameron O-77 balloon | G. M. Westley |
| | G-BIEY | PA-28-151 Warrior | J. A. Pothecary/Shoreham |
| | G-BIFA | Cessna 310R-II | E. A. Pitcher |
| | G-BIFB | PA-28 Cherokee 150 | N. A. Ayub |
| | G-BIFD | R. Commander 114 | D. F. Soul |
| | G-BIFH | Short SD3-30 | Gill Aviation Ltd/Newcastle |
| | G-BIFK | Short SD3-30 | Gill Aviation Ltd/Newcastle |
| | G-BIFN | Bensen B.8M | B. Gunn |
| | G-BIFO | Evans VP-1 | D. J. Rees |
| | G-BIFP | Colt 56C balloon | J. Philp |
| | G-BIFT | Cessna F.150L | Colton Aviation Ltd |
| | G-BIFV | Jodel D.150 | N. A. Smith |
| | G-BIFY | Cessna F.150L | Jureen Aviation |
| | G-BIFZ | Partenavia P.68C | ALY Aviation Ltd/Henstridge |
| | G-BIGD | Cameron V-77 balloon | D. L. Clark *Frog* |
| | G-BIGF | Thunder Ax7-77 balloon | M. D. Stever & C. A. Allen |
| | G-BIGH | Piper J-3C-65 Cub | W. McNally |

| Reg. | Type | Owner or Operator |
|------|------|-------------------|
| G-BIGJ | Cessna F.172M | Clacton Aero Club (1988) Ltd |
| G-BIGK | Taylorcraft BC-12D | H. L. M. & G. R. Williams |
| G-BIGL | Cameron O-65 balloon | P. L. Mossman |
| G-BIGM | Avenger T.200-2112 balloon | M. Murphy |
| G-BIGN | Attic Srs 1 balloon | G. P. Nettleship |
| G-BIGP | Bensen B.8M | R. H. S. Cooper |
| G-BIGR | Avenger T.200-2112 balloon | R. Light |
| G-BIGX | Bensen B.8M | P. R. Moore & M. B. Stone |
| G-BIGY | Cameron V-65 balloon | Dante Balloon Group |
| G-BIGZ | Scheibe SF.25B Falke | G-BIGZ Syndicate |
| G-BIHD | Robin DR.400/160 | Alexander Howden Group Sports & Social Club/Biggin Hill |
| G-BIHE | Cessna FA.152 | Inverness Flying Services Ltd |
| G-BIHF | SE-5A (replica) (F943) | K. J. Garrett *Lady Di*/Booker |
| G-BIHG | PA-28 Cherokee 140 | T. M. Plewman |
| G-BIHH | Sikorsky S-61N | Bristow Helicopters Ltd |
| G-BIHI | Cessna 172M | J. H. Ashley-Rogers |
| G-BIHN | Skyship 500 airship | Airship Industries Ltd/Cardington |
| G-BIHP | Van Den Bemden gas balloon | J. J. Harris |
| G-BIHT | PA-17 Vagabond | G. H. Cork/Burnaston |
| G-BIHU | Saffery S.200 balloon | B. L. King |
| G-BIHW | Aeronca A65TAC Defender | T. J. Ingrouille |
| G-BIHY | Isaacs Fury | P. C. Butler |
| G-BIIA | Fournier RF-3 | T. M. W. Webster |
| G-BIIB | Cessna F.172M | Civil Service Flying Club (Biggin Hill) Ltd |
| G-BIID | PA-18 Super Cub 95 | 875 (Westhill) Squadron ATC/Aberdeen |
| G-BIIE | Cessna F.172P | Shoreham Flight Simulation Ltd/Bournemouth |
| G-BIIF | Fournier RF-4D | J. A. Bridges & J. A. Taylor (G-BVET)/Biggin Hill |
| G-BIIG | Thunder Ax-6-56Z balloon | Chiltern Flyers Ltd |
| G-BIIJ | Cessna F.152 | Leicestershire Aero Club Ltd |
| G-BIIK | M.S.883 Rallye 115 | Chiltern Flyers Ltd |
| G-BIIL | Thunder Ax6-56 balloon | G. W. Reader |
| G-BIIT | PA-28-161 Warrior II | Tayside Aviation Ltd/Dundee |
| G-BIIV | PA-28-181 Archer II | Stratton Motor Co Ltd |
| G-BIIX | Rango NA.12 balloon | Rango Kite Co |
| G-BIIZ | Great Lakes 2T-1A Sport Trainer | J. R. Lindsay/Booker |
| G-BIJB | PA-18 Super Cub 150 | Essex Gliding Club/North Weald |
| G-BIJD | Bo 208C Junior | C. G. Stone |
| G-BIJE | Piper J-3C-65 Cub | R. L. Hayward & A. G. Scott |
| G-BIJS | Luton LA-4A Minor | I. J. Smith |
| G-BIJT | AA-5A Cheetah | Mid-Sussex Timber Co Ltd |
| G-BIJU | CP.301A Emeraude | Eastern Taildraggers Flying Group (G-BHTX) |
| G-BIJV | Cessna F.152 II | Falcon Flying Services/Biggin Hill |
| G-BIJW | Cessna F.152 II | Falcon Flying Services/Biggin Hill |
| G-BIJX | Cessna F.152 II | Civil Service Flying Club (Biggin Hill) Ltd |
| G-BIKA | Boeing 757-236 | British Airways *Dover Castle* |
| G-BIKB | Boeing 757-236 | British Airways *Windsor Castle* |
| G-BIKC | Boeing 757-236 | British Airways *Edinburgh Castle* |
| G-BIKD | Boeing 757-236 | British Airways *Caernarfon Castle* |
| G-BIKE | PA-28R Cherokee Arrow 200 | R. V. Webb Ltd/Elstree |
| G-BIKF | Boeing 757-236 | British Airways *Carrickfergus Castle* |
| G-BIKG | Boeing 757-236 | British Airways *Stirling Castle* |
| G-BIKH | Boeing 757-236 | British Airways *Richmond Castle* |
| G-BIKI | Boeing 757-236 | British Airways *Tintagel Castle* |
| G-BIKJ | Boeing 757-236 | British Airways *Conwy Castle* |
| G-BIKK | Boeing 757-236 | British Airways *Eilean Donan Castle* |
| G-BIKL | Boeing 757-236 | British Airways *Nottingham Castle* |
| G-BIKM | Boeing 757-236 | British Airways *Glamis Castle* |
| G-BIKN | Boeing 757-236 | British Airways *Bodiam Castle* |
| G-BIKO | Boeing 757-236 | British Airways *Harlech Castle* |
| G-BIKP | Boeing 757-236 | British Airways *Enniskillen Castle* |
| G-BIKR | Boeing 757-236 | British Airways *Bamburgh Castle* |
| G-BIKS | Boeing 757-236 | British Airways *Corfe Castle* |
| G-BIKT | Boeing 757-236 | British Airways *Carisbrooke Castle* |
| G-BIKU | Boeing 757-236 | British Airways *Inveraray Castle* |
| G-BIKV | Boeing 757-236 | British Airways *Raglan Castle* |
| G-BIKW | Boeing 757-236 | British Airways *Belvoir Castle* |
| G-BIKX | Boeing 757-236 | British Airways *Warwick Castle* |
| G-BIKY | Boeing 757-236 | British Airways *Leeds Castle* |
| G-BIKZ | Boeing 757-236 | British Airways *Kenilworth Castle* |
| G-BILA | Daletol DM.165L Viking | R. Lamplough (*stored*) |

| Notes | Reg. | Type | Owner or Operator |
|---|---|---|---|
| | G-BILB | WMB.2 Windtracker balloon | B. L. King |
| | G-BILE | Scruggs BL.2B balloon | P. D. Ridout |
| | G-BILF | Practavia Sprite 125 | G. Harfield |
| | G-BILG | Scruggs BL.2B balloon | P. D. Ridout |
| | G-BILI | Piper J-3C-65 Cub (454467) | G-BILI Flying Group |
| | G-BILJ | Cessna FA.152 | Shoreham Flight Simulation Ltd/ Bournemouth |
| | G-BILK | Cessna FA.152 | Exeter Flying Club Ltd |
| | G-BILL | PA-25 Pawnee 235 | Pawnee Aviation |
| | G-BILR | Cessna 152 | Skyviews & General Ltd |
| | G-BILS | Cessna 152 | Skyviews & General Ltd |
| | G-BILU | Cessna 172RG | Full Sutton Flying Centre Ltd |
| | G-BILZ | Taylor JT.1 Monoplane | A. Petherbridge |
| | G-BIMK | Tiger T.200 Srs 1 balloon | M. K. Baron |
| | G-BIMM | PA-18 Super Cub 150 | Clacton Aero Club (1988) Ltd |
| | G-BIMN | Steen Skybolt | C. R. Williamson |
| | G-BIMO | SNCAN Stampe SV-4C | R. A. Roberts |
| | G-BIMT | Cessna FA.152 | Staverton Flying Services Ltd |
| | G-BIMU | Sikorsky S-61N | Bristow Helicopters Ltd |
| | G-BIMX | Rutan Vari-Eze | D. G. Crew/Biggin Hill |
| | G-BIMZ | Beech 76 Duchess | Barrein Engineers Ltd/Lulsgate |
| | G-BINA | Saffery S.9 balloon | A. P. Bashford |
| | G-BINB | WMB.2A Windtracker balloon | S. R. Woolfries |
| | G-BINF | Saffery S.200 balloon | T. Lewis |
| | G-BING | Cessna F.172P | J. E. M. Patrick |
| | G-BINI | Scruggs BL.2C balloon | S. R. Woolfries |
| | G-BINL | Scruggs BL.2B balloon | P. D. Ridout |
| | G-BINM | Scruggs BL.2B balloon | P. D. Ridout |
| | G-BINO | Evans VP-1 | A. M. S. Liggat |
| | G-BINR | Unicorn UE.1A balloon | Unicorn Group |
| | G-BINS | Unicorn UE.2A balloon | Unicorn Group |
| | G-BINT | Unicorn UE.1A balloon | Unicorn Group |
| | G-BINU | Saffery S.200 balloon | T. Lewis |
| | G-BINX | Scruggs BL.2B balloon | P. D. Ridout |
| | G-BINY | Oriental balloon | J. L. Morton |
| | G-BINZ | Rango NA.8 balloon | T. J. Sweeting & M. O. Davies |
| | G-BIOB | Cessna F.172P | Aerofilms Ltd/Elstree |
| | G-BIOC | Cessna F.150L | Seawing Flying Club/Southend |
| | G-BIOE | Short SD3-30 Variant 100 | Gill Aviation Ltd/Newcastle |
| | G-BIOI | Jodel DR.1051/M | H. F. Hambling |
| | G-BIOJ | R. Commander 112TCA | A. T. Dalby |
| | G-BIOK | Cessna F.152 | Tayside Aviation Ltd/Dundee |
| | G-BIOM | Cessna F.152 | Falcon Flying Services/Biggin Hill |
| | G-BION | Cameron V-77 balloon | Flying Doctors Balloon Syndicate |
| | G-BIOO | Unicorn UE.2B balloon | Unicorn Group |
| | G-BIOP | Scruggs BL.2D balloon | J. P. S. Donnellan |
| | G-BIOR | M.S.880B Rallye Club | Aircraft Dept. Royal Aircraft Establishment/ Farnborough |
| | G-BIOU | Jodel D.117A | M. S. Printing & Graphics Machinery Ltd/ Booker |
| | G-BIOW | Slingsby T.67A | A. B. Slinger/Sherburn |
| | G-BIOX | Potter Crompton PRO.1 balloon | G. M. Potter |
| | G-BIPA | AA-5B Tiger | J. Campbell/Walney Island |
| | G-BIPH | Scruggs BL.2B balloon | C. M. Dewsnap |
| | G-BIPI | Everett Blackbird Mk 1 | R. Spall |
| | G-BIPJ | PA-36-375 Brave | G. B. Pearce/Shoreham |
| | G-BIPK | Saffery S.200 balloon | P. J. Kelsey |
| | G-BIPM | Flamboyant Ax7-65 balloon | Pepsi Cola International Ltd/S. Africa |
| | G-BIPN | Fournier RF-3 | S. N. Lawrence |
| | G-BIPO | Mudry/CAARP CAP.20LS-200 | W. Brady/Booker |
| | G-BIPS | SOCATA Rallye 100ST | McAully Flying Group/Little Snoring |
| | G-BIPT | Jodel D.112 | C. R. Davies |
| | G-BIPV | AA-5B Tiger | Solent Flight |
| | G-BIPW | Avenger T.200-2112 balloon | B. L. King |
| | G-BIPY | Bensen B.8 | W. J. Pope |
| | G-BIRA | SOCATA TB.9 Tampico | A. T. Paton |
| | G-BIRD | Pitts S-1C Special | Pitts Artists Flying Group |
| | G-BIRE | Colt 56 Bottle balloon | K. R. Gafney |
| | G-BIRH | PA-18 Super Cub 135 (R-163) | I. R. F. Hammond/Lee-on-Solent |
| | G-BIRI | C.A.S.A. 1.131E Jungmann | M. G. & J. R. Jeffries |
| | G-BIRK | Avenger T.200-2112 balloon | D. Harland |
| | G-BIRL | Avenger T.200-2112 balloon | R. Light |
| | G-BIRM | Avenger T.200-2112 balloon | P. Higgins |

| Reg. | Type | Owner or Operator | Notes |
|------|------|-------------------|-------|
| G-BIRO | Cessna 172P | M. C. Grant | |
| G-BIRP | Arena Mk 17 Skyship balloon | A. S. Viel | |
| G-BIRS | Cessna 182P | John E. Birks & Associates Ltd (G-BBBS) | |
| G-BIRT | Robin R.1180TD | W. D'A. Hall/Booker | |
| G-BIRW | M.S.505 Criquet (F+IS) ★ | Museum of Flight/E. Fortune | |
| G-BIRY | Cameron V-77 balloon | J. J. Winter | |
| G-BIRZ | Zenair CH.250 | A. W. F. Richards | |
| G-BISB | Cessna F.152 II | Sheffield Aero Club Ltd/Netherthorpe | |
| G-BISF | Robinson R-22 | C. R. James | |
| G-BISG | FRED Srs 3 | R. A. Coombe | |
| G-BISH | Cameron O-42 balloon | Zebedee Balloon Service | |
| G-BISJ | Cessna 340A | Billair | |
| G-BISK | R. Commander 112B ★ | P. A. Warner | |
| G-BISL | Scruggs BL.2B balloon | P. D. Ridout | |
| G-BISM | Scruggs BL.2B balloon | P. D. Ridout | |
| G-BISS | Scruggs BL.2C balloon | P. D. Ridout | |
| G-BIST | Scruggs BL.2C balloon | P. D. Ridout | |
| G-BISV | Cameron O-65 balloon | Hylyne Rabbits Ltd | |
| G-BISW | Cameron O-65 balloon | Rango Balloon & Kite Co | |
| G-BISX | Colt 56A balloon | J. R. Gore | |
| G-BISZ | Sikorsky S-76A | Bristow Helicopters Ltd | |
| G-BITA | PA-18 Super Cub 150 | J. & S. A. S. McCullough | |
| G-BITE | SOCATA TB.10 Tobago | M. A. Smith & R. J. Bristow/Fairoaks | |
| G-BITF | Cessna F.152 | Tayside Aviation Ltd/Dundee | |
| G-BITH | Cessna F.152 | Tayside Aviation Ltd/Dundee | |
| G-BITK | FRED Srs 2 | D. J. Wood | |
| G-BITL | Horncastle LL-901 balloon | M. J. Worsdell | |
| G-BITM | Cessna F.172P | D. G. Crabtree/Barton | |
| G-BITO | Jodel D.112D | A. Dunbar/Barton | |
| G-BITR | Sikorsky S-76A | Bristow Helicopters Ltd | |
| G-BITS | Drayton B-56 balloon | M. J. Betts | |
| G-BITW | Short SD3-30 Variant 100 | Celtic Airways Ltd (G-EASI) | |
| G-BITY | FD.31T balloon | A. J. Bell | |
| G-BIUL | Cameron 60 SS balloon | D. C. Patrick-Brown | |
| G-BIUM | Cessna F.152 | Sheffield Aero Club Ltd/Netherthorpe | |
| G-BIUP | SNCAN NC.854S | C. M. Mogg | |
| G-BIUU | PA-23 Aztec 250D ★ | G. Cormack/Glasgow | |
| G-BIUV | H.S.748 Srs 2A | Janes Aviation 748 Ltd (G-AYYH)/ Blackpool | |
| G-BIUW | PA-28-161 Warrior II | D. R. Staley | |
| G-BIUY | PA-28-181 Archer II | W. S. Robertson | |
| G-BIVA | Robin R.2112 | Cotswold Aero Club Ltd/Staverton | |
| G-BIVB | Jodel D.112 | D. H. Anderson | |
| G-BIVC | Jodel D.112 | M. J. Barmby/Cardiff | |
| G-BIVK | Bensen B.8 | J. G. Toy | |
| G-BIVL | Bensen B.8 | R. Gardiner | |
| G-BIVT | Saffery S.80 balloon | L. F. Guyot | |
| G-BIVV | AA-5A Cheetah | W. Dass | |
| G-BIVY | Cessna 172N | Goodwood Aircraft Management Services Ltd | |
| G-BIVZ | D.31A Turbulent | The Tiger Club (1990) Ltd/Headcorn | |
| G-BIWB | Scruggs RS.5000 balloon | P. D. Ridout | |
| G-BIWC | Scruggs RS.5000 balloon | P. D. Ridout | |
| G-BIWD | Scruggs RS.5000 balloon | D. Eaves | |
| G-BIWF | Warren balloon | P. D. Ridout | |
| G-BIWG | Zelenski Mk 2 balloon | P. D. Ridout | |
| G-BIWJ | Unicorn UE.1A balloon | B. L. King | |
| G-BIWK | Cameron V-65 balloon | I. R. Williams & R. G. Bickerdike | |
| G-BIWL | PA-32-301 Saratoga | Harwoods of Essex Ltd | |
| G-BIWN | Jodel D.112 | C. R. Coates | |
| G-BIWP | Mooney M.20J | J. K. McWhinney | |
| G-BIWR | Mooney M.20F | A. C. Brink | |
| G-BIWU | Cameron V-65 balloon | J. T. Whicker & J. W. Unwin | |
| G-BIWW | AA-5 Traveler | B&K Aviation/Cranfield | |
| G-BIWX | AT-16 Harvard IV (FT239) | A. E. Hutton/North Weald | |
| G-BIWY | Westland WG.30 ★ | Instructional airframe/Sherborne | |
| G-BIXA | SOCATA TB.9 Tampico | Lord de Saumarez | |
| G-BIXB | SOCATA TB.9 Tampico | Kitchen Bros/Little Snoring | |
| G-BIXH | Cessna F.152 | Cambridge Aero Club Ltd | |
| G-BIXI | Cessna 172RG Cutlass | J. F. P. Lewis/Sandown | |
| G-BIXJ | Saffery S.40 balloon | T. M. Pates | |
| G-BIXL | P-51D Mustang (472216) | R. Lamplough/North Weald | |
| G-BIXN | Boeing Stearman A.75N1 | I. L. Craig-Wood & ptnrs | |

| Notes | Reg. | Type | Owner or Operator |
|-------|------|------|-------------------|
| | G-BIXR | Cameron A-140 balloon | Skysales Ltd |
| | G-BIXS | Avenger T.200-2112 balloon | M. Stuart |
| | G-BIXV | Bell 212 | Bristow Helicopters Ltd |
| | G-BIXW | Colt 56B balloon | J. R. Birkenhead |
| | G-BIXX | Pearson Srs 2 balloon | D. Pearson |
| | G-BIXZ | Grob G-109 | V. J. R. Day |
| | G-BIYG | Short SD3-30 | Gill Aviation Ltd/Newcastle |
| | G-BIYH | Short SD3-30 | Gill Aviation Ltd/Newcastle |
| | G-BIYI | Cameron V-65 balloon | Sarnia Balloon Group |
| | G-BIYJ | PA-18 Super Cub 95 | S. Russell |
| | G-BIYK | Isaacs Fury | R. S. Martin/Dunkeswell |
| | G-BIYM | PA-32R-301 Saratoga SP | Pinta Investments Ltd |
| | G-BIYO | PA-31-310 Turbo Navajo | Northern Executive Aviation Ltd/ Manchester |
| | G-BIYP | PA-20 Pacer 135 | R. J. Whitcombe |
| | G-BIYR | PA-18 Super Cub 135 | Delta Foxtrot Flying Group/Dunkeswell |
| | G-BIYT | Colt 17A balloon | A. F. Selby |
| | G-BIYU | Fokker S.11.1 Instructor (E-15) | H. R. Smallwood & A. J. Lee/Denham |
| | G-BIYW | Jodel D.112 | Pollard/Balaam/Bye Flying Group |
| | G-BIYX | PA-28 Cherokee 140 | A. Gowlett/Blackpool |
| | G-BIYY | PA-18 Super Cub 95 | A. E. & W. J. Taylor/Ingoldmells |
| | G-BIZF | Cessna F.172P | R. S. Bentley/Bourn |
| | G-BIZG | Cessna F.152 | M. A. Judge |
| | G-BIZI | Robin DR.400/120 | Headcorn Flying School Ltd |
| | G-BIZK | Nord 3202 | A. I. Milne/Swanton Morley |
| | G-BIZM | Nord 3202 | Magnificent Obsessions Ltd |
| | G-BIZN | Slingsby T.67A | L. S. Johnson/Ipswich |
| | G-BIZO | PA-28R Cherokee Arrow 200 | Bowlish Roofing Supplies Ltd |
| | G-BIZR | SOCATA TB.9 Tampico | R. M. Shears (G-BSEC) |
| | G-BIZT | Bensen B.8M | J. Ferguson |
| | G-BIZU | Thunder Ax6-56Z balloon | S. L. Leigh |
| | G-BIZV | PA-18 Super Cub 95 (18-2001) | S. J. Pugh & R. L. Wademan |
| | G-BIZW | Champion 7GCBC Citabria | G. Read & Son |
| | G-BIZY | Jodel D.112 | Wayland Tunley & Associates |
| | | | |
| | G-BJAD | FRED Srs 2 | C. Allison |
| | G-BJAE | Lavadoux Starck AS.80 | D. J. & S. A. E. Phillips/Coventry |
| | G-BJAF | Piper J-3C-65 Cub | P. J. Cottle |
| | G-BJAG | PA-28-181 Archer II | K. F. Hudson & D. J. Casson/Sherburn |
| | G-BJAJ | AA-5B Tiger | A. H. McVicar/Prestwick |
| | G-BJAL | C.A.S.A. 1.131E Jungmann | W. J. Perrins & E. A. C. Elliott |
| | G-BJAN | SA.102-5 Cavalier | J. Powlesland |
| | G-BJAO | Bensen B.8M | G. L. Stockdale |
| | G-BJAP | D.H.82A Tiger Moth | J. A. Pothecary |
| | G-BJAR | Unicorn UE.3A balloon | Unicorn Group |
| | G-BJAS | Rango NA.9 balloon | A. Lindsay |
| | G-BJAV | GY-80 Horizon 160 | T. T. Parr |
| | G-BJAW | Cameron V-65 balloon | G. W. McCarthy |
| | G-BJAX | Pilatus P2-05 (U-108) | Lea Aviation |
| | G-BJAY | Piper J-3C-65 Cub | K. L. Clarke/Ingoldmells |
| | G-BJBI | Cessna 414A | Borfin Ltd/Manchester |
| | G-BJBK | PA-18 Super Cub 95 | M. S. Bird/Old Sarum |
| | G-BJBM | Monnet Sonerai II | J. Pickrell/Southend |
| | G-BJBO | Jodel DR.250/160 | Wiltshire Flying Group |
| | G-BJBP | Beech A200 Super King Air | All Charter Ltd (G-HLUB)/Bournemouth |
| | G-BJBS | Robinson R-22 | R. L. G. Vine |
| | G-BJBV | PA-28-161 Warrior II | C.S.E. Aviation Ltd/Kidlington |
| | G-BJBW | PA-28-161 Warrior II | C.S.E. Aviation Ltd/Kidlington |
| | G-BJBX | PA-28-161 Warrior II | C.S.E. Aviation Ltd/Kidlington |
| | G-BJBY | PA-28-161 Warrior II | C.S.E. Aviation Ltd/Kidlington |
| | G-BJBZ | Rotorway Executive 133 | P. J. D. Kerr |
| | G-BJCA | PA-28-161 Warrior II | D. M. & J. E. Smith |
| | G-BJCD | Bede BD-5BH | Brockmoor-Bede Aircraft (UK) Ltd |
| | G-BJCF | CP.1310-C3 Super Emeraude | K. M. Hodson & C. G. H. Gurney |
| | G-BJCI | PA-18 Super Cub 150 (modified) | The Borders (Milfield) Aero-Tour Club Ltd |
| | G-BJCP | Unicorn UE.2B balloon | Unicorn Group |
| | G-BJCT | Boeing 737-204ADV | Britannia Airways Ltd *The Hon C. S. Rolls* |
| | G-BJCU | Boeing 737-204ADV | Britannia Airways Ltd *Sir Henry Royce* |
| | G-BJCV | Boeing 737-204ADV | Britannia Airways Ltd *Viscount Trenchard* |
| | G-BJCW | PA-32R-301 Saratoga SP | Viscount Chelsea/Kidlington |
| | G-BJDE | Cessna F.172M | H. P. K. Ferdinand/Denham |
| | G-BJDF | M.S.880B Rallye 100T | W. R. Savin & ptnrs |
| | G-BJDI | Cessna FR.182RG | Sunningdale Aviation Services Ltd |

| Reg. | Type | Owner or Operator | Notes |
|---|---|---|---|
| G-BJDK | European E.14 balloon | Aeroprint Tours | |
| G-BJDO | AA-5A Cheetah | Solent Flight | |
| G-BJDT | SOCATA TB.9 Tampico | Tampico Group/Old Sarum | |
| G-BJDW | Cessna F.172M | J. Rae/Ipswich | |
| G-BJEI | PA-18 Super Cub 95 | H. J. Cox | |
| G-BJEL | SNCAN NC.854 | N. F. & S. G. Hunter | |
| G-BJEN | Scruggs RS.5000 balloon | N. J. Richardson | |
| G-BJEO | PA-34-220T Seneca III | D. W. Clark Land Drainage Ltd (G-TOMF) | |
| G-BJES | Scruggs RS.5000 balloon | J. E. Christopher | |
| G-BJEU | Scruggs BL.2D-2 balloon | G. G. Kneller | |
| G-BJEV | Aeronca 11AC Chief (897) | R. F. Willcox | |
| G-BJEX | Bo 208C Junior | G. D. H. Crawford/Thruxton | |
| G-BJFB | Mk 1A balloon | Aeroprint Tours | |
| G-BJFC | European E.8 balloon | P. D. Ridout | |
| G-BJFE | PA-18 Super Cub 95 | J. H. Allistone | |
| G-BJFI | Bell 47G-2A1 | Helicopter Supplies & Engineering Ltd/ Bournemouth | |
| G-BJFL | Sikorsky S-76A | Bristow Helicopters Ltd | |
| G-BJFM | Jodel D.120 | J. V. George & P. A. Smith/Popham | |
| G-BJGC | Mk IV balloon | Windsor Balloon Group | |
| G-BJGD | Mk IV balloon | Windsor Balloon Group | |
| G-BJGE | Thunder Ax3 balloon | K. A. Williams | |
| G-BJGF | Mk 1 balloon | D. & D. Eaves | |
| G-BJGG | Mk 2 balloon | D. & D. Eaves | |
| G-BJGK | Cameron V-77 balloon | A. Simpson & R. Bailey | |
| G-BJGL | Cremer balloon | G. Lowther | |
| G-BJGM | Unicorn UE.1A balloon | D. Eaves & P. D. Ridout | |
| G-BJGO | Cessna 172N | Stratair Ltd/Wellesbourne | |
| G-BJGX | Sikorsky S-76A | Bristow Helicopters Ltd | |
| G-BJGY | Cessna F.172P | Lucca Wines Ltd | |
| G-BJHA | Cremer balloon | G. Cape | |
| G-BJHB | Mooney M.20J | Zitair Flying Club Ltd/Redhill | |
| G-BJHC | Swan 1 balloon | C. A. Swan | |
| G-BJHD | Mk 3B balloon | S. Meagher | |
| G-BJHK | EAA Acro Sport | D. Calabritto | |
| G-BJHL | Osprey 1C balloon | E. Bartlett | |
| G-BJHN | Osprey 1B balloon | J. E. Christopher | |
| G-BJHO | Osprey 1C balloon | G. G. Kneller | |
| G-BJHP | Osprey 1C balloon | N. J. Richardson | |
| G-BJHS | S.25 Sunderland V | Sunderland Ltd | |
| G-BJHT | Thunder Ax7-65 balloon | A. H. & L. Symonds | |
| G-BJHU | Osprey 1C balloon | G. G. Kneller | |
| G-BJHV | Voisin Replica ★ | Brooklands Museum of Aviation/Weybridge | |
| G-BJHW | Osprey 1C balloon | N. J. Richardson | |
| G-BJIA | Allport balloon | D. J. Allport | |
| G-BJIB | D.31 Turbulent | N. H. Lemon | |
| G-BJIC | Dodo 1A balloon | P. D. Ridout | |
| G-BJID | Osprey 1B balloon | P. D. Ridout | |
| G-BJIF | Bensen B.8M | H. Redwin | |
| G-BJIG | Slingsby T.67A | Acebell G-BJIG Syndicate/Redhill | |
| G-BJIR | Cessna 550 Citation II | Gator Aviation Ltd | |
| G-BJIV | PA-18 Super Cub 150 (modified) | Yorkshire Gliding Club (Pty) Ltd/ Sutton Bank | |
| G-BJJE | Dodo Mk 3 balloon | D. Eaves | |
| G-BJJN | Cessna F.172M | Ospreystar Ltd (stored)/Stapleford | |
| G-BJJW | Mk B balloon | S. Meagher | |
| G-BJJX | Mk B balloon | S. Meagher | |
| G-BJJY | Mk B balloon | S. Meagher | |
| G-BJKB | SA.365C-3 Dauphin 2 | Bond Helicopters Ltd | |
| G-BJKF | SOCATA TB.9 Tampico | Manor Promotion Services Ltd/Booker | |
| G-BJKW | Wills Aera II | J. K. S. Wills | |
| G-BJKY | Cessna F.152 | Air Charter & Travel Ltd/Ronaldsway | |
| G-BJLB | SNCAN NC.854S | M. J. Barnaby | |
| G-BJLC | Monnet Sonerai IIL | P. J. Robins & R. King/Sywell | |
| G-BJLE | Osprey 1B balloon | I. Chadwick | |
| G-BJLF | Unicorn UE.1C balloon | I. Chadwick | |
| G-BJLG | Unicorn UE.1B balloon | I. Chadwick | |
| G-BJLH | PA-18 Super Cub 95 (44) | D. S. Kirkham | |
| G-BJLK | Short SD3-30 Variant 100 | Celtic Airways Ltd | |
| G-BJLO | PA-31-310 Turbo Navajo | Linco (Holdings) Ltd | |
| G-BJLU | Featherlight Mk 3 balloon | T. J. Sweeting & N. P. Kemp | |
| G-BJLV | Sphinx balloon | L. F. Guyot | |

# G-BJLX – G-BJTA

| Notes | Reg. | Type | Owner or Operator |
|---|---|---|---|
| | G-BJLX | Cremer balloon | P. W. May |
| | G-BJLY | Cremer balloon | P. Cannon |
| | G-BJMG | European E.26C balloon | D. Eaves & A. P. Chown |
| | G-BJMI | European E.84 balloon | D. Eaves |
| | G-BJMJ | Bensen B.8M | J. I. Hewlett |
| | G-BJML | Cessna 120 | D. F. Lawlor/Inverness |
| | G-BJMO | Taylor JT.1 Monoplane | R. C. Mark |
| | G-BJMR | Cessna 310R | J. McL. Robinson/Sherburn |
| | G-BJMU | European E.157 balloon | A. C. Mitchell |
| | G-BJMV | BAC One-Eleven 531FS | British Air Ferries/Southend |
| | G-BJMW | Thunder Ax8-105 balloon | G. M. Westley |
| | G-BJMX | Jarre JR.3 balloon | P. D. Ridout |
| | G-BJMZ | European EA.8A balloon | P. D. Ridout |
| | G-BJNA | Arena Mk 117P balloon | P. D. Ridout |
| | G-BJND | Osprey Mk 1E balloon | A. Billington & D. Whitmore |
| | G-BJNF | Cessna F.152 | Exeter Flying Club Ltd |
| | G-BJNG | Slingsby T.67A | D. F. Ranger |
| | G-BJNN | PA-38-112 Tomahawk | Scotia Safari Ltd/Prestwick |
| | G-BJNP | Rango NA.32 balloon | N. H. Ponsford |
| | G-BJNX | Cameron O-65 balloon | B. J. Petteford |
| | G-BJNY | Aeronca 11CC Super Chief | P. I. & D. M. Morgans |
| | G-BJNZ | PA-23 Aztec 250F | Leavesden Flight Centre Ltd (G-FANZ) |
| | G-BJOA | PA-28-181 Archer II | Channel Islands Aero Holdings (Jersey) Ltd |
| | G-BJOB | Jodel D.140C | T. W. M. Beck & M. J. Smith |
| | G-BJOE | Jodel D.120A | Forth Flying Group |
| | G-BJOP | BN-2B Islander | Loganair Ltd/Glasgow |
| | G-BJOT | Jodel D.117 | E. Davies |
| | G-BJOV | Cessna F.150K | W. H. Webb & P. F. N. Burrow |
| | G-BJOZ | Scheibe SF.25B Falke | P. W. Hextall |
| | G-BJPB | Osprey Mk 4A balloon | C. B. Rundle |
| | G-BJPI | Bede BD-5G | M. D. McQueen |
| | G-BJPL | Osprey Mk 4A balloon | M. Vincent |
| | G-BJPM | Bursell PW.1 balloon | I. M. Holdsworth |
| | G-BJPV | Haigh balloon | M. J. Haigh |
| | G-BJPW | Osprey Mk 1C balloon | P. J. Cooper & M. Draper |
| | G-BJRA | Osprey Mk 4B balloon | E. Osborn |
| | G-BJRB | European E.254 balloon | D. Eaves |
| | G-BJRC | European E.84R balloon | D. Eaves |
| | G-BJRD | European E.84R balloon | D. Eaves |
| | G-BJRF | Saffery S.80 balloon | C. F. Chipping |
| | G-BJRG | Osprey Mk 4B balloon | A. de Gruchy |
| | G-BJRH | Rango NA.36 balloon | N. H. Ponsford |
| | G-BJRI | Osprey Mk 4D balloon | G. G. Kneller |
| | G-BJRJ | Osprey Mk 4D balloon | G. G. Kneller |
| | G-BJRK | Osprey Mk 1E balloon | G. G. Kneller |
| | G-BJRL | Osprey Mk 4B balloon | G. G. Kneller |
| | G-BJRP | Cremer balloon | M. D. Williams |
| | G-BJRS | Cremer balloon | P. Wallbank |
| | G-BJRT | BAC One-Eleven 528FL | British Airways County of South Glamorgan |
| | G-BJRU | BAC One-Eleven 528FL | British Airways County of West Glamorgan |
| | G-BJRV | Cremer balloon | M. D. Williams |
| | G-BJRW | Cessna U.206G | A. I. Walgate & Son Ltd |
| | G-BJRY | PA-28-151 Warrior | Routair Aviation Services Ltd/Southend |
| | G-BJRZ | Partenavia P.68C | Air Kilroe Ltd/Manchester |
| | G-BJSA | BN-2A Islander | Foxair/Glasgow |
| | G-BJSC | Osprey Mk 4D balloon | N. J. Richardson |
| | G-BJSD | Osprey Mk 4D balloon | N. J. Richardson |
| | G-BJSE | Osprey Mk 1E balloon | J. E. Christopher |
| | G-BJSF | Osprey Mk 4B balloon | N. J. Richardson |
| | G-BJSG | V.S.361 Spitfire LF.IXE (ML417) | Patina Ltd/Duxford |
| | G-BJSI | Osprey Mk 1E balloon | N. J. Richardson |
| | G-BJSK | Osprey Mk 4B balloon | J. E. Christopher |
| | G-BJSL | Flamboyant Ax7-65 balloon | Pepsi Cola International Ltd |
| | G-BJSP | Guido 1A Srs 61 balloon | G. A. Newsome |
| | G-BJSR | Osprey Mk 4B balloon | C. F. Chipping |
| | G-BJSS | Allport balloon | D. J. Allport |
| | G-BJST | CCF Harvard 4 (MM53795) | V. Norman & M. Lawrence (stored) |
| | G-BJSU | Bensen B.8M | J. D. Newlyn |
| | G-BJSV | PA-28-161 Warrior II | R. Gilbert & J. Cole |
| | G-BJSW | Thunder Ax7-65 balloon | Sandicliffe Garage Ltd |
| | G-BJSX | Unicorn UE-1C balloon | N. J. Richardson |
| | G-BJSZ | Piper J-3C-65 Cub | H. Gilbert |
| | G-BJTA | Osprey Mk 4B balloon | C. F. Chipping |

| Reg. | Type | Owner or Operator | Notes |
|------|------|-------------------|-------|
| G-BJTB | Cessna A.150M | Clacton Aero Club (1988) Ltd | |
| G-BJTG | Osprey Mk 4B balloon | M. Millen | |
| G-BJTH | Kestrel AC Mk 1 balloon | R. P. Waller | |
| G-BJTK | Taylor JT.1 Monoplane | E. N. Simmons | |
| G-BJTN | Osprey Mk 4B balloon | M. Vincent | |
| G-BJTO | Piper J-3C-65 Cub | K. R. Nunn | |
| G-BJTP | PA-18 Super Cub 95 (115302) | J. T. Parkins | |
| G-BJTV | M.S.880B Rallye Club | E. C. Hender | |
| G-BJTW | European E.107 balloon | C. J. Brealey | |
| G-BJTY | Osprey Mk 4B balloon | A. E. de Gruchy | |
| G-BJUB | BVS Special 01 balloon | P. G. Wild | |
| G-BJUC | Robinson R-22 | The Helicentre/Blackpool | |
| G-BJUD | Robin DR.400/180R | Lasham Gliding Soc Ltd | |
| G-BJUE | Osprey Mk 4B balloon | M. Vincent | |
| G-BJUG | SOCATA TB.9 Tampico | CB Helicopters | |
| G-BJUI | Osprey Mk 4B balloon | B. A. de Gruchy | |
| G-BJUK | Short SD3-30 | Shorts Aircraft Leasing Ltd (G-OCAS) | |
| G-BJUR | PA-38-112 Tomahawk | Truman Aviation Ltd/Tollerton | |
| G-BJUS | PA-38-112 Tomahawk | Panshanger School of Flying | |
| G-BJUU | Osprey Mk 4B balloon | M. Vincent | |
| G-BJUV | Cameron V-20 balloon | Cameron Balloons Ltd | |
| G-BJUW | Osprey Mk 4B balloon | C. F. Chipping | |
| G-BJUX | Bursell balloon | I. M. Holdsworth | |
| G-BJUZ | BAT Mk II balloon | A. R. Thompson | |
| G-BJVA | BAT Mk I balloon | B. L. Thompson | |
| G-BJVC | Evans VP-2 | J. J. Morrissey | |
| G-BJVF | Thunder Ax3 balloon | A. G. R. Calder | |
| G-BJVH | Cessna F.182Q | A. R. G. Brooker Engineering Ltd/ Wellesbourne | |
| G-BJVJ | Cessna F.152 | Cambridge Aero Club Ltd | |
| G-BJVK | Grob G-109 | B. Kimberley/Enstone | |
| G-BJVM | Cessna 172N | G. J. Mendes | |
| G-BJVS | CP.1310-C3 Super Emeraude | A. E. Futter/Norwich | |
| G-BJVT | Cessna F.152 | Cambridge Aero Club Ltd | |
| G-BJVU | Thunder Ax6-56 balloon | G. V. Beckwith | |
| G-BJVV | Robin R.1180 | Medway Flying Group Ltd/Rochester | |
| G-BJVX | Sikorsky S-76A | Bristow Helicopters Ltd | |
| G-BJWC | Saro Skeeter AOP.12 (XK 482)★ | Wilkie Museum Collection/Blackpool | |
| G-BJWH | Cessna F.152 | Biggin Hill School of Flying | |
| G-BJWI | Cessna F.172P | Agricultural & General Aviation Ltd/ Bournemouth | |
| G-BJWJ | Cameron V-65 balloon | R. G. Turnbull & S. G. Forse | |
| G-BJWO | BN-2A-8 Islander | Peterborough Parachute Centre Ltd (G-BAXC)/Sibson | |
| G-BJWT | Wittman W.10 Tailwind | J. F. Bakewell & R. A. Shelley | |
| G-BJWV | Colt 17A balloon | D. T. Meyes | |
| G-BJWW | Cessna F.172N | Air Charter & Travel Ltd/Blackpool | |
| G-BJWX | PA-18 Super Cub 95 | E. T. Webster | |
| G-BJWY | S-55 Whirlwind HAR.21 (WV198) | Wilkie Museum Collection/Blackpool | |
| G-BJWZ | PA-18 Super Cub 95 | G. V. Harfield/Thruxton | |
| G-BJXA | Slingsby T.67A | Comed Aviation Ltd/Blackpool | |
| G-BJXB | Slingsby T.67A | A. K. Halvorsen/Barton | |
| G-BJXK | Fournier RF-5 | G-BJXK Syndicate/Cardiff | |
| G-BJXP | Colt 56B balloon | C. J. Travis | |
| G-BJXR | Auster AOP.9 (XR267) | Cotswold Aircraft Restoration Group | |
| G-BJXU | Thunder Ax7-77 balloon | S. M. Vardey | |
| G-BJXX | PA-23 Aztec 250E | V. Bojovic | |
| G-BJXZ | Cessna 172N | T. M. Jones | |
| G-BJYD | Cessna F.152 II | Cleveland Flying School Ltd/Teesside | |
| G-BJYF | Colt 56A balloon | Hot Air Balloon Co Ltd | |
| G-BJYG | PA-28-161 Warrior II | Browns of Stoke Ltd | |
| G-BJYK | Jodel D.120A | T. Fox & D. A. Thorpe | |
| G-BJYL | BAC One-Eleven 515FB | British Air Ferries (G-AZPE)/Southend | |
| G-BJYM | BAC One-Eleven 531FS | British Air Ferries/Southend | |
| G-BJYN | PA-38-112 Tomahawk | Panshanger School of Flying Ltd (G-BJTE) | |
| G-BJZA | Cameron N-65 balloon | A. D. Pinner | |
| G-BJZB | Evans VP-2 | J. A. McLeod | |
| G-BJZC | Thunder Ax7-65Z balloon | Greenpeace (UK) Ltd/S. Africa | |
| G-BJZF | D.H.82A Tiger Moth | R. Blast | |
| G-BJZK | Cessna T.303 | Landlink Ltd | |
| G-BJZL | Cameron V-65 balloon | S. L. G. Williams | |
| G-BJZN | Slingsby T.67A | D. M. Upfield | |
| G-BJZR | Colt 42A balloon | C. F. Sisson | |

# G-BJZT – G-BKFP

| Notes | Reg. | Type | Owner or Operator |
|---|---|---|---|
| | G-BJZT | Cessna FA.152 | Biggin Hill School of Flying |
| | G-BJZX | Grob G.109 | Oxfordshire Sport Flying Ltd/Enstone |
| | G-BJZY | Bensen B.8MV | D. E. & M. A. Cooke |
| | G-BKAC | Cessna F.150L | Seawing Flying Club Ltd/Southend |
| | G-BKAE | Jodel D.120 | M. P. Wakem |
| | G-BKAF | FRED Srs 2 | L. G. Millen |
| | G-BKAM | Slingsby T.67M Firefly | A. J. Daley & R. K. Warren |
| | G-BKAN | Cessna 340A | Arrows Aviation Co Ltd/Manchester |
| | G-BKAO | Jodel D.112 | R. Broadhead |
| | G-BKAR | PA-38-112 Tomahawk | R. Thomas |
| | G-BKAS | PA-38-112 Tomahawk | K. J. Scott |
| | G-BKAY | R. Commander 114 | The Rockwell Group |
| | G-BKAZ | Cessna 152 | Skyviews & General Ltd |
| | G-BKBD | Thunder Ax3 balloon | G. A. McCarthy |
| | G-BKBF | M.S.894A Rallye Minerva 220 | M. S. Wright |
| | G-BKBH | H.S.125 Srs 600B | Westminster Aviation Ltd (G-BDJE) |
| | G-BKBK | SNCAN Stampe SV-4A | Freshname No77 Ltd |
| | G-BKBN | SOCATA TB.10 Tobago | RFA Flying Club Ltd |
| | G-BKBO | Colt 17A balloon | J. Armstrong & ptnrs |
| | G-BKBP | Bellanca 7GCBC Scout | H. G. Jefferies & Son |
| | G-BKBR | Cameron Chateau 84 SS balloon | Forbes Europe Ltd/France |
| | G-BKBS | Bensen B.8MV | Construction & Site Administration Ltd |
| | G-BKBV | SOCATA TB.10 Tobago | R. M. Messenger |
| | G-BKBW | SOCATA TB.10 Tobago | Merlin Aviation |
| | G-BKCB | PA-28R Cherokee Arrow 200 | Bristol & Wessex Aeroplane Club Ltd |
| | G-BKCC | PA-28 Cherokee 180 | Cowie Aviation Ltd/Staverton |
| | G-BKCE | Cessna F.172P II | Denham School of Flying Ltd |
| | G-BKCF | Rutan LongEz | I. C. Fallows |
| | G-BKCH | Thompson Cassutt | S. C. Thompson/Redhill |
| | G-BKCI | Brügger MB.2 Colibri | E. R. Newall |
| | G-BKCJ | Oldfield Baby Great Lakes | S. V. Roberts/Sleap |
| | G-BKCK | CCF Harvard IV (P5865) | E. T. Webster & A. Haig-Thomas/North Weald |
| | G-BKCL | PA-30 Twin Comanche 160C | T-Comm Aviation Ltd/Leeds |
| | G-BKCN | Currie Wot | S. E. Tomlinson |
| | G-BKCR | SOCATA TB.9 Tampico | Surrey & Kent Flying Club (1982) Ltd/Biggin Hill |
| | G-BKCT | Cameron V-77 balloon | Quality Products General Engineering (Wickwat) Ltd |
| | G-BKCV | EAA Acro Sport II | M. J. Clark |
| | G-BKCW | Jodel D.120A | A. Greene & G. Kerr/Dundee |
| | G-BKCX | Mudry CAARP CAP.10 | Mahon & Associates/Booker |
| | G-BKCY | PA-38-112 Tomahawk II | Wellesbourne Aviation Ltd |
| | G-BKCZ | Jodel D.120A | M. R. Baker/Shoreham |
| | G-BKDC | Monnet Sonerai II | K. McBride |
| | G-BKDD | Bell 206B JetRanger | Dollar Air Services Ltd/Coventry |
| | G-BKDH | Robin DR.400/120 | Wiltshire Aeroplane Club/Old Sarum |
| | G-BKDI | Robin DR.400/120 | Cotswold Aero Club Ltd/Staverton |
| | G-BKDJ | Robin DR.400/120 | Wiltshire Aeroplane Club/Old Sarum |
| | G-BKDK | Thunder Ax7-77Z balloon | A. J. Byrne |
| | G-BKDP | FRED Srs 3 | M. Whittaker |
| | G-BKDR | Pitts S.1S Special | N. A. Bloom |
| | G-BKDT | SE-5A (replica) (F943) ★ | Yorkshire Air Museum/Elvington |
| | G-BKDX | Jodel DR.1050 | T. G. Collins |
| | G-BKEK | PA-32 Cherokee Six 300 | Flyfast Ltd |
| | G-BKEM | SOCATA TB.9 Tampico | C. J. Burt/Biggin Hill |
| | G-BKEP | Cessna F.172M | R. Green/Glasgow |
| | G-BKER | SE-5A (replica) (F5447) | N. K. Geddes |
| | G-BKET | PA-18 Super Cub 95 | H. M. Mackenzie |
| | G-BKEU | Taylor JT.1 Monoplane | R. J. Whybrow & J. M. Springham |
| | G-BKEV | Cessna F.172M | One Zero One Three Ltd |
| | G-BKEW | Bell 206B JetRanger 3 | N. R. Foster |
| | G-BKEX | Rich Prototype glider | D. B. Rich |
| | G-BKEY | FRED Srs 3 | G. S. Taylor |
| | G-BKEZ | PA-18 Super Cub 95 | G. V. Harfield |
| | G-BKFA | Monnet Sonerai IIL | R. F. Bridge |
| | G-BKFC | Cessna F.152 II | Sulby Aerial Surveys Ltd |
| | G-BKFG | Thunder Ax3 balloon | P. Ray |
| | G-BKFI | Evans VP-1 | F. A. R. de Lavergne |
| | G-BKFK | Isaacs Fury II | G. C. Jones |
| | G-BKFM | QAC Quickie | R. Scroby |
| | G-BKFP | Bell 214ST | Bristow Helicopters Ltd |

| Reg. | Type | Owner or Operator | Notes |
|------|------|-------------------|-------|
| G-BKFR | CP.301C Emeraude | C. R. Beard | |
| G-BKFV | Rand KR-2 | F. H. French/Swansea | |
| G-BKFW | P.56 Provost T.1 (XF597) | Slymar Aviation & Services Ltd | |
| G-BKFZ | PA-28R Cherokee Arrow 200 | Shacklewell Flying Group/Leicester | |
| G-BKGA | M.S.892E Rallye 150GT | BJJ Aviation | |
| G-BKGB | Jodel D.120 | R. W. Greenwood | |
| G-BKGC | Maule M.6-235 | Stol-Air Ltd/Sibson | |
| G-BKGD | Westland WG.30 Srs 100 | British International Helicopters Ltd (G-BKBJ)/Aberdeen | |
| G-BKGL | Beech 18 (1164) | The Aircraft Restoration Co/Duxford | |
| G-BKGR | Cameron O-65 balloon | K. Kidner & L. E. More | |
| G-BKGT | SOCATA Rallye 110ST | Long Marston Flying Group | |
| G-BKGW | Cessna F.152-II | Leicestershire Aero Club Ltd | |
| G-BKHA | W.S.55 Whirlwind HAR.10 (XJ763) | C. J. Evans | |
| G-BKHC | W.S.55 Whirlwind HAR.10 (XP328) | Flight C Helicopters Ltd | |
| G-BKHD | Oldfield Baby Great Lakes | P. J. Tanulak | |
| G-BKHE | Boeing 737-204ADV | Britannia Airways Ltd *Sir Francis Chichester* | |
| G-BKHG | Piper J-3C-65 Cub (479766) | K. G. Wakefield | |
| G-BKHL | Thunder Ax9-140 balloon | R. Carr/France | |
| G-BKHP | P.56 Provost T.1 (WW397) | M. J. Crymble/Lyneham | |
| G-BKHR | Luton LA-4 Minor | A. C. P. de Labat | |
| G-BKHT | BAe 146-100 | British Aerospace PLC | |
| G-BKHW | Stoddard-Hamilton Glasair SH.2RG | N. Clayton | |
| G-BKHX | Bensen B.8M | D. H. Greenwood | |
| G-BKHY | Taylor JT.1 Monoplane | M. C. Holmes & A. Shuttleworth | |
| G-BKHZ | Cessna F.172P | Warwickshire Flying Training Centre Ltd | |
| G-BKIA | SOCATA TB.10 Tobago | D. H. Barton/Redhill | |
| G-BKIB | SOCATA TB.9 Tampico | A. J. Baggerley & F. D. J. Simmons/ Goodwood | |
| G-BKIC | Cameron V-77 balloon | C. A. Butler | |
| G-BKIE | Short SD3-30 Variant 100 | BAC Leasing/Express Air (G-SLUG/ G-METP/G-METO) | |
| G-BKIF | Fournier RF-6B | G. G. Milton | |
| G-BKII | Cessna F.172M | M. S. Knight/Goodwood | |
| G-BKIJ | Cessna F.172M | V. Speck | |
| G-BKIK | Cameron DG-10 airship | Airspace Outdoor Advertising Ltd | |
| G-BKIM | Unicorn UE.5A balloon | I. Chadwick & K. H. Turner | |
| G-BKIN | Alon A.2A Aircoupe | P. A. Williams & M. Quinn/Blackbushe | |
| G-BKIR | Jodel D.117 | R. Shaw & D. M. Hardaker/Sherburn | |
| G-BKIS | SOCATA TB.10 Tobago | Ospreystar Ltd | |
| G-BKIT | SOCATA TB.9 Tampico | Kit Aviation Club/Southend | |
| G-BKIU | Colt 17A balloon | Robert Pooley Ltd | |
| G-BKIV | Colt 21A balloon | Colt Balloons Ltd | |
| G-BKIX | Cameron V-31 balloon | G. Stevens | |
| G-BKIY | Thunder Ax3 balloon | A. Hornak | |
| G-BKIZ | Cameron V-31 balloon | A. P. S. Cox | |
| G-BKJB | PA-18 Super Cub 135 | Cormack (Aircraft Services) Ltd/Glasgow | |
| G-BKJD | Bell 214ST | Bristow Helicopters Ltd | |
| G-BKJE | Cessna 172N | The G-BKJE Group | |
| G-BKJF | M.S.880B Rallye 100T | Nova Flying Group | |
| G-BKJG | BN-2B-21 Islander | Pilatus BN Ltd/Bembridge | |
| G-BKJR | Hughes 269C | March Helicopters Ltd/Sywell | |
| G-BKJS | Jodel D.120A | S. Walmsley | |
| G-BKJT | Cameron O-65 balloon | K. A. Ward | |
| G-BKJW | PA-23 Aztec 250E | Alan Williams Entertainments Ltd | |
| G-BKKN | Cessna 182R | R. A. Marven/Elstree | |
| G-BKKO | Cessna 182R | B. & G. Jebson Ltd/Crosland Moor | |
| G-BKKR | Rand KR-2 | D. Beale & S. P. Gardner | |
| G-BKKZ | Pitts S-1D Special | G. C. Masterton | |
| G-BKLB | R. S2R Thrush Commander | Ag-Air | |
| G-BKLC | Cameron V-56 balloon | M. A. & J. R. H. Ashworth | |
| G-BKLJ | Westland Scout AH.1 ★ | Wilkie Museum Collection/Blackpool | |
| G-BKLM | Thunder Ax9-140 balloon | Aerial Promotions Balloon Club | |
| G-BKLO | Cessna F.172M | Stapleford Flying Club Ltd | |
| G-BKLP | Cessna F.172N | Pagodaplan Ltd | |
| G-BKMA | Mooney M.20J Srs 201 | Foxtrot Whisky Aviation | |
| G-BKMB | Mooney M.20J Srs 201 | W. A. Cook & ptnrs/Sherburn | |
| G-BKMD | SC.7 Skyvan Srs 3 | Army Parachute Association/Netheravon | |
| G-BKMG | Handley Page O/400 (replica) | Paralyser Group | |
| G-BKMH | Flamboyant Ax7-65 balloon | Pepsi-Cola International Ltd/S. Africa | |
| G-BKMI | V.S.359 Spitfire HF VIII (MV154) | Aerial Museum (North Weald) Ltd | |
| G-BKMK | PA-38-112 Tomahawk | Misty Isle Aviation Ltd/Glasgow | |

| Notes | Reg. | Type | Owner or Operator |
|-------|------|------|-------------------|
| | G-BKMM | Cessna 180K | M. Kirk |
| | G-BKMN | BAe 146-100 | British Aerospace PLC (G-ODAN) |
| | G-BKMR | Thunder Ax3 balloon | B. F. G. Ribbans |
| | G-BKMT | PA-32R-301 Saratoga SP | Severn Valley Aviation Group |
| | G-BKMX | Short SD3-60 | Manx Airlines Ltd/Ronaldsway |
| | G-BKNA | Cessna 421 | Young Investments Ltd |
| | G-BKNB | Cameron V-42 balloon | D. N. Close |
| | G-BKND | Colt 56A balloon | Flying Colours Balloon Group |
| | G-BKNH | Boeing 737-210 | Curzon Trustees Ltd |
| | G-BKNI | GY-80 Horizon 160D | A. Hartigan & ptnrs/Fenland |
| | G-BKNL | Cameron D-96 airship | Drawarm Ltd |
| | G-BKNN | Cameron Minar E Pakistan balloon | Forbes Europe Ltd/France |
| | G-BKNO | Monnet Sonerai IIL | M. D. Hughes |
| | G-BKNY | Bensen B.8MPV | D. A. C. MacCormack |
| | G-BKNZ | CP.301A Emeraude | R. Evernden/Barton |
| | G-BKOA | SOCATA M.S.893E Rallye 180GT | P. J. Clegg |
| | G-BKOB | Z.326 Trener Master | W. G. V. Hall |
| | G-BKOR | Barnes 77 balloon | Robert Pooley Ltd |
| | G-BKOT | Wassmer WA.81 Piranha | R. Skingley & B. N. Rolfe |
| | G-BKOU | P.84 Jet Provost T.3 (XN637) | A. Topen/Cranfield |
| | G-BKOV | Jodel DR.220A | Merlin Flying Club Ltd/Hucknall |
| | G-BKOW | Colt 77A balloon | Hot Air Balloon Co Ltd |
| | G-BKPA | Hoffman H-36 Dimona | A. Mayhew |
| | G-BKPB | Aerosport Scamp | E. D. Burke |
| | G-BKPC | Cessna A.185F | Black Knights Parachute Centre |
| | G-BKPD | Viking Dragonfly | E. P. Browne & G. J. Sargent |
| | G-BKPE | Jodel DR.250/160 | J. S. & J. D. Lewer |
| | G-BKPG | Luscombe Rattler Strike | Luscombe Aircraft Ltd |
| | G-BKPK | John McHugh Gyrocopter | J. C. McHugh |
| | G-BKPM | Schempp-Hirth HS.5 Nimbus 2 | J. L. Rolls |
| | G-BKPN | Cameron N-77 balloon | R. H. Sanderson |
| | G-BKPS | AA-5B Tiger | Earthline Ltd |
| | G-BKPT | M.H.1521M Broussard (192) | R. M. Johnston |
| | G-BKPV | Stevex 250.1 | A. F. Stevens |
| | G-BKPW | Boeing 767-204 | Britannia Airways Ltd *The Earl Mountbatten of Burma*/Luton |
| | G-BKPX | Jodel D.120A | N. H. Martin |
| | G-BKPY | Saab 91B/2 Safir (56321)★ | Newark Air Museum Ltd |
| | G-BKPZ | Pitts S-1T Special | P. R. Rutterford/Redhill |
| | G-BKRA | NA T-6G Texan (51-15227) | Pulsegrove Ltd/Shoreham |
| | G-BKRB | Cessna 172N | Saunders Caravans Ltd |
| | G-BKRF | PA-18 Super Cub 95 | K. M. Bishop |
| | G-BKRG | Beechcraft C-45G | Aces High Ltd/North Weald |
| | G-BKRH | Brügger MB.2 Colibri | M. R. Benwell |
| | G-BKRI | Cameron V-77 balloon | J. R. Lowe & R. J. Fuller |
| | G-BKRJ | Colt 105A balloon | Owners Abroad Group PLC |
| | G-BKRK | SNCAN Stampe SV-4C | J. M. Alexander & ptnrs/Aberdeen |
| | G-BKRL | Chichester-Miles Leopard | Chichester-Miles Consultants Ltd |
| | G-BKRM | Boeing 757-236 | — |
| | G-BKRN | Beechcraft D.18S ★ | S. Topen/Cranfield |
| | G-BKRR | Cameron N-56 balloon | S. L. G. Williams |
| | G-BKRS | Cameron V-56 balloon | D. N. & L. J. Close |
| | G-BKRU | Ensign Crossley Racer | M. Crossley |
| | G-BKRV | Hovey Beta Bird | A. V. Francis |
| | G-BKRW | Cameron O-160 balloon | Bondbaste Ltd |
| | G-BKRX | Cameron O-160 balloon | Bondbaste Ltd |
| | G-BKRZ | Dragon 77 balloon | J. R. Barber |
| | G-BKSC | Saro Skeeter AOP.12 (XN351) | R. A. L. Falconer |
| | G-BKSD | Colt 56A balloon | M. J. & G. C. Casson |
| | G-BKSE | QAC Quickie Q.2 | M. D. Burns |
| | G-BKSH | Colt 21A balloon | J. Bartholomew & D. L. Smith |
| | G-BKSJ | Cameron N-108 balloon | Cameron Balloons Ltd |
| | G-BKSP | Schleicher ASK.14 | J. H. Bryson |
| | G-BKSR | Cessna 550 Citation II | Metropolitan Guernsey Ltd |
| | G-BKSS | Jodel D.150 | D. H. Wilson-Spratt/Ronaldsway |
| | G-BKST | Rutan Vari-Eze | R. Towle |
| | G-BKSX | SNCAN Stampe SV-4C | C. A. Bailey & J. A. Carr |
| | G-BKSZ | Cessna P.210N | Blessvale Ltd |
| | G-BKTA | PA-18 Super Cub 95 | K. E. Chapman/Southend |
| | G-BKTH | CCF Hawker Sea Hurricane IB (Z7015) | Shuttleworth Trust/Duxford |
| | G-BKTM | PZL SZD-45A Ogar | Ogar Syndicate |
| | G-BKTR | Cameron V-77 balloon | R. W. Keron |

| Reg. | Type | Owner or Operator | Notes |
|------|------|-------------------|-------|
| G-BKTS | Cameron O-65 balloon | C. H. Pearce & Sons (Contractors) Ltd | |
| G-BKTU | Colt 56A balloon | E. Ten Houten | |
| G-BKTV | Cessna F.152 | London Flight Centre Ltd/Stansted | |
| G-BKTY | SOCATA TB.10 Tobago | B. M. & G. M. McClelland | |
| G-BKTZ | Slingsby T.67M Firefly | E. Hopper (G-SFTV) | |
| G-BKUE | SOCATA TB.9 Tampico | W. J. Moore/Kirkbride | |
| G-BKUJ | Thunder Ax6-56 balloon | R. J. Bent | |
| G-BKUR | CP.301A Emeraude | R. Wells & H. V. Hunter | |
| G-BKUS | Bensen B.8M | G. F. Gardener | |
| G-BKUU | Thunder Ax7-77-1 balloon | City of London Balloon Group | |
| G-BKUY | BAe Jetstream 3102 | British Aerospace PLC/Hatfield | |
| G-BKVA | SOCATA Rallye 180T | Buckminster Gliding Club Syndicate | |
| G-BKVB | SOCATA Rallye 110ST | Martin Ltd/Biggin Hill | |
| G-BKVC | SOCATA TB.9 Tampico | Martin Ltd/Biggin Hill | |
| G-BKVE | Rutan Vari-Eze | R. M. Smith (G-EZLT) | |
| G-BKVF | FRED Srs 3 | D. Coging | |
| G-BKVG | Scheibe SF.25E Super Falke | G-BKVG Ltd | |
| G-BKVK | Auster AOP.9 (WZ662) | J. D. Butcher | |
| G-BKVL | Robin DR.400/160 | The Cotswold Aero Club Ltd/Staverton | |
| G-BKVM | PA-18 Super Cub 150 | D. G. Caffrey | |
| G-BKVN | PA-23 Aztec 250F | B. A. Eastwell/Shoreham | |
| G-BKVO | Pietenpol Air Camper | G. H. & M. G. A. Phillipson | |
| G-BKVP | Pitts S-1D Special | P. J. Leggo | |
| G-BKVR | PA-28 Cherokee 140 | D. P. Alexander | |
| G-BKVS | Bensen B.8M | V. Scott | |
| G-BKVT | PA-23 Aztec 250E | Express Bond Ltd (G-HARV) | |
| G-BKVV | Beech 95-B55 Baron | L. Mc. G. Tulloch | |
| G-BKVW | Airtour 56 balloon | L. D. & H. Vaughan | |
| G-BKVX | Airtour 56 balloon | E. G. Woolnough | |
| G-BKVY | Airtour 31 balloon | Airtour Balloon Co Ltd | |
| G-BKVZ | Boeing 767-204 | Britannia Airways Ltd *Sir Winston Churchill* | |
| G-BKWB | EMB-110P2 Bandeirante | Alexandra Aviation Ltd (G-CHEV) | |
| G-BKWD | Taylor JT.2 Titch | E. Shouler | |
| G-BKWE | Colt 17A balloon | Hot-Air Balloon Co Ltd | |
| G-BKWG | PZL-104 Wilga 35A | Machinery International Ltd | |
| G-BKWI | Pitts S-2A | R. A. Seeley/Denham | |
| G-BKWP | Thunder Ax7-77 balloon | G. V. Beckwith | |
| G-BKWR | Cameron V-65 balloon | K. J. Foster | |
| G-BKWW | Cameron O-77 balloon | A. M. Marten | |
| G-BKWY | Cessna F.152 | Cambridge Aero Club | |
| G-BKXA | Robin R.2100 | G. J. Anderson & ptnrs | |
| G-BKXC | Cameron V-77 balloon | P. Sarretti | |
| G-BKXD | SA.365N Dauphin 2 | Bond Helicopters Ltd | |
| G-BKXE | SA.365N Dauphin 2 | Bond Helicopters Ltd | |
| G-BKXF | PA-28R Cherokee Arrow 200 | P. L. Brunton | |
| G-BKXG | Cessna T.303 | Wilton Construction Ltd | |
| G-BKXL | Cameron Bottle 70 balloon | Cameron Balloons Ltd | |
| G-BKXM | Colt 17A balloon | R. G. Turnbull | |
| G-BKXN | ICA IS-28M2A | British Aerospace PLC/Filton | |
| G-BKXO | Rutan LongEz | P. J. Wareham | |
| G-BKXP | Auster AOP.6 | B. J. & W. J. Ellis | |
| G-BKXR | D.31A Turbulent | M. B. Hill | |
| G-BKXT | Cameron D-50 airship | Cameron Balloons Ltd | |
| G-BKXX | Cameron V-65 balloon | J. D. Pilkington | |
| G-BKYA | Boeing 737-236 | British Airways Birmingham *River Derwent* | |
| G-BKYB | Boeing 737-236 | British Airways Birmingham *River Stour* | |
| G-BKYC | Boeing 737-236 | British Airways Birmingham *River Wye* | |
| G-BKYD | Boeing 737-236 | British Airways Birmingham *River Conwy* | |
| G-BKYE | Boeing 737-236 | British Airways Birmingham *River Lagan* | |
| G-BKYF | Boeing 737-236 | British Airways Birmingham *River Spey* | |
| G-BKYG | Boeing 737-236 | British Airways Birmingham *River Exe* | |
| G-BKYH | Boeing 737-236 | British Airways Birmingham *River Dart* | |
| G-BKYI | Boeing 737-236 | British Airways *River Waveney* | |
| G-BKYJ | Boeing 737-236 | British Airways Birmingham *River Neath* | |
| G-BKYK | Boeing 737-236 | British Airways *River Foyle* | |
| G-BKYL | Boeing 737-236 | British Airways Birmingham *River Isis* | |
| G-BKYM | Boeing 737-236 | British Airways Birmingham *River Cam* | |
| G-BKYN | Boeing 737-236 | British Airways Birmingham *River Ayr* | |
| G-BKYO | Boeing 737-236 | British Airways Manchester *River Kennet* | |
| G-BKYP | Boeing 737-236 | British Airways Manchester *River Ystwyth* | |
| G-BKZA | Cameron N-77 balloon | University of Bath Students Union | |
| G-BKZB | Cameron V-77 balloon | A. J. Montgomery | |
| G-BKZE | AS.332L Super Puma | British International Helicopters/Aberdeen | |

| Notes | Reg. | Type | Owner or Operator |
|-------|------|------|-------------------|
| | G-BKZF | Cameron V-56 balloon | G. M. Hobster |
| | G-BKZG | AS.332L Super Puma | British International Helicopters/Aberdeen |
| | G-BKZH | AS.332L Super Puma | British International Helicopters/Aberdeen |
| | G-BKZI | Bell 206B JetRanger 2 | Western Air Trading Ltd/Thruxton |
| | G-BKZJ | Bensen B.8MV | J. C. Birdsall |
| | G-BKZR | Short SD3-60 Variant 100 | Streamline Aviation (G-OAEX/G-SALU)/ Exeter |
| | G-BKZT | FRED Srs 2 | M. G. Rusby |
| | G-BKZV | Bede BD-4A | A. L. Bergamasco/Headcorn |
| | G-BKZY | Cameron N-77 balloon | W. Counties Automobile Co Ltd |
| | G-BLAA | Fournier RF-5 | A. D. Wren/Southend |
| | G-BLAC | Cessna FA.152 | Howells Group PLC |
| | G-BLAD | Thunder Ax7-77-1 balloon | P. J. Bish |
| | G-BLAF | Stolp SA.900 V-Star | P. R. Skeels |
| | G-BLAG | Pitts S-1D Special | R. G. Gee & E. H. Williams |
| | G-BLAH | Thunder Ax7-77-1 balloon | T. Donnelly |
| | G-BLAI | Monnet Sonerai IIL | T. Simpson |
| | G-BLAM | Jodel DR.360 | B. F. Baldock |
| | G-BLAT | Jodel D.150 | D. J. Dulborough & A. J. Court |
| | G-BLAW | PA-28-181 Archer II | Luton Flight Training Ltd |
| | G-BLAX | Cessna FA.152 | Shoreham Flight Simulation Ltd/ Bournemouth |
| | G-BLAY | Robin HR.100/200B | B. A. Mills |
| | G-BLCA | Bell 206B JetRanger 3 | R.M.H. Stainless Ltd |
| | G-BLCC | Thunder Ax7-77Z balloon | P. Hassell Ltd |
| | G-BLCF | EAA Acro Sport 2 | M. J. Watkins & ptnrs |
| | G-BLCG | SOCATA TB.10 Tobago | Charlie Golf Flying Group (G-BHES)/ Shoreham |
| | G-BLCH | Colt 56D balloon | Balloon Flights Club Ltd |
| | G-BLCI | EAA Acro Sport | M. R. Holden |
| | G-BLCK | V.S.361 Spitfire F.IX (TE566) | Historic Aircraft Collection Ltd |
| | G-BLCM | SOCATA TB.9 Tampico | Repclif Aviation Ltd/Liverpool |
| | G-BLCT | Jodel DR.220 2+2 | H. W. Jemmett |
| | G-BLCU | Scheibe SF.25B Falke | Falke Syndicate |
| | G-BLCV | Hoffman H-36 Dimona | Charlie Victor Motor Glider Group |
| | G-BLCW | Evans VP-1 | K. D. Pearce |
| | G-BLCY | Thunder Ax7-65Z balloon | Thunder Balloons Ltd |
| | G-BLDB | Taylor JT.1 Monoplane | C. J. Bush |
| | G-BLDC | K&S Jungster 1 | A. W. Brown |
| | G-BLDD | WAG-Aero CUBy AcroTrainer | C. A. Laycock |
| | G-BLDE | Boeing 737-2E7 | Curzon Trustees Ltd |
| | G-BLDG | PA-25 Pawnee 260C | Ouse Gliding Club Ltd/Rufforth |
| | G-BLDH | BAC One-Eleven 475EZ | World Oil & Gas Resources Ltd |
| | G-BLDK | Robinson R-22 | J. A. Boardman/Barton |
| | G-BLDL | Cameron Truck 56 balloon | Cameron Balloons Ltd |
| | G-BLDN | Rand KR-2 | G. R. Burgess |
| | G-BLDP | Slingsby T.67M Firefly | Sherburn Aero Club Ltd |
| | G-BLEB | Colt 69A balloon | I. R. M. Jacobs |
| | G-BLEC | BN-2B-27 Islander | LEC Refrigeration PLC (G-BJBG) |
| | G-BLEJ | PA-28-161 Warrior II | Eglinton Flying Club Ltd |
| | G-BLEL | Price Ax7-77-245 balloon | T. S. Price |
| | G-BLEP | Cameron V-65 balloon | D. Chapman |
| | G-BLES | Stolp SA.750 Acroduster Too | T. W. Harris |
| | G-BLET | Thunder Ax7-77-1 balloon | Servatruc Ltd |
| | G-BLEW | Cessna F.182Q | Interair Aviation Ltd/Bournemouth |
| | G-BLEY | SA.365N Dauphin 2 | Bond Helicopters Ltd |
| | G-BLEZ | SA.365N Dauphin 2 | Bond Helicopters Ltd |
| | G-BLFE | Cameron Sphinx SS balloon | Forbes Europe Inc |
| | G-BLFF | Cessna F.172M | Air Advertising UK Ltd |
| | G-BLFJ | F.27 Friendship Mk 100 | Air UK Ltd (G-OMAN/G-SPUD)/Norwich |
| | G-BLFT | P.56 Provost T.1 (WV686) | B. W. H. Parkhouse |
| | G-BLFW | AA-5 Traveler | Grumman Club |
| | G-BLFY | Cameron V-77 balloon | A. N. F. Pertwee |
| | G-BLFZ | PA-31-310 Turbo Navajo C | Cheveley Air Services |
| | G-BLGB | Short SD3-60 | Loganair Ltd/Glasgow |
| | G-BLGH | Robin DR.300/180R | Booker Gliding Club Ltd |
| | G-BLGM | Cessna 425 | M. J. L. Batt |
| | G-BLGO | Bensen B.8M | F. Vernon |
| | G-BLGR | Bell 47G-4A | Autair Ltd |
| | G-BLGS | SOCATA Rallye 180T | Lasham Gliding Society Ltd |
| | G-BLGT | PA-18 Super Cub 95 | T. A. Reed/Dunkeswell |
| | G-BLGV | Bell 206B JetRanger | Part Reward Ltd |

| Reg. | Type | Owner or Operator | Notes |
|------|------|-------------------|-------|
| G-BLGW | F.27 Friendship Mk 200 | Air UK Ltd *Louis Marchesi*/Norwich | |
| G-BLGX | Thunder Ax7-65 balloon | Harper & Co (Glasgow) Ltd | |
| G-BLHA | Thunder Ax10-160 balloon | Thunder Balloons Ltd | |
| G-BLHB | Thunder Ax10-160 balloon | Thunder Balloons Ltd | |
| G-BLHF | Nott-Cameron ULD-2 balloon | J. R. P. Nott | |
| G-BLHH | Jodel DR.315 | G. G. Milton | |
| G-BLHI | Colt 17A balloon | Newbury Ballooning Co Ltd | |
| G-BLHJ | Cessna F.172P | P. P. D. Howard-Johnston/Edinburgh | |
| G-BLHK | Colt 105A balloon | Hale Hot-Air Balloon Club | |
| G-BLHM | PA-18 Super Cub 95 | B. N. C. Mogg | |
| G-BLHN | Robin HR.100/285 | H. M. Bouquiere/Biggin Hill | |
| G-BLHR | GA-7 Cougar | Fotex Aviation Ltd | |
| G-BLHS | Bellanca 7ECA Citabria | J. W. Platten & E. J. Timmins | |
| G-BLHW | Varga 2150A Kachina | D. M. Jagger | |
| G-BLID | D.H.112 Venom FB.50 (J-1605) ★ | P. G. Vallance Ltd/Charlwood | |
| G-BLIE | D.H.112 Venom FB.50 | R. J. Everett | |
| G-BLIG | Cameron V-65 balloon | W. Davison | |
| G-BLIH | PA-18 Super Cub 135 | I. R. F. Hammond | |
| G-BLIK | Wallis WA-116/F/S | K. H. Wallis | |
| G-BLIP | Cameron N-77 balloon | L. A. Beardall & G. R. Hunt | |
| G-BLIT | Thorp T-18 CW | K. B. Hallam | |
| G-BLIW | P.56 Provost T.51 (177) | Pulsegrove Ltd (*stored*)/Shoreham | |
| G-BLIX | Saro Skeeter Mk 12 (XL809) | A. P. Nowicki | |
| G-BLIY | M.S.892A Rallye Commodore | A. J. Brasher & K. R. Haynes | |
| G-BLJD | Glaser-Dirks DG.400 | G. G. Hearne & M. I. Gee | |
| G-BLJE | AB-206B JetRanger | Nexgen Ltd | |
| G-BLJF | Cameron O-65 balloon | C. Dupernex & L. Kindley | |
| G-BLJG | Cameron N-105 balloon | J. W. Cato | |
| G-BLJH | Cameron N-77 balloon | Phillair | |
| G-BLJI | Colt 105A balloon | Tempowish Ltd | |
| G-BLJJ | Cessna 305 Bird Dog | P. Dawe | |
| G-BLJM | Beech 95-B55 Baron | Elstree Aircraft Hire Ltd | |
| G-BLJN | Nott-Cameron ULD-1 balloon | J. R. P. Nott | |
| G-BLJO | Cessna F.152 | Redhill School of Flying Ltd | |
| G-BLJP | Cessna F.150L | Three Counties Aero Engineering Ltd/ Lasham | |
| G-BLKA | D.H.112 Venom FB.54 (WR410) | A. Topen/Cranfield | |
| G-BLKF | Thunder Ax10-160 balloon | Thunder Balloons Ltd | |
| G-BLKG | Thunder Ax10-160 balloon | Thunder Balloons Ltd | |
| G-BLKH | Thunder Ax10-160 balloon | Thunder Balloons Ltd | |
| G-BLKI | Thunder Ax10-160 balloon | Thunder Balloons Ltd | |
| G-BLKJ | Thunder Ax7-65 balloon | D. T. Watkins | |
| G-BLKK | Evans VP-1 | R. W. Burrows | |
| G-BLKL | D.31 Turbulent | D. L. Ripley | |
| G-BLKM | Jodel DR.1051 | T. C. Humphreys | |
| G-BLKP | BAe Jetstream 3102 | British Aerospace PLC/Warton | |
| G-BLKU | Colt 56 SS balloon | Hot-Air Balloon Co Ltd | |
| G-BLKY | Beech 95-58 Baron | Kebbell Holdings Ltd/Leavesden | |
| G-BLKZ | Pilatus P2-05 | Autokraft Ltd | |
| G-BLLA | Bensen B.8M | K. T. Donaghey | |
| G-BLLB | Bensen B.8M | D. H. Moss | |
| G-BLLD | Cameron O-77 balloon | I. O. Gracie | |
| G-BLLE | Cameron 60 Burger King SS balloon | Burger King UK Ltd | |
| G-BLLH | Jodel DR.220A 2+2 | D. R. Scott-Longhurst & V. D. Stotter | |
| G-BLLM | PA-23 Aztec 250E | C. & M. Thomas (G-BBNM)/Cardiff | |
| G-BLLN | PA-18 Super Cub 95 | A. L. Hall-Carpenter | |
| G-BLLO | PA-18 Super Cub 95 | D. G. & M. G. Marketts | |
| G-BLLP | Slingsby T.67B | Devon School of Flying/Dunkeswell | |
| G-BLLR | Slingsby T.67B | Trent Air Services Ltd/Cranfield | |
| G-BLLS | Slingsby T.67B | Chikka Ltd | |
| G-BLLT | AA-5B Tiger | Alpha Welding & Engineering Ltd | |
| G-BLLV | Slingsby T.67B | R. L. Brinklow | |
| G-BLLW | Colt 56B balloon | J. C. Stupples | |
| G-BLLZ | Rutan LongEz | G. E. Relf & ptnrs | |
| G-BLMA | Zlin 326 Trener Master | G. P. Northcott/Shoreham | |
| G-BLMC | Avro 698 Vulcan B.2A (XM575) ★ | Aeropark/E. Midlands | |
| G-BLME | Robinson R-22 | Skyline Helicopters Ltd | |
| G-BLMG | Grob G.109B | Mike Golf Syndicate | |
| G-BLMI | PA-18 Super Cub 95 | B. J. Borsberry | |
| G-BLMN | Rutan LongEz | G-BLMN Flying Group | |
| G-BLMP | PA-17 Vagabond | M. Austin/Popham | |
| G-BLMR | PA-18 Super Cub 150 | South Midlands Commercial Aviation | |

| Notes | Reg. | Type | Owner or Operator |
|---|---|---|---|
| | | | School Ltd |
| | G-BLMT | PA-18 Super Cub 135 | I. S. Runnalls |
| | G-BLMV | Jodel DR.1051 | S. Windsor |
| | G-BLMW | T.66 Nipper 3 | S. L. Millar |
| | G-BLMX | Cessna FR.172H | C. J. W. Littler/Felthorpe |
| | G-BLMZ | Colt 105A balloon | M. J. Hutchins |
| | G-BLNB | V.802 Viscount | British Air Ferries (G-AOHV)/Southend |
| | G-BLNJ | BN-2B-26 Islander | Loganair Ltd/Glasgow |
| | G-BLNO | FRED Srs 3 | L. W. Smith |
| | G-BLNW | BN-2B-27 Islander | Loganair Ltd/Glasgow |
| | G-BLOA | V.806 Viscount Freightmaster II | British Air Ferries (G-AOYJ) *Viscount Jock Bryce OBE*/Southend |
| | G-BLOB | Colt 31A balloon | Jacques W. Soukup Ltd |
| | G-BLOE | PA-31-350 Navajo Chieftain | PW Cleaning Services Ltd (G-NITE) |
| | G-BLOJ | Thunder Ax7-77 Srs 1 balloon | J. W. Cato |
| | G-BLOK | Colt 77A balloon | D. L. Clark *Spritsa* |
| | G-BLOL | SNCAN Stampe SV-4A | Skysport Engineering Ltd |
| | G-BLOO | Sopwith Dove Replica | Skysport Engineering Ltd |
| | G-BLOR | PA-30 Twin Comanche 160 | J. A. Burton |
| | G-BLOS | Cessna 185A (also flown with floats) | E. Brun |
| | G-BLOT | Colt Ax6-56B balloon | H. J. Anderson |
| | G-BLOU | Rand KR-2 | D. Cole |
| | G-BLOV | Colt Ax5-42 Srs 1 balloon | Thunder & Colt Ltd |
| | G-BLPA | Piper J-3C-65 Cub | G. A. Card |
| | G-BLPB | Turner TSW Hot Two Wot | J. R. Woolford |
| | G-BLPE | PA-18 Super Cub 95 | A. Haig-Thomas |
| | G-BLPF | Cessna FR.172G | W. A. F. Cuninghame |
| | G-BLPG | J/1N Alpha (16693) | Q. J. Ball (G-AZIH) |
| | G-BLPH | Cessna FRA.150L | New Aerobat Group/Shoreham |
| | G-BLPI | Slingsby T.67B | Keepcase Ltd |
| | G-BLPK | Cameron V-65 balloon | A. J. & C. P. Nicholls |
| | G-BLPM | AS.332L Super Puma | Bristow Helicopters Ltd |
| | G-BLPP | Cameron V-77 balloon | L. P. Purfield |
| | G-BLPV | Short SD3-60 Variant 100 | Loganair Ltd/Glasgow |
| | G-BLRC | PA-18 Super Cub 135 | Grays (Pakefield) Ltd |
| | G-BLRD | MBB Bo.209 Monsun 150FV | M. D. Ward |
| | G-BLRF | Slingsby T.67C | Bristow Helicopters Ltd/Redhill |
| | G-BLRG | Slingsby T.67B | Devon School of Flying/Dunkeswell |
| | G-BLRH | Rutan LongEz | G. L. Thompson |
| | G-BLRJ | Jodel DR.1051 | M. P. Hallam |
| | G-BLRL | CP.301C-1 Emeraude | M. Howells/Barton |
| | G-BLRM | Glaser-Dirks DG.400 | D. J. Barke |
| | G-BLRN | D.H.104 Dove 8 (WB531) | C.W. Simpson/Exeter |
| | G-BLRP | FMA IA.58A Pucará | R. J. H. Butterfield |
| | G-BLRT | Short SD3-60 Variant 100 | Shorts Aircraft Financing Ltd |
| | G-BLRW | Cameron 77 Elephant SS balloon | Forbes Europe Inc/France |
| | G-BLRX | SOCATA TB.9 Tampico | Wiselock Ltd/Elstree |
| | G-BLRY | AS.332L Super Puma | Bristow Helicopters Ltd |
| | G-BLRZ | SOCATA TB.9 Tampico | Aldred Associates Ltd |
| | G-BLSC | Consolidated PBY-5A Catalina (JV928) | J. P. Warren Wilson/Duxford |
| | G-BLSD | D.H.112 Venom FB.55 (J-1758) | Aces High Ltd/North Weald |
| | G-BLSF | AA-5A Cheetah | J. P. E. Walsh (G-BGCK) |
| | G-BLSH | Cameron V-77 balloon | C. N. Luffingham |
| | G-BLSJ | Thunder Ax8-90 balloon | Thunder Balloons Ltd |
| | G-BLSK | Colt 77A balloon | Solarmoor Ltd |
| | G-BLSM | H.S.125 Srs 700B | Dravidian Air Services Ltd/Heathrow |
| | G-BLSN | Colt AS-56 airship | Flying Pictures (Balloons) Ltd |
| | G-BLSO | Colt AS-42 airship | Huntair Ltd/Germany |
| | G-BLST | Cessna 421C | Cecil Aviation Ltd/Cambridge |
| | G-BLSU | Cameron A-210 balloon | Skysales Ltd |
| | G-BLSX | Cameron O-105 balloon | B. J. Petteford |
| | G-BLTA | Thunder Ax7-77A | K. A. Schlussler |
| | G-BLTC | D.31 Turbulent | G. P. Smith & A. W. Burton |
| | G-BLTF | Robinson R-22A | J. Holt |
| | G-BLTG | WAR Sea Fury (WJ237) | A. N. R. Houghton & D. H. Nourish |
| | G-BLTK | R. Commander 112TC | B. Rogalewski/Denham |
| | G-BLTM | Robin HR.200/100 | B. D. Balcanquall |
| | G-BLTN | Thunder Ax7-65 balloon | J. A. Liddle |
| | G-BLTO | Short SD3-60 Variant 100 | Lynrise Aircraft Financing Ltd |
| | G-BLTP | H.S.125 Srs 700B | Dravidian Air Services Ltd/Heathrow |
| | G-BLTR | Scheibe SF.25B Falke | V. Mallon/Germany |

| Reg. | Type | Owner or Operator | Notes |
|------|------|-------------------|-------|
| G-BLTS | Rutan LongEz | R. W. Cutler | |
| G-BLTT | Slingsby T.67B | S. E. Marples | |
| G-BLTU | Slingsby T.67B | The Neiderhein Powered Flying Club/ Germany | |
| G-BLTV | Slingsby T.67B | Trent Air Services Ltd/Cranfield | |
| G-BLTW | Slingsby T.67B | Devon School of Flying/Dunkeswell | |
| G-BLTZ | SOCATA TB.10 Tobago | Martin Ltd/Biggin Hill | |
| G-BLUA | Robinson R-22 | J. R. Budgen | |
| G-BLUE | Colting Ax7-77A balloon | R. H. Etherington | |
| G-BLUI | Thunder Ax7-65 balloon | S. Johnson | |
| G-BLUJ | Cameron V-56 balloon | J. N. W. West | |
| G-BLUK | Bond Sky Dancer | J. Owen | |
| G-BLUL | Jodel DR.1051/M1 | J. Owen | |
| G-BLUM | SA.365N Dauphin 2 | Bond Helicopters Ltd | |
| G-BLUO | SA.365N Dauphin 2 | Bond Helicopters Ltd | |
| G-BLUP | SA.365N Dauphin 2 | Bond Helicopters Ltd | |
| G-BLUV | Grob G.109B | Go-Grob Ltd | |
| G-BLUX | Slingsby T.67M | Slingsby Aviation Ltd/Kirkbymoorside | |
| G-BLUY | Colt 69A balloon | The Balloon Goes Up Ltd | |
| G-BLUZ | D.H.82B Queen Bee (LF858) | B. Bayes | |
| G-BLVA | Airtour AH-56 balloon | Airtour Balloon Co Ltd | |
| G-BLVB | Airtour AH-56 balloon | Airtour Balloon Co Ltd | |
| G-BLVC | Airtour AH-31 balloon | Airtour Balloon Co Ltd | |
| G-BLVI | Slingsby T.67M | Slingsby Aviation Ltd/Kirkbymoorside | |
| G-BLVK | CAARP CAP-10B | E. K. Coventry/Earls Colne | |
| G-BLVL | PA-28-161 Warrior II | C.S.E. Aviation Ltd/Kidlington | |
| G-BLVN | Cameron N-77 balloon | B. Hodge | |
| G-BLVS | Cessna 150M | W. Lancs Aero Club Ltd/Woodvale | |
| G-BLVW | Cessna F.172H | R. & D. Holloway Ltd | |
| G-BLWB | Thunder Ax6-56 balloon | J. R. Tonkin/Norwich | |
| G-BLWD | PA-34-200T Seneca | C.S.E. Aviation Ltd/Kidlington | |
| G-BLWE | Colt 90A balloon | Huntair Ltd/Germany | |
| G-BLWF | Robin HR.100/210 | K. J. Weston | |
| G-BLWH | Fournier RF-6B-100 | Gloster Aero Club Ltd/Staverton | |
| G-BLWM | Bristol M.1C (replica) (C4994) ★ | RAF Museum/Hendon | |
| G-BLWP | PA-38-112 Tomahawk | A. Dodd/Booker | |
| G-BLWT | Evans VP-1 | C. J. Bellworthy | |
| G-BLWV | Cessna F.152 | Redhill Flying Club | |
| G-BLWW | Taylor Mini Imp Model C | M. K. Field | |
| G-BLWX | Cameron N-56 balloon | W. Evans | |
| G-BLWY | Robin 2161D | A. Spencer & D. A. Rolfe | |
| G-BLXA | SOCATA TB.20 Trinidad | Shropshire Aero Club Ltd | |
| G-BLXF | Cameron V-77 balloon | G. McFarland | |
| G-BLXG | Colt 21A balloon | E. J. A. Macholc | |
| G-BLXH | Fournier RF-3 | A. Rawicz-Szczerbo | |
| G-BLXI | CP.1310-C3 Super Emeraude | RAE Bedford Flying Club | |
| G-BLXK | Agusta-Bell 205 | Autair Helicopters Ltd | |
| G-BLXO | Jodel D.150 | P. R. Powell | |
| G-BLXP | PA-28R Cherokee Arrow 200 | A. M. Bailey & T. A. Shears | |
| G-BLXR | AS.332L Super Puma | Bristow Helicopters Ltd | |
| G-BLXS | AS.332L Super Puma | Bristow Helicopters Ltd | |
| G-BLXT | RAF SE-5A (B4863) ★ | Museum of Army Flying/Middle Wallop | |
| G-BLXX | PA-23 Aztec 250F | Falcon Flying Service (G-PIED)/Biggin Hill | |
| G-BLXY | Cameron V-65 balloon | Gone With The Wind Ltd/Tanzania | |
| G-BLYC | PA-38-112 Tomahawk | Liverpool Flying School Ltd | |
| G-BLYD | SOCATA TB.20 Trinidad | Gourmet Trotters | |
| G-BLYE | SOCATA TB.10 Tobago | G. Hatton | |
| G-BLYJ | Cameron V-77 balloon | E. E. Clark & J. A. Lomas | |
| G-BLYK | PA-34-220T Seneca III | P. G. Somers | |
| G-BLYP | Robin 3000/120 | Lydd Air Training Centre Ltd | |
| G-BLYR | Airtour AH-77B balloon | Airtour Balloon Co Ltd | |
| G-BLYT | Airtour AH-77 balloon | Airtour Balloon Co Ltd | |
| G-BLYY | PA-28-181 Archer II | A. C. Clarke | |
| G-BLZA | Scheibe SF.25B Falke | P. Downes & D. Gardner | |
| G-BLZB | Cameron N-65 balloon | D. Bareford | |
| G-BLZD | Robin R.1180T | Berkshire Aviation Services Ltd | |
| G-BLZE | Cessna F.152 | Flairhire Ltd (G-CSSC)/Redhill | |
| G-BLZF | Thunder Ax7-77 balloon | H. M. Savage | |
| G-BLZH | Cessna F.152 | Biggin Hill School of Flying | |
| G-BLZM | Rutan LongEz | Zulu Mike Group | |
| G-BLZN | Bell 206B JetRanger | Helicopter Services | |
| G-BLZP | Cessna F.152 | E. Midlands Flying School Ltd | |
| G-BLZR | Cameron A-140 balloon | Clipper Worldwide Trading/Venezuela | |

| Notes | Reg. | Type | Owner or Operator |
|---|---|---|---|
| | G-BLZS | Cameron O-77 balloon | M. M. Cobbold |
| | G-BLZT | Short SD3-60 | Jersey European Airways Ltd |
| | G-BMAA | Douglas DC-9-15 | British Midland Airways Ltd *The Shah Diamond*/(G-BFIH)/E. Midlands |
| | G-BMAB | Douglas DC-9-15 | British Midland Airways Ltd *The Great Mogul Diamond*/E. Midlands |
| | G-BMAC | Douglas DC-9-15 | British Midland Airways Ltd *The Eugenie Diamond*/E. Midlands |
| | G-BMAD | Cameron V-77 balloon | F. J. J. Fielder |
| | G-BMAF | Cessna 180F | P. Channon |
| | G-BMAG | Douglas DC-9-15 | British Midland Airways Ltd *The Nassak Diamond*/E. Midlands |
| | G-BMAH | Douglas DC-9-14 | British Midland Airways Ltd *The Florentine Diamond*/E. Midlands |
| | G-BMAI | Douglas DC-9-14 | British Midland Airways Ltd *The Star of Este Diamond*/E. Midlands |
| | G-BMAK | Douglas DC-9-30 | British Midland Airways Ltd *The Stewart Diamond*/E. Midlands |
| | G-BMAL | Sikorsky S-76A | Bond Helicopters Ltd |
| | G-BMAM | Douglas DC-9-30 | British Midland Airways Ltd *The Cullinan Diamond*/E. Midlands |
| | G-BMAO | Taylor JT.1 Monoplane | V. A. Wordsworth |
| | G-BMAR | Short SD3-60 | Loganair Ltd (G-BLCR)/Glasgow |
| | G-BMAV | AS.350B Ecureuil | Southern Trust Co Ltd/Jersey |
| | G-BMAX | FRED Srs 2 | D. A. Arkley |
| | G-BMAY | PA-18 Super Cub 135 | R. W. Davies |
| | G-BMBB | Cessna F.150L | Dacebow Aviation |
| | G-BMBC | PA-31-350 Navajo Chieftain | Comed Aviation Ltd/Blackpool |
| | G-BMBE | PA-46-310P Malibu | Barfax Distributing Co Ltd & Glasdon Group Ltd/Blackpool |
| | G-BMBI | PA-31-350 Navajo Chieftain | Ennemix Holdings Ltd/E. Midlands |
| | G-BMBJ | Schempp-Hirth Janus CM | RAF Germany Gliding Assoc |
| | G-BMBS | Colt 105A balloon | H. G. Davies |
| | G-BMBT | Thunder Ax8-90 balloon | Capital Balloon Club Ltd |
| | G-BMBW | Bensen B.80 | M. Vahdat |
| | G-BMBY | Beech A36 Bonanza | Arthur Webb Engineers Ltd/Birmingham |
| | G-BMBZ | Scheibe SF.25E Super Falke | Buckminster Super Falke Syndicate |
| | G-BMCC | Thunder Ax7-77 balloon | H. N. Harben Ltd |
| | G-BMCD | Cameron V-65 balloon | M. C. Drye |
| | G-BMCG | Grob G.109B | Lagerholm Finnimport Ltd/Booker |
| | G-BMCI | Cessna F.172H | A. B. Davis/Edinburgh |
| | G-BMCJ | PA-31-350 Navajo Chieftain | Chelsea Land (Finance) Ltd |
| | G-BMCK | Cameron O-77 balloon | D. L. Smith |
| | G-BMCM | Grob G.109B | C. J. Partridge/Blackbushe |
| | G-BMCN | Cessna F.152 | Lincoln Aero Club Ltd/Sturgate |
| | G-BMCO | Colomban MC.15 Cri-Cri | G. P. Clarke/Enstone |
| | G-BMCS | PA-22 Tri-Pacer 135 | C. J. Weaver |
| | G-BMCV | Cessna F.152 | Leicestershire Aero Club Ltd |
| | G-BMCW | AS.332L Super Puma | Bristow Helicopters Ltd |
| | G-BMCX | AS.332L Super Puma | Bristow Helicopters Ltd |
| | G-BMDB | SE-5A (replica) (F235) | D. Biggs |
| | G-BMDC | PA-32-301 Saratoga | Maclaren Aviation/Newcastle |
| | G-BMDD | Slingsby T.29 | A. R. Worters |
| | G-BMDE | Pientenpol Air Camper | D. Silsbury |
| | G-BMDF | Boeing 737-2E7 | Capita Ltd |
| | G-BMDH | Cameron O-105 balloon | Buddy Bombard Balloons Ltd/France |
| | G-BMDI | Thunder Ax8-105Z balloon | Buddy Bombard Balloons Ltd/France |
| | G-BMDJ | Price Ax7-77S balloon | T. S. Price/Holland |
| | G-BMDK | PA-34-220T Seneca III | A1 Air Ltd |
| | G-BMDO | ARV Super 2 | R. Lloyd |
| | G-BMDP | Partenavia P.64B Oscar 200 | D. Foey |
| | G-BMDS | Jodel D.120 | J. V. Thompson |
| | G-BMDV | Bell 47G-5 | Trent Air Services Ltd/Cranfield |
| | G-BMDW | Dangerous Sports Club/Colt Hoppalong 1 balloon | D. A. C. Kirke |
| | G-BMDY | GA-7 Cougar | P. J. Bristow |
| | G-BMEA | PA-18 Super Cub 95 | C. L. Towell |
| | G-BMEB | Rotorway Scorpion 145 | I. M. Bartlett |
| | G-BMEE | Cameron O-105 balloon | A. G. R. Calder/Los Angeles |
| | G-BMEG | SOCATA TB.10 Tobago | G. H. N. & R. V. Chamberlain |
| | G-BMEH | Jodel Special Super Mascaret | W. Coupar Ltd |
| | G-BMEJ | PA-28R Cherokee Arrow 200 | London Flight Centre (Stansted) Ltd |

| Reg. | Type | Owner or Operator | Notes |
|------|------|-------------------|-------|
| G-BMEK | Mooney M.20K | Atlantic Film Investments Ltd/USA | |
| G-BMET | Taylor JT.1 Monoplane | M. K. A. Blyth | |
| G-BMEU | Isaacs Fury II | A. W. Austin | |
| G-BMEV | PA-32RT-300T Turbo Lance II | Danton Aviation Ltd | |
| G-BMEX | Cessna A.150K | S. G. Eldred & N. A. M. Brain | |
| G-BMFD | PA-23 Aztec 250F | Rangemile Ltd (G-BGYY)/Coventry | |
| G-BMFG | Dornier Do.27A-4 (3460) | R. F. Warner | |
| G-BMFI | PZL SZD-45A Ogar | Marrix Ltd/Redhill | |
| G-BMFL | Rand KR-2 | E. W. B. Comber & M. F. Leusby | |
| G-BMFN | QAC Quickie Tri-Q.200 | A. W. Webster | |
| G-BMFP | PA-28-161 Warrior II | Bravo-Mike-Fox-Papa Group | |
| G-BMFT | H.S.748 Srs 2A | Business Air Ltd/Aberdeen | |
| G-BMFU | Cameron N-90 balloon | J. J. Rudoni | |
| G-BMFW | Hughes 369E | Ford Helicopters Ltd | |
| G-BMFY | Grob G.109B | P. J. Shearer | |
| G-BMFZ | Cessna F.152 | Cornwall Flying Club Ltd | |
| G-BMGB | PA-28R Cherokee Arrow 200 | Malmesbury Specialist Cars | |
| G-BMGC | Fairey Swordfish Mk II (W5856) | FAA Museum (on rebuild)/Yeovilton | |
| G-BMGD | Colt 17A balloon | Airbureau Ltd | |
| G-BMGG | Cessna 152 | Falcon Flying Services/Biggin Hill | |
| G-BMGH | PA-31-325 Turbo Navajo C/R | Jet West Ltd/Exeter | |
| G-BMGP | Hughes 269C | Orion Atlantic Ltd | |
| G-BMGR | Grob G.109B | M. Clarke & D. S. Hawes | |
| G-BMGT | Cessna 310R | Air Service Training Ltd/Perth | |
| G-BMGV | Robinson R-22 | D. L. Weldon | |
| G-BMGY | Lake LA-4-200 Buccaneer | M. A. Ashmole (G-BWKS/G-BDDI) | |
| G-BMHA | Rutan LongEz | S. F. Elvins | |
| G-BMHC | Cessna U.206G | Clacton Aero Club (1988) Ltd | |
| G-BMHJ | Thunder Ax7-65 balloon | M. G. Robinson | |
| G-BMHK | Cameron V-77 balloon | E. Evans & J. Wilkinson | |
| G-BMHL | Wittman W.8 Tailwind | T. G. Hoult | |
| G-BMHN | Robinson R-22A | Fulford Builders (York) Ltd | |
| G-BMHR | Grob G.109B | HRN Aviation Ltd | |
| G-BMHS | Cessna F.172M | Tango X-Ray Flying Group | |
| G-BMHT | PA-28RT-201T Turbo Arrow IV | Relay Services Ltd | |
| G-BMHX | Short SD3-60 | Loganair Ltd/Glasgow | |
| G-BMHZ | PA-28RT-201T Turbo Arrow IV | M. A. Grayburn | |
| G-BMIA | Thunder Ax8-90 balloon | A. G. R. Calder/Los Angeles | |
| G-BMIB | Bell 206B JetRanger | Lee Aviation Ltd/Booker | |
| G-BMID | Jodel D.120 | P. D. Smoothy | |
| G-BMIF | AS.350B Ecureuil | Colt Car Co Ltd/Staverton | |
| G-BMIG | Cessna 172N | J. R. Nicholls/Conington | |
| G-BMIM | Rutan LongEz | R. M. Smith | |
| G-BMIO | Stoddard-Hamilton Glasair RG | A. H. Carrington | |
| G-BMIP | Jodel D.112 | M. T. Kinch | |
| G-BMIR | Westland Wasp HAS.1 (XT788) | M. Windley | |
| G-BMIS | Monnet Sonerai II | B. A. Bower/Thruxton | |
| G-BMIV | PA-28R-201T Turbo Arrow III | Maurice Mason Ltd | |
| G-BMIW | PA-28-181 Archer II | Oldbus Ltd | |
| G-BMIY | Oldfield Baby Great Lakes | J. B. Scott (G-NOME) | |
| G-BMJA | PA-32R-301 Saratoga SP | Continental Cars (Stansted) Ltd | |
| G-BMJB | Cessna 152 | Bobbington Air Training School Ltd/ Halfpenny Green | |
| G-BMJC | Cessna 152 | Cambridge Aero Club Ltd | |
| G-BMJD | Cessna 152 | Fife Airport Management Ltd | |
| G-BMJG | PA-28R Cherokee Arrow 200 | D. J. D. Ritchie & ptnrs/Elstree | |
| G-BMJL | R. Commander 114 | H. Snelson | |
| G-BMJM | Evans VP-1 | C. A. Macleod | |
| G-BMJN | Cameron O-65 balloon | E. J. A. Machole | |
| G-BMJO | PA-34-220T Seneca III | B. Walker & Co (Dursley) Ltd & John Ward (Holdings) Ltd | |
| G-BMJR | Cessna T.337H | John Roberts Services Ltd (G-NOVA) | |
| G-BMJS | Thunder Ax7-77 balloon | Foulger Transport Ltd | |
| G-BMJT | Beech 76 Duchess | Mike Osborne Properties Ltd | |
| G-BMJW | NA AT-6D Harvard III (EZ259) | J. Woods | |
| G-BMJX | Wallis WA-116X | K. H. Wallis | |
| G-BMJY | Yakolev C18M | R. Lamplough/North Weald | |
| G-BMJZ | Cameron N-90 balloon | Bristol University Hot Air Ballooning Soc | |
| G-BMKB | PA-18 Super Cub 135 | Medway Flight Training/Rochester | |
| G-BMKC | Piper J-3C-65 Cub (329854) | R. J. H. Springall | |
| G-BMKD | Beech C90A King Air | A. E. Bristow | |
| G-BMKE | PA-28RT-201 Arrow IV | AT Aviation Ltd/Cardiff | |
| G-BMKF | Jodel DR.221 | L. Gilbert | |

| Notes | Reg. | Type | Owner or Operator |
|---|---|---|---|
| | G-BMKG | PA-38-112 Tomahawk | R. J. Hickson |
| | G-BMKH | Colt 105A balloon | Scotia Balloons Ltd |
| | G-BMKI | Colt 21A balloon | Thunder & Colt Ltd |
| | G-BMKJ | Cameron V-77 balloon | R. C. Thursby |
| | G-BMKK | PA-28R Cherokee Arrow 200 | J. H. Hutchinson |
| | G-BMKM | AB-206B JetRanger 3 | Fizzle Ltd |
| | G-BMKO | PA-28-181 Archer II | Moulin Ltd |
| | G-BMKP | Cameron V-77 balloon | Jacques W. Soukup Enterprises Ltd |
| | G-BMKR | PA-28-161 Warrior II | Field Flying Group (G-BGKR)/Goodwood |
| | G-BMKV | Thunder Ax7-77 balloon | A. Hornak & M. J. Nadel |
| | G-BMKW | Cameron V-77 balloon | A. C. Garnett |
| | G-BMKX | Cameron 77 Elephant SS balloon | Cameron Balloons Ltd |
| | G-BMKY | Cameron O-65 balloon | K. M. Taylor & A. R. Rich |
| | G-BMLB | Jodel D.120A | W. O. Brown |
| | G-BMLC | Short SD3-60 Variant 100 | Loganair Ltd/Glasgow |
| | G-BMLH | Mooney M.20C | G. D. Bowd |
| | G-BMLJ | Cameron N-77 balloon | C. J. Dunkley |
| | G-BMLK | Grob G.109B | Brams Syndicate |
| | G-BMLL | Grob G.109B | A. H. R. Stansfield |
| | G-BMLP | Boeing 727-264 | Capita Ltd |
| | G-BMLS | PA-28R-201 Arrow III | Faukland Flyers Ltd |
| | G-BMLT | Pietenpol Air Camper | W. E. R. Jenkins |
| | G-BMLU | Colt 90A balloon | Danish Catering Services Ltd |
| | G-BMLV | Robinson R-22A | Skyline Helicopters Ltd/Booker |
| | G-BMLW | Cameron V-65 balloon | M. L. & L. P. Willoughby |
| | G-BMLX | Cessna F.150L | S. G. P. Foster/Headcorn |
| | G-BMLY | Grob G.109B | P. H. Yarrow & D. G. Margetts |
| | G-BMLZ | Cessna 421C | Jet West Ltd (G-OTAD/G-BEVL)/Exeter |
| | G-BMMC | Cessna T310Q | Cooper Clegg Ltd |
| | G-BMMD | Rand KR-2 | R. S. Stoddart-Stones |
| | G-BMMF | FRED Srs 2 | J. M. Jones |
| | G-BMMG | Thunder Ax 7-77 balloon | G. V. Beckwith |
| | G-BMMI | Pazmany PL.4 | M. K. Field |
| | G-BMMJ | Siren PIK-30 | J. P. Greig |
| | G-BMMK | Cessna 182P | M. S. Knight/Goodwood |
| | G-BMML | PA-38-112 Tomahawk | Cumbernauld Aviation Ltd |
| | G-BMMM | Cessna 152 | Luton Flight Training Ltd |
| | G-BMMN | Thunder Ax8-105 balloon | R. C. Weyda |
| | G-BMMP | Grob G.109B | B. F. Fraser-Smith & B. F. Pearson |
| | G-BMMR | Dornier Do.228-200 | Suckling Airways Ltd/Cambridge |
| | G-BMMU | Thunder Ax8-105 balloon | H. C. Wright |
| | G-BMMV | ICA-Brasov IS-28M2A | T. Cust |
| | G-BMMW | Thunder Ax7-77 balloon | P. A. Georges |
| | G-BMMX | ICA-Brasov IS-28M2A | G-BMMX Syndicate |
| | G-BMMY | Thunder Ax7-77 balloon | D. A. Lawson |
| | G-BMNF | Beech B200 Super King Air | Bernard Matthews PLC/Norwich |
| | G-BMNL | PA-28R Cherokee Arrow 200 | I. H. Nettleton |
| | G-BMNP | PA-38-112 Tomahawk | APB Leasing Ltd/Welshpool |
| | G-BMNT | PA-34-220T Seneca III | Airpart Supply Ltd |
| | G-BMNV | SNCAN Stampe SV-4D | Wessex Aviation & Transport Ltd |
| | G-BMNW | PA-31-350 Navajo Chieftain | Crosswind Consultants |
| | G-BMNX | Colt 56A balloon | J. H. Dryden |
| | G-BMNY | Everett gyroplane | G. Jenkis-Lover |
| | G-BMNZ | Cessna U206F | Macpara Ltd/Shobdon |
| | G-BMOE | PA-28R Cherokee Arrow 200 | B. J. Mason/Shoreham |
| | G-BMOF | Cessna U206G | Integrated Hydraulics Ltd |
| | G-BMOG | Thunder Ax7-77A balloon | P. J. Burn |
| | G-BMOH | Cameron N-77 balloon | P. J. Marshall & M. A. Clarke |
| | G-BMOI | Partenavia P.68B | Simmette Ltd |
| | G-BMOJ | Cameron V-56 balloon | S. R. Bridge |
| | G-BMOK | ARV Super 2 | P. E. Barker |
| | G-BMOL | PA-23 Aztec 250D | LDL Enterprises (G-BBSR)/Elstree |
| | G-BMOM | ICA-Brasov IS-28M2A | Brasov Flying Group |
| | G-BMOO | FRED Srs 2 | N. Purllant |
| | G-BMOP | PA-28R-201T Turbo Arrow III | Coleridge Self Service/Cardiff |
| | G-BMOT | Bensen B.8M | R. S. W. Jones |
| | G-BMOV | Cameron O-105 balloon | C. Gillott |
| | G-BMOX | Hovey Beta Bird | A. K. Jones |
| | G-BMPA | G.159 Gulfstream 1 | — |
| | G-BMPC | PA-28-181 Archer II | C. J. & R. J. Barnes |
| | G-BMPD | Cameron V-65 balloon | D. E. & J. M. Hartland |
| | G-BMPL | OA.7 Optica | Lovaux Ltd/Bournemouth |
| | G-BMPP | Cameron N-77 balloon | Sarnia Balloon Group |

| Reg. | Type | Owner or Operator | Notes |
|------|------|-------------------|-------|
| G-BMPR | PA-28R-201 Arrow III | AH Flight Services Ltd | |
| G-BMPS | Strojnik S-2A | G. J. Green | |
| G-BMPY | D.H.82A Tiger Moth | S. M. F. Eisenstein | |
| G-BMRA | Boeing 757-236 | British Airways *Beaumaris Castle* | |
| G-BMRB | Boeing 757-236 | British Airways *Colchester Castle* | |
| G-BMRC | Boeing 757-236 | British Airways *Rochester Castle* | |
| G-BMRD | Boeing 757-236 | British Airways *Bothwell Castle* | |
| G-BMRE | Boeing 757-236 | British Airways *Killyleagh Castle* | |
| G-BMRF | Boeing 757-236 | British Airways *Hever Castle* | |
| G-BMRG | Boeing 757-236 | British Airways *Caerphilly Castle* | |
| G-BMRH | Boeing 757-236 | British Airways *Norwich Castle* | |
| G-BMRI | Boeing 757-236 | British Airways *Tonbridge Castle* | |
| G-BMRJ | Boeing 757-236 | British Airways *Old Wardour Castle/ Caledonian Airways Loch Tummel* | |
| G-BMRK | Boeing 757-236 | British Airways | |
| G-BMRL | Boeing 757-236 | British Airways | |
| G-BMRM | Boeing 757-236 | British Airways | |
| G-BMSA | Stinson HW.75 Voyager | M. A. Thomas (G-BCUM)/Barton | |
| G-BMSB | V.S.509 Spitfire IX (MJ627) | M. S. Bayliss (G-ASOZ) | |
| G-BMSC | Evans VP-2 | E. J. Bedser | |
| G-BMSD | PA-28-181 Archer II | Courtridge Ltd | |
| G-BMSE | Valentin Taifun 17E | A. J. Nurse | |
| G-BMSF | PA-38-112 Tomahawk | N. Bradley/Leeds | |
| G-BMSG | Saab 32A Lansen ★ | Aces High Ltd/Cranfield | |
| G-BMSI | Cameron N-105 balloon | Direction Air Conditioning Ltd | |
| G-BMSK | Hoffman H-36 Dimona | J. P. Kovacs | |
| G-BMSL | FRED Srs 3 | A. C. Coombe | |
| G-BMSR | G.159 Gulfstream 1 | — | |
| G-BMST | Cameron N-31 balloon | Hot Air Balloon Co Ltd | |
| G-BMSU | Cessna 152 | G-BMSU Group | |
| G-BMSX | PA-30 Twin Comanche 160 | M. Sparks/Bristol | |
| G-BMSY | Cameron A-140 balloon | GT Flying Clubs Ltd | |
| G-BMSZ | Cessna 152 | Aerohire Ltd | |
| G-BMTA | Cessna 152 | Turnhouse Flying Club | |
| G-BMTB | Cessna 152 | J. A. Pothecary/Shoreham | |
| G-BMTJ | Cessna 152 | Creaton Aviation Services Ltd | |
| G-BMTK | Cessna 152 | Galaxy Enterprises Ltd | |
| G-BMTL | Cessna 152 | Agricultural & General Aviation/ Bournemouth | |
| G-BMTN | Cameron O-77 balloon | Industrial Services (MH) Ltd | |
| G-BMTO | PA-38-112 Tomahawk | Galaxy Enterprises Ltd | |
| G-BMTP | PA-38-112 Tomahawk | R. A. Wakefield | |
| G-BMTR | PA-28-161 Warrior II | London Flight Centre (Stansted) Ltd | |
| G-BMTS | Cessna 172N | Luton Flight Training Ltd | |
| G-BMTU | Pitts S-1E Special | O. R. Howe | |
| G-BMTW | PA-31-350 Navajo Chieftain | Air Northwest Ltd | |
| G-BMTX | Cameron V-77 balloon | J. A. Langley | |
| G-BMTY | Colt 77A balloon | L. D. Ormerod | |
| G-BMUD | Cessna 182P | J. P. Edwards | |
| G-BMUG | Rutan LongEz | P. Richardson & J. Shanley | |
| G-BMUH | Bensen B.8MR | A. Shuttleworth | |
| G-BMUI | Brügger MB.2 Colibri | D. Adlington | |
| G-BMUJ | Colt Drachenfisch balloon | Air 2 Air Ltd | |
| G-BMUK | Colt UFO balloon | Air 2 Air Ltd | |
| G-BMUL | Colt Kindermond balloon | Air 2 Air Ltd | |
| G-BMUN | Cameron Harley 78 balloon | Forbes Europe Inc/France | |
| G-BMUO | Cessna A.152 | Redhill Flying Club | |
| G-BMUR | Cameron gas airship | Cameron Balloons Ltd | |
| G-BMUT | PA-34-200T Seneca II | G. G. Long | |
| G-BMUU | Thunder Ax7-77 balloon | Thunder & Colt Ltd | |
| G-BMUZ | PA-28-161 Warrior II | Newcastle-upon-Tyne Aero Club Ltd | |
| G-BMVA | Schiebe SF.25B Falke | C. A. Simmonds | |
| G-BMVB | Cessna 152 | Howells Group PLC | |
| G-BMVE | PA-28RT-201 Arrow IV | F. E. Gooding/Biggin Hill | |
| G-BMVG | QAC Quickie Q.1 | P. M. Wright | |
| G-BMVI | Cameron O-105 balloon | Heart of England Balloons | |
| G-BMVJ | Cessna 172N | G & B Aviation Ltd/Coventry | |
| G-BMVK | PA-38-112 Tomahawk | Airways Aero Associations Ltd/Booker | |
| G-BMVL | PA-38-112 Tomahawk | Airways Aero Associations Ltd/Booker | |
| G-BMVM | PA-38-112 Tomahawk | Airways Aero Associations Ltd/Booker | |
| G-BMVO | Cameron O-77 balloon | Warners Motors (Leasing) Ltd | |
| G-BMVS | Cameron 77 SS balloon | Shellrise Ltd/Miami | |
| G-BMVT | Thunder Ax7-77A balloon | M. L. & L. P. Willoughby | |

| Notes | Reg. | Type | Owner or Operator |
|---|---|---|---|
| | G-BMVU | Monnet Moni | F. S. Beckett |
| | G-BMVV | Rutan Vari-Viggen | G. B. Roberts |
| | G-BMVW | Cameron O-65 balloon | S. P. Richards |
| | G-BMVX | M.S.733 Alcyon Srs 1 | J. D. Read |
| | G-BMVZ | Cameron 66 Cornetto SS balloon | Gone With The Wind Ltd |
| | G-BMWA | Hughes 269C | JKG Air Services |
| | G-BMWE | ARV Super 2 | N. R. F. McNally |
| | G-BMWF | ARV Super 2 | ARV Aviation Ltd/Sandown |
| | G-BMWG | ARV Super 2 | Falstaff Finance Ltd/Sandown |
| | G-BMWJ | ARV Super 2 | Mid-West Aero Engines Ltd |
| | G-BMWM | ARV Super 2 | R. Scroby |
| | G-BMWN | Cameron 80 SS Temple balloon | Forbes Europe Inc/France |
| | G-BMWP | PA-34-200T Seneca II | R. H. Steward |
| | G-BMWR | R. Commander 112A | M. & J. Edwards |
| | G-BMWU | Cameron N-42 balloon | The Hot Air Balloon Co Ltd |
| | G-BMWV | Putzer Elster B | E. A. J. Hibberd |
| | G-BMWX | Robinson R-22B | LTG Motors (Baldock) |
| | G-BMXA | Cessna 152 | Chamberlain Leasing |
| | G-BMXB | Cessna 152 | Semloch Aviation Services/Andrewsfield |
| | G-BMXC | Cessna 152 | Vectair Aviation Ltd |
| | G-BMXD | F.27 Friendship Mk 500 | Air UK Ltd *Victor Hugo*/Norwich |
| | G-BMXH | Robinson R-22HP | R. H. Ryan |
| | G-BMXJ | Cessna F.150L | J. W. G. Ellis |
| | G-BMXL | PA-38-112 Tomahawk | Airways Aero Associations Ltd/Booker |
| | G-BMXW | D.H.C.6 Twin Otter 310 | Loganair Ltd/Glasgow |
| | G-BMXX | Cessna 152 | Aerohire Ltd/Halfpenny Green |
| | G-BMXY | Scheibe SF.25B Falke | Marrix Ltd |
| | G-BMYA | Colt 56A balloon | Flying Pictures (Balloons) Ltd |
| | G-BMYC | SOCATA TB.10 Tobago | E. A. Grady |
| | G-BMYD | Beech A36 Bonanza | Seabeam Airways Ltd |
| | G-BMYE | BAe 146-200 | British Aerospace PLC (G-WAUS/ G-WISC)/Hatfield |
| | G-BMYF | Bensen B.8M | T. H. G. Russell |
| | G-BMYG | Cessna F.152 | Rolim Ltd/Aberdeen |
| | G-BMYI | AA-5 Traveler | W. C. & S. C. Westran |
| | G-BMYJ | Cameron V-65 balloon | S. M. Antony & R. J. Christopher |
| | G-BMYK | BAe ATP/Jetstream 61 | British Midland Airways Ltd/E. Midlands |
| | G-BMYM | BAe ATP/Jetstream 61 | British Midland Airways Ltd/E. Midlands |
| | G-BMYN | Colt 77A balloon | J. D. Shapland & ptnrs |
| | G-BMYP | Fairey Gannet AEW.3 (XL502) | R. King |
| | G-BMYR | Robinson R-22 | Ranger Helicopters Ltd/Manchester |
| | G-BMYS | Thunder Ax7-77Z balloon | J. E. Weidema/Holland |
| | G-BMYU | Jodel D.120 | I. A. Marsh/Elstree |
| | G-BMYV | Bensen B.8M | R. G. Cotman |
| | G-BMYW | Hughes 269C | William Tomkins Ltd |
| | G-BMZA | Air Command 503 Commander | R. W. Husband |
| | G-BMZB | Cameron N-77 balloon | D. C. Eager |
| | G-BMZC | Cessna 421C | Gilchrist Enterprises |
| | G-BMZD | Beech C90 King Air | Colt Transport Ltd |
| | G-BMZE | SOCATA TB.9 Tampico | Air Touring Club Ltd/Biggin Hill |
| | G-BMZF | Mikoyan Gurevich MiG-15 (1420) ★ | FAA Museum/Yeovilton |
| | G-BMZG | QAC Quickie Q.2 | K. W. Brooker |
| | G-BMZH | Cameron A-140 balloon | The Balloon Stable Ltd |
| | G-BMZJ | Colt 400A balloon | Thunder & Colt Ltd |
| | G-BMZN | Everett gyroplane | R. J. Brown |
| | G-BMZP | Everett gyroplane | B. C. Norris |
| | G-BMZS | Everett gyroplane | C. W. Cload |
| | G-BMZV | Cessna 172P | Shoreham Flight Simulation/Bournemouth |
| | G-BMZW | Bensen B.8 | P. D. Widdicombe |
| | G-BMZX | Wolf W-II Boredom Fighter (146-11042) | A. R. Meakin & S. W. Watkins |
| | G-BMZZ | Stephens Akro Z | P. G. Kynsey & J. Harper/Redhill |
| | G-BNAA | V.806 Viscount | British Air Ferries (G-AOYH)/Southend |
| | G-BNAB | GA-7 Cougar | BLS Aviation Ltd (G-BGYP)/Elstree |
| | G-BNAD | Rand KR-2 | P. J. Brookman |
| | G-BNAG | Colt 105A balloon | R. W. Batcholer |
| | G-BNAH | Colt Paper Bag SS balloon | Thrustell Ltd |
| | G-BNAI | Wolf W-II Boredom Fighter (146-11083) | P. J. D. Gronow |
| | G-BNAJ | Cessna 152 | G. Duncan |
| | G-BNAL | F.27 Friendship Mk 600 | Air UK Ltd/Norwich |

| Reg. | Type | Owner or Operator | Notes |
|------|------|-------------------|-------|
| G-BNAN | Cameron V-65 balloon | A. M. Lindsay | |
| G-BNAO | Colt AS-105 airship | Heather Flight Ltd | |
| G-BNAP | Colt 240A balloon | Heather Flight Ltd | |
| G-BNAR | Taylor JT.1 Monoplane | C. J. Smith | |
| G-BNAU | Cameron V-65 balloon | J. Buckle | |
| G-BNAW | Cameron V-65 balloon | A. Walker | |
| G-BNAY | Grob G.109B | Microperm Ltd | |
| G-BNBJ | AS.355F-1 Twin Squirrel | Coln Helicopters Ltd | |
| G-BNBL | Thunder Ax7-77 balloon | J. R. Henderson | |
| G-BNBM | Colt 90A balloon | Huntair Ltd | |
| G-BNBR | Cameron N-90 balloon | Morning Star Motors Ltd | |
| G-BNBU | Bensen B.8MV | R. Retallick | |
| G-BNBV | Thunder Ax7-77 balloon | J. M. Robinson | |
| G-BNBW | Thunder Ax7-77 balloon | I. S. & S. W. Watthews | |
| G-BNBY | Beech 95-B55A Baron | C. Wright (G-AXXR) | |
| G-BNBZ | LET L-200D Morava | M. Emery & C. A. Suckling/Redhill | |
| G-BNCA | Lightning F.2A ★ | P. Hoar/Cranfield | |
| G-BNCB | Cameron V-77 balloon | Tyred & Battered Balloon Group | |
| G-BNCC | Thunder Ax7-77 balloon | C. J. Burnhope | |
| G-BNCG | QAC Quickie Q.2 | T. F. Francis | |
| G-BNCH | Cameron V-77 balloon | Royal Engineers Balloon Club | |
| G-BNCJ | Cameron V-77 balloon | I. S. Bridge | |
| G-BNCK | Cameron V-77 balloon | G. Randall/Germany | |
| G-BNCL | WG.13 Lynx HAS.2 (XX469) ★ | Wilkie Museum Collection/Blackpool | |
| G-BNCM | Cameron N-77 balloon | S. & A. Stone Ltd | |
| G-BNCN | Glaser-Dirks DG.400 | M. C. Costin | |
| G-BNCO | PA-38-112 Tomahawk | Cambrian Flying Club/Swansea | |
| G-BNCR | PA-28-161 Warrior II | Airways Aero Associations Ltd/Booker | |
| G-BNCS | Cessna 180 | C. Elwell Transport Ltd | |
| G-BNCU | Thunder Ax7-77 balloon | J. A. Lister | |
| G-BNCV | Bensen B.8 | L. W. Cload | |
| G-BNCW | Boeing 767-204 | Britannia Airways Ltd/Luton | |
| G-BNCX | Hunter T.7 | Lovaux Ltd | |
| G-BNCY | F.27 Friendship Mk 500 | Air UK Ltd *Lillie Langtry*/Norwich | |
| G-BNCZ | Rutan LongEz | R. M. Bainbridge/Sherburn | |
| G-BNDG | Wallis WA-201/R Srs1 | K. H. Wallis | |
| G-BNDH | Colt 21A balloon | Hot-Air Balloon Co Ltd | |
| G-BNDM | Short SD3-60 Variant 100 | Titan Airways Ltd/Stansted | |
| G-BNDN | Cameron V-77 balloon | J. A. Smith | |
| G-BNDO | Cessna 152 II | V. B. Cheesewright | |
| G-BNDP | Brügger MB.2 Colibri | D. A. Peet | |
| G-BNDR | SOCATA TB.10 Tobago | CTR Plastics Ltd | |
| G-BNDS | PA-31-350 Navajo Chieftain | Solomon Investment Co Ltd | |
| G-BNDT | Brügger MB.2 Colibri | T. C. Bayes | |
| G-BNDV | Cameron N-77 balloon | R. Jones | |
| G-BNDW | D.H.82A Tiger Moth | N. D. Welch | |
| G-BNDY | Cessna 425-1 | Standard Aviation Ltd/Newcastle | |
| G-BNED | PA-22 Tri-Pacer 135 | P. Storey | |
| G-BNEE | PA-28R-201 Arrow III | Britannic Management (Aviation) Ltd | |
| G-BNEF | PA-31-310 Turbo Navajo B | Seraph Aviation/Shoreham | |
| G-BNEI | PA-34-200T Seneca II | A. Bucknole | |
| G-BNEJ | PA-38-112 Tomahawk | V. C. & S. G. Swindell | |
| G-BNEK | PA-38-112 Tomahawk | Pool Aviation Ltd/Welshpool | |
| G-BNEL | PA-28-161 Warrior II | J. A. Pothecary/Shoreham | |
| G-BNEN | PA-34-200T Seneca II | Aerohire Ltd/Halfpenny Green | |
| G-BNEO | Cameron V-77 balloon | J. G. O'Connell | |
| G-BNEP | PA-34-220T Seneca III | Handhorn Ltd/Blackpool | |
| G-BNER | PA-34-200T Seneca II | Compass Peripherial Systems Ltd | |
| G-BNES | Cameron V-77 balloon | G. Wells | |
| G-BNET | Cameron O-84 balloon | J. Bennett & Son (Insurance Brokers) Ltd | |
| G-BNEU | Colt 105A balloon | I. Lilja | |
| G-BNEV | Viking Dragonfly | N. W. Eyre | |
| G-BNEX | Cameron O-120 balloon | The Balloon Club Ltd | |
| G-BNFG | Cameron O-77 balloon | Capital Balloon Club Ltd | |
| G-BNFI | Cessna 150J | M. Jackson | |
| G-BNFK | Cameron 89 Egg SS balloon | Forbes Europe Inc/France | |
| G-BNFL | WHE Airbuggy | Roger Savage (Photography) (G-AXXN) | |
| G-BNFM | Colt 21A balloon | M. E. Dworksi | |
| G-BNFN | Cameron N-105 balloon | Air 2 Air Ltd | |
| G-BNFO | Cameron V-77 balloon | D. C. Patrick-Brown | |
| G-BNFP | Cameron O-84 balloon | A. J. & E. J. Clarke | |
| G-BNFR | Cessna 152 II | London Flight Centre (Stansted) Ltd | |
| G-BNFS | Cessna 152 II | London Flight Centre (Stansted) Ltd | |

| Notes | Reg. | Type | Owner or Operator |
|---|---|---|---|
| | G-BNFU | Colt 105A balloon | Basemore Ltd |
| | G-BNFV | Robin DR.400/120 | P. D. W. King |
| | G-BNFW | H.S.125 Srs 700B | British Aerospace PLC |
| | G-BNFY | Cameron N-77 balloon | Holker Estates Ltd |
| | G-BNGC | Robinson R-22 | T. J. Clark |
| | G-BNGD | Cessna 152 | AV Aviation Ltd |
| | G-BNGE | Auster AOP.6 (TW536) | R. W. W. Eastman |
| | G-BNGJ | Cameron V-77 balloon | Latham Timber Centres (Holdings) Ltd |
| | G-BNGL | Boeing 737-3Y0 | Inter European Airways Ltd/Cardiff |
| | G-BNGM | Boeing 737-3Y0 | Inter European Airways Ltd/Cardiff |
| | G-BNGN | Cameron V-77 balloon | A. R. & L. J. McGregor |
| | G-BNGO | Thunder Ax7-77 balloon | J. S. Finlan |
| | G-BNGP | Colt 77A balloon | Headland Services Ltd |
| | G-BNGR | PA-38-112 Tomahawk | Teesside Flight Centre Ltd |
| | G-BNGS | PA-38-112 Tomahawk | Frontline Aviation Ltd/Teesside |
| | G-BNGT | PA-28-181 Archer II | Berry Air/Edinburgh |
| | G-BNGV | ARV Super 2 | A. S. Faiers |
| | G-BNGW | ARV Super 2 | Southern Gas Turbines Ltd |
| | G-BNGX | ARV Super 2 | Southern Gas Turbines Ltd |
| | G-BNGY | ARV Super 2 | N. R. F. McNally (G-BMWL) |
| | G-BNHB | ARV Super 2 | Super Two Group |
| | G-BNHC | ARV Super 2 | M. J. Snelling |
| | G-BNHD | ARV Super 2 | Aviation (Scotland) Ltd |
| | G-BNHE | ARV Super 2 | Aviation (Scotland) Ltd |
| | G-BNHF | Cameron N-31 balloon | P. G. Dunnington |
| | G-BNHG | PA-38-112 Tomahawk | D. A. Whitmore |
| | G-BNHH | Thunder Ax7-77 balloon | Gee-Tee Signs Ltd |
| | G-BNHI | Cameron V-77 balloon | Phillair |
| | G-BNHJ | Cessna 152 | DLM (Flying School) Ltd |
| | G-BNHK | Cessna 152 | Osprey Flying Club/Cranfield |
| | G-BNHL | Colt 90 Beer Glass SS balloon | G. V. Beckwith |
| | G-BNHN | Colt Aerial Bottle SS balloon | The Balloon Stable Ltd |
| | G-BNHO | Thunder Ax7-77 balloon | M. J. Forster |
| | G-BNHP | Saffrey S.330 balloon | N. H. Ponsford *Alpha II* |
| | G-BNHR | Cameron V-77 balloon | P. C. Waterhouse |
| | G-BNHT | Fournier RF-3 | B. Brown |
| | G-BNHV | Thunder Ax10-180 balloon | Thunder & Colt Ltd |
| | G-BNIB | Cameron A-105 balloon | A. G. E. Faulkner |
| | G-BNID | Cessna 152 | Mercia Aircraft Leasing & Sales Ltd/Coventry |
| | G-BNIE | Cameron O-160 balloon | Bristol Balloons |
| | G-BNIF | Cameron O-56 balloon | D. V. Fowler |
| | G-BNII | Cameron N-90 balloon | DW (Direct Wholesale) PLC |
| | G-BNIJ | SOCATA TB.10 Tobago | Alandi Investments Ltd |
| | G-BNIK | Robin HR.200/120 | W. C. Smeaton/Popham |
| | G-BNIM | PA-38-112 Tomahawk | F. R. H. Parker |
| | G-BNIN | Cameron V-77 balloon | Cloud Nine Balloon Group |
| | G-BNIO | Luscombe 8A Silvaire | P. T. Szluha |
| | G-BNIP | Luscombe 8A Silvaire | D. R. C. Hunter & S. Maric |
| | G-BNIT | Bell 206B JetRanger | Black Isle Helicopters Ltd |
| | G-BNIU | Cameron O-77 balloon | A. J. Matthews & D. S. Dunlop |
| | G-BNIV | Cessna 152 | Aerohire Ltd/Halfpenny Green |
| | G-BNIW | Boeing Stearman PT-17 | Lintally Ltd/E. Midlands |
| | G-BNIX | EMB-110P1 Bandeirante | Aeroservices (E. Midlands) Ltd |
| | G-BNJA | WAG-Aero Wag-a-Bond | J. A. Hutchings |
| | G-BNJB | Cessna 152 | Klingair Ltd/Conington |
| | G-BNJC | Cessna 152 | Stapleford Flying Club Ltd |
| | G-BNJD | Cessna 152 | J. A Pothecary/Shoreham |
| | G-BNJE | Cessna A.152 | Seawing Flying Club Ltd/Southend |
| | G-BNJF | PA-32RT-300 Lance II | Biggles Aviation Ltd |
| | G-BNJG | Cameron O-77 balloon | A. M. Figiel |
| | G-BNJH | Cessna 152 | Turnhouse Flying Club |
| | G-BNJJ | Cessna 152 | Merrett Aviation Ltd |
| | G-BNJK | Macavia BAe 748 Turbine Tanker | Macavia International Ltd |
| | G-BNJL | Bensen B.8 | T. G. Ogilvie |
| | G-BNJM | PA-28-161 Warrior II | Teesside Flight Centre Ltd |
| | G-BNJO | QAC Quickie Q.2 | J. D. McKay |
| | G-BNJR | PA-28RT-201T Turbo Arrow IV | Intelligent Micro Software Ltd |
| | G-BNJT | PA-28-161 Warrior II | Airways Aero Associations Ltd/Booker |
| | G-BNJU | Cameron 80 Bust SS balloon | Forbes Europe Inc/France |
| | G-BNJX | Cameron N-90 balloon | Mars UK Ltd |
| | G-BNKC | Cessna 152 | Herefordshire Aero Club Ltd/Shobdon |
| | G-BNKD | Cessna 172N | Bristol Flying Centre Ltd |

| Reg. | Type | Owner or Operator | Notes |
|---|---|---|---|
| G-BNKE | Cessna 172N | Jacques Hall & Co Ltd | |
| G-BNKF | Colt AS-56 airship | Formtrack Ltd | |
| G-BNKG | Alexander Todd Steen Skybolt | Cavendish Aviation Ltd (G-RATS/G-RHFI) | |
| G-BNKH | PA-38-112 Tomahawk | Goodwood Terrena Ltd | |
| G-BNKI | Cessna 152 | RAF Halton Aeroplane Club Ltd | |
| G-BNKL | Beech 95-58PA Baron | E. L. Klinge/Fairoaks | |
| G-BNKP | Cessna 152 | Clacton Aero Club (1988) Ltd | |
| G-BNKR | Cessna 152 | Fife Airport Management Ltd | |
| G-BNKS | Cessna 152 | Shropshire Aero Club Ltd/Shobdon | |
| G-BNKT | Cameron O-77 balloon | British Airways PLC | |
| G-BNKV | Cessna 152 | I. C. Adams & Vectair Aviation Ltd | |
| G-BNKW | PA-38-112 Tomahawk | D. M. MacLean | |
| G-BNKX | Robinson R-22 | AM Helicopter Leasing | |
| G-BNKZ | Hughes 369HS | Reeds Motor Co/Sywell | |
| G-BNLA | Boeing 747-436 | British Airways City of London | |
| G-BNLB | Boeing 747-436 | British Airways City of Edinburgh | |
| G-BNLC | Boeing 747-436 | British Airways City of Cardiff | |
| G-BNLD | Boeing 747-436 | British Airways City of Belfast | |
| G-BNLE | Boeing 747-436 | British Airways City of Newcastle | |
| G-BNLF | Boeing 747-436 | British Airways City of Leeds | |
| G-BNLG | Boeing 747-436 | British Airways City of Southampton | |
| G-BNLH | Boeing 747-436 | British Airways City of Westminster | |
| G-BNLI | Boeing 747-436 | British Airways City of Sheffield | |
| G-BNLJ | Boeing 747-436 | British Airways City of Nottingham | |
| G-BNLK | Boeing 747-436 | British Airways City of Bristol | |
| G-BNLL | Boeing 747-436 | British Airways City of Leicester | |
| G-BNLM | Boeing 747-436 | British Airways City of Durham | |
| G-BNLN | Boeing 747-436 | British Airways City of Portsmouth | |
| G-BNLO | Boeing 747-436 | British Airways City of Dundee | |
| G-BNLP | Boeing 747-436 | British Airways City of Aberdeen | |
| G-BNLR | Boeing 747-436 | British Airways City of Hull | |
| G-BNLS | Boeing 747-436 | British Airways City of Chester | |
| G-BNLT | Boeing 747-436 | British Airways City of Lincoln | |
| G-BNLU | Boeing 747-436 | British Airways City of Bangor | |
| G-BNLV | Boeing 747-436 | British Airways City of Exeter | |
| G-BNLW | Boeing 747-436 | British Airways City of Norwich | |
| G-BNLX | Boeing 747-436 | British Airways City of Worcester | |
| G-BNLY | Boeing 747-436 | British Airways City of Swansea | |
| G-BNLZ | Boeing 747-436 | British Airways City of Perth | |
| G-BNMA | Cameron O-77 balloon | Flying Colours Balloon Group | |
| G-BNMB | PA-28-151 Warrior | Angelchain Ltd/Manchester | |
| G-BNMC | Cessna 152 | M. L. Jones | |
| G-BNMD | Cessna 152 | T. M. Jones | |
| G-BNME | Cessna 152 | L. V. Atkinson | |
| G-BNMF | Cessna 152 | Aerohire Ltd | |
| G-BNMG | Cameron V-77 balloon | Windsor Life Assurance Co Ltd | |
| G-BNMH | Pietenpol Air Camper | N. M. Hitchman | |
| G-BNMI | Colt Flying Fantasy SS balloon | Air 2 Air Ltd | |
| G-BNMK | Dornier Do.27A-1 | G. Machie | |
| G-BNML | Rand KR-2 | R. J. Smyth | |
| G-BNMN | PA-28R-201 Arrow III | T. W. Pullin | |
| G-BNMO | Cessna TR.182RG | G-BNMO Flying Group | |
| G-BNMP | Cessna R.182RG | P. M. Breton | |
| G-BNMX | Thunder Ax7-77 balloon | S. A. D. Beard | |
| G-BNNA | Stolp SA.300 Starduster Too | D. F. Simpson | |
| G-BNNB | PA-34-200 Seneca II | Shoreham Flight Simulation/Bournemouth | |
| G-BNNC | Cameron N-77 balloon | T. M. McCoy/Barrow | |
| G-BNNE | Cameron N-77 balloon | The Balloon Stable Ltd | |
| G-BNNF | SA.315B Alouette III Lama | Dollar Air Services Ltd/Coventry | |
| G-BNNG | Cessna T.337D | Somet Ltd (G-COLD) | |
| G-BNNI | Boeing 727-276 | Arkia Leasing Ltd | |
| G-BNNJ | Boeing 737-3Q8 | British Airways | |
| G-BNNK | Boeing 737-4Q8 | British Airways | |
| G-BNNL | Boeing 737-4Q8 | British Airways | |
| G-BNNO | PA-28-161 Warrior II | W. Lancs Aero Club Ltd/Woodvale | |
| G-BNNR | Cessna 152 | Interair (Aviation) Ltd/Bournemouth | |
| G-BNNS | PA-28-161 Warrior II | P. A. Lancaster | |
| G-BNNT | PA-28-151 Warrior | S. T. Gilbert & ptnrs | |
| G-BNNU | PA-38-112 Tomahawk | APB Leasing Ltd/Welshpool | |
| G-BNNX | PA-28R-201T Turbo Arrow III | C. Dugard Ltd/Shoreham | |
| G-BNNY | PA-28-161 Warrior II | Falcon Flying Services/Biggin Hill | |
| G-BNNZ | PA-28-161 Warrior II | D. Heater/Fairoaks | |
| G-BNOA | PA-38-112 Tomahawk | Aerohire Ltd/Halfpenny Green | |

| Notes | Reg. | Type | Owner or Operator |
|---|---|---|---|
| | G-BNOB | Wittman W.8 Tailwind | M. Robson-Robinson |
| | G-BNOD | PA-28-161 Warrior II | BAe Flying College/Prestwick |
| | G-BNOE | PA-28-161 Warrior II | BAe Flying College/Prestwick |
| | G-BNOF | PA-28-161 Warrior II | BAe Flying College/Prestwick |
| | G-BNOG | PA-28-161 Warrior II | BAe Flying College/Prestwick |
| | G-BNOH | PA-28-161 Warrior II | BAe Flying College/Prestwick |
| | G-BNOI | PA-28-161 Warrior II | BAe Flying College/Prestwick |
| | G-BNOJ | PA-28-161 Warrior II | BAe Flying College/Prestwick |
| | G-BNOK | PA-28-161 Warrior II | BAe Flying College/Prestwick |
| | G-BNOL | PA-28-161 Warrior II | BAe Flying College/Prestwick |
| | G-BNOM | PA-28-161 Warrior II | BAe Flying College/Prestwick |
| | G-BNON | PA-28-161 Warrior II | BAe Flying College/Prestwick |
| | G-BNOO | PA-28-161 Warrior II | BAe Flying College/Prestwick |
| | G-BNOP | PA-28-161 Warrior II | BAe Flying College/Prestwick |
| | G-BNOR | PA-28-161 Warrior II | BAe Flying College/Prestwick |
| | G-BNOS | PA-28-161 Warrior II | BAe Flying College/Prestwick |
| | G-BNOT | PA-28-161 Warrior II | BAe Flying College/Prestwick |
| | G-BNOU | PA-28-161 Warrior II | BAe Flying College/Prestwick |
| | G-BNOV | PA-28-161 Warrior II | BAe Flying College/Prestwick |
| | G-BNOW | PA-28-161 Warrior II | BAe Flying College/Prestwick |
| | G-BNOX | Cessna R.182 | R. Evans/Swansea |
| | G-BNOY | Colt 90A balloon | Huntair Ltd |
| | G-BNOZ | Cessna 152 | Pool Aviation Ltd/Welshpool |
| | G-BNPD | PA-23 Aztec 250E | Cormack (Aircraft Services) Ltd/Glasgow |
| | G-BNPE | Cameron N-77 balloon | Kent Garden Centres Ltd |
| | G-BNPF | Slingsby T.31M | S. Luck & ptnrs |
| | G-BNPH | P.66 Pembroke C.1 (WV740) | R. J. F. Parker/Denham |
| | G-BNPI | Colt 21A balloon | Airship & Balloon Co ltd |
| | G-BNPK | Cameron DP-70 airship | Cameron Balloons Ltd |
| | G-BNPL | PA-38-112 Tomahawk | Tomahawk Aviation Ltd/Leavesden |
| | G-BNPM | PA-38-112 Tomahawk | Papa Mike Aviation Ltd/Leavesden |
| | G-BNPN | PA-28-181 Archer II | Sherani Aviation/Elstree |
| | G-BNPO | PA-28-181 Archer II | Leavesden Flight Centre Ltd |
| | G-BNPT | PA-38-112 Tomahawk II | Cumbernauld Aviation Ltd |
| | G-BNPV | Bowers Flybaby 1A | J. G. Day |
| | G-BNPY | Cessna 152 | Doncaster Aero Club Ltd |
| | G-BNPZ | Cessna 152 | Bristol Flying Centre Ltd |
| | G-BNRA | SOCATA TB.10 Tobago | G. P. Marriott & M. W. J. Chappell |
| | G-BNRC | AB-206A JetRanger | M. & P. Food Products Ltd |
| | G-BNRD | AB-206A JetRanger | H. Ingham Developments Ltd |
| | G-BNRE | AB-206A JetRanger | Tindon Ltd/Little Snoring |
| | G-BNRF | PA-28-181 Archer II | G-Air Ltd/Goodwood |
| | G-BNRG | PA-28-161 Warrior II | RAF Brize Norton Flying Club Ltd |
| | G-BNRH | Beech 95-E55 Baron | Nairn Flying Services Ltd/Inverness |
| | G-BNRI | Cessna U.206G | Target Technology Ltd |
| | G-BNRK | Cessna 152 | Redhill Flying Club |
| | G-BNRL | Cessna 152 | J. R. Nicholls/Sibson |
| | G-BNRP | PA-28-181 Archer II | Atomchoice Ltd/Goodwood |
| | G-BNRR | Cessna 172P | Skyhawk Group |
| | G-BNRU | Cameron V-77 balloon | M. A. Mueller |
| | G-BNRW | Colt 69A balloon | Callers Pegasus Travel Service Ltd |
| | G-BNRX | PA-34-200T Seneca II | Futurama Signs Ltd |
| | G-BNRY | Cessna 182Q | Reefly Ltd |
| | G-BNRZ | Robinson R-22B | W. Jorden-Millers Ltd |
| | G-BNSG | PA-28R-201 Arrow III | Armada Aviation Ltd/Redhill |
| | G-BNSH | Sikorsky S-76A | Bond Helicopters Ltd |
| | G-BNSI | Cessna 152 | Interair (Aviation) Ltd |
| | G-BNSL | PA-38-112 Tomahawk II | M. H. Kleiser |
| | G-BNSM | Cessna 152 | Cornwall Flying Club Ltd/Bodmin |
| | G-BNSN | Cessna 152 | M. K. Barnes & G. N. Olson/Bristol |
| | G-BNSO | Slingsby T.67M Mk II | Trent Air Services Ltd/Cranfield |
| | G-BNSP | Slingsby T.67M | Trent Air Services Ltd/Cranfield |
| | G-BNSR | Slingsby T.67M | Trent Air Services Ltd/Cranfield |
| | G-BNSS | Cessna 150M | Interair (Aviation) Ltd |
| | G-BNST | Cessna 172N | E. J. H. Morgan |
| | G-BNSU | Cessna 152 | Channel Aviation Ltd/Bourn |
| | G-BNSV | Cessna 152 | Channel Aviation Ltd/Bourn |
| | G-BNSW | Cessna 152 | One Zero One Three Ltd |
| | G-BNSY | PA-28-161 Warrior II | Carill Aviation Ltd/Southampton |
| | G-BNSZ | PA-28-161 Warrior II | Carill Aviation Ltd/Southampton |
| | G-BNTC | PA-28RT-201T Turbo Arrow IV | Techspan Aviation Ltd/Booker |
| | G-BNTD | PA-28-161 Warrior II | S. S. Copsey/Ipswich |
| | G-BNTE | FFA AS.202/18A4 Wren | BAe Flying College Ltd/Prestwick |

| Reg. | Type | Owner or Operator | Notes |
|------|------|-------------------|-------|
| G-BNTF | FFA AS.202/18A4 Wren | BAe Flying College Ltd/Prestwick | |
| G-BNTG | FFA AS.202/18A4 Wren | BAe Flying College Ltd/Prestwick | |
| G-BNTH | FFA AS.202/18A4 Wren | BAe Flying College Ltd/Prestwick | |
| G-BNTI | FFA AS.202/18A4 Wren | BAe Flying College Ltd/Prestwick | |
| G-BNTJ | FFA AS.202/18A4 Wren | BAe Flying College Ltd/Prestwick | |
| G-BNTK | FFA AS.202/18A4 Wren | BAe Flying College Ltd/Prestwick | |
| G-BNTL | FFA AS.202/18A4 Wren | BAe Flying College Ltd/Prestwick | |
| G-BNTM | FFA AS.202/18A4 Wren | BAe Flying College Ltd/Prestwick | |
| G-BNTN | FFA AS.202/18A4 Wren | BAe Flying College Ltd/Prestwick | |
| G-BNTO | FFA AS.202/18A4 Wren | BAe Flying College Ltd/Prestwick | |
| G-BNTP | Cessna 172N | Howells Group PLC | |
| G-BNTS | PA-28RT-201T Turbo Arrow IV | Nasire Ltd | |
| G-BNTT | Beech 76 Duchess | L. & J. Donne | |
| G-BNTW | Cameron V-77 balloon | I. R. Comley | |
| G-BNTX | Short SD3-30 Variant 100 | Shorts Aircraft Leasing Ltd (G-BKDN) | |
| G-BNTY | Short SD3-30 Variant 100 | Shorts Aircraft Leasing Ltd (G-BKDO) | |
| G-BNTZ | Cameron N-77 balloon | Balloon Team | |
| G-BNUC | Cameron O-77 balloon | T. J. Bucknall | |
| G-BNUG | Cameron O-105 balloon | Thunder & Colt Ltd | |
| G-BNUH | Cameron O-105 balloon | Thunder & Colt Ltd | |
| G-BNUI | Rutan Vari-Eze | T. N. F. Skead | |
| G-BNUL | Cessna 152 | Osprey Air Services Ltd | |
| G-BNUN | Beech 95-58PA Baron | British Midland Airways Ltd/E. Midlands | |
| G-BNUO | Beech 76 Duchess | B. & W. Aircraft Ltd | |
| G-BNUR | Cessna 172E | A. P. Howells | |
| G-BNUS | Cessna 152 | Stapleford Flying Club Ltd | |
| G-BNUT | Cessna 152 Turbo | Stapleford Flying Club Ltd | |
| G-BNUU | PA-44-180T Turbo Seminole | TEL (IOM) Ltd/Ronaldsway | |
| G-BNUV | PA-23 Aztec 250F | L. J. Martin | |
| G-BNUX | Hoffmann H-36 Dimona | K. H. Abel | |
| G-BNUY | PA-38-112 Tomahawk II | AT Aviation Ltd/Cardiff | |
| G-BNUZ | Robinson R-22B | J. C. Reid | |
| G-BNVB | AA-5A Cheetah | W. J. Siertsema & A. M. Glazer | |
| G-BNVD | PA-38-112 Tomahawk | Channel Aviation Ltd | |
| G-BNVE | PA-28-181 Archer II | Tewin Aviation/Panshanger | |
| G-BNVF | Robinson R-22B | Jetbury Ltd | |
| G-BNVG | ARV Super 2 | ARV Aviation Ltd/Sandown | |
| G-BNVH | ARV Super 2 | ARV Aviation Ltd/Sandown | |
| G-BNVI | ARV Super 2 | Adrianair Ltd | |
| G-BNVJ | ARV Super 2 | Aviation (Scotland) Ltd | |
| G-BNVT | PA-28R-201T Turbo Arrow III | Victor Tango Group | |
| G-BNVV | Cameron DG-19 gas airship | US Skyship (UK) Ltd | |
| G-BNVZ | Beech 95-B55 Baron | C. A. Breeze/Barton | |
| G-BNWA | Boeing 767-336ER | British Airways *City of Brussels* | |
| G-BNWB | Boeing 767-336ER | British Airways *City of Paris* | |
| G-BNWC | Boeing 767-336ER | British Airways *City of Frankfurt* | |
| G-BNWD | Boeing 767-336ER | British Airways *City of Copenhagen* | |
| G-BNWE | Boeing 767-336ER | British Airways *City of Lisbon* | |
| G-BNWF | Boeing 767-336ER | British Airways *City of Milan* | |
| G-BNWG | Boeing 767-336ER | British Airways *City of Strasbourg* | |
| G-BNWH | Boeing 767-336ER | British Airways *City of Rome* | |
| G-BNWI | Boeing 767-336ER | British Airways *City of Madrid* | |
| G-BNWJ | Boeing 767-336ER | British Airways *City of Athens* | |
| G-BNWK | Boeing 767-336ER | British Airways *City of Amsterdam* | |
| G-BNWL | Boeing 767-336ER | British Airways *City of Luxembourg* | |
| G-BNWM | Boeing 767-336ER | British Airways *City of Toulouse* | |
| G-BNWN | Boeing 767-336ER | British Airways *City of Berlin* | |
| G-BNWO | Boeing 767-336ER | British Airways *City of Barcelona* | |
| G-BNWP | Boeing 767-336ER | British Airways *City of Dublin* | |
| G-BNWR | Boeing 767-336ER | British Airways *City of Hamburg* | |
| G-BNWS | Boeing 767-336ER | British Airways *City of Oporto* | |
| G-BNWT | Boeing 767-336ER | British Airways *City of Cork* | |
| G-BNWU | Boeing 767-336ER | British Airways *City of Turin* | |
| G-BNWV | Boeing 767-336ER | British Airways *Cty of Bonn* | |
| G-BNWW | Boeing 767-336ER | British Airways *City of Bordeaux* | |
| G-BNWX | Boeing 767-336ER | British Airways | |
| G-BNWY | Boeing 767-336ER | British Airways | |
| G-BNWZ | Boeing 767-336ER | British Airways | |
| G-BNXA | BN-2A Islander | Atlantic Air Transport Ltd/Coventry | |
| G-BNXC | Cessna 152 | Sir W. G. Armstrong-Whitworth Flying Group/Coventry | |
| G-BNXD | Cessna 172N | Interair (Aviation) Ltd/Bournemouth | |
| G-BNXE | PA-28-161 Warrior II | Rugby Autobody Repairs | |

| Notes | Reg. | Type | Owner or Operator |
|---|---|---|---|
| | G-BNXF | Bell 206B JetRanger | P. Pilkington & K. M. Armitage |
| | G-BNXG | Cameron DP-70 airship | Rexstyle Ltd |
| | G-BNXI | Robin DR.400/180R | London Gliding Club Ltd/Dunstable |
| | G-BNXK | Nott-Cameron ULD-3 balloon | J. R. P. Nott |
| | G-BNXM | Glaser-Dirks DG.400 | D. Hodgson & J. McCormack |
| | G-BNXM | PA-18 Super Cub 95 | G-BNXM Group |
| | G-BNXO | Colt 21A balloon | Thunder & Colt Ltd |
| | G-BNXR | Cameron O-84 balloon | J. A. & N. J. Ballard Gray |
| | G-BNXS | Cessna 404 | Turnbull Associates |
| | G-BNXT | PA-28-161 Warrior II | Falcon Flying Services/Biggin Hill |
| | G-BNXU | PA-28-161 Warrior II | Friendly Warrior Group |
| | G-BNXV | PA-38-112 Tomahawk | Falcon Flying Services/Biggin Hill |
| | G-BNXX | SOCATA TB.20 Trinidad | D. M. Carr |
| | G-BNXZ | Thunder Ax7-77 balloon | Hale Hot Air Balloon Group |
| | G-BNYA | Short SD3-30 Variant 100 | Steamline Aviation (G-BKSU)/Exeter |
| | G-BNYB | PA-28-201T Turbo Dakota | Blackpool Air Centre |
| | G-BNYD | Bell 206B JetRanger | Sterling Helicopters Ltd |
| | G-BNYJ | Cessna 421B | Charles Robertson (Developments) Ltd |
| | G-BNYK | PA-38-112 Tomahawk | APB Leasing Ltd/Welshpool |
| | G-BNYL | Cessna 152 | APB Leasing Ltd/Welshpool |
| | G-BNYM | Cessna 172N | N. B. Lindley |
| | G-BNYN | Cessna 152 | Redhill Flying Club |
| | G-BNYO | Beech 76 Duchess | Skyhawk Ltd |
| | G-BNYP | PA-28-181 Archer II | R. D. Cooper/Cranfield |
| | G-BNYS | Boeing 767-204 | Britannia Airways Ltd/Luton |
| | G-BNYU | Faithfull Ax7-61A balloon | M. L. Faithfull |
| | G-BNYV | PA-38-112 Tomahawk | Channel Aviation Ltd |
| | G-BNYX | Denney Aerocraft Kitfox | R. W. Husband |
| | G-BNYY | PA-28RT-201T Turbo Arrow IV | Kendrick Construction Ltd |
| | G-BNYZ | SNCAN Stampe SV-4E | Tapestry Colour Ltd |
| | G-BNZB | PA-28-161 Warrior II | Falcon Flying Services/Biggin Hill |
| | G-BNZC | D.H.C.1 Chipmunk 22 (671) | The Aircraft Restoration Co (G-ROYS)/Duxford |
| | G-BNZF | Grob G.109B | N. Adam |
| | G-BNZG | PA-28RT-201T Turbo Arrow IV | Trinity Garage (Gainsborough) Ltd |
| | G-BNZJ | Colt 21A balloon | Willowbest Ltd |
| | G-BNZK | Thunder Ax7-77 balloon | P. M. Davies & D. R .Groves |
| | G-BNZL | Rotorway Scorpion 133 | J. R. Wraight |
| | G-BNZM | Cessna T.210N | Stansted Fluid Power (Products) Ltd |
| | G-BNZO | Rotorway Executive | M. G. Wiltshire |
| | G-BNZR | FRED Srs 2 | R. M. Waugh |
| | G-BNZS | Mooney M.20K | D. G. Millington |
| | G-BNZV | PA-25 Pawnee 235 | Northumbria Soaring Co Ltd |
| | G-BNZX | PA-34-200T Seneca II | Chaseside Holdings Ltd |
| | G-BNZZ | PA-28-161 Warrior II | J. P. Alexander/Denham |
| | G-BOAA | Concorde 102 | British Airways (G-N94AA) |
| | G-BOAB | Concorde 102 | British Airways (G-N94AB) |
| | G-BOAC | Concorde 102 | British Airways (G-N81AC) |
| | G-BOAD | Concorde 102 | British Airways (G-N94AD) |
| | G-BOAE | Concorde 102 | British Airways (G-N94AE) |
| | G-BOAF | Concorde 102 | British Airways (G-N94AF/G-BFKX) |
| | G-BOAG | Concorde 102 | British Airways (G-BFKW) |
| | G-BOAH | PA-28-161 Warrior II | Denham School of Flying Ltd |
| | G-BOAI | Cessna 152 | G. Duncan |
| | G-BOAK | PA-22 Tri-Pacer 150 | M. A. Watts |
| | G-BOAL | Cameron V-65 balloon | A. M. Lindsay |
| | G-BOAM | Robinson R-22B | Bristow Helicopters Ltd/Redhill |
| | G-BOAN | PA-30 Twin Comanche 160B | R. L. C. Appleton |
| | G-BOAO | Thunder Ax7-77 balloon | D. V. Fowler |
| | G-BOAS | Air Command 503 Commander | R. Robinson |
| | G-BOAU | Cameron V-77 balloon | G. T. Barstow |
| | G-BOAY | D.H.C.7-110 Dash Seven | British Midland Airways |
| | G-BOAZ | D.H.C.7-102 Dash Seven | British Midland Airways |
| | G-BOBA | PA-28R-201 Arrow III | GNJ Engineering Ltd |
| | G-BOBB | Cameron O-120 balloon | J. M. Albury |
| | G-BOBC | BN-2T Islander | Rhine Army Parachute Association (G-BJYZ) |
| | G-BOBD | Cameron O-160 balloon | A. C. K. Rawson & J. J. Rudoni |
| | G-BOBE | Cameron O-160 balloon | Heart of England Balloon Club |
| | G-BOBF | Brügger MB.2 Colibri | R. Bennett |
| | G-BOBG | Jodel D.150 | C. A. Laycock |
| | G-BOBH | Airtour AH-77 balloon | Airtour Balloon Co Ltd |

| Reg. | Type | Owner or Operator | Notes |
|------|------|-------------------|-------|
| G-BOBJ | PA-38-112 Tomahawk | Air Touring Services Ltd/Biggin Hill | |
| G-BOBK | PA-38-112 Tomahawk | Air Touring Services Ltd/Biggin Hill | |
| G-BOBL | PA-38-112 Tomahawk | Salcombe Crane Hire Ltd | |
| G-BOBN | Cessna 310R | Edinburgh Air Charter Ltd | |
| G-BOBR | Cameron N-77 balloon | C. Bradley | |
| G-BOBS | Quickie Q.2 | P. Wilkinson | |
| G-BOBT | Stolp SA.300 Starduster Too | A. M. Bailey & T. A. Shears | |
| G-BOBU | Colt 90A balloon | Thunder & Colt Ltd | |
| G-BOBV | Cessna F.150M | T. M. & A. Poppleton/Doncaster | |
| G-BOBX | G.159 Gulfstream 1 ★ | Airport Fire Section/Birmingham | |
| G-BOBY | Monnet Sonerai II | R. G. Hallam (*stored*)/Sleap | |
| G-BOBZ | PA-28-181 Archer II | Trustcomms International Ltd | |
| G-BOCB | H.S.125 Srs 1B/522 | MAGEC Aviation Ltd (G-OMCA/ G-DJMJ/G-AWUF)/Luton | |
| G-BOCC | PA-38-112 Tomahawk | Goodwood Terrena Ltd | |
| G-BOCD | Grob G.115 | Landlink PLC | |
| G-BOCF | Colt 77A balloon | P. S. J. Mason | |
| G-BOCG | PA-34-200T Seneca II | Airways Flight Training (Exeter) Ltd | |
| G-BOCH | PA-32 Cherokee Six 300 | Basic Vale Ltd | |
| G-BOCI | Cessna 140A | D. Nieman | |
| G-BOCK | Sopwith Triplane (replica) (N6290) | Shuttleworth Trust/O. Warden | |
| G-BOCL | Slingsby T.67C | C.S.E. Aviation Ltd/Kidlington | |
| G-BOCM | Slingsby T.67C | C.S.E. Aviation Ltd/Kidlington | |
| G-BOCN | Robinson R-22B | J. Bignall | |
| G-BOCP | PA-34-220T Seneca III | BAe Flying College Ltd/Prestwick | |
| G-BOCR | PA-34-220T Seneca III | BAe Flying College Ltd/Prestwick | |
| G-BOCS | PA-34-220T Seneca III | BAe Flying College Ltd/Prestwick | |
| G-BOCT | PA-34-220T Seneca III | BAe Flying College Ltd/Prestwick | |
| G-BOCU | PA-34-220T Seneca III | BAe Flying College Ltd/Prestwick | |
| G-BOCV | PA-34-220T Seneca III | BAe Flying College Ltd/Prestwick | |
| G-BOCW | PA-34-220T Seneca III | BAe Flying College Ltd/Prestwick | |
| G-BOCX | PA-34-220T Seneca III | BAe Flying College Ltd/Prestwick | |
| G-BOCY | PA-34-220T Seneca III | BAe Flying College Ltd/Prestwick | |
| G-BODA | PA-28-161 Warrior II | C.S.E. Aviation Ltd/Kidlington | |
| G-BODB | PA-28-161 Warrior II | C.S.E. Aviation Ltd/Kidlington | |
| G-BODC | PA-28-161 Warrior II | C.S.E. Aviation Ltd/Kidlington | |
| G-BODD | PA-28-161 Warrior II | C.S.E. Aviation Ltd/Kidlington | |
| G-BODE | PA-28-161 Warrior II | C.S.E. Aviation Ltd/Kidlington | |
| G-BODF | PA-28-161 Warrior II | C.S.E. Aviation Ltd/Kidlington | |
| G-BODG | Slingsby T.31 Motor Cadet III | H. P. Vox | |
| G-BODH | Slingsby T.31 Motor Cadet III | H. P. Vox | |
| G-BODI | Stoddard-Hamilton Glasair III | Jackson Barr Ltd | |
| G-BODK | Rotorway Scorpion 133 | J. Brannigan | |
| G-BODL | Steen Skybolt | K. E. Armstrong | |
| G-BODM | PA-28 Cherokee 180 | Bristol & Wessex Aeroplane Club Ltd | |
| G-BODN | PA-28R-201 Arrow III | N. M. G. Pearson/Bristol | |
| G-BODO | Cessna 152 | A. R. Sarson | |
| G-BODP | PA-38-112 Tomahawk | N. C. Gray | |
| G-BODR | PA-28-161 Warrior II | Airways Aero Associations Ltd/Booker | |
| G-BODS | PA-38-112 Tomahawk | Ipswich School of Flying Ltd | |
| G-BODT | Jodel D.18 | L. D. McPhillips | |
| G-BODU | Scheibe SF.25C | Monica English Memorial Trust | |
| G-BODW | Bell 206B JetRanger | Wood Hall Helicopters Ltd | |
| G-BODX | Beech 76 Duchess | Neric Ltd | |
| G-BODY | Cessna 310R | Atlantic Air Transport Ltd/Coventry | |
| G-BODZ | Robinson R-22B | Langley Construction Ltd | |
| G-BOEC | PA-38-112 Tomahawk | R. A. Wakefield | |
| G-BOED | Cameron Opera House SS balloon | Cameron Balloons Ltd | |
| G-BOEE | PA-28-181 Archer II | T. B. Parmenter | |
| G-BOEH | Jodel DR.340 | Piper Flyers Group | |
| G-BOEK | Cameron V-77 balloon | A. J. E. Jones | |
| G-BOEM | Aerotek-Pitts S-2A | Walsh Bros (Tunneling) Ltd | |
| G-BOEN | Cessna 172M | G-BOEN Group | |
| G-BOER | PA-28-161 Warrior II | M. & W. Fraser-Urquhart | |
| G-BOES | Cessna FA.152 | J. R. Nicholls (G-FLIP) | |
| G-BOET | PA-28RT-201 Arrow IV | IBEC (Holdings) Ltd (G-IBEC)/Liverpool | |
| G-BOEW | Robinson R-22B | Bristow Helicopters Ltd/Redhill | |
| G-BOEX | Robinson R-22B | Bristow Helicopters Ltd/Redhill | |
| G-BOEY | Robinson R-22B | Bristow Helicopters Ltd/Redhill | |
| G-BOEZ | Robinson R-22B | Bristow Helicopters Ltd/Redhill | |
| G-BOFA | Robinson R-22 | Panair Ltd | |

| Notes | Reg. | Type | Owner or Operator |
|---|---|---|---|
| | G-BOFB | Sikorsky S-76A | Bond Helicopters Ltd |
| | G-BOFC | Beech 76 Duchess | Wickenby Aviation Ltd |
| | G-BOFD | Cessna U.206G | D. M. Penny |
| | G-BOFE | PA-34-200T Seneca II | E. C. English |
| | G-BOFF | Cameron N-77 balloon | Systems-80 Double Glazing Ltd & N. M. Gabriel |
| | G-BOFL | Cessna 152 | Coventry (Civil) Aviation Ltd |
| | G-BOFM | Cessna 152 | Coventry (Civil) Aviation Ltd |
| | G-BOFO | Ultimate Aircraft 10-200 | M. Werdmuller |
| | G-BOFV | PA-44-180 Seminole | Stapleford Flying Club Ltd |
| | G-BOFW | Cessna A.150M | Three Counties Aero Engineering Ltd/Lasham |
| | G-BOFX | Cessna A.150M | Shropshire Aero Club Ltd/Sleap |
| | G-BOFY | PA-28 Cherokee 140 | Bristol & Wessex Aeroplane Club Ltd |
| | G-BOFZ | PA-28-161 Warrior II | R. W. Harris |
| | G-BOGB | Hawker Tempest II replica | D. L. Riley |
| | G-BOGC | Cessna 152 | Skyviews & General Ltd/Leeds |
| | G-BOGG | Cessna 152 | J. S. & S. Peplow |
| | G-BOGI | Robin DR.400/180 | Shepair Ltd |
| | G-BOGK | ARV Super 2 | D. R. Trouse |
| | G-BOGL | Thunder Ax7-77 balloon | Thunder & Colt Ltd |
| | G-BOGM | PA-28RT-201T Turbo Arrow IV | RJP Aviation |
| | G-BOGO | PA-32R-301T Saratoga SP | S. D. Cole |
| | G-BOGP | Cameron V-77 balloon | The Wealden Balloon Group |
| | G-BOGR | Colt 180A balloon | The Balloon Club of Great Britain Ltd |
| | G-BOGT | Colt 77A balloon | The Hot Air Balloon Co Ltd |
| | G-BOGV | Air Command 532 Elite | G. M. Hobman |
| | G-BOGW | Air Command 532 Elite | K. Ashford |
| | G-BOGY | Cameron V-77 balloon | Dante Balloon Group |
| | G-BOHA | PA-28-161 Warrior II | London Flight Centre (Stansted) Ltd |
| | G-BOHD | Colt 77A balloon | B. L. Alderson & D. B. Court |
| | G-BOHF | Thunder Ax8-84 balloon | Slater Hogg & Howison Ltd |
| | G-BOHG | Air Command 532 Elite | T. E. McDonald |
| | G-BOHH | Cessna 172N | J. S. Baxter |
| | G-BOHI | Cessna 152 | Clacton Aero Club (1988) Ltd |
| | G-BOHJ | Cessna 152 | F. E. P. Holmes |
| | G-BOHL | Cameron A-120 balloon | T. J. Bucknall |
| | G-BOHM | PA-28 Cherokee 180 | M. J. Anthony & B. Keogh |
| | G-BOHN | PA-38-112 Tomahawk | AT Aviation Ltd |
| | G-BOHO | PA-28-161 Warrior II | Egressus Flying Club |
| | G-BOHR | PA-28-151 Warrior | L. T. Evans |
| | G-BOHS | PA-38-112 Tomahawk | Falcon Flying Services/Biggin Hill |
| | G-BOHT | PA-38-112 Tomahawk | Falcon Flying Services/Biggin Hill |
| | G-BOHU | PA-38-112 Tomahawk | Ambrit Ltd & Peter Smith Photography |
| | G-BOHV | Wittman W.8 Tailwind | R. A. Povall |
| | G-BOHW | Van's RV-4 | R. W. H. Cole |
| | G-BOHX | PA-44-180 Seminole | K. D. & D. C. Horton |
| | G-BOIA | Cessna 180K | R. E. Styles & ptnrs |
| | G-BOIB | Wittman W.10 Tailwind | P. H. Lewis |
| | G-BOIC | PA-28R-201T Turbo Arrow III | M. J. Pearson |
| | G-BOID | Bellanca 7ECA Citabria | T. M. Cammidge |
| | G-BOIF | Beech 95-B55 Baron | Air Transport Services Ltd |
| | G-BOIG | PA-28-161 Warrior II | D. Vallence-Pell/Jersey |
| | G-BOIH | Pitts S-1E Special | S. L. Goldspink |
| | G-BOII | Cessna 172N | Trevair Group/Bournemouth |
| | G-BOIJ | Thunder Ax7-77 balloon | R. A. Hughes |
| | G-BOIK | Air Command 503 Commander | D. W. Smith |
| | G-BOIL | Cessna 172N | Upperstack Ltd |
| | G-BOIM | Cessna 150M | E. Alexander |
| | G-BOIN | Bellanca 7ECA Citabria | J. R. Dobson |
| | G-BOIO | Cessna 152 | AV Aviation Ltd |
| | G-BOIP | Cessna 152 | Stapleford Flying Club Ltd |
| | G-BOIR | Cessna 152 | Shropshire Aero Club Ltd/Sleap |
| | G-BOIS | PA-31 Turbo Navajo | Air Care (South West) Ltd (G-AYNB) |
| | G-BOIT | SOCATA TB.10 Tobago | CB Helicopters |
| | G-BOIU | SOCATA TB.10 Tobago | Portman Welbeck Ltd |
| | G-BOIV | Cessna 150M | Andrewsfield Pension Scheme |
| | G-BOIW | Cessna 152 | London Flight Centre (Stansted) Ltd |
| | G-BOIX | Cessna 172N | JR Flying Ltd |
| | G-BOIY | Cessna 172N | London Flight Centre (Stansted) Ltd |
| | G-BOIZ | PA-34-200T Seneca II | Northumbria Aviation Ltd |
| | G-BOJB | Cameron V-77 balloon | K. L. Heron & R. M. Trotter |
| | G-BOJD | Cameron V-77 balloon | L. H. Ellis |

| Reg. | Type | Owner or Operator |
|------|------|-------------------|
| G-BOJE | PA-28-236 Dakota | M. J. Martin |
| G-BOJF | Air Command 532 Elite | P. J. Davies |
| G-BOJH | PA-28R Cherokee Arrow 200 | P. S. Kirby |
| G-BOJI | PA-28RT-201 Arrow IV | Market Penetration Services Ltd |
| G-BOJJ | BAe 146-300 | British Aerospace PLC/Hatfield |
| G-BOJK | PA-34-220T Seneca III | Redhill Flying Club (G-BRUF) |
| G-BOJL | M.S.885 Super Rallye | J. Rees |
| G-BOJM | PA-28-181 Archer II | H. Skelton |
| G-BOJO | Colt 120A balloon | M. G. Ferguson |
| G-BOJR | Cessna 172P | Exeter Flying Club Ltd |
| G-BOJS | Cessna 172P | J. D. Beckett/Exeter |
| G-BOJU | Cameron N-77 balloon | M. A. Scholes |
| G-BOJW | PA-28-161 Warrior II | Piper Warrior G-BJOW Flying Group |
| G-BOJX | PA-28-181 Archer II | Southern Air Ltd/Shoreham |
| G-BOJY | PA-28-161 Warrior II | Southern Air Ltd/Shoreham |
| G-BOJZ | PA-28-161 Warrior II | Southern Air Ltd/Shoreham |
| G-BOKA | PA-28-201T Turbo Dakota | CBG Aviation Ltd/Biggin Hill |
| G-BOKB | PA-28-161 Warrior II | Southern Air Ltd/Shoreham |
| G-BOKE | PA-34-200T Seneca II | Gwent Plant Sales |
| G-BOKF | Air Command 532 Elite | D. Beevers |
| G-BOKG | Slingsby T.31 Motor Cadet III | A. M. Witt |
| G-BOKH | Whittaker MW.7 | M. W. J. Whittaker |
| G-BOKI | Whittaker MW.7 | R. K. Willcox |
| G-BOKJ | Whittaker MW.7 | M. N. Gauntlett |
| G-BOKK | PA-28-161 Warrior II | C. J. Freeman/Headcorn |
| G-BOKL | PA-28-161 Warrior II | BAe Flying College Ltd/Prestwick |
| G-BOKM | PA-28-161 Warrior II | BAe Flying College Ltd/Prestwick |
| G-BOKN | PA-28-161 Warrior II | BAe Flying College Ltd/Prestwick |
| G-BOKO | PA-28-161 Warrior II | BAe Flying College Ltd/Prestwick |
| G-BOKP | PA-28-161 Warrior II | BAe Flying College Ltd/Prestwick |
| G-BOKR | PA-28-161 Warrior II | BAe Flying College Ltd/Prestwick |
| G-BOKS | PA-28-161 Warrior II | BAe Flying College Ltd/Prestwick |
| G-BOKT | PA-28-161 Warrior II | BAe Flying College Ltd/Prestwick |
| G-BOKU | PA-28-161 Warrior II | BAe Flying College Ltd/Prestwick |
| G-BOKW | Bo 208C Junior | R. A. Farrington (G-BITT) |
| G-BOKX | PA-28-161 Warrior II | W. P. J. Jackson |
| G-BOKY | Cessna 152 | London Flight Centre (Stansted) Ltd |
| G-BOLA | Agusta A.109A II | All Charter Ltd |
| G-BOLB | Taylorcraft BC-12-65 | G-BOLB Flying Group |
| G-BOLC | Fournier RF-6B-100 | W. H. Hendy |
| G-BOLD | PA-38-112 Tomahawk | B. R. Pearson & B. F. Fraser-Smith/ Eaglescott |
| G-BOLE | PA-38-112 Tomahawk | M. W. Kibble & E. A. Minard |
| G-BOLF | PA-38-112 Tomahawk | Teesside Flight Centre Ltd |
| G-BOLG | Bellanca 7KCAB Citabria | B. R. Pearson/Eaglescott |
| G-BOLI | Cessna 172P | Boli Flying Club |
| G-BOLJ | GA-7 Cougar | M. A. Hales |
| G-BOLL | Lake LA-4 Skimmer | S. D. Foster |
| G-BOLN | Colt 21A balloon | Airship & Balloon Co Ltd |
| G-BOLO | Bell 206B JetRanger | Hargreaves Construction Co Ltd/ Shoreham |
| G-BOLP | Colt 21A balloon | Airship & Balloon Co Ltd |
| G-BOLR | Colt 21A balloon | Airship & Balloon Co Ltd |
| G-BOLS | FRED Srs 2 | I. F. Vaughan |
| G-BOLT | R. Commander 114 | R. D. Rooke/Elstree |
| G-BOLU | Robin R.3000/120 | Classair |
| G-BOLV | Cessna 152 | London Flight Centre (Stansted) Ltd |
| G-BOLW | Cessna 152 | Seawing Flying Club Ltd/Southend |
| G-BOLX | Cessna 172N | London Flight Centre (Stansted) Ltd |
| G-BOLY | Cessna 172N | London Flight Centre (Headcorn) Ltd |
| G-BOLZ | Rand KR-2 | B. Normington |
| G-BOMB | Cussutt Racer | P. P. Chapman/Biggin Hill |
| G-BOML | Hispano HA.1112MIL (—) | R. G. Hanna/Duxford |
| G-BOMN | Cessna 150F | D. G. Williams & B. L. Wratten |
| G-BOMO | PA-38-112 Tomahawk | Aerohire Ltd/Halfpenny Green |
| G-BOMP | PA-28-181 Archer II | Falcon Flying Services/Biggin Hill |
| G-BOMS | Cessna 172N | Osprey Air Services Ltd/Cranfield |
| G-BOMT | Cessna 172N | Herefordshire Aero Club Ltd/Shobdon |
| G-BOMU | PA-28-181 Archer II | RJ Aviation/Blackbushe |
| G-BOMY | PA-28-161 Warrior II | Carill Aviation Ltd/Southampton |
| G-BOMZ | PA-38-112 Tomahawk | BOMZ Aviation/White Waltham |
| G-BONC | PA-28RT-201 Arrow IV | Modern Air |
| G-BOND | Sikorsky S-76A | Manchester Helicopter Centre/Barton |

| Notes | Reg. | Type | Owner or Operator |
|-------|------|------|-------------------|
| | G-BONE | Pilatus P2-06 (U-142) | D. C. R. Writer |
| | G-BONG | Enstrom F-28A | Run Length Ltd |
| | G-BONH | Enstrom F-28A | Nord Angleterre Specialiste Aviation |
| | G-BONK | Colt 180A balloon | Wye Valley Aviation Ltd |
| | G-BONO | Cessna 172N | M. Rowe/Sywell |
| | G-BONP | CFM Streak Shadow | CFM Metal-Fax Ltd |
| | G-BONR | Cessna 172N | Atlaslocal Ltd/Biggin Hill |
| | G-BONS | Cessna 172N | BONS Group/Leavesden |
| | G-BONT | Slingsby T.67M Mk II | Slingsby Aviation Ltd/Kirkbymoorside |
| | G-BONU | Slingsby T.67B | Slingsby Aviation Ltd/Kirkbymoorside |
| | G-BONV | Colt 17A balloon | Bryant Group PLC |
| | G-BONW | Cessna 152 | Lincoln Aero Club Ltd/Sturgate |
| | G-BONY | Denney Aerocraft Kitfox | Penny Hydraulics Ltd |
| | G-BONZ | Beech V35B Bonanza | P. M. Coulten |
| | G-BOOB | Cameron N-65 balloon | I. J. Sadler |
| | G-BOOC | PA-18 Super Cub 150 | R. R. & S. A. Marriott |
| | G-BOOD | Slingsby T.31M Motor Tutor | G. F. M. Garner |
| | G-BOOE | GA-7 Cougar | G. L. Cailes |
| | G-BOOF | PA-28-181 Archer II | Golf Boof Group |
| | G-BOOG | PA-28RT-201T Turbo Arrow IV | A. W. D. Perkins & J. C. Walton |
| | G-BOOH | Jodel D.112 | M. J. Hayman |
| | G-BOOI | Cessna 152 | Stapleford Flying Club Ltd |
| | G-BOOJ | Air Command 532 Elite | G. Snook |
| | G-BOOL | Cessna 172N | AVA Flyers/Biggin Hill |
| | G-BOOM | Hunter T.7 | Hunter Wing Ltd/Bournemouth |
| | G-BOON | PA-32RT-300 Lance II | G-BOON Ltd/Luton |
| | G-BOOO | Brügger MB .2 Colibri | D. G. Cole |
| | G-BOOP | Cameron N-90 balloon | The Hot Air Balloon Co Ltd (G-BOMX) |
| | G-BOOS | Colt 240A balloon | Thunder & Colt Ltd |
| | G-BOOT | Colt 240A balloon | Thunder & Colt Ltd |
| | G-BOOU | Cameron N-77 balloon | Aqualisa Products Ltd |
| | G-BOOV | AS.355F-2 Twin Squirrel | Merseyside Police Authority |
| | G-BOOW | Aerosport Scamp | B. I. Turner |
| | G-BOOX | Rutan LongEz | I. R. Thomas & I. R. Wilde |
| | G-BOOZ | Cameron N-77 balloon | J. E. F. Kettlety |
| | G-BOPA | PA-28-181 Archer II | J. E. Strutt (London) Ltd |
| | G-BOPB | Boeing 767-204ER | Britannia Airways Ltd *Captain Sir Ross Smith*/Luton |
| | G-BOPC | PA-28-161 Warrior II | Channel Aviation Ltd |
| | G-BOPD | Bede BD-4 | S. T. Dauncey |
| | G-BOPG | Cessna 182Q | J. Tomkins |
| | G-BOPH | Cessna TR.182RG | E. A. L. Sturmer |
| | G-BOPL | PA-28-161 Warrior II | Cambrian Flying Club/Swansea |
| | G-BOPN | Brooklands OA.7 Optica | Lovaux Ltd/Bournemouth |
| | G-BOPT | Grob G.115 | Howells Group PLC |
| | G-BOPU | Grob G.115 | Howells Group PLC |
| | G-BOPV | PA-34-200T Seneca II | Tewin Aviation |
| | G-BOPW | Cessna A.152 | Northamptonshire School of Flying Ltd/Sywell |
| | G-BOPX | Cessna A.152 | Osprey Air Services Ltd/Cranfield |
| | G-BOPZ | Cameron DP-70 airship | The Hot Air Balloon Co Ltd (G-BOMW) |
| | G-BORA | Colt 77A balloon | Cala Homes (Southern) Ltd |
| | G-BORB | Cameron V-77 balloon | M. H. Wolff |
| | G-BORC | Colt 180A balloon | Airship & Balloon Co Ltd |
| | G-BORD | Thunder Ax7-77 balloon | D. D. Owen |
| | G-BORE | Colt 77A balloon | Little Secret Hot-Air Balloon Group |
| | G-BORG | Campbell Cricket | N. G. Bailey |
| | G-BORH | PA-34-200T Seneca II | C. Dugard Ltd & SCA Ltd |
| | G-BORI | Cessna 152 | Staryear Ltd |
| | G-BORJ | Cessna 152 | APB Leasing Ltd/Welshpool |
| | G-BORK | PA-28-161 Warrior II | J. A. Hilton/Coventry |
| | G-BORL | PA-28-161 Warrior II | D. C. Harry |
| | G-BORM | H.S.748 Srs 2B | *(stored)*/Exeter |
| | G-BORN | Cameron N-77 balloon | I. Chadwick |
| | G-BORO | Cessna 152 | Seal Executive Aircraft Ltd |
| | G-BORP | PA-46-310P Malibu | SMC Aviation Ltd/Southend |
| | G-BORR | Thunder Ax8-90 balloon | W. J. Harris |
| | G-BORS | PA-28-181 Archer II | Modern Air/Panshanger |
| | G-BORT | Colt 77A balloon | I. E. A. Joslyn/Germany |
| | G-BORV | Bell 206B JetRanger 2 | P. V. Doman |
| | G-BORW | Cessna 172P | Briter Aviation Ltd/Coventry |
| | G-BORY | Cessna 150L | Airspeed Aviation Ltd |
| | G-BOSA | Boeing 737-204ADV | Santa Fe Aviation Leasing Ltd (G-BAZI) |

| Reg. | Type | Owner or Operator | Notes |
|------|------|-------------------|-------|
| G-BOSB | Thunder Ax7-77 balloon | M. Gallagher | |
| G-BOSC | Cessna U.206G | A. J. Buczkowski/Cranfield | |
| G-BOSD | PA-34-200T Seneca II | Barnes Olson Aeroleasing Ltd | |
| G-BOSE | PA-28-181 Archer II | M. A. Bath | |
| G-BOSF | Colt 69A balloon | Airship & Balloon Co Ltd | |
| G-BOSG | Colt 17A balloon | Airship & Balloon Co Ltd | |
| G-BOSH | Thunder Ax8-84 balloon | Ace Balloons (Bath) Ltd | |
| G-BOSJ | Nord 3400 | A. J. Cowan & H. A. Shillingford | |
| G-BOSM | Jodel DR.253B | J. Cantellow | |
| G-BOSO | Cessna A.152 | Redhill Flying Club | |
| G-BOSP | PA-28-151 Warrior | M. E. Williams/Andrewsfield | |
| G-BOSR | PA-28 Cherokee 140 | R. D. Cornish | |
| G-BOSU | PA-28 Cherokee 140 | M. A. Roberts | |
| G-BOSV | Cameron V-77 balloon | K. H. Greenaway | |
| G-BOTB | Cessna 152 | Stapleford Flying Club Ltd | |
| G-BOTD | Cameron O-105 balloon | P. J. Beglan | |
| G-BOTE | Thunder Ax8-90 balloon | R. S. Hunjan | |
| G-BOTF | PA-28-151 Warrior | G-BOTF Group/Southend | |
| G-BOTG | Cessna 152 | Donington Aviation Ltd/E. Midlands | |
| G-BOTH | Cessna 182Q | G-BOTH Group | |
| G-BOTI | PA-28-151 Warrior | Tango India Flying Group/Biggin Hill | |
| G-BOTK | Cameron O-105 balloon | F. R. & V. L. Higgins | |
| G-BOTM | Bell 206B JetRanger 2 | Spiritbusy Ltd | |
| G-BOTN | PA-28-161 Warrior II | W. Lancashire Aero Club Ltd/Woodvale | |
| G-BOTO | Bellanca 7ECA Citabria | G-BOTO Group | |
| G-BOTP | Cessna 150J | R. E. Thorne | |
| G-BOTS | Hughes 269C | Horizon Helicopters | |
| G-BOTT | Rand KR-2 | M. D. Ott & M. R. Hutchins | |
| G-BOTU | Piper J-3C-65 Cub | T. L. Giles | |
| G-BOTV | PA-32RT-300 Lance II | Robin Lance Aviation Association Ltd | |
| G-BOTW | Cameron V-77 balloon | D. N. Malcolm | |
| G-BOTY | Cessna 150J | T. J. C. Darby & G. Webster | |
| G-BOTZ | Bensen B.80R | C. Jones | |
| G-BOUD | PA-38-112 Tomahawk | K. & C. J. Powell/Southend | |
| G-BOUE | Cessna 172N | E. Alexander | |
| G-BOUF | Cessna 172N | Amber Valley Aviation | |
| G-BOUH | Cessna 172RG | M. G. Fountain | |
| G-BOUI | PA-28-236 Dakota | M. Mansworth | |
| G-BOUJ | Cessna 150M | J. B. Mills | |
| G-BOUK | PA-34-200T Seneca II | Airtime (Hampshire) Ltd | |
| G-BOUL | PA-34-200T Seneca II | C.S.E. Aviation Ltd/Kidlington | |
| G-BOUM | PA-34-200T Seneca II | C.S.E. Aviation Ltd/Kidlington | |
| G-BOUN | Rand KR-2 | W. J. Allan | |
| G-BOUP | PA-28-161 Warrior II | C.S.E. Aviation Ltd/Kidlington | |
| G-BOUR | PA-28-161 Warrior II | C.S.E. Aviation Ltd/Kidlington | |
| G-BOUS | PA-28RT-201 Arrow IV | Hamilton Compass Aviation Ltd | |
| G-BOUT | Colomban MC.12 Cri-Cri | C. K. Farley | |
| G-BOUV | Bensen B.8R | P. Wilkinson | |
| G-BOUZ | Cessna 150G | G. Webster & T. J. C. Darby | |
| G-BOVA | PA-31-310 Turbo Navajo C | Birmingham Aviation Ltd (G-BECP) | |
| G-BOVB | PA-15 Vagabond | Oscar Flying Group/Shoreham | |
| G-BOVC | Everett gyroplane | J. W. Highton | |
| G-BOVG | Cessna F.172H | The G-BOVG Group | |
| G-BOVH | PA-28-161 Warrior II | R. W. Tebby | |
| G-BOVK | PA-28-161 Warrior II | Hamilton Compass Aviation Ltd | |
| G-BOVL | SNCAN Stampe SV-4C | I. M. White | |
| G-BOVP | Air Command 532 Elite | C. K. Park | |
| G-BOVR | Robinson R-22 | P. J. Homan | |
| G-BOVS | Cessna 150M | V. B. Cheesewright | |
| G-BOVT | Cessna 150M | R. G. Moss | |
| G-BOVU | Stoddard-Hamilton Glasair III | W. N. Blair-Hickman | |
| G-BOVV | Cameron V-77 balloon | J. P. Clifford | |
| G-BOVW | Colt 69A balloon | V. Hyland | |
| G-BOVX | Hughes 269C | McIntyre Aviation Ltd/Staverton | |
| G-BOVY | Hughes 269C | R. C. Button | |
| G-BOWA | Thunder Ax8-90 balloon | T. C. Hinton | |
| G-BOWB | Cameron V-77 balloon | R. C. Stone | |
| G-BOWC | Cessna 150J | G-BOWC Flying Group/Southend | |
| G-BOWD | Cessna F.337G | Badgehurst Ltd (G-BLSB) | |
| G-BOWE | PA-34-200T Seneca II | C.S.E. Aviation Ltd/Kidlington | |
| G-BOWK | Cameron N-90 balloon | S. R. Bridge | |
| G-BOWL | Cameron V-77 balloon | Matrix Computers Ltd | |
| G-BOWM | Cameron V-56 balloon | C. G. Caldecott & G. Pitt | |

| Notes | Reg. | Type | Owner or Operator |
|---|---|---|---|
| | G-BOWN | PA-12 Super Cruiser | F. E. P. Holmes/Andrewsfield |
| | G-BOWO | Cessna R.182 | Kenbal Properties Ltd |
| | G-BOWP | Jodel D.120A | A. G. Gedney & ptnrs/Sibson |
| | G-BOWR | Boeing 737-3Q8 | British Airways |
| | G-BOWS | Cessna 150M | Semloh Aviation Services/Andrewsfield |
| | G-BOWT | Stolp SA.300 Starduster Too | F. E. P. Holmes/Andrewsfield |
| | G-BOWU | Cameron O-84 balloon | Raybrake & Co Ltd |
| | G-BOWV | Cameron V-65 balloon | C. P. R. & S. J. Baxter |
| | G-BOWY | PA-28RT-201T Turbo Arrow IV | M. Gardner |
| | G-BOWZ | Benson B.80V | W. M. Day |
| | G-BOXA | PA-28-161 Warrior II | CI Aero Holdings Ltd |
| | G-BOXB | PA-28-161 Warrior II | CI Aero Holdings Ltd |
| | G-BOXC | PA-28-161 Warrior II | CI Aero Holdings Ltd |
| | G-BOXG | Cameron O-77 balloon | S. J. Butler |
| | G-BOXH | Pitts S-1S Special | S. Fenwick |
| | G-BOXJ | Piper J-3C-65 Cub | J. L. Quick & A. J. P. Jackson/Biggin Hill |
| | G-BOXK | Slingsby T.67C | Slingsby Aviation Ltd/Kirkbymoorside |
| | G-BOXN | Robinson R-22B | Conguess Aviation Ltd |
| | G-BOXR | GA-7 Cougar | Campbell Air Services Ltd/Booker |
| | G-BOXS | Hughes 269C | Ford Helicopters Ltd |
| | G-BOXT | Hughes 269C | Elite Helicopters Ltd |
| | G-BOXU | AA-5B Tiger | J. J. Woodhouse |
| | G-BOXV | Pitts S-1S Special | G. R. Clark |
| | G-BOXW | Cassutt Racer Srs IIIM | D. I. Johnson |
| | G-BOXX | Robinson R-22B | J. D. Forbes-Nixon & G. E. Mendham |
| | G-BOXY | PA-28-181 Archer II | Sheffield Aero Club Ltd/Netherthorpe |
| | G-BOYB | Cessna A.152 | Northamptonshire School of Flying Ltd/ Sywell |
| | G-BOYC | Robinson R-22B | Northern Helicopters (Leeds) Ltd |
| | G-BOYE | Cessna TR.182RG | S. K. & W. J. Boettcher |
| | G-BOYF | Sikorsky S-76B | Darley Steel Management Co Ltd |
| | G-BOYH | PA-28-151 Warrior | Superpause Ltd/Booker |
| | G-BOYI | PA-28-161 Warrior II | Rankart Ltd/Kidlington |
| | G-BOYK | Montgomerie-Benson B.8 | H. P. Latham |
| | G-BOYL | Cessna 152 | Sandtoft Air Services (1985) Ltd |
| | G-BOYM | Cameron O-84 balloon | Frontline Distribution Ltd |
| | G-BOYO | Cameron V-20 balloon | Cameron Balloons Ltd |
| | G-BOYP | Cessna 172N | Guildtons Ltd |
| | G-BOYR | Cessna F.337G | Bournewood Aviation |
| | G-BOYS | Cameron N-77 balloon | The Independent Balloon Co Ltd |
| | G-BOYT | PA-38-112 Tomahawk | APB Leasing Ltd/Welshpool |
| | G-BOYU | Cessna A.150L | Flightwheel Group |
| | G-BOYV | PA-28R-201T Turbo Arrow III | P. R. Goldsworthy |
| | G-BOYX | Robinson R-22B | R. Towle |
| | G-BOYY | Cameron A-105 balloon | Hoyers (UK) Ltd |
| | G-BOYZ | Laser Z.200 | M. G. Jefferies |
| | G-BOZI | PA-28-161 Warrior II | Klingair Ltd/Conington |
| | G-BOZK | AS.332L Super Puma | British International Helicopters Ltd |
| | G-BOZL | Bell 206B JetRanger | Ernest George Aviation Ltd |
| | G-BOZM | PA-38-112 Tomahawk | S. J. Green |
| | G-BOZN | Cameron N-77 balloon | Calarel Developments Ltd |
| | G-BOZO | AA-5B Tiger | Becketts Honda Car Centre Ltd |
| | G-BOZP | Beech 76 Duchess | Millhouse Developments Ltd |
| | G-BOZR | Cessna 152 | Interair (Aviation) Ltd/Bournemouth |
| | G-BOZS | Pitts S-1C Special | R. J. & M. B. Trickey |
| | G-BOZT | PA-28-181 Archer II | Andrews Aviation Ltd |
| | G-BOZU | Sparrow Hawk Mk II | R. V. Phillimore |
| | G-BOZV | CEA DR.340 Major | EH Group |
| | G-BOZW | Benson B.8M | M. E. Wills |
| | G-BOZX | Robinson R-22B | Rentatruck (Self Drive) Ltd |
| | G-BOZY | Cameron RTW-120 balloon | G. C. Ludlow |
| | G-BOZZ | AA-5B Tiger | Solent Tiger Group/Southampton |
| | G-BPAA | Acro Advanced | Acro Engines & Airframes Ltd |
| | G-BPAB | Cessna 150M | A. & B. Aviation/Earls Colne |
| | G-BPAC | PA-28-161 Warror II | G. G. Pratt |
| | G-BPAE | Cameron V-77 balloon | C. Dunseath |
| | G-BPAF | PA-28-161 Warrior II | Hendafern Ltd |
| | G-BPAG | Bellanca 8KCAB Decathlon | Deltaflight Ltd |
| | G-BPAH | Colt 69A balloon | International Distillers & Vintners Ltd |
| | G-BPAI | Bell 47F-2A1 | Fizzle Ltd |
| | G-BPAJ | D.H.82A Tiger Moth | P. A. Jackson (G-AOIX) |
| | G-BPAL | D.H.C.1 Chipmunk (WG350) | D. F. Ranger (G-BCYE) |

## UK IN-SEQUENCE

| Reg. | Type | Owner or Operator | Notes |
|------|------|-------------------|-------|
| G-BPAM | Jodel D.150A | A. J. Symes-Bullen | |
| G-BPAO | Air Command 503 Commander | D. J. Sagar | |
| G-BPAS | SOCATA TB.20 Trinidad | South East Aviation Ltd | |
| G-BPAU | PA-28-161 Warrior II | Lapwing Flying Group Ltd/Denham | |
| G-BPAV | FRED Srs 2 | P. A. Valentine | |
| G-BPAW | Cessna 150M | Skegness Air Taxi Service Ltd | |
| G-BPAX | Cessna 150M | Barry Aviation Ltd | |
| G-BPAY | PA-28-181 Archer II | C. Rees | |
| G-BPBA | Benson B.8 | M. E. Green | |
| G-BPBB | Evans VP-2 | J. S. & J. D. Penny | |
| G-BPBG | Cessna 152 | Atlantic Air Transport Ltd/Coventry | |
| G-BPBI | Cessna 152 | B. W. Wells & Burbage Farms Ltd | |
| G-BPBJ | Cessna 152 | A. Windley/Tattershall | |
| G-BPBK | Cessna 152 | B. W. Wells & Burbage Farms Ltd | |
| G-BPBM | PA-28-161 Warrior II | Sandtoft Air Services (1985) Ltd | |
| G-BPBO | PA-28RT-201T Turbo Arrow IV | Arrow Associates/Bournemouth | |
| G-BPBR | PA-38-112 Tomahawk | A.T. Aviation Ltd/Cardiff | |
| G-BPBU | Cameron V-77 balloon | G-BPBU Skymaid Balloon | |
| G-BPBV | Cameron V-77 balloon | J. E. Smith | |
| G-BPBW | Cameron O-105 balloon | R. J. Mansfield | |
| G-BPBX | Cameron V-77 balloon | A. R. M. Hill & C. J. Bell (G-BPCU) | |
| G-BPBY | Cameron V-77 balloon | T. J. & K. A. Brewster (G-BPCS) | |
| G-BPBZ | Thunder Ax7-77 balloon | Wye Valley Aviation Ltd | |
| G-BPCA | BN-2B Islander | Loganair Ltd (G-BLNX)/Glasgow | |
| G-BPCE | Stolp SA.300 Starduster Too | R. E. Todd | |
| G-BPCF | Piper J-3C-65 Cub | A. J. Cook | |
| G-BPCG | Colt AS-80 airship | Willowbest Ltd | |
| G-BPCI | Cessna R.172K | B. E. Simpson | |
| G-BPCJ | Cessna 150J | C. R. Hughes & B. E. Simpson | |
| G-BPCK | PA-28-161 Warrior II | C. R. Hughes & B. E. Simpson | |
| G-BPCL | SA Bulldog Srs 120/128 | Isohigh Ltd/Denham | |
| G-BPCM | Rotorway Executive | Normans (Burton-on-Trent) Ltd | |
| G-BPCN | Cameron A-160 balloon | Golf Centres Balloons Ltd | |
| G-BPCR | Mooney M.20K | T. & R. Harris | |
| G-BPCV | Montgomerie Bensen MB.8R | J. Fisher | |
| G-BPCW | Slingsby T.31 Motor Cadet III | P. C. Williams | |
| G-BPCX | PA-28-236 Dakota | P. Hartley | |
| G-BPCY | PA-34-200T Seneca | Compton Abbas Airfield Ltd | |
| G-BPDA | H.S.748 Srs 2A | Janes Aviation Ltd (G-GLAS)/Blackpool | |
| G-BPDD | Colt 240A balloon | Heather Flight Ltd | |
| G-BPDE | Colt 56A balloon | J. W. Weidema | |
| G-BPDF | Cameron V-77 balloon | Boyson Construction Ltd | |
| G-BPDG | Cameron V-77 balloon | A. & M. A. Dunning | |
| G-BPDJ | Chris Tena Mini Coupe | Air Time Acquisition Ltd | |
| G-BPDK | Sorrell SNS-7 Hyperbipe | A. J. Cable/Barton | |
| G-BPDM | C.A.S.A. 1.131E Jungmann (E3B-369) | Spanish Acquisition/Shoreham | |
| G-BPDN | PA-28R-201 Arrow III | J. M. C. Crompton | |
| G-BPDS | PA-28-161 Warrior II | Hendafern Ltd | |
| G-BPDT | PA-28-161 Warrior II | Hendafern Ltd | |
| G-BPDU | PA-28-161 Warrior II | Hendafern Ltd | |
| G-BPDV | Pitts S-1S Special | D. Clarke | |
| G-BPDY | Westland-Bell 47G-3B1 | Howden Helicopters/Spaldington | |
| G-BPDZ | Cessna 340A | J. G. Kelwick | |
| G-BPEA | Boeing 757-236ER | Caledonian Airways Ltd *Loch of the Clans* | |
| G-BPEB | Boeing 757-236ER | Caledonian Airways Ltd *Loch Lomond* | |
| G-BPEC | Boeing 757-236ER | Caledonian Airways Ltd *Loch Katrine* | |
| G-BPED | Boeing 757-236ER | Caledonian Airways Ltd *Loch Sheil/ Blair Castle* | |
| G-BPEE | Boeing 757-236ER | Caledonian Airways Ltd *Loch Tay* | |
| G-BPEF | Boeing 757-236ER | Caledonian Airways Ltd (G-BOHC) | |
| G-BPEG | Boeing 757-236ER | Caledonian Airways Ltd (G-BNSE) | |
| G-BPEH | Boeing 757-236ER | Caledonian Airways Ltd | |
| G-BPEI | Boeing 757-236ER | Caledonian Airways Ltd | |
| G-BPEJ | — | Caledonian Airways Ltd | |
| G-BPEK | — | Caledonian Airways Ltd | |
| G-BPEL | PA-28-151 Warrior | R. W. Harris & A. J. Jahanfar | |
| G-BPEM | Cessna 150K | G. P. Robinson & R. G. Lindsey | |
| G-BPEO | Cessna 152 | R. W. Harris & A. J. Jahanfar | |
| G-BPER | PA-38-112 Tomahawk | E. Midlands Flying School Ltd | |
| G-BPES | PA-38-112 Tomahawk | Sherwood Flying Club Ltd/Tollerton | |
| G-BPEW | Robinson R-22B | Trade Photographic Services Ltd | |
| G-BPEZ | Colt 77A balloon | A. Stace | |

| Notes | Reg. | Type | Owner or Operator |
|---|---|---|---|
| | G-BPFA | Knight GK-2 Swallow | G. Knight & D. G. Pridham |
| | G-BPFB | Colt 77A balloon | S. Ingram |
| | G-BPFC | Mooney M.20C | Kington Building Supplies Ltd & RV Engineering Ltd |
| | G-BPFD | Jodel D.112 | K. Manley |
| | G-BPFE | Lightning T.5 (XS452) | Ruanil Investments Ltd/Cranfield |
| | G-BPFF | Cameron DP-70 airship | Cameron Balloons Ltd |
| | G-BPFG | SOCATA TB.20 Trinidad | F. T. Arnold |
| | G-BPFH | PA-28-161 Warrior II | M. H. Kleiser |
| | G-BPFI | PA-28-181 Archer II | R. N. Dixon-Smith & B. M. Chilvers |
| | G-BPFJ | Cameron 90 Can SS balloon | The Hot-Air Balloon Co Ltd |
| | G-BPFK | Bensen B.8M | J. W. Birkett |
| | G-BPFL | Davis DA-2 | C. A. Lightfoot |
| | G-BPFM | Aeronca 7AC Champion | Foxtrot Mike Group |
| | G-BPFR | Short SD3-60 Variant 100 | Shorts Aircraft Financing Ltd |
| | G-BPFS | Short SD3-60 Variant 100 | Lynrise Aircraft Financing Ltd (G-REGN/ G-OCIA) |
| | G-BPFV | Boeing 767-204ER | Britannia Airways Ltd/Luton |
| | G-BPFX | Colt 21A balloon | The Hot-Air Balloon Co Ltd |
| | G-BPFY | Consolidated PBY-6A Catalina | D. W. Arnold/Biggin Hill |
| | G-BPFZ | Cessna 152 | J. J. Baumhardt/Southend |
| | G-BPGA | Mooney M.20J | Medallionair Ltd |
| | G-BPGB | Cessna 150J | Skegness Air Taxi Service Ltd |
| | G-BPGC | Air Command 532 Elite | E. C. E. Brown |
| | G-BPGD | Cameron V-65 balloon | Gone With The Wind Ltd |
| | G-BPGE | Cessna U.206C | The Scottish Parachute Club |
| | G-BPGF | Thunder Ax7-77 balloon | Mill Bros Ltd |
| | G-BPGH | EAA Acro Sport 2 | G. M. Bradley |
| | G-BPGI | Colt 69A balloon | Thunder & Colt Ltd |
| | G-BPGJ | Colt 31A balloon | Thunder & Colt Ltd |
| | G-BPGK | Aeronca 7AC Chamption | T. M. Williams |
| | G-BPGL | PA-28 Cherokee 180 | C. N. Ellerbrook |
| | G-BPGM | Cessna 152 | Westward Airways (Land's End) Ltd |
| | G-BPGN | Cameron 90 Tractor SS balloon | Cameron Balloons Ltd |
| | G-BPGU | PA-28-181 Archer II | G. Underwood |
| | G-BPGV | Robinson R-22B | Featureford Ltd |
| | G-BPGX | SOCATA TB.9 Tampico | CB Helicopters |
| | G-BPGY | Cessna 150H | Three Counties Aero Engineering Ltd/ Lasham |
| | G-BPGZ | Cessna 150G | D. F. & B. L. Sperring |
| | G-BPHB | PA-28-161 Warrior II | Channel Islands Aero Holdings (Jersey) Ltd |
| | G-BPHC | Cameron N-42 balloon | P. J. Marshall & M. A. Clarke |
| | G-BPHE | PA-28-161 Warrior II | Pool Aviation Ltd/Welshpool |
| | G-BPHF | AB-206A JetRanger | RCR Aviation Ltd/Southampton |
| | G-BPHG | Robin DR.400/180 | K. J. & M. B. White/Redhill |
| | G-BPHH | Cameron V-77 balloon | C. J. Madigan |
| | G-BPHJ | Cameron V-77 balloon | C. W. Brown |
| | G-BPHK | Whittaker MW.7 | R. V. Hogg |
| | G-BPHL | PA-28-161 Warrior II | Teesside Flight Centre Ltd |
| | G-BPHM | Beech A36 Bonanza | A. P. Vonk |
| | G-BPHO | Taylorcraft BC-12D | J. Roberts |
| | G-BPHP | Taylorcraft BC-12-65 | D. C. Stephens |
| | G-BPHR | D.H.82A Tiger Moth (A17-48) | N. Parry |
| | G-BPHS | Cessna 152 | Keywise Multinational Ltd |
| | G-BPHT | Cessna 152 | A. E. Kedros |
| | G-BPHU | Thunder Ax7-77 balloon | R. P. Waite |
| | G-BPHW | Cessna 140 | J. A. Pothecary |
| | G-BPHX | Cessna 140 | Ark Ltd |
| | G-BPHY | Cameron 110 Cow SS balloon | Cameron Balloons Ltd |
| | G-BPHZ | M.S.505 Criquet (TA+RC) | The Aircraft Restoration Co/Duxford |
| | G-BPIC | AB-206B JetRanger 3 | Heliwork Services Ltd |
| | G-BPID | PA-28-161 Warrior II | P. M. Ireland |
| | G-BPIE | Bell 206B JetRanger | BLS Aviation Ltd/Elstree |
| | G-BPIF | Bensen-Parsons 2 seat | N. J. Stoneham |
| | G-BPIH | Rand KR-2 | J. R. Rowley |
| | G-BPII | Denney Aerocraft Kitfox | J. K. Cross |
| | G-BPIJ | Brantly B.2B | R. B. Payne |
| | G-BPIK | PA-38-112 Tomahawk | Cumbernauld Aviation Ltd |
| | G-BPIL | Cessna 310B | A. L. Brown & R. A. Parsons |
| | G-BPIM | Cameron N-77 balloon | Thermalite Ltd |
| | G-BPIN | Glaser-Dirks DG.400 | M. P. Seth-Smith & J. N. Stevenson |
| | G-BPIO | Cessna F.152 II | S. Harcourt |
| | G-BPIP | Slingsby T.31 Motor Cadet III | J. H. Beard |

| Reg. | Type | Owner or Operator | Notes |
|------|------|-------------------|-------|
| G-BPIR | Scheibe SF.25E Super Falke | Coventry Gliding Club Ltd | |
| G-BPIU | PA-28-161 Warrior II | I. R. Jones & P. C. Rowlands | |
| G-BPIV | Bristol 149 Bolingbroke Mk IVT | The Aircraft Restoration Co/Duxford | |
| G-BPIY | Cessna 152 | J. J. Baumhardt | |
| G-BPIZ | AA-5B Tiger | D. A. Horsley | |
| G-BPJA | Beech 95-58 Baron | Morse Computers Ltd | |
| G-BPJB | Schweizer 269C | J. F. Britten | |
| G-BPJC | Robinson R-22B | Leicester Helicopters Ltd | |
| G-BPJD | SOCATA Rallye 110ST | C. G. Wheeler | |
| G-BPJE | Cameron A-105 balloon | J. S. Eckersley | |
| G-BPJF | PA-38-112 Tomahawk | Air Yorkshire Ltd | |
| G-BPJG | PA-18 Super Cub 150 | Trent Valley Aerotowing Ltd | |
| G-BPJH | PA-18 Super Cub 95 | P. J. Heron | |
| G-BPJK | Colt 77A balloon | Akal Ltd | |
| G-BPJL | Cessna 152 | London Flight Centre (Headcorn) Ltd | |
| G-BPJN | Jodel D.18 | J. A. Nugent | |
| G-BPJO | PA-28-161 Cadet | C.S.E. Aviation Ltd/Kidlington | |
| G-BPJP | PA-28-161 Cadet | C.S.E. Aviation Ltd/Kidlington | |
| G-BPJR | PA-28-161 Cadet | C.S.E. Aviation Ltd/Kidlington | |
| G-BPJS | PA-28-161 Cadet | C.S.E. Aviation Ltd/Kidlington | |
| G-BPJU | PA-28-161 Cadet | C.S.E. Aviation Ltd/Kidlington | |
| G-BPJV | Taylorcraft F-21 | TC Flying Group | |
| G-BPJW | Cessna A.150K | Pan Air Ltd | |
| G-BPJZ | Cameron O-160 balloon | M. L. Gabb | |
| G-BPKF | Grob G.115 | Tayside Aviation Ltd/Dundee | |
| G-BPKH | Robinson R-22B | Findon Air Services | |
| G-BPKI | EAA Acro Sport 1 | D. T. Kaberry | |
| G-BPKJ | Colt AS-80 Mk II airship | Thunder & Co Ltd | |
| G-BPKK | Denney Aerocraft Kitfox | T. P. Eglinton & N. E. Whiteman | |
| G-BPKL | Mooney M.20J | Astraflight Ltd | |
| G-BPKM | PA-28-161 Warrior II | M. J. Greasby | |
| G-BPKN | Colt AS-80 Mk II airship | C. Turnbull | |
| G-BPKO | Cessna 140 | I. R. March | |
| G-BPKR | PA-28-151 Warrior | R. R. Harris | |
| G-BPKS | Stolp SA.300 Starduster Too | J. A. Hubner | |
| G-BPLA | Boeing 737-2K2 | Britannia Airways Ltd *Sir Stanley Matthews* | |
| G-BPLE | Cameron A-160 balloon | Balloons & Airships International Ltd | |
| G-BPLF | Cameron V-77 balloon | C. L. Luffingham | |
| G-BPLG | Morane-Saulnier M.S.317 | F. A. Anderson | |
| G-BPLH | Jodel DR.1051 | M. N. King | |
| G-BPLI | Colt 77A balloon | Yanin International Ltd | |
| G-BPLJ | Colt 90A balloon | Thunder & Colt Ltd | |
| G-BPLM | AIA Stampe SV-4C | C. J. Jesson/Redhill | |
| G-BPLU | Thunder Ax10-160 balloon | Subsearch Ltd | |
| G-BPLV | Cameron V-77 balloon | Jessops (Tailors) Ltd | |
| G-BPLY | Pitts S-2B Special | D. A. Hammant | |
| G-BPLZ | Hughes 369HS | Neil Brown Engineering Ltd | |
| G-BPMB | Maule M5-235C Lunar Rocket | A. P. Le Coyte | |
| G-BPMC | Air Command 503 Commander | M. A. Cheshire | |
| G-BPMD | Boeing Stearman A.75L-3 (320) | M. G. Saunders/White Waltham | |
| G-BPME | Cessna 152 | London Flight Centre (Headcorn) Ltd | |
| G-BPMF | PA-28-151 Warrior | Logtrip Ltd | |
| G-BPMG | Bensen B.8MR | P. Doherty | |
| G-BPMH | Schempp-Hirth Nimbus 3DM | Southern Sailplanes | |
| G-BPMI | Colt 56A balloon | Thunder & Colt Ltd | |
| G-BPMJ | Colt 56A balloon | Thunder & Colt Ltd | |
| G-BPML | Cessna 172M | J. M. Gale & R. D. Andrews | |
| G-BPMM | Champion 7ECA Citabria | D. M. Griffiths | |
| G-BPMN | Aerocar Super Coot Model A | P. Napp | |
| G-BPMO | Cessna 150M | S. L. Mills | |
| G-BPMP | Douglas C-47A-50-DL (224211) | Atlantic Air Transport Ltd/Coventry | |
| G-BPMR | PA-28-161 Warrior II | McIntyre Aviation/Staverton | |
| G-BPMU | Nord 3202B | John Durkin Technical Services Ltd (G-BIZJ) | |
| G-BPMV | PA-28-161 Warrior II | J. W. Donald | |
| G-BPMW | QAC Quickie Q.2 | C. W. Tattersall (G-OICI/G-OGKN) | |
| G-BPMX | ARV Super 2 | G-BPMX Flying Group | |
| G-BPMY | Cameron A-120 balloon | British School of Ballooning | |
| G-BPNA | Cessna 150L | C. M. Vlieland-Boddy/Compton Abbas | |
| G-BPNC | Rotorway Executive | S. J. Hanson | |
| G-BPND | Boeing 727-2D3 | Capita Ltd | |
| G-BPNF | Robinson R-22B | K. N. Tolley | |
| G-BPNG | Bell 206B JetRanger 2 | Tindon Ltd (G-ORTC) | |

| Notes | Reg. | Type | Owner or Operator |
|---|---|---|---|
| | G-BPNI | Robinson R-22B | Arrowbury Ltd |
| | G-BPNL | QAC Quickie Q.2 | J. Catley |
| | G-BPNN | Bensen B.8MR | M. E. Vahdat |
| | G-BPNO | Zlin Z.326 Trener Master | J. A. S. Bailey & S. T. Logan |
| | G-BPNS | Boeing 727-277 | Capita Ltd |
| | G-BPNT | BAe 146-300 | British Aerospace PLC |
| | G-BPNU | Thunder Ax7-77 balloon | J. Fenton |
| | G-BPNY | Boeing 727-230 | Capita Ltd |
| | G-BPNZ | Boeing 737-4Q8 | British Airways |
| | G-BPOA | Gloster Meteor T.7 (WF877) | Aces High Ltd/North Weald |
| | G-BPOB | Sopwith Camel F.1 (replica) (B2458) | Bianchi Aviation Film Services Ltd/ Booker |
| | G-BPOD | Stolp SA.300 Starduster Too | A. T. Fines |
| | G-BPOE | Colt 77A balloon | Albatross Aviation Ltd |
| | G-BPOF | Robinson R-22B | R. D. Masters |
| | G-BPOL | Pietenpol Air Camper | G. W. Postance |
| | G-BPOM | PA-28-161 Warrior II | McIntyre Aviation/Staverton |
| | G-BPON | PA-34-200T Seneca II | London Flight Centre Air Charter Ltd |
| | G-BPOO | Montgomerie Bensen B.8MR | M. E. Vahdat |
| | G-BPOR | Bell 206B JetRanger 2 | Thetford Compactors Finance Ltd |
| | G-BPOS | Cessna 150M | Lanx Engineering Ltd |
| | G-BPOT | PA-28-181 Archer II | Cumbernauld Aviation Ltd |
| | G-BPOU | Luscombe 8A Silvaire | E. T. Wicks |
| | G-BPOV | Cameron 90 Magazine SS balloon | Forbes Europe Inc/France |
| | G-BPOX | Enstrom 280C Shark | J. Evans |
| | G-BPOY | Enstrom F-28A | M. & P. Food Products Ltd |
| | G-BPOZ | Enstrom F-28A | M. & P. Food Products Ltd |
| | G-BPPA | Cameron O-65 balloon | Rix Petroleum Ltd |
| | G-BPPB | PA-34-220T Seneca III | A. Smith |
| | G-BPPD | PA-38-112 Tomahawk | AT Aviation Ltd/Cardiff |
| | G-BPPE | PA-38-112 Tomahawk | Norwich School of Flying |
| | G-BPPF | PA-38-112 Tomahawk | A. N. Doughty |
| | G-BPPG | PA-38-112 Tomahawk | AT Aviation Ltd/Cardiff |
| | G-BPPI | Colt 180A balloon | A. Faulkner |
| | G-BPPJ | Cameron A-180 Balloon | H. R. Evans |
| | G-BPPK | PA-28-151 Warrior | Balgold Ltd |
| | G-BPPL | Enstrom F-28A | M. & P. Food Products Ltd |
| | G-BPPM | Beech B200 Super King Air | Gama Aviation Ltd/Fairoaks |
| | G-BPPN | Cessna F.182Q | Hunt Norris Ltd |
| | G-BPPO | Luscombe 8A Silvaire | M. J. Negus |
| | G-BPPP | Cameron V-77 balloon | P. F. Smart |
| | G-BPPR | Air Command 532 Elite | T. D. Inch |
| | G-BPPS | Mudry CAARP CAP.21 | BAC Aviation Ltd/Earls Colne |
| | G-BPPU | Air Command 532 Elite | J. Hough |
| | G-BPPW | Schweizer 269C | K. W. Harding |
| | G-BPPX | Schweizer 269C | Lakeside Helicopters Ltd |
| | G-BPPY | Hughes 269B | R. W. Carr & C. F. Collier |
| | G-BPPZ | Taylorcraft BC-12D | Zulu Warriors Flying Group |
| | G-BPRA | Aeronca 11AC Chief | D. F. Micklethwait |
| | G-BPRC | Cameron Elephant SS balloon | Cameron Balloons Ltd |
| | G-BPRD | Pitts S-1C Special | S. M. Trickey |
| | G-BPRI | AS.355F-1 Twin Squirrel | American Aviation Technologies Ltd |
| | G-BPRJ | AS.355F-1 Twin Squirrel | G. Greenall |
| | G-BPRL | AS.355F-1 Twin Squirrel | Wood Hall Helicopters Ltd |
| | G-BPRM | Cessna F.172L | A. J. Moseley (G-AZKG) |
| | G-BPRN | PA-28-161 Warrior II | Air Navigation & Trading Co Ltd/Blackpool |
| | G-BPRO | Cessna A.150K | Armphase Ltd |
| | G-BPRP | Cessna 150E | P. G. Powter/Shoreham |
| | G-BPRR | Rand KR-2 | M. W. Albery |
| | G-BPRS | Air Command 532 Elite | B. K. Snoxall |
| | G-BPRT | Piel CP.328 | N. Reddish |
| | G-BPRV | PA-28-161 Warrior II | AT Aviation Ltd/Cardiff |
| | G-BPRX | Aeronca 11AC Chief | R. D. Ward & J. M. Taylor |
| | G-BPRY | PA-28-161 Warrior II | B. McIntyre |
| | G-BPRZ | Robinson R-22A | Bristol Rotary Training Ltd |
| | G-BPSA | Luscombe 8A Silvaire | K. P. Gorman/Staverton |
| | G-BPSB | Air Command 532 Elite | D. K. Duckworth |
| | G-BPSE | NA AT-6D Harvard (483009) | Aces High Ltd/North Weald |
| | G-BPSH | Cameron V-77 balloon | P. G. Hossack |
| | G-BPSI | Thunder Ax10-160 balloon | Airborne Adventures Ltd |
| | G-BPSJ | Thunder Ax6-56 balloon | Thunder & Colt Ltd |
| | G-BPSK | Montgomerie Bensen B.8M | R. J. Mann |
| | G-BPSL | Cessna 177 | I. P. Burnett & ptnrs/White Waltham |

| Reg. | Type | Owner or Operator | Notes |
|------|------|-------------------|-------|
| G-BPSO | Cameron N-90 balloon | L. A. Sadler & K. J. Holt | |
| G-BPSP | Cameron 90 Ship SS balloon | Forbes Europe Inc/France | |
| G-BPSR | Cameron V-77 balloon | K. J. A. Maxwell | |
| G-BPSS | Cameron A-120 balloon | J. P. Clifford | |
| G-BPSV | Cessna F.406 Caravan II | Air Corbière Ltd/Coventry | |
| G-BPSW | Cessna F.406 Caravan II | Directflight Ltd/Norwich | |
| G-BPSX | Cessna F.406 Caravan II | Directflight Ltd/Norwich | |
| G-BPSY | Grob G.115 | Soaring (Oxford) Ltd | |
| G-BPSZ | Cameron N-180 balloon | The Balloon Club Ltd | |
| G-BPTA | Stinson 108-2 | D. N. H. Martin/Booker | |
| G-BPTB | Boeing Stearman A.75N1 (442) | Aero Vintage Ltd | |
| G-BPTC | Taylorcraft BC-12D | J. R. Surbey | |
| G-BPTD | Cameron V-77 balloon | J. Lippett | |
| G-BPTE | PA-28-181 Archer II | London Flight Centre (Stansted) Ltd | |
| G-BPTF | Cessna 152 | London Flight Centre (Stansted) Ltd | |
| G-BPTG | R. Commander 112TC | G. J. Deadman | |
| G-BPTH | Air Command 532 Elite | R. Wheeler | |
| G-BPTI | SOCATA TB.20 Trinidad | Lyndon Scaffolding Hire Ltd/Birmingham | |
| G-BPTL | Cessna 172N | Cleveland Flying School Ltd/Teesside | |
| G-BPTM | Pitts S-1T Special | RPM Aviation Ltd | |
| G-BPTO | Zenith CH.200-AA | B. Philips | |
| G-BPTP | Robinson R-22 | Sarahs Lakeland Fudge | |
| G-BPTS | C.A.S.A. 1.131E Jungmann | Aerobatic Displays Ltd/Booker | |
| G-BPTT | Robin DR.400/120 | The Cotswold Aero Club Ltd/Staverton | |
| G-BPTU | Cessna 152 | Flyteam Aviation Ltd | |
| G-BPTV | Bensen B.8 | L. Chiappi | |
| G-BPTW | Cameron A-160 balloon | Newbury Ballooning Co Ltd | |
| G-BPTX | Cameron O-120 balloon | J. M. Langley | |
| G-BPTZ | Robinson R-22B | J. Luccetti | |
| G-BPUA | EAA P-2 Biplane | G. H. Cork | |
| G-BPUB | Cameron V-31 balloon | M. T. Evans | |
| G-BPUC | QAC Quickie Q.200 | R. Wells | |
| G-BPUD | Ryan PT-22 (I-492) | R. I. Warman | |
| G-BPUE | Air Command 532 Elite | R. A. Fazackerley | |
| G-BPUF | Thunder Ax6-56Z balloon | R. C. & M. A. Trimble | |
| G-BPUG | Air Command 532 Elite | T. A. Holmes | |
| G-BPUH | Cameron A-180 balloon | Golf Centres Balloons Ltd | |
| G-BPUI | Air Command 532 Elite | M. A. Turner | |
| G-BPUJ | Cameron N-90 balloon | Touch Panel Products Ltd | |
| G-BPUL | PA-18 Super Cub 150 | Crissair Ltd | |
| G-BPUM | Cessna R.182RG | R. H. Stradling | |
| G-BPUP | Whittaker MW-7 | J. H. Beard | |
| G-BPUR | Piper J-3L-65 Cub | J3 Group | |
| G-BPUS | Rans S.9 | P. M. Shipman | |
| G-BPUU | Cessna 140 | R. Crossland/Exeter | |
| G-BPUW | Colt 90A balloon | Huntair Ltd | |
| G-BPUX | Cessna 150J | H. H. Goodman | |
| G-BPUY | Cessna 150K | M. Hewison/Luton | |
| G-BPUZ | Cessna 150M | Pektron Ltd | |
| G-BPVA | Cessna 172F | J. E. Stevens | |
| G-BPVC | Cameron V-77 balloon | Courtaulds PLC | |
| G-BPVE | Bleriot 1909 replica | Bianchi Aviation Film Services Ltd/Booker | |
| G-BPVH | Cub Aircraft J-3C-65 Prospector | D. E. Cooper-Maguire | |
| G-BPVI | PA-32R-301 Saratoga SP | J. D. Macpherson | |
| G-BPVJ | Cessna 152 | D. C. Fieldhouse | |
| G-BPVK | Varga 2150A Kachina | H. W. Hall | |
| G-BPVM | Cameron V-77 balloon | Royal Engineers Balloon Club | |
| G-BPVN | PA-32R-301T Turbo Saratoga SP | Hero Aviation/Stapleford | |
| G-BPVO | Cassutt Racer IIIM | Lanx Engineering Ltd | |
| G-BPVT | Thunder Ax7-65 balloon | Anglia Balloon School Ltd | |
| G-BPVU | Thunder Ax7-77 balloon | J. Burlinson | |
| G-BPVW | C.A.S.A. 1.131E Jungmann | S. A. W. Becker/Goodwood | |
| G-BPVX | Cassutt Racer IIIM | A. A. A. White/Manchester | |
| G-BPVY | Cessna 172D | C. A. Morris | |
| G-BPVZ | Luscombe 8E Silvaire | W. E. Gillham & P. Ryman | |
| G-BPWA | PA-28-161 Warrior II | Mid America UK Ltd | |
| G-BPWC | Cameron V-77 balloon | H. B. Roberts | |
| G-BPWD | Cessna 120 | Peregrine Flying Group | |
| G-BPWE | PA-28-161 Warrior II | AT Aviation Ltd/Cardiff | |
| G-BPWF | PA-28 Cherokee 140 ★ | (static display)/ATC Swindon | |
| G-BPWG | Cessna 150M | C. J. Allen | |
| G-BPWH | Robinson R-22B | R. H. Everett | |
| G-BPWI | Bell 206B JetRanger 2 | Lakeside Helicopters Ltd | |

| Notes | Reg. | Type | Owner or Operator |
|-------|------|------|-------------------|
| | G-BPWK | Sportavia Fournier RF-5B | S. L. Reed |
| | G-BPWM | Cessna 150L | Lanx Engineering Ltd |
| | G-BPWN | Cessna 150L | Premier Plane Leasing Co Ltd |
| | G-BPWO | Cessna 150L | Pektron Ltd |
| | G-BPWP | Rutan LongEz | J. F. O'Hara & A. J. Voyle |
| | G-BPWR | Cessna R.172K | A. M. Skelton |
| | G-BPWS | Cessna 172P | Holmes Rentals |
| | G-BPWT | Cameron DG-19 airship | Airspace Outdoor Advertising Ltd |
| | G-BPWV | Colt 56A balloon | W. D. Young |
| | G-BPWW | Piaggio FWP.149D | I. H. Leach-Allen |
| | G-BPWX | Montgomerie Bensen B.8MR | M. S. Lloyd |
| | G-BPWY | Isaacs Fury II | R. J. Knights |
| | G-BPWZ | PA-28-161 Warrior II | Hamilton Compass Aviation Ltd |
| | G-BPXA | PA-28-181 Archer II | Cherokee Flying Group/Netherthorpe |
| | G-BPXB | Glaser-Dirks DG.400 | G. S. Griffiths |
| | G-BPXE | Enstrom 280C Shark | P. Lancaster |
| | G-BPXF | Cameron V-65 balloon | D. Pascall |
| | G-BPXG | Colt 42A balloon | Cooper Group Ltd |
| | G-BPXH | Colt 17A balloon | Gone With The Wind Ltd |
| | G-BPXI | PA-23 Aztec 250F | A. R. D. Knott/Elstree |
| | G-BPXJ | PA-28RT-201T Turbo Arrow IV | Grumman Travel (Surrey) Ltd |
| | G-BPXP | Thunder Ax10-160 balloon | Wellfarrow Ltd |
| | G-BPXX | PA-34-200T Seneca II | Hockstar Ltd |
| | G-BPXY | Aeronca 11AC Chief | S. Hawksworth |
| | G-BPXZ | Cameron V-77 balloon | M. D. Hammond |
| | G-BPYA | Rotorway Executive | Orchard Engineering Co Ltd |
| | G-BPYB | Air Command 532 Elite | P. J. Houtman |
| | G-BPYC | Cessna 310R | Air Service Training Ltd/Perth |
| | G-BPYH | Robinson R-22B | Status Investments Ltd |
| | G-BPYI | Cameron O-77 balloon | Macleod Garage Ltd |
| | G-BPYJ | Wittman W.8 Tailwind | J. Dixon |
| | G-BPYK | Thunder Ax7-77 balloon | A. R. Swinnerton |
| | G-BPYL | Hughes 369D | Aly Aviation Ltd/Henstridge |
| | G-BPYN | Piper J-3C-65 Cub | The Aquila Group/White Waltham |
| | G-BPYO | PA-28-181 Archer II | Premier Flight Services Ltd |
| | G-BPYP | Cameron O-105 balloon | Newbury Ballooning Co Ltd |
| | G-BPYR | PA-31-310 Turbo Navajo | Multi Ltd (G-ECMA) |
| | G-BPYS | Cameron O-77 balloon | D. J. Goldsmith |
| | G-BPYT | Cameron V-77 balloon | Skylite Aviation Ltd |
| | G-BPYV | Cameron V-77 balloon | M. E. Weston |
| | G-BPYW | Air Command 532 Elite | W. V. Tatters |
| | G-BPYX | Robinson R-22B | Glentworth Scottish Farms Ltd |
| | G-BPYY | Cameron A-180 balloon | Sky Balloon Co |
| | G-BPYZ | Thunder Ax7-77 balloon | J. E. Astall |
| | G-BPZA | Luscombe 8A Silvaire | T. P. W. Hyde |
| | G-BPZB | Cessna 120 | C. Grime & J. Cook |
| | G-BPZC | Luscombe 8A Silvaire | C. C. & J. M. Lovell |
| | G-BPZD | SNCAN NC.858S | G. Richards |
| | G-BPZE | Luscombe 8E Silvaire | WFG Luscombe Associates |
| | G-BPZF | PA-46-310P Malibu | Jenrick Engineering Services Ltd |
| | G-BPZG | PA-28R-201T Turbo Arrow III | Salborne Farms Ltd |
| | G-BPZI | Christen Eagle II | S. D. Quigley |
| | G-BPZK | Cameron O-120 balloon | D. L. Smith |
| | G-BPZM | PA-28RT-201 Arrow IV | J. H. Kimber (G-ROYW/G-CRTI) |
| | G-BPZN | Cessna T.303 | R. S. Williams & S. B. Danser (G-RSUL) |
| | G-BPZO | Cameron N-90 balloon | Seaward PLC |
| | G-BPZP | Robin DR.400/180R | Tatenhill Aviation |
| | G-BPZS | Colt 105A balloon | The Balloon Club of GB Ltd |
| | G-BPZT | Cameron N-90 balloon | Peter Lane Transport Ltd |
| | G-BPZU | Scheibe SF.25C Falke | G-BPZU Group |
| | G-BPZW | SOCATA TB.20 Trinidad | Air Touring Services Ltd/Biggin Hill |
| | G-BPZX | Cessna 152 | Woodward & Co (Sheffield) Ltd |
| | G-BPZY | Pitts S-1C Special | J. S. Mitchell |
| | G-BPZZ | Thunder Ax8-105 balloon | Breachwood Motors Ltd |
| | G-BRAA | Pitts S-1C Special | C. Davidson |
| | G-BRAB | BAe 146-300 | British Air Ferries/Stansted |
| | G-BRAE | Colt 69A balloon | Jentime Ltd |
| | G-BRAF | V.S.394 Spitfire FR.XVIII (SM969) | D. W. Arnold/Biggin Hill |
| | G-BRAJ | Cameron V-77 balloon | H. R. Evans |
| | G-BRAK | Cessna 172N | C. Docketty |
| | G-BRAL | G.159 Gulfstream 1 | Ford Motor Co Ltd/Stansted |
| | G-BRAM | Mikoyan MiG-21PF (503) | Aces High Ltd/North Weald |

| Reg. | Type | Owner or Operator | Notes |
|------|------|-------------------|-------|
| G-BRAP | Thermal Aircraft 104 | Thermal Aircraft | |
| G-BRAR | Aeronca 7AC Champion | G-BRAR Group | |
| G-BRAV | PA-23 Aztec 250E | Hartfield Aviation Ltd (G-BBCM) | |
| G-BRAW | Pitts S-1 Special | P. G. Bond & P. B. Hunter | |
| G-BRAX | Payne Knight Twister 85B | R. Earl | |
| G-BRBA | PA-28-161 Warrior II | Hendafern Ltd | |
| G-BRBB | PA-28-161 Warrior II | D. P. Hughes | |
| G-BRBC | NA T-6G Texan | A. P. Murphy | |
| G-BRBD | PA-28-151 Warrior | B. E. Simpson & C. R. Hughes | |
| G-BRBE | PA-28-161 Warrior II | P. A. Lancaster/Compton Abbas | |
| G-BRBF | Cessna 152 | Cumbria Aero Club/Carlisle | |
| G-BRBG | PA-28 Cherokee 180 | Anderson MacArthur & Co | |
| G-BRBH | Cessna 150H | P. J. Webb/Elstree | |
| G-BRBI | Cessna 172N | D. T. Searchfield/Blackbushe | |
| G-BRBJ | Cessna 172M | L. C. MacKnight/Elstree | |
| G-BRBK | Robin DR.400/180 | R. Kemp | |
| G-BRBL | Robin DR.400/180 | Crown Export Services | |
| G-BRBM | Robin DR.400/180 | R. W. Davies/Headcorn | |
| G-BRBN | Pitts S-1S Special | D. R. Evans | |
| G-BRBO | Cameron V-77 balloon | Matrix Computers Ltd | |
| G-BRBP | Cessna 152 | Staverton Flying Services Ltd | |
| G-BRBR | Cameron V-77 balloon | 1066 Balloon Group | |
| G-BRBS | Bensen B.8M | J. Simpson | |
| G-BRBT | Trotter Ax3-20 balloon | R. M. Trotter | |
| G-BRBU | Colt 17A balloon | Airship & Balloon Co Ltd | |
| G-BRBV | Piper J-4A Cub Coupé | J. Schonburg | |
| G-BRBW | PA-28 Cherokee 140 | Cherokee Cruiser Aircraft Group | |
| G-BRBX | PA-28-181 Archer II | M. J. Ireland | |
| G-BRBY | Robinson R-22B | Adern Sales Ltd | |
| G-BRBZ | Beech 400 Beechjet | Bass PLC | |
| G-BRCA | Jodel D.112 | D. I. Walker & W. H. Sherlock | |
| G-BRCC | Cessna 152 | Falcon Flying Services/Biggin Hill | |
| G-BRCD | Cessna A.152 | D. E. Simmons/Shoreham | |
| G-BRCE | Pitts S-1C Special | R. O. Rogers | |
| G-BRCF | Montgomerie-Bensen B.8 | J. S. Walton | |
| G-BRCG | Grob G.109 | Oxfordshire Sportflying Ltd/Enstone | |
| G-BRCI | Pitts S-1 Special | R. N. Crosland | |
| G-BRCJ | Cameron NS-20 balloon | Cameron Balloons Ltd | |
| G-BRCL | Colt Flying Hat SS balloon | Jentime Ltd | |
| G-BRCM | Cessna 172L | S. G. E. Plessis & D. C. C. Handley | |
| G-BRCO | Cameron NS-20 balloon | Flying Pictures Ltd | |
| G-BRCP | Enstrom F-28F | Southern Air Ltd/Shoreham | |
| G-BRCR | Cameron V-77 balloon | E. E. Clark | |
| G-BRCS | Colt 105A balloon | Jentime Ltd | |
| G-BRCT | Denney Aerocraft Kitfox | Wessex Aviation & Transport Ltd | |
| G-BRCV | Aeronca 7AC Champion | A. P. Wellings/Sandown | |
| G-BRCW | Aeronca 11AC Chief | R. B. McComish | |
| G-BRCX | Colt 105A balloon | Jentime Ltd | |
| G-BRDB | Zenair CH.701 STOL | D. L. Botwell | |
| G-BRDC | Thunder Ax7-77 balloon | N. J. Morley & D. M. Levene | |
| G-BRDD | Avions Mudry CAP.10B | R. D. Dickson/Gamston | |
| G-BRDE | Thunder Ax7-77 balloon | C. C. Brash | |
| G-BRDF | PA-28-161 Warrior II | W. London Aero Services Ltd/White Waltham | |
| G-BRDG | PA-28-161 Warrior II | W. London Aero Services Ltd/White Waltham | |
| G-BRDJ | Luscombe 8A Silvaire | C. C. & J. M. Lovell | |
| G-BRDL | Bell 206B JetRanger | Clyde Helicopters Ltd | |
| G-BRDM | PA-28-161 Warrior II | W. London Aero Services Ltd/White Waltham | |
| G-BRDN | M.S.880B Rallye Club | C. R. Owen | |
| G-BRDO | Cessna 177B | Cardinal Group | |
| G-BRDP | Colt Jumbo SS balloon | Airship & Balloon Co Ltd | |
| G-BRDS | Colt Flying Coke Can SS balloon | Thunder & Colt Ltd | |
| G-BRDT | Cameron DP-70 airship | M. M. Cobbold | |
| G-BRDU | Cameron DG-14 airship | Cameron Balloons Ltd | |
| G-BRDV | Viking Wood Products Spitfire Prototype replica (K5054) | C. Du Cros | |
| G-BRDW | PA-24 Comanche 180 | I. P. Gibson/Switzerland | |
| G-BREA | Bensen B.8M | R. Firth | |
| G-BREB | Piper J-3C-65 Cub | C. Parr & I. Watts | |
| G-BREE | Whittaker MW.7 | R. H. Y. Farrer | |
| G-BREH | Cameron V-65 balloon | A. E. & L. C. Rogers | |
| G-BREK | Piper J-3C-65 Cub | C. Parr & I. Watts | |
| G-BREL | Cameron O-77 balloon | A. J. Moore & D. J. Green | |
| G-BREM | Air Command 532 Elite | Modern Air | |

| Notes | Reg. | Type | Owner or Operator |
|---|---|---|---|
| | G-BREP | PA-28RT-201 Arrow IV | P. G. McQuaid |
| | G-BRER | Aeronca 7AC Champion | A. J. O'Shea |
| | G-BREU | Montgomerie-Bensen B.8 | M. A. Hayward |
| | G-BREX | Cameron O-84 balloon | Ovolo Ltd |
| | G-BREY | Taylorcraft BC-12D | BREY Group |
| | G-BREZ | Cessna 172M | B. J. Tucker |
| | G-BRFA | PA-31-350 Navajo Chieftain | Sunseeker Leisure PLC (G-BREW) |
| | G-BRFB | Rutan LongEz | R. A. Gardiner |
| | G-BRFC | P.57 Sea Prince T.1 (WP321) | Rural Naval Air Service/Bourn |
| | G-BRFE | Cameron V-77 balloon | N. J. Appleton |
| | G-BRFF | Colt 90A balloon | Amber Valley Aviation |
| | G-BRFH | Colt 90A balloon | Polydron UK Ltd |
| | G-BRFI | Aeronca 7DC Champion | I. J. Boyd & D. J. McCooke |
| | G-BRFJ | Aeronca 11AC Chief | C. M. G. Ellis |
| | G-BRFK | Colt Flying Drinks Can SS balloon | Thunder & Colt Ltd |
| | G-BRFL | PA-38-112 Tomahawk | Technology & Marketing Ltd |
| | G-BRFM | PA-28-161 Warrior II | GCJ Moffatt & Co Ltd |
| | G-BRFN | PA-38-112 Tomahawk | Technology & Marketing Ltd |
| | G-BRFO | Cameron V-77 balloon | Hedge Hoppers Balloon Group |
| | G-BRFP | Schweizer 269C | Daedalus Aviation Ltd |
| | G-BRFR | Cameron N-105 balloon | Flying Pictures (Balloons) Ltd |
| | G-BRFS | Cameron N-90 balloon | Flying Pictures (Balloons) Ltd |
| | G-BRFU | Fouga CM.170 Magister (MT-11) | P. F. A. Hoar/Cranfield |
| | G-BRFW | Montgomerie-Bensen B.8 Two Seat | J. M. Montgomerie |
| | G-BRFX | Pazmany PL.4A | D. E. Hills |
| | G-BRGD | Cameron O-84 balloon | J. R. H. & M. A. Ashworth |
| | G-BRGE | Cameron N-90 balloon | Oakfield Farm Products Ltd |
| | G-BRGF | Luscombe 8E Silvaire | M. H. Wood |
| | G-BRGG | Luscombe 8A Silvaire | M. P. & V. H. Weatherby |
| | G-BRGI | PA-28 Cherokee 180 | Golf India Aviation Ltd |
| | G-BRGJ | PA-28-151 Warrior | D. D. Stone |
| | G-BRGN | BAe Jetstream 3102 | British Aerospace PLC (G-BLHC)/ Prestwick |
| | G-BRGO | Air Command 532 Elite | D. A. Wood |
| | G-BRGP | Colt Flying Stork SS balloon | Thunder & Colt Ltd |
| | G-BRGT | PA-32 Cherokee Six 260 | M. J. Smith & P. Cowley |
| | G-BRGW | GY-201 Minicab | R. G. White |
| | G-BRGX | Rotorway Executive | D. W. J. Lee |
| | G-BRHA | PA-32RT-300 Lance II | ACG Building Contractors |
| | G-BRHB | Boeing Stearman B.75N1 | D. Calabritto |
| | G-BRHC | Cameron V-77 balloon | Golf Centres Balloons Ltd |
| | G-BRHE | Piper J-3C-65 Cub | S. M. Kearney |
| | G-BRHG | Colt 90A balloon | Bath University Students Union |
| | G-BRHH | Cameron 106 Cow SS balloon | Cameron Ballons Ltd |
| | G-BRHI | Bell 206B JetRanger 3 | Highland Properties Ltd |
| | G-BRHJ | PA-34-200T Seneca II | Draycott Seneca Group |
| | G-BRHK | Colt GA-42 airship | Thunder & Colt Ltd |
| | G-BRHL | Montgomerie-Bensen B.8M | N. D. Marshall |
| | G-BRHM | Bensen B.8M | P. M. Crook |
| | G-BRHN | Robinson R-22B | Barhale Surveying Ltd |
| | G-BRHO | PA-34-200 Seneca | D. A. Lewis/Luton |
| | G-BRHP | Aeronca O-58B Grasshopper (31923) | J. G. Townsend |
| | G-BRHR | PA-38-112 Tomahawk | Hamilton Compass Aviation Ltd |
| | G-BRHS | PA-38-112 Tomahawk | Hamilton Compass Aviation Ltd |
| | G-BRHT | PA-38-112 Tomahawk | Hamilton Compass Aviation Ltd |
| | G-BRHU | Montgomerie-Bensen B.8MR | G. L. & S. R. Moon |
| | G-BRHW | D.H.82A Tiger Moth | P. J. & A. J. Borsberry |
| | G-BRHX | Luscombe 8E Silvaire | J. Lakin |
| | G-BRHY | Luscombe 8E Silvaire | D. Lofts & A. R. W. Taylor |
| | G-BRHZ | Stephens Akro Astro 235 | N. M. Bloom & ptnrs |
| | G-BRIA | Cessna 310L | R. C. Pugsley |
| | G-BRIB | Cameron N-77 balloon | D. Stitt |
| | G-BRID | Cessna U.206A | Emair Bridlington Ltd |
| | G-BRIE | Cameron N-77 balloon | Vokins Estates Ltd |
| | G-BRIF | Boeing 767-204ER | Britannia Airways Ltd/Luton |
| | G-BRIG | Boeing 767-204ER | Britannia Airways Ltd/Luton |
| | G-BRIH | Taylorcraft BC-12D | G. J. Taylor |
| | G-BRII | Zenair CH.600 Zodiac | A. C. Bowdrey |
| | G-BRIJ | Taylorcraft F-19 | K. E. Ballington |
| | G-BRIK | T.66 Nipper 3 | C. W. R. Piper |
| | G-BRIL | Piper J-5A Cub Cruiser | M. Stow |

| Reg. | Type | Owner or Operator | Notes |
|------|------|-------------------|-------|
| G-BRIM | Cameron O-160 balloon | Golf Centres Balloons Ltd | |
| G-BRIN | SOCATA TB.20 Trinidad | Fletcher Group Holidays Ltd | |
| G-BRIO | Turner Super T-40A | D. McIntyre | |
| G-BRIR | Cameron V-56 balloon | Century Factors Ltd | |
| G-BRIS | Steen Skybolt | Eriskay Atlantic Ltd | |
| G-BRIT | Cessna 421C | Coppersmith Ltd | |
| G-BRIV | SOCATA TB.9 Tampico | CB Group Ltd/Biggin Hill | |
| G-BRIW | Hughes 269C | Belmont Press Ltd | |
| G-BRIY | Taylorcraft DF-65 (42-58678) | J. A. Rollason/North Weald | |
| G-BRIZ | D.31 Turbulent | M. C. Hunt | |
| G-BRJA | Luscombe 8A Silvaire | C. W. Thirtle | |
| G-BRJB | Zenair CH.600 Zodiac | E. G. Brown | |
| G-BRJC | Cessna 120 | One Twenty Group | |
| G-BRJK | Luscombe 8A Silvaire | C. J. L. Peat | |
| G-BRJL | PA-15 Vagabond | D. D. Saint | |
| G-BRJM | Cameron A-210 balloon | R. S. Hunjan | |
| G-BRJN | Pitts S-1C Special | G-BRJN Group | |
| G-BRJR | PA-38-112 Tomahawk | Chester Aviation Ltd | |
| G-BRJT | Cessna 150H | Technology & Marketing Ltd | |
| G-BRJU | PA-28-151 Warrior | Newcastle-upon-Tyne Aero Club Ltd | |
| G-BRJV | PA-28-161 Cadet | Newcastle-upon-Tyne Aero Club Ltd | |
| G-BRJW | Bellanca 7GCBC Citabria | H. W. Weston/Staverton | |
| G-BRJX | Rand KR-2 | C. Willcocks | |
| G-BRJY | Rand KR-2 | A. J. Wilkinson & R. P. H. Hancock | |
| G-BRKA | Luscombe 8F Silvaire | C. H. J. Andrews | |
| G-BRKB | Cameron N-65 balloon | M. C. Bradley/Hong Kong | |
| G-BRKC | J/1 Autocrat | J. W. Conlon | |
| G-BRKD | Piaggio FWP.149D | Operation Ability Ltd | |
| G-BRKE | Hawker Sea Hurricane XIIA (BW853) | AJD Engineering Ltd | |
| G-BRKH | PA-28-236 Dakota | P. A. Wright & D. Rawlley | |
| G-BRKJ | Stoddard-Hamilton Glasair III | R. F. E. Simard | |
| G-BRKL | Cameron H-34 balloon | Cameron Balloons Ltd | |
| G-BRKN | Robinson R-22 Mariner | P. M. Webber/Greece | |
| G-BRKO | Oldfield Baby Great Lakes | C. Wren | |
| G-BRKP | Colt 31A balloon | Bavarian Balloon Co Ltd | |
| G-BRKR | Cessna 182R | A. R. D. Brooker | |
| G-BRKS | Air Command 532 Elite | G. Sandercock | |
| G-BRKT | PA-28-161 Warrior II | Leisure World (Holdings) Ltd | |
| G-BRKW | Cameron V-77 balloon | M. W. A. Shemilt | |
| G-BRKX | Air Command 532 Elite | K. Davis | |
| G-BRKY | Viking Dragonfly Mk II | G. D. Price | |
| G-BRKZ | Air Command 532 Elite | S. C. West | |
| G-BRLB | Air Command 532 Elite | D. Wilson | |
| G-BRLC | Thunder Ax7-77 balloon | Fuji Photo Film (UK) Ltd | |
| G-BRLD | Robinson R-22B | Future Music (Chelmsford) Ltd | |
| G-BRLE | PA-28-181 Archer II | Charles Clowes (Estates) Co Ltd | |
| G-BRLF | Campbell Cricket | D. Wood | |
| G-BRLG | PA-28RT-201T Turbo Arrow IV | Specialist Welding & Metallurgical Services Ltd | |
| G-BRLH | Air Command 532 Elite | Childs Garages (Sherborne) Ltd | |
| G-BRLI | Piper J-5A Cub Cruiser | A. E. Poulson | |
| G-BRLJ | Evans VP-2 | R. L. Jones | |
| G-BRLK | Air Command 532 Elite | G. L. Hunt | |
| G-BRLL | Cameron A-105 balloon | Adventure Flights Ltd | |
| G-BRLM | BAe 146-100 | British Aerospace PLC | |
| G-BRLO | PA-38-112 Tomahawk | Scotia Safari Ltd/Prestwick | |
| G-BRLP | PA-38-112 Tomahawk | Lightstrong Ltd | |
| G-BRLR | Cessna 150G | D. C. Maxwell | |
| G-BRLS | Thunder Ax7-77 balloon | E. C. Meek | |
| G-BRLT | Colt 77A balloon | D. Bareford | |
| G-BRLU | Cameron H-24 balloon | Airspace Outdoor Advertising Ltd | |
| G-BRLV | CCF Harvard IV (93542) | B. C. Abela | |
| G-BRLW | Cessna 150M | Visionkind Ltd | |
| G-BRLX | Cameron N-77 balloon | National Power | |
| G-BRLY | BAe ATP/Jetstream 61 | British Aerospace PLC | |
| G-BRMA | W.S.51 Dragonfly HR.5 (WG719) ★ | International Helicopter Museum/ Weston-s-Mare | |
| G-BRMB | B.192 Belvedere HC.1 (XG452) ★ | International Helicopter Museum/ Weston-s-Mare | |
| G-BRMC | Stampe et Renard SV-4B | E. K. Coventry | |
| G-BRMD | Cameron O-160 balloon | Ballooning Endeavours Ltd | |
| G-BRME | PA-28-181 Archer II | S. Edgar | |

| Notes | Reg. | Type | Owner or Operator |
|---|---|---|---|
| | G-BRMF | Bell 206B JetRanger 3 | Heliwork Services Ltd/Thruxton |
| | G-BRMG | V.S.384 Seafire XVII (SX336) | P. J. Wood |
| | G-BRMH | Bell 206B JetRanger 2 | RCR Aviation Ltd (G-BBUX) |
| | G-BRMI | Cameron V-65 balloon | M. Davies |
| | G-BRMJ | PA-38-112 Tomahawk | P. H. Rogers/Coventry |
| | G-BRML | PA-38-112 Tomahawk | P. H. Rogers/Coventry |
| | G-BRMM | Air Command 532 Elite | R. de Serville |
| | G-BRMN | Thunder Ax7-77 balloon | G. Restell & R. Higham |
| | G-BRMS | PA-28RT-201 Arrow IV | Fleetbridge Ltd |
| | G-BRMT | Cameron V-31 balloon | R. M. Trotter & K. L. Heron |
| | G-BRMU | Cameron V-77 balloon | K. J. & G. R. Ibbotson |
| | G-BRMV | Cameron O-77 balloon | P. D. Griffiths |
| | G-BRMW | Whittaker MW.7 | M. R. Grunwell |
| | G-BRMY | Short SD3-60 | Short Bros PLC/Belfast City |
| | G-BRNA | Short SD3-60 | Short Bros PLC/Belfast City |
| | G-BRNB | Short SD3-60 | Short Bros PLC/Belfast City |
| | G-BRNC | Cessna 150M | Mercia Aircraft Leasing Ltd |
| | G-BRND | Cessna 152 | Mercia Aircraft Leasing Ltd |
| | G-BRNE | Cessna 152 | Aerohire Ltd/Halfpenny Green |
| | G-BRNJ | PA-38-112 Tomahawk | S. Eddison |
| | G-BRNK | Cessna 152 | Sheffield Aero Club Ltd/Netherthorpe |
| | G-BRNL | Cessna 172P | B. W. Wells |
| | G-BRNM | Chichester-Miles Leopard | Chichester-Miles Consultants Ltd |
| | G-BRNN | Cessna 152 | Sheffield Aero Club Ltd/Netherthorpe |
| | G-BRNP | Rotorway Executive | C. A. Laycock |
| | G-BRNR | Schweizer 269C | C.S.E. Aviation Ltd/Kidlington |
| | G-BRNS | Avid Flyer | Ladel Ltd |
| | G-BRNT | Robin DR.400/180 | M. J. Cowham |
| | G-BRNU | Robin DR.400/180 | Pranconic Ltd |
| | G-BRNV | PA-28-181 Archer II | Valley Flying Co Ltd |
| | G-BRNW | Cameron V-77 balloon | N. Robertson & G. Smith |
| | G-BRNX | PA-22 Tri-Pacer 150 | R. S. Tomlinson & B. Yager |
| | G-BRNY | Thunder Ax6-56A balloon | P. A. Clent |
| | G-BRNZ | PA-32 Cherokee Six 300B | IML Aviation Ltd |
| | G-BROB | Cameron V-77 balloon | R. W. Richardson |
| | G-BROE | Cameron N-65 balloon | R. H. Sanderson |
| | G-BROF | Air Command 532 Elite | M. J. Hoskins |
| | G-BROG | Cameron V-65 balloon | R. Kunert |
| | G-BROH | Cameron O-90 balloon | A. & W. Derbyshire |
| | G-BROI | CFM Streak Shadow Srs SA | G. W. Rowbotham |
| | G-BROJ | Colt 31A balloon | Airship & Balloon Co Ltd |
| | G-BROL | Colt AS-80 Mk II airship | Wellfarrow Ltd |
| | G-BROM | ICA IS-282MA | Kent Motor Gliding & Soaring Centre |
| | G-BROO | Luscombe 8A Silvaire | Bedwell Hey Flying Group |
| | G-BROP | Van's RV-4 | K. E. Armstrong |
| | G-BROR | Piper J-3C-65 Cub | White Hart Flying Group |
| | G-BROS | Cameron O-84 balloon | Airship Shop Ltd |
| | G-BROV | Colt 105A balloon | Thunder & Colt Ltd |
| | G-BROW | Colt 90A balloon | Thunder & Colt Ltd |
| | G-BROX | Robinson R-22B | Freshname No 77 Ltd |
| | G-BROY | Cameron V-77 balloon | Zebedee Balloon Service |
| | G-BROZ | PA-18 Super Cub 150 | P. G. Kynsey |
| | G-BRPE | Cessna 120 | C. Briggs |
| | G-BRPF | Cessna 120 | D. Sharp |
| | G-BRPG | Cessna 120 | I. C. Lomax |
| | G-BRPH | Cessna 120 | T. W. Greaves |
| | G-BRPI | Pitts S-1C Special | J. C. Lister |
| | G-BRPJ | Cameron N-90 balloon | Paul Johnson Cars Ltd |
| | G-BRPK | PA-28 Cherokee 140 | Gütersloh Flying Club/Germany |
| | G-BRPL | PA-28 Cherokee 140 | Comed Aviation Ltd/Blackpool |
| | G-BRPM | T.66 Nipper 3 | T. C. Horner |
| | G-BRPN | Enstrom F-28C | Manchester Helicopter Centre/Barton |
| | G-BRPO | Enstrom 280C | R. Moffett |
| | G-BRPP | Brookland Hornet | D. E. Cox |
| | G-BRPR | Aeronca O-58B Grasshopper (43-1952) | N. Davis |
| | G-BRPS | Cessna 177B | C. R. Goforth |
| | G-BRPT | Rans S.10 Sakota | P. A. Aston |
| | G-BRPU | Beech 76 Duchess | Hamilton Compass Aviation Ltd |
| | G-BRPV | Cessna 152 | Coventry (Civil) Aviation Ltd |
| | G-BRPX | Taylorcraft BC-12D | M. J. Brett |
| | G-BRPY | PA-15 Vagabond | J. P. Esson |
| | G-BRPZ | Luscombe 8A Silvaire | J. D. Rooney/Goodwood |

| Reg. | Type | Owner or Operator | Notes |
|------|------|-------------------|-------|
| G-BRRA | V.S.361 Spitfire LF.IX | Historic Aircraft Collection Ltd | |
| G-BRRB | Luscombe 8E Silvaire | D. J. Willison | |
| G-BRRD | Scheibe SF.25B Falke | K. E. Ballington | |
| G-BRRE | Colt 77A balloon | P. Patel | |
| G-BRRF | Cameron O-77 balloon | Mid-Bucks Farmers Balloon Group | |
| G-BRRG | Glaser-Dirks DG.500M | A. W. White | |
| G-BRRJ | PA-28RT-201T Turbo Arrow IV | M. & E. Machinery Ltd | |
| G-BRRK | Cessna 182Q | Clacton Aviation | |
| G-BRRL | PA-18 Super Cub 95 | T. J. McRae | |
| G-BRRM | PA-28-161 Cadet | R. H. Sellier | |
| G-BRRN | PA-28-161 Warrior II | C. J. & L. M. Worsley | |
| G-BRRO | Cameron N-77 balloon | Newbury Building Soc | |
| G-BRRP | Pitts S-1S Special | J. E. Sweetman/Hong Kong | |
| G-BRRR | Cameron V-77 balloon | L. M. Heal & A. P. Wilcox | |
| G-BRRS | Pitts S-1C Special | R. C. Atkinson | |
| G-BRRT | C.A.S.A. 1-131E Jungmann | R. A. L. Hubbard/Syerston | |
| G-BRRU | Colt 90A balloon | Thunder & Colt Ltd | |
| G-BRRW | Cameron O-77 balloon | D. V. Fowler | |
| G-BRRX | Hughes 369HS | Valiant Press Ltd | |
| G-BRRY | Robinson R-22B | Bristow Helicopters Ltd/Redhill | |
| G-BRRZ | Robinson R-22B | Phoenix Group | |
| G-BRSA | Cameron N-56 balloon | C. Wilkinson | |
| G-BRSC | Rans S.10 Sakota | M. A. C. Stephenson | |
| G-BRSD | Cameron V-77 balloon | T. J. Porter & J. E. Kelly | |
| G-BRSE | PA-28-161 Warrior II | Air Service Training Ltd/Perth | |
| G-BRSF | V.S.361 Spitfire F.IX (RR232) | Sussex Spraying Services Ltd | |
| G-BRSG | PA-28-161 Cadet | Denham School of Flying Ltd | |
| G-BRSH | C.A.S.A. 1-131E Jungmann | M. G. Searley | |
| G-BRSI | PA-28-161 Cadet | Denham School of Flying Ltd | |
| G-BRSJ | PA-38-112 Tomahawk | Pool Aviation Ltd/Welshpool | |
| G-BRSK | Boeing Stearman N2S-3 (180) | Wymondham Engineering | |
| G-BRSL | Cameron N-56 balloon | S. Budd | |
| G-BRSN | Rand-Robinson KR-2 | K. W. Darby | |
| G-BRSO | CFM Streak Shadow Srs SA | D. J. Smith | |
| G-BRSP | Air Command 532 Elite | D. R. G. Griffith | |
| G-BRSW | Luscombe 8A Silvaire | J. Regan | |
| G-BRSX | PA-15 Vagabond | C. Milne-Fowler | |
| G-BRSY | Hatz CB-1 | G. A. Barrett & Son | |
| G-BRSZ | MEM RSZ-05/1 balloon | Zebedee Balloon Service | |
| G-BRTA | PA-38-112 Tomahawk | R. A. Wakefield | |
| G-BRTB | Bell 206B JetRanger 2 | Harris Technology Ltd | |
| G-BRTC | Cessna 150G | Thorpe Air Ltd/Goodwood | |
| G-BRTD | Cessna 152 II | Thorpe Air Ltd/Goodwood | |
| G-BRTH | Cameron A-180 balloon | The Ballooning Business Ltd | |
| G-BRTJ | Cessna 150F | Cubitt Aviation/Foulsham | |
| G-BRTK | Boeing Stearman E.75 (217786) | J. K. & S. L. Avis | |
| G-BRTL | Hughes 369E | P. C. Shann Management & Research Ltd | |
| G-BRTM | PA-28-161 Warrior II | Air Service Training Ltd/Perth | |
| G-BRTN | Beech 95-B58 Baron | Colneway Ltd | |
| G-BRTO | Cessna 152 | Galaxy Enterprises Ltd | |
| G-BRTP | Cessna 152 | Anglia Aviation Ltd | |
| G-BRTR | Colt GA-42 airship | Thunder & Colt Ltd | |
| G-BRTS | Bell 206B JetRanger 3 | Norwich Aviation Ltd | |
| G-BRTT | Schweizer 269C | Fairthorpe Ltd/Denham | |
| G-BRTV | Cameron O-77 balloon | C. Vening | |
| G-BRTW | Glaser-Dirks DG.400 | I. J. Carruthers | |
| G-BRTX | PA-28-151 Warrior | T. Gracey | |
| G-BRTZ | Slingsby T.31 Motor Cadet III | M. N. Martin | |
| G-BRUA | Cessna 152 | C. M. Vlieland-Boddy/Compton Abbas | |
| G-BRUB | PA-28-161 Warrior II | Flytrek Ltd/Bournemouth | |
| G-BRUD | PA-28-181 Archer II | Wilkins & Wilkins Special Auctions Ltd | |
| G-BRUE | Cameron V-77 balloon | B. J. Newman & P. L. Harrison | |
| G-BRUG | Luscombe 8E Silvaire | P. A. Cain & N. W. Barratt | |
| G-BRUH | Colt 105A balloon | D. C. Chipping | |
| G-BRUI | PA-44-180 Seminole | Bath Stone Co Ltd | |
| G-BRUJ | Boeing Stearman A.75N1 | Early Birds Ltd/Staverton | |
| G-BRUL | Thunder Ax8-105 balloon | H. C. J. Williams | |
| G-BRUM | Cessna A.152 | Aerohire Ltd/Halfpenny Green | |
| G-BRUN | Cessna 120 | O. C. Brun (G-BRDH) | |
| G-BRUO | Taylor JT.1 Monoplane | G. Verity | |
| G-BRUR | Grob G.115 | Risestat Ltd | |
| G-BRUS | Cessna 140 | M. J. Fogarty | |
| G-BRUT | Thunder Ax8-90 balloon | Moet & Chandon (London) Ltd | |

| Notes | Reg. | Type | Owner or Operator |
|---|---|---|---|
| | G-BRUU | EAA Biplane Model P.1 | M. J. Fogarty |
| | G-BRUV | Cameron V-77 balloon | T. W. & R. F. Benbrook |
| | G-BRUX | PA-44-180 Seminole | Hambrair Ltd/Tollerton |
| | G-BRUZ | Raven Europe FS-57A balloon | R. H. Etherington |
| | G-BRVA | Nord 3202B-1 | Cavok Ltd (G-BIZL) |
| | G-BRVB | Stolp SA.300 Starduster Too | R. W. Davies |
| | G-BRVC | Cameron N-180 balloon | The Apollo Balloon Co Ltd |
| | G-BRVE | Beech D.17S | Intrepid Aviation Co/North Weald |
| | G-BRVF | Colt 77A balloon | Airborne Adventures Ltd |
| | G-BRVG | NA SNJ-7 Texan (27) | Intrepid Aviation Co/North Weald |
| | G-BRVH | Smyth Model S Sidewinder | I. S. Bellamy |
| | G-BRVI | Robinson R-22B | Burnell Helicopters Ltd |
| | G-BRVJ | Slingsby T.31 Motor Cadet III | B. Outhwaite |
| | G-BRVK | Cameron A-210 Balloon | The Balloon Club Ltd |
| | G-BRVL | Pitts S-1C Special | I. Duncan |
| | G-BRVN | Thunder Ax7-77 balloon | J. T. Hughes Ltd |
| | G-BRVO | AS.350B Ecureuil | Radstrong Ltd/Booker |
| | G-BRVR | Barnett J4B-2 | Ilkeston Contractors |
| | G-BRVS | Barnett J4B-2 | Ilkeston Contractors |
| | G-BRVT | Pitts S-2B Special | C. J. & M. D. Green |
| | G-BRVU | Colt 77A balloon | H. C. J. Williams |
| | G-BRVV | Colt 56B balloon | S. J. Hollingsworth |
| | G-BRVX | Cameron A-210 balloon | Bath Hot Air Balloon Club Ltd |
| | G-BRVY | Thunder Ax8-90 balloon | G. E. Morris |
| | G-BRVZ | Jodel D.117 | J.G. Patton |
| | G-BRWA | Aeronca 7AC Champion | D. D. Smith & J. R. Edwards |
| | G-BRWB | NA T-6G Texan (51-14526) | Aircraft Restorations Ltd/Duxford |
| | G-BRWC | Cessna 152 | T. Hayselden (Doncaster) Ltd |
| | G-BRWD | Robinson R22B | Odanrose Ltd |
| | G-BRWF | Thunder Ax7-77 | D. J. Greaves |
| | G-BRWH | Cameron N-77 | D. J. Usher |
| | G-BRWI | Short SD3-60 Variant 300 | Short Bros PLC/Belfast City |
| | G-BRWJ | Short SD3-60 Variant 300 | Short Bros PLC/Belfast City |
| | G-BRWK | Short SD3-60 Variant 300 | Short Bros PLC/Belfast City |
| | G-BRWL | Short SD3-60 Variant 300 | Short Bros PLC/Belfast City |
| | G-BRWM | Short SD3-60 Variant 300 | Short Bros PLC/Belfast City |
| | G-BRWO | PA-28 Cherokee 140 | ML Associates |
| | G-BRWP | CFM Streak Shadow Srs SA | A. D. Stewart |
| | G-BRWR | Aeronca 11AC Chief | P. G. Peal |
| | G-BRWT | Scheibe SF.25C Falke | Brompton Promotions Ltd |
| | G-BRWU | Luton LA-4A Minor | R. B. Webber & P. K. Pike |
| | G-BRWV | Brügger MB.2 Colibri | S. J. McCollum |
| | G-BRWX | Cessna 172P | D. A. Abels |
| | G-BRWY | Cameron H-34 balloon | Cameron Balloons Ltd |
| | G-BRWZ | Cameron 90 Macaw SS balloon | Forbes Europe Inc/France |
| | G-BRXA | Cameron O-120 balloon | A. F. Green |
| | G-BRXB | Thunder Ax7-77 balloon | H. Peel |
| | G-BRXC | PA-28-161 Warrior II | Air Service Training Ltd/Perth |
| | G-BRXD | PA-28-181 Archer II | Gosky Aviation Ltd |
| | G-BRXE | Taylorcraft BC-12D | V. H. Spencer |
| | G-BRXF | Aeronca 11AC Chief | G. G. Pugh/Stapleford |
| | G-BRXG | Aeronca 7AC Champion | X-Ray Golf Flying Group |
| | G-BRXH | Cessna 120 | J. N. Pittock & A. P. Fox |
| | G-BRXK | Soko P-2 Kraguj | Cavok Ltd |
| | G-BRXL | Aeronca 11AC Chief (42-78044) | R. L. Jones |
| | G-BRXN | Montgomerie-Bensen B.8MR | J. C. Aitken |
| | G-BRXO | PA-34-200T Seneca II | Aviation Services Ltd |
| | G-BRXP | SNCAN Stampe SV-4C (modified) | P. G. Kavanagh & D. T. Kaberry |
| | G-BRXS | Howard Special T Minus | H. C. Cox |
| | G-BRXV | Robinson R-22B | E. Wootton |
| | G-BRXW | PA-24 Comanche 260 | The Oak Group |
| | G-BRXX | Colt 180A balloon | J. P. Clifford |
| | G-BRXY | Pietenpol Air Camper | A. E. Morris |
| | G-BRYA | D.H.C.7-110 Dash Seven | Brymon European Airways Ltd *City of Paris* |
| | G-BRYB | D.H.C.7-110 Dash Seven | Brymon European Airways Ltd *City of Plymouth* |
| | G-BRYC | D.H.C.7-110 Dash Seven | Brymon European Airways Ltd *City of London* |
| | G-BRYD | D.H.C.7-110 Dash Seven | Brymon European Airways Ltd *City of Exeter* |
| | G-BRYE | D.H.C.7-102 Dash Seven | Brymon European Airways Ltd *City of Aberdeen* |

| Reg. | Type | Owner or Operator | Notes |
|---|---|---|---|
| G-BRYG | D.H.C.8-102A Dash Eight | Brymon European Airways Ltd *City of Bristol* | |
| G-BRYH | D.H.C.8-102A Dash Eight | Brymon European Airways Ltd *City of Edinburgh* | |
| G-BRYI | D.H.C.8-311 Dash Eight | Brymon European Airways Ltd *City of Glasgow* | |
| G-BRYJ | D.H.C.8-311 Dash Eight | Brymon European Airways Ltd | |
| G-BRYK | — | Brymon European Airways Ltd | |
| G-BRYM | — | Brymon European Airways Ltd | |
| G-BRYN | SOCATA TB.20 Trinidad | Jones & Bradbourn (Guernsey) Ltd | |
| G-BRYO | — | Brymon European Airways Ltd | |
| G-BRYP | — | Brymon European Airways Ltd | |
| G-BRZA | Cameron O-77 balloon | L. & R. J. Mold | |
| G-BRZB | Cameron A-105 balloon | Headland Services Ltd | |
| G-BRZC | Cameron N-90 balloon | Flying Pictures (Balloons) Ltd | |
| G-BRZD | Hapi Cygnet SF-2A | L. G. Millen | |
| G-BRZE | Thunder Ax7-77 balloon | G. V. Beckwith | |
| G-BRZG | Enstrom F-28A | Chart Planes Inland Ltd | |
| G-BRZI | Cameron N-180 balloon | Pegasus Balloon Co Ltd | |
| G-BRZK | Stinson 108-2 | F. H. Wheeler & G. P. A. Elborough | |
| G-BRZL | Pitts S-1D Special | R. G. Tomlinson | |
| G-BRZO | Jodel D.18 | J. D. Anson | |
| G-BRZP | PA-28-161 Warrior II | Air Service Training Ltd/Perth | |
| G-BRZR | PA-22 Tri-Pacer 150 | W. Treacy | |
| G-BRZS | Cessna 172P | YP Flying Group/Blackpool | |
| G-BRZT | Cameron V-77 balloon | B. Drawbridge | |
| G-BRZU | Colt Flying Cheese SS balloon | Willow Best Ltd | |
| G-BRZV | Colt Flying Apple SS balloon | Thrust Drive Ltd | |
| G-BRZW | Rans S.10 Sakota | D. L. Davies | |
| G-BRZX | Pitts S-1S Special | G-BRZX Group | |
| G-BRZZ | CFM Streak Shadow | P. R. Oakes | |
| G-BSAB | PA-46-350P Malibu Mirage | D. O. Hooper | |
| G-BSAI | Stoddard-Hamilton Glasair III | K. J. & P. J. Whitehead | |
| G-BSAJ | C.A.S.A. 1-131E Jungmann | P. G. Kynsey/Redhill | |
| G-BSAK | Colt 21A balloon | Airship & Balloon Co Ltd | |
| G-BSAO | Steen Skybolt | S. F. Elvins | |
| G-BSAR | Air Command 532 Elite | S. A. Ryder | |
| G-BSAS | Cameron V-65 balloon | M. P. G. Papworth | |
| G-BSAT | PA-28-181 Archer II | A1 Aircraft Ltd/Biggin Hill | |
| G-BSAU | Enstrom F-28F | Southern Air Ltd/Shoreham | |
| G-BSAV | Thunder Ax7-77 balloon | E. A. Evans & ptnrs | |
| G-BSAW | PA-28-161 Warrior II | Carill Aviation Ltd/Southampton | |
| G-BSAX | Piper J-3C-65 Cub | Crop Aviation (UK) Ltd | |
| G-BSAY | Cessna 172M | D. B. Zabel | |
| G-BSAZ | Denney Aerocraft Kitfox | P. E. Hinkley | |
| G-BSBA | PA-28-161 Warrior II | P. A. Lancaster/White Waltham | |
| G-BSBB | CCF Harvard IV | Pulsegrove Ltd/Thruxton | |
| G-BSBD | NA T-6G Texan | Pulsegrove Ltd/Thruxton | |
| G-BSBE | CCF Harvard IV | Pulsegrove Ltd/Thruxton | |
| G-BSBF | CCF Harvard IV | Pulsegrove Ltd/Thruxton | |
| G-BSBG | CCF Harvard IV | Pulsegrove Ltd/Thruxton | |
| G-BSBH | Short SD3-30★ | Ulster Aviation Soc Museum *(stored)* | |
| G-BSBI | Cameron O-77 balloon | Calibre Motor Co Ltd | |
| G-BSBK | Colt 105A balloon | Zebra Balloons | |
| G-BSBM | Cameron N-77 balloon | Nuclear Electric | |
| G-BSBN | Thunder Ax7-77 balloon | B. Pawson | |
| G-BSBP | Jodel D.18 | R. T. Pratt | |
| G-BSBR | Cameron V-77 balloon | B. Bromiley | |
| G-BSBT | Piper J-3C-65 Cub | M. B. & L. J. Proudfoot | |
| G-BSBU | Firefly 8B | A. R. Peart | |
| G-BSBV | Rans S.10 Sakota | Sportair UK Ltd | |
| G-BSBW | Bell 206B JetRanger 3 | Leeds Central Helicopters | |
| G-BSBX | Montgomerie-Bensen B.8MR | B. Ibbott | |
| G-BSBY | Cessna 150L | M. Entwistle | |
| G-BSBZ | Cessna 150M | M. Entwistle | |
| G-BSCA | Cameron N-90 balloon | P. J. Marshall & M. A. Clarke | |
| G-BSCB | Air Command 532 Elite | P. H. Smith | |
| G-BSCC | Colt 105A balloon | A. F. Selby | |
| G-BSCD | Hughes 269C | McIntyre Aviation Ltd | |
| G-BSCE | Robinson R-22B | S. B. Evans & G. F. Burridge | |
| G-BSCF | Thunder Ax7-77 balloon | V. P. Gardiner | |
| G-BSCG | Denney Aerocraft Kitfox | A. C. & T. G. Pinkstone | |

| Notes | Reg. | Type | Owner or Operator |
|-------|------|------|-------------------|
| | G-BSCH | Denney Aircraft Kitfox | Baldoon Leisure Flying Co Ltd |
| | G-BSCI | Colt 77A balloon | F. W. Farnsworth Ltd |
| | G-BSCK | Cameron H-24 balloon | J. D. Shapland |
| | G-BSCL | Robinson R-22B | Ketton Holdings Ltd |
| | G-BSCM | Denney Aircraft Kitfox | R. Wheeler |
| | G-BSCN | SOCATA TB.20 Trinidad | T. & G. Engineering Co Ltd & P. W. Huntley |
| | G-BSCO | Thunder Ax7-77 balloon | F. J. Whalley |
| | G-BSCP | Cessna 152 | Doncaster Aero Club Ltd |
| | G-BSCR | Cessna 172M | Halsmith (Aircraft Sales) Ltd |
| | G-BSCS | PA-28-181 Archer II | Wing Task Ltd |
| | G-BSCV | PA-28-161 Warrior II | Southwood Flying Group/Southend |
| | G-BSCW | Taylorcraft BC-65 | J. W. Heale |
| | G-BSCX | Thunder Ax8-105 balloon | Balloon Flights Club Ltd |
| | G-BSCY | PA-28-151 Warrior | S. G. P. Fowler |
| | G-BSCZ | Cessna 152 | London Flight Centre (Stansted) Ltd |
| | G-BSDA | Taylorcraft BC-12D | J. F. Morris |
| | G-BSDB | Pitts S-1C Special | M. K. Whitaker |
| | G-BSDC | — | |
| | G-BSDD | Denney Aircraft Kitfox | J. Windmill |
| | G-BSDF | Cameron N-105 balloon | G. V. Beckwith |
| | G-BSDG | Robin DR.400/180 | B. Hodge |
| | G-BSDH | Robin DR.400/180 | R. L. Brucciani |
| | G-BSDI | Corben Junior Ace Model E | J. Pearson/Eaglescott |
| | G-BSDJ | Piper J-4E Cub Coupé | J. Pearson/Eaglescott |
| | G-BSDK | Piper J-5A Cub Cruiser | B. F. T. Kitt & B. P. Young |
| | G-BSDL | SOCATA TB.10 Tobago | Delta Lima Group |
| | G-BSDN | PA-34-200T Seneca II | Belso Aviation Ltd |
| | G-BSDO | Cessna 152 | Bath Stone Co Ltd |
| | G-BSDP | Cessna 152 | Lincoln Aero Club Ltd/Sturgate |
| | G-BSDS | Boeing Stearman E.75 (118) | E. Hopper |
| | G-BSDU | Bell 206B JetRanger 3 | RJS Aviation Ltd |
| | G-BSDV | Colt 31A balloon | Airship & Balloon Co Ltd |
| | G-BSDW | Cessna 182P | Kerygma Trust |
| | G-BSDX | Cameron V-77 balloon | D. K. Fish |
| | G-BSDY | Beech 58 Baron | Astra Aviation Ltd |
| | G-BSEA | Thunder Ax7-77 balloon | R. Titterton |
| | G-BSED | PA-22 Tri-Pacer 160 (modified) | Pacer Group |
| | G-BSEE | Rans S.9 | P. M. Semler |
| | G-BSEF | PA-28 Cherokee 180 | Prestwick Pilots Group |
| | G-BSEG | Ken Brock KB-2 | H. A. Bancroft-Wilson |
| | G-BSEH | Cameron V-77 balloon | G. V. Beckwith |
| | G-BSEI | Cameron N-90 balloon | Flying Pictures (Balloons) Ltd |
| | G-BSEJ | Cessna 150M | Hollyclass Ltd |
| | G-BSEK | Robinson R-22 | Skyline Helicopters Ltd |
| | G-BSEL | Slingsby T.61G Super Falke | RAFGSA/Hullavington |
| | G-BSEM | Cameron 90 Four-Pack SS balloon | Flying Pictures (Balloons) Ltd |
| | G-BSEN | Colt 31A balloon | Thunder & Colt Ltd |
| | G-BSEP | Cessna 172 | B. Myers & C. H. Moore/Doncaster |
| | G-BSER | PA-28 Cherokee 160 | Yorkair Ltd/Leeds |
| | G-BSES | Denney Aircraft Kitfox | M. Albert-Brecht & J. J. M. Donnelly |
| | G-BSET | B.206 Srs 1 Basset | Beagle Basset Ltd/Shoreham |
| | G-BSEU | PA-28-181 Archer II | Euro Aviation 91 Ltd |
| | G-BSEV | Cameron O-77 balloon | UK Transplant Co-ordinators Assoc |
| | G-BSEW | Sikorsky S-76A | Bond Helicopters Ltd |
| | G-BSEX | Cameron A-180 balloon | Heart of England Balloons |
| | G-BSEY | Beech A36 Bonanza | K. Phillips Ltd |
| | G-BSEZ | Air Command 532 Elite | D. S. Robinson |
| | G-BSFA | Aero Designs Pulsar | S. A. Gill |
| | G-BSFB | C.A.S.A. 1.131E Jungmann 2000 | J. A. Sykes |
| | G-BSFD | Piper J-3C-65 Cub | E. C. English |
| | G-BSFE | PA-38-112 Tomahawk II | D. J. Campbell |
| | G-BSFF | Robin DR.400/180R | Lasham Gliding Soc Ltd |
| | G-BSFJ | Thunder Ax8-105 balloon | Airborne Adventures Ltd |
| | G-BSFK | PA-28-161 Warrior II | Air Service Training Ltd/Perth |
| | G-BSFM | Cameron 82 Cheese SS balloon | Gone With The Wind Ltd |
| | G-BSFN | SE.313B Alouette II | M & P Food Products Ltd |
| | G-BSFO | Cameron 60 House SS balloon | Clipsal UK Ltd |
| | G-BSFP | Cessna 152 | J. R. Nicholls |
| | G-BSFR | Cessna 152 | Galair Ltd |
| | G-BSFS | SE.313B Alouette II | M & P Food Products Ltd |
| | G-BSFT | PA-31 Turbo Navajo | SFT Aviation Ltd (G-AXYC)/Bournemouth |
| | G-BSFU | SE.313B Alouette II | M & P Food Products Ltd |

| Reg. | Type | Owner or Operator | Notes |
|------|------|-------------------|-------|
| G-BSFV | Woods Woody Pusher | C. W. N. Huke | |
| G-BSFW | PA-15 Vagabond | J. R. Kimberley | |
| G-BSFX | Denney Aerocraft Kitfox | D. A. McFadyean | |
| G-BSFY | Denney Aerocraft Kitfox | J. R. Howard | |
| G-BSGB | Gaertner Ax4 Skyranger balloon | B. Gaertner | |
| G-BSGC | PA-18 Super Cub 95 | G. Churchill | |
| G-BSGD | PA-28 Cherokee 180 | R. J. Cleverley | |
| G-BSGF | Robinson R-22B | Garingdell Aviation Ltd | |
| G-BSGG | Denney Aerocraft Kitfox | C. G. Richardson | |
| G-BSGH | Airtour AH-56B balloon | Airtour Balloon Co Ltd | |
| G-BSGJ | Monnet Sonerai 2 | A. N. Burrows | |
| G-BSGK | PA-34-200T Seneca II | J. A. Burrett & P. A. Greenhalgh | |
| G-BSGL | PA-28-161 Warrior II | Keywest Air Charter Ltd/Liverpool | |
| G-BSGM | Cameron V-77 balloon | 5th Regiment Royal Artillery | |
| G-BSGN | PA-28-151 Warrior | J. R. Whetlor & M. Gipps/Denham | |
| G-BSGP | Cameron N-65 balloon | Haywards Heath Building Soc | |
| G-BSGR | Boeing Stearman E.75 | A. G. Dunkerley | |
| G-BSGS | Rans S.10 Sakota | R. Handley | |
| G-BSGT | Cessna T.210N | B. J. Sharpe/Booker | |
| G-BSGV | Rotorway Executive | D. T. Price | |
| G-BSGY | Thunder Ax7-77 balloon | Thunder & Colt Ltd | |
| G-BSHA | PA-34-200T Seneca II | Warrior Aircraft Sales & Leasing Ltd | |
| G-BSHB | Colt 69A balloon | Airship & Balloon Co Ltd | |
| G-BSHC | Colt 69A balloon | Airship & Balloon Co Ltd | |
| G-BSHD | Colt 69A balloon | Airship & Balloon Co Ltd | |
| G-BSHE | Cessna 152 | J. A. Pothecary/Shoreham | |
| G-BSHH | Luscombe 8E Silvaire | Golf Centres Balloons Ltd | |
| G-BSHI | Luscombe 8F Silvaire | W. H. J. Knowles | |
| G-BSHJ | Luscombe 8E Silvaire | C. R. M. Hart & S. J. Turner | |
| G-BSHK | Denney Aerocraft Kitfox | A. E. Cree & G. J. Cuzzocrea | |
| G-BSHM | Slingsby T.31 Motor Cadet III | R. R. Hadley | |
| G-BSHN | Cessna 152 | C. Walsh | |
| G-BSHO | Cameron V-77 balloon | T. P. Barlass & D. J. Duckworth | |
| G-BSHP | PA-28-161 Warrior II | Air Service Training Ltd/Perth | |
| G-BSHR | Cessna F.172N | H. Rothwell (G-BFGE)/Blackpool | |
| G-BSHS | Colt 105A balloon | Prescott Hot Air Balloon Ltd | |
| G-BSHT | Cameron V-77 balloon | ECM Construction Ltd | |
| G-BSHV | PA-18 Super Cub 135 | Fen Tigers Flying Group | |
| G-BSHW | Hawker Tempest II | D. N. H. Martin | |
| G-BSHX | Enstrom F-28A | Manchester Helicopter Centre/Barton | |
| G-BSHY | EAA Acro Sport 1 | A. W. Hughes & R. J. Hodder | |
| G-BSHZ | Enstrom F-28F | Heliway Aviation | |
| G-BSIB | PA-28-161 Warrior II | Bobbington Air Training School Ltd | |
| G-BSIC | Cameron V-77 balloon | P. D. Worthy | |
| G-BSIE | Enstrom 280FX | Richard Mullock Homes Ltd | |
| G-BSIF | Denney Aerocraft Kitfox | R. M. Kimbell & M. H. Wylde | |
| G-BSIG | Colt 21A balloon | Thunder & Colt Ltd | |
| G-BSIH | Rutan LongEz | W. S. Allen | |
| G-BSII | PA-34-200T Seneca II | N. H. N. Gardner | |
| G-BSIJ | Cameron V-77 balloon | A. S. Jones | |
| G-BSIK | Denney Aerocraft Kitfox | I. A. Davies & B. Barr | |
| G-BSIL | Colt 120A balloon | A. Bolger | |
| G-BSIM | PA-28-181 Archer II | E. Midlands Aircraft Hire Ltd | |
| G-BSIN | Robinson R-22B | Solent Projects Ltd | |
| G-BSIO | Cameron 80 Shed SS balloon | Furness Building Soc | |
| G-BSIP | Cameron V-77 balloon | R. S. Ham | |
| G-BSIR | Cessna 340 | Airmaster Aviation Ltd/Cardiff | |
| G-BSIT | Robinson R-22B | P. R. Earp | |
| G-BSIU | Colt 90A balloon | Thunder & Colt Ltd | |
| G-BSIW | BAe Jetstream 3100 | Manx Airlines (Europe) Ltd/Cardiff | |
| G-BSIY | Schleicher ASK.14 | H. F. Lamprey | |
| G-BSIZ | PA-28-181 Archer II | Firmdale Ltd | |
| G-BSJA | Cameron N-77 balloon | N. Sanders (G-SPAR) | |
| G-BSJB | Bensen B.8 | J. W. Limbrick | |
| G-BSJC | Bell 206B JetRanger 3 | JETC Helicopters | |
| G-BSJU | Cessna 150M | Fox Aviation Ltd/E. Midlands | |
| G-BSJV | Cessna 172N | Local Basic Ltd | |
| G-BSJW | Everett Srs 2 gyroplane | A. R. Willis | |
| G-BSJX | PA-28-161 Warrior II | Border Air Training Ltd/Ronaldsway | |
| G-BSJY | Murphy Renegade II | J. Hatswell | |
| G-BSJZ | Cessna 150J | M. Tye | |
| G-BSKA | Cessna 150M | K. J. Farrance | |
| G-BSKB | — | — | |

| Notes | Reg. | Type | Owner or Operator |
|---|---|---|---|
| | G-BSKC | PA-38-112 Tomahawk | Bath Stone Co Ltd |
| | G-BSKD | Cameron V-77 balloon | P. Thomas |
| | G-BSKF | Schweizer 269C | J. W. Sandle |
| | G-BSKG | Maule MXT-7-180 | Beeches Auto Services |
| | G-BSKH | Cessna 421C | Bristol & Mendip Estates Ltd |
| | G-BSKI | Thunder Ax8-90 balloon | G-BSKI Balloon Group |
| | G-BSKJ | Mooney M.20J | M. C. Wroe |
| | G-BSKK | PA-38-112 Tomahawk | Falcon Flying Services/Biggin Hill |
| | G-BSKL | PA-38-112 Tomahawk | Falcon Flying Services/Biggin Hill |
| | G-BSKN | Grob G.109B | C. S. Faber |
| | G-BSKO | Maule MXT-7-180 | G. B. Esslemont |
| | G-BSKP | V.S.379 Spitfire F.XIV | Historic Aircraft Collection Ltd |
| | G-BSKR | Rand Robinson KR-2 | T. D. Saveker |
| | G-BSKS | Nieuport 28C-1 | Historic Aircraft Collection Ltd |
| | G-BSKT | Maule MXT-7-180 | D. D. Smith |
| | G-BSKU | Cameron O-84 balloon | Alfred Bagnall & Sons (West) Ltd |
| | G-BSKV | PA-28-181 Archer II | BAe Flying College Ltd/Prestwick |
| | G-BSKW | PA-28-181 Archer II | BAe Flying College Ltd/Prestwick |
| | G-BSKX | PA-28-181 Archer II | BAe Flying College Ltd/Prestwick |
| | G-BSLA | Robin DR.400/180 | A. B. McCoig/Biggin Hill |
| | G-BSLC | Robinson R-22B | Modern Air/Fowlmere |
| | G-BSLD | PA-28RT-201 Arrow IV | Actionwings Ltd |
| | G-BSLE | PA-28-161 Warrior II | Air Service Training Ltd/Perth |
| | G-BSLF | Robinson R-22B | Arian Helicopters Ltd |
| | G-BSLG | Cameron A-180 balloon | West Country Balloons |
| | G-BSLH | C.A.S.A. 1-131E Jungmann 2000 | P. Warden |
| | G-BSLI | Cameron V-77 balloon | J. D. C. & F. E. Bevan |
| | G-BSLJ | Denney Aerocraft Kitfox | A. F. Reid |
| | G-BSLK | PA-28-161 Warrior II | R. A. Rose |
| | G-BSLM | PA-28 Cherokee 160 | E. Sussex Aviation/Shoreham |
| | G-BSLN | Thunder Ax10-180 balloon | Albatross Aviation Ltd |
| | G-BSLO | Cameron A-180 balloon | Adventure Balloon Co Ltd |
| | G-BSLT | PA-28-161 Warrior II | Warrior Aircraft Sales & Leasing Ltd |
| | G-BSLU | PA-28 Cherokee 140 | Warrior Aircraft Sales & Leasing Ltd |
| | G-BSLV | Enstrom 280FX | Kendrick Construction Ltd |
| | G-BSLW | Bellanca 7ECA Citabria | A. A. & J. A. Killerby/Shoreham |
| | G-BSLX | WAR Focke-Wulf Fw.190 (4+) | E. Sussex Aviation/Shoreham |
| | G-BSLY | Colt AS-80 GD airship | Huntair Ltd |
| | G-BSMA | Colt Flying Open Book SS balloon | Jentime Ltd |
| | G-BSMB | Cessna U.206E | Army Parachute Association/Netheravon |
| | G-BSMD | Nord 1101 Noralpha | Rare Aeroplane Soc |
| | G-BSME | Bo 208C Junior | D. J. Hampson |
| | G-BSMF | Avro 652A Anson C.19 (TX183) | G. M. K. Fraser |
| | G-BSMG | Montgomerie-Bensen B.8M | A. C. Timperley |
| | G-BSMH | Colt 240A balloon | Formtrack Ltd |
| | G-BSMJ | — | — |
| | G-BSMK | Cameron O-84 balloon | J. C. Reavley |
| | G-BSML | Schweizer 269C | Nunkeeling Ltd |
| | G-BSMM | Colt 31A balloon | D. V. Fowler |
| | G-BSMN | CFM Streak Shadow | K. Daniels |
| | G-BSMO | Denney Aerocraft Kitfox | G-BSMO Group |
| | G-BSMP | PA-34-220T Seneca III | Gabriel Enterprises Ltd |
| | G-BSMS | Cameron V-77 balloon | C. D. Howes |
| | G-BSMT | Rans S.10 Sakota | N. Woodworth |
| | G-BSMU | Rans S.6 | W. D. Walker (G-MWJE) |
| | G-BSMV | PA-17 Vagabond (modified) | A. Cheriton |
| | G-BSMX | Bensen B.8MR | J. S. E. McGregor |
| | G-BSMZ | PA-28-161 Warrior II | Air Service Training Ltd/Perth |
| | G-BSND | Air Command 532 Elite | B. J. Castle |
| | G-BSNE | Luscombe 8A Silvaire | Aerolite Luscombe Group |
| | G-BSNF | Piper J-3C-65 Cub | D. A. Hammant |
| | G-BSNG | Cessna 172N | A. J. & P. C. Macdonald |
| | G-BSNI | Bensen B.8V | B. D. Gibbs |
| | G-BSNJ | Cameron N-90 balloon | D. P. H. Smith |
| | G-BSNL | Bensen B.8MR | A. C. Breane |
| | G-BSNN | Rans S.10 Sakota | S. Adams |
| | G-BSNO | Denney Aerocraft Kitfox | A. G. V. McClintock |
| | G-BSNP | PA-28-201T Turbo Arrow III | V. Dowd/Stapleford |
| | G-BSNR | BAe 146-300A | Trident Aviation Leasing Services Ltd |
| | G-BSNS | BAe 146-300A | Trident Aviation Leasing Services Ltd |
| | G-BSNT | Luscombe 8A Silvaire | B. J. Robe |
| | G-BSNU | Colt 105A balloon | Sun Life Assurance Soc PLC |
| | G-BSNV | Boeing 737-4Q8 | British Airways |

| Reg. | Type | Owner or Operator | Notes |
|---|---|---|---|
| G-BSNW | Boeing 737-4Q8 | British Airways | |
| G-BSNX | PA-28-181 Archer II | Lotus Air | |
| G-BSNY | Bensen B.8M | A. S. Deakin | |
| G-BSNZ | Cameron O-105 balloon | Aire Valley Balloons | |
| G-BSOE | Luscombe 8A Silvaire | S. B. Marsden | |
| G-BSOF | Colt 25A Mk II balloon | Thunder & Colt Ltd | |
| G-BSOG | Cessna 172M | B. Chapman & A. R. Budden | |
| G-BSOI | AS.332L Super Puma | Bristow Helicopters Ltd | |
| G-BSOJ | Thunder Ax7-77 balloon | P. J. S. & S. Hughes | |
| G-BSOK | PA-28-161 Warrior II | Hallmark Aviation | |
| G-BSOM | Glaser-Dirks DG.400 | G-BSOM Group | |
| G-BSON | Green S.25 | J. J. Green | |
| G-BSOO | Cessna 172F | Double Oscar Flying Group | |
| G-BSOR | CFM Streak Shadow Srs SA | J. P. Sorenson | |
| G-BSOT | PA-38-112 Tomahawk II | Misty Isle Aviation Ltd/Glasgow | |
| G-BSOU | PA-38-112 Tomahawk II | Misty Isle Aviation Ltd/Glasgow | |
| G-BSOV | PA-38-112 Tomahawk II | Misty Isle Aviation Ltd/Glasgow | |
| G-BSOW | PA-32R Cherokee Lance 300 | Halsmith (Aircraft Sales) Ltd | |
| G-BSOX | Luscombe 8A Silvaire | D. Gill | |
| G-BSOY | PA-34-220T Seneca III | BAe Flying College Ltd/Prestwick | |
| G-BSOZ | PA-28-161 Warrior II | Moray Flying Club Ltd/Kinloss | |
| G-BSPA | QAC Quickie Q.2 | M. Ward | |
| G-BSPB | Thunder Ax8-84 balloon | Nigs Pertwee Ltd | |
| G-BSPC | Jodel D.140C | B. E. Cotton/Headcorn | |
| G-BSPE | Cessna F.172P | P. & M. Jones/Denham | |
| G-BSPF | Cessna T.303 | B. M. Cane | |
| G-BSPG | PA-34-200T Seneca II | C. M. Vlieland-Boddy/Compton Abbas | |
| G-BSPI | PA-28-161 Warrior II | Snapfleet Ltd/Wellesbourne | |
| G-BSPJ | Bensen B.8 | P. Soanes | |
| G-BSPK | Cessna 195A | Walavia | |
| G-BSPL | CFM Streak Shadow Srs SA | MEL (Aviation Oxygen) Ltd | |
| G-BSPM | PA-28-161 Warrior II | W. London Aero Services Ltd/ White Waltham | |
| G-BSPN | PA-28R-201T Turbo Arrow III | R. G. & W. Allison | |
| G-BSPT | BN-2B-26 Islander | Pilatus BN Ltd/Bembridge | |
| G-BSPW | Light Aero Avid Flyer C | P. D. Wheatland | |
| G-BSPX | Lancair 320 | C. H. Skelt | |
| G-BSPY | BN-2A Islander | Glassbrush Ltd (G-AXYM) | |
| G-BSPZ | PA-28-161 Warrior II | Air Service Training Ltd/Perth | |
| G-BSRC | Cessna 150M | R. W. Boote | |
| G-BSRD | Cameron N-105 balloon | J. R. Joiner | |
| G-BSRG | Robinson R-22B | Meridian Helicopters | |
| G-BSRH | Pitts S-1C Special | J. R. Groom/Biggin Hill | |
| G-BSRI | Lancair 235 | G. Lewis | |
| G-BSRJ | Colt AA-1050 balloon | Thunder & Colt Ltd | |
| G-BSRK | ARV Super 2 | J. K. Davies | |
| G-BSRL | Everett Srs 2 gyroplane | R. F. E. Burley | |
| G-BSRP | Rotorway Executive | J. P. Dennison | |
| G-BSRR | Cessna 182Q | Comet Aviation Ltd | |
| G-BSRT | Denney Aerocraft Kitfox | L. A. James | |
| G-BSRU | BAe 146-200 | British Aerospace PLC (G-OSKI) | |
| G-BSRV | BAe 146-200 | British Aerospace PLC (G-OSUN) | |
| G-BSRX | CFM Streak Shadow | R. G. M. Proost | |
| G-BSRY | Cessna F.406 Caravan II | Bob Crowe Aircraft Sales Ltd | |
| G-BSRZ | Air Command 532 Elite 2-seat | A. S. G. Crabb | |
| G-BSSA | Luscombe 8E Silvaire | Punters Promotions Ltd/Denham | |
| G-BSSB | Cessna 150L | D. T. A. Rees | |
| G-BSSC | PA-28-161 Warrior II | Air Service Training Ltd/Perth | |
| G-BSSE | PA-28 Cherokee 140 | Severn Aircraft Co | |
| G-BSSF | Denney Aerocraft Kitfox | D. M. Orrock | |
| G-BSSI | Rans S.6 Coyote II | D. A. Farnworth (G-MWJA) | |
| G-BSSJ | FRED Srs 2 | R. F. Jopling | |
| G-BSSK | QAC Quickie Q.2 | D. G. Greatrex | |
| G-BSSN | Air Command 532 Elite 2-seat | R. C. Bettany | |
| G-BSSO | Cameron O-90 balloon | J. N. H. Purvis | |
| G-BSSP | Robin DR.400/180R | Soaring (Oxford) Ltd | |
| G-BSSR | PA-28-151 Warrior | G. Webster & R. J. Sixsmith | |
| G-BSST | Concorde 002★ | FAA Museum/Yeovilton | |
| G-BSSV | CFM Streak Shadow | R. W. Payne | |
| G-BSSW | PA-28-161 Warrior II | MJ Leasing/Cardiff | |
| G-BSSX | PA-28-161 Warrior II | Airpart Supply Ltd/Booker | |
| G-BSSY | Polikarpov Po-2W | Sussex Spraying Services Ltd | |
| G-BSSZ | Thunder Ax8-90 balloon | Capital Balloon Club Ltd | |

| Notes | Reg. | Type | Owner or Operator |
|---|---|---|---|
| | G-BSTC | Aeronca 11AC Chief | B. Bridgman & N. J. Mortimore |
| | G-BSTE | AS.355F-2 Twin Squirrel | McAlpine Helicopters Ltd |
| | G-BSTH | PA-25 Pawnee 235 | Scottish Gliding Union Ltd |
| | G-BSTI | Piper J-3C-65 Cub | I. Fraser & G. L. Nunn |
| | G-BSTJ | D.H.82A Tiger Moth | R. F. Harvey |
| | G-BSTK | Thunder Ax8-90 balloon | M. Williams |
| | G-BSTL | Rand Robinson KR-2 | T. M. Scale |
| | G-BSTM | Cessna 172L | G-BSTM Group/Cambridge |
| | G-BSTO | Cessna 152 | I. Taylor |
| | G-BSTP | Cessna 152 | FR Aviation Ltd/Bournemouth |
| | G-BSTR | AA-5 Traveler | James Allan (Aviation & Engineering) Ltd |
| | G-BSTS | Schleicher ASW.20L | T. I. Gardiner |
| | G-BSTT | Rans S.6 Coyote II | M. W. Holmes |
| | G-BSTU | Cessna P.210N | Boomselect Ltd |
| | G-BSTV | PA-32 Cherokee Six 300 | J. V. Hudson |
| | G-BSTY | Thunder Ax8-90 balloon | J. W. Cato |
| | G-BSTZ | PA-28 Cherokee 140 | Air Navigation & Trading Co Ltd/Blackpool |
| | G-BSUA | Rans S.6 Coyote II | P. S. Dopson & A. J. Todd |
| | G-BSUB | Colt 77A balloon | W. Country Marketing & Licensing Ltd |
| | G-BSUD | Luscombe 8A Silvaire | A. Corrigan |
| | G-BSUE | Cessna U.206G | R. A. Robinson |
| | G-BSUF | PA-32RT-300 Lance II | HPS Aviation |
| | G-BSUH | Cessna 140 | J. C. Greenslade |
| | G-BSUI | Robinson R-22B | C. T. Norman |
| | G-BSUJ | Brügger MB.2 Colibri | M. A. Farrelly |
| | G-BSUK | Colt 77A balloon | K. J. Foster |
| | G-BSUM | Scheibe SF.27MB | M Syndicate |
| | G-BSUO | Scheibe SF.25C Falke | British Gliding Association Ltd |
| | G-BSUR | Rotorway Executive 90 | N. J. Betmell |
| | G-BSUS | Taylor JT.1 Monoplane | R. Parker |
| | G-BSUT | Rans S.6 Coyote II | P. J. Clegg |
| | G-BSUU | Colt 180A balloon | J. P. Clifford |
| | G-BSUV | Cameron O-77 balloon | R. Moss |
| | G-BSUW | PA-34-200T Seneca II | Berry Air |
| | G-BSUX | Carlson Sparrow II | J. Stephenson |
| | G-BSUZ | Denney Aerocraft Kitfox | E. T. Wicks |
| | G-BSVA | Christen A.1 Husky | STOL Aviation Ltd |
| | G-BSVB | PA-28-181 Archer II | Redhill Flying Club |
| | G-BSVC | Cameron A-120 balloon | First Class Ballooning Ltd |
| | G-BSVE | Binder CP.301S Smaragd | B. F. Arnall |
| | G-BSVF | PA-28-161 Warrior II | Airways Aero Associations Ltd/Booker |
| | G-BSVG | PA-28-161 Warrior II | Airways Aero Associations Ltd/Booker |
| | G-BSVH | Piper J-3C-65 Cub | A. R. Meakin |
| | G-BSVI | PA-16 Clipper | Knight Flying Group |
| | G-BSVJ | — | — |
| | G-BSVK | Denney Aerocraft Kitfox Mk 2 | B. W. Davies |
| | G-BSVM | PA-28-161 Warrior II | Falcon Flying Services/Biggin Hill |
| | G-BSVN | Thorp T-18 | J. H. Kirkham |
| | G-BSVO | Sikorsky S-61N | Bristow Helicopters Ltd |
| | G-BSVP | PA-23 Aztec 250 | Time Electronics Ltd/Biggin Hill |
| | G-BSVR | Schweizer 269C | Nunkeeling Ltd |
| | G-BSVS | Robin DR.400/100 | J. Macdonald |
| | G-BSVU | Stemme S.10 | Sonic Aviation Ltd |
| | G-BSVV | PA-38-112 Tomahawk | A. J. & C. C. Leicester |
| | G-BSVW | PA-38-112 Tomahawk | Aeroleasing Ltd/Coventry |
| | G-BSVX | PA-38-112 Tomahawk | Aeroleasing Ltd/Coventry |
| | G-BSVY | PA-38-112 Tomahawk | Aeroleasing Ltd/Coventry |
| | G-BSVZ | Pietenpol Air Camper | A. F. Cashin |
| | G-BSWA | Luscombe 8A Silvaire | J. W. Street |
| | G-BSWB | Rans S.10 Sakota | F. A. Hewitt |
| | G-BSWC | Boeing Stearman E.75 (112) | R. J. & N. R. Lancaster |
| | G-BSWE | PA-18 Super Cub 150 | William Mark Holdings Ltd |
| | G-BSWF | PA-16 Clipper | T. M. Storey |
| | G-BSWG | PA-17 Vagabond | J. P. Taylor |
| | G-BSWH | Cessna 152 | Swansea Aviation Ltd |
| | G-BSWI | Rans S.10 Sakota | A. Gault |
| | G-BSWJ | Cameron O-77 balloon | T. Charlwood |
| | G-BSWK | Robinson R-22B | Clarity Aviation Ltd |
| | G-BSWM | Slingsby T.61F | L. J. McKelvie |
| | G-BSWN | BN-2B-26 Islander | Pilatus BN Ltd/Bembridge |
| | G-BSWR | BN-2B-26 Islander | Police Authority for Northern Ireland |
| | G-BSWS | BN-2B-26 Islander | Pilatus BN Ltd/Bembridge |
| | G-BSWV | Cameron N-77 balloon | Leicester Mercury Ltd |

| Reg. | Type | Owner or Operator | Notes |
|------|------|-------------------|-------|
| G-BSWW | Cameron O-105 balloon | R. B. & R. A. Naylor | |
| G-BSWX | Cameron V-90 balloon | Cameron Balloons Ltd | |
| G-BSWY | Cameron N-77 balloon | Nottingham Building Soc | |
| G-BSXA | PA-28-161 Warrior II | Hillvine Ltd | |
| G-BSXB | PA-28-161 Warrior II | Hillvine Ltd | |
| G-BSXC | PA-28-161 Warrior II | Hillvine Ltd | |
| G-BSXD | Soko P-2 Kraguj (30146) | C. J. Pearce | |
| G-BSXE | Bell 206B JetRanger | Sterling Helicopters Ltd | |
| G-BSXF | Cameron A-180 balloon | Gone With The Wind Ltd | |
| G-BSXG | Cessna 150K | Midair Aviation Ltd/Bournemouth | |
| G-BSXH | Pitts S-1 Special | A. Howard | |
| G-BSXI | Mooney M.20E | Halsmith (Aircraft Sales) Ltd | |
| G-BSXM | Cameron V-77 balloon | C. A. Oxby | |
| G-BSXN | Robinson R-22B | J. G. Gray | |
| G-BSXP | Air Command 532 Elite | B. J. West | |
| G-BSXR | Air Command 532 Elite | T. Wing | |
| G-BSXS | PA-28-181 Archer II | Pipe-Air Ltd | |
| G-BSXT | Piper J-5A Cub Cruiser | M. G. & K. J. Thompson | |
| G-BSXW | PA-28-161 Warrior II | Cloudshire Ltd/Wellesbourne | |
| G-BSXX | Whittaker MW.7 | H. J. Stanley | |
| G-BSXY | Oldfield Baby Great Lakes | B. Freeman-Jones | |
| G-BSYA | Jodel D.18 | S. Harrison | |
| G-BSYB | Cameron N-120 balloon | Cameron Balloons Ltd | |
| G-BSYC | PA-32R-300 Lance | Arrow Aviation | |
| G-BSYD | Cameron A-180 balloon | A. A. Brown | |
| G-BSYE | Cessna 140 | P. E. Villiers | |
| G-BSYF | Luscombe 8A Silvaire | M. K. Whitaker | |
| G-BSYG | PA-12 Super Cruiser | M. K. Whitaker | |
| G-BSYH | Luscombe 8A Silvaire | N. R. Osborne | |
| G-BSYI | AS.355F-1 Twin Squirrel | Lynton Aviation Ltd/Denham | |
| G-BSYJ | Cameron N-77 balloon | Chub Fire Ltd | |
| G-BSYK | PA-38-112 Tomahawk | Joyset Ltd | |
| G-BSYL | PA-38-112 Tomahawk | Joyset Ltd | |
| G-BSYM | PA-38-112 Tomahawk | Joyset Ltd | |
| G-BSYO | Piper J-3C-65 Cub | A. Eastelow | |
| G-BSYP | Bensen B.8M | A. T. Pocklington | |
| G-ASYT | BAe 146-300A | Trident Aviation Leasing Services Ltd | |
| G-BSYU | Robin DR.400/180 | P. A. Desoutter | |
| G-BSYV | Cessna 150M | Howells Group PLC | |
| G-BSYW | Cessna 150M | Howells Group PLC | |
| G-BSYX | Cessna 152 | Howells Group PLC | |
| G-BSYY | PA-28-161 Warrior II | Air Service Training Ltd/Perth | |
| G-BSYZ | PA-28-161 Warrior II | Air Service Training Ltd/Perth | |
| G-BSZB | Stolp SA.300 Starduster Too | Cambrian Flying Club/Swansea | |
| G-BSZC | Beech C-45H | A. A. Hodgson | |
| G-BSZD | Robin DR.400/180 | Trantshore Ltd | |
| G-BSZF | Jodel DR.250/160 | J. B. Randle | |
| G-BSZG | Stolp SA.100 Starduster | S. W. Watkins | |
| G-BSZH | Thunder Ax7-77 balloon | M. S. Drinkwater | |
| G-BSZI | Cessna 152 | Eglinton Flying Club Ltd | |
| G-BSZJ | PA-28-181 Archer II | R. D. Fuller | |
| G-BSZL | Colt 77A balloon | Airship & Balloon Co Ltd | |
| G-BSZM | Bensen B.8 | J. H. H. Turner | |
| G-BSZN | Bucker Bu133D-1 Jungmeister | V. Lindsay | |
| G-BSZO | Cessna 152 | Cloudshire Ltd/Wellesbourne | |
| G-BSZR | PA-28RT-201T Turbo Arrow IV | Venuetime Ltd | |
| G-BSZS | Robinson R-22B | South West Helicopters Ltd | |
| G-BSZT | PA-28-161 Warrior II | Lynair Aviation & Franchi Aviation Ltd | |
| G-BSZU | Cessna 150F | L. A. Maynard | |
| G-BSZV | Cessna 150F | Midair Aviation Ltd/Bournemouth | |
| G-BSZW | Cessna 152 | Midair Aviation Ltd/Bournemouth | |
| G-BSZX | Cessna 150M | Midair Aviation Ltd/Bournemouth | |
| G-BSZY | Cameron A-180 balloon | Bryant Group PLC | |
| G-BTAA | EMB-110P1 Bandeirante | Alexandra Aviation Ltd (G-BHJY) | |
| G-BTAB | BAe 125 Srs 800B | Abbey Investments Co Ltd (G-BOOA) | |
| G-BTAD | Macair Merlin | A. T. & M. R. Dowie | |
| G-BTAF | PA-28-181 Archer II | Enpar (North) Ltd | |
| G-BTAG | Cameron O-77 balloon | H. Phethean & R. A. Shapland | |
| G-BTAH | Bensen B.8A | T. B. Johnson | |
| G-BTAJ | PA-34-200T Seneca II | Ravenair Aircraft Engineering Ltd/ Manchester | |
| G-BTAK | EAA Acro Sport 2 | P. G. Harrison | |

| Notes | Reg. | Type | Owner or Operator |
|---|---|---|---|
| | G-BTAL | Cessna F.152 | Thanet Flying Club/Manston |
| | G-BTAM | PA-28-181 Archer II | RJH Air Services Ltd/Fowlmere |
| | G-BTAN | Thunder Ax7-65Z balloon | C. Wilkinson |
| | G-BTAO | Cameron A-180 balloon | R. M. Bishop & D. C. La Beaume |
| | G-BTAP | PA-38-112 Tomahawk | I. J. McGarrigle |
| | G-BTAR | PA-38-112 Tomahawk | Rhodair Maintenance Ltd/Cardiff |
| | G-BTAS | PA-38-112 Tomahawk | Rhodair Maintenance Ltd/Cardiff |
| | G-BTAT | Denny Aerocraft Kitfox | Fast Ford Centre Ltd |
| | G-BTAU | Thunder Ax7-77 balloon | Thunder & Colt Ltd |
| | G-BTAV | Colt 105A balloon | D. C. Chipping |
| | G-BTAW | PA-28-161 Warrior II | Enpar (North) Ltd |
| | G-BTAX | PA-31-350 Navajo Chieftain | Jet West Ltd/Exeter |
| | G-BTAY | — | — |
| | G-BTAZ | Evans VP-2 | G. S. Poulter |
| | G-BTBA | Robinson R-22B | Forestdale Hotels Ltd |
| | G-BTBB | Thunder Ax8-105 balloon | Scotia Balloons Ltd |
| | G-BTBC | PA-28-161 Warrior II | M. J. L. Macdonald |
| | G-BTBD | MBB Bo 105D | Bond Helicopters Ltd |
| | G-BTBE | — | — |
| | G-BTBF | Super Koala | E. A. Taylor (G-MWOZ) |
| | G-BTBG | Denny Aerocraft Kitfox | J. Catley |
| | G-BTBH | Ryan ST3KR | Ryan Group |
| | G-BTBI | WAR P-47 Thunderbolt (replica) (85) | J. Berry |
| | G-BTBJ | Cessna 195B | P. G. Galumbo |
| | G-BTBK | Cessna 152 | R. P. Schaak |
| | G-BTBL | Montgomerie-Bensen B.8MR | R. de H. Dobree-Carey |
| | G-BTBN | Denney Aerocraft Kitfox | Avon Valley Flying Group |
| | G-BTBO | Cameron N-77 balloon | Cameron Balloons Ltd |
| | G-BTBP | Cameron N-90 balloon | Gone With The Wind Ltd |
| | G-BTBR | Cameron DP-80 airship | Cameron Balloons Ltd |
| | G-BTBS | Cameron N-180 balloon | G. Scaife & B. Smith |
| | G-BTBT | PA-32R-301 Saratogo SP | B. Taylor |
| | G-BTBU | PA-18 Super Cub 150 | Acebell Aviation Ltd & H. J. Rose |
| | G-BTBV | Cessna 140 | A. Brinkley |
| | G-BTBW | Cessna 120 | A. Brinkley |
| | G-BTBX | Piper J-3C-65 Cub | Henlow Taildraggers |
| | G-BTBY | PA-17 Vagabond | M. M. Wallis |
| | G-BTCA | PA-32R-300 Lance | P. Taylor |
| | G-BTCB | Air Command 582 Sport | G. Scurrah |
| | G-BTCC | Grumman F6F-5 Hellcat (19) | Patina Ltd/Duxford |
| | G-BTCD | P-51D-25-NA Mustang (463221) | Patina Ltd/Duxford |
| | G-BTCE | Cessna 152 | S. T. Miller |
| | G-BTCF | CFM Streak Shadow | P. Crossman |
| | G-BTCH | Luscombe 8E Silvaire | P. D. Sparling |
| | G-BTCI | PA-17 Vagabond | F. M. Ward |
| | G-BTCJ | Luscombe 8C Silvaire | C. C. & J. M. Lovell |
| | G-BTCK | Cameron A-210 balloon | P. J. D. Kerr & A. J. Street |
| | G-BTCL | Cameron A-210 balloon | P. J. D. Kerr & A. J. Street |
| | G-BTCM | Cameron N-90 balloon | W. I. Hooker |
| | G-BTCN | Cameron A-300 balloon | Cameron Balloons Ltd |
| | G-BTCO | FRED Srs 2 | I. P. Manley |
| | G-BTCR | Rans S.10 Sakota | S. H. Barr |
| | G-BTCS | Colt 90A balloon | D. N. Belton |
| | G-BTCT | AS.332L Super Puma | Bristow Helicopters Ltd |
| | G-BTCU | WSK PZL Antonov An-2T (77) | Wessex Aviation & Transport Ltd |
| | G-BTCW | Cameron A-180 balloon | Bristol Balloons |
| | G-BTCX | Hunter F.4 | Gray Tuplin Ltd |
| | G-BTCY | Hunter F.4 | Gray Tuplin Ltd |
| | G-BTCZ | Cameron 84 Chateau SS balloon | Forbes Europe Inc/France |
| | G-BTDA | Slingsby T.61G | RAFGSA/Bicester |
| | G-BTDB | Cameron A-180 balloon | Cameron Balloons Ltd |
| | G-BTDC | Denney Aerocraft Kitfox | D. Collinson |
| | G-BTDD | CFM Streak Shadow | S. J. Evans |
| | G-BTDE | Cessna C-165 | G. S. Moss |
| | G-BTDF | Luscombe 8A Silvaire | M. Stow |
| | G-BTDG | Colt 105A balloon | Thunder & Colt Ltd |
| | G-BTDH | P.56 Provost T.1 (WV666) | Pulsegrove Ltd/Shoreham |
| | G-BTDI | Robinson R-22B | A. Palmer |
| | G-BTDJ | Cessna T.303 | European Aviation Services Ltd |
| | G-BTDK | Cessna 421C | RK Carbon Fibre Ltd/Manchester |
| | G-BTDN | Denney Aerocraft Kitfox | A. B. Butler |
| | G-BTDP | TBM-3R Avenger (53319) | A. Haig-Thomas/North Weald |

| Reg. | Type | Owner or Operator | Notes |
|------|------|-------------------|-------|
| G-BTDR | Aero Designs Pulsar | R. M. Hughes | |
| G-BTDS | Colt 77A balloon | C. P. Witter Ltd | |
| G-BTDT | C.A.S.A. 1-131E Jungmann | T. A. Reed | |
| G-BTDU | Robin DR.400/180 | N. French | |
| G-BTDV | PA-28-161 Warrior II | R. E. Thorne | |
| G-BTDW | Cessna 152 II | J. A. Blenkharn/Carlisle | |
| G-BTDX | PA-18 Super Cub 150 | Acebell Aviation Ltd/Redhill | |
| G-BTDY | PA-18 Super Cub 150 | Rodger Aircraft Ltd | |
| G-BTDZ | C.A.S.A. 1-131E Jungmann 2000 | R. J. Pickin | |
| G-BTEA | Cameron N-105 balloon | Southern Balloon Group | |
| G-BTEE | Cameron O-120 balloon | W. H. & J. P. Morgan | |
| G-BTEF | Pitts S-1 Special | Northwest Aerobatics | |
| G-BTEH | Colt 77A balloon | Thunder & Colt Ltd | |
| G-BTEI | Everett Srs 3 gyroplane | J. W. Highton | |
| G-BTEJ | Boeing 757-208 | Britannia Airways Ltd *David Livingstone* | |
| G-BTEK | SOCATA TB.20 Trinidad | Air Touring Services Ltd/Biggin Hill | |
| G-BTEL | CFM Streak Shadow | J. E. Eatwell | |
| G-BTEN | Thunder Ax7-77 balloon | T. W. Dawson | |
| G-BTEO | Cameron V-90 balloon | Cameron Balloons Ltd | |
| G-BTEP | Cameron DP-80 airship | Cameron Balloons Ltd | |
| G-BTER | Cessna 150J | Universal Air Services Ltd/Sywell | |
| G-BTES | Cessna 150H | Universal Air Services Ltd/Sywell | |
| G-BTET | Piper J-3C-65 Cub | W. F. Crozier | |
| G-BTEU | SA.365N-2 Dauphin | Bond Helicopters Ltd | |
| G-BTEV | PA-38-112 Tomahawk | T. R. Blockley & J. Mingay/Cardiff | |
| G-BTEW | Cessna 120 | Tindon Ltd/Little Snoring | |
| G-BTEX | PA-28 Cherokee 140 | McAully Flying Group Ltd/Little Snoring | |
| G-BTFA | Denney Aerocraft Kitfox | K. R. Peek | |
| G-BTFB | Cameron DG-14 airship | Cameron Balloons Ltd | |
| G-BTFC | Cessna F.152 II | Tayside Aviation Ltd | |
| G-BTFD | Colt AS-105 airshiip Mk II | Media Fantasy Aviation UK Ltd | |
| G-BTFE | Bensen-Parsons 2-seat gyroplane | I. Brewster | |
| G-BTFF | Cessna T.310R II | Rajmech Ltd | |
| G-BTFG | Boeing Stearman A.75N1 (441) | S. J. Ellis | |
| G-BTFJ | PA-15 Vagabond | Eastbach Aircraft Preservation | |
| G-BTFK | Taylorcraft BC-12D | J. J. Penney | |
| G-BTFL | Aeronca 11AC Chief | BTFL Group | |
| G-BTFM | Cameron O-105 balloon | Edinburgh University Hot Air Balloon Club | |
| G-BTFN | Beech F33C Bonanza | Robert Hinton Design & Creative Communications Ltd | |
| G-BTFO | PA-28-161 Warrior II | Flyfar Ltd | |
| G-BTFP | PA-38-112 Tomahawk | Teesside Flight Centre Ltd | |
| G-BTFR | Colt AS-105 airship | Heather Flight Ltd | |
| G-BTFS | Cessna A.150M | Birmingham Airport Flying Group | |
| G-BTFT | Beech 58 Baron | Roseberry Management Ltd | |
| G-BTFU | Cameron N-90 balloon | J. J. Rudoni & A. C. K. Rawson | |
| G-BTFV | Whittaker MW.7 | S. J. Luck | |
| G-BTFW | Montgomerie-Bensen B.8MR | A. Mansfield | |
| G-BTFX | Bell 206B JetRanger 2 | J. Selwyn Smith (Shepley)/Ltd | |
| G-BTFY | Bell 206B JetRanger 2 | R & M International Helicopters Ltd | |
| G-BTFZ | Cameron A-120 balloon | A. G. E. Faulkner | |
| G-BTGA | Boeing Stearman A.751N1 | J. C. Lister | |
| G-BTGC | PA-38-112 Tomahawk | R. E. Wooldridge & T. Hayselden (Doncaster) Ltd | |
| G-BTGD | Rand-Robinson KR-2 | D. W. Mullin | |
| G-BTGE | PA-28-181 Archer II | J. Sieker | |
| G-BTGG | Rans S.10 Sakota | A. R. Cameron | |
| G-BTGH | Cessna 152 | R. S. Trayhurn & P. D. Myson | |
| G-BTGI | Rearwin 175 Skyranger | A. H. Hunt/St Just | |
| G-BTGJ | Smith DSA-1 Miniplane | G. J. Knowles | |
| G-BTGK | PA-28-161 Warrior II | S. Dorrington | |
| G-BTGL | Light Aero Avid Flyer | A. J. Maxwell | |
| G-BTGM | Aeronca 7AC Champion | Claybourn Garages Ltd | |
| G-BTGN | Cessna 310R | Air Service Training Ltd/Perth | |
| G-BTGO | PA-28 Cherokee 140 | Hadleyridge Ltd | |
| G-BTGP | Cessna 150M | Billins Air Services Ltd | |
| G-BTGR | Cessna 152 II | A. J. Gomes | |
| G-BTGS | Stolp SA.300 Starduster Too | T. G. Solomon (G-AYMA)/Shoreham | |
| G-BTGT | CFM Streak Shadow | M. P. Allinson (G-MWPY) | |
| G-BTGU | PA-34-200T Seneca III | Carill Aviation Ltd | |
| G-BTGV | PA-34-200T Seneca II | Hollowbrook Flying Group | |
| G-BTGW | Cessna 152 II | Stapleford Flying Club Ltd | |
| G-BTGX | Cessna 152 II | Stapleford Flying Club Ltd | |

| Notes | Reg. | Type | Owner or Operator |
|---|---|---|---|
| | G-BTGY | PA-28-161 Warrior II | Stapleford Flying Club Ltd |
| | G-BTGZ | PA-28-181 Archer II | Express Aviation Marketing/Biggin Hill |
| | G-BTHA | Cessna 182P | N. J. Douglas |
| | G-BTHB | Bell 212 | Autair Helicopters Ltd |
| | G-BTHC | Bell 212 | Autair Helicopters Ltd |
| | G-BTHD | Yakolev Yak-3U | Patina Ltd/Duxford |
| | G-BTHE | Cessna 150L | Humberside Police Flying Club |
| | G-BTHF | Cameron V-90 balloon | N. J. & S. J. Langley |
| | G-BTHH | Jodel DR.100A | H. R. Leefe & D. J. Williams |
| | G-BTHI | Robinson R-22B | A. M. Green |
| | G-BTHJ | Evans VP-2 | C. J. Moseley |
| | G-BTHK | Thunder Ax7-77 balloon | Krauss Maffei (UK) Ltd |
| | G-BTHM | Thunder Ax8-105 balloon | Anglia Balloons |
| | G-BTHN | Murphy Renegade 912 | F. A. Purvis |
| | G-BTHP | Thorp T.211 | Arrow Air Sales/Shipdham |
| | G-BTHR | SOCATA TB.10 Tobago | CB Helicopters |
| | G-BTHU | Light Aero Avid Flyer | M. Morris |
| | G-BTHV | MBB Bo 105DBS/4 | Bond Helicopers Ltd |
| | G-BTHW | Beech F33C Bonanza | Robin Lance Aviation Associates Ltd |
| | G-BTHX | Colt 105A balloon | R. Ollier |
| | G-BTHY | Bell 206B JetRanger 3 | J. W. Sandle |
| | G-BTHZ | Cameron V-56 balloon | C. N. Marshall |
| | G-BTIB | Dassault Falcon 900B | Glaxo Holdings Ltd |
| | G-BTIC | PA-22 Tri-Pacer 150 | Yorkshire Commercial Properties Ltd |
| | G-BTID | PA-28-161 Warrior II | Halsmith (Aircraft Sales) Ltd |
| | G-BTIE | SOCATA TB.10 Tobago | Rotaters Ltd/Machester |
| | G-BTIF | Denney Aerocraft Kitfox | C. R. Thompson |
| | G-BTIG | Montgomerie-Bensen B.8MR | D. Beevers |
| | G-BTIH | PA-28-151 Warrior | MPM Aviation |
| | G-BTII | AA-5B Tiger | B. D. Greenwood |
| | G-BTIJ | Luscombe 8E Silvaire | C. P. Wadlow |
| | G-BTIK | Cessna 152 | B. R. Pearson/Eaglescott |
| | G-BTIL | PA-38-112 Tomahawk | B. R. Pearson/Eaglescott |
| | G-BTIM | PA-28-161 Cadet | Mid-Sussex Timber Co Ltd |
| | G-BTIN | Cessna 150C | Cormack (Aircraft Services) Ltd |
| | G-BTIO | SNCAN Stampe SV-4C | L. J. & A. A. Rice |
| | G-BTIP | Denney Aerocraft Kitfox | P. A. Hardy |
| | G-BTIR | Denney Aerocraft Kitfox Mk 2 | Bluetit Group |
| | G-BTIS | AS.355F-1 Twin Squirrel | Walsh Aviation (G-TALI) |
| | G-BTIU | M.S.892A Rallye Commodore 150 | W. H. Cole |
| | G-BTIV | PA-28-161 Warrior II | Warrior Group/Eaglescott |
| | G-BTIW | Jodel DR.1050/M1 | P. A. Hardy |
| | G-BTIX | Cameron V-77 balloon | S. A. Simington |
| | G-BTIZ | Cameron A-105 balloon | A. Faulkner |
| | G-BTJA | Luscombe 8E Silvaire | M. W. & L. M. Rudkin |
| | G-BTJB | Luscombe 8E Silvaire | M. Loxton |
| | G-BTJC | Luscombe 8F Silvaire | S. C. & M. Goddard |
| | G-BTJD | Thunder Ax8-90 balloon | T. C. Restell |
| | G-BTJE | Hiller UH-12E4 | T. J. Clark |
| | G-BTJF | Thunder Ax10-180 balloon | Airborne Adventures Ltd |
| | G-BTJG | BAe 146-300A | Trident Aviation Leasing Services Ltd |
| | G-BTJH | Cameron O-77 balloon | H. Stringer |
| | G-BTJI | Beech F33C Bonanza | Neil Brown Engineering Ltd |
| | G-BTJJ | PA-38-112 Tomahawk | Ravenair Training Ltd/Manchester |
| | G-BTJK | PA-38-112 Tomahawk | Network Enterprise International Ltd |
| | G-BTJL | PA-38-112 Tomahawk | Ravenair Training Ltd/Manchester |
| | G-BTJN | Montgomerie-Bensen B.8MR | A. Hamilton |
| | G-BTJO | Thunder Ax9-140 balloon | Abbey Plant Co Ltd |
| | G-BTJS | Montgomerie-Bensen B.8M | T. C. Jackson |
| | G-BTJT | BAe 146-300 | British Aerospace PLC |
| | G-BTJU | Cameron V-90 balloon | C. W. Jones (Flooring) Ltd |
| | G-BTJV | PZL SZD-50-3 Puchacz | Kent Gliding Club Ltd |
| | G-BTJX | Rans S.10 Sakota | M. Goacher |
| | G-BTJY | Bell 212 | Ostermans Aero (UK) Ltd |
| | G-BTJZ | Taylorcraft BC-12D-1 | K. E. Ballington |
| | G-BTKA | Piper J-5A Cub Cruiser | S. J. Rudkin |
| | G-BTKB | Renegade Spirit 912 | G. S. Blundell |
| | G-BTKD | Denney Aerocraft Kitfox | J. F. White |
| | G-BTKE | Colt 90A balloon | N. C. Lindsay |
| | G-BTKG | Light Aero Avid Flyer | P. R. Snowden |
| | G-BTKH | Colt GA-42 airship | Thunder & Colt Ltd |
| | G-BTKI | NA T-6G Texan | P. S. & S. M. Warner |
| | G-BTKJ | G.44 Widgeon | B. J. Snoxall |

| Reg. | Type | Owner or Operator |
|------|------|-------------------|
| G-BTKK | Colt 240A balloon | Heather Flight Ltd |
| G-BTKL | MBB Bo 105DB-4 | Veritair Ltd/Cardiff |
| G-BTKN | Cameron O-120 balloon | The Ballooning Business Ltd |
| G-BTKO | Cameron A-180 balloon | Balloon Flights International Ltd |
| G-BTKP | CFM Streak Shadow | K. S. Woodward |
| G-BTKS | Rans S.10 Sakota | J. R. I. Rolfe & ptnrs |
| G-BTKT | PA-28-161 Warrior II | C. R. Herbert |
| G-BTKU | Cameron A-105 balloon | Champagne Flights International Ltd |
| G-BTKV | PA-22 Tri-Pacer 160 | M. Hanna |
| G-BTKW | Cameron O-105 balloon | P. Spellward |
| G-BTKX | PA-28-181 Archer II | Goldhawk Aviation |
| G-BTKY | PA-28-181 Archer II | Commanche Travel Ltd/Elstree |
| G-BTKZ | Cameron V-77 balloon | S. P. Richards |
| G-BTLA | Sikorsky S-76B | Falcon of Friendship Ltd |
| G-BTLB | Wassmer WA.52 Europa | M. D. O'Brien/Shoreham |
| G-BTLC | SA.365N2 Dauphin 2 | Bond Helicopters Ltd |
| G-BTLE | PA-31-350 Navajo Chieftain | Orient Aviation Ltd |
| G-BTLF | Enstrom 280 | M. A. Crook |
| G-BTLG | PA-28R Cherokee Arrow 200 | A. P. Reilly |
| G-BTLI | Scheibe SF.25B Falke | S. F. Duerden/Germany |
| G-BTLL | Pilatus P3-05 | D. L. Masters/Biggin Hill |
| G-BTLM | PA-22 Tri-Pacer 160 | F & H (Aircraft) Ltd |
| G-BTLN | Cessna T.303 | Pektron Ltd |
| G-BTLP | AA-1C Lynx | Partlease Ltd |
| G-BTLR | SA.365N2 Dauphin 2 | McAlpine Helicopters Ltd/Hayes |
| G-BTLY | BN-2B-26 Islander | Pilatus BN Ltd/Bembridge |
| G-BTMA | Cessna 172N | Cheshire Air Training School (Merseyside) Ltd |
| G-BTMB | Colt 120A balloon | Pickstead Ltd |
| G-BTMC | Colt 120A balloon | Pickstead Ltd |
| G-BTMF | Taylorcraft BC-12D | C. M. Churchill/Cambridge |
| G-BTMH | Colt 90A balloon | Douwe Egberts UK Ltd |
| G-BTMJ | Maule MX-7-180 | C. M. McGill |
| G-BTMK | Cessna R.172K XP | Strand Coachworks |
| G-BTML | Cameron 90 Rupert Bear SS balloon | Flying Pictures (Balloons) Ltd |
| G-BTMM | Cameron N-105 balloon | M. F. Glue |
| G-BTMN | Thunder Ax9-120 S2 balloon | Aerial Display Co Ltd |
| G-BTMO | Colt 69A balloon | Thunder & Colt Ltd |
| G-BTMP | Everett Srs 2 gyroplane | D. G. Hill |
| G-BTMR | Cessna 172M | Cumbria Aero Club/Carlisle |
| G-BTMS | Light Aero Avid Flyer | M. J. Schyns |
| G-BTMT | Denney Aerocraft Kitfox | Skulk Flying Group |
| G-BTMV | Everett Srs 2 gyroplane | L. Armes |
| G-BTMW | Zenair CH.701 STOL | L. Lewis |
| G-BTMX | Denney Aerocraft Kitfox Mk 3 | M. E. F. Reynolds |
| G-BTMY | Cameron 80 Train SS balloon | Cameron Balloons Ltd |
| G-BTMZ | PA-38-112 Tomahawk | T. Drew |
| G-BTNA | Robinson R-22B | MG Group Ltd |
| G-BTNB | Robinson R-22B | Davron Aviation |
| G-BTNC | AS.365N-2 Dauphin 2 | Bond Helicopters Ltd |
| G-BTND | PA-38-112 Tomahawk | S. Edmunds |
| G-BTNE | PA-28-161 Warrior II | Cloudshire Ltd |
| G-BTNH | PA-28-161 Warrior II | C. R. Herbert |
| G-BTNJ | Cameron V-90 balloon | P. L. Harrison & B. J. Newman |
| G-BTNL | Thunder Ax10-180 balloon | Airships Ltd |
| G-BTNM | AS.355F-2 Twin Squirrel | McAlpine Helicopters Ltd/Hayes |
| G-BTNN | Colt 21A balloon | Thunder & Colt Ltd |
| G-BTNO | Aeronca 7AC Champion | November Oscar Group/Netherthorpe |
| G-BTNP | Light Aero Avid Flyer Commuter | N. Evans |
| G-BTNR | Denney Aerocraft Kitfox Mk 3 | J. W. G. Ellis |
| G-BTNS | PZL-104 Wilga 80 | R. W. Husband |
| G-BTNT | PA-28-151 Warrior | Britannia Airways Ltd/Luton |
| G-BTNU | BAe 146-300 | British Aerospace PLC (G-BSLS) |
| G-BTNV | PA-28-161 Warrior II | D. K. Oakeley & A. M. Dawson |
| G-BTNW | Rans S.6-ESA Coyote II | G. N. J. King & K. J. Dixon |
| G-BTNX | Colt 105A balloon | Thunder & Colt Ltd |
| G-BTNY | Fairchild M-62A | C. L. H. Parr |
| G-BTNZ | AS.332L-1 Super Puma | British International Helicopters Ltd |
| G-BTOA | Mong Sport MS-2 | M. J. Cook |
| G-BTOC | Robinson R-22B | T. Kressner |
| G-BTOD | PA-38-112 Tomahawk | V. F. & J. A. Shirley |
| G-BTOG | D.H.82A Tiger Moth | P. T. Szluha |

| Notes | Reg. | Type | Owner or Operator |
|---|---|---|---|
| | G-BTOH | Cameron A-105 balloon | R. E. Jones |
| | G-BTOI | Cameron N-77 balloon | The Nestle Co Ltd |
| | G-BTOJ | Mooney M.10 Cadet | D. W. Vernon |
| | G-BTOL | Denney Aerocraft Kitfox Mk 3 | C. R. Phillips |
| | G-BTON | PA-28 Cherokee 140 | W. A. & K. C. Ryan |
| | G-BTOO | Pitts S-1C Special | F. Sharples/Sandown |
| | G-BTOP | Cameron V-77 balloon | J. J. Winter |
| | G-BTOR | Lancair 320 | R. W. Fairless |
| | G-BTOS | Cessna 140 | G. N. Smith |
| | G-BTOT | PA-15 Vagabond | M. Stow |
| | G-BTOU | Cameron O-120 balloon | Balloon-A-Drome Ltd |
| | G-BTOW | SOCATA Rallye 180GT | Cambridge University Gliding Trust Ltd |
| | G-BTOX | Aero Designs Pulsar | J. K. McWhinney |
| | G-BTOZ | Thunder Ax9-120 S2 balloon | H. G. Davies |
| | G-BTPA | BAe ATP/Jetstream 61 | British Airways *Strathblane*/Glasgow |
| | G-BTPB | Cameron N-105 balloon | Test Valley Balloon Group |
| | G-BTPC | BAe ATP/Jetstream 61 | British Airways *Strathallan*/Glasgow |
| | G-BTPD | BAe ATP/Jetstream 61 | British Airways *Strathconon*/Glasgow |
| | G-BTPE | BAe ATP/Jetstream 61 | British Airways *Strathdon*/Glasgow |
| | G-BTPF | BAe ATP/Jetstream 61 | British Airways *Strathlarn*/Glasgow |
| | G-BTPG | BAe ATP/Jetstream 61 | British Airways *Strathfillan*/Glasgow |
| | G-BTPH | BAe ATP/Jetstream 61 | British Airways *Strathhaver*/Glasgow |
| | G-BTPJ | BAe ATP/Jetstream 61 | British Airways *Strathpeffer*/Glsagow |
| | G-BTPK | BAe ATP/Jetstream 61 | British Airways *Strathrannoch*/Glasgow |
| | G-BTPL | BAe ATP/Jetstream 61 | British Airways *Strathspey*/Glasgow |
| | G-BTPM | BAe ATP/Jetstream 61 | British Airways *Strathory*/Glasgow |
| | G-BTPN | BAe ATP/Jetstream 61 | British Airways *Strathbrora*/Glasgow |
| | G-BTPO | BAe ATP/Jetstream 61 | British Airways *Strathclyde*/Glasgow |
| | G-BTPP | — | — |
| | G-BTPR | — | — |
| | G-BTPS | — | — |
| | G-BTPT | Cameron N-77 balloon | Derbyshire Building Soc |
| | G-BTPV | Colt 90A balloon | Airship & Balloon Co Ltd |
| | G-BTPX | Thunder Ax8-90 balloon | J. L. Guy |
| | G-BTPZ | Isaacs Fury II | P. D. Holt |
| | G-BTRA | Denney Aerocraft Kitfox Mk 3 | T. P. Spurge |
| | G-BTRB | Colt Mickey Mouse SS balloon | Wellfarrow Ltd |
| | G-BTRC | Light Aero Avid Speedwing | A. A. Craig |
| | G-BTRE | Cessna F.172H | Hero Aviation/Stapleford |
| | G-BTRF | Aero Designs Pulsar | C. Smith |
| | G-BTRG | Aeronca 65C Super Chief | H. J. Cox |
| | G-BTRH | Aeronca 7AC Champion | H. J. Cox |
| | G-BTRI | Aeronca 11CC Super Chief | H. J. Cox |
| | G-BTRJ | Boeing Stearman B.75N1 | G. L. Carpenter |
| | G-BTRK | PA-28-161 Warrior II | C. R. Herbert |
| | G-BTRL | Cameron N-105 balloon | J. Lippett |
| | G-BTRN | Thunder Ax9-120 S2 balloon | Solar Communications Ltd |
| | G-BTRO | Thunder Ax8-90 balloon | Capital Balloon Club Ltd |
| | G-BTRP | Hughes 369E | Southern Air Ltd/Shoreham |
| | G-BTRR | Thunder Ax7-77 balloon | S. M. Roberts |
| | G-BTRS | PA-28-161 Warrior II | Actionwings Ltd/Barton |
| | G-BTRT | PA-28R Cherokee Arrow 200-II | C. E. Yates |
| | G-BTRU | Robin DR.400/180 | R. & M. Engineering Ltd |
| | G-BTRV | Boeing Stearman B.75N1 | J. M. & R. J. Knights |
| | G-BTRW | Slingsby T.61F Venture T.2 | B. Kerby & G. Grainer |
| | G-BTRX | Cameron V-77 balloon | R. P. Jones & N. P.Hemsley |
| | G-BTRY | PA-28-161 Warrior II | Air Service Training Ltd/Perth |
| | G-BTRZ | Jodel D.18 | R. M. Johnson & R. Collin |
| | G-BTSA | Cessna 150K | M. E. Bartlett |
| | G-BTSB | Corben Baby Ace D | W. R. Savin |
| | G-BTSC | Evans VP-2 | B. P. Irish |
| | G-BTSD | Midget Mustang | R. Fitzpatrick |
| | G-BTSE | — | — |
| | G-BTSG | Cessna 414A | Kingsway Furniture PLC (G-BTFH) |
| | G-BTSI | BAe 125-1000 | Shell Aircraft Ltd/Heathrow |
| | G-BTSJ | PA-28-161 Warrior II | Plymouth School of Flying Ltd |
| | G-BTSK | Beech F33C Bonanza | R. N. Goode/White Waltham |
| | G-BTSL | Cameron Glass SS balloon | M. R. Humphrey & J. R .Clifton |
| | G-BTSM | Cessna 180A | C. Couston |
| | G-BTSN | Cessna 150G | H. W. & R. W. Sage |
| | G-BTSO | Cessna 150M | H. W. & R. W. Sage |
| | G-BTSP | Piper J-3C-65 Cub | H. W. & R. W. Sage |
| | G-BTSR | Aeronca 11AC Chief | H. W. & R. W. Sage |

| Reg. | Type | Owner or Operator | Notes |
|------|------|-------------------|-------|
| G-BTSS | Colt Flying Shopping Trolley SS balloon | Jentime Ltd | |
| G-BTST | Bensen B.9 | V. Scott | |
| G-BTSU | Bensen B.8MR | B. T. Goggin | |
| G-BTSV | Denney Aerocraft Kitfox Mk 3 | D. J. Sharland | |
| G-BTSW | Colt AS-80 Mk II airship | Huntair Ltd | |
| G-BTSX | Thunder Ax7-77 balloon | C. Moris-Gallimore | |
| G-BTSY | Lightning F.6 | Lightning Association | |
| G-BTSZ | Cessna 177A | W. B. Pope | |
| G-BTTA | Hawker Sea Fury FB.10 (WH589) | R. G. Hanna/Duxford | |
| G-BTTB | Cameron V-90 balloon | Royal Engineers Balloon Club | |
| G-BTTD | Montgomerie-Bensen B.8M | K. J. Parker | |
| G-BTTE | Cessna 150L | I. J. Lawson | |
| G-BTTH | Beech F33C Bonanza | N. K. Mere/Germany | |
| G-BTTI | Thunder Ax8-90 balloon | Capital Balloon Club Ltd | |
| G-BTTJ | Thunder Ax9-120 S2 balloon | G. D. & L. Fitzpatrick | |
| G-BTTK | Thunder Ax8-105 balloon | Tempowish Ltd | |
| G-BTTL | Cameron V-90 balloon | A. J. Baird | |
| G-BTTN | V.S.349 Spitfire Vb (BL628) | Aerofab Restorations | |
| G-BTTP | BAe 146-300 | Trident Aviation Leasing Services Ltd | |
| G-BTTR | Aerotek Pitts S-2A Special | Ebork Ltd | |
| G-BTTS | Colt 77A balloon | Rutland Balloon Club | |
| G-BTTU | Cameron V-90 balloon | Heather Flight Ltd | |
| G-BTTV | Schweizer 269C | C.S.E. Aviation Ltd/Kidlington | |
| G-BTTW | Thunder Ax7-77 balloon | Thunder & Colt Ltd | |
| G-BTTY | Denney Aerocraft Kitfox Mk 2 | K. J. Fleming | |
| G-BTTZ | Slingsby T.61F Venture T.2 | I. R. F. Hammond | |
| G-BTUA | Slingsby T.61F Venture T.2 | M. W. Olliver | |
| G-BTUB | Yakolev C.11 | M. G. & J. R. Jefferies | |
| G-BTUC | EMB-312 Tucano | Short Bros PLC/Belfast City | |
| G-BTUD | CFM Image | D. G. Cook (G-MWPV) | |
| G-BTUG | SOCATA Rallye 180T | Lasham Gliding Soc | |
| G-BTUH | Cameron N-65 balloon | B. J. Godding | |
| G-BTUJ | Thunder Ax9-120 balloon | R. T. Revel | |
| G-BTUK | Aerotek Pitts S-2A Special | Wickenby Aviation Ltd | |
| G-BTUL | Aerotek Pitts S-2A Special | C. & S. Aviation | |
| G-BTUM | Piper J-3C-65 Cub | B. G. Ell | |
| G-BTUN | Colt Flying Drinks Can SS balloon | BIAS UK Ltd | |
| G-BTUR | PA-18 Super Cub 95 (modified) | G. Cormack/Glasgow | |
| G-BTUS | Whittaker MW.7 | J. F. Bakewell | |
| G-BTUT | PA-34-200T Seneca II | A. G. Norman-Thorpe | |
| G-BTUU | Cameron O-120 balloon | Henley-on-Thames Air Balloons | |
| G-BTUV | Aeronca A65TAC Defender | J. T. Ingrouille | |
| G-BTUW | PA-28-151 Warrior | J. Robinson | |
| G-BTUX | AS.365N-2 Dauphin 2 | Bond Helicopters Ltd/Aberdeen | |
| G-BTUY | BAe 146-300 | British Aerospace PLC | |
| G-BTUZ | American General AG-5B Tiger | The Cabair Group Ltd/Elstree | |
| G-BTVA | Thunder Ax7-77 balloon | C. E. Wood | |
| G-BTVB | Everett Srs 3 gyroplane | J. Pumford | |
| G-BTVC | Denney Aercoraft Kitfox Mk 2 | R. Swinden | |
| G-BTVE | Hawker Demon | Aero Vintage Ltd | |
| G-BTVF | Rotorway Executive 90 | E. P. Sadler | |
| G-BTVG | Cessna 140 | V. C. Gover | |
| G-BTVH | Colt 77A balloon | D. N. & L. J. Close (G-ZADT/G-ZBCA) | |
| G-BTVJ | BN-2B-26 Islander | Pilatus BN Ltd/Bembridge | |
| G-BTVK | BN-2B-26 Islander | Pilatus BN Ltd/Bembridge | |
| G-BTVL | BN-2B-26 Islander | Pilatus BN Ltd/Bembridge | |
| G-BTVM | BN-2B-26 Islander | Pilatus BN Ltd/Bembridge | |
| G-BTVN | BN-2B-26 Islander | Pllatus BN Ltd/Bembridge | |
| G-BTVP | Currie Wot | B. V. Mayo & V. Panteli | |
| G-BTVR | PA-28 Cherokee 140 | West of Scotland Flying Club Ltd | |
| G-BTVS | AS.355F-1 Twin Squirrel | BLS Aviation Ltd (G-STVE/G-TOFF/ G-BKJX) | |
| G-BTVU | Robinson R-22B | Sloane Helicopters Ltd/Sywell | |
| G-BTVV | Cessna F.337G | Taylor Aircraft Services | |
| G-BTVW | Cessna 152 | Cloudshire Ltd | |
| G-BTVX | Cessna 152 | Cloudshire Ltd | |
| G-BTVY | Cessna 402B | R. K. Spence | |
| G-BTWB | Denney Aerocraft Kitfox Mk 3 | J. E. Tootell (G-BTTM) | |
| G-BTWC | Slingsby T.61F Venture T.2 | RAFGSA/Bicester | |
| G-BTWD | Slingsby T.61F Venture T.2 | York Gliding Centre | |
| G-BTWE | Slingsby T.61F Venture T.2 | RAFGSA/Bicester | |
| G-BTWF | D.H.C.1 Chipmunk 22 | J. A. & V. G. Sims | |

| Notes | Reg. | Type | Owner or Operator |
|---|---|---|---|
| | G-BTWG | Thunder Ax10-160 S2 balloon | W. O. T. Holmes & R. J. Barr |
| | G-BTWH | Thunder Ax7-77 balloon | Jim Barker Motor Factor |
| | G-BTWI | EAA Acro Sport 1 | Detail Offers Ltd |
| | G-BTWJ | Cameron V-77 balloon | F. W. Barnes |
| | G-BTWK | Colt 210A balloon | Airship & Balloon Co Ltd |
| | G-BTWL | WAG-Aero Acro Sport Trainer | D. H. Tonkin |
| | G-BTWM | Cameron V-77 balloon | D. I. Gray-Fisk |
| | G-BTWN | Maule MXT-7-180 | MLP Aviation Ltd/Elstree |
| | G-BTWO | — | |
| | G-BTWP | Robinson R-22B | Sloane Helicopters Ltd/Sywell |
| | G-BTWR | Bell P-63A-7-BE Kingcobra | Patina Ltd/Duxford |
| | G-BTWS | Thunder Ax7-77 balloon | Bavarian Balloon Co Ltd |
| | G-BTWU | PA-22 Tri-Pacer 135 | G. A. Bentley |
| | G-BTWV | Cameron O-90 balloon | Bodkin House Hotel |
| | G-BTWW | AB-206B JetRanger 2 | Dollar Air Services Ltd/Coventry |
| | G-BTWX | SOCATA TB.9 Tampico | Air Touring Services Ltd/Biggin Hill |
| | G-BTWY | Aero Designs Pulsar | J. J. Pridal & A. K. Pirie |
| | G-BTWZ | Rans S.10 Sakota | D. G. Hey |
| | G-BTXB | Colt 77A balloon | Unigas Ltd |
| | G-BTXC | Team Minimax | M. H. D. Soltau (G-MWFC) |
| | G-BTXD | Rans S.6-ESA Coyote II | M. Isterling |
| | G-BTXF | Cameron V-90 balloon | Gone With The Wind Ltd |
| | G-BTXH | Colt AS-56 airship | Huntair Ltd |
| | G-BTXI | Noorduyn AT-16 Harvard IIB | Patina Ltd/Duxford |
| | G-BTXK | Thunder Ax7-65 balloon | E. J. Jacobs |
| | G-BTXM | Colt 21A balloon | Airship & Balloon Co Ltd |
| | G-BTXN | BAe 146-300 | Trident Aviation Leasing Services Ltd |
| | G-BTXP | Cameron RX-100 balloon | Cameron Balloons Ltd |
| | G-BTXR | Cassutt Racer | J. Cull/Popham |
| | G-BTXS | Cameron O-120 balloon | Southern Balloon Group |
| | G-BTXT | Maule MXT-7-180 | R. G. Humphries |
| | G-BTXU | Cameron A-210 balloon | P. J. D. Kerr & A. J. Street |
| | G-BTXV | Cameron A-210 balloon | The Ballooning Business Ltd |
| | G-BTXW | Cameron V-77 balloon | K. W. Scott |
| | G-BTXX | Bellanca 8KCAB Decathlon | Sherwood Flying Club Ltd |
| | G-BTXZ | Zenair CH.250 | B. F. Arnall |
| | G-BTYC | Cessna 150L | JJ Aviation |
| | G-BTYD | Cameron N-90 balloon | S. J. Colin |
| | G-BTYE | Cameron A-180 balloon | Fight Flight |
| | G-BTYF | Thunder Ax10-180 S2 balloon | Champagne Flights International Ltd |
| | G-BTYH | Pottier P.80S | R. Pickett |
| | G-BTYI | PA-28-181 Archer II | Premier Flight Services Ltd |
| | G-BTYJ | Schleicher ASH.25 | T. I. Gardiner |
| | G-BTYK | Cessna 310R | R. J. Lane & D. R. C. Knight |
| | G-BTYL | Hunter T.7 | Cubitt Aviation Ltd/Foulsham |
| | G-BTYT | Cessna 152 | M. J. Green |
| | G-BTYV | Fokker Dr.1 (replica) (152/17) | A. E. Hutton/North Weald |
| | G-BTYW | Cessna 120 | P. J. Singleton & C. J. Archer |
| | G-BTYX | Cessna 140 | P. J. Singleton & C. J. Archer |
| | G-BTYY | Curtiss Robin C-2 | R. R. L. Windus |
| | G-BTYZ | Colt 210A balloon | T. M. Donnelly |
| | G-BTZA | Beech F33A Bonanza | G-BTZA Group/Edinburgh |
| | G-BTZB | Yakovlev Yak-50 | Patina Ltd/Duxford |
| | G-BTZC | Colt 90A balloon | P. J. Harlow |
| | G-BTZD | Yakovlev Yak-1 | Historic Aircraft Collection Ltd |
| | G-BTZE | LET Yakovlev C.11 | Bianchi Aviation Film Services Ltd/Booker |
| | G-BTZF | Boeing 737-204ADV | Britannia Airways Ltd *Sir Alliot Verdon Roe* (G-BKHF)/Luton |
| | G-BTZL | Oldfield Baby Lakes | J. M. Roach |
| | G-BTZO | SOCATA TB.20 Trinidad | C.S.E. Aviation Ltd/Kidlington |
| | G-BTZP | SOCATA TB.9 Tampico | C.S.E. Aviation Ltd/Kidlington |
| | G-BTZR | Colt 77B balloon | P. J. Fell |
| | G-BTZS | Colt 77B balloon | Thunder & Colt Ltd |
| | G-BTZU | Cameron Concept SS balloon | Gone With The Wind Ltd |
| | G-BTZV | Cameron V-77 balloon | A. W. Sumner |
| | G-BTZW | Piper J-3C-65 Cub | D. A. Woodhams |
| | G-BTZX | Piper J-3C-65 Cub | D. A. Woodhams & J. T. Coulthard |
| | G-BTZY | Colt 56A balloon | T. M. Donnelly |
| | G-BTZZ | CFM Streak Shadow | D. R. Stennett |
| | | | |
| | G-BUAA | Corben Bay Ace D | B. F. Hill |
| | G-BUAB | Aeronca 11AC Chief | J. Reed |
| | G-BUAC | Slingsby T.31 Motor Cadet III | D. A. Wilson |

| Reg. | Type | Owner or Operator | Notes |
|------|------|-------------------|-------|
| G-BUAD | Colt AS-105 Mk II airship | Thunder & Colt Ltd | |
| G-BUAE | Thunder Ax8-105 S2 balloon | T. Donnelly | |
| G-BUAF | Cameron N-77 balloon | S. J. Colin | |
| G-BUAG | Jodel D.18 | A. L. Silcox | |
| G-BUAH | Rotorway Executive 90 | I. L. Griffith | |
| G-BUAI | Everett Srs 3 gyroplane | P. Stanlake | |
| G-BUAJ | Cameron N-90 balloon | J. R. & S. J. Huggins | |
| G-BUAK | Thunder Ax8-105 S2 balloon | G. D. & L. Fitzpatrick | |
| G-BUAL | Colt 105A balloon | H. C. J. Williams | |
| G-BUAM | Cameron V-77 balloon | Broadland Balloons Ltd | |
| G-BUAN | Cessna 172N | Bell Aviation | |
| G-BUAO | Luscombe 8A Silvaire | G. H. Matthews | |
| G-BUAR | V.S.358 Seafire IIIc (PP972) | Precious Metals Ltd | |
| G-BUAS | Thunder Ax10-180 S2 balloon | Scotair Balloons | |
| G-BUAT | Thunder Ax9-120 balloon | J. Fenton | |
| G-BUAU | Cameron A-180 balloon | GT Flying Club Ltd | |
| G-BUAV | Cameron O-105 balloon | K. D. Johnson | |
| G-BUAW | Pitts S-1C Special | E. J. Hedges | |
| G-BUAX | Rans S.10 Sakota | J. W. Topham | |
| G-BUAY | Cameron A-210 balloon | Ballooning World Ltd | |

G-BRVE, Beech D.17S. *AJW*

| Notes | Reg. | Type | Owner or Operator |
|---|---|---|---|
| | G-BUBA | PA-18 Super Cub 150 | B. Jackson |
| | G-BUBB | Light Aero Avid Flyer | D. Hookins |
| | G-BUBC | QAC Quickie Tri-Q.200 | D. J. Clarke |
| | G-BUBD | BN-2B-26 Islander | Pilatus BN Ltd/Bembridge |
| | G-BUBE | BN-2B-26 Islander | Pilatus BN Ltd/Bembridge |
| | G-BUBF | BN-2B-26 Islander | Pilatus BN Ltd/Bembridge |
| | G-BUBG | BN-2B-26 Islander | Pilatus BN Ltd/Bembridge |
| | G-BUBH | BN-2B-26 Islander | Pilatus BN Ltd/Bembridge |
| | G-BUBI | BN-2B-26 Islander | Pilatus BN Ltd/Bembridge |
| | G-BUBJ | BN-2B-26 Islander | Pilatus BN Ltd/Bembridge |
| | G-BUBK | BN-2B-26 Islander | Pilatus BN Ltd/Bembridge |
| | G-BUBL | Thunder Ax8-105 balloon | Moet & Chandon (London) Ltd |
| | G-BUBM | BN-2B-26 Islander | Pilatus BN Ltd/Bembridge |
| | G-BUBN | BN-2B-26 Islander | Pilatus BN Ltd/Bembridge |
| | G-BUBO | BN-2B-26 Islander | Pilatus BN Ltd/Bembridge |
| | G-BUBP | BN-2B-26 Islander | Pilatus BN Ltd/Bembridge |
| | G-BUBS | — | |
| | G-BUBT | Stoddard-Hamilton Glasair IIRGS | M. D. Evans |
| | G-BUBU | PA-34-220T Seneca III | Brinor (Holdings) Ltd/Ipswich |
| | G-BUBW | Robinson R-22B | Forth Helicopters |
| | G-BUBX | Cameron O-120 balloon | Wheathill Leisure Ltd |
| | G-BUBY | Thunder Ax8-105 S2 balloon | T. M. Donnelly |
| | G-BUCA | Cessna A.150K | A. Bucknole |
| | G-BUCB | Cameron H-34 balloon | Flying Pictures (Balloons) Ltd |
| | G-BUCC | C.A.S.A. 1.131E Jungmann (BU+EM) | E. J. F. McEntee (G-BUEM) |
| | G-BUCD | Colt 120A balloon | Bavarian Balloon Co Ltd |
| | G-BUCG | Schleicher ASW.20L (modified) | W. B. Andrews |
| | G-BUCH | Stinson V-77 Reliant | Rare Aeroplane Soc |
| | G-BUCI | Auster AOP.9 (XP242) | Historic Aircraft Flight Reserve Collection/ Middle Wallop |
| | G-BUCJ | D.H.C.2 Beaver 1 (XP772) | Historic Aircraft Flight Reserve Collection/ Middle Wallop |
| | G-BUCK | C.A.S.A. 1.131E Jungmann (BU+CK) | Jungmann Flying Group/White Waltham |
| | G-BUCL | Robinson R-22B | Crispian Motor Co Ltd |
| | G-BUCM | Hawker Sea Fury FB.11 | Patina Ltd/Duxford |
| | G-BUCO | Pietenpol Air Camper | A. James |
| | G-BUCP | BAe 125 Srs 800B | CIBC Finance Ltd |
| | G-BUCS | Cessna 150F | A. Bucknole |
| | G-BUCT | Cessna 150L | A. Bucknole |
| | G-BUDA | Slingsby T.61F Venture T.2 | RAF Germany Gliding Association |
| | G-BUDB | Slingsby T.61F Venture T.2 | RAF Germany Gliding Association |
| | G-BUDC | Slingsby T.61F Venture T.2 | D. Collinson |
| | G-BUDD | Team Minimax Z | M. A. J. Hutt (G-MWZM) |
| | G-BUDE | PA-22 Tri-Pacer 135 (tailwheel) | B. A. Bower/Thruxton |
| | G-BUDF | Rand-Robinson KR-2 | J. B. McNab |
| | G-BUDH | Light Aero Avid Flyer | D. Cowen |
| | G-BUDI | Aero Designs Pulsar | R. W. L. Oliver |
| | G-BUDK | Thunder Ax7-77 balloon | C. J. Warriner |
| | G-BUDL | Auster 3 | M. Pocock |
| | G-BUDM | Colt Flying Hand SS balloon | BIAS (UK) Ltd |
| | G-BUDN | Cameron 30 Shoe SS balloon | Converse Europe Ltd |
| | G-BUDO | PZL-110 Koliber 150 | P. C. Dimond |
| | G-BUDR | Denney Aerocraft Kitfox Mk 3 | N. J. Wills |
| | G-BUDS | Rand Robinson KR-2 | D. W. Munday |
| | G-BUDT | Slingsby T.61F Venture T.2 | G-BUDT Group |
| | G-BUDU | Cameron V-77 balloon | T. M. G. Amery |
| | G-BUDV | Cameron A-210 balloon | Bridges Van Hire Ltd |
| | G-BUDW | Brügger MB.2 Colibri | J. M. Hoblyn |
| | G-BUDX | Boeing 757-236 | Ambassador Airlines Ltd/Nationair (C-FNXY) |
| | G-BUDY | Colt 17A balloon | Bondbaste Ltd |
| | G-BUDZ | Boeing 757-236 | Ambassador Airlines Ltd |
| | G-BUEA | Aerospatiale ATR-42-300 | CityFlyer Express Ltd/Gatwick |
| | G-BUEB | Aerospatiale ATR-42-300 | CityFlyer Express Ltd/Gatwick |
| | G-BUEC | Van's RV-6 | D. W. Richardson & R. D. Harper |
| | G-BUED | Slingsby T.61F Venture T.2 | SE Kent Civil Service Flying Club |
| | G-BUEE | Cameron A-210 balloon | Bristol Balloons |
| | G-BUEF | Cessna 152 | Three Counties Aero Engineering Ltd/ Lasham |
| | G-BUEG | Cessna 152 | Three Counties Aero Engineering Ltd/ Lasham |

| Reg. | Type | Owner or Operator | Notes |
|------|------|-------------------|-------|
| G-BUEI | Thunder Ax8-105 balloon | Anglia Balloons | |
| G-BUEJ | Colt 77B balloon | P. M. Taylor | |
| G-BUEK | Slingsby T.61F Venture T.2 | P. B. Duhig & W. Retzler | |
| G-BUEL | Colt Bottle II SS balloon | Jentime Ltd | |
| G-BUEN | VPM M.14 Scout | A. T. Wortley | |
| G-BUEO | Maule MX-7-180 | Aeromarine Ltd | |
| G-BUEP | Maule MX-7-180 | Aeromarine Ltd | |
| G-BUER | Robinson R-22B | Masters Managerial Services Ltd | |
| G-BUES | Cameron N-77 balloon | Bath City Council-Parks Section | |
| G-BUET | Colt Flying Drinks Can SS balloon | Flying Pictures (Balloons) Ltd | |
| G-BUEU | Colt 21A balloon | Flying Pictures (Balloons) Ltd | |
| G-BUEW | Rans S.6 Coyote II | D. J. O'Gorman (G-MWYF) | |
| G-BUEX | Schweizer 269C | Ollier Aviation Ltd (G-HFLR) | |
| G-BUEZ | Hunter F.6A | Old Flying Machine Co Ltd/Duxford | |
| G-BUFA | Cameron R-77 balloon | Noble Advertures Ltd | |
| G-BUFB | Cameron R-77 balloon | Noble Advertures Ltd | |
| G-BUFC | Cameron R-77 balloon | Noble Advertures Ltd | |
| G-BUFD | Cameron R-77 balloon | Noble Advertures Ltd | |
| G-BUFE | Cameron R-77 balloon | Noble Advertures Ltd | |
| G-BUFG | Slingsby T.61F Venture T.2 | P. K. J. Spencer & R. I. Davidson | |
| G-BUFH | PA-28-161 Warrior II | A. Tootell | |
| G-BUFI | BAe 146-100 | British Aerospace PLC | |
| G-BUFJ | Cameron V-90 balloon | Whitebread Hop Farm | |
| G-BUFK | Cassutt Racer IIIM | D. I. H. Johnstone & W. T. Barnard | |
| G-BUFL | BAe Jetstream 3102 | British Aerospace PLC | |
| G-BUFN | Slingsby T.61F Venture T.2 | BUFN Group | |
| G-BUFO | Cameron 70 UFO SS balloon | Airship & Balloon Co Ltd | |
| G-BUFP | Slingsby T.61F Venture T.2 | Venture Group | |
| G-BUFR | Slingsby T.61F Venture T.2 | Marchington Gliding Club Ltd | |
| G-BUFT | Cameron O-120 balloon | Hot Airlines Ltd | |
| G-BUFU | Colt 105A balloon | Basemore Ltd | |
| G-BUFV | Light Aero Avid Flyer | S. C. Ord | |
| G-BUFX | Cameron N-90 balloon | Kerridge Computer Co Ltd | |
| G-BUFY | PA-28-161 Warrior II | B. Powell/Biggin Hill | |
| G-BUGA | — | | |
| G-BUGB | Stolp SA.750 Acroduster Too | D. Burnham | |
| G-BUGC | Jurca MJ.5 Sirocco | A. Burani (G-BWDJ) | |
| G-BUGD | Cameron V-77 balloon | Cameron Balloons Ltd | |
| G-BUGE | Bellanca 7GCAA Cltabria | Welsh Dragon Aviation Ltd | |
| G-BUGF | Cameron A-210 balloon | Adventure Ballooning | |
| G-BUGG | Cessna 150F | A. Passfield | |
| G-BUGH | Rans S.10 Sakota | D. T. Smith | |
| G-BUGI | Evans VP-2 | R. G. Boyes | |
| G-BUGJ | Robin DR.400/180 | Alfred Graham Ltd | |
| G-BUGL | Slngisby T.61F Venture T.2 | VMG Group | |
| G-BUGM | CFM Streak Shadow | J. A. & W. J. de Gier | |
| G-BUGN | Colt 210A balloon | Balloon Club of GB Ltd | |
| G-BUGO | Colt 56B balloon | D. W. & P. Allum | |
| G-BUGP | Cameron V-77 balloon | G. J. & R. Plant | |
| G-BUGR | — | | |
| G-BUGS | Cameron V-77 balloon | A Load of Hot Air | |
| G-BUGT | Slingsby T.61F Venture T.2 | J. F. R. Jones | |
| G-BUGU | | | |
| G-BUGV | Slingsby T.61F Venture T.2 | J. E. Doleac | |
| G-BUGW | Slingsby T.61F Venture T.2 | F. W. Cater & Son Ltd | |
| G-BUGX | M.S.880B Rallye Club | The Rallye Group | |
| G-BUGY | Cameron V-65 balloon | Dante Balloon Group | |
| G-BUGZ | Slingsby T.61F Venture T.2 | Dishforth Flying Club | |
| G-BUHA | Slingsby T.61F Venture T.2 | A. W. Swales | |
| G-BUHB | BAe 146-300 | Trident Aviation Leasing Services Ltd (G-BSYS) | |
| G-BUHC | BAe 146-300 | Trident Aviation Leasing Services Ltd (G-BTMI) | |
| G-BUHD | BAe 146-300 | — | |
| G-BUHE | BAe 146-300 | — | |
| G-BUHF | BAe 146-300 | — | |
| G-BUHG | BAe 146-300 | — | |
| G-BUHH | — | | |
| G-BUHI | Boeing 737- | — | |
| G-BUHJ | Boeing 737- | — | |
| G-BUHK | Boeing 737-4Q8 | — | |
| G-BUHL | Boeing 737- | — | |
| G-BUHM | Cameron V-77 balloon | L. A. Watts | |

| Notes | Reg. | Type | Owner or Operator |
|---|---|---|---|
| | G-BUHN | Cameron N-90 balloon | Cameron Balloons Ltd |
| | G-BUHO | Cessna 140 | D. F. Cumberlidge |
| | G-BUHP | Flyair 1100 | R. White |
| | G-BUHR | Slingsby T.61F Venture T.2 | Lleweni Parc Ltd |
| | G-BUHS | Stoddard-Hamilton Glasair SH-TD-1 | S. J. Marsh |
| | G-BUHT | Cameron A-210 balloon | British School of Ballooning |
| | G-BUHU | Cameron N-105 balloon | Flying Pictures (Balloons) Ltd |
| | G-BUHW | BAe 146-300 | British Aerospace PLC |
| | G-BUHX | Robinson R-22B | Rotaflite Helicopter Sales |
| | G-BUHY | Cameron A-210 balloon | Adventure Balloon Co Ltd |
| | G-BUHZ | Cessna 120 | N. R. Hunt |
| | G-BUIA | Colt 77B balloon | R. A. Riley |
| | G-BUIB | MBB Bo 105DBS/4 | Bond Helicopters Ltd (G-BDYZ) |
| | G-BUIC | Denney Aerocraft Kitfox Mk 2 | C. R. Northrop & B. M. Chilvers |
| | G-BUID | BAe 125 Srs 800B | Corporate Jets Ltd/Hatfield |
| | G-BUIE | Cameron N-90 balloon | Flying Pictures (Balloons) Ltd |
| | G-BUIF | PA-28-161 Warior II | Newcastle upon Tyne Aero Club Ltd |
| | G-BUIG | Campbell Cricket | T. A. Holmes |
| | G-BUIH | Slingsby T.61F Venture T.2 | Yorkshire Gliding Club (Pty) Ltd |
| | G-BUII | Cameron A-210 balloon | Aire Valley Balloons |
| | G-BUIJ | PA-28-161 Warrior II | Tradecliff Ltd |
| | G-BUIK | PA-28-161 Warrior II | I. H. Webb |
| | G-BUIL | CFM Streak Shadow | P. N. Bevan & L. M. Poor |
| | G-BUIM | BAe 125 Srs 800B | United Bank of Kuwait PLC |
| | G-BUIN | Thunder Ax7-77 balloon | Free Flight Aerostat Group |
| | G-BUIO | BAe Jetstream 3202 | Barclays Canada Leasing Corporation |
| | G-BUIP | Denney Aerocraft Kitfox Mk 2 | Avcomm Developments Ltd |
| | G-BUIR | Light Aero Avid Speedwing Mk 4 | K. N. Pollard |
| | G-BUIS | Rotorway Executive 90 | Exec Helicopters Ltd |
| | G-BUIT | Denney Aerocraft Kitfox Mk 3 | S. Collins |
| | G-BUIU | Cameron V-90 balloon | Prescott Hot Air Balloons Ltd |
| | G-BUIV | SA.313B Alouette II | M. & P. Food Products Ltd |
| | G-BUIW | Robinson R-22B | Findon Air Services/Shoreham |
| | G-BUIX | BAe 125-1000B | Corporate Jets Ltd/Hatfield |
| | G-BUIY | BAe 125 Srs 800B | Corporate Jets Ltd/Hatfield |
| | G-BUIZ | Cameron N-90 balloon | Airship & Balloon Co Ltd |
| | G-BUJA | Slingsby T.61F Venture T.2 | RAFGSA/Bicester |
| | G-BUJB | Slingsby T.61F Venture T.2 | Falke Syndicate |
| | G-BUJC | Partenavia P.68C | Intradco Cargo Services Ltd |
| | G-BUJD | Robinson R-22B | Ocean Shields Ltd |
| | G-BUJE | Cessna 177B | Chartwade Ltd/Blackbushe |
| | G-BUJF | AS.355N Twin Squirrel | McAlpine Helicopters Ltd/Hayes |
| | G-BUJG | AS.350B-2 Ecureuil | R. J. & E. M. Frost (G-HEAR) |
| | G-BUJH | Colt 77B balloon | A. D. Watt & ptnrs |
| | G-BUJI | Slingsby T.61F Venture T.2 | F. J. Shevill |
| | G-BUJJ | Light Aero Avid Flyer | A. C. Debrett |
| | G-BUJK | Montgomerie-Bensen B.8MR | J. M. Montgomerie |
| | G-BUJL | Aero Designs Pulsar | J. J. Lynch |
| | G-BUJM | Cessna 120 | De Cadenet Engineering Ltd/Shipdham |
| | G-BUJN | Cessna 172N | De Cadenet Engineering Ltd/Shipdham |
| | G-BUJO | PA-28-161 Warrior II | De Cadenet Engineering Ltd/Shipdham |
| | G-BUJP | PA-28-161 Warrior II | De Cadenet Engineering Ltd/Shipdham |
| | G-BUJR | Cameron A-180 balloon | W. I. Hooker & C. Parker |
| | G-BUJS | Colt 17A balloon | Thunder & Colt Ltd |
| | G-BUJT | BAe Jetstream 3100 | British Aerospace PLC/Prestwick |
| | G-BUJU | Cessna 150H | T. F. Slowen |
| | G-BUJV | Light Aero Avid Speedwing Mk 4 | D. N. Anderson |
| | G-BUJW | Thunder Ax8-90 balloon | R. T. Fagan |
| | G-BUJX | Slingsby T.61F Venture T.2 | Glaser-Dirks UK/Rufforth |
| | G-BUJY | D.H.82A Tiger Moth | Aero Vintage Ltd |
| | G-BUJZ | Rotorway Executive 90 | T. W. Aisthorpe & R. J. D. Crick |
| | G-BUKA | Fairchild SA227AC Metro III | Air Corbière Ltd/Coventry |
| | G-BUKB | Rans S.10 Sakota | M. K. Blatch & M. P. Lee |
| | G-BUKC | Cameron A-180 balloon | Cloud Nine Balloon Co |
| | G-BUKE | Boeing Stearman A.75N1 | R. G. Rance |
| | G-BUKF | Denney Aerocraft Kitfox Mk 4 | M. R. Crosland |
| | G-BUKG | Robinson R-22B | Streamline Aviation Ltd |
| | G-BUKH | D.31 Turbulent | J. S. Smith |
| | G-BUKI | Thunder Ax7-77 balloon | Adventure Aloft |
| | G-BUKK | Bucker Bu133 Jungmeister (U-80) | E. J. F. McEntee/White Waltham |
| | G-BUKL | Brantly B.2B | Helihire Ltd |
| | G-BUKM | Pilatus P3-05 | A. L. Hall-Carpenter/Shipdham |

| Reg. | Type | Owner or Operator | Notes |
|------|------|-------------------|-------|
| G-BUKN | PA-15 Vagabond | M. R. Masters | |
| G-BUKO | Cessna 120 | N. G. Abbott | |
| G-BUKP | Denney Aerocraft Kitfox Mk 2 | T. D. Reid | |
| G-BUKR | M.S.880B Rallye Club 100T | D. Sharp | |
| G-BUKS | Colt 77B balloon | R. & M. Bairstow | |
| G-BUKT | Luscombe 8A Silvaire | R. C. Steel | |
| G-BUKU | Luscombe 8E Silvaire | R. C. Steel | |
| G-BUKV | Colt AS-105 Mk II airship | Magictheme Management Ltd | |
| G-BUKX | PA-28-161 Warrior II | Creswick Air Ltd | |
| G-BUKY | CCF Harvard IVM | P. R. Monk & A. C. Savage | |
| G-BUKZ | Evans VP-2 | P. R. Farnell | |
| G-BULA | Cameron 77 Raindrop SS balloon | Cameron Balloons Ltd | |
| G-BULB | Thunder Ax7-77 balloon | Shiltons of Rothbury | |
| G-BULC | Light Aero Avid Flyer Mk 4 | A. G. Batchelor | |
| G-BULD | Cameron N-105 balloon | S. D. Baker | |
| G-BULE | Price TPB.2 balloon | A. G. R. Calder | |
| G-BULF | Colt 77A balloon | M. V. Farrant | |
| G-BULG | Van's RV-4 | J. R. Ware | |
| G-BULH | Cessna 172N | B. R. Gaunt | |
| G-BULI | BAe 125-1000B | Corporate Jets Ltd/Hatfield | |
| G-BULJ | CFM Steak Shadow | C. C. Brown | |
| G-BULK | Thunder Ax9-120 S2 balloon | Rapidflame Ltd | |
| G-BULL | SA Bulldog 120/128 | J. D. Richardson | |
| G-BULM | Aero Designs Pulsar | W. R. Davis-Smith | |
| G-BULN | Colt 210A balloon | H. G. Davies | |
| G-BULO | Luscombe 8A Silvaire | J. R. Kimberley | |
| G-BULP | Thunder Ax9-120 S2 balloon | Regency Balloons Ltd | |
| G-BULR | PA-28 Cherokee 140 | Peter Collier Aviation Ltd/Ipswich | |
| G-BULS | Cameron A-210 balloon | Airship & Balloon Co Ltd | |
| G-BULT | Campbell Cricket | A. T. Pocklington | |
| G-BULU | Short S.312 Tucano T.1 | Short Bros PLC/Belfast City | |
| G-BULV | Aeronca 11AC Chief | M. R. Masters | |
| G-BULW | Rans S.10 Sakota | V. G. Gale | |
| G-BULX | Robinson R-22B | Sloane Helicopters Ltd/Sywell | |
| G-BULY | Light Aero Avid Flyer | M. O. Breen | |
| G-BULZ | Denney Aerocraft Kitfox Mk 2 | D. J. Dumolo & C. R. Barnes | |
| G-BUMP | PA-28-181 Archer II | M. Dunlop | |
| G-BUNB | Slingsby T.61F Venture T.2 | RAFGSA Cranwell Gliding Club | |
| G-BUNC | PZL-104 Wilga 35 | R. R. Walters | |
| G-BUND | PA-28RT-201T Turbo Arrow IV | W. S. Stanley | |
| G-BUNE | Colt Flying Drinks Can SS balloon | Pepsi Cola Overseas Ltd | |
| G-BUNF | Colt Flying Drinks Can SS balloon | Pepsi Cola Overseas Ltd | |
| G-BUNG | Cameron N-77 balloon | T. S. King | |
| G-BUNH | PA-28RT-201T Turbo Arrow IV | A. Tootell | |
| G-BUNI | Cameron 90 Bunny SS balloon | Virgin Airship & Balloon Co Ltd | |
| G-BUNJ | Squarecraft SA.102-5 Cavalier | J. A. Smith | |
| G-BUNL | H.S.125 Srs 700B | Corporate Jets Ltd/Hatfield | |
| G-BUNM | Denney Aerocraft Kitfox Mk 3 | P. J. Carter | |
| G-BUNN | Whittaker MW.6-S Fatboy Flyer | M. R. Grunwell | |
| G-BUNO | Lancair 320 | J. Softley | |
| G-BUNR | PA-34-200T Seneca II | Impatex Air Service Ltd | |
| G-BUNS | Cessna F.150K | R. W. H. Cole | |
| G-BUNT | AIA Stampe SV-4C | J. F. Graham (G-AYCK) | |
| G-BUNU | Bell 206L-3 LongRanger 3 | Forward Trust Ltd (G-GWIN) | |
| G-BUNV | Thunder Ax7-77 balloon | P. J. Waller | |
| G-BUNW | BAe 125-1000B | Corporate Jets Ltd/Hatfield | |
| G-BUNX | Cameron V-77 balloon | J. H. Bailey | |
| G-BUNZ | Thunder Ax10-180 S2 balloon | T. M. Donnelly | |
| G-BUOA | Whittaker MW.6-S Fatboy Flyer | D. A. Izod | |
| G-BUOB | CFM Streak Shadow | A. M. Simmons | |
| G-BUOC | Cameron A-210 balloon | G. N. & K. A. Connolly | |
| G-BUOD | SE-5A (replica) | M. D. Waldron | |
| G-BUOE | Cameron V-90 balloon | Dusters & Co | |
| G-BUOF | D.62B Condor | K. Jones | |
| G-BUOG | Colt 90A balloon | Scotair Balloons | |
| G-BUOH | Jet Hawk Ducted Fan Trainer | C. Herbert | |
| G-BUOI | PA-20 Pacer | L. G. Applebeck | |
| G-BUOJ | Cessna 172N | Skytronics Ltd | |
| G-BUOK | Rans S.6-ESA Coyote II | M. Morris | |
| G-BUOL | Denney Aerocraft Kitfox Mk 3 | J. G. D. Barbour | |
| G-BUOM | D.H.C.6 Twin Otter 210 | Baltic Asset Finance Ltd (G-DOSH) | |
| G-BUON | Light Aero Avid Aerobat | I. A. J. Lappin | |
| G-BUOO | — | — | |

| Notes | Reg. | Type | Owner or Operator |
|-------|------|------|-------------------|
| | G-BUOP | Skycycle D.2 airship | G. E. Dorrington |
| | G-BUOR | C.A.S.A. 1-131E Jungmann 2000 | M. J. Aherne |
| | G-BUOS | V.S.394 Spitfire FR.XVIII | A. J. Reynard & Park Avenue Investments Ltd |
| | G-BUOT | Colt 77A balloon | Thunder & Colt Ltd |
| | G-BUOU | Colt 90A balloon | Thunder & Colt Ltd |
| | G-BUOW | Aero Designs Pulsar XP | M. P. Allinson |
| | G-BUOX | Cameron V-77 balloon | R. M. Pursey & C. M. Richardson |
| | G-BUOY | SA.315B Alouette III | Dollar Air Services Ltd/Coventry |
| | G-BUOZ | Thunder Ax10-180 balloon | Ashleader Ltd |
| | G-BUPA | Rutan LongEz | M. D. Faiers |
| | G-BUPB | Stolp SA.300 Starduster Too | Nationwide Aerial Promotions Ltd |
| | G-BUPC | Rollason Beta B.2 | C. A. Rolph |
| | G-BUPD | Cameron N-90 balloon | Cameron Balloons Ltd |
| | G-BUPE | Cameron N-90 balloon | Cameron Balloons Ltd |
| | G-BUPF | Bensen B.8R | G. M. Hobman |
| | G-BUPG | Cessna 180K | T. P. A. Norman |
| | G-BUPH | Colt 25A balloon | Wellfarrow Ltd |
| | G-BUPI | Cameron V-77 balloon | S. A. Masey (G-BOUC) |
| | G-BUPJ | Fournier RF-4D | M. R. Shelton |
| | G-BUPK | AS.350B Ecureuil | L. Keating |
| | G-BUPM | VPM M.16 Tandem Trainer | A. T. Wortley |
| | G-BUPN | PA-46-350P Malibu | K. Fletcher/Coventry |
| | G-BUPO | Zlin Z.526F | Aerobuild Ltd/Gransden |
| | G-BUPP | Cameron V-42 balloon | J. A. Hibberd |
| | G-BUPR | Jodel D.18 | R. W. Burrows |
| | G-BUPS | Aérospatiale ATR-42-300 | CityFlyer Express Ltd/Gatwick |
| | G-BUPT | Cameron O-105 balloon | Chiltern Balloons |
| | G-BUPU | Thunder Ax7-77 balloon | R. C. Barkworth & D. G. Maguire |
| | G-BUPV | Great Lakes 2T-1A | R. J. Fray |
| | G-BUPW | Denney Aerocraft Kitfox Mk 3 | D. Sweet |
| | G-BUPX | Robin DR.400/180 | Ambrion Aviation Engineering/Leavesden |
| | G-BUPY | Commander 114B | CB Helicopters |
| | G-BUPZ | Colt AS-105 Mk II airship | Thunder & Colt Ltd |
| | G-BURA | Thunder Ax8-105 S2 balloon | Airship Shop Ltd |
| | G-BURB | Denney Aerocraft Kitfox Mk 3 | G. J. Langston |
| | G-BURC | — | — |
| | G-BURD | Cessna F.172N | RJS Aviation Ltd |
| | G-BURE | Jodel D.9 | L. J. Kingsford |
| | G-BURF | Rand KR-2 | P. J. H. Moorhouse & B. L. Hewart |
| | G-BURG | Colt 77A balloon | S. J. Humphreys |
| | G-BURH | Cessna 150E | J. J. Woodhouse |
| | G-BURI | Enstrom F-28C | F. B. Holben |
| | G-BURJ | H.S.748 Srs 2A | Clewer Aviation Ltd |
| | G-BURK | Luscombe 8A Silvaire | M. Stow |
| | G-BURL | Colt 105A balloon | Scotia Balloons Ltd |
| | G-BURM | Canberra TT.18 | A. R. Mitchell |
| | G-BURN | Cameron O-120 balloon | I. Bentley |
| | G-BURO | PZL-104 Wilga 80 | S. F. Elvins |
| | G-BURP | Rotorway Executive 90 | A. G. A. Edwards |
| | G-BURR | Auster AOP.9 | R. P. D. Folkes |
| | G-BURS | Sikorsky S-76A | Lynton Aviation Ltd (G-OHTL) |
| | G-BURT | PA-28-161 Warrior II | I. P. Stockwell |
| | G-BURU | BAe Jetstream 3202 | British Aerospace PLC |
| | G-BURV | BAe 125 Srs 800B | Corporate Jets Ltd |
| | G-BURW | Light Aero Avid Speedwing | A. Charlton |
| | G-BURX | Re-registered G-NPNP | |
| | G-BURY | Cessna 152 | M. L. Grunnill |
| | G-BURZ | Hawker Nimrod | Aero Vintage Ltd |
| | G-BUSA | — | — |
| | G-BUSB | Airbus A.320-111 | British Airways |
| | G-BUSC | Airbus A.320-111 | British Airways |
| | G-BUSD | Airbus A.320-111 | British Airways |
| | G-BUSE | Airbus A.320-111 | British Airways *Isles of Scilly* |
| | G-BUSF | Airbus A.320-111 | British Airways |
| | G-BUSG | Airbus A.320-211 | British Airways |
| | G-BUSH | Airbus A.320-211 | British Airways |
| | G-BUSI | Airbus A.320-211 | British Airways *Isle of Anglesey* |
| | G-BUSJ | Airbus A.320-211 | British Airways *Island of Sark* |
| | G-BUSK | Airbus A.320-211 | British Airways *Island of Guernsey* |
| | G-BUSL | Boeing 737-33A | TNT European Airlines Ltd |
| | G-BUSM | Boeing 737-33A | TNT European Airlines Ltd |
| | G-BUSN | Rotorway Executive 90 | B. Seymour |

| Reg. | Type | Owner or Operator | Notes |
|------|------|-------------------|-------|
| G-BUSP | Cameron Cart SS balloon | Cameron Balloons Ltd | |
| G-BUSR | Aero Designs Pulsar | S. S. Bateman & R. A. Watts | |
| G-BUSS | Cameron 90 Bus SS balloon | A. G. E. Faulkner | |
| G-BUST | Lancair IV | C. C. Butt | |
| G-BUSU | Colt 42A balloon | Thunder & Colt Ltd | |
| G-BUSV | Colt 105A balloon | Thunder & Colt Ltd | |
| G-BUSW | R. Commander 114 | K. Costello | |
| G-BUSX | Learjet 35A | Skytech Aviation Services Ltd (G-NEVL) | |
| G-BUSY | Thunder Ax6-56A balloon | M. S. Drinkwater | |
| G-BUSZ | Light Aero Avid Speedwing Mk 4 | G. N. S. Farrant | |
| G-BUTA | C.A.S.A. 1-131E Jungmann 2000 | K. D. Dunkerley | |
| G-BUTB | CFM Streak Shadow | F. A. H. Ashmead | |
| G-BUTC | Cyclone AX3/582 | N. R. Beale (G-MYHO) | |
| G-BUTD | Van's RV-6 | N. Reddish | |
| G-BUTE | Anderson EA-1 Kingfisher | T. C. Crawford (G-BRCK) | |
| G-BUTF | Aeronca 11AC Chief | M. R. Masters | |
| G-BUTG | Zenair CH.601HD | J. M. Scott | |
| G-BUTH | — | — | |
| G-BUTI | Firefly 7-15 balloon | A. C. Debrett | |
| G-BUTJ | Cameron O-77 balloon | A. J. A. Bubb | |
| G-BUTK | Rebel | D. Webb | |
| G-BUTL | PA-24 Comanche 250 | D. Buttle (G-ARLB)/Blackbushe | |
| G-BUTM | Rans S.6-116 | M. Rudd | |
| G-BUTN | MBB Bo 105DBS/4 | Bond Helicopters Ltd | |
| G-BUTO | — | — | |
| G-BUTP | — | — | |
| G-BUTR | — | — | |
| G-BUTS | — | — | |
| G-BUTT | Cessna FA.150K | C. R. Guggenheim (G-AXSJ) | |
| G-BUTU | OA.7 Optica Srs 300 | FLS Aerospace (Lovaux) Ltd/Bournemouth | |
| G-BUTV | OA.7 Optica Srs 300 | FLS Aerospace (Lovaux) Ltd/Bournemouth | |
| G-BUTW | — | — | |
| G-BUTX | — | — | |
| G-BUTY | Brügger MB.2 Colibri | R. M. Lawday | |
| G-BUTZ | — | — | |
| G-BUUM | PA-28RT-201 Arrow IV | Bluebird Flying Group | |
| G-BUUT | Interavia 70TA | Aero Vintage Ltd | |
| G-BUYI | Thunder Ax7-77 balloon | Chelmsford Management Ltd | |
| G-BUZI | AS.355F-1 Twin Squirrel | Sarpedon Ltd | |
| G-BUZZ | AB-206B JetRanger | Crest Fame Ltd | |
| G-BVAH | Denney Aerocraft Kitfox Mk 3 | V. A. Hutchinson | |
| G-BVAN | M.S.892E Rallye 150 | C. D. Weiswall | |
| G-BVAX | Colt 77A balloon | Vax Appliances Ltd | |
| G-BVER | D.H.C.2 Beaver 1 (XV268) | A. F. Allen (G-BTDM) | |
| G-BVHM | PA-38-112 Tomahawk | Linkcrest Ltd (G-DCAN) | |
| G-BVMM | Robin HR.200/100 | M. G. Owne | |
| G-BVMZ | Robin HR.100/210 | Chiltern Handbags (London) Ltd | |
| G-BVNM | Boeing 737-4S3 | British Airways (G-BPKA) | |
| G-BVNN | Boeing 737-4S3 | British Airways (G-BPKB) | |
| G-BVNO | Boeing 737-4S3 | British Airways (G-BPKE) | |
| G-BVPI | Evans VP-1 | C. M. Gibson | |
| G-BVPM | Evans VP-2 | P. Marigold | |

# Out-of-Sequence Registrations

| Notes | Reg. | Type | Owner or Operator |
|---|---|---|---|
| | G-BWAC | Waco YKS-7 | J. R. D. Bygraves |
| | G-BWAS | PA-31-350 Navajo Chieftain | BWOC Ltd/Bristol |
| | G-BWAY | Beech A36 Bonanza | Vuewood Ltd |
| | G-BWBW | Cameron A-180 balloon | Ballooning World Ltd |
| | G-BWCI | Light Aero Avid Flyer | R. A. Kilvington |
| | G-BWDT | PA-34-220T Seneca II | A. J. Wickenden (G-BKHS) |
| | G-BWEC | Cassutt-Colson Variant | N. R. Thomason & M. P. J. Hill |
| | G-BWFJ | Evans VP-1 | G. F. Kennedy |
| | G-BWHY | Robinson R-22 | R. E. Benke |
| | G-BWJB | Thunder Ax8-105 balloon | Justerini & Brooks Ltd Whiskey J. & B. |
| | G-BWKK | Auster AOP.9 (XP279) | R. W. Fairless & D. R. White |
| | G-BWMA | Colt 105A balloon | Bristol & West Motor Auction Ltd |
| | G-BWMB | Jodel D.119 | K. Jarman & KM Services Ltd |
| | G-BWMP | Gulfstream 695A | R. B. Tyler (Plant) Ltd |
| | G-BWMR | Robinson R-22B | Bowmur Haulage Co Ltd |
| | G-BWOC | PA-31-350 Navajo Chieftain | BWOC Ltd |
| | G-BWSI | K&S SA.102.5 Cavalier | B. W. Shaw |
| | G-BWTX | PA-42-720 Cheyenne III | Broome & Wellington (Aviation) Ltd |
| | G-BWVE | Bell 206B JetRanger | Willow Vale Electronics Ltd (G-BOSX) |
| | G-BWWJ | Hughes 269C | Dave Nieman Models Ltd (G-BMYZ) |
| | G-BWWW | BAe Jetstream 3102 | British Aerospace PLC/Dunsfold |
| | G-BXAX | Cameron N-77 balloon | Flying Pictures Ltd |
| | G-BXPS | PA-23 Aztec 250C | N. H. Bailey (G-AYLI) |
| | G-BXVI | V.S.361 Spitfire F.XVI (RW386) | D. Arnold |
| | G-BYAA | Boeing 767-204ER | Britannia Airways Ltd/Luton |
| | G-BYAB | Boeing 767-204ER | Britannia Airways Ltd/Luton |
| | G-BYAC | Boeing 757-204ER | Britannia Airways Ltd/Luton |
| | G-BYAD | Boeing 757-204ER | Britannia Airways Ltd/Luton |
| | G-BYAE | Boeing 757-204ER | Britannia Airways Ltd/Luton |
| | G-BYAF | Boeing 757-204 | Britannia Airways Ltd/Luton |
| | G-BYAG | Boeing 757-204 | Britannic Airways Ltd/Luton |
| | G-BYAH | Boeing 757-204 | Britannia Airways Ltd/Luton |
| | G-BYAI | Boeing 757-204 | Britannia Airways Ltd/Luton |
| | G-BYAJ | Boeing 757-28AER | Britannia Airways Ltd/Luton |
| | G-BYAK | Boeing 757-28AER | Britannia Airways Ltd/Luton |
| | G-BYAL | Boeing 757-28AER | Britannia Airways Ltd/Luton |
| | G-BYEE | Mooney M.20K | Axe & Status Ltd |
| | G-BYIJ | C.A.S.A. 1-131E Jungmann 2000 | K. B. Palmer |
| | G-BYLL | F.8L Falco | N. J. Langrick/Sherburn |
| | G-BYLS | Bede BD-4 | G. H. Bayliss |
| | G-BYNG | Cessna T.303 | J. M. E. Byng (G-PTWB) |
| | G-BYOL | Cessna 340A | Jetline Ltd |
| | G-BYRD | Mooney M.20K | V. J. Holden/Teesside |
| | G-BYRE | Rans S.10 Sakota | R. J. & M. B. Trickey |
| | G-BYRN | PA-31-350 Navajo Chieftain | Byrne Group PLC (G-YLAN) |
| | G-BYSE | AB-206B JetRanger 2 | Bewise Ltd (G-BFND) |
| | G-BYSL | Cameron O-56 balloon | Charles of the Ritz Ltd |
| | G-BYTE | Robinson R-22B | Datel Electronics Ltd |
| | G-BZBH | Thunder Ax6-65 balloon | R. B. & G. Clarke |
| | G-BZKK | Cameron V-56 balloon | P. J. Green & C. Bosley Gemini II |
| | G-BZZZ | Enstrom F-28C-UK | Chartec Ltd (G-BBBZ) |
| | G-CAFZ | PA-31-350 Navajo Chieftain | London Flight Centre (Stansted) Ltd (G-BPPT) |
| | G-CALL | PA-23 Aztec 250F | Woodgate Aviation Ltd/Ronaldsway |
| | G-CALV | PA-39 Twin Comanche 160 C/R | Rhoburt Ltd (G-AZFO) |
| | G-CAMM | Hawker Cygnet (replica) | D. M. Cashmore |
| | G-CAPT | Taylor JT.2 Titch | V. W. B. Davies (G-BTJM) |
| | G-CARS | Pitts S-2A Special (replica) ★ | Toyota Ltd |
| | G-CAXF | Cameron O-77 balloon | R. D. & S. J. Sarjeant |
| | G-CAYN | Dornier Do.228-201 | Cayenne Ltd (G-MLNR) |
| | G-CBEA | BAe Jetstream 3102-01 | Brymon European Airways Ltd |
| | G-CBIL | Cessna 182K | K. A. Clarke/Newcastle |
| | G-CBJB | Sikorsky S-76A | Bond Helicopters Ltd |
| | G-CBKT | Cameron O-77 balloon | Caledonian Airways Ltd |
| | G-CBOR | Cessna F.172N | P. Seville |
| | G-CCAR | Cameron N-77 balloon | The Colt Car Co Ltd |
| | G-CCAT | AA-5A Cheetah | BLS Aviation Ltd (G-OAJH/G-KILT/ G-BJFA)/Elstree |

146

| Reg. | Type | Owner or Operator | Notes |
|------|------|-------------------|-------|
| G-CCCC | Cessna 172H | K. E. Wilson | |
| G-CCDI | Cameron N-77 balloon | Charles Church Developments PLC | |
| G-CCOL | AA-5A Cheetah | Lowlog Ltd (G-BIVU) | |
| G-CCON | Beech F33C Bonanza | P. J. Withinshaw | |
| G-CCOZ | Monnet Sonerai II | P. R. Cozens | |
| G-CCUB | Piper J-3C-65 Cub | Cormack (Aircraft Services) Ltd | |
| G-CCVV | V.S.379 Spitfire FR.XIV | Charles Church Displays Ltd | |
| G-CDBS | MBB Bo 105DBS | Bond Helicopters Ltd/Aberdeen | |
| G-CDET | Culver LCA Cadet | H. B. Fox/Booker | |
| G-CDGA | Taylor JT.1 Monoplane | R. M. Larimore | |
| G-CDGL | Saffery S.330 balloon | C. J. Dodd & G. J. Luckett *Penny* | |
| G-CDON | PA-28-161 Warrior II | East Midlands Flying Club PLC | |
| G-CDRU | C.A.S.A. 1-131E Jungmann | P. Cunniff/White Waltham | |
| G-CEAS | HPR-7 Herald 214 | Channel Express (Air Services) Ltd (G-BEBB)/Bournemouth | |
| G-CEGA | PA-34-200T Seneca II | Hendefern Ltd | |
| G-CEJA | Cameron V-77 balloon | N. L. Jaques (G-BTOF) | |
| G-CELL | PA-32R-301 Saratoga SP | CEL Electronics Ltd | |
| G-CERT | Mooney M.20K | Fairline Boats PLC/Conington | |
| G-CETC | Aeronca 15AC Sedan | J. W. Scale | |
| G-CEXP | HPR-7 Herald 209 | Channel Express (Air Services) Ltd (G-BFRJ)/Bournemouth | |
| G-CEXS | L.188C Electra | Channel Express (Air Services) Ltd/ Bournemouth | |
| G-CFBI | Colt 56A balloon | G. A. Fisher | |
| G-CFLT | AS.355F-1 Twin Squirrel | Osten Airfinance Ltd (G-BNBI) | |
| G-CFLY | Cessna 172F | I. Hughes & B. T. Williams | |
| G-CGCG | Robinson R-22B | J .M. Henderson | |
| G-CGHM | PA-28 Cherokee 140 | CGH Managements Ltd/Elstree | |
| G-CGOD | Cameron N-77 balloon | Abbey Plant Co Ltd | |
| G-CHAA | Cameron O-90 balloon | Cloudhoppers Ltd | |
| G-CHAL | Robinson R-22B | Cabair Helicopters Ltd/Elstree | |
| G-CHAM | Cameron 90 Pot SS balloon | Nestlé UK Ltd | |
| G-CHAR | Grob G.109B | RAFGSA/Bicester | |
| G-CHAS | PA-28-181 Archer II | C. H. Elliott | |
| G-CHEM | PA-34-200T Seneca II | ML Associates | |
| G-CHIK | Cessna F.152 | Stapleford Flying Club Ltd (G-BHAZ) | |
| G-CHIL | Robinson R-22HP | Skyline Helicopters Ltd | |
| G-CHIP | PA-28-181 Archer II | C. M. Hough/Fairoaks | |
| G-CHIS | Robinson R-22B | Bradmore Helicopter Leasing | |
| G-CHLT | Stemme S.10 | F. C. Y. Cheung/Hong Kong | |
| G-CHMP | Bellanca 7ECA Citabria | J. T. Parkins | |
| G-CHOK | Cameron V-77 balloon | K. W. Overton | |
| G-CHOP | Westland-Bell 47G-3B1 | Wessex Air Contracts Ltd | |
| G-CHRP | Colt Flying Book SS balloon | Chronicle Communications Ltd | |
| G-CHRR | Colt Flying Book SS balloon | Chronicle Communications Ltd | |
| G-CHSR | BAe 146-200 | British Aerospace PLC | |
| G-CHTA | AA-5A Cheetah | Rapid Spin Ltd (G-BFRC)/Biggin Hill | |
| G-CHTT | Varga 2150A Kachina | C.H.T. Trace | |
| G-CHUB | Colt N-51 balloon | Chubb Fire Security Ltd | |
| G-CHUK | Cameron O-77 balloon | Converse Europe Ltd | |
| G-CHYL | Robinson R-22B | L. M. Dresher | |
| G-CIAS | BN-2B-21 Islander | Channel Island Air Search Ltd (G-BKJM) | |
| G-CICI | Cameron R-15 balloon | Ballooning Endeavours Ltd | |
| G-CIII | Oldfield Baby Great Lakes | G. Cooper | |
| G-CIPI | AJEP Wittman W.8 Tailwind | G. J. Z. Cipirski (G-AYDU)/Biggin Hill | |
| G-CITI | Cessna 501 Citation | Messenger Group PLC | |
| G-CITY | PA-31-350 Navajo Chieftain | Woodgate Aviation Ltd/Ronaldsway | |
| G-CIVA | Boeing 747-436 | British Airways | |
| G-CIVB | Boeing 747-436 | British Airways | |
| G-CIVC | Boeing 747-436 | British Airways | |
| G-CJBC | PA-28 Cherokee 180 | J. B. Cave/Halfpenny Green | |
| G-CJCI | Pilatus P2-06 (CC+43) | Charles Church Displays Ltd | |
| G-CJET | Learjet 35A | Interflight (Learjet) Ltd (G-SEBE/G-ZIPS/ G-ZONE)/Gatwick | |
| G-CJIM | Taylor JT.1 Monoplane | J. Crawford | |
| G-CJUD | Denney Aerocraft Kitfox | C. W. Judge | |
| G-CJWS | PA-34-200T Seneca II | P. R. & M. R. Parr | |
| G-CKEN | Wombat autogyro | K. H. Durran | |
| G-CLAC | PA-28-161 Warrior II | J. D. Moonie | |
| G-CLEA | PA-28-161 Warrior II | Creative Logistics Enterprises & Aviation Ltd & R. J. Harrison | |

| Notes | Reg. | Type | Owner or Operator |
|---|---|---|---|
| | G-CLEM | Bo 208A2 Junior | A. W. Webster (G-ASWE) |
| | G-CLIC | Cameron N-105 balloon | Matrix Computer Maintenance Ltd |
| | G-CLIK | PA-18 Super Cub 95 | N. J. R. Empson/Ipswich |
| | G-CLIV | PA-28R-201T Turbo Arrow III | C. R. Harrisson |
| | G-CLOS | PA-34-200 Seneca II | Greenclose Aviation Services Ltd/ Bournemouth |
| | G-CLRL | Agusta A.109A-II | MDFC Asset Finance Ltd (G-EJCB) |
| | G-CLUB | Cessna FRA.150M | J. J. Woodhouse |
| | G-CLUE | PA-34-200T Seneca II | Bristol Office Machines Ltd |
| | G-CLUX | Cessna F.172N | J. & K. Aviation/Liverpool |
| | G-CLYV | Robinson R-22B | C. A. Ecroyd |
| | G-CMDR | R. Commander 114 | J. D. Hallahan & G. C. Bishop |
| | G-CMGC | PA-25 Pawnee 235 | Midland Gliding Club Ltd (G-BFEX) |
| | G-CNIS | Partenavia P.68B | Beechair Ltd (G-BJOF/G-PAUL) |
| | G-CNMF | BAe 146-200 | Air UK Ltd *Vincent Van Gogh*/Norwich |
| | G-COCO | Cessna F.172M | P. C. Sheard & R. C. Larder |
| | G-COES | McD Douglas MD-83 | Airtours International Aviation Ltd |
| | G-COIN | Bell 206B JetRanger 2 | British Helicopter Service |
| | G-COKE | Cameron O-65 balloon | M. C. Bradley |
| | G-COLA | Beech F33C Bonanza | John Bradley & Barry Ltd and J. A. Kelman (G-BUAZ) |
| | G-COLL | Enstrom 280C-UK-2 Shark | Estate Computer Systems Ltd |
| | G-COLR | Colt 69A balloon | Graeme Scaife Productions Ltd |
| | G-COMB | PA-30 Twin Comanche 160B | J. T. Bateson (G-AVBL)/Ronaldsway |
| | G-COMM | PA-23 Aztec 250C | M. G. Wild (G-AZMG) |
| | G-COMP | Cameron N-90 balloon | Computacenter Ltd |
| | G-CONC | Cameron N-90 balloon | British Airways |
| | G-COOK | Cameron N-77 balloon | IAZ (International) Ltd |
| | G-COOP | Cameron N-31 balloon | Aire Valley Balloons |
| | G-COPS | Piper J-3C-65 Cub | R. W. Sproat & C. E. Simpson |
| | G-COPY | AA-5A Cheetah | Emberden Ltd (G-BIEU)/Biggin Hill |
| | G-CORC | Bell 206B JetRanger 2 | Air Corcoran Ltd (G-CJHI/G-BBFB) |
| | G-CORD | Slingsby T.66 Nipper 3 | B. A. Wright (G-AVTB) |
| | G-CORK | Air Command 532 Elite | D. N. B. McCorquodale |
| | G-COTT | Cameron 60 Cottage SS balloon | Nottingham Hot-Air Balloon Club |
| | G-COWE | Beech C90A King Air | Cowie Aviation Ltd/Newcastle |
| | G-COWS | ARV Super 2 | T. C. Harrold (G-BONB) |
| | G-COYS | Colt 42A balloon | Thunder & Colt Ltd |
| | G-CPCD | CEA DR.221 | G-CPCD Flying Group |
| | G-CPEL | Boeing 757-236 | British Airways (G-BRJE) *Walmer Castle* |
| | G-CPFC | Cessna F.152 | Falcon Flying Services/Biggin Hill |
| | G-CPLI | Robinson R-22B | Thurston Helicopters (Engineering) Ltd |
| | G-CPTL | Short SD3-60 | Shorts Aircraft Financing Ltd (G-BOFI) |
| | G-CPTM | PA-28-151 Warrior | T. J. Mackay & C. M. Pollett (G-BTOE) |
| | G-CPTS | AB-206B JetRanger 2 | A. R. B. Aspinall |
| | G-CRAK | Cameron N-77 balloon | Mobile Windscreens Ltd |
| | G-CRAN | Robin R.1180T | D. S. Watson |
| | G-CRAY | Robinson R-22B | W. H. Grimshaw |
| | G-CRES | Denney Aerocraft Kitfox | R. J. Cresswell |
| | G-CRIC | Colomban MC.15 Cri-Cri | A. B. Cameron |
| | G-CRIL | R. Commander 112B | Rockwell Aviation Group/Cardiff |
| | G-CRIS | Taylor JT.1 Monoplane | C. R. Steer |
| | G-CRML | Cessna 414A | Fairport Ltd |
| | G-CRUS | Cessna T.303 | B. A. Groves |
| | G-CRUZ | Cessna T.303 | Bank Farm Ltd |
| | G-CRZY | Thunder Ax8-105 balloon | R. Carr (G-BDLP)/France |
| | G-CSBM | Cessna F.150M | Galaxy Enterprises Ltd |
| | G-CSCS | Cessna F.172N | Conegate Ltd |
| | G-CSFC | Cessna 150L | Shropshire Aero Club Ltd |
| | G-CSFT | PA-23 Aztec 250D | Islerealm Ltd (G-AYKU) |
| | G-CSJH | BAe 146-200 | British Aerospace PLC |
| | G-CSNA | Cessna 421C | Zulu Airlines Ltd |
| | G-CSZB | V.807B Viscount | British Air Ferries *Viscount Scotland* (G-AOXU)/Southend |
| | G-CTCL | SOCATA TB.10 Tobago | Merryfield Leasing Ltd (G-BSIV) |
| | G-CTIX | V.S.509 Spitfire T.IX (PT462) | Charles Church Displays Ltd |
| | G-CTKL | CCF Harvard IV (54137) | G. J. & S. P. Keegan |
| | G-CTOY | Denney Aerocraft Kitfox Mk 3 | G. S. Cass |
| | G-CTRN | Enstrom F-28C-UK | Manchester Helicopter Centre/Barton |
| | G-CTRX | H.P.137 Jetstream 200 | Centrax Ltd (G-BCWW/G-AXUN)/Exeter |
| | G-CUBB | PA-18 Super Cub 180 | G. J. Busby/Booker |
| | G-CUBI | PA-18 Super Cub 135 (51-15673) | T. Watson |
| | G-CUBJ | PA-18 Super Cub 150 | A. K. Leasing (Jersey) Ltd |

| Reg. | Type | Owner or Operator | Notes |
|------|------|-------------------|-------|
| G-CUGA | GA-7 Cougar | Teesside Flight Centre Ltd | |
| G-CULL | Bell 206B JetRanger | Dollar Air Services Ltd (G-BEWY)/ Coventry | |
| G-CURE | Colt 77A balloon | Flying Pictures (Balloons) Ltd | |
| G-CWAG | F. 8L Falco | C. C. Wagner | |
| G-CWOT | Currie Wot | D. A. Lord | |
| G-CXCX | Cameron N-90 balloon | Cathay Pacific Airways (London) Ltd | |
| G-CYLS | Cessna T.303 | Gledhill Water Storage Ltd & M. F. Joseph (G-BKXI)/Blackpool | |
| G-CYMA | GA-7 Cougar | Cyma Petroleum Ltd (G-BKOM)/Elstree | |
| G-CZAR | Cessna 560 Citation V | Aviation Beauport Ltd/Jersey | |
| G-DAAH | PA-28RT-201T Turbo Arrow IV | R. Peplow | |
| G-DAAL | Avro 748 Srs 1A | Alexandra Aviation Ltd (G-BEKG/G-VAJK) | |
| G-DAAM | Robinson R-22B | A. A. Macaskill | |
| G-DACA | P.57 Sea Prince T.1 ★ | P. G. Vallance Ltd/Charlwood | |
| G-DACC | Cessna 401B | Niglon Ltd (G-AYOU)/Birmingham | |
| G-DADS | Hughes 369HS | B. Wronski | |
| G-DAFT | AS.355F-2 Twin Squirrel | Powersense Ltd (G-BNNN)/Hayes | |
| G-DAJB | Boeing 757-2T7 | Monarch Airlines Ltd/Luton | |
| G-DAKS | Dakota 3 (TS423) | Aces High Ltd/North Weald | |
| G-DAMI | Robinson R-22B | Aramerco Ltd | |
| G-DAND | SOCATA TB.10 Tobago | Whitemoor Engineering Co Ltd | |
| G-DANN | Stampe SV-4B | I. M. White | |
| G-DAPH | Cessna 180K | M. R. L. Astor | |
| G-DARA | PA-34-220T Seneca III | P. Hartley | |
| G-DARE | PA-34-200T Seneca II | Diamond Airways Ltd (G-WOTS/G-SEVL) | |
| G-DARL | PA-28 Cherokee 180C | A. R. Liyanage | |
| G-DARR | Cessna 421C | Booth Plant & Equipment Hire Ltd (G-BNEZ) | |
| G-DASH | R. Commander 112A | Josef D. J. Jons & Co Ltd (G-BDAJ) | |
| G-DASI | Short SD3-60 | Air UK Ltd (G-BKKW)/Norwich | |
| G-DASU | Cameron V-77 balloon | D. & L. S. Litchfield | |
| G-DAVE | Jodel D.112 | D. A. Porter/Sturgate | |
| G-DBAF | BAC One-Eleven 201AC | British Air Ferries Ltd (G-ASJG)/Stansted | |
| G-DBAL | H.S.125 Srs 3B | Osprey Aviation Ltd (G-BSAA) | |
| G-DBAR | Beech 200 Super King Air | Brown & Root (UK) Ltd | |
| G-DBII | Cessna 560 Citation V | Artix Ltd | |
| G-DCAC | McD Douglas MD-83 | Airtours International Aviation Ltd | |
| G-DCCH | MBB Bo 105D | Devon & Cornwall Police Authority | |
| G-DCCI | BAe 125-1000B | Consolidated Contractors International (UK) Ltd (G-BUPL) | |
| G-DCEA | PA-34-200T Seneca II | M. J. Greasby | |
| G-DCIO | Douglas DC-10-30 | British Airways *Epping Forest*/Gatwick | |
| G-DCKK | Cessna F.172N | A. R. Mead/Clacton | |
| G-DCOX | PA-31-310 Turbo Navajo | Porten Holdings Ltd | |
| G-DCSW | PA-32R-301 Saratoga SP | Samworth Bros Ltd | |
| G-DCXL | Jodel D.140C | P. Underhill | |
| G-DDAY | PA-28R-201T Turbo Arrow III | W. Haynes (G-BPDO) | |
| G-DDCD | D.H.104 Dove 8 | C. Daniel (G-ARUM)/Biggin Hill | |
| G-DDMV | NA T-6G Texan | E. A. Morgan | |
| G-DEBB | Beech 35-B33 Debonair | Spitfire Aviation Ltd/Bournemouth | |
| G-DEJL | Robinson R-22B | D. E. J. Lomas | |
| G-DELB | Robinson R-22B | Osprey Helicopters Ltd | |
| G-DELI | Thunder Ax7-77 balloon | Heather Flight Ltd | |
| G-DELL | Robinson R-22B | Delta Helicopters Ltd/Luton | |
| G-DELS | Robin DR.400/180 | W. D. Nightingale | |
| G-DELT | Robinson R-22B | Mortec Services | |
| G-DEMH | Cessna F.172M (modified) | M. Hammond (G-BFLO) | |
| G-DEMO | BN-2T Islander | Pilatus BN Ltd (G-BKEA)/Bembridge | |
| G-DENS | Binder CP.301S Smaragd | W. St G. V. Stoney | |
| G-DENW | PA-44-180 Seminole | D. A. Woodhams | |
| G-DERV | Cameron Truck SS balloon | J. M. Percival | |
| G-DESI | Aero Designs Pulsar XP | D. F. Gaughan | |
| G-DESS | Mooney M.20J | W. E. Newnes | |
| G-DEVS | PA-28 Cherokee 180 | 180 Group (G-BGVJ) | |
| G-DEXP | ARV Super 2 | J. P. Jenkins | |
| G-DEXY | Beech E90 King Air | Tornado Ltd | |
| G-DFLT | Cessna F.406 Caravan II | Direct Flight Ltd/Norwich | |
| G-DFLY | PA-38-112 Tomahawk | I. R. March & N. W. Woodward | |
| G-DFVA | Cessna R.172K | R. A. Plowright | |
| G-DGDG | Glaser-Dirks DG.400/17 | DG400 Flying Group/Lasham | |
| G-DGLD | HPR-7 Herald 214 | Channel Express Group (Air Services) Ltd (G-BAVX)/Bournemouth | |

| Notes | Reg. | Type | Owner or Operator |
|---|---|---|---|
| | G-DGWW | Rand Robinson KR-2 | W. Wilson |
| | G-DHCB | D.H.C.2 Beaver 1 | Sealife Ltd (G-BTDL) |
| | G-DHCI | D.H.C.1 Chipmunk 22 | C. J. Crooks (G-BBSE) |
| | G-DHSW | Boeing 737-3Y0 | Monarch Airlines/EuroBerlin |
| | G-DHTM | D.H.82A Tiger Moth replica | E. G. Waite-Roberts |
| | G-DHVV | D.H.115 Vampire T.55 | Lindsay Wood Promotions Ltd |
| | G-DHWW | D.H.115 Vampire T.55 | Lindsay Wood Promotions Ltd |
| | G-DHXX | D.H.100 Vampire FB.6 | Lindsay Wood Promotions Ltd |
| | G-DHZZ | D.H.115 Vampire T.55 (U-1230) | Lindsay Wood Promotions Ltd |
| | G-DIAL | Cameron N-90 balloon | Datacentre Ltd |
| | G-DIAT | PA-28 Cherokee 140 | RAF Benevolent Fund's IAT/Bristol & Wessex Aeroplane Club (G-BCGK)/ Lulsgate |
| | G-DICK | Thunder Ax6-56Z balloon | R. D. Sargeant |
| | G-DIME | R. Commander 114 | Badminton Horse Boxes Ltd |
| | G-DINA | AA-5B Tiger | Warwickshire Aerocentre Ltd/Birmingham |
| | G-DING | Colt 77A balloon | G. J. Bell |
| | G-DINT | B.156 Beaufighter 1F | T. E. Moore |
| | G-DIPI | Cameron Tub SS balloon | Airship & Balloon Co Ltd |
| | G-DIPS | Taylor JT.1 Monoplane | B. J. Halls |
| | G-DIPZ | Colt 17A balloon | Airship & Balloon Co Ltd |
| | G-DIRE | Robinson R-22B | Direct Self Drive Ltd |
| | G-DIRK | Glaser-Dirks DG.400 | D. M. Chalmers |
| | G-DIRT | Thunder Ax7-77Z balloon | R. J. Ngbaronye |
| | G-DISC | Cessna U.206A | I. A. Louttit (G-BGWR)/Exeter |
| | G-DISK | PA-24 Comanche 250 | M. A. McLoughlin (G-APZG)/Booker |
| | G-DISO | Jodel D.150 | P. F. Craven & J. H. Shearer |
| | G-DIVA | Cessna R.172K XPII | R. A. Plowright & J. A. Kaye/Biggin Hill |
| | G-DIWY | PA-32 Cherokee Six 300 | Industrial Foam Systems Ltd |
| | G-DIZO | Jodel D.120A | D. Aldersea (G-EMKM) |
| | G-DIZY | PA-28R-201T Turbo Arrow III | Medway Arrow Group |
| | G-DJEM | AS.350B Ecureuil | Maynard & Harris Plastics Ltd (G-ZBAC/ G-SEBI/G-BMCU) |
| | G-DJHB | Beech A23-19 Musketeer | M. J. Wells (G-AZZE) |
| | G-DJIM | MHCA-I | J. Crawford |
| | G-DJJA | PA-28-181 Archer II | S. J. Lucas |
| | G-DJLW | H.S.125 Srs 3B/RA | Lindsay Wood Promotions Ltd (G-AVVB) |
| | G-DJNH | Denney Aerocraft Kitfox | D. J. N. Hall |
| | G-DKDP | Grob G.109 | Diss Aviation Ltd/Tibenham |
| | G-DKGF | Viking Dragonfly | K. G. Fathers |
| | G-DLDL | Robinson R-22B | D. A. Lawson |
| | G-DLOM | SOCATA TB.20 Trinidad | J. N. A. Adderley/Guernsey |
| | G-DLTA | Slingsby T.67M Firefly | Firefly Aerial Promotions Ltd (G-SFTX) |
| | G-DLTI | Robinson R-22B | D. L. Taylor |
| | G-DMCH | Hiller UH-12E | D. McK. Carnegie & ptnrs |
| | G-DMCS | PA-28R Cherokee Arrow 200-II | D. L. Johns & F. K. Parker (G-CPAC) |
| | G-DNCS | PA-28R-201T Turbo Arrow III | BRT Arrow Ltd/Barton |
| | G-DNLB | MBB Bo 105DBS/4 | Bond Helicopters Ltd (G-BUDP) |
| | G-DNLD | Cameron 97 Donald SS balloon | The Walt Disney Co Ltd |
| | G-DNVT | G.1159C Gulfstream IV | Shell Aircraft Ltd/Heathrow |
| | G-DOCA | Boeing 737-436 | British Airways *River Ballinderry* |
| | G-DOCB | Boeing 737-436 | British Airways *River Bush* |
| | G-DOCC | Boeing 737-436 | British Airways *Rver Afric* |
| | G-DOCD | Boeing 737-436 | British Airways *River Aire* |
| | G-DOCE | Boeing 737-436 | British Airways *River Alness* |
| | G-DOCF | Boeing 737-436 | British Airways *River Beaully* |
| | G-DOCG | Boeing 737-436 | British Airways *River Blackwater* |
| | G-DOCH | Boeing 737-436 | British Airways *River Brue* |
| | G-DOCI | Boeing 737-436 | British Airways *River Carron* |
| | G-DOCJ | Boeing 737-436 | British Airways *River Glass* |
| | G-DOCK | Boeing 737-436 | British Airways *River Lochay* |
| | G-DOCL | Boeing 737-436 | British Airways *River Lune* |
| | G-DOCM | Boeing 737-436 | British Airways *River Meon* |
| | G-DOCN | Boeing 737-436 | British Airways *River Ottery* |
| | G-DOCO | Boeing 737-436 | British Airways *River Parrett* |
| | G-DOCP | Boeing 737-436 | British Airways *River Swift* |
| | G-DOCR | Boeing 737-436 | British Airways *River Tavy* |
| | G-DOCS | Boeing 737-436 | British Airways *River Teifi* |
| | G-DOCT | Boeing 737-436 | British Airways *River Tene* |
| | G-DOCU | Boeing 737-436 | British Airways *River Teviot* |
| | G-DOCV | Boeing 737-436 | British Airways *River Thurso* |
| | G-DOCW | Boeing 737-436 | British Airways *River Till* |

| Reg. | Type | Owner or Operator | Notes |
|------|------|-------------------|-------|
| G-DOCX | Boeing 737-436 | British Airways *River Tirry* | |
| G-DOCY | Boeing 737-436 | British Airways *River Weaver* | |
| G-DOCZ | Boeing 737-436 | British Airways *River Wharfe* | |
| G-DODD | Cessna F.172P-II | K. Watts/Elstree | |
| G-DODS | PA-46-310P Malibu | HPM Investments Ltd | |
| G-DOFY | Bell 206B JetRanger 3 | Cinnamond Ltd | |
| G-DOGS | Cessna R.182RG | P. Bennett & J. R. Shawe | |
| G-DONS | PA-28RT-201T Turbo Arrow IV | D. J. Murphy | |
| G-DOOR | M.S.893E Rallye 180GT | Lynair Flying Group | |
| G-DOOZ | AS.355F-2 Twin Squirrel | Lynton Aviation Ltd (G-BNSX) | |
| G-DORB | Bell 206B JetRanger 3 | Dorb Crest Homes Ltd | |
| G-DORK | EMB-110P1 Bandeirante | Aero Services (E. Midlands) Ltd | |
| G-DOVE | Cessna 182Q | P. J. Contracting | |
| G-DOWN | Colt 31A | M. Williams | |
| G-DPPS | AS.355N Twin Squirrel | Dyfed-Powys Police Authority | |
| G-DRAC | Cameron Dracula Skull SS balloon | Shiplake Investments Ltd | |
| G-DRAI | Robinson R-22B | D. R. Anthony Builders Ltd | |
| G-DRAW | Colt 77A balloon | Readers Digest Association Ltd | |
| G-DRAY | Taylor JT.1 Monoplane | L. J. Dray | |
| G-DRGN | Cameron N-105 balloon | W. I. Hooker & C. Parker | |
| G-DRJC | Boeing 757-2T7 | Monarch Airlines Ltd/Luton | |
| G-DRNT | Sikorsky S-76A | Bond Helicopters Ltd/Aberdeen | |
| G-DROP | Cessna U.206C | I. A. Louttit (G-UKNO/G-BAMN) | |
| G-DRSV | CEA DR.315 (modified) | R. S. Voice | |
| G-DRYI | Cameron N-77 balloon | J. Barbour & Sons Ltd | |
| G-DRZF | CEA DR.360 | C. A. Parker/Sywell | |
| G-DSAM | AS.350B Ecureuil | PLM Helicopters Ltd | |
| G-DSGN | Robinson R-22B | William Towns Ltd | |
| G-DTOO | PA-38-112 Tomahawk | A. Todd | |
| G-DUCH | Beech 76 Duchess | C. D. Weiswall | |
| G-DUDS | C.A.S.A. 1-131E Jungmann 2000 | D. H. Pattison | |
| G-DUET | Wood Duet | C. Wood | |
| G-DUGY | Emstrom 280C-UK-2 Shark | Pool Helicopter Services UK Ltd (G-BEEL) | |
| G-DUNN | Zenair CH.250 | A. Dunn | |
| G-DURX | Thunder 77A balloon | V. Trimble | |
| G-DUST | Stolp SA.300 Starduster Too | J. V. George | |
| G-DUVL | Cessna F.172N | A. J. Simpson/Denham | |
| G-DVON | D.H.104 Devon C.2 (VP955) | C. L. Thatcher | |
| G-DWHH | Boeing 737-2T7 | Monarch Airlines Ltd/Luton | |
| G-DXRG | Cameron 105 Agfa SS balloon | Cameron Balloons Ltd | |
| G-DYNE | Cessna 414 | Commair Aviation Ltd/E. Midlands | |
| G-DYOU | PA-38-112 Tomahawk | Airways Aero Associations Ltd/Booker | |
| G-EAGL | Cessna 421C | Premi-Air Management/Leeds | |
| G-EBJI | Hawker Cygnet (replica) | A. V. Francis | |
| G-ECAV | Beech 200 Super King Air | GEC Avionics Ltd/Rochester | |
| G-ECBH | Cessna F.150K | Air Fenland Ltd | |
| G-ECGC | Cessna F.172N-II | Leicestershire Aero Club Ltd | |
| G-ECGO | Bo208C Junior | M. F. R. B. Collett | |
| G-ECHO | Enstrom 280C-UK-2 Shark | ALP Electrical (Maidenhead) Ltd (G-LONS/ G-BDIB)/White Waltham | |
| G-ECJM | PA-28R-201T Turbo Arrow III | Regishire Ltd (G-FESL/G-BNRN) | |
| G-ECKO | Colt 180A balloon | T. Donnelly | |
| G-ECOS | AS.355F-1 Twin Squirrel | Golden Harvest Ltd (G-DOLR/G-BPVB) | |
| G-ECOX | Grega GN.1 Air Camper | H. C. Cox | |
| G-EDDI | Robinson R-22B | Serve Offer Ltd | |
| G-EDEN | SOCATA TB.10 Tobago | N. G. Pistol & ptnrs | |
| G-EDGE | Jodel D.150 | A. D. Edge | |
| G-EDIT | Beech B95 TravelAir | Warrior Aircraft Sales & Leasing Ltd (G-AXUX) | |
| G-EDNA | PA-38-112 Tomahawk | Ravenair Trading Ltd/Manchester | |
| G-EDOT | Cessna T.337D | A. Brinkley (G-BJIY) | |
| G-EDRY | Cessna T.303 | Pat Eddery Ltd | |
| G-EEEE | Slingsby T.31 Motor Glider | R. F. Selby | |
| G-EEGE | Robinson R-22A | The Helicentre (G-BKZK)/Blackpool | |
| G-EEGL | Christen Eagle II | A. J. Wilson | |
| G-EENY | GA-7 Cougar | BLS Aviation Ltd/Elstree | |
| G-EEUP | SNCAN Stampe SV-4C | A. M. Wajih | |
| G-EEVS | Agusta A.109A Srs II | Wilkes Asset Management Ltd (G-OTSL) | |
| G-EEZE | Rutan Vari-Eze | A. J. Nurse | |
| G-EFSM | Slingsby T.67M-260 | Slingsby Aviation Ltd (G-BPLK) | |
| G-EFTE | Bolkow Bo 207 | N. J. Heaton | |

| Notes | Reg. | Type | Owner or Operator |
|---|---|---|---|
| | G-EGAP | Sequoia F.8L Falco | E. G. A. Prance |
| | G-EGEE | Cessna 310Q | A. J. Fuller & ptnrs (G-AZVY) |
| | G-EGEL | Christen Eagle II | D. J. Daly |
| | G-EGGS | Robin DR.400/180 | R. Foot |
| | G-EGJA | SOCATA TB.20 Trinidad | D. A. Williamson/Alderney |
| | G-EGLD | PA-28-161 Cadet | J. Appleton |
| | G-EGLE | Christen Eagle II | R. L. Mitcham & H. Odone/Elstree |
| | G-EHAP | Sportavia-Pützer RF.7 | R. G. Boyes |
| | G-EHBJ | C.A.S.A. 1-131E Jungmann 2000 | Mangreen Holdings Ltd |
| | G-EHIL | Westland-Agusta EH.101 | Westland Helicopters Ltd/Yeovil |
| | G-EHMM | Robin DR.400/180R | Booker Gliding Club Ltd |
| | G-EIIR | Cameron N-77 balloon | Major C. J. T. Davey *Silver Jubilee* |
| | G-EIST | Robinson R-22B | European Executive Ltd |
| | G-EITE | Luscombe 8A Silvaire | D. L. Eite |
| | G-EIWT | Cessna FR.182RG | P. P. D. Howard-Johnston/Edinburgh |
| | G-EJET | Cessna 550 Citation II | North West Property Management Ltd (G-DJBE) |
| | G-EJGO | Z.226HE Trener | N. J. Radford |
| | G-ELBC | PA-34-200 Seneca II | Stapleford Flying Club Ltd (G-BANS) |
| | G-ELDG | Douglas DC-9-32 | British Midland Airways Ltd *The Orloff Diamond*/E. Midlands |
| | G-ELDH | Douglas DC-9-32 | British Midland Airways Ltd *The Hastings Diamond*/E. Midlands |
| | G-ELDI | Douglas DC-9-32 | British Midland Airways Ltd *The Regent Diamond*/E. Midlands |
| | G-ELEC | Westland WG.30 Srs 200 | Westland Helicopters Ltd (G-BKNV)/Yeovil |
| | G-ELFI | Robinson R-22B | P. J. Paine |
| | G-ELIZ | Denney Aerocraft Kitfox | A. J. Ellis |
| | G-ELMH | NA AT-6D Harvard III | M. Hammond |
| | G-ELRA | BAe 125-1000 | British Aerospace PLC |
| | G-EMAK | PA-28R-201 Arrow III | Arrow Aircraft Group/E. Midlands |
| | G-EMAZ | PA-28-181 Archer II | Emmair Ltd |
| | G-EMER | PA-34-200 Seneca II | Clydeside Surveys Ltd/Glasgow |
| | G-EMMA | Cessna F.182Q | Watkiss Group Aviation |
| | G-EMMS | PA-38-112 Tomahawk | Ravenair Trading Ltd/Manchester |
| | G-EMMY | Rutan Vari-Eze | M. J. Tooze |
| | G-EMSY | D.H.82A Tiger Moth | B. E. Micklewright (G-ASPZ) |
| | G-ENAM | Cessna 340A | Freeway Rentals Ltd |
| | G-ENCE | Partenavia P.68B | P. Davies(G-OROY/G-BFSU) |
| | G-ENIE | Tipsy T.66 Nipper 3 | I. D. Daniels |
| | G-ENII | Cessna F.172M | J. Howley |
| | G-ENNA | PA-28-161 Warrior II | A. J. Wood |
| | G-ENNY | Cameron V-77 balloon | B. G. Jones |
| | G-ENOA | Cessna F.172F | M. K. Acors (G-ASZW) |
| | G-ENRY | Cameron N-105 balloon | Numatic International Ltd |
| | G-ENSI | Beech F33A Bonanza | Special Analysis & Simulation Technology Ltd |
| | G-ENUS | Cameron N-90 balloon | The Hot-Air Balloon Co Ltd |
| | G-EOFF | Taylor JT.2 Titch | G. H. Wylde |
| | G-EORG | PA-38-112 Tomahawk | Airways Aero Association/Booker |
| | G-EPDI | Cameron N-77 balloon | R. Moss |
| | G-ERIC | R. Commander 112TC | P. P. Patterson/Newcastle |
| | G-ERIK | Cameron N-77 balloon | Cultural Resource Management Ltd |
| | G-ERIX | Boeing Stearman A75N-1 | E. E. Rix |
| | G-ERMO | ARV Super 2 | Kenbal Properties Ltd & J. O. Hodgson (G-BMWK) |
| | G-ERMS | Thunder AS-33 airship | B. R. & M. Boyle |
| | G-ERNI | PA-28-181 Archer II | E. L. Collins (G-OSSY) |
| | G-EROS | Cameron H-34 balloon | Evening Standard Co Ltd |
| | G-ERRY | AA-5B Tiger | P. D. Cullen (G-BFMJ) |
| | G-ERTY | D.H.82A Tiger Moth (R4897) | R. F. Tolhurst (G-ANDC) |
| | G-ESSX | PA-28-161 Warrior II | AT Aviation Ltd (G-BHYY)/Cardiff |
| | G-ESTE | AA-5A Cheetah | McGeoghan Plant Hire & Excavations Ltd (G-GHNC) |
| | G-ETBY | PA-32 Cherokee Six 260 | Yarnhaven Ltd (G-AWCY) |
| | G-ETCD | Colt 77A balloon | Philips Electronics Ltd |
| | G-ETDA | PA-28-161 Warrior II | T. Griffiths |
| | G-ETDB | PA-38-112 Tomahawk | R. A. Wakefield |
| | G-ETDC | Cessna 172P | Osprey Air Services Ltd |
| | G-ETFT | Colt Financial Times SS balloon | Financial Times Ltd (G-BSGZ) |
| | G-ETIN | Robinson R-22B | E. & I. Whitmore |
| | G-EURA | Agusta-Bell 47J-2 | E. W. Schnedlitz (G-ASNV) |
| | G-EVAN | Taylor JT.2 Titch | E. Evans |

| Reg. | Type | Owner or Operator | Notes |
|------|------|-------------------|-------|
| G-EVER | Robinson R-22B | Everards Brewery Ltd | |
| G-EWBJ | SOCATA TB.10 Tobago | Longslow Dairy Ltd | |
| G-EWEL | Sikorsky S-76A | Ratners Group PLC | |
| G-EWFN | SOCATA TB-20 Trinidad | Trinidair Ltd (G-BRTY) | |
| G-EWIZ | Pitts S-2E Special | R. H. Jago | |
| G-EXEC | PA-34-200 Seneca | S. J. Green | |
| G-EXEL | EMB-120RT Brasilia | Air Exel (UK) Ltd/Luton | |
| G-EXEX | Cessna 404 | Atlantic Air Transport Ltd/Coventry | |
| G-EXIT | M.S.893E Rallye 180GT | G-Exit Ltd/Rochester | |
| G-EXLR | BAe 125-1000B | British Aerospace PLC | |
| G-EXOR | Robinson R-22B | Ex-Or Ltd (G-CMCM) | |
| G-EXPR | Colt 90A balloon | L. P. Purfield & S. A. Burnett | |
| G-EXTR | Extra EA.260 | D. M. Britten | |
| G-EYCO | Robin DR.400/180 | L. M. Gould | |
| G-EYES | Cessna 402C | Air Corbiere (G-BLCE)/Coventry | |
| G-EYRE | Bell 206L-1 LongRanger | Hideroute Ltd (G-STVI) | |
| G-EZEE | Rutan Vari-Eze | D. & M. Schwier | |
| G-EZIO | EMB-120RT Brasilia | — | |
| G-EZOS | Rutan Vari-Eze | O. Smith/Tees-side | |
| G-FABB | Cameron V-77 balloon | V. P. F. Haines | |
| G-FABM | Beech 95-B55 Baron | F. B. Miles (G-JOND/G-BMVC) | |
| G-FAGN | Robinson R-22B | C. R. Weldon | |
| G-FAIR | SOCATA TB.10 Tobago | Sally Marine Ltd/Guernsey | |
| G-FALC | Aeromere F.8L Falco | P. W. Hunter (G-AROT)/Elstree | |
| G-FAMY | Maule M5-180C | Land Reclamation (Southern) Ltd | |
| G-FANC | Fairchild 24R-46 Argus III | J. I. Hyslop | |
| G-FANG | AA-5A Cheetah | Church & Co | |
| G-FANL | Cessna FR.172K XP-II | J. Woodhouse & Co/Staverton | |
| G-FANN | H.S.125 Srs 600B | Osprey Aviation Ltd (G-BARR) | |
| G-FARM | SOCATA Rallye 235GT | Bristol Cars Ltd | |
| G-FARO | Aero Designs Star-Lite SL.1 | M. K. Faro | |
| G-FARR | Jodel D.150 | G. H. Farr | |
| G-FASL | BAe 125 Srs 800B | Fisons PLC/E. Midlands | |
| G-FAST | Cessna 337G | Seillans Land Investigations Ltd | |
| G-FAYE | Cessna F.150M | Cheshire Air Training School Ltd/Liverpool | |
| G-FBIX | D.H.100 Vampire FB.9 (WL505) | D. G. Jones | |
| G-FBMB | Canadair CL.600-2B16 Challenger | Challenger Aviation Ltd | |
| G-FBWH | PA-28R Cherokee Arrow 180 | F. A. Short | |
| G-FCHJ | Cessna 340A | P. L. & M. J. E. Builder (G-BJLS) | |
| G-FCSP | Robin DR.400/180 | FCS Photochemicals | |
| G-FDGM | Beech B60 Duke | Parissi Air Ltd/Perth | |
| G-FEBE | Cessna 340A | R. H. Everett | |
| G-FELT | Cameron N-77 balloon | Allan Industries Ltd | |
| G-FENI | Robinson R-22B | I. Fenwick | |
| G-FFBR | Thunder Ax8-105 balloon | Fuji Photo Film (UK) Ltd | |
| G-FFEN | Cessna F.150M | Suffolk Aero Club Ltd/Ipswich | |
| G-FFLT | H.S.125 Srs 600B | Albion Aviation Management Ltd | |
| G-FFOR | Cessna 310R | Air Service Training Ltd (G-BMGF)/Perth | |
| G-FFRA | Dassault Falcon 20DC | FR Aviation Ltd/Bournemouth | |
| G-FFTI | SOCATA TB.20 Trinidad | Blicqair Ltd | |
| G-FFTN | Bell 206B JetRanger | Kensington Aviation Ltd | |
| G-FFWD | Cessna 310R | Keef & Co Ltd (G-TVKE/G-EURO) | |
| G-FGID | FG-1D Corsair (88297) | Patina Ltd/Duxford | |
| G-FHAS | Scheibe SF.25E Super Falke | Burn Gliding Club Ltd | |
| G-FIAT | PA-28 Cherokee 140 | RAF Benevolent Fund's IAT/ Bristol & Wessex Aeroplane Club (G-BBYW)/Lulsgate | |
| G-FIFI | SOCATA TB.20 Trinidad | D. J. & M. Gower (G-BMWS) | |
| G-FIGA | Cessna 152 | G & B Aviation Ltd/Coventry | |
| G-FIGB | Cessna 152 | G & B Aviation Ltd/Coventry | |
| G-FIJR | L.188C Electra | Hunting Cargo Airlines Ltd | |
| G-FIJV | L.188C Electra | Hunting Cargo Airlines Ltd | |
| G-FILE | PA-34-200T Seneca | Baltic Industrial Supply Co Ltd | |
| G-FILO | Robin DR.400/180 | F. Friedenberg | |
| G-FIND | Cessna F.406 Caravan II | Air Corbiere Ltd/Coventry | |
| G-FINN | Cameron 90 Reindeer SS balloon | Forbes Europe Inc/France | |
| G-FINS | AB-206B JetRanger 2 | Brian Seedle Helicopters (G-FSCL) | |
| G-FISH | Cessna 310R-II | Bostonair Ltd/Humberside | |
| G-FISK | Pazmany PL-4A | K. S. Woodard | |
| G-FISS | Robinson R-22B | B. G. & D. Bushell | |
| G-FIST | Fieseler Fi.156C Storch | Aero Vintage Ltd | |
| G-FIZZ | PA-28-161 Warrior II | Arrow Air Centre Ltd/Shipdham | |

| Notes | Reg. | Type | Owner or Operator |
|---|---|---|---|
| | G-FJMS | Partenavia P.68B | F. J. M. Sanders (G-SVHA) |
| | G-FKKM | PA-28RT-201T Turbo Arrow IV | D. J. Kaye |
| | G-FLAG | Colt 77A balloon | Thunder & Colt Ltd |
| | G-FLAK | Beech 95-E55 Baron | J. K. Horne |
| | G-FLCA | Fleet Model 80 Canuck | E. C. Taylor |
| | G-FLCO | Sequoia F.8L Falco | J. B. Mowforth |
| | G-FLEA | SOCATA TB.10 Tobago | Fleair Trading Co/Biggin Hill |
| | G-FLEN | PA-28-161 Warrior II | Winchfield Enterprises Ltd |
| | G-FLII | GA-7 Cougar | BLS Aviation Ltd (G-GRAC)/Elstree |
| | G-FLIK | Pitts S.1S Special | R. P. Millinship |
| | G-FLPI | R. Commander 112A | L. Freeman & Son/Newcastle |
| | G-FLTI | Beech F90 King Air | Flightline Ltd/Southend |
| | G-FLTY | EMB-110P1 Bandeirante | Flightline Ltd (G-ZUSS/G-REGA)/ Southend |
| | G-FLUG | Gyroflug SC.01B-160 Speed Canard | ITPS Ltd/Cranfield |
| | G-FLUT | Stitts SA.6B Flut-R-Bug | B. J. Towers |
| | G-FLYA | Mooney M.20J | Flya Aviation Ltd |
| | G-FLYI | PA-34-200 Seneca | BLS Aviation Ltd (G-BHVO)/Elstree |
| | G-FLYR | AB-206B JetRanger 2 | Kwik Fit Euro Ltd (G-BAKT) |
| | G-FLYV | Slingsby T.67M-200 | Firefly Aerial Promotions Ltd |
| | G-FMAL | AB-206A JetRanger | Catto Helicopters (G-RIAN/G-BHSG) |
| | G-FMAM | PA-28-151 Warrior | Essex Radio PLC (G-BBXV)/Southend |
| | G-FMUS | Robinson R-22 | Cormack (Aircraft Services) Ltd (G-BJBT)/ Glasgow |
| | G-FNLD | Cessna 172N | Papa Hotel Flying Group |
| | G-FNLY | Cessna F.172M | London Aviation Ltd (G-WACX/G-BAEX)/ Biggin Hill |
| | G-FOEL | PA-31-350 Navajo Chieftain | Oxaero (G-BBXR)/Kidlington |
| | G-FOGG | Cameron N-90 balloon | J. P. E. Money-Kyrle |
| | G-FOLD | Light Aero Avid Speedwing | S. R. Winder |
| | G-FOLY | Aerotek Pitts S-2A Modified | A. A. Laing |
| | G-FOOD | Beech B200 Super King Air | Specbridge Ltd/Gamston |
| | G-FOPP | Lancair 320 | Airsport (UK) Ltd |
| | G-FORC | SNCAN Stampe SV-4C | G. Pullan |
| | G-FORD | SNCAN Stampe SV-4B | P. Meeson & R. A. J. Spurrell/ White Waltham |
| | G-FORE | Bell 47G-4A | London Aviation Ltd/Biggin Hill |
| | G-FOTO | PA-E23 Aztec 250F | Aerofilms Ltd (G-BJDH/G-BDXV)/ Leavesden |
| | G-FOWL | Colt 90A balloon | Chesterfield Cold Storage Ltd |
| | G-FOXA | PA-28-161 Cadet | Leicestershire Aero Club Ltd |
| | G-FOXC | Denney Aerocraft Kitfox | Junipa Sales (Aviation) Ltd |
| | G-FOXD | Denney Aerocraft Kitfox | M. Hanley |
| | G-FOXE | Denney Aerocraft Kitfox | K. M. Pinkard |
| | G-FOXG | Denney Aerocraft Kitfox | Kitfox Group |
| | G-FOXI | Denney Aerocraft Kitfox | B. Johns |
| | G-FOXS | Denney Aerocraft Kitfox | S. P. Watkins & C. C. Rea |
| | G-FOXX | Denney Aerocraft Kitfox | R. O. F. Harper |
| | G-FOXZ | Denney Aerocraft Kitfox | M. Smalley & ptnrs |
| | G-FPCL | GA-7 Cougar | Eurowide Ltd |
| | G-FPEL | Schweizer 269C | Central Communications Group |
| | G-FRAA | Dassault Falcon 20F | FR Aviation Ltd/Bournemouth |
| | G-FRAB | Dassault Falcon 20F | FR Aviation Ltd/Bournemouth |
| | G-FRAC | Dassault Falcon 20F | FR Aviation Ltd/Bournemouth |
| | G-FRAD | Dassault Falcon 20E | FR Aviation Ltd (G-BCYF)/Bournemouth |
| | G-FRAE | Dassault Falcon 20E | FR Aviation Ltd/Bournemouth |
| | G-FRAF | Dassault Falcon 20E | FR Aviation Ltd/Bournemouth |
| | G-FRAG | PA-32 Cherokee Six 300E | W. R. Bridges/Southend |
| | G-FRAH | Dassault Falcon 20DC | FR Aviation Ltd/Bournemouth |
| | G-FRAI | Dassault Falcon 20E | FR Aviation Ltd/Bournemouth |
| | G-FRAJ | Dassault Falcon 20E | FR Aviation Ltd/Bournemouth |
| | G-FRAK | Dassault Falcon 20DC | FR Aviation Ltd/Bournemouth |
| | G-FRAN | Piper J-3C-90 Cub (480321) | Essex L-4 Group (G-BIXY) |
| | G-FRAO | Dassault Falcon 20DC | FR Aviation Ltd/Bournemouth |
| | G-FRAS | Dassault Falcon 20C | FR Aviation Ltd/Bournemouth |
| | G-FRAT | Dassault Falcon 20C | FR Aviation Ltd/Bournemouth |
| | G-FRAU | Dassault Falcon 20C | FR Aviation Ltd/Bournemouth |
| | G-FRAV | Dassault Falcon 20ECM | FR Aviation Ltd/Bournemouth |
| | G-FRAW | Dassault Falcon 20ECM | FR Aviation Ltd/Bournemouth |
| | G-FRAX | Cessna 441 | FR Aviation Ltd (G-BMTZ)/Bournemouth |
| | G-FRAY | Cassutt IIIM (modified) | C. I. Fray |
| | G-FRAZ | Cessna 441 | FR Aviation Ltd/Bournemouth |

| Reg. | Type | Owner or Operator | Notes |
|---|---|---|---|
| G-FRCE | H.S. Gnat T.1 | Butane Buzzard Aviation Corporation Ltd | |
| G-FREE | Pitts S-2A Special | Pegasus Flying Group/Fairoaks | |
| G-FRJB | Britten Sheriff SA-1 ★ | Aeropark/E. Midlands | |
| G-FRST | PA-44-180T Turbo Seminole | WAM (GB) Ltd | |
| G-FRYS | Christen Eagle II | R. W. J. Foster | |
| G-FSDC | Enstrom 280C-UK Shark | J. Collins (G-BKTG) | |
| G-FSDG | AB-206B JetRanger | Flair (Soft Drinks) Ltd (G-ROOT/G-JETR) | |
| G-FSDH | Hughes 269A | West Country Aviation Ltd | |
| G-FSDT | Hughes 269A | S. G. Oliphant-Hope/Shoreham | |
| G-FSII | Gregory Free Spirit Mk II | M. J. Gregory & R. P. Hallam | |
| G-FSIX | Lightning F.6 | B. J. Pover | |
| G-FSPL | PA-32R Cherokee Lance 300 | J. D. L. Richardson & Goodridge (UK) Ltd | |
| G-FTAX | Cessna 421C | Jet West Ltd (G-BFFM)/Exeter | |
| G-FTFT | Colt Financial Times SS balloon | Financial Times Ltd | |
| G-FTIL | Robin DR.400/180R | C. C. Blakey | |
| G-FTIM | Robin DR.400/100 | P. D. W. King/Kidlington | |
| G-FTIN | Robin DR.400/100 | G. D. Clark & M. J. D. Theobold | |
| G-FTWO | AS.355F-2 Twin Squirrel | McAlpine Helicopters Ltd (G-OJOR/ G-BMUS)/Hayes | |
| G-FUEL | Robin DR.400/180 | R. Darch/Compton Abbas | |
| G-FUGA | Fouga CM.170R Magister | Royalair Services Ltd (G-BSCT) | |
| G-FUJI | Fuji FA.200-180 | R. Gizzi | |
| G-FULL | PA-28R Cherokee Arrow 200-II | Fuller Aviation (G-HWAY/G-JULI) | |
| G-FUND | Thunder Ax7-65Z balloon | Soft Sell Ltd | |
| G-FUZY | Cameron N-77 balloon | Allan Industries Ltd | |
| G-FUZZ | PA-18 Super Cub 95 | G. W. Cline | |
| G-FWPW | PA-28-236 Dakota | P. A. & F. C. Winters | |
| G-FWRP | Cessna 421C | Aerienne Ltd/Southampton | |
| G-FXII | V.S.366 Spitfire F.XII (EN224) | P. R. Arnold | |
| G-FXIV | V.S.379 Spitfire FR.XIV (MV370) | R. Lamplough | |
| G-FZZI | Cameron H-34 balloon | Airship & Balloon Co Ltd | |
| G-FZZY | Colt 69A balloon | Hot-Air Balloon Co Ltd | |
| G-FZZZ | Colt 56A balloon | Hot-Air Balloon Co Ltd | |
| G-GABD | GA-7 Cougar | Scotia Safari Ltd/Prestwick | |
| G-GACA | P.57 Sea Prince T.1 ★ | P. G. Vallance Ltd/Charlwood | |
| G-GAGA | AA-5B Tiger | S. Spier (G-BGPG) | |
| G-GAJB | AA-5B Tiger | G. A. J. Bowles (G-BHZN) | |
| G-GALA | PA-28 Cherokee 180 | E. Alexander | |
| G-GAMA | Beech 95-58 Baron | Gama Aviation Ltd (G-BBSD)/Fairoaks | |
| G-GAME | Cessna T.303 | Street Construction (Wigan) Ltd | |
| G-GANE | Sequoia F.8L Falco | S. J. Gane | |
| G-GANJ | Fournier RF-6B-100 | Soaring Equipment Ltd/Coventry | |
| G-GARY | Cessna TR.182RG II | G. Hitchen | |
| G-GASC | Hughes 369HS | Crewhall Ltd (G-WELD/G-FROG) | |
| G-GASP | PA-28-181 Archer II | G-GASP Flying Group | |
| G-GASS | Thunder Ax7-77 balloon | Travel Gas (Midlands) Ltd | |
| G-GAUL | Cessna 550 Citation II | Chauffair Leasing Ltd | |
| G-GAWA | Cessna 140 | R. A. Page (G-BRSM) | |
| G-GAYL | Learjet 35A | Northern Executive Aviation Ltd (G-ZING)/ Manchester | |
| G-GAZA | SA.341G Gazelle 1 | Stratton Motor Co (Norfolk) Ltd (G-RALE/ G-SFTG) | |
| G-GAZI | SA.341G Gazelle 1 | Stratton Motor Co (Norfolk) Ltd & UCC International Group Ltd (G-BKLU) | |
| G-GAZZ | SA.341G Gazelle 1 | Stratton Motor Co (Norfolk) Ltd & UCC International Group Ltd | |
| G-GBAO | Robin R.1180TD | J. Kay-Movat | |
| G-GBLR | Cessna F.150L | Blue Max Flying Group | |
| G-GBSL | Beech 76 Duchess | R. M. Jones (G-BGVG) | |
| G-GBUE | Robin DR.400/120A | G. Higgins & ptnrs (G-BPXD) | |
| G-GCAA | PA-28R Cherokee Arrow 200 | Southern Air Ltd/Shoreham | |
| G-GCAB | PA-30 Twin Comanche 180 | Southern Air Ltd/Shoreham | |
| G-GCAT | PA-28 Cherokee 140B | F. C. Odie (G-BFRH) | |
| G-GCCL | Beech 76 Duchess | Multirun Ltd | |
| G-GCJL | BAe Jetstream 4100 | British Aerospace PLC/Prestwick | |
| G-GCKI | Mooney M.20K | A. L. Burton & A. J. Daly | |
| G-GCNZ | Cessna 150M | Firecrest Aviation Ltd/Leavesden | |
| G-GDAM | PA-18 Super Cub 135 | G. D. A. Martin | |
| G-GDAY | Robinson R-22B | K. Shaw/Norwich | |
| G-GDOG | PA-28R Cherokee Arrow 200-II | E. J. Percival (G-BDXW) | |
| G-GEAR | Cessna FR.182Q | B. C. J. Lovrey/White Waltham | |
| G-GEDS | AS.350B Ecureuil | Direct Produce Supplies Ltd (G-HMAN/ G-SKIM/G-BIVP) | |

| Notes | Reg. | Type | Owner or Operator |
|---|---|---|---|
| | G-GEEE | Hughes 369HS | B. P. Stein (G-BDOY) |
| | G-GEEP | Robin R.1180T | Organic Concentrates Ltd/Booker |
| | G-GEES | Cameron N-77 balloon | Mark Jarvis Ltd *Mark Jarvis* |
| | G-GEEZ | Cameron N-77 balloon | Charnwood Forest Turf Accountants Ltd |
| | G-GEIL | BAe 125 Srs 800B | Heron Corporation PLC |
| | G-GEMS | Thunder Ax8-90 S2 balloon | Alexander The Jewellers Ltd (G-BUNP) |
| | G-GEOF | Pereira Osprey 2 | G. Crossley |
| | G-GEUP | Cameron N-77 balloon | D. P. & B. O. Turner |
| | G-GFAB | Cameron N-105 balloon | The Andrew Brownsword Collection Ltd |
| | G-GFCA | PA-28-161 Cadet | Swallow Aviation Ltd/Staverton |
| | G-GFCB | PA-28-161 Cadet | S. F. Tebby & Sons |
| | G-GFCC | PA-28-161 Cadet | Swallow Aviation Ltd/Staverton |
| | G-GFCD | PA-34-220T Seneca III | BWOC Ltd (G-KIDS)/Staverton |
| | G-GFCE | PA-28-161 Warrior II | Swallow Aviation Ltd (G-BNJP)/Staverton |
| | G-GFCF | PA-28-161 Cadet | Swallow Aviation Ltd (G-RHBH)/Staverton |
| | G-GFLY | Cessna F.150L | W. Lancs Aero Club Ltd/Woodvale |
| | G-GFRY | Bell 206L-3 LongRanger | Turbine Helicopters Ltd |
| | G-GGCC | AB-206B JetRanger 2 | Hampton Printing (Bristol) Ltd (G-BEHG) |
| | G-GGGG | Thunder Ax7-77A balloon | T. A. Gilmour |
| | G-GGOW | Colt 77A balloon | City of Glasgow District Council |
| | G-GHCL | Bell 206B JetRanger 2 | Grampian Helicopter Charter Ltd (G-SHVV) |
| | G-GHIA | Cameron N-120 balloon | Bristol Street Motors (Cheltenham) Ltd |
| | G-GHIN | Thunder Ax7-77 balloon | G. M. Ghinn |
| | G-GHRW | PA-28RT-201 Arrow IV | Leavesden Flight Centre Ltd (G-ONAB/G-BHAK) |
| | G-GIGI | M.S.893A Rallye Commodore | P. J. C. Phillips (G-AYVX) |
| | G-GIII | G.1159A Gulfstream 3 | Aravco Ltd (G-BSAN)/Heathrow |
| | G-GILY | Robinson R-22B | Reynard Racing Cars Ltd |
| | G-GIRO | Schweizer 269C | D. E. McDowell |
| | G-GJCB | BAe 125 Srs 800B | J. C. Bamford Excavators Ltd |
| | G-GJCD | Robinson R-22B | A. G. Forshaw |
| | G-GLAM | BAe Jetstream 3102 | Manx Airlines Ltd (G-IBLX)/Ronaldsway |
| | G-GLAW | Cameron N-90 balloon | George Law Ltd |
| | G-GLED | Cessna 150M | Firecrest Aviation Ltd/Leavesden |
| | G-GLOR | Cessna 425 | Calmcraft Ltd |
| | G-GLOS | H.P.137 Jetstream 200 | British Aerospace PLC (G-BCGU/G-AXRI) |
| | G-GLOW | AS.355-1 Twin Squirrel | Coalite Group PLC (G-PAPA/G-MCAH/G-CNET) |
| | G-GLUE | Cameron N-65 balloon | L. J. M. Muir & G. D. Hallett |
| | G-GMAX | SNCAN Stampe SV-4C | Glidegold Ltd (G-BXNW) |
| | G-GMJM | McD Douglas MD-83 | Airtours International Aviation Ltd |
| | G-GMPA | AS.355F-2 Twin Squirrel | Greater Manchester Police Authority (G-BPOI) |
| | G-GMSI | SOCATA TB.9 Tampico | ML Associates |
| | G-GNAT | H.S. Gnat T.1 (XS101) | Ruanil Investments Ltd/Cranfield |
| | G-GNSY | HPR-7 Herald 209 | Channel Express (Air Services) Ltd (G-BFRK)/Bournemouth |
| | G-GNTA | SAAB SF.340A | Business Air Ltd/Aberdeen |
| | G-GNTB | SAAB SF.340A | Business Air Ltd/Aberdeen |
| | G-GNTC | SAAB SF.340A | Business Air Ltd/Aberdeen |
| | G-GNTD | SAAB SF.340A | Business Air Ltd/Aberdeen |
| | G-GNTE | SAAB SF.340A | Business Air Ltd/Aberdeen |
| | G-GNTF | — | |
| | G-HRVD | CCF Harvard IV | M. Slater (G-BSBC) |
| | G-GOBP | Bell 206B JetRanger 2 | Clyde Helicopters Ltd (G-BOUY) |
| | G-GOBT | Colt 77A balloon | British Telecom PLC |
| | G-GOCC | AA-5A Cheetah | Lowlog Ltd (G-BPIX) |
| | G-GOCX | Cameron N-90 balloon | Cathay Pacific Airways Ltd |
| | G-GOGO | Hughes 369D | A. W. Alloys Ltd |
| | G-GOLD | Thunder Ax6-56A balloon | Joseph Terry & Sons Ltd |
| | G-GOLF | SOCATA TB.10 Tobago | E. H. Scamell & ptnrs |
| | G-GOMM | PA-32R Cherokee Lance 300 | A. Kazaz/Leicester |
| | G-GONE | D.H.112 Venom FB.50 | J. E. Davies |
| | G-GOOS | Cessna F.182Q | S. W. B. Parkinson |
| | G-GORE | CFM Streak Shadow | D. N. & E. M. Gore |
| | G-GOSS | Jodel DR.221 | D. Folens |
| | G-GOZO | Cessna R.182 | Transmatic Fyllan Ltd (G-BJZO)/Cranfield |
| | G-GPMW | PA-28RT-201T Turbo Arrow IV | M. Worrall & ptnrs |
| | G-GPST | Phillips ST.1 Speedtwin | P. J. C. Philips |
| | G-GRAM | PA-31-350 Navajo Chieftain | Superpower Air Services Ltd (G-BRHF) |

| Reg. | Type | Owner or Operator | Notes |
|------|------|-------------------|-------|
| G-GRAY | Cessna 172N | Truman Aviation Ltd/Tollerton | |
| G-GREG | Jodel DR.220 2+2 | J. T. Wilson | |
| G-GREN | Cessna T.310R | Elvedale Holding Ltd | |
| G-GRID | AS.355F-1 Twin Squirrel | National Grid Co PLC | |
| G-GRIF | R. Commander 112TCA | M. J. Chilton (G-BHXC) | |
| G-GROW | Cameron N-77 balloon | Derbyshire Building Society | |
| G-GSFC | Robinson R-22B | Weller Helicopters Ltd | |
| G-GSML | Enstrom 280C-UK | Guardwell Security Management Ltd (G-BNNV) | |
| G-GTAX | PA-31-350 Navajo Chieftain | Jet West Ltd (G-OIAS)/Exeter | |
| G-GTHM | PA-38-112 Tomahawk | Truman Aviation Ltd/Tollerton | |
| G-GTPL | Mooney M.20K | W. R. Emberton/Spain | |
| G-GUCK | Beech C23 Sundowner 180 | G-GUCK Group (G-BPYG) | |
| G-GUNN | Cessna F.172H | J. G. Gunn (G-AWGC) | |
| G-GUNS | Cameron V-77 balloon | Royal School of Artillery Hot Air Balloon Club | |
| G-GURL | Cameron A-210 balloon | Hot Airlines Ltd | |
| G-GUYI | PA-28-181 Archer II | B. Butler | |
| G-GUYS | PA-34-200T Seneca | H. Jowett & Co Ltd (G-BMWT) | |
| G-GWEN | Cessna F.172M | R. E. Youngsworth (G-GBLP) | |
| G-GWHH | AS.355F Twin Squirrel | Wimpey Homes Holdings Ltd (G-BKUL) | |
| G-GWIL | AS.350B Ecureuil | Talan Ltd | |
| G-GWIT | Cameron O-84 balloon | M. A. Campbell | |
| G-GWIZ | Colt Clown SS balloon | Oxford Promotions (UK) Ltd | |
| G-GWYN | Cessna F.172M | Gwyn Aviation | |
| G-GYAV | Cessna 172N | Southport & Merseyside Aero Club (1979) Ltd | |
| G-GYMM | PA-28R Cherokee Arrow 200 | D. M. Ball (G-AYWW) | |
| G-GYRO | Bensen B.8 | N. A. Pitcher & A. L. Howell | |
| G-GZDO | Cessna 172N | Cambridge Hall Aviation | |
| G-HAEC | CAC-18 Mustang 23 (472917) | R. G. Hanna/Duxford | |
| G-HAGT | Airbus A.320-212 | Excalibur Airways Ltd/E. Midlands | |
| G-HAIG | Rutan LongEz | P. N. Haigh | |
| G-HAJJ | Glaser-Dirks DG.400 | P. W. Endean | |
| G-HALC | PA-28R Cherokee Arrow 200 | Halcyon Aviation Ltd | |
| G-HALL | PA-22 Tri-Pacer 160 | F. P. Hall (G-ARAH) | |
| G-HALP | SOCATA TB.10 Tobago | D. Halpera (G-BITD)/Elstree | |
| G-HAMA | Beech 200 Super King Air | Gama Aviation Ltd/Fairoaks | |
| G-HAMI | Fuji FA.200-180 | Hamilton Rentals (UK) Ltd (G-OISF/G-BAPT) | |
| G-HAMP | Bellanca 7ACA Champ | R. J. Grimstead | |
| G-HANS | Robin DR.400 2+2 | Headcorn Flying School Ltd | |
| G-HAPR | B.171 Sycamore HR.14 (XG547) ★ | International Helicopter Museum/Weston-s-Mare | |
| G-HARE | Cameron N-77 balloon | M. A. Pratt & N. I. Cakebread | |
| G-HARF | G.1159C Gulfstream 4 | Fayair (Jersey) Ltd | |
| G-HARH | Sikorsky S-76B | Fayair (Jersey) 1984 Ltd | |
| G-HART | Cessna 152 | Atlantic Air Transport Ltd/Coventry | |
| G-HASL | AA-5A Cheetah | D.B.G. Ltd (G-BGSL)/(stored) | |
| G-HATZ | Hatz CB-1 | J. Pearson | |
| G-HAZE | Thunder Ax8-90 balloon | H. A. Ingham | |
| G-HBAC | AS.355F-1 Twin Squirrel | BAC Ltd (G-HJET) | |
| G-HBUG | Cameron N-90 balloon | Thorn EMI Computeraid (G-BRCN) | |
| G-HCRP | McD Douglas MD-83 | Airtours International Aviation Ltd | |
| G-HCSL | PA-34-220T Seneca III | Hollowbrook Computer Services Ltd | |
| G-HCTL | PA-31-350 Navajo Chieftain | Field Aircraft Services (Heathrow) Ltd (G-BGOY) | |
| G-HDBC | H.S.748 Srs 2B | BAF Aircraft Engineering Ltd/Southend | |
| G-HDBD | H.S.748 Srs 2B | British Aerospace PLC/Woodford | |
| G-HDEW | PA-32R-301 Saratoga SP | Lord Howard de Walden (G-BRGZ) | |
| G-HEAD | Colt 56 balloon | Colt Balloons Ltd | |
| G-HELE | Bell 206B JetRanger 3 | B. E. E. Smith (G-OJFR) | |
| G-HELI | Saro Skeeter Mk 12 (XM556) ★ | International Helicopter Museum/Weston-s-Mare | |
| G-HELN | PA-18 Super Cub 95 | J. J. Anziani (G-BKDG)/Booker | |
| G-HELP | Colt 17A balloon | Airship & Balloon Co Ltd | |
| G-HELV | D.H.115 Vampire T.55 (U-1215) | Hunter Wing Ltd | |
| G-HELX | Cameron N-31 balloon | Hot-Air Balloon Co Ltd | |
| G-HEMS | SA.365N Dauphin 2 | Express Newspapers PLC | |
| G-HENS | Cameron N-65 balloon | Horrells Dairies Ltd | |
| G-HENY | Cameron V-77 balloon | R. S. D'Alton | |
| G-HERA | Robinson R-22B | J. Malcolm | |
| G-HERB | PA-28R-201 Arrow III | D. I. Weidner | |

| Notes | Reg. | Type | Owner or Operator |
|---|---|---|---|
| | G-HERO | PA-32RT-300 Lance II | R. P. Thomas & C. Moore(G-BOGN) |
| | G-HERS | Jodel D.18 | A. Usherwood |
| | G-HEVY | Boeing 707-324C | HeavyLift Cargo Airlines Ltd/Stansted |
| | G-HEWI | Piper J-3C-90 Cub | Denham Grasshopper Group (G-BLEN) |
| | G-HEWS | Hughes 369D ★ | Spares use/Sywell |
| | G-HEYY | Cameron 77 Bear SS balloon | Hot-Air Balloon Co Ltd George |
| | G-HFBM | Curtiss Robin C-2 | Colin Crabbe Holdings Ltd |
| | G-HFCA | Cessna A.150L | Horizon Flying Club Ltd/Ipswich |
| | G-HFCB | Cessna F.150L | Horizon Flying Club Ltd (G-AZVR)/Ipswich |
| | G-HFCI | Cessna F.150L | Horizon Flying Club Ltd/Ipswich |
| | G-HFCL | Cessna F.152 | Horizon Flying Club Ltd (G-BGLR)/Ipswich |
| | G-HFCT | Cessna F.152 | Stapleford Flying Club Ltd |
| | G-HFIX | V.S.361 Spitfire HF.IXe (MJ730) | D. W. Pennell (G-BLAS) |
| | G-HFLA | Schweizer 269C | Sterling Helicopters Ltd/Norwich |
| | G-HFTG | PA-23 Aztec 250E | Clacton Aero Club (1988) Ltd (G-BSOB/ G-BCJR) |
| | G-HGAS | Cameron V-77 balloon | Handygas Ltd |
| | G-HGPI | SOCATA TB.20 Trinidad | M. J. Jackson/Bournemouth |
| | G-HHUN | Hunter F.4 | Hunter Wing Ltd/Bournemouth |
| | G-HIEL | Robinson R-22B | Hields Aviation |
| | G-HIER | Bell 206B JetRanger 3 | Rentatruck Self Drive Ltd (G-BRFD) |
| | G-HIHI | PA-32R-301 Saratoga SP | D. R. Reynolds/Cranfield |
| | G-HILS | Cessna F.172H | London Aviation Group (G-AWCH) |
| | G-HILT | SOCATA TB.10 Tobago | P. J. Morrison |
| | G-HINT | Cameron N-90 balloon | Hinton Garage Bath Ltd |
| | G-HIPO | Robinson R-22B | Hippo Helicopters Ltd (G-BTGB) |
| | G-HIRE | GA-7 Cougar | London Aerial Tours Ltd (G-BGSZ)/ Biggin Hill |
| | G-HISS | Aerotek Pitts S-2A Special | S. Byers (G-BLVU) |
| | G-HIVA | Cessna 337A | High Voltage Applications Ltd (G-BAES) |
| | G-HIVE | Cessna F.150M | M. P. Lynn (G-BCXT)/Sibson |
| | G-HJSS | AIA Stampe SV-4C (modified) | H. J. Smith (G-AZNF) |
| | G-HLFT | SC.5 Belfast 2 | HeavyLift Cargo Airlines Ltd/Stansted |
| | G-HLIX | Cameron 80 Oil Can balloon | Hot-Air Balloon Co Ltd |
| | G-HMBB | MBB BK-117B-1C | MBB Helicopter Systems Ltd |
| | G-HMES | PA-28-161 Warrior II | Cleveland Flying School Ltd/Teesside |
| | G-HMJB | PA-34-220T Seneca III | M. Gavaghan |
| | G-HMMM | Cameron N-65 balloon | S. Moss |
| | G-HMPH | Bell 206B JetRanger 2 | Mightycraft Ltd (G-BBUY) |
| | G-HMPT | AB-206B JetRanger 2 | Kensington Aviation Ltd |
| | G-HNRY | Cessna 650 Citation III | Quantel Ltd/Biggin Hill |
| | G-HNTR | Hunter T.7 (XL572) ★ | Hunter Wing Ltd/Bournemouth |
| | G-HOBO | Denney Aerocraft Kitfox Mk 4 | W. M. Hodgkins & C. A. Boswell |
| | G-HOCK | PA-28 Cherokee 180 | Arabact Ltd (G-AVSH) |
| | G-HOFM | Cameron N-56 balloon | Hot-Air Balloon Co Ltd |
| | G-HOHO | Colt Santa Claus SS balloon | Oxford Promotions (UK) Ltd |
| | G-HOLY | ST.10 Diplomate | Sussex Spraying Services Ltd/Shoreham |
| | G-HOME | Colt 77A balloon | Anglia Balloon School Tardis |
| | G-HONK | Cameron O-105 balloon | T. F. W. Dixon & Son Ltd |
| | G-HOOV | Cameron N-56 balloon | H. R. Evans |
| | G-HOPE | Beech F33A Bonanza | Hurn Aviation Ltd |
| | G-HOPI | Cameron N-42 balloon | Cameron Balloons Ltd |
| | G-HOPS | Thunder Ax8-90 balloon | A. C. Munn |
| | G-HORN | Cameron V-77 balloon | Travel Gas (Midlands) Ltd |
| | G-HOST | Cameron N-77 balloon | D. Grimshaw |
| | G-HOTI | Colt 77A balloon | R. Ollier |
| | G-HOTT | Cameron O-120 balloon | D. L. Smith |
| | G-HOTZ | Colt 77B balloon | C. J. & S. M. Davies |
| | G-HOUS | Colt 31A balloon | Anglia Balloons Ltd |
| | G-HOWE | Thunder Ax7-77 balloon | M. F. Howe |
| | G-HPAA | BN-2B-26 Islander | Hampshire Police Authority (Air Support Unit) (G-BSWP) |
| | G-HPLC | Sikorsky S-76B | Air Hanson Ltd/Blackbushe |
| | G-HPVC | Partenavia P.68 Victor | Airtime (Hampshire) Ltd |
| | G-HRAY | AB-206B JetRanger 3 | Hecray Co Ltd (G-VANG/G-BIZA) |
| | G-HRHI | B.206 Srs 1 Basset (XS770) | Universal Salvage (Holdings) Ltd |
| | G-HRIO | Robin HR.100/120 | R. L. & G. M. Bagnall |
| | G-HRIS | Cessna P210N | Birmingham Aviation Ltd |
| | G-HRLK | SAAB 91D/2 Safir | Sylmar Aviation & Services Ltd (G-BRZY) |
| | G-HRLM | Brügger MB.2 Colibri | R. A. Harris |
| | G-HROI | R. Commander 112A | H. R. Oldland |
| | G-HRON | D.H.114 Heron 2 | St Helena Airways Ltd (G-AORH) |
| | G-HRVD | CCF Harvard IV | M. Slater (G-BSBC) |

| Reg. | Type | Owner or Operator | Notes |
|------|------|-------------------|-------|
| G-HRZN | Colt 77A balloon | A. J. Spindler | |
| G-HSDW | Bell 206B JetRanger | Winfield Shoe Co Ltd | |
| G-HSHS | Colt 105A balloon | H. & S. Aviation Ltd | |
| G-HTAX | PA-31-350 Navajo Chieftain | Jet Navaid Ltd/Exeter | |
| G-HTPS | SA. 341G Gazelle 1 | ITPS Ltd (G-BRNI) | |
| G-HTRF | Robinson R-22B | Ellmar Plant Hire Ltd | |
| G-HUBB | Partenavia P.68B | G-HUBB Ltd | |
| G-HUCH | Cameron 80 Carrots SS balloon | Airship & Balloon Co Ltd (G-BYPS) | |
| G-HUEY | Bell UH-1H | Butane Buzzard Aviation Corporation Ltd | |
| G-HUFF | Cessna 182P | A. E. G. Cousins | |
| G-HULL | Cessna F.150M | A. D. McLeod | |
| G-HUMF | Robinson R-22B | R. A. Wright | |
| G-HUMT | Bell 206B JetRanger | H. J. Walters | |
| G-HUNY | Cessna F.150G | T. J. Lynn (G-AVGL) | |
| G-HURI | CCF Hawker Hurricane IIB (Z7381) | Patina Ltd/Duxford | |
| G-HURN | Robinson R-22B | Yorkshire Helicopter Centre Ltd | |
| G-HURR | Hawker Hurricane XIIB (BE417) | Autokraft Ltd | |
| G-HURY | Hawker Hurricane IV (KZ321) | D. W. Arnold/Biggin Hill | |
| G-HUTT | Denney Aerocraft Kitfox | B. W. Davies | |
| G-HVDM | V.S.361 Spitfire F.IX (H-25) | DSG (Guernsey) Ltd/Holland | |
| G-HVRD | PA-31-350 Navajo Chieftain | London Flight Centre Air Charter Ltd (G-BEZU) | |
| G-HVRS | Robinson R-22B | Northern Helicopters (Leeds) Ltd | |
| G-HWBK | Agusta A.109A | Camlet Helicopters Ltd | |
| G-HWKN | PA-31P Pressurised Navajo | Industrial Marketing Group | |
| G-HWKR | Colt 90A balloon | P. A. Henderson | |
| G-HYGA | BAe 125 Srs 800B | Helpfactor Ltd | |
| G-HYLT | PA-32R-301 Saratoga SP | R. G. Moggridge | |
| G-HYPO | Colt 180A balloon | The Balloon Club of GB Ltd | |
| G-IAMP | Cameron H-34 balloon | Air 2 Air Ltd | |
| G-IBET | Cameron 70 Can SS balloon | M. R. Humphrey & J. R. Clifton | |
| G-IBFW | PA-28R-201 Arrow III | Speedway Car & Van Hire Ltd | |
| G-IBTX | Boeing 737-2M8 | GB Airways Ltd (G-BTEB)/Gatwick | |
| G-ICED | Cessna 501 Citation | Iceland Frozen Foods PLC/Chester | |
| G-ICES | Thunder Ax6-56 balloon | British Balloon Museum & Library Ltd | |
| G-IDDI | Cameron N-77 balloon | Allen & Harris Ltd | |
| G-IDDY | D.H.C.1 Super Chipmunk | A. J. E. Ditheridge (G-BBMS) | |
| G-IDEA | AA-5A Cheetah | Lowlog Ltd (G-BGNO) | |
| G-IDJB | Cessna 150L | R. J. Browne | |
| G-IDUP | Enstrom 280C Shark | Stephenson Marine Ltd (G-BRZF) | |
| G-IDWR | Hughes 369HS | Ryburn Air Ltd (G-AXEJ) | |
| G-IEAA | Boeing 737-33A | Inter European Airways Ltd/Cardiff | |
| G-IEAB | Boeing 757-23A | Inter European Airways Ltd/Cardiff | |
| G-IEAC | Boeing 757-236 | Inter European Airways Ltd/Cardiff | |
| G-IEAD | Boeing 757-236 | stored (G-BRJG)/Teesside | |
| G-IEAE | Boeing 737-4S3 | Inter European Airways Ltd (G-BRKF)/ Cardiff | |
| G-IEPF | Robinson R-22B | V. T. Nash | |
| G-IEYE | Robin DR, 400/180 | J. S. Haslam | |
| G-IFIT | PA-31-350 Navajo Chieftain | Cook Aviation Services Ltd (G-NABI/ G-MARG) | |
| G-IFLI | AA-5A Cheetah | ABC Aviation Ltd | |
| G-IFLP | PA-34-200T Seneca II | Golf-Sala Ltd | |
| G-IFOX | Robinson R-22B | Munn & Chapman Ltd | |
| G-IFTA | PA-31-350 Navajo Chieftain | Heston Investments Ltd (G-BAVM) | |
| G-IFTD | Cessna 404 | Tristar Cars Ltd (G-BKUN) | |
| G-IGAR | PA-31-310 Turbo Navajo C | BWOC Ltd | |
| G-IGEL | Cameron N-90 balloon | Computacenter Ltd | |
| G-IGHA | PA-34-220T Seneca III | Cormack (Aircraft Sales) Ltd (G-IPUT) | |
| G-IGLA | Colt 240A balloon | P. J. Stapley | |
| G-IGLE | Cameron V-90 balloon | A. A. Laing | |
| G-IHSA | Robinson R-22B | R. J. Everett | |
| G-IHSB | Robinson R-22B | Swift Helicopters Ltd | |
| G-IIAC | Aeronca 11AC Chief | Bailey Aviation Ltd (G-BTPY) | |
| G-IIAN | Aero Designs Pulsar | I. G. Harrison | |
| G-IIBD | PA-44-180T Seminole | H. S. Davies | |
| G-IIIG | Boeing Stearman A.75N1 | Aerosuperbatics Ltd (G-BSDR)/Staverton | |
| G-IIII | Aerotek Pitts S-2B Special | B. K. Lecomber | |
| G-IIIL | Pitts S-1T Special | Skylark Aerobatics | |
| G-IIIT | Aerotek Pitts S-2A Special | Aerobatic Displays Ltd | |
| G-IIIX | Pitts S-1S Special | J. E. R. Seeger (G-LBAT/G-UCCI/G-BIYN) | |
| G-IINA | AS.350B-2 Ecureuil | Endeavour Aviation Ltd | |

| Notes | Reg. | Type | Owner or Operator |
|---|---|---|---|
| | G-IIRB | Bell 206B JetRanger 3 | Robard Consultants Ltd |
| | G-IITI | Extra EA.300 | Aerobatic Displays Ltd/Booker |
| | G-IJAC | Light Aero Avid Speedwing Mk 4 | I. J. A. Charlton |
| | G-IJOE | PA-28RT-201T Turbo Arrow IV | Scotlandair Ltd/Glasgow |
| | G-IJRC | Robinson R-22B | J. R. Clark Ltd (G-BTJP) |
| | G-IJYS | BAe Jetstream 3102 | Jackie Stewart (G-BTZT) |
| | G-IKBP | PA-28-161 Warrior II | Hendafern Ltd/Shoreham |
| | G-IKIS | Cessna 210M | A. C. Davison |
| | G-ILES | Cameron O-90 balloon | G. N. Lantos |
| | G-ILLE | Boeing Stearman A.75L3 (379) | M. H. Pendlebury |
| | G-ILLS | H.S.125 Srs 3B | S. Gill (G-AVRF)/Luton |
| | G-ILLY | PA-28-181 Archer II | A. G. & K. M. Spiers |
| | G-ILSE | Corby CJ-1 Starlet | S. Stride |
| | G-ILTS | PA-32 Cherokee Six 300 | Fadmoor Flying Group (G-CVOK) |
| | G-ILYS | Robinson R-22B | G. K. Ryatt |
| | G-IMAG | Colt 77A balloon | Flying Pictures (Balloons) Ltd |
| | G-IMLH | Bell 206A JetRanger 3 | Subaru (UK) Ltd |
| | G-IMLI | Cessna 310Q | P. D. Carne (G-AZYK) |
| | G-IMPW | PA-32-301 Saratoga SP | C. M. Juggins |
| | G-IMPX | R. Commander 112B | P. A. Day |
| | G-IMPY | Light Aero Avid Flyer C | T. R. C. Griffin |
| | G-INAV | Aviation Composites Mercury | Europa Aviation Ltd |
| | G-INCA | Glaser-Dirks DG.400 | H. W. Ober |
| | G-INCH | Montgomerie-Bensen B.8MR | I. H. C. Branson (G-BRES) |
| | G-INDC | Cessna T.303 | Howarth Timber (Aircharters) Ltd |
| | G-INGA | Thunder Ax8-84 balloon | M. L. J. Ritchie |
| | G-INGB | Robinson R-22B | Motor Care |
| | G-INNY | SE-5A (replica) (F5459) | R. M. Ordish/Old Sarum |
| | G-INOW | Monnet Moni | T. W. Clark |
| | G-INTC | Robinson R-22B | Intec Project Engineering Ltd |
| | G-IOOI | Robin DR.400/160 | Freshname No 77 Ltd |
| | G-IOSI | Jodel DR.1051 | A. Burbidge & R. Slater |
| | G-IPEC | SIAI-Marchetti S.205-18F | P. M. Wright (G-AVEG) |
| | G-IPSI | Grob G.109B | G-IPSI Ltd (G-BMLO) |
| | G-IPSY | Rutan Vari-Eze | R. A. Fairclough/Biggin Hill |
| | G-IRIS | AA-5B Tiger | E. I. Bett (G-BIXU) |
| | G-IRLS | Cessna FR.172J | R. C. Chapman |
| | G-IRLY | Colt 90A balloon | S. A. Burnett & L. P. Purfield |
| | G-IRPC | Cessna 182Q | R. P. Carminke (G-BSKM) |
| | G-ISCA | PA-28RT-201 Arrow IV | D. J. & P. Pay |
| | G-ISEB | Agusta A.109A II | Air Hanson Aircraft Sales Ltd (G-IADT/ G-HCBA)/Blackbushe |
| | G-ISEE | BAe 146-200 | British Aerospace PLC |
| | G-ISEH | Cessna 182R | SEH (Holdings) Ltd (G-BIWS)/Ipswich |
| | G-ISIS | D.H.82A Tiger Moth | D. R. & M. Wood (G-AODR) |
| | G-ISLE | Short SD3-60 | Manx Airlines Ltd/(G-BLEG)/Ronaldsway |
| | G-ISMO | Robinson R-22B | LGH Aviation Ltd/Bournemouth |
| | G-ISTT | Thunder Ax8-84 balloon | RAF Halton Hot Air Balloon Club |
| | G-ITDA | PA-32R-301 Saratoga SP | ITD Aviation Ltd |
| | G-ITPS | Pilatus PC-6/B2-H2 Turbo Porter | ITPS Ltd/Cranfield |
| | G-ITTU | PA-23 Aztec 250E | D. Byrne & M. Cummings (G-BCSW) |
| | G-IVAC | Airtour AH-77B balloon | D. A. Haward/Germany |
| | G-IVAN | Shaw TwinEze | I. Shaw |
| | G-IVAR | Yakovlev Yak-50 | I. G. Anderson |
| | G-IVOR | Aeronca 11AC Chief | South Western Aeronca Group |
| | G-IWON | Cameron V-90 balloon | D. P. P. Jenkinson (G-BTCV) |
| | G-IZEL | SA.341G Gazelle 1 | Fairview Securities (Investments) Ltd (G-BBHW) |
| | G-IZMO | Thunder Ax8-90 balloon | Landrell Fabric Engineering Ltd |
| | G-JACT | Partenavia P.68C | JCT 600 Ltd (G-NVIA)/Leeds |
| | G-JAKE | D.H.C.1 Chipmunk 22 | J. M. W. Henstock (G-BBMY) Netherthorpe |
| | G-JANA | PA-28-181 Archer II | Croaker Aviation/Stapleford |
| | G-JANB | Colt Flying Bottle SS balloon | Justerini & Brooks Ltd |
| | G-JANE | Cessna 340A | John Hewitson Ltd |
| | G-JANN | PA-34-220T Seneca III | J. A. Powell |
| | G-JANS | Cessna FR.172J | I. G. Aizlewood/Luton |
| | G-JANT | PA-28-181 Archer II | Janair Aviation Ltd |
| | G-JARA | Robinson R-22B | J. A. R. Allwright |
| | G-JASE | PA-28-161 Warrior II | J. T. Matthews |
| | G-JASP | PA-23 Turbo Aztec 250E | Landsurcon (Air Survey) Ltd/Staverton |
| | G-JAZZ | AA-5A Cheetah | Jazz Club |
| | G-JBDH | Robin DR.400/180 | D. Hoolahan/Biggin Hill |

| Reg. | Type | Owner or Operator | Notes |
|------|------|-------------------|-------|
| G-JBET | Beech F33A Bonanza | J. Bett/Glasgow | |
| G-JBJB | Colt 69A balloon | Justerini & Brooks Ltd | |
| G-JBPR | Wittman W.10 Tailwind | P. A. Rose & J. P. Broadhurst | |
| G-JBWI | Robinson R-22B | N. J. Wagstaff Leasing | |
| G-JCAS | PA-28-181 Archer II | Charlie Alpha Ltd | |
| G-JCJC | Colt Flying Jeans SS balloon | J. C. Balloon Co Ltd | |
| G-JCUB | PA-18 Super Cub 135 | Piper Cub Consortium Ltd/Jersey | |
| G-JDEE | SOCATA TB.20 Trinidad | Melville Associates Ltd (G-BKLA) | |
| G-JDHI | Enstrom F-28C-UK | B. J. W. Carter (G-BCOT) | |
| G-JDIX | Mooney M.20B | J. E. Dixon (G-ARTB) | |
| G-JDLI | Jodel D.150 | K. F. & R. Richardson | |
| G-JDTI | Cessna 421C | Eastfield Air Ltd/Sturgate | |
| G-JEAA | F.27 Friendship Mk 500F | Jersey European Airways Ltd | |
| G-JEAB | F.27 Friendship Mk 500F | Jersey European Airways Ltd | |
| G-JEAD | F.27 Friendship Mk 500 | Jersey European Airways Ltd | |
| G-JEAE | F.27 Friendship Mk 500 | Jersey European Airways Ltd | |
| G-JEAF | F.27 Friendship Mk 500 | Jersey European Airways Ltd | |
| G-JEAG | F.27 Friendship Mk 500 | Jersey European Airways Ltd | |
| G-JEAH | F.27 Friendship Mk 500 | Jersey European Airways Ltd | |
| G-JEAI | F.27 Friendship Mk 500 | Jersey European Airways Ltd | |
| G-JEAN | Cessna 500 Citation | Foster Associates Ltd | |
| G-JEET | Cessna FA.152 | Luton Flight Training (G-BHMF) | |
| G-JEFF | PA-38-112 Tomahawk | R. J. Alford | |
| G-JENA | Mooney M.20K | P. Leverkuehn/Biggin Hill | |
| G-JENI | Cessna R.182 | R. A. Bentley | |
| G-JENN | AA-5B Tiger | Clamair Aviation Ltd | |
| G-JENS | SOCATA Rallye 100ST | Palmer Pastoral Co Ltd (G-BDEG) | |
| G-JENY | Baby Great Lakes | J. M. C. Pothecary | |
| G-JERS | Robinson R-22B | Ravenheat Manufacturing Ltd | |
| G-JERY | AB-206B JetRanger 2 | J. J. Woodhouse (G-BDBR) | |
| G-JETA | Cessna 550 Citation II | IDS Aircraft Ltd/Heathrow | |
| G-JETB | Cessna 550 Citation II | European Jet Ltd | |
| G-JETC | Cessna 550 Citation II | Colt Car Co Ltd/Staverton | |
| G-JETE | Cessna 500 Citation | IDS Aircraft Ltd (G-BCKM)/Heathrow | |
| G-JETH | Hawker Sea Hawk FGA.6 ★ | P. G. Vallance Ltd/Charlwood | |
| G-JETI | BAe 125 Srs 800B | Alkharafi Aviation Ltd | |
| G-JETK | BAe 125 Srs 800B | Tiger Aviation Ltd (G-GSAM) | |
| G-JETM | Gloster Meteor T.7 (VZ638) ★ | P. G. Vallance Ltd/Charlwood | |
| G-JETN | Learjet 35A | Heathrow Jet Centre Ltd (G-JJSG) | |
| G-JETP | P.84 Jet Provost T.52A (T.4) | Hunter Wing Ltd/Bournemouth | |
| G-JETX | Bell 206B JetRanger | Tripgate Ltd | |
| G-JFWI | Cessna F.172N | Staryear Ltd | |
| G-JGAL | Beech E90 King Air | Vaux (Aviation) Ltd/Newcastle | |
| G-JGCL | Cessna 414A | M. J. Holt | |
| G-JGMN | C.A.S.A. 1-131E Jungmann 2000 | P. D. Scandrett/Staverton | |
| G-JHAN | Beech B200 Super King Air | John Hanson Services Ltd | |
| G-JHAS | Schweizer 269C | Albany Helicopters Ltd | |
| G-JHEW | Robinson R-22B | Burbage Farms Ltd | |
| G-JILL | R. Commander 112TCA | Hanover Aviation/Elstree | |
| G-JIMS | Cessna 340A-II | Cox-Johnston Management Services Ltd (G-PETE)/Dundee | |
| G-JJAN | PA-28-181 Archer II | Redhill Flying Club | |
| G-JLEE | AB-206B JetRanger 3 | Lee Aviation Ltd (G-JOKE/G-CSKY G-TALY) | |
| G-JLHS | Beech A36 Bonanza | J. L. Hopkins/Guernsey | |
| G-JLMW | Cameron V-77 balloon | The Apollo Balloon Co Ltd | |
| G-JLRW | Beech 76 Duchess | Moorfield Developments Ltd/Elstree | |
| G-JMAC | BAe Jetstream 4100 | British Aerospace PLC (G-JAMD/G-JXLI) | |
| G-JMAT | Schweizer 269C | John Matchett Ltd | |
| G-JMDD | Cessna 340A | Thoroughbred Technology Ltd | |
| G-JMDI | Schweizer 269C | Norvic House Ltd (G-FLAT) | |
| G-JMHB | Robin DR.400/140 | TMA Associates Ltd/Biggin Hill | |
| G-JMTS | Robin DR.400/180 | J. R. Whiting | |
| G-JMTT | PA-28R-201T Turbo Arrow III | E. W. Passmore (G-BMHM) | |
| G-JNNB | Colt 90A balloon | Justerini & Brooks Ltd | |
| G-JODL | Jodel DR.1050/M | M. D. Mold | |
| G-JODY | Bell 206B JetRanger 3 | Maztest Motors Ltd | |
| G-JOEY | BN-2A Mk III-2 Trislander | Aurigny Air Services (G-BDGG) Guernsey | |
| G-JOIN | Cameron V-65 balloon | Derbyshire Building Society | |
| G-JOJO | Cameron A-210 balloon | Worcester Balloons | |
| G-JOLY | Cessna 120 | J. D. Tarrant/Bristol | |
| G-JONE | Cessna 172M | A. Pierce | |
| G-JONI | Cessna FA.152 | Luton Flight Training Ltd (G-BFTU) | |
| G-JONN | Bell 206L-1 LongRanger | Veritair Ltd/Cardiff | |

## G-JONO – G-KINE

| Notes | Reg. | Type | Owner or Operator |
|---|---|---|---|
| | G-JONO | Colt 77A balloon | The Sandcliffe Motor Group |
| | G-JONS | PA-31-350 Navajo Chieftain | Echocliff Properties Ltd |
| | G-JONZ | Cessna 172P | Jonesco (Preston) Ltd |
| | G-JOSH | Cameron N-105 balloon | GT Flying Clubs Ltd |
| | G-JOYC | Beech F33A Bonanza | Dunmhor Transport Ltd |
| | G-JOYT | PA-28-181 Archer II | S. W. Taylor (G-BOVO)/Redhill |
| | G-JSCL | Rans S.10 Sakota | D. L. Davies |
| | G-JSMC | McD Douglas MD-83 | Airtours International Aviation Ltd |
| | G-JSON | Cameron N-105 balloon | J. Bennett & Son (Insurance Brokers) Ltd |
| | G-JSSD | SA. Jetstream 3001 | British Aerospace (G-AXJZ)/Prestwick |
| | G-JTCA | PA-23 Aztec 250E | J. D. Tighe (G-BBCU)/Sturgate |
| | G-JTWO | Piper J-2 Cub | A. T. Hooper & C. C. Silk (G-BPZR) |
| | G-JTYE | Aeronca 7AC Champion | J. Tye |
| | G-JUDE | CEA DR.400/180 | R. G. Carrell |
| | G-JUDI | AT-6D Harvard III (FX301) | A. A. Hodgson |
| | G-JUDY | AA-5A Cheetah | Brandon Aviation/Biggin Hill |
| | G-JUIN | Cessna 303 | M. J. Newman/Denham |
| | G-JUNG | C.A.S.A. 1.131E Jungmann 1000 | K. H. Wilson |
| | G-JURE | SOCATA TB.10 Tobago | J. & C. A. Ure |
| | G-JURG | R. Commander 114A | Jurgair Ltd |
| | G-JVAJ | PA-31T1 Cheyenne | Jacques Vert PLC |
| | G-JVJA | Partenavia P.68C | Twinflite Aviation Ltd (G-BMEI) |
| | G-JVMD | Cessna 172M | Brandon Aviation (G-BNTV) |
| | G-JVMR | Partenavia P.68B | Sonardyne Ltd (G-JCTI/G-OJOE) Blackbushe |
| | G-JWBB | Jodel DR.1050 | J. E. Worthy & B. F. Baldock (G-LAKI) |
| | G-JWDG | AA-5A Cheetah | JWDG Aviation (G-OCML/G-JAVA) |
| | G-JWDS | Cessna F.150G | London Aerial Tours Ltd (G-AVNB) |
| | G-JWFT | Robinson R-22B | Tukair Aircraft Charter |
| | G-JWIV | Jodel DR.1051 | R. A. Bragger |
| | G-JWSD | Robinson R-22B | J. W. Sparrow Developments Ltd |
| | G-KAFE | Cameron N-65 balloon | Hot-Air Balloon Co Ltd |
| | G-KAIR | PA-28-181 Archer II | Academy Lithoplates Ltd/Aldergrove |
| | G-KARI | Fuji FA.200-160 | I. Mansfield & F. M. Fiore (G-BBRE) |
| | G-KART | PA-28-161 Warrior II | Newcastle-upon-Tyne Aero Club Ltd |
| | G-KARY | Fuji FA.200-180AO | C. J. Zetter (G-BEYP) |
| | G-KASS | H.S.125 Srs 3B | Baltic Leasing (March) Ltd (G-AVPE) |
| | G-KATE | Westland WG.30 Srs 100 | (stored)/Penzance |
| | G-KATH | Cessna P.210N | S. P. Woods |
| | G-KATS | PA-28 Cherokee 140 | Ipswich School of Flying Ltd (G-BIRC) |
| | G-KAWA | Denney Aerocraft Kitfox | T. W. Maton |
| | G-KBKB | Thunder Ax8-90 S2 balloon | G. Boulden |
| | G-KBPI | PA-28-161 Warrior II | Hendafern Ltd (G-BFSZ)/Shoreham |
| | G-KCAS | Beech 95-B55 Baron | M. J. & J. D. Crymble |
| | G-KCIG | Sportavia RF-5B | Exeter Sperber Syndicate |
| | G-KDET | PA-28-161 Cadet | Rapidspin Ltd/Biggin Hill |
| | G-KDFF | Scheibe SF.25E Super Falke | M. Lee & K. Dudley |
| | G-KDIX | Jodel D.9 Bebe | D. J. Wells |
| | G-KEAA | Beech 65-70 Queen Air | D. Cockburn (G-REXP/G-AYPC) |
| | G-KEAB | Beech 65-B80 Queen Air ★ | Instructional airframe/Shoreham |
| | G-KEAC | Beech 65-A80 Queen Air | D. Cockburn (G-REXY/G-AVNG) |
| | G-KEEN | Stolp SA.300 Starduster Too | Holland Aerobatics Ltd |
| | G-KEMC | Grob G.109 | Eye-Fly Ltd |
| | G-KENB | Air Command 503 Commander | K. Brogden |
| | G-KENI | Rotorway Executive | P. J. Clegg |
| | G-KENM | Luscombe 8A Silvaire | K. McNaughton |
| | G-KENN | Robinson R-22B | Echo Helicopters |
| | G-KERC | SNCAN NC.854S | E. H. Gould |
| | G-KERY | PA-28 Cherokee 180 | Lanafast Ltd (G-ATWO) |
| | G-KEST | Steen Skybolt | S. Thursfield & K. E. Eld |
| | G-KEVN | Robinson R-22B | K. P. Gallen (G-BONX) |
| | G-KEYB | Cameron O-84 balloon | B. P. Key |
| | G-KEYS | PA-23 Aztec 250F | Wards Aviation Ltd |
| | G-KEYY | Cameron N-77 balloon | Business Design Group Ltd (G-BORZ) |
| | G-KFIT | Beech F90 King Air | Kwik Fit Euro Ltd (G-BHUS)/Edinburgh |
| | G-KFOX | Denney Aerocraft Kitfox | C. H. T. Trace |
| | G-KFZI | KFZ-1 Tigerfalke | L. R. Williams |
| | G-KHRE | M.S.893E Rallye 150SV | B. Proctor/Dunkeswell |
| | G-KIAM | Grob G.109B | D. T. Hulme |
| | G-KILY | Robinson R-22A | Julians Supermarket Ltd |
| | G-KIMB | Robin DR.340/140 | R. M. Kimbell |
| | G-KINE | AA-5A Cheetah | Walsh Aviation |

| Reg. | Type | Owner or Operator | Notes |
|------|------|-------------------|-------|
| G-KINK | Cessna 340 | Hulbert of Dudley (Holdings) Ltd (G-PLEV) | |
| G-KIRK | Piper J-3C-65 Cub | M. J. Kirk | |
| G-KISS | Rand KR-2 | E. A. Rooney | |
| G-KITE | PA-28-181 Archer II | World Business Publications Ltd/Elstree | |
| G-KITF | Denney Aerocraft Kitfox | Junipa Sales Aviation Ltd | |
| G-KITI | Pitts S-2E Special | P. A. Grant | |
| G-KITY | Denney Aerocraft Kitfox | Kitfox KFM Group | |
| G-KIWI | Cessna 404 Titan | Aviation Beauport Ltd (G-BHNI) | |
| G-KJET | Beech B90 King Air | Ashcombe Ltd (G-AXFE) | |
| G-KKDL | SOCATA TB.20 Trinidad | Egerton Hospital Equipment Ltd (G-BSHU) | |
| G-KKES | SOCATA TB.20 Trinidad | Kestrel Shipping Ltd (G-BTLH)/Biggin Hill | |
| G-KLAY | Enstrom 280C Shark | Redhill Helicopter Centre (G-BGZD) | |
| G-KLIK | Air Command 532 Elite | Roger Savage (Photography) | |
| G-KMAC | Bell 206B JetRanger | Specbridge Ltd | |
| G-KMAM | Airbus A.320-212 | Excalibur Airways Ltd/E. Midlands | |
| G-KNAP | PA-28-161 Warrior II | R. E. Knapton (G-BIUX)/Finmere | |
| G-KNDY | Bell 206B JetRanger 3 | ASP Helicopter Co Ltd | |
| G-KNIT | Robinson R-22B | BHM Knitwear Ltd | |
| G-KNOW | PA-32 Cherokee Six 300 | P. H. Knowland | |
| G-KODA | Cameron O-77 balloon | United Photofinishers Ltd | |
| G-KOLI | PZL-110 Koliber 150 | T. D. A. George & F. H. Buckland | |
| G-KOLY | Enstrom F-28C-UK | K. M. & H. Bowen (G-WWUK/G-BFFN) | |
| G-KOOL | D.H.104 Devon C.2 ★ | E. Surrey Technical College/nr Redhill | |
| G-KORN | Cameron 70 Brentzen SS balloon | Cameron Balloons Ltd | |
| G-KOTA | PA-28-236 Dakota | JF Packaging | |
| G-KRII | Rand KR-2 | M. R. Cleveley | |
| G-KRIS | Maule M5-235C Lunar Rocket | M. G. Pickering | |
| G-KSVB | PA-24 Comanche 260 | C. M. Gill (G-ENIU/G-AVJU) | |
| G-KTEE | Cameron V-77 balloon | D. C. & N. P. Bull | |
| G-KUKU | Pfalzkuku (BS676) | A. D. Lawrence | |
| G-KUTU | Quickie Q.2 | R. Nash & J. Parkinson | |
| G-KWAX | Cessna 182E Skylane | A. R. Carrillo & J. E. Brewis | |
| G-KWIK | Partenavia P.68B | Travelair UK Ltd | |
| G-KWKI | QAC Quickie Q.200 | B. M. Jackson | |
| G-KYIN | Cessna 421C | Firlea Ltd (G-OAKS) | |
| | | | |
| G-LACA | PA-28-161 Warrior II | Light Planes (Lancashire) Ltd/Barton | |
| G-LACB | PA-28-161 Warrior II | Light Planes (Lancashire) Ltd/Barton | |
| G-LACR | Denney Aerocraft Kitfox | C. M. Rose | |
| G-LADE | PA-32 Cherokee Six 300E | A. G. & D. Webb | |
| G-LADN | PA-28-161 Warrior II | A. J. Diplock (G-BOLK)/Biggin Hill | |
| G-LADS | R. Commander 114 | D. F. Soul | |
| G-LAGR | Cameron N-90 balloon | Bass & Tennent Sales Ltd | |
| G-LAIN | Robinson R-22B | R&R Developments Ltd | |
| G-LAIR | Stoddard-Hamilton Glasair IIS | D. L. Swallow | |
| G-LAKC | Cessna 404 Titan II | Lakeside Aviation Ltd (G-BKTW/G-WTVE)/ Aberdeen | |
| G-LAKD | Cessna 404 Titan II | Lakeside Aviation Ltd (G-BKWA/G-BELV)/ Aberdeen | |
| G-LAKE | Lake LA.250 | Stanford Ltd | |
| G-LAKH | BAe Jetstream 3102 | Lakeside Aviation Ltd (G-BUFM/Aberdeen | |
| G-LAMS | Cessna F.152 | J. J. Baumhardt/Southend | |
| G-LANC | Avro 683 Lancaster X (KB889) ★ | Imperial War Museum/Duxford | |
| G-LAND | Robinson R-22B | Charter Group PLC | |
| G-LANE | Cessna F.172N | G. C. Bantin | |
| G-LANG | Denney Aerocraft Kitfox | J. W. Lang | |
| G-LARA | Robin DR.400/180 | K. D. Brackwell | |
| G-LARE | PA-39 Twin Comanche C/R | J. R. W. Keates/Biggin Hill | |
| G-LARK | Helton Lark 95 | J. Fox | |
| G-LASR | Stoddard-Hamilton Glasair II | P. Taylor | |
| G-LASS | Rutan Vari-Eze | S. Roberts | |
| G-LAXO | Agusta A.109C | Glaxo Holdings Ltd | |
| G-LAZR | Cameron O-77 balloon | Laser Civil Engineering Ltd | |
| G-LBCS | Colt 31A balloon | Airship & Balloon Co Ltd | |
| G-LBLI | Lindstrand LBL-105A balloon | Lindstrand Balloons Ltd | |
| G-LBMM | PA-28-161 Warrior II | M. C. Lawton | |
| G-LBRC | PA-28RT-201 Arrow IV | D. J. V. Morgan & J. C. Lloyd | |
| G-LCIO | Colt 240A balloon | Star Micronics UK Ltd | |
| G-LCGL | CLA.7 Swift (replica) | J. M. Greenland | |
| G-LCOK | Colt 69A balloon | Hot-Air Balloon Co Ltd (G-BLWI) | |
| G-LDYS | Colt 56A balloon | A. Green | |
| G-LEAM | PA-28-236 Dakota | South Yorkshire Caravans Ltd (G-BHLS) | |
| G-LEAN | Cessna FR.182 | J. G. Hogg (G-BGAP)/Biggin Hill | |

| Notes | Reg. | Type | Owner or Operator |
|---|---|---|---|
| | G-LEAP | BN-2T Islander | Army Parachute Association (G-BLND)/Netheravon |
| | G-LEAR | Learjet 35A | Northern Executive Aviation Ltd/Manchester |
| | G-LEAU | Cameron N-31 balloon | P. L. Mossman |
| | G-LECA | AS.355F-1 Twin Squirrel | S. W. Electricity Board (G-BNBK)/Bristol |
| | G-LEDN | Short SD3-30 Variant 100 | Titan Airways Ltd (G-BIOF)/Stansted |
| | G-LEED | Denney Aerocraft Kitfox Mk 2 | G. T. Leedham |
| | G-LEES | Glaser-Dirks DG.400 | T. B. Sargeant & C. A. Marren |
| | G-LEEZ | Bell 206L-1 LongRanger 2 | RJS Aviation Ltd (G-BPCT)/Halfpenny Green |
| | G-LEGO | Cameron O-77 balloon | C. H. Pearce Construction PLC |
| | G-LEGS | Short SD3-60 | Manx Airlines Ltd (G-BLEF)/Ronaldsway |
| | G-LEIC | Cessna FA.152 | Leicestershire Aero Club Ltd |
| | G-LEND | Cameron N-77 balloon | Southern Finance Co Ltd |
| | G-LENN | Cameron V-56 balloon | Anglia Balloon School Ltd |
| | G-LENS | Thunder Ax7-77Z balloon | Big Yellow Balloon Group |
| | G-LEON | PA-31-350 Navajo Chieftain | Prospair Aircharter Ltd/Birmingham |
| | G-LEOS | Robin DR.400/120 | P. G. Newens |
| | G-LEPF | Fairchild 24R-46A Argus III | J. M. Greenland |
| | G-LEPI | Colt 160A balloon | Thunder & Colt Ltd |
| | G-LEVI | Aeronca 7AC Champion | L. Perry & J. P. A. Pumphrey |
| | G-LEXI | Cameron N-77 balloon | Sedgemoor 500 Balloon Group |
| | G-LEZE | Rutan LongEz | K. G. M. Loyal & ptnrs |
| | G-LFIX | V.S.509 Spitfire T.IX (ML407) | C. S. Grace |
| | G-LFSA | PA-38-112 Tomahawk | Liverpool Flying School Ltd (G-BSFC) |
| | G-LFSI | PA-28 Cherokee 140 | Liverpool Flying School Ltd (G-AYKV) |
| | G-LGIO | Colt 240A balloon | Aerial Display Co |
| | G-LIAM | Aerotek Pitts S-2A Special | L. P. McGuinness |
| | G-LIAN | Robinson R-22B | Cotwell Air Services |
| | G-LIBB | Cameron V-77 balloon | B. G. Glibbery |
| | G-LIBS | Hughes 369HS | G. Hinckley & P. Bourdeix |
| | G-LICK | Cessna 172N | Dacebow Aviation (G-BNTR) |
| | G-LIDA | Hoffmann HK-36R Super Dimona | Aeromarine Ltd |
| | G-LIDE | PA-31-350 Navajo Chieftain | Woodgate Executive Air Charter Ltd |
| | G-LIFE | Thunder Ax6-56Z balloon | M. J. & J. Evans |
| | G-LIGG | Cessna F.182Q | Hi-Travel Ltd (G-THAM) |
| | G-LIMA | R. Commander 114 | Tricolore Ltd/Biggin Hill |
| | G-LINC | Hughes 369HS | Fairglobe Ltd |
| | G-LIOA | Lockheed 10A Electra ★ (NC5171N) | Science Museum/Wroughton |
| | G-LION | PA-18 Super Cub 135 (542457 R-167) | A. W. Kennedy |
| | G-LIOT | Cameron O-77 balloon | D. Eliot |
| | G-LIPE | Robinson R-22B | Sloane Helicopters Ltd & Westleigh Construction Ltd (G-BTXJ) |
| | G-LIPP | BN-2T Turbine Islander | Rhine Army Parachute Association (G-BKJG) |
| | G-LISA | Steen Skybolt | T. C. Humphreys |
| | G-LITE | R. Commander 112A | J. Males |
| | G-LITZ | Pitts S-1 Special | J. A. Hughes |
| | G-LIZA | Cessna 340A | M. D. Joy (G-BMDM) |
| | G-LIZI | PA-28 Cherokee 160 | J. A. & J. Saunders (G-ARRP) |
| | G-LIZY | Westland Lysander III (V9300) ★ | G. A. Warner/Duxford |
| | G-LJET | Learjet 35A | Tiger Aviation Ltd/Gatwick |
| | G-LOAG | Cameron N-77 balloon | Matthew Gloag & Son Ltd |
| | G-LOAN | Cameron N-77 balloon | Newbury Building Soc |
| | G-LOCH | Piper J-3C-90 Cub | J. M. Greenland |
| | G-LOGA | BAe ATP/Jetstream 61 | Loganair Ltd/Glasgow |
| | G-LOGB | BAe ATP/Jetstream 61 | Loganair Ltd/Glasgow |
| | G-LOGC | BAe ATP/Jetstream 61 | Loganair Ltd (G-OLCC)/Glasgow |
| | G-LOGD | BAe ATP/Jetstream 61 | Loganair Ltd (G-OLCD)/Glasgow |
| | G-LOGE | BAe ATP/Jetstream 61 | Loganair Ltd (G-BMYL)/Glasgow |
| | G-LOGJ | BAe Jetstream 4102 | Loganair Ltd/Glasgow |
| | G-LOGK | BAe Jetstream 4102 | Loganair Ltd/Glasgow |
| | G-LOGL | BAe Jetstream 4102 | Loganair Ltd/Glasgow |
| | G-LOGP | BAe Jetstream 3102 | Loganair Ltd (G-BPZJ)/Glasgow |
| | G-LOGR | BAe Jetstream 3102 | Loganair Ltd (G-BRGR)/Glasgow |
| | G-LOGS | Robinson R-22B | M. Chantler & ptnrs |
| | G-LOGT | BAe Jetstream 3102 | Loganair Ltd (G-BSFH)/Glasgow |
| | G-LOGU | BAe Jetstream 3102 | Loganair Ltd (G-BRGL)/Glasgow |
| | G-LOGV | BAe Jetstream 3102 | Loganair Ltd (G-BSZK)/Glasgow |
| | G-LOLL | Cameron V-77 balloon | Gone With The Wind Ltd |
| | G-LOLY | AS.350B Ecureuil | Tyne Tees Helicopter Centre |

| Reg. | Type | Owner or Operator | Notes |
|------|------|-------------------|-------|
| G-LONG | Bell 206L LongRanger | Walsh Aviation | |
| G-LOOP | Pitts S-1C Special | B. G. Salter | |
| G-LOOT | EMB-110P1 Bandeirante | Tech Air (Cambridge) Ltd (G-BNOC) | |
| G-LORD | PA-34-200T Seneca II | Aerohire Ltd/Halfpenny Green | |
| G-LORI | H.S.125 Srs 403B | Re-Enforce Trading Co Ltd (G-AYOJ) | |
| G-LORT | Light Aero Avid Speedwing 4 | G. E. Laucht | |
| G-LORY | Thunder Ax4-31Z balloon | A. J. Moore | |
| G-LOSM | Gloster Meteor NF.11 (WM167) | Hunter Wing Ltd/Bournemouth | |
| G-LOSS | Cameron N-77 balloon | D. K. Fish | |
| G-LOTI | Bleriot XI (replica) ★ | Brooklands Museum Trust Ltd | |
| G-LOUI | Extra EA.300 | L. C. A. Knapp (G-OHER) | |
| G-LOUP | Partenavia P.68B | M. H. Wolff (G-OCAL/G-BGMY) | |
| G-LOVX | Cessna 441 Conquest | Hustlepon Ltd/(G-BLCJ) | |
| G-LOWA | Colt 77A balloon | The Hot-Air Balloon Co Ltd | |
| G-LOWE | Monnet Sonerai II | J. L. Kinch | |
| G-LOYA | Cessna FR.172J | T. R. Scorer (G-BLVT) | |
| G-LOYD | SA.341G Gazelle 1 | Appollo Manufacturing (Derby) Ltd (G-SFTC) | |
| G-LPGO | Cameron V-77 balloon | J. Walter Thompson Co Ltd | |
| G-LRBJ | BAe 125-1000B | British Aerospace PLC | |
| G-LRII | Bell 206L LongRanger | Carroll Aircraft Operational Services Ltd | |
| G-LSFI | AA-5A Cheetah | D. P. Williams (G-BGSK) | |
| G-LSHI | Colt 77A balloon | Lambert Smith Hampton Ltd | |
| G-LSLH | Schweizer 269C | Homewood Park (Helicopters) Ltd | |
| G-LSMI | Cessna F.152 | Semloh Aviation Services/Andrewsfield | |
| G-LTNG | Lightning T.5 (XS451) | Lightning Flying Club | |
| G-LUAR | SOCATA TB.10 Tobago | CB Air Ltd | |
| G-LUBE | Cameron N-77 balloon | A. C. K. Rawson | |
| G-LUCA | Thunder Ax7-77Z balloon | R. De-Leyser | |
| G-LUCE | Cameron A-210 balloon | Aerial Promotions Ltd | |
| G-LUCK | Cessna F.150M | S. J. Tolhurst | |
| G-LUCS | Colt 90A balloon | Bavarian Balloon Co Ltd | |
| G-LUED | Aero Designs Pulsar | R. & H. D. Blamires | |
| G-LUFT | Pützer Elster C | Bath Stone Co Ltd (G-BOPY) | |
| G-LUGG | Colt 21A balloon | S. P. Richards | |
| G-LUKE | Rutan LongEz | S. G. Busby | |
| G-LULU | Grob G.109 | A. P. Bowden | |
| G-LUNA | PA-32RT-300T Turbo Lance II | E. Cliffe/Norwich | |
| G-LUSC | Luscombe 8E Silvaire | M. Fowler | |
| G-LUSI | Luscombe 8E Silvaire | R. J. Walker & J. Wrayton/O. Sarum | |
| G-LUST | Luscombe 8E Silvaire | M. Griffiths | |
| G-LUXE | BAe 146-300 | British Aerospace PLC (G-SSSH)/Hatfield | |
| G-LYDD | PA-31 Turbo Navajo | Janes Aviation Ltd (G-BBDU)/Blackpool | |
| G-LYNN | PA-32RT-300 Lance II | Crosswind Aviation Ltd (G-BGNV)/Leeds | |
| G-LYNS | Cessna F.177RG | G. R. E. & G. Evans (G-BDCM) | |
| G-LYNX | Westland WG.13 Lynx | Westland Helicopters Ltd/Yeovil | |
| G-LYTE | Thunder Ax7-77 balloon | G. M. Bulmer | |
| G-MAAC | Advanced Airship Corporation ANR-1 | Advanced Airship Corporation Ltd | |
| G-MABI | Cessna F.150L | Shobdon Aircraft Maintenance (G-BGOJ) | |
| G-MACH | SIAI-Marchetti SF.260 | Cheyne Motors Ltd/Popham | |
| G-MACK | PA-28R Cherokee Arrow 200-II | Mitchell Aircraft | |
| G-MAFE | Dornier Do.228-202K | FR Aviation Ltd (G-OALF/G-MLDO)/ Bournemouth | |
| G-MAFF | BN-2T Islander | FR Aviation Ltd (G-BJEO)/Bournemouth | |
| G-MAFI | Dornier Do.228-200 | FR Aviation Ltd/Bournemouth | |
| G-MAGG | Pitts S-1SE Special | C. A. Boardman | |
| G-MAGY | AS.350B Ecureuil | Quantel Ltd (G-BIYC) | |
| G-MAIR | PA-34-200T Seneca II | D. C. Massey | |
| G-MAJS | Airbus A.300-605R | Monarch Airlines Ltd/Luton | |
| G-MALA | PA-28-181 Archer II | H. Burtwhistle & Son (G-BIIU) | |
| G-MALC | AA-5 Traveler | B. P. Hogan (G-BCPM) | |
| G-MALK | Cessna F.172N | K. M. Drewitt & J. G. Jackson/Liverpool | |
| G-MALS | Mooney M.20K-231 | C. J. Davy/Biggin Hill | |
| G-MALT | Colt Flying Hop balloon | H. de Bock | |
| G-MAMO | Cameron V-77 balloon | The Marble Mosaic Co Ltd | |
| G-MANN | SA.341G Gazelle 1 | First City Air PLC (G-BKLW) | |
| G-MANX | FRED Srs 2 | T. A. Timms | |
| G-MAPR | Beech A36 Bonanza | Openair Ltd | |
| G-MARC | AS.350B Ecureuil | Gabriel Enterprises Ltd (G-BKHU) | |
| G-MARE | Schweizer 269C | The Earl of Caledon | |
| G-MARR | Cessna 421C | Levenmere Ltd (G-JTIE/G-RBBE) | |

| Notes | Reg. | Type | Owner or Operator |
|---|---|---|---|
| | G-MASA | Air & Space 18A gyroplane | M. A. Schumann (G-MELI) |
| | G-MASC | Jodel D.150A | K. F. & R. Richardson |
| | G-MASH | Westland Bell 47G-4A | T. S. Martin (G-AXKU) |
| | G-MASL | Mooney M.20J | Beta Trading Ltd |
| | G-MATE | Moravan Zlin Z.50LS | V. S. E. Norman |
| | G-MATI | Stolp SA.300 Starduster Too | M. R. Clark & J. McM. Rosser/Newcastle |
| | G-MATP | BAe ATP/Jetstream 61 | British Aerospace PLC/Prestwick |
| | G-MATS | Colt GA-42 airship | Imperial Airships Ltd |
| | G-MATT | Robin R.2160 | Sierra Flying Group (G-BKRC)/Newcastle |
| | G-MATZ | PA-28 Cherokee 140 | Midland Air Training School (G-BASI) |
| | G-MAUK | Colt 77A balloon | Airship & Balloon Co Ltd |
| | G-MAVI | Robinson R-22B | Yorkshire Helicopter Centre Ltd/Doncaster |
| | G-MAWL | Maule M4-210C Rocket | D. Group |
| | G-MAXI | PA-34-200T Seneca II | C. W. Middlemass |
| | G-MAXW | Short SD3-60 Variant 100 | Euroworld Airways Ltd (G-BLPY)/Gatwick |
| | G-MAYO | PA-28-161 Warrior II | Jermyk Engineering/Fairoaks |
| | G-MCAR | PA-32 Cherokee Six 300D | Miller Aerial Spraying Ltd (G-LADA/ G-AYWK)/Wickenby |
| | G-MCBP | AIA Stampe SV-4C | Stampe Flying Group (G-BALA) |
| | G-MCKE | Boeing 757-28A | Monarch Airlines Ltd/Luton |
| | G-MCOX | Fuji FA.200-180AO | W. Surrey Engineering (Shepperton) Ltd |
| | G-MCPI | Bell 206B JetRanger 3 | D. A. C. Pipe (G-ONTB) |
| | G-MDAC | PA-28-181 Archer II | B. R. McKay/Bournemouth |
| | G-MDAS | PA-31-310 Turbo Navajo C | Universal Data Technology Ltd (G-BCJZ) |
| | G-MDKD | Robinson R-22B | D. K. Duckworth |
| | G-MDTV | Cameron N-105 balloon | Ideas Factory |
| | G-MEAH | PA-28R Cherokee Arrow 200-II | E. J. Meah (G-BSNM) |
| | G-MEAN | Agusta A.109A | Castle Air Charters Ltd (G-BRYL/G-ROPE/ G-OAMH) |
| | G-MEAT | Robinson R-22B | St Merryn Meat Ltd |
| | G-MEBC | Cessna 310-1 | P. H. Johnson (G-ROGA/G-ASVV) |
| | G-MEGA | PA-28R-201T Turbo Arrow III | Travelworth Ltd |
| | G-MELD | AA-5A Cheetah | Fletcher Aviation Ltd (G-BHCB)/Blackbushe |
| | G-MELT | Cessna F.172H | Vectair Aviation Ltd (G-AWTI) |
| | G-MELV | SOCATA Rallye 235E | Wallis & Sons Ltd (G-BIND) |
| | G-MEME | PA-28R-201 Arrow III | Henry J. Clare Ltd |
| | G-MERC | Colt 56A balloon | Castles Northgate Ltd |
| | G-MERG | Mooney M.20J | Corporate Acquisitions Ltd |
| | G-MERI | PA-28-181 Archer II | Scotia Safari Ltd/Glasgow |
| | G-MERL | PA-28RT-201 Arrow IV | M. Giles |
| | G-MERV | PA-28-161 Warrior II | M. N. Choules |
| | G-META | Bell 222 | The Metropolitan Police/Lippitts Hill |
| | G-METB | Bell 222 | The Metropolitan Police/Lippitts Hill |
| | G-METC | Bell 222 | The Metropolitan Police (G-JAMC)/ Lippitts Hill |
| | G-METE | Gloster Meteor F.8 | Air Support Aviation Systems Ltd |
| | G-METR | Cessna 414A | Hunting Aircraft Ltd/Biggin Hill |
| | G-MEUP | Cameron A-120 balloon | N. J. Tovey |
| | G-MFHL | Robinson R-22B | MFH Ltd |
| | G-MFLI | Cameron V-90 balloon | J. M. Percival |
| | G-MFMF | Bell 206B JetRanger 3 | S.W. Electricity Board (G-BJNJ)/Bristol |
| | G-MFMM | Scheibe SF.25C Falke | S. Lancs Falke Syndicate |
| | G-MHBD | Cameron O-105 balloon | K. Hull |
| | G-MHCA | Enstrom F-28C-UK | Trimcares Ltd (G-SHWW/G-SMUJ/G-BHTF) |
| | G-MHIH | H.S. 125 Srs 700B | Queens Moat Houses PLC (G-BKAA) |
| | G-MICH | Robinson R-22B | A. P. Codling (G-BNKY) |
| | G-MICK | Cessna F.172N | G-MICK Flying Group |
| | G-MICY | Everett Srs 1 gyroplane | D. M. Hughes |
| | G-MIDG | Midget Mustang | C. E. Bellhouse |
| | G-MIFF | Robin DR.400/180 | G. E. Bickerton |
| | G-MIGI | Colt 105A balloon | British School of Ballooning |
| | G-MIKE | Brookland Hornet | M. H. J. Goldring |
| | G-MIKY | Cameron 90 Mickey SS balloon | The Walt Disney Co Ltd |
| | G-MILE | Cameron N-77 balloon | Miles Air Ltd |
| | G-MIMI | SOCATA TB.20 Trinidad | T. J. & P. S. Gower/Biggin Hill |
| | G-MINI | Currie Wot | D. Collinson |
| | G-MINS | Nicollier HN.700 Menestrel II | B. J. Little |
| | G-MINT | Pitts S-1S Special | T. G. Sanderson/Tollerton |
| | G-MINX | Bell 47G-4A | R. F. Warner (G-FOOR) |
| | G-MISR | Robinson R-22B | Wallis & Son Ltd |
| | G-MISS | Taylor JT.2 Titch | A. Brennan |
| | G-MIST | Cessna T.210K | J. Summers (G-AYGM) |
| | G-MITR | Maule MXT-7-180 | A. Mitrega |

| Reg. | Type | Owner or Operator | Notes |
|------|------|-------------------|-------|
| G-MITS | Cameron N-77 balloon | Colt Car Co Ltd | |
| G-MITZ | Cameron N-77 balloon | Colt Car Co Ltd | |
| G-MKAK | Colt 77A balloon | Airship & Balloon Co Ltd | |
| G-MKIX | V.S.361 Spitfire F.IX (NH238) | D. W. Arnold | |
| G-MKVB | V.S.349 Spitfire LF.VB (BM597) | T. Routis | |
| G-MKVI | D.H. Vampire FB.6 | T. C. Topen/Cranfield | |
| G-MKXI | V.S.365 Spitfire PR.XI (PL965) | C. P. B. Horsley | |
| G-MLAS | Cessna 182E | *Parachute jump trainer*/St Merryn | |
| G-MLBU | PA-46-310P Malibu | Northern Scaffold Group Ltd | |
| G-MLFF | PA-23 Aztec 250E | Brands Hatch Circuit Ltd (G-WEBB/ G-BJBU) | |
| G-MLGL | Colt 21A balloon | Colt Balloons Ltd | |
| G-MLWI | Thunder Ax7-77 balloon | M. L. & L. P. Willoughby | |
| G-MOAC | Beech F33A Bonanza | Chalkfarm Productions Ltd | |
| G-MOAK | Schempp-Hirth Nimbus 3DM | P. W. Lever | |
| G-MOAT | Beech 200 Super King Air | Thurston Aviation (Stansted) Ltd | |
| G-MOFF | Cameron O-77 balloon | D. M. Moffat | |
| G-MOGG | Cessna F.172N | I. Grimshaw (G-BHDY) | |
| G-MOGI | AA-5A Cheetah | TL Aviation Ltd (G-BFMU) | |
| G-MOGY | Robinson R-22B | Hireheli Ltd | |
| G-MOHR | Cameron 105 Sarotti balloon | Cameron Balloons Ltd | |
| G-MOLE | Taylor JT.2 Titch | S. R. Mowle | |
| G-MOLL | PA-32-301T Turbo Saratoga | K. Morrissey | |
| G-MOLY | PA-23 Apache 160 | R. R. & M. T. Thorogood (G-APFV)/St Just | |
| G-MONA | M.S.880B Rallye Club | G. L. Thomas | |
| G-MONB | Boeing 757-2T7ER | Monarch Airlines Ltd/Luton | |
| G-MONC | Boeing 757-2T7 | Monarch Airlines Ltd/Luton | |
| G-MOND | Boeing 757-2T7 | Monarch Airlines Ltd/Luton | |
| G-MONE | Boeing 757-2T7ER | Monarch Airlines Ltd/Luton | |
| G-MONF | Boeing 737-3Y0 | Monarch Airlines Ltd/EuroBerlin | |
| G-MONG | Boeing 737-3Y0 | Monarch Airlines Ltd/EuroBerlin | |
| G-MONH | Boeing 737-3Y0 | Monarch Airlines Ltd/EuroBerlin | |
| G-MONI | Monnet Moni | R. J. Baron | |
| G-MONJ | Boeing 757-2T7ER | Monarch Airlines Ltd/Luton | |
| G-MONK | Boeing 757-2T7ER | Monarch Airlines Ltd/Luton | |
| G-MONM | Boeing 737-3Y0 | Monarch Airlines Ltd | |
| G-MONN | Boeing 737-33A | Monarch Airlines Ltd/EuroBerlin | |
| G-MONP | Boeing 737-33A | Monarch Airlines Ltd/EuroBerlin | |
| G-MONR | Airbus A.300-650R | Monarch Airlines Ltd/Luton | |
| G-MONS | Airbus A.300-605R | Monarch Airlines Ltd/Luton | |
| G-MONV | Boeing 737-33A | Monarch Airlines Ltd/Luton | |
| G-MONX | Airbus A.320-211 | Monarch Airlines Ltd/Luton | |
| G-MONY | Airbus A.320-211 | Monarch Airlines Ltd/Luton | |
| G-MOON | Mooney M.20K | M. A. Eccles | |
| G-MOOR | SOCATA TB.10 Tobago | G. A. Moore (G-MILK) | |
| G-MOOS | P.56 Provost T.1 | T. J. Hanna (G-BGKA) | |
| G-MOTH | D.H.82A Tiger Moth (K2567) | M. C. Russell/Duxford | |
| G-MOTO | PA-24 Comanche 160 | C. C. Letchford & A. J. Redknapp (G-EDHE/ G-ASFH) | |
| G-MOTT | Light Aero Avid Speedwing | Avid Aircraft Ltd | |
| G-MOUL | Maule M6-235 | B. C. Abela | |
| G-MOUR | H.S. Gnat T.1 (XR991) | D. J. Gilmour | |
| G-MOUS | Cameron 90 Mickey SS balloon | The Walt Disney Co Ltd | |
| G-MOVI | PA-32R-301 Saratoga SP | Peter Walker (Heritage) Ltd (G-MARI) | |
| G-MOZZ | Avions Mudry CAP.10B | Brandzone Ltd | |
| G-MPBH | Cessna FA.152 | Metropolitan Police Flying Club (G-FLIC/ G-BILV) | |
| G-MPCU | Cessna 402B | Atlantic Air Transport Ltd/Coventry | |
| G-MPWH | Rotorway Executive | MPW Aviation Ltd | |
| G-MPWI | Robin HR.100/210 | Propwash Investments Ltd/Cardiff | |
| G-MPWT | PA-34-220T Seneca III | MPW Aviation Ltd | |
| G-MRCI | Sequoia F.8L Falco | M. R. Clark | |
| G-MRPP | PA-34-220T Seneca III | P. E. Pearce | |
| G-MRSL | Robin DR.400/180 | I. A. S. Laidlaw (G-BUAP) | |
| G-MRSN | Robinson R-22B | P. J. Marson | |
| G-MRST | PA-28RT-201 Arrow IV | Winchfield Enterprises Ltd | |
| G-MRTY | Cameron N-77 balloon | R. A. & P. G. Vale | |
| G-MSDJ | AS.350B-1 Ecureuil | Denis Ferranti Hoverknights Ltd (G-BPOH) | |
| G-MSFC | PA-38-112 Tomahawk | Sherwood Flying Club Ltd/Tollerton | |
| G-MSFY | H.S.125 Srs 700B | Mohamed Said Fakhry/Heathrow | |
| G-MTLE | Cessna 501 Citation | Talan Ltd (G-GENE) | |
| G-MUFF | AS.355F-1 Twin Squirrel | Lynton Aviation Ltd (G-CORR) | |
| G-MUIL | Cessna 172M | Torosay Sandpit Ltd | |

| Notes | Reg. | Type | Owner or Operator |
|-------|------|------|-------------------|
| | G-MUIR | Cameron V-65 balloon | L. C. M. Muir |
| | G-MULL | Douglas DC-10-30 | British Airways *New Forest*/Gatwick |
| | G-MUMS | PA-28-161 Warrior II | A. J. Wood |
| | G-MUNI | Mooney M.20J | Danyderwen Consultants Co Ltd |
| | G-MURF | AA-5B Tiger | D. Collins (G-JOAN/G-BFML) |
| | G-MUSO | Rutan LongEz | M. Moran |
| | G-MUTE | Colt 31A balloon | Redmalt Ltd |
| | G-MXVI | V.S.361 Spitfire LF.XVIe (TE184) | Myrick Aviation Services Ltd |
| | G-NAAT | H.S. Gnat T.1 (XM697) | Hunter Wing Ltd/Bournemouth |
| | G-NABS | Robinson R-22B | Arian Helicopters Ltd |
| | G-NACA | Norman NAC.2 Freelance 180 | Aeronortec Ltd |
| | G-NACI | Norman NAC.1 Srs 100 | I. J. Blackwood |
| | G-NACL | Norman NAC.6 Fieldmaster | EPA Aircraft Co Ltd (G-BNEG) |
| | G-NACM | Norman NAC.6 Fieldmaster | EPA Aircraft Co Ltd |
| | G-NACN | Norman NAC.6 Fieldmaster | EPA Aircraft Co Ltd |
| | G-NACO | Norman NAC.6 Fieldmaster | EPA Aircraft Co Ltd |
| | G-NACP | Norman NAC.6 Fieldmaster | EPA Aircraft Co Ltd |
| | G-NAIL | Cessna 340A | Parelarch Ltd (G-DEXI) |
| | G-NALI | Cessna 152 | Galaxy Enterprises Ltd (G-BHVM) |
| | G-NASA | Lockheed T-33A-5-LO (91007) | A. S. Topen (G-TJET)/Cranfield |
| | G-NASH | AA-5A Cheetah | M. J. Dant/Southampton |
| | G-NATT | R. Commander 114A | Northgleam Ltd |
| | G-NATX | Cameron O-65 balloon | A. Faulkner |
| | G-NATY | H. S. Gnat T.1 (XR537) | F. C. Hackett-Jones |
| | G-NAVO | PA-31-325 Navajo C/R | Shoprite Aviation Ltd |
| | G-NAZO | PA-31-310 Navajo B | Pathway Holdings Ltd (G-AZIM) |
| | G-NBDD | Robin DR.400/180 | D. Dufton/Sherburn |
| | G-NBSI | Cameron N-77 balloon | Nottingham Hot-Air Balloon Club |
| | G-NCUB | Piper J-3C-65 Cub | N. Thomson (G-BGXV)/Norwich |
| | G-NDGC | Grob G.109 | C. H. Appleyard |
| | G-NDNI | NDN-1 Firecracker | Norman Marsh Aircraft Ltd |
| | G-NDRW | Colt AS-80 Mk II airship | Huntair Ltd |
| | G-NEAL | PA-32 Cherokee Six 260 | VSD Group (G-BFPY) |
| | G-NEEL | Rotorway Executive 90 | P. N. Haigh |
| | G-NEEP | Bell 206B JetRanger | Dollar Air Services Ltd/Coventry |
| | G-NEGS | Thunder Ax7-77 balloon | R. Holden |
| | G-NEIL | Thunder Ax3 balloon | Islington Motors (Trowbridge) Ltd |
| | G-NEPB | Cameron N-77 balloon | The Post Office |
| | G-NEVL | Learjet 35A | Skytech Aviation Services Ltd |
| | G-NEWR | PA-31-350 Navajo Chieftain | Eastern Air Executive Ltd/Sturgate |
| | G-NEWS | Bell 206B JetRanger 3 | Peter Press Ltd |
| | G-NEWT | Beech 35 Bonanza | D. W. Mickleburgh (G-APVW) |
| | G-NGBI | AA-5B Tiger | G-NGBI Group (G-JAKK/G-BHWI)/Southend |
| | G-NGRM | Spezio DAL.1 | C. D. O'Malley |
| | G-NHRH | PA-28 Cherokee 140 | H. Dodd |
| | G-NHVH | Maule M5-235C Lunar Rocket | Commercial Go-Karts Ltd/Exeter |
| | G-NICH | Robinson R-22B | Panair Ltd |
| | G-NICK | PA-18 Super Cub 95 | J. G. O'Donnell & I. Woolacott |
| | G-NICO | Robinson R-22B | H. J. Pessall |
| | G-NIFR | Beech 76 Duchess | Transair (UK) Ltd/Fairoaks |
| | G-NIGE | Luscombe 8E Silvaire | Pullmerit Ltd (G-BSHG) |
| | G-NIGS | Thunder Ax7-65 balloon | A. N. F. Pertwee |
| | G-NIKD | Cameron O-120 balloon | D. S. King |
| | G-NIKE | PA-28-181 Archer II | Key Properties Ltd/White Waltham |
| | G-NIKI | Robinson R-22B | N. M. Leatherhead |
| | G-NIKY | PA-31-350 Navajo Chieftain | Ashcombe Ltd (G-BPAR) |
| | G-NIMO | Colt 105A balloon | Thunder & Colt Ltd |
| | G-NINA | PA-28-161 Warrior II | Bailey Aviation Ltd (G-BEUC) |
| | G-NIOS | PA-32R-301 Saratoga SP | Metafin Holdings Ltd |
| | G-NISR | R. Commander 690A | Z. I. Bilbeisi |
| | G-NITA | PA-28 Cherokee 180 | Dove Naish & Ptnrs (G-AVVG) |
| | G-NIUK | Douglas DC-10-30 | British Airways *Cairn Edward Forest*/Gatwick |
| | G-NJAG | Cessna 207 | G. H. Nolan Ltd |
| | G-NJML | PA-34-220T Seneca III | Oxford Management Ltd |
| | G-NJSH | Robinson R-22B | T. F. Hawes |
| | G-NNAC | PA-18 Super Cub 135 | P. A. Wilde |
| | G-NOBI | Spezio Sport HES-1 | M. R. Clark |
| | G-NODE | AA-5B Tiger | Curd & Green Ltd/Elstree |
| | G-NODY | American General AG-5B Tiger | Curd & Green Ltd |
| | G-NOHB | PA-34-220T Seneca III | Malcolm (UK) Ltd |

| Reg. | Type | Owner or Operator | Notes |
|------|------|-------------------|-------|
| G-NOIR | Bell 222 | Arlington Securities Ltd (G-OJLC/G-OSEB/G-BNDA) | |
| G-NONI | AA-5 Traveler | E. B. Landsler (G-BBDA) | |
| G-NORD | SNCAN NC.854 | W. J. McCollum | |
| G-NOTR | McD MD-520N NOTAR | Air Hanson | |
| G-NOTT | Nott ULD-2 balloon | J. R. P. Nott | |
| G-NOVO | Colt AS-56 airship | Thunder & Colt Ltd | |
| G-NPWR | Cameron RX-100 balloon | Nuclear Electric PLC | |
| G-NRDC | NDN-6 Fieldmaster | EPA Aircraft Co Ltd | |
| G-NSGI | Cessna 421C | Northern Scaffold Group PLC | |
| G-NSTG | Cessna F.150F | N. S. T. Griffin (G-ATNI)/Blackpool | |
| G-NTBI | Bell 206B JetRanger 3 | E. Midlands Helicopters Ltd | |
| G-NTOO | SA.365N-2 Dauphin 2 | Bond Helicopters Ltd | |
| G-NTWO | SA.365N-2 Dauphin 2 | Bond Helicopters Ltd | |
| G-NUIG | Beech C90-1 King Air | Norwich Union Fire Insurance Soc (G-BKIP) | |
| G-NUTZ | AS.355F-1 Twin Squirrel | Cotfast Ltd (G-BLRI) | |
| G-NWNW | Cameron V-90 balloon | Royal Mail | |
| G-NWPA | AS.355F-1 Twin Squirrel | McAlpine Helicopters Ltd (G-NAAS/G-BPRG) | |
| G-NWPR | Cameron N-77 balloon | Post Office N.W. Postal Board | |
| G-NYTE | Cessna F.337G | Photoair (G-BATH) | |
| G-NZGL | Cameron O-105 balloon | P. G. & P. M. Vale | |
| G-NZSS | Boeing Stearman N2S-5 (343251) | Pacific Shelf 331 Ltd | |
| G-OAAC | Airtour AH-77B balloon | Army Air Corps | |
| G-OAAL | PA-38-112 Tomahawk | Cumbernauld Aviation Ltd | |
| G-OAAS | Short SD3-60 Variant 100 | Aurigny Air Services Ltd (G-BLIL)/Guernsey | |
| G-OABC | Colt 69A balloon | Airship & Balloon Co Ltd | |
| G-OABG | Hughes 369E | A. B. Gee of Ripley | |
| G-OABY | AB-206B JetRanger 2 | Michael A. Lenihan & Associates Ltd (G-BCWM) | |
| G-OACE | Valentin Taifun 17E | J. E. Dallison | |
| G-OADY | Beech 76 Duchess | Citation Leasing Ltd | |
| G-OAFC | Airtour 56AH balloon | P. J. Donnellan & L. A. Watts | |
| G-OAFT | Cessna 152 | L. E. Steynor (G-BNKM) | |
| G-OAFY | SA.341G Gazelle 1 | R. J. Best (G-SFTH/G-BLAP) | |
| G-OAHC | Beech F33C Bonanza | Clacton Aero Club (1988) Ltd (G-BTTF) | |
| G-OAHF | Boeing 757-27B | Britannia Airways Ltd/Luton | |
| G-OAHK | Boeing 757-23A | Britannia Airways Ltd/Luton | |
| G-OAKC | PA-31-350 Navajo Chieftain | Air Kilroe Ltd (G-WSSC)/Manchester | |
| G-OAKI | BAe Jetstream 3102 | Air Kilroe Ltd/Manchester | |
| G-OAKJ | BAe Jetstream 3200 | Air Kilroe Ltd (G-BOTJ)/Manchester | |
| G-OAKL | Beech 200 Super King Air | Air Kilroe Ltd (G-BJZG)/Manchester | |
| G-OAKM | Beech 200 Super King Air | Air Kilroe Ltd (G-BCUZ)/Manchester | |
| G-OALD | SOCATA TB.20 Trinidad | Mike Little Preparations Ltd | |
| G-OALS | Colt Football SS balloon | Polecroft Ltd | |
| G-OAMG | Bell 206B JetRanger 3 | Alan Mann Helicopters Ltd/Fairoaks | |
| G-OAMY | Cessna 152 | Warwickshire Flying Training Centre Ltd/Birmingham | |
| G-OANC | PA-28-161 Warrior II | Woodvale Aviation Co Ltd (G-BFAD) | |
| G-OANI | PA-28-161 Warrior II | J. A. Caliva | |
| G-OANT | PA-23 Aztec 250 | Air Navigation & Trading Ltd (G-TRFM)/Blackpool | |
| G-OAPR | Brantly B.2B | Helicopter International Magazine/Weston-s-Mare | |
| G-OAPW | Glaser-Dirks DG.400 | A. P. Walsh | |
| G-OARV | ARV Super 2 | P. R. Snowden | |
| G-OASH | Robinson R-22B | A. S. Hawkridge | |
| G-OATP | BAe ATP/Jetstream 61 | Manx Airlines Ltd (G-BZWW)/*King Godred Crovan 1079-1095*/Ronaldsway | |
| G-OATS | PA-38-112 Tomahawk | Truman Aviation Ltd/Tollerton | |
| G-OATV | Cameron V-77 balloon | Gone With The Wind Ltd | |
| G-OAUS | Sikorsky S-76A | Darley Stud Management Co Ltd | |
| G-OAVX | Beech 200 Super King Air | ATS Vulcan Ltd (G-IBCA/G-BMCA) | |
| G-OAWY | Cessna 340A | Industrial Alum Ltd | |
| G-OBAA | Beech B200 Super King Air | BAA PLC | |
| G-OBAL | Mooney M.20J | Britannia Airways Ltd/Luton | |
| G-OBAN | Jodel D.140B | PIK Transport Ltd (G-ATSU) | |
| G-OBBC | Colt 90A balloon | R. A. & M. A. Riley | |
| G-OBEA | BAe Jetstream 3102-01 | Brymon European Airways Ltd *City of Cork* | |
| G-OBED | PA-34-200T Seneca II | V. J. Holden/Newcastle | |
| G-OBEL | Cessna 500 Citation | Gator Aviation Ltd (G-BOGA) | |
| G-OBEY | PA-23 Aztec 250C | Creaton Aircraft Services (G-BAAJ) | |

| Notes | Reg. | Type | Owner or Operator |
|---|---|---|---|
| | G-OBHD | Short SD3-60 Variant 100 | Jersey European Airways Ltd (G-BNDK) |
| | G-OBHX | Cessna F.172H | Jones Aviation Sales Ltd (G-AWMU) |
| | G-OBIL | Robinson R-22B | Pentech |
| | G-OBLC | Beech 76 Duchess | Multirun Ltd |
| | G-OBLK | Short SD3-60 Variant 100 | Jersey European Airways Ltd (G-BNDI) |
| | G-OBLT | BAe 125 Srs 800B | P. Thomas |
| | G-OBMC | Boeing 737-33A | British Midland Airways Ltd/E. Midlands |
| | G-OBMD | Boeing 737-33A | British Midland Airways Ltd/E. Midlands |
| | G-OBMF | Boeing 737-4Y0 | British Midland Airways Ltd/E. Midlands |
| | G-OBMG | Boeing 737-4Y0 | British Midland Airways Ltd/E. Midlands |
| | G-OBMH | Boeing 737-33A | British Midland Airways Ltd/E. Midlands |
| | G-OBMJ | Boeing 737-33A | British Midland Airways Ltd/E. Midlands |
| | G-OBMK | Boeing 737-4S3 | British Midland Airways Ltd/E. Midlands |
| | G-OBML | Boeing 737-3Q8 | British Midland Airways Ltd (G-KKUH)/ E. Midlands |
| | G-OBMM | Boeing 737-4Y0 | British Midland Airways Ltd/E. Midlands |
| | G-OBMN | Boeing 737-46B | British Midland Airways Ltd (G-BOPJ)/ E. Midlands |
| | G-OBMO | Boeing 737-4Q8 | British Midland Airways Ltd/E. Midlands |
| | G-OBMP | Boeing 737-3Y0 | British Midland Airways Ltd/E. Midlands |
| | G-OBMS | Cessna F.172N | D. Beverley & W. F. van Schoten |
| | G-OBMW | AA-5 Traveler | Fretcourt Ltd (G-BDFV) |
| | G-OBOH | Short SD3-60 | Jersey European Airways (G-BNDJ) |
| | G-OBSF | AA-5A Cheetah | Lowlog Ltd (G-ODSF/G-BEUW) |
| | G-OBSV | Partenavia P.68B Observer | Porton Holdings Ltd |
| | G-OBUD | Colt 69A balloon | Hot-Air Balloon Co Ltd |
| | G-OBUY | Colt 69A balloon | Airship & Balloon Co Ltd |
| | G-OBWA | BAC One-Eleven 518FG | British Air Ferries (G-BDAT/G-AYOR) |
| | G-OBWB | BAC One-Eleven 518FG | British Air Ferries (G-BDAS/G-AXMH) |
| | G-OBWC | BAC One-Eleven 520FN | British Air Ferries (G-BEKA) |
| | G-OBWD | BAC One-Eleven 518FG | British Air Ferries (G-BDAE/G-AXMI) |
| | G-OBWE | BAC One-Eleven | British Air Ferries |
| | G-OBWF | — | — |
| | G-OBWG | — | — |
| | G-OBWH | — | — |
| | G-OCAA | H.S. 125 Srs 700B | MAGEC Aviation Ltd (G-BHLF)/Luton |
| | G-OCAD | Sequoia F.8L Falco | Falco Flying Group |
| | G-OCAR | Colt 77A balloon | M. D. Cookson |
| | G-OCAT | Eiri PIK-20E | W. A. D. Thorp/Doncaster |
| | G-OCBA | H.S.125 Srs 3B | Westminster Aviation Ltd (G-MRFB/ G-AZVS) |
| | G-OCBB | Bell 206B JetRanger 2 | CG Group Ltd (G-BASE) |
| | G-OCBC | Cameron A-120 balloon | Corporate Balloon Co |
| | G-OCCA | PA-32R-301 Saratoga SP | CC Aviation Ltd (G-BRIX)/Elstree |
| | G-OCCC | BAe 125 Srs 800B | Consolidated Contractors International |
| | G-OCCI | BAe 125 Srs 800B | Consolidated Contractors International (UK) Ltd |
| | G-OCDB | Cessna 550 Citation II | Paycourt Ltd (G-ELOT) |
| | G-OCDS | Aviamilano F.8L Falco II | P. J. Collins (G-VEGL) |
| | G-OCFR | Learjet 35A | Chauffair (CI) Ltd (G-VIPS/G-SOVN/ G-PJET) |
| | G-OCGJ | Robinson R-22B | Pyramid Aviation Ltd/Halfpenny Green |
| | G-OCHL | Bell 206B JetRanger 3 | Brikos Air Ltd |
| | G-OCJK | Schweizer 269C | M. D. Thorpe |
| | G-OCJR | SA.341G Gazelle 1 | Reeds Motor Co (G-BRGS) |
| | G-OCJS | Cameron V-90 balloon | C. J. Sandell |
| | G-OCND | Cameron O-77 balloon | D. P. H. Smith & Dalby |
| | G-OCNW | BAC One-Eleven 201AC | British Air Ferries (G-ASJH)/Stansted |
| | G-OCPC | Cessna FA.152 | Westward Airways (Lands End) Ltd/St Just |
| | G-OCPI | Cessna 500 Citation | Cooling Power Industries Ltd (G-OXEC) |
| | G-OCPL | AA-5A Cheetah | BLS Aviation Ltd (G-RCPW/G-BERM) |
| | G-OCPS | Colt 120A balloon | CPS Fuels Ltd |
| | G-OCRI | Colomban MC.15 Cri-Cri | M. J. J. Dunning |
| | G-OCTA | BN-2A Mk III-2 Trislander | Aurigny Air Services Ltd (G-BCXW) |
| | G-OCTI | PA-32 Cherokee Six 260 | J. K. Sharkey (G-BGZX)/Elstree |
| | G-OCTU | PA-28-161 Cadet | J. P. Alexander |
| | G-OCUB | Piper J-3C-90 Cub | C. A. Foss & P. A. Brook/Shoreham |
| | G-OCWC | AA-5A Cheetah | Garrick Aviation (G-WULL) |
| | G-OCWT | AS.350B-2 Ecureuil | Carter Wind Turbines (Aviation) Ltd |
| | G-ODAD | Colt 77A balloon | K. Meehan |
| | G-ODAH | Aerotek-Pitts S.2A Special | R. Khatami (G-BDKS) |
| | G-ODAM | AA-5A Cheetah | D. Hilditch/Elstree |
| | G-ODAY | Cameron N-56 balloon | C. O. Day (Estate Agents) |

| Reg. | Type | Owner or Operator |
|---|---|---|
| G-ODEL | Falconar F-11-3 | G. F. Brummell |
| G-ODEN | PA-28-161 Cadet | J. Appleton |
| G-ODER | Cameron O-77 balloon | W. H. Morgan |
| G-ODHL | Cameron N-77 balloon | DHL International (UK) Ltd |
| G-ODIL | Bell 206B JetRanger | Yorkshire Helicopter Centre Ltd |
| G-ODIR | PA-23 Aztec 250D | Metstar Ltd (G-AZGB) |
| G-ODIS | Cameron Cabin SS balloon | Cameron Balloons Ltd |
| G-ODIY | Colt 69A balloon | Flying Pictures (Balloons) Ltd |
| G-ODJP | Robinson R-22 | R. E. Todd |
| G-ODLG | D.H.114 Heron 2 | RSJ Aviation International Ltd (G-ARKU) |
| G-ODLY | Cessna 310J | R. J. Huband (G-TUBY/G-ASZZ) |
| G-ODMC | AS.350B-1 Ecureuil | D. M. Coombs (G-BPVF) |
| G-ODMM | PA-31-350 Navajo Chieftain | Warwickshire Flying Training Centre Ltd/ Birmingham |
| G-ODNP | Cessna 310R | Bostonair Ltd/Humberside |
| G-OEAC | Mooney M.20J | Trifik Services Ltd |
| G-OECH | AA-5A Cheetah | G. W. Plowman & Sons Ltd (G-BKBE) |
| G-OEDB | PA-38-112 Tomahawk | Air Delta Bravo Ltd (G-BGGJ)/Elstree |
| G-OEDP | Cameron N-77 balloon | M. J. Betts & Eastern Counties Newspapers |
| G-OEEC | Short SD3-60 Variant 100 | Shorts Aircraft Financing Ltd (G-BPKY) |
| G-OEGG | Cameron 65 Egg SS balloon | Airship & Balloon Co Ltd |
| G-OENT | Cessna F.152 | M. Entwistle (G-OBAT) |
| G-OEXC | Airbus A.320-212 | Excalibur Airways Ltd/E. Midlands |
| G-OEYE | Rans S.10 Sakota | J. D. Haslam |
| G-OFCM | Cessna F172L | F. C. M Aviation Ltd (G-AZUN)/Guernsey |
| G-OFBJ | Thunder Ax7-77 balloon | N. D. Hicks |
| G-OFER | PA-18 Super Cub 150 | M. S. W. Meagher |
| G-OFHJ | Cessna 441 | Tilling Associates Ltd (G-HSON) |
| G-OFIT | SOCATA TB.10 Tobago | G. S.M. Brain (G-BRIU) |
| G-OFIZ | Cameron 80 Can SS balloon | Airship & Balloon Co Ltd |
| G-OFJS | Robinson R-22B | F. J. Saunders (G-BNXJ) |
| G-OFLG | SOCATA TB.10 Tobago | Studley Pool Management Ltd (G-JMWT) |
| G-OFLI | Colt 105A balloon | Airship & Balloon Co Ltd |
| G-OFLT | EMB-110P1 Bandeirante | Flightline Ltd (G-MOBL)/Southend |
| G-OFLY | Cessna 210L | A. P. Mothew/Stapleford |
| G-OFOR | Thunder Ax3 balloon | A. Walker |
| G-OFOX | Denney Aerocraft Kitfox | P. R. Skeels |
| G-OFRB | Everett gyroplane | Roger Savage (Photography) |
| G-OFRH | Cessna 421C | S. J. K. Walker & A. A. George (G-NORX) |
| G-OFRT | L.188C Electra | Channel Express (Air Services) Ltd/ Bournemouth |
| G-OFTI | PA-28 Cherokee 140 | FTI Aviation Ltd (G-BRKU)/Biggin Hill |
| G-OFUN | Valentin Taifun 17E | J. A. Sangster/Booker |
| G-OGAR | PZL SZD-45A Ogar | N. C. Grayson |
| G-OGAS | Westland WG.30 Srs 100 | (stored) (G-BKNW)/Penzance |
| G-OGCA | PA-28-161 Warrior II | GC Aviation Partnership/Belfast |
| G-OGCI | Short SD3-60 Variant 100 | Short Bros PLC (G-BNBD)/Belfast City |
| G-OGEM | PA-28-181 Archer II | GEM Rewinds Ltd |
| G-OGET | PA-39 Twin Comanche 160 C/R | P. G. Kitchingman (G-AYXY) |
| G-OGGS | Thunder Ax8-84 balloon | G. Gamble & Sons (Quorn) Ltd |
| G-OGJS | Puffer Cozy | G. J. Stamper |
| G-OGOA | AS.350B Ecureuil | Lomas Helicopters Ltd (G-PLMD/G-NIAL) |
| G-OGOB | Schweizer 269C | Lomas Helicopters (Training) Ltd (G-GLEE/ G-BRUW) |
| G-OGOC | Robinson R-22B | M. Horn & Rainbow Wholesale Suppliers Ltd (G-HODG) |
| G-OGOS | Everett Autogyro | R. Abercrombie |
| G-OGRV | PA-31-350 Navajo Chieftain | A. N. J. & S. L. Palmer (G-BMPX) |
| G-OGTS | Air Command 532 Elite | GTS Engineering (Coventry) Ltd |
| G-OHCA | SC.5 Belfast (XR363) | HeavyLift Cargo Airlines Ltd/Southend |
| G-OHEA | H.S.125 Srs 3B/RA | Rogers Aviation Sales Ltd (G-AVRG)/ Cranfield |
| G-OHHL | Robinson R-22B | Hillar Helicopters Ltd |
| G-OHIM | Extra EA.300 | R. N. Boode/White Waltham |
| G-OHMS | AS.355F-1 Twin Squirrel | S.W. Electricity PLC |
| G-OHOG | PA-28 Cherokee 140 | C. R. Guggenheim (G-AVFY) |
| G-OHOP | PA-31 Turbo Navjo | Salon Aviation Ltd (G-BEYY) |
| G-OHOT | V.813 Viscount | British Air Ferries/(G-BMAT/G-AZLT)/ Southend |
| G-OIAN | M.S.880B Rallye Club | Ian Richard Transport Services Ltd |
| G-OIBM | R. Commander 114 | South Coast Computers Ltd (G-BLVZ) |
| G-OIBO | PA-28 Cherokee 180 | J. D. Skidmore (G-AVAZ) |
| G-OICS | Bell 206A JetRanger | Industrial Control Services PLC |

| Notes | Reg. | Type | Owner or Operator |
|---|---|---|---|
| | G-OIDW | Cessna F.150GF | I. D. Wakeling |
| | G-OIEA | PA-31P Pressurised Navajo | Inter European Airways Ltd (G-BBTW)/ Cardiff |
| | G-OIFM | Cameron 90 Dude SS balloon | Air 2 Air Ltd |
| | G-OIGS | Enstrom F-28C | I. R. Gowrie-Smith |
| | G-OIII | BAe 146-300 | British Aerospace PLC |
| | G-OIMC | Cessna 152 | E. Midlands Flying School Ltd |
| | G-OING | AA-5A Cheetah ★ | Abraxas Aviation Ltd (G-BFPD)/Denham |
| | G-OINK | Piper J-3C-65 Cub | A. R. Harding (G-BILD/G-KERK) |
| | G-OIOI | EH Industries EH.101 | Westland Helicopters Ltd/Yeovil |
| | G-OISO | Cessna FRA.150L | Crisptime Ltd (G-BBJW) |
| | G-OITN | AS.355F-1 Twin Squirrel | Independent Television News Ltd |
| | G-OJAC | Mooney M.20J | Hornet Engineering Ltd |
| | G-OJAE | Hughes 269C | Draycott Ltd |
| | G-OJAV | BN-2A Mk III-2 Trislander | Willow Air Ltd (G-BDOS)/Southend |
| | G-OJAY | EMB-110PI Bandeirante | J&J Air Charters Ltd/Exeter |
| | G-OJBA | Beech B200 Super King Air | M1 Machinery Ltd/Luton |
| | G-OJBM | Cameron N-90 balloon | JMB Communications Ltd |
| | G-OJCB | AB-206B JetRanger 2 | Yorkshire Helicopter Centre Ltd |
| | G-OJCM | Rotorway Executive 90 | J. C. Mead & N. Rogers |
| | G-OJCW | PA-32RT-300 Lance II | M. J. Metham/Blackbushe |
| | G-OJDC | Thunder Ax7-77 balloon | J. Crosby |
| | G-OJET | BAe 146-100 | British Aerospace PLC (G-BRJS/G-OBAF/ G-SCHH) |
| | G-OJIM | PA-28R-201T Turbo Arrow III | Motomecca Spares Ltd |
| | G-OJJB | Mooney M.20K | Jeff Brown (Aviation Services) |
| | G-OJMR | Airbus A.300-605R | Monarch Airlines Ltd/Luton |
| | G-OJON | Taylor JT.2 Titch | J. H. Fell |
| | G-OJPI | Robinson R-22B | JPI Group Ltd |
| | G-OJSY | Short SD3-60 | Business Air Ltd (G-BKKT)/Aberdeen |
| | G-OJVH | Cessna F.150H | Yorkshire Light Aircraft Ltd (G-AWJZ)/ Leeds |
| | G-OJVI | Robinson R-22B | JV Investments Ltd (G-OJVJ) |
| | G-OJWS | PA-28-161 Warrior II | Metacomco PLC |
| | G-OKAG | PA-28R Cherokee Arrow 180 | N. F. & B. R. Green/Stapleford |
| | G-OKAT | AS.350B Ecureuil | Tom Walkinshaw Racing Ltd (G-BGIM) |
| | G-OKAY | Pitts S-1E Special | Aerial & Aerobatic Service/Booker |
| | G-OKBT | Colt 25A Mk II balloon | British Telecommunications PLC |
| | G-OKCC | Cameron N-90 balloon | Kerridge Computer Co Ltd |
| | G-OKEN | PA-28R-201T Turbo Arrow III | K. Hassall |
| | G-OKEY | Robinson R-22B | Key Properties Ltd |
| | G-OKIS | Tri Kis | B. W. Davies |
| | G-OKIT | Rotorway Executive | P. T. Waldron |
| | G-OKYA | Cameron V-77 balloon | 14/20 Kings Hussars |
| | G-OKYM | PA-28 Cherokee 140 | D. Hotham (G-AVLS) |
| | G-OLAF | Beech C90 King Air | Westair Flying Services Ltd (G-BFVX)/ Blackpool |
| | G-OLAH | Short SD3-60 Variant 100 | Gill Aviation Ltd (G-BPCO/G-RMSS/ G-BKKU) |
| | G-OLAU | Robinson R-22B | P. M. Green |
| | G-OLBA | Short SD3-60 Variant 100 | Shorts Aircraft Financing Ltd (G-BOFG) |
| | G-OLBC | PA-23 Aztec 250 | Falcon Flying Services (G-BHCT)/ Biggin Hill |
| | G-OLCA | BAe 146-200 | British Aerospace PLC |
| | G-OLCB | BAe 146-200 | British Aerospace PLC |
| | G-OLDE | Cessna 421C | R. & M. International Helicopters Ltd (G-BBSV) |
| | G-OLDN | Bell 206L LongRanger | Gulfstream Air Services (UK) Ltd (G-TBCA/G-BFAL) |
| | G-OLDY | Luton LA-5 Major | M. P. & A. P. Sargent |
| | G-OLEE | Cessna F.152 | Aerohire Ltd/Halfpenny Green |
| | G-OLES | Partenavia P.68C | D. Henrikson (G-JAJV) |
| | G-OLFC | PA-38-112 Tomahawk | T. F. L. Hayes (G-BGZG) |
| | G-OLFI | Robinson R-22B | Candover Management Services Ltd (G-BRKI) |
| | G-OLFR | H.S. 125 Srs 403B | Osprey Aviation Ltd (G-BRXR/G-AXYJ)/ Southend |
| | G-OLFT | R. Commander 114 | B. C. Richens (G-WJMN)/Redhill |
| | G-OLIZ | Robinson R-22B | P & I Data Services Ltd |
| | G-OLLE | Cameron O-84 balloon | N. A. Robertson |
| | G-OLLI | Cameron O-31 SS balloon | N. A. Robertson |
| | G-OLLY | PA-31-350 Navajo Chieftain | Barnes Olsen Aeroleasing Ltd (G-BCES) |
| | G-OLMA | Partenavia P.68B | C. M. Evans (G-BGBT) |

| Reg. | Type | Owner or Operator | Notes |
|------|------|-------------------|-------|
| G-OLRT | Robinson R-22B | B. D. Smith | |
| G-OLSC | Cessna 182A | M. E. Mortlock & D. L. Turner (G-ATNU)/ Pampisford | |
| G-OLTN | Short SD3-60 Variant 100 | Shorts Aircraft Financing Ltd (G-BOFH) | |
| G-OLUM | Robinson R-22B | N. J. Hopkinson | |
| G-OLVR | FRED Srs 2 | A. R. Oliver | |
| G-OMAC | Cessna FR.172E | R. Knox & R. Conway | |
| G-OMAF | Dornier Do.228-200 | FR Aviation Ltd/Bournemouth | |
| G-OMAR | PA-34-220T Seneca III | Redhill Flying Club | |
| G-OMAT | PA-28 Cherokee 140 | Midland Air Training School (G-JIMY/ G-AYUG)/Coventry | |
| G-OMAX | Brantly B.2B | P. D. Benmax (G-AVJN) | |
| G-OMCL | Cessna 550 Citation II | Quantel Ltd/Biggin Hill | |
| G-OMDH | Hughes 369E | Stilgate Ltd/Booker | |
| G-OMEC | AB-206B JetRanger 3 | Kallas Ltd (G-OBLD) | |
| G-OMED | AA-5B Tiger | Caslon Ltd (G-BERL)/Elstree | |
| G-OMGA | H.S.125 Srs 600B/2 | MAGEC Aviation Ltd (G-BSHL/G-BBMD)/ Luton | |
| G-OMGB | H.S.125 Srs 600B | MAGEC Aviation Ltd (G-BKBM/G-BCCL)/ Luton | |
| G-OMGC | H.S.125 Srs 600B | MAGEC Aviation Ltd (G-BKCD/G-BDOA) | |
| G-OMGE | BAe 125 Srs 800B | GEC Marconi Ltd (G-BTMG)/Luton | |
| G-OMHC | PA-28RT-201 Arrow IV | M. H. Cundley/Redhill | |
| G-OMID | H.S. 125 Srs 700B | Alpha Aviation Ltd (G-UKCA) | |
| G-OMIG | Aero-Vodochody MiG-15UTI | G. P. Hinkley/Shoreham | |
| G-OMIL | Beech 58 Baron | Millhouse Aviation Ltd | |
| G-OMJB | Bell 206B JetRanger | Martin Brundle (Overseas) Ltd | |
| G-OMJT | Rutan LongEz | M. J. Timmons | |
| G-OMKF | Aero Designs Pulsar | M. K. Faro | |
| G-OMMC | Mooney M.20J | A. D. Russell/Bourn | |
| G-OMNI | PA-28R Cherokee Arrow 200D | D. J. Warner & J. B. A. Ainsworth | |
| G-OMOG | AA-5A Cheetah | Popham Flight (G-BHWR) | |
| G-OMRB | Cameron V-77 balloon | M. R. Bayne | |
| G-OMRG | Hoffmann H-36 Dimona | M. R. Grimwood (G-BLHG) | |
| G-ONAF | Naval Aircraft Factory N3N-1 | P. M. H. Threadway | |
| G-ONCL | Colt 77A balloon | N. C. Lindsay | |
| G-ONEA | Beech 200 Super King Air | Northern Executive Aviation Ltd/ Manchester | |
| G-ONHH | Forney F-1A Aircoupe | H. Dodd (G-ARHA) | |
| G-ONKA | Aeronca K | L. D. Chapman | |
| G-ONOR | Cessna 425 | Rockville Investments (Jersey) Ltd (G-BKSA) | |
| G-ONOW | Bell 206A JetRanger 2 | P. D. & S. J. Hughes (G-AYMX) | |
| G-ONPI | Thunder Ax10-160 balloon | Ballooning World Ltd | |
| G-ONZO | Cameron N-77 balloon | J. A. Kershaw | |
| G-OOAA | Airbus A.320-231 | Air 2000 Ltd/Manchester | |
| G-OOAB | Airbus A.320-231 | Air 2000 Ltd/Manchester | |
| G-OOAC | Airbus A.320-231 | Air 2000 Ltd/Manchester | |
| G-OOAD | Airbus A.320-231 | Air 2000 Ltd/Manchester | |
| G-OODE | SNCAN Stampe SV-4C (G) | The Biplane Co Ltd (G-AZNN) | |
| G-OODI | Pitts S-1D Special | I. R. B. Frank (G-BBBU) | |
| G-OODW | PA-28-181 Archer II | Goodwood Terrena Ltd | |
| G-OOFI | Cameron N-77 balloon | I. Fishwick | |
| G-OOGA | GA-7 Cougar | Denham School of Flying Ltd | |
| G-OOJB | Cessna 421C | Ferron Trading Ltd (G-BKSO) | |
| G-OOLE | Cessna 172M | P. S. Eccersley (G-BOSI) | |
| G-OOLI | Robinson R-22B | Wyatt Air Partnership (G-DMCD) | |
| G-OONE | Mooney M.20J | N. Skipworth/Booker | |
| G-OONI | Thunder Ax7-77 balloon | Fivedata Ltd | |
| G-OONS | AB-206B JetRanger 3 | Bellini Aviation Ltd | |
| G-OONY | PA-28-161 Warrior II | D. A. Field & P. B. Jenkins | |
| G-OOOA | Boeing 757-28AER | Air 2000/Canada 3000 (C-FOOA) | |
| G-OOOB | Boeing 757-28AER | Air 2000/Canada 3000 (C-FOOB) | |
| G-OOOC | Boeing 757-28AER | Air 2000/Canada 3000 | |
| G-OOOD | Boeing 757-28AER | Air 2000/Canada 3000 (C-FXOD) | |
| G-OOOG | Boeing 757-23AER | Air 2000 Ltd/Manchester | |
| G-OOOH | Boeing 757-23AER | Air 2000 Ltd/Manchester | |
| G-OOOI | Boeing 757-23AER | Air 2000 Ltd/Manchester | |
| G-OOOJ | Boeing 757-23AER | Air 2000 Ltd/Manchester | |
| G-OOOM | Boeing 757-225 | Air 2000 Ltd/Manchester | |
| G-OOOO | Mooney M.20J | Michael Jackson Motors Ltd | |
| G-OOOS | Boeing 757-236 | Air 2000 Ltd (G-BRJD)/Manchester | |
| G-OOOT | Boeing 757-236ER | Air 2000 Ltd (G-BRJJ)/Manchester | |

# G-OOOU – G-OSDI

| Notes | Reg. | Type | Owner or Operator |
|---|---|---|---|
| | G-OOOU | Boeing 757-2Y0ER | Air 2000 Ltd/Manchester |
| | G-OOOV | Boeing 757-225 | Air 2000 Ltd/Manchester |
| | G-OOOW | Boeing 757-225 | Air 2000 Ltd/Manchester |
| | G-OOOX | Boeing 757-2Y0 | Air 2000 Ltd/Manchester |
| | G-OOSE | Rutan Vari-Eze | J. A. Towers |
| | G-OOUT | Colt Flying Shuttlecock SS balloon | Shiplake Investments Ltd |
| | G-OOXP | Pulsar XP | GW Associates Ltd |
| | G-OPAC | Robinson R-22B | Crest Engineering Ltd |
| | G-OPAG | PA-34-200 Seneca II | A. H. Lavender (G-BNGB) |
| | G-OPAL | Robinson R-22B | Service Graphics Ltd |
| | G-OPAM | Cessna F.152 | PJC Leasing Ltd (G-BFZS)/Stapleford |
| | G-OPAT | Beech 76 Duchess | Ray Holt (Land Drainage) Ltd/(G-BHAO) |
| | G-OPBH | Aero Designs Pulsar | P B. Hutchinson |
| | G-OPED | Partenavia P.68B | Pedley Woodwork Ltd/(G-BFKP) |
| | G-OPFC | BAe 125-1000 | British Aerospace PLC |
| | G-OPIB | Lightning F.6 | B. J. Pover |
| | G-OPIG | ARV Super 2 | C. R. Guggenheim (G-BMSJ) |
| | G-OPIK | Eiri PIK-20E | K. & S. C. A. Dudley |
| | G-OPIT | CFM Streak Shadow Srs SA | L. W. Opit |
| | G-OPIX | Cessna 180K | Steve Bicknell Productions Ltd |
| | G-OPJC | Cessna 152 | PJC Leasing Ltd/Stapleford |
| | G-OPJD | PA-28RT-201T Turbo Arrow IV | M. P. Hughes |
| | G-OPKF | Cameron 90 Bowler SS balloon | Flying Pictures (Balloons) Ltd |
| | G-OPLC | D.H.104 Dove 8 | RSJ Aviation International Ltd (G-BLRB) |
| | G-OPOL | H.S.125 Srs F3B/RA | Launchroy Ltd (G-BXPU/G-IBIS/G-AXPU)/Luton |
| | G-OPOP | Enstrom 280C-UK-2 Shark | Crewhall Ltd (G-OFED) |
| | G-OPPL | AA-5A Cheetah | London School of Flying Ltd (G-BGNN)/Elstree |
| | G-OPPP | EMB-110P1 Bandeirante | Streamline Aviation/E. Midlands |
| | G-OPPS | Mudry CAP.231 | Bianchi Aviation Film Services Ltd/Booker |
| | G-OPRA | PA-31 Turbo Navajo | Prospair Aircharter Ltd (G-VICK/G-AWED) |
| | G-OPRO | MDH Hughes 369E | Prodrive Ltd |
| | G-OPSF | PA-38-112 Tomahawk | Neric Ltd (G-BGZI)/Pahshanger |
| | G-OPST | Cessna 182R | Lota Ltd/Shoreham |
| | G-OPUP | B.121 Pup 2 | P. W. Hunter (G-AXEU) |
| | G-OPWK | AA-5A Cheetah | A. H. McVicar (G-OAEL)/Prestwick |
| | G-OPWS | Mooney M.20K | A. C. Clarke |
| | G-ORAF | CFM Streak Shadow | G. A. & S. M. Taylor |
| | G-ORAY | Cessna F.182Q II | S. E. Ward & Sons (Engineers) Ltd (G-BHDN) |
| | G-ORBY | Sukhoi Su-26MX | R. N. Goode/White Waltham |
| | G-ORCE | Cessna 550 Citation II | Oracle Corporation UK Ltd (G-MINE) |
| | G-ORCL | Cessna 421C | Oracle Corporation UK Ltd |
| | G-ORDN | PA-31R Cherokee Arrow 200-II | M. T. Coppen (G-BAJT) |
| | G-ORDO | PA-30 Twin Comanche B | A. C. & A. M. Gordon |
| | G-ORED | BN-2T Islander | The Red Devils (G-BJYW)/Farnborough |
| | G-OREG | BN-2A Mk III-1 Trislander | Industrial Marketing Group Ltd (G-OAVW/G-AZLJ) |
| | G-OREX | Short SD3-60 Variant 100 | Euroworld Airways Ltd (G-BMHY)/Gatwick |
| | G-OREY | Cameron O-90 balloon | S. L. Cuhat |
| | G-ORFC | Jurca MJ.5 Sirocco | D. J. Phillips |
| | G-ORFE | Cameron 76 Golf SS balloon | Balloon-A-Drome Ltd |
| | G-ORJB | Cessna 500 Citation | L'Equipe Air Ltd (G-OKSP) |
| | G-ORJS | Bell 206L-3 LongRanger | Carr Aviation |
| | G-ORJW | Laverda F.8L Falco Srs 4 | W. R. M. Sutton |
| | G-ORMB | Robinson R-22B | R. M. Bailey |
| | G-OROB | Robinson R-22B | Corniche Helicopters (G-TBFC) |
| | G-OROD | PA-18 Super Cub 150 | R. J. O. Walker |
| | G-ORON | Cameron 77A balloon | A. M. Rocliffe |
| | G-OROZ | AS.350B-2 Ecureuil | Flightpaths Ltd |
| | G-ORPR | Cameron O-77 balloon | Outright PR Ltd |
| | G-ORSJ | D.H.114 Heron 2 | RSJ Aviation International Ltd (G-ARKW) |
| | G-ORSP | Beech A36 Bonanza | R. G. O'Rourke |
| | G-ORTM | Glaser-Dirks DG.400 | I. Godfrey |
| | G-ORVB | McCulloch J-2 | R. V. Bowles (G-BLGI/G-BKKL) |
| | G-ORZZ | Robinson R-22B | Heliyorks Flight Training Ltd |
| | G-OSAB | Enstrom 280FX | Goadby Air Services Ltd |
| | G-OSAL | Cessna 421C | Cityshare Ltd |
| | G-OSAS | BAe 146-200 | British Aerospace PLC |
| | G-OSCB | Colt 90A balloon | J. Willis |
| | G-OSCC | PA-32 Cherokee Six 300 | Plant Aviation Ltd (G-BGFD)/Elstree |
| | G-OSDI | Beech 95-58 Baron | K. L. Hawes (G-BHFY) |

174

| Reg. | Type | Owner or Operator | Notes |
|---|---|---|---|
| G-OSEA | BN-2B-26 Islander | W. T. Johnson & Sons (Huddersfield) Ltd (G-BKOL) | |
| G-OSEE | Robinson R-22B | E. Midlands Helicopters | |
| G-OSFC | Cessna F.152 | Stapleford Flying Club Ltd (G-BIVJ) | |
| G-OSHC | Hughes 269C | S. G. Good | |
| G-OSHD | Hughes 269B | Mussett Helicopters Ltd | |
| G-OSIB | Bell 206L-1 LongRanger 2 | Cardale Doors Ltd (G-LEIS) | |
| G-OSIX | PA-32 Cherokee Six 260 | Strata Surveys Ltd (G-AZMO) | |
| G-OSKY | Cessna 172M | G-OSKY (1990) | |
| G-OSLO | Schwiezer 269C | Metham Aviation Ltd | |
| G-OSNB | Cessna 550 Citation II | Scottish & Newcastle Breweries PLC (G-JFRS) | |
| G-OSND | Cessna FRA.150M | Barmoor Aviation (G-BDOU) | |
| G-OSOO | Hughes 369E | Malcolm Wilson (Motorsport) Ltd | |
| G-OSPS | PA-18 Super Cub 95 | J. W. Macleod | |
| G-OSST | Colt 77A balloon | British Airways PLC | |
| G-OSTC | AA-5A Cheetah | C. B. Dew | |
| G-OTAL | ARV Super 2 | Cyclone Hovercraft Ltd (G-BNZG) | |
| G-OTAM | Cessna 172M | T. W. Woods | |
| G-OTBY | PA-32 Cherokee Six 300 | GOTBY Ltd | |
| G-OTEL | Thunder Ax8-90 balloon | Stakis Hotels & Inns Ltd | |
| G-OTHE | Enstrom 280C-UK Shark | The Engineering Co Ltd (G-OPJT/G-BKCO) | |
| G-OTIM | Bensen B.8MV | T. J. Deane | |
| G-OTOE | Aeronca 7AC Champion | J. M. Gale (G-BRWW) | |
| G-OTOW | Cessna 175BX | G-OTOW Flying Group (G-AROC) | |
| G-OTRG | Cessna TR.182RG | A. Hopper | |
| G-OTSB | BN-2A Mk III-2 Trislander | Aurigny Air Services Ltd (G-BDTO) | |
| G-OTSW | Pitts S-1E Special | R. A. Bowes (G-BLHE) | |
| G-OTTO | Cameron 82 Katalog SS balloon | Cameron Balloons Ltd | |
| G-OTUG | PA-18 Super Cub 150 | B. Walker & Co (Dursley) Ltd | |
| G-OTVS | BN-2T Islander | Headcorn Parachute Club Ltd (G-BPBN/G-BCMY) | |
| G-OTWO | Rutan Defiant | D. G. Foreman | |
| G-OTYJ | PA-28-161 Cadet | Holmes Rentals (G-OLSF) | |
| G-OUAE | Cameron 90 Wimmi Airbus SS balloon | Airship & Balloon Co Ltd | |
| G-OULD | Gould Mk I balloon | C. A. Gould | |
| G-OUSA | Colt 105A balloon | Continental Airlines Inc | |
| G-OUVI | Cameron O-105 balloon | Bristol University Hot Air Ballooning Soc | |
| G-OVAA | Colt Jumbo SS balloon | Airship & Balloon Co Ltd | |
| G-OVAN | SC.7 Skyvan 3 Variant 100 | Peterborough Parachute Centre (G-AYZA)/Sibson | |
| G-OVAX | Colt AS-80 Mk II airship | Vax Appliances Ltd | |
| G-OVFM | Cessna 120 | Industrial Foam Systems Ltd | |
| G-OVFR | Cessna F.172N | C. & A. Jenkins Ltd | |
| G-OVID | Light Aero Avid Flyer | M. Stow | |
| G-OVMC | Cessna F.152 II | Staverton Flying Services Ltd | |
| G-OVNE | Cessna 401A | M. A. Billings/Ipswich | |
| G-OVNR | Robinson R-22B | R. A. Kingston & R. Ballard | |
| G-OWAC | Cessna F.152 | Barnes Olson Aeroleasing Ltd (G-BHEB) | |
| G-OWAK | Cessna F.152 | Falcon Flying Services (G-BHEA) | |
| G-OWAR | PA-28-161 Warrior II | Bickertons Aerodromes Ltd | |
| G-OWEL | Colt 105A balloon | Autohaus of Aylesbury Ltd | |
| G-OWEN | K & S Jungster | R. C. Owen | |
| G-OWGC | Slingsby T.61F Venture T.2 | Wolds Gliding Club Ltd | |
| G-OWIN | BN-2A-8 Islander | UK Parachute Services Ltd (G-AYXE) | |
| G-OWIZ | Luscombe 8A Silvaire | J. Wilson & J. V. George | |
| G-OWLC | PA-31 Turbo Navajo | D. S. A. Warwick & P. M. Doran (G-AYFZ) | |
| G-OWNR | Beech 200 Super King Air | Owners Abroad Group PLC/Luton | |
| G-OWVA | PA-28 Cherokee 140 | Woodvale Aviation Co Ltd | |
| G-OWWF | Colt 2500A balloon | Virgin Atlantic Airways Ltd | |
| G-OWYN | Aviamilano F.14 Nibbio | J. R. Wynn | |
| G-OXLI | BAe Jetstream 4100 | British Aerospace PLC/Prestwick | |
| G-OXRG | Colt Film Can SS balloon | Flying Pictures (Balloons) Ltd | |
| G-OXTC | PA-23 Aztec 250D | Falcon Flying Services (G-AZOD)/Biggin Hill | |
| G-OXVI | V.S.361 Spitfire LF.XVIe (TD248) | BAC Aviation Ltd | |
| G-OYAK | Yakovlev C-11 | E. K. Coventry | |
| G-OZLN | Zlin Z.242L | C.S.E. Aviation Ltd/Kidlington | |
| G-OZOI | Cessna R.182 | Velcourt (East) Ltd (G-ROBK) | |
| G-OZUP | Colt 77A balloon | Yanin International Ltd | |
| G-PACE | Robin R.1180T | Millicron Instruments Ltd/Coventry | |

| Notes | Reg. | Type | Owner or Operator |
|---|---|---|---|
| | G-PACL | Robinson R-22B | R. Richardson |
| | G-PADI | Cameron V-77 balloon | T. R. Duffell |
| | G-PALM | PA-34-200T Seneca II | A. M. B. Hedegard |
| | G-PALS | Enstrom 280C-UK-2 Shark | Sonus Wholesale Audio Products |
| | G-PAMI | AS.355F-1 Twin Squirrel | Lynton Aviation Ltd (G-BUSA) |
| | G-PAMS | PA-60 Aerostar 601P | Averglen Ltd (G-GAIR) |
| | G-PAPU | Beech 58PA Baron | ADL Aviation Ltd (G-NIPU) |
| | G-PARA | Cessna 207 | Paraski/Swansea |
| | G-PARI | Cessna 172RG Cutlass | Applied Signs Ltd |
| | G-PARR | Cameron 90 Bottle SS balloon | Airship & Balloon Co Ltd |
| | G-PART | Partenavia P.68B | Phlight Avia Ltd/Coventry |
| | G-PASA | MBB Bo 105D | Medical Aviation Services Ltd (G-BGWP)/ Shoreham |
| | G-PASB | MBB Bo 105D | Medical Aviation Services Ltd (G-BDMC)/ Shoreham |
| | G-PASC | MBB Bo 105DBS/4 | Police Aviation Services Ltd (G-BNPS) |
| | G-PASD | MBB Bo 105DBS/4 | Police Aviation Services Ltd (G-BNRS) |
| | G-PASE | AS.355F-1 Twin Squirrel | Police Aviation Services Ltd |
| | G-PASF | AS.355F-1 Twin Squirrel | Police Aviation Services Ltd (G-SCHU) |
| | G-PASG | MBB Bo 105DBS/4 | Medical Aviation Services Ltd (G-MHSL) |
| | G-PASV | BN-2B-21 Islander | Medical Aviation Services Ltd (G-BKJH) |
| | G-PASX | MBB Bo 105DBS/4 | Police Aviation Services Ltd |
| | G-PASY | BN-2A-26 Islander | Medical Aviation Services Ltd(G-BPCB/ G-BEXA/G-MALI/G-DIVE)/Shoreham |
| | G-PATY | Colt Flying Sausage balloon | Colt Balloons Ltd |
| | G-PAWL | PA-28 Cherokee 140 | A. M. & D. Fitton (G-AWEU) |
| | G-PAWS | AA-5A Cheetah | J. Tolhurst |
| | G-PAXX | PA-20 Pacer 135 | D. W. & M. R. Grace |
| | G-PAZY | Pazmany PL.4A | A. Louth (G-BLAJ) |
| | G-PBBT | Cameron N-56 balloon | Test Valley Balloon Club |
| | G-PBHF | Robinson R-22B | Broughton-Hall Security Fencing |
| | G-PBWH | BAe 125 Srs 800B | Lynton Aviation Ltd |
| | G-PCUB | PA-18 Super Cub 135 | M. J. Wilson/Redhill |
| | G-PDHJ | Cessna T.182R | P. G. Vallance Ltd |
| | G-PDOC | PA-44-180 Seminole | Medicare (G-PVAF) |
| | G-PDON | WMB.2 Windtracker balloon | P. Donnellan |
| | G-PDSI | Cessna 172N | Don-Air Flying Club/Lasham |
| | G-PEAL | Aerotek Pitts S-2A | Plymouth Executive Aviation Ltd |
| | G-PEAT | Cessna 421B | Forest City Export Ltd (G-BBIJ)/Manchester |
| | G-PEEL | BAe ATP/Jetstream 61 | Manx Airlines Ltd/*King Somerled (1158-1164)*/Ronaldsway |
| | G-PEET | Cessna 401A | Air & General Services Ltd |
| | G-PEGG | Colt 90A balloon | Michael Pegg Partnership Ltd |
| | G-PEGI | PA-34-200T Seneca II | Tayflite Ltd |
| | G-PEKT | SOCATA TB.20 Trinidad | Premier Plane Leasing Co Ltd |
| | G-PELE | Cameron 80 Pele SS balloon | Cameron Balloons Ltd |
| | G-PELI | Pelican Club GS | Pelican Aircraft Ltd |
| | G-PENN | AA-5B Tiger | Compair |
| | G-PENY | Sopwith LC-1T Triplane (5492) | J. S. Penny |
| | G-PERL | Robinson R-22B | R. Fawcett |
| | G-PERR | Cameron 60 Bottle SS balloon ★ | British Balloon Museum |
| | G-PERS | Colt Soapbox SS balloon | G. V. Beckwith |
| | G-PEST | Hawker Tempest II | Autokraft Ltd |
| | G-PETR | PA-28 Cherokee 140 | E. W. Keeble/Ipswich (G-BCJL) |
| | G-PFAA | EAA Biplane Model P | E. W. B. Comber |
| | G-PFAB | Colomban MC.15 Cri-Cri | P. Fabish |
| | G-PFAC | FRED Srs 2 | G. R. Yates |
| | G-PFAD | Wittman W.8 Tailwind | M. R. Stamp |
| | G-PFAF | FRED Srs 2 | M. S. Perkins |
| | G-PFAG | Evans VP-1 | P. A. Evans |
| | G-PFAH | Evans VP-1 | J. A. Scott |
| | G-PFAI | Clutton EC.2 Easy Too | G. W. Cartledge |
| | G-PFAL | FRED Srs 2 | J. McD. Robinson |
| | G-PFAO | Evans VP-1 | P. W. Price |
| | G-PFAP | Currie Wot/SE-5A (C1904) | J. M. Alcock/Syerston |
| | G-PFAR | Isaacs Fury II (K2059) | C. J. Repik |
| | G-PFAT | Monnet Sonerai II | H. B. Carter |
| | G-PFAU | Rand KR-2 | D. E. Peace |
| | G-PFAW | Evans VP-1 | R. F. Shingler |
| | G-PFAY | EAA Biplane | A. K. Lang & A. L. Young |
| | G-PHIL | Brookland Hornet | A. J. Philpotts |
| | G-PHON | Cameron Phone SS balloon | Redmalt Ltd (G-BTEY) |
| | G-PHSI | Colt 90A balloon | P. H. Strickland & Simpson (Piccadilly) Ltd |

| Reg. | Type | Owner or Operator | Notes |
|------|------|-------------------|-------|
| G-PHTG | SOCATA TB.10 Tobago | O. Jerome | |
| G-PIAF | Thunder Ax7-65 balloon | Ballooning Adventures Ltd | |
| G-PICS | Cessna 182F | D. A. Cresswell (G-ASHO) | |
| G-PICT | Colt 180A balloon | Scotia Balloons | |
| G-PIEL | CP.301A Emeraude | P. R. Thorne (G-BARY) | |
| G-PIES | Thunder Ax7-77Z balloon | Pork Farms Ltd | |
| G-PIGS | SOCATA Rallye 150ST | Boonhill Flying Group (G-BDWB) | |
| G-PIKE | Robinson R-22 Mariner | M. D. Cook | |
| G-PIKK | PA-28 Cherokee 140 | L. P. & I. Keegan (G-AVLA) | |
| G-PINE | Thunder Ax8-90 balloon | J. A. Pine | |
| G-PINT | Cameron 65 Barrel SS balloon | D. K. Fish | |
| G-PIPE | Cameron N-56 Pipe SS balloon | Carreras Rothmans Ltd | |
| G-PIPS | Van's RV-4 | C. J. Marsh | |
| G-PITS | Pitts S-2AE Special | D. Rolfe | |
| G-PITZ | Pitts S-2A Special | A. K. Halvorsen | |
| G-PIXS | Cessna 336 | D. A. Cresswell | |
| G-PJCB | Agusta A.109A-II | J. C. Bamford Excavators Ltd | |
| G-PJMD | Hughes 369D | Dodici Ltd (G-BMJV) | |
| G-PJRT | BAe Jetstream 4100 | British Aerospace PLC/Prestwick | |
| G-PKBD | Douglas DC-9-32 | British Midland Airways Ltd *The Jubilee Diamond*/E. Midlands | |
| G-PKBE | Douglas DC-9-32 | British Midland Airways Ltd *The Excelsior Diamond*/E. Midlands | |
| G-PKBM | Douglas DC-9-32 | British Midland Airways Ltd *The Tiffany Diamond*/E. Midlands | |
| G-PLAN | Cessna F.150L | Howells Group PLC | |
| G-PLAS | GA-7 Cougar | S. J. A. Smith (G-BGHL)/Biggin Hill | |
| G-PLAX | AS.355F-1 Twin Squirrel | Dollar Air Services (G-BPMT) | |
| G-PLAY | Robin R.2100A | Cotswold Aero Club Ltd/Staverton | |
| G-PLEE | Cessna 182Q | W. J. & M. Barnes | |
| G-PLIV | Pazmany PL.4 | B. P. North | |
| G-PLMA | AS.350B Ecureuil | PLM Helicopters Ltd (G-BMMA) | |
| G-PLMB | AS.350B Ecureuil | PLM Helicopters Ltd (G-BMMB) | |
| G-PLMC | AS.350B Ecureuil | PLM Helicopters Ltd (G-BKUM) | |
| G-PLME | AS.350B-1 Ecureuil | PLM Helicopters Ltd (G-BONN) | |
| G-PLMF | AS.350B-1 Ecureuil | PLM Helicopters Ltd | |
| G-PLOW | Hughes 269B | Sulby Aerial Surveys Ltd (G-AVUM) | |
| G-PLUG | Colt 105A balloon | Eastern Electricity PLC | |
| G-PLUS | PA-34-200T Seneca II | C. G. Strasser/Jersey | |
| G-PLYD | SOCATA TB.20 Trinidad | Crocker Air Services/Biggin Hill | |
| G-PMAM | Cameron V-65 balloon | P. A. Meecham | |
| G-PMNL | Extra EA.230 | Flight Rise Ltd/Redhill | |
| G-PNAV | PA-31P Pressurised Navajo | Tech Air (Cambridge) Ltd | |
| G-POAH | Sikorsky S-76B | P&O Aviation Ltd | |
| G-POLO | PA-31-350 Navajo Chieftain | Aircam Technical Services/Teesside | |
| G-POLY | Cameron N-77 balloon | Empty Wallets Balloon Group | |
| G-POND | Oldfield Baby Lakes | C. R. Weldon | |
| G-PONY | Colt 31A balloon | Ace Balloons (Bath) Ltd | |
| G-POOH | Piper J-3C-65 Cub | P. & H. Robinson | |
| G-POOL | ARV Super 2 | Falstaff Finance Ltd (G-BNHA) | |
| G-POPA | Beech A36 Bonanza | R. G. Jones | |
| G-POPE | Eiri PIK-20E-1 | C. J. Hadley | |
| G-POPI | SOCATA TB.10 Tobago | Rocol Aviation Ltd (G-BKEN) | |
| G-POPP | Colt 105A balloon | Flying Pictures (Balloons) Ltd | |
| G-POPS | PA-34-220T Seneca III | Continental Aero & Marine Ltd | |
| G-PORK | AA-5B Tiger | J. W. & B. A. Flint (G-BFHS) | |
| G-PORT | Bell 206B JetRanger 3 | C. Clark | |
| G-POSH | Colt 56A balloon | Columna Ltd (G-BMPT) | |
| G-POSN | BAe 125 Srs 800B | P&O Containers (Assets) Ltd | |
| G-POST | EMB-110P1 Bandeirante | David Martin Couriers Ltd | |
| G-POTS | Cessna FA.150K | L. J. Potts (G-AYUY) | |
| G-POWL | Cessna 182R | Glasdon Group Ltd/Blackpool | |
| G-PPLH | Robinson R-22B | Henderson Financial Management Ltd | |
| G-PPLI | Pazmany PL.1 | G. Anderson | |
| G-PPPE | Colt 77A balloon | Thunder & Colt Ltd | |
| G-PPPP | Denney Aerocraft Kitfox | W. J. Dale | |
| G-PRAG | Brügger MB.2 Colibri | D. Frankland & ptnrs | |
| G-PRIM | PA-38-112 Tomahawk | Braddock Ltd | |
| G-PRIT | Cameron N-90 balloon | J. M. Albury | |
| G-PRNT | Cameron V-90 balloon | GS Print (West Midlands) Ltd | |
| G-PROP | AA-5A Cheetah | Photonic Science Ld (G-BHKU) | |
| G-PROV | P.84 Jet Provost T.52A (T.4) | Hunter Wing Ltd/Bournemouth | |
| G-PRTT | Cameron N-31 balloon | J. M. Albury | |

177

| Notes | Reg. | Type | Owner or Operator |
|---|---|---|---|
| | G-PRUE | Cameron O-84 balloon | Lalondes Residential Ltd |
| | G-PRXI | V.S.365 Spitfire PR.XI (PL983) | D. W. Arnold/Biggin Hill |
| | G-PSCI | Bell 206B JetRanger 3 | Scammell Properties Ltd (G-BOKD) |
| | G-PSVS | Beech 95-58 Baron | Stesco Ltd/Guernsey |
| | G-PTER | Beech C90 King Air | Moseley Group (PSV) Ltd (G-BIEE) |
| | G-PTRE | SOCATA TB.20 Trinidad | Solving Systems Ltd (G-BNKU) |
| | G-PTWO | Pilatus P2-05 (U-110) | C. M. Lee |
| | G-PUBS | Colt 56 Glass SS balloon | The Balloonatics |
| | G-PUDD | Robinson R-22B | Riggarna UK Ltd |
| | G-PUFF | Thunder Ax7-77A balloon | Intervarsity Balloon Club *Puffin II* |
| | G-PULS | Aero Designs Pulsar | M. J. McBride |
| | G-PUMA | AS.332L Super Puma | Bond Helicopters Ltd |
| | G-PUMB | AS.332L Super Puma | Bond Helicopters Ltd |
| | G-PUMD | AS.332L Super Puma | Bond Helicopters Ltd |
| | G-PUME | AS.332L Super Puma | Bond Helicopters Ltd |
| | G-PUMG | AS.332L Super Puma | Bond Helicopters Ltd |
| | G-PUMH | AS.332L Super Puma | Bond Helicopters Ltd |
| | G-PUMI | AS.332L Super Puma | Bond Helicopters Ltd |
| | G-PUMJ | AS.332L Super Puma | Bond Helicopters Ltd (G-BLZJ) |
| | G-PUMK | AS.332L Super Puma | Bond Helicopters Ltd |
| | G-PUML | AS.332L Super Puma | Bond Helicopters Ltd |
| | G-PUNK | Thunder Ax8-105 balloon | G. E. Harris |
| | G-PURE | Cameron 70 Can SS balloon | The Hot-Air Balloon Co Ltd |
| | G-PURR | AA-5A Cheetah | D. T. Smith (G-BJDN) |
| | G-PURS | Rotorway Executive | J. E. Houseman |
| | G-PUSH | Rutan LongEz | E. G. Peterson |
| | G-PUSI | Cessna T.303 | W. R. Swinburn Ltd |
| | G-PUSS | Cameron N-77 balloon | Bristol Balloons |
| | G-PYRO | Cameron N-65 balloon | N. A. Mitchell |
| | | | |
| | G-RAAD | Mooney M.20L | As-Al Ltd |
| | G-RAAR | BAe 125 Srs 800B | Osprey Executive Aviation Ltd/Southend |
| | G-RACA | P.57 Sea Prince T.1 ★ | Stratford Aircraft Collection/Long Marston |
| | G-RACH | Robinson R-22B | Oaks Construction & Civil Engineering Ltd |
| | G-RACO | PA-28R Cherokee Arrow 200-II | Graco Group Ltd |
| | G-RAEM | Rutan LongEz | G. F. H. Singleton |
| | G-RAFA | Grob G.115 | RAF College Flying Club Ltd/Cranwell |
| | G-RAFB | Grob G.115 | RAF College Flying Club Ltd/Cranwell |
| | G-RAFC | Robin R.2112 | S. J. Cropley |
| | G-RAFE | Thunder Ax7-77 balloon | N. A. Fishlock |
| | G-RAFF | Learjet 35A | Graff Aviation Ltd/Heathrow |
| | G-RAFG | Slingsby T.67C | S. J. Donkin |
| | G-RAFI | P.84 Jet Provost T.4 | R. M. Muir |
| | G-RAFT | Rutan LongEz | H. C. Mackinnon |
| | G-RAFW | Mooney M.20E | S. L. Monksfield (G-ATHW) |
| | G-RAIL | Colt 105A balloon | Ballooning World Ltd |
| | G-RAIN | Maule M5-235C Lunar Rocket | D. S. McKay & J. A. Rayment/ Hinton-in-the-Hedges |
| | G-RALI | Hughes 369HS | Kallas Ltd (G-BLKO) |
| | G-RAMI | Bell 206B JetRanger 3 | R. & M. International Helicopters Ltd |
| | G-RAMP | Piper J-3C-65 Cub | K. N. Whittall |
| | G-RAMS | PA-32R-301 Saratoga SP | Peacock & Archer Ltd/Manchester |
| | G-RAND | Rand KR-2 | R. L. Wharmby |
| | G-RANS | Rans S.10 Sakota | J. D. Weller |
| | G-RANZ | Rans S-10 Sakota | B. A. Phillips |
| | G-RAPE | Colt 300A balloon | Adventure Balloon Co Ltd |
| | G-RAPH | Cameron O-77 balloon | P. H. Jenkins |
| | G-RAPP | Cameron H-34 balloon | Cameron Balloons Ltd |
| | G-RARE | Thunder Ax5-42 SS balloon | International Distillers & Vintners Ltd |
| | G-RASC | Evans VP-2 | R. A. Codling |
| | G-RATE | AA-5A Cheetah | GP Services (G-BIFF) |
| | G-RAVI | Colt 300A balloon | R. S. Hunjan |
| | G-RAVL | H.P.137 Jetstream Srs 200 | Cranfield Institute of Technology (G-AWVK) |
| | G-RAYA | Denney Aerocraft Kitfox Mk 4 | A. K. Ray |
| | G-RAYS | Zenair CH.250 | R. E. Delves |
| | G-RBIN | Robin DR.400/2+2 | Headcorn Flying School Ltd |
| | G-RBOS | Colt AS-105 airship ★ | Science Museum/Wroughton |
| | G-RBOW | Thunder Ax-7-65 balloon | P. G. & S. D. Viney |
| | G-RBUT | Hughes 369HS | R. C. Button |
| | G-RCDI | H.S.125 Srs 700B | Aravco Ltd (G-BJDJ)/Heathrow |
| | G-RCED | R. Commander 114 | Echo Delta Ltd |
| | G-RCMF | Cameron V-77 balloon | Mouldform Ltd |
| | G-RDCI | R. Commander 112A | A. C. Hendriksen (G-BFWG) |

| Reg. | Type | Owner or Operator | Notes |
|---|---|---|---|
| G-RDON | WMB.2 Windtracker balloon | P. J. Donnellan (G-BICH) | |
| G-READ | Colt 77A balloon | CB Helicopters Ltd | |
| G-REAP | Pitts S-1S Special | P. N. Davies | |
| G-REAT | GA-7 Cougar | Denham School of Flying Ltd | |
| G-REBE | Bensen B.8MR | Chartersteps Ltd | |
| G-REBI | Colt 90A balloon | United Friendly Insurance PLC (G-BOYD) | |
| G-REBL | Hughes 269B | M. I. Edwards | |
| G-RECK | PA-28 Cherokee 140B | Phoenix Aviation Services Ltd (G-AXJW) | |
| G-RECO | Jurca MJ-5L Sirocco | J. D. Tseliki | |
| G-REEK | AA-5A Cheetah | Velopend Ltd | |
| G-REEN | Cessna 340 | E. & M. Green (G-AZYR)/Guernsey | |
| G-REES | Jodel D.140C | W. H. Greenwood | |
| G-REFI | Enstrom 280C-UK | Nash & Partners Ltd | |
| G-REGS | Thunder Ax7-77 balloon | M. E. Gregory | |
| G-REID | Rotorway Scorpion 133 | G. F. Burridge & S. B. Evans | |
| G-REIS | PA-28R-201T Turbo Arrow III | G. Webster & J. D. Caudwell | |
| G-REME | Cessna 152 (tailwheel) | Roger Clark Mechanical Engineering Ltd | |
| G-RENE | Renegade 912 | D. Evans | |
| G-RENO | SOCATA TB.10 Tobago | Lamond Ltd | |
| G-RENT | Robinson R-22B | Rentatruck Self Drive Ltd | |
| G-REPM | PA-38-112 Tomahawk | Nultree Ltd | |
| G-REST | Beech P35 Bonanza | C. R. Taylor (G-ASFJ) | |
| G-RETA | C.A.S.A. 1.131 Jungmann | J. S. Allison (G-BGZC)/Denham | |
| G-REVS | Bell 206B JetRanger | Helispeed Ltd (G-AWOL) | |
| G-REXS | PA-28-181 Archer II | Channel Islands Aero Holdings (Jersey) Ltd | |
| G-REZE | Rutan Vari-Eze | S. D. Brown & S. P. Evans | |
| G-RFAB | Cessna 182R | La Patron Holdings Ltd (G-BIXT) | |
| G-RFIL | Colt 77A balloon | The Aerial Display Co Ltd | |
| G-RFSB | Sportavia RF-5B | S. W. Brown | |
| G-RGUS | Fairchild 24R-46A Argus 3 (44-83184) | R. C. Handcraft/Shoreham | |
| G-RHCC | PA-31-350 Navajo Chieftain | Monde-Air Aviation Ltd/Leavesden | |
| G-RHCN | Cessna FR.182RG | R. H. C. Neville | |
| G-RHHT | PA-32RT-300 Lance II | R. W. Struth & ptnrs | |
| G-RICC | AS.350B-2 Ecureuil | McAlpine Helicopters Ltd & Gabriel Enterprises Ltd (G-BTXA) | |
| G-RICH | Cessna F.152 | Ford Equipment Hire | |
| G-RICK | Beech 95-B55 Baron | James Jack (Invergordon) Ltd (G-BAAG) | |
| G-RIDE | Stephens Akro | R. Mitchell/Coventry | |
| G-RIDS | Lancair 235 | R. Y. Kendal | |
| G-RIFA | SA.341G Gazelle 1 | Air & General Services Ltd (G-ORGE/G-BBHU) | |
| G-RIFB | Hughes 269C | Air & General Services Ltd | |
| G-RIGB | Thunder Ax7-77 balloon | Antrum & Andrews Ltd | |
| G-RIGS | PA-60 Aerostar 601P | Rig Design Services Group Ltd/Fairoaks | |
| G-RILL | Cessna 421C | Maxwell Restaurants Ltd (G-BGZM)/Elstree | |
| G-RILY | Monnet Sonerai II | R. Wheeler | |
| G-RIND | Cessna 335 | ATA Grinding Processes/Leavesden | |
| G-RINO | Thunder Ax7-77 balloon | D. J. Head | |
| G-RISE | Cameron V-77 balloon | D. L. Smith | |
| G-RIST | Cessna 310R-II | Air Service Training Ltd (G-DATS)/Perth | |
| G-RJAH | Boeing Stearman A.75N1 | R. J. Horne | |
| G-RJER | McD Douglas MD-83 | Airtours International Aviation Ltd | |
| G-RJMI | AA-5A Cheetah | Garrick Aviation | |
| G-RJMS | PA-28R-201 Arrow III | M. G. Hill | |
| G-RJWW | Maule M5-235C Lunar Rocket | Paw Flying Services Ltd (G-BRWG) | |
| G-RLFI | Cessna FA.152 | Tayside Aviation Ltd (G-DFTS)/Dundee | |
| G-RLMC | Cessna 421C | R. D. Lygo | |
| G-RMCT | Short SD3-60 Variant 100 | BAC Leasing/Express Air (G-BLPU) | |
| G-RMGN | AS.355F-1 Twin Squirrel | Firstearl Ltd (G-BMCY) | |
| G-RNAS | D.H.104 Sea Devon C.20 (XK896) | D. W. Hermiston-Hooper/Staverton | |
| G-RNGR | AB-206B JetRanger 3 | Unicorn Software Ltd | |
| G-RNIE | Cameron 70 Ball SS balloon | Airship & Balloon Co Ltd | |
| G-RNLI | V.S.236 Walrus 1 | R. E. Melton | |
| G-RNRM | Cessna A.185F | RN & R. Marines Sport Parachute Association | |
| G-RNTV | PA-30 Twin Comanche 160C | W. L. Vaughan (G-AXDL) | |
| G-ROAR | Cessna 401 | Aviation (Scotland) Ltd (G-BZFL/G-AWSF) | |
| G-ROBB | Grob G.109B | A. P. Mayne | |
| G-ROBI | Grob G.109B | A. W. McGarrigle/Cardiff | |
| G-ROBN | Robin R.1180T | J. G. Beaumont | |
| G-ROBO | Robinson R-22B | Cabair Air Taxis Ltd/Elstree | |

179

| Notes | Reg. | Type | Owner or Operator |
|---|---|---|---|
| | G-ROBS | Robinson R-22B | Corniche Helicopters (G-BPDH) |
| | G-ROBY | Colt 17A balloon | Airship & Balloon Co Ltd |
| | G-ROCH | Cessna T.303 | R. S. Bentley |
| | G-ROCK | Thunder Ax7-77 balloon | The Long Rake Spar Co Ltd |
| | G-ROCR | Schweizer 269C | KC Holdings |
| | G-RODD | Cessna 310R II | R. J. Herbert Engineering Ltd (G-TEDD/ G-MADI) |
| | G-RODI | Isaacs Fury (K3731) | M. R. Baker/Shoreham |
| | G-RODS | A-Bell 206B JetRanger 2 | Crook & Son (G-NOEL/G-BCWN) |
| | G-RODY | Bell 206A JetRanger | Crook & Son (G-ROGR/G-AXMM) |
| | G-ROGG | Robinson R-22B | Catto Helicopters |
| | G-ROLA | PA-34-200T Seneca | Highsteeple Ltd |
| | G-ROLF | PA-32R-301 Saratoga SP | P. F. Larkins |
| | G-ROLL | Pitts S-2A Special | RPM Aviation Ltd/Guernsey |
| | G-ROLO | Robinson R-22B | Osprey Helicopters Ltd |
| | G-ROMA | Hughes 369S | Helicopters (Northern) Ltd (G-ROPI/ G-ONPP)/Blackpool |
| | G-RONG | PA-28R Cherokee Arrow 200-II | W. R. Griffiths |
| | G-RONI | Cameron V-77 balloon | R. E. Simpson |
| | G-RONS | Robin DR.400/180 | R. & K. Baker |
| | G-RONT | Enstrom F-28A | R. Thomas (G-BDAW) |
| | G-RONW | FRED Srs 2 | K. Atkinson |
| | G-ROOF | Brantly B.2B | S. Lee (G-AXSR) |
| | G-ROOK | Cessna F.172P | Crop Aviation (UK) Ltd |
| | G-ROPA | Europa | R. G. Gray |
| | G-RORO | Cessna 337B | C. Keane (G-AVIX) |
| | G-RORY | Piaggio FW P.149D | R. McCarthy (G-TOWN)/Booker |
| | G-ROSE | Evans VP-1 | W. K. Rose |
| | G-ROSI | Thunder Ax7-77 balloon | Scotia Balloons Ltd |
| | G-ROSY | Robinson R-22B | Aquaprint Ltd |
| | G-ROTI | Luscombe 8A Silvaire | A. L. Chapman & ptnrs |
| | G-ROTO | Rotorway Executive 90 | S. R. Porter |
| | G-ROTR | Brantly B.2B | GP Services |
| | G-ROTS | CFM Streak Shadow Srs SA | H. R. Cayzer |
| | G-ROUP | Cessna F.172M | Stapleford Flying Club Ltd (G-BDPH) |
| | G-ROUS | PA-34-200T Seneca II | C.S.E. Aviation Ltd/Kidlington |
| | G-ROUT | Robinson R-22B | Hooley Bridge Helicopter Services |
| | G-ROVE | PA-18 Super Cub 135 | Cormack (Aircraft Services) Ltd/Glasgow |
| | G-ROWL | AA-5B Tiger | Aviation Simulation/Biggin Hill |
| | G-ROWN | Beech 200 Super King Air | Chauffair Ltd (G-BHLC) |
| | G-ROWS | PA-28-151 Warrior | Mustarrow Ltd |
| | G-ROYZ | PA-34-200T Seneca II | R. L. West (G-GALE) |
| | G-ROZY | Cameron R.36 balloon | Jacques W. Soukup Ltd |
| | G-RPEZ | Rutan LongEz | B. A. Fairston & D. Richardson |
| | G-RRRR | Privateer Motor Glider | R. F. Selby |
| | G-RRSG | Thunder Ax7-77 balloon | M. T. Stevens |
| | G-RRTM | Sikorsky S-70C | Rolls-Royce PLC/Filton |
| | G-RSSF | Denney Aerocraft Kitfox Mk 2 | R. W. Somerville |
| | G-RSWW | Robinson R-22B | Woodstock Enterprises |
| | G-RUBB | AA-5B Tiger | R. Bessant |
| | G-RUBI | Thunder Ax7-77 balloon | Warren & Johnson |
| | G-RUBY | PA-28RT-201T Turbo Arrow IV | Arrow Aircraft Group (G-BROU) |
| | G-RUDD | Cameron V-65 balloon | N. A. Apsey |
| | G-RUDI | QAC Quickie Q.2 | R. Brandenberger |
| | G-RUGB | Cameron 89 Egg SS balloon | The Hot-Air Balloon Co Ltd |
| | G-RUIA | Cessna F.172M | F. Daly |
| | G-RUMN | AA-1A Trainer | G. J. Richardson |
| | G-RUMP | Robinson R-22B | I. P. Crane |
| | G-RUNT | Cassutt Racer IIIM | S. B. Jones |
| | G-RUSO | Robinson R-22B | Universal Salvage (Holdings) Ltd |
| | G-RUSS | Cessna 172N | Leisure Lease/Southend |
| | G-RWHC | Cameron A-180 balloon | Hourds Ltd |
| | G-RWIN | Rearwin 175 | G. Kay |
| | G-RWSS | Denney Aerocraft Kitfox | R. W. Somerville |
| | G-RWWW | W.S.55 Whirlwind HCC.12 (XR486) | R. Windley |
| | G-RZZB | Robinson R-22B | Heli-Link Ltd |
| | G-SAAB | R. Commander 112TC | R. R. White (G-BEFS) |
| | G-SAAM | Cessna T.182R | Hopstop Ltd (G-TAGL)/Elstree |
| | G-SABA | PA-28R-201T Turbo Arrow III | G. I. Cooper (G-BFEN) |
| | G-SABR | NA F-86A Sabre (8178) | Golden Apple Operations Ltd |
| | G-SACB | Cessna F.152 II | Westward Airways (Land's End) Ltd (G-BFRB)/St Just |

| Reg. | Type | Owner or Operator | Notes |
|------|------|-------------------|-------|
| G-SACD | Cessna F.172H | Northbrook College of Design & Technology (G-AVCD)/Shoreham | |
| G-SACE | Cessna F.150L | Arrow Aircraft Group (G-AZLK) | |
| G-SACF | Cessna 152 II | T. M. & M. L. Jones | |
| G-SACI | PA-28-161 Warrior II | Southern Air Ltd/Shoreham | |
| G-SACO | PA-28-161 Warrior II | Southern Air Ltd/Shoreham | |
| G-SACR | PA-28-161 Cadet | Sherburn Aero Club Ltd | |
| G-SACS | PA-28-161 Cadet | Sherburn Aero Club Ltd | |
| G-SACT | PA-28-161 Cadet | Sherburn Aero Club Ltd | |
| G-SACU | PA-28-161 Cadet | Sherburn Aero Club Ltd | |
| G-SACZ | PA-28-161 Warrior II | Southern Air Ltd/Shoreham | |
| G-SADE | Cessna F.150L | Bath Stone Co Ltd (G-AZJW) | |
| G-SAFE | Cameron N-77 balloon | Nottingham Hot Air Balloon Club | |
| G-SAGA | Grob G.109B | G-GROB Ltd/Booker | |
| G-SAGE | Luscombe 8A Silvaire | S. J. Sage (G-AKTL) | |
| G-SAHI | Trago Mills SAH-1 | Lovaux Ltd/Bournemouth | |
| G-SAIR | Cessna 421C | Air Support Aviation Services Ltd | |
| G-SALA | PA-32 Cherokee Six 300E | Stonebold Ltd | |
| G-SALI | Cessna 421C | Rapid 3864 Ltd/Luton | |
| G-SALL | Cessna F.150L (Tailwheel) | J. A. Millar-Craig & M. R. Shelton | |
| G-SALS | Cessna 421C | Michael A. Leniham & Associates Ltd (G-BEFT) | |
| G-SAMA | PA-31-350 Navajo Chieftain | Asseman Ltd | |
| G-SAMG | Grob G.109B | RAFGSA/Bicester | |
| G-SAMM | Cessna 340A | M. R. Cross | |
| G-SAMS | M.S.880B Rallye Club | K. Lewis | |
| G-SAMZ | Cessna 150D | N. E. Sames (G-ASSO) | |
| G-SANB | Beech E90 King Air | ITPS Ltd (G-BGNU)/Cranfield | |
| G-SAND | Schweizer 269C | Aerocroft Ltd | |
| G-SARA | PA-28-181 Archer II | L. C. MacKnight | |
| G-SARH | PA-28-161 Warrior II | Bath Stone Co Ltd | |
| G-SARO | Saro Skeeter Mk 12 (XL812) | F. F. Chamberlain | |
| G-SASU | AS.355F-1 Twin Squirrel | Gulf & UK Industrial Consultants Ltd (G-BSSM/G-BMTC/G-BKUK) | |
| G-SATI | Cameron 105 Sphere SS balloon | Cameron Balloons Ltd | |
| G-SATL | Cameron 105 Sphere SS balloon | Cameron Balloons Ltd | |
| G-SAUF | Colt 90A balloon | K. H. Medau | |
| G-SAVE | PA-31-350 Navajo Chieftain | Osten Airfinance Ltd | |
| G-SBAS | Beech B200 Super King Air | Bond Helicopters (G-BJJV)/Aberdeen | |
| G-SBAC | Short SD3-60 Variant 100 | BAC Leasing Ltd/Gill Aviation (G-BLEE) | |
| G-SBLT | Steen Skybolt | M. A. McCallum & H. Lees | |
| G-SBUS | BN-2A-26 Islander | Isles of Scilly Skybus Ltd (G-BMMH)/St Just | |
| G-SCAN | Vinten-Wallis WA-116/100 | K. H. Wallis | |
| G-SCAT | Cessna F.150F | Cheshire Air Training School (Merseyside) Ltd (G-ATRN)/Liverpool | |
| G-SCFO | Cameron O-77 balloon | M. K. Grigson | |
| G-SCPL | PA-28 Cherokee 140 | Hillvine Ltd (G-BPVL)/Staverton | |
| G-SCSR | Airbus A.320-212 | Excalibur Airways Ltd/E. Midlands | |
| G-SCTT | HPR-7 Herald 210 | Channel Express (Air Services) Ltd (G-ASPJ)/Bournemouth | |
| G-SCUB | PA-18 Super Cub 135 (542447) | N. D. Needham Farms | |
| G-SCUH | Boeing 737-3Q8 | British Airways | |
| G-SDEV | D.H.104 Sea Devon C.20 (XK895) | P. C. Gill & W. Gentle | |
| G-SDLW | Cameron O-105 balloon | P. J. Smart | |
| G-SEAB | Republic RC-3 Seabee | B. A. Farries | |
| G-SEAH | Hawker Sea Hawk FB.3 | Jet Heritage Ltd/Bournemouth | |
| G-SEAI | Cessna U.206G | Seaplane Safaris (Scotland) Ltd | |
| G-SEAS | PA-31-310 Navajo | Sea Surveillance Ltd | |
| G-SEAT | Colt 42 balloon | Airship & Balloon Co Ltd | |
| G-SEED | Piper J-3C-65 Cub | J. H. Seed | |
| G-SEEK | Cessna T.210N | Melrose Pigs Ltd | |
| G-SEGA | Cameron 90 Sonic SS balloon | Virgin Airship & Balloon Co Ltd | |
| G-SEGO | Robinson R-22B | G. Seago | |
| G-SEJW | PA-28-161 Warrior II | Truman Aviation Ltd/Tollerton | |
| G-SELL | Robin DR.400/180 | L. S. Thorne | |
| G-SEND | Colt 90A balloon | Redmalt Ltd | |
| G-SEPT | Cameron N-105 balloon | Deproco UK Ltd | |
| G-SERA | Enstrom F-28A-UK | W. R. Pitcher (G-BAHU) | |
| G-SERL | SOCATA TB.10 Tobago | R. J. & G. Searle (G-LANA)/Biggin Hill | |
| G-SETA | AS.355F-1 Twin Squirrel | McAlpine Helicopters Ltd (G-NEAS/ G-CMMM/G-BNBJ) | |
| G-SEVA | SE-5A (replica) (F141) | I. D. Gregory | |
| G-SEVE | Cessna 172N | S. Patterson | |

| Notes | Reg. | Type | Owner or Operator |
|---|---|---|---|
| | G-SEWL | PA-28-151 Warrior | A. R. Sewell & Sons/Andrewsfield |
| | G-SEXI | Cessna 172M | B. Powell/Biggin Hill |
| | G-SEXY | AA-1 Yankee | H. Morris (G-AYLM) |
| | G-SFHR | PA-23 Aztec 250F | E. L. Becker & J. Harper (G-BHSO) |
| | G-SFPA | Cessna F.406 | Scottish Fisheries Protection Agency |
| | G-SFPB | Cessna F.406 | Scottish Fisheries Protection Agency |
| | G-SFRY | Thunder Ax7-77 balloon | R. J. Fry |
| | G-SFTZ | Slingsby T.67M Firefly | Mega Yield Ltd |
| | G-SGAS | Colt 77A balloon | Avongas Ltd |
| | G-SHAA | Enstrom 280-UK | Manchester Helicopter Centre/Barton |
| | G-SHAW | PA-30 Twin Comanche 160B | PTC Ltd |
| | G-SHCC | AB-206B JetRanger 2 | Yorkshire Helicopter Centre Ltd |
| | G-SHDD | Enstrom F-28C | R. B. Sandell (G-BNBS) |
| | G-SHED | PA-28-181 Archer II | S. V. Smeeth (G-BRAU) |
| | G-SHEL | Cameron O-56 balloon | The Shell Company of Hong Kong Ltd |
| | G-SHFL | Cameron N-77 balloon | M. C. Bradley/Hong Kong |
| | G-SHGG | Enstrom 280C Shark | Haversham Helicopters Ltd |
| | G-SHIP | PA-23 Aztec 250F ★ | Midland Air Museum/Coventry |
| | G-SHIV | GA-7 Cougar | Westley Aviation Services |
| | G-SHKK | Hughes 269A | Starline Helicopters Ltd |
| | G-SHNN | Enstrom 280C | CJ Services |
| | G-SHOO | Hughes TH-55A | Starline Helicopters Ltd |
| | G-SHOP | H.S. 125 Srs F400B | GB Dee Knitwear Ltd (G-BTUF) |
| | G-SHOT | Cameron V-77 balloon | Bucks Hot-Air Balloon Group |
| | G-SHOW | M.S.733 Alycon | Vintage Aircraft Team/Cranfield |
| | G-SHPP | Hughes TH-55A | R. P. Bateman & A. C. Braithwaite |
| | G-SHRL | Jodel D.18 | K. Fern |
| | G-SHRR | AB-206B JetRanger 2 | Woodhey Helicopters (G-FSDA/G-AWJW) |
| | G-SHSS | Enstrom 280C-UK Shark | M. E. Mortlock (G-BENO) |
| | G-SHUG | PA-28R-201T Turbo Arrow III | N. E. Rennie |
| | G-SHUU | Enstrom 280C-UK-2 Shark | S. E. Hobbs (UK) Ltd (G-OMCP/ G-KENY/G-BJFG) |
| | G-SHZZ | Bell 206B JetRanger 3 | Corporate Enterprises Ltd (G-BNUW) |
| | G-SIAN | Cameron V-77 balloon | S. M. Jones |
| | G-SIGN | PA-39 Twin Comanche 160 C/R | Comanche Travel Ltd/Elstree |
| | G-SING | Beech B60 Duke | Sasha Fashions International Ltd/ Leavesden |
| | G-SION | PA-38-112 Tomahawk II | Bath Stone Co Ltd |
| | G-SIPA | SIPA 903 | T. J. McRae (G-BGBM) |
| | G-SITE | AS.355F-1 Twin Squirrel | Bridge Street Nominees Ltd (G-BPHC) |
| | G-SIXC | Douglas DC-6A | Atlantic Air Transport Ltd/Coventry |
| | G-SIXX | Colt 77A balloon | G. E. Harris & S. C. Kinsey |
| | G-SIZL | Bell 206B JetRanger 3 | P. G. Osborn (G-BOSW) |
| | G-SJAB | PA-39 Twin Comanche 160 C/R | Foyle Flyers Ltd |
| | G-SJGM | Cessna 182R | Crystal Air Ltd |
| | G-SKAN | Cessna F.172M | R. Mitchell & J. D. Walton (G-BFKT) |
| | G-SKIL | Cameron N-77 balloon | Flying Pictures (Balloons) Ltd |
| | G-SKIP | Cameron N-77 balloon | Skipton Building Soc |
| | G-SKKA | PA-31 Turbo Navajo | J. J. Baumhardt (G-FOAL/G-RMAE/ G-BAEG) |
| | G-SKKB | PA-31 Turbo Navajo | Bulldog Aviation Ltd/(G-BBDS)/Earls Colne |
| | G-SKKC | Cessan 404 | J. J. Baumhardt (G-OHUB)/Southend |
| | G-SKSA | Airship Industries SKS.500 | Airship Industries Ltd/Cardington |
| | G-SKSC | Airship Industries SKS.600 | Interport Marine Agencies Ltd |
| | G-SKSG | Airship Industries SKS.600/03 | Interport Marine Agencies Ltd |
| | G-SKYD | Pitts S-2B Special | Skydancer Aviation Ltd |
| | G-SKYE | Cessna TU.206G | RAF Sport Parachute Association |
| | G-SKYH | Cessna 172N | Elgor Hire Purchase & Credit Ltd/ Southend |
| | G-SKYI | Air Command 532 Elite | Skyrider Aviation Ltd |
| | G-SKYM | Cessna F.337E | Bencray Ltd (G-AYHW) (stored)/Blackpool |
| | G-SKYP | Cameron A-120 balloon | PSH Skypower Ltd |
| | G-SKYR | Cameron A-180 balloon | PSH Skypower Ltd |
| | G-SKYS | Cameron O-84 balloon | J. R. Christopher |
| | G-SLAC | Cameron N-77 balloon | The Scottish Life Assurance Co |
| | G-SLCI | Thunder Ax8-90 balloon | S. L. Cuhat |
| | G-SLEA | Mudry/CAARP CAP.10B | P. D. Southerington/Sturgate |
| | G-SLII | Cameron O-90 balloon | R. B. & A. M. Harris |
| | G-SLIM | Colt 56A balloon | Hot-Air Balloon Co Ltd |
| | G-SLYN | PA-28-161 Warrior II | G. E. Layton |
| | G-SMAF | Sikorsky S-76A | Fayair (Jersey) 1984 Ltd |
| | G-SMAX | Cameron O-105 balloon | Cameron Balloons Ltd |
| | G-SMHK | Cameron D-38 airship | San Miguel Brewery Ltd |

| Reg. | Type | Owner or Operator | Notes |
|---|---|---|---|
| G-SMIG | Cameron O-65 balloon | Hong Kong Balloon & Airship Club | |
| G-SMJJ | Cessna 414A | Gull Air Ltd/Guernsey | |
| G-SMTC | Colt Flying Hut SS balloon | Shiplake Investments Ltd | |
| G-SMTH | PA-28 Cherokee 140 | D. M. Banner (G-AYJS) | |
| G-SNAP | Cameron V-77 balloon | P. A. George | |
| G-SNAX | Colt 69A balloon | Derwent Valley Foods Ltd | |
| G-SNDY | Piper J-3C-65 Cub | R. R. K. Mayall | |
| G-SNOW | Cameron V-77 balloon | M. J. Snow | |
| G-SOAR | Eiri PIK-20E | F. W. Fay | |
| G-SOAS | PA-60 Aerostar 601P | Kenilgate Ltd | |
| G-SOFA | Cameron N-65 balloon | GT Flying Club Ltd | |
| G-SOFI | PA-60 Aerostar 601P (Machen Superstar II) | Allzones Travel Ltd/Biggin Hill | |
| G-SOFT | Thunder Ax7-77 balloon | Bristol Software Factory Ltd | |
| G-SOLA | Aero Designs Star-Lite SL.1 | P. Clifton & A. Clarke | |
| G-SOLD | Robinson R-22A | Travel Management Ltd | |
| G-SOLO | Pitts S-2S Special | Landitfast Ltd | |
| G-SONA | SOCATA TB.10 Tobago | J. Greenwood (G-BIBI) | |
| G-SONY | Aero Commander 200D | General Airline Ltd (G-BGPS) | |
| G-SOOE | Hughes 369E | Arrow Aviation Co Ltd/Manchester | |
| G-SOOM | Glaser-Dirks DG.500M | Glaser-Dirks UK | |
| G-SOOS | Colt 21A balloon | P. J. Stapley | |
| G-SOOT | PA-28 Cherokee 180 | Thornton Browne Ltd (G-AVNM)/Exeter | |
| G-SORT | Cameron N-90 balloon | The Post Office | |
| G-SOUL | Cessna 310R | Atlantic Air Transport Ltd/Coventry | |
| G-SPAM | Light Aero Avid Aerobat | C. M. Hicks | |
| G-SPEY | AB-206B JetRanger 3 | Castle Air Charters Ltd (G-BIGO) | |
| G-SPIN | Pitts S-2A Special | R. P. Grace & P. L. Goldberg | |
| G-SPIT | V.S.379 Spitfire FR.XIV (MV293) | Patina Ltd (G-BGHB)/Duxford | |
| G-SPOL | MBB Bo 105CBS/4 | Clyde Helicopters Ltd | |
| G-SSBS | Colting Ax77 balloon | K. J. & M. E. Gregory | |
| G-SSFS | H.S. 748 Srs 2B | British Aerospace PLC (G-BJTM) | |
| G-SSFT | PA-28-161 Warrior II | SFT Aviation Ltd (G-BHIL)/Bournemouth | |
| G-SSJT | Cessna 210L | J. Taylor | |
| G-SSKY | BN-2B-26 Islander | Isles of Scilly Skybus Ltd (G-BSWT) | |
| G-SSOZ | Cessna 550 Citation II | Arrows Aviation Co Ltd | |
| G-SSRS | Cessna 172N | Romair | |
| G-SSWV | Sportavia Fournier RF-5B | J. L. Collins & J. A. Melville | |
| G-STAG | Cameron O-65 balloon | Holker Estates Ltd | |
| G-STAK | Bell 206B JetRanger 2 | Tyringham Charter & Group Services Ltd (G-BNIS) | |
| G-STAN | F.27 Friendship Mk.200 | Air UK *Jimmy Saville OBE*/Norwich | |
| G-STAT | Cessna U.206F | SMK Engineers Ltd | |
| G-STAV | Cameron O-84 balloon | Nestle UK Ltd | |
| G-STEF | Hughes 369HS | D. J. L. Wood (G-BKTK) | |
| G-STEN | Stemme S.10 | W. A. H. Kahn | |
| G-STEP | Schweizer 269C | M. D. Thorpe | |
| G-STEV | Jodel DR.221 | S. W. Talbot/Long Marston | |
| G-STMI | Robinson R-22B | J. N. & C. J. Carter | |
| G-STMP | SNCAN Stampe SV-4A | W. R. Partridge | |
| G-STOX | Bell 206B JetRanger 2 | Tickstop Ltd (G-BNIR) | |
| G-STOY | Robinson R-22B | Tickstop Ltd | |
| G-STRK | CFM Streak Shadow Srs SA | M. E. Dodd | |
| G-STST | Bell 206B JetRanger 3 | Petrochemical Supplies Ltd | |
| G-STUA | Aerotek Pitts S-2A Special (modified) | Aero-Balance Aviation/White Waltham | |
| G-STVN | HPR-7 Herald 210 | Channel Express (Air Services) Ltd /Bournemouth | |
| G-STWO | ARV Super 2 | Aviation (Scotland) Ltd | |
| G-STYL | Pitts S-1S Special | B. MacMillan | |
| G-SUIT | Cessna 210N | Edinburgh Air Centre Ltd | |
| G-SUKI | PA-38-112 Tomahawk | Bath Stone Co Ltd (G-BPNV) | |
| G-SULL | PA-32R-301 Saratoga SP | B. R. Chaplin | |
| G-SULY | Monnet Moni | M. J. Sullivan | |
| G-SUMT | Robinson R-22B | Frankham Bros Ltd (G-BUKD) | |
| G-SUPA | PA-18 Super Cub 150 | Crop Aviation (UK) Ltd | |
| G-SURG | PA-30 Twin Comanche 160B | A. R. Taylor (G-VIST/G-AVHZ) | |
| G-SUSI | Cameron V-77 balloon | H. S. & C. J. Dryden | |
| G-SUSY | P-51D-25-NA Mustang (472773) | P. J. Morgan | |
| G-SUZI | Beech 95-B55 Baron | Bebecar (UK) Ltd (G-BAXR) | |
| G-SUZN | PA-28-161 Warrior II | Bath Stone Co Ltd | |
| G-SUZY | Taylor JT.1 Monoplane | E. J. Blackoe | |
| G-SVIV | SNCAN Stampe SV-4C | A. J. Clarry & S. F. Bancroft | |

| Notes | Reg. | Type | Owner or Operator |
|---|---|---|---|
| | G-SVJM | AS.355F-1 Twin Squirrel | UB Air Ltd & Jensen & Nicholson Ltd (G-BOPS) |
| | G-SVSS | Beech C90A King Air | Terry Coleman (UK) Ltd (G-OAKZ) |
| | G-SWAG | EMB-110P1 Bandeirante | Tech Air (Cambridge) Ltd (G-CLAW) |
| | G-SWEB | Cameron N-90 balloon | Air 2 Air Ltd |
| | G-SWET | Cessna 500 Citation | GB Dee Knitwear Ltd |
| | G-SWFT | Beech 200 Super King Air | Airswift Ltd (G-SIBE/G-MCEO/G-BILY) |
| | G-SWIF | V.S.541 Swift F.7 | Jet Heritage Ltd/Bournemouth |
| | G-SWIM | Taylor Coot Amphibian (modified) | R. J. Hopkins |
| | G-SWIS | D.H.100 Vampire F.6 (J-1149) | Hunter Wing Ltd/Bournemouth |
| | G-SWOT | Currie Super Wot (C3011) | J. D. Haslam |
| | G-SWPR | Cameron N-56 balloon | A. Brown |
| | G-SYFW | Focke-Wulf Fw.190 replica (2+1) | M. R. Parr |
| | | | |
| | G-TACK | Grob G.109B | Oval (275) Ltd/Bristol |
| | G-TAFF | C.A.S.A. 1.131 Jungmann | A. Horsfall (G-BFNE) |
| | G-TAFY | Piper J-3F-65 Cub | C. P. Goodley |
| | G-TAGS | PA-28-161 Warrior II | Air Service Training Ltd/Perth |
| | G-TAIL | Cessna 150J | Routair Aviation Services Ltd/Southend |
| | G-TAIR | PA-34-200T Seneca II | Wessex Mouldings Ltd |
| | G-TAMY | Cessna 421B | Malcolm Enamellers (Midlands) Ltd |
| | G-TAPE | PA-23 Aztec 250D | Merlix Ltd (G-AWVW) |
| | G-TART | PA-28-236 Dakota | Withercourt Ltd |
| | G-TATT | GY-20 Minicab | L. Tattershall |
| | G-TAXI | PA-23 Aztec 250E | Yorkair Ltd/Leeds |
| | G-TAYI | Grob G.115 | Tayside Aviation Ltd (G-DODO)/Dundee |
| | G-TAYS | Cessna F.152 | Tayside Aviation Ltd (G-LFCA)/Dundee |
| | G-TBAC | Short SD3-60 Variant 100 | BAC Leasing Ltd/Gill Aviation (G-BMNK) |
| | G-TBAG | Murphy Renegade 1 | M. R. Tetley |
| | G-TBIO | SOCATA TB.10 Tobago | R. A. Perrot |
| | G-TBIX | MDH Hughes 369E | Weetabix Ltd/Sywell |
| | G-TBXX | SOCATA TB.20 Trinidad | J. D. Moore |
| | G-TBZO | SOCATA TB.20 Trinidad | D. L. Clarke & J. S. Monk |
| | G-TCAN | Colt 69A balloon | Thunder & Colt Ltd |
| | G-TCAR | Robin HR.100/210 | Gibad Aviation Ltd |
| | G-TCMP | Robinson R-22B | M. S. Wilford |
| | G-TCSL | R. Commander 112A | Trans-Channel Services Ltd |
| | G-TCTC | PA-28RT-201 Arrow IV | Terry Coleman (UK) Ltd |
| | G-TCUB | Piper J-3C-65 Cub | J. C. R. Rogers |
| | G-TDFS | IMCO Callair A.9 | Dollarhigh Ltd (G-AVZA) |
| | G-TEAC | AT-6C Harvard IIA (889696) | E. C. English/North Weald |
| | G-TEAL | Thurston TSC-1A1 | K. Heeley |
| | G-TECC | Aeronca 7AC Champion | T. E. C. Cushing/Little Snoring |
| | G-TECH | R. Commander 114 | P. A. Reed (G-BEDH)/Denham |
| | G-TECK | Cameron V-77 balloon | G. M. N. Spencer |
| | G-TEDF | Cameron N-90 balloon | Fort Vale Engineering Ltd |
| | G-TEDS | SOCATA TB.10 Tobago | E. W. Lyon (G-BHCO) |
| | G-TEDY | Evans VP-1 | C. J. D. Edwards (G-BHGN) |
| | G-TEEM | PA-32R Cherokee Six 300 | Madgwick International (Holdings) Ltd |
| | G-TEFC | PA-28 Cherokee 140 | A. R. Knight |
| | G-TEFH | Cessna 500 Citation | Birmingham Aviation Ltd (G-BCII) |
| | G-TELL | Cessna 421C | Holding & Barnes Ltd |
| | G-TELY | Agusta A.109A-II | Castle Air Charters Ltd |
| | G-TEMP | PA-28 Cherokee 180 | BEV Piper Group (G-AYBK)/Andrewsfield |
| | G-TEMT | Hawker Tempest II | Autokraft Ltd |
| | G-TENT | J/1N Alpha | R. Callaway-Lewis (G-AKJU) |
| | G-TERI | Beech F33A Bonanza | T. & D. E. Beanland/Jersey |
| | G-TERY | PA-28-181 Archer II | T. Barlow (G-BOXZ)/Barton |
| | G-TESS | Quickie Q.2 | D. Evans |
| | G-TEST | PA-34-200 Seneca | Stapleford Flying Club Ltd (G-BLCD) |
| | G-TEWS | PA-28 Cherokee 140 | M. J. & M. J. Tew (G-KEAN/G-AWTM) |
| | G-TFCI | Cessna FA.152 | Tayside Aviation Ltd/Dundee |
| | G-TFRB | Air Command 532 Elite | F. R. Blennerhassett |
| | G-TFOX | Denney Aerocraft Kitfox Mk 2 | F. A. Roberts |
| | G-TFUN | Valentin Taifun 17E | NW Taifun Group |
| | G-TGAS | Cameron O-160 balloon | G. A. Fisher |
| | G-TGER | AA-5B Tiger | A. Wuensche (G-BFZP) |
| | G-THCL | Cessna 550 Citation II | Tower House Consultants Ltd |
| | G-THEA | Boeing Stearman E.75 | L. M. Walton |
| | G-THGS | SA.365N-1 Dauphin 2 | HeavyLift Cargo Airlines Ltd (G-BPOJ) |
| | G-THLS | MBB Bo 105DBS/4 | Bond Helicopters Ltd |
| | G-THOM | Thunder Ax6-56 balloon | T. H. Wilson |
| | G-THOR | Thunder Ax8-105 balloon | N. C. Faithful/*Turncoat* |

| Reg. | Type | Owner or Operator | Notes |
|---|---|---|---|
| G-THOS | Thunder Ax7-77 balloon | Thos Wood & Son (Builders) Ltd | |
| G-THSL | PA-28R-201 Arrow III | G. Fearnley/Southend | |
| G-THUR | Beech 200 Super King Air | Thurston Aviation (Stansted) Ltd | |
| G-TIBC | Cameron A-180 balloon | Aerial Promotions Ltd | |
| G-TICK | Cameron V-77 balloon | T. J. Tickler | |
| G-TIDS | Jodel D.150 | J. B. Dovey/Ipswich | |
| G-TIGA | D.H.82A Tiger Moth | D. E. Leatherland (G-AOEG) | |
| G-TIGB | AS.332L Super Puma | Bristow Helicopters Ltd (G-BJXC) | |
| G-TIGC | AS.332L Super Puma | Bristow Helicopters Ltd (G-BJYH) | |
| G-TIGE | AS.332L Super Puma | Bristow Helicopters Ltd (G-BJYJ) | |
| G-TIGF | AS.332L Super Puma | Bristow Helicopters Ltd | |
| G-TIGG | AS.332L Super Puma | Bristow Helicopters Ltd | |
| G-TIGI | AS.332L Super Puma | Bristow Helicopters Ltd | |
| G-TIGK | AS.332L Super Puma | Bristow Helicopters Ltd | |
| G-TIGL | AS.332L Super Puma | Bristow Helicopters Ltd | |
| G-TIGM | AS.332L Super Puma | Bristow Helicopters Ltd | |
| G-TIGO | AS.332L Super Puma | Bristow Helicopters Ltd | |
| G-TIGP | AS.332L Super Puma | Bristow Helicopters Ltd | |
| G-TIGR | AS.332L Super Puma | Bristow Helicopters Ltd | |
| G-TIGS | AS.332L Super Puma | Bristow Helicopters Ltd | |
| G-TIGT | AS.332L Super Puma | Bristow Helicopters Ltd | |
| G-TIGU | AS.332L Super Puma | Bristow Helicopters Ltd | |
| G-TIGV | AS.332L Super Puma | Bristow Helicopters Ltd | |
| G-TIGW | AS.332L Super Puma | Bristow Helicopters Ltd | |
| G-TIGZ | AS.332L Super Puma | British International Helicopters Ltd | |
| G-TIII | Aerotek Pitts S-2A | Aerobatic Displays Ltd (G-BGSE)/Booker | |
| G-TILE | Robinson R-22B | S. Lee | |
| G-TILL | Robinson R-22B | G. Till | |
| G-TILT | Bell 206B JetRanger 3 | Alan Mann Helicopters Ltd (G-BRJO) | |
| G-TIMB | Rutan Vari-Eze | T. M. Bailey (G-BKXJ) | |
| G-TIME | Ted Smith Aerostar 601P | J. J. Donn | |
| G-TIMJ | Rand KR-2 | N. Seaton | |
| G-TIMK | PA-28-181 Archer II | T. Baker | |
| G-TIMM | Folland Gnat T.1 | T. J. Manna/Leavesden | |
| G-TIMP | Aeronca 7BCM Champion | T. E. Phillips | |
| G-TIMS | Falconar F-12A | T. Sheridan | |
| G-TIMW | PA-28 Cherokee 140C | W. H. Sanders (G-AXSH) | |
| G-TINA | SOCATA TB.10 Tobago | A. Lister | |
| G-TINS | Cameron N-90 balloon | Bass & Tennent Sales Ltd | |
| G-TJHI | Cessna 500 Citation | Trustair Ltd (G-CCCL/G-BEIZ) | |
| G-TKPZ | Cessna 310R | Auxili-Air Aviation Ltd (G-BRAH)/ Humberside | |
| G-TKYO | Boeing 747-212B | Virgin Atlantic Airways Ltd *Maiden Japan* | |
| G-TLOL | Cessna 421C | Littlewoods Organisation Ltd/Liverpool | |
| G-TLTD | Cessna 182Q | Gray Tuplin Ltd | |
| G-TMKI | P.56 Provost T.1 | T. J. Manna/Leavesden | |
| G-TMMC | AS.355F-1 Twin Squirrel | The Colt Car Co Ltd (G-JLCO) | |
| G-TNTA | BAe 146-200QT | TNT Express Worldwide Ltd | |
| G-TNTB | BAe 146-200QT | TNT Express Worldwide Ltd | |
| G-TNTD | BAe 146-200QT | TNT Express Worldwide Ltd (G-BOMJ) | |
| G-TNTE | BAe 146-300QT | TNT Express Worldwide Ltd (G-BRPW) | |
| G-TNTG | BAe 146-300QT | TNT Express Worldwide Ltd (G-BSUY) | |
| G-TNTK | BAe 146-300QT | TNT Express Worldwide Ltd (G-BSXL) | |
| G-TNTL | BAe 146-300QT | TNT Express Worldwide Ltd (G-BSGI) | |
| G-TNTM | BAe 146-300QT | TNT Express Worldwide Ltd (G-BSLZ) | |
| G-TNTN | Thunder Ax6-56 balloon | D. P. & A. Dickinson | |
| G-TOAD | Jodel D.140B | Mothballs Ltd | |
| G-TOAK | SOCATA TB.20 Trinidad | Self Adhesive Fixings Ltd | |
| G-TOBA | SOCATA TB.10 Tobago | E. Downing | |
| G-TOBE | PA-28R Cherokee Arrow 200 | J. Bradley & Barry Ltd (G-BNRO) | |
| G-TOBI | Cessna F.172K | G. Hall (G-AYVB) | |
| G-TODD | ICA IS-28M2A | C. I. Roberts & C. D. King | |
| G-TOFT | Colt 90A balloon | Norwest Holst Construction Ltd | |
| G-TOGA | PA-32-301 Saratoga | Toga Flying Four Group | |
| G-TOMI | H.S.125 Srs 600B | Falcon Jet Centre Ltd(G-BBEP/G-BJOY)/ Heathrow | |
| G-TOMS | PA-38-112 Tomahawk | R. J. Alford | |
| G-TOMY | Mitsubishi Mu.300 Diamond | Lynton Aviation Ltd | |
| G-TONE | Pazmany PL.4 | J. A. Walmsley | |
| G-TONI | Cessna 421C | M. Scott | |
| G-TONW | McD Douglas MD-83 | Airtours International Aviation Ltd | |
| G-TOOL | Thunder Ax8-105 balloon | W. J. Honey | |
| G-TOPS | AS.355F-1 Twin Squirrel | ICS Worldwide Couriers Ltd (G-BPRH) | |

| Notes | Reg. | Type | Owner or Operator |
|---|---|---|---|
| | G-TORE | P.84 Jet Provost T.3A (XM405) | Butane Buzzard Aviation Corpn Ltd |
| | G-TOTO | Cessna F.177RG | C. R. & J. Cox (G-OADE/G-AZKH) |
| | G-TOTY | Robinson R-22B | Northern Helicopters Ltd |
| | G-TOUR | Robin R.2112 | Barnes Martin Ltd |
| | G-TOWS | PA-25 Pawnee 260 | Blackpool & Fylde Gliding Club Ltd |
| | G-TOYS | Enstrom 280C-UK-2 Shark | B. Murphy (G-BISE) |
| | G-TPHK | BAe 125 Srs 800B | Tiphook PLC (G-FDSL)/Biggin Hill |
| | G-TREE | Bell 206B JetRanger 3 | LGH Aviation Ltd |
| | G-TREK | Jodel D.18 | R. H. Mole |
| | G-TREN | Boeing 737-4S3 | British Airways (G-BRKG) |
| | G-TRIC | D.H.C.1 Chipmunk 22A | D. M. Barnett (G-AOSZ) |
| | G-TRIK | Bell 206B JetRanger 2 | Annabelle Casion Ltd (G-BMWY) |
| | G-TRIM | Monnet Moni | J. E. Bennell |
| | G-TRIN | SOCATA TB.20 Trinidad | South East Aviation Ltd |
| | G-TRIO | Cessna 172M | Biggin Hill School of Flying (G-BNXY) |
| | G-TRIP | PA-32R-301 Saratoga SP | C. P. Lockyer (G-HOSK) |
| | G-TRIX | V.S.509 Spitfire T.IX (PV202) | R. A. Roberts |
| | G-TROP | Cessna 310R | R. P. Nash/Norwich |
| | G-TRUC | Cassutt Speed One | J. A. H. Chadwick |
| | G-TRUK | Stoddard-Hamilton Glasair RG | Compustar Ltd |
| | G-TRUX | Colt 77A balloon | Highway Truck Rental Ltd |
| | G-TSAM | BAe 125 Srs 800B | British Aerospace PLC/Hatfield |
| | G-TSFT | PA-28-161 Warrior II | SFT Aviation Ltd (G-BLDJ)/Bournemouth |
| | G-TSGJ | PA-28-181 Archer II | Golf Juliet Flying Club |
| | G-TSIX | AT-6C Harvard IIA | D. Taylor/E. Midlands |
| | G-TTAM | Taylor JT.2 Titch | A. J. Manning |
| | G-TTEL | PA-E23 Aztec 250D | Target Technology Electronics Ltd (G-BBXE) |
| | G-TTHC | Robinson R-22B | Paul Hopper Entertainments Ltd |
| | G-TTPT | McD Douglas MD-83 | Airtours International Aviation Ltd |
| | G-TTWO | Colt 56A balloon | P. N. Tilney |
| | G-TUBS | Beech 65-80 Queen Air | A. H. Bowers (G-ASKM)/Staverton |
| | G-TUDR | Cameron V-77 balloon | Jacques W. Soukup Ltd |
| | G-TUGG | PA-18 Super Cub 150 | Ulster Gliding Club Ltd |
| | G-TUKE | Robin DR.400/160 | Tukair/Headcorn |
| | G-TURB | D.31 Turbulent | A. Ryan-Fecitt |
| | G-TURK | Cameron 80 Sultan SS balloon | Forbes Europe Inc/France |
| | G-TURN | Steen Skybolt | M. Hammond |
| | G-TVMM | Cessna 310Q | TVMM Aviation Ltd (G-CETA/G-BBIM) |
| | G-TVSI | Campbell Cricket | W. H. Beevers (G-AYHH) |
| | G-TVTV | Cameron 90 TV SS balloon | Cameron Balloons Ltd |
| | G-TWEL | PA-28-181 Archer II | Universal Salvage (Holdings) Ltd |
| | G-TWEY | Colt 69A balloon | British Telecom Thameswey |
| | G-TWIN | PA-44-180 Seminole | Leavesden Flight Centre Ltd |
| | G-TWIZ | R. Commander 114 | B. C. & P. M. Cox/Biggin Hill |
| | G-TYGA | AA-5B Tiger | Hovemere Ltd (G-BHNZ)/Biggin Hill |
| | G-TYRE | Cessna F.172M | Staverton Flying Services Ltd |
| | G-UBBE | Cameron Clown SS balloon | Cameron Balloons Ltd |
| | G-UDAY | Robinson R-22B | Oakover Holdings Ltd |
| | G-UERN | BN-2B-26 Islander | Air & General Services Ltd (G-BHXI) |
| | G-UEST | Bell 206B JetRanger 2 | Leisure & Retail Consultants Ltd (G-ROYB/G-BLWU) |
| | G-UFLY | Cessna F.150H | Westair Flying Services Ltd (G-AVVY)/Blackpool |
| | G-UIDA | Aero Designs Star-Lite SL.1 | I. J. Widger (G-BRKK) |
| | G-UIDE | Jodel D.120 | S. T. Gilbert/Popham |
| | G-UIET | BAe ATP/Jetstream 61 | Manx Airlines Ltd/*King Reginald (1187-1229)*/Ronaldsway |
| | G-UILD | Grob G.109B | Runnymede Consultants Ltd |
| | G-UKAC | BAe 146-300 | Air UK Ltd/Stansted |
| | G-UKAG | BAe 146-300 | Air UK Ltd/Stansted |
| | G-UKFA | Fokker 100 | Air UK Ltd/Stansted |
| | G-UKFB | Fokker 100 | Air UK Ltd/Stansted |
| | G-UKFC | Fokker 100 | Air UK Ltd/Stansted |
| | G-UKFD | Fokker 100 | Air UK Ltd/Stansted |
| | G-UKFE | Fokker 100 | Air UK Ltd/Stansted |
| | G-UKHP | BAe 146-300 | Air UK Ltd/Stansted |
| | G-UKID | BAe 146-300 | Air UK Ltd/Stansted |
| | G-UKJF | BAe 146-100 | Air UK Ltd/Stansted |
| | G-UKLA | Boeing 737-4Y0 | Air UK Leisure Ltd *St Andrew*/Stansted |
| | G-UKLB | Boeing 737-4Y0 | Air UK Leisure Ltd *St Bernard*/Stansted |
| | G-UKLC | Boeing 737-42C | Air UK Leisure Ltd *St Christopher*/Stansted |

| Reg. | Type | Owner or Operator | Notes |
|------|------|-------------------|-------|
| G-UKLD | Boeing 737-42C | Air UK Leisure Ltd St David/Stansted | |
| G-UKLE | Boeing 737-4Y0 | Air UK Leisure Ltd St Emilion/Stansted | |
| G-UKLF | Boeing 737-42C | Air UK Leisure Ltd St Francis/Stansted | |
| G-UKLG | Boeing 737-42C | Air UK Leisure Ltd St George/Stansted | |
| G-UKLH | Boeing 767-3Q8ER | Air UK Leisure Ltd/Stansted | |
| G-UKLI | Boeing 767-3Q8ER | Air UK Leisure Ltd/Stansted | |
| G-UKLN | BAe 146-200 | Air UK Ltd (G-BNKJ)/Stansted | |
| G-UKNZ | Colt Flying Harp SS balloon | Flying Pictures Ltd | |
| G-UKPC | BAe 146-100 | Air UK Ltd (G-BKXZ)/Stansted | |
| G-UKRB | Colt 105A balloon | Airship & Balloon Co Ltd | |
| G-UKRC | BAe 146-300 | Air UK Ltd (G-BSMR)/Stansted | |
| G-UKRH | BAe 146-200 | Air UK Ltd/(G-BRNG)/Stansted | |
| G-UKSC | BAe 146-300 | Air UK Ltd/Stansted | |
| G-ULIA | Cameron V-77 balloon | J. & R. Bayly | |
| G-UMBO | Thunder Ax7-77A balloon | Airship & Balloon Co Ltd | |
| G-UMMI | PA-31-310 Turbo Navjo | Everts Balloon Co Ltd (G-BGSO) | |
| G-UNDY | Cessna 340 | Morris Cohen (Underwear) Ltd (G-BBNR) | |
| G-UNIK | AB-206B JetRanger 2 | First City Air PLC (G-TPPH/G-BCYP) | |
| G-UNIP | Cameron Oil Container SS balloon | Flying Pictures (Balloons) Ltd | |
| G-UNST | Beech F33C Bonanza | I. G. Meredith | |
| G-UPCC | Robinson R-22B | Deltair Ltd (G-MUSS) | |
| G-UPDN | Cameron V-65 balloon | R. J. O. Evans | |
| G-UPMW | Robinson R-22B | M. Wood Haulage | |
| G-UPPP | Colt 77A balloon | M. Williams | |
| G-UPPY | Cameron DP-80 balloon | Jacques W. Soukup Enterprises Ltd | |
| G-UPUP | Cameron V-77 balloon | S. F. Burden | |
| G-UROP | Beech 95-B55 Baron | Pooler International Ltd | |
| G-URRR | Air Command 582 Sport | L. Armes | |
| G-USAM | Cameron Uncle Sam SS balloon | Jacques W. Soukup Enterprises Ltd | |
| G-USGB | Colt 105A balloon | Thunder & Colt Ltd | |
| G-USIL | Thunder Ax7-77 balloon | Capital Balloon Club Ltd | |
| G-USMC | Cameron 90 Chestie SS balloon | Jacques W. Soukup Enterprises Ltd | |
| G-USSR | Cameron 90 Doll SS balloon | Jacques W. Soukup Enterprises Ltd | |
| G-USSY | PA-28-181 Archer II | Western Air Training Ltd/Thruxton | |
| G-USTI | Cameron H-34 balloon | Allen & Harris Ltd | |
| G-USTV | Messerschmitt Bf.109G-2 (6) | Imperial War Museum/Duxford | |
| G-USTY | FRED Srs 2 | K. Jones | |
| G-UTSI | Rand KR-2 | K. B. Gutridge | |
| G-UTSY | PA-28R-201 Arrow III | D. G. Perry//Stapleford | |
| G-UTZY | SA.341G Gazelle 1 | Davinci Aviation Ltd (G-BKLV) | |
| G-UZEL | SA.341G Gazelle 1 | Kepak Ltd (G-BRNH) | |
| G-UZLE | Colt 77A balloon | Flying Pictures (Balloons) Ltd | |
| G-VAGA | PA-15 Vagabond | E. J. McEntee/White Waltham | |
| G-VAJT | M.S.894E Rallye 220GT | R. W. B. Rolfe | |
| G-VANS | Van's RV-4 | T. R. Grief | |
| G-VARG | Varga 2150A Kachina | J. Hannibal/Halfpenny Green | |
| G-VAUK | PA-31-350 Navajo Chieftain | John Mowlem & Co PLC (G-GWEA) | |
| G-VAUN | Cessna 340 | F. E. Peacock & Son (Thorney) Ltd | |
| G-VCJH | Robinson R-22B | Great Northern Helicopters Ltd | |
| G-VCSI | Rotorway Executive | Qual-Rect Ltd | |
| G-VDIR | Cessna T.310R | Van Diemen International Racing Ltd | |
| G-VELA | SIAI-Marchetti S.205-22R | D. P. & P. A. Dawson | |
| G-VENI | D.H.112 Venom FB.50 | Source Premium & Promotional Consultants Ltd | |
| G-VERT | Bell 222 | Arlington Securities PLC (G-JLBZ/G-BNDB) | |
| G-VGIN | Boeing 747-243B | Virgin Atlantic Airways Ltd Scarlet Lady/ Gatwick | |
| G-VHFA | PA-23 Aztec 250 | Hartfield Aviation Ltd (G-BZFE/G-AZFE) | |
| G-VIBA | Cameron DP-80 airship | Jacques W. Soukup Enterprises Ltd | |
| G-VICC | PA-28-161 Warrior II | V. G. Lamb (G-JFHL) | |
| G-VICM | Beech F33C Bonanza | Charles W. Michie Ltd | |
| G-VIDI | D.H.112 Venom FB.50 (WE402) | Source Premium & Promotional Consultants Ltd | |
| G-VIEW | Vinten-Wallis WA-116/100 | K. H. Wallis | |
| G-VIII | V. S. Spitfire LF.VIII (MT719) | Reynard Racing Cars Ltd/Duxford | |
| G-VIKE | Bellanca 1730A Viking | Peter Dolan & Co Ltd | |
| G-VIPI | BAe 125 Srs 800B | Yeates of Leicester Ltd | |
| G-VIRG | Boeing 747-287B | Virgin Atlantic Airways Ltd Maiden Voyager/ Gatwick | |
| G-VISA | Cessna A.152 | K. W. Felton | |
| G-VITE | Robin R.1180T | G-VITE Flying Group | |
| G-VIVA | Thunder Ax7-65 balloon | J. G. Spearing | |

| Notes | Reg. | Type | Owner or Operator |
|---|---|---|---|
| | G-VIXN | D.H.110 Sea Vixen FAW.2 (XS587) ★ | P. G. Vallance Ltd/Charlwood |
| | G-VIZZ | Sportavia RS.180 Sportsman | Exeter Fournier Group |
| | G-VJAI | GA-7 Cougar | UB Air Ltd (G-OCAB/G-BICF)/Elstree |
| | G-VJAY | H.S.125 Srs F400B | Jensen & Nicholson (S) Pte Ltd (G-AYLG) |
| | G-VJCB | Agusta A.109A II | J. C. Bamford Excavators Ltd (G-BOUA) |
| | G-VJCT | Partenavia P.68C | Montrose Leasing Ltd |
| | G-VJET | Avro 698 Vulcan B.2 (XL426) | R. E. Jacobsen |
| | G-VJFK | Boeing 747-238B | Virgin Atlantic Airways Ltd/Gatwick |
| | G-VJIM | Colt 77 Jumbo Jim SS balloon | Airship & Balloon Co Ltd |
| | G-VLAD | Yakovlev Yak-50 | W. J. J. Kamper |
| | G-VLAX | Boeing 747-238B | Virgin Atlantic Airways Ltd *California Girl*/Gatwick |
| | G-VMAX | Mooney M.20K | Glidegold Ltd |
| | G-VMDE | Cessna P.210N | Royton Express Deliveries (Welwyn) Ltd |
| | G-VMIA | Boeing 747-123 | Virgin Atlantic Airways Ltd (G-HIHO) |
| | G-VMJM | SOCATA TB.10 Tobago | J. H. Michaels (G-BTOK) |
| | G-VNOM | D.H.112 Venom FB.50 | A. Topen/Cranfield |
| | G-VODA | Cameron N-77 balloon | Racal Telecom PLC |
| | G-VOID | PA-28RT-201 Arrow IV | Newbus Aviation Ltd |
| | G-VOLT | Cameron N-77 balloon | National Power |
| | G-VOYG | Boeing 747-283B | Virgin Atlantic Airways Ltd (G-BMGS) |
| | G-VPII | Evans VP-2 | V. D. J. Hitchings (G-EDIF) |
| | G-VPLC | Beech 200 Super King Air | Vickers Shipbuilding & Engineering Ltd |
| | G-VRES | Beech A200 Super King Air | Northern Executive Aviation Ltd/Manchester |
| | G-VRGN | Boeing 747-212B | Virgin Atlantic Airways Ltd *Maid of Honour* |
| | G-VRVI | Cameron O-90 balloon | Cooling Services Ltd |
| | G-VSOP | Cameron 60 Bottle SS balloon | J. R. Parkington & Co Ltd |
| | G-VTAX | PA-31-350 Navajo Chieftain | Jet West Ltd/Exeter |
| | G-VTII | D.H.115 Vampire T.11 (WZ507) | J. Turnbull & ptnrs/Cranfield |
| | G-VTOL | H.S. Harrier T.52 ★ | Brooklands Museum of Aviation/Weybridge |
| | G-VULC | Avro 698 Vulcan B.2 (XM655) | R. E. Jacobsen |
| | G-VVBK | PA-34-200T Seneca II | Computaplane Ltd (G-BSBS/G-BDRI) |
| | G-VVIP | Cessna 421C | Capital Trading Aviation Ltd (G-BMWB) |
| | G-WAAC | Cameron N-56 balloon | Newbury Ballooning Co Ltd |
| | G-WACA | Cessna F.152 | Wycombe Air Centre Ltd |
| | G-WACB | Cessna F.152 | Wycombe Air Centre Ltd |
| | G-WACC | Cessna F.152 | Wycombe Air Centre Ltd |
| | G-WACE | Cessna F.152 | Wycombe Air Centre Ltd |
| | G-WACF | Cessna 152 | Wycombe Air Centre Ltd |
| | G-WACG | Cessna F.152 | Wycombe Air Centre Ltd |
| | G-WACH | Cessna FA.152 | Wycombe Air Centre Ltd |
| | G-WACI | Beech 76 Duchess | Wycombe Air Centre Ltd |
| | G-WACJ | Beech 76 Duchess | Wycombe Air Centre Ltd |
| | G-WACK | Short SD3-60 Variant 100 | Loganair Ltd (G-BMAJ)/Glasgow |
| | G-WACL | Cessna F.172N | Wycombe Air Centre Ltd (G-BHGG) |
| | G-WACO | Waco UPF-7 | RGV (Aircraft Services) & Co/Staverton |
| | G-WACP | PA-28 Cherokee 180 | RAF Halton Aeroplane Club Ltd |
| | G-WACR | PA-28 Cherokee 180 | Wycombe Air Centre Ltd (G-BCZF) |
| | G-WACS | Cessna F.152 | RAF Halton Aeroplane Club Ltd |
| | G-WACT | Cessna F.152 II | Hartmann Ltd (G-BKFT)/Booker |
| | G-WACU | Cessna FA.152 | Hartmann Ltd (G-BJZU)/Booker |
| | G-WACW | Cessna 172P | Wycombe Air Centre Ltd |
| | G-WACY | Cessna F.172P | Wycombe Air Centre Ltd |
| | G-WACZ | Cessna F.172M | Wycombe Air Centre Ltd (G-BCUK) |
| | G-WAGI | Robinson R-22B | J. Wagstaff |
| | G-WAIR | PA-32-301 Saratoga | Ware Aviation Ltd |
| | G-WAIT | Cameron V-77 balloon | G. & D. A. Waite |
| | G-WALL | Beech 95-58PA Baron | MLP Aviation Ltd/Elstree |
| | G-WALS | Cessna A.152 | Redhill Flying Club |
| | G-WALT | Cameron Flying Castle SS balloon | Cameron Balloons Ltd |
| | G-WARD | Taylor JT.1 Monoplane | G. D. & P. J. Ward |
| | G-WARE | PA-28-161 Warrior II | W. J. Ware |
| | G-WARI | PA-28-161 Warrior II | Abraxas Aviation Ltd |
| | G-WARK | Schweizer 269C | Warwickshire Constabulary |
| | G-WARR | PA-28-161 Warrior II | T. J. & G. M. Laundy |
| | G-WASH | Noble 1250 balloon | Noble Adventures Ltd |
| | G-WASP | Brantly B.2B | W. C. Evans & M. L. Morris (G-ASXE) |
| | G-WATH | Colt 77A balloon | Ballooning Adventures Ltd |
| | G-WATS | PA-34-220T Seneca III | Aerohire Ltd (G-BOVJ)/Halfpenny Green |

| Reg. | Type | Owner or Operator | Notes |
|------|------|-------------------|-------|
| G-WATT | Cameron Cooling Tower SS balloon | National Power | |
| G-WATZ | PA-28-151 Warrior | Air Nova/Liverpool | |
| G-WAWL | BAe Jetstream 4102 | Manx Airlines Ltd | |
| G-WAWR | BAe Jetstream 4102 | Manx Airlines Ltd | |
| G-WAYR | BAe Jetstream 4102 | Manx Airlines Ltd | |
| G-WAVE | Grob G.109B | M. L. Murdoch/Cranfield | |
| G-WBAT | Wombat gyroplane | C. D. Julian (G-BSID) | |
| G-WBPR | BAe 125 Srs 800B | Trusthouse Forte PLC/Heathrow | |
| G-WBTS | Falconair F-11 | W. C. Brown (G-BDPL) | |
| G-WCAT | Colt Flying Mitt SS balloon | Interline Develoments Ltd | |
| G-WCEI | M.S.894E Rallye 220GT | R. A. L. Lucas (G-BAOC) | |
| G-WDEB | Thunder Ax-7-77 balloon | W. de Bock | |
| G-WEEZ | Mooney M.20J | Weyland Ltd | |
| G-WELA | SA.341G Gazelle 1 | Weller Helicopters Ltd (G-SFTD/G-RIFC) | |
| G-WELI | Cameron N-77 balloon | M. A. Shannon | |
| G-WELL | Beech E90 King Air | CEGA Aviation Ltd/Goodwood | |
| G-WELS | Cameron N-65 balloon | K. J. Vickery | |
| G-WEND | PA-28RT-201 Arrow IV | Chingford Magnetic Signs | |
| G-WENT | BAe Jetstream 3102 | Manx Airlines Ltd (G-IBLW)/Ronaldsway | |
| G-WERY | SOCATA TB.20 Trinidad | Wery Flying Group/Sherburn | |
| G-WEST | Agusta A.109A | Westland Helicopters Ltd/Yeovil | |
| G-WESX | CFM Streak Shadow | Wessex Aviation Ltd | |
| G-WETI | Cameron N-31 balloon | C. A. Butter & J. J. T. Cooke | |
| G-WGCS | PA-18 Super Cub 95 | T. M. Storey/Shoreham | |
| G-WGEL | Boeing 737-2U4 | Capita Ltd (G-ILFC/G-BOSL) | |
| G-WGSC | Pilatus PC-6/B2-H4 Turbo Porter | D. M. Penny | |
| G-WHAT | Colt 77A balloon | Thunder & Colt Ltd | |
| G-WHFO | Colt 10 Bottle SS balloon | Airship & Balloon Co Ltd (G-BUCN) | |
| G-WHIM | Colt 77A balloon | D. L. Morgan | |
| G-WHIR | Montgomerie Bensen B.8MR | A. P. Barden (G-BROT) | |
| G-WHIZ | Pitts S-1 Special | K. M. McLeod | |
| G-WHIZ† | V.701 Viscount ★ | Saltwell Park (G-AMOE)/Gateshead | |
| G-WHOW | Thunder Ax7-65 balloon | Thunder & Colt Ltd | |
| G-WHRL | Schweizer 269C | Aviation Metals Ltd | |
| G-WICK | Partenavia P.68B | J. C. Taylor (G-BGFZ) | |
| G-WIEN | Rans S.10 Sakota | N. P. Rieser | |
| G-WILD | Pitts S-1T Special | G. H. Wilson | |
| G-WILI | PA-32R-301 Saratoga SP | Minster Enterprises Ltd | |
| G-WILY | Rutan LongEz | G. V. Waters | |
| G-WIMP | Colt 56A balloon | C. Wolstenholme *Wimp* | |
| G-WINE | Thunder Ax-77Z balloon | R. Brooker | |
| G-WINK | AA-5B Tiger | B. St J. Cooke | |
| G-WINS | PA-32 Cherokee Six 300 | First Time Racing Ltd | |
| G-WIRE | AS.355F-1 Twin Squirrel | National Grid Co PLC (G-CEGB/G-BLJL) | |
| G-WIRL | Robinson R-22B | T. Goring | |
| G-WISH | Lindstrand LBL Cake SS balloon | Lindstrand Balloons Ltd | |
| G-WIZO | PA-34-220T Seneca III | Extrajet Ltd | |
| G-WIZZ | AB-206B JetRanger 2 | Lateq Aviation Ltd | |
| G-WMCC | BAe Jetstream 3102 | Brymon European Airways Ltd *City of Newcastle* (G-TALL) | |
| G-WMPA | AS.355F-2 Twin Squirrel | W. Midlands Police Authority/Birmingham | |
| G-WMTM | AA-5B Tiger | T. & W. E. Menham/Biggin Hill | |
| G-WOLF | PA-28 Cherokee 140 | P. R. Wernham | |
| G-WOOD | Beech 95-B55A Baron | T. D. Broadhurst (G-AYID) | |
| G-WOSP | Bell 206B JetRanger 3 | Lakeside Helicopters Ltd | |
| G-WOTG | BN-2T Islander | RAF Sport Parachute Association (G-BJYT) | |
| G-WOZA | PA-32RT-300 Lance II | K. T. P. Ratcliffe (G-BYBB) | |
| G-WRCF | Beech 200 Super King Air | W. R. C. M. Foyle/Luton | |
| G-WREN | Pitts S-2A Special | Northamptonshire School of Flying Ltd/ Sywell | |
| G-WRFM | Enstrom 280C-UK Shark | Southern Air Ltd (G-CTSI/G-BKIO)/ Shoreham | |
| G-WRIT | Thunder Ax7-77A balloon | J. Edge | |
| G-WRLD | Cameron R-15 balloon | Cameron Balloons Ltd | |
| G-WRMN | Glaser-Dirks DG.400 | W. R. McNair | |
| G-WROX | PA-31-350 Navajo Chieftain | Levenmere Ltd (G-BNZI) | |
| G-WSEC | Enstrom F-28C | R. J. Everett (G-BONF) | |
| G-WSFT | PA-23 Aztec 250F | SFT Aviation Ltd (G-BTHS)/Bournemouth | |
| G-WSKY | Enstrom 280C-UK-2 Shark | GTS Engineering (Coventry) Ltd (G-BEEK) | |
| G-WSSL | PA-31-350 Navajo Chieftain | Compass Aviation Ltd | |
| G-WTBC | Partenavia P.68C | Wild Touch Aviazione Ltd (G-SITU/G-NEWU/ G-BHJX) | |

| Notes | Reg. | Type | Owner or Operator |
|---|---|---|---|
| | G-WTFA | Cessna F.182P | David Martin Couriers Ltd |
| | G-WULF | WAR Focke-Wulf Fw.190 (08) | P. C. Logsdon |
| | G-WWII | V.S. 379 Spitfire XIV (SM832) | Patina Ltd/Duxford |
| | G-WYCH | Cameron 90 Witch SS balloon | Jacques W. Soukup Enterprises Ltd |
| | G-WYLX | Cessna 550 Citation II | Citation Lesaing Ltd (G-JETD) |
| | G-WYMP | Cessna F.150J | L. Scattergood & R. Hall (G-BAGW) |
| | G-WYNN | Rand KR-2 | W. Thomas |
| | G-WYNS | Aero Designs Pulsar XP | G. Griffith |
| | G-WYNT | Cameron N-56 balloon | Jacques W. Soukup Enterprises Ltd |
| | G-WYPA | MBB Bo 105DBS/4 | W. Yorkshire Police Authority |
| | G-WYTE | Bell 47G-2A-1 | Howden Helicopters/Spaldington |
| | G-WYZZ | Air Command 532 Elite | C. H. Gem (G-BPAK) |
| | G-WZZZ | Colt AS-56 airship | Hot-Air Balloon Co Ltd |
| | | | |
| | G-XALP | Schweizer 269C | R. F. Jones |
| | G-XCUB | PA-18 Super Cub 150 | M. C. Barraclough |
| | G-XGBE | Cessna 340A | G. B. Express Ltd (G-MAGS) |
| | G-XIIX | Robinson R-22B | G. Clarke |
| | G-XLXL | Robin DR.400/160 | Reinsurance Flying Group (G-BAUD) |
| | G-XPOL | AS.355F-1 Twin Squirrel | Aeromega Ltd (G-BPRF) |
| | G-XPXP | Aero Designs Pulsar XP | B. J. Edwards |
| | G-XRAY | Rand KR-2 | R. S. Smith |
| | G-XRMC | BAe 125 Srs 800B | RMC Group Services Ltd |
| | G-XSFT | PA-23 Aztec 250F | SFT Aviation Ltd (G-CPPC/G-BGBH)/ Bournemouth |
| | G-XSKY | Cameron N-77 balloon | Birds Eye Walls Ltd |
| | G-XTRA | Extra EA.230 | Firebird Aerobatics Ltd/Booker |
| | G-XVIA | V.S.361 Spitfire LF.XVIe (RW382) | Historic Flying Ltd |
| | G-XVIE | V.S.361 Spitfire LF.XVIe | Historic Flying Ltd |
| | G-XXIV | AB-206B JetRanger 3 | Defence Products Ltd |
| | | | |
| | G-YAWW | PA-28R-201T Turbo Arrow III | Barton Aviation Ltd |
| | G-YBAA | Cessna FR.172J | J. Blackburn |
| | G-YEOM | PA-31-350 Navajo Chieftain | Foster Yeoman Ltd/Exeter |
| | G-YEWS | Rotorway Executive | D. G. Pollard |
| | G-YIII | Cessna F.150L | Skyviews & General Ltd/Sherburn |
| | G-YNOT | D.62B Condor | T. Littlefair (G-AYFH) |
| | G-YOGI | Robin DR.400/140B | R. M. Gosling (G-BDME) |
| | G-YORK | Cessna F.172M | H. G. Keighley/Sherburn |
| | G-YOTT | Cessna 425 | E. & M. Green (G-NORC)/Guernsey |
| | G-YPSY | Andreasson BA-4B | H. P. Burrill |
| | G-YRAT | VPM M.16 Tandem Trainer | A. J. Unwin |
| | G-YRIL | Luscombe 8E Silvaire | C. Potter |
| | G-YROI | Air Command Commander 532 | W. B. Lumb |
| | G-YROS | Bensen B.80-D | C. Tuxworth |
| | G-YROY | Montgomerie Bensen B.8MR | R. D. Armishaw |
| | G-YSFT | PA-23 Aztec 250F | SFT Aviation Ltd (G-BEJT)/Bournemouth |
| | G-YSKY | PA-31-350 Navajo Chieftain | J. J. Baumhardt/Southend |
| | G-YTWO | Cessna F.172M | Sherburn Aero Club Ltd |
| | G-YUCS | PA-32R-301 Saratoga SP | Eastman Securities Ltd (G-BSOL) |
| | G-YUGO | H.S.125 Srs 1B/R-522 | RCR Aviation Ltd (G-ATWH) |
| | G-YULL | PA-28 Cherokee 180E | Lansdowne Chemical Co (G-BEAJ)/ Kidlington |
| | G-YUMM | Cameron N-90 balloon | Wunderbar Ltd |
| | G-YUPI | Cameron N-90 balloon | H. C. Wright |
| | G-YURO | Europa | Europa Aviation Ltd |
| | | | |
| | G-ZACH | Robin DR.400/100 | G. de Botton (G-FTIO) |
| | G-ZAIR | Zenair CH 601HD | C. B. Shaw |
| | G-ZAND | Robinson R-22B | R. Bean Commercial Vehicles |
| | G-ZAPC | Short SD3-30 Variant 100 | Titan Airways Ltd (G-RNMO/G-BFZW)/ Stansted |
| | G-ZAPD | Short SD3-60 Variant 100 | Titan Airways Ltd (G-OLGW/G-BOFK)/ Stansted |
| | G-ZARA | Nord 3400 | D. E. Bain & ptnrs |
| | G-ZARI | AA-5B Tiger | P. L. Pilch (G-BHVY)/Biggin Hill |
| | G-ZAZA | PA-18 Super Cub 95 | Airbourne Taxi Services Ltd |
| | G-ZBRA | Thunder Ax10-160 balloon | Zebra Ballooning |
| | G-ZEBO | Thunder Ax8-105 S2 balloon | Air Hops Ltd |
| | G-ZEBR | Colt 210A balloon | Zebra Ballooning Ltd |
| | G-ZELL | SA.341G Gazelle 1 | D. K. Shead |
| | G-ZEPI | Colt GA-42 airship | Imperial Airships Ltd (G-ISPY) |
| | G-ZEPY | Colt GA-42 airship | Thunder & Colt Ltd (G-BSCU) |

| Reg. | Type | Owner or Operator | Notes |
|------|------|-------------------|-------|
| G-ZERO | AA-5B Tiger | Snowadem Ltd/Luton | |
| G-ZFDB | AS.355F-1 Twin Squirrel | Haydon-Baillie Naval & Aircraft Museum (G-BLEV)/Southampton | |
| G-ZIGG | Robinson R-22B | Uriah Woodhead & Son Ltd | |
| G-ZIGI | Robin DR.400/180 | J. Nivison | |
| G-ZIPI | Robin DR.400/180 | Stahl Engineering Co Ltd/Headcorn | |
| G-ZIPP | Cessna E.310Q | Zipp Aviation Ltd (G-BAYU) | |
| G-ZIPY | Wittman W.8 Tailwind | M. J. Butler | |
| G-ZLIN | Z.526 Trener Master | R. P. Hallam | |
| G-ZSFT | PA-23 Aztec 250 | SFT Aviation Ltd (G-SALT/G-BGTH)/ Bournemouth | |
| G-ZSOL | Zlin Z.50L | A. J. E. Ditheridge | |
| G-ZULU | PA-28-161 Warrior II | Denham School of Flying Ltd | |
| G-ZUMP | Cameron N-77 balloon | Allen & Harris Ltd | |
| G-ZZIP | Mooney M.20J | D. A. H. Dixon | |

# Toy Balloons

| Reg. | Type | Owner or Operator |
|---|---|---|
| G-FYAK | European E.21 | J. E. Christopher |
| G-FYAN | Williams | M. D. Williams |
| G-FYAO | Williams | M. D. Williams |
| G-FYAT | Osprey Mk 4D | L. A. Cotgrove |
| G-FYAU | Williams MK 2 | M. D. Williams |
| G-FYAV | Osprey Mk 4E2 | C. D. Egan & C. Stiles |
| G-FYAZ | Osprey Mk 4D2 | M. A. Roblett |
| G-FYBA | Portswood Mk XVI | C. R. Rundle |
| G-FYBD | Osprey Mk 1E | M. Vincent |
| G-FYBE | Osprey Mk 4D | M. Vincent |
| G-FYBF | Osprey Mk V | M. Vincent |
| G-FYBG | Osprey Mk 4G2 | M. Vincent |
| G-FYBH | Osprey Mk 4G | M. Vincent |
| G-FYBI | Osprey Mk 4H | M. Vincent |
| G-FYBP | European E.84PW | D. Eaves |
| G-FYBR | Osprey Mk 4G2 | A. J. Pugh |
| G-FYBU | Portswood Mk XVI | M. A. Roblett |
| G-FYBX | Portswood Mk XVI | I. Chadwick |
| G-FYCC | Osprey Mk 4G2 | A. Russell |
| G-FYCL | Osprey Mk 4G | P. J. Rogers |
| G-FYCN | Osprey Mk 4D | C. F. Chipping |
| G-FYCO | Osprey Mk 4B | C. F. Chipping |
| G-FYCP | Osprey Mk 1E | C. F. Chipping |
| G-FYCR | Osprey MK 4D | C. F. Chipping |
| G-FYCT | Osprey Mk 4D | S. T. Wallbank |
| G-FYCU | Osprey Mk 4D | G. M. Smith |
| G-FYCV | Osprey Mk 4D | M. Thomson |
| G-FYCW | Osprey Mk 4D | M. L. Partridge |
| G-FYCZ | Osprey Mk 4D2 | P. Middleton |
| G-FYDC | European EDH-1 | D. Eaves & H. Goddard |
| G-FYDD | Osprey Mk 4D | A. C. Mitchell |
| G-FYDF | Osprey Mk 4D | K. A. Jones |
| G-FYDI | Williams Westwind Two | M. D. Williams |
| G-FYDK | Williams Westwind Two | M. D. Williams |
| G-FYDM | Williams Westwind Four | M. D. Williams |
| G-FYDN | European 8C | P. D. Ridout |
| G-FYDO | Osprey Mk 4D | N. L. Scallan |
| G-FYDP | Williams Westwind Three | M. D. Williams |
| G-FYDS | Osprey Mk 4D | N. L. Scallan |
| G-FYDW | Osprey Mk 4B | R. A. Balfre |
| G-FYEB | Rango Rega | N. H. Ponsford |
| G-FYEG | Osprey Mk 1C | P. E. Prime |
| G-FYEI | Portswood Mk XVI | A. Russell |
| G-FYEJ | Rango NA.24 | N. H. Ponsford |
| G-FYEK | Unicorn UE.1C | D. & D. Eaves |
| G-FYEL | European E.84Z | D. Eaves |
| G-FYEO | Eagle Mk 1 | M. E. Scallon |
| G-FYEV | Osprey Mk 1C | M. E. Scallen |
| G-FYEZ | Firefly Mk 1 | M. E. & N. L. Scallan |
| G-FYFA | European E.84LD | D. Goddard & D. Eaves |
| G-FYFG | European E.84DE | D. Eaves |
| G-FYFH | European E.84DS | D. Eaves |
| G-FYFI | European E.84DS | M. Stelling |
| G-FYFJ | Williams Westland 2 | M. D. Williams |
| G-FYFK | Williams Westland 2 | D. Feasey |
| G-FYFN | Osprey Saturn 2 | J. & M. Woods |
| G-FYFT | Rango NA-32BC | Rango Kite & Balloon Co |
| G-FYFV | Saffrey Grand Edinburgh | I. G. & G. M. McIntosh |
| G-FYFW | Rango NA-55 | Rango Kite & Balloon Co |
| G-FYFY | Rango NA-55RC | A. M. Lindsay |
| G-FYGA | Rango NA-50RC | Rango Kite & Balloon Co |
| G-FYGB | Rango NA-105RC | Rango Kite & Balloon Co |
| G-FYGC | Rango NA-42B | L. J. Wardle |
| G-FYGG | Buz-B20 | D. P. Busby & S. Spink |
| G-FYGH | Busby Buz B.20W | D. P. Busby |
| G-FYGI | Rango NA-55RC | Advertair Ltd |
| G-FYGJ | Airspeed 300 | N. Wells |
| G-FYGK | Rango NA-42POC | Rango Balloon & Kite Co |
| G-FYGL | Glowball | J. J. Noble |

# Microlights

| Reg. | Type | Notes | Reg. | Type | Notes |
|------|------|-------|------|------|-------|
| G-MBAA | Hiway Skytrike Mk 2 | | G-MBEN | Eipper Quicksilver MX | |
| G-MBAB | Hovey Whing-Ding II | | G-MBEP | American Aerolights Eagle | |
| G-MBAD | Weedhopper JC-24A | | G-MBES | Skyhook Cutlass | |
| G-MBAF | R. J. Swift 3 | | G-MBET | MEA Mistral Trainer | |
| G-MBAJ | Chargus T.250 | | G-MBEU | Hiway Demon T.250 | |
| G-MBAL | Hiway Demon | | G-MBEV | Chargus Titan 38 | |
| G-MBAM | Skycraft Scout 2 | | G-MBFA | Hiway Skytrike 250 | |
| G-MBAN | American Aerolights Eagle | | G-MBFE | American Aerolights Eagle | |
| G-MBAR | Skycraft Scout | | G-MBFF | Southern Aerosports | |
| G-MBAS | Typhoon Tripacer 250 | | | Scorpion | |
| G-MBAU | Hiway Skytrike | | G-MBFG | Skyhook Sabre | |
| G-MBAW | Pterodactyl Ptraveller | | G-MBFJ | Chargus Typhoon T.250 | |
| G-MBAZ | Rotec Rally 2B | | G-MBFK | Hiway Demon | |
| G-MBBA | Ultraflight Lazair | | G-MBFM | Hiway Hang Glider | |
| G-MBBB | Skycraft Scout 2 | | G-MBFU | Ultrasports Tripacer | |
| G-MBBG | Weedhopper JC-24B | | G-MBFX | Hiway Skytrike 250 | |
| G-MBBH | Flexiform Sealander 160 | | G-MBFY | Mirage II | |
| G-MBBJ | Hiway Demon Trike | | G-MBFZ | M. S. S. Goldwing | |
| G-MBBM | Eipper Quicksilver MX | | G-MBGA | Solar Wings Typhoon | |
| G-MBBN | Eagle Microlight | | G-MBGB | American Aerolights Eagle | |
| G-MBBT | Ultrasports Tripacer 330 | | G-MBGF | Twamley Sabre | |
| G-MBBU | Southdown Savage | | G-MBGJ | Hiway Skytrike Mk 2 | |
| G-MBBW | Flexiform Hilander | | G-MBGK | Electra Flyer Eagle | |
| G-MBBX | Chargus Skytrike | | G-MBGP | Solar Wings Typhoon | |
| G-MBBY | Flexiform Sealander | | | Skytrike | |
| G-MBBZ | Volmer Jensen VJ-24W | | G-MBGR | Eurowing Goldwing | |
| G-MBCA | Chargus Cyclone T.250 | | G-MBGS | Rotec Rally 2B | |
| G-MBCD | La Mouette Atlas | | G-MBGT | American Aerolights Eagle | |
| G-MBCE | American Aerolights Eagle | | G-MBGV | Skyhook Cutlass | |
| G-MBCF | Pterodactyl Ptraveler | | G-MBGW | Hiway Skytrike | |
| G-MBCG | Ultrasports Tripacer T.250 | | G-MBGX | Southdown Lightning | |
| G-MBCI | Hiway Skytrike | | G-MBGY | Hiway Demon Skytrike | |
| G-MBCJ | Mainair Sports Tri-Flyer | | G-MBHA | Trident Trike | |
| G-MBCK | Eipper Quicksilver MX | | G-MBHC | Chargus Lightning T.250 | |
| G-MBCL | Hiway Demon Triflyer | | G-MBHD | Hiway Vulcan Trike | |
| G-MBCM | Hiway Demon 175 | | G-MBHE | American Aerolights Eagle | |
| G-MBCN | Hiway Super Scorpion | | G-MBHH | Flexiform Sealander | |
| G-MBCO | Flexiform Sealander | | | Skytrike | |
| | Buggy | | G-MBHJ | Hornet Skyhook Cutlass | |
| G-MBCR | Ultraflight Mirage | | G-MBHK | Flexiform Skytrike | |
| G-MBCU | American Aerolights Eagle | | G-MBHP | American Aerolights | |
| G-MBCV | Hiway Skytrike | | | Eagle II | |
| G-MBCX | Airwave Nimrod 165 | | G-MBHT | Chargus T.250 | |
| G-MBCZ | Chargus Skytrike 160 | | G-MBHW | American Aerolights Eagle | |
| G-MBDC | Skyhook Cutlass | | G-MBHX | Pterodactyl Ptraveller | |
| G-MBDD | Skyhook Skytrike | | G-MBHZ | Pterodactyl Ptraveller | |
| G-MBDE | Flexiform Skytrike | | G-MBIA | Flexiform Sealander | |
| G-MBDF | Rotec Rally 2B | | | Skytrike | |
| G-MBDG | Eurowing Goldwing | | G-MBIC | Maxair Hummer | |
| G-MBDH | Hiway Demon Triflyer | | G-MBID | American Aerolights Eagle | |
| G-MBDI | Flexiform Sealander | | G-MBII | Hiway Skytrike | |
| G-MBDJ | Flexiform Sealander | | G-MBIO | American Aerolights Eagle | |
| | Triflyer | | | Z Drive | |
| G-MBDM | Southdown Sigma Trike | | G-MBIT | Hiway Demon Skytrike | |
| G-MBDN | Hornet Atlas | | G-MBIU | Hiway Super Scorpion | |
| G-MBDR | U.A.S. Stormbuggy | | G-MBIV | Flexiform Skytrike | |
| G-MBDU | Chargus Titan 38 | | G-MBIW | Hiway Demon Tri-Flyer | |
| G-MBDW | Ultrasports Tripacer | | | Skytrike | |
| | Skytrike A | | G-MBIY | Ultra Sports | |
| G-MBDX | Electraflyer Eagle | | G-MBIZ | Mainair Tri-Flyer | |
| G-MBDZ | Eipper Quicksilver MX | | G-MBJA | Eurowing Goldwing | |
| G-MBEA | Hornet Nimrod | | G-MBJD | American Aerolights Eagle | |
| G-MBEB | Hiway Skytrike 250 Mk II | | G-MBJE | Airwave Nimrod | |
| G-MBED | Chargus Titan 38 | | G-MBJF | Hiway Skytrike Mk II | |
| G-MBEE | Hiway Super Scorpion | | G-MBJG | Airwave Nimrod | |
| | Skytrike 160 | | G-MBJI | Southern Aerosports | |
| G-MBEG | Eipper Quicksilver MX | | | Scorpion | |
| G-MBEJ | Electraflyer Eagle | | G-MBJK | American Aerolights Eagle | |

| Reg. | Type | Notes | Reg | Type | Notes |
|------|------|-------|-----|------|-------|
| G-MBJL | Airwave Nimrod | | G-MBOR | Chotia 460B Weedhopper | |
| G-MBJM | Striplin Lone Ranger | | G-MBOT | Hiway 250 Skytrike | |
| G-MBJN | Electraflyer Eagle | | G-MBOU | Wheeler Scout | |
| G-MBJO | Birdman Cherokee | | G-MBOV | Southdown Lightning Trike | |
| G-MBJP | Hiway Skytrike | | G-MBOX | American Aerolights Eagle | |
| G-MBJR | American Aerolights Eagle | | G-MBPA | Weedhopper Srs 2 | |
| G-MBJS | Mainair Tri-Flyer | | G-MBPC | American Aerolights Eagle | |
| G-MBJT | Hiway Skytrike II | | G-MBPD | American Aerolights Eagle | |
| G-MBJU | American Eagle 215B | | G-MBPE | Ultrasports Trike | |
| G-MBJZ | Eurowing Catto CP.16 | | G-MBPG | Hunt Skytrike | |
| G-MBKA | Mistral Trainer | | G-MBPJ | Moto-Delta | |
| G-MBKC | Southdown Lightning | | G-MBPL | Hiway Demon | |
| G-MBKD | Chargus T.250 | | G-MBPM | Eurowing Goldwing | |
| G-MBKG | Batchelor-Hunt Skytrike | | G-MBPN | American Aerolights Eagle | |
| G-MBKH | Southdown Skytrike | | G-MBPO | Volnik Arrow | |
| G-MBKS | Hiway Skytrike 160 | | G-MBPS | Gryphon Willpower | |
| G-MBKT | Mitchell Wing B.10 | | G-MBPU | Hiway Demon | |
| G-MBKU | Hiway Demon Skytrike | | G-MBPW | Weedhopper | |
| G-MBKV | Eurowing Goldwing | | G-MBPX | Eurowing Goldwing | |
| G-MBKW | Pterodactyl Ptraveller | | G-MBPY | Ultrasports Tripacer 330 | |
| G-MBKZ | Hiway Skytrike | | G-MBPZ | Flexiform Striker | |
| G-MBLA | Flexiform Skytrike | | G-MBRB | Electraflyer Eagle 1 | |
| G-MBLB | Eipper Quicksilver MX | | G-MBRD | American Aerolights Eagle | |
| G-MBLD | Flexiform Striker | | G-MBRE | Wheeler Scout | |
| G-MBLF | Hiway Demon 195 Tri Pacer | | G-MBRF | Weedhopper 460C | |
| G-MBLH | Flexwing Tri-Flyer 330 | | G-MBRH | Ultraflight Mirage Mk II | |
| G-MBLJ | Eipper Quicksilver MX | | G-MBRK | Huntair Pathfinder | |
| G-MBLK | Southdown Puma | | G-MBRM | Hiway Demon | |
| G-MBLM | Hiway Skytrike | | G-MBRO | Hiway Skytrike 160 | |
| G-MBLN | Pterodactyl Ptraveller | | G-MBRS | American Aerolights Eagle | |
| G-MBLO | Sealander Skytrike | | G-MBRV | Eurowing Goldwing | |
| G-MBLR | Ultrasports Tripacer | | G-MBRZ | Hiway Vulcan 250 | |
| G-MBLS | MEA Mistral | | G-MBSA | Ultraflight Mirage II | |
| G-MBLU | Southdown Lightning L.195 | | G-MBSC | Ultraflight Mirage II | |
| G-MBLV | Ultrasports Hybrid | | G-MBSD | Southdown Puma DS | |
| G-MBLY | Flexiform Sealander Trike | | G-MBSF | Ultraflight Mirage II | |
| G-MBLZ | Southern Aerosports Scorpion | | G-MBSG | Ultraflight Mirage II | |
| G-MBME | American Aerolights Eagle Z Drive | | G-MBSN | American Aerolights Eagle | |
| | | | G-MBSR | Southdown Puma DS | |
| G-MBMG | Rotec Rally 2B | | G-MBSS | Ultrasports Puma 2 | |
| G-MBMJ | Mainair Tri-Flyer | | G-MBST | Mainair Gemini Sprint | |
| G-MBMO | Hiway Skytrike 160 | | G-MBSW | Ultraflight Mirage II | |
| G-MBMR | Ultrasports Tripacer Typhoon | | G-MBSX | Ultraflight Mirage II | |
| | | | G-MBTA | UAS Storm Buggy 5 Mk 2 | |
| G-MBMS | Hornet | | G-MBTB | Davies Tri-Flyer S | |
| G-MBMT | Mainair Tri-Flyer | | G-MBTC | Weedhopper | |
| G-MBMU | Eurowing Goldwing | | G-MBTF | Mainair Tri-Flyer Skytrike | |
| G-MBMW | Solar Wings Typhoon | | G-MBTG | Mainair Gemini | |
| G-MBMZ | Sealander Tripacer | | G-MBTH | Whittaker MW.4 | |
| G-MBNA | American Aerolights Eagle | | G-MBTI | Hovey Whing Ding | |
| G-MBNF | American Aerolights Eagle | | G-MBTJ | Solar Wings Microlight | |
| G-MBNG | Hiway Demon Skytrike | | G-MBTO | Mainair Tri-Flyer 250 | |
| G-MBNH | Southern Airsports Scorpion | | G-MBTS | Hovey WD-II Whing-Ding | |
| | | | G-MBTW | Raven Vector 600 | |
| G-MBNJ | Eipper Quicksilver MX | | G-MBTZ | Huntair Pathfinder | |
| G-MBNK | American Aerolights Eagle | | G-MBUA | Hiway Demon | |
| G-MBNN | Southern Microlight Gazelle P.160N | | G-MBUB | Horne Sigma Skytrike | |
| | | | G-MBUC | Huntair Pathfinder | |
| G-MBNT | American Aerolights Eagle | | G-MBUD | Wheeler Scout Mk III | |
| G-MBNY | Steer Terror Fledge II | | G-MBUE | MBA Tiger Cub 440 | |
| G-MBNZ | Hiway Skytrike Demon | | G-MBUH | Hiway Skytrike | |
| G-MBOA | Flexiform Hilander | | G-MBUI | Wheeler Scout Mk I | |
| G-MBOD | American Aerolights Eagle | | G-MBUK | Mainair 330 Tri Pacer | |
| G-MBOE | Solar Wing Typhoon Trike | | G-MBUL | American Aerolights Eagle | |
| G-MBOF | Pakes Jackdaw | | G-MBUO | Southern Aerosports Scorpion | |
| G-MBOH | Microlight Engineering Mistral | | G-MBUP | Hiway Skytrike | |
| | | | G-MBUT | UAS Storm Buggy | |
| G-MBOK | Dunstable Microlight | | G-MBUZ | Wheeler Scout Mk II | |
| G-MBOM | Hiway Hilander | | G-MBVA | Volmer Jensen VJ-23E | |
| G-MBON | Eurowing Goldwing Canard | | G-MBVC | American Aerolights Eagle | |
| | | | G-MBVH | Mainair Triflyer Striker | |
| | | | G-MBVJ | Skyhook Trike | |

| Reg. | Type | Notes | Reg | Type | Notes |
|------|------|-------|-----|------|-------|
| G-MBVK | Ultraflight Mirage II | | G-MBZZ | Southern Aerosports Scorpion | |
| G-MBVL | Southern Aerosports Scorpion | | G-MGAG | Aviasud Mistral | |
| G-MBVP | Mainair Triflyer 330 Striker | | G-MGOM | Medway Hybred 44XLR | |
| G-MBVR | Rotec Rally 2B | | G-MGOO | Renegade Spirit UK Ltd | |
| G-MBVS | Hiway Skytrike | | G-MGUY | CFM Shadow Srs BD | |
| G-MBVT | American Aerolights Eagle | | G-MGWH | Thruster T.300 | |
| G-MBVU | Flexiform Sealander Triflyer | | | | |
| G-MBVV | Hiway Skytrike | | G-MJAA | Ultrasports Tripacer | |
| G-MBVW | Skyhook TR.2 | | G-MJAB | Ultrasports Skytrike | |
| G-MBVY | Eipper Quicksilver MX | | G-MJAD | Eipper Quicksilver MX | |
| G-MBWA | American Aerolights Eagle | | G-MJAE | American Aerolights Eagle | |
| G-MBWB | Hiway Skytrike | | G-MJAF | Ultrasports Puma 440 | |
| G-MBWD | Rotec Rally 2B | | G-MJAG | Skyhook TR1 | |
| G-MBWE | American Aerolights Eagle | | G-MJAH | American Aerolights Eagle | |
| G-MBWF | Mainair Triflyer Striker | | G-MJAI | American Aerolights Eagle | |
| G-MBWG | Huntair Pathfinder | | G-MJAJ | Eurowing Goldwing | |
| G-MBWH | Designability Duet I | | G-MJAL | Wheeler Scout 3 | |
| G-MBWL | Huntair Pathfinder | | G-MJAM | Eipper Quicksilver MX | |
| G-MBWO | Hiway Demon Skytrike | | G-MJAN | Hiway Skytrike | |
| G-MBWP | Ultrasports Trike | | G-MJAO | Hiway Skytrike | |
| G-MBWR | Hornet | | G-MJAP | Hiway 160 | |
| G-MBWT | Huntair Pathfinder | | G-MJAR | Chargus Titan | |
| G-MBWU | Hiway Demon Skytrike | | G-MJAV | Hiway Demon Skytrike 244cc | |
| G-MBWW | Southern Aerosports Scorpion | | G-MJAZ | Aerodyne Vector 610 | |
| G-MBWX | Southern Aerosports Scorpion | | G-MJBF | Southdown Puma 330 | |
| G-MBWY | American Aerolights Eagle | | G-MJBH | American Aerolights Eagle | |
| G-MBXB | Southdown Sailwings Puma | | G-MJBI | Eipper Quicksilver MX | |
| | | | G-MJBK | Swallow AeroPlane Swallow B | |
| G-MBXE | Hiway Skytrike | | G-MJBL | American Aerolights Eagle | |
| G-MBXF | Hiway Skytrike | | G-MJBN | American Aerolights Eagle | |
| G-MBXI | Hiway Skytrike | | G-MJBS | Ultralight Stormbuggy | |
| G-MBXJ | Hiway Demon Skytrike | | G-MJBT | Eipper Quicksilver MX | |
| G-MBXK | Ultrasports Puma | | G-MJBV | American Aerolights Eagle | |
| G-MBXO | Sheffield Trident | | G-MJBX | Pterodactyl Ptraveller | |
| G-MBXP | Hornet Skytrike | | G-MJBZ | Huntair Pathfinder | |
| G-MBXR | Hiway Skytrike 150 | | G-MJCA | Skyhook Sabre | |
| G-MBXT | Eipper Quicksilver MX2 | | G-MJCB | Hornet 330 | |
| G-MBXW | Hiway Skytrike | | G-MJCC | Ultrasports Puma | |
| G-MBXX | Ultraflight Mirage II | | G-MJCD | Sigma Tetley Skytrike | |
| G-MBYD | American Aerolights Eagle | | G-MJCE | Ultrasports Tripacer | |
| G-MBYF | Skyhook TR2 | | G-MJCF | Maxair Hummer | |
| G-MBYH | Maxair Hummer | | G-MJCG | S.M.C. Flyer Mk 1 | |
| G-MBYI | Ultraflight Lazair | | G-MJCH | Ultraflight Mirage II | |
| G-MBYJ | Hiway Super Scorpion IIC | | G-MJCI | Kruchek Firefly 440 | |
| G-MBYK | Huntair Pathfinder Mk 1 | | G-MJCJ | Hiway Spectrum | |
| G-MBYL | Huntair Pathfinder 330 | | G-MJCK | Southern Aerosports Scorpion | |
| G-MBYM | Eipper Quicksilver MX | | G-MJCL | Eipper Quicksilver MX | |
| G-MBYO | American Aerolights Eagle | | G-MJCN | S.M.C. Flyer Mk 1 | |
| G-MBYR | American Aerolights Eagle | | G-MJCP | Huntair Pathfinder | |
| G-MBYS | Ultraflight Mirage II | | G-MJCU | Tarjani | |
| G-MBYT | Ultraflight Mirage II | | G-MJCW | Hiway Super Scorpion | |
| G-MBYU | American Aerolights Eagle | | G-MJCY | Eurowing Goldwing | |
| G-MBYX | American Aerolights Eagle | | G-MJCZ | Southern Aerosports Scorpion 2 | |
| G-MBYY | Southern Aerosports Scorpion | | G-MJDA | Hornet Trike Executive | |
| G-MBZA | Ultrasports Tripacer 330 | | G-MJDB | Birdman Cherokee | |
| G-MBZB | Hiway Skytrike | | G-MJDE | Huntair Pathfinder | |
| G-MBZF | American Aerolights Eagle | | G-MJDG | Hornet Supertrike | |
| G-MBZG | Twinflight Scorpion 2 seat | | G-MJDH | Huntair Pathfinder | |
| G-MBZH | Eurowing Goldwing | | G-MJDI | Southern Flyer Mk 1 | |
| G-MBZI | Eurowing Goldwing | | G-MJDJ | Hiway Skytrike Demon | |
| G-MBZK | Ultrasports Tripacer 250 | | G-MJDK | American Aerolights Eagle | |
| G-MBZL | Weedhopper | | G-MJDO | Southdown Puma 440 | |
| G-MBZM | UAS Storm Buggy | | G-MJDP | Eurowing Goldwing | |
| G-MBZN | Ultrasports Puma | | G-MJDR | Hiway Demon Skytrike | |
| G-MBZO | Mainair Triflyer 330 | | G-MJDU | Eipper Quicksilver MX2 | |
| G-MBZP | Skyhook TR2 | | G-MJDW | Eipper Quicksilver MX | |
| G-MBZU | Skyhook Sabre C | | G-MJDX | Moyes Mega II | |
| G-MBZV | American Aerolights Eagle | | G-MJDY | Ultrasports Solarwings | |

| Reg. | Type | Notes | Reg | Type | Notes |
|------|------|-------|-----|------|-------|
| G-MJEC | Ultrasports Puma | | G-MJIS | American Aerolights Eagle | |
| G-MJEE | Mainair Triflyer Trike | | G-MJIU | Eipper Quicksilver MX | |
| G-MJEF | Gryphon 180 | | G-MJIV | Pterodactyl Ptraveller | |
| G-MJEG | Eurowing Goldwing | | G-MJIY | Flexiform Voyage | |
| G-MJEH | Rotec Rally 2B | | G-MJIZ | Southdown Lightning | |
| G-MJEJ | American Aerolights Eagle | | G-MJJA | Huntair Pathfinder | |
| G-MJEK | Hiway Demon 330 Skytrike | | G-MJJB | Eipper Quicksilver MX | |
| | | | G-MJJD | Birdman Cherokee | |
| G-MJEL | GMD-01 Trike | | G-MJJF | Sealey | |
| G-MJEO | American Aerolights Eagle | | G-MJJJ | Moyes Knight | |
| G-MJEP | Pterodactyl Ptraveller | | G-MJJK | Eipper Quicksilver MX2 | |
| G-MJER | Flexiform Striker | | G-MJJL | Solar Wings Storm | |
| G-MJET | Stratos Prototype 3 Axis 1 | | G-MJJM | Birdman Cherokee Mk 1 | |
| G-MJEX | Eipper Quicksilver MX | | G-MJJN | Ultrasports Puma | |
| G-MJEY | Southdown Lightning | | G-MJJO | Flexiform Skytrike Dual | |
| G-MJFB | Flexiform Striker | | G-MJJS | Swallow AeroPlane Swallow B | |
| G-MJFD | Ultrasports Tripacer | | | | |
| G-MJFF | Huntair Pathfinder | | G-MJJU | Hiway Demon | |
| G-MJFH | Eipper Quicksilver MX | | G-MJJV | Wheeler Scout | |
| G-MJFI | Flexiform Striker | | G-MJJX | Hiway Skytrike | |
| G-MJFJ | Hiway Skytrike 250 | | G-MJJY | Tirith Firefly | |
| G-MJFK | Flexiform Skytrike Dual | | G-MJJZ | Hiway Demon 175 Skytrike | |
| G-MJFL | Mainair Tri-Flyer 440 | | | | |
| G-MJFM | Huntair Pathfinder | | G-MJKA | Skyhook Sabre Trike | |
| G-MJFO | Eipper Quicksilver MX | | G-MJKB | Striplin Skyranger | |
| G-MJFP | American Aerolights Eagle | | G-MJKC | Mainair Triflyer 330 Striker | |
| G-MJFS | American Aerolights Eagle | | G-MJKE | Mainair Triflyer 330 | |
| G-MJFV | Ultrasports Tripacer | | G-MJKF | Hiway Demon | |
| G-MJFX | Skyhook TR-1 | | G-MJKG | John Ivor Skytrike | |
| G-MJGC | Hornet | | G-MJKH | Eipper Quicksilver MX II | |
| G-MJGD | Huntair Pathfinder | | G-MJKI | Eipper Quicksilver MX | |
| G-MJGE | Eipper Quicksilver MX | | G-MJKJ | Eipper Quicksilver MX | |
| G-MJGG | Skyhook TR-1 | | G-MJKO | Goldmarque 250 Skytrike | |
| G-MJGI | Eipper Quicksilver MX | | G-MJKP | Hiway Super Scorpion | |
| G-MJGL | Chargus Titan 38 | | G-MJKR | Rotec Rally 2B | |
| G-MJGM | Hiway Demon 195 Skytrike | | G-MJKS | Mainair Triflyer | |
| G-MJGN | Greenslade Monotrike | | G-MJKU | Hiway Demon 175 | |
| G-MJGO | Barnes Avon Skytrike | | G-MJKV | Hornet | |
| G-MJGT | Skyhook Cutlass Trike | | G-MJKX | Ultralight Skyrider Phantom | |
| G-MJGV | Eipper Quicksilver MX2 | | | | |
| G-MJGW | Solar Wings Trike | | G-MJKY | Hiway Skytrike | |
| G-MJGX | Ultrasports Puma 250 | | G-MJLA | Ultrasports Puma 2 | |
| G-MJHA | Hiway Skytrike 250 Mk II | | G-MJLB | Ultrasports Puma 2 | |
| G-MJHC | Ultrasports Tripacer 330 | | G-MJLD | Wheeler Scout Mk III | |
| G-MJHE | Hiway Demon Skytrike | | G-MJLF | Southern Microlight Trike | |
| G-MJHF | Skyhook Sailwing Trike | | G-MJLH | American Aerolights Eagle 2 | |
| G-MJHK | Hiway Demon 195 | | | | |
| G-MJHM | Ultrasports Trike | | G-MJLI | Hiway Demon Skytrike | |
| G-MJHN | American Aerolights Eagle | | G-MJLJ | Flexiform Sealander | |
| G-MJHO | Shilling Bumble Bee Srs 1 | | G-MJLL | Hiway Demon Skytrike | |
| G-MJHP | American Aerolights Eagle | | G-MJLM | Mainair Triflyer 250 | |
| G-MJHR | Southdown Lightning | | G-MJLO | Goldmarque Skytrike | |
| G-MJHU | Eipper Quicksilver MX | | G-MJLR | Skyhook SK-1 | |
| G-MJHV | Hiway Demon 250 | | G-MJLS | Rotec Rally 2B | |
| G-MJHW | Ultrasports Puma 1 | | G-MJLT | American Aerolights Eagle | |
| G-MJHX | Eipper Quicksilver MX | | G-MJLU | Skyhook | |
| G-MJHZ | Southdown Sailwings | | G-MJLY | American Aerolights Eagle | |
| G-MJIA | Flexiform Striker | | G-MJMA | Hiway Demon | |
| G-MJIB | Hornet 250 | | G-MJMB | Weedhopper | |
| G-MJIC | Ultrasports Puma 330 | | G-MJME | Ultrasports Tripacer Mega II | |
| G-MJID | Southdown Sailwings Puma DS | | G-MJMM | Chargus Vortex | |
| | | | G-MJMP | Eipper Quicksilver MX | |
| G-MJIE | Hornet 330 | | G-MJMR | Solar Wings Typhoon | |
| G-MJIF | Mainair Triflyer | | G-MJMS | Hiway Skytrike | |
| G-MJIG | Hiway Demon Skytrike | | G-MJMT | Hiway Demon Skytrike | |
| G-MJIH | Ultrasports Tripacer | | G-MJMW | Eipper Quicksilver MX2 | |
| G-MJIJ | Ultrasports Tripacer 250 | | G-MJMX | Ultrasports Tripacer | |
| G-MJIK | Southdown Sailwings Lightning | | G-MJNB | Hiway Skytrike | |
| | | | G-MJNE | Hornet Supreme Dual Trike | |
| G-MJIL | Bremner Mitchell B.10 | | | | |
| G-MJIN | Hiway Skytrike | | G-MJNH | Skyhook Cutlass Trike | |
| G-MJIO | American Aerolights Eagle | | G-MJNK | Hiway Skytrike | |
| G-MJIR | Eipper Quicksilver MX | | G-MJNL | American Aerolights Eagle | |

| Reg. | Type | Notes | Reg | Type | Notes |
|------|------|-------|-----|------|-------|
| G-MJNM | American Aerolights Double Eagle | | G-MJTD | Gardner T-M Scout | |
| G-MJNN | Ultraflight Mirage II | | G-MJTE | Skyrider Airsports Phantom | |
| G-MJNO | American Aerolights Double Eagle | | G-MJTF | Gryphon Wing | |
| | | | G-MJTH | S.M.D. Gazelle | |
| | | | G-MJTI | Huntair Pathfinder II | |
| G-MJNP | American Aerolights Eagle | | G-MJTL | Aerostructure Pipistrelle 2B | |
| G-MJNR | Ultralight Solar Buggy | | G-MJTM | Aerostructure Pipistrelle 2B | |
| G-MJNS | Swallow AeroPlane Swallow B | | G-MJTN | Eipper Quicksilver MX | |
| | | | G-MJTO | Jordan Duet Srs 1 | |
| G-MJNT | Hiway Skytrike | | G-MJTP | Flexiform Striker | |
| G-MJNU | Skyhook Cutlass | | G-MJTR | Southdown Puma DS Mk 1 | |
| G-MJNV | Eipper Quicksilver MX | | G-MJTU | Skyhook Cutlass 185 | |
| G-MJNY | Skyhook Sabre Trike | | G-MJTW | Eurowing Trike | |
| G-MJOA | Chargus T.250 Vortex | | G-MJTX | Skyrider Phantom | |
| G-MJOC | Huntair Pathfinder | | G-MJTY | Huntair Pathfinder | |
| G-MJOD | Rotec Rally 2B | | G-MJTZ | Skyrider Airsports Phantom | |
| G-MJOE | Eurowing Goldwing | | | | |
| G-MJOG | American Aerolights Eagle | | G-MJUB | MBA Tiger Cub 440 | |
| G-MJOI | Hiway Demon | | G-MJUC | MBA Tiger Cub 440 | |
| G-MJOJ | Flexiform Skytrike | | G-MJUE | Southdown Lightning II | |
| G-MJOK | Mainair Triflyer 250 | | G-MJUH | MBA Tiger Cub 440 | |
| G-MJOL | Skyhook Cutlass | | G-MJUI | Flexiform Striker | |
| G-MJOM | Southdown Puma 40F | | G-MJUJ | Eipper Quicksilver Mk II | |
| G-MJOO | Southdown Puma 40F | | G-MJUK | Eipper Quicksilver MX II | |
| G-MJOR | Solair Phoenix | | G-MJUL | Southdown Puma Sprint | |
| G-MJOS | Southdown Lightning 170 | | G-MJUM | Flexiform Striker | |
| G-MJOU | Hiway Demon 175 | | G-MJUO | Eipper Quicksilver MX II | |
| G-MJOV | Solar Wings Typhoon | | G-MJUP | Weedhopper B | |
| G-MJOW | Eipper Quicksilver MX | | G-MJUR | Skyrider Airsports Phantom | |
| G-MJPA | Rotec Rally 2B | | G-MJUS | MBA Tiger Cub 440 | |
| G-MJPC | American Aerolights Double Eagle | | G-MJUT | Eurowing Goldwing | |
| | | | G-MJUU | Eurowing Goldwing | |
| G-MJPD | Hiway Demon Skytrike | | G-MJUW | MBA Tiger Cub 440 | |
| G-MJPE | Hiway Demon Skytrike | | G-MJUX | Skyrider Airsports Phantom | |
| G-MJPG | American Aerolights Eagle 430R | | G-MJUY | Eurowing Goldwing | |
| | | | G-MJUZ | Dragon Srs 150 | |
| G-MJPI | Flexiform Striker | | G-MJVA | Skyrider Airsports Phantom | |
| G-MJPJ | Flexiform Dual Trike 440 | | G-MJVC | Hiway Skytrike | |
| G-MJPK | Hiway Vulcan | | G-MJVE | Hybred Skytrike | |
| G-MJPO | Eurowing Goldwing | | G-MJVF | CFM Shadow | |
| G-MJPS | American Aerolights Eagle 430R | | G-MJVG | Hiway Skytrike | |
| | | | G-MJVJ | Flexiform Striker Dual | |
| G-MJPT | Dragon | | G-MJVL | Flexiform Striker | |
| G-MJPU | Solar Wings Typhoon | | G-MJVM | Dragon 150 | |
| G-MJPV | Eipper Quicksilver MX | | G-MJVN | Ultrasports Puma 440 | |
| G-MJRA | Hiway Demon | | G-MJVP | Eipper Quicksilver MX II | |
| G-MJRE | Hiway Demon | | G-MJVR | Flexiform Striker | |
| G-MJRG | Ultrasports Puma | | G-MJVT | Eipper Quicksilver MX | |
| G-MJRH | Hiway Skytrike | | G-MJVU | Eipper Quicksilver MX II | |
| G-MJRI | American Aerolights Eagle | | G-MJVV | Hornet Supreme Dual | |
| G-MJRK | Flexiform Striker | | G-MJVW | Airwave Nimrod | |
| G-MJRL | Eurowing Goldwing | | G-MJVX | Skyrider Phantom | |
| G-MJRN | Flexiform Striker | | G-MJVY | Dragon Srs 150 | |
| G-MJRO | Eurowing Goldwing | | G-MJVZ | Hiway Demon Tripacer | |
| G-MJRP | Mainair Triflyer 330 | | G-MJWB | Eurowing Goldwing | |
| G-MJRR | Striplin Skyranger Srs 1 | | G-MJWD | Solar Wings Typhoon XL | |
| G-MJRS | Eurowing Goldwing | | G-MJWE | Hiway Demon | |
| G-MJRT | Southdown Lightning DS | | G-MJWF | Tiger Cub 440 | |
| G-MJRU | MBA Tiger Cub 440 | | G-MJWG | MBA Tiger Cub | |
| G-MJRX | Ultrasports Puma II | | G-MJWI | Flexiform Striker | |
| G-MJSA | Mainair 2-Seat Trike | | G-MJWJ | MBA Tiger Cub 440 | |
| G-MJSE | Skyrider Airsports Phantom | | G-MJWK | Huntair Pathfinder | |
| G-MJSF | Skyrider Airsports Phantom | | G-MJWN | Flexiform Striker | |
| G-MJSL | Dragon 200 | | G-MJWO | Hiway Skytrike | |
| G-MJSO | Hiway Skytrike | | G-MJWR | MBA Tiger Cub 440 | |
| G-MJSP | MBA Super Tiger Cub 440 | | G-MJWS | Eurowing Goldwing | |
| G-MJSS | American Aerolights Eagle | | G-MJWU | Maxair Hummer TX | |
| G-MJST | Pterodactyl Praveler | | G-MJWV | Southdown Puma MS | |
| G-MJSU | MBA Tiger Cub | | G-MJWW | MBA Super Tiger Cub 440 | |
| G-MJSV | MBA Tiger Cub | | G-MJWX | Flexiform Striker | |
| G-MJSY | Eurowing Goldwing | | G-MJWY | Flexiform Striker | |
| G-MJSZ | DH Wasp | | G-MJWZ | Ultrasports Panther XL | |
| G-MJTC | Solar Wings Typhoon | | G-MJXA | Flexiform Striker | |

## G-MJXB – G-MMFB

| Reg. | Type | Notes | Reg | Type | Notes |
|---|---|---|---|---|---|
| G-MJXB | Eurowing Goldwing | | G-MMBC | Hiway Super Scorpion | |
| G-MJXD | MBA Tiger Cub 440 | | G-MMBD | Spectrum 330 | |
| G-MJXE | Hiway Demon | | G-MMBE | MBA Tiger Cub 440 | |
| G-MJXF | MBA Tiger Cub 440 | | G-MMBF | American Aerolights Eagle | |
| G-MJXJ | MBA Tiger Cub 440 | | G-MMBH | MBA Super Tiger Cub 440 | |
| G-MJXM | Hiway Skytrike | | G-MMBJ | Solar Wings Typhoon | |
| G-MJXR | Huntair Pathfinder II | | G-MMBK | American Aerolights Eagle | |
| G-MJXS | Huntair Pathfinder II | | G-MMBL | Southdown Puma | |
| G-MJXT | Phoenix Falcon 1 | | G-MMBN | Eurowing Goldwing | |
| G-MJXV | Flexiform Striker | | G-MMBS | Flexiform Striker | |
| G-MJXX | Flexiform Striker Dual | | G-MMBT | MBA Tiger Cub 440 | |
| G-MJXY | Hiway Demon Skytrike | | G-MMBU | Eipper Quicksilver MX II | |
| G-MJXZ | Hiway Demon | | G-MMBV | Huntair Pathfinder | |
| G-MJYA | Huntair Pathfinder | | G-MMBW | MBA Tiger Cub 440 | |
| G-MJYC | Ultrasports Panther XL Dual 440 | | G-MMBX | MBA Tiger Cub 440 | |
| | | | G-MMBY | Solar Wings Panther | |
| G-MJYD | MBA Tiger Cub 440 | | G-MMBZ | Solar Wings Typhoon P | |
| G-MJYF | Mainair Gemini Flash | | G-MMCD | Southdown Lightning DS | |
| G-MJYG | Skyhook Orion Canard | | G-MMCE | MBA Tiger Cub 440 | |
| G-MJYI | Mainair Triflyer | | G-MMCF | Solar Wings Panther 330 | |
| G-MJYJ | MBA Tiger Cub 440 | | G-MMCG | Eipper Quicksilver MX I | |
| G-MJYL | Airwave Nimrod | | G-MMCI | Southdown Puma Sprint | |
| G-MJYM | Southdown Puma Sprint | | G-MMCJ | Flexiform Striker | |
| G-MJYP | Mainair Triflyer 440 | | G-MMCM | Southdown Puma Sprint | |
| G-MJYR | Catto CP.16 | | G-MMCN | Solar Wings Storm | |
| G-MJYS | Southdown Puma Sprint | | G-MMCO | Southdown Sprint | |
| G-MJYT | Southdown Puma Sprint | | G-MMCR | Eipper Quicksilver MX | |
| G-MJYV | Mainair Triflyer 2 Seat | | G-MMCS | Southdown Puma Sprint | |
| G-MJYW | Wasp Gryphon III | | G-MMCV | Solar Wings Typhoon III | |
| G-MJYX | Mainair Triflyer | | G-MMCX | MBA Super Tiger Cub 440 | |
| G-MJYY | Hiway Demon | | G-MMCY | Flexiform Striker | |
| G-MJYZ | Flexiform Striker | | G-MMCZ | Flexiform Striker | |
| G-MJZA | MBA Tiger Cub | | G-MMDB | La Mouette Atlas | |
| G-MJZB | Flexiform Striker Dual | | G-MMDC | Eipper Quicksilver MXII | |
| G-MJZC | MBA Tiger Cub 440 | | G-MMDD | Huntair Pathfinder | |
| G-MJZD | Mainair Gemini Flash | | G-MMDE | Solar Wings Typhoon | |
| G-MJZE | MBA Tiger Cub 440 | | G-MMDF | Southdown Lightning II | |
| G-MJZF | La Mouette Atlas 16 | | G-MMDG | Eurowing Goldwing | |
| G-MJZG | Mainair Triflyer 440 | | G-MMDH | Manta Fledge 2B | |
| G-MJZH | Southdown Lightning 195 | | G-MMDI | Hiway Super Scorpion | |
| G-MJZI | Eurowing Goldwing | | G-MMDJ | Solar Wings Typhoon | |
| G-MJZJ | Hiway Cutlass Skytrike | | G-MMDK | Flexiform Striker | |
| G-MJZK | Southdown Puma Sprint 440 | | G-MMDN | Flexiform Striker | |
| | | | G-MMDO | Southdown Sprint | |
| G-MJZL | Eipper Quicksilver MX II | | G-MMDP | Southdown Sprint | |
| G-MJZO | Flexiform Striker | | G-MMDR | Huntair Pathfinder II | |
| G-MJZP | MBA Tiger Cub 440 | | G-MMDS | Ultrasports Panther XLS | |
| G-MJZT | Flexiform Striker | | G-MMDT | Flexiform Striker | |
| G-MJZU | Flexiform Striker | | G-MMDU | MBA Tiger Cub 440 | |
| G-MJZW | Eipper Quicksilver MX II | | G-MMDV | Ultrasports Panther | |
| G-MJZX | Maxair Hummer TX | | G-MMDW | Pterodactyl Pfledgling | |
| G-MJZZ | Skyhook Cutlass | | G-MMDX | Solar Wings Typhoon | |
| G-MMAC | Dragon Srs 150 | | G-MMDY | Southdown Puma Sprint | |
| G-MMAE | Dragon Srs 150 | | G-MMDZ | Flexiform Dual Strike | |
| G-MMAG | MBA Tiger Cub 440 | | G-MMEB | Hiway Super Scorpion | |
| G-MMAH | Eipper Quicksilver MX II | | G-MMEE | American Aerolights Eagle | |
| G-MMAI | Dragon Srs 150 | | G-MMEF | Hiway Super Scorpion | |
| G-MMAJ | Mainair Tri-Flyer 440 | | G-MMEG | Eipper Quicksilver MX | |
| G-MMAK | MBA Tiger Cub 440 | | G-MMEI | Hiway Demon | |
| G-MMAL | Flexiform Striker Dual | | G-MMEJ | Flexiform Striker | |
| G-MMAM | MBA Tiger Cub 440 | | G-MMEK | Solar Wings Typhoon XL2 | |
| G-MMAN | Flexiform Striker | | G-MMEL | Solar Wings Typhoon XL2 | |
| G-MMAO | Southdown Puma Sprint | | G-MMEM | Solar Wings Typhoon XL2 | |
| G-MMAP | Hummer TX | | G-MMEN | Solar Wings Typhoon XL2 | |
| G-MMAR | Southdown Puma Sprint | | G-MMEP | MBA Tiger Cub 440 | |
| G-MMAS | Southdown Sprint | | G-MMES | Southdown Puma Sprint | |
| G-MMAT | Southdown Puma Sprint | | G-MMET | Skyhook Sabre TR-1 Mk II | |
| G-MMAU | Flexiform Rapier | | G-MMEU | MBS Tiger Cub 440 | |
| G-MMAW | Mainair Rapier | | G-MMEW | MBA Tiger Cub 440 | |
| G-MMAX | Flexiform Striker | | G-MMEX | Solar Wings Sprint | |
| G-MMAZ | Southdown Puma Sprint | | G-MMEY | MBA Tiger Cub 440 | |
| G-MMBA | Hiway Super Scorpion | | G-MMEZ | Southdown Puma Sprint | |
| G-MMBB | American Aerolights Eagle | | G-MMFB | Flexiform Striker | |

| Reg. | Type | Notes | Reg. | Type | Notes |
|------|------|-------|------|------|-------|
| G-MMFC | Flexiform Striker | | | 440 | |
| G-MMFD | Flexiform Striker | | G-MMJG | Mainair Tri-Flyer 440 | |
| G-MMFE | Flexiform Striker | | G-MMJH | Southdown Puma Sprint | |
| G-MMFG | Flexiform Striker | | G-MMJJ | Solar Wings Typhoon | |
| G-MMFI | Flexiform Striker | | G-MMJK | Hiway Demon | |
| G-MMFJ | Flexiform Striker | | G-MMJL | Flexiform 1+1 Sealander | |
| G-MMFK | Flexiform Striker | | G-MMJM | Southdown Puma Sprint | |
| G-MMFL | Flexiform Striker | | G-MMJN | Eipper Quicksilver MX II | |
| G-MMFM | Piranha Srs 200 | | G-MMJO | MBA Tiger Cub 440 | |
| G-MMFN | MBA Tiger Cub 440 | | G-MMJS | MBA Tiger Cub | |
| G-MMFS | MBA Tiger Cub 440 | | G-MMJT | Southdown Puma Sprint | |
| G-MMFT | MBA Tiger Cub 440 | | G-MMJU | Hiway Demon | |
| G-MMFW | Skyhook Cutlass | | G-MMJV | MBA Tiger Cub 440 | |
| G-MMFX | MBA Tiger Cub 440 | | G-MMJW | Southdown Puma Sprint | |
| G-MMFY | Flexiform Dual Striker | | G-MMJX | Teman Mono-Fly | |
| G-MMFZ | AES Sky Ranger | | G-MMJY | MBA Tiger Cub 440 | |
| G-MMGA | Bass Gosling | | G-MMJZ | Skyhook Pixie | |
| G-MMGB | Southdown Puma Sprint | | G-MMKA | Ultrasports Panther Dual | |
| G-MMGC | Southdown Puma Sprint | | G-MMKB | Ultralight Flight Mirage II | |
| G-MMGD | Southdown Puma Sprint | | G-MMKC | Southdown Puma Sprint | |
| G-MMGE | Hiway Super Scorpion | | G-MMKD | Southdown Puma Sprint | |
| G-MMGF | MBA Tiger Cub 440 | | G-MMKE | Birdman Chinook WT-11 | |
| G-MMGL | MBA Tiger Cub 440 | | G-MMKF | Ultrasports Panther Dual | |
| G-MMGN | Southdown Puma Sprint | | | 440 | |
| G-MMGO | MBA Tiger Cub 440 | | G-MMKG | Solar Wings Typhoon XL | |
| G-MMGP | Southdown Puma Sprint | | G-MMKH | Solar Wings Typhoon XL | |
| G-MMGR | Flexiform Dual Striker | | G-MMKI | Ultrasports Panther 330 | |
| G-MMGS | Solar Wings Panther Dual | | G-MMKJ | Ultrasports Panther 330 | |
| G-MMGT | Solar Wings Typhoon | | G-MMKK | Mainair Flash | |
| G-MMGU | Flexiform Sealander | | G-MMKL | Mainair Flash | |
| G-MMGV | Whittaker MW.5 Sorcerer | | G-MMKM | Flexiform Dual Striker | |
| G-MMGX | Southdown Puma | | G-MMKO | Southdown Puma Sprint | |
| G-MMGY | Dean Piranha 1000 | | G-MMKP | MBA Tiger Cub 440 | |
| G-MMHA | Skyhook TR-1 Pixie | | G-MMKR | Southdown Lightning DS | |
| G-MMHB | Skyhook TR-1 Pixie | | G-MMKS | Southdown Lightning 195 | |
| G-MMHD | Hiway Demon 175 | | G-MMKT | MBA Tiger Cub 440 | |
| G-MMHE | Southdown Puma Sprint | | G-MMKU | Southdown Puma Sprint | |
| G-MMHF | Southdown Puma Sprint | | G-MMKV | Southdown Puma Sprint | |
| G-MMHG | Solar Wings Storm | | G-MMKW | Solar Wings Storm | |
| G-MMHJ | Flexiform Hilander | | G-MMKY | Jordan Duet | |
| G-MMHK | Hiway Super Scorpion | | G-MMKZ | Ultrasports Puma 440 | |
| G-MMHL | Hiway Super Scorpion | | G-MMLB | MBA Tiger Cub 440 | |
| G-MMHM | Goldmarque Gyr | | G-MMLD | Solar Wings Typhoon S | |
| G-MMHP | Hiway Demon | | G-MMLE | Eurowing Goldwing SP | |
| G-MMHR | Southdown Puma Sprint | | G-MMLF | MBA Tiger Cub 440 | |
| G-MMHS | SMD Viper | | G-MMLG | Solar Wings Typhoon XL | |
| G-MMHT | Flexiform Viper | | G-MMLH | Hiway Demon | |
| G-MMHX | Hornet Invader 440 | | G-MMLI | Solar Wings Typhoon S | |
| G-MMHY | Hornet Invader 440 | | G-MMLK | MBA Tiger Cub 440 | |
| G-MMHZ | Solar Wings Typhoon XL | | G-MMLL | Midland Ultralights Sirocco | |
| G-MMIB | MEA Mistral | | G-MMLM | MBA Tiger Cub 440 | |
| G-MMIC | Luscombe Vitality | | G-MMLN | Skyhook Pixie | |
| G-MMID | Flexiform Dual Striker | | G-MMLO | Skyhook Pixie | |
| G-MMIE | MBA Tiger Cub 440 | | G-MMLP | Southdown Sprint | |
| G-MMIF | Wasp Gryphon | | G-MMLV | Southdown Puma 330 | |
| G-MMIH | MBA Tiger Cub 440 | | G-MMLX | Ultrasports Panther | |
| G-MMII | Southdown Puma Sprint | | G-MMLZ | Mainair Tri-Flyer | |
| | 440 | | G-MMMB | Mainair Tri-Flyer | |
| G-MMIJ | Ultrasports Tripacer | | G-MMMD | Flexiform Dual Striker | |
| G-MMIL | Eipper Quicksilver MX II | | G-MMMG | Eipper Quicksilver MXL | |
| G-MMIM | MBA Tiger Cub 440 | | G-MMMH | Hadland Willow | |
| G-MMIO | Huntair Pathfinder II | | G-MMMI | Southdown Lightning | |
| G-MMIR | Mainair Tri-Flyer 440 | | G-MMMJ | Southdown Sprint | |
| G-MMIS | Hiway Demon | | G-MMMK | Hornet Invader | |
| G-MMIV | Southdown Puma Sprint | | G-MMML | Dragon 150 | |
| G-MMIW | Southdown Puma Sprint | | G-MMMN | Ultrasports Panther Dual | |
| G-MMIX | MBA Tiger Cub 440 | | | 440 | |
| G-MMIY | Eurowing Goldwing | | G-MMMP | Flexiform Dual Striker | |
| G-MMIZ | Southdown Lightning II | | G-MMMR | Flexiform Striker | |
| G-MMJC | Southdown Sprint | | G-MMMS | MBA Tiger Cub 440 | |
| G-MMJD | Southdown Puma Sprint | | G-MMMT | Hornet Sigma | |
| G-MMJE | Southdown Puma Sprint | | G-MMMU | Skyhook Cutlass CD | |
| G-MMJF | Ultrasports Panther Dual | | G-MMMV | Skyhook Cutlass Dual | |

| Reg. | Type | Notes | Reg | Type | Notes |
|------|------|-------|-----|------|-------|
| G-MMMW | Flexiform Striker | | G-MMSR | MBA Tiger Cub 440 | |
| G-MMMX | Hornet Nimrod | | G-MMSS | Solar Wings Panther 330 | |
| G-MMNA | Eipper Quicksilver MX II | | G-MMST | Southdown Puma Sprint | |
| G-MMNB | Eipper Quicksilver MX | | G-MMSV | Southdown Puma Sprint | |
| G-MMNC | Eipper Quicksilver MX | | G-MMSW | MBA Tiger Cub 440 | |
| G-MMND | Eipper Quicksilver MX II-Q2 | | G-MMSZ | Medway Half Pint | |
| G-MMNE | Eipper Quicksilver MX II | | G-MMTA | Ultrasports Panther XL | |
| G-MMNF | Hornet | | G-MMTC | Ultrasports Panther Dual | |
| G-MMNG | Solar Wings Typhoon XL | | G-MMTD | Mainair Tri-Flyer 330 | |
| G-MMNN | Buzzard | | G-MMTE | Mainair Gemini | |
| G-MMNP | Ultrasports Panther 250 | | G-MMTF | Southdown Puma Sprint | |
| G-MMNS | Mitchell U-2 Super Wing | | G-MMTG | Mainair Gemini | |
| G-MMNT | Flexiform Striker | | G-MMTH | Southdown Puma Sprint | |
| G-MMNU | Ultrasports Panther | | G-MMTI | Southdown Puma Sprint | |
| G-MMNW | Mainair Tri-Flyer 330 | | G-MMTJ | Southdown Puma Sprint | |
| G-MMNX | Solar Wings Panther XL | | G-MMTK | Medway Hybred | |
| G-MMOB | Southdown Sprint | | G-MMTL | Mainair Gemini | |
| G-MMOD | MBA Tiger Cub 440 | | G-MMTM | Mainair Tri-Flyer 440 | |
| G-MMOF | MBA Tiger Cub 440 | | G-MMTO | Mainair Tri-Flyer | |
| G-MMOG | Huntair Pathfinder | | G-MMTR | Ultrasports Panther | |
| G-MMOH | Solar Wings Typhoon XL | | G-MMTS | Solar Wings Panther XL | |
| G-MMOI | MBA Tiger Cub 440 | | G-MMTT | Solar Wings Panther XL | |
| G-MMOK | Solar Wings Panther XL | | G-MMTV | American Aerolights Eagle | |
| G-MMOL | Skycraft Scout R3 | | G-MMTX | Mainair Gemini 440 | |
| G-MMOO | Southdown Storm | | G-MMTY | Fisher FP.202U | |
| G-MMOW | Mainair Gemini Flash | | G-MMTZ | Eurowing Goldwing | |
| G-MMOX | Mainair Gemini Flash | | G-MMUA | Southdown Puma Sprint | |
| G-MMOY | Mainair Gemini Sprint | | G-MMUB | Ultrasports Tripacer 250 | |
| G-MMPD | Mainair Tri-Flyer | | G-MMUC | Mainair Gemini 440 | |
| G-MMPE | Eurowing Goldwing | | G-MMUE | Mainair Gemini Flash | |
| G-MMPG | Southdown Puma | | G-MMUG | Mainair Tri-Flyer | |
| G-MMPH | Southdown Puma Sprint | | G-MMUH | Mainair Tri-Flyer | |
| G-MMPI | Pterodactyl Ptraveller | | G-MMUJ | Southdown Puma Sprint 440 | |
| G-MMPJ | Mainair Tri-Flyer 440 | | | | |
| G-MMPL | Flexiform Dual Striker | | G-MMUK | Mainair Tri-Flyer | |
| G-MMPN | Chargus T250 | | G-MMUL | Ward Elf E.47 | |
| G-MMPO | Mainair Gemini Flash | | G-MMUM | MBA Tiger Cub 440 | |
| G-MMPR | Dragon 150 | | G-MMUN | Ultrasports Panther Dual XL | |
| G-MMPT | SMD Gazelle | | G-MMUO | Mainair Gemini Flash | |
| G-MMPU | Ultrasports Tripacer 250 | | G-MMUP | Airwave Nimrod 140 | |
| G-MMPW | Airwave Nimrod | | G-MMUS | Mainair Gemini | |
| G-MMPX | Ultrasports Panther Dual 440 | | G-MMUU | ParaPlane PM-1 | |
| | | | G-MMUV | Southdown Puma Sprint | |
| G-MMPZ | Teman Mono-Fly | | G-MMUW | Mainair Gemini Flash | |
| G-MMRA | Mainair Tri-Flyer 250 | | G-MMUX | Mainair Gemini | |
| G-MMRC | Southdown Lightning | | G-MMVA | Southdown Puma Sprint | |
| G-MMRD | Skyhook Cutlass CD | | G-MMVC | Ultrasports Panther XL | |
| G-MMRF | MBA Tiger Cub 440 | | G-MMVG | MBA Tiger Cub 440 | |
| G-MMRH | Hiway Demon | | G-MMVH | Southdown Raven | |
| G-MMRI | Skyhook Sabre | | G-MMVI | Southdown Puma Sprint | |
| G-MMRJ | Solar Wings Panther XL | | G-MMVJ | Southdown Puma Sprint | |
| G-MMRK | Ultrasports Panther XL | | G-MMVL | Ultrasports Panther XL-S | |
| G-MMRL | Solar Wings Panther XL | | G-MMVM | Whiteley Orion 1 | |
| G-MMRN | Southdown Puma Sprint | | G-MMVN | Solar Wings Typhoon | |
| G-MMRO | Mainair Gemini 440 | | G-MMVO | Southdown Puma Sprint | |
| G-MMRP | Mainair Gemini | | G-MMVP | Mainair Gemini Flash | |
| G-MMRT | Southdown Puma Sprint | | G-MMVR | Hiway Skytrike 1 | |
| G-MMRU | Tirith Firebird FB-2 | | G-MMVS | Skyhook Pixie | |
| G-MMRV | MBA Tiger Cub 440 | | G-MMVT | Mainair Gemini Flash | |
| G-MMRW | Flexiform Dual Striker | | G-MMVW | Skyhook Pixie | |
| G-MMRX | Willmot J.W.1 | | G-MMVX | Southdown Puma Sprint | |
| G-MMRY | Chargus T.250 | | G-MMVY | American Aerolights Eagle | |
| G-MMRZ | Ultrasports Panther Dual 440 | | G-MMVZ | Southdown Puma Sprint | |
| | | | G-MMWA | Mainair Gemini Flash | |
| G-MMSA | Ultrasports Panther XL | | G-MMWB | Huntair Pathfinder II | |
| G-MMSC | Mainair Gemini | | G-MMWC | Eipper Quicksilver MXII | |
| G-MMSE | Eipper Quicksilver MX | | G-MMWF | Hiway Skytrike 250 | |
| G-MMSG | Solar Wings Panther XL | | G-MMWG | Greenslade Mono-Trike | |
| G-MMSH | Solar Wings Panther XL | | G-MMWH | Southdown Puma Sprint 440 | |
| G-MMSM | Mainair Gemini Flash | | | | |
| G-MMSN | Mainair Gemini | | G-MMWI | Southdown Lightning | |
| G-MMSO | Mainair Tri-Flyer 440 | | G-MMWJ | Pterodactyl Ptraveler | |
| G-MMSP | Mainair Gemini Flash | | G-MMWK | Hiway Demon | |

| Reg. | Type | Notes | Reg | Type | Notes |
|---|---|---|---|---|---|
| G-MMWL | Eurowing Goldwing | | G-MNAF | Solar Wings Panther XL | |
| G-MMWN | Ultrasports Tripacer | | G-MNAG | Hiway Skytrike 1 | |
| G-MMWO | Ultrasports Panther XL | | G-MNAH | Solar Wings Panther XL | |
| G-MMWP | American Aerolights Eagle | | G-MNAI | Ultrasports Panther XL-S | |
| G-MMWS | Mainair Tri-Flyer | | G-MNAJ | Solar Wings Panther XL-S | |
| G-MMWT | CFM Shadow | | G-MNAK | Solar Wings Panther XL-S | |
| G-MMWX | Southdown Puma Sprint | | G-MNAL | MBA Tiger Cub 440 | |
| G-MMWY | Skyhook Pixie | | G-MNAM | Solar Wings Panther XL-S | |
| G-MMWZ | Southdown Puma Sprint | | G-MNAN | Solar Wings Panther XL-S | |
| G-MMXC | Mainair Gemini Flash | | G-MNAO | Solar Wings Panther XL-S | |
| G-MMXD | Mainair Gemini Flash | | G-MNAR | Solar Wings Panther XL-S | |
| G-MMXE | Mainair Gemini Flash | | G-MNAT | Solar Wings Pegasus XL-R | |
| G-MMXG | Mainair Gemini Flash | | G-MNAU | Solar Wings Pegasus XL-R | |
| G-MMXH | Mainair Gemini Flash | | G-MNAV | Southdown Puma Sprint | |
| G-MMXI | Horizon Prototype | | G-MNAW | Solar Wings Pegasus XL-R | |
| G-MMXJ | Mainair Gemini Flash | | G-MNAX | Solar Wings Pegasus XL-R | |
| G-MMXK | Mainair Gemini Flash | | G-MNAY | Ultrasports Panther XL-S | |
| G-MMXL | Mainair Gemini Flash | | G-MNAZ | Solar Wings Pegasus XL-R | |
| G-MMXM | Mainair Gemini Flash | | G-MNBA | Solar Wings Pegasus XL-R | |
| G-MMXN | Southdown Puma Sprint | | G-MNBB | Solar Wings Pegasus XL-R | |
| G-MMXO | Southdown Puma Sprint | | G-MNBC | Solar Wings Pegasus XL-R | |
| G-MMXP | Southdown Puma Sprint | | G-MNBD | Mainair Gemini Flash | |
| G-MMXR | Southdown Puma DS | | G-MNBE | Southdown Puma Sprint | |
| G-MMXT | Mainair Gemini Flash | | G-MNBF | Mainair Gemini Flash | |
| G-MMXU | Mainair Gemini Flash | | G-MNBG | Mainair Gemini Flash | |
| G-MMXV | Mainair Gemini Flash | | G-MNBH | Southdown Puma Sprint | |
| G-MMXW | Mainair Gemini | | G-MNBI | Ultrasports Panther XL | |
| G-MMXX | Mainair Gemini | | G-MNBJ | Skyhook Pixie | |
| G-MMXZ | Eipper Quicksilver MXII | | G-MNBK | Hiway Skytrike | |
| G-MMYA | Solar Wings Pegasus XL | | G-MNBL | American Aerolights Z Eagle | |
| G-MMYB | Solar Wings Pegasus XL | | | | |
| G-MMYD | CFM Shadow Srs B | | G-MNBM | Southdown Puma Sprint | |
| G-MMYF | Southdown Puma Sprint | | G-MNBN | Mainair Gemini Flash | |
| G-MMYI | Southdown Puma Sprint | | G-MNBP | Mainair Gemini Flash | |
| G-MMYJ | Southdown Puma Sprint | | G-MNBR | Mainair Gemini Flash | |
| G-MMYK | Southdown Puma Sprint | | G-MNBS | Mainair Gemini Flash | |
| G-MMYL | Cyclone 70 | | G-MNBT | Mainair Gemini Flash | |
| G-MMYN | Ultrasports Panther XL | | G-MNBU | Mainair Gemini Flash | |
| G-MMYO | Southdown Puma Sprint | | G-MNBV | Mainair Gemini Flash | |
| G-MMYR | Eipper Quicksilver MXII | | G-MNBW | Mainair Gemini Flash | |
| G-MMYS | Southdown Puma Sprint | | G-MNBY | Mainair Gemini | |
| G-MMYT | Southdown Puma Sprint | | G-MNCA | Hiway Demon 175 | |
| G-MMYU | Southdown Puma Sprint | | G-MNCB | Mainair Gemini Flash | |
| G-MMYV | Webb Trike | | G-MNCD | Harmsworth Trike | |
| G-MMYY | Southdown Puma Sprint | | G-MNCF | Mainair Gemini Flash | |
| G-MMYZ | Southdown Puma Sprint | | G-MNCG | Mainair Gemini Flash | |
| G-MMZA | Mainair Gemini Flash | | G-MNCH | Lancashire Micro Trike 330 | |
| G-MMZB | Mainair Gemini Flash | | G-MNCI | Southdown Puma Sprint | |
| G-MMZC | Mainair Gemini Flash | | G-MNCJ | Mainair Gemini Flash | |
| G-MMZE | Mainair Gemini Flash | | G-MNCK | Southdown Puma Sprint | |
| G-MMZF | Mainair Gemini Flash | | G-MNCL | Southdown Puma Sprint | |
| G-MMZG | Ultrasports Panther XL-S | | G-MNCM | CFM Shadow Srs B | |
| G-MMZH | Ultrasports Tripacer | | G-MNCO | Eipper Quicksilver MXII | |
| G-MMZI | Medway 130SX | | G-MNCP | Southdown Puma Sprint | |
| G-MMZJ | Mainair Gemini Flash | | G-MNCR | Flexiform Striker | |
| G-MMZK | Mainair Gemini Flash | | G-MNCS | Skyrider Airsports Phantom | |
| G-MMZL | Mainair Gemini Flash | | G-MNCU | Medway Hybred | |
| G-MMZM | Mainair Gemini Flash | | G-MNCV | Medway Typhoon XL | |
| G-MMZN | Mainair Gemini Flash | | G-MNCW | Hornet Dual Trainer | |
| G-MMZO | Microflight Spectrum | | G-MNCX | Mainair Gemini Flash | |
| G-MMZP | Ultrasports Panther XL | | G-MNCZ | Solar Wings Pegasus XL | |
| G-MMZR | Southdown Puea Sprint | | G-MNDA | Thruster TST | |
| G-MMZS | Eipper Quicksilver MX1 | | G-MNDB | Southdown Puma Sprint | |
| G-MMZU | Southdown Puma DS | | G-MNDC | Mainair Gemini Flash | |
| G-MMZV | Mainair Gemini Flash | | G-MNDD | Mainair Scorcher Solo | |
| G-MMZW | Southdown Puma Sprint | | G-MNDE | Medway Half Pint | |
| G-MMZX | Southdown Puma Sprint | | G-MNDF | Mainair Gemini Flash | |
| G-MMZY | Ultrasports Tripacer 330 | | G-MNDG | Southdown Puma Sprint | |
| G-MMZZ | Maxair Hummer | | G-MNDH | Hiway Skytrike | |
| G-MNAA | Striplin Sky Ranger | | G-MNDI | MBA Tiger Cub 440 | |
| G-MNAC | Mainair Gemini Flash | | G-MNDM | Mainair Gemini Flash | |
| G-MNAD | Mainair Gemini Flash | | G-MNDO | Mainair Flash | |
| G-MNAE | Mainair Gemini Flash | | G-MNDP | Southdown Puma Sprint | |

# G-MNDU – G-MNJZ

| Reg. | Type | Notes | Reg | Type | Notes |
|------|------|-------|-----|------|-------|
| G-MNDU | Midland Sirocco 377GB | | G-MNHJ | Solar Wings Pegasus XL-R | |
| G-MNDV | Midland Sirocco 377GB | | G-MNHK | Solar Wings Pegasus XL-R | |
| G-MNDW | Midland Sirocco 377GB | | G-MNHL | Solar Wings Pegasus XL-R | |
| G-MNDY | Southdown Puma Sprint | | G-MNHM | Solar Wings Pegasus XL-R | |
| G-MNDZ | Southdown Puma Sprint | | G-MNHN | Solar Wings Pegasus XL-R | |
| G-MNEF | Mainair Gemini Flash | | G-MNHP | Solar Wings Pegasus XL-R | |
| G-MNEG | Mainair Gemini Flash | | G-MNHR | Solar Wings Pegasus XL-R | |
| G-MNEH | Mainair Gemini Flash | | G-MNHS | Solar Wings Pegasus XL-R | |
| G-MNEI | Medway Hybred 440 | | G-MNHT | Solar Wings Pegasus XL-R | |
| G-MNEK | Medway Half Pint | | G-MNHU | Solar Wings Pegasus XL-R | |
| G-MNEL | Medway Half Pint | | G-MNHV | Solar Wings Pegasus XL-R | |
| G-MNEM | Solar Wings Pegasus Dual | | G-MNHW | Medway Half Pint | |
| G-MNEN | Southdown Puma Sprint | | G-MNHX | Solar Wings Typhoon S4 | |
| G-MNEO | Southdown Raven | | G-MNHZ | Mainair Gemini Flash | |
| G-MNEP | Aerostructure Pipstrelle P.2B | | G-MNIA | Mainair Gemini Flash | |
| G-MNER | CFM Shadow Srs B | | G-MNIB | American Aerolights Eagle 215B | |
| G-MNET | Mainair Gemini Flash | | G-MNID | Mainair Gemini Flash | |
| G-MNEV | Mainair Gemini Flash | | G-MNIE | Mainair Gemini Flash | |
| G-MNEW | Mainair Tri-Flyer | | G-MNIF | Mainair Gemini Flash | |
| G-MNEX | Mainair Gemini Flash | | G-MNIG | Mainair Gemini Flash | |
| G-MNEY | Mainair Gemini Flash | | G-MNIH | Mainair Gemini Flash | |
| G-MNEZ | Skyhook TR1 Mk 2 | | G-MNII | Mainair Gemini Flash | |
| G-MNFA | Solar Wings Typhoon | | G-MNIL | Southdown Puma Sprint | |
| G-MNFB | Southdown Puma Sprint | | G-MNIM | Maxair Hummer | |
| G-MNFC | Midland Ultralights Sirocco 377GB | | G-MNIN | Designability Duet | |
| G-MNFE | Mainair Gemini Flash | | G-MNIO | Mainair Gemini Flash | |
| G-MNFF | Mainair Gemini Flash | | G-MNIP | Mainair Gemini Flash | |
| G-MNFG | Southdown Puma Sprint | | G-MNIR | Skyhook Pixie 130 | |
| G-MNFH | Mainair Gemini Flash | | G-MNIS | CFM Shadow Srs B | |
| G-MNFI | Medway Half Pint | | G-MNIT | Aerial Arts 130SX | |
| G-MNFJ | Mainair Gemini Flash | | G-MNIU | Solar Wings Pegasus Photon | |
| G-MNFK | Mainair Gemini Flash | | | | |
| G-MNFL | AMF Chevron | | G-MNIV | Solar Wings Typhoon | |
| G-MNFM | Mainair Gemini Flash | | G-MNIW | Airwave Nimrod 165 | |
| G-MNFN | Mainair Gemini Flash | | G-MNIX | Mainair Gemini Flash | |
| G-MNFP | Mainair Gemini Flash | | G-MNIY | Skyhook Pixie Zipper | |
| G-MNFR | Wright Tri-Flyer | | G-MNIZ | Mainair Gemini Flash | |
| G-MNFT | Mainair Gemini Flash | | G-MNJA | Southdown Lightning | |
| G-MNFV | Ultrasports Trike | | G-MNJB | Southdown Raven | |
| G-MNFW | Medway Hybred 44XL | | G-MNJC | MBA Tiger Cub 440 | |
| G-MNFX | Southdown Puma Sprint | | G-MNJD | Southdown Puma Sprint | |
| G-MNFY | Hornet 250 | | G-MNJE | Southdown Puma Sprint | |
| G-MNFZ | Southdown Puma Sprint | | G-MNJF | Dragon 150 | |
| G-MNGA | Aerial Arts Chaser 110SX | | G-MNJG | Mainair Tri-Flyer | |
| G-MNGB | Mainair Gemini Flash | | G-MNJH | Solar Wings Pegasus Flash | |
| G-MNGD | Quest Air Services | | G-MNJI | Solar Wings Pegasus Flash | |
| G-MNGF | Solar Wings Pegasus | | | | |
| G-MNGG | Solar Wings Pegasus XL-R | | G-MNJJ | Solar Wings Pegasus Flash | |
| G-MNGH | Skyhook Pixie | | | | |
| G-MNGJ | Skyhook Zipper | | G-MNJK | Solar Wings Pegasus Flash | |
| G-MNGK | Mainair Gemini Flash | | G-MNJL | Solar Wings Pegasus Flash | |
| G-MNGL | Mainair Gemini Flash | | | | |
| G-MNGM | Mainair Gemini Flash | | G-MNJM | Solar Wings Pegasus Flash | |
| G-MNGN | Mainair Gemini Flash | | | | |
| G-MNGO | Solar Wings Storm | | G-MNJN | Solar Wings Pegasus Flash | |
| G-MNGR | Southdown Puma Sprint | | | | |
| G-MNGS | Southdown Puma 330 | | G-MNJO | Solar Wings Pegasus Flash | |
| G-MNGT | Mainair Gemini Flash | | | | |
| G-MNGU | Mainair Gemini Flash | | G-MNJP | Solar Wings Pegasus Flash | |
| G-MNGW | Mainair Gemini Flash | | | | |
| G-MNGX | Southdown Puma Sprint | | G-MNJR | Solar Wings Pegasus Flash | |
| G-MNGY | Hiway Skytrike 160 | | | | |
| G-MNGZ | Mainair Gemini Flash | | G-MNJS | Southdown Puma Sprint | |
| G-MNHB | Solar Wings Pegasus XL-R | | G-MNJT | Southdown Raven | |
| G-MNHC | Solar Wings Pegasus XL-R | | G-MNJU | Mainair Gemini Flash | |
| G-MNHD | Solar Wings Pegasus XL-R | | G-MNJV | Medway Half Pint | |
| G-MNHE | Solar Wings Pegasus XL-R | | G-MNJW | Mitchell Wing B10 | |
| G-MNHF | Solar Wings Pegasus XL-R | | G-MNJX | Medway Hybred 44XL | |
| G-MNHG | Solar Wings Pegasus XL-R | | G-MNJY | Medway Half Pint | |
| G-MNHH | Solar Wings Panther XL-S | | G-MNJZ | Aerial Arts Alpha 130SX | |
| G-MNHI | Solar Wings Pegasus XL-R | | | | |

| Reg. | Type | Notes | Reg | Type | Notes |
|---|---|---|---|---|---|
| G-MNKA | Solar Wings Pegasus Photon | | G-MNMV | Mainair Gemini Flash | |
| G-MNKB | Solar Wings Pegasus Photon | | G-MNMW | Aerotech MW.6 Merlin | |
| | | | G-MNMY | Cyclone 70 | |
| G-MNKC | Solar Wings Pegasus Photon | | G-MNNA | Southdown Raven | |
| | | | G-MNNB | Southdown Raven | |
| G-MNKD | Solar Wings Pegasus Photon | | G-MNNC | Southdown Raven | |
| | | | G-MNND | Solar Wings Pegasus Flash | |
| G-MNKE | Solar Wings Pegasus Photon | | G-MNNE | Mainair Gemini Flash | |
| | | | G-MNNF | Mainair Gemini Flash | |
| G-MNKG | Solar Wings Pegasus Photon | | G-MNNG | Solar Wings Photon | |
| | | | G-MNNI | Mainair Gemini Flash | |
| G-MNKH | Solar Wings Pegasus Photon | | G-MNNJ | Mainair Gemini Flash | |
| | | | G-MNNK | Mainair Gemini Flash | |
| G-MNKI | Solar Wings Pegasus Photon | | G-MNNL | Mainair Gemini Flash | |
| | | | G-MNNM | Mainair Scorcher Solo | |
| G-MNKJ | Solar Wings Pegasus Photon | | G-MNNN | Southdown Raven | |
| | | | G-MNNO | Southdown Raven | |
| G-MNKK | Solar Wings Pegasus Photon | | G-MNNP | Mainair Gemini Flash | |
| | | | G-MNNR | Mainair Gemini Flash | |
| G-MNKL | Mainair Gemini Flash | | G-MNNS | Eurowing Goldwing | |
| G-MNKM | MBA Tiger Cub 440 | | G-MNNT | Medway Hybred 44XLR | |
| G-MNKN | Skycraft Scout Mk III | | G-MNNU | Mainair Gemini Flash | |
| G-MNKO | Solar Wings Pegasus Flash | | G-MNNV | Mainair Gemini Flash | |
| G-MNKP | Solar Wings Pegasus Flash | | G-MNNY | Solar Wings Pegasus Flash | |
| G-MNKR | Solar Wings Pegasus Flash | | G-MNNZ | Solar Wings Pegasus Flash | |
| G-MNKS | Solar Wings Pegasus Flash | | G-MNPA | Solar Wings Pegasus Flash | |
| G-MNKT | Solar Wings Typhoon S4 | | G-MNPB | Solar Wings Pegasus Flash | |
| G-MNKU | Southdown Puma Sprint | | G-MNPC | Mainair Gemini Flash | |
| G-MNKV | Solar Wings Pegasus Flash | | G-MNPD | Midland Ultralights 130SX | |
| G-MNKW | Solar Wings Pegasus Flash | | G-MNPF | Mainair Gemini Flash | |
| G-MNKX | Solar Wings Pegasus Flash | | G-MNPG | Mainair Gemini Flash | |
| G-MNKY | Southdown Raven | | G-MNPH | Flexiform Dual Striker | |
| G-MNKZ | Southdown Raven | | G-MNPI | Southdown Pipistrelle 2C | |
| G-MNLB | Southdown Raven X | | G-MNPL | Ultrasports Panther 330 | |
| G-MNLC | Southdown Raven | | G-MNPP | Romain Cobra Biplane | |
| G-MNLE | Southdown Raven X | | G-MNPR | Hiway Demon 175 | |
| G-MNLH | Romain Cobra Biplane | | G-MNPV | Mainair Scorcher Solo | |
| G-MNLI | Mainair Gemini Flash | | G-MNPW | AMF Chevron | |
| G-MNLK | Southdown Raven | | G-MNPX | Mainair Gemini Flash | |
| G-MNLL | Southdown Raven | | G-MNPY | Mainair Scorcher Solo | |
| G-MNLM | Southdown Raven | | G-MNPZ | Mainair Scorcher Solo | |
| G-MNLN | Southdown Raven | | G-MNRA | CFM Shadow Srs B | |
| G-MNLO | Southdown Raven | | G-MNRD | Ultraflight Lazair | |
| G-MNLP | Southdown Raven | | G-MNRE | Mainair Scorcher Solo | |
| G-MNLS | Southdown Raven | | G-MNRF | Mainair Scorcher Solo | |
| G-MNLT | Southdown Raven | | G-MNRG | Mainair Scorcher Solo | |
| G-MNLU | Southdown Raven | | G-MNRI | Hornet Dual Trainer | |
| G-MNLV | Southdown Raven | | G-MNRJ | Hornet Dual Trainer | |
| G-MNLW | Medway Halt Pint | | G-MNRK | Hornet Dual Trainer | |
| G-MNLX | Mainair Gemini Flash | | G-MNRL | Hornet Dual Trainer | |
| G-MNLY | Mainair Gemini Flash | | G-MNRM | Hornet Dual Trainer | |
| G-MNLZ | Southdown Raven | | G-MNRN | Hornet Dual Trainer | |
| G-MNMA | Solar Wings Pegasus Flash | | G-MNRP | Southdown Raven | |
| G-MNMB | Solar Wings Pegasus Flash | | G-MNRR | Southdown Raven X | |
| G-MNMC | Southdown Puma MS | | G-MNRS | Southdown Raven | |
| G-MNMD | Southdown Raven | | G-MNRT | Midland Ultralights Sirocco | |
| G-MNME | Hiway Skytrike | | G-MNRU | Midland Ultralights Sirocco | |
| G-MNMF | Maxair Hummer TX | | G-MNRW | Mainair Gemini Flash II | |
| G-MNMG | Mainair Gemini Flash | | G-MNRX | Mainair Gemini Flash II | |
| G-MNMH | Mainair Gemini Flash | | G-MNRY | Mainair Gemini Flash | |
| G-MNMI | Mainair Gemini Flash | | G-MNRZ | Mainair Scorcher Solo | |
| G-MNMJ | Mainair Gemini Flash | | G-MNSA | Mainair Gemini Flash | |
| G-MNMK | Solar Wings Pegasus XL-R | | G-MNSB | Southdown Puma Sprint | |
| | | | G-MNSD | Solar Wings Typhoon | |
| G-MNML | Southdown Puma Sprint | | G-MNSE | Mainair Gemini Flash | |
| G-MNMM | Aerotech MW.5 Sorcerer | | G-MNSF | Hornet Dual Trainer | |
| G-MNMN | Medway Hybred 44XLR | | G-MNSH | Solar Wings Pegasus Flash II | |
| G-MNMO | Mainair Gemini Flash | | | | |
| G-MNMR | Solar Wings Typhoon 180 | | G-MNSI | Mainair Gemini Flash | |
| G-MNMS | Wheeler Scout | | G-MNSJ | Mainair Gemini Flash | |
| G-MNMT | Southdown Raven | | G-MNSK | Hiway Skytrike | |
| G-MNMU | Southdown Raven | | G-MNSL | Southdown Raven X | |
| | | | G-MNSM | Hornet Demon | |

| Reg. | Type | Notes | Reg | Type | Notes |
|---|---|---|---|---|---|
| G-MNSN | Solar Wings Pegasus Flash II | | G-MNVK | CFM Shadow Srs B | |
| G-MNSP | Aerial Arts 130SX | | G-MNVL | Medway Half Pint | |
| G-MNSR | Mainair Gemini Flash | | G-MNVM | Southdown Raven X | |
| G-MNSS | American Aerolights Eagle | | G-MNVN | Southdown Raven X | |
| G-MNST | Vector 600 | | G-MNVO | Hovey Whing-Ding II | |
| G-MNSV | CFM Shadown Srs B | | G-MNVP | Southdown Raven X | |
| G-MNSW | Southdown Raven X | | G-MNVR | Mainair Gemini Flash II | |
| G-MNSX | Southdown Raven X | | G-MNVS | Mainair Gemini Flash II | |
| G-MNSY | Southdown Raven X | | G-MNVT | Mainair Gemini Flash II | |
| G-MNSZ | Noble Hardman Snowbird | | G-MNVU | Mainair Gemini Flash II | |
| G-MNTB | Solar Wings Typhoon S4 | | G-MNVW | Mainair Gemini Flash II | |
| G-MNTC | Southdown Raven X | | G-MNVY | Solar Wings Pegasus Photon | |
| G-MNTD | Aerial Arts Chaser 110SX | | | | |
| G-MNTE | Southdown Raven X | | G-MNVZ | Solar Wings Pegasus Photon | |
| G-MNTF | Southdown Raven X | | | | |
| G-MNTG | Southdown Raven X | | G-MNWA | Southdown Raven X | |
| G-MNTH | Mainair Gemini Flash | | G-MNWB | Thruster TST | |
| G-MNTI | Mainair Gemini Flash | | G-MNWC | Mainair Gemini Flash II | |
| G-MNTK | CFM Shadow Srs B | | G-MNWD | Mainair Gemini Flash | |
| G-MNTL | Arbee Wasp Gryphon | | G-MNWF | Southdown Raven X | |
| G-MNTM | Southdown Raven X | | G-MNWG | Southdown Raven X | |
| G-MNTN | Southdown Raven X | | G-MNWH | Aerial Arts 130SX | |
| G-MNTO | Southdown Raven X | | G-MNWI | Mainair Gemini Flash II | |
| G-MNTP | CFM Shadow Srs B | | G-MNWJ | Mainair Gemini Flash II | |
| G-MNTS | Mainair Gemini Flash II | | G-MNWK | CFM Shadow Srs B | |
| G-MNTT | Medway Half Pint | | G-MNWL | Aerial Arts 130SX | |
| G-MNTU | Mainair Gemini Flash II | | G-MNWM | CFM Shadow Srs B | |
| G-MNTV | Mainair Gemini Flash II | | G-MNWN | Mainair Gemini Flash II | |
| G-MNTW | Mainair Gemini Flash II | | G-MNWO | Mainair Gemini Flash II | |
| G-MNTX | Mainair Gemini Flash II | | G-MNWP | Solar Wings Pegasus Flash II | |
| G-MNTY | Southdown Raven X | | | | |
| G-MNTZ | Mainair Gemini Flash II | | G-MNWR | Medway Hybred 44LR | |
| G-MNUA | Mainair Gemini Flash II | | G-MNWT | Southdown Raven | |
| G-MNUB | Mainair Gemini Flash II | | G-MNWU | Solar Wings Pegasus Flash II | |
| G-MNUC | Solar Wings Pegasus Flash II | | | | |
| | | | G-MNWV | Solar Wings Pegasus Flash II | |
| G-MNUD | Solar Wings Pegasus Flash II | | | | |
| | | | G-MNWW | Solar Wings Pegasus XL-R | |
| G-MNUE | Solar Wings Pegasus Flash II | | G-MNWX | Solar Wings Pegasus XL-R | |
| | | | G-MNWY | CFM Shadown Srs B | |
| G-MNUF | Mainair Gemini Flash II | | G-MNWZ | Mainair Gemini Flash II | |
| G-MNUG | Mainair Gemini Flash II | | G-MNXA | Southdown Raven X | |
| G-MNUH | Southdown Raven X | | G-MNXB | Solar Wings Photon | |
| G-MNUI | Skyhook Cutlass Dual | | G-MNXC | Aerial Arts 110SX | |
| G-MNUJ | Solar Wings Pegasus Photon | | G-MNXD | Southdown Raven | |
| | | | G-MNXE | Southdown Raven X | |
| G-MNUK | Midland Ultralights SX130 | | G-MNXF | Southdown Raven | |
| G-MNUL | Midland Ultralights SX130 | | G-MNXG | Southdown Raven X | |
| G-MNUM | Southdown Puma Sprint | | G-MNXI | Southdown Raven X | |
| G-MNUO | Mainair Gemini Flash II | | G-MNXJ | Medway Half Pint | |
| G-MNUP | Mainair Gemini Flash II | | G-MNXK | Medway Half Pint | |
| G-MNUR | Mainair Gemini Flash II | | G-MNXM | Medway Hybred 44XLR | |
| G-MNUS | Mainair Gemini Flash II | | G-MNXN | Medway Hybred 44XLR | |
| G-MNUT | Southdown Raven X | | G-MNXO | Medway Hybred 44XLR | |
| G-MNUU | Southdown Raven X | | G-MNXP | Solar Wings Pegasus Flash II | |
| G-MNUV | Southdown Raven X | | | | |
| G-MNUW | Southdown Raven X | | G-MNXR | Mainair Gemini Flash II | |
| G-MNUX | Solar Wings Pegasus XL-R | | G-MNXS | Mainair Gemini Flash II | |
| G-MNUY | Mainair Gemini Flash II | | G-MNXT | Mainair Gemini Flash II | |
| G-MNUZ | Mainair Gemini Flash II | | G-MNXU | Mainair Gemini Flash II | |
| G-MNVA | Solar Wings Pegasus XL-R | | G-MNXX | CFM Shadow Srs BD | |
| G-MNVB | Solar Wings Pegasus XL-R | | G-MNXY | Whittaker MW.5 Sorcerer | |
| G-MNVC | Solar Wings Pegasus XL-R | | G-MNXZ | Whittaker MW.5 Sorcerer | |
| G-MNVE | Solar Wings Pegasus XL-R | | G-MNYA | Solar Wings Pegasus Flash II | |
| G-MNVF | Solar Wings Pegasus Flash II | | | | |
| | | | G-MNYB | Solar Wings Pegasus XL-R | |
| G-MNVG | Solar Wings Pegasus Flash II | | G-MNYC | Solar Wings Pegasus XL-R | |
| | | | G-MNYD | Aerial Arts 110SX Chaser | |
| G-MNVH | Solar Wings Pegasus Flash II | | G-MNYE | Aerial Arts 110SX Chaser | |
| | | | G-MNYF | Aerial Arts 110SX Chaser | |
| G-MNVI | CFM Shadow Srs B | | G-MNYG | Southdown Raven | |
| G-MNVJ | CFM Shadow Srs B | | G-MNYH | Southdown Puma Sprint | |

| Reg. | Type | Notes |
|---|---|---|
| G-MNYI | Southdown Raven X | |
| G-MNYJ | Mainair Gemini Flash II | |
| G-MNYK | Mainair Gemini Flash II | |
| G-MNYL | Southdown Raven X | |
| G-MNYM | Southdown Raven X | |
| G-MNYO | Southdown Raven X | |
| G-MNYP | Southdown Raven X | |
| G-MNYS | Southdown Raven X | |
| G-MNYT | Solar Wings Pegasus XL-R | |
| G-MNYU | Solar Wings Pegasus XL-R | |
| G-MNYV | Solar Wings Pegasus XL-R | |
| G-MNYW | Solar Wings Pegasus XL-R | |
| G-MNYX | Solar Wings Pegasus XL-R | |
| G-MNYY | Solar Wings Pegasus Flash II | |
| G-MNYZ | Solar Wings Pegasus Flash II | |
| G-MNZA | Solar Wings Pegasus Flash II | |
| G-MNZB | Mainair Gemini Flash II | |
| G-MNZC | Mainair Gemini Flash II | |
| G-MNZD | Mainair Gemini Flash II | |
| G-MNZE | Mainair Gemini Flash II | |
| G-MNZF | Mainair Gemini Flash II | |
| G-MNZG | Aerial Arts 110SX | |
| G-MNZH | AMF Chevron 2-32 | |
| G-MNZI | Prone Power Typhoon 2 | |
| G-MNZJ | CFM Shadow Srs BD | |
| G-MNZK | Solar Wings Pegasus XL-R | |
| G-MNZL | Solar Wings Pegasus XL-R | |
| G-MNZM | Solar Wings Pegasus XL-R | |
| G-MNZN | Solar Wings Pegasus Flash II | |
| G-MNZO | Solar Wings Pegasus Flash II | |
| G-MNZP | CFM Shadow Srs B | |
| G-MNZR | CFM Shadown Srs BD | |
| G-MNZS | Aerial Arts 130SX | |
| G-MNZU | Eurowing Goldwing | |
| G-MNZV | Southdown Raven X | |
| G-MNZW | Southdown Raven X | |
| G-MNZX | Southdown Raven X | |
| G-MNZY | Striker Tri-Flyer 330 | |
| G-MNZZ | CFM Shadow Srs B | |
| G-MTAA | Solar Wings Pegasus XL-R | |
| G-MTAB | Mainair Gemini Flash II | |
| G-MTAC | Mainair Gemini Flash II | |
| G-MTAD | Mainair Gemini Skyflash | |
| G-MTAE | Mainair Gemini Flash II | |
| G-MTAF | Mainair Gemini Flash II | |
| G-MTAG | Mainair Gemini Flash II | |
| G-MTAH | Mainair Gemini Flash II | |
| G-MTAI | Solar Wings Pegasus XL-R | |
| G-MTAJ | Solar Wings Pegasus XL-R | |
| G-MTAK | Solar Wings Pegasus XL-R | |
| G-MTAL | Solar Wings Photon | |
| G-MTAM | Solar Wings Pegasus Flash | |
| G-MTAO | Solar Wings Pegasus XL-R | |
| G-MTAP | Southdown Raven X | |
| G-MTAR | Mainair Gemini Flash II | |
| G-MTAS | Whittaker MW.5 Sorcerer | |
| G-MTAT | Solar Wings Pegasus XL-R | |
| G-MTAU | Solar Wings Pegasus XL-R | |
| G-MTAV | Solar Wings Pegasus XL-R | |
| G-MTAW | Solar Wings Pegasus XL-R | |
| G-MTAX | Solar Wings Pegasus XL-R | |
| G-MTAY | Solar Wings Pegasus XL-R | |
| G-MTAZ | Solar Wings Pegasus XL-R | |
| G-MTBA | Solar Wings Pegasus XL-R | |
| G-MTBB | Southdown Raven X | |
| G-MTBC | Mainair Gemini Flash II | |
| G-MTBD | Mainair Gemini Flash II | |
| G-MTBE | CFM Shadow Srs BD | |
| G-MTBF | Mirage Mk II | |
| G-MTBG | Mainair Gemini Flash II | |
| G-MTBH | Mainair Gemini Flash II | |
| G-MTBI | Mainair Gemini Flash II | |
| G-MTBJ | Mainair Gemini Flash II | |
| G-MTBK | Southdown Raven X | |
| G-MTBL | Solar Wings Pegasus XL-R | |
| G-MTBM | Airwave Nimrod | |
| G-MTBN | Southdown Raven X | |
| G-MTBO | Southdown Raven X | |
| G-MTBP | Aerotech MW.5 Sorcerer | |
| G-MTBR | Aerotech MW.5 Sorcerer | |
| G-MTBS | Aerotech MW.5 Sorcerer | |
| G-MTBT | Aerotech MW.5 Sorcerer | |
| G-MTBU | Solar Wings Pegasus XL-R | |
| G-MTBV | Solar Wings Pegasus XL-R | |
| G-MTBW | Mainair Gemini Flash II | |
| G-MTBX | Mainair Gemini Flash II | |
| G-MTBY | Mainair Gemini Flash II | |
| G-MTBZ | Southdown Raven X | |
| G-MTCA | CFM Shadow Srs B | |
| G-MTCB | Snowbird Mk III | |
| G-MTCC | Mainair Gemini Flash II | |
| G-MTCD | Southdown Raven X | |
| G-MTCE | Mainair Gemini Flash II | |
| G-MTCG | Solar Wings Pegasus XL-R | |
| G-MTCH | Solar Wings Pegasus XL-R | |
| G-MTCJ | Aerial Arts Avenger | |
| G-MTCK | Solar Wings Pegasus Flash | |
| G-MTCL | Southdown Raven X | |
| G-MTCM | Southdown Raven X | |
| G-MTCN | Solar Wings Pegasus XL-R | |
| G-MTCO | Solar Wings Pegasus XL-R | |
| G-MTCP | Aerial Arts Chaser 110SX | |
| G-MTCR | Solar Wings Pegasus XL-R | |
| G-MTCT | CFM Shadow Srs BD | |
| G-MTCU | Mainair Gemini Flash II | |
| G-MTCV | Microflight Spectrum | |
| G-MTCW | Mainair Gemini Flash | |
| G-MTCX | Solar Wings Pegasus XL-R | |
| G-MTCY | Southdown Raven X | |
| G-MTCZ | Ultrasports Tripacer 250 | |
| G-MTDA | Hornet Dual Trainer | |
| G-MTDB | Owen Pola Mk 1 | |
| G-MTDC | Owen Pola Mk 1 | |
| G-MTDD | Aerial Arts Chaser 110SX | |
| G-MTDE | American Aerolights 110SX | |
| G-MTDF | Mainair Gemini Flash II | |
| G-MTDG | Solar Wings Pegasus XL-R | |
| G-MTDH | Solar Wings Pegasus XL-R | |
| G-MTDI | Solar Wings Pegasus XL-R | |
| G-MTDJ | Medway Hybred 44XL | |
| G-MTDK | Aerotech MW.5 Sorcerer | |
| G-MTDL | Solar Wings Pegasus XL-R | |
| G-MTDM | Mainair Gemini Flash II | |
| G-MTDN | Ultraflight Lazair IIIE | |
| G-MTDO | Eipper Quicksilver MXII | |
| G-MTDP | Solar Wings Pegasus XL-R | |
| G-MTDR | Mainair Gemini Flash II | |
| G-MTDS | Solar Wings Photon | |
| G-MTDT | Solar Wings Pegasus XL-R | |
| G-MTDU | CFM Shadow Srs BD | |
| G-MTDV | Solar Wings Pegasus XL-R | |
| G-MTDW | Mainair Gemini Flash II | |
| G-MTDX | CFM Shadow Srs BD | |
| G-MTDY | Mainair Gemini Flash II | |
| G-MTDZ | Eipper Quicksilver MXII | |
| G-MTEA | Solar Wings Pegasus XL-R | |
| G-MTEB | Solar Wings Pegasus XL-R | |
| G-MTEC | Solar Wings Pegasus XL-R | |

| Reg. | Type | Notes | Reg | Type | Notes |
|------|------|-------|-----|------|-------|
| G-MTED | Solar Wings Pegasus XL-R | | G-MTHM | Solar Wings Pegasus XL-R | |
| G-MTEE | Solar Wings Pegasus XL-R | | G-MTHN | Solar Wings Pegasus XL-R | |
| G-MTEF | Solar Wings Pegasus XL-R | | G-MTHO | Solar Wings Pegasus XL-R | |
| G-MTEG | Mainair Gemini Flash II | | G-MTHP | Solar Wings Pegasus XL-R | |
| G-MTEH | Mainair Gemini Flash II | | G-MTHS | CFM Shadow Srs BD | |
| G-MTEJ | Mainair Gemini Flash II | | G-MTHT | CFM Shadow Srs BD | |
| G-MTEK | Mainair Gemini Flash II | | G-MTHU | Hornet Dual Trainer | |
| G-MTEL | Mainair Gemini Flash II | | G-MTHV | CFM Shadow Srs BD | |
| G-MTEM | Mainair Gemini Flash II | | G-MTHW | Mainair Gemini Flash II | |
| G-MTEN | Mainair Gemini Flash II | | G-MTHX | Mainair Gemini Flash IIA | |
| G-MTEO | Midland Ultralight Sirocco 337 | | G-MTHY | Mainair Gemini Flash IIA | |
| | | | G-MTHZ | Mainair Gemini Flash IIA | |
| G-MTER | Solar Wings Pegasus XL-R | | G-MTIA | Mainair Gemini Flash IIA | |
| G-MTES | Solar Wings Pegasus XL-R | | G-MTIB | Mainair Gemini Flash IIA | |
| G-MTET | Solar Wings Pegasus XL-R | | G-MTIC | Mainair Gemini Flash IIA | |
| G-MTEU | Solar Wings Pegasus XL-R | | G-MTID | Southdown Raven X | |
| G-MTEV | Solar Wings Pegasus XL-R | | G-MTIE | Solar Wings Pegasus XL-R | |
| G-MTEW | Solar Wings Pegasus XL-R | | G-MTIF | Solar Wings Pegasus XL-R | |
| G-MTEX | Solar Wings Pegasus XL-R | | G-MTIG | Solar Wings Pegasus XL-R | |
| G-MTEY | Mainair Gemini Flash II | | G-MTIH | Solar Wings Pegasus XL-R | |
| G-MTEZ | Ultraflight Lazair IIIE | | G-MTII | Solar Wings Pegasus XL-R | |
| G-MTFA | Solar Wings Pegasus XL-R | | G-MTIJ | Solar Wings Pegasus XL-R | |
| G-MTFB | Solar Wings Pegasus XL-R | | G-MTIK | Southdown Raven X | |
| G-MTFC | Medway Hybred 44XLR | | G-MTIL | Mainair Gemini Flash IIA | |
| G-MTFE | Solar Wings Pegasus XL-R | | G-MTIM | Mainair Gemini Flash IIA | |
| G-MTFF | Mainair Gemini Flash II | | G-MTIN | Solar Wings Pegasus XL-R | |
| G-MTFG | AMF Chevvron 232 | | G-MTIO | Solar Wings Pegasus XL-R | |
| G-MTFH | Aerotech MW.5B Sorcerer | | G-MTIP | Solar Wings Pegasus XL-R | |
| G-MTFI | Mainair Gemini Flash II | | G-MTIR | Solar Wings Pegasus XL-R | |
| G-MTFJ | Mainair Gemini Flash II | | G-MTIS | Solar Wings Pegasus XL-R | |
| G-MTFL | AMF Lazair IIIE | | G-MTIT | Solar Wings Pegasus XL-R | |
| G-MTFM | Solar Wings Pegasus XL-R | | G-MTIU | Solar Wings Pegasus XL-R | |
| G-MTFN | Aerotech MW.5 Sorcerer | | G-MTIV | Solar Wings Pegasus XL-R | |
| G-MTFO | Solar Wings Pegasus XL-R | | G-MTIW | Solar Wings Pegasus XL-R | |
| G-MTFP | Solar Wings Pegasus XL-R | | G-MTIX | Solar Wings Pegasus XL-R | |
| G-MTFR | Solar Wings Pegasus XL-R | | G-MTIY | Solar Wings Pegasus XL-R | |
| G-MTFS | Solar Wings Pegasus XL-R | | G-MTIZ | Solar Wings Pegasus XL-R | |
| G-MTFT | Solar Wings Pegasus XL-R | | G-MTJA | Mainair Gemini Flash IIA | |
| G-MTFU | CFM Shadow Series BD | | G-MTJB | Mainair Gemini Flash IIA | |
| G-MTFX | Mainair Gemini Flash | | G-MTJC | Mainair Gemini Flash IIA | |
| G-MTFY | CFM Shadow Srs BD | | G-MTJD | Mainair Gemini Flash IIA | |
| G-MTFZ | CFM Shadow Srs BD | | G-MTJE | Mainair Gemini Flash IIA | |
| G-MTGA | Mainair Gemini Flash | | G-MTJF | Mainair Gemini Flash IIA | |
| G-MTGB | Thruster TST Mk 1 | | G-MTJG | Medway Hybred 44XLR | |
| G-MTGC | Thruster TST Mk 1 | | G-MTJH | Solar Wings Pegasus Flash | |
| G-MTGD | Thruster TST Mk 1 | | | | |
| G-MTGE | Thruster TST Mk 1 | | G-MTJI | Raven X | |
| G-MTGF | Thruster TST Mk 1 | | G-MTJK | Mainair Gemini Flash IIA | |
| G-MTGH | Mainair Gemini Flash IIA | | G-MTJL | Mainair Gemini Flash IIA | |
| G-MTGI | Solar Wings Pegasus XL-R | | G-MTJM | Mainair Gemini Flash IIA | |
| G-MTGJ | Solar Wings Pegasus XL-R | | G-MTJN | Midland Ultralights Sirocco 377GB | |
| G-MTGK | Solar Wings Pegasus XL-R | | | | |
| G-MTGL | Solar Wings Pegasus XL-R | | G-MTJP | Medway Hybred 44XLR | |
| G-MTGM | Solar Wings Pegasus XL-R | | G-MTJR | Solar Wings Pegasus XL-R | |
| G-MTGO | Mainair Gemini Flash | | G-MTJS | Solar Wings Pegasus XL-Q | |
| G-MTGP | Thruster TST Mk 1 | | | | |
| G-MTGR | Thruster TST Mk 1 | | G-MTJT | Mainair Gemini Flash IIA | |
| G-MTGS | Thruster TST Mk 1 | | G-MTJV | Mainair Gemini Flash IIA | |
| G-MTGT | Thruster TST Mk 1 | | G-MTJW | Mainair Gemini Flash IIA | |
| G-MTGU | Thruster TST Mk 1 | | G-MTJX | Hornet Dual Trainer | |
| G-MTGV | CFM Shadow Srs BD | | G-MTJY | Mainair Gemini Flash IIA | |
| G-MTGX | Hornet Dual Trainer | | G-MTJZ | Mainair Gemini Flash IIA | |
| G-MTGY | Southdown Lightning | | G-MTKA | Thruster TST Mk 1 | |
| G-MTHB | Aerotech MW.5B Sorcerer | | G-MTKB | Thruster TST Mk 1 | |
| G-MTHC | Raven X | | G-MTKD | Thruster TST Mk 1 | |
| G-MTHD | Hiway Demon 195 | | G-MTKE | Thruster TST Mk 1 | |
| G-MTHF | Solar Wings Pegasus XL-R | | G-MTKG | Solar Wings Pegasus XL-R | |
| G-MTHG | Solar Wings Pegasus XL-R | | G-MTKH | Solar Wings Pegasus XL-R | |
| G-MTHH | Solar Wings Pegasus XL-R | | G-MTKI | Solar Wings Pegasus XL-R | |
| G-MTHI | Solar Wings Pegasus XL-R | | G-MTKJ | Solar Wings Pegasus XL-R | |
| G-MTHJ | Solar Wings Pegasus XL-R | | G-MTKK | Solar Wings Pegasus XL-R | |
| G-MTHK | Solar Wings Pegasus XL-R | | G-MTKM | Gardner T-M Scout S.2 | |
| G-MTHL | Solar Wings Pegasus XL-R | | G-MTKN | Mainair Gemini Flash IIA | |

| Reg. | Type | Notes | Reg | Type | Notes |
|---|---|---|---|---|---|
| | | | | Q | |
| G-MTKO | Mainair Gemini Flash IIA | | G-MTNR | Thruster TST Mk 1 | |
| G-MTKP | Solar Wings Pegasus XL-R | | G-MTNS | Thruster TST Mk 1 | |
| G-MTKR | CFM Shadow Srs BD | | G-MTNT | Thruster TST Mk 1 | |
| G-MTKS | CFM Shadow Srs BD | | G-MTNU | Thruster TST Mk 1 | |
| G-MTKU | CFM Shadow Srs BD | | G-MTNV | Thruster TST Mk 1 | |
| G-MTKV | Mainair Gemini Flash | | G-MTNW | Thruster TST Mk 1 | |
| G-MTKW | Mainair Gemini Flash IIA | | G-MTNX | Mainair Gemini Flash II | |
| G-MTKX | Mainair Gemini Flash IIA | | G-MTNY | Mainair Gemini Flash IIA | |
| G-MTKY | Mainair Gemini Flash IIA | | G-MTNZ | Solar Wings Pegasus XL-Q | |
| G-MTKZ | Mainair Gemini Flash IIA | | G-MTOA | Solar Wings Pegasus XL-R | |
| G-MTLA | Mainair Gemini Flash IIA | | G-MTOB | Solar Wings Pegasus XL-R | |
| G-MTLB | Mainair Gemini Flash IIA | | G-MTOC | Solar Wings Pegasus XL-R | |
| G-MTLC | Mainair Gemini Flash IIA | | G-MTOD | Solar Wings Pegasus XL-R | |
| G-MTLD | Mainair Gemini Flash IIA | | G-MTOE | Solar Wings Pegasus XL-R | |
| G-MTLE | See main Register | | G-MTOF | Solar Wings Pegasus XL-R | |
| G-MTLG | Solar Wings Pegasus XL-R | | G-MTOG | Solar Wings Pegasus XL-R | |
| G-MTLH | Solar Wings Pegasus XL-R | | G-MTOH | Solar Wings Pegasus XL-R | |
| G-MTLI | Solar Wings Pegasus XL-R | | G-MTOI | Solar Wings Pegasus XL-R | |
| G-MTLJ | Solar Wings Pegasus XL-R | | G-MTOJ | Solar Wings Pegasus XL-R | |
| G-MTLK | Raven X | | G-MTOK | Solar Wings Pegasus XL-R | |
| G-MTLL | Mainair Gemini Flash IIA | | G-MTOL | Solar Wings Pegasus XL-R | |
| G-MTLM | Thruster TST Mk 1 | | G-MTOM | Solar Wings Pegasus XL-R | |
| G-MTLN | Thruster TST Mk 1 | | G-MTON | Solar Wings Pegasus XL-R | |
| G-MTLO | Thruster TST Mk 1 | | G-MTOO | Solar Wings Pegasus XL-R | |
| G-MTLP | Thruster TST Mk 1 | | G-MTOP | Solar Wings Pegasus XL-R | |
| G-MTLR | Thruster TST Mk 1 | | G-MTOR | Solar Wings Pegasus XL-R | |
| G-MTLS | Solar Wings Pegasus XL-R | | G-MTOS | Solar Wings Pegasus XL-R | |
| G-MTLT | Solar Wings Pegasus XL-R | | G-MTOT | Solar Wings Pegasus XL-R | |
| G-MTLU | Solar Wings Pegasus XL-R | | G-MTOU | Solar Wings Pegasus XL-R | |
| G-MTLV | Solar Wings Pegasus XL-R | | G-MTOV | Solar Wings Pegasus XL-R | |
| G-MTLW | Solar Wings Pegasus XL-R | | G-MTOW | Solar Wings Pegasus XL-R | |
| G-MTLX | Medway Hybred 44XLR | | G-MTOX | Solar Wings Pegasus XL-R | |
| G-MTLY | Solar Wings Pegasus XL-R | | G-MTOY | Solar Wings Pegasus XL-R | |
| G-MTLZ | Whittaker MW.5 Sorceror | | G-MTOZ | Solar Wings Pegasus XL-R | |
| G-MTMA | Mainair Gemini Flash IIA | | G-MTPA | Mainair Gemini Flash IIA | |
| G-MTMB | Mainair Gemini Flash IIA | | G-MTPB | Mainair Gemini Flash IIA | |
| G-MTMC | Mainair Gemini Flash IIA | | G-MTPC | Raven X | |
| G-MTMD | Whittaker MW.6 Merlin | | G-MTPE | Solar Wings Pegasus XL-R | |
| G-MTME | Solar Wings Pegasus XL-R | | G-MTPF | Solar Wings Pegasus XL-R | |
| G-MTMF | Solar Wings Pegasus XL-R | | G-MTPG | Solar Wings Pegasus XL-R | |
| G-MTMG | Solar Wings Pegasus XL-R | | G-MTPH | Solar Wings Pegasus XL-R | |
| G-MTMH | Solar Wings Pegasus XL-R | | G-MTPI | Solar Wings Pegasus XL-R | |
| G-MTMI | Solar Wings Pegasus XL-R | | G-MTPJ | Solar Wings Pegasus XL-R | |
| G-MTMJ | Maxair Hummer | | G-MTPK | Solar Wings Pegasus XL-R | |
| G-MTMK | Raven X | | G-MTPL | Solar Wings Pegasus XL-R | |
| G-MTML | Mainair Gemini Flash IIA | | G-MTPM | Solar Wings Pegasus XL-R | |
| G-MTMM | CFM Shadow Srs BD | | G-MTPN | Solar Wings Pegasus XL-Q | |
| G-MTMO | Raven X | | G-MTPO | Solar Wings Pegasus XL-Q | |
| G-MTMP | Hornet Dual Trainer/Raven | | G-MTPP | Solar Wings Pegasus XL-R | |
| G-MTMR | Hornet Dual Trainer/Raven | | G-MTPR | Solar Wings Pegasus XL-Q | |
| G-MTMT | Mainair Gemini Flash IIA | | G-MTPS | Solar Wings Pegasus XL-Q | |
| G-MTMU | Mainair Gemini Flash IIA | | G-MTPT | Thruster TST Mk Mk 1 | |
| G-MTMV | Mainair Gemini Flash IIA | | G-MTPU | Thruster TST Mk 1 | |
| G-MTMW | Mainair Gemini Flash IIA | | G-MTPV | Thruster TST Mk 1 | |
| G-MTMX | CFM Shadow Srs BD | | G-MTPW | Thruster TST Mk 1 | |
| G-MTMY | CFM Shadow Srs BD | | G-MTPX | Thruster TST Mk 1 | |
| G-MTMZ | CFM Shadow Srs BD | | G-MTPY | Thruster TST Mk 1 | |
| G-MTNB | Raven X | | G-MTPZ | Solar Wings Pegasus XL-R | |
| G-MTNC | Mainair Gemini Flash IIA | | G-MTRA | Mainair Gemini Flash IIA | |
| G-MTND | Medway Hybred 44XLR | | G-MTRB | Mainair Gemini Flash IIA | |
| G-MTNE | Medway Hybred 44XLR | | G-MTRC | Midlands Ultralights Sirocco 377GB | |
| G-MTNF | Medway Hybred 44XLR | | | | |
| G-MTNG | Mainair Gemini Flash IIA | | G-MTRD | Midlands Ultralights Sirocco 377GB | |
| G-MTNH | Mainair Gemini Flash IIA | | | | |
| G-MTNI | Mainair Gemini Flash IIA | | G-MTRE | Whittaker MW.6 Merlin | |
| G-MTNJ | Mainair Gemini Flash IIA | | G-MTRF | Mainair Gemini Flash IIA | |
| G-MTNK | Weedhopper JC-24B | | G-MTRG | Mainair Gemini Flash IIA | |
| G-MTNL | Mainair Gemini Flash IIA | | G-MTRH | Hiway Demon | |
| G-MTNM | Mainair Gemini Flash IIA | | G-MTRJ | AMF Chevvron 232 | |
| G-MTNN | Mainair Gemini Flash IIA | | G-MTRK | Hornet Dual Trainer | |
| G-MTNO | Solar Wings Pegasus XL-Q | | G-MTRL | Hornet Dual Trainer | |
| G-MTNP | Solar Wings Pegasus XL- | | G-MTRM | Solar Wings Pegasus XL-R | |

| Reg. | Type | Notes | Reg. | Type | Notes |
|------|------|-------|------|------|-------|
| G-MTRN | Solar Wings Pegasus XL-R | | G-MTUR | Solar Wings Pegasus XL-Q | |
| G-MTRO | Solar Wings Pegasus XL-R | | G-MTUS | Solar Wings Pegasus XL-Q | |
| G-MTRP | Solar Wings Pegasus XL-R | | G-MTUT | Solar Wings Pegasus XL-Q | |
| G-MTRR | Solar Wings Pegasus XL-R | | G-MTUU | Mainair Gemini Flash IIA | |
| G-MTRS | Solar Wings Pegasus XL-R | | G-MTUV | Mainair Gemini Flash IIA | |
| G-MTRT | Raven X | | G-MTUX | Medway Hybred 44XLR | |
| G-MTRU | Solar Wings Pegasus XL-Q | | G-MTUY | Solar Wings Pegasus XL-Q | |
| G-MTRV | Solar Wings Pegasus XL-Q | | G-MTUZ | Hornet Dual Trainer | |
| G-MTRW | Raven X | | G-MTVA | Solar Wings Pegasus XL-R | |
| G-MTRX | Whittaker MW.5 Sorceror | | G-MTVB | Solar Wings Pegasus XL-R | |
| G-MTRY | Noble Hardman Snowbird IV | | G-MTVC | Solar Wings Pegasus XL-R | |
| G-MTRZ | Mainair Gemini Flash IIA | | G-MTVE | Solar Wings Pegasus XL-R | |
| G-MTSA | Mainair Gemini Flash IIA | | G-MTVF | Solar Wings Pegasus XL-R | |
| G-MTSB | Mainair Gemini Flash IIA | | G-MTVG | Mainair Gemini Flash IIA | |
| G-MTSC | Mainair Gemini Flash IIA | | G-MTVH | Mainair Gemini Flash IIA | |
| G-MTSD | Raven X | | G-MTVI | Mainair Gemini Flash IIA | |
| G-MTSE | Flexiform Striker | | G-MTVJ | Mainair Gemini Flash IIA | |
| G-MTSF | Aerial Arts Chaser 110SX | | G-MTVK | Solar Wings Pegasus XL-R | |
| G-MTSG | CFM Shadow Srs BD | | G-MTVL | Solar Wings Pegasus XL-R | |
| G-MTSH | Thruster TST Mk 1 | | G-MTVM | Solar Wings Pegasus XL-R | |
| G-MTSI | Thruster TST Mk 1 | | G-MTVN | Solar Wings Pegasus XL-R | |
| G-MTSJ | Thruster TST Mk 1 | | G-MTVO | Solar Wings Pegasus XL-R | |
| G-MTSK | Thruster TST Mk 1 | | G-MTVP | Thruster TST Mk 1 | |
| G-MTSL | Thruster TST Mk 1 | | G-MTVR | Thruster TST Mk 1 | |
| G-MTSM | Thruster TST Mk 1 | | G-MTVS | Thruster TST Mk 1 | |
| G-MTSN | Solar Wings Pegasus XL-R | | G-MTVT | Thruster TST Mk 1 | |
| G-MTSO | Solar Wings Pegasus XL-R | | G-MTVU | Thruster TST Mk 1 | |
| G-MTSP | Solar Wings Pegasus XL-R | | G-MTVV | Thruster TST Mk 1 | |
| G-MTSR | Solar Wings Pegasus XL-R | | G-MTVX | Solar Wings Pegasus XL-Q | |
| G-MTSS | Solar Wings Pegasus XL-R | | G-MTVY | Solar Wings Pegasus XL-Q | |
| G-MTST | Thruster TST Mk 1 | | G-MTVZ | Powerchute Raider | |
| G-MTSU | Solar Wings Pegasus XL-R | | G-MTWA | Solar Wings Pegasus XL-R | |
| G-MTSV | Solar Wings Pegasus XL-R | | G-MTWB | Solar Wings Pegasus XL-R | |
| G-MTSX | Solar Wings Pegasus XL-R | | G-MTWC | Solar Wings Pegasus XL-R | |
| G-MTSY | Solar Wings Pegasus XL-R | | G-MTWD | Solar Wings Pegasus XL-R | |
| G-MTSZ | Solar Wings Pegasus XL-R | | G-MTWE | Solar Wings Pegasus XL-R | |
| G-MTTA | Solar Wings Pegasus XL-R | | G-MTWF | Mainair Gemini Flash IIA | |
| G-MTTB | Solar Wings Pegasus XL-R | | G-MTWG | Mainair Gemini Flash IIA | |
| G-MTTC | Solar Wings Pegasus XL-R | | G-MTWH | CFM Shadow Srs BD | |
| G-MTTD | Solar Wings Pegasus XL-R | | G-MTWK | CFM Shadow Srs BD | |
| G-MTTE | Solar Wings Pegasus XL-R | | G-MTWL | CFM Shadow Srs BD | |
| G-MTTF | Aerotech MW.6 Merlin | | G-MTWM | CFM Shadow Srs BD | |
| G-MTTG | Excalibur TriPacer 250 | | G-MTWN | CFM Shadow Srs BD | |
| G-MTTH | CFM Shadow Srs BD | | G-MTWO | Weedhopper JC-24B | |
| G-MTTI | Mainair Gemini Flash IIA | | G-MTWP | CFM Shadow Srs BD | |
| G-MTTK | Southdown Lightning DS | | G-MTWR | Mainair Gemini Flash IIA | |
| G-MTTL | Hiway Sky-Trike | | G-MTWS | Mainair Gemini Flash IIA | |
| G-MTTM | Mainair Gemini Flash IIA | | G-MTWW | Solar Wings Typhoon | |
| G-MTTN | Ultralight Flight Phantom | | G-MTWX | Mainair Gemini Flash IIA | |
| G-MTTO | Mainair Gemini Flash IIA | | G-MTWY | Thruster TST Mk 1 | |
| G-MTTP | Mainair Gemini Flash IIA | | G-MTWZ | Thruster TST Mk 1 | |
| G-MTTR | Mainair Gemini Flash IIA | | G-MTXA | Thruster TST Mk 1 | |
| G-MTTS | Mainair Gemini Flash IIA | | G-MTXB | Thruster TST Mk 1 | |
| G-MTTU | Solar Wings Pegasus XL-R | | G-MTXC | Thruster TST Mk 1 | |
| G-MTTW | Mainair Gemini Flash IIA | | G-MTXD | Thruster TST Mk 1 | |
| G-MTTX | Solar Wings Pegasus XL-Q | | G-MTXE | Hornet Dual Trainer | |
| G-MTTY | Solar Wings Pegasus XL-Q | | G-MTXG | Solar Wings Pegasus XL-Q | |
| G-MTTZ | Solar Wings Pegasus XL-Q | | G-MTXH | Solar Wings Pegasus XL-Q | |
| G-MTUA | Solar Wings Pegasus XL-R | | G-MTXI | Solar Wings Pegasus XL-Q | |
| G-MTUB | Thruster TST Mk 1 | | G-MTXJ | Solar Wings Pegasus XL-Q | |
| G-MTUC | Thruster TST Mk 1 | | G-MTXK | Solar Wings Pegasus XL-Q | |
| G-MTUD | Thruster TST Mk 1 | | | | |
| G-MTUE | Thruster TST Mk 1 | | G-MTXL | Noble Hardman Snowbird Mk IV | |
| G-MTUF | Thruster TST Mk 1 | | | | |
| G-MTUG | Thruster TST Mk 1 | | G-MTXM | Mainair Gemini Flash IIA | |
| G-MTUH | Solar Wings Pegasus XL-R | | G-MTXO | Whittaker MW.6 | |
| G-MTUI | Solar Wings Pegasus XL-R | | G-MTXP | Mainair Gemini Flash IIA | |
| G-MTUJ | Solar Wings Pegasus XL-R | | G-MTXR | CFM Shadow Srs BD | |
| G-MTUK | Solar Wings Pegasus XL-R | | G-MTXS | Mainair Gemini Flash IIA | |
| G-MTUL | Solar Wings Pegasus XL-R | | | | |
| G-MTUN | Solar Wings Pegasus XL-Q | | | | |
| G-MTUO | Solar Wings Pegasus XL-Q | | | | |
| G-MTUP | Solar Wings Pegasus XL-Q | | | | |

| Reg. | Type | Notes | Reg | Type | Notes |
|------|------|-------|-----|------|-------|
| G-MTXT | MBA Tiger Cub 440 | | G-MVAS | Solar Wings Pegasus XL-R | |
| G-MTXU | Noble Hardman Snowbird Mk IV | | G-MVAT | Solar Wings Pegasus XL-R | |
| | | | G-MVAU | Solar Wings Pegasus XL-R | |
| G-MTXV | Noble Hardman Snowbird Mk IV | | G-MVAV | Solar Wings Pegasus XL-R | |
| | | | G-MVAW | Solar Wings Pegasus XL-Q | |
| G-MTXW | Noble Hardman Snowbird Mk IV | | G-MVAX | Solar Wings Pegasus XL-Q | |
| | | | G-MVAY | Solar Wings Pegasus XL-Q | |
| G-MTXY | Hornet Dual Trainer | | G-MVAZ | Solar Wings Pegasus XL-Q | |
| G-MTXZ | Mainair Gemini Flash IIA | | G-MVBA | Solar Wings Pegasus XL-Q | |
| G-MTYA | Solar Wings Pegasus XL-Q | | G-MVBB | CFM Shadow Srs BD | |
| G-MTYC | Solar Wings Pegasus XL-Q | | G-MVBC | Aerial Arts Tri-Flyer 130SX | |
| G-MTYD | Solar Wings Pegasus XL-Q | | G-MVBD | Mainair Gemini Flash IIA | |
| G-MTYE | Solar Wings Pegasus XL-Q | | G-MVBE | Mainair Scorcher | |
| G-MTYF | Solar Wings Pegasus XL-Q | | G-MVBF | Mainair Gemini Flash IIA | |
| G-MTYG | Solar Wings Pegasus XL-Q | | G-MVBG | Mainair Gemini Flash IIA | |
| G-MTYH | Solar Wings Pegasus XL-Q | | G-MVBH | Mainair Gemini Flash IIA | |
| G-MTYI | Solar Wings Pegasus XL-Q | | G-MVBI | Mainair Gemini Flash IIA | |
| G-MTYK | Solar Wings Pegasus XL-Q | | G-MVBJ | Solar Wings Pegasus XL-R | |
| G-MTYL | Solar Wings Pegasus XL-Q | | G-MVBK | Mainair Gemini Flash IIA | |
| G-MTYM | Solar Wings Pegasus XL-Q | | G-MVBL | Mainair Gemini Flash IIA | |
| G-MTYN | Solar Wings Pegasus XL-Q | | G-MVBM | Mainair Gemini Flash IIA | |
| G-MTYO | Solar Wings Pegasus XL-Q | | G-MVBN | Mainair Gemini Flash IIA | |
| G-MTYP | Solar Wings Pegasus XL-Q | | G-MVBO | Mainair Gemini Flash IIA | |
| G-MTYR | Solar Wings Pegasus XL-Q | | G-MVBP | Thruster TST Mk 1 | |
| G-MTYS | Solar Wings Pegasus XL-Q | | G-MVBR | Thruster TST Mk 1 | |
| G-MTYT | Solar Wings Pegasus XL-Q | | G-MVBS | Thruster TST Mk 1 | |
| G-MTYU | Solar Wings Pegasus XL-Q | | G-MVBT | Thruster TST Mk 1 | |
| G-MTYV | Raven X | | G-MVBU | Thruster TST Mk 1 | |
| G-MTYW | Raven X | | G-MVBY | Solar Wings Pegasus XL-R | |
| G-MTYX | Raven X | | G-MVBZ | Solar Wings Pegasus XL-R | |
| G-MTYY | Solar Wings Pegasus XL-R | | G-MVCA | Solar Wings Pegasus XL-R | |
| G-MTZA | Thruster TST Mk 1 | | G-MVCB | Solar Wings Pegasus XL-R | |
| G-MTZB | Thruster TST Mk 1 | | G-MVCC | CFM Shadow Srs BD | |
| G-MTZC | Thruster TST Mk 1 | | G-MVCD | Medway Hybred 44XLR | |
| G-MTZD | Thruster TST Mk 1 | | G-MVCE | Mainair Gemini Flash IIA | |
| G-MTZE | Thruster TST Mk 1 | | G-MVCF | Mainair Gemini Flash IIA | |
| G-MTZF | Thruster TST Mk 1 | | G-MVCH | Noble Hardman Snowbird Mk IV | |
| G-MTZG | Mainair Gemini Flash IIA | | | | |
| G-MTZH | Mainair Gemini Flash IIA | | G-MVCI | Noble Hardman Snowbird Mk IV | |
| G-MTZI | Solar Wings Pegasus XL-R | | | | |
| G-MTZJ | Solar Wings Pegasus XL-R | | G-MVCJ | Noble Hardman Snowbird Mk IV | |
| G-MTZK | Solar Wings Pegasus XL-R | | | | |
| G-MTZL | Mainair Gemini Flash IIA | | G-MVCL | Solar Wings Pegasus XL-Q | |
| G-MTZM | Mainair Gemini Flash IIA | | G-MVCM | Solar Wings Pegasus XL-Q | |
| G-MTZN | Mainair Gemini Flash IIA | | G-MVCN | Solar Wings Pegasus XL-Q | |
| G-MTZO | Mainair Gemini Flash IIA | | G-MVCO | Solar Wings Pegasus XL-Q | |
| G-MTZP | Solar Wings Pegasus XL-Q | | G-MVCP | Solar Wings Pegasus XL-Q | |
| G-MTZR | Solar Wings Pegasus XL-Q | | G-MVCR | Solar Wings Pegasus XL-Q | |
| G-MTZS | Solar Wings Pegasus XL-Q | | G-MVCS | Solar Wings Pegasus XL-Q | |
| G-MTZT | Solar Wings Pegasus XL-Q | | G-MVCT | Solar Wings Pegasus XL-Q | |
| G-MTZU | Solar Wings Pegasus XL-Q | | G-MVCV | Solar Wings Pegasus XL-Q | |
| G-MTZV | Mainair Gemini Flash IIA | | G-MVCW | CFM Shadow Srs BD | |
| G-MTZW | Mainair Gemini Flash IIA | | G-MVCY | Mainair Gemini Flash IIA | |
| G-MTZX | Mainair Gemini Flash IIA | | G-MVCZ | Mainair Gemini Flash IIA | |
| G-MTZY | Mainair Gemini Flash IIA | | G-MVDA | Mainair Gemini Flash IIA | |
| G-MTZZ | Mainair Gemini Flash IIA | | G-MVDB | Medway Hybred 44XLR | |
| G-MVAA | Mainair Gemini Flash IIA | | G-MVDC | Medway Hybred 44XLR | |
| G-MVAB | Mainair Gemini Flash IIA | | G-MVDD | Thruster TST Mk 1 | |
| G-MVAC | CFM Shadow Srs BD | | G-MVDE | Thruster TST Mk 1 | |
| G-MVAD | Mainair Gemini Flash IIA | | G-MVDF | Thruster TST Mk 1 | |
| G-MVAF | Southdown Puma Sprint | | G-MVDG | Thruster TST Mk 1 | |
| G-MVAG | Thruster TST Mk 1 | | G-MVDH | Thruster TST Mk 1 | |
| G-MVAH | Thruster TST Mk 1 | | G-MVDI | Thruster TST Mk 1 | |
| G-MVAI | Thruster TST Mk 1 | | G-MVDJ | Medway Hybred 44XLR | |
| G-MVAJ | Thruster TST Mk 1 | | G-MVDK | Aerial Arts Chaser S | |
| G-MVAK | Thruster TST Mk 1 | | G-MVDL | Aerial Arts Chaser S | |
| G-MVAL | Thruster TST Mk 1 | | G-MVDM | Aerial Arts Chaser S | |
| G-MVAM | CFM Shadow Srs BD | | G-MVDN | Aerial Arts Chaser S | |
| G-MVAN | CFM Shadow Srs BD | | G-MVDO | Aerial Arts Chaser S | |
| G-MVAO | Mainair Gemini Flash IIA | | G-MVDP | Aerial Arts Chaser S | |
| G-MVAP | Mainair Gemini Flash IIA | | G-MVDR | Aerial Arts Chaser S | |
| G-MVAR | Solar Wings Pegasus XL-R | | G-MVDS | Hiway Skytrike | |
| | | | G-MVDT | Mainair Gemini Flash IIA | |

| Reg. | Type | Notes | Reg | Type | Notes |
|------|------|-------|-----|------|-------|
| G-MVDU | Solar Wings Pegasus XL-R | | G-MVGW | Solar Wings Pegasus XL-Q | |
| G-MVDV | Solar Wings Pegasus XL-R | | G-MVGX | Solar Wings Pegasus XL-Q | |
| G-MVDW | Solar Wings Pegasus XL-R | | G-MVGY | Medway Hybred 44XL | |
| G-MVDX | Solar Wings Pegasus XL-R | | G-MVGZ | Ultraflight Lazair IIIE | |
| G-MVDY | Solar Wings Pegasus XL-R | | G-MVHA | Aerial Arts Chaser S | |
| G-MVDZ | Solar Wings Pegasus XL-R | | G-MVHB | Powerchute Raider | |
| G-MVEA | Solar Wings Pegasus XL-R | | G-MVHC | Powerchute Raider | |
| G-MVEB | Solar Wings Pegasus XL-R | | G-MVHD | CFM Shadow Srs BD | |
| G-MVEC | Solar Wings Pegasus XL-R | | G-MVHE | Mainair Gemini Flash IIA | |
| G-MVED | Solar Wings Pegasus XL-R | | G-MVHF | Mainair Gemini Flash IIA | |
| G-MVEE | Medway Hybred 44XLR | | G-MVHG | Mainair Gemini Flash IIA | |
| G-MVEG | Solar Wings Pegasus XL-R | | G-MVHH | Mainair Gemini Flash IIA | |
| G-MVEH | Mainair Gemini Flash IIA | | G-MVHI | Thruster TST Mk 1 | |
| G-MVEI | CFM Shadow Srs BD | | G-MVHJ | Thruster TST Mk 1 | |
| G-MVEJ | Mainair Gemini Flash IIA | | G-MVHK | Thruster TST Mk 1 | |
| G-MVEK | Mainair Gemini Flash IIA | | G-MVHL | Thruster TST Mk 1 | |
| G-MVEL | Mainair Gemini Flash IIA | | G-MVHM | Whittaker MW.5 Sorcerer | |
| G-MVEN | CFM Shadow Srs BD | | G-MVHN | Aerial Arts Chaser S | |
| G-MVEO | Mainair Gemini Flash IIA | | G-MVHO | Solar Wings Pegasus XL-Q | |
| G-MVEP | Mainair Gemini Flash IIA | | G-MVHP | Solar Wings Pegasus XL-Q | |
| G-MVER | Mainair Gemini Flash IIA | | G-MVHR | Solar Wings Pegasus XL-Q | |
| G-MVES | Mainair Gemini Flash IIA | | G-MVHS | Solar Wings Pegasus XL-Q | |
| G-MVET | Mainir Gemini Flash IIA | | G-MVHU | Solar Wings Pegasus XL-Q | |
| G-MVEV | Mainair Gemini Flash IIA | | G-MVHV | Solar Wings Pegasus XL-Q | |
| G-MVEW | Mainair Gemini Flash IIA | | G-MVHW | Solar Wings Pegasus XL-Q | |
| G-MVEX | Solar Wings Pegasus XL-Q | | G-MVHX | Solar Wings Pegasus XL-Q | |
| G-MVEY | Solar Wings Pegasus XL-Q | | G-MVHY | Solar Wings Pegasus XL-Q | |
| G-MVEZ | Solar Wings Pegasus XL-Q | | G-MVHZ | Hornet Dual Trainer | |
| G-MVFA | Solar Wings Pegasus XL-Q | | G-MVIA | Solar Wings Pegasus XL-R | |
| G-MVFB | Solar Wings Pegasus XL-Q | | G-MVIB | Mainair Gemini Flash IIA | |
| G-MVFC | Solar Wings Pegasus XL-Q | | G-MVIC | Mainair Gemini Flash IIA | |
| G-MVFD | Solar Wings Pegasus XL-Q | | G-MVID | Aerial Arts Chaser S | |
| G-MVFE | Solar Wings Pegasus XL-Q | | G-MVIE | Aerial Arts Chaser S | |
| G-MVFF | Solar Wings Pegasus XL-Q | | G-MVIF | Medway Hybred 44XLR | |
| G-MVFG | Solar Wings Pegasus XL-Q | | G-MVIG | CFM Shadow Srs B | |
| G-MVFH | CFM Shadow Srs BD | | G-MVIH | Mainair Gemini Flash IIA | |
| G-MVFJ | Thruster TST Mk 1 | | G-MVIL | Noble Hardman Snowbird Mk IV | |
| G-MVFK | Thruster TST Mk 1 | | | | |
| G-MVFL | Thruster TST Mk 1 | | G-MVIM | Noble Hardman Snowbird Mk IV | |
| G-MVFM | Thruster TST Mk 1 | | | | |
| G-MVFN | Thruster TST Mk 1 | | G-MVIN | Noble Hardman Snowbird Mk IV | |
| G-MVFO | Thruster TST Mk 1 | | | | |
| G-MVFP | Solar Wings Pegasus XL-R | | G-MVIO | Noble Hardman Snowbird Mk IV | |
| G-MVFR | Solar Wings Pegasus XL-R | | | | |
| G-MVFS | Solar Wings Pegasus XL-R | | G-MVIP | AMF Chevvron 232 | |
| G-MVFT | Solar Wings Pegasus XL-R | | G-MVIR | Thruster TST Mk 1 | |
| G-MVFU | Solar Wings Pegasus XL-R | | G-MVIS | Thruster TST Mk 1 | |
| G-MVFV | Solar Wings Pegasus XL-R | | G-MVIU | Thruster TST Mk 1 | |
| G-MVFW | Solar Wings Pegasus XL-R | | G-MVIV | Thruster TST Mk 1 | |
| G-MVFX | Solar Wings Pegasus XL-R | | G-MVIW | Thruster TST Mk 1 | |
| G-MVFY | Solar Wings Pegasus XL-R | | G-MVIX | Mainair Gemini Flash IIA | |
| G-MVFZ | Solar Wings Pegasus XL-R | | G-MVIY | Mainair Gemini Flash IIA | |
| G-MVGA | Aerial Arts Chaser S | | G-MVIZ | Mainair Gemini Flash IIA | |
| G-MVGB | Medway Hybred 44XLR | | G-MVJA | Mainair Gemini Flash IIA | |
| G-MVGC | AMF Chevvron 232 | | G-MVJB | Mainair Gemini Flash IIA | |
| G-MVGD | AMF Chevvron 232 | | G-MVJC | Mainair Gemini Flash IIA | |
| G-MVGE | AMF Chevvron 232 | | G-MVJD | Solar Wings Pegasus XL-R | |
| G-MVGF | Aerial Arts Chaser S | | G-MVJE | Mainair Gemini Flash IIA | |
| G-MVGG | Aerial Arts Chaser S | | G-MVJF | Aerial Arts Chaser S | |
| G-MVGH | Aerial Arts Chaser S | | G-MVJG | Aerial Arts Chaser S | |
| G-MVGI | Aerial Arts Chaser S | | G-MVJH | Aerial Arts Chaser S | |
| G-MVGJ | Aerial Arts Chaser S | | G-MVJI | Aerial Arts Chaser S | |
| G-MVGK | Aerial Arts Chaser S | | G-MVJJ | Aerial Arts Chaser S | |
| G-MVGL | Medway Hybred 44XLR | | G-MVJK | Aerial Arts Chaser S | |
| G-MVGM | Mainair Gemini Flash IIA | | G-MVJL | Mainair Gemini Flash IIA | |
| G-MVGN | Solar Wings Pegasus XL-R | | G-MVJM | Microflight Spectrum | |
| G-MVGO | Solar Wings Pegasus XL-R | | G-MVJN | Solar Wings Pegasus XL-Q | |
| G-MVGR | Solar Wings Pegasus XL-R | | | | |
| G-MVGS | Solar Wings Pegasus XL-R | | G-MVJO | Solar Wings Pegasus XL-Q | |
| G-MVGT | Solar Wings Pegasus XL-Q | | | | |
| G-MVGU | Solar Wings Pegasus XL-Q | | G-MVJP | Solar Wings Pegasus XL-Q | |
| G-MVGV | Solar Wings Pegasus XL-Q | | | | |

| Reg. | Type | Notes | Reg | Type | Notes |
|------|------|-------|-----|------|-------|
| G-MVJR | Solar Wings Pegasus XL-Q | | G-MVMX | Mainair Gemini Flash IIA | |
| G-MVJS | Solar Wings Pegasus XL-Q | | G-MVMY | Mainair Gemini Flash IIA | |
| G-MVJT | Solar Wings Pegasus XL-Q | | G-MVMZ | Mainair Gemini Flash IIA | |
| G-MVJU | Solar Wings Pegasus XL-Q | | G-MVNA | Powerchute Raider | |
| G-MVJV | Solar Wings Pegasus XL-Q | | G-MVNB | Powerchute Raider | |
| G-MVJW | Solar Wings Pegasus XL-Q | | G-MVNC | Powerchute Raider | |
| G-MVJX | Solar Wings Pegasus XL-Q | | G-MVND | Powerchute Raider | |
| G-MVJZ | Birdman Cherokee | | G-MVNE | Powerchute Raider | |
| G-MVKA | Medway Hybred 44XLR | | G-MVNF | Powerchute Raider | |
| G-MVKB | Medway Hybred 44XLR | | G-MVNI | Powerchute Raider | |
| G-MVKC | Mainair Gemini Flash IIA | | G-MVNJ | Powerchute Raider | |
| G-MVKE | Solar Wings Pegasus XL-R | | G-MVNK | Powerchute Raider | |
| G-MVKF | Solar Wings Pegasus XL-R | | G-MVNL | Powerchute Raider | |
| G-MVKG | Solar Wings Pegasus XL-R | | G-MVNM | Mainair Gemini Flash IIA | |
| G-MVKH | Solar Wings Pegasus XL-R | | G-MVNN | Whittaker MW.5 (K) Sorcerer | |
| G-MVKI | Solar Wings Pegasus XL-R | | | | |
| G-MVKJ | Solar Wings Pegasus XL-R | | G-MVNO | Aerotech MW.5 (K) Sorcerer | |
| G-MVKK | Solar Wings Pegasus XL-R | | | | |
| G-MVKL | Solar Wings Pegasus XL-R | | G-MVNP | Aerotech MW.5 (K) Sorcerer | |
| G-MVKM | Solar Wings Pegasus XL-R | | | | |
| G-MVKN | Solar Wings Pegasus XL-Q | | G-MVNR | Aerotech MW.5 (K) Sorcerer | |
| G-MVKO | Solar Wings Pegasus XL-Q | | | | |
| G-MVKP | Solar Wings Pegasus XL-Q | | G-MVNS | Aerotech MW.5 (K) Sorcerer | |
| G-MVKR | Solar Wings Pegasus XL-Q | | | | |
| G-MVKS | Solar Wings Pegasus XL-Q | | G-MVNT | Whittaker MW.5 (K) Sorcerer | |
| G-MVKT | Solar Wings Pegasus XL-Q | | | | |
| G-MVKU | Solar Wings Pegasus XL-Q | | G-MVNU | Aerotech MW.5 Sorcerer | |
| G-MVKV | Solar Wings Pegasus XL-Q | | G-MVNV | Aerotech MW.5 Sorcerer | |
| G-MVKW | Solar Wings Pegasus XL-Q | | G-MVNW | Mainair Gemini Flash IIA | |
| G-MVKX | Solar Wings Pegasus XL-Q | | G-MVNX | Mainair Gemini Flash IIA | |
| G-MVKY | Aerial Arts Chaser S | | G-MVNY | Mainair Gemini Flash IIA | |
| G-MVKZ | Aerial Arts Chaser S | | G-MVNZ | Mainair Gemini Flash IIA | |
| G-MVLA | Aerial Arts Chaser S | | G-MVOA | Aerial Arts Alligator | |
| G-MVLB | Aerial Arts Chaser S | | G-MVOB | Mainair Gemini Flash IIA | |
| G-MVLC | Aerial Arts Chaser S | | G-MVOD | Aerial Arts Chaser 110SX | |
| G-MVLD | Aerial Arts Chaser S | | G-MVOE | Solar Wings Pegasus XL-R | |
| G-MVLE | Aerial Arts Chaser S | | G-MVOF | Mainair Gemini Flash IIA | |
| G-MVLF | Aerial Arts Chaser S | | G-MVOG | Huntair Pathfinder Mk 1 | |
| G-MVLG | Aerial Arts Chaser S | | G-MVOH | CFM Shadow Srs B | |
| G-MVLH | Aerial Arts Chaser S | | G-MVOI | Noble Hardman Snowbird Mk IV | |
| G-MVLJ | CFM Shadow Srs B | | | | |
| G-MVLL | Mainair Gemini Flash IIA | | G-MVOJ | Noble Hardman Snowbird Mk IV | |
| G-MVLM | Solar Wings Pegasus Bandit | | | | |
| | | | G-MVOK | Noble Hardman Snowbird Mk IV | |
| G-MVLP | CFM Shadow Srs BD | | | | |
| G-MVLR | Mainair Gemini Flash IIA | | G-MVOL | Noble Hardman Snowbird Mk IV | |
| G-MVLS | Aerial Arts Chaser S | | | | |
| G-MVLT | Aerial Arts Chaser S | | G-MVOM | Medway Hybred 44XLR | |
| G-MVLU | Aerial Arts Chaser S | | G-MVON | Mainair Gemini Flash IIA | |
| G-MVLW | Aerial Arts Chaser S | | G-MVOO | AMF Chevvron 232 | |
| G-MVLX | Solar Wings Pegasus XL-Q | | G-MVOP | Aerial Arts Chaser S | |
| G-MVLY | Solar Wings Pegasus XL-Q | | G-MVOR | Mainair Gemini Flash IIA | |
| G-MVLZ | Solar Wings Pegasus XL-Q | | G-MVOS | Southdown Raven | |
| G-MVMA | Solar Wings Pegasus XL-Q | | G-MVOT | Thruster TST Mk 1 | |
| G-MVMB | Solar Wings Pegasus XL-Q | | G-MVOU | Thruster TST Mk 1 | |
| G-MVMC | Solar Wings Pegasus XL-Q | | G-MVOV | Thruster TST Mk 1 | |
| G-MVMD | Powerchute Raider | | G-MVOW | Thruster TST Mk 1 | |
| G-MVME | Thruster TST Mk 1 | | G-MVOX | Thruster TST Mk 1 | |
| G-MVMG | Thruster TST Mk 1 | | G-MVOY | Thruster TST Mk 1 | |
| G-MVMI | Thruster TST Mk 1 | | G-MVPA | Mainair Gemini Flash IIA | |
| G-MVMJ | Thruster TST Mk 1 | | G-MVPB | Mainair Gemini Flash IIA | |
| G-MVMK | Medway Hybred 44XLR | | G-MVPC | Mainair Gemini Flash IIA | |
| G-MVML | Aerial Arts Chaser S | | G-MVPD | Mainair Gemini Flash IIA | |
| G-MVMM | Aerial Arts Chaser S | | G-MVPE | Mainair Gemini Flash IIA | |
| G-MVMN | Mainair Gemini Flash IIA | | G-MVPF | Medway Hybred 44XLR | |
| G-MVMO | Mainair Gemini Flash IIA | | G-MVPG | Medway Hybred 44XLR | |
| G-MVMP | Eipper Quicksilver MXII | | G-MVPH | Whittaker MW.6 Merlin | |
| G-MVMR | Mainair Gemini Flash IIA | | G-MVPI | Mainair Gemini Flash IIA | |
| G-MVMT | Mainair Gemini Flash IIA | | G-MVPJ | Rans S.5 | |
| G-MVMU | Mainair Gemini Flash IIA | | G-MVPK | CFM Shadow Srs B | |
| G-MVMV | Aerotech MW.5 (K) Sorcerer | | G-MVPL | Medway Hybred 44XLR | |
| | | | G-MVPM | Whittaker MW.6 Merlin | |
| G-MVMW | Mainair Gemini Flash IIA | | G-MVPN | Whittaker MW.6 Merlin | |

# G-MVPO – G-MVXW

**MICROLIGHTS**

| Reg. | Type | Notes | Reg | Type | Notes |
|---|---|---|---|---|---|
| G-MVPO | Mainair Gemini Flash IIA | | G-MVUF | Solar Wings Pegasus XL-Q | |
| G-MVPR | Solar Wings Pegasus XL-Q | | G-MVUG | Solar Wings Pegasus XL-Q | |
| G-MVPS | Solar Wings Pegasus XL-Q | | G-MVUH | Solar Wings Pegasus XL-Q | |
| G-MVPT | Solar Wings Pegasus XL-Q | | G-MVUI | Solar Wings Pegasus XL-Q | |
| G-MVPU | Solar Wings Pegasus XL-Q | | G-MVUJ | Solar Wings Pegasus XL-Q | |
| G-MVPV | Solar Wings Pegasus XL-Q | | G-MVUK | Solar Wings Pegasus XL-Q | |
| G-MVPW | Solar Wings Pegasus XL-R | | G-MVUL | Solar Wings Pegasus XL-Q | |
| G-MVPX | Solar Wings Pegasus XL-Q | | G-MVUM | Solar Wings Pegasus XL-Q | |
| G-MVPY | Solar Wings Pegasus XL-Q | | G-MVUN | Solar Wings Pegasus XL-Q | |
| G-MVPZ | Rans S.5 | | G-MVUO | AMF Chevvron 232 | |
| G-MVRA | Mainair Gemini Flash IIA | | G-MVUP | Aviasud Mistral | |
| G-MVRB | Mainair Gemini Flash IIA | | G-MVUR | Hornet ZA | |
| G-MVRC | Mainair Gemini Flash IIA | | G-MVUS | Aerial Arts Chaser S | |
| G-MVRD | Mainair Gemini Flash IIA | | G-MVUT | Aerial Arts Chaser S | |
| G-MVRE | CFM Shadow Srs BD | | G-MVUU | Hornet R-ZA | |
| G-MVRF | Rotec Rally 2B | | G-MVVG | Medway Hybred 44XLR | |
| G-MVRG | Aerial Arts Chaser S | | G-MVVG | Medway Hybred 44XLR | |
| G-MVRH | Solar Wings Pegasus XL-Q | | G-MVVH | Medway Hybred 44XLR | |
| G-MVRJ | Solar Wings Pegasus XL-Q | | G-MVVI | Medway Hybred 44XLR | |
| G-MVRK | Solar Wings Pegasus XL-Q | | G-MVVJ | Medway Hybred 44XLR | |
| G-MVRL | Aerial Arts Chaser S | | G-MVVK | Solar Wings Pegasus XL-R | |
| G-MVRM | Mainair Gemini Flash IIA | | G-MVVM | Solar Wings Pegasus XL-R | |
| G-MVRN | Rans S.4 Coyote | | G-MVVN | Solar Wings Pegasus XL-Q | |
| G-MVRO | CFM Shadow Srs BD | | G-MVVP | Solar Wings Pegasus XL-Q | |
| G-MVRP | CFM Shadow Srs BD | | G-MVVR | Medway Hybred 44XLR | |
| G-MVRR | CFM Shadow Srs BD | | G-MVVS | Southdown Puma Sprint | |
| G-MVRT | CFM Shadow Srs BD | | G-MVVT | CFM Shadow Srs BD | |
| G-MVRU | Solar Wings Pegasus XL-Q | | G-MVVU | Aerial Arts Chaser S | |
| G-MVRV | Powerchute Kestrel | | G-MVVV | AMF Chevvron 232 | |
| G-MVRW | Solar Wings Pegasus XL-Q | | G-MVVW | Aerial Arts Chaser S | |
| G-MVRX | Solar Wings Pegasus XL-Q | | G-MVVZ | Powerchute Raider | |
| G-MVRY | Medway Hybred 44XLR | | G-MVWA | Powerchute Raider | |
| G-MVRZ | Medway Hybred 44XLR | | G-MVWB | Powerchute Raider | |
| G-MVSA | Solar Wings Pegasus XL-Q | | G-MVWE | Powerchute Raider | |
| G-MVSB | Solar Wings Pegasus XL-Q | | G-MVWF | Powerchute Raider | |
| G-MVSC | Solar Wings Pegasus XL-Q | | G-MVWH | Powerchute Raider | |
| G-MVSD | Solar Wings Pegasus XL-Q | | G-MVWI | Powerchute Raider | |
| G-MVSE | Solar Wings Pegasus XL-Q | | G-MVWJ | Powerchute Raider | |
| G-MVSG | Aerial Arts Chaser S | | G-MVWK | Powerchute Raider | |
| G-MVSI | Medway Hybred 44XLR | | G-MVWL | Powerchute Raider | |
| G-MVSJ | Aviasud Mistral 532 | | G-MVWM | Powerchute Raider | |
| G-MVSK | Aerial Arts Chaser S | | G-MVWN | Thruster T.300 | |
| G-MVSL | Aerial Arts Chaser S | | G-MVWO | Thruster T.300 | |
| G-MVSM | Midland Ultralights Sirocco | | G-MVWP | Thruster T.300 | |
| G-MVSN | Mainair Gemini Flash IIA | | G-MVWR | Thruster T.300 | |
| G-MVSO | Mainair Gemini Flash IIA | | G-MVWS | Thruster T.300 | |
| G-MVSP | Mainair Gemini Flash IIA | | G-MVWU | Medway Hybred 44XLR | |
| G-MVSR | Medway Hybred 44XLR | | G-MVWV | Medway Hybred 44XLR | |
| G-MVSS | Hornet RS-ZA | | G-MVWW | Aviasud Mistral 532 | |
| G-MVST | Mainair Gemini Flash IIA | | G-MVWX | Microflight Spectrum | |
| G-MVSU | Microflight Spectrum | | G-MVWZ | Aviasud Mistral | |
| G-MVSV | Mainair Gemini Flash IIA | | G-MVXA | Whittaker MW.6 Merlin | |
| G-MVSW | Solar Wings Pegasus XL-Q | | G-MVXB | Mainair Gemini Flash IIA | |
| G-MVSX | Solar Wings Pegasus XL-Q | | G-MVXC | Mainair Gemini Flash IIA | |
| G-MVSY | Solar Wings Pegasus XL-Q | | G-MVXD | Medway Hybred 44XLR | |
| G-MVSZ | Solar Wings Pegasus XL-Q | | G-MVXE | Medway Hybred 44XLR | |
| G-MVTA | Solar Wings Pegasus XL-Q | | G-MVXF | Weedhopper JC-31A | |
| G-MVTC | Mainair Gemini Flash IIA | | G-MVXG | Aerial Arts Chaser S | |
| G-MVTD | Whittaker MW.6 Merlin | | G-MVXH | Microflight Spectrum | |
| G-MVTE | Whittaker MW.6 Merlin | | G-MVXI | Medway Hybred 44XLR | |
| G-MVTF | Aerial Arts Chaser S | | G-MVXJ | Medway Hybred 44XLR | |
| G-MVTG | Solar Wings Pegasus XL-Q | | G-MVXK | Medway Hybred 44XLR | |
| G-MVTI | Solar Wings Pegasus XL-Q | | G-MVXL | Thruster TST Mk 1 | |
| G-MVTJ | Solar Wings Pegasus XL-Q | | G-MVXM | Medway Hybred 44XLR | |
| G-MVTK | Solar Wings Pegasus XL-Q | | G-MVXN | Aviasud Mistral | |
| G-MVTL | Aerial Arts Chaser S | | G-MVXO | Aerial Arts Chaser S | |
| G-MVTM | Aerial Arts Chaser S | | G-MVXP | Aerial Arts Chaser S | |
| G-MVUA | Mainair Gemini Flash IIA | | G-MVXR | Mainair Gemini Flash IIA | |
| G-MVUB | Thruster T.300 | | G-MVXS | Mainair Gemini Flash IIA | |
| G-MVUC | Medway Hybred 44XLR | | G-MVXT | Mainair Gemini Flash IIA | |
| G-MVUD | Medway Hybred 44XLR | | G-MVXU | Aviasud Mistral | |
| G-MVUE | Solar Wings Pegasus XL-Q | | G-MVXV | Aviasud Mistral | |
| | | | G-MVXW | Rans S.4 Coyote | |

| Reg. | Type | Notes | Reg | Type | Notes |
|------|------|-------|-----|------|-------|
| G-MVXX | AMF Chevvron 232 | | G-MWAO | Thruster T.300 | |
| G-MVXY | AMF Paracat 1-24 | | G-MWAP | Thruster T.300 | |
| G-MVXZ | Minimax | | G-MWAR | Thruster T.300 | |
| G-MVYA | Aerial Arts Chaser S | | G-MWAS | Thruster T.300 | |
| G-MVYB | Solar Wings Pegasus XL-Q | | G-MWAT | Solar Wings Pegasus XL-Q | |
| G-MVYC | Solar Wings Pegasus XL-Q | | G-MWAU | Mainair Gemini Flash IIA | |
| G-MVYD | Solar Wings Pegasus XL-Q | | G-MWAV | Solar Wings Pegasus XL-R | |
| G-MVYE | Thruster TST Mk 1 | | G-MWAW | Whittaker MW.6 Merlin | |
| G-MVYG | Hornet R-ZA | | G-MWBH | Hornet RS-ZA | |
| G-MVYH | Hornet R-ZA | | G-MWBI | Medway Hybred 44XLR | |
| G-MVYI | Hornet R-ZA | | G-MWBJ | Medway Sprint | |
| G-MVYJ | Hornet R-ZA | | G-MWBK | Solar Wings Pegasus XL-Q | |
| G-MVYK | Hornet R-ZA | | G-MWBL | Solar Wings Pegasus XL-Q | |
| G-MVYM | Hornet R-ZA | | G-MWBM | Hornet RS-ZA | |
| G-MVYN | Hornet R-ZA | | G-MWBN | Hornet RS-ZA | |
| G-MVYO | Hornet R-ZA | | G-MWBO | Rans S.4 | |
| G-MVYP | Medway Hybred 44XLR | | G-MWBP | Hornet RS-ZA | |
| G-MVYR | Medway Hybred 44XLR | | G-MWBR | Hornet RS-ZA | |
| G-MVYS | Mainair Gemini Flash IIA | | G-MWBS | Hornet RS-ZA | |
| G-MVYT | Noble Hardman Snowbird Mk IV | | G-MWBU | Hornet RS-ZA | |
| | | | G-MWBV | Hornet RS-ZA | |
| G-MVYU | Noble Hardman Snowbird Mk IV | | G-MWBW | Hornet RS-ZA | |
| | | | G-MWBX | Hornet RS-ZA | |
| G-MVYV | Noble Hardman Snowbird Mk IV | | G-MWBY | Hornet RS-ZA | |
| | | | G-MWBZ | Hornet RS-ZA | |
| G-MVYW | Noble Hardman Snowbird Mk IV | | G-MWCA | Hornet RS-ZA | |
| | | | G-MWCB | Solar Wings Pegasus XL-Q | |
| G-MVYX | Noble Hardman Snowbird Mk IV | | G-MWCC | Solar Wings Pegasus XL-R | |
| | | | G-MWCE | Mainair Gemini Flash IIA | |
| G-MVYY | Aerial Arts Chaser S508 | | G-MWCF | Solar Wings Pegasus XL-R | |
| G-MVYZ | CFM Shadow Srs BD | | G-MWCG | Microflight Spectrum | |
| G-MVZA | Thruster T.300 | | G-MWCH | Rans S.6 | |
| G-MVZB | Thruster T.300 | | G-MWCI | Powerchute Kestrel | |
| G-MVZC | Thruster T.300 | | G-MWCJ | Powerchute Kestrel | |
| G-MVZD | Thruster T.300 | | G-MWCK | Powerchute Kestrel | |
| G-MVZE | Thruster T.300 | | G-MWCL | Powerchute Kestrel | |
| G-MVZF | Thruster T.300 | | G-MWCM | Powerchute Kestrel | |
| G-MVZG | Thruster T.300 | | G-MWCN | Powerchute Kestrel | |
| G-MVZH | Thruster T.300 | | G-MWCO | Powerchute Kestrel | |
| G-MVZI | Thruster T.300 | | G-MWCP | Powerchute Kestrel | |
| G-MVZJ | Solar Wings Pegasus XL-Q | | G-MWCR | Southdown Puma Sprint | |
| G-MVZK | Challenger II | | G-MWCS | Powerchute Kestrel | |
| G-MVZL | Solar Wings Pegasus XL-Q | | G-MWCU | Solar Wings Pegasus XL-R | |
| G-MVZM | Aerial Arts Chaser S | | G-MWCV | Solar Wings Pegasus XL-Q | |
| G-MVZN | Aerial Arts Chaser S | | G-MWCW | Mainair Gemini Flash IIA | |
| G-MVZO | Medway Hybred 44XLR | | G-MWCX | Medway Hybred 44XLR | |
| G-MVZP | Renegade Spirit UK | | G-MWCY | Medway Hybred 44XLR | |
| G-MVZR | Aviasud Mistral | | G-MWCZ | Medway Hybred 44XLR | |
| G-MVZS | Mainair Gemini Flash IIA | | G-MWDA | Jakeway Powered Parachute | |
| G-MVZT | Solar Wings Pegasus XL-Q | | G-MWDB | CFM Shadow Srs BD | |
| G-MVZU | Solar Wings Pegasus XL-Q | | G-MWDC | Solar Wings Pegasus XL-R | |
| G-MVZV | Solar Wings Pegasus XL-Q | | G-MWDD | Solar Wings Pegasus XL-Q | |
| G-MVZW | Hornet R-ZA | | G-MWDE | Hornet RS-ZA | |
| G-MVZX | Renegade Spirit UK | | G-MWDF | Hornet RS-ZA | |
| G-MVZY | Aerial Arts Chaser S | | G-MWDG | Hornet RS-ZA | |
| G-MVZZ | AMF Chevvron 232 | | G-MWDH | Hornet RS-ZA | |
| G-MWAA | Medway Hybred 44XLR | | G-MWDI | Hornet RS-ZA | |
| G-MWAB | Mainair Gemini Flash IIA | | G-MWDJ | Mainair Gemini Flash IIA | |
| G-MWAC | Solar Wings Pegasus XL-Q | | G-MWDK | Solar Wings Pegasus XL-R | |
| G-MWAD | Solar Wings Pegasus XL-Q | | G-MWDL | Solar Wings Pegasus XL-R | |
| G-MWAE | CFM Shadow Srs BD | | G-MWDM | Renegade Spirit UK | |
| G-MWAF | Solar Wings Pegasus XL-R | | G-MWDN | CFM Shadow Srs BD | |
| | | | G-MWDO | Spencer Cub | |
| G-MWAG | Solar Wings Pegasus XL-R | | G-MWDP | Thruster TST Mk 1 | |
| | | | G-MWDS | Thruster T.300 | |
| G-MWAH | Hornet RS-ZA | | G-MWDZ | Eipper Quicksilver MXL II | |
| G-MWAI | Solar Wings Pegasus XL-R | | G-MWEA | Mosler Motors N.3 Pup | |
| | | | G-MWEE | Solar Wings Pegasus XL-Q | |
| G-MWAJ | Renegade Spirit UK | | G-MWEF | Solar Wings Pegasus XL-Q | |
| G-MWAL | Solar Wings Pegasus XL-Q | | G-MWEG | Solar Wings Pegasus XL-Q | |
| | | | G-MWEH | Solar Wings Pegasus XL-Q | |
| G-MWAM | Thruster T.300 | | G-MWEI | Mainair Gemini Flash IIA | |
| G-MWAN | Thruster T.300 | | | | |

| Reg. | Type | Notes | Reg | Type | Notes |
|---|---|---|---|---|---|
| G-MWEK | Whittaker MW.5 Sorcerer | | G-MWHL | Solar Wings Pegasus XL-Q | |
| G-MWEL | Mainair Gemini Flash IIA | | G-MWHM | Whittaker MW.6 Merlin | |
| G-MWEM | Medway Hybred 44XLR | | G-MWHO | Mainair Gemini Flash IIA | |
| G-MWEN | CFM Shadow Srs BD | | G-MWHP | Rans S.6 | |
| G-MWEO | Whittaker MW.5 Sorcerer | | G-MWHR | Mainair Gemini Flash IIA | |
| G-MWEP | Rans S.4 | | G-MWHS | AMF Chevvron 232 | |
| G-MWER | Solar Wings Pegasus XL-Q | | G-MWHT | Solar Wings Pegasus Quasar | |
| G-MWES | Rans S.4 | | | | |
| G-MWET | Hornet RS-ZA | | G-MWHU | Solar Wings Pegasus Quasar | |
| G-MWEU | Hornet RS-ZA | | | | |
| G-MWEV | Hornet RS-ZA | | G-MWHV | Solar Wings Pegasus Quasar | |
| G-MWEY | Hornet RS-ZA | | | | |
| G-MWEZ | CFM Shadow Srs CD | | G-MWHW | Solar Wings Pegasus XL-Q | |
| G-MWFA | Solar Wings Pegasus XL-R | | G-MWHX | Solar Wings Pegasus XL-Q | |
| G-MWFB | CFM Shadow Srs BD | | G-MWHY | Mainair Gemini Flash IIA | |
| G-MWFD | Team Minimax | | G-MWHZ | Trion J-1 | |
| G-MWFE | Robin 330/Lightning 195 | | G-MWIA | Mainair Gemini Flash IIA | |
| G-MWFF | Rans S.4 | | G-MWIB | Aviasud Mistral | |
| G-MWFG | Powerchute Kestrel | | G-MWIC | Whittaker MW.5 Sorcerer | |
| G-MWFH | Powerchute Kestrel | | G-MWID | Solar Wings Pegasus XL-Q | |
| G-MWFI | Powerchute Kestrel | | G-MWIE | Solar Wings Pegasus XL-Q | |
| G-MWFK | Powerchute Kestrel | | G-MWIF | Rans S.6 | |
| G-MWFL | Powerchute Kestrel | | G-MWIG | Mainair Gemini Flash IIA | |
| G-MWFN | Powerchute Kestrel | | G-MWIH | Mainair Gemini Flash IIA | |
| G-MWFO | Solar Wings Pegasus XL-R | | G-MWII | Medway Hybred 44XLR | |
| G-MWFP | Solar Wings Pegasus XL-R | | G-MWIJ | Medway Hybred 44XLR | |
| G-MWFS | Solar Wings Pegasus XL-Q | | G-MWIK | Medway Hybred 44XLR | |
| G-MWFT | MBA Tiger Cub 440 | | G-MWIL | Medway Hybred 44XLR | |
| G-MWFU | Quad City Challenger II UK | | G-MWIM | Solar Wings Pegasus Quasar | |
| G-MWFV | Quad City Challenger II UK | | G-MWIN | Mainair Gemini Flash IIA | |
| | | | G-MWIO | Rans S.4 | |
| G-MWFW | Rans S.4 | | G-MWIP | Whittaker MW.6 Merlin | |
| G-MWFX | Quad City Challenger II UK | | G-MWIR | Solar Wings Pegasus XL-Q | |
| | | | G-MWIS | Solar Wings Pegasus XL-Q | |
| G-MWFY | Quad City Challenger II UK | | G-MWIT | Solar Wings Pegasus XL-Q | |
| | | | G-MWIU | Solar Wings Pegasus XL-Q | |
| G-MWFZ | Quad City Challenger II UK | | G-MWIV | Mainair Gemini Flash IIA | |
| | | | G-MWIW | Solar Wings Pegasus Quasar | |
| G-MWGA | Rans S.5 | | | | |
| G-MWGB | Medway Hybred 44XLR | | G-MWIX | Solar Wings Pegasus Quasar | |
| G-MWGC | Medway Hybred 44XLR | | | | |
| G-MWGD | Medway Hybred 44XLR | | G-MWIY | Solar Wings Pegasus Quasar | |
| G-MWGE | Medway Hybred 44XLR | | | | |
| G-MWGF | Renegade Spirit UK | | G-MWIZ | CFM Shadow Srs BD | |
| G-MWGG | Mainair Gemini Flash IIA | | G-MWJC | Solar Wings Pegasus Quasar | |
| G-MWGI | Whittaker MW.5 (K) Sorcerer | | | | |
| | | | G-MWJD | Solar Wings Pegasus Quasar | |
| G-MWGJ | Whittaker MW.5 (K) Sorcerer | | G-MWJF | CFM Shadow Srs BD | |
| | | | G-MWJG | Solar Wings Pegasus XL-R | |
| G-MWGK | Whittaker MW.5 (K) Sorcerer | | G-MWJH | Solar Wings Pegasus Quasar | |
| G-MWGL | Solar Wings Pegasus XL-Q | | | | |
| G-MWGM | Solar Wings Pegasus XL-Q | | G-MWJI | Solar Wings Pegasus Quasar | |
| G-MWGN | Rans S.4 | | | | |
| G-MWGO | Aerial Arts Chaser 110SX | | G-MWJJ | Solar Wings Pegasus Quasar | |
| G-MWGP | Renegade Spirit UK | | | | |
| G-MWGR | Solar Wings Pegasus XL-Q | | G-MWJK | Solar Wings Pegasus Quasar | |
| G-MWGT | Powerchute Kestrel | | | | |
| G-MWGU | Powerchute Kestrel | | G-MWJL | AMF Chevvron 232 | |
| G-MWGV | Powerchute Kestrel | | G-MWJM | AMF Chevvron 232 | |
| G-MWGW | Powerchute Kestrel | | G-MWJN | Solar Wings Pegasus XL-Q | |
| G-MWGY | Powerchute Kestrel | | G-MWJO | Solar Wings Pegasus XL-Q | |
| G-MWGZ | Powerchute Kestrel | | G-MWJP | Medway Hybred 44XLR | |
| G-MWHC | Solar Wings Pegasus XL-Q | | G-MWJR | Medway Hybred 44XLR | |
| G-MWHD | Microflight Spectrum | | G-MWJS | Solar Wings Pegasus Quasar | |
| G-MWHE | Microflight Spectrum | | | | |
| G-MWHF | Solar Wings Pegasus XL-Q | | G-MWJT | Solar Wings Pegasus Quasar | |
| G-MWHG | Solar Wings Pegasus XL-Q | | | | |
| G-MWHH | Team Minimax | | G-MWJU | Solar Wings Pegasus Quasar | |
| G-MWHI | Mainair Gemini Flash IIA | | | | |
| G-MWHJ | Solar Wings Pegasus XL-Q | | G-MWJV | Solar Wings Pegasus Quasar | |
| G-MWHK | Renegade Spirit UK | | | | |

| Reg. | Type | Notes |
|---|---|---|
| G-MWJW | Whittaker MW.5 Sorcerer | |
| G-MWJX | Medway Puma Sprint | |
| G-MWJY | Mainair Gemini Flash IIA | |
| G-MWJZ | CFM Shadow Srs CD | |
| G-MWKA | Renegade Spirit UK | |
| G-MWKE | Hornet R-ZA | |
| G-MWKO | Solar Wings Pegasus XL-Q | |
| G-MWKP | Solar Wings Pegasus XL-Q | |
| G-MWKW | Microflight Spectrum | |
| G-MWKX | Microflight Spectrum | |
| G-MWKY | Solar Wings Pegasus XL-Q | |
| G-MWKZ | Solar Wings Pegasus XL-Q | |
| G-MWLA | Rans S.4 | |
| G-MWLB | Medway Hybred 44XLR | |
| G-MWLC | Medway Hybred 44XLR | |
| G-MWLD | CFM Shadow Srs BD | |
| G-MWLE | Solar Wings Pegasus XL-R | |
| G-MWLF | Solar Wings Pegasus XL-R | |
| G-MWLG | Solar Wings Pegasus XL-R | |
| G-MWLH | Solar Wings Pegasus XL-R | |
| G-MWLI | Solar Wings Pegasus Quasar | |
| G-MWLJ | Solar Wings Pegasus Quasar | |
| G-MWLK | Solar Wings Pegasus Quasar | |
| G-MWLL | Solar Wings Pegasus XL-Q | |
| G-MWLM | Solar Wings Pegasus XL-Q | |
| G-MWLN | Whittaker MW.6-S Fatboy Flyer | |
| G-MWLO | Whittaker MW.6 Merlin | |
| G-MWLP | Mainair Gemini Flash IIA | |
| G-MWLR | Mainair Gemini Flash IIA | |
| G-MWLS | Medway Hybred 44XLR | |
| G-MWLT | Mainair Gemini Flash IIA | |
| G-MWLU | Solar Wings Pegasus XL-R | |
| G-MWLW | Team Minimax | |
| G-MWLX | Mainair Gemini Flash IIA | |
| G-MWLY | Rans S.4 | |
| G-MWLZ | Rans S.4 | |
| G-MWMA | Powerchute Kestrel | |
| G-MWMB | Powerchute Kestrel | |
| G-MWMC | Powerchute Kestrel | |
| G-MWMD | Powerchute Kestrel | |
| G-MWME | Powerchute Kestrel | |
| G-MWMF | Powerchute Kestrel | |
| G-MWMG | Powerchute Kestrel | |
| G-MWMH | Powerchute Kestrel | |
| G-MWMI | Solar Wings Pegasus Quasar | |
| G-MWMJ | Solar Wings Pegasus Quasar | |
| G-MWMK | Solar Wings Pegasus Quasar | |
| G-MWML | Solar Wings Pegasus Quasar | |
| G-MWMM | Mainair Gemini Flash IIA | |
| G-MWMN | Solar Wings Pegasus XL-Q | |
| G-MWMO | Solar Wings Pegasus XL-Q | |
| G-MWMP | Solar Wings Pegasus XL-Q | |
| G-MWMR | Solar Wings Pegasus XL-R | |
| G-MWMS | Mainair Gemini Flash | |
| G-MWMT | Mainair Gemini Flash IIA | |
| G-MWMU | CFM Shadow Srs CD | |
| G-MWMV | Solar Wings Pegasus XL-R | |
| G-MWMW | Renegade Spirit UK | |
| G-MWMX | Mainair Gemini Flash IIA | |
| G-MWMY | Mainair Gemini Flash IIA | |
| G-MWMZ | Solar Wings Pegasus XL-Q | |
| G-MWNA | Solar Wings Pegasus XL-Q | |

| Reg | Type | Notes |
|---|---|---|
| G-MWNB | Solar Wings Pegasus XL-Q | |
| G-MWNC | Solar Wings Pegasus XL-Q | |
| G-MWND | Tiger Cub Developments RL.5A | |
| G-MWNE | Mainair Gemini Flash IIA | |
| G-MWNF | Renegade Spirit UK | |
| G-MWNG | Solar Wings Pegasus XL-Q | |
| G-MWNH | Powerchute Mk III | |
| G-MWNK | Solar Wings Pegasus Quasar | |
| G-MWNL | Solar Wings Pegasus Quasar | |
| G-MWNM | Solar Wings Pegasus Quasar | |
| G-MWNN | Solar Wings Pegasus Quasar | |
| G-MWNO | AMF Chevvron 232 | |
| G-MWNP | AMF Chevvron 232 | |
| G-MWNR | Renegade Spirit UK | |
| G-MWNS | Mainair Gemini Flash IIA | |
| G-MWNT | Mainair Gemini Flash IIA | |
| G-MWNU | Mainair Gemini Flash IIA | |
| G-MWNV | Powerchute Kestrel | |
| G-MWNW | Powerchute Kestrel | |
| G-MWNX | Powerchute Kestrel | |
| G-MWNY | Powerchute Kestrel | |
| G-MWNZ | Powerchute Kestrel | |
| G-MWOA | Powerchute Kestrel | |
| G-MWOB | Powerchute Kestrel | |
| G-MWOC | Powerchute Kestrel | |
| G-MWOD | Powerchute Kestrel | |
| G-MWOE | Powerchute Kestrel | |
| G-MWOF | Microflight Spectrum | |
| G-MWOH | Solar Wings Pegasus XL-R | |
| G-MWOI | Solar Wings Pegasus XL-R | |
| G-MWOJ | Mainair Gemini Flash IIA | |
| G-MWOK | Mainair Gemini Flash IIA | |
| G-MWOL | Mainair Gemini Flash IIA | |
| G-MWOM | Solar Wings Pegasus Quasar TC | |
| G-MWON | CFM Shadow Srs CD | |
| G-MWOO | Renegade Spirit UK | |
| G-MWOP | Solar Wings Pegasus Quasar | |
| G-MWOR | Solar Wings Pegasus XL-Q | |
| G-MWOS | Cosmos Chronos | |
| G-MWOT | Icarus Covert Insertion & Recovery Vehicle | |
| G-MWOU | Medway Hybred 44XLR | |
| G-MWOV | Whittaker MW.6 Merlin | |
| G-MWOW | CFM Shadow Srs B | |
| G-MWOX | Solar Wings Pegasus XL-Q | |
| G-MWOY | Solar Wings Pegasus XL-Q | |
| G-MWPA | Mainair Gemini Flash IIA | |
| G-MWPB | Mainair Gemini Flash IIA | |
| G-MWPC | Mainair Gemini Flash IIA | |
| G-MWPD | Mainair Gemini Flash IIA | |
| G-MWPE | Solar Wings Pegasus XL-Q | |
| G-MWPF | Mainair Gemini Flash IIA | |
| G-MWPG | Microflight Spectrum | |
| G-MWPH | Microflight Spectrum | |
| G-MWPI | Microflight Spectrum | |
| G-MWPJ | Solar Wings Pegasus XL-Q | |
| G-MWPK | Solar Wings Pegasus XL-Q | |
| G-MWPL | MBA Tiger Cub 440 | |
| G-MWPM | Medway Flaven | |
| G-MWPN | CFM Shadow Srs CD | |
| G-MWPO | Mainair Gemini Flash IIA | |
| G-MWPP | CFM Streak Shadow (G-BTEM) | |
| G-MWPR | Whittaker MW.6 Merlin | |
| G-MWPS | Renegade Spirit UK | |
| G-MWPT | Hunt Avon Trike | |

| Reg. | Type | Notes | Reg | Type | Notes |
|------|------|-------|-----|------|-------|
| G-MWPU | Solar Wings Pegasus Quasar TC | | G-MWTP | CFM Shadow Srs CD | |
| | | | G-MWTR | Mainair Gemini Flash IIA | |
| G-MWPX | Solar Wings Pegasus XL-R | | G-MWTS | Whittaker MW.6-S Fatboy Flyer | |
| G-MWPZ | Renegade Spirit UK | | | | |
| G-MWRA | Mainair Gemini Flash IIA | | G-MWTT | Rans S.6-ESD Coyote II | |
| G-MWRB | Mainair Gemini Flash IIA | | G-MWTU | Solar Wings Pegasus XL-R | |
| G-MWRC | Mainair Gemini Flash IIA | | G-MWTV | Solar Wings Pegasus XL-R | |
| G-MWRD | Mainair Gemini Flash IIA | | G-MWTW | Whittaker MW.6 Merlin | |
| G-MWRE | Mainair Gemini Flash IIA | | G-MWTX | Medway Hybred 44XLR | |
| G-MWRF | Mainair Gemini Flash IIA | | G-MWTY | Mainair Gemini Flash IIA | |
| G-MWRG | Mainair Gemini Flash IIA | | G-MWTZ | Mainair Gemini Flash IIA | |
| G-MWRH | Mainair Gemini Flash IIA | | G-MWUA | CFM Shadow Srs CD | |
| G-MWRI | Mainair Gemini Flash IIA | | G-MWUB | Solar Wings Pegasus XL-R | |
| G-MWRJ | Mainair Gemini Flash IIA | | G-MWUC | Solar Wings Pegasus XL-R | |
| G-MWRK | Rans S.6 | | G-MWUD | Solar Wings Pegasus XL-R | |
| G-MWRL | CFM Shadow Srs CD | | G-MWUF | Solar Wings Pegasus XL-R | |
| G-MWRM | Medway Hybred 44XLR | | G-MWUG | Solar Wings Pegasus XL-R | |
| G-MWRN | Solar Wings Pegasus XL-R | | G-MWUH | Renegade Spirit UK | |
| G-MWRO | Solar Wings Pegasus XL-R | | G-MWUI | AMF Chevvron 232C | |
| G-MWRP | Solar Wings Pegasus XL-R | | G-MMUJ | Medway Hybred 44XLR | |
| G-MWRR | Mainair Gemini Flash IIA | | G-MWUK | Rans S.6-ESD Coyote II | |
| G-MWRS | Ultravia Super Pelican | | G-MWUL | Rans S.6-ESD Coyote II | |
| G-MWRT | Solar Wings Pegasus XL-R | | G-MWUM | Rans S.6-ESD Coyote II | |
| G-MWRU | Solar Wings Pegasus XL-R | | G-MWUN | Rans S.6-ESD Coyote II | |
| G-MWRV | Solar Wings Pegasus XL-R | | G-MWUO | Solar Wings Pegasus XL-R | |
| G-MWRW | Solar Wings Pegasus XL-Q | | G-MWUP | Solar Wings Pegasus XL-R | |
| G-MWRX | Solar Wings Pegasus XL-Q | | G-MWUR | Solar Wings Pegasus XL-R | |
| G-MWRY | CFM Shadow Srs CD | | G-MWUS | Solar Wings Pegasus XL-R | |
| G-MWRZ | AMF Chevvron 232 | | G-MWUT | Solar Wings Pegasus XL-R | |
| G-MWSA | Team Minimax | | G-MWUU | Solar Wings Pegasus XL-R | |
| G-MWSB | Mainair Gemini Flash IIA | | G-MWUV | Solar Wings Pegasus XL-R | |
| G-MWSC | Rans S.6-ESD Coyote II | | G-MWUW | Solar Wings Pegasus XL-R | |
| G-MWSD | Solar Wings Pegasus XL-Q | | G-MWUX | Solar Wings Pegasus XL-Q | |
| G-MWSE | Solar Wings Pegasus XL-R | | G-MWUY | Solar Wings Pegasus XL-R | |
| G-MWSF | Solar Wings Pegasus XL-R | | G-MWUZ | Solar Wings Pegasus XL-Q | |
| G-MWSG | Solar Wings Pegasus XL-R | | G-MWVA | Solar Wings Pegasus XL-Q | |
| G-MWSH | Solar Wings Pegasus Quasar TC | | G-MWVB | Solar Wings Pegasus XL-R | |
| | | | G-MWVE | Solar Wings Pegasus XL-R | |
| G-MWSI | Solar Wings Pegasus Quasar TC | | G-MWVF | Solar Wings Pegasus XL-R | |
| | | | G-MWVG | CFM Shadow Srs CD | |
| G-MWSJ | Solar Wings Pegasus XL-Q | | G-MWVH | CFM Shadow Srs CD | |
| G-MWSK | Solar Wings Pegasus XL-Q | | G-MWVI | Whittaker MW.6 Merlin | |
| G-MWSL | Mainair Gemini Flash IIA | | G-MWVJ | Mainair Mercury | |
| G-MWSM | Mainair Gemini Flash IIA | | G-MWVK | Mainair Mercury | |
| G-MWSN | Solar Wings Pegasus Quasar TC | | G-MWVL | Rans S.6-ESD Coyote II | |
| | | | G-MWVM | Solar Wings Pegasus Quasar II | |
| G-MWSO | Solar Wings Pegasus XL-R | | | | |
| G-MWSP | Solar Wings Pegasus XL-R | | G-MWVN | Mainair Gemini Flash IIA | |
| G-MWSR | Solar Wings Pegasus XL-R | | G-MWVO | Mainair Gemini Flash IIA | |
| G-MWSS | Medway Hybred 44XLR | | G-MWVP | Renegade Spirit UK | |
| G-MWST | Medway Hybred 44XLR | | G-MWVR | Mainair Gemini Flash IIA | |
| G-MWSU | Medway Hybred 44XLR | | G-MWVS | Mainair Gemini Flash IIA | |
| G-MWSV | Solar Wings Pegasus Quasar TC | | G-MWVT | Mainair Gemini Flash IIA | |
| | | | G-MWVU | Medway Hybred 44XLR | |
| G-MWSW | Whittaker MW.6 Merlin | | G-MWVV | Solar Wings Pegasus XL-Q | |
| G-MWSX | Whittaker MW.5 Sorcerer | | G-MWVW | Mainair Gemini Flash IIA | |
| G-MWSY | Whittaker MW.5 Sorcerer | | G-MWVX | Quad City Challenger II UK | |
| G-MWSZ | CFM Shadow Srs CD | | G-MWVY | Mainair Gemini Flash IIA | |
| G-MWTA | Solar Wings Pegasus XL-Q | | G-MWVZ | Mainair Gemini Flash IIA | |
| G-MWTB | Solar Wings Pegasus XL-Q | | G-MWWA | Solar Wings Pegasus Quasar II | |
| G-MWTC | Solar Wings Pegasus XL-Q | | | | |
| G-MWTD | Spectrum | | G-MWWB | Mainair Gemini Flash IIA | |
| G-MWTE | Spectrum | | G-MWWC | Mainair Gemini Flash IIA | |
| G-MWTF | Mainair Gemini | | G-MWWD | Mainair Gemini Flash IIA | |
| G-MWTG | Mainair Gemini Flash IIA | | G-MWWE | Team Minimax | |
| G-MWTH | Mainair Gemini Flash IIA | | G-MWWF | Kolb Twinstar Mk 3 | |
| G-MWTI | Solar Wings Pegasus XL-Q | | G-MWWG | Solar Wings Pegasus XL-Q | |
| G-MWTJ | CFM Shadow Srs CD | | G-MWWH | Solar Wings Pegasus XL-Q | |
| G-MWTK | Solar Wings Pegasus XL-R | | G-MWWI | Mainair Gemini Flash IIA | |
| G-MWTL | Solar Wings Pegasus XL-R | | G-MWWJ | Mainair Gemini Flash IIA | |
| G-MWTM | Solar Wings Pegasus XL-R | | G-MWWK | Mainair Gemini Flash IIA | |
| G-MWTN | CFM Shadow Srs CD | | G-MWWL | Rans S.6-ESD Coyote II | |
| G-MWTO | Mainair Gemini Flash IIA | | G-MWWM | Kolb Twinstar Mk 2 | |

| Reg. | Type | Notes |
|---|---|---|
| G-MWWN | Mainair Gemini Flash IIA | |
| G-MWWO | Solar Wings Pegasus XL-R | |
| G-MWWP | Rans S.4 | |
| G-MWWR | Spectrum | |
| G-MWWS | Thruster T.300 | |
| G-MWWT | Thruster Super T.300 | |
| G-MWWU | Air Creation Fun 18 GTBI | |
| G-MWWV | Solar Wings Pegasus XL-Q | |
| G-MWWW | Whittaker MW.6-S Fatboy Flyer | |
| G-MWWX | Spectrum | |
| G-MWWY | Spectrum | |
| G-MWWZ | Cyclone Chaser S | |
| G-MWXA | Mainair Gemini Flash IIA | |
| G-MWXB | Mainair Gemini Flash IIA | |
| G-MWXC | Mainair Gemini Flash IIA | |
| G-MWXD | Mainair Gemini Flash IIA | |
| G-MWXE | Flexiform Skytrike | |
| G-MWXF | Mainair Mercury | |
| G-MWXG | Solar Wings Pegasus Quasar IITC | |
| G-MWXH | Solar Wings Pegasus Quasar IITC | |
| G-MWXI | Solar Wings Pegasus Quasar IITC | |
| G-MWXJ | Mainair Mercury | |
| G-MWXK | Mainair Mercury | |
| G-MWXL | Mainair Gemini Flash IIA | |
| G-MWXN | Mainair Gemini Flash IIA | |
| G-MWXO | Mainair Gemini Flash IIA | |
| G-MWXP | Solar Wings Pegasus XL-Q | |
| G-MWXR | Solar Wings Pegasus XL-Q | |
| G-MWXS | Mainair Gemini Flash IIA | |
| G-MWXU | Mainair Gemini Flash IIA | |
| G-MWXV | Mainair Gemini Flash IIA | |
| G-MWXW | Cyclone Chaser S | |
| G-MWXX | Cyclone Chaser S 447 | |
| G-MWXY | Cyclone Chaser S 447 | |
| G-MWXZ | Cyclone Chaser S 508 | |
| G-MWYA | Mainair Gemini Flash IIA | |
| G-MWYB | Solar Wings Pegasus XL-Q | |
| G-MWYC | Solar Wings Pegasus XL-Q | |
| G-MWYD | CFM Shadow Srs C | |
| G-MWYE | Rans S.6-ESD Coyote II | |
| G-MWYF | Rans S.6 | |
| G-MWYG | Mainair Gemini Flash IIA | |
| G-MWYH | Mainair Gemini Flash IIA | |
| G-MWYI | Solar Wings Pegasus Quasar II | |
| G-MWYJ | Solar Wings Pegasus Quasar IITC | |
| G-MWYK | Mainair Gemini Flash IIA | |
| G-MWYL | Mainair Gemini Flash IIA | |
| G-MWYM | Cyclone Chaser S 1000 | |
| G-MWYN | Rans S.6-ESD Coyote II | |
| G-MWYO | CGS Hawk II Arrow | |
| G-MWYP | CGS Hawk I Arrow | |
| G-MWYR | CGS Hawk AG Arrow | |
| G-MWYS | — | |
| G-WMYT | Mainair Gemini Flash IIA | |
| G-MWYU | Solar Wings Pegasus XL-Q | |
| G-WMYV | Mainair Gemini Flash IIA | |
| G-MWYW | Mainair Gemini Flash IIA | |
| G-MWYX | Mainair Gemini Flash IIA | |
| G-MWYY | Mainair Gemini Flash IIA | |
| G-MWYZ | Solar Wings Pegasus XL-Q | |
| G-WMZA | Mainair Mercury | |
| G-MWZB | AMF Chevvron 2-32C | |
| G-MWZC | Mainair Gemini Flash IIA | |
| G-WMZD | Solar Wings Pegasus Quasar IITC | |
| G-MWZE | Solar Wings Pegasus Quasar IITC | |
| G-MWZF | Solar Wings Pegasus Quasar IITC | |
| G-MWZG | Mainair Gemini Flash IIA | |
| G-MWZH | Solar Wings Pegasus XL-R | |
| G-MWZI | Solar Wings Pegasus XL-R | |
| G-MWZJ | Solar Wings Pegasus XL-R | |
| G-MWZK | Solar Wings Pegasus XL-R | |
| G-MWZL | Mainair Gemini Flash IIA | |
| G-MWZN | Mainair Gemini Flash IIA | |
| G-MWZO | Solar Wings Pegasus Quasar IITC | |
| G-MWZP | Solar Wings Pegasus Quasar IITC | |
| G-MWZR | Solar Wings Pegasus Quasar IITC | |
| G-MWZS | Solar Wings Pegasus Quasar IITC | |
| G-MWZT | Solar Wings Pegasus XL-R | |
| G-MWZU | Solar Wings Pegasus XL-R | |
| G-MWZV | Solar Wings Pegasus XL-R | |
| G-MWZW | Solar Wings Pegasus XL-R | |
| G-MWZX | Solar Wings Pegasus XL-R | |
| G-MWZY | Solar Wings Pegasus XL-R | |
| G-MWZZ | Solar Wings Pegasus XL-R | |
| G-MYAA | CFM Shadow Srs CD | |
| G-MYAB | Solar Wings Pegasus XL-R | |
| G-MYAC | Solar Wings Pegasus XL-Q | |
| G-MYAD | Solar Wings Pegasus XL-Q | |
| G-MYAE | Solar Wings Pegasus XL-Q | |
| G-MYAF | Solar Wings Pegasus XL-Q | |
| G-MYAG | Quad City Challenger II | |
| G-MYAH | Whittaker MW.5 Sorcerer | |
| G-MYAI | Mainair Mercury | |
| G-MYAJ | Rans S.6-ESD Coyote II | |
| G-MYAK | Solar Wings Pegasus Quasar IITC | |
| G-MYAL | Rotec Rally 2B | |
| G-MYAM | Renegade Spirit UK | |
| G-MYAN | Whittaker MW.5 (K) Sorcerer | |
| G-MYAO | Mainair Gemini Flash IIA | |
| G-MYAP | Thruster T.300 | |
| G-MYAR | Thruster T.300 | |
| G-MYAS | Mainair Gemini Flash IIA | |
| G-MYAT | Team Minimax | |
| G-MYAU | Mainair Gemini Flash IIA | |
| G-MYAV | Mainair Mercury | |
| G-MYAW | Team Minimax | |
| G-MYAX | Mainair Gemini Flash IIA | |
| G-MYAY | Spectrum | |
| G-MYAZ | Renegade Spirit UK | |
| G-MYBA | Rans S.6-ESD Coyote II | |
| G-MYBB | Drifter | |
| G-MYBC | CFM Shadow Srs CD | |
| G-MYBD | Solar Wings Pegasus Quaser IITC | |
| G-MYBE | Solar Wings Pegasus Quaser IITC | |
| G-MYBF | Solar Wings Pegasus XL-Q | |
| G-MYBG | Solar Wings Pegasus XL-Q | |
| G-MYBH | Quicksilver GT500 | |
| G-MYBI | Rans S.6-ESD Coyote II | |
| G-MYBJ | Mainair Gemini Flash IIA | |
| G-MYBK | Solar Wings Pegasus Quasar IITC | |
| G-MYBL | CFM Shadow Srs C | |
| G-MYBM | Team Minimax | |
| G-MYBN | Hiway Demon 175 | |
| G-MYBO | Solar Wings Pegasus XL-R | |
| G-MYBP | Solar Wings Pegasus XL-R | |
| G-MYBR | Solar Wings Pegasus XL-Q | |
| G-MYBS | Solar Wings Pegasus XL-Q | |
| G-MYBT | Solar Wings Pegasus | |

| Reg. | Type | Notes | Reg | Type | Notes |
|------|------|-------|-----|------|-------|
| | Quasar IITC | | G-MYEL | Solar Wings Pegasus | |
| G-MYBU | Cyclone Chaser S447 | | | Quasar IITC | |
| G-MYBV | Solar Wings Pegasus XL-Q | | G-MYEM | Solar Wings Pegasus | |
| G-MYBW | Solar Wings Pegasus XL-Q | | | Quasar IITC | |
| G-MYBX | Solar Wings Pegasus XL-Q | | G-MYEN | Solar Wings Pegasus | |
| G-MYBY | Solar Wings Pegasus XL-Q | | | Quasar IITC | |
| G-MYBZ | Solar Wings Pegasus XL-Q | | G-MYEO | Solar Wings Pegasus | |
| G-MYCA | Whittaker MW.6 Merlin | | | Quasar IITC | |
| G-MYCB | Cyclone Chaser S 447 | | G-MYEP | CFM Shadow Srs CD | |
| G-MYCC | Renegade Spirit UK | | G-MYER | Cyclone AX3/503 | |
| G-MYCD | CFM Shadow Srs CD | | G-MYES | Rans S.6-ESD Coyote II | |
| G-MYCE | Solar Wings Pegasus | | G-MYET | Whittaker MW.6 Merlin | |
| | Quasar IITC | | G-MYEU | Mainair Gemini Flash IIA | |
| G-MYCF | Solar Wings Pegasus | | G-MYEV | Whittaker MW.6 Merlin | |
| | Quasar IITC | | G-MYEW | Powerchute Kestrel | |
| G-MYCG | Solar Wings Pegasus | | G-MYEX | Powerchute Kestrel | |
| | Quasar IITC | | G-MYEY | Powerchute Kestrel | |
| G-MYCH | Solar Wings Pegasus XL-R | | G-MYEZ | Powerchute Kestrel | |
| G-MYCI | Solar Wings Pegasus XL-R | | G-MYFA | Powerchute Kestrel | |
| G-MYCJ | Mainair Mercury | | G-MYFB | Powerchute Kestrel | |
| G-MYCK | Mainair Gemini Flash IIA | | G-MYFC | Powerchute Kestrel | |
| G-MYCL | Mainair Mercury | | G-MYFD | Powerchute Kestrel | |
| G-MYCM | CFM Shadow Srs CD | | G-MYFE | Rans S.6-ESD Coyote II | |
| G-MYCN | Mainair Mercury | | G-MYFF | – | |
| G-MYCO | Whittaker MW.6 Merlin | | G-MYFG | Hunt Avon Skytrike | |
| G-MYCP | Whittaker MW.6 Merlin | | G-MYFH | Quad City Challenger II | |
| G-MYCR | Mainair Gemini Flash IIA | | G-MYFI | Cyclone AX3/503 | |
| G-MYCS | Mainair Gemini Flash IIA | | G-MYFJ | Solar Wings Pegasus | |
| G-MYCT | Team Minimax | | | Quasar IITC | |
| G-MYCU | Whittaker MW.6 Merlin | | G-MYFK | Solar Wings Pegasus | |
| G-MYCV | Mainair Mercury | | | Quasar IITC | |
| G-MYCW | Powerchute Kestrel | | G-MYFL | Solar Wings Pegasus | |
| G-MYCX | Powerchute Kestrel | | | Quasar IITC | |
| G-MYCY | Powerchute Kestrel | | G-MYFM | Renegade Spirit UK | |
| G-MYCZ | Powerchute Kestrel | | G-MYFN | Rans S.5 | |
| G-MYDA | Powerchute Kestrel | | G-MYFO | Cyclone Chaser S | |
| G-MYDB | Powerchute Kestrel | | G-MYFP | Mainair Gemini Flash IIA | |
| G-MYDC | Mainair Mercury | | G-MYFR | Mainair Gemini Flash IIA | |
| G-MYDD | CFM Shadow Srs CD | | G-MYFS | Solar Wings Pegasus XL-R | |
| G-MYDE | CFM Shadow Srs CD | | G-MYFT | Mainair Scorcher | |
| G-MYDF | Team Minimax | | G-MYFU | Mainair Gemini Flash IIA | |
| G-MYDG | Solar Wings Pegasus XL-R | | G-MYFV | Cyclone AX3/503 | |
| G-MYDH | Solar Wings Pegasus XL-R | | G-MYFW | Cyclone AX3/503 | |
| G-MYDI | Solar Wings Pegasus XL-R | | G-MYFX | – | |
| G-MYDJ | Solar Wings Pegasus XL-R | | G-MYFY | Cyclone AX3/503 | |
| G-MYDK | Rans S.6-ESD Coyote II | | G-MYFZ | Cyclone AX3/503 | |
| G-MYDL | Whittaker MW.5 (K) | | G-MYGA | Solar Wings Pegasus XL-R | |
| | Sorcerer | | G-MYGB | Solar Wings Pegasus XL-R | |
| G-MYDM | Whittaker MW.6-S Fatboy | | G-MYGC | Solar Wings Pegasus XL-R | |
| | Flyer | | G-MYGD | Cyclone AX3/503 | |
| G-MYDN | Quad City Challenger II | | G-MYGE | Whittaker MW.6 Merlin | |
| G-MYDO | Rans S.5 | | G-MYGF | Team Minimax | |
| G-MYDP | Kolb Twinstar Mk 3 | | G-MYGG | Mainair Mercury | |
| G-MYDR | Thruster T.300 | | G-MYGH | Rans S.6-ESD Coyote II | |
| G-MYDS | Quad City Challenger II | | G-MYGI | Cyclone Chaser S447 | |
| G-MYDT | Thruster T.300 | | G-MYGJ | Mainair Mercury | |
| G-MYDU | Thruster T.300 | | G-MYGK | Cyclone Chaser S508 | |
| G-MYDV | Thruster T.300 | | G-MYGL | Team Minimax | |
| G-MYDW | Whittaker MW.6 Merlin | | G-MYGM | Quad City Challenger II | |
| G-MYDX | Rans S.6-ESD Coyote II | | G-MYGN | AMF Chevvron 240 | |
| G-MYDZ | Mignet HM.1000 Balerit | | G-MYGO | CFM Shadow Srs CD | |
| G-MYEA | Solar Wings Pegasus XL-Q | | G-MYGP | Rans S.6-ESD Coyote II | |
| G-MYEB | Solar Wings Pegasus XL-Q | | G-MYGR | Rans S.6-ESD Coyote II | |
| G-MYEC | Solar Wings Pegasus XL-Q | | G-MYGS | Whittaker MW.5 (K) | |
| G-MYED | Solar Wings Pegasus XL-R | | | Sorcerer | |
| G-MYEE | Thruster TST Mk 1 | | G-MYGT | Solar Wings Pegasus XL-R | |
| G-MYEF | – | | G-MYGU | Solar Wings Pegasus XL-R | |
| G-MYEG | Solar Wings Pegasus XL-R | | G-MYGV | Solar Wings Pegasus XL-R | |
| G-MYEH | Solar Wings Pegasus XL-R | | G-MYGW | Solar Wings Pegasus XL-Q | |
| G-MYEI | Cyclone Chaser S447 | | G-MYGX | Solar Wings Pegasus XL-Q | |
| G-MYEJ | Cyclone Chaser S447 | | G-MYGY | Solar Wings Pegasus XL-Q | |
| G-MYEK | Solar Wings Pegasus | | G-MYGZ | Mainair Gemini Flash IIA | |
| | Quaser IITC | | G-MYHA | Solar Wings Pegasus XL-R | |

| Reg. | Type | Notes | Reg | Type | Notes |
|---|---|---|---|---|---|
| G-MYHB | Solar Wings Pegasus XL-R | | | | |
| G-MYHC | Solar Wings Pegasus XL-R | | | | |
| G-MYHD | Solar Wings Pegasus XL-R | | | | |
| G-MYHE | Solar Wings Pegasus XL-R | | | | |
| G-MYHF | Mainair Gemini Flash IIA | | | | |
| G-MYHG | Cyclone AX/503 | | | | |
| G-MYHH | Cyclone AX/503 | | | | |
| G-MYHI | Rans S.6-ESD Coyote II | | | | |
| G-MYHJ | Cyclone AX3/503 | | | | |
| G-MYHK | Rans S.6-ESD Coyote II | | | | |
| G-MYHL | Mainair Gemini Flash IIA | | | | |
| G-MYHM | Cyclone AX3/503 | | | | |
| G-MYHN | Mainair Gemini Flash IIA | | | | |
| G-MYHP | Rans S.6-ESD Coyote II | | | | |
| G-MYHR | Cyclone AX3/503 | | | | |
| G-MYHS | Powerchute Kestrel | | | | |
| G-MYHT | Powerchute Kestrel | | | | |
| G-MYHU | Powerchute Kestrel | | | | |
| G-MYHV | Powerchute Kestrel | | | | |
| G-MYHW | Powerchute Kestrel | | | | |
| G-MYHY | Powerchute Kestrel | | | | |
| G-MYHX | Mainair Gemini Flash IIA | | | | |
| G-MYHZ | Powerchute Kestrel | | | | |
| G-MYIA | Quad City Challenger II | | | | |
| G-MYIB | Powerchute Kestrel | | | | |
| G-MYIC | Powerchute Kestrel | | | | |
| G-MYID | Powerchute Kestrel | | | | |
| G-MYIE | Whittaker MW.6 Merlin | | | | |
| G-MYIF | — | | | | |
| G-MYIG | — | | | | |
| G-MYIH | — | | | | |
| G-MYII | Team Minimax | | | | |
| G-MYIJ | — | | | | |
| G-MYIK | Kolb Twinstar Mk 3 | | | | |
| G-MYIL | — | | | | |
| G-MYIM | — | | | | |
| G-MYIN | — | | | | |
| G-MYIO | — | | | | |
| G-MYIP | — | | | | |
| G-MYIR | — | | | | |
| G-MYIT | — | | | | |
| G-MYIS | Rans S.6-ESD Coyote II | | | | |
| G-MYIU | — | | | | |
| G-MYIV | — | | | | |
| G-MYIW | — | | | | |
| G-MYIX | Quad City Challenger II | | | | |
| G-MYIY | — | | | | |
| G-MYIZ | — | | | | |
| G-MYJE | CFM Shadow Srs CD | | | | |
| G-MYJP | Renegade Spirit UK | | | | |
| G-MYKE | CFM Shadow Srs BD | | | | |
| G-MYNA | CFM Shadow Srs BD | | | | |
| G-MYND | Mainair Gemini Flash IIA | | | | |
| G-MYNX | CFM Streak Shadow Srs S-AI | | | | |
| G-MYOO | Kolb Twinstar Mk 3 | | | | |
| G-MYPG | Solar Wings Pegasus XL-Q | | | | |
| G-MYRK | Renegade Spirit UK | | | | |
| G-MYSL | Avia Sud Mistral | | | | |
| G-MYSP | Rans S.6-ESD Coyote II | | | | |
| G-MYST | Aviasud Mistral | | | | |
| G-MYTH | CFM Shadow Srs BD | | | | |
| G-MZDP | AMF Chevvron 232 | | | | |
| G-MZIP | Renegade Spirit UK | | | | |
| G-MZIZ | Renegade Spirit UK (G-MWGP) | | | | |
| G-MZOO | Renegade Spirit UK | | | | |
| G-MZPJ | Team Minimax | | | | |
| G-MZRS | CFM Shadow Srs CD | | | | |
| G-MZZZ | Whitaker MW.6-S Fatboy Flyer | | | | |

# Military to Civil Cross-Reference

| Serial carried | Civil identity | Serial carried | Civil identity |
|---|---|---|---|
| 5 (Croatian AF) | G-BEDB | 115302 (TP USAAF) | G-BJTP |
| 19 (USN) | G-BTCC | 121714 | NX700HL |
| 23 (USAAC) | N49272 | 151632 (USAAF) | NL9494Z |
| 26 (US) | G-BAVO | 18-2001 (USAAF) | G-BIZV |
| 27 (USN) | G-BRVG | 124485 (DF-A USAAF) | G-BEDF |
| 44 (K-33 USAAF) | G-BJLH | 133722 | NX1337A |
| 45 (Aeronavale) | G-BHFG | 217786 (USAAF) | G-BRTK |
| 75 | G-AFDX | 224211 (M2-Z USAF) | G-BPMP |
| 77 (Soviet AF) | G-BTCU | 226671 (MX-X USAAF) | NX47DD |
| 85 (USAAF) | G-BTBI | 231983 (USAAF) | F-BDRS |
| 112 (USAAC) | G-BSWC | 236800 (A-44 USAAF) | G-BHPK |
| 118 (USAAC) | G-BSDS | 314887 (USAAF) | G-AJPI |
| 120 (Fr AF) | G-AZGC | 315509 (USAAF) | G-BHUB |
| 152/17 | G-ATJM | 329417 (USAAF) | G-BDHK |
| 152/17 | G-BTYV | 329471 (F-44 USAAF) | G-BGXA |
| 157 (Fr AF) | G-AVEB | 329601 (D-44 USAAF) | G-AXHR |
| 168 | G-BFDE | 329854 (R-44 USAAF) | G-BMKC |
| 177 (Irish AC) | G-BLIW | 329934 (B-72 USAAF) | G-BCPH |
| 180 (USN) | G-BRSK | 330485 (C-44 USAAF) | G-AJES |
| 192 (Fr AF) | G-BKPT | 343251 (USAAC) | G-NZSS |
| 208 (USN) | N75664 | 413048 (E-39 USAAF) | G-BCXJ |
| 320 (USAAC) | G-BPMD | 414151 (HO-M USAAF) | NL314BG |
| 361 (USN) | G-ELAN | 430823 | N1042B |
| 379 (USAAC) | G-ILLE | 454467 (J-44 USAAF) | G-BILI |
| 385 (RCAF) | G-BGPB | 454537 (J-04 USAAF) | G-BFDL |
| 422-15 | G-AVJO | 461748 | G-BHDK |
| 425/17 | G-BEFR | 463221 (G4-5 USAAF) | G-BTCD |
| 441 (USN) | G-BTFG | 472216 (HO-L USAAF) | G-BIXL |
| 442 (USN) | G-BPTB | 472773 (AJ-C USAF) | G-SUSY |
| 503 (Hungarian AF) | G-BRAM | 472917 (AJ-A USAF) | G-HAEC |
| 671 (RCAF) | G-BNZC | 479766 (D-63 USAAF) | G-BKHG |
| 855 (USAAC) | N56421 | 474008 (VF-R USAF) | N51RR |
| 897 (USN) | G-BJEV | 480015 (USAAF) | G-AKIB |
| 1164 (USAAC) | G-BKGL | 480133 (B-44 USAAF) | G-BDCD |
| 1411 (US Coast Guard) | N444M | 480321 (H-44 USAAF) | G-FRAN |
| 1420 (Polish AF) | G-BMZF | 480480 (E-44 USAAF) | G-BECN |
| 2345 | G-ATVP | 483009 (USAF) | G-BPSE |
| 2807 (VE-103 USN) | G-BHTH | 41-33275 (CE USAAC) | G-BICE |
| 3066 | G-AETA | 42-58678 (IY USAAC) | G-BRIY |
| 3398 (FrAF) | G-BFYO | 42-78044 (USAAC) | G-BRXL |
| 3460 | G-BMFG | 43-1952 (USAAC) | G-BRPR |
| 4253/18 | G-BFPL | 44-30861 | N9089Z |
| 5492 | G-PENY | 44-79609 (PR USAAF) | G-BHXY |
| 5894 | G-BFVH | 44-80594 (USAAF) | G-BEDJ |
| 7198/18 | G-AANJ | 44-83184 | G-RGUS |
| 7797 (USAAF) | G-BFAF | 45-49192 | N47DD |
| 8178 (FU-178 USAF) | G-SABR | 511335 (VF-S USAAF) | NL1051S |
| 8449M | G-ASWJ | 542447 | G-SCUB |
| 14863 (USAAF) | G-BGOR | 542457 | G-LION |
| 16693 (693 RCAF) | G-BLPG | 542474 (R-184) | G-PCUB |
| 18393 (RCAF) | G-BCYK | 51-14526 (USAF) | G-BRWB |
| 20385 (385 RCAF) | G-BGPB | 51-15227 (USN) | G-BKRA |
| 30146 (Yugoslav Army) | G-BSXD | 51-15673 (USAF) | G-CUBI |
| 31923 (USAAC) | G-BRHP | 54-21261 (USAF) | N33VC |
| 34037 (USAAF) | N9115Z | 607327 (09-L USAAF) | G-ARAO |
| 53319 (319/RB USN) | G-BTDP | 889696 (688 USN) | G-TEAC |
| 54137 (69 USN) | G-CTKL | A16-199 (SF-R RAAF) | G-BEOX |
| 56321 (U-AB RNorAF) | G-BKPY | A17-48 (RAAF) | G-BPHR |
| 67543 (MC-O USAAF) | N3145X | A8226 | G-BIDW |
| 88297 (29 USN) | G-FGID | B1807 | G-EAVX |
| 88439 (USN) | N55JP | B2458 | G-BPOB |
| 91007 (USAF) | G-NASA | B4863 (G) | G-BLXT |
| 93542 (LTA-542 USAF) | G-BRLV | B6291 | G-ASOP |
| 115042 (TA-042 USAF) | G-BGHU | B6401 | G-AWYY |

| Serial carried | Civil identity | Serial carried | Civil identity |
|---|---|---|---|
| B7270 | G-BFCZ | R4907 | G-ANCS |
| C1904 (Z) | G-PFAP | R5086 | G-APIH |
| C3011 (S) | G-SWOT | S1287 | G-BEYB |
| C4994 | G-BLWM | S1579 | G-BBVO |
| D5397/17 | G-BFXL | T5424 | G-AJOA |
| D7889 | G-AANM | T5493 | G-ANEF |
| D8084 | G-ACAA | T5672 | G-ALRI |
| D8096 (D) | G-AEPH | T5854 | G-ANKK |
| E-15 (RNethAF) | G-BIYU | T5879 | G-AXBW |
| E3B-369 (781-32 Span AF) | G-BPDM | T6099 | G-AOGR |
| E449 | G-EBJE | T6269 (FOR-T) | G-AMOU |
| EM-01 (Spanish AF) | G-AAOR | T6313 | G-AHVU |
| F141 (G) | G-SEVA | T6645 | G-AIIZ |
| F235 (B) | G-BMDB | T6818 | G-ANKT |
| F904 | G-EBIA | T6991 | G-ANOR |
| F938 | G-EBIC | T7230 | G-AFVE |
| F939 (6) | G-EBIB | T7281 | G-ARTL |
| F943 | G-BIHF | T7404 | G-ANMV |
| F943 | G-BKDT | T7909 | G-ANON |
| F5447 (N) | G-BKER | T7997 | G-AOBH |
| F5459 (Y) | G-INNY | T9707 | G-AKKR |
| F8010 | G-BDWJ | T9738 | G-AKAT |
| F8614 | G-AWAU | U-80 (Swiss AF) | G-BUKK |
| G-48-1 (Class B) | G-ALSX | U-0247 (Class B identity) | G-AGOY |
| H-25 (RNethAF) | G-HVDM | U-108 (Swiss AF) | G-BJAX |
| H2311 | G-ABAA | U-110 (Swiss AF) | G-PTWO |
| H5199 | G-ADEV | U-142 (Swiss AF) | G-BONE |
| — (I-492 USAAC) | G-BPUD | U-1215 (Swiss AF) | G-HELV |
| J-1149 (Swiss AF) | G-SWIS | U-1230 (Swiss AF) | G-DHZZ |
| J-1605 (Swiss AF) | G-BLID | V1075 | G-AKPF |
| J-1758 (Swiss AF) | G-BLSD | V3388 | G-AHTW |
| J7326 | G-EBQP | V9281 (RU-M) | G-BCWL |
| J9941 (57) | G-ABMR | V9300 (MA-J) | G-LIZY |
| K1786 | G-AFTA | V9441 (AR-A) | G-AZWT |
| K2050 | G-ASCM | W5856 | G-BMGC |
| K2059 | G-PFAR | Z2033 (N/275) | G-ASTL |
| K2567 | G-MOTH | Z7015 | G-BKTH |
| K2568 | G-APMM | Z7197 | G-AKZN |
| K2572 | G-AOZH | Z7381 (XR-T) | G-HURI |
| K3215 | G-AHSA | AP507 (KX-P) | G-ACWP |
| K3731 | G-RODI | AR213 (PR-D) | G-AIST |
| K4235 | G-AHMJ | AR501 (NN-D) | G-AWII |
| K5054 | G-BRDV | BB807 | G-ADWO |
| K5414 (XV) | G-AENP | BE417 (AE-K) | G-HURR |
| L2301 | G-AIZG | BL628 | G-BTTN |
| MM53795 (SC-52 ItAF) | G-BJST | BM597 (PR-O) | G-MKVB |
| N1854 | G-AIBE | BS676 (K-U) | G-KUKU |
| N2308 (HP-B) | G-AMRK | BW853 | G-BRKE |
| N4877 (VX-F) | G-AMDA | DE208 | G-AGYU |
| N5180 | G-EBKY | DE363 | G-ANFC |
| N5182 | G-APUP | DE623 | G-ANFI |
| N5195 | G-ABOX | DE992 | G-AXXV |
| N6290 | G-BOCK | DF128 (RCO-U) | G-AOJJ |
| N6452 | G-BIAU | DF155 | G-ANFV |
| N6466 | G-ANKZ | DF198 | G-BBRB |
| N6532 | G-ANTS | DG590 | G-ADMW |
| N6847 | G-APAL | DR613 | G-AFJB |
| N6848 | G-BALX | EM720 | G-AXAN |
| N6965 (FL-J) | G-AJTW | EM903 | G-APBI |
| N6985 | G-AHMN | EN224 | G-FXII |
| N9191 | G-ALND | EZ259 | G-BMJW |
| N9389 | G-ANJA | FB226 (MT-A) | G-BDWM |
| P5865 (LE-W) | G-BKCK | FE992 | G-BDAM |
| P6382 | G-AJRS | FH153 | G-BBHK |
| R-163 (RNethAF) | G-BIRH | FR870 (GA-S) | NL1009N |
| R-167 (RNethAF) | G-LION | FS728 | G-BAFM |
| R1914 | G-AHUJ | FT239 | G-BIWX |
| R4897 | G-ERTY | FT391 | G-AZBN |

| Serial carried | Civil identity | Serial carried | Civil identity |
|---|---|---|---|
| FX301 (FD-NQ) | G-JUDI | TW384 | G-ANHZ |
| HB275 | N5063N | TW439 | G-ANRP |
| HB751 | G-BCBL | TW467 (ROD-F) | G-ANIE |
| HM580 | G-ACUU | TW511 | G-APAF |
| JV928 (Y) | G-BLSC | TW517 | G-BDFX |
| KB889 (NA-I) | G-LANC | TW536 (TS-V) | G-BNGE |
| KB976 (LQ-K) | G-BCOH | TW591 | G-ARIH |
| KG874 (YS-L) | G-DAKS | TW641 | G-ATDN |
| KL161 (VO-B) | N88972 | TX183 | G-BSMF |
| KZ321 | G-HURY | VF516 | G-ASMZ |
| LB294 | G-AHWJ | VF526 | G-ARXU |
| LB312 | G-AHXE | VF548 | G-ASEG |
| LB375 | G-AHGW | VL348 | G-AVVO |
| LF858 | G-BLUZ | VL349 | G-AWSA |
| LZ766 | G-ALCK | VM360 | G-APHV |
| MD497 | G-ANLW | VP955 | G-DVON |
| MH434 | G-ASJV | VR192 | G-APIT |
| MJ627 | G-BMSB | VR249 | G-APIY |
| MJ730 (GN-F) | G-HFIX | VR259 | G-APJB |
| ML407 (OU-V) | G-LFIX | VS356 | G-AOLU |
| ML417 (2I-T) | G-BJSG | VS610 | G-AOKL |
| MP425 | G-AITB | VS623 | G-AOKZ |
| MT-11 (RBelgAF) | G-BRFU | VX118 | G-ASNB |
| MT438 | G-AREI | VX147 | G-AVIL |
| MT719 (YB-J) | G-VIII | VX926 | G-ASKJ |
| MV154 | G-BKMI | VZ638 | G-JETM |
| MV293 (OI-C) | G-SPIT | VZ728 | G-AGOS |
| MV370 (AV-L) | G-FXIV | WA576 | G-ALSS |
| NF875 (603/CH) | G-AGTM | WA577 | G-ALST |
| NH238 (D-A) | G-MKIX | WB531 | G-BLRN |
| NJ695 | G-AJXV | WB585 (RCU-X) | G-AOSY |
| NJ703 | G-AKPI | WB588 (D) | G-AOTD |
| NJ719 | G-ANFU | WB660 | G-ARMB |
| NM181 | G-AZGZ | WB702 | G-AOFE |
| NP181 | G-AOAR | WB703 | G-ARMC |
| NP184 | G-ANYP | WB763 | G-BBMR |
| NP303 | G-ANZJ | WD286 (J) | G-BBND |
| NX611 | G-ASXX | WD292 | G-BCRX |
| NZ5628 | N240CA | WD305 | G-ARGG |
| PL965 | G-MKVI | WD363 (5) | G-BCIH |
| PL983 | G-PRXI | WD379 (K) | G-APLO |
| PP972 (6M-D) | G-BUAR | WD388 | G-BDIC |
| PT462 | G-CTIX | WD413 | G-BFIR |
| PV202 (VZ-M) | G-TRIX | WE402 | G-VIDI |
| RG333 | G-AIEK | WE569 | G-ASAJ |
| RG333 | G-AKEZ | WF877 | G-BPOA |
| RH377 | G-ALAH | WG307 | G-BCYJ |
| RL962 | G-AHED | WG316 | G-BCAH |
| RM221 | G-ANXR | WG348 | G-BBMV |
| RN218 (N) | G-BBJI | WG350 | G-BPAL |
| RR232 | G-BRSF | WG422 (16) | G-BFAX |
| RR299 (HT-E) | G-ASKH | WG472 | G-AOTY |
| RT486 | G-AJGJ | WG719 | G-BRMA |
| RT520 | G-ALYB | WH589 (115/NW) | G-BTTA |
| RW382 (NG-C) | G-XVIA | WJ237 (113/O) | G-BLTG |
| RW386 | G-BXVI | WJ358 | G-ARYD |
| SM832 | G-WWII | WJ945 | G-BEDV |
| SM969 (D-A) | G-BRAF | WK522 | G-BCOU |
| SX336 | G-BRMG | WK611 | G-ARWB |
| TA634 (8K-K) | G-AWJV | WK622 | G-BCZH |
| TA719 | G-ASKC | WK628 | G-BBMW |
| TD248 | G-OXVI | WL505 | G-FBIX |
| TE184 | G-MXVI | WL626 | G-BHDD |
| TE566 (DU-A) | G-BLCK | WM167 | G-LOSM |
| TJ569 | G-AKOW | WP321 (750/CU) | G-BRFC |
| TJ672 | G-ANIJ | WP788 | G-BCHL |
| TS423 | G-DAKS | WP790 | G-BBNC |
| TS798 | G-AGNV | WP800 (2) | G-BCXN |

# MILITARY/CIVIL CROSS REFERENCE

| Serial carried | Civil identity | Serial carried | Civil identity |
|---|---|---|---|
| WP808 | G-BDEU | XN351 | G-BKSC |
| WP835 | G-BDCB | XN435 | G-BGBU |
| WP843 | G-BDBP | XN437 | G-AXWA |
| WP857 (24) | G-BDRJ | XN441 | G-BGKT |
| WP903 | G-BCGC | XN637 | G-BKOU |
| WP971 | G-ATHD | XP279 | G-BWKK |
| WP977 | G-BHRD | XP282 | G-BGTC |
| WR410 (N) | G-BLKA | XP328 | G-BKHC |
| WT933 | G-ALSW | XP355 | G-BEBC |
| WV198 | G-BJWY | XR240 | G-BDFH |
| WV493 (A-P) | G-BDYG | XR241 | G-AXRR |
| WV666 (O-D) | G-BTDH | XR267 | G-BJXR |
| WV686 | G-BLFT | XR363 | G-OHCA |
| WV740 | G-BNPH | XR486 | G-RWWW |
| WV783 | G-ALSP | XR537 | G-NATY |
| WW397 (N-E) | G-BKHP | XR944 | G-ATTB |
| WZ507 | G-VTII | XR991 | G-MOUR |
| WZ662 | G-BKVK | XS101 | G-GNAT |
| WZ711 | G-AVHT | XS451 | G-LTNG |
| WZ876 | G-BBWN | XS452 (BT) | G-BPFE |
| XF597 (AH) | G-BKFW | XS587 (252/V) | G-VIXN |
| XF690 | G-MOOS | XS770 | G-HRHI |
| XF785 | G-ALBN | XT788 (442) | G-BMIR |
| XF836 (J-G) | G-AWRY | XV268 | G-BVER |
| XF877 (JX) | G-AWVF | XW635 | G-AWSW |
| XG452 | G-BRMB | XW784 | G-BBRN |
| XG547 | G-HAPR | XX469 | G-BNCL |
| XJ389 | G-AJJP | 2+1 (Luftwaffe) | G-SYFW |
| XJ763 | G-BKHA | 4+ (Luftwaffe) | G-BSLX |
| XK416 | G-AYUA | 6+ (Luftwaffe) | G-USTV |
| XK417 | G-AVXY | 08+ (Luftwaffe) | G-WULF |
| XK482 | G-BJWC | 14+ (Luftwaffe) | G-BBII |
| XK895 (19/CU) | G-SDEV | F+IS (Luftwaffe) | G-BIRW |
| XK896 | G-RNAS | BU+CK (Luftwaffe) | G-BUCK |
| XK940 | G-AYXT | BU+EM (Luftwaffe) | G-BUCC |
| XL426 | G-VJET | CC+43 (Luftwaffe) | G-CJCI |
| XL502 | G-BMYP | LG+01 (Luftwaffe) | G-AYSJ |
| XL572 | G-HNTR | NJ+C11 (Luftwaffe) | G-ATBG |
| XL809 | G-BLIX | RF+16 (Luftwaffe) | G-PTWO |
| XL812 | G-SARO | TA+RC (Luftwaffe) | G-BPHZ |
| XM405 (42) | G-TORE | ZA+WN (Luftwaffe) | G-AZMH |
| XM553 | G-AWSV | 6J+PR | G-AWHB |
| XM556 | G-HELI | 97+04 (Luftwaffe) | G-APVF |
| XM575 | G-BLMC | ⊕ (Russian AF) | G-KYAK |
| XM655 | G-VULC | — (Luftwaffe) | G-BOML |
| XM685 (513/PO) | G-AYZJ | 146-11042 (7) | G-BMZX |
| XM697 | G-NAAT | 146-11083 (5) | G-BNAI |

14863 (G-BGOR), AT-6D Harvard III. *AJW*

EI-FKC, Fokker 50. *AJW*

F-GMCD, McD Douglas MD-83. *AJW*

# Overseas Airliner Registrations

(Aircraft included in this section are those most likely to be seen at UK and major European airports on scheduled or charter services.)

| Reg. | Type | Owner or Operator | Notes |
|---|---|---|---|

## A6 (United Arab Emirates

| | | | |
|---|---|---|---|
| A6-EKA | Airbus A.310-304 | Emirate Airlines | |
| A6-EKB | Airbus A.310-304 | Emirate Airlines | |
| A6-EKC | Airbus A.300-605R | Emirate Airlines | |
| A6-EKD | Airbus A.300-605R | Emirate Airlines | |
| A6-EKE | Airbus A.300-605R | Emirate Airlines | |
| A6-EKF | Airbus A.300-605R | Emirate Airlines | |
| A6-EKG | Airbus A.310-308 | Emirate Airlines | |
| A6-EKH | Airbus A.310-308 | Emirate Airlines | |
| A6-EKI | Airbus A.310-308 | Emirate Airlines | |
| A6-EKJ | Airbus A.310-308 | Emirate Airlines | |
| A6-EKK | Airbus A.310-308 | Emirate Airlines | |
| A6-EKL | Airbus A.310-308 | Emirate Airlines | |
| A6-E | Airbus A.300-605R | Emirate Airlines | |
| A6-KUA | Airbus A.310-304 | Kuwait Airways | |
| A6-KUB | Airbus A.310-304 | Kuwait Airways | |
| A6-KUC | Airbus A.310-304 | Kuwait Airways | |
| A6-KUD | Airbus A.310-304 | Kuwait Airways | |
| A6-KUE | Airbus A.310-304 | Kuwait Airways | |

## A40 (Oman)

| | | | |
|---|---|---|---|
| A40-GF | Boeing 767-3P6ER (601) | Gulf Air | |
| A40-GG | Boeing 767-3P6ER (602) | Gulf Air | |
| A40-GH | Boeing 767-3P6ER (603) | Gulf Air | |
| A40-GI | Boeing 767-3P6ER (604) | Gulf Air | |
| A40-GJ | Boeing 767-3P6ER (605) | Gulf Air | |
| A40-GK | Boeing 767-3P6ER (606) | Gulf Air | |
| A40-GL | Boeing 767-3P6ER (607) | Gulf Air | |
| A40-GM | Boeing 767-3P6ER (608) | Gulf Air | |
| A40-GN | Boeing 767-3P6ER (609) | Gulf Air | |
| A40-GO | Boeing 767-3P6ER | Gulf Air | |
| A40-GP | Boeing 767-3P6ER | Gulf Air | |
| A40-GR | Boeing 767-3P6ER | Gulf Air | |
| A40-GS | Boeing 767-3P6ER | Gulf Air | |
| A40-GT | Boeing 767-3P6ER | Gulf Air | |
| A40-GU | Boeing 767-3P6ER | Gulf Air | |
| A40-GV | Boeing 767-3P6ER | Gulf Air | |
| A40-GW | Boeing 767-3P6ER | Gulf Air | |
| A40-GX | Boeing 767-3P6ER | Gulf Air | |
| A40-SO | Boeing 747SP-27 | Oman Royal Flight | |
| A40-SP | Boeing 747SP-27 | Oman Government | |
| A40-TA | L-1011-385 TriStar 200 (105) | Gulf Air | |
| A40-TB | L-1011-385 TriStar 200 (106) | Gulf Air | |
| A40-TT | L-1011-385 TriStar 200 (107) | Gulf Air | |
| A40-TV | L-1011-385 TriStar 200 (108) | Gulf Air | |
| A40-TW | L-1011-385 TriStar 200 (101) | Gulf Air | |
| A40-TX | L-1011-385 TriStar 200 (102) | Gulf Air | |
| A40-TY | L-1011-385 TriStar 200 (103) | Gulf Air | |
| A40-TZ | L-1011-385 TriStar 200 (104) | Gulf Air | |

## AP (Pakistan)

| | | | |
|---|---|---|---|
| AP-AXA | Boeing 707-340C | Pakistan International Airlines | |
| AP-AXG | Boeing 707-340C | Pakistan International Airlines | |
| AP-AYV | Boeing 747-282B | Pakistan International Airlines | |
| AP-AYW | Boeing 747-282B | Pakistan International Airlines | |
| AP-AZW | Boeing 707-351B | Pakistan International Airlines | |
| AP-BAK | Boeing 747-240B (SCD) | Pakistan International Airlines | |
| AP-BAT | Boeing 747-240B (SCD) | Pakistan International Airlines | |
| AP-BBK | Boeing 707-323C | Pakistan International Airlines | |
| AP-BCL | Boeing 747-217B | Pakistan International Airlines | |
| AP-BCM | Boeing 747-217B | Pakistan International Airlines | |
| AP-BCN | Boeing 747-217B | Pakistan International Airlines | |

| Notes | Reg. | Type | Owner or Operator |
|---|---|---|---|
| | AP-BCO | Boeing 747-217B | Pakistan International Airlines |

# B (China/Taiwan)

| | | |
|---|---|---|
| B-160 | Boeing 747-209F (SCD) | China Airlines |
| B-161 | Boeing 747-409 | China Airlines |
| B-162 | Boeing 747-409 | China Airlines |
| B-163 | Boeing 747-409 | China Airlines |
| B-164 | Boeing 747-409 | China Airlines |
| B-165 | Boeing 747-409 | China Airlines |
| B-1862 | Boeing 747SP-09 | China Airlines |
| B-1864 | Boeing 747-209B (SCD) | China Airlines |
| B-1866 | Boeing 747-209B | China Airlines |
| B-1880 | Boeing 747SP-09 | China Airlines |
| B-1886 | Boeing 747-209B | China Airlines |
| B-1888 | Boeing 747-209B | China Airlines |
| B-1894 | Boeing 747-209F (SCD) | China Airlines |
| B-2414 | Boeing 707-3J6C | CAAC/Air China |
| B-2420 | Boeing 707-3J6C | CAAC/Air China |
| B-2438 | Boeing 747SP-J6 | CAAC/Air China |
| B-2442 | Boeing 747SP-J6 | CAAC/Air China |
| B-2443 | Boeing 747-4J6 | CAAC/Air China |
| B-2445 | Boeing 747-4J6 | CAAC/Air China |
| B-2446 | Boeing 747-2J6B (SCD) | CAAC/Air China |
| B-2447 | Boeing 747-4J6 | CAAC/Air China |
| B-2448 | Boeing 747-2J6B (SCD) | CAAC/Air China |
| B-2450 | Boeing 747-2J6B (SCD) | CAAC/Air China |
| B-2452 | Boeing 747SP-J6 | CAAC/Air China |
| B-2454 | Boeing 747SP-27 | CAAC/Air China |
| B-2456 | Boeing 747-4J6 (SCD) | CAAC/Air China |
| B-2458 | Boeing 747-4J6 (SCD) | CAAC/Air China |
| B-2460 | Boeing 747-4J6 (SCD) | CAAC/Air China |
| B-2462 | Boeing 747-2J6F (SCD) | CAAC/Air China |
| B-2464 | Boeing 747-4J6 | CAAC/Air China |
| B-2466 | Boeing 747-4J6 | CAAC/Air China |
| B-16603 | Boeing 767-35EER | EVA Airways |
| B-16605 | Boeing 767-35EER | EVA Airways |

**Note:** China Airlines also operates N4508H and N4522V, both Boeing 747SP-09s.

# C5 (Gambia)

| | | |
|---|---|---|
| C5-GOA | Boeing 707-323B | Air Gambia |
| C5-GOB | Boeing 707-120B | Air Gambia |
| C5-GOC | Boeing 707-321B | Air Gambia |

# C9 (Mozambique)

| | | |
|---|---|---|
| C9-BAE | Ilyushin IL-62M | Linhas Aéreas de Mocambique (LAM) *Mozambique* |
| C9- | Boeing 767-2B1ER | LAM |

**Note:** LAM also operates Boeing 767-2B1ER EI-CEM on lease.

# C-F and C-G (Canada)

| | | |
|---|---|---|
| C-FBCA | Boeing 747-475 (884) | Canadian Airlines International *Grant McConachie* |
| C-FBEF | Boeing 767-233ER (617) | Air Canada |
| C-FBEG | Boeing 767-233ER (618) | Air Canada |
| C-FBEM | Boeing 767-233ER (619) | Air Canada |
| C-FCAB | Boeing 767-375ER (631) | Canadian Airlines International |
| C-FCAE | Boeing 767-375ER (632) | Canadian Airlines International |
| C-FCAF | Boeing 767-375ER (633) | Canadian Airlines International |
| C-FCAG | Boeing 767-375ER (634) | Canadian Airlines International |
| C-FCAJ | Boeing 767-375ER (635) | Canadian Airlines International |
| C-FCAU | Boeing 767-375ER (636) | Canadian Airlines International |
| C-FCRA | Boeing 747-475 (882) | Canadian Airlines International *T. Russ Baker* |
| C-FCWW | Douglas DC-8-55F | ACS of Canada |
| C-FDJC | Boeing 747-1D1 (411) | Nationair |
| C-FDWW | Douglas DC-8-55F | ACS of Canada *Gilles Roudeau* |
| C-FFUN | Boeing 747-1D1 (412) | Nationair |

| Reg. | Type | Owner or Operator | Notes |
|------|------|-------------------|-------|
| C-FIWW | Douglas DC-8-55F | ACS of Canada | |
| C-FNXA | Boeing 747-230B | Nationair | |
| C-FNXP | Boeing 747-212B | Nationair | |
| C-FNXY | Boeing 757-236 | Nationair/Ambassador Airlines (G-BUDZ) | |
| C-FOCA | Boeing 767-375ER (640) | Canadian Airlines International | |
| C-FOOA | Boeing 757-28A | Canada 3000/Air 2000 (G-OOOA) | |
| C-FOOB | Boeing 757-28A | Canada 3000/Air 2000 (G-OOOB) | |
| C-FOOE | Boeing 757-28A | Canada 3000 Airlines | |
| C-FPCA | Boeing 767-375ER (637) | Canadian Airlines International | |
| C-FTCA | Boeing 767-375ER (638) | Canadian Airlines International | |
| C-FTIK | Douglas DC-8-73AF (867) | Air Canada | |
| C-FTIO | Douglas DC-8-73AF (871) | Air Canada | |
| C-FTIQ | Douglas DC-8-73AF (873) | Air Canada | |
| C-FTIR | Douglas DC-8-73AF (874) | Air Canada | |
| C-FTIS | Douglas DC-8-73AF (875) | Air Canada | |
| C-FTNA | L.1011-385 TriStar 150 (501) | Air Transat | |
| C-FTNB | L.1011-385 TriStar 150 (549) | Air Transat | |
| C-FTNC | L.1011-385 TriStar 150 (503) | Air Transat | |
| C-FTOC | Boeing 747-133 (303) | Air Canada | |
| C-FTOD | Boeing 747-133 (304) | Air Canada | |
| C-FTOE | Boeing 747-133 (305) | Air Canada | |
| C-FXCA | Boeing 767-375ER (639) | Canadian Airlines International | |
| C-FXOD | Boeing 757-28A | Canada 3000/Air 2000 (G-OOOD) | |
| C-FXOF | Boeing 757-28A | Canada 3000 Airlines | |
| C-FXOK | Boeing 757-23A | Canada 3000 Airlines | |
| C-FXOO | Boeing 757-28A | Canada 3000 Airlines | |
| C-GAGA | Boeing 747-233B (SCD) (306) | Air Canada | |
| C-GAGB | Boeing 747-233B (SCD) (307) | Air Canada | |
| C-GAGC | Boeing 747-238B (SCD) (308) | Air Canada | |
| C-GAGL | Boeing 747-433 (SCD) (341) | Air Canada | |
| C-GAGM | Boeing 747-433 (SCD) (342) | Air Canada | |
| C-GAGN | Boeing 747-433 (SCD) (343) | Air Canada | |
| C-GAUY | Boeing 767-233 (609) | Air Canada | |
| C-GAVA | Boeing 767-233 (610) | Air Canada | |
| C-GAVC | Boeing 767-233ER (611) | Air Canada | |
| C-GAVF | Boeing 767-233ER (612) | Air Canada | |
| C-GCPC | Douglas DC-10-30 (901) | Canadian Airlines International | |
| C-GCPD | Douglas DC-10-30 (902) | Canadian Airlines International | |
| C-GCPE | Douglas DC-10-30ER (903) | Canadian Airlines International | |
| C-GCPF | Douglas DC-10-30ER (904) | Canadian Airlines International | |
| C-GCPG | Douglas DC-10-30ER (905) | Canadian Airlines International | |
| C-GCPH | Douglas DC-10-30ER (906) | Canadian Airlines International | |
| C-GCPI | Douglas DC-10-30ER (907) | Canadian Airlines International | |
| C-GCPJ | Douglas DC-10-30 (908) | Canadian Airlines International | |
| C-GDSP | Boeing 767-233ER (613) | Air Canada | |
| C-GDSS | Boeing 767-233ER (614) | Air Canada | |
| C-GDSU | Boeing 767-233ER (615) | Air Canada | |
| C-GDSY | Boeing 767-233ER (616) | Air Canada | |
| C-GLCA | Boeing 767-375ER (641) | Canadian Airlines International | |
| C-GMWW | Boeing 747-475 (881) | Canadian Airlines International *Maxwell W. Ward* | |
| C-GMXB | Douglas DC-8-61 (811) | Nationair | |
| C-GMXL | Douglas DC-8-61 (813) | Nationair | |
| C-GMXY | Douglas DC-8-62 (822) | Nationair | |
| C-GNXA | Boeing 747-230B | Nationair | |
| C-GNXB | Boeing 757-236 | Nationair | |
| C-GNXC | Boeing 757-28A (521) | Nationair | |
| C-GNXH | Boeing 747-129 (SCD) (413) | Nationair | |
| C-GNXI | Boeing 757-28A (522) | Nationair | |
| C-GNXU | Boeing 757-28A (523) | Nationair | |
| C-GQBA | Douglas DC-8-63 (806) | Nationair | |
| C-GQBF | Douglas DC-8-63 (807) | Nationair | |
| C-GSCA | Boeing 767-375ER (642) | Canadian Airlines International | |
| C-GTSE | Boeing 757-23A | Air Transat | |
| C-GTSF | Boeing 757-23A | Air Transat | |
| C-GTSZ | L.1011-385 TriStar 100 (548) | Air Transat | |

**Note:** Airline fleet number carried on aircraft is shown in parenthesis. Nationair also operates two Boeing 747-257Bs registered N303TW and N304TW.

# CCCP (CIS)

The country code CCCP officially ceased to exist on 1 January 1993. Many of the registered aircraft using the prefix have been transferred to RA (Russia).

# CN (Morocco)

| Reg. | Type | Owner or Operator |
|------|------|-------------------|
| CN-CCF | Boeing 727-2B6 | Royal Air Maroc *Fez* |
| CN-CCG | Boeing 727-2B6 | Royal Air Maroc *L'Oiseau de la Providence* |
| CN-CCH | Boeing 727-2B6 | Royal Air Maroc *Marrakech* |
| CN-CCW | Boeing 727-2B6 | Royal Air Maroc *Agadir* |
| CN-RMB | Boeing 707-351C | Royal Air Maroc *Tangier* |
| CN-RMC | Boeing 707-351C | Royal Air Maroc *Casablanca* |
| CN-RME | Boeing 747-2B6B (SCD) | Royal Air Maroc |
| CN-RMF | Boeing 737-4B6 | Royal Air Maroc |
| CN-RMG | Boeing 737-4B6 | Royal Air Maroc |
| CN-RMI | Boeing 737-2B6 | Royal Air Maroc *El Ayounne* |
| CN-RMJ | Boeing 737-2B6 | Royal Air Maroc *Oujda* |
| CN-RMK | Boeing 737-2B6 | Royal Air Maroc *Smara* |
| CN-RML | Boeing 737-2B6 | Royal Air Maroc |
| CN-RMM | Boeing 737-2B6C | Royal Air Maroc |
| CN-RMN | Boeing 737-2B6C | Royal Air Maroc |
| CN-RMO | Boeing 727-2B6 | Royal Air Maroc |
| CN-RMP | Boeing 727-2B6 | Royal Air Maroc |
| CN-RMQ | Boeing 727-2B6 | Royal Air Maroc |
| CN-RMR | Boeing 727-2B6 | Royal Air Maroc |
| CN-RMS | Boeing 747SP-44 | Royal Air Maroc |
| CN-RMT | Boeing 757-2B6 | Royal Air Maroc |
| CN-RMU | Boeing 737-53A | Royal Air Maroc |
| CN-RMV | Boeing 737-5B6 | Royal Air Maroc |
| CN-RMW | Boeing 737-5B6 | Royal Air Maroc |
| CN-RMX | Boeing 737-4B6 | Royal Air Maroc |
| CN-RMY | Boeing 737-5B6 | Royal Air Maroc |
| CN-RMZ | Boeing 757-2B6 | Royal Air Maroc |
| CN-RNA | Boeing 737-4B6 | Royal Air Maroc |
| CN-RNB | Boeing 737-5B6 | Royal Air Maroc |

# CS (Portugal)

| Reg. | Type | Owner or Operator |
|------|------|-------------------|
| CS-TEA | L.1011-385 TriStar 500 | TAP — Air Portugal *Luis de Camoes* |
| CS-TEB | L.1011-385 TriStar 500 | TAP — Air Portugal *Infante D. Henrique* |
| CS-TEC | L.1011-385 TriStar 500 | TAP — Air Portugal *Gago Coutinho* |
| CS-TED | L.1011-385 TriStar 500 | TAP — Air Portugal *Bartolomeu de Gusmao* |
| CS-TEE | L.1011-385 TriStar 500 | TAP — Air Portugal *St Antonio de Lisboa* |
| CS-TEF | L.1011-385 TriStar 500 | TAP — Air Portugal *Fernando Pessoa* |
| CS-TEG | L.1011-385 TriStar 500 | TAP — Air Portugal *Eca de Queiroz* |
| CS-TEH | Airbus A.310-304 | TAP — Air Portugal *Bartolomeu Dias* |
| CS-TEI | Airbus A.310-304 | TAP — Air Portugal *Fernao de Magalhaes* |
| CS-TEJ | Airbus A.310-304 | TAP — Air Portugal *Pedro Nunes* |
| CS-TEK | Boeing 737-282 | TAP — Air Portugal *Ponta Delgada* |
| CS-TEL | Boeing 737-282 | TAP — Air Portugal *Funchal* |
| CS-TEM | Boeing 737-282 | TAP — Air Portugal *Setubal* |
| CS-TEN | Boeing 737-282 | TAP — Air Portugal *Braga* |
| CS-TEO | Boeing 737-282 | TAP — Air Portugal *Evora* |
| CS-TEP | Boeing 737-282 | TAP — Air Portugal *Porto* |
| CS-TEQ | Boeing 737-282C | TAP — Air Portugal *Vila Real* |
| CS-TER | Boeing 737-230 | TAP — Air Portugal *Aveiro* |
| CS-TES | Boeing 737-230 | TAP — Air Portugal *Viana do Castelo* |
| CS-TET | Boeing 737-2K9 | Air Atlantis *Viseu* |
| CS-TEU | Boeing 737-2K9 | Air Atlantis *Porto Santo* |
| CS-TEV | Boeing 737-230 | Air Atlantis/Air Portugal |
| CS-TEW | Airbus A.310-304 | TAP — Air Portugal *Vasco da Gama* |
| CS-TEX | Airbus A.310-304 | TAP — Air Portugal *Joao XXI* |
| CS-TIA | Boeing 737-382 | TAP — Air Portugal *Madeira* |
| CS-TIB | Boeing 737-382 | TAP — Air Portugal *Acores* |
| CS-TIC | Boeing 737-382 | TAP — Air Portugal *Algarve* |
| CS-TID | Boeing 737-382 | TAP — Air Portugal *Alto Minho* |
| CS-TIE | Boeing 737-382 | TAP — Air Portugal *Costa Azul* |
| CS-TIF | Boeing 737-3K9 | Air Atlantis |
| CS-TIG | Boeing 737-3K9 | Air Atlantis |
| CS-TIH | Boeing 737-3K9 | Air Atlantis |

| Reg. | Type | Owner or Operator | Notes |
| :--- | :--- | :--- | :--- |
| CS-TII | Boeing 737-382 | Air Atlantis | |
| CS-TIJ | Boeing 737-382 | Air Atlantis | |
| CS-TIK | Boeing 737-382 | TAP — Air Portugal Costa do Estoril | |
| CS-TIL | Boeing 737-382 | TAP — Air Portugal Lisbon | |
| CS-TIM | Boeing 737-3Q8 | Air Atlantis | |
| CS-TKA | Boeing 727-2J4RE | Air Columbus Cristovao Colombo | |
| CS-TKB | Boeing 727-2J4RE | Air Columbus Joao Concalves Zarco | |
| CS-TKC | Boeing 737-33A | Air Columbus Santa Maria | |
| CS-TKD | Boeing 737-33A | Air Columbus | |
| CS-TNA | Airbus A.320-211 | TAP — Air Portugal | |
| CS-TNB | Airbus A.320-211 | TAP — Air Portugal Gil Vicente | |
| CS-TNC | Airbus A.320-211 | TAP — Air Portugal Pero da Covilha | |
| CS-TND | Airbus A.320-211 | TAP — Air Portugal Garcia de Orta | |
| CS-TNE | Airbus A.320-211 | TAP — Air Portugal | |
| CS-TNF | Airbus A.320-211 | TAP — Air Portugal | |
| CS-TPA | Fokker 100 | Portugalia Albatroz | |
| CS-TPB | Fokker 100 | Portugalia Pelicano | |
| CS-TPC | Fokker 100 | Portugalia | |

# CU (Cuba)

| CU-T1208 | Ilyushin IL-62M | Cubana Capt Wifredo Perez | |
| :--- | :--- | :--- | :--- |
| CU-T1209 | Ilyushin IL-62M | Cubana | |
| CU-T1215 | Ilyushin IL-62M | Cubana | |
| CU-T1216 | Ilyushin IL-62M | Cubana | |
| CU-T1217 | Ilyushin IL-62M | Cubana | |
| CU-T1218 | Ilyushin IL-62M | Cubana | |
| CU-T1225 | Ilyushin IL-62M | Cubana | |
| CU-T1226 | Ilyushin IL-62M | Cubana | |
| CU-T1252 | Ilyushin IL-62M | Cubana | |
| CU-T1259 | Ilyushin IL-62M | Cubana | |
| CU-T1280 | Ilyushin IL-62M | Cubana | |
| CU-T1282 | Ilyushin IL-62M | Cubana | |
| CU-T1283 | Ilyushin IL-62M | Cubana | |

# D (Germany)

| D-AARS | F.27 Friendship Mk 600 | Ratioflug | |
| :--- | :--- | :--- | :--- |
| D-AASL | Boeing 737-3M8 | Saarland Airlines | |
| D-ABAB | Boeing 737-4K5 | Air Berlin | |
| D-ABAC | Boeing 737-4Y0 | Air Berlin | |
| D-ABAD | Boeing 737-4Y0 | Air Berlin | |
| D-ABAE | Boeing 737-4Y0 | Air Berlin | |
| D-ABEA | Boeing 737-330 | Lufthansa Saarbrücken | |
| D-ABEB | Boeing 737-330 | Lufthansa Xanten | |
| D-ABEC | Boeing 737-330 | Lufthansa Express Karlsruhe | |
| D-ABED | Boeing 737-330 | Lufthansa Express Hagen | |
| D-ABEE | Boeing 737-330 | Lufthansa Express Ulm | |
| D-ABEF | Boeing 737-330 | Lufthansa Express | |
| D-ABEH | Boeing 737-330 | Lufthansa Express | |
| D-ABEI | Boeing 737-330 | Lufthansa Express | |
| D-ABEK | Boeing 737-330 | Lufthansa Express | |
| D-ABEL | Boeing 737-330 | Lufthansa Express | |
| D-ABEM | Boeing 737-330 | Lufthansa Express | |
| D-ABEN | Boeing 737-330 | Lufthansa Express | |
| D-ABEO | Boeing 737-330 | Lufthansa Express | |
| D-ABEP | Boeing 737-330 | Lufthansa Express | |
| D-ABER | Boeing 737-330 | Lufthansa Express | |
| D-ABES | Boeing 737-330 | Lufthansa Express | |
| D-ABFA | Boeing 737-230 | Lufthansa Regensburg | |
| D-ABFB | Boeing 737-230 | Lufthansa Flensburg | |
| D-ABFC | Boeing 737-230 | Lufthansa Würzburg | |
| D-ABFF | Boeing 737-230 | Lufthansa Gelsenkirchen | |
| D-ABFL | Boeing 737-230 | Lufthansa Coburg | |
| D-ABFM | Boeing 737-230 | Lufthansa Osnabruk | |
| D-ABFN | Boeing 737-230 | Lufthansa Kempten | |
| D-ABFP | Boeing 737-230 | Lufthansa Offenbach | |
| D-ABFR | Boeing 737-230 | Lufthansa Solingen | |
| D-ABFS | Boeing 737-230 | Lufthansa Oldenburg | |
| D-ABFU | Boeing 737-230 | Lufthansa Mülheim a.d.Ruhr | |
| D-ABFW | Boeing 737-230 | Lufthansa Wolfsburg | |
| D-ABFX | Boeing 737-230 | Lufthansa Tübingen | |

| Notes | Reg. | Type | Owner or Operator |
|---|---|---|---|
| | D-ABFY | Boeing 737-230 | Lufthansa *Göttingen* |
| | D-ABFZ | Boeing 737-230 | Lufthansa *Wilhelmshaven* |
| | D-ABGE | Boeing 737-230F | German Cargo |
| | D-ABHE | Boeing 737-230F | German Cargo |
| | D-ABHF | Boeing 737-230 | Lufthansa *Heilbronn* |
| | D-ABHH | Boeing 737-230 | Lufthansa *Marburg* |
| | D-ABHL | Boeing 737-230 | Lufthansa *Worms* |
| | D-ABHM | Boeing 737-230 | Lufthansa *Landshut* |
| | D-ABHN | Boeing 737-230 | Lufthansa *Trier* |
| | D-ABHP | Boeing 737-230 | Lufthansa *Erlangen* |
| | D-ABHR | Boeing 737-230 | Lufthansa *Darmstadt* |
| | D-ABHU | Boeing 737-230 | Lufthansa *Konstanz* |
| | D-ABHW | Boeing 737-230 | Lufthansa *Baden Baden* |
| | D-ABIA | Boeing 737-530 | Lufthansa *Greifswald* |
| | D-ABIB | Boeing 737-530 | Lufthansa *Esslingen* |
| | D-ABIC | Boeing 737-530 | Lufthansa *Krefeld* |
| | D-ABID | Boeing 737-530 | Lufthansa *Aachen* |
| | D-ABIE | Boeing 737-530 | Lufthansa *Hildesheim* |
| | D-ABIF | Boeing 737-530 | Lufthansa *Landau* |
| | D-ABIH | Boeing 737-530 | Lufthansa *Bruchsal* |
| | D-ABII | Boeing 737-530 | Lufthansa *Lörrach* |
| | D-ABIK | Boeing 737-530 | Lufthansa *Rastatt* |
| | D-ABIL | Boeing 737-530 | Lufthansa *Memmingen* |
| | D-ABIM | Boeing 737-530 | Lufthansa *Salzgitter* |
| | D-ABIN | Boeing 737-530 | Lufthansa *Langenhangen* |
| | D-ABIO | Boeing 737-530 | Lufthansa *Wesel* |
| | D-ABIP | Boeing 737-530 | Lufthansa *Oberhausen* |
| | D-ABIR | Boeing 737-530 | Lufthansa *Anklam* |
| | D-ABIS | Boeing 737-530 | Lufthansa *Rendsburg* |
| | D-ABIT | Boeing 737-530 | Lufthansa |
| | D-ABIU | Boeing 737-530 | Lufthansa |
| | D-ABIW | Boeing 737-530 | Lufthansa *Bad Nauheim* |
| | D-ABIX | Boeing 737-530 | Lufthansa *Bamberg* |
| | D-ABIY | Boeing 737-530 | Lufthansa *Wuerzburg* |
| | D-ABIZ | Boeing 737-530 | Lufthansa *Kirchheim unter Teck* |
| | D-ABJA | Boeing 737-530 | Lufthansa *Pforzheim* |
| | D-ABJB | Boeing 737-530 | Lufthansa *Rheine* |
| | D-ABJC | Boeing 737-530 | Lufthansa |
| | D-ABJD | Boeing 737-530 | Lufthansa |
| | D-ABJE | Boeing 737-530 | Lufthansa |
| | D-ABJF | Boeing 737-530 | Lufthansa |
| | D-ABJH | Boeing 737-530 | Lufthansa |
| | D-ABJI | Boeing 737-530 | Lufthansa |
| | D-ABKA | Boeing 737-430 | Lufthansa Express |
| | D-ABKB | Boeing 737-430 | Lufthansa Express |
| | D-ABKC | Boeing 737-430 | Lufthansa Express |
| | D-ABKD | Boeing 737-430 | Lufthansa Express |
| | D-ABKF | Boeing 737-430 | Lufthansa Express |
| | D-ABKK | Boeing 737-430 | Lufthansa Express |
| | D-ABKL | Boeing 737-430 | Lufthansa Express |
| | D-ABMA | Boeing 737-230 | Lufthansa *Idar-Oberstein* |
| | D-ABMB | Boeing 737-230 | Lufthansa *Ingolstadt* |
| | D-ABMC | Boeing 737-230 | Lufthansa *Norderstedt* |
| | D-ABMD | Boeing 737-230 | Lufthansa *Paderborn* |
| | D-ABME | Boeing 737-230 | Lufthansa *Schweinfurt* |
| | D-ABMF | Boeing 737-230 | Lufthansa *Verden* |
| | D-ABNA | Boeing 757-230 | Condor Flugdienst |
| | D-ABNB | Boeing 757-230 | Condor Flugdienst |
| | D-ABNC | Boeing 757-230 | Condor Flugdienst |
| | D-ABND | Boeing 757-230 | Condor Flugdienst |
| | D-ABNE | Boeing 757-230 | Condor Flugdienst |
| | D-ABNF | Boeing 757-230 | Condor Flugdienst |
| | D-ABNH | Boeing 757-230 | Condor Flugdienst |
| | D-ABNI | Boeing 757-230 | Condor Flugdienst |
| | D-ABNK | Boeing 757-230 | Condor Flugdienst |
| | D-ABNL | Boeing 757-230 | Condor Flugdienst |
| | D-ABNM | Boeing 757-230 | Condor Flugdienst |
| | D-ABNN | Boeing 757-230 | Condor Flugdienst |
| | D-ABNO | Boeing 757-230 | Condor Flugdienst |
| | D-ABNS | Boeing 757-230 | Condor Flugdienst |
| | D-ABNX | Boeing 757-230 | Condor Flugdienst |
| | D-ABOA | Boeing 757-230 | Condor Flugdienst |
| | D-ABOB | Boeing 757-230 | Condor Flugdienst |

| Reg. | Type | Owner or Operator | Notes |
|---|---|---|---|
| D-ABOC | Boeing 757-230 | Condor Flugdienst | |
| D-ABOE | Boeing 757-230 | Condor Flugdienst | |
| D-ABOF | Boeing 757-230 | Condor Flugdienst | |
| D-ABOH | Boeing 757-230 | Condor Flugdienst | |
| D-ABTA | Boeing 747-430 (SCD) | Lufthansa *Sachsen* | |
| D-ABTB | Boeing 747-430 (SCD) | Lufthansa *Brandenburg* | |
| D-ABTC | Boeing 747-430 (SCD) | Lufthansa *Mecklenburg-Verpommern* | |
| D-ABTD | Boeing 747-430 (SCD) | Lufthansa *Hamburg* | |
| D-ABTE | Boeing 747-430 (SCD) | Lufthansa *Sachsen-Anhalt* | |
| D-ABTF | Boeing 747-430 (SCD) | Lufthansa *Thüringen* | |
| D-ABTH | Boeing 747-430 (SCD) | Lufthansa | |
| D-ABUA | Boeing 767-330ER | Condor Flugdienst | |
| D-ABUB | Boeing 767-330ER | Condor Flugdienst | |
| D-ABUC | Boeing 767-330ER | Condor Flugdienst | |
| D-ABUD | Boeing 767-330ER | Condor Flugdienst | |
| D-ABUE | Boeing 767-330ER | Condor Flugdienst | |
| D-ABUX | Boeing 767-330ER | Condor Flugdienst | |
| D-ABUY | Boeing 767-330ER | Condor Flugdienst | |
| D-ABUZ | Boeing 767-330ER | Condor Flugdienst | |
| D-ABVA | Boeing 747-430 | Lufthansa *Berlin* | |
| D-ABVB | Boeing 747-430 | Lufthansa *Bonn* | |
| D-ABVC | Boeing 747-430 | Lufthansa *Baden-Württemberg* | |
| D-ABVD | Boeing 747-430 | Lufthansa *Bochum* | |
| D-ABVE | Boeing 747-430 | Lufthansa *Potsdam* | |
| D-ABVF | Boeing 747-430 | Lufthansa *Frankfurt* | |
| D-ABVH | Boeing 747-430 | Lufthansa | |
| D-ABVK | Boeing 747-430 | Lufthansa | |
| D-ABVL | Boeing 747-430 | Lufthansa *Muenchen* | |
| D-ABVN | Boeing 747-430 | Lufthansa | |
| D-ABWA | Boeing 737-330 | Condor Flugdienst *Claus Gillmann* | |
| D-ABWB | Boeing 737-330 | Condor Flugdienst | |
| D-ABWC | Boeing 737-330 | Condor Flugdienst | |
| D-ABWD | Boeing 737-330 | Condor Flugdienst | |
| D-ABWE | Boeing 737-330 | Condor Flugdienst | |
| D-ABWF | Boeing 737-330 | Condor Flugdienst | |
| D-ABWH | Boeing 737-330 | Condor Flugdienst | |
| D-ABXA | Boeing 737-330QC | Lufthansa *Giessen* | |
| D-ABXB | Boeing 737-330 | Lufthansa *Passau* | |
| D-ABXC | Boeing 737-330 | Lufthansa *Delmenhorst* | |
| D-ABXD | Boeing 737-330 | Lufthansa *Siegen* | |
| D-ABXE | Boeing 737-330 | Lufthansa *Hamm* | |
| D-ABXF | Boeing 737-330 | Lufthansa *Minden* | |
| D-ABXH | Boeing 737-330 | Lufthansa *Cuxhaven* | |
| D-ABXI | Boeing 737-330 | Lufthansa *Berchtesgaden* | |
| D-ABXK | Boeing 737-330 | Lufthansa *Ludwigsburg* | |
| D-ABXL | Boeing 737-330 | Lufthansa *Neuss* | |
| D-ABXM | Boeing 737-330 | Lufthansa *Herford* | |
| D-ABXN | Boeing 737-330 | Lufthansa *Böblingen* | |
| D-ABXO | Boeing 737-330 | Lufthansa *Schwäbisch-Gmünd* | |
| D-ABXP | Boeing 737-330 | Lufthansa *Fulda* | |
| D-ABXR | Boeing 737-330 | Lufthansa *Celle* | |
| D-ABXS | Boeing 737-330 | Lufthansa *Sindelfingen* | |
| D-ABXT | Boeing 737-330 | Lufthansa *Reutlingen* | |
| D-ABXU | Boeing 737-330 | Lufthansa *Seeheim-Jugenheim* | |
| D-ABXW | Boeing 737-330 | Lufthansa *Hanau* | |
| D-ABXX | Boeing 737-330 | Lufthansa *Bad Homburg v.d. Höhe* | |
| D-ABXY | Boeing 737-330 | Lufthansa *Hof* | |
| D-ABXZ | Boeing 737-330 | Lufthansa *Bad Mergentheim* | |
| D-ABYJ | Boeing 747-230B (SCD) | Lufthansa *Hessen* | |
| D-ABYK | Boeing 747-230B (SCD) | Lufthansa *Rheinland-Pfalz* | |
| D-ABYL | Boeing 747-230B (SCD) | Lufthansa *Saarland* | |
| D-ABYM | Boeing 747-230B (SCD) | Lufthansa *Schleswig-Holstein* | |
| D-ABYO | Boeing 747-230F (SCD) | Lufthansa *America* | |
| D-ABYP | Boeing 747-230B | Lufthansa *Niedersachen* | |
| D-ABYQ | Boeing 747-230B | Lufthansa *Bremen* | |
| D-ABYR | Boeing 747-230B (SCD) | Lufthansa *Nordrhein-Westfalen* | |
| D-ABYS | Boeing 747-230B (SCD) | Lufthansa *Bayern* | |
| D-ABYT | Boeing 747-230F (SCD) | German Cargo | |
| D-ABYU | Boeing 747-230B (SCD) | Lufthansa *Asia* | |
| D-ABYW | Boeing 747-230F (SCD) | German Cargo | |
| D-ABYX | Boeing 747-230B (SCD) | Lufthansa *Köln* | |
| D-ABYY | Boeing 747-230F (SCD) | German Cargo | |
| D-ABZA | Boeing 747-230F (SCD) | Lufthansa *Düsseldorf* | |

| Notes | Reg. | Type | Owner or Operator |
|-------|------|------|-------------------|
| | D-ABZB | Boeing 747-230F (SCD) | Lufthansa *Europa* |
| | D-ABZC | Boeing 747-230B (SCD) | Lufthansa *Hannover* |
| | D-ABZD | Boeing 747-230B | Lufthansa *Kiel* |
| | D-ABZE | Boeing 747-230B (SCD) | Lufthansa *Stuttgart* |
| | D-ABZF | Boeing 747-230F (SCD) | Lufthansa *Africa* |
| | D-ABZH | Boeing 747-230B | Lufthansa *Bonn* |
| | D-ABZI | Boeing 747-230F (SCD) | Lufthansa *Australia* |
| | D-ACBA | Boeing 737-505 | Lufthansa |
| | D-ACBB | Boeing 737-505 | Lufthansa |
| | D-ACBC | Boeing 737-505 | Lufthansa |
| | D-ACFA | BAe 146-200 | Conti-Flug |
| | D-ACVK | S.E.210 Caravelle 10R | Aero Lloyd *Otto Trump* (stored) |
| | D-ADBA | Boeing 737-3L9 | Deutsche BA |
| | D-ADBB | Boeing 737-3L9 | Deutsche BA |
| | D-ADBC | Boeing 737-3L9 | Deutsche BA |
| | D-ADBD | Boeing 737-3L9 | Deutsche BA |
| | D-ADBE | Boeing 737-3L9 | Deutsche BA |
| | D-ADBF | Boeing 737-3L9 | Deutsche BA |
| | D-ADBG | Boeing 737-3L9 | Deutsche BA |
| | D-ADBO | Douglas DC-10-30 | Lufthansa |
| | D-ADCO | Douglas DC-10-30 | Lufthansa |
| | D-ADDO | Douglas DC-10-30 | Lufthansa *Duisburg* |
| | D-ADEP | F.27 Friendship Mk 600 | Ratioflug |
| | D-ADFO | Douglas DC-10-30 | Lufthansa |
| | D-ADGO | Douglas DC-10-30 | Lufthansa |
| | D-ADHO | Douglas DC-10-30 | Lufthansa |
| | D-ADJO | Douglas DC-10-30 | Lufthansa *Essen* |
| | D-ADKO | Douglas DC-10-30 | Lufthansa *Bremenhaven* |
| | D-ADLO | Douglas DC-10-30 | Lufthansa *Nürnberg* |
| | D-ADMO | Douglas DC-10-30 | Lufthansa *Dortmund* |
| | D-ADPO | Douglas DC-10-30 | Condor Flugdienst |
| | D-ADQO | Douglas DC-10-30 | Condor Flugdienst |
| | D-ADSO | Douglas DC-10-30 | Condor Flugdienst |
| | D-ADUA | Douglas DC-8-73AF | German Cargo |
| | D-ADUC | Douglas DC-8-73AF | German Cargo |
| | D-ADUE | Douglas DC-8-73AF | German Cargo |
| | D-ADUI | Douglas DC-8-73AF | German Cargo |
| | D-ADUO | Douglas DC-8-73AF | German Cargo |
| | D-AELC | F.27 Friendship Mk 600 | WDL |
| | D-AELD | F.27 Friendship Mk 600 | WDL |
| | D-AELE | F.27 Friendship Mk 600 | WDL |
| | D-AERB | McD Douglas MD-11 | LTU |
| | D-AERE | L.1011-385 TriStar 1 | LTU |
| | D-AERL | L.1011-385 TriStar 500 | LTU |
| | D-AERM | L.1011-385 TriStar 1 | LTU |
| | D-AERN | L.1011-385 TriStar 200 | LTU |
| | D-AERP | L.1011-385 TriStar 1 | LTU |
| | D-AERT | L.1011-385 TriStar 500 | LTU |
| | D-AERU | L.1011-385 TriStar 100 | LTU |
| | D-AERV | L.1011-385 TriStar 500 | LTU |
| | D-AERW | McD Douglas MD-11 | LTU |
| | D-AERX | McD Douglas MD-11 | LTU |
| | D-AERY | L.1011-385 TriStar 1 | LTU |
| | D-AERZ | McD Douglas MD-11 | LTU |
| | D-AFFA | Fokker 50 | Lufthansa CityLine |
| | D-AFFB | Fokker 50 | Lufthansa CityLine |
| | D-AFFC | Fokker 50 | Lufthansa CityLine |
| | D-AFFD | Fokker 50 | Lufthansa CityLine |
| | D-AFFI | Fokker 50 | Lufthansa CityLine |
| | D-AFFJ | Fokker 50 | Lufthansa CityLine |
| | D-AFFK | Fokker 50 | Lufthansa CityLine |
| | D-AFFL | Fokker 50 | Lufthansa CityLine |
| | D-AFKC | Fokker 50 | Lufthansa CityLine |
| | D-AFKD | Fokker 50 | Lufthansa CityLine |
| | D-AFKE | Fokker 50 | Lufthansa CityLine |
| | D-AFKF | Fokker 50 | Lufthansa CityLine |
| | D-AFKG | Fokker 50 | Lufthansa CityLine |
| | D-AFKH | Fokker 50 | Lufthansa CityLine |
| | D-AFKI | Fokker 50 | Lufthansa CityLine |
| | D-AFKJ | Fokker 50 | Lufthansa CityLine |
| | D-AFKK | Fokker 50 | Lufthansa CityLine |
| | D-AFKL | Fokker 50 | Lufthansa CityLine |
| | D-AFKM | Fokker 50 | Lufthansa CityLine |

| Reg. | Type | Owner or Operator | Notes |
|------|------|-------------------|-------|
| D-AFKN | Fokker 50 | Lufthansa CityLine | |
| D-AFKO | Fokker 50 | Lufthansa CityLine | |
| D-AFKP | Fokker 50 | Lufthansa CityLine | |
| D-AFKT | Fokker 50 | Lufthansa CityLine | |
| D-AFKU | Fokker 50 | Lufthansa CityLine | |
| D-AFKV | Fokker 50 | Lufthansa CityLine | |
| D-AFKW | Fokker 50 | Lufthansa CityLine | |
| D-AFKX | Fokker 50 | Lufthansa CityLine | |
| D-AFKY | Fokker 50 | Lufthansa CityLine | |
| D-AFKZ | Fokker 50 | Lufthansa CityLine | |
| D-AGEA | Boeing 737-35B | Germania | |
| D-AGEB | Boeing 737-35B | Germania | |
| D-AGEC | Boeing 737-35B | Germania/Condor Flugdienst | |
| D-AGED | Boeing 737-35B | Germania/Condor Flugdienst | |
| D-AGEE | Boeing 737-35B | Germania | |
| D-AGEG | Boeing 737-35B | Germania | |
| D-AGEH | Boeing 737-3L9 | Germania | |
| D-AGEI | Boeing 737-3L9 | Germania | |
| D-AGEJ | Boeing 737-3L9 | Germania | |
| D-AGWB | McD Douglas MD-83 | Aero Lloyd | |
| D-AGWC | McD Douglas MD-83 | Aero Lloyd | |
| D-AHLA | Airbus A.310-304 | Hapag-Lloyd | |
| D-AHLB | Airbus A.310-304 | Hapag-Lloyd | |
| D-AHLC | Airbus A.310-308 | Hapag-Lloyd | |
| D-AHLD | Boeing 737-5K5 | Hapag-Lloyd | |
| D-AHLE | Boeing 737-5K5 | Hapag-Lloyd | |
| D-AHLF | Boeing 737-5K5 | Hapag-Lloyd | |
| D-AHLI | Boeing 737-5K5 | Hapag-Lloyd | |
| D-AHLJ | Boeing 737-4K5 | Hapag-Lloyd | |
| D-AHLK | Boeing 737-4K5 | Hapag-Lloyd | |
| D-AHLL | Boeing 737-4K5 | Hapag-Lloyd | |
| D-AHLN | Boeing 737-5K5 | Hapag-Lloyd | |
| D-AHLO | Boeing 737-4K5 | Hapag-Lloyd | |
| D-AHLP | Boeing 737-4K5 | Hapag-Lloyd | |
| D-AHLQ | Boeing 737-4K5 | Hapag-Lloyd | |
| D-AHLR | Boeing 737-4K5 | Hapag-Lloyd | |
| D-AHLS | Boeing 737-4K5 | Hapag-Lloyd | |
| D-AHLV | Airbus A.310-204 | Hapag-Lloyd | |
| D-AHLW | Airbus A.310-204 | Hapag-Lloyd | |
| D-AHLX | Airbus A.310-204 | Hapag-Lloyd | |
| D-AHLZ | Airbus A.310-204 | Hapag-Lloyd | |
| D-AIAH | Airbus A.300-603 | Lufthansa *Lindau/Bodensee* | |
| D-AIAI | Airbus A.300-603 | Lufthansa *Erbach/Odenwald* | |
| D-AIAK | Airbus A.300-603 | Lufthansa *Kronberg/Taunus* | |
| D-AIAL | Airbus A.300-603 | Lufthansa *Stade* | |
| D-AIAM | Airbus A.300-603 | Lufthansa *Rosenheim* | |
| D-AIAN | Airbus A.300-603 | Lufthansa Express *Nördlingen* | |
| D-AIAP | Airbus A.300-603 | Lufthansa Express *Donauwörth* | |
| D-AIAR | Airbus A.300-603 | Lufthansa *Bingen am Rhein* | |
| D-AIAS | Airbus A.300-603 | Lufthansa *Monchengladbach* | |
| D-AIAT | Airbus A.300-603 | Lufthansa Express | |
| D-AIAU | Airbus A.300-603 | Lufthansa Express | |
| D-AIBA | Airbus A.340-211 | Lufthansa | |
| D-AIBB | Airbus A.340-211 | Lufthansa | |
| D-AIBC | Airbus A.340-211 | Lufthansa | |
| D-AIBD | Airbus A.340-211 | Lufthansa | |
| D-AIBE | Airbus A.340-211 | Lufthansa | |
| D-AIBF | Airbus A.340-211 | Lufthansa | |
| D-AIBH | Airbus A.340-211 | Lufthansa | |
| D-AICA | Airbus A.310-203 | Lufthansa *Neustadt an der Weinstrasse* | |
| D-AICB | Airbus A.310-203 | Lufthansa *Garmisch-Partenkirchen* | |
| D-AICC | Airbus A.310-203 | Lufthansa *Kaiserslautern* | |
| D-AICD | Airbus A.310-203 | Lufthansa *Detmold* | |
| D-AICF | Airbus A.310-203 | Lufthansa *Rüdesheim am Rhein* | |
| D-AICH | Airbus A.310-203 | Lufthansa *Lüneburg* | |
| D-AICK | Airbus A.310-203 | Lufthansa *Westerland/Sylt* | |
| D-AICL | Airbus A.310-203 | Lufthansa *Rothenburg ob der Tauber* | |
| D-AICM | Airbus A.310-203 | Lufthansa | |
| D-AICN | Airbus A.310-203 | Lufthansa *Lübeck* | |
| D-AICP | Airbus A.310-203 | Lufthansa *Bremerhaven* | |
| D-AICR | Airbus A.310-203 | Lufthansa Express *Freudenstadt* | |
| D-AICS | Airbus A.310-203 | Lufthansa Express *Recklinghausen/ Schwarzwald* | |
| D-AIDA | Airbus A.310-304 | Condor Flugdienst/Lufthansa | |

**D**

| Notes | Reg. | Type | Owner or Operator |
|---|---|---|---|
| | D-AIDB | Airbus A.310-304 | Lufthansa *Fürth* |
| | D-AIDC | Airbus A.310-304 | Condor Flugdienst/Lufthansa |
| | D-AIDD | Airbus A.310-304 | Lufthansa *Emden* |
| | D-AIDE | Airbus A.310-304 | Lufthansa *Speyer* |
| | D-AIDF | Airbus A.310-304 | Lufthansa *Aschaffenburg* |
| | D-AIDH | Airbus A.310-304 | Lufthansa *Wetzlar* |
| | D-AIDI | Airbus A.310-304 | Lufthansa *Fellbach* |
| | D-AIDK | Airbus A.310-304 | Lufthansa *Donaueschingen* |
| | D-AIDL | Airbus A.310-304 | Lufthansa *Obersdorf* |
| | D-AIDM | Airbus A.310-304 | Lufthansa *Chemnitz* |
| | D-AIDN | Airbus A.310-304 | Lufthansa *Guetersloh* |
| | D-AIGA | Airbus A.340-311 | Lufthansa |
| | D-AIGB | Airbus A.340-311 | Lufthansa |
| | D-AIGC | Airbus A.340-311 | Lufthansa |
| | D-AIGD | Airbus A.340-311 | Lufthansa |
| | D-AIGF | Airbus A.340-311 | Lufthansa |
| | D-AIGH | Airbus A.340-311 | Lufthansa |
| | D-AIGI | Airbus A.340-311 | Lufthansa |
| | D-AIGK | Airbus A.340-311 | Lufthansa |
| | D-AIPA | Airbus A.320-211 | Lufthansa *Buxtehude* |
| | D-AIPB | Airbus A.320-211 | Lufthansa *Heidelberg* |
| | D-AIPC | Airbus A.320-211 | Lufthansa *Mannheim* |
| | D-AIPD | Airbus A.320-211 | Lufthansa *Freiburg* |
| | D-AIPE | Airbus A.320-211 | Lufthansa *Kassel* |
| | D-AIPF | Airbus A.320-211 | Lufthansa *Leipzig* |
| | D-AIPH | Airbus A.320-211 | Lufthansa *Münster* |
| | D-AIPK | Airbus A.320-211 | Lufthansa *Wiesbaden* |
| | D-AIPL | Airbus A.320-211 | Lufthansa *Ludwigshafen am Rhein* |
| | D-AIPM | Airbus A.320-211 | Lufthansa *Troisdorf* |
| | D-AIPN | Airbus A.320-211 | Lufthansa *Kulmbach* |
| | D-AIPP | Airbus A.320-211 | Lufthansa *Starnberg* |
| | D-AIPR | Airbus A.320-211 | Lufthansa *Kaufbeuren* |
| | D-AIPS | Airbus A.320-211 | Lufthansa *Augsburg* |
| | D-AIPT | Airbus A.320-211 | Lufthansa *Cottbus* |
| | D-AIPU | Airbus A.320-211 | Lufthansa *Dresden* |
| | D-AIPW | Airbus A.320-211 | Lufthansa *Schwerin* |
| | D-AIPX | Airbus A.320-211 | Lufthansa |
| | D-AIPY | Airbus A.320-211 | Lufthansa *Magdeburg* |
| | D-AIPZ | Airbus A.320-211 | Lufthansa *Erfurt* |
| | D-AIQA | Airbus A.320-211 | Lufthansa *Mainz* |
| | D-AIQB | Airbus A.320-211 | Lufthansa *Bielefeld* |
| | D-AIQC | Airbus A.320-211 | Lufthansa *Zwickau* |
| | D-AIQD | Airbus A.320-211 | Lufthansa *Jena* |
| | D-AIQE | Airbus A.320-211 | Lufthansa *Gera* |
| | D-AIQF | Airbus A.320-211 | Lufthansa |
| | D-AIQH | Airbus A.320-211 | Lufthansa |
| | D-AIQK | Airbus A.320-211 | Lufthansa |
| | D-AIQL | Airbus A.320-211 | Lufthansa *Sralsund* |
| | D-AIQM | Airbus A.320-211 | Lufthansa *Nordenham* |
| | D-AIQN | Airbus A.320-211 | Lufthansa |
| | D-AIQP | Airbus A.320-211 | Lufthansa |
| | D-AIQR | Airbus A.320-211 | Lufthansa |
| | D-AIQS | Airbus A.320-211 | Lufthansa |
| | D-AIRA | Airbus A.321-132 | Lufthansa |
| | D-AIRB | Airbus A.321-132 | Lufthansa |
| | D-AIRC | Airbus A.321-132 | Lufthansa |
| | D-AIRD | Airbus A.321-132 | Lufthansa |
| | D-AISY | F.27 Friendship Mk 600 | Ratioflug |
| | D-AJET | BAe 146-200 | Conti-Flug |
| | D-ALLA | Douglas DC-9-32 | Aero Lloyd |
| | D-ALLB | Douglas DC-9-32 | Aero Lloyd |
| | D-ALLC | Douglas DC-9-32 | Aero Lloyd |
| | D-ALLD | McD Douglas MD-83 | Aero Lloyd |
| | D-ALLE | McD Douglas MD-83 | Aero Lloyd |
| | D-ALLF | McD Douglas MD-83 | Aero Lloyd |
| | D-ALLG | McD Douglas MD-87 | Aero Lloyd |
| | D-ALLH | McD Douglas MD-87 | Aero Lloyd |
| | D-ALLI | McD Douglas MD-87 | Aero Lloyd |
| | D-ALLJ | McD Douglas MD-87 | Aero Lloyd |
| | D-ALLK | McD Douglas MD-83 | Aero Lloyd |
| | D-ALLL | McD Douglas MD-83 | Aero Lloyd |
| | D-ALLM | McD Douglas MD-83 | Aero Lloyd |
| | D-ALLN | McD Douglas MD-83 | Aero Lloyd |
| | D-ALLO | McD Douglas MD-83 | Aero Lloyd |

| Reg. | Type | Owner or Operator | Notes |
|------|------|-------------------|-------|
| D-ALLP | McD Douglas MD-83 | Aero Lloyd *Kassel* | |
| D-ALLQ | McD Douglas MD-83 | Aero Lloyd | |
| D-ALLR | McD Douglas MD-83 | Aero Lloyd | |
| D-AMUM | Boeing 757-2G5ER | LTU-Sud | |
| D-AMUN | Boeing 767-3G5ER | LTU-Sud | |
| D-AMUP | Boeing 767-33AER | LTU-Sud | |
| D-AMUR | Boeing 767-3G5ER | LTU-Sud | |
| D-AMUS | Boeing 767-3G5ER | LTU-Sud | |
| D-AMUU | Boeing 757-225 | LTU-Sud | |
| D-AMUV | Boeing 757-2G5ER | LTU-Sud | |
| D-AMUW | Boeing 757-2G5ER | LTU-Sud | |
| D-AMUX | Boeing 757-2G5ER | LTU-Sud | |
| D-AMUY | Boeing 757-2G5ER | LTU-Sud | |
| D-AMUZ | Boeing 757-2G5ER | LTU-Sud | |
| D-ANFA | Aérospatiale ATR-72-202 | Euro Wings | |
| D-ANFB | Aérospatiale ATR-72-202 | Euro Wings | |
| D-ANFC | Aérospatiale ATR-72-202 | Euro Wings | |
| D-ANFD | Aérospatiale ATR-72-202 | Euro Wings | |
| D-ANFE | Aérospatiale ATR-72-202 | Euro Wings | |
| D-ANFF | Aérospatiale ATR-72-202 | Euro Wings | |
| D-ANFG | Aérospatiale ATR-72-202 | Euro Wings | |
| D-ANFH | Aérospatiale ATR-72-202 | Euro Wings | |
| D-ANTJ | BAe 146-200QT | Euro Wings/TNT Express Europe | |
| D-ARJA | Canadair Regional Jet 100ER | Lufthansa CityLine | |
| D-ARJB | Canadair Regional Jet 100ER | Lufthansa CityLine | |
| D-ARJC | Canadair Regional Jet 100ER | Lufthansa CityLine | |
| D-ARJD | Canadair Regional Jet 100ER | Lufthansa CityLine | |
| D-ARJE | Canadair Regional Jet 100ER | Lufthansa CityLine | |
| D-ARJF | Canadair Regional Jet 100ER | Lufthansa CityLine | |
| D-ARJG | Canadair Regional Jet 100ER | Lufthansa CityLine | |
| D-ARJH | Canadair Regional Jet 100ER | Lufthansa CityLine | |
| D-ARJI | Canadair Regional Jet 100ER | Lufthansa CityLine | |
| D-ARJJ | Canadair Regional Jet 100ER | Lufthansa CityLine | |
| D-ARJK | Canadair Regional Jet 100ER | Lufthansa CityLine | |
| D-ARJL | Canadair Regional Jet 100ER | Lufthansa CityLine | |
| D-ARJM | Canadair Regional Jet 100ER | Lufthansa CityLine | |
| D-BAAA | Aerospatiale ATR-42-300 | Euro Wings | |
| D-BAGB | D.H.C.8 Dash Eight | Interot Airways | |
| D-BAKA | F.27 Friendship Mk 100 | WDL | |
| D-BAKI | F.27 Friendship Mk 100 | WDL | |
| D-BAKO | F.27 Friendship Mk 100 | WDL | |
| D-BAKU | F.27 Friendship Mk 200 | WDL | |
| D-BBBB | Aérospatiale ATR-42-300 | Euro Wings | |
| D-BCCC | Aérospatiale ATR-42-300 | Euro Wings | |
| D-BCRM | Aérospatiale ATR-42-300 | Euro Wings | |
| D-BCRN | Aérospatiale ATR-42-300 | Euro Wings | |
| D-BCRO | Aérospatiale ATR-42-300QC | Euro Wings | |
| D-BCRP | Aérospatiale ATR-42-300QC | Euro Wings | |
| D-BCRQ | Aérospatiale ATR-42-300 | Euro Wings | |
| D-BCRR | Aérospatiale ATR-42-300 | Euro Wings | |
| D-BCRS | Aérospatiale ATR-42-300 | Euro Wings | |
| D-BCRT | Aérospatiale ATR-42-300 | Euro Wings | |
| D-BDDD | Aérospatiale ATR-42-300 | Euro Wings | |
| D-BEEE | Aérospatiale ATR-42-300 | Euro Wings | |
| D-BELT | D.H.C.8-311 Dash Eight | Contactair/Lufthansa CityLine | |
| D-BERT | D.H.C.8-103 Dash Eight | Contactair/Lufthansa CityLine | |
| D-BEST | D.H.C.8-103 Dash Eight | Contactair/Lufthansa CityLine | |
| D-BEYT | D.H.C.8-311 Dash Eight | Contactair/Lufthansa CityLine | |
| D-BFFF | Aérospatiale ATR-42-300 | Euro Wings | |
| D-BGGG | Aérospatiale ATR-42-300 | Euro Wings | |
| D-BHHH | Aérospatiale ATR-42-300 | Euro Wings | |
| D-BIER | D.H.C.8-103 Dash Eight | Interot Airways | |
| D-BIII | Aérospatiale ATR-42-300 | Euro Wings | |
| D-BIRT | D.H.C.8-103 Dash Eight | Interot Airways | |
| D-BJJJ | Aérospatiale ATR-42-300 | Euro Wings | |
| D-BKIS | D.H.C.8-311 Dash Eight | Contactair/Lufthansa CityLine | |
| D-BOBA | D.H.C.8-311 Dash Eight | Hamburg Airlines | |
| D-BOBE | D.H.C.8-311 Dash Eight | Hamburg Airlines | |
| D-BOBL | D.H.C.8-102 Dash Eight | Hamburg Airlines | |
| D-BOBO | D.H.C.8-102 Dash Eight | Hamburg Airlines | |
| D-BOBU | D.H.C.8-311 Dash Eight | Hamburg Airlines | |
| D-BOBY | D.H.C.8-102 Dash Eight | Hamburg Airlines | |
| D-CABE | Swearingen SA227AC Metro III | Euro Wings | |

| Notes | Reg. | Type | Owner or Operator |
|---|---|---|---|
| | D-CABI | Swearingen SA227AC Metro III | Euro Wings |
| | D-CALK | Dornier Do.228-202K | Ratioflug |
| | D-CDIA | SAAB SF.340A | Deutsche BA |
| | D-CDIB | SAAB SF.340A | Deutsche BA |
| | D-CDIC | SAAB SF.340A | Deutsche BA |
| | D-CDID | SAAB SF.340A | Deutsche BA |
| | D-CDIE | SAAB SF.340A | Deutsche BA |
| | D-CDIF | SAAB SF.340A | Deutsche BA |
| | D-CDIG | SAAB SF.340A | Deutsche BA |
| | D-CDIH | SAAB SF.340A | Deutsche BA |
| | D-CDIJ | SAAB SF.340A | Deutsche BA |
| | D-CDIZ | Dornier Do.228-201 | Deutsche BA |
| | D-CHOF | Dornier Do.228-202 | Euro Wings |
| | D-CIRB | Beech 1900C-1 | Interot Airways |
| | D-CISA | Beech 1900C | Interot Airways |
| | D-CKVW | Swearingen SA227AC Metro III | Euro Wings |
| | D-CMIC | Dornier Do.228-202K | Ratioflug |
| | D-CONA | BAe Jetstream 3102 | Contactair |
| | D-CONU | BAe Jetstream 3102 | Contactair |

## EC (Spain)

| Notes | Reg. | Type | Owner or Operator |
|---|---|---|---|
| | EC-BIG | Douglas DC-9-32 | Iberia *Villa de Madrid* |
| | EC-BIH | Douglas DC-9-32 | Aviaco |
| | EC-BIJ | Douglas DC-9-32 | Iberia *Santa Cruz de Tenerife* |
| | EC-BIK | Douglas DC-9-32 | Aviaco *Castillo de Guanapay* |
| | EC-BIM | Douglas DC-9-32 | Iberia *Ciudad de Santander* |
| | EC-BIN | Douglas DC-9-32 | Iberia *Palma de Mallorca* |
| | EC-BIO | Douglas DC-9-32 | Aviaco |
| | EC-BIP | Douglas DC-9-32 | Aviaco *Castillo de Monteagudo* |
| | EC-BIR | Douglas DC-9-32 | Iberia |
| | EC-BIS | Douglas DC-9-32 | Iberia |
| | EC-BIT | Douglas DC-9-32 | Iberia |
| | EC-BPG | Douglas DC-9-32 | Iberia *Ciudad de Vigo* |
| | EC-BPH | Douglas DC-9-32 | Iberia *Ciudad de Gerona* |
| | EC-BQT | Douglas DC-9-32 | Iberia *Ciudad de Murcia* |
| | EC-BQU | Douglas DC-9-32 | Iberia *Ciudad de La Coruna* |
| | EC-BQV | Douglas DC-9-32 | Iberia *Ciudad de Ibiza* |
| | EC-BQX | Douglas DC-9-32 | Iberia *Ciudad de Valladolid* |
| | EC-BQY | Douglas DC-9-32 | Aviaco |
| | EC-BQZ | Douglas DC-9-32 | Iberia *Ciudad de Sta Cruz de La Palma* |
| | EC-BRQ | Boeing 747-256B | Iberia *Calderon de la Barca* |
| | EC-BYE | Douglas DC-9-32 | Aviaco |
| | EC-BYF | Douglas DC-9-32 | Aviaco *Hernan Cortes* |
| | EC-BYI | Douglas DC-9-32 | Aviaco *Pedro de Valdivia* |
| | EC-BYJ | Douglas DC-9-32 | Aviaco |
| | EC-CAI | Boeing 727-256 | Iberia *Castilla la Nueva* |
| | EC-CAJ | Boeing 727-256 | Iberia *Cataluna* |
| | EC-CBA | Boeing 727-256 | Iberia *Vascongadas* |
| | EC-CBB | Boeing 727-256 | Iberia *Valencia* |
| | EC-CBC | Boeing 727-256 | Iberia *Navarra* |
| | EC-CBD | Boeing 727-256 | Iberia *Murcia* |
| | EC-CBE | Boeing 727-256 | Iberia *Leon* |
| | EC-CBF | Boeing 727-256 | Iberia *Gran Canaria* |
| | EC-CBG | Boeing 727-256 | Iberia *Extremadura* |
| | EC-CBH | Boeing 727-256 | Iberia *Galicia* |
| | EC-CBI | Boeing 727-256 | Iberia *Asturias* |
| | EC-CBJ | Boeing 727-256 | Iberia *Andalucia* |
| | EC-CBL | Boeing 727-256 | Iberia *Tenerife* |
| | EC-CBM | Boeing 727-256 | Iberia *Castilla La Vieja* |
| | EC-CBO | Douglas DC-10-30 | Iberia *Costa del Sol* |
| | EC-CBP | Douglas DC-10-30 | Iberia *Costa Dorada* |
| | EC-CEZ | Douglas DC-10-30 | Iberia *Costa del Azahar* |
| | EC-CFA | Boeing 727-256 | Iberia *Jerez Xeres Sherry* |
| | EC-CFB | Boeing 727-256 | Iberia *Rioja* |
| | EC-CFC | Boeing 727-256 | Iberia *Tarragona* |
| | EC-CFD | Boeing 727-256 | Iberia *Montilla-Moriles* |
| | EC-CFE | Boeing 727-256 | Iberia *Penedes* |
| | EC-CFF | Boeing 727-256 | Iberia *Valdepenas* |
| | EC-CFG | Boeing 727-256 | Iberia *La Mancha* |
| | EC-CFH | Boeing 727-256 | Iberia *Priorato* |
| | EC-CFI | Boeing 727-256 | Iberia *Carinena* |
| | EC-CFK | Boeing 727-256 | Iberia *Ribeiro* |

| Reg. | Type | Owner or Operator | Notes |
|------|------|-------------------|-------|
| EC-CGN | Douglas DC-9-32 | Aviaco *Martin Alonso Pinzon* | |
| EC-CGO | Douglas DC-9-32 | Aviaco *Pedro Alonso Nino* | |
| EC-CGP | Douglas DC-9-32 | Aviaco *Juan Sebastian Elcano* | |
| EC-CGQ | Douglas DC-9-32 | Aviaco *Alonso de Ojeda* | |
| EC-CGR | Douglas DC-9-32 | Aviaco *Francisco de Orellana* | |
| EC-CID | Boeing 727-256 | Iberia *Malaga* | |
| EC-CIE | Boeing 727-256 | Iberia *Esparragosa* | |
| EC-CLB | Douglas DC-10-30 | Iberia *Costa Blanca* | |
| EC-CLD | Douglas DC-9-32 | Aviaco *Hernando de Soto* | |
| EC-CLE | Douglas DC-9-32 | Aviaco *Juan Ponce de Leon* | |
| EC-CSJ | Douglas DC-10-30 | Iberia *Costa de la Luz* | |
| EC-CSK | Douglas DC-10-30 | Iberia *Cornisa Cantabrica* | |
| EC-CTR | Douglas DC-9-34CF | Iberia | |
| EC-CTS | Douglas DC-9-34CF | Aviaco *Francisco de Pizarro* | |
| EC-CTT | Douglas DC-9-34CF | Iberia | |
| EC-CTU | Douglas DC-9-34CF | Aviaco *Pedro de Alvarado* | |
| EC-DCC | Boeing 727-256 | Iberia *Albarino* | |
| EC-DCD | Boeing 727-256 | Iberia *Chacoli-Txakoli* | |
| EC-DCE | Boeing 727-256 | Iberia *Mentrida* | |
| EC-DDV | Boeing 727-256 | Iberia *Acueducto de Segovia* | |
| EC-DDX | Boeing 727-256 | Iberia *Monasterio de Poblet* | |
| EC-DDY | Boeing 727-256 | Iberia *Cuevas de Altamira* | |
| EC-DDZ | Boeing 727-256 | Iberia *Murallas de Avila* | |
| EC-DEA | Douglas DC-10-30 | Iberia *Rias Gallegas* | |
| EC-DGB | Douglas DC-9-34 | Iberia | |
| EC-DGC | Douglas DC-9-34 | Aviaco *Castillo de Sotomayor* | |
| EC-DGD | Douglas DC-9-34 | Aviaco *Castillo de Arcos* | |
| EC-DGE | Douglas DC-9-34 | Aviaco *Castillo de Bellver* | |
| EC-DHZ | Douglas DC-10-30 | Iberia *Costas Canarias* | |
| EC-DIA | Boeing 747-256B | Iberia *Tirso de Molina* | |
| EC-DIB | Boeing 747-256B | Iberia *Cervantes* | |
| EC-DLC | Boeing 747-256B (SCD) | Iberia *Francisco de Quevedo* | |
| EC-DLD | Boeing 747-256B (SCD) | Iberia *Lupe de Vega* | |
| EC-DLE | Airbus A.300B4-120 | Iberia *Donana* | |
| EC-DLF | Airbus A.300B4-120 | Iberia *Canadas del Teide* | |
| EC-DLG | Airbus A.300B4-120 | Iberia *Las Tablas de Daimiel* | |
| EC-DLH | Airbus A.300B4-120 | Iberia *Aigues Tortes* | |
| EC-DNP | Boeing 747-256B | Iberia *Juan Ramon Jimenez* | |
| EC-DNQ | Airbus A.300B4-120 | Iberia *Islas Cies* | |
| EC-DNR | Airbus A.300B4-120 | Iberia *Ordesa* | |
| EC-EEK | Boeing 747-256B (SCD) | Iberia *Garcia Lorca* | |
| EC-EFX | Boeing 757-2G5 | LTE International Airways *Bluebird I* | |
| EC-EGH | Boeing 757-2G5 | LTE International Airways *Bluebird II* | |
| EC-EHT | McD Douglas MD-83 | Spanair *Sunrise* | |
| EC-EIG | McD Douglas MD-83 | Spanair *Sunlight* | |
| EC-EJQ | McD Douglas MD-83 | Spanair *Sunshine* | |
| EC-EJU | McD Douglas MD-83 | Spanair *Sunbird* | |
| EC-ELM | Douglas DC-8-62F | Cargosur | |
| EC-ELT | BAe 146-200QT | Pan Air Lineas Aéreas/TNT | |
| EC-ELY | Boeing 737-3K9 | Viva Air | |
| EC-EMD | Douglas DC-8-62F | Cargosur | |
| EC-EMT | McD Douglas MD-83 | Aviaco *Puerta de Alcala* | |
| EC-EMX | Douglas DC-8-62F | Cargosur | |
| EC-ENQ | Boeing 757-2G5 | LTE International Airways *Bluebird III* | |
| EC-EOL | Boeing 757-236 | Air Europa | |
| EC-EON | Airbus A.300B4-203 | Iberia *Penalara* | |
| EC-EOO | Airbus A.300B4-203 | Iberia *Covadouga* | |
| EC-EOZ | McD Douglas MD-83 | Spanair *Sunbeam* | |
| EC-EPA | BAe 146-200QT | Pan Air Lineas Aéreas/TNT | |
| EC-EPL | McD Douglas MD-83 | Spanair *Sunseeker* | |
| EC-EQI | Douglas DC-8-62F | Cargosur | |
| EC-ESC | Boeing 757-236ER | Air Europa | |
| EC-ESJ | McD Douglas MD-83 | Spanair *Sunflower* | |
| EC-ETB | Boeing 737-4Y0 | Futura International Airways | |
| EC-ETZ | Boeing 757-225 | LTE International Airways *Bluebird IV* | |
| EC-EUC | McD Douglas MD-87 | Iberia *Ciudad de Burgos* | |
| EC-EUD | McD Douglas MD-87 | Iberia *Ciudad de Toledo* | |
| EC-EUE | McD Douglas MD-87 | Iberia *Ciudad de Sevilla* | |
| EC-EUL | McD Douglas MD-87 | Iberia *Ciudad de Cadiz* | |
| EC-EVB | McD Douglas MD-87 | Iberia *Arrecife de Lanzarote* | |
| EC-EVE | Boeing 737-4Y0 | Futura International Airways | |
| EC-EXF | McD Douglas MD-87 | Iberia *Ciudad de Pamplona* | |
| EC-EXG | McD Douglas MD-87 | Iberia *Ciudad de Almeria* | |

| Notes | Reg. | Type | Owner or Operator |
|---|---|---|---|
| | EC-EXM | McD Douglas MD-87 | Iberia *Ciudad de Zaragoza* |
| | EC-EXN | McD Douglas MD-87 | Iberia *Ciudad de Badajoz* |
| | EC-EXR | McD Douglas MD-87 | Iberia *Ciudad de Oviedo* |
| | EC-EXT | McD Douglas MD-87 | Iberia *Ciudad de Albacete* |
| | EC-EXX | McD Douglas MD-83 | Oasis International Airlines |
| | EC-EXY | Boeing 737-4Y0 | Futura International Airways |
| | EC-EYB | McD Douglas MD-87 | Iberia *Ciudad de Onis* |
| | EC-EYX | McD Douglas MD-87 | Iberia *Ciudad de Caceres* |
| | EC-EYY | McD Douglas MD-87 | Iberia *Ciudad de Barcelona* |
| | EC-EYZ | McD Douglas MD-87 | Iberia *Ciudad de Las Palmas* |
| | EC-EZA | McD Douglas MD-87 | Iberia *Ciudad de Segovia* |
| | EC-EZS | McD Douglas MD-87 | Iberia *Ciudad de Mahon* |
| | EC-EZU | McD Douglas MD-83 | Oasis International Airlines |
| | EC-FAS | Airbus A.320-211 | Iberia *Sierra de Cazorla* |
| | EC-FBP | Boeing 737-4Y0 | Futura International Airways |
| | EC-FBQ | Airbus A.320-211 | Iberia *Montseny* |
| | EC-FBR | Airbus A.320-211 | Iberia *Segura* |
| | EC-FBS | Airbus A.320-211 | Iberia *Timanfaya* |
| | EC-FCB | Airbus A.320-211 | Iberia *Montana de Covadonga* |
| | EC-FCU | Boeing 767-3Y0ER | Spanair *Baleares* |
| | EC-FDA | Airbus A.320-211 | Iberia *Lagunas de Ruidera* |
| | EC-FDB | Airbus A.320-211 | Iberia *Lago de Sanabria* |
| | EC-FEE | Boeing 757-236 | Air Europa |
| | EC-FEF | Boeing 757-236 | Air Europa |
| | EC-FEO | Airbus A.320-211 | Iberia *Delta del Ebro* |
| | EC-FEP | McDouglas MD-83 | Oasis International Airways |
| | EC-FER | Boeing 737-3Q8 | Viva Air |
| | EC-FET | Boeing 737-3Q8 | Viva Air |
| | EC-FEY | McD Douglas MD-87 | Iberia *Ciudad de Jaen* |
| | EC-FEZ | McD Douglas MD-87 | Iberia *Ciudad de Malaga* |
| | EC-FFA | McD Douglas MD-87 | Iberia *Ciudad de Avila* |
| | EC-FFC | Boeing 737-3Q8 | Viva Air |
| | EC-FFH | McD Douglas MD-87 | Iberia *Ciudad de Logrono* |
| | EC-FFI | McD Douglas MD-87 | Iberia *Ciudad de Cuenca* |
| | EC-FFK | Boeing 757-236 | Air Europa |
| | EC-FFN | Boeing 737-36E | Viva Air |
| | EC-FFY | BAe 146-300 | Pan Air Lineas Aéreas/TNT |
| | EC-FGH | Airbus A.320-211 | Iberia *Caldera de Taburiente* |
| | EC-FGM | McD Douglas MD-88 | Aviaco *Torre de Hércules* |
| | EC-FGR | Airbus A.320-211 | Iberia *Dehesa de Moncayo* |
| | EC-FGU | Airbus A.320-211 | Iberia *Sierra Espuna* |
| | EC-FGV | Airbus A.320-211 | Iberia *Monfrague* |
| | EC-FHA | Boeing 767-3Y0ER | Spanair *Canarias* |
| | EC-FHD | McD Douglas MD-87 | Iberia *Ciudad de Leon* |
| | EC-FHG | McD Douglas MD-88 | Aviaco *La Almudiana* |
| | EC-FHK | McD Douglas MD-87 | Iberia *Ciudad de Tarragona* |
| | EC-FHR | Boeing 737-36E | Viva Air |
| | EC-FIA | Airbus A.320-211 | Iberia *Isla de la Cartuja* |
| | EC-FIC | Airbus A.320-211 | Iberia *Sierra de Grazalema* |
| | EC-FIG | McD Douglas MD-88 | Aviaco *Penon de Ifach* |
| | EC-FIH | McD Douglas MD-88 | Aviaco *Albaicin* |
| | EC-FJE | McD Douglas MD-88 | Aviaco *Gibralfaro* |
| | EC-FJQ | McD Douglas MD-82 | Spanair |
| | EC-FJR | Boeing 737-3Y0 | Air Europa |
| | EC-FJZ | Boeing 737-3Y0 | Air Europa |
| | EC-FKC | Boeing 737-3L9 | Air Europa |
| | EC-FKD | Airbus A.320-211 | Iberia *Monte Alhoya* |
| | EC-FKH | Airbus A.320-211 | Iberia *Canon de Rio Lobos* |
| | EC-FKI | Boeing 737-375 | Air Europa |
| | EC-FKJ | Boeing 737-3Y0 | Air Europa |
| | EC-FKS | Boeing 737-3L9 | Air Europa |
| | EC-FLD | Boeing 737-4Y0 | Futura International Airways |
| | EC-FLF | Boeing 737-36E | Viva Air |
| | EC-FLG | Boeing 737-36E | Viva Air |
| | EC-FLK | McD Douglas MD-88 | Aviaco *Palacio de la Magdalena* |
| | EC-FLN | McD Douglas MD-88 | Aviaco *Puerta de Tierra* |
| | EC-FLP | Airbus A.320-211 | Iberia *Torcal de Antequera* |
| | EC-FLQ | Airbus A.320-211 | Iberia *Dunas de Liencres* |
| | EC-FLY | Boeing 757-236 | LTE International Airways |
| | EC-FMJ | Boeing 737-4Y0 | Futura International Airways |
| | EC-FML | Airbus A.320-211 | Iberia *Hayedo de Tejara Negra* |
| | EC-FMN | Airbus A.320-211 | Iberia *Cadi Moixeroi* |
| | EC-FMP | Boeing 737-33A | Viva Air |

## OVERSEAS AIRLINERS

| Reg. | Type | Owner or Operator |
|------|------|-------------------|
| EC-FMQ | Boeing 757-236ER | Air Europa |
| EC-FND | McD Douglas MD-88 | Aviaco |
| EC-FNI | Airbus A.310-324 | Oasis International Airlines |
| EC-FNO | McD Douglas MD-88 | Aviaco *Playa de la Concha* |
| EC-FNR | Airbus A.320-211 | Iberia *Monte de Valle* |
| EC-FNU | McD Douglas MD-83 | Spanair *Sunray* |
| EC- | Boeing 737-3Y0 | Air Europa |
| EC- | Boeing 737-348 | Futura International Airways |
| EC- | Boeing 737-348 | Futura International Airways |
| EC-FOF | McD Douglas MD-88 | Aviaco |
| EC-FOG | McD Douglas MD-88 | Aviaco |
| EC-FOZ | McD Douglas MD-88 | Aviaco *Montjuic* |
| EC-FPD | McD Douglas MD-88 | Aviaco *Ria de Vigo* |

# EI (Republic of Ireland)

Including complete current Irish Civil Register

| Reg. | Type | Owner or Operator |
|------|------|-------------------|
| EI-ABI | D.H.84 Dragon | Aer Lingus *Iolar* (EI-AFK) |
| EI-ADV | PA-12 Super Cruiser | R. E. Levis |
| EI-AFE | Piper J3C-65 Cub | O. Bruton |
| EI-AFF | B.A. Swallow 2 ★ | J. McCarthy |
| EI-AFN | B.A. Swallow 2 ★ | J. McCarthy |
| EI-AGB | Miles M.38 Messenger 4 ★ | J. McLoughlin |
| EI-AGD | Taylorcraft Plus D ★ | H. Wolf |
| EI-AGJ | J/1 Autocrat | W. G. Rafter |
| EI-AHA | D.H.82A Tiger Moth ★ | J. H. Maher |
| EI-AHR | D.H.C.1 Chipmunk 22 ★ | C. Lane |
| EI-AKM | Piper J-3C-65 Cub | Setanta Flying Group |
| EI-ALH | Taylorcraft Plus D | N. Reilly |
| EI-ALP | Avro 643 Cadet | J. C. O'Loughlin |
| EI-ALU | Avro 631 Cadet | M. P. Cahill (*stored*) |
| EI-AMK | J/1 Autocrat | Irish Aero Club |
| EI-AND | Cessna 175A | M. A. Cooke |
| EI-ANT | Champion 7ECA Citabria | S. Donohoe |
| EI-ANY | PA-18 Super Cub 95 | Bogavia Group |
| EI-AOB | PA-28 Cherokee 140 | J. Surdival & ptnrs |
| EI-AOK | Cessna F.172G | R. J. Cloughley & N. J. Simpson |
| EI-AOP | D.H.82A Tiger Moth ★ | Institute of Technology/Dublin |
| EI-AOS | Cessna 310B | Joyce Aviation Ltd |
| EI-APF | Cessna F.150F | L. O. Kennedy |
| EI-APS | Schleicher ASK.14 | SLG Group |
| EI-ARH | Currie Wot/S.E.5 Replica | L. Garrison |
| EI-ARM | Currie Wot/S.E.5 Replica | L. Garrison |
| EI-ARW | Jodel D.R.1050 | P. Walsh & P. Ryan |
| EI-ASD | Boeing 737-248C | Alitalia Cargo |
| EI-ASE | Boeing 737-248C | Alitalia Cargo |
| EI-ASG | Boeing 737-248 ★ | *Instructional airframe*/Dublin |
| EI-ASH | Boeing 737-248 | Aer Lingus *St Eugene* |
| EI-ASI | Boeing 747-148 | Aer Lingus *St Patrick* |
| EI-ASJ | Boeing 747-148 | Aer Lingus *St Colmcille* |
| EI-ASL | Boeing 737-248C | Aer Lingus *St Killian* |
| EI-AST | Cessna F.150H | Liberty Flying Group |
| EI-ATC | Cessna 310G | Iona National Airways Ltd |
| EI-ATJ | B.121 Pup 1 | Wexford Aero Club |
| EI-ATK | PA-28 Cherokee 140 | Mayo Flying Club Ltd |
| EI-ATS | M.S.880B Rallye Club | ATS Group |
| EI-AUC | Cessna FA.150K Aerobat | Kestrel Flying Group |
| EI-AUE | M.S.880B Rallye Club | Kilkenny Flying Club Ltd |
| EI-AUG | M.S.894 Rallye Minerva 220 | K. O'Leary |
| EI-AUJ | M.S.880B Rallye Club | Ormond Flying Club Ltd |
| EI-AUM | J/1 Autocrat | J. G. Rafter |
| EI-AUO | Cessna FA.150K Aerobat | Kerry Aero Club |
| EI-AUS | J/5F Aiglet Trainer | T. Stephens & T. Lennon |
| EI-AUT | Forney F-1A Aircoupe | Joyce Aviation Ltd |
| EI-AUV | PA-23 Aztec 250C | Shannon Executive Aviation |
| EI-AUY | Morane-Saulnier M.S.502 | G. Warner/Duxford |
| EI-AVB | Aeronca 7AC Champion | P. Ryan |
| EI-AVC | Cessna F.337F | 337 Flying Group |
| EI-AVM | Cessna F.150L | P. Kearney |
| EI-AVN | Hughes 369HM | Helicopter Maintenance Ltd |
| EI-AWE | Cessna F.150M | Third Flight Group |
| EI-AWH | Cessna 210J | Cork Flying Club Ltd |

| Notes | Reg. | Type | Owner or Operator |
|---|---|---|---|
| | EI-AWP | D.H.82A Tiger Moth | A. Lyons |
| | EI-AWR | Malmo MFI-9 Junior | M. R. Nesbitt & S. Duignan |
| | EI-AWU | M.S.880B Rallye Club | Longford Aviation Ltd |
| | EI-AWW | Cessna 414 | Shannon Executive Aviation Ltd |
| | EI-AYA | M.S.880B Rallye Club | D. Bothwell & ptnrs |
| | EI-AYB | GY-80 Horizon 180 | Westwing Flying Group |
| | EI-AYD | AA-5 Traveler | P. Howick & ptnrs |
| | EI-AYF | Cessna FRA.150L | Garda Flying Club |
| | EI-AYI | M.S.880B Rallye Club | J. McNamara |
| | EI-AYK | Cessna F.172M | S. T. Scully |
| | EI-AYN | BN-2A Islander | Aer Arran *Inis-Mór* |
| | EI-AYO | Douglas DC-3A ★ | Science Museum, Wroughton |
| | EI-AYR | Schleicher ASK-16 | Kilkenny Airport Ltd |
| | EI-AYS | PA-22 Colt 108 | M. Skelly & R. Hall |
| | EI-AYV | M.S.892A Rallye Commodore 150 | P. Murtagh |
| | EI-AYW | PA-23 Aztec 250 | Chutehall International Ltd |
| | EI-AYY | Evans VP-1 | M. Donoghue |
| | | | |
| | EI-BAF | Thunder Ax6-56 balloon | W. G. Woollett |
| | EI-BAJ | SNCAN Stampe SV-4C | Dublin Tiger Group |
| | EI-BAO | Cessna F.172G | Garda Flying Group |
| | EI-BAR | Thunder Ax8-105 balloon | J. Burke & V. Hourihane |
| | EI-BAS | Cessna F.172M | Falcon Aviation Ltd |
| | EI-BAT | Cessna F.150M | Donegal Aero Club Ltd |
| | EI-BAV | PA-22 Colt 108 | J. Davy |
| | EI-BBC | PA-28 Cherokee 180C | B. Healy |
| | EI-BBD | Evans VP-1 | Volksplane Group |
| | EI-BBE | Champion 7FC Tri-Traveler (tailwheel) | P. Forde & D. Connaire |
| | EI-BBG | M.S.880B Rallye Club | Weston Ltd |
| | EI-BBI | M.S.892 Rallye Commodore | Kilkenny Airport Ltd |
| | EI-BBJ | M.S.880B Rallye Club | Weston Ltd |
| | EI-BBM | Cameron O-65 balloon | Dublin Ballooning Club |
| | EI-BBN | Cessna F.150M | Sligo N.W. Aero Club |
| | EI-BBO | M.S.893E Rallye 180GT | J. G. Lacey & ptnrs |
| | EI-BBV | Piper J-3C-65 Cub | F. Cronin |
| | EI-BCE | BN-2A-26 Islander | Aer Arann |
| | EI-BCF | Bensen B.8M | T. A. Brennan |
| | EI-BCH | M.S.892A Rallye Commodore 150 | The Condor Group |
| | EI-BCJ | F.8L Falco 1 Srs 3 | D. Kelly |
| | EI-BCK | Cessna F.172K | H. Caulfield |
| | EI-BCL | Cessna 182P | Iona National Airways |
| | EI-BCM | Piper J-3C-65 Cub | Kilmoon Flying Group |
| | EI-BCN | Piper J-3C-65 Cub | Snowflake Flying Group |
| | EI-BCO | Piper J-3C-65 Cub | J. Molloy |
| | EI-BCP | D.628 Condor | A. Delaney |
| | EI-BCR | Boeing 737-281 | Aer Lingus *St Oliver Plunkett* |
| | EI-BCS | M.S.880B Rallye Club | Organic Fruit & Vegetables of Ireland Ltd |
| | EI-BCT | Cessna 411A | Avmark (Ireland) Ltd |
| | EI-BCU | M.S.880B Rallye Club | Weston Ltd |
| | EI-BCW | M.S.880B Rallye Club | Kilkenny Flying Club |
| | EI-BCY | Beech 200 Super King Air (232) | Minister of Defence |
| | EI-BDH | M.S.880B Rallye Club | Munster Wings Ltd |
| | EI-BDK | M.S.880B Rallye Club | Limerick Flying Club Ltd |
| | EI-BDL | Evans VP-2 | J. Hackett |
| | EI-BDM | PA-23 Aztec 250D ★ | Industrial Training School |
| | EI-BDP | Cessna 182P | S. Bruton |
| | EI-BDR | PA-28 Cherokee 180 | Cherokee Group |
| | EI-BDY | Boeing 737-2E1 | Aer Lingus Teo *St Brigid* |
| | EI-BEA | M.S.880B Rallye 100ST | Weston Ltd |
| | EI-BEB | Boeing 737-248 | Aer Lingus Teo *(leased in India)* |
| | EI-BEC | Boeing 737-248 | Aer Lingus Teo *(leased in India)* |
| | EI-BED | Boeing 747-130 | Aer Linte Eireann Teo *St Kieran* |
| | EI-BEE | Boeing 737-281 | Aer Lingus Teo *St Cronan* |
| | EI-BEI | — | Aer Lingus Teo |
| | EI-BEJ | — | Aer Lingus Teo |
| | EI-BEN | Piper J-3C-65 Cub | J. J. Sullivan |
| | EI-BEO | Cessna 310Q | Iona National Airways |
| | EI-BEP | M.S.892A Rallye Commodore 150 | H. Lynch & J. O'Leary |
| | EI-BEY | Naval N3N-3 ★ | Huntley & Huntley Ltd |
| | EI-BFF | Beech A.23 Musketeer | E. Hopkins |
| | EI-BFH | Bell 212 | Irish Helicopters Ltd |
| | EI-BFI | M.S.880B Rallye 100ST | J. O'Neill |

| Reg. | Type | Owner or Operator | Notes |
|------|------|-------------------|-------|
| EI-BFJ | Beech A.200 Super King Air (234) | Minister of Defence | |
| EI-BFM | M.S.893E Rallye 235GT | J. K. Group | |
| EI-BFO | Piper J-3C-90 Cub | D. Gordon | |
| EI-BFP | M.S.800B Rallye 100ST | Weston Ltd | |
| EI-BFR | M.S.880B Rallye 100ST | G. P. Moorhead | |
| EI-BFV | M.S.880B Rallye 100T | Ormond Flying Club | |
| EI-BGA | SOCATA Rallye 100ST | J. J. Frew | |
| EI-BGB | M.S.880B Rallye Club | Limerick Flying Club | |
| EI-BGD | M.S.880B Rallye Club | N. Kavanagh | |
| EI-BGG | M.S.892E Rallye 150GT | M. J. Hanlon | |
| EI-BGH | Cessna F.172N | Iona National Airways | |
| EI-BGJ | Cessna F.152 | Hibernian Flying Club | |
| EI-BGO | Canadair CL-44D-4J ★ | Irish Airports Authority/Dublin | |
| EI-BGT | Colt 77A balloon | K. Haugh | |
| EI-BGU | M.S.880B Rallye Club | M. F. Neary | |
| EI-BHB | M.S.887 Rallye 125 | Hotel Bravo Flying Club | |
| EI-BHC | Cessna F.177RG | P. V. Maguire | |
| EI-BHF | M.S.892A Rallye Commodore 150 | B. Mullen | |
| EI-BHI | Bell 206B JetRanger 2 | J. Mansfield | |
| EI-BHK | M.S.880B Rallye Club | J. Lawlor & B. Lyons | |
| EI-BHL | Beech E90 King Air | Stewart Singlam Fabrics Ltd | |
| EI-BHM | Cessna 337E | Positively Belfast | |
| EI-BHN | M.S.893A Rallye Commodore 180 | K. O'Connor | |
| EI-BHO | Sikorsky S-61N | Irish Helicopters Ltd | |
| EI-BHP | M.S.893A Rallye Commodore 180 | Spanish Point Flying Club | |
| EI-BHT | Beech 77 Skipper | Waterford Aero Club | |
| EI-BHV | Champion 7EC Traveler | Condor Group | |
| EI-BHW | Cessna F.150F | R. Sharpe | |
| EI-BHY | SOCATA Rallye 150ST | D. Killian | |
| EI-BIB | Cessna F.152 | Galway Flying Club | |
| EI-BIC | Cessna F.172N | Oriel Flying Group Ltd | |
| EI-BID | PA-18 Super Cub 95 | D. MacCarthy | |
| EI-BIF | SOCATA Rallye 235E | Empire Enterprises Ltd | |
| EI-BIG | Zlin 526 | P. von Lonkhuyzen | |
| EI-BIJ | AB-206B JetRanger 2 | Celtic Helicopters Ltd | |
| EI-BIK | PA-18 Super Cub 180 | Dublin Gliding Club | |
| EI-BIM | M.S.880B Rallye Club | D. Millar | |
| EI-BIO | Piper J-3C-65 Cub | Monasterevin Flying Club | |
| EI-BIR | Cessna F.172M | B. Harrison & ptnrs | |
| EI-BIS | Robin R.1180TD | Robin Aiglon Group | |
| EI-BIT | M.S.887 Rallye 125 | Spanish Point Flying Club | |
| EI-BIU | Robin R.2112A | Wicklow Flying Group | |
| EI-BIV | Bellanca 8KCAB Citabria | Aerocrats Flying Group | |
| EI-BIW | M.S.880B Rallye Club | E. J. Barr | |
| EI-BJA | Cessna FRA.150L | Blackwater Flying Group | |
| EI-BJC | Aeronca 7AC Champion | B. Lyons | |
| EI-BJG | Robin R.1180 | N. Hanley | |
| EI-BJJ | Aeronca 15AC Sedan | A. A. Alderdice & S. H. Boyd | |
| EI-BJK | M.S.880B Rallye 110ST | Jordan Larkin Flying Group | |
| EI-BJL | Cessna 550 Citation II | Helicopter Maintenance Ltd | |
| EI-BJM | Cessna A.152 | Leinster Aero Club | |
| EI-BJO | Cessna R.172K | P. Hogan & G. Ryder | |
| EI-BJS | AA-5B Tiger | P. Morrisey | |
| EI-BJT | PA-38-112 Tomahawk | O. Bruton | |
| EI-BJW | D.H.104 Dove 6 ★ | Waterford Museum | |
| EI-BKC | Aeronca 115AC Sedan | J. Lynch | |
| EI-BKD | Mooney M.20J | Limerick Warehousing Ltd | |
| EI-BKF | Cessna F.172H | M. & M. C. Veale | |
| EI-BKK | Taylor JT.1 Monoplane | Waterford Aero Club | |
| EI-BKM | Zenith CH.200 | D. van de Braam | |
| EI-BKN | M.S.880B Rallye 100ST | Weston Ltd | |
| EI-BKS | Eipper Quicksilver | Irish Microlight Ltd | |
| EI-BKT | AB-206B JetRanger 3 | Irish Helicopters Ltd | |
| EI-BKU | M.S.892A Rallye Commodore 150 | Limerick Flying Club | |
| EI-BLB | SNCAN Stampe SV-4C | J. E. Hutchinson & R. A. Stafford | |
| EI-BLD | Bolkow Bo 105C | Irish Helicopters Ltd | |
| EI-BLE | Eipper Microlight | R. P. St George-Smith | |
| EI-BLG | AB-206B JetRanger 3 | Monarch Property Services Ltd | |
| EI-BLN | Eipper Quicksilver MX | O. J. Conway & B. Daffy | |
| EI-BLO | Catto CP.16 | R. W. Hall | |
| EI-BLR | PA-34-200T Seneca II | R. Paris | |
| EI-BLU | Evans VP-1 | S. Pallister | |
| EI-BLW | PA-23 Aztec 250C | — (stored) | |

241

| Notes | Reg. | Type | Owner or Operator |
|---|---|---|---|
| | EI-BLY | Sikorsky S-61N | Irish Helicopters Ltd |
| | EI-BMA | M.S.880B Rallye Club | W. Rankin & M. Kelleher |
| | EI-BMB | M.S.880B Rallye 100T | Clyde Court Development Ltd |
| | EI-BMC | Hiway Demon Skytrike | S. Pallister |
| | EI-BMF | Laverda F.8L Falco | M. Slazenger & H. McCann |
| | EI-BMH | M.S.880B Rallye Club | N. J. Bracken |
| | EI-BMI | SOCATA TB.9 Tampico | Weston Ltd |
| | EI-BMJ | M.S.880B Rallye 100T | Weston Ltd |
| | EI-BMK | Cessna 310Q | Iona National Airways Ltd |
| | EI-BML | PA-23 Aztec 250 | Bruton Aircraft Engineering Ltd |
| | EI-BMM | Cessna F.152 II | Iona National Airways Ltd |
| | EI-BMN | Cessna F.152 II | Iona National Airways Ltd |
| | EI-BMO | Robin R.2160 | L. Gavin & ptnrs |
| | EI-BMS | Cessna F.177RG | A. M. Smyth |
| | EI-BMU | Monnet Sonerai II | P. Forde & D. Connaire |
| | EI-BMV | AA-5 Traveler | E. Tierney & K. Harold |
| | EI-BMW | Vulcan Air Trike | L. Maddock |
| | EI-BNA | Douglas DC-8-63CF | Aer Turas Teo |
| | EI-BNB | Lake LA-4-200 Buccaneer | L. McNamara & M. Ledwith |
| | EI-BNC | Cessna F.152 | Iona National Airlines |
| | EI-BND | Conroy CL-44-0 | HeavyLift Cargo Airlines Ltd/Stansted |
| | EI-BNF | Goldwing Canard | T. Morelli |
| | EI-BNG | M.S.892A Rallye Commodore 150 | Shannon Executive Aviation |
| | EI-BNH | Hiway Skytrike | M. Martin |
| | EI-BNJ | Evans VP-2 | G. A. Cashman |
| | EI-BNK | Cessna U.206F | Irish Parachute Club Ltd |
| | EI-BNL | Rand KR-2 | K. Hayes |
| | EI-BNP | Rotorway 133 | R. L. Renfroe |
| | EI-BNT | Cvjetkovic CA-65 | B. Tobin & P. G. Ryan |
| | EI-BNU | M.S.880B Rallye Club | P. A. Doyle |
| | EI-BOA | Pterodactyl Ptraveller | A. Murphy |
| | EI-BOE | SOCATA TB.10 Tobago | P. Byron & ptnrs |
| | EI-BOH | Eipper Quicksilver | J. Leech |
| | EI-BOM | Boeing 737-2T4 | Air Tara Ltd (leased to Delta A/L) |
| | EI-BON | Boeing 737-2T4 | Air Tara Ltd (leased to Delta A/L) |
| | EI-BOO | PA-23 Aztec 250C | K. A. O'Connor |
| | EI-BOR | Bell 222 | Westair Ltd |
| | EI-BOV | Rand KR-2 | G. O'Hara & G. Callan |
| | EI-BOX | Duet | K. Riccius |
| | EI-BPB | PA-28R Cherokee Arrow 200 | Rathcoole Flying Club |
| | EI-BPE | Viking Dragonfly | G. Bracken |
| | EI-BPI | EMB-110P1 Bandeirante | Iona National Airways Ltd |
| | EI-BPJ | Cessna 182A | J. Matthews & V. McCarthy |
| | EI-BPL | Cessna F.172K | Phoenix Flying |
| | EI-BPM | AS.350B Ecureuil | Helicopter Maintenance Ltd |
| | EI-BPO | Puma Skytrike | A. Morelli |
| | EI-BPP | Quicksilver MX | J. A. Smith |
| | EI-BPS | PA-30 Twin Comanche 160 | Group Air |
| | EI-BPT | Skyhook Sabre | T. McGrath |
| | EI-BPU | Hiway Demon | A. Channing |
| | EI-BRH | Mainair Gemini Flash | F. Warren & T. McGrath |
| | EI-BRK | Flexiform Trike | L. Maddock |
| | EI-BRO | Cessna F.152 | Iona National Airways |
| | EI-BRS | Cessna P.172D | D. & M. Hillery |
| | EI-BRT | Flexwing M17727 | M. J. McCrystal |
| | EI-BRU | Evans VP-1 | R. Smith & T. Coughlan |
| | EI-BRV | Hiway Demon | M. Garvey & C. Tully |
| | EI-BRW | Ultralight Deltabird | A. & E. Aerosports |
| | EI-BRX | Cessna FRA.150L | Trim Flying Club Ltd |
| | EI-BSB | Jodel D.112 | W. Kennedy |
| | EI-BSC | Cessna F.172N | S. Phelan |
| | EI-BSD | Enstrom F-28A | Clark Aviation |
| | EI-BSF | H.S.748 Srs 1 ★ | S.E. Aviation Museum/Waterford |
| | EI-BSG | Bensen B.80 | J. Todd |
| | EI-BSK | SOCATA TB.9 Tampico | Weston Ltd |
| | EI-BSL | PA-34-220T Seneca | E. L. Symons |
| | EI-BSN | Cameron O-65 balloon | W. Woollett |
| | EI-BSO | PA-28 Cherokee 140B | D. Rooney |
| | EI-BSQ | Thundercolt Ax6-56Z balloon | D. Hooper |
| | EI-BSS | RomBac One-Eleven 561RC | Ryanair Ltd/Tarom (YR-BRB) |
| | EI-BST | Bell 206B JetRanger | Celtic Helicopters Ltd |
| | EI-BSU | Champion 7KCAB | R. Bentley |
| | EI-BSV | SOCATA TB.20 Trinidad | J. Condron |

| Reg. | Type | Owner or Operator | Notes |
|------|------|-------------------|-------|
| EI-BSW | Solar Wings Pegasus XL-R | E. Fitzgerald | |
| EI-BSX | Piper J-3C-65 Cub | J. & T. O'Dwyer | |
| EI-BTN | L.1101-385 TriStar 1 | Air Tara Ltd (leased to Air America) | |
| EI-BTS | Boeing 747-283B | Air Tara Ltd (leased to Philippine A/L) | |
| EI-BTX | McD Douglas MD-82 | Air Tara Ltd (leased to AeroMexico) | |
| EI-BTY | McD Douglas MD-82 | Air Tara Ltd | |
| EI-BUA | Cessna 172M | Skyhawks Flying Club | |
| EI-BUC | Jodel D.9 Bebe | L. Maddock | |
| EI-BUF | Cessna 210N | 210 Group | |
| EI-BUG | SOCATA ST.10 Diplomate | J. Cooke | |
| EI-BUH | Lake LA.4-200 Buccaneer | Derg Aviation (Group) Ltd | |
| EI-BUJ | M.S.892A Rallye Commodore 150 | T. Cunniffe | |
| EI-BUL | MW-5 Sorcerer | J. Conlon | |
| EI-BUM | Cessna 404 | Iona National Airways Ltd | |
| EI-BUN | Beech 76 Duchess | The 172 Flying Group Ltd | |
| EI-BUO | Lavery Sea Hawker | C. Lavery & C. Donaldson | |
| EI-BUR | PA-38-112 Tomahawk | Leoni Aviation Ltd | |
| EI-BUS | PA-38-112 Tomahawk | Leoni Aviation Ltd | |
| EI-BUT | M.S.893A Commodore 180 | T. Keating | |
| EI-BUU | Solar Wings Pegasus XL-R | R. L. T. Hudson | |
| EI-BUV | Cessna 172RG | J. J. Spollen | |
| EI-BUW | Noble Hardman Snowbird IIIA | T.I.F.C. & I.S. Ltd | |
| EI-BUX | Agusta A.109A | Orring Ltd | |
| EI-BUZ | Robinson R-22 | Leoni Aviation Ltd | |
| EI-BVA | Cessna 404 Titan | Iona National Airways Ltd | |
| EI-BVB | Whittaker MW.6 Merlin | R. England | |
| EI-BVC | Cameron N-65 balloon | E. Shepherd | |
| EI-BVE | Jodel D.9 Bebe | J. Greene | |
| EI-BVF | Cessna F.172N | First Phantom Group | |
| EI-BVG | BAC One-Eleven 525FT | Ryanair Ltd/Tarom (YR-BCL) | |
| EI-BVH | RomBac One-Eleven 561RC | Ryanair Ltd | |
| EI-BVI | BAC One-Eleven 525FT | Ryanair Ltd | |
| EI-BVJ | AMF Chevvron 232 | W. T. King & S. G. Dunne | |
| EI-BVK | PA-38 Tomahawk | Shannon Executive Aviation | |
| EI-BVN | Bell 206B Jet Ranger 3 | Helicopter Hire (Ireland) Ltd | |
| EI-BVP | Cessna T.303 | Iona National Airways Ltd | |
| EI-BVQ | Cameron Can SS balloon | T. McCormack | |
| EI-BVS | Cessna 172RG | P. Bruno | |
| EI-BVT | Evans VP-2 | J. J. Sullivan | |
| EI-BVU | Cessna 152 | Iona National Airways Ltd | |
| EI-BVW | Cessna 152 | Iona National Airways Ltd | |
| EI-BVX | EMB-110P1 Bandeirante | Iona National Airways Ltd | |
| EI-BVY | Zenith 200AA-RW | J. Matthews & ptnrs | |
| EI-BVZ | Scheibe SF.25B Falke | D. Lamb & ptnrs | |
| EI-BWD | McD Douglas MD-83 | Air Tara Ltd (leased to BWIA) | |
| EI-BWF | Boeing 747-283B | Air Tara Ltd (leased to Philippine A/L) | |
| EI-BWH | Partenavia P.68C | K. Buckley | |
| EI-BWT | BAC One-Eleven 414ED | Air Tara Ltd | |
| EI-BXA | Boeing 737-448 | Aer Lingus Teo St Conleth | |
| EI-BXB | Boeing 737-448 | Aer Lingus Teo St Gall | |
| EI-BXC | Boeing 737-448 | Aer Lingus Teo St Brendan | |
| EI-BXD | Boeing 737-448 | Aer Lingus Teo St Colman | |
| EI-BXI | Boeing 737-448 | Aer Lingus Teo St Finnian | |
| EI-BXK | Boeing 737-448 | Aer Lingus Teo St Caimin | |
| EI-BXL | — | Aer Lingus Teo | |
| EI-BXN | Boeing 737-448 | Aer Lingus Teo | |
| EI-BXO | Fouga CM.170 Magister | G. W. Connolly | |
| EI-BXP | PA-23 Aztec 250E | Aer Arran | |
| EI-BXR | Aérospatiale ATR-42-300 | GPA Group (leased to Brit Air) | |
| EI-BXS | Aérospatiale ATR-42-300 | GPA Group | |
| EI-BXT | D.62B Condor | J. Sweeney | |
| EI-BXU | PA-28-161 Warrior II | W. T. King | |
| EI-BXX | AB-206B JetRanger | Leoni Aviation Ltd | |
| EI-BXY | Boeing 737-2S3 | GPA Group | |
| EI-BXZ | Flexiwing | R. England | |
| EI-BYA | Thruster TST Mk 1 | E. Fagan | |
| EI-BYC | Bensen B.8MR | C. Kirwan | |
| EI-BYD | Cessna 150J | Kestrel Flying Group | |
| EI-BYE | PA-31-350 Navajo Chieftain | EI-Air Exports Ltd | |
| EI-BYF | Cessna 150M | Twentieth Air Training Group | |
| EI-BYG | SOCATA TB.9 Tampico | Weston Ltd | |
| EI-BYH | Cessna 340A | Claddagh Air Carriers | |
| EI-BYJ | Bell 206B JetRanger | Celtic Helicopters Ltd | |

| Notes | Reg. | Type | Owner or Operator |
|---|---|---|---|
| | EI-BYK | PA-23 Aztec 250E | M. F. Hilary |
| | EI-BYL | Zenith CH.250 | A. Corcoran & J. Martin |
| | EI-BYN | Cessna 550 Citation II | Stickbury Enterprises Ltd |
| | EI-BYO | Aérospatiale ATR-42-300 | GPA Group (leased to Brit Air) |
| | EI-BYS | Robinson R-22B | G. V. Maloney |
| | EI-BYV | Hughes 369D | Irish Helicopters Ltd |
| | EI-BYX | Champion 7GCAA | J. Keane & P. Gallagher |
| | EI-BYY | Piper J-3C-85 Cub | A. J. Haines |
| | EI-BYZ | PA-44-180 Seminole | European College of Aeronautics |
| | EI-BZA | Boeing 747-283B | Air Tara Ltd (leased to Philippine A/L) |
| | EI-BZB | Airbus A.300C4 | GPA Finance (leased to Philippine A/L) |
| | EI-BZE | Boeing 737-3Y0 | GPA Group Ltd (leased to Philippine A/L) |
| | EI-BZF | Boeing 737-3Y0 | GPA Group Ltd (leased to Philippine A/L) |
| | EI-BZH | Boeing 737-3Y0 | GPA Group Ltd (leased to Philippine A/L) |
| | EI-BZI | Boeing 737-3Y0 | GPA Group Ltd (leased to Philippine A/L) |
| | EI-BZJ | Boeing 737-3Y0 | GPA Group Ltd (leased to Philippine A/L) |
| | EI-BZK | Boeing 737-3Y0 | GPA Group Ltd (leased to Philippine A/L) |
| | EI-BZL | Boeing 737-3Y0 | GPA Group Ltd (leased to Philippine A/L) |
| | EI-BZM | Boeing 737-3Y0 | GPA Group Ltd (leased to Philippine A/L) |
| | EI-BZN | Boeing 737-3Y0 | GPA Group Ltd (leased to Philippine A/L) |
| | EI-BZT | Boeing 737-3Y0 | GPA Group Ltd |
| | EI-BZZ | Douglas DC-9-15 | GPA Finance Ltd (stored) |
| | EI-CAA | Cessna FR.172J | A. Ross |
| | EI-CAB | Grob G.115 | European College of Aeronautics |
| | EI-CAC | Grob G.115 | European College of Aeronautics |
| | EI-CAD | Grob G.115 | European College of Aeronautics |
| | EI-CAE | Grob B.115 | European College of Aeronautics |
| | EI-CAF | Bell 206B JetRanger 2 | Irish Helicopters Ltd |
| | EI-CAG | PA-31 Navajo | Leoni Aviation Ltd |
| | EI-CAH | G.1159C Gulfstream 4 | Ardesir Ltd |
| | EI-CAJ | O'Leary Biplane | J. O. Leary |
| | EI-CAK | Douglas DC-8-63AF | Aer Turas Teo |
| | EI-CAL | Boeing 767-3Y0ER | Aer Lingus Teo (leased to Air Aruba) |
| | EI-CAM | Boeing 767-3Y0ER | Aer Lingus Teo |
| | EI-CAN | Aerotech MW.5 Sorcerer | J. Conlon |
| | EI-CAO | Cameron O-84 balloon | K. Haugh |
| | EI-CAP | Cessna R.182RG | Skyline Flight Management Ltd |
| | EI-CAR | Schweizer 269C | Island Helicopters Ltd |
| | EI-CAT | Cessna 421C | S. E. Ryle Ltd |
| | EI-CAU | AMF Chevvron 232 | H. Sydner |
| | EI-CAW | Bell 206B JetRanger | Celtic Helicopters Ltd |
| | EI-CAX | Cessna P.210N | N. Dunne |
| | EI-CAY | Mooney M.20C | Ranger Flights Ltd |
| | EI-CBB | Douglas DC-9-15 | GPA Finance Ltd (stored) |
| | EI-CBC | Aérospatiale ATR-72 | Air Tara Ltd |
| | EI-CBD | Aérospatiale ATR-72 | Air Tara Ltd |
| | EI-CBF | Aérospatiale ATR-42-300 | Air Tara Ltd (leased to Trans World Express) |
| | EI-CBG | Douglas DC-9-51 | GPA Finance Ltd (leased to Hawaiian) |
| | EI-CBH | Douglas DC-9-51 | GPA Finance Ltd (leased to Hawaiian) |
| | EI-CBI | Douglas DC-9-51 | Air Tara Ltd (leased to Hawaiian) |
| | EI-CBJ | D.H.C. 8-102 Dash Eight | GPA Group Ltd (leaesd in Alaska) |
| | EI-CBK | Aérospatiale ATR-42-300 | Air Tara Ltd |
| | EI-CBO | McD Douglas MD-83 | Air Tara Ltd |
| | EI-CBP | Boeing 737-3Y0 | Air Tara Ltd (leased to LAM) |
| | EI-CBQ | Boeing 737-3Y0 | Air Tara Ltd (leased to LAM) |
| | EI-CBR | McD Douglas MD-83 | Irish Aerospace (leased to Avianca) |
| | EI-CBS | McD Douglas MD-83 | Irish Aerospace (leased to Avianca) |
| | EI-CBU | McD Douglas MD-87 | Air Tara Ltd |
| | EI-CBW | Airbus A.300B4-203 | Air Tara Ltd |
| | EI-CBY | McD Douglas MD-83 | Air Tara Ltd (leased to Avianca) |
| | EI-CBZ | McD Douglas MD-83 | Air Tara Ltd (leased to Avianca) |
| | EI-CCA | Beech 19A Musketeer | P. F. McCooke |
| | EI-CCB | PA-44-180 Seminole | European College of Aeronautics |
| | EI-CCC | McD Douglas MD-83 | Irish Aerospace Ltd (leased to Avianca) |
| | EI-CCD | Grob G.115A | European College of Aeronautics |
| | EI-CCE | McD Douglas MD-83 | Irish Aerospace Ltd (leased to Avianca) |
| | EI-CCF | Aeronca 11AC Chief | O. Bruton |
| | EI-CCG | Robinson R-22B | Leoni Aviation Ltd |
| | EI-CCH | Piper J-3C-65 Cub | M. Slattery |
| | EI-CCJ | Cessna 152 | Irish Aero Club |
| | EI-CCK | Cessna 152 | Irish Aero Club |
| | EI-CCL | Cessna 152 | Irish Aero Club |
| | EI-CCM | Cessna 152 | Irish Aero Club |

| Reg. | Type | Owner or Operator | Notes |
|------|------|-------------------|-------|
| EI-CCN | Grob G.115A | European College of Aeronautics | |
| EI-CCO | PA-44-180 Seminole | European College of Aeronautics | |
| EI-CCQ | Slingsby T.31F Motor Cadet | Kerry Aero Club Ltd | |
| EI-CCR | Gulfstream 690D | Earl of Granard | |
| EI-CCT | Robinson R-22B | Air Investments Ltd | |
| EI-CCU | BAC One-Eleven 531FS | Ryanair Ltd | |
| EI-CCV | Cessna R.172K-XP | Kerry Aero Club | |
| EI-CCW | BAC One-Eleven 509EW | Ryanair Ltd | |
| EI-CCX | BAC One-Eleven 531FS | Ryanair Ltd | |
| EI-CCY | AA-1B Trainer | N. & C. Whisler | |
| EI-CCZ | Cessna F.150L | Comprehensive Enterprises Ltd | |
| EI-CDA | Boeing 737-548 | Aer Lingus Teo *St Columba* | |
| EI-CDB | Boeing 737-548 | Aer Lingus Teo *St Albert* | |
| EI-CDC | Boeing 737-548 | Aer Lingus Teo *St Munchin* | |
| EI-CDD | Boeing 737-548 | Aer Lingus Teo *St Macartan* | |
| EI-CDF | Boeing 737-548 | Aer Lingus Teo *St Cronan* | |
| EI-CDG | Boeing 737-548 | Aer Lingus Teo *St Moling* | |
| EI-CDH | Boeing 737-548 | Aer Lingus Teo *St Ronan* | |
| EI-CDI | McD Douglas MD-11 | GPA Group (*leased to Garuda*) | |
| EI-CDJ | McD Douglas MD-11 | GPA Group (*leased to Garuda*) | |
| EI-CDK | McD Douglas MD-11 | GPA Group (*leased to Garuda*) | |
| EI-CDL | McD Douglas MD-11 | GPA Group (*leased to Garuda*) | |
| EI-CDM | McD Douglas MD-11 | GPA Group (*leased to Garuda*) | |
| EI-CDN | McD Douglas MD-11 | GPA Group (*leased to Garuda*) | |
| EI-CDO | BAC One-Eleven 518FG | Ryanair Ltd | |
| EI-CDP | Cessna 182L | O. Bruton | |
| EI-CDQ | SA.300 Starduster Too | J. Keane | |
| EI-CDR | — | — | |
| EI-CDS | Boeing 737-548 | Aer Lingus Teo | |
| EI-CDT | Boeing 737-548 | Aer Lingus Teo | |
| EI-CDU | Cessna 150F | Blue Heron Aircraft Services Ltd | |
| EI-CDV | Cessna 150F | Blue Heron Aircraft Services Ltd | |
| EI-CDW | Robinson R-22B | J. Martyn | |
| EI-CDX | Cessna 210K | Falcon Aviation Ltd | |
| EI-CDY | McD Douglas MD-83 | Irish Aerospace Ltd (*leased to Avianca*) | |
| EI-CDZ | Luscombe 8A Silvaire | S. Bruton | |
| EI-CEB | Airbus A.300B4 | GPA Finance Ltd | |
| EI-CEC | PA-31-350 Navajo Chieftain | M. Knopek | |
| EI-CED | D.H.C.8-311 Dash Eight | GPA Finance Ltd (*leased to Hamburg A/L*) | |
| EI-CEF | Robinson R-22HP | Santail Ltd | |
| EI-CEG | M.S.893A Rallye 180GT | M. Farrelly | |
| EI-CEJ | Robinson R-22B | Helifly Ltd | |
| EI-CEK | McD Douglas MD-83 | Irish Aerospace Ltd | |
| EI-CEL | Rans S.6 Coyote | D. O'Gorman | |
| EI-CEM | Boeing 767-2B1ER | GPA Group (*leased to LAM*) | |
| EI-CEN | Thruster T.300 | J. Conlon | |
| EI-CEO | Boeing 747-259B | GPA Group (*leased to Avianca*) | |
| EI-CEP | McD Douglas MD-83 | Irish Aerospace Ltd | |
| EI-CEQ | McD Douglas MD-83 | Irish Aerospace Ltd (*leased to Avianca*) | |
| EI-CER | McD Douglas MD-83 | Irish Aerospace Ltd (*leased to Avianca*) | |
| EI-CES | Taylorcraft BC-65 | N. O'Brien | |
| EI-CET | L.188CF Electra | El Air Exports | |
| EI-CEX | Lake LA-4-200 | Derg Developments Ltd | |
| EI-CEY | Boeing 757-2Y0 | GPA Group (*leased to Avianca*) | |
| EI-CEZ | Boeing 757-2Y0 | GPA Group (*leased to Avianca*) | |
| EI-CFA | SAAB SF.340B | Aer Lingus Commuter *St Eithne* | |
| EI-CFB | SAAB SF.340B | Aer Lingus Commuter *St Aoife* | |
| EI-CFC | SAAB SF.340B | Aer Lingus Commuter *St Finbarr* | |
| EI-CFD | SAAB SF.340B | Aer Lingus Commuter *St Senan* | |
| EI-CFE | Robinson R-22B | Windsor Motors Ltd | |
| EI-CFF | PA-12 Super Cruiser | J. O'Dwyer & J. Molloy | |
| EI-CFG | CP.301B Emeraude | Southlink Ltd | |
| EI-CFH | PA-12 Super Cruiser | G. Treacy | |
| EI-CFI | PA-34-200T Seneca II | Mockfield Construction | |
| EI-CFJ | — | — | |
| EI-CFK | Varga 2150A Kachina | W. M. Patterson | |
| EI-CFL | — | — | |
| EI-CFM | Cessna 172P | M. P. Cahill | |
| EI-CFN | Cessna 172P | M. P. Cahill | |
| EI-CFO | Piper J-3C-65 Cub | S. Bruton | |
| EI-CFP | Cessna 172P | S. Bruton | |
| EI-CFQ | Boeing 737-3Y0 | Air Tara Ltd (*leased to TEA Basle*) | |
| EI-CFR | Boeing 767-375ER | GPA Group Ltd (*leased to China*) | |

| Notes | Reg. | Type | Owner or Operator |
|-------|------|------|-------------------|
| | EI-CFS | — | — |
| | EI-CFT | — | — |
| | EI-CFV | M.S.880B Rallye Club | Kilkenny Flying Club |
| | EI-CFW | Cameron O-77 balloon | Council for Positively Belfast |
| | EI-CFX | Robinson R-22B | Glenwood Transport |
| | EI-CFY | Cessna 172N | Transatlantic Ferry Services Ltd |
| | EI-CFZ | McD Douglas MD-83 | Irish Aerospace Ltd |
| | EI-CGA | McD Douglas MD-83 | GPA Group Ltd (leased in US) |
| | EI-CGB | Medway Hybred | M. Garvey |
| | EI-CGC | Stinson 108-3 | S. Bruton |
| | EI-CGD | Cessna 172M | Hibernian Flying Club Ltd |
| | EI-CGE | Hiway Demon | T. E. Carr |
| | EI-CGF | Luton LA-5 Major | F. Doyle & J. Duggan |
| | EI-CGG | Ercoupe 415C | Irish Ercoupe Group |
| | EI-CGH | Cessna 210N | J. J. Spollen |
| | EI-CGI | McD Douglas MD-83 | Irish Aerospace Ltd |
| | EI-CGJ | — | — |
| | EI-CGK | Robinson R-22B | Rathcoole Flying Club Ltd |
| | EI-CGL | Solar Wings Pegasus XL-R | Microlight Ltd |
| | EI-CGM | Solar Wings Pegasus XL-R | Microlight Ltd |
| | EI-CGN | Solar Wings Pegasus XL-R | Microlight Ltd |
| | EI-CGO | Douglas DC-8-63AF | Aer Turas Teo |
| | EI-CGP | PA-28 Cherokee 140 | M. Goss |
| | EI-CHL | Bell 206B JetRanger 3 | Celtic Helicopters Ltd |
| | EI-CUB | Piper J-3C-65 Cub | Galway Flying Club |
| | EI-DMI | PA-31-325 Turbo Navajo C | Dawn Meats |
| | EI-EDR | PA-28R Cherokee Arrow 200 | Victor Mike Flying Group Ltd |
| | EI-EEC | PA-23 Aztec 250 | Westair Ltd |
| | EI-EIO | PA-34-200T Seneca II | M. Casey & ptnrs |
| | EI-EXP | Short SD3-30 Variant 100 | EI Air Exports |
| | EI-FKA | Fokker 50 | Aer Lingus Commuter St Fionnan |
| | EI-FKB | Fokker 50 | Aer Lingus Commuter St Fergal |
| | EI-FKC | Fokker 50 | Aer Lingus Commuter St Fidelma |
| | EI-FKD | Fokker 50 | Aer Lingus Commuter St Flannan |
| | EI-FKE | Fokker 50 | Aer Lingus Commuter St Pappin |
| | EI-FKF | Fokker 50 | Aer Lingus Commuter St Ultan |
| | EI-FKG | — | Aer Lingus Commuter |
| | EI-FKH | — | Aer Lingus Commuter |
| | EI-FKI | — | Aer Lingus Commuter |
| | EI-FKJ | — | Aer Lingus Commuter |
| | EI-LMG | Bell 206L-3 LongRanger | Ven Air |
| | EI-PJM | Lake LA-250 Renegade | P. J. McGoldrick |
| | EI-SNN | Cessna 650 Citation III | Westair Aviation Ltd |
| | EI-TCK | Cessna 421A | T. C. Killeen |
| | EI-TKI | Robinson R-22B | Hydraulic Services Ltd |
| | EI-TLA | Douglas DC-8-71F | TransLift Airways Ltd |
| | EI-TLB | Douglas DC-8-71F | TransLift Airways Ltd |
| | EI-TLC | Douglas DC-8-71 | TransLift Airways Ltd |
| | EI-TLD | Douglas DC-8-71 | TransLift Airways Ltd |
| | EI-XMA | Robinson R-22B | Leoni Aviation Ltd |
| | EI-XMC | Robinson R-22B | McAuliffe Photographic Laboratories |

## EL (Liberia)

| | | | |
|-------|------|------|-------------------|
| | EL-AJC | Boeing 707-430 ★ | Airport Fire Services/Bournemouth |
| | EL-AJO | Douglas DC-8-55F | Liberia World Airways |
| | EL-AJQ | Douglas DC-8-54F | Liberia World Airways |
| | EL-AJT | Boeing 707-344B | Liberia World |
| | EL-AKA | Boeing 707-123B | Omega Air |
| | EL-AKB | Boeing 707 | Air Gambia |
| | EL-AKH | Boeing 707-338C | Omega Air |
| | EL-JNS | Boeing 707-323C | Skyair Cargo |
| | EL-ZGS | Boeing 707-309C | Jet Cargo Liberia |

## EP (Iran)

| | | | |
|-------|------|------|-------------------|
| | EP-IAA | Boeing 747SP-86 | Iran Air Fars |
| | EP-IAB | Boeing 747SP-86 | Iran Air Kurdistan |
| | EP-IAC | Boeing 747SP-86 | Iran Air Khuzestan |
| | EP-IAD | Boeing 747SP-86 | Iran Air Rushdie |
| | EP-IAG | Boeing 747-286B (SCD) | Iran Air Azarabadegan |

| Reg. | Type | Owner or Operator |
|---|---|---|
| EP-IAH | Boeing 747-286B (SCD) | Iran Air *Khorasan* |
| EP-IAM | Boeing 747-186B | Iran Air |
| EP-ICA | Boeing 747-2J9F | Iran Air |
| EP-ICC | Boeing 747-2J9F | Iran Air |

# ES (Estonia)

| | | |
|---|---|---|
| ES-AAE | Tupolev Tu-134A | Estonian Air |
| ES-AAF | Tupolev Tu-134A-3 | Estonian Air |
| ES-AAG | Tupolev Tu-134A | Estonian Air |
| ES-AAH | Tupolev Tu-134A | Estonian Air |
| ES-AAI | Tupolev Tu-134A | Estonian Air |
| ES-AAJ | Tupolev Tu-134A | Estonian Air |
| ES-AAK | Tupolev Tu-134A | Estonian Air |
| ES-AAL | Tupolev Tu-134A | Estonian Air |
| ES-AAM | Tupolev Tu-134A | Estonian Air |
| ES-AAO | Tupolev Tu-134A | Estonian Air |
| ES-AAP | Tupolev Tu-134A | Estonian Air |

# ET (Ethiopia)

| | | |
|---|---|---|
| ET-AIE | Boeing 767-260ER | Ethiopian Airlines |
| ET-AIF | Boeing 767-260ER | Ethiopian Airlines |
| ET-AIV | Boeing 707-327C | Ethiopian Airlines |
| ET-AIZ | Boeing 767-260ER | Ethiopian Airlines |
| ET-AJS | Boeing 757-260PF | Ethiopian Airlines |
| ET-AJX | Boeing 757-260ER | Ethiopian Airlines |
| ET-AKC | Boeing 757-260ER | Ethiopian Airlines |
| ET-AKE | Boeing 757-260ER | Ethiopian Airlines |
| ET-AKF | Boeing 757-260ER | Ethiopian Airlines |

# F (France)

| | | |
|---|---|---|
| F-BGNR | V.708 Viscount ★ | Air Service Training Ltd/Perth |
| F-BJEN | S.E.210 Caravelle 10B | Europe Aero Service (*stored*) |
| F-BJTU | S.E.210 Caravelle 10B3 | Air Enterprise |
| F-BMKS | S.E.210 Caravelle 10B | Air Toulouse |
| F-BPJK | Boeing 727-228 | Air France |
| F-BPJR | Boeing 727-228 | Air Charter |
| F-BPJV | Boeing 727-214 | Air Charter |
| F-BPPA | Aero Spacelines Super Guppy-201 | Airbus Industrie *Airbus Skylink 2* |
| F-BPUA | F.27 Friendship Mk 500 | Air France |
| F-BPUB | F.27 Friendship Mk 500 | Air France |
| F-BPUC | F.27 Friendship Mk 500 | Air France |
| F-BPUD | F.27 Friendship Mk 500 | Air France |
| F-BPUE | F.27 Friendship Mk 500 | Air France |
| F-BPUF | F.27 Friendship Mk 500 | Air France |
| F-BPUG | F.27 Friendship Mk 500 | Air France |
| F-BPUH | F.27 Friendship Mk 500 | Air France |
| F-BPUI | F.27 Friendship Mk 500 | Air France |
| F-BPUJ | F.27 Friendship Mk 500 | Air France |
| F-BPUK | F.27 Friendship Mk 500 | Air France |
| F-BPUL | F.27 Friendship Mk 500 | Air France |
| F-BPVA | Boeing 747-128 | Air France |
| F-BPVB | Boeing 747-128 | Air France |
| F-BPVD | Boeing 747-128 | Air France |
| F-BPVE | Boeing 747-128 | Air France |
| F-BPVF | Boeing 747-128 | Air France |
| F-BPVG | Boeing 747-128 | Air France |
| F-BPVH | Boeing 747-128 | Air France |
| F-BPVJ | Boeing 747-128 | Air France |
| F-BPVK | Boeing 747-128 | Air France |
| F-BPVL | Boeing 747-128 | Air France |
| F-BPVM | Boeing 747-128 | Air France |
| F-BPVN | Boeing 747-128 | Air France |
| F-BPVP | Boeing 747-128 | Air France |
| F-BPVR | Boeing 747-228F (SCD) | Air France |
| F-BPVS | Boeing 747-228B (SCD) | Air France |
| F-BPVT | Boeing 747-228B (SCD) | Air France |
| F-BPVU | Boeing 747-228B (SCD) | Air France |
| F-BPVV | Boeing 747-228F (SCD) | Air France |

| Notes | Reg. | Type | Owner or Operator |
|---|---|---|---|
| | F-BPVX | Boeing 747-228B (SCD) | Air France |
| | F-BPVY | Boeing 747-228B | Air France |
| | F-BPVZ | Boeing 747-228F (SCD) | Air France |
| | F-BSUM | F.27 Friendship Mk 500 | Air France |
| | F-BSUN | F.27 Friendship Mk 500 | Air France |
| | F-BSUO | F.27 Friendship Mk 500 | Air France |
| | F-BTDB | Douglas DC-10-30 | Union de Transports Aériens (UTA) |
| | F-BTDC | Douglas DC-10-30 | Union de Transports Aériens (UTA) |
| | F-BTDD | Douglas DC-10-30 | Union de Transports Aériens (UTA) |
| | F-BTDE | Douglas DC-10-30 | Union de Transports Aériens (UTA) |
| | F-BTDG | Boeing 747-3B3 (SCD) | Union de Transports Aériens (UTA) |
| | F-BTDH | Boeing 747-3B3 (SCD) | Union de Transports Aériens (UTA) |
| | F-BTGV | Aero Spacelines Super Guppy-201 | Airbus Industrie *Airbus Skylink 1* |
| | F-BTOA | S.E.210 Caravelle 12 | Air Inter (*stored*) |
| | F-BTOC | S.E.210 Caravelle 12 | Air Inter (*stored*) |
| | F-BTOE | S.E.210 Caravelle 12 | Air Inter (*stored*) |
| | F-BTSC | Concorde 101 | Air France |
| | F-BTSD | Concorde 101 | Air France |
| | F-BTTA | Mercure 100 | Air Inter |
| | F-BTTB | Mercure 100 | Air Inter |
| | F-BTTD | Mercure 100 | Air Inter |
| | F-BTTE | Mercure 100 | Air Inter |
| | F-BTTF | Mercure 100 | Air Inter |
| | F-BTTG | Mercure 100 | Air Inter |
| | F-BTTH | Mercure 100 | Air Inter |
| | F-BTTI | Mercure 100 | Air Inter |
| | F-BTTJ | Mercure 100 | Air Inter |
| | F-BUAE | Airbus A.300B2 | Air Inter |
| | F-BUAF | Airbus A.300B2 | Air Inter |
| | F-BUAG | Airbus A.300B2 | Air Inter |
| | F-BUAH | Airbus A.300B2 | Air Inter |
| | F-BUAI | Airbus A.300B2 | Air Inter |
| | F-BUAJ | Airbus A.300B2 | Air Inter |
| | F-BUAK | Airbus A.300B2 | Air Inter |
| | F-BUAL | Airbus A.300B4 | Air Inter |
| | F-BUAM | Airbus A.300B2 | Air Inter |
| | F-BUAN | Airbus A.300B2 | Air Inter |
| | F-BUAO | Airbus A.300B2 | Air Inter |
| | F-BUAP | Airbus A.300B2 | Air Inter |
| | F-BUAQ | Airbus A.300B4 | Air Inter |
| | F-BUAR | Airbus A.300B4 | Air Inter |
| | F-BUTI | F.28 Fellowship 1000 | T.A.T. European |
| | F-BVFA | Concorde 101 | Air France |
| | F-BVFB | Concorde 101 | Air France |
| | F-BVFC | Concorde 101 | Air France |
| | F-BVFD | Concorde 101 | Air France |
| | F-BVFF | Concorde 101 | Air France |
| | F-BVGA | Airbus A.300B2 | Air France |
| | F-BVGB | Airbus A.300B2 | Air France |
| | F-BVGC | Airbus A.300B2 | Air France |
| | F-BVGD | Airbus A.300B2 | Air Inter |
| | F-BVGE | Airbus A.300B2 | Air Inter |
| | F-BVGF | Airbus A.300B2 | Air Inter |
| | F-BVGG | Airbus A.300B4 | Air France |
| | F-BVGH | Airbus A.300B4 | Air France |
| | F-BVGI | Airbus A.300B4 | Air Charter |
| | F-BVGJ | Airbus A.300B4 | Air France |
| | F-BVGL | Airbus A.300B4 | Air France |
| | F-BVGM | Airbus A.300B4 | Air France |
| | F-BVGN | Airbus A.300B4 | Air France |
| | F-BVGO | Airbus A.300B4 | Air France |
| | F-BVGP | Airbus A.300B4 | Air France |
| | F-BVGQ | Airbus A.300B4 | Air France |
| | F-BVGR | Airbus A.300B4 | Air France |
| | F-BVGT | Airbus A.300B4 | Air Charter |
| | F-BVJL | Beech 99A | T.A.T. European |
| | F-BYAB | F.27 Friendship Mk 600 | Air Jet |
| | | | |
| | F-GATS | EMB-110P2 Bandeirante | Compagnie Air Littoral *Hérault* |
| | F-GBBR | F.28 Fellowship 1000 | T.A.T. European/Air France |
| | F-GBBS | F.28 Fellowship 1000 | T.A.T. European/Air France |
| | F-GBBT | F.28 Fellowship 1000 | T.A.T. European/Air France |
| | F-GBBX | F.28 Fellowship 1000 | T.A.T. European |

| Reg. | Type | Owner or Operator | Notes |
|------|------|-------------------|-------|
| F-GBEA | Airbus A.300B2 | Air Inter | |
| F-GBEB | Airbus A.300B2 | Air Inter | |
| F-GBEC | Airbus A.300B2 | Air France | |
| F-GBEK | Nord 262A | Compagnie Air Littoral | |
| F-GBGA | EMB-110P2 Bandeirante | Brit Air | |
| F-GBLE | EMB-110P2 Bandeirante | Air Atlantique | |
| F-GBME | EMB-110P2 Bandeirante | Air Atlantique | |
| F-GBMG | EMB-110P2 Bandeirante | Brit Air | |
| F-GBOX | Boeing 747-2B3F (SCD) | Air France | |
| F-GBRM | EMB-110P2 Bandeirante | Air Atlantique | |
| F-GBRQ | FH.227B Friendship | T.A.T. European | |
| F-GBRU | F.27J Friendship | T.A.T. European | |
| F-GBRV | F.27J Friendship | ACE Transvalair | |
| F-GBYA | Boeing 737-228 | Air France | |
| F-GBYB | Boeing 737-228 | Air France/Air Charter | |
| F-GBYC | Boeing 737-228 | Air France | |
| F-GBYD | Boeing 737-228 | Air France | |
| F-GBYE | Boeing 737-228 | Air France | |
| F-GBYF | Boeing 737-228 | Air France | |
| F-GBYG | Boeing 737-228 | Air France | |
| F-GBYH | Boeing 737-228 | Air France | |
| F-GBYI | Boeing 737-228 | Air France | |
| F-GBYJ | Boeing 737-228 | Air France | |
| F-GBYK | Boeing 737-228 | Air France | |
| F-GBYL | Boeing 737-228 | Air France | |
| F-GBYM | Boeing 737-228 | Air France | |
| F-GBYN | Boeing 737-228 | Air France | |
| F-GBYO | Boeing 737-228 | Air France | |
| F-GBYP | Boeing 737-228 | Air France | |
| F-GBYQ | Boeing 737-228 | Air France | |
| F-GCBA | Boeing 747-228B | Air France | |
| F-GCBB | Boeing 747-228B (SCD) | Air France | |
| F-GCBD | Boeing 747-228B (SCD) | Air France | |
| F-GCBE | Boeing 747-228F (SCD) | Air France | |
| F-GCBF | Boeing 474-228B (SCD) | Air France | |
| F-GCBG | Boeing 747-228B (SCD) | Air France | |
| F-GCBH | Boeing 747-228B (SCD) | Air France | |
| F-GCBI | Boeing 747-228B (SCD) | Air France | |
| F-GCBJ | Boeing 747-228B (SCD) | Air France | |
| F-GCBK | Boeing 747-228F (SCD) | Air France | |
| F-GCBL | Boeing 747-228F (SCD) | Air France | |
| F-GCBM | Boeing 747-228F | UTA Cargo | |
| F-GCDA | Boeing 727-228 | Europe Aero Service | |
| F-GCDB | Boeing 727-228 | Euralair International | |
| F-GCDC | Boeing 727-228 | Air France | |
| F-GCDD | Boeing 727-228 | Air France | |
| F-GCDE | Boeing 727-228 | Air Charter | |
| F-GCDF | Boeing 727-228 | Air France | |
| F-GCFC | FH.227B Friendship | T.A.T. European/Stellair | |
| F-GCGQ | Boeing 727-227 | Europe Aero Service | |
| F-GCJL | Boeing 737-222 | Euralair International/Air Charter | |
| F-GCJO | FH.227B Friendship | ACE Transvalair | |
| F-GCJV | F.27 Friendship Mk 400 | Air Jet | |
| F-GCLA | EMB-110P1 Bandeirante | Aigle Azur | |
| F-GCLL | Boeing 737-222 | Euralair International/Air Charter | |
| F-GCLM | FH.227B Friendship | ACE Transvalair | |
| F-GCLO | FH.227B Friendship | ACE Transvalair | |
| F-GCMV | Boeing 727-2X3 | Air Charter | |
| F-GCMX | Boeing 727-2X3 | Air Charter | |
| F-GCPT | FH.227B Friendship | T.A.T. European | |
| F-GCPU | FH.227B Friendship | T.A.T. European | |
| F-GCPX | FH.227B Friendship | T.A.T. European | |
| F-GCPY | FH.227B Friendship | T.A.T. European | |
| F-GCQG | Boeing 727-227 | Europe Aero Service | |
| F-GCSL | Boeing 737-222 | Euralair International/Air Charter | |
| F-GCVJ | S.E.210 Caravelle 12 | Air Inter (*stored*) | |
| F-GCVK | S.E.210 Caravelle 12 | Air Inter (*stored*) | |
| F-GCVL | S.E.210 Caravelle 12 | — | |
| F-GCVM | S.E.210 Caravelle 12 | — | |
| F-GDAQ | L.100-30 Hercules | Jet Fret | |
| F-GDFC | F.28 Fellowship 4000 | T.A.T. European/Air France | |
| F-GDFD | F.28 Fellowship 4000 | T.A.T. European/Air France | |
| F-GDFY | S.E.210 Caravelle 10B | — | |

249

| Notes | Reg. | Type | Owner or Operator |
|-------|------|------|-------------------|
| | F-GDFZ | S.E.210 Caravelle 10B | — |
| | F-GDJK | Douglas DC-10-30 | — |
| | F-GDJM | Douglas DC-8-62CF | Cargo Lion |
| | F-GDMR | Swearingen SA.226TC Metro II | Compagnie Air Littoral |
| | F-GDPP | Douglas DC-3C | France DC-3 |
| | F-GDRM | Douglas DC-8-73 | AOM French Airlines/Air Sweden |
| | F-GDSG | UTA Super Guppy | Airbus Industrie *Airbus Skylink 3* |
| | F-GDSK | F.28 Fellowship 4000 | T.A.T. European/Air France |
| | F-GDUS | F.28 Fellowship 2000 | T.A.T. European |
| | F-GDUT | F.28 Fellowship 2000 | T.A.T. European/Air France |
| | F-GDUU | F.28 Fellowship 2000 | T.A.T. European |
| | F-GDUV | F.28 Fellowship 2000 | T.A.T. European |
| | F-GDUY | F.28 Fellowship 4000 | T.A.T. European/Air France |
| | F-GDUZ | F.28 Fellowship 4000 | T.A.T. European/Air France |
| | F-GDXL | Aérospatiale ATR-42-300 | Brit Air |
| | F-GDXT | F.27J Friendship | Stellair |
| | F-GEAI | UTA Super Guppy | Airbus Industrie *Airbus Skylink 4* |
| | F-GECK | F.28 Fellowship 1000 | T.A.T. European/Air France |
| | F-GEGD | Aérospatiale ATR-42-300 | Compagnie Air Littoral |
| | F-GEGE | Aérospatiale ATR-42-300 | Compagnie Air Littoral |
| | F-GEGF | Aérospatiale ATR-42-300 | Compagnie Air Littoral |
| | F-GELG | SAAB SF.340A | Brit Air/Air France |
| | F-GELP | S.E.210 Caravelle | Air Toulouse International |
| | F-GEMA | Airbus A.310-203 | Air France |
| | F-GEMB | Airbus A.310-203 | Air France |
| | F-GEMC | Airbus A.310-203 | Air France |
| | F-GEMD | Airbus A.310-203 | Air France |
| | F-GEME | Airbus A.310-203 | Air France |
| | F-GEMF | Airbus A.310-203 | Air France |
| | F-GEMG | Airbus A.310-203 | Air France |
| | F-GEMN | Airbus A.310-304 | Air France |
| | F-GEMO | Airbus A.310-304 | Air France |
| | F-GEMP | Airbus A.310-304 | Air France |
| | F-GEMQ | Airbus A.310-304 | Air France |
| | F-GEOM | Douglas DC-3C | — |
| | F-GEPC | S.E. 210 Caravelle 10B3 | Air Enterprise |
| | F-GEQJ | Aérospatiale ATR-42-300 | T.A.T. European/Lufthansa CityLine |
| | F-GETB | Boeing 747-3B3 (SCD) | Air France |
| | F-GEXA | Boeing 747-4B3 | Union de Transports Aériens (UTA) |
| | F-GEXB | Boeing 747-4B3 | Union de Transports Aériens (UTA) |
| | F-GEXI | Boeing 737-2L9 | Air Charter/Europe Aero Service |
| | F-GEXJ | Boeing 737-2Q8 | Air Charter/Europe Aero Service |
| | F-GEXX | F.28 Fellowship 1000 | T.A.T. European |
| | F-GEXZ | F.27J Friendship | Stellair |
| | F-GFBA | S.E.210 Caravelle 10B | — |
| | F-GFBZ | SAAB SF.340A | Brit Air |
| | F-GFEN | EMB-120 Brasilia | Compagnie Air Littoral |
| | F-GFEO | EMB-120 Brasilia | Compagnie Air Littoral |
| | F-GFEP | EMB-120 Brasilia | Compagnie Air Littoral |
| | F-GFEQ | EMB-120 Brasilia | Compagnie Air Littoral |
| | F-GFER | EMB-120 Brasilia | Compagnie Air Littoral |
| | F-GFES | Aérospatiale ATR-42-300 | Compagnie Air Littoral |
| | F-GFIN | EMB-120 Brasilia | Compagnie Air Littoral |
| | F-GFJE | Aérospatiale ATR-42-300 | Brit Air/Air France |
| | F-GFJH | Aérospatiale ATR-42-300 | Brit Air/Air France |
| | F-GFJP | Aérospatiale ATR-42-300 | Brit Air/Air France |
| | F-GFJS | F.27 Friendship Mk 600 | Air Jet |
| | F-GFKA | Airbus A.320-111 | Air France *Ville de Paris* |
| | F-GFKB | Airbus A.320-111 | Air France *Ville de Rome* |
| | F-GFKD | Airbus A.320-111 | Air France *Ville de Londres* |
| | F-GFKE | Airbus A.320-111 | Air France *Ville de Bonn* |
| | F-GFKF | Airbus A.320-111 | Air France *Ville de Madrid* |
| | F-GFKG | Airbus A.320-111 | Air France *Ville d'Amsterdam* |
| | F-GFKH | Airbus A.320-211 | Air France *Ville de Bruxelles* |
| | F-GFKI | Airbus A.320-211 | Air France *Ville de Lisbonne* |
| | F-GFKJ | Airbus A.320-211 | Air France *Ville de Copenhagen* |
| | F-GFKK | Airbus A.320-211 | Air France *Ville d'Athenes* |
| | F-GFKL | Airbus A.320-211 | Air France *Ville de Dublin* |
| | F-GFKM | Airbus A.320-211 | Air France *Ville de Luxembourg* |
| | F-GFKN | Airbus A.320-211 | Air France |
| | F-GFKO | Airbus A.320-211 | Air France |
| | F-GFKP | Airbus A.320-211 | Air France *Ville de Nice* |
| | F-GFKQ | Airbus A.320-111 | Air France |

| Reg. | Type | Owner or Operator | Notes |
|------|------|-------------------|-------|
| F-GFKR | Airbus A.320-211 | Air France *Ville de Berlin* | |
| F-GFKS | Airbus A.320-211 | Air France | |
| F-GFKT | Airbus A.320-211 | Air France | |
| F-GFKU | Airbus A.320-211 | Air France | |
| F-GFKV | Airbus A.320-211 | Air France *Ville de Bordeaux* | |
| F-GFKX | Airbus A.320-211 | Air France | |
| F-GFKY | Airbus A.320-211 | Air France *Ville de Toulouse* | |
| F-GFKZ | Airbus A.320-211 | Air France *Ville de Turin* | |
| F-GFLV | Boeing 737-2K5 | Air France/Air Charter | |
| F-GFLX | Boeing 737-2K5 | Air France/Air Charter | |
| F-GFPR | Swearingen SA226AT Merlin IVA | Regional Airlines | |
| F-GFUA | Boeing 737-33A | Air France | |
| F-GFUB | Boeing 737-33A | Air France | |
| F-GFUC | Boeing 737-33A | Air Charter | |
| F-GFUD | Boeing 737-33A | Air France | |
| F-GFUE | Boeing 737-3B3 | Air France | |
| F-GFUF | Boeing 737-3B3 | Air France | |
| F-GFUG | Boeing 737-4B3 | Corsair International | |
| F-GFUH | Boeing 737-4B3 | Corsair International | |
| F-GFUJ | Boeing 737-33A | Air France | |
| F-GFYL | Boeing 737-2A9C | Euralair International/Air Charter | |
| F-GFYN | Aérospatiale ATR-42-300 | Compagnie Air Littoral | |
| F-GFZB | McD Douglas MD-83 | Air Liberte | |
| F-GGBV | SAAB SF.340A | Aigle Azur | |
| F-GGEA | Airbus A.320-111 | Air Inter | |
| F-GGEB | Airbus A.320-111 | Air Inter | |
| F-GGEC | Airbus A.320-111 | Air Inter | |
| F-GGEE | Airbus A.320-111 | Air Inter | |
| F-GGEF | Airbus A.320-111 | Air Inter | |
| F-GGEG | Airbus A.320-111 | Air Inter | |
| F-GGFI | Boeing 737-210C | T.A.T. European | |
| F-GGFJ | Boeing 737-248C | T.A.T. European | |
| F-GGGR | Boeing 727-2H3 | Europe Aero Service *Alsace* | |
| F-GGKD | S.E.210 Caravelle 10B | Air Service Nantes | |
| F-GGLK | Aérospatiale ATR-42-300 | T.A.T. European | |
| F-GGLR | Aérospatiale ATR-42-300 | Brit Air | |
| F-GGMA | McD Douglas MD-83 | AOM French Airlines | |
| F-GGMB | McD Douglas MD-83 | AOM French Airlines | |
| F-GGMC | McD Douglas MD-83 | AOM French Airlines | |
| F-GGMD | McD Douglas MD-83 | Jet Alsace | |
| F-GGME | McD Douglas MD-83 | Jet Alsace | |
| F-GGML | Boeing 737-53A | Euralair International/Air France | |
| F-GGMZ | Douglas DC-10-30 | AOM French Airlines | |
| F-GGPA | Boeing 737-242C | T.A.T. European | |
| F-GGPB | Boeing 737-204C | T.A.T. European | |
| F-GGPC | Boeing 737-204C | T.A.T. European | |
| F-GGPN | FH.227B Friendship | — | |
| F-GGSV | Swearingen SA226TC Metro II | — | |
| F-GGTD | EMB-120RT Brasilia | Air Exel *Nord-Pas de Calais* | |
| F-GGTE | EMB-120RT Brasilia | Air Exel | |
| F-GGTF | EMB-120RT Brasilia | Air Exel | |
| F-GGTP | Boeing 737-217 | Air Service Nantes | |
| F-GHDB | SAAB SF.340A | Brit Air/Air France | |
| F-GHEB | McD Douglas MD-83 | Air Liberte | |
| F-GHEC | McD Douglas MD-83 | Air Liberte | |
| F-GHED | McD Douglas MD-83 | Air Liberte | |
| F-GHEF | Airbus A.300-622R | Air Liberte | |
| F-GHEG | Airbus A.300-622R | Air Liberte | |
| F-GHEI | McD Douglas MD-83 | Air Liberte | |
| F-GHEJ | Airbus A.310-324 | Air Liberte | |
| F-GHEK | McD Douglas MD-83 | Air Liberte | |
| F-GHEX | EMB-120RT Brasilia | Alsavia/T.A.T. European | |
| F-GHEY | EMB-120RT Brasilia | Alsavia/T.A.T. European | |
| F-GHGD | Boeing 767-27EER | Air France/Balkan | |
| F-GHGE | Boeing 767-27EER | Air France/Balkan | |
| F-GHGF | Boeing 767-3Q8ER | Air France | |
| F-GHGG | Boeing 767-3Q8ER | Air France | |
| F-GHGH | Boeing 767-37EER | Air France | |
| F-GHGI | Boeing 767-328ER | Air France | |
| F-GHGJ | Boeing 767-328ER | Air France | |
| F-GHGM | Airbus A.310-304 | — | |
| F-GHGR | Swearingen SA226AT Merlin IVA | Regional Airlines | |
| F-GHHO | McD Douglas MD-83 | Air Liberte | |

| Notes | Reg. | Type | Owner or Operator |
|---|---|---|---|
| | F-GHHP | McD Douglas MD-83 | Air Liberte |
| | F-GHIA | EMB-120RT Brasilia | Compagnie Air Littoral |
| | F-GHIB | EMB-120RT Brasilia | Compagnie Air Littoral |
| | F-GHJE | Aérospatiale ATR-42-300 | Brit Air |
| | F-GHLA | Swearingen SA226AT Merlin IVA | Regional Airlines |
| | F-GHME | Aérospatiale ATR-42-300 | Brit Air |
| | F-GHMI | SAAB SF.340A | Brit Air/Air France |
| | F-GHMJ | SAAB SF.340A | Brit Air |
| | F-GHMK | SAAB SF.340A | Brit Air |
| | F-GHOI | Douglas DC-10-30 | Union de Transports Aériens (UTA) |
| | F-GHOL | Boeing 737-53C | Euralair International/Air France |
| | F-GHPI | Aérospatiale ATR-42-300 | Brit Air |
| | F-GHPK | Aérospatiale ATR-42-300 | Brit Air |
| | F-GHPS | Aérospatiale ATR-42-300 | Brit Air |
| | F-GHPU | Aérospatiale ATR-72-101 | Brit Air |
| | F-GHPV | Aérospatiale ATR-72-101 | Brit Air |
| | F-GHPX | Aérospatiale ATR-72-101 | Brit Air |
| | F-GHPY | Aérospatiale ATR-72-101 | Brit Air |
| | F-GHPZ | Aérospatiale ATR-42-300 | Brit Air |
| | F-GHQA | Airbus A.320-211 | Air Inter |
| | F-GHQB | Airbus A.320-211 | Air Inter |
| | F-GHQC | Airbus A.320-211 | Air Inter |
| | F-GHQD | Airbus A.320-211 | Air Inter |
| | F-GHQE | Airbus A.320-211 | Air Inter |
| | F-GHQF | Airbus A.320-211 | Air Inter |
| | F-GHQG | Airbus A.320-211 | Air Inter |
| | F-GHQH | Airbus A.320-211 | Air Inter |
| | F-GHQI | Airbus A.320-211 | Air Inter |
| | F-GHQJ | Airbus A.320-211 | Air Inter |
| | F-GHQK | Airbus A.320-211 | Air Inter |
| | F-GHQL | Airbus A.320-211 | Air Inter |
| | F-GHQM | Airbus A.320-211 | Air Inter |
| | F-GHQN | Airbus A.320-211 | Air Inter |
| | F-GHQO | Airbus A.320-211 | Air Inter |
| | F-GHQP | Airbus A.320-211 | Air Inter |
| | F-GHQQ | Airbus A.320-211 | Air Inter |
| | F-GHQR | Airbus A.320-211 | Air Inter |
| | F-GHQS | Airbus A.320-211 | Air Inter |
| | F-GHRC | F.27 Friendship Mk 600 | Air Jet |
| | F-GHUL | Boeing 737-53C | Euralair International/Air Charter |
| | F-GHVA | Swearingen SA227AC Metro III | Regional Airlines |
| | F-GHVC | Swearingen SA227AC Metro III | Regional Airlines |
| | F-GHVD | Swearingen SA227AC Metro III | Regional Airlines |
| | F-GHVF | Swearingen SA227AT Merlin IV | Regional Airlines |
| | F-GHVG | Swearingen SA227AC Metro III | Regional Airlines |
| | F-GHVL | Boeing 737-53C | Euralair International/Air France |
| | F-GHVN | Boeing 737-33A | Air France |
| | F-GHVO | Boeing 737-33A | Air France |
| | F-GHVS | SAAB SF.340B | Regional Airlines |
| | F-GHVT | SAAB SF.340B | Regional Airlines |
| | F-GHVU | SAAB SF.340B | Regional Airlines |
| | F-GHXK | Boeing 737-2A1 | Europe Aero Service |
| | F-GHXL | Boeing 737-2S3 | Europe Aero Service/Air Charter |
| | F-GHXM | Boeing 737-53A | Europe Aero Service/Air Charter |
| | F-GHXN | Boeing 737-53A | — |
| | F-GIAH | F.28 Fellowship 1000 | T.A.T. European |
| | F-GIAI | F.28 Fellowship 1000 | T.A.T. European/Stellair |
| | F-GIAJ | F.28 Fellowship 1000 | T.A.T. European |
| | F-GIAK | F.28 Fellowship 1000 | T.A.T. European |
| | F-GIDK | Douglas DC-3C | Air Dakota |
| | F-GIGO | Aérospatiale ATR-72-201 | Compagnie Air Littoral |
| | F-GIGU | Aérospatiale ATR-72-202 | Compagnie Air Littoral |
| | F-GIHR | F.27J Friendship | — |
| | F-GIJS | Airbus A.300B4 | Air Inter |
| | F-GIJT | Airbus A.300B4 | Air Inter |
| | F-GIJU | Airbus A.300B4 | Air Inter |
| | F-GILN | Swearingen SA227AC Metro III | Regional Airlines |
| | F-GIMH | F.28 Fellowship 1000 | T.A.T. European |
| | F-GIMJ | Boeing 747-121 | Corsair International |
| | F-GINL | Boeing 737-53C | Euralair International/Air France |
| | F-GIOA | Fokker 100 | T.A.T. European |
| | F-GIOB | Fokker 100 | T.A.T. European |
| | F-GIOC | Fokker 100 | T.A.T. European |

| Reg. | Type | Owner or Operator | Notes |
|------|------|-------------------|-------|
| F-GIOD | Fokker 100 | T.A.T. European | |
| F-GIOE | Fokker 100 | T.A.T. European | |
| F-GIOF | Fokker 100 | T.A.T. European | |
| F-GIOG | Fokker 100 | T.A.T. European | |
| F-GIOH | Fokker 100 | T.A.T. European | |
| F-GIOI | Fokker 100 | T.A.T. European | |
| F-GIOJ | Fokker 100 | T.A.T. European | |
| F-GIOK | Fokker 100 | T.A.T. European | |
| F-GIOL | Fokker 100 | T.A.T. European | |
| F-GIOV | Fokker 100 | T.A.T. European | |
| F-GIOX | Fokker 100 | T.A.T. European | |
| F-GIRC | Aérospatiale ATR-42-300 | T.A.T. European | |
| F-GISA | Boeing 747-428 (SCD) | Air France | |
| F-GISB | Boeing 747-428 (SCD) | Air France | |
| F-GISC | Boeing 747-428 (SCD) | Air France | |
| F-GISD | Boeing 747-428 (SCD) | Air France | |
| F-GISE | Boeing 747-428 (SCD) | Air France | |
| F-GISF | Boeing 747-428 (SCD) | Air France | |
| F-GISG | Boeing 747-428 (SCD) | Air France | |
| F-GITA | Boeing 747-428 | Air France | |
| F-GITB | Boeing 747-428 | Air France | |
| F-GITC | Boeing 747-428 | Air France | |
| F-GITD | Boeing 747-428 | Air France | |
| F-GITE | Boeing 747-428 | Air France | |
| F-GITF | Boeing 747-428 | Air France | |
| F-GIVA | Boeing 747-428F (SCD) | Air France | |
| F-GJAK | EMB-120RT Brasilia | Compagnie Air Littoral | |
| F-GJDL | Boeing 737-210C | Air Charter/Euralair International | |
| F-GJDM | S.E.210 Caravelle 10B | STAIR | |
| F-GJEG | Beech 1900-1 | T.A.T. European | |
| F-GJNA | Boeing 737-528 | Air France | |
| F-GJNB | Boeing 737-528 | Air France | |
| F-GJNC | Boeing 737-528 | Air France | |
| F-GJND | Boeing 737-528 | Air France | |
| F-GJNE | Boeing 737-528 | Air France | |
| F-GJNF | Boeing 737-528 | Air France | |
| F-GJNG | Boeing 737-528 | Air France | |
| F-GJNH | Boeing 737-528 | Air France | |
| F-GJNI | Boeing 737-528 | Air France | |
| F-GJNJ | Boeing 737-528 | Air France | |
| F-GJNK | Boeing 737-528 | Air France | |
| F-GJNM | Boeing 737-528 | Air France | |
| F-GJTF | EMB-120RT Brasilia | Air Exel | |
| F-GJVA | Airbus A.320-211 | Air Inter | |
| F-GJVB | Airbus A.320-211 | Air Inter | |
| F-GJVC | Airbus A.320-211 | Air Inter | |
| F-GJVD | Airbus A.320-211 | Air Inter | |
| F-GJVE | Airbus A.320-211 | Air Inter | |
| F-GJVF | Airbus A.320-211 | Air Inter | |
| F-GJVG | Airbus A.320-211 | Air Inter | |
| F-GJVH | Airbus A.320-211 | Air Inter | |
| F-GJVZ | Airbus A.320-211 | Air Inter | |
| F-GKCS | Boeing 707-369C | Pan Europe Air | |
| F-GKCT | Boeing 707-369C | Pan Europe Air | |
| F-GKJC | F.27 Friendship Mk 600 | Air Jet | |
| F-GKLJ | Boeing 747-121 | Corsair International | |
| F-GKMY | Douglas DC-10-30 | AOM French Airlines | |
| F-GKNA | Aérospatiale ATR-42-300 | T.A.T. European | |
| F-GKNB | Aérospatiale ATR-42-300 | T.A.T. European | |
| F-GKNC | Aérospatiale ATR-42-300 | T.A.T. European | |
| F-GKND | Aérospatiale ATR-42-300 | T.A.T. European | |
| F-GKNE | Aérospatiale ATR-42-300 | T.A.T. European | |
| F-GKNF | Aérospatiale ATR-42-300 | T.A.T. European | |
| F-GKNG | Aérospatiale ATR-42-300 | T.A.T. European | |
| F-GKNH | Aérospatiale ATR-42-300 | T.A.T. European | |
| F-GKOA | Aérospatiale ATR-72-202 | T.A.T. European | |
| F-GKOB | Aérospatiale ATR-72-202 | T.A.T. European | |
| F-GKOC | Aérospatiale ATR-72-202 | T.A.T. European | |
| F-GKOD | Aérospatiale ATR-72-202 | T.A.T. European | |
| F-GKOE | Aérospatiale ATR-72-202 | T.A.T. European | |
| F-GKOF | Aérospatiale ATR-72-202 | T.A.T. European | |
| F-GKOG | Aérospatiale ATR-72-202 | T.A.T. European | |
| F-GKOH | Aérospatiale ATR-72-202 | T.A.T. European | |

| Notes | Reg. | Type | Owner or Operator |
|---|---|---|---|
| | F-GKOI | Aérospatiale ATR-72-202 | T.A.T. European |
| | F-GKOJ | Aérospatiale ATR-72-202 | T.A.T. European |
| | F-GKOK | Aérospatiale ATR-72-202 | T.A.T. European |
| | F-GKOL | Aérospatiale ATR-72-202 | T.A.T. European |
| | F-GKOM | Aérospatiale ATR-72-202 | T.A.T. European |
| | F-GKON | Aérospatiale ATR-72-202 | T.A.T. European |
| | F-GKST | Beech 1900-1 | Proteus Air System |
| | F-GKTA | Boeing 737-3M8 | — |
| | F-GKTB | Boeing 737-3M8 | — |
| | F-GKTD | Airbus A.310-304 | Sudan Airways |
| | F-GKXA | Airbus A.320-211 | Air France Ville de Nantes |
| | F-GLMX | Douglas DC-10-30 | AOM French Airlines |
| | F-GLNA | Boeing 747-206B | Corsair International |
| | F-GLNI | BAe 146-200 | Air Jet |
| | F-GLTT | Boeing 737-3Y0 | Corsair International |
| | F-GLXH | Boeing 737-2D6 | Europe Aero Service |
| | F-GMCD | McD Douglas MD-83 | Jet Alsace |
| | F-GMDA | Airbus A.330-301 | Air Inter |
| | F-GMDB | Airbus A.330-301 | Air Inter |
| | F-GMDC | Airbus A.330-301 | Air Inter |
| | F-GMPG | Fokker 100 | T.A.T. European |
| | F-GMPP | McD Douglas MD-83 | Jet Alsace |
| | F-GMVH | BAe Jetstream 3100 | Regional Airlines |
| | F-GMVI | BAe Jetstream 3100 | Regional Airlines |
| | F-GMVJ | BAe Jetstream 3100 | Regional Airlines |
| | F-GMVK | BAe Jetstream 3100 | Regional Airlines |
| | F-GMVL | BAe Jetstream 3100 | Regional Airlines |
| | F-GMVM | BAe Jetstream 3100 | Regional Airlines |
| | F-GNBB | Douglas DC-10-30 | — |
| | F-GNFM | Douglas DC-8-71F | Jet Fret |
| | F-GPAN | Boeing 747-2B3F (SCD) | Air France |
| | F-GTNT | BAe 146-200QT | Euralair International/TNT |
| | F-GTNU | BAe 146-200QT | Euralair International/TNT |
| | F-ODJG | Boeing 747-2Q2B | Air Gabon |
| | F-ODLX | Douglas DC-10-30 | AOM French Airlines Diamant |
| | F-ODLY | Douglas DC-10-30 | AOM French Airlines Turquoise |
| | F-ODLZ | Douglas DC-10-30 | AOM French Airlines Saphir |
| | F-ODSV | Airbus A.310-304 | Somali Airlines (to become 6O-SHH) |
| | F-ODVD | Airbus A.310-304 | Royal Jordanian Prince Hashem |
| | F-ODVE | Airbus A.310-304 | Royal Jordanian Princess Iman |
| | F-ODVF | Airbus A.310-304 | Royal Jordanian Princess Raiyah |
| | F-ODVG | Airbus A.310-304 | Royal Jordanian Prince Faisal |
| | F-ODVH | Airbus A.310-304 | Royal Jordanian Prince Hamazeh |
| | F-ODVI | Airbus A.310-304 | Royal Jordanian Princess Haya |
| | F-OGQN | Airbus A.310-304 | Sudan Airways |
| | F-OGQR | Airbus A.310-308 | Aeroflot Rachmaninov |
| | F-OGQS | Airbus A.310-308 | Aeroflot Glinka |
| | F-OGQT | Airbus A.310-308 | Aeroflot Muossorgksi |
| | F-OGQU | Airbus A.310-308 | Aeroflot Skriabin |
| | F-OGYA | Airbus A.320-211 | Royal Jordanian Cairo |
| | F-OGYB | Airbus A.320-211 | Royal Jordanian Baghdad |
| | F-OGYC | Airbus A.320-211 | Royal Jordanian Sanaa |

**Note:** UTA also operates one DC-10-30 registered N54649.

# HA (Hungary)

| | HA-LBI | Tupolev Tu-134A-3 | Malev |
|---|---|---|---|
| | HA-LBK | Tupolev Tu-134A-3 | Malev |
| | HA-LBN | Tupolev Tu-134A-3 | Malev |
| | HA-LBO | Tupolev Tu-134A-3 | Malev |
| | HA-LBP | Tupolev Tu-134A-3 | Malev |
| | HA-LBR | Tupolev Tu-134A-3 | Malev |
| | HA-LCA | Tupolev Tu-154B-2 | Malev Cargo |
| | HA-LCB | Tupolev Tu-154B-2 | Malev |
| | HA-LCE | Tupolev Tu-154B-2 | Malev |
| | HA-LCG | Tupolev Tu-154B-2 | Malev |
| | HA-LCH | Tupolev Tu-154B-2 | Malev |
| | HA-LCM | Tupolev Tu-154B-2 | Malev |
| | HA-LCN | Tupolev Tu-154B-2 | Malev |
| | HA-LCO | Tupolev Tu-154B-2 | Malev |
| | HA-LCP | Tupolev Tu-154B-2 | Malev |

| Reg. | Type | Owner or Operator | Notes |
|------|------|-------------------|-------|
| HA-LCR | Tupolev Tu-154B-2 | Malev | |
| HA-LCU | Tupolev Tu-154B-2 | Malev | |
| HA-LCV | Tupolev Tu-154B-2 | Malev | |
| HA-LEA | Boeing 737-2QB | Malev | |
| HA-LEB | Boeing 737-2M8 | Malev | |
| HA-LEC | Boeing 737-2T5 | Malev | |
| HA-LED | Boeing 737-3Y0 | Malev | |
| HA-LEF | Boeing 737-3Y0 | Malev | |
| HA-LEG | Boeing 737-3Y0 | Malev *Szent Istvan-Sanctus Stephanus* | |
| HA-LHA | Boeing 767-27GER | Malev | |
| HA-LHB | Boeing 767-27GER | Malev | |
| HA-TAB | BAe 146-200QT | TNT/Malev | |

# HB (Switzerland)

| Reg. | Type | Owner or Operator |
|------|------|-------------------|
| HB-AHB | SAAB SF.340A | Crossair |
| HB-AHC | SAAB SF.340A | Crossair |
| HB-AHD | SAAB SF.340A | Crossair |
| HB-AHO | SAAB SF.340A | Crossair |
| HB-AHR | SAAB SF.340A | Crossair |
| HB-AHS | SAAB SF.340A | Crossair |
| HB-AHT | SAAB SF.340A | Crossair |
| HB-AKA | SAAB SF.340B | Crossair |
| HB-AKB | SAAB SF.340B | Crossair |
| HB-AKC | SAAB SF.340B | Crossair |
| HB-AKD | SAAB SF.340B | Crossair |
| HB-AKE | SAAB SF.340B | Crossair |
| HB-AKF | SAAB SF.340B | Crossair |
| HB-AKG | SAAB SF.340B | Crossair |
| HB-AKH | SAAB SF.340B | Crossair |
| HB-AKI | SAAB SF.340B | Crossair |
| HB-AKK | SAAB SF.340B | Crossair |
| HB-AKL | SAAB SF.340B | Crossair |
| HB-AKM | SAAB SF.340B | Crossair |
| HB-AKN | SAAB SF.340B | Crossair |
| HB-AKO | SAAB SF.340B | Crossair |
| HB-AKP | SAAB SF.340B | Crossair |
| HB-IAN | Fokker 50 | Crossair |
| HB-IAO | Fokker 50 | Crossair |
| HB-IAP | Fokker 50 | Crossair |
| HB-IAR | Fokker 50 | Crossair |
| HB-IAS | Fokker 50 | Crossair |
| HB-IBF | Douglas DC-8-63 | ASA Air Starline |
| HB-ICJ | S.E. 210 Caravelle 10B3 | Aero Jet |
| HB-IGC | Boeing 747-357 (SCD) | Swissair *Bern* |
| HB-IGD | Boeing 747-357 (SCD) | Swissair *Basel* |
| HB-IGE | Boeing 747-357 | Swissair *Genéve* |
| HB-IGF | Boeing 747-357 | Swissair *Zürich* |
| HB-IGG | Boeing 747-357 (SCD) | Swissair *Ticino* |
| HB-IIA | Boeing 737-3M8 | TEA Basle |
| HB-IIB | Boeing 737-3M8 | TEA Basle |
| HB-IIC | Boeing 737-3M8 | TEA Basle *Emmental* |
| HB-IKK | McD Douglas MD-82 | Meridiana |
| HB-IKL | McD Douglas MD-82 | Meridiana |
| HB-INA | McD Douglas MD-81 | Swissair *Höri* |
| HB-INB | McD Douglas MD-82 | Balair CTA |
| HB-INC | McD Douglas MD-81 | Swissair *Lugano* |
| HB-IND | McD Douglas MD-81 | Swissair *Bachenbülach* |
| HB-INE | McD Douglas MD-81 | Swissair *Rümlang* |
| HB-INF | McD Douglas MD-81 | Swissair *Appenzell a.Rh.* |
| HB-ING | McD Douglas MD-81 | Swissair *Winkel* |
| HB-INH | McD Douglas MD-81 | Swissair *Winterthur* |
| HB-INI | McD Douglas MD-81 | Swissair *Kloten* |
| HB-INK | McD Douglas MD-81 | Swissair *Opfikon* |
| HB-INL | McD Douglas MD-81 | Swissair *Jura* |
| HB-INM | McD Douglas MD-81 | Swissair *Lausanne* |
| HB-INN | McD Douglas MD-81 | Swissair *Bülach* |
| HB-INO | McD Douglas MD-81 | Swissair *Bellinzona* |
| HB-INP | McD Douglas MD-81 | Swissair *Oberglatt* |
| HB-INR | McD Douglas MD-82 | Balair CTA |
| HB-INS | McD Douglas MD-81 | Swissair *Meyrin* |
| HB-INT | McD Douglas MD-81 | Swissair *Grand-Saconnex* |

| Notes | Reg. | Type | Owner or Operator |
|-------|------|------|-------------------|
| | HB-INU | McD Douglas MD-81 | Swissair *Vernier* |
| | HB-INV | McD Douglas MD-81 | Swissair *Dubendorf* |
| | HB-INW | McD Douglas MD-82 | Balair CTA |
| | HB-INX | McD Douglas MD-81 | Swissair *Wallisellen* |
| | HB-INY | McD Douglas MD-81 | Swissair *Bassersdorf* |
| | HB-INZ | McD Douglas MD-81 | Swissair *Regensdorf* |
| | HB-IPA | Airbus A.310-221 | Swissair *Aargau* |
| | HB-IPB | Airbus A.310-221 | Swissair *Neuchatel* |
| | HB-IPC | Airbus A.310-221 | Swissair *Schwyz* |
| | HB-IPD | Airbus A.310-221 | Swissair *Solothurn* |
| | HB-IPE | Airbus A.310-221 | Swissair *Basel-Land* |
| | HB-IPF | Airbus A.310-322 | Swissair *Glarus* |
| | HB-IPG | Airbus A.310-322 | Swissair *Zug* |
| | HB-IPH | Airbus A.310-322 | Swissair *Appenzell i. Rh* |
| | HB-IPI | Airbus A.310-322 | Swissair *Luzern* |
| | HB-IPK | Airbus A.310-322 | Balair CTA |
| | HB-IPL | Airbus A.310-325 | Balair CTA |
| | HB-IPM | Airbus A.310-325 | Balair CTA |
| | HB-IPN | Airbus A.310-325 | Balair CTA |
| | HB-ISB | Douglas DC-3C | Classic Air |
| | HB-ISC | Douglas DC-3C | Classic Air |
| | HB-ISG | F.27 Friendship Mk 200 | Sunshine Aviation |
| | HB-ISH | F.27 Friendship Mk 200 | Sunshine Aviation *Locarno* |
| | HB-ISX | McD Douglas MD-81 | Swissair *Binningen* |
| | HB-ISZ | McD Douglas MD-83 | Balair CTA |
| | HB-IUA | McD Douglas MD-87 | Balair CTA |
| | HB-IUB | McD Douglas MD-87 | Balair CTA |
| | HB-IUC | McD Douglas MD-87 | Balair CTA |
| | HB-IUD | McD Douglas MD-87 | Balair CTA |
| | HB-IUG | McD Douglas MD-81 | Swissair *Illnau-Effretikon* |
| | HB-IUH | McD Douglas MD-81 | Swissair *Wangen-Brüttisellen* |
| | HB-IUI | McD Douglas MD-83 | Balair CTA |
| | HB-IVA | Fokker 100 | Swissair *Aarau* |
| | HB-IVB | Fokker 100 | Swissair *Biel/Bienne* |
| | HB-IVC | Fokker 100 | Swissair *Chur* |
| | HB-IVD | Fokker 100 | Swissair *Dietlikon* |
| | HB-IVE | Fokker 100 | Swissair *Baden* |
| | HB-IVF | Fokker 100 | Swissair *Sion* |
| | HB-IVG | Fokker 100 | Swissair *Genthod* |
| | HB-IVH | Fokker 100 | Swissair *Stadel* |
| | HB-IVI | Fokker 100 | Swissair *Bellevue* |
| | HB-IVK | Fokker 100 | Swissair *Hochfelden* |
| | HB-IWA | McD Douglas MD-11 | Swissair *Obwalden* |
| | HB-IWB | McD Douglas MD-11 | Swissair *Graubünden* |
| | HB-IWC | McD Douglas MD-11 | Swissair *Vaud* |
| | HB-IWD | McD Douglas MD-11 | Swissair *Thurgau* |
| | HB-IWE | McD Douglas MD-11 | Swissair *Nidwalden* |
| | HB-IWF | McD Douglas MD-11 | Swissair *Schafthausen* |
| | HB-IWG | McD Douglas MD-11 | Swissair *Valais/Wallis* |
| | HB-IWH | McD Douglas MD-11 | Swissair *St Gallen* |
| | HB-IWI | McD Douglas MD-11 | Swissair *Uri* |
| | HB-IWK | McD Douglas MD-11 | Swissair *Fribourg* |
| | HB-IWL | McD Douglas MD-11 | Swissair *Appenzell a.Rh* |
| | HB-IWM | McD Douglas MD-11 | Swissair *Jura* |
| | HB-IWN | McD Douglas MD-11 | Swissair |
| | HB-IXB | BAe 146-200A | Crossair |
| | HB-IXC | BAe 146-200A | Crossair |
| | HB-IXD | BAe 146-200A | Crossair |
| | HB-IXF | BAe RJ85 | Crossair |
| | HB-IXG | BAe RJ85 | Crossair |
| | HB-IXH | BAe RJ85 | Crossair |
| | HB-IXK | BAe RJ85 | Crossair |
| | HB-IXZ | BAe 146-300 | Crossair |
| | HB-IZA | SAAB 2000 | Crossair |
| | HB-IZB | SAAB 2000 | Crossair |
| | HB-IZC | SAAB 2000 | Crossair |
| | HB-IZD | SAAB 2000 | Crossair |
| | HB-IZE | SAAB 2000 | Crossair |
| | HB-IZF | SAAB 2000 | Crossair |
| | HB-IZG | SAAB 2000 | Crossair |
| | HB-IZH | SAAB 2000 | Crossair |

# HK (Colombia)

**Note:** Avianca operates a Boeing 747-259B (SCD) registered EI-CEO.

# HL (Korea)

| | | |
|---|---|---|
| HL7315 | Douglas DC-10-30 | Korean Air |
| HL7316 | Douglas DC-10-30 | Korean Air |
| HL7317 | Douglas DC-10-30 | Korean Air |
| HL7371 | McD Douglas MD-11 | Korean Air |
| HL7372 | McD Douglas MD-11 | Korean Air |
| HL | McD Douglas MD-11 | Korean Air |
| HL | McD Douglas MD-11 | Korean Air |
| HL | McD Douglas MD-11 | Korean Air |
| HL7441 | Boeing 747-230F | Korean Air Cargo |
| HL7443 | Boeing 747-2B5B | Korean Air |
| HL7451 | Boeing 747-2B5F (SCD) | Korean Air Cargo |
| HL7452 | Boeing 747-2B5F (SCD) | Korean Air Cargo |
| HL7453 | Boeing 747-212B | Korean Air |
| HL7454 | Boeing 747-2B5B (SCD) | Korean Air Cargo |
| HL7458 | Boeing 747-2B5F | Korean Air Cargo |
| HL7459 | Boeing 747-2B5F (SCD) | Korean Air Cargo |
| HL7463 | Boeing 747-2B5B | Korean Air |
| HL7464 | Boeing 747-2B5B | Korean Air |
| HL7468 | Boeing 747-3B5 | Korean Air |
| HL7469 | Boeing 747-3B5 | Korean Air |
| HL7470 | Boeing 747-3B5 (SCD) | Korean Air |
| HL7471 | Boeing 747-273C | Korean Air Cargo |
| HL7474 | Boeing 747-2S4F (SCD) | Korean Air Cargo |
| HL7475 | Boeing 747-2B5F (SCD) | Korean Air Cargo |
| HL7476 | Boeing 747-2B5F (SCD) | Korean Air Cargo |
| HL7477 | Boeing 747-4B5 | Korean Air |
| HL7478 | Boeing 747-4B5 | Korean Air |
| HL7479 | Boeing 747-4B5 | Korean Air |
| HL7480 | Boeing 747-4B5 (SCD) | Korean Air |
| HL7481 | Boeing 747-4B5 | Korean Air |
| HL7482 | Boeing 747-4B5 (SCD) | Korean Air |
| HL7483 | Boeing 747-4B5 | Korean Air |
| HL7484 | Boeing 747-4B5 | Korean Air |
| HL7485 | Boeing 747-4B5 | Korean Air |
| HL7486 | Boeing 747-4B5 | Korean Air |
| HL7487 | Boeing 747-4B5 | Korean Air |
| HL7488 | Boeing 747-4B5 | Korean Air |

# HS (Thailand)

| | | |
|---|---|---|
| HS-TGA | Boeing 747-2D7B | Thai Airways International *Visuthakasatriya* |
| HS-TGB | Boeing 747-2D7B | Thai Airways International *Sirisobhakya* |
| HS-TGC | Boeing 747-2D7B | Thai Airways International *Dararasmi* |
| HS-TGD | Boeing 747-3D7 | Thai Airways International *Suchada* |
| HS-TGE | Boeing 747-3D7 | Thai Airways International *Chutamat* |
| HS-TGF | Boeing 747-2D7B | Thai Airways International *Phimara* |
| HS-TGG | Boeing 747-2D7B | Thai Airways International *Sriwanna* |
| HS-TGH | Boeing 747-4D7 | Thai Airways International *Chaiprakarn* |
| HS-TGJ | Boeing 747-4D7 | Thai Airways International *Hariphunchai* |
| HS-TGK | Boeing 747-4D7 | Thai Airways International *Alongkorn* |
| HS-TGL | Boeing 747-4D7 | Thai Airways International |
| HS-TGM | Boeing 747-4D7 | Thai Airways International |
| HS-TGN | Boeing 747-4D7 | Thai Airways International |
| HS-TGO | Boeing 747-4D7 | Thai Airways International *Bowonrangsi* |
| HS-TGS | Boeing 747-2D7B | Thai Airways International *Chainarai* |
| HS-TMA | Douglas DC-10-30ER | Thai Airways International *Kwanmuang* |
| HS-TMB | Douglas DC-10-30ER | Thai Airways International *Thepalai* |
| HS-TMC | Douglas DC-10-30ER | Thai Airways International *Sri Ubon* |

# HZ (Saudi Arabia)

| | | |
|---|---|---|
| HZ-AHA | L.1011-385 TriStar 200 | Saudia — Saudi Arabian Airlines |
| HZ-AHB | L.1011-385 TriStar 200 | Saudia — Saudi Arabian Airlines |
| HZ-AHC | L.1011-385 TriStar 200 | Saudia — Saudi Arabian Airlines |

| Reg. | Type | Owner or Operator |
|------|------|-------------------|
| HZ-AHD | L.1011-385 TriStar 200 | Saudia — Saudi Arabian Airlines |
| HZ-AHE | L.1011-385 TriStar 200 | Saudia — Saudi Arabian Airlines |
| HZ-AHF | L.1011-385 TriStar 200 | Saudia — Saudi Arabian Airlines |
| HZ-AHG | L.1011-385 TriStar 200 | Saudia — Saudi Arabian Airlines |
| HZ-AHH | L.1011-385 TriStar 200 | Saudia — Saudi Arabian Airlines |
| HZ-AHI | L.1011-385 TriStar 200 | Saudia — Saudi Arabian Airlines |
| HZ-AHJ | L.1011-385 TriStar 200 | Saudia — Saudi Arabian Airlines |
| HZ-AHL | L.1011-385 TriStar 200 | Saudia — Saudi Arabian Airlines |
| HZ-AHM | L.1011-385 TriStar 200 | Saudia — Saudi Arabian Airlines |
| HZ-AHN | L.1011-385 TriStar 200 | Saudia — Saudi Arabian Airlines |
| HZ-AHO | L.1011-385 TriStar 200 | Saudia — Saudi Arabian Airlines |
| HZ-AHP | L.1011-385 TriStar 200 | Saudia — Saudi Arabian Airlines |
| HZ-AHQ | L.1011-385 TriStar 200 | Saudia — Saudi Arabian Airlines |
| HZ-AHR | L.1011-385 TriStar 200 | Saudia — Saudi Arabian Airlines |
| HZ-AIA | Boeing 747-168B | Saudia — Saudi Arabian Airlines |
| HZ-AIB | Boeing 747-168B | Saudia — Saudi Arabian Airlines |
| HZ-AIC | Boeing 747-168B | Saudia — Saudi Arabian Airlines |
| HZ-AID | Boeing 747-168B | Saudia — Saudi Arabian Airlines |
| HZ-AIE | Boeing 747-168B | Saudia — Saudi Arabian Airlines |
| HZ-AIF | Boeing 747SP-68 | Saudia — Saudi Arabian Airlines |
| HZ-AIG | Boeing 747-168B | Saudia — Saudi Arabian Airlines |
| HZ-AIH | Boeing 747-168B | Saudia — Saudi Arabian Airlines |
| HZ-AII | Boeing 747-168B | Saudia — Saudi Arabian Airlines |
| HZ-AIJ | Boeing 747SP-68 | Saudi Royal Flight |
| HZ-AIK | Boeing 747-368 | Saudia — Saudi Arabian Airlines |
| HZ-AIL | Boeing 747-368 | Saudia — Saudi Arabian Airlines |
| HZ-AIM | Boeing 747-368 | Saudia — Saudi Arabian Airlines |
| HZ-AIN | Boeing 747-368 | Saudia — Saudi Arabian Airlines |
| HZ-AIO | Boeing 747-368 | Saudia — Saudi Arabian Airlines |
| HZ-AIP | Boeing 747-368 | Saudia — Saudi Arabian Airlines |
| HZ-AIQ | Boeing 747-368 | Saudia — Saudi Arabian Airlines |
| HZ-AIR | Boeing 747-368 | Saudia — Saudi Arabian Airlines |
| HZ-AIS | Boeing 747-368 | Saudia — Saudi Arabian Airlines |
| HZ-AIT | Boeing 747-368 | Saudia — Saudi Arabian Airlines |
| HZ-AIU | Boeing 747-268F (SCD) | Saudia — Saudi Arabian Airlines |
| HZ-AJA | Airbus A.300-620 | Saudia — Saudi Arabian Airlines |
| HZ-AJB | Airbus A.300-620 | Saudia — Saudi Arabian Airlines |
| HZ-AJC | Airbus A.300-620 | Saudia — Saudi Arabian Airlines |
| HZ-AJD | Airbus A.300-620 | Saudia — Saudi Arabian Airlines |
| HZ-AJE | Airbus A.300-620 | Saudia — Saudi Arabian Airlines |
| HZ-AJF | Airbus A.300-620 | Saudia — Saudi Arabian Airlines |
| HZ-AJG | Airbus A.300-620 | Saudia — Saudi Arabian Airlines |
| HZ-AJH | Airbus A.300-620 | Saudia — Saudi Arabian Airlines |
| HZ-AJI | Airbus A.300-620 | Saudia — Saudi Arabian Airlines |
| HZ-AJJ | Airbus A.300-620 | Saudia — Saudi Arabian Airlines |
| HZ-AJK | Airbus A.300-620 | Saudia — Saudi Arabian Airlines |

**Note:** Saudia also operates other aircraft on lease.

# I (Italy)

| | | |
|------|------|-------------------|
| I-AEJB | Boeing 767-283ER | Air Europe SpA |
| I-AEJC | Boeing 767-283ER | Air Europe SpA |
| | | |
| I-BUSB | Airbus A.300B4 | Alitalia *Tiziano* |
| I-BUSC | Airbus A.300B4 | Alitalia *Botticelli* |
| I-BUSD | Airbus A.300B4 | Alitalia *Caravaggio* |
| I-BUSF | Airbus A.300B4 | Alitalia *Tintoretto* |
| I-BUSG | Airbus A.300B4 | Alitalia *Canaletto* |
| I-BUSH | Airbus A.300B4 | Alitalia *Mantegna* |
| I-BUSJ | Airbus A.300B4 | Alitalia *Tiepolo* |
| I-BUSL | Airbus A.300B4 | Alitalia *Pinturicchio* |
| I-BUSM | Airbus A.300B2 | Alitalia *Raffaello* |
| I-BUSN | Airbus A.300B2 | Alitalia *Giotto* |
| I-BUSP | Airbus A.300B4 | Alitalia |
| I-BUSQ | Airbus A.300B4 | Alitalia *Michelangelo* |
| I-BUSR | Airbus A.300B4 | Alitalia *Cimabue* |
| I-BUST | Airbus A.300B4 | Alitalia *Piero della Francesca* |
| | | |
| I-DACM | McD Douglas MD-82 | Aero Trasporti Italiani (ATI) *La Spezia* |
| I-DACN | McD Douglas MD-82 | ATI *Rieti* |
| I-DACP | McD Douglas MD-82 | ATI *Padova* |
| I-DACQ | McD Douglas MD-82 | ATI *Lecce* |
| I-DACR | McD Douglas MD-82 | Alitalia *Carrara* |

| Reg. | Type | Owner or Operator | Notes |
|------|------|-------------------|-------|
| I-DACS | McD Douglas MD-82 | Alitalia *Valtellina* | |
| I-DACT | McD Douglas MD-82 | Alitalia *Maratea* | |
| I-DACU | McD Douglas MD-82 | ATI *Fabriano* | |
| I-DACV | McD Douglas MD-82 | ATI *Riccione* | |
| I-DACW | McD Douglas MD-82 | Alitalia *Vieste* | |
| I-DACX | McD Douglas MD-82 | Alitalia *Piacenza* | |
| I-DACY | McD Douglas MD-82 | Alitalia *Novara* | |
| I-DACZ | McD Douglas MD-82 | ATI *Castelfidardo* | |
| I-DAND | McD Douglas MD-82 | ATI *Bolzano* | |
| I-DANF | McD Douglas MD-82 | ATI *Vicenza* | |
| I-DANG | McD Douglas MD-82 | ATI | |
| I-DANH | McD Douglas MD-82 | Alitalia | |
| I-DANL | McD Douglas MD-82 | Alitalia | |
| I-DANM | McD Douglas MD-82 | Alitalia *Vicenza* | |
| I-DANP | McD Douglas MD-82 | ATI | |
| I-DANQ | McD Douglas MD-82 | ATI | |
| I-DANR | McD Douglas MD-82 | ATI | |
| I-DANU | McD Douglas MD-82 | ATI | |
| I-DANV | McD Douglas MD-82 | Alitalia | |
| I-DANW | McD Douglas MD-82 | Alitalia | |
| I-DAVA | McD Douglas MD-82 | ATI *Cuneo* | |
| I-DAVB | McD Douglas MD-82 | ATI *Ferrara* | |
| I-DAVC | McD Douglas MD-82 | ATI *Lucca* | |
| I-DAVD | McD Douglas MD-82 | ATI *Mantova* | |
| I-DAVF | McD Douglas MD-82 | ATI *Oristano* | |
| I-DAVG | McD Douglas MD-82 | ATI *Pesaro* | |
| I-DAVH | McD Douglas MD-82 | ATI *Salerno* | |
| I-DAVI | McD Douglas MD-82 | Alitalia *Assisi* | |
| I-DAVJ | McD Douglas MD-82 | Alitalia *Parma* | |
| I-DAVK | McD Douglas MD-82 | Alitalia *Pompei* | |
| I-DAVL | McD Douglas MD-82 | ATI *Reggio Calabria* | |
| I-DAVM | McD Douglas MD-82 | Alitalia *Caserta* | |
| I-DAVN | McD Douglas MD-82 | ATI *Volterra* | |
| I-DAVP | McD Douglas MD-82 | ATI *Gorizia* | |
| I-DAVR | McD Douglas MD-82 | ATI | |
| I-DAVS | McD Douglas MD-82 | ATI | |
| I-DAVT | McD Douglas MD-82 | ATI | |
| I-DAVU | McD Douglas MD-82 | ATI | |
| I-DAVV | McD Douglas MD-82 | ATI | |
| I-DAVW | McD Douglas MD-82 | ATI *Camerino* | |
| I-DAVX | McD Douglas MD-82 | ATI *Asti* | |
| I-DAVZ | McD Douglas MD-82 | ATI *Brescia* | |
| I-DAWA | McD Douglas MD-82 | Alitalia *Roma* | |
| I-DAWB | McD Douglas MD-82 | Alitalia *Cagliari* | |
| I-DAWC | McD Douglas MD-82 | Alitalia *Campobasso* | |
| I-DAWD | McD Douglas MD-82 | Alitalia *Catanzaro* | |
| I-DAWE | McD Douglas MD-82 | Alitalia *Milano* | |
| I-DAWF | McD Douglas MD-82 | Alitalia *Firenze* | |
| I-DAWG | McD Douglas MD-82 | Alitalia *L'Aquila* | |
| I-DAWH | McD Douglas MD-82 | Alitalia *Palermo* | |
| I-DAWI | McD Douglas MD-82 | Alitalia *Ancona* | |
| I-DAWJ | McD Douglas MD-82 | Alitalia *Genova* | |
| I-DAWL | McD Douglas MD-82 | Alitalia *Perugia* | |
| I-DAWM | McD Douglas MD-82 | Alitalia *Potenza* | |
| I-DAWO | McD Douglas MD-82 | Alitalia *Bari* | |
| I-DAWP | McD Douglas MD-82 | Alitalia *Torino* | |
| I-DAWQ | McD Douglas MD-82 | Alitalia *Trieste* | |
| I-DAWR | McD Douglas MD-82 | Alitalia *Venezia* | |
| I-DAWS | McD Douglas MD-82 | Alitalia *Aosta* | |
| I-DAWT | McD Douglas MD-82 | ATI *Napoli* | |
| I-DAWU | McD Douglas MD-82 | Alitalia *Bologna* | |
| I-DAWV | McD Douglas MD-82 | ATI *Trento* | |
| I-DAWW | McD Douglas MD-82 | ATI *Riace* | |
| I-DAWY | McD Douglas MD-82 | ATI *Agrigento* | |
| I-DAWZ | McD Douglas MD-82 | ATI *Avellino* | |
| I-DEMC | Boeing 747-243B (SCD) | Alitalia *Taormina* | |
| I-DEMD | Boeing 747-243B (SCD) | Alitalia *Cortina d'Ampezzo* | |
| I-DEMF | Boeing 747-243B (SCD) | Alitalia *Portofino* | |
| I-DEMG | Boeing 747-243B | Alitalia *Cervinia* | |
| I-DEML | Boeing 747-243B | Alitalia *Sorrento* | |
| I-DEMN | Boeing 747-243B | Alitalia *Portocervo* | |
| I-DEMP | Boeing 747-243B | Alitalia *Capri* | |
| I-DEMR | Boeing 747-243F (SCD) | Alitalia *Stresa* | |
| I-DEMS | Boeing 747-243B | Alitalia *Monte Argentario* | |

| Reg. | Type | Owner or Operator |
|------|------|-------------------|
| I-DEMT | Boeing 747-243B (SCD) | Alitalia *Monte Catini* |
| I-DEMV | Boeing 747-243B | Alitalia *Sestriere* |
| I-DEMW | Boeing 747-243B (SCD) | Alitalia *Spoleto* |
| I-DEMX | Boeing 747-230F (SCD) | Alitalia *Ciclop* |
| I-DEMY | Boeing 747-230B | Alitalia *Asolo* |
| I-DIBA | Douglas DC-9-32 | Alitalia *Isola di Capri* |
| I-DIBE | Douglas DC-9-32 | Alitalia *Isola di Murano* |
| I-DIBI | Douglas DC-9-32 | Alitalia *Isola del Giglio* |
| I-DIBL | Douglas DC-9-32 | Alitalia *Isola d'Ischia* |
| I-DIBM | Douglas DC-9-32 | Alitalia *Isola di Panarea* |
| I-DIBP | Douglas DC-9-32 | Alitalia *Isola di Lipari* |
| I-DIBS | Douglas DC-9-32 | Alitalia *Isola d'Elba* |
| I-DIBU | Douglas DC-9-32 | Alitalia *Isola di Pantelleria* |
| I-DIBX | Douglas DC-9-32 | Alitalia *Isola di Giannutri* |
| I-DIKM | Douglas DC-9-32 | Alitalia *Isola di Positano* |
| I-DIKP | Douglas DC-9-32 | Alitalia *Isola di Marettimo* |
| I-DIKR | Douglas DC-9-32 | Alitalia *Piemonte* |
| I-DIZE | Douglas DC-9-32 | Alitalia *Isola della Meloria* |
| I-DUPA | McD Douglas MD-11C | Alitalia *Teatro alla Scala* |
| I-DUPB | McD Douglas MD-11 | Alitalia *Valle dei Templi* |
| I-DUPE | McD Douglas MD-11C | Alitalia *Arena di Verona* |
| I-DUPI | McD Douglas MD-11C | Alitalia *Fontona di Trevi* |
| I-DUPO | McD Douglas MD-11C | Alitalia *Nicolo Paccannini* |
| I-DUPU | McD Douglas MD-11C | Alitalia *Antonio Vivaldi* |
| | | |
| I-FLRV | BAe 146-200 | Meridiana |
| I-FLRW | BAe 146-200 | Meridiana |
| I-FLRX | BAe 146-200 | Meridiana |
| I-FLRZ | BAe 146-200 | Meridiana |
| I-FLYY | Douglas DC-9-51 | Eurofly |
| I-FLYZ | Douglas DC-9-51 | Eurofly |
| | | |
| I-JETA | Boeing 737-229 | Fortune Aviation |
| | | |
| I-RIBQ | Douglas DC-9-32 | Alitalia *Isola di Pianosa* |
| I-RIFB | Douglas DC-9-32 | Alitalia *Abruzzo* |
| I-RIFC | Douglas DC-9-32 | Alitalia *Isola di Lampedusa* |
| I-RIFD | Douglas DC-9-32 | Alitalia *Isola di Montecristo* |
| I-RIFE | Douglas DC-9-32 | Alitalia *Erice* |
| I-RIFG | Douglas DC-9-32 | Alitalia *Isola di Nisida* |
| I-RIFH | Douglas DC-9-32 | Alitalia *Isola di Ponza* |
| I-RIFJ | Douglas DC-9-32 | Alitalia *Isola della Capraia* |
| I-RIFL | Douglas DC-9-32 | Alitalia *Molise* |
| I-RIFM | Douglas DC-9-32 | ATI *Marche* |
| I-RIFP | Douglas DC-9-32 | Alitalia *Veneto* |
| I-RIFS | Douglas DC-9-32 | ATI *Basilicata* |
| I-RIFT | Douglas DC-9-32 | Alitalia *Friuli Venezia Giulia* |
| I-RIFU | Douglas DC-9-32 | ATI *Valle d'Aosta* |
| I-RIFV | Douglas DC-9-32 | ATI *Lazio* |
| I-RIFW | Douglas DC-9-32 | Alitalia *Lombardia* |
| I-RIFY | Douglas DC-9-32 | Alitalia *Puglia* |
| I-RIFZ | Douglas DC-9-32 | Alitalia *Toscana* |
| I-RIKT | Douglas DC-9-32 | ATI *Trento Alto Adige* |
| I-RIKV | Douglas DC-9-32 | Alitalia *Isola di Vulcano* |
| I-RIKZ | Douglas DC-9-32 | Alitalia *Isola di Linosa* |
| I-RIZA | Douglas DC-9-32 | Alitalia *Isola di Palmarola* |
| I-RIZF | Douglas DC-9-32 | Alitalia *Isola di Spargi* |
| I-RIZJ | Douglas DC-9-32 | Alitalia *Umbria* |
| I-RIZL | Douglas DC-9-32 | Alitalia *Romagna* |
| I-RIZN | Douglas DC-9-32 | ATI *Calabria* |
| I-RIZS | Douglas DC-9-32 | ATI *Compania* |
| I-RIZX | Douglas DC-9-32 | Alitalia *Isola di Procida* |
| | | |
| I-SMEA | Douglas DC-9-51 | Meridiana |
| I-SMEE | Douglas DC-9-51 | Meridiana |
| I-SMEI | Douglas DC-9-51 | Meridiana |
| I-SMEJ | Douglas DC-9-51 | Meridiana |
| I-SMEO | Douglas DC-9-51 | Meridiana |
| I-SMEP | McD Douglas MD-82 | Meridiana |
| I-SMER | McD Douglas MD-82 | Meridiana |
| I-SMES | McD Douglas MD-82 | Meridiana |
| I-SMET | McD Douglas MD-82 | Meridiana |
| I-SMEU | Douglas DC-9-51 | Meridiana |
| I-SMEV | McD Douglas MD-82 | Meridiana |

| Reg. | Type | Owner or Operator |
|---|---|---|
| I-SMEZ | McD Douglas MD-82 | Meridiana |
| I-TEAA | Boeing 737-3M8 | TEA Italia |
| I-TEAE | Boeing 737-3M8 | TEA Italia |
| I-TEAI | Boeing 737-3M8 | TEA Italia |
| I-TIAN | Douglas DC-9-15RC | Fortune Aviation |
| I-TIAR | Douglas DC-9-15RC | Fortune Aviation |
| I-TNTC | BAe146-200QT | Mistral Air/TNT |

**Note:** Meridiana also uses two DC-9-82s which retain their Swiss registrations HB-IKK
and HB-IKL. Alitalia Cargo operates two Boeing 737-248s registered EI-ASD and
EI-ASE. Air Europe SpA operates two Boeing 767s registered S7-AAQ and
S7-AAV.

# JA (Japan)

| Reg. | Type | Owner or Operator |
|---|---|---|
| JA8071 | Boeing 747-446 | Japan Airlines |
| JA8072 | Boeing 747-446 | Japan Airlines |
| JA8073 | Boeing 747-446 | Japan Airlines |
| JA8074 | Boeing 747-446 | Japan Airlines |
| JA8075 | Boeing 747-446 | Japan Airlines |
| JA8076 | Boeing 747-446 | Japan Airlines |
| JA8077 | Boeing 747-446 | Japan Airlines |
| JA8078 | Boeing 747-446 | Japan Airlines |
| JA8079 | Boeing 747-446 | Japan Airlines |
| JA8080 | Boeing 747-446 | Japan Airlines |
| JA8081 | Boeing 747-446 | Japan Airlines |
| JA8082 | Boeing 747-446 | Japan Airlines |
| JA8085 | Boeing 747-446 | Japan Airlines |
| JA8086 | Boeing 747-446 | Japan Airlines |
| JA8087 | Boeing 747-446 | Japan Airlines |
| JA8088 | Boeing 747-446 | Japan Airlines |
| JA8089 | Boeing 747-446 | Japan Airlines |
| JA8094 | Boeing 747-481 | All Nippon Airways |
| JA8095 | Boeing 747-481 | All Nippon Airways |
| JA8096 | Boeing 747-481 | All Nippon Airways |
| JA8097 | Boeing 747-481 | All Nippon Airways |
| JA8098 | Boeing 747-481 | All Nippon Airways |
| JA8104 | Boeing 747-246B | Japan Airlines |
| JA8105 | Boeing 747-246B | Japan Airlines |
| JA8106 | Boeing 747-246B | Japan Airlines |
| JA8108 | Boeing 747-246B | Japan Airlines |
| JA8110 | Boeing 747-246B | Japan Airlines |
| JA8111 | Boeing 747-246B | Japan Airlines |
| JA8114 | Boeing 747-246B | Japan Airlines |
| JA8115 | Boeing 747-146A | Japan Airlines |
| JA8116 | Boeing 747-146A | Japan Airlines |
| JA8122 | Boeing 747-246B | Japan Airlines |
| JA8123 | Boeing 747-246F (SCD) | Japan Airlines |
| JA8125 | Boeing 747-246B | Japan Airlines |
| JA8130 | Boeing 747-246B | Japan Airlines |
| JA8131 | Boeing 747-246B | Japan Airlines |
| JA8132 | Boeing 747-246F | Japan Airlines |
| JA8140 | Boeing 747-246B | Japan Airlines |
| JA8141 | Boeing 747-246B | Japan Airlines |
| JA8144 | Boeing 747-246F (SCD) | Japan Airlines |
| JA8149 | Boeing 747-246B | Japan Airlines |
| JA8150 | Boeing 747-246B | Japan Airlines |
| JA8151 | Boeing 747-246F (SCD) | Japan Airlines |
| JA8154 | Boeing 747-246B | Japan Airlines |
| JA8160 | Boeing 747-221F (SCD) | Japan Airlines/JUST |
| JA8161 | Boeing 747-246B | Japan Airlines |
| JA8162 | Boeing 747-246B | Japan Airlines |
| JA8163 | Boeing 747-346 | Japan Airlines |
| JA8165 | Boeing 747-221F (SCD) | Japan Airlines |
| JA8166 | Boeing 747-346 | Japan Airlines |
| JA8169 | Boeing 747-246B | Japan Airlines |
| JA8171 | Boeing 747-246F (SCD) | Japan Airlines |
| JA8173 | Boeing 747-346 | Japan Airlines |
| JA8174 | Boeing 747-281B | All Nippon Airways |
| JA8175 | Boeing 747-281B | All Nippon Airways |
| JA8177 | Boeing 747-346 | Japan Airlines |
| JA8178 | Boeing 747-346 | Japan Airlines |

| Notes | Reg. | Type | Owner or Operator |
|---|---|---|---|
| | JA8179 | Boeing 747-346 | Japan Airlines |
| | JA8180 | Boeing 747-246F (SCD) | Japan Airlines |
| | JA8181 | Boeing 747-281B | All Nippon Airways |
| | JA8182 | Boeing 747-281B | All Nippon Airways |
| | JA8185 | Boeing 747-346 | Japan Airlines |
| | JA8190 | Boeing 747-281B | All Nippon Airways |
| | JA8192 | Boeing 747-2D3B | All Nippon Airways |
| | JA8193 | Boeing 747-212F (SCD) | Japan Airlines |
| | JA8535 | Douglas DC-10-40 | Japan Airlines |
| | JA8538 | Douglas DC-10-40 | Japan Airlines |
| | JA8541 | Douglas DC-10-40 | Japan Airlines |
| | JA8542 | Douglas DC-10-40 | Japan Airlines |
| | JA8543 | Douglas DC-10-40 | Japan Airlines |
| | JA8545 | Douglas DC-10-40 | Japan Airlines |
| | JA8547 | Douglas DC-10-40 | Japan Airlines |
| | JA8901 | Boeing 747-446 | Japan Airlines |
| | JA8902 | Boeing 747-446 | Japan Airlines |
| | JA8906 | Boeing 747-446 | Japan Airlines |
| | JA8907 | Boeing 747-446 | Japan Airlines |
| | JA8958 | Boeing 747-481 | All Nippon Airways |
| | JA8962 | Boeing 747-481 | All Nippon |

**Note:** Japan Airlines also operates a Boeing 747-246F which retains its US registration. N211JL and two 747-346s N212JL and N213JL.

# JY (Jordan)

| | | | |
|---|---|---|---|
| JY-AGA | L.1011-385 TriStar 500 | Royal Jordanian *Amman* | |
| JY-AGB | L.1011-385 TriStar 500 | Royal Jordanian *Princess Alia* | |
| JY-AGC | L.1011-385 TriStar 500 | Royal Jordanian *Princess Zein* | |
| JY-AGD | L.1011-385 TriStar 500 | Royal Jordanian *Prince Ali* | |
| JY-AGE | L.1011-385 TriStar 500 | Royal Jordanian *Princess Aysha* | |
| JY-AJK | Boeing 707-384C | Royal Jordanian *City of Jerash* | |
| JY-AJL | Boeing 707-324C | Royal Jordanian | |
| JY-AJM | Boeing 707-365C | Royal Jordanian Cargo | |
| JY-HKJ | L.1011-385 TriStar 500 | Jordan Government | |

**Note:** Royal Jordanian also operates six A.310-304s registered F-ODVD, F-ODVE, F-ODVF, F-ODVG, F-ODVH and F-ODVI. The marks JY-CAD, JY-CAE, JY-CAF, JY-CAG, JY-CAH and JY-CAI respectively have been reserved for them. Similarly three A.320-211s retain the registrations F-OGYA, F-OGYB and F-OGYC.

# LN (Norway)

| | | | |
|---|---|---|---|
| LN-AKA | F.27 Friendship Mk 200 | Busy Bee | |
| LN-AKB | F.27 Friendship Mk 200 | Busy Bee | |
| LN-AKC | F.27 Friendship Mk 200 | Busy Bee | |
| LN-AKD | F.27 Friendship Mk 200 | Busy Bee | |
| LN-BBA | Fokker 50 | Busy Bee/Norsk Air | |
| LN-BBB | Fokker 50 | Busy Bee | |
| LN-BBC | Fokker 50 | Busy Bee | |
| LN-BBD | Fokker 50 | Busy Bee | |
| LN-BBE | Fokker 50 | Busy Bee | |
| LN-BRA | Boeing 737-405 | Braathens SAFE *Eirik Blodoeks* | |
| LN-BRB | Boeing 737-405 | Braathens SAFE *Inge Bardson* | |
| LN-BRC | Boeing 737-505 | Braathens SAFE | |
| LN-BRD | Boeing 737-505 | Braathens SAFE | |
| LN-BRE | Boeing 737-405 | Braathens SAFE | |
| LN-BRG | Boeing 737-505 | Braathens SAFE | |
| LN-BRI | Boeing 737-405 | Braathens SAFE | |
| LN-BRK | Boeing 737-505 | Braathens SAFE | |
| LN-BRM | Boeing 737-505 | Braathens SAFE | |
| LN-BRN | Boeing 737-505 | Braathens SAFE | |
| LN-BRO | Boeing 737-505 | Braathens SAFE | |
| LN-BRP | Boeing 737-405 | Braathens SAFE *Harold Hardrade* | |
| LN-BRQ | Boeing 737-405 | Braathens SAFE | |
| LN-BRR | Boeing 737-505 | Braathens SAFE | |
| LN-BRS | Boeing 737-505 | Braathens SAFE | |
| LN-BRT | Boeing 737-505 | Braathens SAFE | |
| LN-BRU | Boeing 737-505 | Braathens SAFE | |
| LN-BRV | Boeing 737-505 | Braathens SAFE | |
| LN-FOG | L-188AF Electra | Fred Olsen Airtransport/DHL | |
| LN-FOH | L-188AF Electra | Fred Olsen Airtransport/DHL | |

| Reg. | Type | Owner or Operator |
|------|------|-------------------|
| LN-FOI | L-188CF Electra | Fred Olsen Airtransport/DHL |
| LN-FOL | L-188AF Electra | Fred Olsen Airtransport/EMS |
| LN-KOC | EMB-120RT Brasilia | Norsk Air |
| LN-KOD | EMB-120RT Brasilia | Norsk Air |
| LN-KOE | EMB-120RT Brasilia | Norsk Air |
| LN-MOA | Beech 200 Super King Air | Morefly |
| LN-MOB | Beech 200 Super King Air | Morefly |
| LN-NPD | F-27 Friendship Mk 100 | Air Nordic |
| LN-NPI | F.27 Friendship Mk 100 | Air Nordic |
| LN-NPM | F.27 Friendship Mk 100 | Air Nordic |
| LN-RCC | Boeing 767-283ER | S.A.S. *Freydis Viking* |
| LN-RCD | Boeing 767-383ER | S.A.S. *Gyda Viking* |
| LN-RCE | Boeing 767-383ER | S.A.S. *Aase Viking* |
| LN-RCG | Boeing 767-383ER | S.A.S. *Yrsa Viking* |
| LN-RLA | Douglas DC-9-41 | S.A.S. *Are Viking* |
| LN-RLB | Douglas DC-9-41 | S.A.S. *Arne Viking* |
| LN-RLE | McD Douglas MD-81 | S.A.S. *Trygve Viking* |
| LN-RLH | Douglas DC-9-41 | S.A.S. *Einar Viking* |
| LN-RLN | Douglas DC-9-41 | S.A.S. *Halldor Viking* |
| LN-RLP | Douglas DC-9-41 | S.A.S. *Froste Viking* |
| LN-RLS | Douglas DC-9-41 | S.A.S. *Asmund Viking* |
| LN-RLT | Douglas DC-9-41 | S.A.S. *Audun Viking* |
| LN-RLU | Douglas DC-9-41 | S.A.S. *Eivind Viking* |
| LN-RLX | Douglas DC-9-41 | S.A.S. *Sote Viking* |
| LN-RLZ | Douglas DC-9-41 | S.A.S. *Bodvar Viking* |
| LN-RMA | McD Douglas MD-81 | S.A.S. *Hasting Viking* |
| LN-RMC | McD Douglas MD-87 | S.A.S. |
| LN-RMD | McD Douglas MD-82 | Scanair *Fenge Viking* |
| LN-RMF | McD Douglas MD-83 | Scanair *Piff Viking* |
| LN-RMG | McD Douglas MD-87 | S.A.S. *Snorre Viking* |
| LN-RMH | McD Douglas MD-87 | S.A.S. *Solmund Viking* |
| LN-RMJ | McD Douglas MD-81 | S.A.S. *Rand Viking* |
| LN-RMK | McD Douglas MD-87 | S.A.S. *Ragnhild Viking* |
| LN-RML | McD Douglas MD-81 | S.A.S. *Aud Viking* |
| LN-RMM | McD Douglas MD-81 | S.A.S. *Blenda Viking* |
| LN-RMN | McD Douglas MD-82 | S.A.S. *Ivar Viking* |
| LN-RMO | McD Douglas MD-81 | S.A.S. *Bergljot Viking* |
| LN-RMP | McD Douglas MD-87 | S.A.S. *Reidun Viking* |
| LN-RMR | McD Douglas MD-81 | S.A.S. *Olav Viking* |
| LN-RMS | McD Douglas MD-81 | S.A.S. *Nial Viking* |
| LN-RMT | McD Douglas MD-81 | S.A.S. *Atle Viking* |
| LN-RMU | McD Douglas MD-87 | S.A.S. *Grim Viking* |
| LN-RNB | Fokker 50 | S.A.S. Commuter *Bardufoss* |
| LN-RNC | Fokker 50 | S.A.S. Commuter *Evenes* |
| LN-RND | Fokker 50 | S.A.S. Commuter *Lakselv* |
| LN-RNE | Fokker 50 | S.A.S. Commuter *Alta* |
| LN-RNF | Fokker 50 | S.A.S. Commuter *Kirkenes* |
| LN-RNG | Fokker 50 | S.A.S. Commuter *Bodö* |
| LN-RNH | Fokker 50 | S.A.S. Commuter *Trondheim* |
| LN-SUA | Boeing 737-205 | Braathens SAFE |
| LN-SUE | F.27 Friendship Mk 100 | Busy Bee |
| LN-SUF | F.27 Friendship Mk 100 | Busy Bee |
| LN-WND | Douglas DC-3C | Dakota Norway |

**Note:** Braathens also operates the Boeing 737-205s N73FS, N73TH, N891FS, N7031A and N7031F (ex-LN-SUB, -SUK, -SUJ, -SUH and -SUM respectively).

# LV (Argentina)

| | | |
|------|------|------|
| LV-MLO | Boeing 747-287B | Aerolineas Argentinas |
| LV-MLP | Boeing 747-287B | Aerolineas Argentinas |
| LV-MLR | Boeing 747-287B | Aerolineas Argentinas |
| LV-OEP | Boeing 747-287B | Aerolineas Argentinas |
| LV-OHV | Boeing 747SP-27 | Aerolineas Argentinas |
| LV-OOZ | Boeing 747-287B | Aerolineas Argentinas |
| LV-OPA | Boeing 747-287B | Aerolineas Argentinas |

# LX (Luxembourg)

| | | |
|------|------|------|
| LX-ACV | Boeing 747-271C (SCD) | Cargolux *City of Esch/Alzette* |
| LX-BCV | Boeing 747-271C (SCD) | Cargolux |
| LX-DCV | Boeing 747-228F (SCD) | Cargolux |

| Notes | Reg. | Type | Owner or Operator |
|---|---|---|---|
| | LX-ECV | Boeing 747-271C (SCD) | Cargolux *City of Luxembourg* |
| | LX-LGB | Fokker 50 | Luxair |
| | LX-LGC | Fokker 50 | Luxair *Prince Guillaume* |
| | LX-LGD | Fokker 50 | Luxair *Prince Felix* |
| | LX-LGE | Fokker 50 | Luxair *Prince Louis* |
| | LX-LGF | Boeing 737-4C9 | Luxair *Chateau de Vianden* |
| | LX-LGG | Boeing 737-4C9 | Luxair *Chateau de Bourscheid* |
| | LX-LGH | Boeing 737-2C9 | Luxair *Prince Guillaume* |
| | LX-LGI | Boeing 737-2C9 | Luxair *Princesse Marie-Astrid* |
| | LX-LGK | EMB-120RT Brasilia | Luxair |
| | LX-LGL | EMB-120RT Brasilia | Luxair |
| | LX-LGM | EMB-120RT Brasilia | Luxair |
| | LX-LGO | Boeing 737-5C9 | Luxair |
| | LX-LGP | Boeing 737-5C9 | Luxair |
| | LX-LGX | Boeing 747SP-44 | Luxair |
| | LX-ZCV | Boeing 747-2D3B (SCD) | Cargolux |

## LY (Lithuania)

| | | | |
|---|---|---|---|
| | LY-ABA | Tupolev Tu-134A | Lithuanian Airlines |
| | LY-ABB | Tupolev Tu-134A | Lithuanian Airlines |
| | LY-ABC | Tupolev Tu-134A | Lithuanian Airlines |
| | LY-SBD | Tupolev Tu-134A | Lithuanian Airlines |
| | LY-ABE | Tupolev Tu-134A | Lithuanian Airlines |
| | LY-ABF | Tupolev Tu-134A | Lithuanian Airlines |
| | LY-ABG | Tupolev Tu-134A-3 | Lithuanian Airlines |
| | LY-ABH | Tupolev Tu-134A | Lithuanian Airlines |
| | LY-ABI | Tupolev Tu-134A | Lithuanian Airlines |
| | LY-GPA | Boeing 737-2Q8 | Lithuanian Airlines |

## LZ (Bulgaria)

| | | | |
|---|---|---|---|
| | LZ-ABA | Airbus A.320-231 | Balkan Bulgarian Airlines *Vitosha* |
| | LZ-ABB | Airbus A.320-231 | Balkan Bulgarian Airlines *Rila* |
| | LZ-ABC | Airbus A.320-231 | Balkan Bulgarian Airlines *Rhodope* |
| | LZ-ABD | Airbus A.320-231 | Balkan Bulgarian Airlines *Pirin* |
| | LZ-BAC | Antonov An-12 | Balkan Bulgarian Airlines |
| | LZ-BAE | Antonov An-12 | Balkan Bulgarian Airlines |
| | LZ-BAF | Antonov An-12 | Balkan Bulgarian Airlines |
| | LZ-BEH | Ilyushin IL-18V | Balkan Bulgarian Airlines |
| | LZ-BEI | Ilyushin IL-18V | Balkan Bulgarian Airlines |
| | LZ-BEU | Ilyushin IL-18V | Balkan Bulgarian Airlines |
| | LZ-BOA | Boeing 737-53A | Balkan Bulgarian Airlines |
| | LZ-BOB | Boeing 737-53A | Balkan Bulgarian Airlines |
| | LZ-BOC | Boeing 737-53A | Balkan Bulgarian Airlines |
| | LZ- | Boeing 767-300ER | Balkan Bulgarian Airlines |
| | LZ- | Boeing 767-300ER | Balkan Bulgarian Airlines |
| | LZ-BTA | Tupolev Tu-154B | Balkan Bulgarian Airlines |
| | LZ-BTC | Tupolev Tu-154B | Balkan Bulgarian Airlines |
| | LZ-BTE | Tupolev Tu-154B | Balkan Bulgarian Airlines |
| | LZ-BTF | Tupolev Tu-154B | Balkan Bulgarian Airlines |
| | LZ-BTG | Tupolev Tu-154B | Balkan Bulgarian Airlines |
| | LZ-BTH | Tupolev Tu-154M | Balkan Bulgarian Airlines |
| | LZ-BTI | Tupolev Tu-154M | Balkan Bulgarian Airlines |
| | LZ-BTJ | Tupolev Tu-154B-1 | Palair Macedonian |
| | LZ-BTK | Tupolev Tu-154B | Balkan Bulgarian Airlines |
| | LZ-BTL | Tupolev Tu-154B | Balkan Bulgarian Airlines |
| | LZ-BTM | Tupolev Tu-154B | Balkan Bulgarian Airlines |
| | LZ-BTN | Tupolev Tu-154M | Balkan Bulgarian Airlines |
| | LZ-BTO | Tupolev Tu-154B-1 | Balkan Bulgarian Airlines |
| | LZ-BTP | Tupolev Tu-154B-1 | Balkan Bulgarian Airlines |
| | LZ-BTQ | Tupolev Tu-154M | Balkan Bulgarian Airlines |
| | LZ-BTR | Tupolev Tu-154B-2 | Balkan Bulgarian Airlines |
| | LZ-BTS | Tupolev Tu-154B-2 | Balkan Bulgarian Airlines |
| | LZ-BTT | Tupolev Tu-154B-2 | Balkan Bulgarian Airlines |
| | LZ-BTU | Tupolev Tu-154B-2 | Palair Macedonian |
| | LZ-BTV | Tupolev Tu-154B-2 | Balkan Bulgarian Airlines |
| | LZ-BTW | Tupolev Tu-154M | Balkan Bulgarian Airlines |
| | LZ-BTX | Tupolev Tu-154M | Balkan Bulgarian Airlines |
| | LZ-BTY | Tupolev Tu-154M | Balkan Bulgarian Airlines |
| | LZ-BTZ | Tupolev Tu-154M | Balkan Bulgarian Airlines |
| | LZ-JXA | Airbus A.310-324 | Jes Air |

| Reg. | Type | Owner or Operator | Notes |
|------|------|-------------------|-------|
| LZ-JXB | Airbus A.310-222 | Jes Air | |
| LZ-JXC | Airbus A,310-304 | Jes Air | |
| LZ-MIG | Tupolev Tu-154M | Varna International Airways (VIA) | |
| LZ-MIK | Tupolev Tu-154M | Varna International Airways (VIA) | |
| LZ-MIL | Tupolev Tu-154M | Varna International Airways (VIA) | |
| LZ-MIR | Tupolev Tu-154M | Varna International Airways (VIA) | |
| LZ-MIS | Tupolev Tu-154M | Varna International Airways (VIA) | |
| LZ-SGA | Antonov An-12 | Sofia Air Cargo | |
| LZ-SGB | Antonov An-12 | Sofia Air Cargo | |
| LZ-SGC | Antonov An-12 | Sofia Air Cargo | |
| LZ-TUG | Tupolev Tu-134A-3 | Balkan Bulgarian Airlines | |
| LZ-TUK | Tupolev Tu-134A | Balkan Bulgarian Airlines | |
| LZ-TUM | Tupolev Tu-134A-3 | Balkan Bulgarian Airlines | |
| LZ-TUP | Tupolev Tu-134A | Balkan Bulgarian Airlines | |
| LZ-TUS | Tupolev Tu-134A | Balkan Bulgarian Airlines | |
| LZ-TUT | Tupolev Tu-134A-3 | Balkan Bulgarian Airlines | |
| LZ-TUU | Tupolev Tu-134A-3 | Balkan Bulgarian Airlines | |
| LZ-TUV | Tupolev Tu-134A-3 | Balkan Bulgarian Airlines | |
| LZ-TUZ | Tupolev Tu-134A-3 | Balkan Bulgarian Airlines | |

**Note:** Balkan also operates two Boeing 767-27EERs F-GHGD and F-GHGE on lease from Air France.

# N (USA)

| Reg. | Type | Owner or Operator | Notes |
|------|------|-------------------|-------|
| N14AZ | Boeing 707-336C | Seagreen Air Transport | |
| N21AZ | Boeing 707-351C | Seagreen Air Transport | |
| N25UA | Douglas DC-8-61F | American International Airways | |
| N73FS | Boeing 737-205 | Braathens SAFE *Magnus den Gode* | |
| N73TH | Boeing 737-205 | Braathens SAFE *Magnus Erlingsson* | |
| N105WA | Douglas DC-10-30CF | World Airways | |
| N106WA | Douglas DC-10-30CF | World Airways | |
| N107WA | Douglas DC-10-30CF | World Airways | |
| N108WA | Douglas DC-10-30CF | World Airways | |
| N112WA | Douglas DC-10-30CF | World Airways | |
| N116KB | Boeing 747-312 | Singapore Airlines | |
| N117AA | Douglas DC-10-10ER | American Airlines | |
| N117KC | Boeing 747-312 | Singapore Airlines | |
| N119KE | Boeing 747-312 | Singapore Airlines | |
| N120KF | Boeing 747-312 | Singapore Airlines | |
| N121KG | Boeing 747-312 | Singapore Airlines | |
| N122KH | Boeing 747-312 | Singapore Airlines | |
| N123KJ | Boeing 747-312 | Singapore Airlines | |
| N124KK | Boeing 747-312 | Singapore Airlines | |
| N125AA | Douglas DC-10-10ER | American Airlines | |
| N125KL | Boeing 747-312 | Singapore Airlines | |
| N133JC | Douglas DC-10-40 | Northwest Airlines | |
| N133TW | Boeing 747-156 | Trans World Airlines | |
| N134TW | Boeing 747-156 | Trans World Airlines | |
| N137AA | Douglas DC-10-30 | American Airlines | |
| N138AA | Douglas DC-10-30 | American Airlines | |
| N139AA | Douglas DC-10-30 | American Airlines | |
| N140AA | Douglas DC-10-30 | American Airlines | |
| N140UA | Boeing 747SP-21 | United Airlines | |
| N141AA | Douglas DC-10-30 | American Airlines | |
| N141UA | Boeing 747SP-21 | United Airlines | |
| N141US | Douglas DC-10-40 | Northwest Airlines | |
| N142AA | Douglas DC-10-30 | American Airlines | |
| N142UA | Boeing 747SP-21 | United Airlines | |
| N143AA | Douglas DC-10-30 | American Airlines | |
| N143UA | Boeing 747SP-21 | United Airlines | |
| N144AA | Douglas DC-10-30 | American Airlines | |
| N144JC | Douglas DC-10-40 | Northwest Airlines | |
| N144UA | Boeing 747SP-21 | United Airlines | |
| N145UA | Boeing 747SP-21 | United Airlines | |
| N145US | Douglas DC-10-40 | Northwest Airlines | |
| N146UA | Boeing 747SP-21 | United Airlines | |
| N146US | Douglas DC-10-40 | Northwest Airlines | |
| N147UA | Boeing 747SP-21 | United Airlines | |
| N147US | Douglas DC-10-40 | Northwest Airlines | |
| N148UA | Boeing 747SP-21 | United Airlines | |
| N148US | Douglas DC-10-40 | Northwest Airlines | |
| N149UA | Boeing 747SP-21 | United Airlines | |

N

| Notes | Reg. | Type | Owner or Operator |
|---|---|---|---|
| | N149US | Douglas DC-10-40 | Northwest Airlines |
| | N150US | Douglas DC-10-40 | Northwest Airlines |
| | N151UA | Boeing 747-222B | United Airlines |
| | N151US | Douglas DC-10-40 | Northwest Airlines |
| | N152UA | Boeing 747-222B | United Airlines |
| | N152US | Douglas DC-10-40 | Northwest Airlines |
| | N153UA | Boeing 747-123 | United Airlines |
| | N153US | Douglas DC-10-40 | Northwest Airlines |
| | N154UA | Boeing 747-123 | United Airlines |
| | N154US | Douglas DC-10-40 | Northwest Airlines |
| | N155UA | Boeing 747-123 | United Airlines |
| | N155US | Douglas DC-10-40 | Northwest Airlines |
| | N156UA | Boeing 747-123 | United Airlines |
| | N156US | Douglas DC-10-40 | Northwest Airlines |
| | N157UA | Boeing 747-123 | United Airlines |
| | N157US | Douglas DC-10-40 | Northwest Airlines |
| | N158UA | Boeing 747-238B | United Airlines |
| | N158US | Douglas DC-10-40 | Northwest Airlines |
| | N159UA | Boeing 747-238B | United Airlines |
| | N159US | Douglas DC-10-40 | Northwest Airlines |
| | N160UA | Boeing 747-238B | United Airlines |
| | N160US | Douglas DC-10-40 | Northwest Airlines |
| | N161UA | Boeing 747-238B | United Airlines |
| | N161US | Douglas DC-10-40 | Northwest Airlines |
| | N162US | Douglas DC-10-40 | Northwest Airlines |
| | N163AA | Douglas DC-10-30 | American Airlines |
| | N163UA | Boeing 747-238B | United Airlines |
| | N164AA | Douglas DC-10-30 | American Airlines |
| | N164UA | Boeing 747-238B | United Airlines |
| | N165UA | Boeing 747-238B | United Airlines |
| | N166AA | Douglas DC-10-10ER | American Airlines |
| | N171DN | Boeing 767-332ER | Delta Air Lines |
| | N171UA | Boeing 747-422 | United Airlines *Spirit of Seattle II* |
| | N172DN | Boeing 767-332ER | Delta Air Lines |
| | N172UA | Boeing 747-422 | United Airlines |
| | N173DN | Boeing 767-332ER | Delta Air Lines |
| | N173UA | Boeing 747-422 | United Airlines |
| | N174DN | Boeing 767-332ER | Delta Air Lines |
| | N174UA | Boeing 747-422 | United Airlines |
| | N175DN | Boeing 767-332ER | Delta Air Lines |
| | N175UA | Boeing 747-422 | United Airlines |
| | N176DN | Boeing 767-332ER | Delta Air Lines |
| | N176UA | Boeing 747-422 | United Airlines |
| | N177DN | Boeing 767-332ER | Delta Air Lines |
| | N177UA | Boeing 747-422 | United Airlines |
| | N178DN | Boeing 767-332ER | Delta Air Lines |
| | N178UA | Boeing 747-422 | United Airlines |
| | N179DN | Boeing 767-332ER | Delta Air Lines |
| | N179UA | Boeing 747-422 | United Airlines |
| | N180DN | Boeing 767-332ER | Delta Air Lines |
| | N180UA | Boeing 747-422 | United Airlines |
| | N181DN | Boeing 767-332ER | Delta Air Lines |
| | N181UA | Boeing 747-422 | United Airlines |
| | N182DN | Boeing 767-332ER | Delta Air Lines |
| | N182UA | Boeing 747-422 | United Airlines |
| | N183DN | Boeing 767-332ER | Delta Air Lines |
| | N183UA | Boeing 747-422 | United Airlines |
| | N184DN | Boeing 767-322ER | Delta Air Lines |
| | N184UA | Boeing 747-422 | United Airlines |
| | N185AT | L-1011 TriStar 50 | American Trans Air |
| | N185UA | Boeing 747-422 | United Airlines |
| | N186AT | L.1011 TriStar 50 | American Trans Air |
| | N186UA | Boeing 747-422 | United Airlines |
| | N187AT | L.1011 TriStar 50 | American Trans Air |
| | N187UA | Boeing 747-422 | United Airlines |
| | N188AT | L.1011 TriStar 50 | American Trans Air |
| | N188UA | Boeing 747-422 | United Airlines |
| | N189AT | L.1011 TriStar 50 | American Trans Air |
| | N189UA | Boeing 747-422 | United Airlines |
| | N190AT | L.1011 TriStar 50 | American Trans Air |
| | N190UA | Boeing 747-422 | United Airlines |
| | N191AT | L.1011 TriStar 50 | American Trans Air |
| | N191UA | Boeing 747-422 | United Airlines |

## OVERSEAS AIRLINERS

| Reg. | Type | Owner or Operator | Notes |
|------|------|-------------------|-------|
| N192AT | L.1011 TriStar 50 | American Trans Air | |
| N192UA | Boeing 747-422 | United Airlines | |
| N193AT | L.1011 TriStar 50 | American Trans Air | |
| N193UA | Boeing 747-422 | United Airlines | |
| N195AT | L.1011 TriStar 150 | American Trans Air | |
| N202AE | Boeing 747-2B4B (SCD) | Middle East Airlines | |
| N203AE | Boeing 747-2B4B (SCD) | Middle East Airlines | |
| N204AE | Boeing 747-2B4B (SCD) | Middle East Airlines | |
| N207AE | Boeing 747-211B | Philippine Airlines | |
| N208AE | Boeing 747-211B | Philippine Airlines | |
| N211JL | Boeing 747-246F | Japan Airlines | |
| N211NW | Douglas DC-10-30 | Northwest Airlines | |
| N212JL | Boeing 747-346 | Japan Airlines | |
| N213JL | Boeing 747-346 | Japan Airlines | |
| N220NW | Douglas DC-10-30 | Northwest Airlines | |
| N221NW | Douglas DC-10-30 | Northwest Airlines | |
| N223NW | Douglas DC-10-30 | Northwest Airlines | |
| N224NW | Douglas DC-10-30 | Northwest Airlines | |
| N225NW | Douglas DC-10-30 | Northwest Airlines | |
| N226NW | Douglas DC-10-30 | Northwest Airlines | |
| N227NW | Douglas DC-10-30 | Northwest Airlines | |
| N301FE | Douglas DC-10-30AF | Federal Express | |
| N301TW | Boeing 747-282B | Trans World Airlines *(stored)* | |
| N302FE | Douglas DC-10-30AF | Federal Express | |
| N302TW | Boeing 747-282B | Trans World Airlines *(stored)* | |
| N303FE | Douglas DC-10-30AF | Federal Express | |
| N303TW | Boeing 747-257B | Nationair | |
| N304FE | Douglas DC-10-30AF | Federal Express | |
| N304TW | Boeing 747-257B | Nationair | |
| N305FE | Douglas DC-10-30AF | Federal Express *John David* | |
| N305TW | Boeing 747-284B | Trans World Airlines | |
| N306FE | Douglas DC-10-30AF | Federal Express *John Peter Jr* | |
| N307FE | Douglas DC-10-30AF | Federal Express *Erin Lee* | |
| N308FE | Douglas DC-10-30AF | Federal Express *Ann* | |
| N309FE | Douglas DC-10-30AF | Federal Express *Stacey* | |
| N310FE | Douglas DC-10-30AF | Federal Express *John Shelby* | |
| N311FE | Douglas DC-10-30AF | Federal Express *Abe* | |
| N312AA | Boeing 767-223ER | American Airlines | |
| N312FE | Douglas DC-10-30AF | Federal Express *Angela* | |
| N313AA | Boeing 767-223ER | American Airlines | |
| N313FE | Douglas DC-10-30AF | Federal Express *Brandon Parks* | |
| N314FE | Douglas DC-10-30AF | Federal Express *Caitlin-Ann* | |
| N315AA | Boeing 767-223ER | American Airlines | |
| N315FE | Douglas DC-10-30AF | Federal Express *Kevin* | |
| N316AA | Boeing 767-223ER | American Airlines | |
| N316FE | Douglas DC-10-30AF | Federal Express *Brandon* | |
| N317AA | Boeing 767-223ER | American Airlines | |
| N319AA | Boeing 767-223ER | American Airlines | |
| N319EA | L.1011 TriStar 1 | Rich International Airways | |
| N320AA | Boeing 767-223ER | American Airlines | |
| N320FE | Douglas DC-10-30CF | Federal Express | |
| N321AA | Boeing 767-223ER | American Airlines | |
| N321FE | Douglas DC-10-30CF | Federal Express | |
| N322AA | Boeing 767-223ER | American Airlines | |
| N322FE | Douglas DC-10-30CF | Federal Express *King Frank* | |
| N323AA | Boeing 767-223ER | American Airlines | |
| N324AA | Boeing 767-223ER | American Airlines | |
| N325AA | Boeing 767-223ER | American Airlines | |
| N327AA | Boeing 767-223ER | American Airlines | |
| N328AA | Boeing 767-223ER | American Airlines | |
| N329AA | Boeing 767-223ER | American Airlines | |
| N330AA | Boeing 767-223ER | American Airlines | |
| N332AA | Boeing 767-223ER | American Airlines | |
| N334AA | Boeing 767-223ER | American Airlines | |
| N335AA | Boeing 767-223ER | American Airlines | |
| N336AA | Boeing 767-223ER | American Airlines | |
| N338AA | Boeing 767-223ER | American Airlines | |
| N339AA | Boeing 767-223ER | American Airlines | |
| N341HA | L.188F Electra | Channel Express (Air Services) Ltd/ Bournemouth | |
| N343HA | L.188F Electra | Channel Express (Air Services) Ltd/ Bournemouth | |
| N345HC | Douglas DC-10-30ER | Finnair | |

| Notes | Reg. | Type | Owner or Operator |
|-------|------|------|-------------------|
| | N345JW | Douglas DC-8-63AF | Arrow Air |
| | N351AA | Boeing 767-323ER | American Airlines |
| | N352AA | Boeing 767-323ER | American Airlines |
| | N353AA | Boeing 767-323ER | American Airlines |
| | N354AA | Boeing 767-323ER | American Airlines |
| | N355AA | Boeing 767-323ER | American Airlines |
| | N357AA | Boeing 767-323ER | American Airlines |
| | N358AA | Boeing 767-323ER | American Airlines |
| | N359AA | Boeing 767-323ER | American Airlines |
| | N360AA | Boeing 767-323ER | American Airlines |
| | N361AA | Boeing 767-323ER | American Airlines |
| | N362AA | Boeing 767-323ER | American Airlines |
| | N363AA | Boeing 767-323ER | American Airlines |
| | N366AA | Boeing 767-323ER | American Airlines |
| | N368AA | Boeing 767-323ER | American Airlines |
| | N369AA | Boeing 767-323ER | American Airlines |
| | N370AA | Boeing 767-323ER | American Airlines |
| | N371AA | Boeing 767-323ER | American Airlines |
| | N372AA | Boeing 767-323ER | American Airlines |
| | N373AA | Boeing 767-323ER | American Airlines |
| | N374AA | Boeing 767-323ER | American Airlines |
| | N376AN | Boeing 767-323ER | American Airlines |
| | N377AN | Boeing 767-323ER | American Airlines |
| | N378AN | Boeing 767-323ER | American Airlines |
| | N379AA | Boeing 767-323ER | American Airlines |
| | N380AM | Boeing 767-323ER | American Airlines |
| | N381AN | Boeing 767-323ER | American Airlines |
| | N382AN | Boeing 767-323ER | American Airlines |
| | N383AN | Boeing 767-323ER | American Airlines |
| | N384AA | Boeing 767-323ER | American Airlines |
| | N385AM | Boeing 767-323ER | American Airlines |
| | N386AA | Boeing 767-323ER | American Airlines |
| | N417DG | Douglas DC-10-30 | Aeromexico *Ciudad de Mexico* |
| | N441J | Douglas DC-8-63CF | Arrow Air |
| | N470EV | Boeing 747-273C | Evergreen International Airlines |
| | N471EV | Boeing 747-273C | Evergreen International Airlines |
| | N472EV | Boeing 747-131 | Evergreen International Airlines |
| | N473EV | Boeing 747-121F (SCD) | Evergreen International Airlines |
| | N474EV | Boeing 747-121 | Evergreen International Airlines |
| | N475EV | Boeing 747-121F (SCD) | Evergreen International Airlines |
| | N477EV | Boeing 747SR-46 (SCD) | Evergreen International Airlines |
| | N478EV | Boeing 747SR-46 (SCD) | Evergreen International Airlines |
| | N479EV | Boeing 747-132 (SCD) | Evergreen International Airlines |
| | N480EV | Boeing 747-121 (SCD) | Evergreen International Airlines |
| | N481EV | Boeing 747-132 (SCD) | Evergreen International Airlines |
| | N482EV | Boeing 747-212B (SCD) | Evergreen International Airlines |
| | N485EV | Boeing 747-212B (SCD) | Evergreen International Airlines |
| | N522SJ | L-100-20 Hercules | Southern Air Transport |
| | N601FE | McD Douglas MD-11F | Federal Express *Christy* |
| | N601US | Boeing 747-151 | Northwest Airlines |
| | N602AA | Boeing 747SP-31 | American Airlines |
| | N602FE | McDouglas MD-11F | Federal Express *Malcolm Baldrige* |
| | N602FF | Boeing 747-124 | Tower Air |
| | N602UA | Boeing 767-222ER | United Airlines |
| | N602US | Boeing 747-151 | Northwest Airlines |
| | N603FE | McD Douglas MD-11F | Federal Express *Elizabeth* |
| | N603FF | Boeing 747-130 | Tower Air *Suzie* |
| | N603US | Boeing 747-151 | Northwest Airlines |
| | N604FE | McD Douglas MD-11F | Federal Express *Hollis* |
| | N604FF | Boeing 747-121 | Tower Air |
| | N604US | Boeing 747-151 | Northwest Airlines |
| | N605FE | McD Douglas MD-11F | Federal Express *April Star* |
| | N605FF | Boeing 747-136 | Tower Air |
| | N605UA | Boeing 767-222ER | United Airlines |
| | N605US | Boeing 747-151 | Northwest Airlines |
| | N606FE | McD Douglas MD-11F | Federal Express *Louis III* |
| | N606FF | Boeing 747-136 | Tower Air |
| | N606UA | Boeing 767-222ER | United Airlines *City of Chicago* |
| | N606US | Boeing 747-151 | Northwest Airlines |
| | N607FE | McD Douglas MD-11F | Federal Express *Dana Elena* |
| | N607FF | Boeing 747-121 | Tower Air |
| | N607PE | Boeing 747-238B (022) | Continental Airlines *(to become N50022)* |
| | N607UA | Boeing 767-222ER | United Airlines *City of Denver* |

# OVERSEAS AIRLINERS

| Reg. | Type | Owner or Operator | Notes |
|------|------|-------------------|-------|
| N607US | Boeing 747-151 | Northwest Airlines | |
| N608FE | McD Douglas MD-11F | Federal Express *Scott* | |
| N608FF | Boeing 747-131 | Tower Air | |
| N608UA | Boeing 767-222ER | United Airlines | |
| N608US | Boeing 747-151 | Northwest Airlines | |
| N609UA | Boeing 767-222ER | United Airlines | |
| N609US | Boeing 747-151 | Northwest Airlines | |
| N610UA | Boeing 767-222ER | United Airlines | |
| N610US | Boeing 747-151 | Northwest Airlines | |
| N611UA | Boeing 767-222ER | United Airlines | |
| N611US | Boeing 747-251B | Northwest Airlines | |
| N612US | Boeing 747-251B | Northwest Airlines | |
| N613US | Boeing 747-251B | Northwest Airlines | |
| N614FE | McD Douglas MD-11F | Federal Express | |
| N614US | Boeing 747-251B | Northwest Airlines | |
| N615US | Boeing 747-251B | Northwest Airlines | |
| N616US | Boeing 747-251F (SCD) | Northwest Airlines | |
| N617US | Boeing 747-251F (SCD) | Northwest Airlines | |
| N618US | Boeing 747-251F (SCD) | Northwest Airlines | |
| N619US | Boeing 747-251F (SCD) | Northwest Airlines | |
| N620FE | Boeing 747-133 | Federal Express | |
| N620US | Boeing 747-135 | Northwest Airlines | |
| N621FE | Boeing 747-133 | Federal Express | |
| N621US | Boeing 747-135 | Northwest Airlines | |
| N622US | Boeing 747-251B | Northwest Airlines | |
| N623US | Boeing 747-251B | Northwest Airlines | |
| N624US | Boeing 747-251B | Northwest Airlines | |
| N625FE | Boeing 747-132F (SCD) | Federal Express | |
| N625US | Boeing 747-251B | Northwest Airlines | |
| N626US | Boeing 747-251B | Northwest Airlines | |
| N627US | Boeing 747-251B | Northwest Airlines | |
| N628US | Boeing 747-251B | Northwest Airlines | |
| N629US | Boeing 747-251F (SCD) | Northwest Airlines | |
| N630FE | Boeing 747-124F (SCD) | Federal Express | |
| N630US | Boeing 747-2J9F | Northwest Airlines | |
| N631FE | Boeing 747-249F (SCD) | Federal Express | |
| N631US | Boeing 747-251B | Northwest Airlines | |
| N632FE | Boeing 747-249F (SCD) | Federal Express | |
| N632US | Boeing 747-251B | Northwest Airlines | |
| N633FE | Boeing 747-249F | Federal Express | |
| N633US | Boeing 747-227B | Northwest Airlines | |
| N634US | Boeing 747-227B | Northwest Airlines | |
| N635US | Boeing 747-227B | Northwest Airlines | |
| N636FE | Boeing 747-245F (SCD) | Federal Express | |
| N636US | Boeing 747-251B | Northwest Airlines | |
| N637US | Boeing 747-251B | Northwest Airlines | |
| N638FE | Boeing 747-245F (SCD) | Federal Express | |
| N638US | Boeing 747-251B | Northwest Airlines | |
| N639FE | Boeing 747-2R7F (SCD) | Federal Express | |
| N639US | Boeing 747-251F (SCD) | Northwest Airlines | |
| N640FE | Boeing 747-245F (SCD) | Federal Express | |
| N640US | Boeing 747-251F (SCD) | Northwest Airlines | |
| N641FE | Boeing 747-245F (SCD) | Federal Express | |
| N641UA | Boeing 767-322ER | United Airlines | |
| N642UA | Boeing 767-322ER | United Airlines | |
| N643UA | Boeing 767-322ER | United Airlines | |
| N644UA | Boeing 767-322ER | United Airlines | |
| N645UA | Boeing 767-322ER | United Airlines | |
| N645US | Boeing 767-201ER | USAir *Pride of Piedmont* | |
| N646UA | Boeing 767-322ER | United Airlines | |
| N646US | Boeing 767-201ER | USAir *City of London* | |
| N647UA | Boeing 767-322ER | United Airlines | |
| N647US | Boeing 767-201ER | USAir *City of Charlotte* | |
| N648AU | Boeing 767-322ER | United Airlines | |
| N648US | Boeing 767-201ER | USAir *City of Tampa* | |
| N649UA | Boeing 767-322ER | United Airlines | |
| N649US | Boeing 767-201ER | USAir *City of Los Angeles* | |
| N650UA | Boeing 767-322ER | United Airlines | |
| N650US | Boeing 767-201ER | USAir *Pride of Baltimore* | |
| N651UA | Boeing 767-322ER | United Airlines | |
| N651US | Boeing 767-2B7ER | USAir | |
| N652UA | Boeing 767-322ER | United Airlines | |
| N652US | Boeing 767-2B7ER | USAir | |

| Notes | Reg. | Type | Owner or Operator |
|---|---|---|---|
| | N653UA | Boeing 767-322ER | United Airlines |
| | N653US | Boeing 767-2B7ER | USAir |
| | N654UA | Boeing 767-322ER | United Airlines |
| | N654US | Boeing 767-2B7ER | USAir |
| | N655UA | Boeing 767-322ER | United Airlines |
| | N655US | Boeing 767-2B7ER | USAir *Edwin L. Colodny* |
| | N656UA | Boeing 767-322ER | United Airlines |
| | N657UA | Boeing 767-322ER | United Airlines |
| | N658UA | Boeing 767-322ER | United Airlines |
| | N659UA | Boeing 767-322ER | United Airlines |
| | N660UA | Boeing 767-322ER | United Airlines |
| | N661AV | Douglas DC-8-63AF | Arrow Air |
| | N661UA | Boeing 767-322ER | United Airlines |
| | N661US | Boeing 747-451 | Northwest Airlines |
| | N662UA | Boeing 767-322ER | United Airlines |
| | N662US | Boeing 747-451 | Northwest Airlines |
| | N663UA | Boeing 767-322ER | United Airlines |
| | N663US | Boeing 747-451 | Northwest Airlines |
| | N664UA | Boeing 767-322ER | United Airlines |
| | N664US | Boeing 747-451 | Northwest Airlines |
| | N665UA | Boeing 767-322ER | United Airlines |
| | N665US | Boeing 747-451 | Northwest Airlines |
| | N666UA | Boeing 767-322ER | United Airlines |
| | N666US | Boeing 747-451 | Northwest Airlines |
| | N667US | Boeing 747-451 | Northwest Airlines |
| | N668US | Boeing 747-451 | Northwest Airlines |
| | N669US | Boeing 747-451 | Northwest Airlines |
| | N670US | Boeing 747-451 | Northwest Airlines |
| | N671UP | Boeing 747-123F (SCD) | United Parcel Service |
| | N671US | Boeing 747-451 | Northwest Airlines |
| | N672UP | Boeing 747-123F (SCD) | United Parcel Service |
| | N672US | Boeing 747-451 | Northwest Airlines |
| | N673UP | Boeing 747-123F (SCD) | United Parcel Service |
| | N674UP | Boeing 747-123F (SCD) | United Parcel Service |
| | N675UP | Boeing 747-123F (SCD) | United Parcel Service |
| | N676UP | Boeing 747-123F (SCD) | United Parcel Service |
| | N677UP | Boeing 747-123F (SCD) | United Parcel Service |
| | N681UP | Boeing 747-123F (SCD) | United Parcel Service |
| | N682UP | Boeing 747-121F (SCD) | United Parcel Service |
| | N683UP | Boeing 747-121F (SCD) | United Parcel Service |
| | N724DA | L.1011-385 TriStar 200 | Delta Air Lines |
| | N736DY | L.1011-385 TriStar 250 | Delta Air Lines |
| | N737D | L.1011-385 TriStar 250 | Delta Air Lines |
| | N740DA | L.1011-385 TriStar 250 | Delta Air Lines |
| | N741DA | L.1011-385 TriStar 250 | Delta Air Lines |
| | N741PR | Boeing 747-2F6B | Philippine Airlines |
| | N742PR | Boeing 747-2F6B | Philippine Airlines |
| | N743PR | Boeing 747-2F6B | Philippine Airlines |
| | N744PR | Boeing 747-2F6B | Philippine Airlines |
| | N750AT | Boeing 757-212ER | American Trans Air |
| | N751AT | Boeing 757-212ER | American Trans Air |
| | N751DA | L-1011-385 TriStar 500 | Delta Air Lines |
| | N752AT | Boeing 757-212ER | American Trans Air |
| | N752DA | L-1011-385 TriStar 500 | Delta Air Lines |
| | N753DA | L-1011-385 TriStar 500 | Delta Air Lines |
| | N754AT | Boeing 757-2Q8 | American Trans Air |
| | N754DL | L.1011-385 TriStar 500 | Delta Air Lines |
| | N755AT | Boeing 757-2Q8 | American Trans Air |
| | N755DL | L.1011-385 TriStar 500 | Delta Air Lines |
| | N756DR | L.1011-385 TriStar 500 | Delta Air Lines |
| | N757AT | Boeing 757-212ER | American Trans Air |
| | N759DA | L.1011-385 TriStar 500 | Delta Air Lines |
| | N760DH | L.1011-385 TriStar 500 | Delta Air Lines |
| | N761DA | L.1011-385 TriStar 500 | Delta Air Lines |
| | N762BE | L.1011-385 TriStar 50 | Hawaiian Air *Waikiki* |
| | N762DA | L.1011-385 TriStar 500 | Delta Air Lines |
| | N763DL | L.1011-385 TriStar 500 | Delta Air Lines |
| | N764BE | L.1011-385 TriStar 50 | Hawaiian Air *Wahwaii* |
| | N764DA | L.1011-385 TriStar 500 | Delta Air Lines |
| | N765BE | L.1011-385 TriStar 50 | Hawaiian Air *Kauai* |
| | N765DA | L.1011-385 TriStar 500 | Delta Air Lines |
| | N766BE | L.1011-385 TriStar 50 | Hawaiian Air *Oahu* |
| | N766DA | L.1011-385 TriStar 500 | Delta Air Lines |

| Reg. | Type | Owner or Operator | Notes |
|------|------|-------------------|-------|
| N767DA | L.1011-385 TriStar 500 | Delta Air Lines | |
| N768DL | L.1011-385 TriStar 500 | Delta Air Lines | |
| N769DL | L.1011-385 TriStar 500 | Delta Air Lines | |
| N772CA | Douglas DC-8-62 | Rich International Airways | |
| N784AL | Douglas DC-8-63CF | Arrow Air | |
| N791AL | Douglas DC-8-62AF | Arrow Air | |
| N791FT | Douglas DC-8-73AF | Emery Worldwide | |
| N792FT | Douglas DC-8-73AF | Emery Worldwide | |
| N795FT | Douglas DC-8-73AF | Emery Worldwide | |
| N796AL | Douglas DC-8-63AF | Emery Worldwide | |
| N796FT | Douglas DC-8-73AF | Emery Worldwide | |
| N797AL | Douglas DC-8-63AF | Emery Worldwide | |
| N798AL | Douglas DC-8-62CF | Arrow Air | |
| N799AL | Douglas DC-8-62CF | Arrow Air | |
| N801CK | Douglas DC-8-55F | American International Airways | |
| N801DE | McD Douglas MD-11 | Delta Air Lines | |
| N801PA | Airbus A.310-222 | Delta Air Lines | |
| N801UP | Douglas DC-8-73AF | United Parcel Service | |
| N802BN | Douglas DC-8-62AF | Arrow Air | |
| N802DE | McD Douglas MD-11 | Delta Air Lines | |
| N802PA | Airbus A.310-222 | Delta Air Lines | |
| N802UP | Douglas DC-8-73AF | United Parcel Service | |
| N803DE | McD Douglas MD-11 | Delta Air Lines | |
| N803PA | Airbus A.310-222 | Delta Air Lines | |
| N803UP | Douglas DC-8-63AF | United Parcel Service | |
| N804DE | McD Douglas MD-11 | Delta Air Lines | |
| N804PA | Airbus A.310-222 | Delta Air Lines | |
| N804UP | Douglas DC-8-51 | United Parcel Service | |
| N805CK | Douglas DC-8-51F | American International Airways | |
| N805DE | McD Douglas MD-11 | Delta Air Lines | |
| N805PA | Airbus A.310-222 | Delta Air Lines | |
| N805UP | Douglas DC-8-73CF | United Parcel Service | |
| N806DE | McD Douglas MD-11 | Delta Air Lines | |
| N806PA | Airbus A.310-222 | Delta Air Lines | |
| N806UP | Douglas DC-8-73AF | United Parcel Service | |
| N807CK | Douglas DC-8-55F | American International Airways | |
| N807DE | McD Douglas MD-11 | Delta Air Lines | |
| N807PA | Airbus A.310-222 | Delta Air Lines | |
| N807UP | Douglas DC-8-73AF | United Parcel Service | |
| N808CK | Douglas DC-8-55F | American International Airways | |
| N808DE | McD Douglas MD-11 | Delta Air Lines | |
| N808UP | Douglas DC-8-73AF | United Parcel Service | |
| N809CK | Douglas DC-8-73AF | American International Airways | |
| N809DE | McD Douglas MD-11 | Delta Air Lines | |
| N809UP | Douglas DC-8-73AF | United Parcel Service | |
| N810CK | Douglas DC-8-52F | American International Airways | |
| N810UP | Douglas DC-8-71AF | United Parcel Service | |
| N811CK | Douglas DC-8-63AF | American International Airways | |
| N811PA | Airbus A.310-324 | Delta Air Lines | |
| N811UP | Douglas DC-8-73AF | United Parcel Service | |
| N812CK | Douglas DC-8-61AF | American International Airways | |
| N812PA | Airbus A.310-324 | Delta Air Lines | |
| N812UP | Douglas DC-8-73AF | United Parcel Service | |
| N813CK | Douglas DC-8-61AF | American International Airways | |
| N813PA | Airbus A.310-324 | Delta Air Lines | |
| N813UP | Douglas DC-8-73AF | United Parcel Service | |
| N814PA | Airbus A.310-324 | Delta Air Lines | |
| N814UP | Douglas DC-8-73AF | United Parcel Service | |
| N815EV | Douglas DC-8-73CF | Evergreen International Airlines | |
| N815PA | Airbus A.310-324 | Delta Air Lines | |
| N816EV | Douglas DC-8-73CF | Evergreen International Airlines/TNT | |
| N816PA | Airbus A.310-324 | Delta Air Lines | |
| N817EV | Douglas DC-8-62AF | Evergreen International Airlines | |
| N817PA | Airbus A.310-324 | Delta Air Lines | |
| N818PA | Airbus A.310-324 | Delta Air Lines | |
| N818UP | Douglas DC-8-73AF | United Parcel Service | |
| N819PA | Airbus A.310-324 | Delta Air Lines | |
| N819UP | Douglas DC-8-73AF | United Parcel Service | |
| N820PA | Airbus A.310-324 | Delta Air Lines | |
| N821PA | Airbus A.310-324 | Delta Air Lines | |
| N822PA | Airbus A.310-324 | Delta Air Lines | |
| N823PA | Airbus A.310-324 | Delta Air Lines | |
| N824PA | Airbus A.310-324 | Delta Air Lines | |

| Notes | Reg. | Type | Owner or Operator |
|-------|------|------|-------------------|
| | N825PA | Airbus A.310-324 | Delta Air Lines |
| | N826PA | Airbus A.310-324 | Delta Air Lines |
| | N835AB | Airbus A.310-324 | Delta Air Lines |
| | N836AB | Airbus A.310-324 | Delta Air Lines |
| | N836UP | Douglas DC-8-73AF | United Parcel Service |
| | N837AB | Airbus A.310-324 | Delta Air Lines |
| | N838AB | Airbus A.310-324 | Delta Air Lines |
| | N839AB | Airbus A.310-324 | Delta Air Lines |
| | N840AB | Airbus A.310-324 | Delta Air Lines |
| | N840UP | Douglas DC-8-73AF | United Parcel Service |
| | N841AB | Airbus A.310-324 | Delta Air Lines |
| | N842AB | Airbus A.310-324 | Delta Air Lines |
| | N843AB | Airbus A.310-324 | Delta Air Lines |
| | N851UP | Douglas DC-8-73AF | United Parcel Service |
| | N852UP | Douglas DC-8-73AF | United Parcel Service |
| | N865F | Douglas DC-8-63AF | Emery Worldwide |
| | N866UP | Douglas DC-8-73AF | United Parcel Service |
| | N867BX | Douglas DC-8-63AF | Burlington Express |
| | N867UP | Douglas DC-8-73AF | United Parcel Service |
| | N868BX | Douglas DC-8-63AF | Burlington Express |
| | N868UP | Douglas DC-8-73AF | United Parcel Service |
| | N869BX | Doulgas DC-8-63AF | Burlington Express |
| | N870BX | Doulgas DC-8-63AF | Burlington Express |
| | N870TV | Douglas DC-8-73AF | Emery Worldwide |
| | N871SJ | Douglas DC-8-71AF | Southern Air Transport |
| | N872SJ | Douglas DC-8-71AF | Southern Air Transport |
| | N873SJ | Douglas DC-8-73AF | Southern Air Transport |
| | N874SJ | Douglas DC-8-71AF | Southern Air Transport |
| | N874UP | Douglas DC-8-73AF | United Parcel Service |
| | N875SJ | Douglas DC-8-71AF | Southern Air Transport |
| | N880UP | Douglas DC-8-73AF | United Parcel Service |
| | N891FS | Boeing 737-205 | Braathens SAFE *Magnus Barfot* |
| | N894UP | Douglas DC-8-73AF | United Parcel Service |
| | N901SJ | L.100-30 Hercules | Southern Air Transport |
| | N902SJ | L.100-30 Hercules | Southern Air Transport |
| | N903SJ | L.100-30 Hercules | Southern Air Transport |
| | N904SJ | L.100-30 Hercules | Southern Air Transport |
| | N905SJ | L.100-30 Hercules | Southern Air Transport |
| | N906R | Douglas DC-8-63AF | Emery Worldwide |
| | N906SJ | L.100-30 Hercules | Southern Air Transport |
| | N907SJ | L.100-30 Hercules | Southern Air Transport |
| | N908SJ | L.100-30 Hercules | Southern Air Transport |
| | N909SJ | L.100-30 Hercules | Southern Air Transport |
| | N910SJ | L.100-30 Hercules | Southern Air Transport |
| | N912SJ | L.100-30 Hercules | Southern Air Transport |
| | N916SJ | L.100-30 Hercules | Southern Air Transport |
| | N918SJ | L.100-30 Hercules | Southern Air Transport |
| | N919SJ | L.100-30 Hercules | Southern Air Transport |
| | N920SJ | L.100-30 Hercules | Southern Air Transport |
| | N921R | Douglas DC-8-63AF | Emery Worldwide |
| | N921SJ | L.100-30 Hercules | Southern Air Transport |
| | N923SJ | L.100-30 Hercules | Southern Air Transport |
| | N929R | Douglas DC-8-63AF | Emery Worldwide |
| | N950R | Douglas DC-8-63AF | Emery Worldwide |
| | N951R | Douglas DC-8-63AF | Emery Worldwide |
| | N952R | Douglas DC-8-63AF | Emery Worldwide |
| | N957R | Douglas DC-8-63AF | Emery Worldwide |
| | N959R | Douglas DC-8-63AF | Emery Worldwide |
| | N961R | Douglas DC-8-73AF | Emery Worldwide |
| | N964R | Douglas DC-8-63AF | Emery Worldwide |
| | N990CF | Douglas DC-8-62AF | Emery Worldwide |
| | N993CF | Douglas DC-8-62AF | Emery Worldwide |
| | N994CF | Douglas DC-8-62AF | Emery Worldwide |
| | N995CF | Douglas DC-8-62AF | Emery Worldwide |
| | N996CF | Douglas DC-8-62AF | Emery Worldwide |
| | N997CF | Douglas DC-8-62AF | Emery Worldwide |
| | N998CF | Douglas DC-8-62AF | Emery Worldwide |
| | N1309E | Boeing 747-306 | K.L.M. *Admiral Richard E. Byrd* |
| | N1738D | L.1011-385 TriStar 250 | Delta Air Lines |
| | N1739D | L.1011-385 TriStar 250 | Delta Air Lines |
| | N1750B | McD Douglas MD-11 | American Airlines |
| | N1751A | McD Douglas MD-11 | American Airlines |
| | N1752K | McD Douglas MD-11 | American Airlines |

| Reg. | Type | Owner or Operator | Notes |
|------|------|-------------------|-------|
| N1753 | McD Douglas MD-11 | American Airlines | |
| N1754 | McD Douglas MD-11 | American Airlines | |
| N1755 | McD Douglas MD-11 | American Airlines | |
| N1756 | McD Douglas MD-11 | American Airlines | |
| N1757A | McD Douglas MD-11 | American Airlines | |
| N1758B | McD Douglas MD-11 | American Airlines | |
| N1759 | McD Douglas MD-11 | American Airlines | |
| N1760A | McD Douglas MD-11 | American Airlines | |
| N1761R | McD Douglas MD-11 | American Airlines | |
| N1762B | McD Douglas MD-11 | American Airlines | |
| N1763 | McD Douglas MD-11 | American Airlines | |
| N1764B | McD Douglas MD-11 | American Airlines | |
| N1765B | McD Douglas MD-11 | American Airlines | |
| N1766A | McD Douglas MD-11 | American Airlines | |
| N1767A | McD Douglas MD-11 | American Airlines | |
| N1768D | McD Douglas MD-11 | American Airlines | |
| N1805 | Douglas DC-8-62 | Rich International Airways | |
| N2674U | Douglas DC-8-73AF | Emery Worldwide | |
| N3016Z | Douglas DC-10-30 | Zambia Airways *Nkwazi* | |
| N3024W | Douglas DC-10-30 | Nigeria Airways | |
| N3140D | L.1011-385 TriStar 500 (598) | B.W.I.A. | |
| N4508H | Boeing 747SP-09 | China Airlines | |
| N4522V | Boeing 747SP-09 | China Airlines | |
| N4714U | Boeing 747-122 | United Airlines | |
| N4716U | Boeing 747-122 | United Airlines | |
| N4717U | Boeing 747-122 | United Airlines | |
| N4718U | Boeing 747-122 | United Airlines *Thomas F. Gleed* | |
| N4719U | Boeing 747-122 | United Airlines | |
| N4720U | Boeing 747-122 | United Airlines | |
| N4723U | Boeing 747-122 | United Airlines *William A. Patterson* | |
| N4724U | Boeing 747-122 | United Airlines | |
| N4727U | Boeing 747-122 | United Airlines *Robert E. Johnson* | |
| N4728U | Boeing 747-122 | United Airlines | |
| N4729U | Boeing 747-122 | United Airlines | |
| N4732U | Boeing 747-122 | United Airlines | |
| N4735U | Boeing 747-122 | United Airlines | |
| N4935C | Douglas DC-8-63 | Rich International Airways | |
| N5535 | L.188 Electra | Channel Express (Air Services) Ltd/ Bournemouth | |
| N7031A | Boeing 737-205 | Braathens SAFE *Sigurd Jorsalfar* | |
| N7031F | Boeing 737-205 | Braathens SAFE *Magnus Lagaboter* | |
| N7035T | L.1011-385 TriStar 100 | Trans World Airlines *(stored)* | |
| N7036T | L.1011-385 TriStar 100 | Trans World Airlines | |
| N7375A | Boeing 767-323ER | American Airlines | |
| N7622U | Boeing 727-222 | United Airlines | |
| N7623U | Boeing 727-222 | United Airlines | |
| N7638U | Boeing 727-222 | United Airlines | |
| N7642U | Boeing 727-222 | United Airlines | |
| N7643U | Boeing 727-222 | United Airlines | |
| N7644U | Boeing 727-222 | United Airlines | |
| N7645U | Boeing 727-222 | United Airlines | |
| N7646U | Boeing 727-222 | United Airlines | |
| N7647U | Boeing 727-222 | United Airlines | |
| N7464U | Boeing 727-222 | United Airlines | |
| N7466U | Boeing 727-222 | United Airlines | |
| N8034T | L.1011-385 TriStar 100 | Trans World Airlines *(stored)* | |
| N8089U | Douglas DC-8-71AF | Southern Air Transport | |
| N8097U | Douglas DC-8-71AF | Southern Air Transport | |
| N8228P | Douglas DC-10-30 | Aeromexico *Castillo de Chapultepec* | |
| N8872Z | Boeing 727-225 | Delta Air Lines | |
| N8875Z | Boeing 727-225 | Delta Air Lines | |
| N8879Z | Boeing 727-225 | Delta Air Lines | |
| N8887Z | Boeing 727-225 | Delta Air Lines | |
| N8889Z | Boeing 727-225 | Delta Air Lines | |
| N8890Z | Boeing 727-225 | Delta Air Lines | |
| N8891Z | Boeing 727-225 | Delta Air Lines | |
| N8892Z | Boeing 727-225 | Delta Air Lines | |
| N8968U | Douglas DC-8-62AF | Arrow Air | |
| N8974U | Douglas DC-8-62 | Rich International Airways | |
| N10024 | Boeing 747-238B | Continental Airlines | |
| N12061 | Douglas DC-10-30 | Continental Airlines *Richard M. Adams* | |
| N12064 | Douglas DC-10-30 | Continental Airlines | |
| N13066 | Douglas DC-10-30 | Continental Airlines | |

| Notes | Reg. | Type | Owner or Operator |
|---|---|---|---|
| | N13067 | Douglas DC-10-30 | Continental Airlines |
| | N14062 | Douglas DC-10-30 | Continental Airlines |
| | N14063 | Douglas DC-10-30 | Continental Airlines |
| | N15069 | Douglas DC-10-30 | Continental Airlines |
| | N17010 | Boeing 747-143 | Continental Airlines |
| | N17011 | Boeing 747-143 | Continental Airlines |
| | N17025 | Boeing 747-238B | Continental Airlines |
| | N19072 | Douglas DC-10-30 | Continental Airlines |
| | N31018 | L.1011-385 TriStar 50 | Trans World Airlines |
| | N31019 | L.1011-385 TriStar 50 | Trans World Airlines |
| | N31021 | L.1011-385 TriStar 50 | Trans World Airlines |
| | N31022 | L.1011-385 TriStar 50 | American Trans Air |
| | N31023 | L.1011-385 TriStar 50 | Trans World Airlines |
| | N31024 | L.1011-385 TriStar 50 | Trans World Airlines *(stored)* |
| | N31029 | L.1011-385 TriStar 100 | Trans World Airlines |
| | N31030 | L.1011-385 TriStar 100 | Trans World Airlines *(stored)* |
| | N31031 | L.1011-385 TriStar 100 | Trans World Airlines |
| | N31032 | L.1011-385 TriStar 100 | Trans World Airlines *(stored)* |
| | N31033 | L.1011-385 TriStar 100 | Trans World Airlines *(stored)* |
| | N33021 | Boeing 747-243B | Continental Airlines |
| | N39356 | Boeing 767-323ER | American Airlines |
| | N39364 | Boeing 767-323ER | American Airlines |
| | N39365 | Boeing 767-323ER | American Airlines |
| | N39367 | Boeing 767-323ER | American Airlines |
| | N41020 | L.1011-385 TriStar 50 | Trans World Airlines *(stored)* |
| | N41068 | Douglas DC-10-30 | Continental Airlines |
| | N50022 | Boeing 747-238B | Continental Airlines |
| | N53110 | Boeing 747-131 | Trans World Airlines |
| | N53116 | Boeing 747-131 | Trans World Airlines |
| | N54325 | Boeing 727-231 | Trans World Airlines |
| | N54649 | Douglas DC-10-30 | Union de Transports Aériens (UTA) |
| | N68060 | Douglas DC-10-30 | Continental Airlines *Robert F. Six* |
| | N68065 | Douglas DC-10-30 | Continental Airlines *Robert P. Gallaway* |
| | N78019 | Boeing 747-238B | Continental Airlines |
| | N78020 | Boeing 747-243B | Continental Airlines |
| | N81025 | L.1011-385 TriStar 100 | Trans World Airlines *(stored)* |
| | N81026 | L.1011-385 TriStar 100 | Trans World Airlines *(stored)* |
| | N81027 | L.1011-385 TriStar 50 | Trans World Airlines *(stored)* |
| | N81028 | L.1011-385 TriStar 100 | Trans World Airlines *(stored)* |
| | N93104 | Boeing 747-131 | Trans World Airlines |
| | N93105 | Boeing 747-131 | Trans World Airlines |
| | N93107 | Boeing 747-131 | Trans World Airlines |
| | N93108 | Boeing 747-131 | Trans World Airlines |
| | N93109 | Boeing 747-131 | Trans World Airlines |
| | N93117 | Boeing 747-131 | Trans World Airlines *(stored)* |
| | N93119 | Boeing 747-131 | Trans World Airlines |

## OD (Lebanon)

| | | |
|---|---|---|
| OD-AFD | Boeing 707-3B4C | Middle East Airlines |
| OD-AFE | Boeing 707-3B4C | Middle East Airlines |
| OD-AFM | Boeing 720-023B | Middle East Airlines |
| OD-AFZ | Boeing 720-023B | Middle East Airlines |
| OD-AGB | Boeing 720-023B | Middle East Airlines |
| OD-AGD | Boeing 707-323C | Trans Mediterranean Airways |
| OD-AGF | Boeing 720-047B | Middle East Airlines |
| OD-AGO | Boeing 707-321C | Trans Mediterranean Airways |
| OD-AGP | Boeing 707-321C | Trans Mediterranean Airways |
| OD-AGS | Boeing 707-331C | Trans Mediterranean Airways |
| OD-AGU | Boeing 707-347C | Middle East Airlines |
| OD-AGV | Boeing 707-347C | Middle East Airlines |
| OD-AGX | Boeing 707-327C | Trans Mediterranean Airways |
| OD-AGY | Boeing 707-327C | Trans Mediterranean Airways |
| OD-AHC | Boeing 707-323C | Middle East Airlines |
| OD-AHD | Boeing 707-323C | Middle East Airlines |
| OD-AHE | Boeing 707-323C | Middle East Airlines |
| OD-AHF | Boeing 707-323B | Middle East Airlines |

**Note:** MEA also uses the 747s N202AE, N203AE and N204AE when not on lease and two Airbus A.310s leased from KLM as PH-AGE and PH-AGF.

| Reg. | Type | Owner or Operator | Notes |
|------|------|-------------------|-------|

## OE (Austria)

| | | | |
|------|------|-------------------|-------|
| OE-ILF | Boeing 737-3Z9 | Lauda Air *Bob Marley* | |
| OE-ILG | Boeing 737-3Z9 | Lauda Air *John Lennon* | |
| OE-LAA | Airbus A.310-324 | Austrian Airlines *New York* | |
| OE-LAB | Airbus A.310-324 | Austrian Airlines *Tokyo* | |
| OE-LAC | Airbus A.310-324 | Austrian Airlines *Paris* | |
| OE-LAD | Airbus A.310-324 | Austrian Airlines *Chicago* | |
| OE-LAU | Boeing 767-3Z9ER | Lauda Air *Johann Strauss* | |
| OE-LAW | Boeing 767-3Z9ER | Lauda Air | |
| OE-LAX | Boeing 767-3Z9ER | Lauda Air | |
| OE-LDP | McD Douglas MD-81 | Austrian Airlines *Niederösterreich* | |
| OE-LDR | McD Douglas MD-81 | Austrian Airlines *Wien* | |
| OE-LDS | McD Douglas MD-81 | Austrian Airlines *Burgenland* | |
| OE-LDT | McD Douglas MD-81 | Austrian Airlines *Kärnten* | |
| OE-LDU | McD Douglas MD-81 | Austrian Airlines *Steiermark* | |
| OE-LDV | McD Douglas MD-81 | Austrian Airlines *Oberösterreich* | |
| OE-LDW | McD Douglas MD-81 | Austrian Airlines *Salzburg* | |
| OE-LDX | McD Douglas MD-82 | Austrian Airlines *Tirol* | |
| OE-LDY | McD Douglas MD-82 | Austrian Airlines *Vorarlberg* | |
| OE-LDZ | McD Douglas MD-82 | Austrian Airlines *Graz* | |
| OE-LLH | D.H.C.8-103 Dash Eight | Tyrolean Airways *Stadt Kitzbühel* | |
| OE-LLI | D.H.C.8-102 Dash Eight | Tyrolean Airways | |
| OE-LLK | D.H.C.8-103 Dash Eight | Tyrolean Airways *Stadt Salzburg* | |
| OE-LLL | D.H.C.8-103 Dash Eight | Tyrolean Airways *Stadt Graz* | |
| OE-LLM | D.H.C.8-103 Dash Eight | Tyrolean Airways *Stadt Klagenfurt* | |
| OE-LLN | D.H.C.8-103 Dash Eight | Tyrolean Airways *Stadt Linz* | |
| OE-LLP | D.H.C.8-103 Dash Eight | Tyrolean Airways | |
| OE-LLS | D.H.C.7-102 Dash Seven | Tyrolean Airways *Stadt Innsbruck* | |
| OE-LLU | D.H.C.7-102 Dash Seven | Tyrolean Airways *Stadt Wien* | |
| OE-LLV | D.H.C.8-314 Dash Eight | Tyrolean Airways *Land Tirol* | |
| OE-LLW | D.H.C.8-314 Dash Eight | Tyrolean Airways | |
| OE-LLX | D.H.C.8-314 Dash Eight | Tyrolean Airways | |
| OE-LMA | McD Douglas MD-82 | Austrian Airlines *Linz* | |
| OE-LMB | McD Douglas MD-82 | Austrian Airlines *Eisenstadt* | |
| OE-LMC | McD Douglas MD-82 | Austrian Airlines *Baden* | |
| OE-LMD | McD Douglas MD-83 | Austrian Airlines *Villach* | |
| OE-LME | McD Douglas MD-83 | Austrian Airlines | |
| OE-LMK | McD Douglas MD-87 | Austrian Airlines *St Pölten* | |
| OE-LML | McD Douglas MD-87 | Austrian Airlines *Salzburg* | |
| OE-LMM | McD Douglas MD-87 | Austrian Airlines *Innsbruck* | |
| OE-LMN | McD Douglas MD-87 | Austrian Airlines *Klagenfurt* | |
| OE-LMO | McD Douglas MD-87 | Austrian Airlines *Bregenz* | |
| OE-LNH | Boeing 737-4Z9 | Lauda Air *Elvis Presley* | |
| OE-LNI | Boeing 737-4Z9 | Lauda Air | |

## OH (Finland)

| | | | |
|------|------|-------------------|-------|
| OH-LAA | Airbus A.300B4-203 | Finnair | |
| OH-LAB | Airbus A.300B4-203 | Finnair | |
| OH-LGA | McD Douglas MD-11 | Finnair | |
| OH-LGB | McD Douglas MD-11 | Finnair | |
| OH-LGC | McD Douglas MD-11 | Finnair | |
| OH-LGD | McD Douglas MD-11 | Finnair | |
| OH-LHA | Douglas DC-10-30ER | Finnair *Iso Antti* | |
| OH-LHB | Douglas DC-10-30ER | Finnair | |
| OH-LHD | Douglas DC-10-30ER | Finnair | |
| OH-LHE | Douglas DC-10-30ER | Finnair | |
| OH-LMA | McD Douglas MD-87 | Finnair | |
| OH-LMB | McD Douglas MD-87 | Finnair | |
| OH-LMC | McD Douglas MD-87 | Finnair | |
| OH-LMG | McD Douglas MD-83 | Finnair | |
| OH-LMH | McD Douglas MD-82 | Finnair | |
| OH-LMN | McD Douglas MD-82 | Finnair | |
| OH-LMO | McD Douglas MD-82 | Finnair | |
| OH-LMP | McD Douglas MD-82 | Finnair | |
| OH-LMR | McD Douglas MD-83 | Finnair | |
| OH-LMS | McD Douglas MD-83 | Finnair | |
| OH-LMT | McD Douglas MD-82 | Finnair | |
| OH-LMU | McD Douglas MD-83 | Finnair | |
| OH-LMV | McD Douglas MD-83 | Finnair | |

| Notes | Reg. | Type | Owner or Operator |
|---|---|---|---|
| | OH-LMW | McD Douglas MD-82 | Finnair |
| | OH-LMX | McD Douglas MD-82 | Finnair |
| | OH-LMY | McD Douglas MD-82 | Finnair |
| | OH-LMZ | McD Douglas MD-82 | Finnair |
| | OH-LNB | Douglas DC-9-41 | Finnair |
| | OH-LNC | Douglas DC-9-41 | Finnair |
| | OH-LND | Douglas DC-9-41 | Finnair |
| | OH-LNE | Douglas DC-9-41 | Finnair |
| | OH-LNF | Douglas DC-9-41 | Finnair |
| | OH-LYN | Douglas DC-9-51 | Finnair |
| | OH-LYO | Douglas DC-9-51 | Finnair |
| | OH-LYP | Douglas DC-9-51 | Finnair |
| | OH-LYR | Douglas DC-9-51 | Finnair |
| | OH-LYS | Douglas DC-9-51 | Finnair |
| | OH-LYT | Douglas DC-9-51 | Finnair |
| | OH-LYU | Douglas DC-9-51 | Finnair |
| | OH-LYV | Douglas DC-9-51 | Finnair |
| | OH-LYW | Douglas DC-9-51 | Finnair |
| | OH-LYX | Douglas DC-9-51 | Finnair |
| | OH-LYY | Douglas DC-9-51 | Finnair |
| | OH-LYZ | Douglas DC-9-51 | Finnair |

**Note:** Finnair also operates a DC-10-30ER which retains its US registration N345HC.

## OK (Czech Republic and Slovakia)

| | OK-BYP | Tupolev Tu-154M | Ensor Air |
|---|---|---|---|
| | OK-CFH | Tupolev Tu-134A | Ceskoslovenske Aerolinie (CSA) |
| | OK-EFK | Tupolev Tu-134A | CSA |
| | OK-FBF | Ilyushin IL-62 | CSA |
| | OK-GBH | Ilyushin IL-62 | CSA *Usti Nad Labem* |
| | OK-HFL | Tupolev Tu-134A | CSA |
| | OK-HFM | Tupolev Tu-134A | CSA |
| | OK-IFN | Tupolev Tu-134A | CSA |
| | OK-JBI | Ilyushin IL-62M | CSA *Plzen* |
| | OK-JBJ | Ilyushin IL-62M | CSA *Hradec Kralové* |
| | OK-JGY | Boeing 727-230 | Air Terrex |
| | OK-KBK | Ilyushin IL-62M | CSA *Ceske Budejovice* |
| | OK-KBN | Ilyushin IL-62M | CSA |
| | OK-LCP | Tupolev Tu-154B-2 | Ensor Air |
| | OK-OBL | Ilyushin IL-62M | CSA *Ostrava* |
| | OK-PBM | Ilyushin IL-62M | CSA |
| | OK-TCD | Tupolev Tu-154M | CSA *Trencianské Teplic* |
| | OF-TGX | Boeing 727-51 | Air Terrex |
| | OK-UCE | Tupolev Tu-154M | CSA *Marianské Laze* |
| | OK-UCF | Tupolev Tu-154M | CSA *Smokovec* |
| | OK-VCG | Tupolev Tu-154M | CSA *Luhacovice* |
| | OK-WAA | Airbus A.310-304 | CSA *Praha* |
| | OK-WAB | Airbus A.310-304 | CSA *Bratislava* |
| | OK-XFJ | Boeing 707-331B | Central European Airlines |
| | OK-XGA | Boeing 737-55S | CSA *Plzen* |
| | OK-XGB | Boeing 737-55S | CSA *Olomouc* |
| | OK-XGC | Boeing 737-55S | CSA *Ceske Budejovice* |
| | OK-XGD | Boeing 737-55S | CSA |
| | OK-XGE | Boeing 737-55S | CSA |

## OO (Belgium)

| | OO-DHB | Convair Cv.580 | European Air Transport (DHL) |
|---|---|---|---|
| | OO-DHC | Convair Cv.580 | European Air Transport (DHL) |
| | OO-DHD | Convair Cv.580 | European Air Transport (DHL) |
| | OO-DHE | Convair Cv.580 | European Air Transport (DHL) |
| | OO-DHF | Convair Cv.580 | European Air Transport (DHL) |
| | OO-DHG | Convair Cv.580 | European Air Transport (DHL) |
| | OO-DHH | Convair Cv.580 | European Air Transport (DHL) |
| | OO-DHI | Convair Cv.580 | European Air Transport (DHL) |
| | OO-DHJ | Convair Cv.580 | European Air Transport (DHL) |
| | OO-DHL | Convair Cv.580 | European Air Transport (DHL) |
| | OO-DHM | Boeing 727-31C | European Air Transport (DHL) |
| | OO-DHN | Boeing 727-31C | European Air Transport (DHL) |
| | OO-DHO | Boeing 727-31C | European Air Transport (DHL) |
| | OO-DHP | Boeing 727-35F | European Air Transport (DHL) |

| Reg. | Type | Owner or Operator | Notes |
|---|---|---|---|
| OO-DHQ | Boeing 727-35F | European Air Transport (DHL) | |
| OO-DJA | F.28 Fellowship 3000 | Delta Air Transport | |
| OO-DJB | F.28 Fellowship 4000 | Delta Air Transport | |
| OO-DJE | BAe 146-200 | Delta Air Transport | |
| OO-DJF | BAe 146-200 | Delta Air Transport | |
| OO-DJG | BAe 146-200 | Delta Air Transport | |
| OO-DJH | BAe 146-200 | Delta Air Transport | |
| OO-DJJ | BAe 146-200 | Delta Air Transport | |
| OO-DTF | EMB-120RT Brasilia | Delta Air Transport | |
| OO-DTG | EMB-120RT Brasilia | Delta Air Transport | |
| OO-DTH | EMB-120RT Brasilia | Delta Air Transport | |
| OO-DTI | EMB-120RT Brasilia | Delta Air Transport | |
| OO-DTJ | EMB-120RT Brasilia | Delta Air Transport | |
| OO-DTK | EMB-120RT Brasilia | Delta Air Transport | |
| OO-DTL | EMB-120RT Brasilia | Delta Air Transport | |
| OO-DTN | EMB-120RT Brasilia | Delta Air Transport | |
| OO-DTO | EMB-120RT Brasilia | Delta Air Transport | |
| OO-D | EMB-120RT Brasilia | Delta Air Transport | |
| OO-FEL | F.27 Friendship Mk 500 | Sky Freighters | |
| OO-HUB | Convair Cv.580 | European Air Transport (DHL) | |
| OO-ILI | Boeing 757-23A | Air Belgium | |
| OO-ILJ | Boeing 737-46B | Air Belgium | |
| OO-ING | Airbus A.300B4-103 | European Airlines | |
| OO-JPA | Swearingen SA226AT Merlin IVA | European Air Transport | |
| OO-JPI | Swearingen SA226TC Metro II | European Air Transport | |
| OO-JPN | Swearingen SA226AT Merlin IVA | European Air Transport | |
| OO-LTJ | Boeing 737-3M8 | EuroBelgian Airlines | |
| OO-LTL | Boeing 737-3M8 | EuroBelgian Airlines | |
| OO-LTM | Boeing 737-3M8 | EuroBelgian Airlines | |
| OO-MJE | Boeing 146-200 | DAT Air Meuse | |
| OO-MTD | EMB-120RT Brasilia | DAT Air Meuse | |
| OO-SBJ | Boeing 737-46B | Sobelair *Juliette* | |
| OO-SBM | Boeing 737-429 | Sobelair | |
| OO-SBQ | Boeing 737-229 | Sobelair | |
| OO-SBT | Boeing 737-229 | Sobelair | |
| OO-SBZ | Boeing 737-329 | Sobelair | |
| OO-SCA | Airbus A.310-222 | SABENA | |
| OO-SCB | Airbus A.310-222 | SABENA | |
| OO-SCC | Airbus A.310-322 | SABENA | |
| OO-SCD | Airbus A.340-211 | SABENA/Air France | |
| OO-SCF | Airbus A.340-211 | SABENA/Air France | |
| OO-SCG | Airbus A.340-211 | SABENA/Air France | |
| OO-SCH | Airbus A.340-211 | SABENA/Air France | |
| OO-SDA | Boeing 737-229 | Sobelair | |
| OO-SDD | Boeing 737-229 | Sobelair | |
| OO-SDE | Boeing 737-229 | Sobelair | |
| OO-SDF | Boeing 737-229 | SABENA | |
| OO-SDG | Boeing 737-229 | SABENA | |
| OO-SDJ | Boeing 737-229C | SABENA | |
| OO-SDK | Boeing 737-229C | SABENA | |
| OO-SDL | Boeing 737-229 | SABENA | |
| OO-SDM | Boeing 737-229 | SABENA | |
| OO-SDN | Boeing 737-229 | SABENA | |
| OO-SDO | Boeing 737-229 | SABENA | |
| OO-SDP | Boeing 737-229C | SABENA | |
| OO-SDR | Boeing 737-229C | SABENA | |
| OO-SDV | Boeing 737-329 | SABENA | |
| OO-SDW | Boeing 737-329 | SABENA | |
| OO-SDX | Boeing 737-329 | SABENA | |
| OO-SDY | Boeing 737-329 | SABENA | |
| OO-SGA | Boeing 747-129A (SCD) | SABENA | |
| OO-SGC | Boeing 747-329 (SCD) | SABENA | |
| OO-SGD | Boeing 747-329 (SCD) | SABENA | |
| OO-SLA | Douglas DC-10-30CF | SABENA | |
| OO-SLB | Douglas DC-10-30CF | SABENA | |
| OO-SYA | Boeing 737-329 | SABENA | |
| OO-SYB | Boeing 737-329 | SABENA | |
| OO-SYC | Boeing 737-429 | SABENA | |
| OO-SYD | Boeing 737-429 | SABENA | |
| OO-SYE | Boeing 737-529 | SABENA | |
| OO-SYF | Boeing 737-429 | SABENA | |
| OO-SYG | Boeing 737-529 | SABENA | |

| Notes | Reg. | Type | Owner or Operator |
|---|---|---|---|
| | OO-SYH | Boeing 737-529 | SABENA |
| | OO-SYI | Boeing 737-529 | SABENA |
| | OO-SYJ | Boeing 737-529 | SABENA |
| | OO-SYK | Boeing 737-529 | SABENA |
| | OO-TBI | Boeing 757-236 | Benelux Falcon Service |
| | OO-TEF | Airbus A.300B1 | *stored*/Brussels |

# OY (Denmark)

| Reg. | Type | Owner or Operator |
|---|---|---|
| OY-AZW | Swearingen SA226TC Metro II | Newair of Denmark |
| OY-BDD | Nord 262A-21 | Cimber Air |
| OY-BHT | EMB-110P2 Bandeirante | Muk Air |
| OY-BNM | EMB-110P2 Bandeirante | Muk Air |
| OY-BPB | Douglas DC-3C | Flyvende MuseumsFly |
| OY-BPL | Swearingen SA227AC Metro III | Metro Airways |
| OY-BVF | F.27 Friendship Mk 600 | Aviation Assistance |
| OY-BVH | F.27 Friendship Mk 200 | Aviation Assistance |
| OY-BYN | Swearingen SA226TC Metro II | Muk Air |
| OY-CCN | F.27 Friendship Mk 600 | Alkair |
| OY-CIB | Aérospatiale ATR-42-300 | Cimber Air/Lufthansa CityLine |
| OY-CIC | Aérospatiale ATR-42-300 | Cimber Air/Lufthansa CityLine |
| OY-CID | Aérospatiale ATR-42-300 | Cimber Air/Lufthansa CityLine |
| OY-CIE | Aérospatiale ATR-42-300 | Cimber Air/Lufthansa CityLine |
| OY-CIF | Aérospatiale ATR-42-300 | Cimber Air/Lufthansa CityLine |
| OY-CIG | Aérospatiale ATR-42-300 | Cimber Air/Lufthansa CityLine |
| OY-CIH | Aérospatiale ATR-42-300 | Cimber Air |
| OY-CIJ | Aérospatiale ATR-42-300 | Cimber Air/Lufthansa CityLine |
| OY-CLB | BAe Jetstream 3102 | Newair of Denmark |
| OY-CNA | Airbus A.300B4 | Conair/ZAS Airline of Egypt |
| OY-CND | Airbus A.320-231 | Conair *Merkur* |
| OY-CNE | Airbus A.320-231 | Conair *Jupiter* |
| OY-CNF | Airbus A.320-231 | Conair *Venus* |
| OY-CNG | Airbus A.320-231 | Conair *Mars* |
| OY-CNH | Airbus A.320-231 | Conair *Sirius* |
| OY-CNI | Airbus A.320-231 | Conair *Spica* |
| OY-CNK | Airbus A.300B4 | Conair/ZAS Airline of Egypt |
| OY-CNL | Airbus A.300B4 | Conair |
| OY-CPG | EMB-110P1 Bandeirante | Sun-Air |
| OY-CRR | H.P. 137 Jetstream 1 | Newair of Denmark |
| OY-CRT | H.P. 137 Jetstream 1 | Newair of Denmark |
| OY-EEC | BAe Jetstream 3101 | Sun-Air |
| OY-KAE | Fokker 50 | S.A.S. Commuter *Hans* |
| OY-KAF | Fokker 50 | S.A.S. Commuter *Sigvat* |
| OY-KAG | Fokker 50 | S.A.S. Commuter *Odensis* |
| OY-KAH | Fokker 50 | S.A.S. Commuter *Bjorn* |
| OY-KAI | Fokker 50 | S.A.S. Commuter *Skjold* |
| OY-KAK | Fokker 50 | S.A.S. Commuter *Turid* |
| OY-KDL | Boeing 767-383ER | S.A.S. *Tjodhild Viking* |
| OY-KDM | Boeing 767-383ER | S.A.S. *Inva Viking* |
| OY-KDN | Boeing 767-383ER | S.A.S. *Ulf Viking* |
| OY-KDO | Boeing 767-383ER | S.A.S. *Svea Viking* |
| OY-KGD | Douglas DC-9-21 | S.A.S. *Ubbe Viking* |
| OY-KGE | Douglas DC-9-21 | S.A.S. *Orvar Viking* |
| OY-KGF | Douglas DC-9-21 | S.A.S. *Rolf Viking* |
| OY-KGL | Douglas DC-9-41 | S.A.S. *Angantyr Viking* |
| OY-KGM | Douglas DC-9-41 | S.A.S. *Arnfinn Viking* |
| OY-KGN | Douglas DC-9-41 | S.A.S. *Gram Viking* |
| OY-KGO | Douglas DC-9-41 | S.A.S. *Holte Viking* |
| OY-KGP | Douglas DC-9-41 | S.A.S. *Torbern Viking* |
| OY-KGR | Douglas DC-9-41 | S.A.S. *Holger Viking* |
| OY-KGS | Douglas DC-9-41 | S.A.S. *Hall Viking* |
| OY-KGT | McD Douglas MD-81 | S.A.S. *Hake Viking* |
| OY-KGY | McD Douglas MD-81 | S.A.S. *Rollo Viking* |
| OY-KGZ | McD Douglas MD-81 | S.A.S. *Hagbard Viking* |
| OY-KHC | McD Douglas MD-81 | S.A.S. *Faste Viking* |
| OY-KHE | McD Douglas MD-82 | S.A.S. *Saxo Viking* |
| OY-KHF | McD Douglas MD-87 | S.A.S. *Ragnar Viking* |
| OY-KHG | McD Douglas MD-81 | S.A.S. *Alle Viking* |
| OY-KHI | McD Douglas MD-87 | S.A.S. *Torkel Viking* |
| OY-KHK | McD Douglas MD-81 | S.A.S. *Roald Viking* |
| OY-KHL | McD Douglas MD-81 | S.A.S. *Knud Viking* |
| OY-KHM | McD Douglas MD-81 | S.A.S. *Mette Viking* |

| Reg. | Type | Owner or Operator | Notes |
|------|------|-------------------|-------|
| OY-KHN | McD Douglas MD-81 | S.A.S. *Dan Viking* | |
| OY-KHP | McD Douglas MD-81 | S.A.S. *Arild Viking* | |
| OY-KHR | McD Douglas MD-81 | S.A.S. *Torlild Viking* | |
| OY-KHT | McD Douglas MD-82 | S.A.S. *Gorm Viking* | |
| OY-KHU | McD Douglas MD-87 | S.A.S. *Ravn Viking* | |
| OY-KHW | McD Douglas MD-87 | S.A.S. *Ingemund Viking* | |
| OY-KIA | Douglas DC-9-21 | S.A.S. *Guttorm Viking* | |
| OY-KIB | Douglas DC-9-21 | S.A.S. *Gunder Viking* | |
| OY-KID | Douglas DC-9-21 | S.A.S. *Rane Viking* | |
| OY-KIE | Douglas DC-9-21 | S.A.S. *Skate Viking* | |
| OY-KIF | Douglas DC-9-21 | S.A.S. *Svipdag Viking* | |
| OY-MAC | Boeing 737-5L9 | Maersk Air | |
| OY-MAD | Boeing 737-5L9 | Maersk Air | |
| OY-MAE | Boeing 737-5L9 | Maersk Air | |
| OY-MMG | Fokker 50 | Maersk Air | |
| OY-MMH | Fokker 50 | Maersk Air | |
| OY-MMI | Fokker 50 | Maersk Air | |
| OY-MMJ | Fokker 50 | Maersk Air | |
| OY-MMO | Boeing 737-3L9 | Maersk Air | |
| OY-MMS | Fokker 50 | Maersk Air | |
| OY-MMT | Fokker 50 | Maersk Air | |
| OY-MMU | Fokker 50 | Maersk Air | |
| OY-MMV | Fokker 50 | Maersk Air | |
| OY-MMY | Boeing 737-3L9 | Maersk Air | |
| OY-MMZ | Boeing 737-3L9 | Maersk Air | |
| OY-MUA | EMB-110P1 Bandeirante | Muk Air | |
| OY-MUB | Short SD3-30 | Muk Air | |
| OY-MUF | F.27 Friendship | Newair of Denmark | |
| OY-SAT | Boeing 727-2J4 | Sterling Airways | |
| OY-SBE | Boeing 727-2J4 | Sterling Airways | |
| OY-SBF | Boeing 727-2J4 | Sterling Airways | |
| OY-SBG | Boeing 727-2J4 | Sterling Airways | |
| OY-SBH | Boeing 727-2B7 | Sterling Airways | |
| OY-SBI | Boeing 727-270 | Sterling Airways | |
| OY-SBN | Boeing 727-2B7 | Sterling Airways | |
| OY-SBO | Boeing 727-2K3 | Sterling Airways | |
| OY-SHA | Boeing 757-2J4 | Sterling Airways | |
| OY-SHB | Boeing 757-2J4 | Sterling Airways | |
| OY-SRA | F.27 Friendship Mk 600 | Starair | |
| OY-SRB | F.27 Friendship Mk 600 | Alkair | |
| OY-SRC | F.27 Friendship Mk 600 | Starair | |
| OY-SRR | F.27 Friendship Mk 600 | Starair | |
| OY-SRZ | F.27 Friendship Mk 600 | Starair | |
| OY-STH | S.E.210 Caravelle 10B | Sterling Airways | |
| OY-STI | S.E.210 Caravelle 10B | Sterling Airways | |
| OY-SVF | BAe Jetstream 3102 | Sun Air | |
| OY-SVJ | BAe Jetstream 3101 | Sun Air | |
| OY-SVS | BAe Jetstream 4100 | Sun Air | |
| OY-TOV | Nord 262A-30 | Cimber Air | |

# PH (Netherlands)

| Reg. | Type | Owner or Operator | Notes |
|------|------|-------------------|-------|
| PH-AGA | Airbus A.310-203 | K.L.M. *Rembrandt* | |
| PH-AGB | Airbus A.310-203 | K.L.M. *Jeroen Bosch* | |
| PH-AGC | Airbus A.310-203 | K.L.M. *Albert Cuyp* | |
| PH-AGD | Airbus A.310-203 | K.L.M. *Marinus Ruppert* | |
| PH-AGE | Airbus A.310-203 | Middle East Airlines | |
| PH-AGF | Airbus A.310-203 | Middle East Airlines | |
| PH-AGG | Airbus A.310-203 | K.L.M. *Vincent van Gogh* | |
| PH-AGH | Airbus A.310-203 | K.L.M. *Pieter de Hoogh* | |
| PH-AGI | Airbus A.310-203 | K.L.M. *Jan Toorop* | |
| PH-AGK | Airbus A.310-203 | K.L.M. *Johannes Vermeer* | |
| PH-AHE | Boeing 757-27BER | Air Holland Charter | |
| PH-AHI | Boeing 757-27BER | Air Holland Charter | |
| PH-BDA | Boeing 737-306 | K.L.M. *Willem Barentsz* | |
| PH-BDB | Boeing 737-306 | K.L.M. *Olivier van Noort* | |
| PH-BDC | Boeing 737-306 | K.L.M. *Cornelis De Houteman* | |
| PH-BDD | Boeing 737-306 | K.L.M. *Anthony van Diemen* | |
| PH-BDE | Boeing 737-306 | K.L.M. *Abel J. Tasman* | |
| PH-BDG | Boeing 737-306 | K.L.M. *Michiel A. de Ruyter* | |
| PH-BDH | Boeing 737-306 | K.L.M. *Petrus Plancius* | |
| PH-BDI | Boeing 737-306 | K.L.M. *Maarten H. Tromp* | |

| Notes | Reg. | Type | Owner or Operator |
|---|---|---|---|
| | PH-BDK | Boeing 737-306 | K.L.M. *Jan H. van Linschoten* |
| | PH-BDL | Boeing 737-306 | K.L.M. *Piet Heyn* |
| | PH-BDN | Boeing 737-306 | K.L.M. *Willem van Ruysbroeck* |
| | PH-BDO | Boeing 737-306 | K.L.M. *Jacob van Heemskerck* |
| | PH-BDP | Boeing 737-306 | K.L.M. *Jacob Rogeveen* |
| | PH-BDR | Boeing 737-406 | K.L.M. *Willem C. Schouten* |
| | PH-BDS | Boeing 737-406 | K.L.M. *Jorris van Spilbergen* |
| | PH-BDT | Boeing 737-406 | K.L.M. *Gerrit de Veer* |
| | PH-BDU | Boeing 737-406 | K.L.M. *Marco Polo* |
| | PH-BDW | Boeing 737-406 | K.L.M. *Leifur Eiriksson* |
| | PH-BDY | Boeing 737-406 | K.L.M. *Vasco da Gama* |
| | PH-BDZ | Boeing 737-406 | K.L.M. *Christophorus Columbus* |
| | PH-BFA | Boeing 747-406 | K.L.M. *City of Atlanta* |
| | PH-BFB | Boeing 747-406 | K.L.M. *City of Bangkok* |
| | PH-BFC | Boeing 747-406 (SCD) | K.L.M. *City of Calgary* |
| | PH-BFD | Boeing 747-406 (SCD) | K.L.M. *City of Dubai* |
| | PH-BFE | Boeing 747-406 (SCD) | K.L.M. *City of Melbourne* |
| | PH-BFF | Boeing 747-406 (SCD) | K.L.M. *City of Freetown* |
| | PH-BFG | Boeing 747-406 | K.L.M. *City of Guayaquil* |
| | PH-BFH | Boeing 747-406 (SCD) | K.L.M. *City of Hong Kong* |
| | PH-BFI | Boeing 747-406 (SCD) | K.L.M. *City of Jakarta* |
| | PH-BFK | Boeing 747-406 (SCD) | K.L.M. *City of Karachi* |
| | PH-BFL | Boeing 747-406 | K.L.M. *City of Lima* |
| | PH-BFM | Boeing 747-406 (SCD) | K.L.M. *City of Mexico* |
| | PH-BFN | Boeing 747-406 | K.L.M. *City of Nairobi* |
| | PH-BFO | Boeing 747-406 (SCD) | K.L.M. *City of Orlando* |
| | PH-BFP | Boeing 747-406 (SCD) | K.L.M. |
| | PH-BFR | Boeing 747-406 (SCD) | K.L.M. *City of Rio de Janeiro* |
| | PH-BTA | Boeing 737-406 | K.L.M. *Fernao Magalhaes* |
| | PH-BTB | Boeing 737-406 | K.L.M. *Henry Hudson* |
| | PH-BTC | Boeing 737-406 | K.L.M. *David Livingstone* |
| | PH-BTD | Boeing 737-306 | K.L.M. *James Cook* |
| | PH-BTE | Boeing 737-306 | K.L.M. *Roald Amundsen* |
| | PH-BTF | Boeing 737-406 | K.L.M. *Alexander von Humboldt* |
| | PH-BUH | Boeing 747-306 (SCD) | K.L.M. *Dr Albert Plesman* |
| | PH-BUI | Boeing 747-306 (SCD) | K.L.M. *Wilbur Wright* |
| | PH-BUK | Boeing 747-306 (SCD) | K.L.M. *Louis Blériot* |
| | PH-BUL | Boeing 747-306 (SCD) | K.L.M. *Charles A. Lindbergh* |
| | PH-BUM | Boeing 747-306 (SCD) | K.L.M. *Charles E. Kingsford-Smith* |
| | PH-BUN | Boeing 747-306 (SCD) | K.L.M. *Anthony H. G. Fokker* |
| | PH-BUO | Boeing 747-306 | K.L.M. *Missouri* |
| | PH-BUP | Boeing 747-306 | K.L.M. *The Ganges* |
| | PH-BUR | Boeing 747-306 | K.L.M. *The Indus* |
| | PH-BUU | Boeing 747-306 (SCD) | K.L.M. *Sir Frank Whittle* |
| | PH-BUV | Boeing 747-306 (SCD) | K.L.M. *Sir Geoffrey de Havilland* |
| | PH-BUW | Boeing 747-306 (SCD) | K.L.M. *Leonardo da Vinci* |
| | PH-CHB | F.28 Fellowship 4000 | K.L.M. CityHopper *Birmingham* |
| | PH-CHD | F.28 Fellowship 4000 | K.L.M. CityHopper *Maastricht* |
| | PH-CHF | F.28 Fellowship 4000 | K.L.M. CityHopper *Guernsey* |
| | PH-CHN | F.28 Fellowship 4000 | K.L.M. CityHopper *Belfast* |
| | PH-DDA | Douglas DC-3 | Dutch Dakota Association |
| | PH-DTA | Douglas DC-10-30 | K.L.M. *Johann Sebastian Bach* |
| | PH-DTB | Douglas DC-10-30 | K.L.M. *Ludwig van Beethoven* |
| | PH-DTC | Douglas DC-10-30 | K.L.M. *Frédéric François Chopin* |
| | PH-DTD | Douglas DC-10-30 | K.L.M. *Maurice Ravel* |
| | PH-DTL | Douglas DC-10-30 | K.L.M. *Edvard Hagerup Grieg* |
| | PH-FEY | F.27 Friendship Mk 200 | Celtic Airways |
| | PH-FFF | F.27 Friendship Mk 200 | Celtic Airways |
| | PH-FGE | F.27 Friendship Mk 200 | Celtic Airways |
| | PH-FWS | EMB-110P1 Bandeirante | Freeway Air |
| | PH-FWT | EMB-110P1 Bandeirante | Freeway Air |
| | PH-FXA | Dornier Do.228-202K | Flexair |
| | PH-HVF | Boeing 737-3K2 | Transavia *Johan Cruijff* |
| | PH-HVG | Boeing 737-3K2 | Transavia *Wubbo Ockels* |
| | PH-HVJ | Boeing 737-3K2 | Transavia *Nelli Cooman* |
| | PH-HVM | Boeing 737-3K2 | Transavia |
| | PH-HVN | Boeing 737-3K2 | Transavia |
| | PH-HVT | Boeing 737-3K2 | Transavia |
| | PH-HVV | Boeing 737-3K2 | Transavia |
| | PH-HVW | Boeing 737-3K2 | Transavia |
| | PH-HVX | Boeing 737-3K2 | Transavia |
| | PH-JDV | PA-42 Cheyenne III | BASE Business Airlines |
| | PH-KCA | McD Douglas MD-11 | K.L.M. |

| Reg. | Type | Owner or Operator | Notes |
|------|------|-------------------|-------|
| PH-KCB | McD Douglas MD-11 | K.L.M. | |
| PH-KJA | BAe Jetstream 3108 | BASE Business Airlines | |
| PH-KJB | BAe Jetstream 3108 | BASE Business Airlines | |
| PH-KLC | Fokker 100 | Compagnie Air Littoral/K.L.M. | |
| PH-KLD | Fokker 100 | Compagnie Air Littoral/K.L.M. | |
| PH-KLE | Fokker 100 | Compagnie Air Littoral/K.L.M. | |
| PH-KLG | Fokker 100 | Compagnie Air Littoral/K.L.M. | |
| PH-KLH | Fokker 100 | Compagnie Air Littoral/K.L.M. | |
| PH-KLI | Fokker 100 | Compagnie Air Littoral/K.L.M. | |
| PH-KSA | SAAB SF.340B | K.L.M. CityHopper *Straatsburg* | |
| PH-KSB | SAAB SF.340B | K.L.M. CityHopper *Bristol* | |
| PH-KSC | SAAB SF.340B | K.L.M. CityHopper *Cardiff* | |
| PH-KSD | SAAB SF.340B | K.L.M. CityHopper *Neurenburg* | |
| PH-KSE | SAAB SF.340B | K.L.M. CityHopper *Southampton* | |
| PH-KSF | SAAB SF.340B | K.L.M. CityHopper *Basel* | |
| PH-KSG | SAAB SF.340B | K.L.M. CityHopper *Mulhouse* | |
| PH-KSH | SAAB SF.340B | K.L.M. CityHopper *Hamburg* | |
| PH-KSI | SAAB SF.340B | K.L.M. CityHopper *Eindhoven* | |
| PH-KSK | SAAB SF.340B | K.L.M. CityHopper *Rotterdam* | |
| PH-KSL | SAAB SF.340B | K.L.M. CityHopper *Luxembourg* | |
| PH-KSM | SAAB SF.340B | K.L.M. CityHopper *Malmoe* | |
| PH-KVA | Fokker 50 | K.L.M. CityHopper *Bremen* | |
| PH-KVB | Fokker 50 | K.L.M. CityHopper *Brussels* | |
| PH-KVC | Fokker 50 | K.L.M. CityHopper *Stavanger* | |
| PH-KVD | Fokker 50 | K.L.M. CityHopper *Dusseldorf* | |
| PH-KVE | Fokker 50 | K.L.M. CityHopper *Amsterdam* | |
| PH-KVF | Fokker 50 | K.L.M. CityHopper *Parijs* | |
| PH-KVG | Fokker 50 | K.L.M. CityHopper *Stuttgart* | |
| PH-KVH | Fokker 50 | K.L.M. CityHopper *Hannover* | |
| PH-KVI | Fokker 50 | K.L.M. CityHopper *Bordeaux* | |
| PH-KVK | Fokker 50 | K.L.M. CityHopper *London* | |
| PH-MBP | Douglas DC-10-30CF | Martinair *Hong Kong* | |
| PH-MBT | Douglas DC-10-30CF | Martinair | |
| PH-MCA | Airbus A.310-203 | Martinair *Prins Bernhard* | |
| PH-MCB | Airbus A.310-203CF | Martinair *Prins Maurits* | |
| PH-MCE | Boeing 747-21AC (SCD) | Martinair *Prins van Oranje* | |
| PH-MCF | Boeing 747-21AC (SCD) | Martinair *Prins Claus* | |
| PH-MCG | Boeing 767-31AER | Martinair *Prins Johan Friso* | |
| PH-MCH | Boeing 767-31AER | Martinair *Prins Constantijn* | |
| PH-MCI | Boeing 767-31AER | Martinair | |
| PH-MCK | Boeing 767-31AER | Martinair | |
| PH-MCL | Boeing 767-31AER | Martinair *Koningin Beatrix* | |
| PH-MCM | Boeing 767-31AER | Martinair | |
| PH-MCN | Boeing 747-228F | Martinair | |
| PH-OZA | Boeing 737-3L9 | Air Holland Charter | |
| PH-SDH | D.H.C.8-102 Dash Eight | Schreiner Airways | |
| PH-SDI | D.H.C.8-311A Dash Eight | Schreiner Airways/SABENA | |
| PH-SDJ | D.H.C.8-311A Dash Eight | Schreiner Airways/SABENA | |
| PH-SFA | F.27 Friendship Mk 400 | Schreiner Airways | |
| PH-SFE | F.27 Friendship Mk 300 | Schreiner Airways | |
| PH-SFI | F.27 Friendship Mk 500 | Schreiner Airways | |
| PH-SHC | L.100 Hercules | Schreiner Airways | |
| PH-SHD | L.100 Hercules | Schreiner Airways | |
| PH-TKA | Boeing 757-2K2ER | Transavia | |
| PH-TKB | Boeing 757-2K2ER | Transavia | |
| PH-TKC | Boeing 757-2K2ER | Transavia | |
| PH-TKZ | Boeing 757-236 | Transavia | |
| PH-TVH | Boeing 737-222 | Transavia *Neil Armstrong* | |
| PH-TVP | Boeing 737-2K2 | Transavia | |
| PH-TVR | Boeing 737-2K2 | Transavia | |
| PH-TVS | Boeing 737-2K2 | Transavia | |
| PH-TVX | Boeing 737-2K2 | Transavia/K.L.M. | |
| PH-XLA | EMB-120RT Brasilia | Exel Commuter | |
| PH-XLB | EMB-120RT Brasilia | Exel Commuter | |

**Note:** K.L.M. also operates Boeing 747-306, N1309E.

## PK (Indonesia)

| | | | |
|------|------|-------------------|-------|
| PK-GIA | Douglas DC-10-30 | Garuda Indonesian Airways | |
| PK-GIB | Douglas DC-10-30 | Garuda Indonesian Airways | |
| PK-GIC | Douglas DC-10-30 | Garuda Indonesian Airways | |
| PK-GID | Douglas DC-10-30 | Garuda Indonesian Airways | |

| Notes | Reg. | Type | Owner or Operator |
|---|---|---|---|
| | PK-GIE | Douglas DC-10-30 | Garuda Indonesian Airways |
| | PK-GIF | Douglas DC-10-30 | Garuda Indonesian Airways |
| | PK-GSA | Boeing 747-2U3B | Garuda Indonesian Airways |
| | PK-GSB | Boeing 747-2U3B | Garuda Indonesian Airways |
| | PK-GSC | Boeing 747-2U3B | Garuda Indonesian Airways |
| | PK-GSD | Boeing 747-2U3B | Garuda Indonesian Airways |
| | PK-GSE | Boeing 747-2U3B | Garuda Indonesian Airways |
| | PK-GSF | Boeing 747-2U3B | Garuda Indonesian Airways |
| | PK-PLR | L.100-30 Hercules | HeavyLift Cargo Airlines |
| | PK-PLV | L.100-30 Hercules | HeavyLift Cargo Airlines |
| | PK-PLW | L.100-30 Hercules | HeavyLift Cargo Airlines |

**Note:** The DC-10-30 EI-BZD and MD-11s EI-CDI, EI-CDJ, EI-CDK, EI-CDL, EI-CDM and EI-CDN are also operated by Garuda.

## PP (Brazil)

| | Reg. | Type | Owner or Operator |
|---|---|---|---|
| | PP-VMA | Douglas DC-10-30 | VARIG |
| | PP-VMB | Douglas DC-10-30 | VARIG |
| | PP-VMD | Douglas DC-10-30 | VARIG |
| | PP-VMQ | Douglas DC-10-30 | VARIG |
| | PP-VMT | Douglas DC-10-30F | VARIG Cargo |
| | PP-VMU | Douglas DC-10-30F | VARIG Cargo |
| | PP-VMV | Douglas DC-10-30 | VARIG |
| | PP-VMW | Douglas DC-10-30 | VARIG |
| | PP-VMX | Douglas DC-10-30 | VARIG |
| | PP-VMY | Douglas DC-10-30 | VARIG |
| | PP-VNA | Boeing 747-2L5B (SCD) | VARIG |
| | PP-VNB | Boeing 747-2L5B (SCD) | VARIG |
| | PP-VNC | Boeing 747-2L5B (SCD) | VARIG |
| | PP-VNH | Boeing 747-341 (SCD) | VARIG |
| | PP-VNI | Boeing 747-341 (SCD) | VARIG |
| | PP-VNN | Boeing 767-241ER | VARIG |
| | PP-VNO | Boeing 767-241ER | VARIG |
| | PP-VNP | Boeing 767-241ER | VARIG |
| | PP-NVQ | Boeing 767-241ER | VARIG |
| | PP-VNR | Boeing 767-241ER | VARIG |
| | PP-VNS | Boeing 767-241ER | VARIG |
| | PP-VOA | Boeing 747-341 | VARIG |
| | PP-VOB | Boeing 747-341 | VARIG |
| | PP-VOC | Boeing 747-341 | VARIG |
| | PP-VOI | Boeing 767-341ER | VARIG |
| | PP-VOJ | Boeing 767-341ER | VARIG |
| | PP-VOK | Boeing 767-341ER | VARIG |
| | PP-VOL | Boeing 767-341ER | VARIG |
| | PP-VPG | Boeing 747-441 | VARIG |
| | PP-VPH | Boeing 747-441 | VARIG |
| | PP-VPI | Boeing 747-475 | VARIG |

## RA (Russia)

All aircraft were originally operated by Aeroflot/Russia International using registrations with the country code CCCP. Some have now been transferred to other operators and it is likely that these will acquire new identities. Those known to be with new airlines are shown with a code letter in parenthesis after the type. A – Air Moldova, B – Air Ukraine, C – Azerbayan, E – Armenia, F – Baltic International, G – Georgia, AF – AirFoyle, HV – HeavyLift/Volga Dnepr, H – HeavyLift, J – Harco Air, K – Uzbekistan, L – Aviompex, M – Bosna Air/VB-Air.

| Notes | Reg. | Type | Notes | Reg | Type |
|---|---|---|---|---|---|
| | 65014 | Tu-134A | | 65051 | Tu-134A |
| | 65020 | Tu-134A | | 65054 | Tu-134A |
| | 65024 | Tu-134A | | 65064 | Tu-134A |
| | 65027 | Tu-134A | | 65072 | Tu-134A |
| | 65028 | Tu-134A | | 65073 | Tu-134A |
| | 65035 | Tu-134A | | 65076 | Tu-134A |
| | 65036 | Tu-134A (A) | | 65077 | Tu-134A (B) |
| | 65038 | Tu-134A | | 65087 | Tu-134A |
| | 65042 | Tu-134A | | 65089 | Tu-134A |
| | 65044 | Tu-134A | | 65107 | Tu-134A |
| | 65048 | Tu-134A (B) | | 65119 | Tu-134A |
| | 65049 | Tu-134A | | 65134 | Tu-134A (B) |
| | 65050 | Tu-134A (A) | | 65135 | Tu-134A (B) |

| Reg. | Type | Notes | Reg. | Type | Notes |
|------|------|-------|------|------|-------|
| 65139 | Tu-134A | | 65757 | Tu-134A | |
| 65140 | Tu-134A (A) | | 65758 | Tu-134A | |
| 65141 | Tu-134A | | 65765 | Tu-134A | |
| 65145 | Tu-134A | | 65769 | Tu-134A-3 | |
| 65550 | Tu-134A | | 65770 | Tu-134A-3 | |
| 65551 | Tu-134A | | 65771 | Tu-134A | |
| 65552 | Tu-134A-3 | | 65772 | Tu-134A | |
| 65553 | Tu-134A-3 | | 65777 | Tu-134A-3 | |
| 65554 | Tu-134A-3 | | 65780 | Tu-134A | |
| 65555 | Tu-134A | | 65781 | Tu-134A-3 | |
| 65557 | Tu-134A-3 | | 65782 | Tu-134A | |
| 65601 | Tu-134 | | 65783 | Tu-134A-3 | |
| 65602 | Tu-134 | | 65784 | Tu-134A-3 | |
| 65603 | Tu-134 | | 65785 | Tu-134A-3 | |
| 65604 | Tu-134 | | 65786 | Tu-134A-3 | |
| 65608 | Tu-134A | | 65790 | Tu-134A-3 | |
| 65609 | Tu-134 | | 65791 | Tu-134A (A) | |
| 65611 | Tu-134 | | 65794 | Tu-134A | |
| 65612 | Tu-134 | | 65796 | Tu-134A | |
| 65614 | Tu-134 (J) | | 65801 | Tu-134A | |
| 65615 | Tu-134 | | 65802 | Tu-134A | |
| 65616 | Tu-134 (J) | | 65815 | Tu-134A | |
| 65619 | Tu-134 | | 65835 | Tu-134A | |
| 65620 | Tu-134 | | 65851 | Tu-134A | |
| 65621 | Tu-134 (J) | | 65854 | Tu-134A | |
| 65622 | Tu-134A | | 65862 | Tu-134A | |
| 65623 | Tu-134A (B) | | 65863 | Tu-134A | |
| 65625 | Tu-134 (B) | | 65864 | Tu-134A | |
| 65627 | Tu-134 | | 65872 | Tu-134A | |
| 65628 | Tu-134 | | 65885 | Tu-134A | |
| 65629 | Tu-134 | | 65888 | Tu-134A | |
| 65630 | Tu-134 | | 65891 | Tu-134A | |
| 65631 | Tu-134 | | 65892 | Tu-134A | |
| 65632 | Tu-134 | | 65893 | Tu-134A | |
| 65633 | Tu-134 | | 65894 | Tu-134A | |
| 65634 | Tu-134 | | 65904 | Tu-134A-3 | |
| 65635 | Tu-134 | | 65905 | Tu-134A-3 | |
| 65636 | Tu-134 | | 65911 | Tu-134A-3 | |
| 65637 | Tu-134 | | 65912 | Tu-134A-3 | |
| 65639 | Tu-134 | | 65916 | Tu-134A | |
| 65644 | Tu-134 | | 65919 | Tu-134A | |
| 65645 | Tu-134A | | 65921 | Tu-134A-3 | |
| 65646 | Tu-134A | | 65923 | Tu-134A | |
| 65647 | Tu-134A | | 65926 | Tu-134A | |
| 65649 | Tu-134A | | 65935 | Tu-134A | |
| 65650 | Tu-134A | | 65939 | Tu-134A | |
| 65651 | Tu-134A | | 65951 | Tu-134A | |
| 65652 | Tu-134A | | 65953 | Tu-134A | |
| 65653 | Tu-134A | | 65954 | Tu-134A | |
| 65654 | Tu-134A | | 65955 | Tu-134A | |
| 65655 | Tu-134A | | 65956 | Tu-134A | |
| 65656 | Tu-134A | | 65965 | Tu-134A | |
| 65657 | Tu-134A | | 65967 | Tu-134A-3 | |
| 65658 | Tu-134A | | 65971 | Tu-134A | |
| 65659 | Tu-134A | | 65972 | Tu-134A | |
| 65660 | Tu-134A | | 65974 | Tu-134A | |
| 65661 | Tu-134A | | 65976 | Tu-134A | |
| 65662 | Tu-134A | | 65977 | Tu-134A-3 | |
| 65663 | Tu-134A | | 65978 | Tu-134A-3 | |
| 65664 | Tu-134A | | | | |
| 65665 | Tu-134A | | 76447 | IL-76TD (K) | |
| 65666 | Tu-134A | | 76450 | IL-76TD | |
| 65667 | Tu-134A | | 76454 | IL-76TD | |
| 65669 | Tu-134A | | 76460 | IL-76TD | |
| 65680 | Tu-134A-3 | | 76466 | IL-76TD | |
| 65681 | Tu-134A | | 76467 | IL-76TD | |
| 65697 | Tu-134A | | 76468 | IL-76TD | |
| 65703 | Tu-134A | | 76469 | IL-76TD | |
| 65714 | Tu-134A | | 76470 | IL-76TD | |
| 65717 | Tu-134A-3 | | 76471 | IL-76TD | |
| 65730 | Tu-134A | | 76472 | IL-76TD | |
| 65739 | Tu-134A | | 76473 | IL-76TD | |
| 65750 | Tu-134A | | 76474 | IL-76TD | |

| Notes | Reg. | Type | Notes | Reg | Type |
|-------|------|------|-------|-----|------|
| | 76475 | IL-76TD | | 85011 | Tu-154 |
| | 76476 | IL-76TD | | 85012 | Tu-154 |
| | 76477 | IL-76TD | | 85013 | Tu-154 |
| | 76478 | IL-76TD | | 85014 | Tu-154 |
| | 76479 | IL-76TD | | 85015 | Tu-154 |
| | 76482 | IL-76TD | | 85016 | Tu-154 |
| | 76484 | IL-76TD | | 85017 | Tu-154 |
| | 76485 | IL-76TD | | 85018 | Tu-154 |
| | 76486 | IL-76TD | | 85020 | Tu-154 |
| | 76487 | IL-76TD | | 85021 | Tu-154 |
| | 76488 | IL-76TD | | 85022 | Tu-154 |
| | 76489 | IL-76TD | | 85024 | Tu-154 |
| | 76491 | IL-76TD | | 85025 | Tu-154 |
| | 76493 | IL-76TD | | 85029 | Tu-154 |
| | 76494 | IL-76TD | | 85030 | Tu-154 |
| | 76495 | IL-76TD | | 85031 | Tu-154 |
| | 76496 | IL-76TD | | 85034 | Tu-154 |
| | 76497 | IL-76TD | | 85037 | Tu-154 |
| | 76498 | IL-76TD | | 85038 | Tu-154 |
| | 76499 | IL-76TD | | 85039 | Tu-154 |
| | 76750 | IL-76TD | | 85040 | Tu-154 |
| | 76751 | IL-76TD | | 85041 | Tu-154 |
| | 76752 | IL-76TD | | 85042 | Tu-154 |
| | 76754 | IL-76TD | | 85043 | Tu-154 |
| | 76755 | IL-76TD | | 85044 | Tu-154 |
| | 76756 | IL-76TD | | 85049 | Tu-154 |
| | 76757 | IL-76TD | | 85050 | Tu-154 |
| | 76758 | IL-76TD (H) | | 85051 | Tu-154 |
| | 76761 | IL-76TD | | 85052 | Tu-154 |
| | 76764 | IL-76TD | | 85055 | Tu-154 |
| | 76777 | IL-76TD | | 85056 | Tu-154 |
| | 76780 | IL-76TD | | 85057 | Tu-154 |
| | 76781 | IL-76TD | | 85059 | Tu-154A |
| | 76784 | IL-76TD | | 85060 | Tu-154A |
| | 76785 | IL-76TD | | 85061 | Tu-154A |
| | 76786 | IL-76TD | | 85062 | Tu-154C |
| | 76787 | IL-76TD | | 85063 | Tu-154C |
| | 76788 | IL-76TD | | 85064 | Tu-154A |
| | 76789 | IL-76TD | | 85065 | Tu-154A |
| | 76792 | IL-76TD | | 85066 | Tu-154A |
| | 76794 | IL-76TD | | 85067 | Tu-154C |
| | 76795 | IL-76TD | | 85068 | Tu-154B |
| | 76800 | IL-76TD | | 85069 | Tu-154A |
| | 76801 | IL-76TD | | 85070 | Tu-154A |
| | 76806 | IL-76TD | | 85071 | Tu-154A |
| | 76812 | IL-76TD | | 85072 | Tu-154A |
| | 76814 | IL-76TD | | 85074 | Tu-154A |
| | 76824 | IL-76TD (K) | | 85075 | Tu-154B |
| | 76834 | IL-76TD | | 85076 | Tu-154A |
| | 76835 | IL-76TD | | 85078 | Tu-154A |
| | 76836 | IL-76TD | | 85079 | Tu-154A |
| | 76839 | IL-76TD | | 85080 | Tu-154A |
| | | | | 85081 | Tu-154C |
| | 82007 | An-124 (AF) | | 85082 | Tu-154A |
| | 82008 | An-124 (AF) | | 85083 | Tu-154A |
| | 82009 | An-124 | | 85084 | Tu-154A |
| | 82027 | An-124 (AF) | | 85085 | Tu-154A |
| | 82033 | An-124 | | 85086 | Tu-154A |
| | 82042 | An-124 (HV) | | 85087 | Tu-154A |
| | 82043 | An-124 (HV) | | 85088 | Tu-154A |
| | 82044 | An-124 (HV) | | 85089 | Tu-154A |
| | 82066 | An-124 (B) | | 85090 | Tu-154A |
| | | | | 85091 | Tu-154A |
| | 85001 | Tu-154 | | 85092 | Tu-154B-1 |
| | 85002 | Tu-154 | | 85093 | Tu-154A |
| | 85003 | Tu-154 | | 85094 | Tu-154A |
| | 85004 | Tu-154 | | 85096 | Tu-154B-2 |
| | 85005 | Tu-154 | | 85098 | Tu-154A |
| | 85006 | Tu-154 | | 85099 | Tu-154A |
| | 85007 | Tu-154 | | 85100 | Tu-154A |
| | 85008 | Tu-154 | | 85101 | Tu-154A |
| | 85009 | Tu-154 | | 85103 | Tu-154A |
| | 85010 | Tu-154 | | 85105 | Tu-154A |

| Reg. | Type | Notes | Reg. | Type | Notes |
|------|------|-------|------|------|-------|
| 85106 | Tu-154B-2 | | 85187 | Tu-154B | |
| 85107 | Tu-154A | | 85188 | Tu-154B | |
| 85108 | Tu-154A | | 85189 | Tu-154B | |
| 85109 | Tu-154B-1 | | 85190 | Tu-154B | |
| 85110 | Tu-154A | | 85191 | Tu-154B | |
| 85111 | Tu-154A | | 85192 | Tu-154B | |
| 85112 | Tu-154A | | 85193 | Tu-154B | |
| 85113 | Tu-154A | | 85194 | Tu-154B | |
| 85114 | Tu-154A | | 85195 | Tu-154B | |
| 85115 | Tu-154A | | 85196 | Tu-154B | |
| 85116 | Tu-154A | | 85197 | Tu-154B | |
| 85117 | Tu-154A | | 85198 | Tu-154B | |
| 85118 | Tu-154B | | 85199 | Tu-154B | |
| 85119 | Tu-154A | | 85200 | Tu-154B | |
| 85120 | Tu-154B | | 85201 | Tu-154B | |
| 85121 | Tu-154B | | 85202 | Tu-154B | |
| 85122 | Tu-154B | | 85203 | Tu-154B | |
| 85123 | Tu-154B | | 85204 | Tu-154B | |
| 85124 | Tu-154B | | 85205 | Tu-154B | |
| 85125 | Tu-154B | | 85206 | Tu-154B | |
| 85129 | Tu-154B | | 85207 | Tu-154B | |
| 85130 | Tu-154B | | 85210 | Tu-154B | |
| 85131 | Tu-154B | | 85211 | Tu-154B | |
| 85132 | Tu-154B | | 85212 | Tu-154B | |
| 85134 | Tu-154B | | 85213 | Tu-154B | |
| 85135 | Tu-154B | | 85214 | Tu-154B | |
| 85136 | Tu-154B | | 85215 | Tu-154B | |
| 85137 | Tu-154B | | 85216 | Tu-154B | |
| 85138 | Tu-154B | | 85217 | Tu-154B | |
| 85139 | Tu-154B | | 85218 | Tu-154B | |
| 85140 | Tu-154B | | 85219 | Tu-154B | |
| 85141 | Tu-154B | | 85220 | Tu-154B | |
| 85142 | Tu-154B | | 85221 | Tu-154B | |
| 85143 | Tu-154B | | 85223 | Tu-154B | |
| 85145 | Tu-154B | | 85226 | Tu-154B | |
| 85146 | Tu-154B | | 85227 | Tu-154B | |
| 85147 | Tu-154B | | 85228 | Tu-154B | |
| 85148 | Tu-154B | | 85229 | Tu-154B-1 | |
| 85149 | Tu-154B | | 85230 | Tu-154B-1 | |
| 85150 | Tu-154B | | 85231 | Tu-154B-1 | |
| 85151 | Tu-154B | | 85232 | Tu-154B-1 | |
| 85152 | Tu-154B | | 85233 | Tu-154B-1 | |
| 85153 | Tu-154B | | 85235 | Tu-154B-1 | |
| 85154 | Tu-154B | | 85236 | Tu-154B-1 | |
| 85155 | Tu-154B | | 85237 | Tu-154B-1 | |
| 85156 | Tu-154B | | 85238 | Tu-154B-1 | |
| 85157 | Tu-154B | | 85240 | Tu-154B-1 | |
| 85158 | Tu-154B | | 85241 | Tu-154B-1 | |
| 85160 | Tu-154B | | 85242 | Tu-154B-1 | |
| 85162 | Tu-154B | | 85243 | Tu-154B-1 | |
| 85163 | Tu-154B | | 85244 | Tu-154B-1 | |
| 85164 | Tu-154B | | 85245 | Tu-154B-1 | |
| 85165 | Tu-154B | | 85246 | Tu-154B-1 | |
| 85166 | Tu-154B | | 85247 | Tu-154B-1 | |
| 85167 | Tu-154B | | 85248 | Tu-154B-1 | |
| 85168 | Tu-154B | | 85249 | Tu-154B-1 | |
| 85169 | Tu-154B | | 85250 | Tu-154B-1 | |
| 85170 | Tu-154B | | 85251 | Tu-154B-1 | |
| 85171 | Tu-154B | | 85252 | Tu-154B-1 | |
| 85172 | Tu-154B | | 85253 | Tu-154B-1 | |
| 85173 | Tu-154B | | 85255 | Tu-154B-1 | |
| 85174 | Tu-154B | | 85256 | Tu-154B-1 | |
| 85176 | Tu-154B | | 85257 | Tu-154B-1 | |
| 85177 | Tu-154B | | 85259 | Tu-154B-1 | |
| 85178 | Tu-154B | | 85260 | Tu-154B-1 | |
| 85179 | Tu-154B (B) | | 85261 | Tu-154B-1 | |
| 85180 | Tu-154B | | 85263 | Tu-154B-1 | |
| 85181 | Tu-154B | | 85264 | Tu-154B-1 | |
| 85182 | Tu-154B | | 85265 | Tu-154B-1 | |
| 85183 | Tu-154B | | 85266 | Tu-154B-1 | |
| 85184 | Tu-154B | | 85267 | Tu-154B-1 | |
| 85185 | Tu-154B | | 85268 | Tu-154B-1 | |
| 85186 | Tu-154B | | 85269 | Tu-154B-1 | |

| Notes | Reg. | Type | Notes | Reg | Type |
|---|---|---|---|---|---|
| | 85270 | Tu-154B-1 | | 85350 | Tu-154B-2 (B) |
| | 85271 | Tu-154B-1 | | 85351 | Tu-154B-2 |
| | 85272 | Tu-154B-1 | | 85352 | Tu-154B-2 |
| | 85273 | Tu-154B-1 | | 85353 | Tu-154B-2 |
| | 85274 | Tu-154B-1 | | 85354 | Tu-154B-2 |
| | 85275 | Tu-154B-1 | | 85355 | Tu-154B-2 |
| | 85276 | Tu-154B-1 | | 85356 | Tu-154B-2 |
| | 85277 | Tu-154B-1 | | 85357 | Tu-154B-2 |
| | 85279 | Tu-154B-1 | | 85358 | Tu-154B-2 |
| | 85280 | Tu-154B-1 | | 85359 | Tu-154B-2 |
| | 85281 | Tu-154B-1 | | 85360 | Tu-154B-2 |
| | 85283 | Tu-154B-1 | | 85361 | Tu-154B-2 |
| | 85284 | Tu-154B-1 | | 85362 | Tu-154B-2 |
| | 85285 | Tu-154B-1 | | 85363 | Tu-154B-2 |
| | 85286 | Tu-154B-1 | | 85364 | Tu-154B-2 |
| | 85287 | Tu-154B-1 | | 85365 | Tu-154B-2 |
| | 85288 | Tu-154B-1 | | 85366 | Tu-154B-2 |
| | 85289 | Tu-154B-1 | | 85367 | Tu-154B-2 |
| | 85290 | Tu-154B-1 | | 85368 | Tu-154B-2 |
| | 85291 | Tu-154B-1 | | 85369 | Tu-154B-2 |
| | 85292 | Tu-154B-2 | | 85370 | Tu-154B-2 |
| | 85293 | Tu-154B-1 | | 85371 | Tu-154B-2 |
| | 85294 | Tu-154B-1 | | 85372 | Tu-154B-2 |
| | 85295 | Tu-154B-1 | | 85373 | Tu-154B-2 |
| | 85296 | Tu-154B-1 | | 85374 | Tu-154B-2 |
| | 85297 | Tu-154B-1 | | 85375 | Tu-154B-2 |
| | 85298 | Tu-154B-1 | | 85376 | Tu-154B-2 |
| | 85299 | Tu-154B-1 | | 85377 | Tu-154B-2 |
| | 85300 | Tu-154B-2 | | 85378 | Tu-154B-2 (B) |
| | 85301 | Tu-154B-2 | | 85379 | Tu-154B-2 (B) |
| | 85302 | Tu-154B-2 | | 85380 | Tu-154B-2 |
| | 85303 | Tu-154B-2 | | 85381 | Tu-154B-2 |
| | 85304 | Tu-154B-2 | | 85382 | Tu-154B-2 |
| | 85305 | Tu-154B-2 | | 85383 | Tu-154B-2 |
| | 85306 | Tu-154B-2 | | 85384 | Tu-154B-2 (A) |
| | 85307 | Tu-154B-2 | | 85385 | Tu-154B-2 |
| | 85308 | Tu-154B-2 | | 85386 | Tu-154B-2 |
| | 85309 | Tu-154B-2 | | 85387 | Tu-154B-2 |
| | 85310 | Tu-154B-2 | | 85388 | Tu-154B-2 |
| | 85311 | Tu-154B-2 | | 85389 | Tu-154B-2 |
| | 85312 | Tu-154B-2 | | 85390 | Tu-154B-2 |
| | 85313 | Tu-154B-2 | | 85391 | Tu-154B-2 |
| | 85314 | Tu-154B-2 | | 85392 | Tu-154B-2 |
| | 85315 | Tu-154B-2 | | 85393 | Tu-154B-2 |
| | 85316 | Tu-154B-2 | | 85394 | Tu-154B-2 |
| | 85318 | Tu-154B-2 | | 85395 | Tu-154B-2 |
| | 85319 | Tu-154B-2 | | 85396 | Tu-154B-2 |
| | 85321 | Tu-154B-2 | | 85397 | Tu-154B-2 |
| | 85322 | Tu-154B-2 | | 85398 | Tu-154B-2 |
| | 85323 | Tu-154B-2 | | 85399 | Tu-154B-2 |
| | 85324 | Tu-154B-2 | | 85400 | Tu-154B-2 |
| | 85327 | Tu-154B-2 | | 85401 | Tu-154B-2 |
| | 85328 | Tu-154B-2 | | 85402 | Tu-154B-2 |
| | 85329 | Tu-154B-2 | | 85403 | Tu-154B-2 |
| | 85330 | Tu-154B-2 | | 85404 | Tu-154B-2 |
| | 85331 | Tu-154B-2 | | 85405 | Tu-154B-2 (A) |
| | 85332 | Tu-154B-2 | | 85406 | Tu-154B-2 |
| | 85333 | Tu-154B-2 | | 85407 | Tu-154B-2 |
| | 85334 | Tu-154B-2 | | 85409 | Tu-154B-2 |
| | 85335 | Tu-154B-2 | | 85410 | Tu-154B-2 |
| | 85336 | Tu-154B-2 | | 85411 | Tu-154B-2 |
| | 85337 | Tu-154B-2 | | 85412 | Tu-154B-2 |
| | 85338 | Tu-154B-2 | | 85414 | Tu-154B-2 |
| | 85339 | Tu-154B-2 | | 85416 | Tu-154B-2 |
| | 85340 | Tu-154B-2 | | 85417 | Tu-154B-2 |
| | 85341 | Tu-154B-2 | | 85418 | Tu-154B-2 |
| | 85343 | Tu-154B-2 | | 85419 | Tu-154B-2 |
| | 85344 | Tu-154B-2 | | 85421 | Tu-154B-2 |
| | 85345 | Tu-154B-2 | | 85423 | Tu-154B-2 |
| | 85346 | Tu-154B-2 | | 85424 | Tu-154B-2 |
| | 85347 | Tu-154B-2 | | 85425 | Tu-154B-2 |
| | 85348 | Tu-154B-2 | | 85426 | Tu-154B-2 |
| | 85349 | Tu-154B-2 | | 85427 | Tu-154B-2 |

| Reg. | Type | Notes | Reg. | Type | Notes |
|------|------|-------|------|------|-------|
| 85429 | Tu-154B-2 | | 85510 | Tu-154B-2 | |
| 85430 | Tu-154B-2 | | 85511 | Tu-154B-2 | |
| 85431 | Tu-154B-2 | | 85512 | Tu-154B-2 | |
| 85432 | Tu-154B-2 | | 85513 | Tu-154B-2 | |
| 85433 | Tu-154B-2 | | 85514 | Tu-154B-2 | |
| 85434 | Tu-154B-2 | | 85516 | Tu-154B-2 | |
| 85435 | Tu-154B-2 | | 85518 | Tu-154B-2 | |
| 85436 | Tu-154B-2 | | 85519 | Tu-154B-2 | |
| 85437 | Tu-154B-2 | | 85520 | Tu-154B-2 | |
| 85438 | Tu-154B-2 | | 85521 | Tu-154B-2 | |
| 85439 | Tu-154B-2 | | 85522 | Tu-154B-2 | |
| 85440 | Tu-154B-2 | | 85523 | Tu-154B-2 | |
| 85441 | Tu-154B-2 | | 85524 | Tu-154B-2 | |
| 85442 | Tu-154B-2 | | 85525 | Tu-154C-2 | |
| 85443 | Tu-154B-2 | | 85526 | Tu-154B-2 | |
| 85444 | Tu-154B-2 | | 85527 | Tu-154B-2 | |
| 85445 | Tu-154B-2 | | 85529 | Tu-154B-2 | |
| 85446 | Tu-154B-2 | | 85530 | Tu-154B-2 | |
| 85448 | Tu-154B-2 | | 85532 | Tu-154B-2 | |
| 85449 | Tu-154B-2 | | 85533 | Tu-154B-2 | |
| 85450 | Tu-154B-2 | | 85534 | Tu-154B-2 | |
| 85451 | Tu-154B-2 | | 85535 | Tu-154B-2 | |
| 85452 | Tu-154B-2 | | 85536 | Tu-154B-2 | |
| 85453 | Tu-154B-2 | | 85537 | Tu-154B-2 | |
| 85454 | Tu-154B-2 | | 85538 | Tu-154B-2 | |
| 85455 | Tu-154B-2 | | 85539 | Tu-154B-2 | |
| 85456 | Tu-154B-2 | | 85540 | Tu-154B-2 | |
| 85457 | Tu-154B-2 | | 85542 | Tu-154B-2 | |
| 85458 | Tu-154B-2 | | 85545 | Tu-154B-2 | |
| 85459 | Tu-154B-2 | | 85547 | Tu-154B-2 (G) | |
| 85460 | Tu-154B-2 | | 85548 | Tu-154B-2 | |
| 85461 | Tu-154B-2 | | 85549 | Tu-154B-2 | |
| 85462 | Tu-154B-2 | | 85550 | Tu-154B-2 | |
| 85463 | Tu-154B-2 | | 85551 | Tu-154B-2 | |
| 85464 | Tu-154B-2 | | 85552 | Tu-154B-2 | |
| 85465 | Tu-154B-2 | | 85553 | Tu-154B-2 | |
| 85466 | Tu-154B-2 | | 85554 | Tu-154B-2 | |
| 85467 | Tu-154B-2 | | 85555 | Tu-154B-2 | |
| 85468 | Tu-154B-2 | | 85556 | Tu-154B-2 | |
| 85469 | Tu-154B-2 | | 85557 | Tu-154B-2 | |
| 85470 | Tu-154B-2 | | 85558 | Tu-154B-2 | |
| 85471 | Tu-154B-2 | | 85559 | Tu-154B-2 | |
| 85472 | Tu-154B-2 | | 85560 | Tu-154B-2 | |
| 85475 | Tu-154B-2 | | 85561 | Tu-154B-2 | |
| 85476 | Tu-154B-2 | | 85562 | Tu-154B-2 | |
| 85477 | Tu-154B-2 | | 85563 | Tu-154B-2 | |
| 85478 | Tu-154B-2 | | 85564 | Tu-154B-2 | |
| 85479 | Tu-154B-2 | | 85565 | Tu-154B-2 | |
| 85480 | Tu-154B-2 | | 85566 | Tu-154B-2 | |
| 85481 | Tu-154B-2 | | 85567 | Tu-154B-2 | |
| 85482 | Tu-154B-2 | | 85568 | Tu-154B-2 | |
| 85485 | Tu-154B-2 | | 85570 | Tu-154B-2 | |
| 85486 | Tu-154B-2 | | 85571 | Tu-154B-2 | |
| 85487 | Tu-154B-2 | | 85572 | Tu-154B-2 | |
| 85489 | Tu-154B-2 | | 85573 | Tu-154B-2 | |
| 85490 | Tu-154B-2 | | 85574 | Tu-154B-2 | |
| 85491 | Tu-154B-2 | | 85575 | Tu-154B-2 | |
| 85492 | Tu-154B-2 | | 85577 | Tu-154B-2 | |
| 85494 | Tu-154B-2 | | 85578 | Tu-154B-2 | |
| 85495 | Tu-154B-2 | | 85579 | Tu-154B-2 | |
| 85496 | Tu-154B-2 (G) | | 85580 | Tu-154B-2 | |
| 85497 | Tu-154B-2 | | 85581 | Tu-154B-2 | |
| 85498 | Tu-154B-2 | | 85582 | Tu-154B-2 | |
| 85499 | Tu-154B-2 | | 85583 | Tu-154B-2 | |
| 85500 | Tu-154B-2 | | 85584 | Tu-154B-2 | |
| 85501 | Tu-154B-2 | | 85585 | Tu-154B-2 | |
| 85502 | Tu-154B-2 | | 85586 | Tu-154B-2 | |
| 85503 | Tu-154B-2 | | 85587 | Tu-154B-2 | |
| 85504 | Tu-154B-2 | | 85588 | Tu-154B-2 | |
| 85505 | Tu-154B-2 | | 85589 | Tu-154B-2 | |
| 85506 | Tu-154B-2 | | 85590 | Tu-154B-2 | |
| 85507 | Tu-154B-2 | | 85591 | Tu-154B-2 | |
| 85508 | Tu-154B-2 | | 85592 | Tu-154B-2 | |
| 85509 | Tu-154B-2 | | 85593 | Tu-154B-2 | |

| Notes | Reg. | Type | Notes | Reg | Type |
|---|---|---|---|---|---|
| | 85594 | Tu-154B-2 | | 85672 | Tu-154M |
| | 85595 | Tu-154B-2 | | 85675 | Tu-154M |
| | 85596 | Tu-154B-2 | | 85676 | Tu-154M |
| | 85597 | Tu-154B-2 | | 85677 | Tu-154M |
| | 85598 | Tu-154B-2 | | 85678 | Tu-154M |
| | 85600 | Tu-154B-2 | | 85679 | Tu-154M |
| | 85601 | Tu-154B-2 | | 85680 | Tu-154M |
| | 85602 | Tu-154B-2 | | 85681 | Tu-154M |
| | 85603 | Tu-154B-2 | | 85682 | Tu-154M |
| | 85604 | Tu-154B-2 | | 85683 | Tu-154M |
| | 85605 | Tu-154B-2 | | 85684 | Tu-154M |
| | 85606 | Tu-154B-2 | | 85685 | Tu-154M |
| | 85607 | Tu-154B-2 | | 85686 | Tu-154M |
| | 85608 | Tu-154B-2 | | 85687 | Tu-154M |
| | 85609 | Tu-154M | | 85688 | Tu-154M |
| | 85610 | Tu-154M | | 85689 | Tu-154M |
| | 85611 | Tu-154M | | 85690 | Tu-154M |
| | 85612 | Tu-154M | | 85691 | Tu-154M |
| | 85613 | Tu-154M | | 85692 | Tu-154M |
| | 85614 | Tu-154M | | 85693 | Tu-154M |
| | 85616 | Tu-154M | | 85694 | Tu-154M |
| | 85617 | Tu-154M | | 85695 | Tu-154M |
| | 85618 | Tu-154M | | 85696 | Tu-154M |
| | 85619 | Tu-154M | | 85697 | Tu-154M |
| | 85621 | Tu-154M (M) | | 85698 | Tu-154M |
| | 85622 | Tu-154M | | 85699 | Tu-154M |
| | 85623 | Tu-154M | | 85700 | Tu-154M |
| | 85624 | Tu-154M (M) | | 85706 | Tu-154M |
| | 85625 | Tu-154M | | 85708 | Tu-154M |
| | 85626 | Tu-154M | | 85712 | Tu-154M |
| | 85627 | Tu-154M | | 85713 | Tu-154M |
| | 85628 | Tu-154M | | 85714 | Tu-154M |
| | 85629 | Tu-154M | | 85715 | Tu-154M (F) |
| | 85630 | Tu-154M (L) | | 85717 | Tu-154M |
| | 85631 | Tu-154M (L) | | 85724 | Tu-154M |
| | 85632 | Tu-154M | | 85725 | Tu-154M |
| | 85633 | Tu-154M | | 85737 | Tu-154M |
| | 85634 | Tu-154M | | | |
| | 85635 | Tu-154M | | 86000 | IL-86 |
| | 85636 | Tu-154M | | 86002 | IL-86 |
| | 85637 | Tu-154M | | 86003 | IL-86 |
| | 85638 | Tu-154M | | 86004 | IL-86 |
| | 85639 | Tu-154M | | 86005 | IL-86 |
| | 85640 | Tu-154M | | 86006 | IL-86 |
| | 85641 | Tu-154M | | 86007 | IL-86 |
| | 85642 | Tu-154M | | 86008 | IL-86 |
| | 85643 | Tu-154M | | 86009 | IL-86 |
| | 85644 | Tu-154M | | 86010 | IL-86 |
| | 85645 | Tu-154M | | 86011 | IL-86 |
| | 85646 | Tu-154M | | 86012 | IL-86 |
| | 85647 | Tu-154M | | 86013 | IL-86 |
| | 85648 | Tu-154M | | 86014 | IL-86 |
| | 85649 | Tu-154M | | 86015 | IL-86 |
| | 85650 | Tu-154M | | 86016 | IL-86 |
| | 85651 | Tu-154M | | 86017 | IL-86 |
| | 85652 | Tu-154M | | 86018 | IL-86 |
| | 85653 | Tu-154M | | 86050 | IL-86 |
| | 85654 | Tu-154M | | 86051 | IL-86 |
| | 85655 | Tu-154M | | 86052 | IL-86 |
| | 85656 | Tu-154M | | 86053 | IL-86 |
| | 85657 | Tu-154M | | 86054 | IL-86 |
| | 85658 | Tu-154M | | 86055 | IL-86 |
| | 85659 | Tu-154M | | 86056 | IL-86 |
| | 85660 | Tu-154M | | 86057 | IL-86 |
| | 85661 | Tu-154M | | 86058 | IL-86 |
| | 85662 | Tu-154M | | 86059 | IL-86 |
| | 85663 | Tu-154M | | 86060 | IL-86 |
| | 85665 | Tu-154M | | 86061 | IL-86 |
| | 85666 | Tu-154M | | 86062 | IL-86 |
| | 85667 | Tu-154M | | 86063 | IL-86 |
| | 85668 | Tu-154M | | 86064 | IL-86 |
| | 85669 | Tu-154M | | 86065 | IL-86 |
| | 85670 | Tu-154M | | 86066 | IL-86 |
| | 85671 | Tu-154M | | 86067 | IL-86 |

| Reg. | Type | Notes | Reg. | Type | Notes |
|------|------|-------|------|------|-------|
| 86068 | IL-86 | | 86465 | IL-62M | |
| 86069 | IL-86 | | 86466 | IL-62MK | |
| 86070 | IL-86 | | 86467 | IL-62MK (B) | |
| 86071 | IL-86 | | 86468 | IL-62MK | |
| 86072 | IL-86 | | 86469 | IL-62M | |
| 86073 | IL-86 | | 86471 | IL-62M | |
| 86074 | IL-86 | | 86472 | IL-62M | |
| 86075 | IL-86 | | 86473 | IL-62M | |
| 86076 | IL-86 | | 86474 | IL-62M | |
| 86077 | IL-86 | | 86475 | IL-62M | |
| 86078 | IL-86 | | 86476 | IL-62M | |
| 86079 | IL-86 | | 86477 | IL-62M | |
| 86080 | IL-86 | | 86478 | IL-62M | |
| 86081 | IL-86 | | 86479 | IL-62M | |
| 86082 | IL-86 | | 86480 | IL-62M | |
| 86083 | IL-86 | | 86481 | IL-62M | |
| 86084 | IL-86 | | 86482 | IL-62M | |
| 86085 | IL-86 | | 86483 | IL-62M | |
| 86086 | IL-86 | | 86484 | IL-62M | |
| 86087 | IL-86 | | 86485 | IL-62M | |
| 86088 | IL-86 | | 86486 | IL-62M | |
| 86089 | IL-86 | | 86487 | IL-62M | |
| 86090 | IL-86 | | 86488 | IL-62M | |
| 86091 | IL-86 | | 86489 | IL-62M | |
| 86092 | IL-86 | | 86490 | IL-62M | |
| 86093 | IL-86 | | 86491 | IL-62M | |
| 86094 | IL-86 | | 86492 | IL-62M | |
| 86095 | IL-86 | | 86493 | IL-62M | |
| 86096 | IL-86 | | 86494 | IL-62M | |
| 86097 | IL-86 | | 86495 | IL-62M | |
| 86098 | IL-86 | | 86496 | IL-62M | |
| 86099 | IL-86 | | 86497 | IL-62M | |
| 86100 | IL-86 | | 86498 | IL-62M | |
| 86101 | IL-86 | | 86499 | IL-62M | |
| 86102 | IL-86 | | 86500 | IL-62M | |
| 86103 | IL-86 | | 86501 | IL-62M | |
| 86104 | IL-86 | | 86502 | IL-62M | |
| 86105 | IL-86 | | 86503 | IL-62M | |
| 86106 | IL-86 | | 86504 | IL-62M | |
| 86107 | IL-86 | | 86505 | IL-62M | |
| 86108 | IL-86 | | 86506 | IL-62M | |
| 86109 | IL-86 | | 86507 | IL-62M | |
| 86110 | IL-86 | | 86508 | IL-62M | |
| 86111 | IL-86 | | 86509 | IL-62M | |
| 86112 | IL-86 | | 86510 | IL-62M | |
| 86113 | IL-86 | | 86511 | IL-62M | |
| 86114 | IL-86 | | 86512 | IL-62M | |
| 86115 | IL-86 | | 86514 | IL-62M | |
| 86116 | IL-86 | | 86515 | IL-62M | |
| 86117 | IL-86 | | 86516 | IL-62M | |
| 86118 | IL-86 | | 86517 | IL-62MK | |
| 86119 | IL-86 | | 86518 | IL-62M | |
| 86120 | IL-86 | | 86519 | IL-62M | |
| 86121 | IL-86 | | 86520 | IL-62MK | |
| 86122 | IL-86 | | 86521 | IL-62M | |
| 86123 | IL-86 | | 86522 | IL-62M | |
| 86132 | IL-62M (B) | | 86523 | IL-62M | |
| 86134 | IL-62M (B) | | 86524 | IL-62M | |
| 86135 | IL-62M (B) | | 86527 | IL-62MK | |
| | | | 86528 | IL-62MK | |
| 86450 | IL-62 | | 86529 | IL-62MK | |
| 86451 | IL-62 | | 86530 | IL-62MK | |
| 86452 | IL-62M | | 86531 | IL-62M | |
| 86453 | IL-62M | | 86532 | IL-62MK | |
| 86454 | IL-62M | | 86533 | IL-62M | |
| 86455 | IL-62M | | 86534 | IL-62MK | |
| 86457 | IL-62M | | 86535 | IL-62M | |
| 86458 | IL-62M | | 86536 | IL-62M | |
| 86459 | IL-62M | | 86537 | IL-62M | |
| 86460 | IL-62 | | 86538 | IL-62M | |
| 86461 | IL-62 | | 86539 | IL-62MK | |
| 86462 | IL-62M | | 86540 | IL-62M | |
| 86463 | IL-62M | | 86554 | IL-62M | |
| 86464 | IL-62M | | 86555 | IL-62M | |

| Notes | Reg. | Type | Notes | Reg | Type |
|---|---|---|---|---|---|
| | 86558 | IL-62M | | 86666 | IL-62 |
| | 86565 | IL-62M | | 86667 | IL-62 |
| | 86573 | IL-62M | | 86668 | IL-62 |
| | 86574 | IL-62M | | 86669 | IL-62 |
| | 86575 | IL-62M (K) | | 86670 | IL-62 |
| | 86576 | IL-62M | | 86673 | IL-62M |
| | 86577 | IL-62M | | 86674 | IL-62 |
| | 86578 | IL-62M | | 86675 | IL-62 |
| | 86579 | IL-62M | | 86676 | IL-62 |
| | 86580 | IL-62M (B) | | 86677 | IL-62 |
| | 86581 | IL-62M (B) | | 86678 | IL-62 |
| | 86582 | IL-62M (B) | | 86679 | IL-62 |
| | 86605 | IL-62 | | 86680 | IL-62 |
| | 86606 | IL-62 | | 86681 | IL-62 |
| | 86608 | IL-62 | | 86682 | IL-62 |
| | 86609 | IL-62 | | 86683 | IL-62 |
| | 86610 | IL-62 | | 86684 | IL-62 |
| | 86611 | IL-62 | | 86685 | IL-62 |
| | 86612 | IL-62 | | 86686 | IL-62 |
| | 86614 | IL-62 | | 86687 | IL-62 |
| | 86615 | IL-62 | | 86688 | IL-62 |
| | 86616 | IL-62 | | 86689 | IL-62 |
| | 86617 | IL-62 | | 86690 | IL-62 |
| | 86618 | IL-62M | | 86691 | IL-62 |
| | 86619 | IL-62M | | 86692 | IL-62M |
| | 86620 | IL-62M | | 86693 | IL-62M |
| | 86621 | IL-62M | | 86694 | IL-62 |
| | 86622 | IL-62M | | 86695 | IL-62 |
| | 86623 | IL-62M | | 86696 | IL-62 |
| | 86624 | IL-62M | | 86697 | IL-62 |
| | 86648 | IL-62 | | 86698 | IL-62 |
| | 86649 | IL-62 | | 86699 | IL-62 |
| | 86652 | IL-62 | | 86700 | IL-62M |
| | 86653 | IL-62 | | 86701 | IL-62M |
| | 86654 | IL-62 | | 86702 | IL-62M |
| | 86655 | IL-62 | | 86703 | IL-62M |
| | 86656 | IL-62M | | 86704 | IL-62M |
| | 86657 | IL-62 | | 86705 | IL-62M |
| | 86658 | IL-62M | | 86706 | IL-62M |
| | 86659 | IL-62M | | 86708 | IL-62MK |
| | 86661 | IL-62 | | 86709 | IL-62MK |
| | 86662 | IL-62 | | 86710 | IL-62MK |
| | 86663 | IL-62 | | 86711 | IL-62M |
| | 86664 | IL-62 | | 86712 | IL-62M |
| | 86665 | IL-62 | | | |

**Note:** Aeroflot also operates Airbus A.310-308s registered F-OGQR, F-OGQS, F-OGQT and F-OGQU

| Notes | Reg. | Type | Owner or Operator |
|---|---|---|---|

## RP (Philippines)

**Note:** Philippine Airlines operates four Boeing 747-2F6Bs which retain their U.S. identities N741PR, N742PR, N743PR and N744PR, two 747-283Bs registered EI-BTS and EI-BZA and two 747-211Bs registered N207AE and N208AE.

## S2 (Bangladesh)

| | | |
|---|---|---|
| S2-ACO | Douglas DC-10-30 | Bangladesh Biman *The City of Hazrat-Shah Makhdoom (R.A.)* |
| S2-ACP | Douglas DC-10-30 | Bangladesh Biman *The City of Dhaka* |
| S2-ACQ | Douglas DC-10-30 | Bangladesh Biman *The City of Hz Shah Jalal (R.A.)* |
| S2-ACR | Douglas DC-10-30 | Bangladesh Biman *The New Era* |

## S7 (Seychelles)

| | | |
|---|---|---|
| S7-AAQ | Boeing 767-35H | Air Europe SpA |
| S7-AAS | Boeing 767-2Q8ER | Air Seychelles *Aldabra* |
| S7-AAV | Boeing 767-35H | Air Europe SpA |

## SE (Sweden)

| | | |
|---|---|---|
| SE-CFP | Douglas DC-3 | Flygande Veteraner *Fridtjof Viking* |

| Reg. | Type | Owner or Operator | Notes |
|---|---|---|---|
| SE-DAK | Douglas DC-9-41 | S.A.S. *Ragnvald Viking* | |
| SE-DAP | Douglas DC-9-41 | S.A.S. *Torgils Viking* | |
| SE-DAR | Douglas DC-9-41 | S.A.S. *Agnar Viking* | |
| SE-DAS | Douglas DC-9-41 | S.A.S. *Garder Viking* | |
| SE-DAU | Douglas DC-9-41 | S.A.S. *Hadding Viking* | |
| SE-DAW | Douglas DC-9-41 | S.A.S. *Gotrik Viking* | |
| SE-DAX | Douglas DC-9-41 | S.A.S. *Helsing Viking* | |
| SE-DBM | Douglas DC-9-41 | S.A.S. *Ossur Viking* | |
| SE-DBO | Douglas DC-9-21 | S.A.S. *Siger Viking* | |
| SE-DDP | Douglas DC-9-41 | S.A.S. *Brun Viking* | |
| SE-DDR | Douglas DC-9-41 | S.A.S. | |
| SE-DDS | Douglas DC-9-41 | S.A.S. *Alrik Viking* | |
| SE-DDT | Douglas DC-9-41 | S.A.S. *Amund Viking* | |
| SE-DEI | BAe 146-200QT | City Air Scandinavia/TNT | |
| SE-DFR | McD Douglas MD-81 | S.A.S. *Ingjald Viking* | |
| SE-DFS | McD Douglas MD-82 | S.A.S. | |
| SE-DFT | McD Douglas MD-82 | S.A.S. *Assur Viking* | |
| SE-DFU | McD Douglas MD-82 | S.A.S. *Vegard Viking* | |
| SE-DFX | McD Douglas MD-82 | S.A.S. | |
| SE-DFY | McD Douglas MD-81 | S.A.S. *Ottar Viking* | |
| SE-DGA | F.28 Fellowship 1000 | Linjeflyg/S.A.S. | |
| SE-DGC | F.28 Fellowship 1000 | Linjeflyg/S.A.S. | |
| SE-DGE | F.28 Fellowship 4000 | Linjeflyg/S.A.S. | |
| SE-DGF | F.28 Fellowship 4000 | Linjeflyg/S.A.S. | |
| SE-DGG | F.28 Fellowship 4000 | Linjeflyg/S.A.S. | |
| SE-DGH | F.28 Fellowship 4000 | Linjeflyg/S.A.S. | |
| SE-DGI | F.28 Fellowship 4000 | Linjeflyg/S.A.S. | |
| SE-DGK | F.28 Fellowship 4000 | Linjeflyg/S.A.S. | |
| SE-DGL | F.28 Fellowship 4000 | Linjeflyg/S.A.S. | |
| SE-DGM | F.28 Fellowship 4000 | Linjeflyg/S.A.S. | |
| SE-DGN | F.28 Fellowship 4000 | Linjeflyg/S.A.S. | |
| SE-DGO | F.28 Fellowship 4000 | Linjeflyg/S.A.S. | |
| SE-DGP | F.28 Fellowship 4000 | Linjeflyg/S.A.S. | |
| SE-DGR | F.28 Fellowship 4000 | Linjeflyg/S.A.S. | |
| SE-DGS | F.28 Fellowship 4000 | Linjeflyg/S.A.S. | |
| SE-DGT | F.28 Fellowship 4000 | Linjeflyg/S.A.S. | |
| SE-DGU | F.28 Fellowship 4000 | Linjeflyg/S.A.S. | |
| SE-DGX | F.28 Fellowship 4000 | Linjeflyg/S.A.S. | |
| SE-DHB | McD Douglas MD-83 | Transwede | |
| SE-DHC | McD Douglas MD-83 | Transwede | |
| SE-DHD | McD Douglas MD-83 | Transwede | |
| SE-DHG | McD Douglas MD-87 | Transwede | |
| SE-DHI | McD Douglas MD-87 | Transwede | |
| SE-DHN | McD Douglas MD-83 | Transwede | |
| SE-DHS | Douglas DC-10-10 | Scanair *Baloo* | |
| SE-DHT | Douglas DC-10-10 | Scanair *Dumbo* | |
| SE-DHU | Douglas DC-10-10 | Scanair *Bamse* | |
| SE-DHX | Douglas DC-10-10 | (leased to Sun Country) | |
| SE-DHY | Douglas DC-10-10 | Scanair *Snoopy* | |
| SE-DHZ | Douglas DC-10-10 | Scanair *Moby Dick* | |
| SE-DIA | McD Douglas MD-81 | S.A.S. *Ulvrik Viking* | |
| SE-DIB | McD Douglas MD-87 | S.A.S. *Varin Viking* | |
| SE-DIC | McD Douglas MD-87 | S.A.S. *Grane Viking* | |
| SE-DID | McD Douglas MD-82 | S.A.S. | |
| SE-DIF | McD Douglas MD-87 | S.A.S. *Hjorulv Viking* | |
| SE-DIH | McD Douglas MD-87 | S.A.S. *Slagfinn Viking* | |
| SE-DII | McD Douglas MD-81 | S.A.S. *Sigtrygg Viking* | |
| SE-DIK | McD Douglas MD-82 | S.A.S. *Stenkil Viking* | |
| SE-DIL | McD Douglas MD-81 | S.A.S. *Tord Viking* | |
| SE-DIM | BAe 146-300QT | City Air Scandinavia/TNT | |
| SE-DIN | McD Douglas MD-81 | S.A.S. *Eskil Viking* | |
| SE-DIP | McD Douglas MD-87 | S.A.S. *Jarl Viking* | |
| SE-DIR | McD Douglas MD-81 | S.A.S. *Nora Viking* | |
| SE-DIS | McD Douglas MD-81 | S.A.S. *Sigmund Viking* | |
| SE-DIT | BAe 146-300QT | City Air Scandinavia/TNT | |
| SE-DIU | McD Douglas MD-87 | S.A.S. *Torsten Viking* | |
| SE-DIX | McD Douglas MD-81 | S.A.S. *Adils Viking* | |
| SE-DIY | McD Douglas MD-81 | S.A.S. *Albin Viking* | |
| SE-DIZ | McD Douglas MD-82 | S.A.S. *Sigyn Viking* | |
| SE-DKO | Boeing 767-383ER | S.A.S. *Ingegerd Viking* | |
| SE-DKP | Boeing 767-283ER | S.A.S. *Sigrid Viking* | |
| SE-DKU | Boeing 767-383ER | S.A.S. *Tor Viking* | |
| SE-DKX | Boeing 767-383ER | S.A.S. *Sven Viking* | |

| Notes | Reg. | Type | Owner or Operator |
|---|---|---|---|
| | SE-DLC | Douglas DC-9-41 | S.A.S. *Eiliv Viking* |
| | SE-DLD | Boeing 737-205 | Air Sweden |
| | SE-DLG | Boeing 737-3Q8 | Air Sweden |
| | SE-DLH | Douglas DC-8-71 | Air Sweden |
| | SE-DLM | Douglas DC-8-71AF | Air Sweden |
| | SE-DLN | Boeing 737-3Y0 | — |
| | SE-DLO | Boeing 737-3Y0 | — |
| | SE-DLP | Boeing 737-205 | Air Sweden *Irish Rainbow* |
| | SE-DLS | McD Douglas MD-83 | Transwede |
| | SE-DLU | McD Douglas MD-83 | Transwede |
| | SE- | McD Douglas MD-83 | Transwede |
| | SE- | McD Douglas MD-83 | Transwede |
| | SE-DMA | McD Douglas MD-87 | S.A.S. |
| | SE-DMB | McD Douglas MD-81 | S.A.S. |
| | SE-DMD | McD Douglas MD-81 | S.A.S. |
| | SE-DME | McD Douglas MD-81 | S.A.S. |
| | SE-DNA | Boeing 737-59D | Linjeflyg/S.A.S. |
| | SE-DNB | Boeing 737-59D | Linjeflyg/S.A.S. |
| | SE-DNC | Boeing 737-53A | Linjeflyg/S.A.S. |
| | SE-DND | Boeing 737-59D | Linjeflyg/S.A.S. |
| | SE-DNE | Boeing 737-59D | Linjeflyg/S.A.S. |
| | SE-DNF | Boeing 737-5Q8 | Linjeflyg/S.A.S. |
| | SE-DNG | Boeing 737-5Q8 | Linjeflyg/S.A.S. |
| | SE-DNH | Boeing 737-5Q8 | Linjeflyg/S.A.S. |
| | SE-DNI | Boeing 737-59D | Linjeflyg/S.A.S. |
| | SE-DNK | Boeing 737-59D | Linjeflyg/S.A.S. |
| | SE-DNL | Boeing 737-59D | Linjeflyg/S.A.S. |
| | SE-DN | Boeing 737-59D | Linjeflyg/S.A.S. |
| | SE-DOB | Boeing 767-383ER | S.A.S. *Helga Viking* |
| | SE-DOC | Boeing 767-383ER | S.A.S. *Gudrun Viking* |
| | SE-DPA | Boeing 737-33A | Falcon Cargo |
| | SE-DPB | Boeing 737-33A | Falcon Cargo |
| | SE-DPC | Boeing 737-33A | Falcon Cargo |
| | SE-DPH | McD Douglas MD-83 | Scanair |
| | SE-DPI | McD Douglas MD-83 | Scanair *Puff* |
| | SE-DPN | Boeing 737-3G7 | Air Sweden |
| | SE-DPO | Boeing 737-3G7 | Air Sweden |
| | SE-DRA | BAe 146-200 | City Air Scandinavia |
| | SE-DRB | BAe 146-200 | City Air Scandinavia |
| | SE-IVR | L-188CF Electra | Falcon Cargo |
| | SE-IVS | L-188CF Electra | Falcon Cargo |
| | SE-IVT | L-188CF Electra | Falcon Cargo |
| | SE-IZU | L-188CF Electra | Falcon Cargo |
| | SE-KBP | FH.227E Friendship | Sweden Airways |
| | SE-KBR | FH.227B Friendship | Sweden Airways |
| | SE-KGA | FH.227B Friendship | Sweden Airways |
| | SE-KGB | FH.227B Friendship | Sweden Airways |
| | SE-LFA | Fokker 50 | S.A.S. Commuter *Jorund* |
| | SE-LFB | Fokker 50 | S.A.S. Commuter *Sture* |
| | SE-LFC | Fokker 50 | S.A.S. Commuter *Ylva* |
| | SE-LFK | Fokker 50 | S.A.S. Commuter *Alvar* |
| | SE-LFN | Fokker 50 | S.A.S. Commuter *Edmund* |
| | SE-LFO | Fokker 50 | S.A.S. Commuter *Folke* |
| | SE-LFP | Fokker 50 | S.A.S. Commuter *Ingemar* |
| | SE-LFR | Fokker 50 | S.A.S. Commuter *Vagn* |
| | SE-LFS | Fokker 50 | S.A.S. Commuter *Vigge* |

## SL (Slovenia)

| | | | |
|---|---|---|---|
| | SL-AAA | Airbus A.310-231 | Adria Airways (YU-AOA) |
| | SL-AAB | Airbus A.310-231 | Adria Airways (YU-AOD) |
| | SL-AAC | Airbus A.310-231 | Adria Airways (YU-AOE |
| | SL-ABA | McD Douglas MD-82 | Adria Airways (YU-ANB) |
| | SL-ABB | McD Douglas MD-82 | Adria Airways (YU-ANC) |
| | SL-ABC | McD Douglas MD-82 | Adria Airways (YU-ANG) |
| | SL-ABD | McD Douglas MD-82 | Adria Airways (YU-ANO) |
| | SL-ABE | McD Douglas MD-81 | Adria Airways (YU-AJZ) |
| | SL-ABF | Douglas DC-9-32 | Adria Airways (YU-AHJ) |
| | SL-ABG | Douglas DC-9-33RC | Adria Airways (YU-AHW) |
| | SL-ABH | Douglas DC-9-32 | Adria Airways (YU-AJF) |

# SP (Poland)

| Reg. | Type | Owner or Operator |
|------|------|-------------------|
| SP-LCA | Tupolev Tu-154M | Polskie Linie Lotnicze (LOT) |
| SP-LCB | Tupolev Tu-154M | LOT |
| SP-LCC | Tupolev Tu-154M | LOT |
| SP-LCD | Tupolev Tu-154M | LOT |
| SP-LCE | Tupolev Tu-154M | LOT |
| SP-LCF | Tupolev Tu-154M | LOT |
| SP-LCG | Tupolev Tu-154M | LOT |
| SP-LCH | Tupolev Tu-154M | LOT |
| SP-LCI | Tupolev Tu-154M | LOT |
| SP-LCK | Tupolev Tu-154M | LOT |
| SP-LCL | Tupolev Tu-154M | LOT |
| SP-LCM | Tupolev Tu-154M | LOT |
| SP-LCN | Tupolev Tu-154M | LOT |
| SP-LCO | Tupolev Tu-154M | LOT |
| SP-LHA | Tupolev Tu-134A | LOT |
| SP-LHB | Tupolev Tu-134A | LOT |
| SP-LHC | Tupolev Tu-134A | LOT |
| SP-LHD | Tupolev Tu-134A | LOT |
| SP-LHE | Tupolev Tu-134A | LOT |
| SP-LHF | Tupolev Tu-134A | LOT |
| SP-LHG | Tupolev Tu-134A | LOT |
| SP-LKA | Boeing 737-55D | LOT |
| SP-LKB | Boeing 737-55D | LOT |
| SP-LKC | Boeing 737-55D | LOT |
| SP-LKD | Boeing 737-55D | LOT |
| SP-LKE | Boeing 737-55D | LOT |
| SP-LLA | Boeing 737-45D | LOT |
| SP-LLB | Boeing 737-45D | LOT |
| SP-LLC | Boeing 737-45D | LOT |
| SP-LLD | Boeing 737-45D | LOT |
| SP-LOA | Boeing 767-25DER | LOT *Gneizao* |
| SP-LOB | Boeing 767-25DER | LOT *Kracow* |
| SP-LPA | Boeing 767-35DER | LOT *Warszawa* |

# ST (Sudan)

| Reg. | Type | Owner or Operator |
|------|------|-------------------|
| ST-AFA | Boeing 707-3J8C | Sudan Airways |
| ST-AFB | Boeing 707-3J8C | Sudan Airways |
| ST-AIX | Boeing 707-369C | Sudan Airways |
| ST-AKW | Boeing 707-330C | Transarabian Air Transport |
| ST-AMF | Boeing 707-321C | Transarabian Air Transport |
| ST-NSR | Boeing 707-330B | Sudan Airways |

**Note:** Sudan Airways also operates an A.310-304 which retains the registration F-OGQN and named *Khartoum*. The airline also leases the A.310-304 F-GKTD.

# SU (Egypt)

| Reg. | Type | Owner or Operator |
|------|------|-------------------|
| SU-AOU | Boeing 707-366C | EgyptAir Cargo *Khopho* |
| SU-APD | Boeing 707-366C | EgyptAir *Khafrah* |
| SU-AVX | Boeing 707-366C | EgyptAir *Tutankhamun* |
| SU-AVY | Boeing 707-366C | EgyptAir *Akhenaton* |
| SU-AVZ | Boeing 707-366C | EgyptAir *Mena* |
| SU-AXK | Boeing 707-366C | EgyptAir *Seti I* |
| SU-BCB | Airbus A.300B4 | EgyptAir *Osiris* |
| SU-BCC | Airbus A.300B4 | EgyptAir *Nout* |
| SU-BDF | Airbus A.300B4 | EgyptAir *Hathor* |
| SU-BLL | Boeing 737-4Y0 | Transmed |
| SU-DAA | Boeing 707-351C | ZAS Airline of Egypt |
| SU-DAC | Boeing 707-336C | ZAS Airline of Egypt |
| SU-DAL | McD Douglas MD-83 | ZAS Airline of Egypt |
| SU-DAM | McD Douglas MD-83 | ZAS Airline of Egypt |
| SU-DAO | McD Douglas MD-87 | ZAS Airline of Egypt |
| SU-DAP | McD Douglas MD-87 | ZAS Airline of Egypt |
| SU-DAQ | McD Douglas MD-87 | ZAS Airline of Egypt |
| SU-GAH | Boeing 767-266ER | EgyptAir *Nefertiti* |
| SU-GAI | Boeing 767-266ER | EgyptAir *Nefertari* |
| SU-GAJ | Boeing 767-266ER | EgyptAir *Tiye* |
| SU-GAL | Boeing 747-366 (SCD) | EgyptAir *Hatshepsut* |

| Notes | Reg. | Type | Owner or Operator |
|---|---|---|---|
| | SU-GAM | Boeing 747-366 (SCD) | EgyptAir *Cleopatra* |
| | SU-GAO | Boeing 767-366ER | EgyptAir *Ramses II* |
| | SU-GAP | Boeing 767-366ER | EgyptAir *Thutmosis III* |
| | SU-GAR | Airbus A.300-622R | EgyptAir *Zoser* |
| | SU-GAS | Airbus A.300-622R | EgyptAir *Cheops* |
| | SU-GAT | Airbus A.300-622R | EgyptAir *Chephren* |
| | SU-GAU | Airbus A.300-622R | EgyptAir *Mycerinus* |
| | SU-GAV | Airbus A.300-622R | EgyptAir *Menes* |
| | SU-GAW | Airbus A.300-622R | EgyptAir *Ahmuse* |
| | SU-GAX | Airbus A.300-622R | EgyptAir *Tut-Ankh-Amun* |
| | SU-GAY | Airbus A.300-622R | EgyptAir *Seti I* |
| | SU-GAZ | Airbus A.300-622R | EgyptAir |
| | SU-GBA | Airbus A.320-231 | EgyptAir *Aswan* |
| | SU-GBB | Airbus A.320-231 | EgyptAir *Luxor* |
| | SU-GBC | Airbus A.320-231 | EgyptAir *Hurghada* |
| | SU-GBD | Airbus A.320-231 | EgyptAir *Taba* |
| | SU-GBE | Airbus A.320-231 | EgyptAir *El Alamein* |
| | SU-GBF | Airbus A.320-231 | EgyptAir *Sharm El Sheikh* |
| | SU-GBG | Airbus A.320-231 | EgyptAir |
| | SU-OAA | Ilyushin IL-76TD | Cairo Charter & Cargo Airlines |
| | SU-OAB | Ilyushin IL-76TD | Cairo Charter & Cargo Airlines |
| | SU-OAC | Tupolev Tu-154M | Cairo Charter & Cargo Airlines |
| | SU-OAD | Tupolev Tu-154M | Cairo Charter & Cargo Airlines |
| | SU-RAA | Airbus A.320-231 | Shorouk Air |
| | SU-RAB | Airbus A.320-231 | Shorouk Air |

**Note:** ZAS also operates the A.300s OY-CNA and OY-CNK on lease from Conair.

## SX (Greece)

| | | | |
|---|---|---|---|
| | SX-BCA | Boeing 737-284 | Olympic Airways *Apollo* |
| | SX-BCB | Boeing 737-284 | Olympic Airways *Hermes* |
| | SX-BCC | Boeing 737-284 | Olympic Airways *Hercules* |
| | SX-BCD | Boeing 737-284 | Olympic Airways *Hephaestus* |
| | SX-BCE | Boeing 737-284 | Olympic Airways *Dionysus* |
| | SX-BCF | Boeing 737-284 | Olympic Airways *Poseidon* |
| | SX-BCG | Boeing 737-284 | Olympic Airways *Phoebus* |
| | SX-BCH | Boeing 737-284 | Olympic Airways *Triton* |
| | SX-BCI | Boeing 737-284 | Olympic Airways *Proteus* |
| | SX-BCK | Boeing 737-284 | Olympic Airways *Nereus* |
| | SX-BCL | Boeing 737-284 | Olympic Airways *Isle of Thassos* |
| | SX-BEB | Airbus A.300B4 | Olympic Airways *Odysseus* |
| | SX-BEC | Airbus A.300B4 | Olympic Airways *Achilleus* |
| | SX-BED | Airbus A.300B4 | Olympic Airways *Telemachus* |
| | SX-BEE | Airbus A.300B4 | Olympic Airways *Nestor* |
| | SX-BEF | Airbus A.300B4 | Olympic Airways *Ajax* |
| | SX-BEG | Airbus A.300B4 | Olympic Airways *Diomedes* |
| | SX-BEH | Airbus A.300B4 | Olympic Airways *Peleus* |
| | SX-BEI | Airbus A.300B4 | Olympic Airways *Neoptolemos* |
| | SX-BEK | Airbus A.300-605R | Olympic Airlines *Macedonia* |
| | SX-BEL | Airbus A.300-605R | Olympic Airlines |
| | SX-BEM | Airbus A.300-605R | Olympic Airlines |
| | SX-BEN | Airbus A.300-605R | Olympic Airlines |
| | SX-BKA | Boeing 737-484 | Olympic Airways *Vergina* |
| | SX-BKB | Boeing 737-484 | Olympic Airways *Olynthos* |
| | SX-BKC | Boeing 737-484 | Olympic Airways *Philipoli* |
| | SX-BKD | Boeing 737-484 | Olympic Airways *Amphipoli* |
| | SX-BKE | Boeing 737-484 | Olympic Airways *Stagira* |
| | SX-BKF | Boeing 737-484 | Olympic Airways *Dion* |
| | SX-CBA | Boeing 727-284 | Olympic Airways *Mount Olympus* |
| | SX-CBB | Boeing 727-284 | Olympic Airways *Mount Pindos* |
| | SX-CBC | Boeing 727-284 | Olympic Airways *Mount Parnassus* |
| | SX-CBD | Boeing 727-284 | Olympic Airways *Mount Helicon* |
| | SX-CBE | Boeing 727-284 | Olympic Airways *Mount Athos* |
| | SX-CBF | Boeing 727-284 | Olympic Airways *Mount Taygetus* |
| | SX-CBG | Boeing 727-230 | Olympic Airways *Mount Menalon* |
| | SX-CBH | Boeing 727-230 | Olympic Airways *Mount Vermio* |
| | SX-CBI | Boeing 727-230 | Greek Government (VIP) |
| | SX-OAB | Boeing 747-284B | Olympic Airways *Olympic Eagle* |
| | SX-OAC | Boeing 747-212B | Olympic Airways *Olympic Spirit* |
| | SX-OAD | Boeing 747-212B | Olympic Airways *Olympic Flame* |
| | SX-OAE | Boeing 747-212B | Olympic Airways *Olympic Peace* |

| Reg. | Type | Owner or Operator | Notes |
|---|---|---|---|

## TC (Turkey)

| Reg. | Type | Owner or Operator |
|---|---|---|
| TC-ABA | S.E.210 Caravelle 10B1R | Istanbul Airlines *Mine* |
| TC-ACA | Boeing 737-4Y0 | Istanbul Airlines |
| TC-ADA | Boeing 737-4Y0 | Istanbul Airlines |
| TC-AFM | Boeing 737-4Q8 | Pegasus Airlines |
| TC-AFN | Boeing 727-230 | Istanbul Airlines |
| TC-AFO | Boeing 727-230 | Istanbul Airlines |
| TC-AFP | Boeing 727-230 | Istanbul Airlines |
| TC-AFR | Boeing 727-230 | Istanbul Airlines |
| TC-AFT | Boeing 727-230 | Istanbul Airlines |
| TC-AGA | Boeing 737-4Y0 | Istanbul Airlines |
| TC-AKA | S.E.210 Caravelle 10B1R | Istanbul Airlines *Gül* |
| TC-ALA | S.E.210 Caravelle 10B1R | Istanbul Airlines *Orkide* |
| TC-ALB | Boeing 727-230 | Albatross Air *Tan & Can* |
| TC- | McD Douglas MD-82 | Albatross Air |
| TC- | McD Douglas MD-82 | Albatross Air |
| TC-ALF | Boeing 727-230 | Air Alfa *Sena* |
| TC-ASA | S.E.210 Caravelle 10B1R | Istanbul Airlines *Nergis* |
| TC-CYO | Boeing 737-3H9 | Bosphorus Airways *Hakan* |
| TC-GRA | Tupolev Tu-154M | Greenair *Cappadocia* |
| TC-GRB | Tupolev Tu-154M | Greenair *Perestroika* |
| TC-GRC | Tupolev Tu-154M | Greenair *Fenerbahce* |
| TC-GRD | Tupolev Tu-134A-3 | Greenair *Besiktas* |
| TC-GRE | Tupolev Tu-134A-3 | Greenair *Galatasary* |
| TC-GUL | Boeing 757-225 | Birgenair |
| TC-JAB | Douglas DC-9-32 | Türk Hava Yollari (THY) *Bogazici* |
| TC-JAD | Douglas DC-9-32 | Türk Hava Yollari (THY) *Anadolu* |
| TC-JAE | Douglas DC-9-32 | Türk Hava Yollari (THY) *Trakya* |
| TC-JAF | Douglas DC-9-32 | Türk Hava Yollari (THY) *Ege* |
| TC-JAG | Douglas DC-9-32 | Türk Hava Yollari (THY) *Akdeniz* |
| TC-JAK | Douglas DC-9-32 | Türk Hava Yollari (THY) *Karadeniz* |
| TC-JAL | Douglas DC-9-32 | Türk Hava Yollari (THY) *Halic* |
| TC-JBF | Boeing 727-2F2 | Türk Hava Yollari (THY) *Adana* |
| TC-JBG | Boeing 727-2F2 | Türk Hava Yollari (THY) |
| TC-JBJ | Boeing 727-2F2 | Türk Hava Yollari (THY) *Yaruvatan* |
| TC-JBK | Douglas DC-9-32 | Türk Hava Yollari (THY) *Aydin* |
| TC-JBL | Douglas DC-9-32 | Türk Hava Yollari (THY) *Gediz* |
| TC-JBM | Boeing 727-2F2 | Türk Hava Yollari (THY) *Menderes* |
| TC-JCA | Boeing 727-2F2 | Türk Hava Yollari (THY) *Edirne* |
| TC-JCB | Boeing 727-2F2 | Türk Hava Yollari (THY) *Kars* |
| TC-JCD | Boeing 727-2F2 | Türk Hava Yollari (THY) *Sinop* |
| TC-JCE | Boeing 727-2F2 | Türk Hava Yollari (THY) *Hatay* |
| TC-JCK | Boeing 727-243 | Türk Hava Yollari (THY) *Erciyes* |
| TC-JCL | Airbus A.310-203 | Türk Hava Yollari (THY) *Seyhan* |
| TC-JCM | Airbus A.310-203 | Türk Hava Yollari (THY) *Ceyhan* |
| TC-JCN | Airbus A.310-203 | Türk Hava Yollari (THY) *Dicle* |
| TC-JCO | Airbus A.310-203 | Türk Hava Yollari (THY) *Firat* |
| TC-JCR | Airbus A.310-203 | Türk Hava Yollari (THY) *Kizilirmak* |
| TC-JCS | Airbus A.310-203 | Türk Hava Yollari (THY) *Yesilirmak* |
| TC-JCU | Airbus A.310-203 | Türk Hava Yollari (THY) *Sakarya* |
| TC-JCV | Airbus A.310-304 | Türk Hava Yollari (THY) *Aras* |
| TC-JCY | Airbus A.310-304 | Türk Hava Yollari (THY) *Coruh* |
| TC-JCZ | Airbus A.310-304 | Türk Hava Yollari (THY) *Ergene* |
| TC-JDA | Airbus A.310-304ET | Türk Hava Yollari (THY) *Aksu* |
| TC-JDB | Airbus A.310-304ET | Türk Hava Yollari (THY) *Goksu* |
| TC-JDC | Airbus A.310-304ET | Türk Hava Yollari (THY) *Meric* |
| TC-JDD | Airbus A.310-304ET | Türk Hava Yollari (THY) *Dalaman* |
| TC-JDE | Boeing 737-4Y0 | Türk Hava Yollari (THY) |
| TC-JDF | Boeing 737-4Y0 | Türk Hava Yollari (THY) *Ayvalik* |
| TC-JDG | Boeing 737-4Y0 | Türk Hava Yollari (THY) |
| TC-JDH | Boeing 737-4Y0 | Türk Hava Yollari (THY) |
| TC-JDI | Boeing 737-4Q8 | Türk Hava Yollari (THY) |
| TC-JDT | Boeing 737-4Y0 | Türk Hava Yollari (THY) *Istanbul* |
| TC-JDU | Boeing 737-5Y0 | Türk Hava Yollari (THY) *Bursa* |
| TU-JDV | Boeing 737-5Y0 | Türk Hava Yollari (THY) *Trabzon* |
| TC-JDY | Boeing 737-4Y0 | Türk Hava Yollari (THY) *Ankara* |
| TC-JDZ | Boeing 737-4Y0 | Türk Hava Yollari (THY) *Izmir* |
| TC-JFA | Boeing 727-264 | Türk Hava Yollari (THY) *Ortaköy* |
| TC-JFB | Boeing 727-264 | Türk Hava Yollari (THY) *Vaniköy* |
| TC- | Boeing 747-212B | Türk Hava Yollari (THY) |
| TC-JUP | Boeing 737-205 | Sultan Air |

| Notes | Reg. | Type | Owner or Operator |
|---|---|---|---|
| | TC-JUR | Boeing 737-205 | Sultan Air |
| | TC-JUV | Airbus A.300B4-203 | Sultan Air |
| | TC-MAB | Douglas DC-8-61 | Birgenair |
| | TC-MIO | Boeing 737-3H9 | Bosphorus Airways *Kaan* |
| | TC-ONA | Airbus A.320-211 | Onur Airways |
| | TC-ONB | Airbus A.320-211 | Onur Airways *Ertug* |
| | TC-RTU | McD Douglas MD-83 | TUR European Airways |
| | TC-RUT | Boeing 727-230 | TUR European Airways |
| | TC-SUN | Boeing 737-3Y0 | Sun Express |
| | TC-SUP | Boeing 737-3Y0 | Sun Express |
| | TC-SUR | Boeing 737-3Y0 | Sun Express |
| | TC-TCA | Boeing 727-230 | TUR European Airways |
| | TC-TCB | Boeing 727-230 | TUR European Airways |
| | TC-TRU | McD Douglas MD-83 | TUR European Airways |
| | TC-TUR | Boeing 727-230 | TUR European Airways |
| | TC-VAA | Boeing 737-248 | Sultan Air |
| | TC-VAB | Boeing 737-248 | VIP Air/Sultan Air |

# TF (Iceland)

| | | | |
|---|---|---|---|
| | TF-ABG | L-1011-385 TriStar | Atlanta Icelandic |
| | TF-ABH | Boeing 737-222 | Atlanta Icelandic |
| | TF-ABJ | Boeing 737-201C | Atlanta Icelandic/Finnair Cargo |
| | TF-ABT | Boeing 737-205C | Atlanta Icelandic/Finnair Cargo *Spirit of Nome 1924 Alaska* |
| | TF-FIA | Boeing 737-408 | Icelandair *Aldis* |
| | TF-FIB | Boeing 737-408 | Icelandair *Eydis* |
| | TF-FIC | Boeing 737-408 | Icelandair *Vedis* |
| | TF-FID | Boeing 737-408 | Icelandair |
| | TF-FIH | Boeing 757-208ER | Icelandair *Hafdis* |
| | TF-FII | Boeing 757-208ER | Icelandair *Fanndis* |
| | TF-FIR | Fokker 50 | Icelandair *Asdis* |
| | TF-FIS | Fokker 50 | Icelandair *Sigdis* |
| | TF-FIT | Fokker 50 | Icelandair *Freydis* |
| | TF-FIU | Fokker 50 | Icelandair *Valdis* |

# TJ (Cameroon)

| | | | |
|---|---|---|---|
| | TJ-CAB | Boeing 747-2H7B (SCD) | Cameroon Airlines *Mont Cameroun* |

# TR (Gabon)

| | | | |
|---|---|---|---|
| | TR-LBV | L-100-30 Hercules | Air Gabon Cargo |

**Note:** Air Gabon operates Boeing 747-2Q2B F-ODJG for which the registration TR-LXK has been reserved.

# TS (Tunisia)

| | | | |
|---|---|---|---|
| | TS-IEC | Boeing 737-3H9 | Tunis Air |
| | TS-IED | Boeing 737-3H9 | Tunis Air |
| | TS-IMA | Airbus A.300B4 | Tunis-Air *Amilcar* |
| | TS-IMB | Airbus A.320-211 | Tunis-Air *Fahrat Hached* |
| | TS-IMC | Airbus A.320-211 | Tunis-Air *7 Novembre* |
| | TS-IMD | Airbus A.320-211 | Tunis-Air *Khereddine* |
| | TS-IME | Airbus A.320-211 | Tunis-Air |
| | TS-IMF | Airbus A.320-211 | Tunis Air *Jerba* |
| | TS- | Airbus A.320-211 | Tunis Air |
| | TS-IOC | Boeing 737-2H3 | Tunis-Air *Salammbo* |
| | TS-IOD | Boeing 737-2H3C | Tunis-Air *Bulla Regia* |
| | TS-IOE | Boeing 737-2H3 | Tunis-Air *Zarzis* |
| | TS-IOF | Boeing 737-2H3 | Tunis-Air *Sousse* |
| | TS-IOG | Boeing 737-5H3 | Tunis-Air *Sfax* |
| | TS-IOH | Boeing 737-5H3 | Tunis-Air |
| | TS-JEA | Boeing 727-2H9 | Tunis Air |
| | TS-JEB | Boeing 727-2H9 | Tunis Air |
| | TS-JHN | Boeing 727-2H3 | Tunis-Air *Carthago* |
| | TS-JHQ | Boeing 727-2H3 | Tunis-Air *Tozeur-Nefta* |
| | TS-JHR | Boeing 727-2H3 | Tunis-Air *Bizerte* |
| | TS-JHS | Boeing 727-2H3 | Tunis-Air *Kairouan* |
| | TS-JHT | Boeing 727-2H3 | Tunis-Air *Sidi Bousaid* |
| | TS-JHU | Boeing 727-2H3 | Tunis-Air *Hannibal* |

| Reg. | Type | Owner or Operator | Notes |
|------|------|-------------------|-------|
| TS-JHV | Boeing 727-2H3 | Tunis-Air *Jugurtha* | |
| TS-JHW | Boeing 727-2H3 | Tunis-Air *Ibn Khaldoun* | |

## TU (Ivory Coast)

| | | | |
|------|------|-------------------|-------|
| TU-TAC | Airbus A.310-304 | Air Afrique | |
| TU-TAD | Airbus A.310-304 | Air Afrique | |
| TU-TAE | Airbus A.310-304 | Air Afrique | |
| TU-TAF | Airbus A.310-304 | Air Afrique | |
| TU-TAG | Airbus A.310-304 | Air Afrique | |
| TU-TAL | Douglas DC-10-30 | Air Afrique *Libreville* | |
| TU-TAM | Douglas DC-10-30 | Air Afrique | |
| TU-TAN | Douglas DC-10-30 | Air Afrique *Niamey* | |
| TU-TAO | Airbus A.300B4-203 | Air Afrique *Nouackchott* | |
| TU-TAS | Airbus A.300B4-203 | Air Afrique *Bangui* | |
| TU-TAT | Airbus A.300B4-203 | Air Afrique | |

## UR (Ukraine)

| | | | |
|------|------|-------------------|-------|
| UR-GAA | Boeing 737-4Y0 | Air Ukraine International | |
| UR-GAB | Boeing 737-4Y0 | Air Ukraine International | |

## V2 (Antigua)

**Note:** Seagreen Air Transport operates two Boeing 707s registered N14AZ and N21AZ.

## V5 (Namibia)

| | | | |
|------|------|-------------------|-------|
| V5-SPF | Boeing 747SP-44 | Air Namibia | |

## V8 (Brunei)

| | | | |
|------|------|-------------------|-------|
| V8-RBA | Boeing 757-2M6ER | Royal Brunei Airlines | |
| V8-RBB | Boeing 757-2M6ER | Royal Brunei Airlines | |
| V8-RBC | Boeing 757-2M6ER | Royal Brunei Airlines | |
| V8-RBD | Boeing 767-284ER | Royal Brunei Airlines | |
| V8-RBE | Boeing 767-33AER | Royal Brunei Airlines | |
| V8-RBF | Boeing 767-33AER | Royal Brunei Airlines | |
| V8-RBG | Boeing 767-33AER | Royal Brunei Airlines | |

## VH (Australia)

| | | | |
|------|------|-------------------|-------|
| VH-EBA | Boeing 747-238B | QANTAS Airways *City of Ipswich* | |
| VH-EBQ | Boeing 747-238B | QANTAS Airways *City of Bunbury* | |
| VH-EBR | Boeing 747-238B | QANTAS Airways *City of Mt Gambier* | |
| VH-EBS | Boeing 747-238B | QANTAS Airways *City of Broken Hill* | |
| VH-EBT | Boeing 747-338 | QANTAS Airways *City of Wagga Wagga* | |
| VH-EBU | Boeing 747-338 | QANTAS Airways *City of Warrnambool* | |
| VH-EBV | Boeing 747-338 | QANTAS Airways *Geraldton* | |
| VH-EBW | Boeing 747-338 | QANTAS Airways *City of Tamworth* | |
| VH-EBX | Boeing 747-338 | QANTAS Airways *City of Wodonga* | |
| VH-EBY | Boeing 747-338 | QANTAS Airways *City of Mildura* | |
| VH-OJA | Boeing 747-438 | QANTAS Airways *City of Canberra* | |
| VH-OJB | Boeing 747-438 | QANTAS Airways *City of Sydney* | |
| VH-OJC | Boeing 747-438 | QANTAS Airways *City of Melbourne* | |
| VH-OJD | Boeing 747-438 | QANTAS Airways *City of Brisbane* | |
| VH-OJE | Boeing 747-438 | QANTAS Airways *City of Adelaide* | |
| VH-OJF | Boeing 747-438 | QANTAS Airways *City of Perth* | |
| VH-OJG | Boeing 747-438 | QANTAS Airways *City of Hobart* | |
| VH-OJH | Boeing 747-438 | QANTAS Airways *City of Darwin* | |
| VH-OJI | Boeing 747-438 | QANTAS Airways *Longreach* | |
| VH-OJJ | Boeing 747-438 | QANTAS Airways *Winton* | |
| VH-OJK | Boeing 747-438 | QANTAS Airways *City of Newcastle* | |
| VH-OJL | Boeing 747-438 | QANTAS Airways *City of Sale* | |
| VH-OJM | Boeing 747-438 | QANTAS Airways *City of Gosford* | |
| VH-OJN | Boeing 747-438 | QANTAS Airways *City of Dubbo* | |
| VH-OJO | Boeing 747-438 | QANTAS Airways *City of Toowoomba* | |
| VH-OJP | Boeing 747-438 | QANTAS Airways *City of Albury* | |
| VH-OJQ | Boeing 747-438 | QANTAS Airways *City of Mandurah* | |
| VH-OJR | Boeing 747-438 | QANTAS Airways *City of Bathurst* | |

## VR-H (Hong Kong)

| | | |
|---|---|---|
| VR-HIA | Boeing 747-267B | Cathay Pacific Airways |
| VR-HIB | Boeing 747-267B | Cathay Pacific Airways |
| VR-HIC | Boeing 747-267B | Cathay Pacific Airways |
| VR-HID | Boeing 747-267B | Cathay Pacific Airways |
| VR-HIE | Boeing 747-267B | Cathay Pacific Airways |
| VR-HIF | Boeing 747-267B | Cathay Pacific Airways |
| VR-HIH | Boeing 747-267B (SCD) | Cathay Pacific Cargo |
| VR-HII | Boeing 747-367 | Cathay Pacific Airways |
| VR-HIJ | Boeing 747-367 | Cathay Pacific Airways |
| VR-HIK | Boeing 747-367 | Cathay Pacific Airways |
| VR-HKB | Boeing 747-200 | Air Hong Kong |
| VR-HKG | Boeing 747-267B | Cathay Pacific Airways |
| VR-HKM | Boeing 747-132F | Air Hong Kong |
| VR-HKN | Boeing 747-132F | Air Hong Kong |
| VR-HK | Boeing 747-121F | Air Hong Kong |
| VR-HOL | Boeing 747-367 | Cathay Pacific Airways |
| VR-HOM | Boeing 747-367 | Cathay Pacific Airways |
| VR-HON | Boeing 747-367 | Cathay Pacific Airways |
| VR-HOO | Boeing 747-467 | Cathay Pacific Airways |
| VR-HOP | Boeing 747-467 | Cathay Pacific Airways |
| VR-HOR | Boeing 747-467 | Cathay Pacific Airways |
| VR-HOS | Boeing 747-467 | Cathay Pacific Airways |
| VR-HOT | Boeing 747-467 | Cathay Pacific Airways |
| VR-HOU | Boeing 747-467 | Cathay Pacific Airways |
| VR-HOV | Boeing 747-467 | Cathay Pacific Airways |
| VR-HOW | Boeing 747-467 | Cathay Pacific Airways |
| VR-HOX | Boeing 747-467 | Cathay Pacific Airways |
| VR-HOY | Boeing 747-467 | Cathay Pacific Airways |
| VR-HOZ | Boeing 747-467 | Cathay Pacific Airways |
| VR-HUA | Boeing 747-467 | Cathay Pacific Airways |
| VR-HUB | Boeing 747-467 | Cathay Pacific Airways |
| VR-HUD | Boeing 747-467 | Cathay Pacific Airways |
| VR-HUE | Boeing 747-467 | Cathay Pacific Airways |
| VR-HUF | Boeing 747-467 | Cathay Pacific Airways |
| VR-HUG | Boeing 747-467 | Cathay Pacific Airways |
| VR-HVX | Boeing 747-267F (SCD) | Cathay Pacific Airways |
| VR-HVY | Boeing 747-236F (SCD) | Cathay Pacific Airways *Hong Kong Jumbo* |
| VR-HVZ | Boeing 747-267F (SCD) | Cathay Pacific Airways |

## VT (India)

| | | |
|---|---|---|
| VT-EBE | Boeing 747-237B | Air-India *Shahjehan* |
| VT-EBN | Boeing 747-237B | Air-India *Rajendra Chola* |
| VT-EBO | Boeing 747-237B | Air-India *Vikramaditya* |
| VT-EDU | Boeing 747-237B | Air-India *Akbar* |
| VT-EFJ | Boeing 747-237B | Air-India *Chandragupta* |
| VT-EFU | Boeing 747-237B | Air-India *Krishna Deva Raya* |
| VT-EGA | Boeing 747-237B | Air-India *Samudra Gupta* |
| VT-EGB | Boeing 747-237B | Air-India *Mahendra Varman* |
| VT-EGC | Boeing 747-237B | Air-India *Harsha Vardhana* |
| VT-EJG | Airbus A.310-304 | Air-India *Vamuna* |
| VT-EJH | Airbus A.310-304 | Air-India *Tista* |
| VT-EJI | Airbus A.310-304 | Air-India *Saraswati* |
| VT-EJJ | Airbus A.310-304 | Air-India *Beas* |
| VT-EJK | Airbus A.310-304 | Air-India *Gomti* |
| VT-EJL | Airbus A.310-304 | Air-India *Sabarmati* |
| VT-ENQ | Boeing 747-212B | Air-India *Himalaya* |
| VT-EPW | Boeing 747-337 (SCD) | Air-India *Shivaji* |
| VT-EPX | Boeing 747-337 (SCD) | Air-India *Narasimha Varman* |
| VT-EQS | Airbus A.310-304 | Air-India *Krishna* |
| VT-EQT | Airbus A.310-304 | Air-India *Narmada* |
| VT-ESM | Boeing 747-437 | Air India |

**Note:** Air-India Cargo operates Douglas DC-8s and Boeing 747s on lease from various airlines.

## XA (Mexico)

| | | |
|---|---|---|
| XA-AMR | Douglas DC-10-30 | Aeromexico |
| XA-RIY | Douglas DC-10-30 | Aeromexico *Jose Marie Morelos* |

**Note:** Aeromexico also operates DC-10-30s N8228P *Castillo de Chapultepec* and N417DG *Ciudad de Mexico*.

## XT (Burkina Faso)

| | | | |
|---|---|---|---|
| XT-ABX | Boeing 707-336C | Naganagani | |

## YI (Iraq)

| | | |
|---|---|---|
| YI-AGE | Boeing 707-370C | Iraqi Airways |
| YI-AGF | Boeing 707-370C | Iraqi Airways |
| YI-AGG | Boeing 707-370C | Iraqi Airways |
| YI-AGK | Boeing 727-270 | Iraqi Airways Ninevah |
| YI-AGL | Boeing 727-270 | Iraqi Airways Basrah |
| YI-AGM | Boeing 727-270 | Iraqi Airways Al Habbania |
| YI-AGN | Boeing 747-270C (SCD) | Iraqi Airways Tigris |
| YI-AGO | Boeing 747-270C (SCD) | Iraqi Airways Euphrates |
| YI-AGP | Boeing 747-270C (SCD) | Iraqi Airways Shat-al-Arab |
| YI-AGQ | Boeing 727-270 | Iraqi Airways Ataameem |
| YI-AGR | Boeing 727-270 | Iraqi Airways Babylon |
| YI-AGS | Boeing 727-270 | Iraqi Airways |
| YI-AKO | Ilyushin IL-76M | Iraqi Airways |
| YI-AKQ | Ilyushin IL-76M | Iraqi Airways |
| YI-AKT | Ilyushin IL-76M | Iraqi Airways |
| YI-AKU | Ilyushin IL-76M | Iraqi Airways |
| YI-AKV | Ilyushin IL-76M | Iraqi Airways |
| YI-AKW | Ilyushin IL-76M | Iraqi Airways |
| YI-AKX | Ilyushin IL-76M | Iraqi Airways |
| YI-ALP | Ilyushin IL-76M | Iraqi Airways |
| YI-ALQ | Ilyushin IL-76MD | Iraqi Airways |
| YI-ALR | Ilyushin IL-76MD | Iraqi Airways |
| YI-ALS | Ilyushin IL-76MD | Iraqi Airways |
| YI-ALT | Ilyushin IL-76MD | Iraqi Airways |
| YI-ALU | Ilyushin IL-76MD | Iraqi Airways |
| YI-ALV | Ilyushin IL-76MD | Iraqi Airways |
| YI-ALW | Ilyushin IL-76MD | Iraqi Airways |
| YI-ALX | Ilyushin IL-76MD | Iraqi Airways |
| YI-ANA | Ilyushin IL-76MD | Iraqi Airways |
| YI-ANB | Ilyushin IL-76MD | Iraqi Airways |
| YI-ANC | Ilyushin IL-76MD | Iraqi Airways |
| YI-AND | Ilyushin IL-76MD | Iraqi Airways |
| YI-ANE | Ilyushin IL-76MD | Iraqi Airways |
| YI-ANF | Ilyushin IL-76MD | Iraqi Airways |
| YI-ANG | Ilyushin IL-76MD | Iraqi Airways |
| YI-ANH | Ilyushin IL-76MD | Iraqi Airways |
| YI-ANI | Ilyushin IL-76MD | Iraqi Airways |

## YK (Syria)

| | | |
|---|---|---|
| YK-AGA | Boeing 727-294 | Syrian Arab Airlines October 6 |
| YK-AGB | Boeing 727-294 | Syrian Arab Airlines Damascus |
| YK-AGC | Boeing 727-294 | Syrian Arab Airlines Palmyra |
| YK-AHA | Boeing 747SP-94 | Syrian Arab Airlines 16 Novembre |
| YK-AHB | Boeing 747SP-94 | Syrian Arab Airlines Arab Solidarity |
| YK-AIA | Tupolev Tu-154M | Syrian Arab Airlines |
| YK-AIB | Tupolev Tu-154M | Syrian Arab Airlines |
| YK-AIC | Tupolev Tu-154M | Syrian Arab Airlines |
| YK-ATA | Ilyushin IL-76M | Syrian Arab Airlines |
| YK-ATB | Ilyushin IL-76M | Syrian Arab Airlines |
| YK-ATC | Ilyushin IL-76M | Syrian Arab Airlines |
| YK-ATD | Ilyushin IL-76M | Syrian Arab Airlines |

## YL (Latvia)

| | | |
|---|---|---|
| YL-LAB | Tupolev Tu-154B-2 | Latavio |
| YL-LAE | Tupolev Tu-154B-2 | Baltic International |
| YL-LBI | Tupolev Tu-154B-3 | Latavio |
| YL-LBK | Tupolev Tu-134B-3 | Baltic International |
| YL-LBM | Tupolev Tu-134B-3 | Baltic International |

## YR (Romania)

| | | |
|---|---|---|
| YR-ABA | Boeing 707-3K1C | Tarom |
| YR-ABC | Boeing 707-3K1C | Tarom |

| Notes | Reg. | Type | Owner or Operator |
|---|---|---|---|
| | YR-ABM | Boeing 707-321C | Tarom |
| | YR-ABN | Boeing 707-321C | Tarom |
| | YR-BCI | BAC One-Eleven 525FT | Tarom |
| | YR-BCJ | BAC One-Eleven 525FT | Tarom |
| | YR-BCK | BAC One-Eleven 525FT | Tarom |
| | YR-BCL | BAC One-Eleven 525FT | Tarom/Ryanair Ltd (EI-BVG) |
| | YR-BCN | BAC One-Eleven 525FT | Tarom |
| | YR-BCO | BAC One Eleven 525FT | Tarom |
| | YR-BRA | RomBac One-Eleven 561RC | Tarom |
| | YR-BRB | RomBac One-Eleven 561RC | Tarom/Ryanair Ltd (EI-BSS) |
| | YR-BRC | RomBac One-Eleven 561RC | Tarom |
| | YR-BRD | RomBac One-Eleven 561RC | Tarom |
| | YR-BRF | RomBac One-Eleven 561RC | Tarom |
| | YR-BRG | RomBac One-Eleven 561RC | Tarom/Ryanair Ltd (EI-BVH) |
| | YR- | Boeing 737-38J | Tarom |
| | YR- | Boeing 737-38J | Tarom |
| | YR- | Boeing 737-38J | Tarom |
| | YR- | Boeing 737-38J | Tarom |
| | YR-IMF | Ilyushin IL-18V | Tarom |
| | YR-IMG | Ilyushin IL-18V | Tarom |
| | YR-IMJ | Ilyushin IL-18D | Tarom |
| | YR-IML | Ilyushin IL-18D | Tarom |
| | YR-IRA | Ilyushin IL-62 | Tarom |
| | YR-IRB | Ilyushin IL-62 | Tarom |
| | YR-IRC | Ilyushin IL-62 | Tarom |
| | YR-IRD | Ilyushin IL-62M | Tarom |
| | YR-IRE | Ilyushin IL-62M | Tarom |
| | YR-LCA | Airbus A.310-325 | Tarom *Transilvania* |
| | YR-LCB | Airbus A.310-325 | Tarom *Moldova* |
| | YR-LCC | Airbus A.310-325 | Tarom |
| | YR-TPA | Tupolev Tu-154B | Tarom |
| | YR-TPB | Tupolev Tu-154B | Tarom |
| | YR-TPC | Tupolev Tu-154B | Tarom |
| | YR-TPD | Tupolev Tu-154B | Tarom |
| | YR-TPE | Tupolev Tu-154B-1 | Tarom |
| | YR-TPF | Tupolev Tu-154B-1 | Tarom |
| | YR-TPG | Tupolev Tu-154B-1 | Tarom |
| | YR-TPI | Tupolev Tu-154B-2 | Tarom |
| | YR-TPK | Tupolev Tu-154B-2 | Tarom |
| | YR-TPL | Tupolev Tu-154B-2 | Tarom |

## YU (Yugoslavia)

| | | | |
|---|---|---|---|
| | YU-AHN | Douglas DC-9-32 | Jugoslovenski Aerotransport (JAT) |
| | YU-AHU | Douglas DC-9-32 | JAT |
| | YU-AHV | Douglas DC-9-32 | JAT |
| | YU-AJH | Douglas DC-9-32 | JAT |
| | YU-AJI | Douglas DC-9-32 | JAT |
| | YU-AJJ | Douglas DC-9-32 | JAT |
| | YU-AJK | Douglas DC-9-32 | JAT |
| | YU-AJL | Douglas DC-9-32 | JAT |
| | YU-AJM | Douglas DC-9-32 | JAT |
| | YU-AKB | Boeing 727-2H9 | JAT/Air Commerce |
| | YU-AKD | Boeing 727-2L8 | Aviogenex *Split* |
| | YU-AKE | Boeing 727-2H9 | JAT/Genius Air |
| | YU-AKF | Boeing 727-2H9 | JAT/Genius Air |
| | YU-AKG | Boeing 727-2H9 | JAT |
| | YU-AKH | Boeing 727-2L8 | Aviogenex *Dubrovnik* |
| | YU-AKI | Boeing 727-2H9 | JAT |
| | YU-AKJ | Boeing 727-2H9 | JAT |
| | YU-AKM | Boeing 727-243 | Aviogenex *Pula* |
| | YU-AMB | Douglas DC-10-30 | JAT *Edvard Rusijan* |
| | YU-AND | Boeing 737-3H9 | JAT |
| | YU-ANF | Boeing 737-3H9 | JAT |
| | YU-ANI | Boeing 737-3H9 | JAT |
| | YU-ANK | Boeing 737-3H9 | JAT |
| | YU-ANP | Boeing 737-2K3 | Aviogenex *Zadar* |
| | YU-ANU | Boeing 737-2K3 | Aviogenex *Tivat* |
| | YU-ANV | Boeing 737-3H9 | JAT |
| | YU-AOF | Boeing 737-2K5 | Aviogenex |

**Note:** Both JAT and Aviogenex have been affected by the war in Yugoslavia with aircraft grounded or leased out.

# YV (Venezuela)

| | | |
|---|---|---|
| YV-134C | Douglas DC-10-30 | VIASA |
| YV-135C | Douglas DC-10-30 | VIASA |
| YV-136C | Douglas DC-10-30 | VIASA |
| YV-137C | Douglas DC-10-30 | VIASA |
| YV-138C | Douglas DC-10-30 | VIASA |

# Z (Zimbabwe)

| | | |
|---|---|---|
| Z-WKS | Boeing 707-330B | Air Zimbabwe |
| Z-WKU | Boeing 707-330B | Air Zimbabwe |
| Z-WMJ | Douglas DC-8-55F | Affretair *Captain Jack Malloch* |
| Z-WPE | Boeing 767-2N0ER | Air Zimbabwe *Victoria Falls* |
| Z-WPF | Boeing 767-2N0ER | Air Zimbabwe *Chimanimani* |
| Z-WSB | Douglas DC-8-55F | Affretair |

# ZK (New Zealand)

| | | |
|---|---|---|
| ZK-NBS | Boeing 747-419 | Air New Zealand *Mataatua* |
| ZK-NBT | Boeing 747-419 | Air New Zealand |
| ZK-NBU | Boeing 747-419 | Air New Zealand |
| ZK-NZV | Boeing 747-219B | Air New Zealand *Aotea* |
| ZK-NZW | Boeing 747-219B | Air New Zealand *Tainui* |
| ZK-NZY | Boeing 747-219B | Air New Zealand *Te Arawa* |
| ZK-NZZ | Boeing 747-219B | Air New Zealand |

# ZP (Paraguay)

| | | |
|---|---|---|
| ZP-CCE | Boeing 707-321B | Lineas Aéreas Paraguayas |
| ZP-CCF | Boeing 707-321B | Lineas Aéreas Paraguayas |
| ZP-CCG | Boeing 707-321B | Lineas Aéreas Paraguayas |
| ZP-CCH | Douglas DC-8-63 | Lineas Aéreas Paraguayas |

# ZS (South Africa)

| | | |
|---|---|---|
| ZS-SAL | Boeing 747-244B | South African Airways *Tafelberg* |
| ZS-SAM | Boeing 747-244B | South African Airways *Drakensberg* |
| ZS-SAN | Boeing 747-244B | South African Airways *Lebombo* |
| ZS-SAO | Boeing 747-244B | South African Airways *Magaliesberg* |
| ZS-SAP | Boeing 747-244B | South African Airways *Swartberg* |
| ZS-SAR | Boeing 747-244B (SCD) | South African Airways *Waterberg* |
| ZS-SAT | Boeing 747-344 | South African Airways *Johannesburg* |
| ZS-SAU | Boeing 747-344 | South African Airways *Cape Town* |
| ZS-SAV | Boeing 747-444 | South African Airways *Durban* |
| ZS-SAW | Boeing 747-444 | South African Airways *Bloemfontein* |
| ZS-SAX | Boeing 747-444 | South African Airways |
| ZS-SPE | Boeing 747-SP-44 | South African Airways |

# 3B (Mauritius)

| | | |
|---|---|---|
| 3B-NAG | Boeing 747SP-44 | Air Mauritius *Chateau du Reduit* |
| 3B-NAJ | Boeing 747SP-44 | Air Mauritius *Chateau Mon Plaisir* |
| 3B-NAK | Boeing 767-23BER | Air Mauritius *City of Curepipe* |
| 3B-NAL | Boeing 767-23BER | Air Mauritius *City of Port Louis* |
| 3B-NAQ | Boeing 747SP-27 | Air Mauritius *Chateau Benares* |

# 3D (Swaziland)

| | | |
|---|---|---|
| 3D-ASB | Boeing 707-323C | Air Swazi Cargo |

# 4R (Sri Lanka)

| | | |
|---|---|---|
| 4R-ULA | L.1011-385 TriStar 500 | Air Lanka |
| 4R-ULB | L.1011-385 TriStar 500 | Air Lanka |
| 4R-ULC | L.1011-385 TriStar 100 | Air Lanka *City of Jayawardanapura* |
| 4R-ULE | L.1011-385 TriStar 50 | Air Lanka *City of Ratnapura* |

| Notes | Reg. | Type | Owner or Operator |
|---|---|---|---|
| | 4R-ULM | L.1011-385 TriStar 200 | Air Lanka |
| | 4R-ULN | L.1011-385 TriStar 200 | Air Lanka |

## 4X (Israel)

| Reg. | Type | Owner or Operator |
|---|---|---|
| 4X-ABN | Boeing 737-258 | El Al/Arkia |
| 4X-ABO | Boeing 737-258 | El Al/Arkia |
| 4X-ATF | Boeing 707-321B | Arkia |
| 4X-ATX | Boeing 707-358C | El Al/Arkia |
| 4X-AXA | Boeing 747-258B | El Al |
| 4X-AXB | Boeing 747-258B | El Al |
| 4X-AXC | Boeing 747-258B | El Al |
| 4X-AXD | Boeing 747-258C | El Al Cargo Air Lines |
| 4X-AXF | Boeing 747-258C | El Al |
| 4X-AXH | Boeing 747-258B | El Al |
| 4X-AXQ | Boeing 747-238B | El Al |
| 4X-AXZ | Boeing 747-124F (SCD) | El Al |
| 4X-EAA | Boeing 767-258 | El Al |
| 4X-EAB | Boeing 767-258 | El Al |
| 4X-EAC | Boeing 767-258ER | El Al |
| 4X-EAD | Boeing 767-258ER | El Al |
| 4X-EBL | Boeing 757-258 | El Al |
| 4X-EBM | Boeing 757-258 | El Al |
| 4X-EBR | Boeing 757-258 | El Al |
| 4X-EBS | Boeing 757-258ER | El Al |
| 4X-EBT | Boeing 757-258ER | El Al |
| 4X-EBU | Boeing 757-258 | El Al |
| 4X-EBV | Boeing 757-258 | El Al |
| 4X-ELA | Boeing 747-458 | El Al |
| 4X-ELB | Boeing 747-458 | El Al |

## 5A (Libya)

| Reg. | Type | Owner or Operator |
|---|---|---|
| 5A-DAI | Boeing 727-224 | Libyan Arab Airlines |
| 5A-DAK | Boeing 707-3L5C | Libyan Arab Airlines |
| 5A-DIB | Boeing 727-2L5 | Libyan Arab Airlines |
| 5A-DIC | Boeing 727-2L5 | Libyan Arab Airlines |
| 5A-DID | Boeing 727-2L5 | Libyan Arab Airlines |
| 5A-DIE | Boeing 727-2L5 | Libyan Arab Airlines |
| 5A-DIF | Boeing 727-2L5 | Libyan Arab Airlines |
| 5A-DIG | Boeing 727-2L5 | Libyan Arab Airlines |
| 5A-DIH | Boeing 727-2L5 | Libyan Arab Airlines |
| 5A-DII | Boeing 727-2L5 | Libyan Arab Airlines |
| 5A-DJM | Boeing 707-321B | Libyan Arab Airlines |
| 5A-DJU | Boeing 707-351C | Libyan Arab Airlines |

**Note:** Services to the UK suspended.

## 5B (Cyprus)

| Reg. | Type | Owner or Operator |
|---|---|---|
| 5B-DAG | BAC One Eleven 537GF | Cyprus Airways |
| 5B-DAH | BAC One Eleven 537GF | Cyprus Airways |
| 5B-DAJ | BAC One Eleven 537GF | Cyprus Airways |
| 5B-DAQ | Airbus A.310-203 | Cyprus Airways Soli |
| 5B-DAR | Airbus A.310-203 | Cyprus Airways |
| 5B-DAS | Airbus A.310-203 | Cyprus Airways Salamis |
| 5B-DAT | Airbus A.320-231 | Cyprus Airways Praxandros |
| 5B-DAU | Airbus A.320-231 | Cyprus Airways |
| 5B-DAV | Airbus A.320-231 | Cyprus Airways Kinyras |
| 5B-DAW | Airbus A.320-231 | Cyprus Airways Agapinor |
| 5B-DAX | Airbus A.310-204 | Cyprus Airways Engomi |
| 5B-DAZ | Boeing 707-328C | Avistar/Tramson Airlines |
| 5B-DBA | Airbus A.320-231 | Cyprus Airways Evagoras |
| 5B-DBB | Airbus A.320-231 | Eurocypria Airways Akamas |
| 5B-DBC | Airbus A.320-231 | Eurocypria Airways |
| 5B-DBD | Airbus A.320-231 | Cyprus Airways |

## 5N (Nigeria)

| Reg. | Type | Owner or Operator |
|---|---|---|
| 5N-ABK | Boeing 707-3F9C | Nigeria Airways |
| 5N-ANN | Douglas DC-10-30 | Nigeria Airways Yunkari |

| Reg. | Type | Owner or Operator | Notes |
|------|------|-------------------|-------|
| 5N-AOM | BAC One-Eleven 420EL | Okada Air | |
| 5N-AOP | BAC One-Eleven 320AZ | Okada Air | |
| 5N-AOQ | Boeing 707-355C | Okada Air | |
| 5N-AOS | BAC One-Eleven 420EL | Okada Air | |
| 5N-AOZ | BAC One-Eleven 320AZ | Okada Air | |
| 5N-ARQ | Boeing 707-338C | DAS Air Cargo | |
| 5N-ATY | Douglas DC-8-55F | Flash Airlines | |
| 5N-ATZ | Douglas DC-8-55F | Flash Airlines | |
| 5N-AUE | Airbus A.310-222 | Nigeria Airways *River Yobe* | |
| 5N-AUF | Airbus A.310-222 | Nigeria Airways | |
| 5N-AUG | Airbus A.310-222 | Nigeria Airways *Lekki Peninsula* | |
| 5N-AUH | Airbus A.310-222 | Nigeria Airways *Rima River* | |
| 5N-AWE | Douglas DC-8-55F | Kabo Air | |
| 5N-AWO | Boeing 707-321C | G.A.S. Air | |
| 5N-AXQ | BAC One-Eleven 432FD | Okada Air | |
| 5N-AYR | BAC One-Eleven 409AY | Okada Air | |
| 5N-AYS | BAC One-Eleven 416EK | Okada Air | |
| 5N-AYT | BAC One-Eleven 416EK | Okada Air | |
| 5N-AYU | BAC One-Eleven 401AK | Okada Air | |
| 5N-AYV | BAC One-Eleven 408EF | Okada Air | |
| 5N-BBB | L.1011-385 TriStar 100 | ADC Airlines | |
| 5N-BIN | BAC One-Eleven 539GL | Okada Air | |
| 5N-EDO | Boeing 747-146 | Okada Air | |
| 5N-EHI | BAC One-Eleven 401AK | Okada Air | |
| 5N-JIL | Boeing 707-351C | Foremost Aviation | |
| 5N-MZE | BAC One-Eleven 304AX | Okada Air | |
| 5N-NRC | BAC One-Eleven 217EA | Okada Air | |
| 5N-OKA | BAC One-Eleven 424EU | Okada Air | |
| 5N-OMO | BAC One-Eleven 301AG | Okada Air | |
| 5N-ORO | BAC One-Eleven 539GL | Okada Air | |
| 5N-OSA | BAC One-Eleven 510ED | Okada Air | |
| 5N-OVE | BAC One-Eleven 304AX | Okada Air | |
| 5N-SDP | BAC One-Eleven 217EA | Okada Air | |
| 5N-USE | BAC One-Eleven 510ED | Okada Air | |

**Note:** Nigeria Airways operates a DC-10-30 which retains its US identity N3024W (5N-AUI reserved)

# 5R (Madagascar)

| | | |
|------|------|------|
| 5R-MFT | Boeing 747-2B2B (SCD) | Air Madagascar *Tolom Piavotana* |

# 5X (Uganda)

| | | |
|------|------|------|
| 5X-UCF | L-100-30 Hercules | Uganda Air Cargo *The Silver Lady* |
| 5X-UCM | Boeing 707-324C | Uganda Airlines |

# 5Y (Kenya)

| | | |
|------|------|------|
| 5Y-ANA | Boeing 707-328C | Yana Air Cargo |
| 5Y-AXM | Boeing 707-330B | African Airlines International |
| 5Y-AXW | Boeing 707-321B | African Airlines International |
| 5Y-BEL | Airbus A.310-304 | Kenya Airways *Nyayo Star* |
| 5Y-BEN | Airbus A.310-304 | Kenya Airways *Harambee Star* |
| 5Y-BFT | Airbus A.310-304 | Kenya Airways *Uhuru Star* |
| 5Y-BGI | Boeing 757-23A | Kenya Airways *Jamhuri Star* |
| 5Y-BHG | Boeing 757-23A | Kenya Airways *Umoja Star* |
| 5Y-ZEB | Douglas DC-8-63 | African Safari Airways |

**Note:** African Safari also operates DC-8-63 which carries the registration HB-IBF.

# 6O (Somalia)

| | | |
|------|------|------|
| 6O-SHH | Airbus A.310-304 | Somali Airlines |

**Note:** The A.310 may retain its French identity F-ODSV

# 6Y (Jamaica)

**Note:** Air Jamaica operates its UK services jointly with British Airways.

# 7O (Yemen)

| | | |
|------|------|------|
| 7O-ACT | Tupolev Tu-154M | Alyemda |
| 7O-ACV | Boeing 727-2N8 | Yemenia |
| 7O-ACW | Boeing 727-2N8 | Yemenia |

| Notes | Reg. | Type | Owner or Operator |
|-------|------|------|-------------------|
| | 7O-ACX | Boeing 727-2N8 | Yemenia |
| | 7O-ACY | Boeing 727-2N8 | Yemenia |
| | 7O-ADA | Boeing 727-2N8 | Yemenia |

## 7T (Algeria)

| | | | |
|-------|------|------|-------------------|
| | 7T-VEA | Boeing 727-2D6 | Air Algerie *Tassili* |
| | 7T-VEB | Boeing 727-2D6 | Air Algerie *Hoggar* |
| | 7T-VED | Boeing 737-2D6C | Air Algerie *Atlas Saharien* |
| | 7T-VEE | Boeing 737-2D6C | Air Algerie *Oasis* |
| | 7T-VEF | Boeing 737-2D6 | Air Algerie *Saoura* |
| | 7T-VEG | Boeing 737-2D6 | Air Algerie *Monts des Ouleds Neils* |
| | 7T-VEH | Boeing 737-2D6 | Air Algerie *Lalla Khadidja* |
| | 7T-VEI | Boeing 727-2D6 | Air Algerie *Djebel Amour* |
| | 7T-VEJ | Boeing 737-2D6 | Air Algerie *Chrea* |
| | 7T-VEK | Boeing 737-2D6 | Air Algerie *Edough* |
| | 7T-VEL | Boeing 737-2D6 | Air Algerie *Akfadou* |
| | 7T-VEM | Boeing 727-2D6 | Air Algerie *Mont du Ksall* |
| | 7T-VEN | Boeing 737-2D6 | Air Algerie *La Soummam* |
| | 7T-VEO | Boeing 737-2D6 | Air Algerie *La Titteri* |
| | 7T-VEP | Boeing 727-2D6 | Air Algerie *Mont du Tessala* |
| | 7T-VEQ | Boeing 727-2D6 | Air Algerie *Le Zaccar* |
| | 7T-VER | Boeing 727-2D6 | Air Algerie *Le Souf* |
| | 7T-VES | Boeing 737-2D6C | Air Algerie *Le Tadmaït* |
| | 7T-VET | Boeing 727-2D6 | Air Algerie *Georges du Rhumel* |
| | 7T-VEU | Boeing 727-2D6 | Air Algerie *Djurdjura* |
| | 7T-VEV | Boeing 727-2D6 | Air Algerie |
| | 7T-VEW | Boeing 727-2D6 | Air Algerie |
| | 7T-VEX | Boeing 727-2D6 | Air Algerie *Djemila* |
| | 7T-VEY | Boeing 737-2D6 | Air Algerie *Rhoufi* |
| | 7T-VEZ | Boeing 737-2T4 | Air Algerie *Monts du Daia* |
| | 7T-VJA | Boeing 737-2T4 | Air Algerie *Monts des Babors* |
| | 7T-VJB | Boeing 737-2T4 | Air Algerie *Monts des Bibons* |
| | 7T-VJC | Airbus A.310-203 | Air Algerie |
| | 7T-VJD | Airbus A.310-203 | Air Algerie |
| | 7T-VJE | Airbus A.310-203 | Air Algerie/Libyan Arab |
| | 7T-VJF | Airbus A.310-203 | Air Algerie/Libyan Arab |
| | 7T-VJG | Boeing 767-3D6 | Air Algerie |
| | 7T-VJH | Boeing 767-3D6 | Air Algerie |
| | 7T-VJI | Boeing 767-3D6 | Air Algerie |

## 9A (Croatia)

| | | | |
|-------|------|------|-------------------|
| | 9A-CTA | Boeing 737-230 | Croatia Airlines |
| | 9A-CTB | Boeing 737-230 | Croatia Airlines |
| | 9A-CTC | Boeing 737-230 | Croatia Airlines |
| | 9A- | Boeing 737- | Croatia Airlines |
| | 9A- | Boeing 737- | Croatia Airlines |
| | 9A- | Boeing 737- | Croatia Airlines |
| | 9A- | Douglas DC-10-30 | Croatia Airlines |
| | 9A- | Douglas DC-10-30 | Croatia Airlines |

## 9G (Ghana)

| | | | |
|-------|------|------|-------------------|
| | 9G-ADM | Boeing 707-321C | African Airlines International |
| | 9G-ANA | Douglas DC-10-30 | Ghana Airways |
| | 9G-MKA | Douglas DC-8-55F | MK Air Cargo |
| | 9G-ONE | Boeing 707-379C | Phoenix Aviation |
| | 9G-TWO | Boeing 707-336C | Phoenix Aviation |

## 9H (Malta)

| | | | |
|-------|------|------|-------------------|
| | 9H-ABA | Boeing 737-2Y5 | Air Malta *Manuel de Vilhena* |
| | 9H-ABC | Boeing 737-2Y5 | Air Malta *Claude de la Sengle* |
| | 9H-ABF | Boeing 737-2Y5 | Air Malta *Manuel Pinto* |
| | 9H-ABG | Boeing 737-2Y5 | Air Malta *Jean de Lavalette* |
| | 9H-ABP | Airbus A.320-211 | Air Malta *Nicholas de Cottoner* |
| | 9H-ABQ | Airbus A.320-211 | Air Malta *Hughes Loubenx de Verdelle* |
| | 9H-ABR | Boeing 737-5Y5 | Air Malta |
| | 9H-ABS | Boeing 737-5Y5 | Air Malta |
| | 9H-ABT | Boeing 737-5Y5 | Air Malta |

**Note:** Air Malta also operates other aircraft on lease during the summer.

| Reg. | Type | Owner or Operator | Notes |
|------|------|-------------------|-------|

# 9J (Zambia)

| | | |
|---|---|---|
| 9J-AFL | Douglas DC-8-71 | Zambia Airways |
| 9J-AFO | Boeing 757-23APF | Zambia Airways |

**Note:** Zambia Airways operates DC-10-30 N3016Z *Nkwazi* on lease.

# 9K (Kuwait)

| | | |
|---|---|---|
| 9K-ADA | Boeing 747-269B (SCD) | Kuwait Airways *Al Sabahiya* |
| 9K-ADB | Boeing 747-269B (SCD) | Kuwait Airways *Al Jaberiya* |
| 9K-ADC | Boeing 747-269B (SCD) | Kuwait Airways *Al Murbarakiya* |
| 9K-ADD | Boeing 747-269B (SCD) | Kuwait Airways *Al Salmiya* |
| 9K-AHA | Airbus A.310-222 | Kuwait Airways *Al-Jahra* |
| 9K-AHB | Airbus A.310-222 | Kuwait Airways *Gharnada* |
| 9K-AHC | Airbus A.310-222 | Kuwait Airways *Kadhma* |
| 9K-AHD | Airbus A.310-222 | Kuwait Airways *Failaka* |
| 9K-AHE | Airbus A.310-222 | Kuwait Airways *Burghan* |
| 9K-AHI | Airbus A.300-620C | Kuwait Airways *Ali-Rawdhatain* |
| 9K-AIA | Boeing 767-269ER | Kuwait Airways *Alriggah* |
| 9K-AIC | Boeing 767-269ER | Kuwait Airways *Garouh* |
| 9K-ALC | Airbus A.310-308 | Kuwait Airways |
| 9K-A | Airbus A.310-308 | Kuwait Airways |
| 9K-AMA | Airbus A.300-605R | Kuwait Airways |
| 9K-A | Airbus A.300-605R | Kuwait Airways |
| 9K-A | Airbus A.300-605R | Kuwait Airways |

**Note:** Five A.310s registered A6-KUA, A6-KUB, A6-KUC, A6-KUD and A6-KUE are also operated by Kuwait Airways.

# 9M (Malaysia)

| | | |
|---|---|---|
| 9M-MHG | Boeing 747-219B | Malaysian Airliine System |
| 9M-MHI | Boeing 747-236B | Malaysian Airline System |
| 9M-MHJ | Boeing 747-236B | Malaysian Airline System |
| 9M-MHK | Boeing 747-3H6 (SCD) | Malaysian Airline System |
| 9M-MHL | Boeing 747-4H6 (SCD) | Malaysian Airline System |
| 9M-MHM | Boeing 747-4H6 (SCD) | Malaysian Airline System |
| 9M-MHN | Boeing 747-4H6 | Malaysian Airline System |
| 9M-MHO | Boeing 747-4H6 | Malaysian Airline System *Alor Setar* |
| 9M-MPA | Boeing 747-4H6 | Malaysian Airline System |
| 9M-MPB | Boeing 747-4H6 | Malaysian Airline System |
| 9M-MPC | Boeing 747-4H6 | Malaysian Airline System |
| 9M-MPD | Boeing 747-4H6 | Malaysian Airline System |
| 9M-MPE | Boeing 747-4H6 | Malaysian Airline System |
| 9M-MPF | Boeing 747-4H6 | Malaysian Airline System |

# 9N (Nepal)

| | | |
|---|---|---|
| 9N-ACA | Boeing 757-2F8 | Royal Nepal Airlines |
| 9N-ACB | Boeing 757-2F8C | Royal Nepal Airlines *Gandaki* |

# 9Q (Zaïre)

| | | |
|---|---|---|
| 9Q-CBW | Boeing 707-329C | Scibe Airlift Zaïre |
| 9Q-CJW | Boeing 707-321C | ACS Air Charter |
| 9Q-CLI | Douglas DC-10-30 | Air Zaïre *Mont Ngaliema* |
| 9Q-CLV | Douglas DC-8-54F | Air Zaïre |
| 9Q-CSB | Boeing 707-373C | Sicotra Aviation |
| 9Q-CTK | Boeing 707-436 | ACS Air Charter |
| 9Q-CVH | Douglas DC-8-55F | ACS Air Charter |

# 9V (Singapore)

| | | |
|---|---|---|
| 9V-SKA | Boeing 747-312 | Singapore Airlines |
| 9V-SKD | Boeing 747-312 | Singapore Airlines |
| 9V-SKM | Boeing 747-312 (SCD) | Singapore Airlines |
| 9V-SKN | Boeing 747-312 (SCD) | Singapore Airlines |
| 9V-SKP | Boeing 747-312 (SCD) | Singapore Airlines |
| 9V-SKQ | Boeing 747-212F (SCD) | Singapore Airlines |
| 9V-SMA | Boeing 747-412 | Singapore Airlines |

| Notes | Reg. | Type | Owner or Operator |
|---|---|---|---|
| | 9V-SMB | Boeing 747-412 | Singapore Airlines |
| | 9V-SMC | Boeing 747-412 | Singapore Airlines |
| | 9V-SMD | Boeing 747-412 | Singapore Airlines |
| | 9V-SME | Boeing 747-412 | Singapore Airlines |
| | 9V-SMF | Boeing 747-412 | Singapore Airlines |
| | 9V-SMG | Boeing 747-412 | Singapore Airlines |
| | 9V-SMH | Boeing 747-412 | Singapore Airlines |
| | 9V-SMI | Boeing 747-412 | Singapore Airlines |
| | 9V-SMJ | Boeing 747-412 | Singapore Airlines |
| | 9V-SMK | Boeing 747-412 | Singapore Airlines |
| | 9V-SML | Boeing 747-412 | Singapore Airlines |
| | 9V-SMM | Boeing 747-412 | Singapore Airlines |
| | 9V-SMN | Boeing 747-412 | Singapore Airlines |
| | 9V-SMO | Boeing 747-412 | Singapore Airlines |
| | 9V-SMP | Boeing 747-412 | Singapore Airlines |
| | 9V-SMQ | Boeing 747-412 | Singapore Airlines |
| | 9V-SMR | Boeing 747-412 | Singapore Airlines |
| | 9V-SMS | Boeing 747-412 | Singapore Airlines |
| | 9V-SMT | Boeing 747-412 | Singapore Airlines |
| | 9V-SMU | Boeing 747-412 | Singapore Airlines |
| | 9V-SMV | Boeing 747-412 | Singapore Airlines |
| | 9V-SMW | Boeing 747-412 | Singapore Airlines |
| | 9V-SQP | Boeing 747-212B | Singapore Airlines |
| | 9V-SQQ | Boeing 747-212B | Singapore Airlines |
| | 9V-SQR | Boeing 747-212B | Singapore Airlines |
| | 9V-SQS | Boeing 747-212B | Singapore Airlines |
| | 9V-SQT | Boeing 747-245F (SCD) | Singapore Airlines |
| | 9V-SQU | Boeing 747-245F (SCD) | Singapore Airlines |

**Note:** Singapore Airlines also operates Boeing 747-312 N116KB, N117KC, N119KE, N120KF, N121KG, N122KH, N123KJ, N124KK and N125KL.

# 9XR (Rwanda)

| | | | |
|---|---|---|---|
| 9XR-JA | Boeing 707-328C | | Air Rwanda |

# 9Y (Trinidad and Tobago)

| | | | |
|---|---|---|---|
| 9Y-TGJ | L.1011 TriStar 500 (595) | | B.W.I.A. *Flamingo* |
| 9Y-TGN | L.1011 TriStar 500 (596) | | B.W.I.A. |
| 9Y-THA | L.1011 TriStar 500 (597) | | B.W.I.A. |

**Note:** B.W.I.A. also operates a TriStar 500 which retains its US registration N3140D (598).

# Overseas Registrations

Aircraft included in this section are those based in the UK but which retain their non-British identities.

| Reg. | Type | Owner or Operator | Notes |
|------|------|-------------------|-------|
| A40-AB | V.1103 VC10 ★ | Brooklands Museum (G-ASIX) | |
| CF-EQS | Boeing-Stearman PT-17 ★ | Imperial War Museum/Duxford | |
| CF-KCG | Grumman TBM-3E Avenger AS.3★ | Imperial War Museum/Duxford | |
| D-HMQV | Bolkow Bo 102 ★ | International Helicopter Museum (IHM)/ Weston-s-Mare | |
| D-IFSB | D.H.104 Dove 6★ | Mosquito Aircraft Museum | |
| F-BDRS | Boeing B-17G (231983) ★ | Imperial War Museum/Duxford | |
| F-BMCY | Potez 840° | Sumburgh Fire Service | |
| N1MF | Cessna 421B | Pelmont Aviation Inc/Cranfield | |
| N2FU | Learjet 35A | Motor Racing Developments Inc | |
| N14KH | Christen Eagle II | R. Frohmayer | |
| N15AW | Cessna 500 Citation | A. W. Alloys Ltd | |
| N15SC | Learjet 35A | Sea Containers Associates/Luton | |
| N18E | Boeing 247D ★ | Science Museum/Wroughton | |
| N18V | Beech D.17S Traveler (PB1) | R. Lamplough | |
| N33VC | Lockheed T-33A (54-21261) | Old Flying Machine Co/Duxford | |
| N34AB | Beech T-34 Mentor | Warbirds of GB Ltd | |
| N47DD | Republic P-47D Thunderbolt (45-49192)★ | Imperial War Museum/Duxford | |
| N49UR | Canadair CL.601 Challenger | Kingson Corporation | |
| N51RR | P-51D Mustang (474008) | D. Gilmour/North Weald | |
| N59NA | Douglas C-47A | Aces High Ltd (G-AKNB)/North Weald | |
| N71AF | R. Commander 680W | Metropolitan Aviation | |
| N153JS | Nieuport 24 (replica) | A. E. Hutton/North Weald | |
| N154JS | Airco D.H.5 (replica) | A. E. Hutton/North Weald | |
| N158C | S.24 Sandringham (VH-BRC) ★ | Southampton Hall of Aviation | |
| N167F | P-51D Mustang (473877) | RLS 51 Ltd/Duxford | |
| N179NP | Vought F4U-7 Corsair | D. W. Arnold/Biggin Hill | |
| N232J | Hawker Sea Fury FB.11 | R. Lamplough/North Weald | |
| N240CA | F-4U-4B Corsair (NZ5628) | R. Hanna/Duxford | |
| N260QB | Pitts S-2S Special | D. Baker | |
| N365F | Hawker Sea Fury FB.10 | J. Bradshaw | |
| N416FS | F-100F Super Sabre | Flight Refuelling Ltd/Bournemouth | |
| N417FS | F-100F Super Sabre | Flight Refuelling Ltd/Bournemouth | |
| N418FS | F-100F Super Sabre | Flight Refuelling Ltd/Bournemouth | |
| N425EE | Cessna 425 | J. W. MacDonald | |
| N444M | Grumman G.44 Widgeon (1411) | M. Dunkerley/Biggin Hill | |
| N490CC | Cessna 551 Citation II | A. W. Alloys Ltd | |
| N500LN | Howard 500 | D. Baker | |
| N535SM | R. Commander 680 | J. E. Tuberty | |
| N707TJ | Boeing Stearman A.75N1 | V. S. E. Norman (Crunchie) | |
| N903FR | Dassault Falcon 20DC | Flight Refuelling Ltd/Bournemouth | |
| N904FR | Dassault Falcon 20DC | Flight Refuelling Ltd/Bournemouth | |
| N907FR | Dassault Falcon 20DC | Flight Refuelling Ltd/Bournemouth | |
| N908FR | Dassault Falcon 20DC | Flight Refuelling Ltd/Bournemouth | |
| N909FR | Dassault Falcon 20DC | Flight Refuelling Ltd/Bournemouth | |
| N909WJ | FM-2 Wildcat | D. W. Arnold/Biggin Hill | |
| N999PJ | M.S.760 Paris 2 | Aces High Ltd/North Weald | |
| N1042B | B-25J Mitchell (430823) | Aces High Ltd/North Weald | |
| N1051S | P-51D-25-NA Mustang (511371) | Myrick Aviation/Leavesden | |
| N1344 | Ryan PT-22 | H. Mitchell | |
| N1447C | Cessna 150L | US Embassy Flying Club/Denham | |
| N1755C | Cessna 180 | Alconbury Aero Club | |
| N2700 | Fairchild C-119G | Aces High Ltd (G-BLSW)/North Weald | |
| N2929W | PA-28-151 Warrior | R. Lobell | |
| N3145X | P-38J Lightning (67543) | Fighter Collection/Duxford | |
| N3600X | Dassault Falcon 10 | Xerox Corporation/Heathrow | |
| N3851Q | Cessna 172K | Bentwaters Aero Club/Woodbridge | |
| N3983N | Agusta A.109A | NSM Aviation | |
| N4151D | TF-51D Mustang | Warbirds of GB Ltd | |
| N4306Z | PA-28 -161 Warrior II | USAF Aero Club/Upper Heyford | |
| N4565L | Douglas DC.3 | Hibernian Dakota Flight Ltd/Ipswich | |
| N4596N | Boeing Stearman PT-13D | N. Mason & D. Gilmour/North Weald | |
| N4712V | Boeing Stearman PT-13D | Wessex Aviation & Transport Ltd | |
| N4727V | Spad S.VII (S4523) | Imperial War Museum/Duxford | |
| N4806E | Douglas A-26C Invader ★ | R. & R. Cadman/Southend | |
| N5063N | Beech D.18S (HB275) | Harvard Formation Team (G-BKGM) | |
| N5237V | Boeing B-17G (483868) ★ | RAF Museum/Hendon | |
| N5824H | PA-38 Tomahawk | Lakenheath Aero Club | |
| N6178C | F7F-3 Tigercat | Planesailing Air Displays/Duxford | |

307

| Notes | Reg. | Type | Owner or Operator |
|---|---|---|---|
| | N6268 | Travel Air Model 2000 | Personal Plane Services Ltd |
| | N6526D | P-51D Mustang ★ | RAF Museum/Henlow |
| | N7614C | B-25J Mitchell | Imperial War Museum/Duxford |
| | N7777G | L.749A Constellation ★ | Science Museum (G-CONI)/Wroughton |
| | N8155E | Mooney M.20A | D. Skans |
| | N8389H | Beech C-45 | Bar-Belle Aviation Ltd |
| | N9043 | Stolp SA.301 Starduster Too | J. McTaggart |
| | N9089Z | TB-25J Mitchell (44-30861)★ | Aces High Ltd (G-BKXW)/North Weald |
| | N9115Z | TB-25N Mitchell (34037) ★ | RAF Museum/Hendon |
| | N9606H | Fairchild M.62A Cornell ★ | Rebel Air Museum/Earls Colne |
| | N9950 | P-40N Kittyhawk | D. W. Arnold/Biggin Hill |
| | N26178 | Cessna 550 Citation II | A. W. Alloys Ltd |
| | N26634 | PA-24 Comanche 250 | P. Biggs (G-BFKR) |
| | N30228 | Piper J-3C-65 Cub | C. Morris |
| | N33600 | Cessna L-19A Bird Dog (111989) ★ | Museum of Army Flying/Middle Wallop |
| | N43069 | PA-28-161 Warrior II | Lakenheath Aero Club |
| | N49272 | Ryan PT-23 (23) | H. Mitchell |
| | N50993 | Ryan PT-22 | V. S. E. Norman |
| | N53091 | Boeing Stearman A.75N1 | Eastern Stearman Ltd |
| | N53127 | Boeing Stearman A.75N1 | — |
| | N54426 | Boeing Stearman A.75N1 | R. Simpson |
| | N54922 | Boeing Stearman N25-4 | V. S. E. Norman (Crunchie) |
| | N56028 | Ryan PT-22 | V. S. E. Norman |
| | N56421 | Ryan PT-22 (855) | PT Flight/Cosford |
| | N58566 | BT-13 Valiant | PT Flight/Cosford |
| | N70290 | B.121 Pup | Lakenheath Aero Club |
| | N75664 | Boeing Stearman E.75N1 (208) | — |
| | N88972 | B-25D-30-ND Mitchell (KL161) | Fighter Collection/Duxford |
| | N90005 | G.1159A Gulfstream 4 | Siebe PLC |
| | N91437 | PA-38-112 Tomahawk | Lakenheath Aero Club |
| | N91457 | PA-38-112 Tomahawk | Lakenheath Aero Club |
| | N91590 | PA-38-112 Tomahawk | Lakenheath Aero Club |
| | N91764 | Cessna 152 II (tailwheel) | Wessex Aviation & Transport Ltd |
| | N96240 | Beech D.18S | J. Hawke (G-AYAH) |
| | N99153 | T-28C Trojan ★ | Norfolk & Suffolk Aviation Museum/Flixton |
| | NC5171N | Lockheed 10A Electra ★ | Science Museum (G-LIOA)/Wroughton |
| | NC15214 | Waco UKC-S | P. H. McConnell/White Waltham |
| | NC16403 | Cessna C.34 Airmaster | Kennet Aircraft Ltd (G-BSEB) |
| | NL314BG | P-51D Mustang (414151) | D. W. Arnold/Biggin Hill |
| | NL1009N | P-40N Kittyhawk (FR870) | B. J. S. Grey/Duxford |
| | NL9494Z | TB-25N Mitchell (151632) | Visionair Ltd |
| | NX11SN | Yakolev C-11 | Old Flying Machine Co/Duxford |
| | NX47DD | Republic P-47D Thunderbolt (226671) | The Fighter Collection/Duxford |
| | NX55JP | FG-1D Corsair | Old Flying Machine Co/Duxford |
| | NX700HL | F8F-2B Bearcat (121714) | B. J. S. Grey/Duxford |
| | NX800H | F8F-2 Bearcat | D. W. Arnold/Biggin Hill |
| | NX1337A | F4U-7 Corsair (133722) | L. M. Walton/Duxford |
| | NX49092 | F4U-4 Corsair | D. W. Arnold/Biggin Hill |
| | VH-BRC | See N158C | |
| | VH-SNB | D.H.84 Dragon ★ | Museum of Flight/E. Fortune |
| | VH-UTH | GAL Monospar ST-12 ★ | Newark Air Museum (stored) |
| | VR-BEP | WS.55 Whirlwind 3 ★ | East Midlands Aeropark (G-BAMH) |
| | VR-BET | WS.55 Whirlwind 3 ★ | IHM (G-ANJV)/Weston-s-Mare |
| | VR-BEU | WS.55 Whirlwind 3 ★ | IHM (G-ATKV)/Weston-s-Mare |
| | VR-BJI | Lockheed Jetstar | Denis Vanguard International Ltd |
| | VR-BKC | Boeing 727-1H2 | USAL Inc |
| | VR-BKY | H.S.125 Srs F.3B | Corporate Jet Services |
| | VR-BKZ | H.S.125 Srs 700A | Dennis Vanguard International |
| | VR-BLA | Canadair CL.600.2A12 Challenger | Granaway Ltd |
| | VR-BLP | BAe 125 Srs 800A | BP Flight Operations Ltd |
| | VR-BLQ | BAe 125 Srs 800A | BP Flight Operations Ltd |
| | VR-BLR | G.1159C Gulfstream IV | BP Flight Operations Ltd |
| | VR-BLT | Dassault Falcon 50 | Triair (Bermuda) Ltd |
| | VR-BLX | F.27 Friendship Mk 400 | BP Flight Operations Ltd |
| | VR-BLY | F.27 Friendship Mk 400 | BP Flight Operations Ltd |
| | VR-BLZ | F.27 Friendship Mk 400 | BP Flight Operations Ltd |
| | VR-BOO | McD Douglas MD-87 | Ford Motor Co Ltd/Stansted |
| | VR-BOP | McD Douglas MD-87 | Ford Motor Co Ltd/Stansted |
| | VR-CBE | Boeing 727-46 | Resebury Corporation |
| | VR-CRB | Boeing 727-089 | Jade Air Leasing |
| | VR-CSH | Beech 350 Super King Air | United Biscuits Ltd |
| | 5N-ABW | Westland Widgeon 2 ★ | IHM (G-AOZE)/Weston-s-Mare |

# Radio Frequencies

The frequencies used by the larger airfields/airports are listed below. Abbreviations used: TWR — Tower, APP — Approach, A/G — Air-ground advisory. It is possible for changes to be made from time to time with the frequencies allocated which are all quoted in Megahertz (MHz).

| Airfield | TWR | APP | A/G |
|---|---|---|---|
| Aberdeen | 118.1 | 120.4 | |
| Aldergrove | 118.3 | 120.0 | |
| Alderney | 125.35 | | |
| Andrewsfield | | | 130.55 |
| Audley End | | | 122.35 |
| Barton | | | 122.7 |
| Barrow | | | 123.2 |
| Belfast City | 130.75 | 130.85 | |
| Bembridge | | | 123.25 |
| Biggin Hill | 134.8 | 129.4 | |
| Birmingham | 118.3 | 131.325 | |
| Blackbushe | | | 122.3 |
| Blackpool | 118.4 | 135.95 | |
| Bodmin | | | 122.7 |
| Booker | | | 126.55 |
| Bourn | | | 129.8 |
| Bournemouth | 125.6 | 119.625 | |
| Bristol | 133.85 | 132.4 | |
| Cambridge | 122.2 | 123.6 | |
| Cardiff | 125.0 | 125.85 | |
| Carlisle | | | 123.6 |
| Compton Abbas | | | 122.7 |
| Conington | | | 129.725 |
| Coventry | 119.25 | 122.0 | |
| Cranfield | 123.2 | 122.85 | |
| Denham | | | 130.725 |
| Doncaster | | | 122.9 |
| Dundee | 122.9 | | |
| Dunkeswell | | | 123.475 |
| Dunsfold | 124.32 | 119.825 | |
| Duxford | | | 122.075 |
| East Midlands | 124.0 | 120.125 | |
| Edinburgh | 118.7 | 121.2 | |
| Elstree | | | 122.4 |
| Exeter | 119.8 | 128.15 | |
| Fairoaks | | | 123.425 |
| Felthorpe | | | 123.5 |
| Fenland | | | 122.925 |
| Filton | 124.95 | 122.725 | |
| Gamston | | | 130.47 |
| Gatwick | 134.225 | 128.575 | |
| Glasgow | 118.8 | 119.1 | |
| Goodwood | 120.65 | 122.45 | |
| Guernsey | 119.95 | 128.65 | |
| Halfpenny Green | | | 123.0 |
| Hatfield | 130.8 | 123.35 | |
| Haverfordwest | | | 122.2 |
| Hawarden | 124.95 | 123.35 | |
| Hayes Heliport | | | 123.65 |
| Headcorn | | | 122.0 |
| Heathrow | 118.7 | 119.2 | |
| | 118.5 | 119.5 | |
| Hethel | | | 122.35 |
| Hucknall | | | 130.8 |
| Humberside | 118.55 | 124.675 | |
| Ingoldmells | | | 130.45 |
| Inverness | 122.6 | | |
| Ipswich | 118.325 | | |
| Jersey | 119.45 | 120.3 | |
| Kidlington | 118.875 | 125.325 | |
| Land's End | 130.7 | | |
| Leavesden | 122.15 | | |
| Leeds | 120.3 | 123.75 | |
| Leicester | | | 122.25 |
| Liverpool | 118.1 | 119.85 | |
| London City | 118.075 | 128.05 | |
| Long Marston | | | 130.1 |
| Luton | 120.2 | 128.75 | |
| Lydd | 120.7 | 131.3 | |
| Manchester | 118.625 | 119.4 | |
| Manston | 128.775 | 126.35 | |
| Netherthorpe | | | 123.575 |
| Newcastle | 119.7 | 126.35 | |
| North Denes | | | 120.45 |
| North Weald | | | 123.525 |
| Norwich | 124.25 | 119.35 | |
| Perth | 119.8 | 122.3 | |
| Plymouth | 122.6 | 133.55 | |
| Popham | | | 129.8 |
| Prestwick | 118.15 | 120.55 | |
| Redhill | 120.275 | | |
| Rochester | | | 122.25 |
| Ronaldsway | 118.9 | 120.85 | |
| Sandown | | | 123.5 |
| Seething | | | 122.6 |
| Sherburn | | | 122.6 |
| Shipdham | | | 123.05 |
| Shobdon | | | 123.5 |
| Shoreham | 125.4 | 123.15 | |
| Sibson | | | 122.3 |
| Sleap | | | 122.45 |
| Southampton | 118.2 | 131.0 | |
| Southend | 127.725 | 128.95 | |
| Stansted | 118.15 | 125.55 | |
| Stapleford | | | 122.8 |
| Staverton | 125.65 | 122.9 | |
| Sumburgh | 118.25 | 123.15 | |
| Swansea | 119.7 | | |
| Swanton Morley | | | 123.5 |
| Sywell | | | 122.7 |
| Teesside | 119.8 | 118.85 | |
| Thruxton | | | 130.45 |
| Tollerton | | | 122.8 |
| Wellesbourne | | | 130.45 |
| White Waltham | | | 122.6 |
| Wick | 119.7 | | |
| Wickenby | | | 122.45 |
| Woodford | 126.925 | 130.05 | |
| Yeovil | 125.4 | 130.8 | |

# Airline Flight Codes

Three-letter flight codes are now in general use. Those listed below identify both UK and overseas carriers appearing in the book.

| Code | Airline | | Code | Airline | | Code | Airline | |
|---|---|---|---|---|---|---|---|---|
| AAF | Aigle Azur | F | CSA | Czech A/L | OK | LOT | Polish A/L (LOT) | SP |
| AAG | Air Atlantique | G | CTA | CTA | HB | LTE | LTE | EC |
| AAL | American A/L | N | CTN | Croatia A/L | 9A | LTS | LTU Sud | D |
| AAN | Oasis | EC | CYP | Cyprus A/W | 5B | LTU | LTU | D |
| ABB | Air Belgium | OO | DAH | Air Algerie | 7T | MAH | Malev | HA |
| ABR | Air Hunting | G | DAL | Delta A/L | N | MAS | Malaysian A/L | 9M |
| ACA | Air Canada | C | DAT | Delta Air Transport | OO | MAU | Air Mauritius | 3B |
| ACF | Air Charter Intl | F | DLH | Lufthansa | D | MDN | Meridiana | EC |
| ADR | Adria A/W | SL | DMA | Maersk Air | OY | MEA | Middle East A/L | OD |
| AEA | Air Europa | EC | DQI | Cimber Air | OY | MNX | Manx A/L | G |
| AEF | Aero Lloyd | D | DYA | Alyemda | 7O | MON | Monarch A/L | G |
| AFL | Aeroflot | CCCP | EGY | Egypt Air | SU | MOR | Morefly | LN |
| AFM | Affretair | Z | EIA | Evergreen Intl | N | MPH | Martinair | PH |
| AFR | Air France | F | EIN | Aer Lingus | EI | NAD | Nobleair | TC |
| AGX | Aviogenex | YU | ELY | El Al | 4X | NAW | Newair | OY |
| AHK | Air Hong Kong | VR-H | ETH | Ethiopian A/L | ET | NEX | Northern Executive | G |
| AIA | Air Atlantis | CS | EUI | Euralair | F | NGA | Nigeria A/W | 5N |
| AIC | Air-India | VT | EWW | Emery | N | NSA | Nile Safaris | ST |
| AIH | Airtours | G | EXS | Channel Express | G | NWA | Northwest A/L | N |
| ALK | Air Lanka | 4R | EXX | Air Exel UK | G | NXA | Nationair | C |
| AMC | Air Malta | 9H | FDE | Federal Express | N | OAL | Olympic A/L | SX |
| AMM | Air 2000 | G | FIN | Finnair | OH | OYC | Conair | OY |
| AMT | American Trans Air | N | FOB | Ford | G | PAL | Philippine A/L | RP |
| ANA | All Nippon A/W | JA | FOF | Fred Olsen | LN | PGA | Portugalia | CS |
| ANZ | Air New Zealand | ZK | FUA | Futura | EC | PGT | Pegasus | TC |
| AOM | Air Outre Mer | F | FXY | Flexair | PH | PIA | Pakistan Intl | AP |
| APW | Arrow Air | N | GBL | GB Airways | G | QFA | Qantas | VH |
| ARG | Argentine A/W | LV | GEC | German Cargo | D | QSC | African Safaris | 5Y |
| ATI | ATI | I | GFA | Gulf Air | A40 | RAM | Royal Air Maroc | CN |
| ATT | Aer Turas | EI | GFG | Germania | D | RBA | Royal Brunei | V8 |
| AUA | Austrian A/L | OE | GHA | Ghana A/W | 9G | RIA | Rich Intl | N |
| AUR | Aurigny A/S | G | GIA | Garuda | PK | RJA | Royal Jordanian | JY |
| AVA | Avianca | HK | GIL | Gill Air | G | RNA | Royal Nepal A/L | 9N |
| AWC | Titan A/W | G | GNT | Business Air | G | ROT | Tarom | YR |
| AYC | Aviaco | EC | GRN | Greenair | TC | RWD | Air Rwanda | 9XR |
| AZA | Alitalia | I | HAL | Hawaiian Air | N | RYR | Ryanair | EI |
| AZI | Air Zimbabwe | Z | HAS | Hamburg A/L | D | SAA | South African A/W | ZS |
| AZR | Air Zaire | 9Q | HLA | HeavyLift | G | SAB | Sabena | OO |
| BAC | BAC Leasing | G | HLF | Hapag-Lloyd | D | SAS | SAS | SE OY LN |
| BAF | British Air Ferries | G | IAW | Iraqi A/W | YI | SAW | Sterling A/W | OY |
| BAL | Britannia A/L | G | IBE | Iberia | EC | SAY | Suckling A/W | G |
| BAW | British Airways | G | ICE | Icelandair | TF | SDI | Saudi | HZ |
| BBB | Balair | HB | IEA | Inter European | G | SEY | Air Seychelles | S7 |
| BBC | Bangladesh Biman | S2 | INS | Instone A/L | G | SIA | Singapore A/L | 9V |
| BCS | European A/T | OO | IRA | Iran Air | EP | SJM | Southern AT | N |
| BEA | Brymon European | G | IST | Istanbul A/L | TC | SLA | Sobelair | OO |
| BEE | Busy Bee | LN | ITF | Air Inter | F | SPP | Spanair | EC |
| BER | Air Berlin | N | JAL | Japan A/L | JA | STR | Stellair | F |
| BIH | British Intl Heli | G | JAT | JAT | YU | SUD | Sudan A/W | ST |
| BMA | British Midland | G | JAV | Janes Aviation | G | SUT | Sultan Air | TC |
| BRA | Braathens | LN | JEA | Jersey European A/W | G | SWE | Swedair | SE |
| BWA | BWIA | 9Y | KAC | Kuwait A/W | 9K | SWR | Swissair | HB |
| BZH | Brit Air | F | KAL | Korean Air | HL | SXS | Sun Express | TC |
| CCA | CAAC | B | KAR | Kar-Air | OH | SYR | Syrian Arab | YK |
| CDN | Canadian A/L Intl | C | KIS | Contactair | D | TAP | Air Portugal | CS |
| CFE | City Flyer | G | KLM | KLM | PH | TAR | Tunis Air | TS |
| CFG | Condor | D | KQA | Kenya A/W | 5Y | TAT | TAT | F |
| CIC | Celtic Air | G | LAA | Libyan Arab A/L | 5A | TCT | TUR European | TC |
| CKT | Caledonian | G | LAZ | Bulgarian A/L | LZ | THA | Thai A/W Intl | HS |
| CLH | Lufthansa CityLine | D | LDA | Lauda Air | OE | THG | Thurston | G |
| CLX | Cargolux | LX | LEI | Air UK Leisure | G | THY | Turkish A/L | TC |
| CMM | Canada 3000 A/L | C | LGL | Luxair | LX | TLE | Air Toulouse | F |
| CNB | Air Columbus | CS | LIB | Air Liberte | F | TMA | Trans Mediterranean | OD |
| COA | Continental A/L | N | LIN | Linjeflyg | SE | TOW | Tower Air | N |
| CPA | Cathay Pacific | VR-H | LIT | Air Littoral | F | TRA | Transavia | PH |
| CRL | Corse Air | F | LKA | Alkair | OY | TSC | Air Transat | C |
| CRX | Crossair | HB | LOG | Loganair | G | TSW | TEA Basle | HB |

# AIRLINE FLIGHT CODES

| | | | | | | | | | |
|---|---|---|---|---|---|---|---|---|---|
| WA | TWA | N | ULE | Air UK Leisure | G | VIV | Viva Air | EC | |
| WE | Transwede | SE | UPA | Air Foyle | G | VKG | Scanair | SE OY LN | |
| YR | Tyrolean | OE | UPS | United Parcels | N | VRG | Varig | PP | |
| AE | Emirates A/L | A6 | USA | USAir | N | WDL | WDL | D | |
| AL | United A/L | N | UTA | UTA | F | WOA | World A/W | N | |
| GA | Uganda A/L | 5X | UYC | Cameroon A/L | TJ | ZAC | Zambia A/W | 9J | |
| KA | Air UK | G | VIA | Viasa | YV | ZAS | ZAS A/L of Egypt | SU | |
| KR | Air Ukraine | UR | VIR | Virgin Atlantic | G | | | | |

OK-XGB, Boeing 737-55S. *AJW*

SL-ABH, Douglas DC-9-32. *AJW*

# British Aircraft Preservation Council Register

The British Aircraft Preservation Council was formed in 1967 to co-ordinate the works of all bodies involved in the preservation, restoration and display of historical aircraft. Membership covers the whole spectrum of national, Service, commercial and voluntary groups, and meetings are held regularly at the bases of member organisations. The Council is able to provide a means of communication, helping to resolve any misunderstandings or duplication of effort. Every effort is taken to encourage the raising of standards of both organisation and technical capacity amongst the member groups to the benfit of everyone interested in aviation. To assist historians, the B.A.P.C. register has been set up and provides an identity for those aircraft which do not qualify for a Service serial or inclusion in the UK Civil Register.

Aircraft on the current B.A.P.C. Register are as follows:

| Notes | Reg. | Type | Owner or Operator |
|---|---|---|---|
| | 6 | Roe Triplane Type IV (replica) | Greater Manchester Museum of Science & Technology |
| | 7 | Southampton University MPA | Southampton Hall of Aviation |
| | 8 | Dixon ornithopter | The Shuttleworth Trust |
| | 9 | Humber Monoplane (replica) | Airport Terminal/Birmingham |
| | 10 | Hafner R.II Revoplane | Museum of Army Flying/Middle Wallop |
| | 12 | Mignet HM.14 | Museum of Flight/E. Fortune |
| | 13 | Mignet HM.14 | Brimpex Metal Treatments |
| | 14 | Addyman standard training glider | N. H. Ponsford |
| | 15 | Addyman standard training glider | The Aeroplane Collection Ltd |
| | 16 | Addyman ultra-light aircraft | N. H. Ponsford |
| | 17 | Woodhams Sprite | The Aeroplane Collection Ltd |
| | 18 | Killick MP Gyroplane | N. H. Ponsford |
| | 19 | Bristol F.2b | Brussels Air Museum |
| | 20 | Lee-Richards annular biplane (replica) | Newark Air Musem |
| | 21 | Thruxton Jackaroo | M. J. Brett |
| | 22 | Mignet HM.14 (G-AEOF) | Aviodome/Schiphol, Holland |
| | 25 | Nyborg TGN-III glider | Midland Air Museum |
| | 27 | Mignet HM.14 | M. J. Abbey |
| | 28 | Wright Flyer (replica) | Bygone Times Antique Warehouse/ Eccleston |
| | 29 | Mignet HM.14 (replica) (G-ADRY) | Brooklands Museum of Aviation/ Weybridge |
| | 32 | Crossley Tom Thumb | Midland Air Museum |
| | 33 | DFS.108-49 Grunau Baby IIb | Russavia Collection |
| | 34 | DFS.108-49 Grunau Baby IIb | D. Elsdon |
| | 35 | EoN primary glider | Russavia Collection |
| | 36 | Fieseler Fi.103 (V-1) (replica) | Kent Battle of Britain Museum/Hawkinge |
| | 37 | Blake Bluetit | The Shuttleworth Trust |
| | 38 | Bristol Scout replica (A1742) | *Stored*/Wroughton |
| | 40 | Bristol Boxkite (replica) | Bristol City Museum |
| | 41 | B.E.2C (replica) (6232) | Historical Aircraft Museum/RAF St Athan |
| | 42 | Avro 504 (replica) (H1968) | Historical Aircraft Museum/RAF St Athan |
| | 43 | Mignet HM.14 | Lincolnshire Aviation Museum |
| | 44 | Miles Magister (L6906) | Berkshire Aviation Group (G-AKKY)/ Woodley |
| | 45 | Pilcher Hawk (replica) | Stanford Hall Museum |
| | 46 | Mignet HM.14 | Alan McKechnie Racing Ltd |
| | 47 | Watkins Monoplane | Historical Aircraft Museum/RAF St Athan |
| | 48 | Pilcher Hawk (replica) | Glasgow Museum of Transport |
| | 49 | Pilcher Hawk | Royal Scottish Museum/Edinburgh |
| | 50 | Roe Triplane Type 1 | Science Museum/S. Kensington |
| | 51 | Vickers Vimy IV | Science Museum/S. Kensington |
| | 52 | Lilienthal glider | Science Museum Store/Hayes |
| | 53 | Wright Flyer (replica) | Science Museum/S. Kensington |
| | 54 | JAP-Harding monoplane | Science Museum/S. Kensington |
| | 55 | Levavasseur Antoinette VII | Science Museum/S. Kensington |
| | 56 | Fokker E.III (210/16) | Science Museum/S. Kensington |
| | 57 | Pilcher Hawk (replica) | Science Museum/S. Kensington |
| | 58 | Yokosuka MXY7 Ohka 11 (15-1585) | FAA Museum/Yeovilton |
| | 59 | Sopwith Camel (replica) (D3419) | Historical Aircraft Museum/RAF St Athan |
| | 60 | Murray M.1 helicopter | The Aeroplane Collection Ltd |
| | 61 | Stewart man-powered ornithopter | Lincolnshire Aviation Museum |
| | 62 | Cody Biplane (304) | Science Museum/S. Kensington |
| | 63 | Hurricane (replica) (L1592) | Kent Battle of Britain Museum/Hawkinge |
| | 64 | Hurricane (replica) (P3059) | Kent Battle of Britain Museum/Hawkinge |

| Reg. | Type | Owner or Operator | Notes |
|---|---|---|---|
| 5 | Spitfire (replica) (DW-K) | Kent Battle of Britain Museum/Hawkinge | |
| 6 | Bf 109 (replica) (1480) | Kent Battle of Britain Museum/Hawkinge | |
| 7 | Bf 109 (replica) (14) | Kent Battle of Britain Museum/Hawkinge | |
| 8 | Hurricane (replica) (H3426) | Midland Air Museum | |
| 9 | Spitfire (replica) (QV-K) | Kent Battle of Britain Museum/Hawkinge | |
| 0 | Auster AOP.5 (TJ398) | Aircraft Preservation Soc of Scotland | |
| 1 | Spitfire (replica) (P8140) | Norfolk & Suffolk Aviation Museum | |
| 2 | Hurricane (replica) (V7767) | N. Weald Aircraft Restoration Flight | |
| 3 | Hurricane (replica) | Queens Head/Bishops Stortford | |
| 4 | Bf 109 (replica) (6357-6) | Kent Battle of Britain Museum/Hawkinge | |
| 5 | Mignet HM.14 (G-AEFG) | N. H. Ponsford | |
| 6 | Mignet HM.14 (G-AFFI) | Yorkshire Air Museum/Elvington | |
| 7 | Mignet HM.14 (replica) (G-ADRG) | Stratford Aircraft Collection | |
| 9 | Fiat G.46-4 (MM53211) | British Air Reserve/Lympne | |
| 0 | Airspeed Horsa (KJ351) | Museum of Army Flying/Middle Wallop | |
| 1 | Hawkridge Dagling | Russavia Collection | |
| 2 | Hawker Hind (Afghan) | RAF Museum/Hendon | |
| 3 | Kawasaki Ki-100-1b | Aerospace Museum/Cosford | |
| 4 | Nakajima Ki-46 (Dinah III) | Historical Aircraft Museum/RAF St Athan | |
| 5 | Weir W-2 autogyro | Museum of Flight/E. Fortune | |
| 6 | de Havilland Tiger Moth (replica) | Yorkshire Aircraft Preservation Soc | |
| 7 | Bristol Babe (replica) (G-EASQ) | Bomber County Museum/Hemswell | |
| 8 | Fokker Dr 1 (replica) (102/18) | FAA Museum/Yeovilton | |
| 9 | Cayley glider (replica) | Greater Manchester Museum of Science & Technology | |
| 0 | Colditz Cock (replica) | Imperial War Museum/Duxford | |
| 1 | Fieseler Fi 103 (V.1) | Lashenden Air Warfare Museum | |
| 2 | Fieseler Fi 103 (V.1) | Historical Aircraft Museum/RAF St Athan | |
| 3 | Fieseler Fi 103 (V.1) | Imperial War Museum/Duxford | |
| 4 | Fieseler Fi 103 (V.1) | Aerospace Museum/Cosford | |
| 5 | Gizmer autogyro | F. Fewsdale | |
| 6 | Brown helicopter | NE Aircraft Museum | |
| 7 | Luton L.A.4A Minor | NE Aircraft Museum | |
| 8 | Yokosuka MXY7 Ohka 11 | Greater Manchester Museum of Science & Technology | |
| 9 | Yokosuka MXY7 Ohka 11 | Aerospace Museum/Cosford | |
| 00 | Clarke glider | RAF Museum/Hendon | |
| 01 | Mignet HM.14 | Lincolnshire Aviation Museum | |
| 03 | Pilcher glider (replica) | Personal Plane Services Ltd | |
| 05 | Blériot XI (replica) | Aviodome/Schiphol, Holland | |
| 06 | Blériot XI | RAF Museum/Hendon | |
| 07 | Blériot XXVII | RAF Museum/Hendon | |
| 08 | Fairey Swordfish IV (HS503) | Cosford Aerospace Museum | |
| 09 | Slingsby Kirby Cadet TX.1 | RAF Museum/Henlow store | |
| 0 | Fokker D.VII replica (static) (5125) | — | |
| 1 | Sopwith Triplane replica (static) (N5492) | FAA Museum/Yeovilton | |
| 2 | D.H.2 replica (static) (5964) | Museum of Army Flying/Middle Wallop | |
| 3 | S.E.5A replica (static) (B4863) | — | |
| 4 | Vickers Type 60 Viking (static) (G-EBED) | Brooklands Museum of Aviation/ Weybridge | |
| 5 | Mignet HM.14 | Essex Aviation Group/Andrewsfield | |
| 6 | Santos-Dumont Demoiselle (replica) | Cornwall Aero Park/Helston | |
| 7 | B.E.2C (replica) | N. Weald Aircraft Restoration Flight | |
| 8 | Albatros D.V. (replica) (C19/18) | S. Yorks Aviation Soc/Firbeck | |
| 9 | Bensen B.7 | N.E. Aircraft Museum | |
| 20 | Mignet HM.14 (G-AEJZ) | Bomber County Museum/Hemswell | |
| 21 | Mignet HM.14 (G-AEKR) | S. Yorks Aviation Soc/Firbeck | |
| 22 | Avro 504 (replica) | British Broadcasting Corp | |
| 23 | Vickers FB.5 Gunbus (replica) | A. Topen (*stored*)/Cranfield | |
| 24 | Lilienthal Glider Type XI (replica) | Science Museum/S. Kensington | |
| 25 | Clay Cherub (G-BDGP) | B. R. Clay | |
| 26 | D.31 Turbulent (static) | Midland Air Museum store | |
| 27 | Halton Jupiter MPA | Shuttleworth Trust | |
| 28 | Watkinson Cyclogyroplane Mk IV | International Helicopter Museum/ Weston-s-Mare | |
| 29 | Blackburn 1911 Monoplane (replica) | Cornwall Aero Park/Helston store | |
| 30 | Blackburn 1912 Monoplane (replica) | Cornwall Aero Park/Helston store | |
| 31 | Pilcher Hawk (replica) | C. Paton | |
| 32 | Blériot XI (G-BLXI) | Musée de L'Automobile/France | |

| Notes | Reg. | Type | Owner or Operator |
|---|---|---|---|
| | 133 | Fokker Dr 1 (replica) (425/17) | Newark Air Museum |
| | 134 | Pitts S-2A static (G-CARS) | Toyota Ltd/Sywell |
| | 135 | Bristol M.1C (replica) (C4912) | — |
| | 136 | Deperdussin Seaplane (replica) | — |
| | 137 | Sopwith Baby Floatplane (replica) (8151) | — |
| | 138 | Hansa Brandenburg W.29 Floatplane (replica) (2292) | — |
| | 139 | Fokker Dr 1 (replica) 150/17 | — |
| | 140 | Curtiss R3C-2 Floatplane (replica) | Planes of Fame Museum/Chino, Ca |
| | 141 | Macchi M.39 Floatplane (replica) | Planes of Fame Museum/Chino, Ca |
| | 142 | SE-5A (replica) (F5459) | Cornwall Aero Park/Helston |
| | 143 | Paxton MPA | R. A. Paxton/Staverton |
| | 144 | Weybridge Mercury MPA | Cranwell Gliding Club |
| | 145 | Oliver MPA | D. Oliver (stored)/Warton |
| | 146 | Pedal Aeronauts Toucan MPA | Shuttleworth Trust |
| | 147 | Bensen B.7 | Norfolk & Suffolk Aviation Museum |
| | 148 | Hawker Fury II (replica) (K7271) | Aerospace Museum/Cosford |
| | 149 | Short S.27 (replica) | FAA Museum (stored)/Yeovilton |
| | 150 | SEPECAT Jaguar GR.1 (replica) (XX724) | RAF Exhibition Flight |
| | 151 | SEPECAT Jaguar GR.1 (replica) (XZ363) | RAF Exhibition Flight |
| | 152 | BAe Hawk T.1 (replica) (XX163) | RAF Exhibition Flight |
| | 153 | Westland WG.33 | IHM/Weston-s-Mare |
| | 154 | D.31 Turbulent | Lincolnshire Aviation Museum |
| | 155 | Panavia Tornado GR.1 (replica) (ZA600) | RAF Exhibition Flight |
| | 156 | Supermarine S-6B (replica) (S1595) | Planes of Fame Museum/Chino, Ca |
| | 157 | Waco CG-4A | Pennine Aviation Museum |
| | 158 | Fieseler Fi 103 (V.1) | Joint Bomb Disposal School/Chattenden |
| | 159 | Yokosuka MXY7 Ohka 11 | Joint Bomb Disposal School/Chattenden |
| | 160 | Chargus 108 hang glider | Museum of Flight/E. Fortune |
| | 161 | Stewart Ornithopter Coppelia | Bomber County Museum |
| | 162 | Goodhart Newbury Manflier MPA | Science Museum/Wroughton |
| | 163 | AFEE 10/42 Rotabuggy (replica) | Museum of Army Flying/Middle Wallop |
| | 164 | Wight Quadruplane Type 1 (replica) | Wessex Aviation Soc/Wimborne |
| | 165 | Bristol F.2b (E2466) | RAF Museum/Hendon |
| | 167 | S.E.5A replica | Newark Air Museum |
| | 168 | D.H.60G Moth static replica (G-AAAH) | Hilton Hotel/Gatwick |
| | 169 | SEPECAT Jaguar GR.1 (static replica) (XX110) | No 1 S. of T.T. RAF Halton |
| | 170 | Pilcher Hawk (replica) | A. Gourlay/Strathallan |
| | 171 | BAe Hawk T.1 (replica) (XX297) | RAF Exhibition Flight/Abingdon |
| | 172 | Chargus Midas Super 8 hang glider | Science Museum/Wroughton |
| | 173 | Birdman Promotions Grasshopper | Science Museum/Wroughton |
| | 174 | Bensen B.7 | Science Museum/Wroughton |
| | 175 | Volmer VJ-23 Swingwing | Greater Manchester Museum of Science & Technology |
| | 176 | SE-5A (replica) (A4850) | S. Yorks Aviation Soc/Firbeck |
| | 177 | Avro 504K (replica) (G1381) | Brooklands Museum of Aviation/ Weybridge |
| | 178 | Avro 504K (replica) (E373) | Bygone Times Antique Warehouse/ Eccleston, Lancs |
| | 179 | Sopwith Camel (replica) | N. Weald Aircraft Restoration Flight |
| | 180 | McCurdy Silver Dart (replica) | RAF Museum/Cardington |
| | 181 | RAF B.E.2b (replica) | RAF Museum/Cardington |
| | 182 | Wood Ornithopter | Greater Manchester Museum of Science & Technology |
| | 183 | Zurowski ZP.1 | Newark Air Museum |
| | 184 | Spitfire IX (replica) (EN398) | Aces High Ltd/North Weald |
| | 185 | Waco CG-4A (243809) | Museum of Army Flying/Middle Wallop |
| | 186 | D.H.82B Queen Bee (K3584) | Mosquito Aircraft Museum |
| | 187 | Roe Type 1 biplane (replica) | Brooklands Museum of Aviation/ Weybridge |
| | 188 | McBroom Cobra 88 | Science Museum/Wroughton |
| | 189 | Blériot XI (replica) | |
| | 190 | Spitfire (replica) (K5054) | Biggin Hill Museum |
| | 191 | BAe Harrier GR.5 (replica) (ZD472) | RAF Exhibition Flight |
| | 192 | Weedhopper JC-24 | The Aeroplane Collection |

| eg. | Type | Owner or Operator | Notes |
|---|---|---|---|
| 93 | Hovey WD-11 Whing Ding | The Aeroplane Collection | |
| 94 | Santos Dumont Demoiselle (replica) | Brooklands Museum of Aviation/ Weybridge | |
| 95 | Moonraker 77 hang glider | Museum of Flight/E. Fortune | |
| 96 | Sigma 2M hang glider | Museum of Flight/E. Fortune | |
| 97 | Cirrus III hang glider | Museum of Flight/E. Fortune | |
| 98 | Fieseler Fi.103 (V-1) | Imperial War Museum/Lambeth | |
| 99 | Fieseler Fi.103 (V-1) | Science Museum/S. Kensington | |
| 00 | Bensen B.7 | K. Fern Collection/Stoke | |
| 04 | McBroom Hang Glider | The Aeroplane Collection | |
| 08 | SE-5A (replica) (2700) | Prince's Mead Shopping Precinct/ Farnborough | |
| 09 | Spitfire IX (replica) | Museum of D-Day Aviation/Appledram, West Sussex | |
| 10 | Avro 504J (replica) | Southampton Hall of Aviation | |

**ote:** Registrations/Serials carried are mostly false identities. MPA = Man Powered Aircraft.

H-XLA, EMB-120RT Brasilia. *AJW*

6-EKB, Airbus A310-304. *AJW*

G-BNNA, Stolp SA.300 Starduster Too. AJW

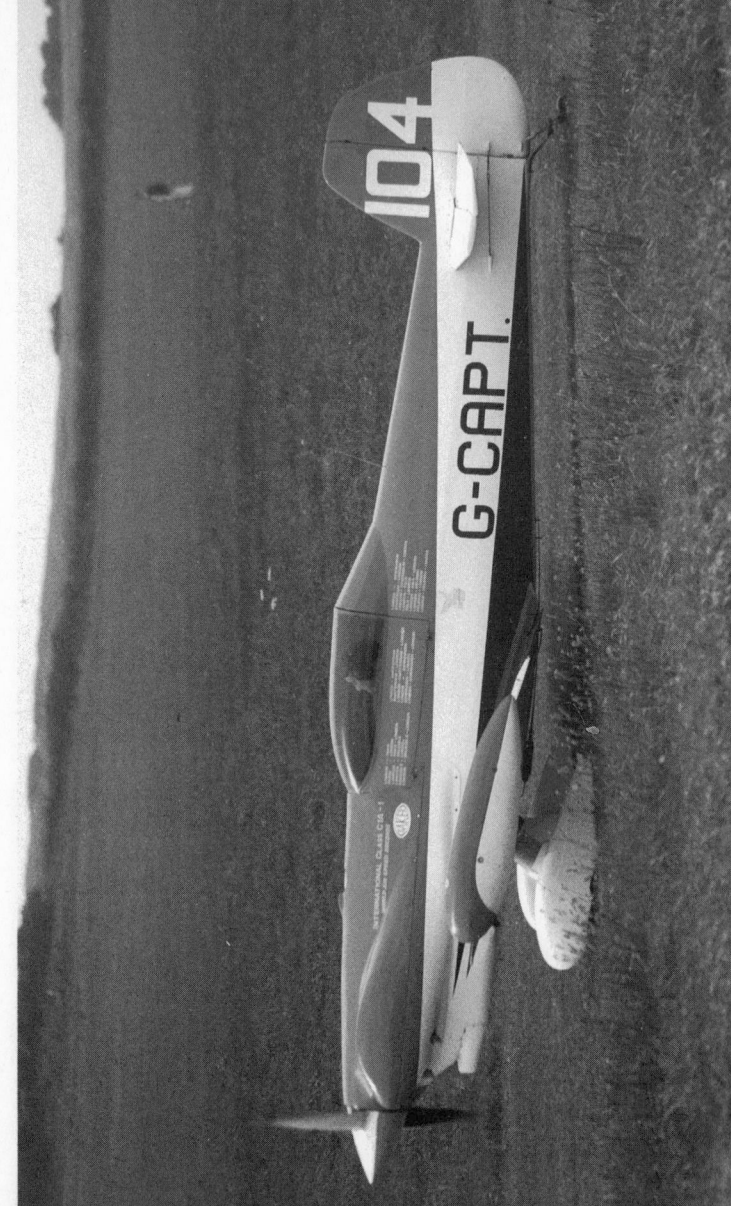

G-GNTB, SAAB SF.340A. A/W

319

G-HEVY, Boeing 707-423C. AJW

321

G-OOOH, Boeing 757-28AER. AJW

323

EC-FHA, Boeing 767-3Y0ER. A/W

JA8161, Boeing 747-246B. AJW

N603FF, Boeing 747-130. AJW

SE-DRA, BAe-146-200, AJW

# Future Allocations Log (In-Sequence)

The grid provides the facility to record future in-sequence registrations as they are issued or seen. To trace a particular code, refer to the left hand column which contains the three letters following the G pre-fix. The final letter can be found by reading across the columns headed A to Z. For example, the box for G-BUZD is located five rows down (BUZ) and then four across to the D column.

| G- | A | B | C | D | E | F | G | H | I | J | K | L | M | N | O | P | R | S | T | U | V | W | X | Y | Z |
|----|---|---|---|---|---|---|---|---|---|---|---|---|---|---|---|---|---|---|---|---|---|---|---|---|---|
| BUV | | | | | | | | | | | | | | | | | | | | | | | | | |
| BUW | | | | | | | | | | | | | | | | | | | | | | | | | |
| BUX | | | | | | | | | | | | | | | | | | | | | | | | | |
| BUY | | | | | | | | | | | | | | | | | | | | | | | | | |
| BUZ | | | | | | | | | | | | | | | | | | | | | | | | | |
| BVA | | | | | | | | | | | | | | | | | | | | | | | | | |
| BVB | | | | | | | | | | | | | | | | | | | | | | | | | |
| BVC | | | | | | | | | | | | | | | | | | | | | | | | | |
| BVD | | | | | | | | | | | | | | | | | | | | | | | | | |
| BVE | | | | | | | | | | | | | | | | | | | | | | | | | |
| BVF | | | | | | | | | | | | | | | | | | | | | | | | | |
| BVG | | | | | | | | | | | | | | | | | | | | | | | | | |
| BVH | | | | | | | | | | | | | | | | | | | | | | | | | |
| BVI | | | | | | | | | | | | | | | | | | | | | | | | | |
| BVJ | | | | | | | | | | | | | | | | | | | | | | | | | |
| BVK | | | | | | | | | | | | | | | | | | | | | | | | | |
| BVL | | | | | | | | | | | | | | | | | | | | | | | | | |
| BVM | | | | | | | | | | | | | | | | | | | | | | | | | |
| BVN | | | | | | | | | | | | | | | | | | | | | | | | | |
| BVO | | | | | | | | | | | | | | | | | | | | | | | | | |
| BVP | | | | | | | | | | | | | | | | | | | | | | | | | |
| BVR | | | | | | | | | | | | | | | | | | | | | | | | | |
| BVS | | | | | | | | | | | | | | | | | | | | | | | | | |
| BVT | | | | | | | | | | | | | | | | | | | | | | | | | |
| BVU | | | | | | | | | | | | | | | | | | | | | | | | | |
| BVV | | | | | | | | | | | | | | | | | | | | | | | | | |
| BVW | | | | | | | | | | | | | | | | | | | | | | | | | |
| BVX | | | | | | | | | | | | | | | | | | | | | | | | | |
| BVY | | | | | | | | | | | | | | | | | | | | | | | | | |
| BVZ | | | | | | | | | | | | | | | | | | | | | | | | | |
| BWA | | | | | | | | | | | | | | | | | | | | | | | | | |
| BWB | | | | | | | | | | | | | | | | | | | | | | | | | |
| BWC | | | | | | | | | | | | | | | | | | | | | | | | | |
| BWD | | | | | | | | | | | | | | | | | | | | | | | | | |
| BWE | A | B | C | D | E | F | G | H | I | J | K | L | M | N | O | P | R | S | T | U | V | W | X | Y | Z |

Credit: *Wal Gandy*

# Future Allocations Log (Out-of-Sequence)

This grid can be used to record out-of-sequence registrations as they are issued or seen. The first column is provided for the ranges prefixed with G-B, ie from G-BUxx to G-Bxx. The remaining columns cover the sequences from G-Cxxx to G-Zxxx and in this case it is necessary to insert the last three letters in the appropriate section.

| G-B | G-C | G-E | G-G | G-J | G-L | G-N | G-O | G-P | G-S | G-U |
|-----|-----|-----|-----|-----|-----|-----|-----|-----|-----|-----|
| | | | | | | | | | | |
| | | | | | | | | | | |
| | | | | | | | | | | |
| | | | | | | | | | | |
| | | | | | | | | | | G-V |
| | | | | | | | | | | |
| | G-D | G-F | G-H | | G-M | G-O | | | | |
| | | | | | | | | | | |
| | | | | | | | | | | |
| | | | | | | | | | | |
| | | | | | | | | | | |
| | | | | G-K | | | | | | |
| | | | | | | | | | | G-W |
| | | | | | | | | | | |
| | | | | | | | | | | |
| | | | | | | | | | | |
| | | | | | | | | G-R | | |
| | | | | | | | | | | |
| | | | | | | | | | G-T | |
| | | | | | | | | | | G-X |
| | | | | | | | | | | |
| | | | | | | | | | | |
| G-C | G-E | G-G | G-I | G-L | G-N | | | | | |
| | | | | | | | | | | G-Y |
| | | | | | | | | | | |
| | | | | | | | | | | |
| | | | | | | | | | | |
| | | | | | | | | | | |
| | | | | | | | | | | G-Z |
| | | | | | | | | | | |
| | | | | | | | | | | |
| | | | | | | | | | | |
| | | | | | | | | | | |

# Overseas Airliners Registration Log

This grid may be used to record airliner registrations not included in the main section

| Reg | Type | Operator |
|-----|------|----------|
| | | |
| | | |
| | | |
| | | |
| | | |
| | | |
| | | |
| | | |
| | | |
| | | |
| | | |
| | | |
| | | |
| | | |
| | | |
| | | |
| | | |
| | | |
| | | |
| | | |
| | | |
| | | |
| | | |
| | | |
| | | |
| | | |
| | | |
| | | |
| | | |
| | | |
| | | |
| | | |
| | | |
| | | |
| | | |
| | | |
| | | |
| | | |
| | | |
| | | |
| | | |
| | | |
| | | |
| | | |
| | | |

# Addenda

**New or restored British registrations**

| Reg. | Type | Owner or Operator | Notes |
|------|------|-------------------|-------|
| G-AJWB | M.38 Messenger 2A | P. G. Lee | |
| G-ANKL | D.H. 82A Tiger Moth | J. D. Souch | |
| G-BGJL | Bell 212 | Bristow Helicopters Ltd | |
| G-BOPO | OA.7 Optica Srs 300 | FLS Aerospace (Lovaux) Ltd | |
| G-BOPP | OA.7 Optica Srs 300 | FLS Aerospace (Lovaux) Ltd | |
| G-BOPR | OA.7 Optica Srs 300 | FLS Aerospace (Lovaux) Ltd | |
| G-BWLY | Rotorway Executive 90 | P. W. & I. P. Bewley | |
| G-DTCP | PA-32R Cherokee Lance 300 | Campbell Aviation Ltd (G-TEEM) | |
| G-DWIA | Chilton D.W.1A | D. Elliott | |
| G-EGUL | Christen Eagle II | P. N. Davis (G-FRYS) | |
| G-ENTW | Cessna F.152 | M. Entwistle (G-BFLK) | |
| G-HORS | Cameron Horse SS balloon | Cameron Balloons Ltd | |
| G-IEAF | Airbus A.320-231 | Inter European Airways Ltd/Cardiff | |
| G-IEAG | Airbus A.320-231 | Inter European Airways Ltd/Cardiff | |
| G-IIIR | Pitts S-1 Special | R. O. Rogers | |
| G-JHSX | BAe 125 Srs 800A | Corporate Jets Ltd/Hatfield | |
| G-LBLZ | Lindstrand LBL-105A balloon | Lindstrand Balloons Ltd | |
| G-LILI | Cessna 425 | Ortac Air Ltd (G-YOTT/G-NORC) | |
| G-MADD | Robinson R-22B | Great Excitement Ltd (G-MEAT) | |
| G-NPNP | Cameron N-105 balloon | Air 2 Air Ltd | |
| G-OBAT | Cessna F.152 | M. & M. Entwistle (G-OENT) | |
| G-ODJH | Mooney M.20C | D. J. Hockings (G-BMLH) | |
| G-OEBA | Robin DR.400/140B | EB Aviation (G-JMHB) | |
| G-OILX | AS. 355F-1 Twin Squirrel | Firstearl Ltd (G-RMGN/G-BMCY) | |
| G-OKED | Cessna 150L | Midair Aviation Ltd/Bournemouth | |
| G-OMMM | Colt 90A balloon | 3M Health Care Ltd | |
| G-ONAV | PA-31-310 Turbo Navajo C | Panther Aviation Ltd (G-IGAR) | |
| G-OPDS | Denney Aerocraft Kitfox | P. D. Sparling | |
| G-OSFT | PA-31-310 Turbo Navajo C | SFT Aviation Ltd (G-MDAS/G-BCJZ)/ Bournemouth | |
| G-PYLN | Cameron Pylon SS balloon | Air 2 Air Ltd (G-BUSO) | |
| G-RMGW | Denney Aerocraft Kitfox | G. H. Gilmour-White | |
| G-RONC | Aeronca 11AC Chief | M. R. Masters (G-BULV) | |
| G-RVVI | Van's RV-6 | J. E. Alsford & J. N. Parr | |
| G-TAFI | Bücker Bu133 Jungmeister | A. J. E. Smith | |
| G-TOBA | SOCATA TB.10 Tobago | E. Downing | |

**Cancellations**

G-AVIO, G-AWXO, G-AXNC, G-AXTI, G-BDAE, G-BFLK, G-BKXC, G-BMGP, G-BMLH, G-BNVF, G-BOYE, G-BRCL, G-BRCS, G-BRCX, G-BRHH, G-BROS, G-BSFT, G-BSMA, G-BSWE, G-BTBK, G-BTDJ, G-BTLR, G-BULI, G-BULV, G-BUNU, G-BUOM, G-BUPK, G-BURH, G-BURX, G-EEGE, G-FMUS, G-FRYS, G-HYPO, G-IFTD, G-IGAR, G-JERY, G-JMBH, G-JONS, G-MDAS, G-MEAT, G-MIGI, G-MURF, G-NEVL, G-OAKM, G-OENT, G-OMCL, G-PEET, G-RMGN, G-SHSS, G-TEEM, G-UKNZ, G-VAUK, G-YOTT

**New overseas registrations**

| Notes | Reg. | Type | Owner or Operator |
|---|---|---|---|
| | C-FTOB | Boeing 747-133 | Nationair |
| | D-BKIR | D.H.C.8-311 Dash Eight | Contactair/Lufthansa CityLine |
| | EC-FQB | Boeing 737-4YO | Air Europa |
| | OY-EDB | BAe Jetstream 3103 | Sun-Air |
| | RA-82045 | An-124 | HeavyLift/Volga Dnepr |
| | RA-85804 | Tupolev Tu-154B-2 | Aeroflot |
| | RP-C5745 | Boeing 747-212B | Philippine Airlines |
| | SE-DPP | L.1011-385 Tri-Star 100 | Air Sweden |
| | SE-DPR | L.1011-385 TriStar 100 | Air Sweden |
| | TC-ONC | Airbus A.320-211 | Onur Airways |
| | TF-ABD | Boeing 737-204 | Atlanta Icelantic |
| | VT-ESN | Boeing 747-437 | Air India |
| | VT-ESO | Boeing 747-437 | Air India |
| | VT-ESP | Boeing 747-437 | Air India |
| | 9V-SMY | Boeing 747-412 | Singapore Airlines |
| | 9V-SMZ | Boeing 747-412 | Singapore Airlines |

**Cancellations**

EC-CAJ, EC-CBB, EC-CBL, EC-CBM, F-BPJV, F-GGTP, F-GMCD, HS-TMA, HS-TMB, HS-TMC, LZ-JXA, N621FE, N7035T, N31033, OY-CNL, PH-DTL, SU-AOU, SU-AVX, SU-AVY, YR-ABM, ZS-SAR, 5X-UCM, 9V-SQP

# Monthly news & aircraft movements throughout the UK

Over 500 pages every year, packed with regular national UK movement reports, airline news, military aviation and overflight listings. Add comprehensive Heathrow movement lists, a full UK register update and illustrate with photographs and you have the best magazine of its type. All this for just £14.00 per year.

To commence membership from January 1993 send £14.00 to SAS (CAM offer), 271 Birchanger Lane, Birchanger, Bishop's Stortford, Herts CM23 5QP. Or to join during the year, simply send £1.20 per month of 1993 remaining. As well as postal subscription to the magazine you will also be entitled to discounts at the Society shop (open Sundays at Stansted Airport) which stocks a range of books, models, registers and magazines.

## The essential magazine for the aircraft enthusiast

## Just £14 p.a.

# Stansted Aviation Society